ISBN 978-1-5280-2169-2
PIBN 10902499

English
Français
Deutsche
Italiano
Español
Português

www.forgottenbooks.com

Mythology Photography **Fiction**
Fishing Christianity **Art** Cooking
Essays Buddhism Freemasonry
Medicine **Biology** Music **Ancient
Egypt** Evolution Carpentry Physics
Dance Geology **Mathematics** Fitness
Shakespeare **Folklore** Yoga Marketing
Confidence Immortality Biographies
Poetry **Psychology** Witchcraft
Electronics Chemistry History **Law**
Accounting **Philosophy** Anthropology
Alchemy Drama Quantum Mechanics
Atheism Sexual Health **Ancient History**
Entrepreneurship Languages Sport
Paleontology Needlework Islam
Metaphysics Investment Archaeology
Parenting Statistics Criminology
Motivational

THE SPIRIT OF MISSIONS

AN ILLUSTRATED MONTHLY REVIEW
OF CHRISTIAN MISSIONS

Vol. LXXV.   **January,** 1910   No. 1

THE PROGRESS OF THE KINGDOM

THIS somewhat hackneyed phrase represents the wish that will pass from lip to lip and from heart to heart at this season. That in most cases it is a sincere wish we are glad to believe. The majority of the world really wants the rest of the world to have a Happy New Year. Not least of all does THE SPIRIT OF MISSIONS fervently desire this blessing for its readers.

"A Happy New Year!"

But we wish far more than is ordinarily conveyed by the words of the old greeting. We would put into them a prayer for the true happiness of all men, and for the coming of the "year of the redeemed." If this be the burden of the words, then there emerges a seeming paradox; for we cannot make the wish in the narrow sense and in the wider sense at the same time. We cannot honestly desire that our readers may be comfortable and smug and self-congratulatory while the happiness of the greater part of the world waits upon our activity in the extension of the Kingdom. The "Happy New Year" which we wish for each one of you is that which will surely be found by the man who has placed himself in line with the eternal purposes of God, and is realizing the mission upon which the Christian soul is sent into a world where the Incarnate Christ waits to be made manifest to all His children.

THERE can scarcely be any among our readers who remember receiving the first copy of THE SPIRIT OF MISSIONS. If there should happen to be one, we should like to be informed of it, but as the last issue closes the seventy-fourth year of the periodical we greatly doubt whether any living person can claim to have read the little pamphlet of thirty-two pages which appeared in January, 1836, "issued by the authority of the Board of Missions and edited under its direction."

Seventy-four Years

Those pages lie before us now, and it is refreshing to see how, even from the first—with that new baptism of missionary inspiration which showed its fruits in the consecration of Jackson Kemper as the first missionary bishop in 1835—there was sounded forth the true note that "in her missionary organization the Church herself undertakes the conversion of the world. Engaging in so great a work, in the name and strength of her divine and glorious

(7)

Head, her appeal is made to all who in the sacrament of baptism have bound themselves to be His soldiers until death, to come up to His help against the mighty."

For this purpose THE SPIRIT OF MISSIONS was established, and its appeal was made to the clergy that they bear to their people the story of the missionaries' toils and successes, "to thus instruct their understandings in the nature, to fix upon their consciences the responsibility, and to engage their hearts in the sublime, self-sacrificing charity of the missionary enterprise."

Good, sound words these, written by some hand long since crumbled into dust, but still representing the purpose and aim which THE SPIRIT OF MISSIONS has steadily kept in view during its seventy-four years of life.

Then and Now

In its day the little pamphlet, of which it is recorded that "the editor is authorized to make each number from sixteen to thirty-two pages, in his discretion," did not unworthily represent the aspirations and enthusiasms of the Church. Certainly there are in its pages many signs of vigorous life and high ambition.

The mission to Greece, long since discontinued, represents our greatest effort at that time in the foreign field, but there is a note to the effect that "Messrs. Lockwood and Hanson, missionaries to China, have arrived on the distant shore to which they have gone forth at the call of the Church to preach the Gospel." In Africa a single colored man, James M. Thompson, is recorded as "the head of a school about to be established." The Rev. Horatio Southgate, Jr., is spoken of as conducting "an exploring missionary agency in Persia," and last among the foreign mission fields we find Texas, with the word "Vacant" written against it.

The claims of the "Far" West are heard in letters from Tennessee, Indiana, Michigan and Kentucky. Bishop Otey,

of Tennessee, assures us that Memphis is "likely to become a place of great commercial importance, being finely situated on the Mississippi River," while the Rev. Isaac W. Hallam, "missionary to Chicago," says that during the last quarter he has confined his labors to Chicago and added four to the number of communicants there. He is convinced that missionaries of the Church should be immediately stationed at several places, "of which," he says, "I select Milwalky. It is situated in the Ouisconson territory, on the shores of Lake Michigan, about eighty miles from Chicago. In the opinion of many judicious persons it will be very little inferior to the last-named place. Twenty-five miles this side of Milwalky is Root River (the present Racine); the two might be united at present under one station."

The membership of the Board of Missions is interesting: The Rt. Rev. William White was president, and what was probably a majority of the bishops of the Church constituted the remaining Episcopal membership—among them Griswold, Philander Chase, Onderdonk, John Henry Hopkins, G. W. Doane and Jackson Kemper. Scarcely less interesting is the list of missionaries in the employment of the Board, whose names, with their stations, are published in detail, the total number being thirty-three clergy, four laymen and nine women.

There is, of course, a striking contrast between the present issue of our periodical as it begins its seventy-fifth year and that other issue with which it began its existence, but it is not greater than the contrast between the present Church, with its numbers, power, and wealth, its scores of missionary stations and hundreds of missionaries, and the dauntless little handful which represented the Church in that day. But the finest thing of all is the spirit which breathes through the old-fashioned and somewhat stilted sentences of these pioneers of the Church. It may be questioned whether with all that we have gained we have not lost something of their indomitable earnestness and cheerful self-sacrifice.

The Seventy-fifth Year

There is nothing to show what was the circulation of our first issue. The Editor *does* record the fact that "of the present issue a very large edition is printed as a specimen of the magazine. It will be continued monthly, in the same form, and varying in size from sixteen to thirty-two pages, at *one dollar per annum*, payable *always in advance*. The propriety of this condition will appear to all who consider the very low price at which it is put."

And still we are publishing the magazine at a dollar per annum, and still we are asking payment in advance, and still we are urging upon our readers that "it ought to be, by the large number of its subscribers and the certainty of its income, a source of profit to the missionary enterprise."

Just here emerges a consideration worthy of attention. Unquestionably this magazine should be more than self-supporting; beyond doubt it ought to reach the homes of the majority of our communicants, yet seventy-four years find us with only about thirty thousand subscribers and the publication does not yet pay expenses. Seventy-five thousand would be a moderate number of subscribers for a Church which has 900,000 communicants. Is there any hope that by the end of our seventy-fifth year we might reach some such number? If each subscriber would produce another, the thing would be well-nigh accomplished, and a respectable revenue for mission work realized. It would seem that such an advance were well within the limits of possibility.

With this suggestion, and bespeaking the cordial co-operation and friendly kindness of all our readers, we enter upon the seventy-fifth year of the life of THE SPIRIT OF MISSIONS. May its one hundred and fiftieth year witness as great an advance over to-day as that which is chronicled above!

A Missionary Meeting in a City Hall

A MISSIONARY meeting in the city hall of an American city would cause no little comment — possibly even consternation in some quarters. Yet that is what happened at the Mansion House in London recently. The Society for the Propagation of the Gospel took this method of making known to London business men the need for vigorous extension in the field and larger support at home. The Lord Mayor of London presided and expressed the hope that a Mansion House missionary meeting would in future be an annual event. One of the speakers at the meeting was Professor Honda, of Tokyo, who has been sent by his government to study teaching methods in England and America. Professor Honda told this incident concerning the coming of the Gospel to modern Japan:

"In 1854 our treaty was signed with the United States of America, followed by other Powers in rapid succession. In the same year, before the treaty was made with your country [England], a British man-of-war came to Nagasaki; a detachment of soldiers was despatched with a view to expel the unwelcome visitor, and the officer in command, Murata by name, went one day to this English ship on official business. He found a curious book floating on the water, picked it up and learned from his Dutch interpreter that it was the Bible of the Western religion of universal brotherhood. His curiosity was raised to the highest pitch and he began to study it through a Chinese translation. Eight years later, hearing of a Protestant missionary in Nagasaki, Murata sent his English-speaking relative to Dr. Verbeck, a Dutch gentleman, to clear up points of doubt in the sacred book. For nearly three years this messenger used to travel backward and forward between Sag and Nagasaki, a distance of two days' journey on foot. In 1866 Murata, with his younger brother, and the interpreting relative were baptized by the same missionary. Thus the first Protestant convert of Japan was made through the English Bible picked up in the harbor of Nagasaki."

O NE of the significant events of each January is the observance of the missionary day for Sunday-schools on the Second Sunday
The Sunday-school Missionary Day after Epiphany. Last year more than a thousand schools kept the day by using the form of service provided by the Board of Missions. In the last few weeks hundreds of packages of the service leaflet have been shipped to all parts of the country. In some cities union services are to be held. In many a small outpost where the members of the school have never seen another Church school the day will be kept with the same spirit of love and good will.

A FEW days ago this letter reached the office of the London Missionary Society:

"DEAR SIR:
Individual Gifts   "I enclose £2,000 for your society. Please send receipt and enter as from 'A Friend,' and don't mention my name either in committee or otherwise.

"Yours faithfully,
"_____ _____

"This is instead of the £100 I have given you the last two or three years."

This is a striking instance of the application of the counsel "Let not thy left hand know what thy right hand doeth." More than that, it is an inspiring instance of a right hand that is really doing something. The Society for the Propagation of the Gospel also acknowledges the receipt, from an anonymous donor, of what it has come to regard as an annual gift of £1,000.

It rarely happens that the Board of Missions is able to announce similar gifts from living donors. Yet it is be-

coming increasingly evident that the work of the American Church at home and abroad cannot be worthily done unless the offerings of congregations are largely supplemented from individuals. Scores of parishes include among their members men and women who can give much more than they ought to give through the offering to meet the apportionment. In not a few instances a dozen persons or more could each give more than the amount apportioned to the whole congregation. To do so would obviously be unwise, since it would weaken the sense of responsibility on the part of others. Having given a due share through the congregational offering, there is still the opportunity of making personal offerings to meet the general obligations—the payment of salaries, the maintenance of schools and hospitals—and to provide for extension. Such individual offerings go to the credit of the diocese as a whole, and aid it in meeting the diocesan apportionment.

A larger number of people are claiming this privilege. So the apportionment plan seems to be stimulating both corporate and personal giving. While introducing system it in no wise necessarily does away with the cherished ideal of "free-will offerings." We wish that all who make personal offerings could realize as we do what their gifts accomplish in enabling the Board of Missions to extend aid to many vigorous enterprises whose requests for help to render larger service it would otherwise be compelled to refuse.

O UR next issue—that for the month of February—will be the annual Children's Number. For the ninth time this special issue is
The Annual Children's Number sent forth to the Church. That it is of value, and in some measure at least accomplishes the purpose which it has in view, is indicated by the steady and continuous growth made from year

to year in the edition published. Last year 140,000 copies were issued, and a number of belated orders could not be filled. This year every endeavor is being made to get the orders in early and thus escape the unpleasant predicament of being obliged to say "No" to good friends who send a requisition for additional copies. The number sold this year ought to reach 150,000.

It would be an unwise policy to give too great a foretaste of the good things which will be found in the Children's Number for this year; but without betraying confidence we may just drop a hint that there are some little Filipino chaps who will dance through its pages, while the almond-eyed children of Japan and China will vie with the Indian boys of Alaska in securing the attention of our readers. Nor will the healthy, hearty children of the western mission field be forgotten, though they may not excite the eager interest which the small boy always feels when he encounters "something about Indians." Our cover also will, we believe, tell a story of its own which will appeal to the old as well as the young.

Our Little Salesmen
Of course everyone knows that the Children's Number of THE SPIRIT OF MISSIONS is disposed of largely by the children of the Sunday-schools, and the Editor desires to tell them how greatly he appreciates what they have done in this way. Without their co-operation, their fresh interest and vivid enthusiasm, his work would be largely in vain. The eager rush for copies of the Children's Number has become a yearly feature marking the Sunday before Lent in many of our Sunday-schools, and we are convinced that thousands in our congregations have come into more intelligent touch with the missionary enterprise of the Church because, moved by the appeal in the bright face of some child, they have purchased a copy of our Children's Number. The work therefore

is not simply one for revenue, but is itself a missionary enterprise, and as such we believe it distinctly worth doing. To each of the little missionaries who will this year help us to carry far and wide the tidings of what the Church is trying to do on behalf of Her Master's little ones, we send our best wishes and express our heartfelt appreciation.

NINETEEN hundred and nine has many notable achievements to its credit. Only once before in a single calendar year have so *The Gift* many recruits been *of Lives* added to the staff of our distant missions. The Church is giving more largely of her best life. The quality is better as the quantity is greater than in the past. It is no reflection upon that past and it is no cause for special congratulation in the present that our representatives are better trained and equipped for the tasks to which we send them than were their predecessors. The same thing holds true in every profession. The physician of 1909 is better trained for the battle against disease than the physician of 1859. The average lawyer of to-day is better equipped than his counterpart of half a century ago. The modern business man accomplishes as a matter of course tasks that would have appalled the merchant of the old school. So naturally we expect the present-day missionary to have a more complete and thorough equipment than most of the pioneers. Well will it be for the cause they love if they can always show the same devout purpose, the same readiness to make sacrifices, the same desire to bring blessing to the souls of men as shaped the lives of the men and women who went to the front a generation or two ago. Still better will it be for the cause to which all of us are committed if we can even measurably display in our own home-lived lives the qualities which our friends of to-day are manifesting in many a trying place.

THE SANCTUARY OF MISSIONS

O GOD, our help in ages past,
Our hope for years to come,
Be Thou our guide while life shall
last,
And our eternal home.

—*Isaac Watts.*

O TEACH us to number our
days: that we may apply
our hearts unto wisdom."—Psa. xc.
12.

THANKSGIVINGS

"We thank Thee"—
For the memories of "the days of
old, and the years that are past."
For the opportunities of growth
and service which await us in the
New Year.
For the good witness borne to
Thy Truth by our mission in Brazil.
(Page 16.)
For the work of faithful men in
the religious upbuilding of the great
Northwest. (Page 21.)
For our opportunities to protect
and strengthen Thy little ones, and
to save by Thy word of power the
backward peoples of the earth.
(Pages 26 and 36.)
For the way in which Thou dost
still work with Thy messengers,
"confirming the word with signs fol-
lowing." (Pages 35 and 42.)
For the great awakening to re-
sponsibility among Christian laymen. (Page 44.)

INTERCESSIONS

"That it may please Thee"—
To use us during the coming year
as instruments whereby Thou wilt
bring "light to them that sit in darkness, and guide their feet into the
way of peace."
To bring in "the year of Thy redeemed," and to hasten Thy Kingdom.
So to stir the hearts of Thy people that they may gladly give to
Thy messengers the equipment
which shall aid them in accomplishing Thy work.

To cheer the hearts of all those
who preach Thy Gospel everywhere
—especially Thy servants in the Republic of Brazil.
To protect the defenceless and
strengthen the weak and the
tempted, softening the hearts of
those who do them wrong. (Page
28.)
To lead those who teach the
young into a better knowledge of
and zeal for the establishment of
Thy Kingdom in all the earth.
(Page 32.)
To move many to offer themselves as heralds of the glad tidings
of the Incarnate Christ.

PRAYERS

FOR THE NEW YEAR

O LORD JESUS CHRIST, we
offer Thee ourselves and
all that we are and have. We
beseech Thee to use our poverty,
our ignorance and our weakness. Come Thou, and rule in all
our hearts by Thy sacred presence,
making us to depart from sin and to
be wholly Thine; and may Thy
Kingdom grow in our hearts day by
day, Who livest and reignest with
the Father and the Holy Ghost, One
God world without end. *Amen.*"

O GOD of endless years; Give
to each of us, in this little
day of life which remains, some
share in the working out of Thy
eternal purposes for men. Show us
where we may stand in the battle,
and arm us for the fight. Fill our
weakness with Thy strength; touch
our hearts with Thy love; gird us
with a measure of Thy great patience, and cheer us with the confidence of final victory through
Thee. That so, through the life
which we now live in the flesh, there
may shine some token of Thy presence; to our own eternal benefit and
to the blessing of our fellow-men;
through Him Who is the Captain of
our Salvation, and the rich reward
of those who give their lives to
Him, Thy Son, Jesus Christ, our
Lord.

The great charm of the Passeio Publico is a broad promenade built up along the water's edge

BRAZIL AND OUR MISSION

By Bishop L. L. Kinsolving

BRAZIL is the largest of the South American republics and covers an area equal to that of the United States of America plus another Texas.

It was discovered in 1500 by Pedro Alvares Cabral soon after the first discovery of the continent, and was ceded to Portugal, partly by right of discovery, partly by a papal decree which gave all land to the west of a certain meridian to Spain, all east to Portugal. Consequently the language of Brazil is Portuguese, not Spanish, as is the case with all the other South American republics.

Settlements were made very early along the coast, that at Bahia dating from 1532, more than thirty years before St. Augustine was founded by the Spanish, and three-fourths of a century before the English came to Jamestown.

Slavery was introduced early into Brazil, and there was always a great deal of intermarriage between the Portuguese settlers and the aboriginal Indians and the Negroes. The Indians are now pushed back into the interior and number about a million of the 16,000,000 of the population of Brazil.

Brazil was a Portuguese colony until 1821, when she declared her independence and afterward invited a member of the Royal House of Bragança to be her king. During her colonial period the Dutch tried to establish colonies in the North, but were driven out, also the Spanish Jesuits in the South. There was in Rio Bay an attempted Huguenot settlement headed by the Marquis de Villegaignon, which was entirely unsuccessful, so that Brazil remained in the hands of the Portuguese. During the Napoleonic wars the court of Portugal established itself in Brazil, where it continued until the peninsula was free from the Corsican's sway.

(13)

Brazil had two emperors: Dom Pedro I. and Dom Pedro II.—the last being a most liberal ruler, deeply interested in the progress of his people, who introduced many reforms and innovations. Slavery was abolished in 1870. At first only those born after a certain date were to be free, but later all were emancipated, no compensation being made their owners; which measure, being the pet scheme of the Princess Isabella, Dom Pedro's heir, is said by many to be the chief cause of the revolt against the throne in 1889, which resulted in the banishment of the royal family from Brazil and the establishment of a republic.

It is the Brazilians' boast that they have never been conquered in warfare. In addition to their colonial warfare, they were victorious during the empire over Paraguay, and showed great bravery, determination and military capacity.

In the early days of the republic there were many short revolutions, for although independence itself was achieved without bloodshed, there was at first much friction between the army and navy, and much political intrigue. Since 1895, however, the government has been stable, the constitution being modelled · after that of the United States. Many former monarchists have become reconciled to the existing order and are holding prominent positions under the government, notably Sr. Joaquim Nabuco, Ambassador at Washington, and Barão do Rio Branco, the Secretary of State in this and a former cabinet.

Geographical Features

Brazil is one of the richest countries of the world in natural advantages. She lies between 5° north to 32° south of the equator, the latter being about the latitude of Savannah.

Her products are inexhaustible, the rubber in the Amazon valley supplying a great part of the world's needs. Further down her coast sugar is the export, then coffee, which furnishes two-thirds of that consumed by the world. Further

south still is the great cattle state which furnishes bones, hoofs and hides to Europe and America. Rice and cotton are other exports.

Brazil's mineral wealth has as yet only been touched, gold silver and diamond mines being worked· in the State of Minas Geraes, while coal is found in other States.

Only the fringe of states along the coast have as yet been populated. The interior is a pathless wild, a plateau for the most part, covered with virgin forest abounding in beautiful cabinet woods. Possibly because Brazil has no western coast there is no transcontinental railway and no way of reaching her westernmost State, Matto Grosso, except by boat · down the coast, then up its branch, the Paraguay River. A railway in the direction of Matto Grosso and Goyaz is now projected, however. Most of the travel in Brazil is done by steamer, along the coast, up the rivers and lakes, and sometimes by stage coach and horseback, there being comparatively few railways in the country.

Social and Religious Conditions

To within a few years of the establishment of the republic education was entirely in the hands of the Roman Church, which was the State Church, and there is as yet 80 per cent. of illiteracy. Now, however, a public school system has been established throughout the country, which is not obligatory, but much appreciated.

The Roman Catholic form of the Christian faith has always been the nominal religion of the people. In the old days foreigners desirous of building churches for themselves were only allowed to do so on condition that the building should bear no tower, steeple or bell, and should not be ecclesiastical in appearance. They were also forbidden to proselytize.

Brazilians are extremely patriotic, hospitable and courteous, and conservative

The bamboos here are fifty feet high. Their feathery arms interlock and make regal avenues which shield one from the heat of the sun

to a fault. They have great poetic, musical and oratorical gifts. While proud of their connection with Portugal and her record in furnishing the pathfinders of the seas in olden days, the discoveries of the sea passages round the world to east and west—one voyage being commemorated in that great epic, the Lusiadas of Camoens—the Brazilians are most of all proud of their own country and birthright.

There have been foreign immigrations, notably the German in the State of Rio Grande do Sul, and the Italian in São Paulo, but these become absorbed after the third generation, generally.

Brazilian men often go to Europe and the States to complete their studies, especially the professions. The girls are more often taught at home by foreign governesses and are not required to follow the solid studies very far, though the accomplishments—music, languages, painting—are often kept up after the

girl has finished her course. In a convent school in São Paulo, however, I found a high standard, and girls of fourteen were studying Latin as in the States.

Girls marry young in this tropical country. In the old days eleven and thirteen were not an uncommon age for a bride, but now sixteen, seventeen and eighteen are more usual.

The coast is fringed with picturesque towns of varying size and importance, Rio de Janeiro, the capital, being, by reason of its natural advantages, one of the most beautiful cities in the world. It lies on the shores of a land-locked bay, large enough to anchor all the navies of the nations, and is flanked by a lofty range of mountains of irregular shape, some of them 4,000 feet high, covered with tropical vegetation, and with an atmosphere and coloring like that of Italy. The buildings add much to the picturesqueness, being—as in all

Brazil—of stucco in true rainbow colors —red, pink, blue, green, yellow and white. Brazilians find our towns in the States so "sad looking" they say, being of almost uniform color, and that generally sombre brick.

Other important towns are Pará, at the mouth of the Amazon, Manaos, Bahia, Pernambuco, Santos, São Paulo, Porto Alegre and Rio Grande do Sul, the latter the seaport of the State of the same name.

The Church's Mission in Brazil

In 1889 two young men of the Theological Seminary of Virginia, hearing of the corrupt form of Roman Catholicism practised in Brazil and desirous of offering a purer form of our faith to a people who were being stifled under superstition, volunteered to carry the Church's message to Brazil. They were sent out by the American Church Missionary Society, Auxiliary to the Board of Missions, an organization resembling the missionary societies of our Mother Church of England, with a layman as president, and then supporting missions in Cuba and the domestic fields. This Society was in 1906 taken over with all its responsibilities, by the Board of Missions. The two young men were the Rev. J. W. Morris and the Rev. L. L. Kinsolving, the latter of whom was in 1899 consecrated first bishop to Brazil.

They found spiritual affairs worse even than reported—an immoral and negligent priesthood; the grossest superstition among the adherents to the Roman Catholic Church, who. in their worship of the *images* of their patron saints and of the Virgin were almost as literally "bowing down to wood and stone" as any pagan in the Orient; an appalling percentage of illegitimacy, caused in large measure by the enormous marriage fees exacted by the clergy; and among the educated classes, especially among the men, a complete indifference to things spiritual, the philosophy of Auguste Comte being substituted for religion, and in many cases free-masonry

taking its place while spiritualism was making an active propaganda.

Large churches were scattered through the land, built by the government during the empire, but rarely were they frequented except for some "festa" (festival), while more rarely still was the Gospel of Christ preached from the pulpits. There were no Sunday-schools for the instruction of the young, the Bible was a forbidden book—only a few years ago there was an "*auto de fé*" of Bibles in the public square of Pernambuco, ordered by the Roman archbishop.

The two pioneer missionaries on arriving in Brazil, spent six months in a little interior town in São Paulo, living in a Brazilian family to learn the language, themselves the only English-speaking people in the place. They received much kindness at the hands of the Presbyterian missionaries, who advised them to begin work in Porto Alegre, the capital of the State of Rio Grande, where to their knowledge there was no other Protestant work. It was afterward found that a Methodist work had been undertaken there. The Presbyterians had a small work at Rio Grande, the seaport of the State, which two years later was handed over to our missionaries in the truest spirit of Christian unity.

The two pioneers rented a house on a good street of Porto Alegre—a busy city of 100,000 inhabitants, a miniature Rio in beauty—where they fitted up the large front room as a chapel, and then had cards printed announcing that services would be held there on the next Sunday. These they distributed among the neighboring families and then waited for Sunday, praying God's blessing on their efforts.

From this small beginning has grown the present Egreja Brasileira Episcopal (Brazilian Episcopal Church) with its twenty clergy, fifteen of whom are native Brazilians, its communicant list of over 1,000, its baptized members numbering 3,000, its congregations of over 5,000. There are twenty-six mission stations in the State of Rio Grande do Sul, two in

CHURCH AND BISHOP'S HOUSE FROM PUBLIC GARDEN, RIO GRANDE DO SUL

the City of Rio de Janeiro, started this year, Santos and São Paulo only awaiting suitable men to have the Church's standard unfolded there, while a mission in Pernambuco, endorsed by the English Bishop of the Falkland Islands, is asking to be taken over. There are two more now in construction, and a theological school for the training of the native clergy. There are two branches of the Woman's Auxiliary and several branches of the St. Andrew's Brotherhood.

Each year the clergy and lay delegates meet in council, presided over by the bishop, to discuss plans for the further development of the work. Last year the native church contributed over $12,000.

The great need now is for schools—parish schools where the younger generation growing up in the Church may be trained.

Time and space fail to tell the many interesting incidents and encouraging proofs of God's blessing on the work. There has been no proselytizing—there has been no need. No individual undermining of anyone's sincere faith, however mistaken, has been attempted. Only Christ's pure Gospel has been proclaimed, the Bible and Prayer Book have been freely scattered abroad, and the missionaries' homes have been centres of Christian life, that all who will may read.

We count as among the greatest results of our work that the Roman Church in Brazil is no longer so grossly neglectful of her people as before: that where our clergy have their homes, public opinion demands that the Roman Catholic priests lead moral lives; that Roman Catholic Sunday-schools have been started; that long silent churches are now open for prayer and praise; that interest in religion is being revived, however slowly and imperfectly, in the Roman form.

And above all we are thankful that no controversy has embittered our nineteen years of work for the Master of Peace and that there has been no cause given to the modern philosophers, infidels and agnostics of Brazil to say, "See how these Christians hate one another!"

AN IDAHO PACK TRAIN ON THE TRAIL

BY TRAIL AND RAIL IN IDAHO

By the Right Reverend James Bowen Funsten

BISHOP OF IDAHO

FORTY-FIVE years have passed since that bright day—made glorious by the sunshine of the far Northwest—when two travellers on horseback, leading their pack animals, passed down the hard trail that follows the Burnt River as it goes through its narrow canyons to the point where it empties into the Snake. Both these travellers were men well on toward middle life. One was Bishop Scott, of Oregon, the other St. Michael Fackler, who was to be the first Church missionary in what is now known as the State of Idaho. It was a hard, dusty journey, full of privations, promising but small returns for strenuous effort. Their objective point was the great mining camp of the Boise basin, in which had gathered a heterogeneous population, and where was located a typical mining town called Idaho City. The discovery of placer gold

in large quantities brought together hundreds of men from all parts of the West. To plant the Church idea in such a community was no easy task, but good Bishop Scott was willing to do his part, though his stay was brief on account of sickness. He left his companion of that journey to do what proved to be his life-work.

There are those still living who love to talk of the godly St. Michael Fackler, and to tell how, from Boise City as a centre, he visited adjacent camps, riding alone across the plains, sleeping on the ground at night, joyfully doing the work of a pioneer missionary. With his own hands he helped to build the little church, still preserved, which was the only church building Bishop Tuttle found in all his great district of Idaho, Montana and Utah when he came to the West in 1867.

(19)

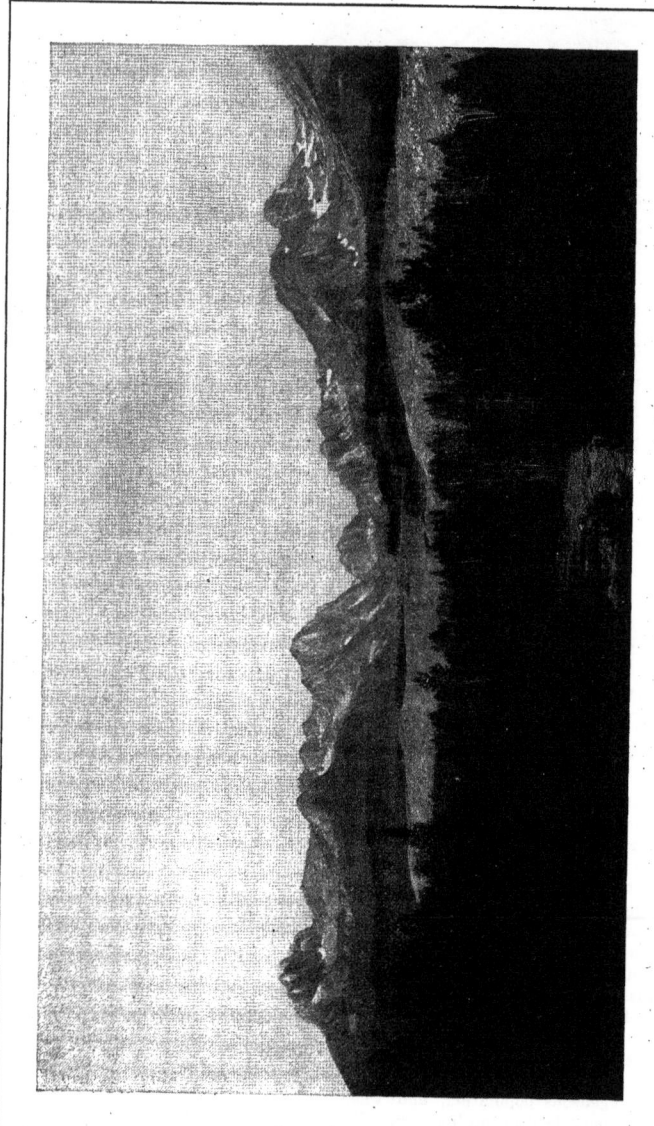

ALONG THE RANGE OF THE SAWTOOTH MOUNTAINS

(20)

It was a day of thrilling adventures, in which one recalls in panoramic form visions of stage-coaches jostling over rough mountain roads; stage drivers, laconic, resourceful, courageous; carrying rugged passengers, a motley crowd of miners, frontiersmen and gamblers, moving about from camp to camp; lonely roadhouses and mining communities; with our sturdy Bishop Tuttle and his little band of workers mingling in the scene, preaching the Gospel, joyfully bearing privations for the Master's sake. The whole work seemed migratory, and the day of permanent things far away.

The larger part of Idaho appeared hopelessly sterile, its miles of sage-brush, like the armies of the desert king, flaunting gray banners of defiance to advancing civilization. Few churches were built in Idaho during those days. Why should they be? The mining camp, with its placer claims, was of necessity largely a temporary community. There were no railroads, and the little hamlets on the stage line did not demand church buildings, so that as late as 1886 all Idaho had only five small, inexpensive churches. Still, Bishop Tuttle and his corps of workers were laying solid foundations. We wish we could mention each one of these men by name, but it is impossible. We must think of them as men with big brains, big hearts, and fine digestion.

Under Bishop Scott the Church was on horseback, and moved along the trail to do her mission; under Bishop Tuttle she commences to ride onward in the stage-coach; and now she is rolling over mountain and plain by the force of the majestic steam engine. She began with a few scattered villages; now she is trying to reach the communities that have grown out of the development of the marvellous resources of the great West.

In 1887 Bishop Talbot was placed in charge of Wyoming and Idaho. It was a vast Rocky Mountain field, with but a comparatively small population. The work each year required hundreds of miles of travel, and it still had enough of pioneer conditions in staging and horseback riding to tax to the limit even Bishop Talbot's splendid physique. He remained in charge of the field for eleven years, establishing mission churches in many of the small railroad towns that had grown up along the Oregon Short Line in southern Idaho, and in the more permanent mining camps, and some of the small towns of northern Idaho. He also started St. Margaret's School for girls, and very wisely chose Miss Frances M. Buchan, an educator of unusual ability, as the first principal. Bishop Talbot's activity, enterprise and ability are too well known in the Church to need any comment here. While his residence was at Laramie, 800 miles east of Boise City, his work for Idaho and that of those missionaries who helped him is gratefully remembered, and without it our present work, difficult as it now is, would be even more perplexing.

Up to the period of the Spanish-American War in 1898, American Church life was comparatively insulated. Some interest was manifested in the foreign field, but the great West, into which thousands of people were pouring, occupied a large place in the public mind, and gathered around itself an atmosphere of romance, adventure and achievement, which made it a matter of deep interest to the people of the East. Weird stories, humorous situations, grotesque incongruities, as brought out in the story of the missionary, won many a friend to the cause of missions in the West. But when America came into its world-wide position, and had its island possessions to deal with, a new chapter opened, in which the picturesqueness and the need of foreign lands claimed a large hold on the attention of the Church. This is as it should be, for every part of our country will get its uplift from the advance of the whole, and it would be fatal to any Church to narrow its sympathies, as it would also to any part of the world to be the favored child in the Church family. Nevertheless, we are passing through a great constructive age in the West at this time, which probably more than ever

The Government is doing such things as this for the irrigation of Idaho

demands the loving care and helpfulness of the Church in the older communities of the country.

From a religious standpoint the work is as strenuous in the West at this time as in the foreign field; the cost of living has in many cases doubled in the last ten years, while all the prosperity of America has left missionaries' salaries all about the same. The problem is a very difficult one for bishop and missionaries, but we must make the best of our conditions and do our duty. We shall for a few years have to struggle with the financial and other problems growing out of the frontier conditions of the country and the comparatively small number of people interested in the Church; but let it be remembered that we will surely, if we are persevering, get a large control over coming generations. These will love the Church and be loyal supporters.

So much has been said of the wonderful development of the West in recent years that some of the earnest Church people of the East have felt disposed to diminish their gifts to the great western home mission field. But speaking from my experience in Idaho—applicable, I know, to every western field and missionary bishop—it is absolutely necessary to have liberal help for a few years to come, until things can be gotten upon a more solid foundation. Whatever our theories may be of the case, there is not a single one of us but feels the tremendous weight of responsibility in this newer part of America, where well-equipped towns, with large mercantile establishments and often good public schools, are rising up in a comparatively short time from the arid plains, brought into being by the magic touch of irrigation. But we must not estimate financial resources available for the Church on the basis of the picturesque magazine article. If I could get local offerings on the basis of western optimism my burdens would be far lighter. The truth is that most of our people are comparatively new to the

(22)

country, and the bishop's greatest opportunity is generally where he has to deal with the man who has a desert homestead, or the people who have large families and small salaries, or professional people just starting in life — people living under conditions where their incomes are small and living expenses large, and from whom it is impossible to expect what is needed to erect in their community at once a church and rectory, and also to support a clergyman to minister among them.

For example, in one section where there has been a great reclamation work done by the Government, and large irrigation plants introduced by private enterprise, ten towns have grown up in the last seven years. I have been forced to see to the erection of seven buildings in that section, and we have now three clergymen, who have to be partly supported, laboring there among the people. Every missionary put in the field is a good investment for the Church, because he wins his own way into the hearts of the people, and thus links the community to Christ and His Church. It is a false economy at this day of wonderful opportunities to withhold men and money if we are going to be in earnest with our home missionary work.

Speaking of Idaho in particular, though by the blessing of God we have met with some success, it is still a great pioneer mission field, in which bishop and missionaries alike must toil on with slow and painful steps in the path of progress. The towns are small; incomes are often inadequate; the people preoccupied with worldly things, a few of them bringing a religious taste cultivated in a great city, and developed with the environment of some splendid plant, into the narrow surroundings of a western village, torturing with unreasonable idealism some faithful minister who is trying to do his best.

We have to work with the conditions suggested by the romantic pursuits of ranchers and cowboys, of sheep-herders and miners, of forest-rangers and soldiers, Mormons and Indians, of young men from the East in search of experience, of merchants who have moved in with their families to try their fortunes in a new country—all thoroughly American life, with its vigor and its defects, and with its future of great promise in a business way.

Along the educational line we have our St. Margaret's School for girls, in which last year we had 158 enrolled. Young girls come to the institution from

ST. MARGARET'S SCHOOL, BOISE

the ranches and from the mines. They come to find a new vision of womanhood and grasp with their young hands the torch of religion with which to light their paths. They become our missionaries, our Churchwomen, our Christian mothers, our Sunday-school superintendents and organists. The school has been more than doubled in size; the debt for construction which I found upon it has been paid, but we need scholarships to help some of these young girls; we need money to pay for absolutely necessary additions and better equipment. We need also the gift of a chapel for the services to be rendered with the solemnity that cannot be obtained in a study-hall.

The hospital is another way in which we are trying to meet the mission problem. St. Luke's Hospital and Nurses' Training School at Boise, Ida., was started seven years ago. No one can realize the struggle we have had to maintain this institution, yet we have taken care of 3,000 people; we have erected the buildings, where there are fifty beds, and where we have had under our training in the nurses' school twenty-five young Idaho women who are giving their lives to the cause of nursing. The work is widening every day, but its widening responsibility compels me to think of the enlargement of its resources. The hospital needs another cottage that will cost at least $5,000; it needs three or four beds endowed after the manner of the one

given by that splendid Churchwoman of Cincinnati, which meant a $5,000 endowment. An elevator was needed, but more than half of its cost has been supplied.

We have also to deal with the Indian problem. Our work among the Shoshones and Bannocks at Fort Hall Reservation is most interesting, and needs the sympathy of the Church as a whole, but we cannot treat of this part of the field in the present article.

We have twenty clergymen where we had only half that number a few years ago. Forty buildings have gone up, most of them without debt. Our communicants have increased, and our offerings have multiplied many times. But these figures are valuable only by comparison. The work in the great new State of Idaho has just begun. A railroad man said to me some time ago: "Idaho is destined to be one of the greatest States west of the Mississippi." Since then in the southern part of Idaho, which is as large as the State of New York, the whole valley of the Snake is being developed by governmental reclamation, and the effect of irrigation and electric power has meant the awakening of a new life, and a promise of the growth of the small towns that are now being planted into important centres of population in the near future. The central part of Idaho, with its mighty mountains, rising up in some cases to 12,000 or 14,000 feet, has rich mineral deposits, and its uplands

(24)

TWIN FALLS, IDAHO

An example of the magnificent natural resources in the way of water-power which make the future of Idaho so promising

are being used for summer pastures of cattle and sheep, and here in winter are laid up the treasures of snow, which, melting, gives the water in summer for irrigation. This part of Idaho, with its wonderful mountain scenery, has an area which is equal to the State of West Virginia; while "the Panhandle," in which are many thriving little towns, is largely covered with timber, though it also has some of the best agricultural and mining districts in the whole state. Counting from the Salmon River north to the British Columbia line, the area of this part of Idaho would be about twice the size of the State of Maryland, making the whole State twice as large as Pennsylvania.

Every year with the increase of railroad facilities our opportunity will grow greater and greater of accomplishing what we all long to see—a strong, self-supporting work in this new state of the great Northwest, which promises to be the home of a vigorous and prosperous type of American people. We believe in this future. During these days of foundation-laying in Idaho, and in all the

great states of the new West, we need the sympathy, prayers and material aid of the people of the Church.

ON THE BIG LOST RIVER

Chief Engineer Henderson, of the Big Lost River proje t, Judge Malsbary, of Cincinnati, and the Bishop of Idaho

THE CURE FOR DISCOURAGEMENT

By *Archdeacon Stuck*

Tortella Hall, Nenana

WHEN I come away from a visit to Nenana and sit down to write about it, I have to watch my words. If I gave myself free rein I should grow extravagant and those who read would discount what I write. I itched to be at it at Tanana, so soon as I got to my typewriter again, but I restrained myself and held off these two months, and am set down to it now in the quiet of my fine new study at Fort Yukon, furnished beyond anything you ever saw at an Alaskan mission, out of money given specifically "for Miss Woods's comfort"! She bought the stuff herself—and what can I do about it?

Let us go back to St. Mark's mission and school at Nenana. Here are twenty odd children, of both sexes and all ages, most of them full-blooded natives, some of them half-breeds. The girls have a large dormitory, with neat cots set in a row, on one side of the house, and the boys have a room just like it on the other side of the house, and underneath the dormitories is one very large dining and living room, with kitchen and store-room at one end and Miss Farthing's room and the teacher's room at the other end. Put a wide porch all round and that is all

there is to "Tortella Hall." It is well planned and well built, and is far and away the most convenient and spacious structure of its kind in all our mission work. It was built by the Rev. Mr. Betticher, our missionary in charge of the Tanana valley, out of the $5,000 given from the Men's Thank-offering.

I have told all this in as few words as possible because it is the background of the story, and, while backgrounds may not be interesting, they are necessary. Stories about people are always more or less interesting, and this is a story about a person. "Tortella Hall" and the thicket of spruce around it, and the dormitories and the children, and the native village hard by, and the Tanana River running swiftly in front, and the great bluffs across the river, from which on a clear day you can get a glorious view of Mt. McKinley—these are the setting of the story.

It is a principle of my philosophy that there is no such thing as an indispensable person, so I suppose if there had been no Miss Farthing the Nenana enterprise would have managed without her; but sometimes one is confronted with facts that jar one's philosophy. It is hard to think of anyone else doing that work, hard to believe that anyone else could do that work as well as she does it. If there is any greater joy than knowing that one is exactly where one belongs, and that the work one is doing is exactly the work that one is best suited to, then I hope that some day Miss Farthing may have that greater joy, whatever it may be. For all who have been to Nenana know that she is the right woman in the right place, with her hands full and overflowing, of just the tasks she loves to do most, and knows how to do best.

Since the word "savage" comes from the Latin *"silva,"* a tree, and meant originally simply "forest dweller," I have no etymological objection to the term as applied to the Yukon Indian. In that sense I am a savage myself a great part of the year. But if the term is used with its ordinary implication of ferocity and bloodthirstiness, then it is absurd to apply it to them. They are not, and never were, I am convinced, ferocious or brutal, whoever may write to the contrary notwithstanding. They are a gentle and mild people. But, of course, they are an uncultivated and unpolished people also. You must not look for urbanity in *any* sort of savage, you know. Naturally they have none of the white man's politeness. Their own language has no terms of courtesy. In this part of the river the native word for "thank you" is *merci*, which they learned from the French Canadian *voyageurs*, who were the first white men to make their acquaintance. In their own tongue is no such expression. As you would expect, they are for the most part stolid and rough and without any refinements of speech or personal habit. A hasty observer might say of them as the young midshipman said of

Justin, the oldest boy of the mission

the natives of a Fiji island whose manners and customs he was sent to report on: "Manners they have none, and their customs are beastly."

But I do not think that you would find a higher degree of politeness and courtesy in any similar number of white children in any school anywhere than you will find amongst Miss Farthing's children at Nenana. That is the first thing that strikes a visitor. They are taught and trained to be polite. If you rose to leave the room and there was any child, even the youngest, present, he would dart ahead and open the door for you before you could get to it, and stand with a smile until you had passed out. If you were a guest at her table you would find

A corner of the boys' dormitory

the boys jealous which one should have the honor of putting your chair beneath you when you seated yourself. If you spoke to one of the boys outdoors he would take off his cap when he replied. When you arose you would be greeted with a cheery "Good morning" from every member of the household, and at night each one would come and take leave of you with a smiling, if shy, "Good night." To find children thus transformed, to find those who by nature and early breeding are such strangers to all the little courtesies of life, now so naturally and spontaneously courteous, is altogether charming,

The secret of it and the motive of it is the secret and the motive of all true politeness—love. The devotion with which Miss Farthing inspires these boys and girls of the forest is wonderful. Great hulking fellows of sixteen and seventeen and eighteen, wild-run all their lives, hunters with a tale of big game to their credit, some of them, that would make an Eastern sportsman envious, unaccustomed to any restraint at all and commonly chafing at the slightest, fly at her word, at her look, to do her bidding.

"Thy Servant David," with the cat that froze its ears

They fawn upon her with their eyes. They are the knights and champions of this gray-haired lady, and would serve her on bended knee like a princess of the olden time, if she would let them. I never go there but I marvel at it. I have never seen anything just like it in my life before. What a supreme power is inherent in a gentlewoman when it is consecrated by love!

And how they learn, with the great incentive in the breast of each one of them, to please Miss Farthing! They will write you letters, if you will give them any encouragement, that will surprise you. I hear from them all the time and never fail to answer them, whether my important "outside" letters get answered or not. They give me chronicles of their little world with all the gusto of new-found expression. "Justin has killed another moose." Good news that for the mission larder, somewhat of the slimmest this winter with so many unexpected additions to the family; meat for nigh a month, I judge. "David" ("Thy Servant David" he is called at the mission, from a verse in the psalter the day he arrived) "has learned to walk on his hands." That is a legacy from Dr. Burke's visit last summer. "Johnny Lije has got sword and is drilling boys." Johnny Lije is from Tanana, near the military post of Fort Gibbon, and Johnny Lije is evidently enamored of the army.

"Timothy ran away from school to village, so Miss Farthing she tie him with little rope and another boy he lead him to school." That little scamp! I gathered him up with three others, nay, four, and took him to Nenana and turned him over to Miss Farthing "for keeps"—the most roguish little rascal, with big black laughing eyes and dimples in his cheeks, and his mouth full of cursing and swearing that he does not know the meaning of. Poor little wild half-breed! I don't know whether he is six or seven, and his mother doesn't either. I don't know who his father was, and his mother doesn't either. Watch his transformation! Red pepper on his tongue every time he says a naughty word—and by this time he has forgotten them all. "To-night he ask Miss Farthing to take off rope, he no more run away." I am looking forward to hugging the dear little chap and singing "I went to the animal fair" to him, which was his delight on the way up.

What a problem our half-breeds are! And what a damning responsibility these reckless white men have hanging over

Photo by Arthur Wright

SOME OF THE BOYS AND GIRLS

SOME OF THE GIRLS AT PLAY
Laura, "the little mother," holding the swing, is the first girl Miss Farthing took

their heads. I take shame to myself when I see a child with white blood in his veins growing up in more utter neglect and ignorance than even the Indian children. I picked up one on the Yukon this summer, a gentle, shy, well-grown lad of sixteen, who can neither read nor write. Yes, I sent him to Nenana too, and I will venture that by this time he is one of Miss Farthing's most loyal henchmen. An ever-generous lady in Alaska, who used to be connected with our mission work, gave me $50 toward his support, which is half what he will cost us this year. And a kindly steamboat agent gave him free passage to the school, that the *Pelican* might not have to make another trip up there with him, and burn 100 gallons of gasoline at sixty-five cents a gallon.

Can you understand my strong desire and temptation every time I find a bright, neglected child with no possible useful or honorable future, to snatch him or her up and add another to the family at Nenana? There is no other school to which they can be sent. Anvik is 500 miles away and, for the Middle River, practically out of the question. Until that school was started at Nenana there was practically no place where a child could be sent, save here and there to a missionary's own family. Moreover, I covet for them just the influence that dominates that school, which I have tried to give some conception of.

I go here and there amongst our native peoples and my heart is sore at what I see and hear. The progressive drunkenness and corruption, the weakness in the face of temptation, the undermining of the stalwart qualities of the Indian nature—these things are thrust upon my notice at place after place. And sometimes I get discouraged. Sometimes the prospect looks gloomy and my heart sinks. Then I go to Nenana. And at Nenana I find the Cure for Discouragement. I find boys who know what temptation is and who have yielded to it again and again, now resolutely resisting it. I find girls training to be virtuous women and good housewives, and boys with their ideal of womankind so raised that they will never be content to wive with girls who are are not chaste and domesticated. I find the precepts of Christian morality so carefully instilled that the tone of the children themselves reflects them. No foolish attempt is here to make imitation white men and white

(29)

The smaller boys at St. Mark's, Nenana

women out of children whom God made Indian; no foolish attempt to wean them away from their natural food and their natural avocations. Good Indians—that is the aim; clean, God-fearing, self-respecting Alaskan Indians.

For it is my firm and sustaining conviction that God desires to keep His Indians on the Yukon River, and that He has sent us into the land to save them alive for Him. As I see it, their only chance of salvation lies with us. I believe the same conviction animates the heart and consecrates the labor of almost every worker in the Alaskan mission field. We feel that we are charged with the future of these people. And I tell Miss Farthing that she and her school are the hope of the Middle Yukon Indian —the "Indian Hope." I wrote to the committee of the Thank-offering fund after my first visit to the school that "Wisdom is justified of her children." Now I write to them that they "builded better than they knew" or dreamed.

In about three weeks' time I start out once more on my winter journey, and I am glad of it and looking forward to it. I am afraid that all this unwonted luxury of Morris chairs and "mission" furniture, and carpet on the floor, and cathedral etchings on the wall, and gasoline-

pressure-lighting-system that turns night into day, will undermine my constitution and make me languid and self-indulgent again. I am glad that they are here, but I am glad to get away from them. Arthur will come back from Tanana with my dogs over the first good ice, and I strike across the wilderness 200 miles to the Koyukuk River, and I hope to spend Christmas at the Allakaket. You may know I am looking forward to that.

The next place I am keenly looking forward to is Nenana. I want to see those boys gather round Miss Farthing again with the love in their eyes. I want to hear their fresh voices raised again, clear and sweet, in the evening hymn. I want to hear them join intelligently and reverently in the family worship. I want to hear Justin tell how he killed that moose. I want to see Johnny Lije drilling his recruits. I want to snatch up Timothy and "Thy servant David" and the other little chaps and romp all over the house with them. I want to see that old chief Henry, who stubbornly opposed Miss Farthing and "made medicine" against her, eating out of her hand.

Did you hear how she invaded the midnight pavilion of the old conjurer in the midst of his conjurations—the very figure of Righteous Indignation—and tossed his paraphernalia outside and laid her trusty stick across the backs of those present, till they fled, panic-stricken? I make no apology that I thought of our Lord and the scourge of small cords He used on occasion, when I heard of it. It "hath given such a blow as shall not be healed" to the lingering survival of that tyrannical superstition. The younger villagers chuckle over the jest of it to this day. Does anybody think it was unladylike? On the contrary, it was precisely a thing that

only a gentlewoman could do. No man living could have done it with like effect, nor any woman save one of her complete self-possession and devotion.

I hope to get to Nenana sometime in February—but you never can tell. If anyone would like to hear more about Nenana and the "Indian Hope" that it enshrines, I shall have lots of news then. Meanwhile the children are eating up the "grub" fast, and I hope those who back our work with their purses and their prayers will not forget them.

MISSION STUDY IN THE SUNDAY-SCHOOL

By the Reverend Malcolm Taylor

THE place that the study of missions will occupy in the Sunday-school will depend upon the ideal that underlies the work of the school. Is the purpose of the school to give information regarding the facts and teachings of the Bible and the Church, or does it seek by means of such instruction to lead up to confirmation and active and intelligent membership in the Church, or has it some goal beyond confirmation? The ideal which underlies the thought of this paper, and which is being worked out in the school whose work is here described, is that the goal of Sunday-school instruction is the making of missionaries, the development in its members of the missionary spirit. For the missionary spirit, as here conceived, is the apex of the pyramid of the Christian life, and toward its development all lines of instruction, and the motives for Christian profession as presented in confirmation, should be made to converge.

How, then, shall such an ideal be attained? Naturally, by a curriculum that has the missionary motive continually in mind. But there is no such curriculum. Our Sunday-school text-books and leaflets are not written from the missionary point of view. There are definite courses in missions, but no system of lessons with the mis-

sionary spirit permeating all the courses. Such a curriculum we eagerly look for; but in the meantime, with the best graded courses now available, how may the study of missions be made effective so as to produce in the scholar the conviction that the Christian profession and missionary activity are one, and lead him to an intelligent and ardent love for the missionary work of the Church?

In the school under discussion there is, in the first place, regular missionary instruction on one Sunday in each month by the superintendent and others from the platform to the Primary, Junior and Senior departments. This instruction is given at the close of the lesson for about fifteen minutes and follows a carefully devised plan, the course being varied from year to year, and including missionary biography, survey of particular fields, etc. The prayers and hymns on that Sunday are missionary, and the day is clearly marked in its emphasis. In addition, special offerings are taken for missionary work, scholarships in mission schools are undertaken, and the mite-box Lenten offering is emphasized.

These methods are simple and have a permanent place in the ideal school; but if missionary instruction is to be thorough it must be made a part of the work of the teacher. Two methods have been tried, both of which have worked well. One is to give the teacher a text-book on missions, divided into short lessons, one of which is to be taught each Sunday after the regular lesson for the day. The difficulty here is the fact that many teachers have neither the necessary information nor love for missions to make such teaching effective. If this difficulty can be overcome this method is, I believe, the best. The other alternative is the special mission teacher who takes one class each Sunday and gives in place of the regular lesson a lesson on missions, following, of course, a definite scheme, with lessons adapted to the varying ages of the scholars. Here the teacher has the entire recitation period at his disposal; but the instruction is not continuous and tends to be regarded as merely "an extra" and not of fundamental importance. It is possible to combine these two methods by having a special teacher for certain grades and throwing the responsibility upon the regular teachers in other grades.

The missionary teacher should be specially prepared. In the school described three of the teachers have been sent to the summer conference at Silver Bay, and have in the ten days of study there found a training which has made them very effective teachers of missions. We have discovered at Silver Bay the key to the chief difficulty—the lack of knowledge on the part of the teachers. This is equally true of superintendents, whose instruction to the school as a whole will be limited in its effectiveness by their own knowledge and enthusiasm regarding the missionary work of the Church.

By these methods, all of which have been tested—missionary instruction by the superintendent, the intelligent use of offerings, instruction by special teachers and missionary instruction by the regular teachers—the missionary motive may be given something of its rightful place in the work of the school. But all such instruction should find practical application in the daily life of the scholars. Nor should their participation in missionary service be confined to gifts of

money, valuable as such gifts are when accompanied by adequate instruction as to the needs and character of the work for which the money is given. To move the scholars to feelings of pity, or sympathy, or aspiration, by presenting the needs, the heroism or the sacrifice of Christian missions, and yet fail to give these feelings expression in action, is to invite ultimate indifference and seriously to cripple the child's own emotional life.

It is here that missionary instruction needs the aid of psychology. It must seek to evoke self-activity and afford an opportunity to express in action every ideal that is seen. The ways in which this may be done vary so greatly with the conditions of any particular school that definite suggestions are difficult, and the applications of the missionary ideals must be left largely to the inventiveness of the individual teachers and superintendents. Missionary organizations which undertake definite work are always helpful. The Junior Auxiliary—or, for boys, an organization like the Brotherhood of St. Paul or the Knights of King Arthur—offers splendid opportunities. Then there are visits to sick companions, to the lonely or unfortunate; helpfulness in the homes and other forms of active missionary work.

Confirmation in such a school would be presented as involving consecration to the missionary ideal, and in such a way that the Christian profession and missionary activity are seen to be inseparable. Actual participation in direct missionary work would be held up as the noblest expression of discipleship.

Such a school, with the missionary ideal as the centre of all its teaching and activity, may or may not make missionaries; but at least it will make that fundamental identification of the Christian profession with missionary activity which was so characteristic of the teaching of Christ; for the spirit of Christ is the spirit of missions, and the more our children are filled with missionary enthusiasm the more like Him will they become.

A TYPICAL CHINESE HOUSEBOAT

These boats are used everywhere for navigating the rivers and inland canals of China

COUNTRY WORK FROM A HOUSEBOAT

By the Reverend Henry A. McNulty

ONE who has never had the opportunity of being brought into close contact with either the Chinese country or people may think that both are dull and uninteresting. But such an one has never had the privilege of a house-boat trip through the network of canals to the north of Soochow, nor the chance of meeting the Chinese at close range—else his opinion both of country and people would be utterly altered. The country is very beautiful and the people bright, full of energy, and altogether good fun, so that a halo is not necessary for one who undertakes work among them. At least such was the vivid impression left on a newcomer in the Chinese mission after a five-days' house-boat trip in May with the Rev. R. C. Wilson. Mr. Wilson has under his charge some forty towns and villages in the country above Soochow, and these he visits in turn, covering as much territory as he can by a trip of five days in each week.

We started from Soochow on Saturday and were towed by a puffing little steamer to the picturesque walled city of Zangzok, where in a Chinese house we spent Sunday. Not idly, either, on Mr. Wilson's part; for the city of Zangzok is really the centre from which he works among the villages; and here first Mr. Wilson's two guests (the Rev. Mr. Sinclair from Yangchow had joined us to study Mr. Wilson's methods of reaching the country people)—here first we caught a glimpse of his way of working. While he himself preached or celebrated the Holy Communion, he none the less threw a great part of the responsibility on the catechists with whom he was working, giving them a chance to assist in the services and to address the people, and to talk over with them their difficulties or encouragements. It was never Mr. Wil-

son first and the work second; but everywhere the Master's message presented by
the Chinese to their own people, Mr.
Wilson meantime watching over and
encouraging them as he trained them to
bear their own burdens.

At Zangzok we hired a house-boat for
the rest of our trip. This sounds more
aristocratic than it really is. The fact is
that this is positively the only way of
travelling in the country districts of the
Yang-tse delta, as there are no roads and,
therefore, no means of conveyance except
boats. This sounds almost impossible,
but it is not, as the canals are everywhere. True, there are paths through the
richly-cultivated fields; but these are
merely for the convenience of the farmers on whose land the crops are growing.

Our party as we left Zangzok consisted
of two Chinese—one a catechist and the
other a colporteur; ourselves—three foreigners—the two boatmen and our cook.
The Chinese workers occupied the first
section of our thirty-foot boat, the foreigners the second, the cook and boatmen
the third. And so we travelled, taking
our meals and sleeping on board; sometimes riding on the boat, sometimes
walking through the bridle-paths. We
slept on the floor of the boat; and the
meals we ate were cooked in a Standard
Oil five-gallon can, which our ingenious
cook had transformed in a marvellous
way into a cooking range, producing
therefrom delicious biscuits and many
other good things. The country through
which we travelled was wonderfully
green and fertile. It was too early for
the rice, but grain and beans and
many other things were growing on
all sides, interspersed with great
groves of mulberry trees; for this
country is the centre of the silk
industry and the mulberry leaves were
just beginning to be stripped from the
trees to feed the as yet tiny but voracious
silk-worms. From the flat valley rose the
curious trello; while every little while
some old picturesque stone bridge, with
the trees on either bank, would add a
beauty to the picture that one does not

pressing upon us, we would sing some hymns together. The preaching followed this, our Chinese helpers sometimes being the only ones to speak; but generally Mr. Wilson would begin or close the meeting by some message that it was in his heart to give; while Mr. Sinclair would often speak, in spite of the fact that the Mandarin dialect was not wholly understood by the people of this section of China. At times Mr. Wilson would ask me to say a word in English, which he would interpret to the wondering crowd around us.

One had to be in the midst of it all in order fully to appreciate it: the eager, listening faces; the little children who would crowd in to touch the violin, or stand staring within two feet of us; the earnest appeals from the Chinese speakers—for one can tell something of that, even though the words are still quite unintelligible; the more than happy faces of the Christians in the towns where a little Christian community was being built up; all and everything gave an inspiration to the scene that can hardly be imagined by those who have not seen it. But it did not, in face of those listening crowds and Chinese Christians, seem a hopeless task to make them at last learn to love the truth of the Gospel message. For there was no opposition, no sneering. It seemed as though they greatly wanted to hear what it was these three strange foreigners and their companions had to bring to them. The contrast was great between this message and that which must have come to the crowds of worshippers we saw in a Buddhist temple on the top of a beautiful hill which we climbed the third day. Such hideous idols, such filth and squalor; and yet a desire for something which religion alone could express, as the women in priestess' garb and bound feet prostrated themselves again and again before the idols. What they were seeking, and seeking at no little cost, was that which Mr. Wilson was striving with all his might to bring to them.

Striving and succeeding, too, for in the village at the foot of this same mountain we held a service; and here, with the crowd still pressing around—some from mere curiosity, but many from a deeper sense of what it all meant—two men came forward and were received by baptism into Christ's Church; while the other Christians, some of whom had come from miles and miles away to be present at the service, lifted up their voices in thanksgiving to God. It did not matter that the tune they sang had no note of what we should call music; it was truest music in the Heavenly Father's ears. 36039

And once more, in the last village which it was our privilege to visit on this trip, the Church's life was manifested. Here we had a kind of chapel—how different from chapels at home it would be hard to explain. But in this chapel all preparations had been made for a Communion service. Amid the crowds upon crowds who had come, the Gospel message was first preached; then hymns were sung. I never heard such strange singing; it had no tune, and it entirely drowned the violin, yet it did not make one smile—and after that, in perfect silence the people stayed, while Mr. Wilson read the words of the Communion Office, and perhaps fifteen or twenty received from his hands the Bread of Life. It was a fitting climax to this glimpse into real missionary work; for it was truly great work, done quickly but well.

As we took our boat and turned our faces again toward Soochow Mr. Wilson's two guests felt that their eyes had been opened to see great things, and as we sailed homeward that night through the beautiful, peaceful country, it did not seem an impossible dream that the peace of God should, in some not distant day, keep the hearts and minds of these, His so great people, in the knowledge and love of Him and of His Son, Jesus Christ our Lord.

ON THE UPPER NANTAHALA RIVER

IN THE SAPPHIRE COUNTRY

By the Reverend Theodore Andrews

THE Sapphire Country! The very name calls up pictures of rare gems flashing in the sunlight; or it may bring before the mind's eye a glimpse of glorious blue skies, where the light breeze blows the summer clouds across to the bluer mountains in the distance. It is no error to apply this name to Macon County, North Carolina.

About sixty miles southwest of Asheville it lies, encircled by the Blue Ridge and its flanking spurs, the Cowee and Nantahala Mountains; one of the most isolated and yet one of the fairest valleys in the southern Appalachians. The Little Tennessee marks a shining course, flowing northward through the valley. Near the little town of Franklin, the cold waters of the Cullasagee or "Sugar Fork" mingle with the more placid stream. This exuberant stream rises high up on the craggy slopes of Whitesides, and comes roaring down in fall

after fall of unharnessed strength; the upper, or "Dry Falls," where one may walk dry-shod beneath the cataract, being one of the sights of the mountains.

The rocks of the whole region are unusually rich in gems and valuable minerals: Mica, kaolin, talc, corundum and many others almost unique in this country, have been yielded up. The red clay of the valleys is not so good for farming; the real wealth of the soil is in the magnificent timber of the north and west slopes—an asset, sad to relate, that is rapidly being depleted without much regard for the future.

But it is with the people themselves that we have most to do. They are of splendid stock, remarkable even among the sturdy folk of the mountains; their ancestors, of Scotch, English or German descent, wended their way hither from east of the mountains or from Tennessee. And although the Yankee visitor judges by a pretty strict standard, he

(36)

A TYPICAL VIEW OF THE MOUNTAIN COUNTRY

will easily notice the contrast between these comfortable-looking farms and the thin acres of most of the mountain regions. Yet one cannot help feeling here, as elsewhere, that a *little* progress, like a *little* learning, is a dangerous thing.

It was thirty years ago when the Rev. J. A. Deal began the Church's work in this country. Young, enthusiastic, and full of energy, he fought the good fight against obstacles which few to-day can

The Rev. J. A. Deal and his grandson

realize. To-day eight missions exist which are the result of his labors—a chain extending seventy miles from east to west across these mountains. Such a far-reaching group could only be made effective and permanent with the assistance of associate priests. But the field was remote, and assistants, as well as funds for their support, hard to secure; the spiritual care of so many churches in a rugged country, through all kinds of weather, was bound to tell on the health and strength of any man; and to-day several of these churches are closed and silent.

When I came to the field last June, I was struck by the unfailing optimism of the man who had ministered there so long. The attractive though simple church buildings testify to his love for the work of his life. I trust that, under God, this faith may find fruition, and that He will "stablish the thing that He hath wrought in us."

As now constituted, the Franklin Associate Mission comprises six churches; of these one is the colored chapel, and another (All Saints', Irena), is so remote that it cannot be served by the present staff.

St. Agnes's, "our town church," was built in Franklin twenty years before the railroad came. Here, with a population of 800, town conditions and prob-

(37)

St. Agnes's Church, Franklin   *St. John's Church, Nonah*

TWO NORTH CAROLINA MOUNTAIN CHURCHES

lems are already evident; the non-church-going element; the young man with nowhere to spend his evenings; the summer or other transient visitor, who is very apt to seek out our Church, no matter what his affiliation may be at home. All this points the need for some definite institutional work; for Franklin, like so many other Southern country towns, wants just that moral force which only a living, working Church can give.

Five miles south is St. George's, near Prentiss, on the new railroad. Here, in a little frame building in an old field, is one of our most hopeful Church centres. In connection with the church we have a day-school, where some sixty young folk supplement the four months of the district school by four more months with us; our two teachers are full of faith and enthusiasm, and the building is sadly crowded. We are hoping for the $1,000 necessary to put up a school and club house; and then we shall be able to reserve the church building for religious services only. The possibility of a little choir at this mission is not very remote.

Near "Nonah Farm," eight miles west at the foot of the "big mountains," is St. John's. This was Mr. Deal's first work; and his influence may be seen to-day in the lives of many who are not called by our name. But the shifting tides of mountain population have left the little

church building stranded, and the present settlement is a mile to the south. Our faithful communicants have assisted nobly in our necessary removal into new quarters; though many sacred ties bound them to the little building across the creek. More distant still is Ascension Church, at Slagle on the Nantahala River; the permanent population is small, but many summer visitors go there.

The colored work must not be forgotten. There are about 1,000 Negroes in the vicinity of Franklin—a large number for the mountains. At St. Cyprian's Church we have a faithful colored deacon, who not only ministers in the church on Sundays but during the week is in charge of the mission's furniture shop as well. The cabinet-work made here has a local reputation that is all the more well-earned when one realizes that this man knew nothing about carpentry when he first came to take charge of the mission. The mission's day-school is attended by about fifty children.

This is largely a record of schemes and prospects, is it not? But, people of the Church, it is your prayers, your help, your work, which will have part in making such plans into realities; which will enable the mountain people to understand more fully what it means to be "inheritors of the kingdom of heaven." They *will* come to realize it—if *we* do.

NEW BUILDING FOR WOMEN'S WORK, JUST COMPLETED

THE GOSPEL IN WUSIH

By the Reverend G. F. Mosher

THE evangelistic work in Wusih is carried on in the city in four places—the mission compound, two preaching-halls, and the dispensary. The beginning of the future parish centre is the compound, where all services are held in the temporary chapel, and from which the work radiates to the other parts of the city and to the country.

Mr. Tsang and his family live inside the north gate of the city on the main street in a very crowded, busy section. The front of the house is used as a preaching-hall. The house is a wretched one, and if it could be avoided no one would be asked to live there. Moreover, the preaching-hall itself is a small, dismal room, too dark to be used except at night, when it can be lighted with a lamp. And yet, the city is so crowded in that section and it is so difficult, if not impossible, to find buildings for rent that it has not been possible to find a better place without leaving that part of the city entirely—a thing that cannot be thought of, as it is the most important place in Wusih for such work. Mr. Tsang preaches there regularly every night that he is at home, excepting on Sunday.

Mr. Tsu has his quarters in the preaching-hall in about the centre of the city on the street leading to the west gate, which is crowded day and night with passers-by. The building is small, but with only an unmarried man living in it affords very satisfactory quarters. A good-sized room on the street is fitted up as a preaching-hall; the front part of the second floor is divided into two small rooms, one being used as a library and reading-room and the other as a bedroom for any of our people from the country whom Mr. Tsu may wish to keep over night. The hall and reading-room are in constant use, and a number of men have been brought into the Church there this year. Such a reading-room has long been planned for this station,

and the way in which it has been used
since opened has proven its value.

In the dispensary there are prayers
every morning, attended by the doctors
and employees and as many of the patients as are able to come in. Four
times weekly these prayers are led by the
doctors and twice by the evangelistic
staff. There is a catechist specially appointed for work in the dispensary. He
attends every morning and afternoon,
speaking to the in-patients and those
who call for private consultation with
the doctor in the morning, and preaching in the clinic in the afternoon. Mrs:
Sung also frequently attends the clinic
and talks to the women, though her duties as the only Bible-woman in the station prevent her being there daily.

There have been, during the year, two
rather striking cases of whole families
joining the Church because of work done
in the dispensary. A little boy who has
been in St. Andrew's School for some
years lives but a short distance from the
dispensary, His mother was very ill
with chronic malaria—too ill to go to the
dispensary for treatment and too poor
to pay the fees for an out-call. When
Mrs. Sung reported the case to Dr. Lee
he kindly visited the woman in her home
without charge, and gave her both treatment and medicine. She was cured, and
almost immediately afterward she, with
her mother, two daughters and one son,
began coming to church. They have all
been made catechumens, and at Christmas time we hope to have them baptized.
The other case was also brought about
through a little boy: Mrs. Sung helped
to rent a room for him where he could
be near the dispensary and go for daily
treatment. In this way she became acquainted with the family, with the result
that some two weeks ago no less than
ten names were handed in—the boy's
own family, including his father and
mother, with some friends, all of whom
have come frequently to church since.
There seems to be no reason for doubting
that at the expiration of the usual six
months' probation all, or nearly all, of

MRS. TSU, OF LOK-CHUI-JAU, AND HER
DAUGHTER-IN-LAW

The former when very ill greatly desired baptism. Her happiness on receiving it doubtless had much to do with her recovery. The daughter-in-law is also under treatment and nearly well after three operations

amount each week or each month. This is collected by two men appointed for that purpose, and applied as far as it will go on the regular running expenses. At present, the sexton's wages and a few of the lesser expenses are paid from this fund.

During Advent and Lent mite-chests furnished by the Board of Missions are distributed, and the offerings at Christmas are for foreign, and at Easter for domestic missions. At Christmas the apportionment of $20 (Mexican) is first paid, and the balance is then given to some object abroad—this year to St. Augustine's School, Raleigh, N. C. At Easter the bishop is requested to suggest the object to which the offering shall be devoted. Last year it was sent to the new work in Yangchow, and this year it was given to our own dispensary. The

two offerings this year were respectively $60.47 and $65.01.

The members of the Men's Auxiliary have during the year gone to various places to preach, and the Auxiliary itself has raised $32 (Mexican) for missionary purposes. The Woman's Auxiliary has held regular weekly meetings, doing some needed local work and raising $47 (Mexican) for their annual offering.

This year has seen the first steps taken toward parish organization. On St. Andrew's Day a meeting of the baptized Christians was held, and, after a brief statement of the history of the work in the station and of the nature of a parish, two treasurers were elected to collect and care for all church subscriptions, and instructions were given them as to how the money should be used. In the nature of things there was no action that could be taken at the first meeting other than this, of caring for the subscriptions. It is, however, a longer step than it might seem to the casual observer who does not understand how in mission work every detail depends entirely upon the foreign missionary until this first step can be taken. And other steps follow rapidly.

In the summer of 1908 the Parish House—so-called—was completed. It consists of two guest-rooms on the ground floor—one for men and one for women—with a covered passage ten feet wide between. On the second floor, where there are eventually to be seven bedrooms, for the accommodation of men from the country whom we hope can come for station classes in the winters, is the temporary chapel, forty-seven feet long and twenty-five feet wide. Here all the church services are held. On Easter Day an attendance of 153—the largest for the year—packed every available foot.

The experience in Wusih would seem to prove that in a work such as this the attendance at services is influenced not a little by the size of the church building. For the seven years—nearly—that the chapel occupied a ten by thirty-foot room in the rented school building the attendance was small, though toward the end it tended to crowd us out; for the six months that it occupied the parlor and dining-room of the mission residence there was a perceptible increase; since it has been in its present quarters the attendance has doubled, and is still growing.

At the present time a building for all of the woman's work is just being completed, at a cost of about $1,800 gold. A guest-room 25x20, a girls' day-school 16x23 feet, a dining-room and a small servant's room fill the first floor. On the second floor there are three larger rooms on the front side, to be occupied by Mrs. Sung, another Bible-woman and the girls' teacher, when the latter two shall come. Back of a hall running the width of the building are four small bedrooms that are to be used for women from the country who will come for instruction in the winters as the men do in the other building. For the present Mr. Tsang is to bring his family to this building for the summer months, removing back to his preaching-hall in September.

On St. Andrew's Day a large temple bell, over four feet high and weighing nearly 1,000 pounds, cast here in Wusih, was given by Mrs. Mosher in memory of her brother, Lewis Stewart, who died a year ago. The bell has a beautiful tone, and when the tower now building for it—which is double the height of the one that has been tried for several months—is finished, the sound of the bell will carry for a long distance.

Recent gifts are: A new stereopticon, with acetylene generator, which will be useful in the evangelistic work; also a Singer sewing-machine, which is to be placed in the new women's guest-room, under the care of Mrs. Sung, for the use of our Christian women. Nearly all of the women do all of their own sewing, and some of them make their living by it. If their burdens are lightened and their pitifully small incomes increased a little by this means, at the same time that they learn to make themselves at home in the guest-room, the gift will be

of great value to us. Through the kindness of Bishop Graves, who applied some of his special gifts to it, a gate-house and chair-house have been erected, and the main gate rebuilt after being damaged by the burning of the mat-shed that did temporary service for several months.

I must tell you about a family in Lok-chui-jau, all communicants, who are well-to-do farmers, and have offered a piece of land at the edge of the village, which it is hoped will be transferred to the mission shortly. The Wusih branch of the "Emmanuel Movement" had an unintentional beginning in this family. The mother was very ill, probably with typhoid fever, unconscious a part of the time, and being dieted by the country doctor (?) on olives and raw pears. Her one desire was that she might receive baptism before she died, and I went and administered it to her. She recovered. Some fifteen months later the step-grandson of another farmer, also a communicant, was brought to the dispensary, anæmic and weak, for treatment; and baptism was asked for for him so that he might get strong and well, and be able to work on the farm. This was felt to be one duty more than baptism could rightly be called upon to perform, and the request was refused, though the people were told frankly that they should pray as well as obey the doctor. The boy has since become well, and has been baptized. It will, perhaps, be the end of this sort of Emmanuel Movement.

The growth in the work in Wusih, as far as figures can show it, will be seen in my report. What this fails to show, however, is the gradual growth of the Christian environment — a very real thing, and one which is seen easily by the missionaries living in close contact with the people. For example, while there have been six baptisms less this year than last, there have been five more infant baptisms—and the coming of the infant means that the father has interested the rest of his family. The infant of a Christian father is baptized immediately when desired, and it nearly al-

FOUR GENERATIONS OF CHRISTIANS AT WUSIH

ways means that the whole family is coming. It may be stated as an axiom of mission work that three persons in one family is evidence of more solid growth than five persons in five families would be; that the family and not the father shall be considered the *unit*, is the desire of every missionary heart. Again, a hopeful sign is found in the fact that not only do the seven confirmations during the year show the largest number in any year yet, but that in the past three years of twenty adults baptized fifteen have already been confirmed. This is a healthy proportion.

I feel as I write that the work grows, steadily and solidly, though slowly, and that after a few more years we shall have such a foundation that the growth will be in geometrical rather than as now in arithmetical progression. There is every reason for confidence and hope.

AN EXPLANATION

DESIRING to introduce and make familiar to our Church people the names and faces of those who are their representatives abroad, we give from time to time in THE SPIRIT OF MISSIONS brief sketches and pictures of the new volunteers for distant fields. Like all who attempt to introduce persons they do not know to people who do not know them, it occasionally happens that THE SPIRIT OF MISSIONS finds itself in error. Such an instance occurred in our November number, when good Bishop Cheshire, opening the magazine, was confronted with an absolutely strange person purporting to be his eldest daughter. Who that person really is, the Editor has not yet himself discovered, but we have the testimony of the bishop and of a photograph that it is *not* Miss

Miss Elizabeth T. Cheshire

Elizabeth Cheshire. To rectify our mistake as far as possible, we are printing in this issue pictures of the two daughters of the Bishop of North Carolina, who have just taken up work in China—Miss Elizabeth T. Cheshire, who is at St. Hilda's School, and Miss Annie W. Cheshire, who has gone to Wusih.

Miss Annie W. Cheshire

Surely, the example of the clergy in giving their own sons and daughters to the work of the Church's Mission, not fearing for them the hardships and lack of worldly recompense which in the work of the ministry they have themselves experienced, ought to be an inspiration and a rebuke to the parents who sometimes would withhold this greatest and best gift.

A NATIONAL MISS

UNDER THE AUSPICES OF

FROM October 16th to December 14th conventions of the Laymen's Missionary Movement were held in these eighteen centres: Buffalo, Bristol, Tenn., Cleveland, Richmond, Worcester, Providence, Boston, Washington, D. C., Baltimore, Philadelphia, Harrisburg, Scranton, Hartford, Portland, Me., Reading, Detroit, Syracuse, Schenectady.

They were attended by nearly 25,000 enrolled members, each of whom paid the $1 registration fee for the convention privileges, and by several thousand other men who did not register, but showed their good will and interest by coming to one or more of the sessions.

Some Churchmen Who Took Part

Churchmen, both clerical and lay, took a prominent part in the preparations for most of the meetings and on the convention programmes. In Richmond and Philadelphia the chairman of the executive committees were Churchmen. In Washington the chairman of the general committee was a Churchman. In Washington, too, Bishop Harding, the Rev. Dr. McKim and several of the clergy took a large share in all things connected with the convention, and before its close Bishop Harding was recognized as the leader of the occasion. In Worcester, Bishop Vinton presided at the sectional conference of Churchmen. Bishop Talbot's presence and addresses at Scranton and Reading were most stimulating. In the latter city he conducted the daily devotional services for the convention in connection with the week of prayer. Bishop Williams carried the Detroit convention to a high plane at its first session by an address

A Typical Laymen's Convention

The conventions have followed a common plan. The first session has been a men's supper or dinner, informal and simple in character. Each man paid for his ticket. This relieved him from any sense of obligation and emphasized the importance of the occasion. For it is a demonstrated fact that what a man pays is much more likely to enlist his interest than what is given him. In most instances the largest places available were inadequate to accommodate all the men who wished to attend this opening dinner. In Baltimore 1,500 men were present; in Philadelphia more than 1,300; in Detroit 1,000. Places no larger than Scranton and Harrisburg found it possible to bring together 900 men, with more wishing to come but unable to secure accommodations. In Syracuse 1,200 men were seated at the tables in the spacious new gymnasium of Syracuse University, but 200 others had to be provided for in another building, joining the main body later for the speaking. Quite apart from anything else these dinners did good in supplying an ocular demonstration of the virility of the Christian forces of a city. They brought men of various communions together in helpful comradeship. They were often the means whereby men who knew each other in business learned that they had an unsuspected common interest. But the real purpose of the occasion was to assemble a large and representative company of men before whom might be laid some of the outstanding facts of the missionary enterprise. After addresses on the attitude of the mission boards to the Laymen's Movement, and on the relation of men to the mission of the Christian Church, Mr. J. Campbell White, General Secretary of the Movement, generally spoke on "America's World Responsibility." By a masterly massing of facts and figures he would show what is being attempted in the foreign field to-day, how inadequate it is to give all men a chance to hear the Gospel in this generation, what needs to be done and what is the share of American Christians in meeting that need. This address, illustrated and enforced by charts, has made a profound impression upon thousands of men and has brought them back to discuss what they could do to discharge their responsibility.

A Statistical Reminder

The necessity for more vigorous effort was made plain, too, by the statistical card which each man found at his plate. It showed the amounts given by the congregations of the city, grouped by communions, for current expenses, for home missions and other benevolent objects and for foreign missions, with the number of communicants and the annual *per capita* gift for work abroad. Here is a typical card showing the facts in a city which shall be nameless:

	No. of Communicants	Congregational Expenses	Missionary and Educational Work in America	Foreign Missions	Average Per Capita Foreign Missions
Baptist	6,043	$54,015	$10,222	$3,163	$0.52
Christian	537	7,200	1,950	3,100	5.77
Church of Christ	500	3,529	24	381	.76
Congregational	2,285	53,071	16,221	2,682	1.17
Dutch Reformed Church in America	110	2,300	205	100	.91
Episcopal	7,546	77,919	12,134	2,727	.36
Evangelical Association	400	5,954	422	97	.24
Evangelical Lutheran	1,344	10,174	696	306	.23
German Evangelical Synod of N. A.	6,633	31,079	2,523	419	.06
Free Methodist	125	1,340	227	214	1.71
Methodist Episcopal	8,387	73,908	21,722	7,972	.95
Presbyterian	9,275	113,726	37,678	10,898	1.17
Reformed Episcopal	70	956	71	70	1.00
Reformed Church in U. S. A.	441	2,322	235	141	.32
United Presbyterian	625	4,084	1,819	289	.46
Total	44,321	$441,577	$106,149	$32,559	$0.74

The average *per capita* gift for work
abroad from congregations of the Church,
as shown on this card, is somewhat
higher than in a number of other cities,
and considerably lower than in two or
three. The lowest *per capita* for the
Church in the eighteen cities was
24 cents; the highest $1.94. These
included offerings from all sources—congregations, individuals, Sunday-schools,
branches of the Woman's Auxiliary and
for "specials." A huge screen with these
figures painted upon it hung before the
convention during its sessions.

The first morning was generally given
to addresses by missionaries from the
field, telling of conditions, achievements
and needs. In the afternoon plans for
bringing a congregation to its highest
missionary efficiency were discussed—
such as the formation of a vigorous missionary committee, the distribution of
literature, the promotion of mission
study and intercession. Then followed a
discussion on an adequate plan of missionary finance in which the advantages
of a weekly offering for missionary work
were convincingly set forth. At night addresses on particular fields and general
subjects helped to deepen the impressions
made during the day sessions.

On the second morning the personal
responsibility of men to render Christian
service was enforced, ending with the
consideration of the question, "What
should this convention undertake to do?"
At this time there was introduced a
series of resolutions prepared by the local
executive committee on the preceding
day after a careful survey of the situation. These resolutions named a sum
which it was recommended that all congregations should endeavor to give during the next twelve months, and suggested plans for accomplishing the result.

These resolutions were referred to the
conferences held in the afternoon, when
the men of each communion met to consider what they would do to insure larger
offerings from their congregations. Each
conference decided upon an amount it
would recommend should be given. At
the final convention session in the evening reports from these conferences were

people have been as large, perhaps larger, to foreign missions than those of any other parish in this diocese; but through the influence of this Movement, and through the diligent canvass of a committee of twenty-one laymen, re-enforcing the message of the pulpit, it looks as if the gifts of this parish to missions, domestic and foreign, would be, for the year ending next Advent, at least three times as large as last year.

"I consider the spiritual influence of the Movement of still greater importance; in particular it has distinctly brightened the horizon for Christian unity."

Bishop Talbot voices the experience and the hope of many Churchmen when he says:

"The work of the Laymen's Missionary Movement, both at Scranton and Reading, two of our largest centres of population, was most inspiring and helpful. I found myself constantly regretting that every clergyman and layman in my diocese could not be present, and catch the contagion and uplift of the Movement. I regard it as the most hopeful and significant movement of our time. Heartily endorsed by all of our Church papers in England and America, and by our Board of Missions, it gives our Church a unique opportunity of leadership in a world-wide crusade for missions. May its influence widen until every clergyman and layman is reached."

Dr. Matthew D. Mann, the distinguished surgeon of Buffalo, says of the convention there:

"The Laymen's Missionary Convention produced a most profound impression on the religious life of Buffalo. Never have the men of our own Church been so deeply stirred as they have been by this Movement. The clergy, almost without exception, took a great interest in the meetings, and there was a large attendance of our laymen, 212 having registered as delegates.

"There was nothing said or done at any of the meetings to arouse any feeling of opposition or to offend any prejudice or cherished belief. The utmost harmony prevailed, and we all met on the common ground of being followers of the same Master and being concerned in the extension of His Kingdom."

Richmond's Good Work

Richmond has done the most complete work so far in connection with this national Movement. The 925 members of the Richmond convention found that 33,000 communicants gave last year $36,000 to foreign missions, an average of $1.09 *per capita*. They determined to work for an advance to $60,000 for the next twelve months. Within a few days after the convention adjourned congregational meetings of men were held to plan for a canvass of each congregation to secure subscriptions on a weekly basis, payable, weekly, monthly, quarterly or annually, as the donor preferred. In less than a month the committees reported subscriptions totalling more than $62,000, with a number of reports still to be made.

In one of our Church congregations the first two men approached subscribed as much as the whole congregation gave last year, while the first seventeen subscriptions amounted to more than twice as much as the congregation gave last year. All the Church congregations were asked to increase from about $7,000 to $14,000 for foreign missions. They not only expected to do this, but to give $8,000 for domestic missions, too. Local work in city and diocesan missions is feeling the stimulus of this enlarged giving for work at a distance, and the outlook is for greatly increased gifts for Church extension work in Virginia as well as more money for congregational expenses.

The Winter and Spring Campaign

Early in January the national campaign reopens in New York and then extends west and south. With a brief break in Holy Week and at Easter the conventions will continue through April and will lead up to the great national congress in Chicago, May 3d to 6th, when fully 5,000 commissioners from all parts of the country are expected. The places and dates of the coming conventions are:

January
New York City, 9-16
Greensboro, N. C., 12-14
Columbia, S. C., 17-19.
Pittsburgh, Pa., 20-23
Macon, Ga., 21-23
Wheeling, W. Va., 25-27
Dayton, O., 25-27
Huntington, W. Va., 27-28
Cincinnati, O., 28-30
Nashville, Tenn., 28-30

February
Louisville, Ky., 1-3
Jacksonville and Tampa, Fla., 1-3
St. Louis, Mo., 3-6
Montgomery, Ala., 4-6
Memphis, Tenn., 8-10
Jackson, Miss., 8-10
Little Rock, Ark., 11-13
New Orleans, La., 12-15
Oklahoma, Okla., 15-17
Shreveport, La., 16-17
Wichita, Kan., 18-20
Houston, Tex., 18-20
Topeka, Kan., 22-24
San Antonio, Tex., 22-24
Kansas City, Mo., 24-27
El Paso, Tex., 27-March 1

March
Colorado Springs, Col., 2-4
Denver, Col., 3-6
Phœnix, Ariz., 4-6
Salt Lake City, Utah, 8-10
Los Angeles, Cal., 8-10
Fresno, Cal., 12-14
Cheyenne, Wyo., 13-14
Sacramento, Cal., 14-16
Lincoln, Neb., 15-17
San Francisco, Cal., 17-20
Omaha, Neb., 18-20
Sioux City, Ia., 22-24
Mitchell, S. D., 29-31
Portland, Ore., 29-31

April
Davenport, Ia., 1-3
Moline and Rock Island, Ill., 1-3
Tacoma, Wash., 1-3
Seattle, Wash., 2-5
Milwaukee, Wis., 5-7
Peoria, Ill., 8-10
Spokane, Wash., 8-10
Indianapolis, Ind., 12-14
Butte, Mont., 12-14
Billings, Mont., 15-17
Fargo, N. D., 19-21
Duluth, Minn., 22-24
St. Paul, Minn., 26-28

May 3d-6th—National Missionary Congress, Chicago, Ill.

THE AMERICAN CHURCH INSTITUTE FOR NEGROES

By the Reverend Samuel H. Bishop, Secretary

THE Institute having determined to extend its work by entering into relation with three schools in addition to those for which it has been working since its organization in February, 1906, the Board of the Institute asks the courtesy of THE SPIRIT OF MISSIONS for a brief restatement of its purposes and work.

As stated in its first announcement its purpose was the supervision of the educational work conducted under the auspices of the Church among the Negroes. It was to enter as soon as possible into some kind of organic relationship with the various schools established either by the dioceses or by Church men and women, in order that a collective unity might be given to the work and that the Church might become conscious of her responsibility for the uplift, moral and spiritual, of the Negroes, as well as of her opportunity to aid in their practical training for useful life.

Up to the date of the recent action of the Institute's Board it has confined its work to three schools: St. Paul's Normal and Industrial School, Lawrenceville, Va., that school being primarily industrial and normal; St. Augustine's School, Raleigh, N. C., representing normal, academic and collegiate training; and the Bishop Payne Divinity-school, Petersburg, Va., representing

for the normal department; and it is now about to erect a new domestic science building at St. Paul's.

To aid in carrying out these suggestions of improvement and to help bear the expense involved, the Institute has appropriated to the schools something over $67,000. The Institute has attempted to help these three schools to a grade of work such as that being done by the best schools in the South; and it believes that these schools are deserving of the same kind of support from Churchmen which Hampton and Tuskegee are getting from their constituencies.

BOOK NOTICE

WINNERS OF THE WORLD. By Mary T. and William E. Gardner. Old Corner Book Store, Boston, Mass. Paper, 35 cents. On sale at Educational Department, Church Missions House, 281 Fourth Avenue, New York.

"WHAT will stir the hearts of our boys and girls?" That is the question which Sunday-school teachers and Junior Auxiliary leaders are always asking as they look for missionary textbooks, and that is the question which Mr. and Mrs. Gardner have most successfully answered in "Winners of the World." In a little book of only 238 pages there is told the story of the world being won for Christ. "The course centres about an outline map of the world and each lesson deals with some heroic character or characters, who as Christian soldiers aim to win the peoples of a certain country to Christ." Boys and girls, quick to give hero-worship, can hardly fail to be stirred to interest and one hopes to action by the story of Christian heroes such as St. Paul, Boniface, Carey, Judson, Gardiner, Livingstone, Mackay, Paton, Patteson, Ingle and many others, told as they are in this book. Teachers and leaders who want to make the boys and girls "see the world, part of it won, part of it waiting for Christ," will find "Winners of the World" a most helpful and successful text-book.

A CONSECRATI

THE eleventh annual Council of the Brazilian Episcopal Church met on the 15th of October in Pelotas, with an attendance of sixteen out of our twenty clergy. On Friday and Saturday, the first two days, the meetings were held in the now disused Chapel of the Redeemer; but the sessions of Monday, Tuesday and Wednesday in the new church.

On Sunday, the Nineteenth after Trinity, October 17th, the Church of the Redeemer "was consecrated by the bishop and fifteen clergy"—as a daily paper put it. The procession passed from the robing-room to the tower entrance, where they were met by the vestry and lay delegates. The service, taken from the Prayer Book, had been printed previously on leaflets and distributed. It was heartily rendered by the large congregation present. The sentence of consecration was read by the Rev. John G. Meem, B.SC., the preacher being the Rev. Wm. Cabell Brown, D.D., epistoler, the Rev. W. M. M. Thomas, B.A., gospeller, the Rev. A. V. Cabral. Morning Prayer was read by the younger clergy who had been connected with the parish, the Rev. Messrs. Cunha, Krischke, Silva, Mello and Ferreira. The bishop was celebrant and the number of communicants between 100 and 200, while the church was more than comfortably filled by the congregation.

At 3 P.M. there was again assembled a large congregation at the children's service at which addresses were made by the Rev. Mr. Krischke (formerly a Sunday-school boy in Pelotas), the Rev. Mr. Guimarães, of Bagé, and the bishop. At 7:30 Evening Prayer was said, and the Rev. A. V. Cabral, of Trinity, Porto Alegre, preached. In the translated phrase of the chief daily paper of Pelotas: "After the magnificent sermon of our distinguished fellow-citizen, his Excellency, Bishop Kinsolving, began

(50)

measures 28 metres (93½ feet) in length of nave, by 11 metres (37½ feet) in breadth. The choir is 7x7 metres (23½x23½ feet), thus giving a total length of 116½ feet, interior measurement. It affords a seating capacity of somewhat less than 400. The tower rises to the height of 27½ metres (91¾ feet). Except the single tubular chime, which came from England, and the windows, which came from the United States, everything needed for the construction of the church was supplied here. The tubular chime measures 3 metres in length and weighs 220 pounds. The windows are of beautiful tones and have appropriate symbols and texts. At night, when illuminated, both symbols and texts are clearly visible to all passers-by.

Procession of clergy entering the church at the time of the convocation

"The master brick-layer was Senhor Francisco Marques and the chief carpenter was Senhor Polybio Ribeiro. The engineer-architect was the Rev. Dr. John G. Meem, who besides his course of theology is a graduate of civil engineering. The beautiful Church of the Redeemer is a work of art and adds greatly to the attractiveness of our city."

The funds for the erection of the new church came from three sources: First, from the offerings of the congregation, which they have accumulated with signal self-devotion during many years past; second, from two generous offerings, one by a communicant in Norfolk, ·Va., more than seven years since, and another by Mrs. E. Walpole Warren, of New York, in memory of her husband, under whose mission-preaching Mr. Meem was led to the ministry of the Church; and lastly, from the Men's Thank-offering in Richmond.

As compared with the cost of Trinity Church, Porto Alegre, and of the Church of the Saviour, Rio Grande, the new church is a marvel of economy, due to Mr. Meem's wise and efficient oversight. A year was spent in its construction, which is likewise a marvel of rapidity in this land of *festina lente.* In the deepest sense of the words the church is the product of Mr. Meem's brain and heart and prayers. Every brick and arch and

beam was laid under his personal direction. He was the sole designer, architect and constructor. With a few bricklayers and carpenters he has achieved a structure whose grace and beauty excite the highest praise, whose exterior and interior are inspiringly expressive of the spirit of worship and devotion, and whose strength betokens endurance for generations.

From Sunday to Wednesday, inclusive, services were held each evening by the bishop and clergy, the preacher being one of the visitors. Large congregations continued to the end. On the evening of St. Luke's Day a sermon of signal lucidity and historic grasp was preached by the Rev. J. Mozart de Mello on the credal text: "I believe in the Holy Catholic Church." The daily papers gave several columns each day to the council and published excerpts of the sermons preached. The comments made on council and church were kindly and generous.

The following is taken from the close of a two-column article in the *Diario Popular,* and is said to be from the pen of a young army officer (a member of the Methodist communion): "And now as the splendid result of such efforts for the propagation of its blessed seed, the Brazilian Episcopal Church erects in the heart of this city of rich traditions an imperishable monument of victory, the holy temple of its superb faith.

"As a Christian and a Brazilian I rejoice with a just and uplifted joy in beholding this temple of divine reconciliation, with its strong tower pointing silently to God. It affords an edifying lesson of the vanity of the passing things of the world and of the attainable aspiration for things moral and sublime.

"May there fall upon it, along with the night dews and the diamond shafts of starlight, the blessings of heaven above; and may it be to the people of Pelotas a preponderating factor of moral progress and edification.

"May there gather in the near future under its high-arched roof multitudes, as in the primitive times of the Christian apostolate, thirsty for the words of con-solation and love, evangelization and peace, humility and concord, which He holds for all sinners Who was yet without sin and Who is the Way, the Truth and the Life."

These frequent quotations from the press give, I think, in most signal fashion, the local point of view—which is, after all, what we most wish to ascertain. What such a solemnity means to ourselves we already know. The impression it makes upon those among whom we labor demonstrates if there be any correlation between our inner consciousness and external environment.

It seems legitimate to conclude that the Church here is not merely a voice crying in the wilderness with no answer save its own echo. Voices from the desert call back to us. They show susceptibility to the age-long Catholic methods and message. They betoken new visions of the new day.

NEWS AND NOTES

IN an article in the August number of THE SPIRIT OF MISSIONS the Rev. Edward P. Newton, of Valdez, describing the work of the Red Dragon Inn at Cordova, said: "The reading table at the Red Dragon is not so well stocked with magazines and papers as I wish it were. At Valdez I am much better supplied, and the opposite should be the case, as the Red Dragon has ten to one as many visitors as the Valdez rectory."

Mr. Newton now writes: "Mr. Ziegler has been a bit snowed under by the generous response to the August appeal. We have to call in a wagon to handle our mail now. I was in Cordova the first of the month and we sorted, packed and sent out eight sacks of reading matter. It took four of us an afternoon to do this. The prompt and generous response to the appeal was most gratifying as showing the real interest of people in the men in Alaska and in our work."

THE Rev. W. W. Steel, Archdeacon of Havana, who has been in this country securing funds to replace church buildings destroyed in the Isle of Pines and on the western end of Cuba by a recent hurricane, writes, just as he is starting back to the field: "The more I hear from Guaniguanico the worse the story grows. About all the people lost their homes and much property; some were personally injured—many were out in the terrible storm all night, and yet when they wrote me about the disaster all they said was: 'The chapel was destroyed in the storm; what shall we do about the next service?' Not a word about their own sufferings and loss!' Archdeacon Steel secured nearly $2,000 which will do much toward helping to meet the situation, though it will not fully cover all that ought to be done at present.

MR. WILLIAM B. CLEVELAND, Jr., of Houston, Tex., who has been acting as the treasurer of the fund for the relief of the famine-stricken people of Mexico, acknowledges the receipt to December 9th of $2,812.87. This has been entirely expended in the purchase of supplies. Through the kindness of two Houston business men, everything has been purchased at wholesale rates, and has been shipped into Mexico without charge.

¶

AT a recent week-day Communion service in Yampa, a small town in Routt County, Col., held by the Bishop of Western Colorado, one of the worshippers was a young Irishman from a ranch seventy miles away, who had come to the town for some farm implements. It was the first service this young Churchman had been able to attend since his coming from Ireland, more than a year and a half before. His ranch is thirty miles from the nearest post-office. This service was also the first Communion service held in this part of the state for six months.

¶

THE rector of St. James's church, Pulaski, in the Diocese of Central New York, has adopted an interesting plan for circulating missionary information. He has ordered one hundred copies of THE SPIRIT OF MISSIONS each month for the next year and proposes to bind it with the monthly issues of the diocesan magazine and of his own parish paper. The plan is worth while. How many others will try it?

¶

A VERY large congregation was present in St. James's Cathedral, Toronto, Canada, on November 30th, when the Rev. W. C. White was consecrated Bishop of Honan, China, being the first Missionary Bishop sent abroad by the Canadian Church. The service was fully choral, and the ceremonial was carried out in the usual manner, with all the dignity and grace which the ritual

prescribes. Archbishop Matheson, of Rupert's Land, officiated, and the other bishops assisting were Bishop Farthing, of Montreal; Bishop Du Moulin, of Niagara; Bishop Mills, of Ontario; Bishop Sweeney, and Bishop Reeve, of Toronto.

¶

A RECTOR in Massachusetts writes: "This none too strong parish was blessed of God last year in giving outside the parish the exact amount that was spent within the parish, and help in the way of speakers from the Missions House will keep them to at least that this year."

¶

JUST before Christmas this pleasant message reached the Editor from the other side of the Atlantic: "I have pleasure in enclosing $1 for my 1910 subscription. I have been a subscriber to THE SPIRIT OF MISSIONS for about thirty years and would be very sorry to be without it. I think it becomes more interesting every year."

¶

BISHOP KNIGHT, who has just returned from a visit to the Canal Zone, reports the confirmation of 221 candidates, all but thirteen Negroes.

¶

AT the meeting of the Missionary Council of the Department of New York and New Jersey, held at Utica, N. Y., on October 27th, the following memorial was introduced by the Rev. Dr. Alsop, and by vote was referred to the Board of Missions with an expression of the sympathy of the Council:

WHEREAS, arrangements entered into between Turkey and the other Signatory Powers in the formation of the Treaty of Berlin, in 1878, provided for the introduction of definite forms in the administration of the Turkish Government, so far as the protection of Christians was concerned, these reforms to be superintended by some of the Signatory Powers; and

WHEREAS, these arrangements
have not been carried out, but
many thousands of Christians,
mostly Armenians, have been
barbarously murdered by Moslems, with little protest from
outside except expressions of
sympathy for the sufferers; and
WHEREAS, these conditions
have long been a flaunting disgrace before the civilized
world; and
WHEREAS, the time has now
passed for the mere passing of
resolutions,
We, the members of this
council, call these facts to the
definite attention of the governments of Christendom, and especially the Signatory Powers of
the Berlin Treaty, and urge
them to take into most careful
consideration these conditions,
with a view to effective action
that shall afford protection in
Turkey to the Armenians as a
race and to Christians as a
whole.

¶

THE Church Laymen's Union plans
to hold a missionary conference in
Pittsburgh, February 25th to 27th, 1910.
The conference "will be held, not to hear
addresses intended to inspire and inform, but to plan how laymen may best
help their rectors in their own parishes,
their bishops in their own dioceses, the
Board of Missions in its work throughout the world."

¶

Appreciation from Alaska, or anywhere else, is
always welcome. Deaconess Carter, of Allakaket, says:

OUR Indians would rather have a
copy of THE SPIRIT OF MISSIONS to
look at and talk over than any book or
magazine we can give them. I do not
mean that they can read it, but they love
to look at the pictures and ask questions about them. And we are very fortunate in having three or four copies
coming, but you know up here we are
usually three or four months behind.

for $100,000 with which to create a fund in memory of the Board's late Treasurer, the income thereof to be at the disposal of the Board to meet its obligations.

The Advisory Committee, reporting upon an exhaustive statement for the Treasurer concerning the multiplicity of special appeals, recommended, and the Board adopted, a resolution providing that "no new appeals for specials should be authorized by the Board under present conditions."

The Rev. H. Percy Silver notified the Board of his acceptance of his election as secretary of the Department of the Southwest (No. VII). Upon nomination of the Missionary Council of the Department of New England (No. I), the election of the Rev. William E. Gardner, of St. James's Church, Cambridge, as Department Secretary was approved.

The Board had before it many communications from bishops in this country and, wherever possible, took affirmative action. An appropriation of $1,500 was made to the Missionary District of South Dakota to make possible the addition of a general missionary to the staff.

Additional appropriations were also made to St. Paul's, Lawrenceville; St. Augustine's, Raleigh; St. Mary's, Vicksburg; St. Mark's, Birmingham, and to the Diocese of East Carolina for educational work among the Negroes.

Upon the request of the Bishop of Kyoto, the name of St. Agnes's School, Kyoto, was changed to "The Girls' High School of the City of Peace," this being the official name under which the school has always been registered in the Japanese Department of Education.

The Bishops of Asheville and Kyoto addressed the Board upon special needs in their districts, and their requests were referred to the Committee on New Appropriations.

The Bishop of Newark, the Rev. Dr.

Alsop and Mr. Elihu Chauncey were appointed to represent the Board, with the secretaries, at the conference of the secretaries and members of foreign mission boards, to be held in New York, January 12th to 14th. The Corresponding Secretary was appointed to represent the Board at the meetings of the Home Missions Council *vice* the former General Secretary.

To Mr. John Marston, who, with the late George C. Thomas, shared in the inauguration of the Sunday-school Lenten Offering, this message was sent:

> *Resolved:* That the Board of Missions sends its hearty congratulations to Mr. John Marston upon the seventy-sixth anniversary of his birth on December 15th, with the assurance of its hope that his life may be spared for many years, and of its profound gratitude for the great service rendered by him to the Church in sharing with the late Treasurer of the Board of Missions in the inauguration of the Sunday-school Lenten Offering.

This resolution with regard to Archdeacon Thomson was also unanimously adopted:

> WHEREAS, St. Thomas's Day, December 21st, marks the fiftieth anniversary of the arrival in China of the Venerable Elliot H. Thomson, Archdeacon of Shanghai,
>
> *Resolved:* That the Board of Missions, on behalf of the Church in the United States, records its thanks to God for giving long life to this devoted servant and enabling him to render such long continued and self-sacrificing service on behalf of others; that it records its deep appreciation of the spirit of self-forgetfulness, of care for others, and of high devotion to duty that have marked Archdeacon Thomson's entire career in the Chinese empire; that to its congratulations

MISSIONARY SPEAKERS

FOR the convenience of those arranging missionary meetings, the following list of clergy and other missionary workers available as speakers is published:

When no address is given, requests for the services of these speakers should be addressed to the Corresponding Secretary, 281 Fourth Avenue, New York.

Department Secretaries

Department 1. The Rev. William E. Gardner, Secretary-elect. Enters upon his duties February 1st. Cambridge, Mass.

Department 2. Cared for at present by secretaries at the Church Missions House.

Department 3. The Rev. Thomas J. Garland, Secretary, Church House, Philadelphia.

Department 4. The Rev. R. W. Patton, care of the Rev. C. B. Wilmer, D.D., 412 Courtland Street, Atlanta, Ga.

Department 5. The Rev. John Henry Hopkins, D.D., 703 Ashland Boulevard, Chicago.

Department 6. The Rev. C. C. Rollit, Secretary, 4416 Upton Avenue, South, Minneapolis, Minn.

Department 7. The Rev. H. Percy Silver, Secretary. Address for the present, 281 Fourth Avenue, New York.

Department 8. The Rev. L. C. Sanford, 1215 Sacramento Street, San Francisco, Cal.

Alaska

Miss Isabel M. Emberley, of Fairbanks.

South Dakota

Bishop Johnson.

Wyoming

Bishop Thomas.

China

SHANGHAI:

The Rev. F. L. Hawks Pott, D.D., of Shanghai.

Mrs. Pott.

The Rev. John W. Nichols, of Shanghai. Available in Department 8. Address: 1215 Sacramento Street, San Francisco, Cal.

Dr. Angie M. Myers, of Shanghai.

Miss Margaret E. Bender, of Shanghai.

HANKOW:

The Rev. Arthur M. Sherman, of Hankow.

The Rev. A. A. Gilman, of Changsha. Available for State of Nebraska during January.

The Rev. R. C. Wilson, of Zangzok. Available for Department 4 during January, February and March.

Japan

Bishop Partridge, of Kyoto.

The Rev. I. H. Correll, D.D., of Osaka.

The Rev. Roger A. Walke, of St. Paul's College, Tokyo.

The Rev. Isaac Dooman, of Wakayama.

The Rev. W. J. Cuthbert, of Kyoto.

Deaconess Anna L. Ranson, of Sendai.

The Philippines

The Rev. Hobart E. Studley, of Manila.

Work Among Negroes in the South

The Rev. S. H. Bishop, Secretary of the American Church Institute for Negroes, 500 West 122d Street, New York.

Archdeacon Russell, of St. Paul's, Lawrenceville, Va., and the Rev. A. B. Hunter, of St. Augustine's, Raleigh, N. C., are always ready to take appointments, especially when a number of engagements in the same neighborhood can be grouped.

ANNOUNCEMENTS

CONCERNING THE MISSIONARIES

Porto Rico

THE REV. F. A. WARDEN, on leave of absence for three months, sailed from San Juan by the steamer *Philadelphia* on December 8th and arrived at New York on the 13th.

THE REV. E. H. EDSON, returning because of illness in his family, sailed from San Juan by the steamer *Coamo* on December 1st and arrived at New York on the 6th. His wife and daughter preceded him. At the meeting on December 14th the Board of Missions accepted Mr. Edson's resignation to date from March 1st.

The Philippines

MISS ELIZABETH GIBSON, who was appointed as a missionary nurse at the meeting of the Board on September 28th, left San Antonio on December 16th and sailed from San Francisco by the steamer *Mongolia* on the 21st.

Shanghai

MRS. F. R. GRAVES, returning to the field, left Chicago on December 14th and sailed from San Francisco by the steamer *Mongolia* on the 21st.

MISS E. M. A. CARTWRIGHT, who was appointed on October 12th, sailed from London by the steamer *Sicilia* on October 23d and arrived at Shanghai December 9th.

MRS. LILIAN P. FREDERICKS, who spent a portion of her furlough in Europe, sailed from Glasgow by the steamer *Columbia* December 4th and arrived at New York on the 13th.

Hankow

THE REV. and MRS. JAMES JACKSON, returning after furlough, sailed from

London for Shanghai by the steamer *Nyanza* on December 4th.

MISS REBECCA R. HALSEY, returning to New York by way of Europe, sailed by the German Mail steamer which left Shanghai on November 13th.

MISS SADA C. TOMLINSON, coming home because of the illness of her mother, sailed from Shanghai for Vancouver by the steamer *Monteagle* on November 24th.

Tokyo

THE REV. JAMES CHAPPELL, on regular furlough, with his wife and two children sailed from Yokohama by the *Sado Maru* on November 24th, for England.

DR. THEODORE BLISS and wife left their home, Schenectady, N. Y., on December 24th, intending to sail from San Francisco by the steamer *Korea* on January 7th. Dr. Bliss is to be associated in the work at St. Luke's Hospital, Tokyo.

Kyoto

MISS MABEL L. BACON left Santa Barbara on December 23d and sailed from San Francisco by the *Tenyo Maru* on the 28th, for Kobe.

Cuba

AT the meeting of the Board of Missions on December 14th the employment by Bishop Knight of Mrs. L. Mendez as teacher in the Guantanamo school *vice* Mrs. Giribet, was approved.

THE REV. H. PERCY SILVER, who has accepted his election as Secretary of the Seventh Department, arrived in New York on January 1st. After two weeks spent in preparation he plans to go directly to the Seventh Department and begin his work.

THE WOMAN'S AUXILIARY
To the Board of Missions

OLD-TIME DAKOTAS

THE BEGINNINGS AND PROGRESS OF WOMAN'S WORK AMONG THE DAKOTAS

By Mrs. H. Burt

[A paper read at All Saints' School, Sioux Falls,
South Dakota, on the evening of October 11, 1909.]

WOMEN had a share in the earliest work of our Church for the Dakota tribe. There were three who entered upon this work, in Minnesota, as early as 1858, but work in this State was suddenly interrupted by what is known as the Minnesota Outbreak, and four years later we find most of the Santee·part of the Sioux tribe settled on their present location close to the northern boundary of Nebraska. The work prospered more and more, until the handful of Christians became three congregations, and there was a flourishing and well-filled boarding-school for girls, called St. Mary's.

Meantime, their neighbors, the Yanktons, impressed by what they saw, urgently asked for a missionary. In answer to the call the Rev. J. W. Cook came to them, and remained till the day of his death. Large numbers were in attendance upon the services and day-school from the first. Two Sisters, trained at the Bishop Potter Memorial House, Philadelphia, Sister Anna Prichard and Sister Lizzie Stitler, afterwards Mrs. Cleveland, were among the ladies associated with the work, also Miss Anna Baker, afterward Mrs. Gregory, and Miss Hicks, afterward Mrs. Cook. During 1871 Miss West was with them part of the time. She and Sister Lizzie, with the help of Mrs. Daniel Hemans, wife of the native deacon, for interpreter, instituted meetings for the instruction and improvement of the women. The next year a sewing-school was started by the ladies of the Mission, as-

(59)

sisted by Mrs. Gasman, wife of the agent, and Mrs. Canfield, the agency carpenter's wife, two earnest Church-women. Here the women and girls were taught to cut out and sew garments, to knit, and piece quilts, and the result of their work was given to them.

After nearly two years of faithful work in the Yankton Mission Sister Lizzie was asked to help do a woman's part in the establishment of a Mission in the entirely new and unbroken field of Lower Brulé. Miss Leigh was with her, and the Rev. Mr. Cleveland was placed in charge of the Mission, with Mr. Walter Hall to assist him. Mr. Cleveland gives us a breezy account of their life there, as follows:

In October, 1872, Miss Leigh, my wife and myself began work at Lower Brulé, and the mere presence of these brave women was in itself a work of grace and a power for good among the wild occupants of the camp near by. We were the suburbanites to the tented city where dwelt and schemed old Iron Nation, Medicine Bull, Little Pheasant, Tobacco Mouth and many other leaders of the proud Burnt Thighs, their tribal name. But while yet the missionary's hands were tied for lack of any way to take hold, and his mouth dumb, not having acquired the *iapi* of the urbanites, these "daughters of Jerusalem" lit and kept burning a light in the strange little mission house—the light of a clean, well-ordered, cheery, civilized and Christian home in a dark place. In my opinion, that was the light which first struck in among those who there, given over wholly to the joy of their own city—the feast, the dance, gambling, war and lust—sat in darkness and the shadow of death. It was the first glimmer, coming not from the lips of the preacher but from the example of these women; reflecting that True Light that lighteth every man that cometh into the world, and shineth ever more and more, as we have seen it doing through the instrumentality of others like-minded in their labor of love among the Sioux, unto the perfect day. All it was possible for them to do in that crude time was in the simplest manner to let their light shine before savages, that they might see their good works, and, later on, learn to glorify their Father and our Father which is in Heaven. They did their commonplace work of decent housekeeping under manifold trials and handicaps. Of each it was true, "She hath done what she could," but it was arranged for them that their abundant grace in doing that little faithfully should, through the thanksgiving of many, redound to the glory of God.

There were, moreover, no circuses to visit cities in those lands, so it was arranged for us all that, quite involuntarily, we should constitute ourselves into a counter attraction to the harmful amusements which beguiled dull hours in the Red Man's camp. Not being gifted otherwise in that line, we resolved ourselves (or were constituted willy-nilly) into a white-skinned, marvellously-garmented menagerie in a wooden cage with glass-covered openings on all sides. Day after day we drew the crowds, and window panes were smirched as painted faces gathered round, darkening the rooms, while eager, wondering eyes stared in unabashed to watch each move of the animals: how the squaws handled the outlandish implements—especially in the kitchen—how they put dishes and things around on a table, then sat on chairs (what nonsense!) and served their braves, etc., etc. My! wasn't it a show! What grins, laughter, jokes and fun on both sides of the glass!

Soon, however, it was possible to tempt a few youngsters inside and to start a little school. Here Miss Leigh was in her element. Nothing much could be taught, to be sure, but it was wonderful how quickly the Indian children, and adults too, picked up the tunes and words of hymns in their own tongue, and Miss Leigh, even as they, never tired, or showed it if she did. The whole hymn book was A. B. C. to her, and the organ a part of herself, and she was always ready to comply at any call, always willing hour after hour to play another tune, and yet another. There was work that told, and told mightily. She took the situation as it was, and gracefully did what she could. In fact, those last words cover about all there was that any of us could do "those days." There was no possible way of organizing guilds or the like, then; one just had to peck at the barbarous mass here and there. Samuel Medicine Bull was the first-fruit of Miss Leigh's teaching at Lower Brulé, and what is above given will serve as descriptive of the beginnings of the women's work in other new fields. At Old Spotted Tail, Rosebud, later, Miss Leigh had Miss Sophie Pendleton for an associate in the work, while Mrs. Cleveland, for the most part, "did the other things." Why, you know yourself how it used to be, and that there was enough work all the time to keep those good pioneer women from ever being dull, though often very tired. The Rev. Joseph Marshall, Miss Leigh's crack schoolboy at Beaver Creek, was one fruit of her labors there.

THE VISITING PRESIDENT

By Marie J. Hopkins,

Travelling Missionary and formerly President of the Chicago Branch

THE life of the visiting president is far from monotonous. She might be a tourist, seeing Europe in the most approved American fashion, so varied is the experience of each day. For there are city parishes and country parishes; vigorous Auxiliary branches and those that are just learning to walk in the missionary way; knots of women in leisurely rural circles and groups of two or three, who are certainly faithful in good works, since, upon their capable shoulders falls the entire burden of Church work, parochial and diocesan, as well as that of the wider outlook that is most truly missionary. And there are those regions—ay, there's the rub!—where missionary zeal, if, indeed, it ever existed, is falling into gray ashes, where the faint glow is fading away, where people will have "none of missions."

Every visiting president learns, first of all, in her alphabet of "symptoms," that the branches that need her presence most, want her least. This paradoxical condition furnishes mental pabulum most stimulating kind to enliven many an hour of travel, as she returns from some distant visit and busily plans others. In facing bravely the difficulty of reaching such branches, she would do well to hang above her desk, and to ponder upon these sacred words, "God is a righteous Judge, strong and patient, and God is provoked every day." She cannot allow herself to be provoked into petty feeling by any woman or set of women in the diocese. If she has "feelings," it would be better for her to resign at once. No one with "feelings" can do God's work well. If she approaches each individual case that puzzles her, with prayer and consecration, the way will open and

THE TOWN HALL IN X—— WHERE MARY STUART RECEIVED SLIGHT ATTENTION

light will come, and her map of "undiscovered country," bearing the names of many parishes and missions in the diocese without working Auxiliary branches, will show such gains that she will feel like a Peary, with the coveted North Pole in sight.

The responsibilities of a visiting president may prove, at times, burdensome, but her joys are superlative. She makes and cements intimate personal friendships among the choicest spirits in the diocese, nay, in the whole round world— Churchwomen, pledged to the cause of missions. In her travels she carries the missionary utterance as her main object, never, for one moment, forgetting that she is a messenger; but she also finds time for the Church supper of rural communities; she even lectures on timely topics of the day in localities not lecture-ridden, and she enjoys the hospitable farm-house dinner, where, perhaps, a dozen women have come to greet her, having gathered from the vast prairie for many miles around, as loyal to the missionary call as were the devoted followers of grim Roderick Dhu, when his fiery signal summoned them to gather for warfare.

Nor is the lightsome play of humor lacking in the experience of a visiting president. The writer of these words well recalls one meeting in the little village of X——, which boasts the richest of cream and the purest of air and half a thousand inhabitants. The loyal Auxiliary branch in this delightful spot had planned festivities that should last an entire day, to celebrate the visit of their diocesan president. The town hall had been rented, where an Auxiliary meeting was scheduled for the morning, to be followed by a turkey dinner at noon, and a lecture on "Mary, Queen of Scots" in the afternoon, the sum charged for the dinner including the lecture also, for "good measure." The president confessed to a tickling of vanity in her very human heart, when over one-third of the entire population of X—— gathered for the dinner and the subsequent lecture, but her vanity was shortlived. Upon inquiring in a casual way whether any Roman Catholics were in the audience, she was told that about thirty of the most prominent Romanists in the county were before her. Imagine her consternation, for she had made of the ill-fated Mary a peg on which to hang the entire English Reformation! Hastily did she repair to some secluded spot, and glance over her notes, and it is needless to say that she gave another lecture with the inoffensive title of "Lights and Shades of Foreign Travel," in which she referred to Mary as a "beautiful but unfortunate queen"! With the proceeds in cash of that day, the branch at X—— more than paid its missionary pledges.

Concentration is the watchword of the hour, and in a large diocese no gatherings are quite as ideal as the smaller meetings that include several neighboring parishes or missions, and that rejoice in the name of "sectional meetings," so called from the sectional bookcases so widely advertised. One ideal sectional meeting was held in the month of roses in the garden-like villa of Z——. All along the trolley line that balmy June morning, prosaic passengers sleepily rubbed their eyes, for at every station they beheld groups of bright, eager women, with "Auxiliary" writ large on their faces, while all the carriages of Z——, the hostesses attired in white, were waiting to welcome the travellers after their ride through verdant fields. The church at Z—— is a tiny one, nestling under lofty trees, beside a great family estate, to whose fair mistress the little building, dating from the time when Z—— boasted but a handful of people, owes existence.

A flag hung over the door of the church, as we passed under the arched gate and entered the flower-laden interior. Every seat was filled, and there were chairs in the aisles, as we joined in the simple service that ushered in our sectional meeting. The rector of the parish welcomed us, and the missionary addresses were given by neighboring clergymen, whose delegates sat proudly in the congregation. Roll call showed over one hundred delegates present, representing some ten or twelve branches. Luncheon was served in a spacious home near the church, and the president's rule that none but the simplest meal should be served was right royally disobeyed. The lawn and gardens were a real benison to those who had come from city streets, and the lace-like shower that fell for a few minutes during the noon hour was a blessing in disguise, as it made the women hasten indoors for the social chat

that is such a feature of our sectional meetings.

With the usual preliminaries of reports and statistics, the afternoon session began, and then came that opportunity so highly prized by the members of a great diocesan branch—time to discuss ways and means, methods and pledges. The large annual and semi-annual meetings give time for only the briefest summaries, and it is to the sectional meeting we have learned to turn for the valuable information brought out in the reports. One by one, in orderly array, did each branch present report its work in money and boxes for the previous year. Each report showed strong points and weak points, and interest was at fever heat to know how one branch had given such a large sum to the United Offering, and how another had raised double the amount of any other branch, for the diocesan pledges. Quick and fast came question and answer at that precious sectional meeting, when missionary zeal and enthusiasm soared far above all cut-and-dried rules of order. This president counted herself fortunate when she could crowd in two offerings in one day, and the money side of a sectional meeting was thus a powerful object-lesson to those faint-hearted women who hate to ask for money. Dimes and quarters and dollars literally rained into the little alms-basins, the women showing their eagerness to give "something," no matter how small the sum.

All things must come to an end, and so did our day at Z——. The president presided, watch in hand, for she had promised that the meeting should close in time for the afternoon car that should take every delegate home in time for dinner. The last missionary hymn was sung, hasty farewells were said, and we left the little church to the birds and the purple shades of evening, a tear in the eye and a song in the heart, as we thought of one whole perfect day in perfect June devoted to the greatest work in all the world, the missionary work of our beloved Church.

WOMAN'S AUXILIARY PAPERS

NO. IV: DIOCESAN OFFICERS

DIOCESAN Officers of the Woman's Auxiliary number in its ninety-two branches very nearly 1,000. In a few branches there are less than half a dozen, in some there are twenty, thirty, even fifty and over. Some of these are appointed by the bishops, some chosen by the branch, some elected by the branch have this election then confirmed by the bishop, of some it is difficult to learn just how and by whom they are elected or appointed. Branches where this is the case should especially notice that the resolution on representation adopted at the last triennial explicitly states·that officers entitled to take part in the next triennial conference must have been "elected or appointed at the last annual meeting of their branches."

But, however elected or appointed diocesan officers may be, it is certainly important they should understand before accepting election or appointment, something of what that acceptance should involve. Every diocesan officer should know what the Woman's Auxiliary is: A helper to the Board of Missions of the Church as a whole; an association formed to extend through every diocese and missionary district, through every parish and mission, to gather into its membership all women old and young throughout the Church, with a Junior Department to enlist the young girls and children even from the day of baptism.

The new diocesan officer therefore will look at once to see how many parishes and missions in her own diocese have parish branches of the Auxiliary, and, together, the diocesan officers of a branch will plan and work to increase that number.

The diocesan officer will inform herself as to the obligations of the Auxiliary: She will study, so that she may not be confused between appropriations and apportionments, designated contributions and specials; with her fellow-officers she will note what has been apportioned to

her own diocesan branch for General Missions, and will learn what regularly given designated contributions count on this, and together the officers will distribute the apportionment among the parish branches, suggesting a definite proportion of it to each.

The diocesan officer will know the United Offering; its story, that she may tell it to others, its purpose, that ·she may inform and stimulate them, íts methods of collection, that she may train them in continuous and thankful giving. She should not only take, but carefully read and keep on file, THE SPIRIT OF MISSIONS, the Reports of the· Missionary Society and the Auxiliary, and the leaflets of the Auxiliary. She should study how Auxiliary work along all its lines—devotional, educational and practical—may be developed; adding to the box work of early Auxiliary days, and to the loving gifts in response to special appeals, the habit of conscientious giving from instructed principle for the mission work as one great whole, enlisting for General Missions and the United Offering, the rank and file of all Auxiliary givers, while gathering one by one the names of women able to give largely, who shall agree to welcome the visits of missionaries representing special work approved by the Board, to listen willingly to the opportunities of which they tell, and to give largely of their abundance. To the frequent meeting, with its constant claim on the live missionary as a speaker, she should add the normal study class in which selected pupils from the parish branches · shall come for definite training in the conduct of mission study classes in their parishes, learning how to gain and to give information and enthusiasm without overtaxing the time and strength of missionaries at home on furlough. The Quiet Day, with its set hours of prayer and spiritual instruction, she should supplement by the use at parish meetings of the Sanctuary of Missions printed monthly in THE SPIRIT OF MISSIONS, and with the encouragement of constant intercession in the parish branches, for all missionaries and missionary needs brought to their notice, and with continual remembrance of and thanksgiving for blessings bestowed. And, in view, of the future opened before us through the object of the United Offering, the diocesan officer should keep in mind, and keep in the minds of the parochial officers within the diocese, the realization that the best gift to the mission field is the missionary herself; encouraging in all parishes and missions continued search for and constant watchfulness over those young people who, trained habitually in the missionary spirit and taught by practical work in Sunday-school and hospital and neighborhood ministries, how to serve Christ in the person of the ignorant and the poor, shall there get their first lessons to be practised in the lifelong service in the mission field itself. Such a diocesan officer as has been pictured here is the one who is the true helper of the Board of Missions and in the missionary society whose representative the Board of Missions is; and the responsibility thus laid upon her will be all the better fulfilled if, in her own person as a member of Christ's Body, the Church, she exemplifies the Love which made her what she is, by showing it to those among whom she lives in deeds of personal service in their behalf.

HINTS FOR JUNIOR LEADERS

OUR Junior leaders are certainly realizing more and more how important the work is, and as they appreciate this they will think more often and more seriously of their responsibility. And surely the responsibilities and privileges of Junior service are among the greatest in the Church to-day. To-day we see clearer than ever before how true it is that "the fields are white to harvest," that we lack only the laborers to be sent out; how

nothing prevents the Church from taking "the world for Christ," but the fact that there is not an adequate force to send to the front. It is given to Junior leaders to find and train a part of the force, which surely in the next generation will "move like a mighty army" to fulfil the Church's mission. How can we best go about this work? Here are a few simple hints or suggestions for Junior Diocesan Leaders:

1. *Study how to use time.* We are not to "save" time. No one should accept an office unless she is willing to give much time and thought; unless, as far as possible, her Junior work, next to her home, is her first consideration.

2. *Find, use and pass on the best methods.* Do not be content to use the second best, or methods because they are the "things always done." Keep in touch with the new ways of educating and training children.

3. *Plan all the work far enough ahead.* Many a plan might be carried out successfully if only it had been begun earlier, but is spoiled or marred by being rushed through.

4. *Choose and train leaders.* The most important work diocesan leaders have is not to teach the rank and file, but to prepare and train the officers. It is better to train ten leaders than to interest one hundred children.

5. *Have Normal Study Mission Classes.* This is a practical way of training your leaders, and you will find that the best way to bring about a general study of missions is to do all in your power to persuade to join these classes leaders who will pledge themselves in their turn to teach their branches.

6. *Use your officers.* Do not do all the work. The more others are given to do the more interest they will take in the work. There are some things which you, as leader, can do better than any one else, but do not do what can be given them to do. See that they feel that they are responsible for the growth of the whole and that you depend on them for advice and co-operation.

7. *Let your work be both intensive*

and extensive. There is a very real danger in going to the extreme in either direction. Try therefore to do intensive
work first, making the branches which
already exist worthy of existence. When
you have done this do not be satisfied because you have some good branches; this
is the time to gain others of the same
kind.

8. *Make use of personal visits and interviews.* A talk will often accomplish
more than a letter. Let each parish
leader feel that you are interested in *her*
branch, and that you have an intelligent
knowledge of *her* work and *her* problems.
Above all things be sympathetic.

9. *Emphasize essentials.* Never be
afraid of putting the work on too high a
plane, but in addresses and interviews
dwell on essentials, and non-essentials
will take care of themselves.

10. *Try never to hurry away after a
meeting.* You can often accomplish
much after your special part in it is done
by staying to meet the officers and children.

11. *Don't be afraid to try new plans.*
Nothing is more striking than to find, as
one often does, that the thing you only
dreamed of doing and had not dared
think possible, was the very thing the
Auxiliary was most ready to help you
carry out.

12. *Guard the spirit in which you do
your work.* Remember we are not responsible for *success,* that is God's part.
We must never allow ourselves to get
worried or distracted, but do our work
quietly without feeling hurried, and we
will both do better work and avoid
breaking down, for He will give us
strength, since we and our work are both
His.

THE DECEMBER CON-
FERENCE

MRS. NEILSON, President of the
Pennsylvania Branch, presided
over the December conference of dioc-
esan officers, on Thursday the 16th.
Thirty officers were present: Central
New York, 1; Connecticut, 3; Long
Island, 3; Louisiana, 1; Maryland,
1; Newark, 4—1 Junior; New Jersey, 2;

(67)

ACKNOWLEDGMENT OF OFFERINGS

Offerings are asked to sustain missions in thirty missionary districts in the United States, Africa, China, Japan, Brazil, Mexico and Cuba; also work in the Haitien Church; in forty-two dioceses, including missions to the Indians and to the Colored People; to pay the salaries of thirty-two bishops, and stipends to 2,253 missionary workers, domestic and foreign; also two general missionaries to the Swedes and two missionaries among deaf-mutes in the Middle West and the South; and to support schools, hospitals and orphanages. With all remittances the name of the Diocese and Parish should be given. Remittances, when practicable, should be by Check or Draft, and should always be made payable to the order of George Gordon King, Treasurer, and sent to him, Church Missions House, 281 Fourth Avenue, New York. Remittances in Bank Notes are not safe unless sent in Registered Letters.

The Treasurer of the Board of Missions acknowledges the receipt of the following from November 1st to December 1st, 1909

* Lenten and Easter Offering from the Sunday-school Auxiliary.

NOTE.—*The items in the following pages marked "Sp." are Specials which do not aid the Board in meeting its appropriations. In the heading for each Diocese the total marked "Ap." is the amount which does aid the Board of Missions in meeting its appropriations. Wherever the abbreviation "Wo. Aux." precedes the amount, the offering is through a branch of the Woman's Auxiliary*

Home Dioceses

Alabama
Ap. $65.00; *Sp.* $165.37

ANNISTON—*Grace*: Gen............	50 00
BIRMINGHAM—*St. Mary's*: Sp. for Tsu Property Fund, Kyoto............	65 37
COAL VALLEY—*Mission*: Gen.......	4 50
FLORENCE—*Trinity Church*: Gen.....	3 00
TALLADEGA—*St. Peter's*: Gen.......	7 50
MISCELLANEOUS—Bishop Beckwith, Sp. for Tsu Property Fund, Kyoto....	100 00

Albany
Ap. $395.11; *Sp.* $126.00

ALBANY—*All Saints' Cathedral*: Gen..	105 01
COHOES—*St. John's*: Gen..........	8 05
EAST LINE—*St. John's*: Gen........	12 50
FORT EDWARD—*St. James's*: Gen....	3 70
HUDSON—*Christ Church*: Sp. for Bishop Griswold, Salina............	25 00
MECHANICSVILLE—*St. Luke's*: Gen...	13 54
OGDENSBURG—*St. John's* S. S.*: Gen.	62 61
POTSDAM — *Trinity Church*: Indian, $7.10 (Frn., $12.60, Apportionment, 1908-09); "T. Streatfield Clarkson" (In Memoriam) (Graduate) scholarship, $60; "Levinus Clarkson" (In Memoriam) (Graduate) scholarship, $60......................	139 70
ROUSE'S POINT—*Christ Church*: Gen.	15 00
SCHENECTADY — Miss Florence C. Strong, Sp. for Mexican famine sufferers	1 00
SOUTH CAIRO—"Cash," Frn.........	35 00
TROY—George B. Cluett, Sp. for St. John's College Expansion Fund....	100 00

Arkansas
Sp. $1.00

MARIANNA—*St. Andrew's*: Dudley S. Clark, Sp. for Church Extension Fund, Porto Rico................	1 00

(68)

Atlanta
Ap. $396.54; *Sp.* $100.00

ATHENS — *Emmanuel Church*: Dom. and Frn., $5....................	39 5
ATLANTA—*Church of the Holy Comforter*: Dom..............	10 0
FORT VALLEY—*St. Andrew's*: Dom., $2.26; Frn., $2.25.............	4 5
COLLEGE PARK—*St. John's*: Dom....	10 0
MACON—*Christ Church*: (Apportionment, 1908-09) Gen.............	225 0
MARIETTA—*St. James's*: For Deaf-Mutes	2 5
TALLAPOOSA—*St. Ignatius's*: Gen.....	5 0
MISCELLANEOUS—Through Right Rev. C. H. Nelson, Sp. for Dr. Correll's work, Kyoto...............	100 0

Bethlehem
Ap. $370.75; *Sp.* $174.14

ATHENS—*Trinity Church*: Gen.......	17 0
DORRANCETON—*Grace Chapel S. S.*: Frn.	30 1
DRIFTON—*St. James's*: Sp. for Dr. Correll's work at Tsu, Kyoto........	141 1
HAZLETON—*St. Peter's*: Domestic Missionary, $13.90, Wo. Aux., $23, Junior Aux., $10, Sp. for Tsu Property Fund, Kyoto................	46 9
READING—*St. Mary's Chapel*: Gen....	5 0
SCRANTON—*Church of the Good Shepherd*: Gen.....................	50 0
St. Luke's: Indian, $36.16; Gen., $6..	42 1
WILKES-BARRE—*St. Stephen's S. S.*: Frn., $22.57; "St. Stephen's" scholarship, St. Hilda's School, Wuchang, Hankow, $50; "St. Peter's" scholarship, St. Agnes's School, Kyoto, $50; "St. Stephen's" scholarship, Cape Palmas Orphan Asylum, Africa, $50; "St. Stephen's" scholarship, High School, Africa, $40.....	212 t

California

Ap. $37.59 ; *Sp.* $174.05

ALAMEDA Co.—Wo. Aux., Sp. for Catechist School Fund, Shanghai...... 12 00
KING CITY—*St. Mark's*: Gen........ 4 00
MILL VALLEY—*Church of Our Saviour*: Gen...................... 7 50
OAKLAND—*St. Paul's*: Sp. for work in Utah 55 95
SAN FRANCISCO—*Grace*: Sp. for Catechist School Fund, Shanghai, $50 ; Wo. Aux., Sp. for Utah, $15....... 65 00
St. John's: Gen.................... 6 09
St. Luke's: Wo. Aux., Sp. for Catechist School Fund, Shanghai...... 10 00
St. Stephen's: Sp. for Utah.......... 11 10
SAN RAFAEL—*St. Paul's*: Gen...... 20 00
MISCELLANEOUS—"A Friend," Sp. for Catechist School Fund, Shanghai... 19 00
"A Friend," Sp. for Bishop Spalding's work, Utah................. 1 00

Central New York

Ap. $70.15

HOMER—*Calvary*: Gen............. 15 00
PHOENIX—*St. John's*: Gen.......... 8 00
SYRACUSE—*Calvary*: Gen........... 21 00
Grace: Gen...................... 5 00
UTICA—*Grace*: Gen............... 10 00
St. Andrew's; Dom., $3.50; Gen., $7.65 11 15

Chicago

Ap. $205.15

CHICAGO—*Calvary*: Wo. Aux., Gen... 1 00
Christ Church: Gen............... 35 15
Church of Our Saviour: Gen........ 41 38
St. Barnabas's: Gen.............. 14 85
St. Luke's: Gen................. 10 67
St. Paul's: Mrs. W. C. Wheelock, Gen. 75 00
St. Philip's: Dom. and Frn.......... 1 85
St. James's: Wo. Aux., Evening Guild, Gen. 5 00
CHICAGO LAWN—*St. Elizabeth's*: Dom. and Frn...................... 2 60
DUNDEE—*St. James's*: Gen.......... 7 50
EVANSTON—*St. Matthew's*: Gen...... 5 15
HINSDALE—*Grace*: Wo. Aux., Gen.... 5 00

Connecticut

Ap. $214.68 ; *Sp.* $791.25

BLACK HALL—*Guild Room Mission*: Gen. 5 13
BRISTOL—*Trinity Church*: Dom. and Frn. 5 00
CHESTER—*St. Luke's S. S.*: (Additional) Gen................... 1 00
EAST HADDAM—Rev. Dr. F. C. H. Wendel, Colored, $1 ; Mrs. F. C. H. Wendel, Sp. for St. Agnes's Hospital, Raleigh, North Carolina, $1....... 2 00
GUILFORD—"G.," Alaska............ 6 00
HARTFORD—*St. John's*: Sp. for St. John's College Expansion Fund, Shanghai 25 00
Trinity Church: D. G. Littlejohn, $5, "S. M. B.," $20, "A Friend," $10, "A Member," $10, "A Member," $5, Sp. for Expansion Fund, St. John's University, Shanghai............ 50 00
MARBLEDALE—*St. Andrew's*: "A Member," Sp. for famine sufferers in Mexico 2 00
MERIDEN—*All Saints' S. S.*: Gen.... 21 00
St. Andrew's: Colored, $4.50; G. M. Curtis, Sp. for Church Extension Fund, Porto Rico, $5........... 9 50
NEW HAVEN—*St. Paul's*: George S. Armstrong, Sp. for St. John's College Expansion Fund, Shanghai... 50 00
NEW LONDON—Wo. Aux., annual meet-

ing, Sp. for St. John's University Expansion Fund, Shanghai........ 80 00
NORWALK—*Grace*: Gen............ 15 00
POMFRET — *Christ Church*: Dom., $28.16 ; Frn., $28.16............ 56 32
RIDGEFIELD — *St. Stephen's*: "A Friend," Sp. for Church Extension Fund, Porto Rico, $50 ; Girls' Sewing-class, Gen., $5.25........... 55 25
SHELTON—Mission Study Class, Sp. for St. Margaret's School Bed Fund, Tokyo 17 25
TORRINGTON—"A Friend," Sp. for relief work, Mexico.............. 1 00
WATERBURY—*St. John's*: Alaska..... 67 35
MISCELLANEOUS — Litchfield Archdeaconry, Wo. Aux., Gen.......... 18 13
Wo. Aux., "A Member," Sp. for St. John's College Expansion Fund, Shanghai 10 00
"Friend of the late Treasurer, Mr. Thomas," Sp. for Bishop Thomas, Wyoming, toward support of his clergy 500 00
"R.," "From Three Friends," Gen.. 9 00

Dallas

Ap. $27.35 ; *Sp.* $10.00

ABILENE—*Heavenly Rest*: Wo. Aux., Gen. 12 35
FORT WORTH—*St. Andrew's*: Wo. Aux., Indian, $10 ; Sp. for St. Mary's-on-the-Mountain, Sewanee, Tennessee, $10.................. 20 00
Trinity Church: Junior Aux., Gen... 5 00

Delaware

Ap. $138.01

MIDDLETOWN—*St. Anne's*: Gen...... 3 00
NEWARK—*St. Thomas's*: (Apportionment, 1908-09) Gen........... 20 00
WILMINGTON — *Immanuel Church*: Dom. 115 01

Duluth

Ap. $398.89

ALEXANDRIA—*Emmanuel Church*: Gen. 2 10
BEAULIEU—*Epiphany*: Gen.......... 3 90
BENA—*St. Matthew's*: Gen.......... 2 75
BEND OF THE RIVER—*St. Philip's*: Gen. 3 00
BRAINERD—*St. Paul's*: Gen......... 4 45
BRECKENRIDGE—*St. Paul's*: Gen.... 1 00
BROWN'S VALLEY—*St. Luke's*: Gen... 1 05
CASS LAKE—*Prince of Peace*: Gen... 4 25
CROOKSTON—*Christ Church*: Gen.... 22 42
DETROIT—*St. Luke's*: Gen......... 5 05
DULUTH—*St. John's*: Gen......... 4 11
St. Paul's: Wo. Aux., Colored, $25 ; school work in China, $25........ 50 00
Trinity Church: Dom.............. 197 00
EAGLE BEND—*Emmanuel Church*: Gen 3 50
GLENWOOD—*St. Paul's*: Gen........ 71
GRACEVILLE—*Gethsemane*: Gen...... 3 00
HIBBING—*Christ Church*: Gen...... 9 50
LAKE PARK—*St. John's*: Gen....... 2 85
MELROSE—*Trinity Church*: Gen..... 2 15
MOOREHEAD—*St. John's*: Gen...... 8 00
NORTHOME—Gen.................. 1 25
ORTONVILLE—*St. John's*: Gen...... 75
PAYNESVILLE—*St. Stephen's*: Gen... 75
PINE POINT—*Breck Memorial*: Gen.. 3 75
RED LAKE—*St. John's*: Gen........ 10 50
REDLEY—*St. Antipas's*: Gen...... 6 75
ST. VINCENT—*Christ Church*: Gen.... 4 00
SAUK CENTRE—*Good Samaritan*: Gen. 3 40
STAPLES—*St. Alban's*: Gen........ 7 75
TENSTRIKE—Gen................. 2 00
TWIN LAKES—*Samuel Memorial*: Gen. 7 50
TWO HARBORS—*St. Paul's*: Gen..... 3 85
WADENA—*St. Helena's*: Gen........ 8 85
WILLOW RIVER—*St. Jude's*: Gen..... 5 00

East Carolina

Ap. $73.91

EDENTON—Convocation, Gen......... 22 60
HERTFORD—*Holy Trinity Church*: Wo.
Aux., Alaska, $1'; China, $1; Japan,
$1; Gen., $1.................... 4 00
NEW BERNE—*Christ Church*: Wo.
Aux., Gen.................... 5 00
WASHINGTON—*St. Peter's*: Wo. Aux.,
Gen. 5 00
WILMINGTON—*St. James's*: $25, Mrs.
Walter L. Parsley, $5, "A Member,"
$3, Gen.......................... 33 00
WOODVILLE—*Grace*: Gen........... 4 31

Fond du Lac

Ap. $42.30

ASHLAND—*St. Andrew's*: Gen....... 1 40
PLYMOUTH—*St. Paul's*: Dom........ 35 90
WAUSAU—*St. John's*: Gen........... 5 00

Georgia

Ap. $31.10

SAVANNAH—*St. John's*: Wo. Aux.,
salary of Miss Crummer, Shanghai.. 25 00
St. Paul's: Wo. Aux., Gen......... 6 10

Harrisburg

Ap. $345.68 ; *Sp.* $4.87

GALETON—*Church of the Good Shep-
herd*: Gen..................... 1 15
HARRISBURG—*St. Andrew's*: Gen..... 109 16
LANCASTER—*St. James's*: Dom. and
Frn., $177.07 ; Medical Missions in
Alaska, $25.................... 202 07
PARADISE—*All Saints'*: Gen........ 5 00
SELINS GROVE—*All Saints'*: Gen..... 5 15
SHAMOKIN — *Trinity Church*: Gen.,
$10 ; S. S., Sp. for Equipment Fund,
Ichang, Hankow, $4.87.......... 14 87
WELLSBORO—*St. Paul's*: Dom., $5;
Frn., $5....................... 10 00
WESTFIELD—*St. John's*: Gen........ 3 15

Indianapolis

Ap. $4.00

MADISON—*Christ Church*: Gen...... 4 00

Iowa

Ap. $9.00

DES MOINES—*St. Paul's*: Gen....... 4 00
DUBUQUE—*St. John's*: Salary of Rev.
Mr. Nieh, Hanchuan, Hankow..... 5 00

Kansas

Ap. $24.00

FORT RILEY—*Mission*: Gen.......... 19 00
KANSAS CITY—*St. Paul's*: Gen...... 5 00

Kansas City

Ap. $75.00

ST. JOSEPH—*Christ Church*: Gen..... 75 00

Kentucky

Ap. $173.91 ; *Sp.* $14.72

LOUISVILLE — *Advent*: Junior Aux.,
Gen........................... 7 00
Epiphany: Wo. Aux., Gen.......... 15 00
Grace: Junior Aux., Gen.......... 5 00
St. Andrew's: (Apportionment, 1908-
09) Gen.. $130.26; Wo. Aux.,
Brazil, $12.50.................. 142 76
St. Peter's: Junior Aux., Gen...... 2 15
St. Thomas's: Junior Aux., Gen.... 2 00
Wo. Aux., Sp. for St. Elizabeth's
Hospital Building Fund, Shanghai.. 14 72

Lexington

Ap. $10.00; *Sp.* $25.00

DANVILLE—*Trinity Church*: Gen.... 5 00

ELIZABETHTOWN—*Christ Church*: Gen. 5
LEXINGTON—*Christ Church Cathedral*:
Wo. Aux., Sp. for life insurance of
Rev. C. H. Evans, Tokyo.......... 25

Long Island

Ap. $408.53 ; *Sp.* $339.50

BELLPORT—*Christ Church*: Gen...... 5
BROOKLYN—*Church of St. Mark*: Dom.
and Frn....................... 18
St. Ann's: William G. Low, Sp. for
famine sufferers, Mexico, $250; Wo.
Aux., Sp. for Rev. C. E. Betticher,
Jr., Fairbanks, Alaska, for door and
window of native cabin, $10....... 260
St. George's S. S.: For "St. George's"
scholarship, St. John's University,
Shanghai 50
St. Jude's: Wo. Aux., Sp. for Domes-
tic Contingent Fund............. 2
St. Philip's (Dyker Heights): Gen.. 12
BROOKLYN — "Anonymous," Sp. for
Mexican Famine Fund............ 25
FLUSHING—*St. George's*: Dom...... 91
GARDEN CITY—C. P. Turner, Frn.,
$50 ; Boone College, Wuchang, Han-
kow, $50...................... 100
ROCKAWAY—*Trinity Church*: Gen.... 30
ROSLYN—*Trinity Church*: Dom. and
Frn........................... 100
ST. JAMES—*St. James's*: Wo. Aux.,
Sp. at discretion of Mrs. F. R.
Graves, Shanghai............... 50
MISCELLANEOUS—Mrs. Paulding, Wo.
Aux., Sp. for Mrs. F. R. Graves,
for furnishing the Mrs. Scheres-
chewsky Memorial Station School,
Shanghai 2

Los Angeles

Ap. $16.80 ; *Sp.* $117.20

LOS ANGELES—*St. Paul's Cathedral*:
Wo. Aux., Sp. for Bishop Spalding,
Utah 25
MONTECITO — *All Saints'-by-the-Sea*:
Gen........................... 16
PASADENA—*All Saints'*: Wo. Aux., Sp.
for Bishop Scadding, Oregon...... 50
SAN DIEGO—H. N. Manney, Sp. for
Bishop Whipple Memorial, Havana,
Cuba 10
TERMINAL — *St. Michael and All
Angels'*: Gen.................. 10
MISCELLANEOUS—Wo. Aux., Sp. for
Bishop Spalding, Utah........... 32

Louisiana

Ap. $356.35 ; *Sp.* $2.00

AMITE—*Incarnation*: Wo. Aux., Mrs.
Evans's salary, Alaska, $1; Miss
Suthon's salary, Kyoto, $1........ 2
HOUMA—*St. Matthew's*: Wo. Aux., Sp.
for St. James's Church, Mesilla
Park, New Mexico............... 2
NEW ORLEANS — *Annunciation*: Wo.
Aux., Miss Suthon's salary, Kyoto..
Christ Church: Wo. Aux., Gen., $2;
Miss Suthon's salary, Kyoto, 50
cts........................... 2
St. John's: Wo. Aux., Miss Evans's
salary, Alaska, 25 cts.; Miss Su-
thon's salary, Kyoto, $1; Gen.,
25 cts........................ i
St. Paul's: Wo. Aux., Miss Evans's
salary, Alaska, $2; Miss Suthon's
salary, Kyoto, $6.25; Gen., $310.. 318
Trinity Church: Wo. Aux., Miss
Suthon's salary, Kyoto........... 5
THIBODAUX—*St. John's*: Wo. Aux.,
Miss Suthon's salary, Kyoto, $4.20;
Gen., $2...................... 6
MISCELLANEOUS — Babies' Branch,
Jack Eastwood Memorial, for Japan
Kindergarten 20

Maryland

Ap. $191.05; *Sp.* $205.32

ANNE ARUNDEL CO. — *St. Anne's Parish*: Gen.................... 50 00
BALTIMORE—*St. Paul's Parish*: (In Memoriam) "L. C. A.," Dom...... 5 00
Grace: Wo. Aux., Sp. for St. Luke's Hospital, Tokyo................. 5 00
Memorial: Wo. Aux., Sp. for Bishop Whipple Memorial, Havana, Cuba.. 10 00
Mt. Calvary: Wo. Aux., Sp. for Miss Ridgely's house, Cape Mount, West Africa 10 00
"A Friend," Gen................... 25 00
"H. W. A.," Sp. for Rev. Mr. Ancell, Shanghai.................. 10 00
"A Friend," Sp. for St. Margaret's School Building Fund, Tokyo...... 1 00
BALTIMORE CO.—*Reisterstown Parish*: Gen. 41 05
Oldfields School (Glencoe): Sp. for St. Margaret's School Building Fund, Tokyo 17 32
St. Mark's-on-the-Hill (Pikesville): Wo. Aux., Sp. for Miss Ridgely's house, Cape Mount, West Africa... 10 00
Trinity Church (Towson): Wo. Aux., Sp. for Miss Ridgely's house, Cape Mount, West Africa............ 75 00
Church of the Holy Comforter (Lutherville): Wo. Aux., Sp. for Rev. J. R. Ellis, Elliston, Virginia.. 17 00
Epiphany S. S. (Ready Avenue): Sp. for "Weston O'Brien Harding" scholarship, Mr. Standing's School, Soo-chow, Shanghai............. 35 00
FREDERICK CO.—*Zion* (Urbana): Dom. and Frn.................... 10 00
HOWARD CO.—*St. John's* (Ellicott City): Wo. Aux., Indian, $2.50; Colored, $5; Frn., $2.50; Sp. for famine sufferers, Mexico, $10...... 20 00
Trinity Church (Elkridge): Wo. Aux., "Paid" scholarship, Boone University, Wuchang, Hankow.......... 50 00
MISCELLANEOUS—Wo. Aux., Sp. for St. James's Church, Mesilla Park, New Mexico.................... 5 00

Massachusetts

Ap. $563.95; *Sp.* $995.25

AMESBURY—*St. James's*: Gen....... 9 55
ARLINGTON—*St. John's*: M. Wharton Bickley, Sp. for Rev. Edmund J. Lee's work, Anking, Hankow...... 10 00
BOSTON—*Advent*: Wo. Aux., "Member," Sp. for Rev. Nathan Matthews's Trade-school, Cape Mount, West Africa................... 1 90
St. Paul's: Wo. Aux., salary of Nathan Matthews, Cape Mount, West Africa. 20 00
St. Margaret's (Brighton): The Girls' Friendly Society, Sp. for salary of deacon, for Rev. S. C. Hughson, O. H. C., St. Andrew's School, Sewanee, Tennessee............ 5 00
Trinity Church: Hon. Charles R. Codman, Sp. for Church Extension Fund, Porto Rico, $25; Wo. Aux., "A Member," Sp. for life insurance of Rev. F. E. Lund, Hankow, $50.. "Friends," Sp. for St. John's College Expansion Fund, Shanghai... 75 00
BROOKLINE—*Church of Our Saviour*: Wo. Aux., salary of Rev. Nathan Matthews, Cape Mount, West Africa. 5 35
FALL RIVER—*St. John's*: Babies' Branch, Gen.................. 10 00
FALMOUTH—*St. Barnabas's*: Gen...., 10 50
MATTAPOISETT—*St. Philip's*: Wo. Aux., Sp. for Deaconess Carter's work, Alaska 9 00
                                            5 00

NEW BEDFORD—*Grace*: Frn., $146.73; "A Friend," Sp. for Church Extension Fund, Porto Rico, $10........ 156 73
NEWBURYPORT — *St. Paul's*: (Apportionment, 1908-09) Gen.......... 231 55
NEWTON — *St. John's* (Newtonville): Miss Harriet M. Swasey, Sp. for Bishop Rowe, Alaska............ 5 00
Trinity Church (Centre): Gen....... 66 62
"A Friend" (Highlands), Sp. for St. Margaret's School, Tokyo, Building Fund 1 00
TAUNTON—Mrs. Arthur V. Goss, Sp. for benefit of the children of St. John's-in-the-Wilderness, Alaska... 18 00
MISCELLANEOUS—Wo. Aux., St. Luke's Hospital, Tokyo (of which from "A Friend," $5, Mrs. Babcock, $5); Sp. for Rev. Nathan Matthews's Trade-school, Cape Mount (of which from "A Friend," $275, "A Member of the Wo. Aux.," $275); anniversary offering, November 3d, Sp. for Bishop Brooke's Hospital, Oklahoma, $117; Sp. for Dr. Pott, St. John's University, Shanghai, $117; Sp. for hospital, Manila, Philippine Islands, $25; Colored Committee, Sp. for Miss Dickerman's salary, St. Paul's School, Lawrenceville, Southern Virginia, $50.; Colored Missions, Vicksburg, Mississippi, $25; Spartanburg, South Carolina, $25.. 919 00

Michigan

Ap. $130.82; *Sp.* $80.50

ADRIAN—*Christ Church*: Wo. Aux., salary of Miss Bull, Kyoto, $1; Sp. for Foreign Life Insurance Fund, 50 cts...................... 1 50
CARO—*Trinity Church*: Gen.......... 6 25
DETROIT—*Grace*: Wo. Aux., "Personal," Sp. for Mrs. Littell's work, Hankow 5 00
St. John's: Wo. Aux., Mrs. Henry P. Baldwin, Sp. for Rev. Nathan Matthews, Cape Mount, Liberia, West Africa, for equipment of infirmary, $25; Mrs. Minor, Sp. for Girls' School, Havana, Cuba, $10; Sp. for Rev. H. C. Parke, Waynesville, Asheville, $10................ 45 00
St. Paul's: Wo. Aux., salary of Miss Bull, Kyoto................ 50 00
St. Thomas's: Wo. Aux., Gen........ 1 00
Wo. Aux., Sp. for St. Elizabeth's Hospital Building Fund, Shanghai. 18 00
GRASS LAKE—*St. Mary's*: Wo. Aux., salary of Miss Bull, Kyoto........ 2 00
HUDSON—*St. Paul's*: Gen.......... 1 00
JACKSON—*St. Paul's*: Wo. Aux., salary of Miss Bull, Kyoto, $20; "Harris Memorial" scholarship, St. John's University, Shanghai, $10; Sp. for Foreign Life Insurance Fund, $5 .... 35 00
MT. CLEMENS—*Grace*: Gen.......... 3 07
Wo. Aux., Gen............... 12 00
TRENTON—*St. Thomas's*: Wo. Aux., salary of Miss Bull, Kyoto, $2; "Harris Memorial" scholarship, St. John's University, Shanghai, $1; "J. H. Johnson" scholarship, St. Andrew's School, Mexico, $2....... 5 00
VASSAR—*St. John's*: Gen.......... 50
YPSILANTI—*St. Luke's*: Wo. Aux., Alaska, $10; Gen., $2; salary of Miss Bull, Kyoto, $5; "Harris Memorial" scholarship, St. John's University, Shanghai, $2; Sp. for Foreign Life Insurance Fund, $2; Sp. for Mrs. Littell's work, Hankow, "Personal," $5.................. 26 00

Michigan City

Ap. $12.93 ; *Sp.* $5.00

FORT WAYNE—*Trinity Church* ; Babies'
Branch, Gen......................   7 43
GARY—*Christ Church* : Babies' Branch,
Gen.......................   2 50
LAPORTE—*St. Paul's* : Wo. Aux., Sp.
for Bishop Rowe's work, Alaska....   5 00
MICHIGAN CITY — *Trinity Church* :
Junior Aux., Gen.................   3 00

Milwaukee

Ap. $102.53 ; *Sp.* $4.50

MADISON — *Grace S. S.* : The Bishop
Partridge class, Sp. at discretion of
Bishop Williams, Kyoto...........   4 50
RACINE—*St. Luke's* : Gen............   102 53

Minnesota

Ap. $440.99 ; *Sp.* $25.00

ST. PAUL—*St. Clement's* : Junior Aux.,
support of bed in the Elizabeth
Bunn Memorial Hospital, Wuchang,
Hankow 25 00
WABASHA—James G. Laurence, Sp. for
Bishop Whipple Memorial, Havana,
Cuba 25 00
MISCELLANEOUS—Wo. Aux., Sybil Car-
ter Memorial, for Supply Fund, St.
John's-in-the-Wilderness, A l a s k a,
$208 ; Frn., $77.99 ; "Bishop Whip-
ple" scholarship, $40, "Bishop Gil-
bert" scholarship, $40, both in St.
Hilda's School, Wuchang, Hankow ;
"Cora R. Brunson" scholarship, St.
Mary's Hall, Shanghai, $50.......   415 99

Mississippi

Ap. $16.80 ; *Sp.* $18.50

ABERDEEN—*St. John's* : Gen..........   1 30
JACKSON—Mrs. E. L. Ragland, Gen..   1 00
LEXINGTON—*St. Mary's* : Wo. Aux.,
Sp. for Domestic Contingent Fund..   18 50
VARDEN — *St. Clement's* : Wo. Aux.,
Gen. 3 50
WILCZINSKI—*All Saints'* : Wo. Aux.,
Gen. 1 00
WINONA — *Immanuel Church* : Wo.
Aux., Gen....................   10 00

Missouri

Ap. $147.95 ; *Sp.* $6.25

ST. LOUIS—*St. Peter's* : Dom., $42.45 ;
Frn., $42.45....................   84 90
Trinity Church : Gen...............   63 50
"A Friend," Wo. Aux., Sp. for Bish-
op Graves, Shanghai.............   6 25

Montana

Ap. $26.00

DILLON—*St. James's* : Gen...........   26 00

Newark

Ap. $1,238.49 ; *Sp.* $323.00

ALLENDALE—*Epiphany Mission* : Gen..   1 40
COYTESVILLE—*St. Stephen's* : Gen....   2 40
ENGLEWOOD—*St. Paul's* : Gen.......   27 75
GRANTWOOD—*Trinity Church S. S.* :
Gen. 6 10
JERSEY CITY—*St. John's* : Gen.......   57 43
MONTCLAIR—*St. Luke's* : Dom........   410 77
Caroline B. Brown, Sp. for Arch-
deacon Stuck, for industrial training
of natives, Alaska..............   100 00
St. James's (Upper) : Mrs. H. W.
Calef, Sp. for Expansion Fund, St.
John's University, Shanghai.......   5 00
NEWARK—*St. Barnabas's* : Gen.......   300 00
PATERSON—*St. Paul's* : Gen.........   132 64
SHORT HILLS—*Christ Church* : Dom.,

1,259 00

9 36

35 00

10 00

220 .00

15 00

225 00

17 50

3,911 67

50 00
55 23

5.00

112 00

50 00

5 00

op Horner, Asheville, $50......... 100 00
Trinity Church: German Mission, Gen. 5 00
Trinity Chapel: Dom., $100; Frn.,
$100 .... 200 00
"Eight men of the General Theological Seminary," Sp. for Rev. F. C.
Meredith, Philippines.............. 100 .00
George Zabriskie, Sp. for chancel
furniture, St. Timothy's Church,
Tokyo 89 00
"A Friend," Wo. Aux., Sp. for Domestic Contingent Fund........ ... 50 00
"A Friend," Wo. Aux., "Marie Antoinette Whitlock" scholarship, St.
Hilda's School, Wuchang, Hankow.. 50 00
Miss Livingston, Sp. for famine sufferers, Mexico.................... 50 00
Boys of Riverdale School, Sp. for
famine sufferers, Mexico.......... 25 00
Miss Wisner, Sp. for infirmary in
Africa, in charge of Rev. N. Matthews 20 00
The Misses Moore (Richmond), Wo.
Aux., Sp. for Rev. Yoshimichi
Sugiura, Tokyo.................... 10 00
Mrs. M. M. Robinson (Riverdale-on-the-Hudson), Sp. for Bishop Aves,
famine sufferers, Mexico.......... 5 00
John E. Roberts, Sp. for famine sufferers, Mexico.................... 5 00
OSSINING—Deaconess Mary Kneeves,
Wo. Aux., Gen.................... 55
PELHAM MANOR—*Christ Church*: Wo.
Aux., Miss Schuyler, $10, Miss S.
F. de Luze, $5, Mrs. Gill, $5, Mrs.
Miller, $5, Sp. for Good Shepherd
Hospital, Fort Defiance, Arizona... 25 00
POUGHKEEPSIE—*Christ Church*: Gen.. 30 00
RYE—*Christ Church*: W. V. Brady,
Sp. for Expansion Fund, St. John's
University, Shanghai, $2; Wo. Aux.,
Sp. for Bishop Restarick, Honolulu,
for furnishing the Priory, $158;
Mrs. Titus, Sp. for Rev. N. Matthews, for equipment of infirmary,
Cape Mount, Africa, $5............ 165 00
YONKERS—*St. Andrew's*: Gen........ 68 13
MISCELLANEOUS—Domestic Committee,
Wo. Aux., Seaman's Missions in
Honolulu, $300; toward expenses of
school, San Juan, Porto Rico, $400. 700 00
"A Diocesan Officer," Wo. Aux., Sp.
for Industrial School, under Mrs.
Matthews, Cape Mount, Africa..... 500 00
"C." Gen.......................... 25 00
"A Member," Wo. Aux., Sp. for
Building Fund, Dr. Lee's Hospital,
Wusih, Shanghai................ 1,000 00

North Carolina
Ap. $65.37; *Sp.* $18.50,
CHARLOTTE—*St. Peter's*: Wo. Aux.,
Alaska 5 00
DURHAM—*St. Philip's*: Wo. Aux., salary of Miss Annie Cheshire, Shanghai, $5; Miss Elizabeth Cheshire's
work, Hankow, $5; Gen., $5....... 15 00
GREENSBORO—*St. Andrew's*: Wo. Aux.,
Alaska, $2; Sp. at Bishop Rowe's
disposal, Alaska, $6.............. 8 00
St. Barnabas's: Wo. Aux., Alaska, $5;
salary of Miss Babcock, Tokyo, $2.. 7 00
HENDERSON — *Holy Innocents'*: Wo.
Aux., Miss Hick's work, Philippines,
$5; salary of Miss Babcock, Tokyo,
$5 .... 10 00
HILLSBORO—*St. Matthew's*: Wo. Aux.,
Alaska, 17 cts.; salary of Miss Babcock, Tokyo, $1.50; Sp. at Bishop
Gray's disposal, Southern Florida,
$2.50 .... 4 17
LAWRENCE—*Grace*: Wo. Aux., salary
of Miss Annie Cheshire, Shanghai.. 2 70
LITTLETON—*St. Alban's*: Wo. Aux.,
salary of Miss Annie Cheshire,

74 Acknowledgments

Shanghai, $5; Gen., $10......... 15 00
ROCKY MOUNT—*Church of the Good
Shepherd*: Wo. Aux., Sp. for "Lind-
say Patton" scholarship, at Bishop
McKim's disposal, Tokyo.......... 5 00
SOUTHERN PINES—*Emmanuel Church*:
Wo. Aux., Alaska, $1; salary of
Miss Babcock, Tokyo, $1; Sp. at
Bishop Gray's disposal, Southern
Florida, $2; Sp. for "Bishop Ches-
hire" scholarship, Holy Trinity Or-
phanage, Tokyo, $3............... 7 00
WADESBORO—*Calvary*: Wo. Aux., sal-
ary of Miss Babcock, Tokyo, $1;
Gen., $4.....................:..... 5 00

Ohio
Ap. $62.32; *Sp.* $47.00
CANTON—*St. Paul's*: Gen........... 11 25
CLEVELAND — *St. Agnes's*: Deaf-Mute
Mission, Gen.................... 2 07
St. Paul's: Wo. Aux., East Oklahoma,
$5; "Ohio" scholarship, St. Eliza-
beth's School, South Dakota, $5;
salary of Miss Elwin, Shanghai, $5.
Wo. Aux., Sp. for St. Elizabeth's 15 00
Hospital, Building Fund, Shanghai. 15 00
EAST LIVERPOOL—*St. Stephen's*: Gen. 5 00
TOLEDO—*St. John's*: Gen............ 9 00
St. Mark's: Wo. Aux., salary of Miss
Elwin, Shanghai................. 20 00
Wo. Aux., Sp. for St. Elizabeth's
Hospital, Building Fund, Shanghai. 32 00

Oregon
Sp. $20.39
PORTLAND—*St. David's*: Sp. for Utah.. 20 39

Pennsylvania
Ap. $2,720.96; *Sp.* $4,412.46
AMBLER — *Trinity Church*: Through
Wo. Aux., "Kinsolving" scholarship,
Brazil 2 00
ARDMORE—*St. Mary's*: Indian Hope
Association, Indian............... 5 00
Mrs. Wellins, Sp. for Bishop Knight,
for rebuilding of chapels, Isle of
Pines, Cuba..................... 15 00
W. H. Miller, Sp. for Isle of Pines
chapels, Cuba.................... 3 00
BALA—Mrs. George Roberts, Sp. for
rebuilding chapels, Isle of Pines,
Cuba 10 00
BRISTOL—*St. Paul's*: Sp. for Tsu
Building Fund, Kyoto.............. 15 45
BRYN MAWR—*Church of the Redeemer*:
Rev. James Houghton, Sp. for re-
building chapels, Isle of Pines, Cuba,
$15; through Wo. Aux., Hooker
Memorial School, Mexico, $50; Sp.
for Dr. I. H. Correll, Tsu Building
Fund, Kyoto, $5; Sp. for Foreign
Life Insurance Fund, $5........... 75 00
CHELTENHAM—*St. Paul's*: Through
Wo. Aux., Sp. Dr. I. H. Correll
Bldg. Fund, Tsu, Kyoto, $5; Indian
Hope Association, Indian, $5...... 10 00
COATESVILLE—*Trinity Church*: Sp. for
rebuilding chapels, Isle of Pines,
Cuba, $152...................... 152 00
ELKVIEW—Mrs. J. W. Gibson, Gen..... 5 00
HAVERFORD—Mr. and Mrs. Allen Evans,
Sp. for rebuilding chapels, Isle of
Pines, Cuba..................... 100 00
JENKINTOWN—*Church of Our Saviour*:
Gen., $902; Sp. Rev. W. W. Steel,
Cuba, $5........................ 907 00
NEWTOWN—*St. Luke's*: Gen.......... 21 50
NORRISTOWN—*All Saints'*: Gen....... 39 70
PERKIOMEN—*St. James's*: Gen....... 50
PHILADELPHIA—*Advocate*: "A Mem-
ber," Sp. St. John's College Expan-
sion Fund, Shanghai.............. 1 00

Atonement (Memorial): Sp, Tsu Prop-
erty Fund, Kyoto................
Calvary (Germantown): Through Wo.
Aux., Sp. "Philadelphia" scholarship,
St. Mary's Orphanage, Shanghai, $5;
Sp. Foreign Life Insurance, $5; Sp.
nurse's salary, St. Luke's Hospital,
Shanghai, $5; "Kinsolving" scholar-
ship, Brazil, $5; Indian Hope Asso-
ciation, Indian, $5...............
Calvary (Northern Liberties): Gen....
Christ Church Chapel: Through Wo.
Aux., Sp. Bishop Knight to rebuild
chapel, Isle of Pines, Cuba........
Christ Church: Wo. Aux. (German-
town), Sp. Miss Ridgely's new
house, Cape Mount, Africa, $3; Sp.
nurse's salary, St. Luke's Hospital,
Shanghai, $5; Sp. for Dr. I. H. Cor-
rell Building Fund, Tsu, Kyoto, $5..
Epiphany: Through Wo. Aux., Mrs.
Tsu Bible-women, salary, Shanghai.
Grace: Miss Elizabeth Davis, Gen.,
$1; through Wo. Aux., Sp. for For-
eign Life Insurance, $2.50; Sp. for
Dr. I. H. Correll Building Fund,
Tsu, Kyoto, $5...................
Grace (Mt. Airy): Dom., $113.14;
through Wo. Aux., Sp. for For-
eign Insurance, $3; "Dr. Twing"
(Memorial) scholarship, St. John's
University, Shanghai, $5; S. S.,
Archdeacon Russell's Colored work
at Lawrenceville, Southern Virginia,
$25 ....
Holy Apostles': Through Wo. Aux.,
"Bishop Stevens" scholarship, St.
John's University, Shanghai, $5;
"Anna M. Stevens Memorial" schol-
arship, Girls' Training Institute,
West Africa, $5; Sp. for Miss
Ridgely's new house, Cape Mount,
Africa, $5; Sp. for Bishop Knight,
to rebuild chapels, Isle of Pines,
Cuba, $5.......................
Holy Trinity Church: Miss Clyde, Sp.
for St. John's University, Expansion
Fund, Shanghai, $25; through Wo.
Aux., "Kinsolving" scholarship, Bra-
zil, $5; Sp. for Bishop Knight, to re-
build chapels, Isle of Pines, Cuba,
$2; S. S., "Lemuel Coffin" scholar-
ship, High School, Africa, $40; "Al-
exander Brown" scholarship, Girls'
Training Institute, Africa, $25; Chi-
nese S. S., "Gertrude Fau" (Me-
morial) scholarship, St. Hilda's
School, Wuchang, Hankow, $50...
Holy Trinity Memorial Chapel:
Through Wo. Aux., Sp. for Miss
Ridgely's new house, Capt Mount, Africa,
$5; Sp. for Bishop Knight, to rebuild
chapels, Isle of Pines, Cuba, $25...
Incarnation: Dr. Pott, Shanghai,
$17.08; Dr. Pott, St. John's Col-
lege, Shanghai, $5................
Prince of Peace Chapel: Through Wo.
Aux., Sp. for "John W. Wood" schol-
arship, Guantanamo, Cuba.........
Resurrection: $32.26, S. S.,* $18.05,
Sp. for Tsu Property Fund, Kyoto..
St. Anna's: Sp. for Miss Ridgely's new
house, Cape Mount, Africa........
St. Elizabeth's: Girls' Friendly So-
ciety, Sp. for salary of deacon, for
Rev. S. C. Hughson, O.H.C., St. An-
drew's School, Sewanee, Tennessee.
St. James's: Mrs. William P. Ellison,
Sp. for St. John's University, Ex-
pansion Fund, Shanghai, $20; In-
dian Hope Association, Indian, $18..
St. Jude and the Nativity: Through
Wo. Aux., Sp. for Foreign Life In-
surance Fund...................
St. Luke's (Germantown): Sp. for
Isle of Pines chapels, Cuba, $82.90;

through Wo. Aux., No. 1, Sp. for Dr. I. H. Correll, Building Fund, Tsu, Kyoto, $5; Sp. for Miss Ridgely's new house, Cape Mount, Africa, $5; No. 2, Sp. for Bishop Knight, to rebuild chapels, Isle of Pines, $5..... 97 90
St. Luke and the Epiphany: Through Wo. Aux., Sp. for Foreign Life Insurance Fund.................... 4 00
St. Mark's: Through Wo. Aux., Sp. for Boone College Library, Hankow, $250; Sp. for Dr. Jefferys, St. Luke's Hospital, Shanghai, $250.... 500 00
St. Martin's-in-the-Fields: Sp. for rebuilding chapels, Isle of Pines, Cuba. 200 00
St. Mary's (West): Through Wo. Aux., Sp. for Mrs. Bull, for orphan baby, Osaka, Kyoto.................... 25 00
St. Matthias's: Through Wo. Aux., Sp. for Bishop Knight, to rebuild chapels, Isle of Pines, Cuba, $16; "Kinsolving" scholarship, Brazil, $2; Training-school, Sendai, Tokyo. 20 00
St. Paul's (Chestnut Hill): Dom., $395.75; Wo. Aux., Sp. for rebuilding chapels, Isle of Pines, Cuba, $125 .... 520 75
St. Paul's (Overbrook): Dom., $6; Through Wo. Aux., Sp. for Foreign Life Insurance Fund, $5......... 11 00
St. Philip's S. S.: Sp. for Tsu Property Fund, Kyoto............... 100 00
St. Stephen's: Sp. for Isle of Pines, Cuba, $55.25; Indian Hope Association, Indian, $20................. 75 25
St. Timothy's (Roxborough): Wo. Aux., Sp. for Mrs. Thomas C. Wetmore, Arden, Asheville................ 10 00
Church of the Saviour: Sp. for rebuilding chapels, Isle of Pines, Cuba, $77.54; through Wo. Aux., "Kinsolving" scholarship, Brazil, $5; Sp. for rebuilding chapels, Isle of Pines, Cuba, $5................. 87 54
Through Wo. Aux., "A Delegate to the Foreign Committee," Sp. for Bishop Knight, to rebuild chapels, Isle of Pines, Cuba............... 50 00
Cuban Guild, Sp. for rebuild chapels, Cuba..................... 100 00
Church Club Honorium, Sp. for St. John's University, Expansion Fund, Shanghai 50 00
W. A. "M.," Gen................ 500 00
"Cash," "A. F.," Sp. for Rev. A. A. Gilman, Changsha, Hankow, $100; Sp. for Archdeacon Steel, rebuilding chapels, Isle of Pines, Cuba, $100.. 200 00
John Baird, Sp. for Isle of Pines chapels, Cuba................... 100 00
Mrs. John Markoe, Sp. for Mexican famine sufferers.............. 100 00
The Misses Blanchard, Sp. for rebuilding Isle of Pines chapels, Cuba. 100 00
A. V. Spooner, "Thank-offering," Sp. for Christian Church at Southern Mountain, Hankow, $50; St. Margaret's School, Tokyo, $25....... 75 00
George Wharton Pepper, Sp. for Bishop Whipple Memorial, Havana, Cuba 25 00
Andrew A. Blain, Sp. for Church Extension Fund, Porto Rico...... 25 00
Mrs. E. A. Coxe, Sp. for Tsu Property Fund, Kyoto.............. 25 00
Miss Cox, Sp. for Isle of Pines chapels, Cuba................... 5 00
Mrs. Smith, Sp. for Isle of Pines chapels, Cuba................... 5 00
Mrs. Comegys (Chestnut Hill): Sp. for rebuilding chapels, Isle of Pines, Cuba 5 00
PHOENIXVILLE—St. Peter's: Sp. for rebuilding chapels, Isle of Pines, Cuba 70 00
ROSEMONT—Church of the Good Shep-

herd: Sp. for rebuilding chapels, Isle of Pines, Cuba.............. 48 50
WAYNE—St. Mary's Memorial: Sp. for Dr. Correll, Kyoto, $16; through Wo. Aux., "W. Beaumont Whitney" scholarship, Havana, Cuba, $5..... 21 00
WEST CHESTER—Holy Trinity Church: Through Wo. Aux., Training-school, Sendai, Tokyo, $15; Sp. for Dr. I. H. Correll, Tsu Building Fund, Kyoto, $15; Miss Harriet Baldwin, "Foreign Committee" scholarship, St. Hilda's School, Wuchang, Hankow, $10; Training-school for Bible-women, Hankow, $10; "Dr. Twing Memorial" scholarship, St. John's University, Shanghai, $10........ 60 00
WYNCOTE—All Hallows': Gen........ 215 29
MISCELLANEOUS — Wo. Aux., Gen., $100; "A Member," Sp. for Industrial School, Cape Mount, Africa, Rev. Nathan Matthews, $100; Foreign Committee, Sp. for rebuilding chapels, Isle of Pines, Cuba, $25... 225 00
"A. T. A.," Sp. for St. John's College, Expansion Fund, Shanghai.... 1,000 00
"M.," St. John's College, Expansion Fund, Shanghai.................. 500 00

Pittsburgh

Ap. $209.20; *Sp.* $177.22

BROWNSVILLE—Wo. Aux., Miss Hogg, Sp. for Miss Mann, Tokyo........ 50 00
DU BOIS—Church of Our Saviour: Gen. 22 30
MEADVILLE—Christ Church: Wo. Aux., Gen. 10 50
McKEESPORT—St. Stephen's: Dom. and Frn. 6 40
PITTSBURGH—St. Andrew's: Daughters of the King, Sp. for Tsu Property Fund, Kyoto, $15; school, Sp. for Bishop Van Buren's Hospital, Porto Rico, $21................... 36 00
St. Peter's: $50, S. S., $4.82, Sp. for Tsu Building Fund, Kyoto........ 54 82
SMETHPORT—St. Luke's: Gen......... 15 00
TARENTUM—St. Barnabas's S. S.: Sp. for Rev. R. E. Wood, Hankow..... 1 40
UNIONTOWN—St. Peter's: Dom. and Frn., $150; Daughters of the King, Rev. G. B. Benedict, Aux. Cayes, Haiti, West Indies, $5........... 155 00
MISCELLANEOUS—Wo. Aux., Sp. for Bishop Aves, Mexico, for famine sufferers 25 00
Branch Wo. Aux., "C. K. E.," Sp. for Bishop Rowe, Alaska........... 10 00

Quincy

Ap. $64.75

GALVA—Holy Communion: Gen....... 5 00
LEWISTOWN—St. James's S. S.: Gen.. 1 30
PEORIA—St. Paul's: Gen............ 15 40
QUINCY—St. John's Cathedral: Gen... 3 05
ROCK ISLAND—Trinity Church: Gen.. 35 00

Rhode Island

Ap. $276.82

ASHTON—St. John's: Junior Aux., Alaska 5 00
MANVILLE—Emmanuel Church: Gen... 34 82
PROVIDENCE — All Saints' Memorial: Dom., $35; Frn., $35............ 70 00
St. John's: Dom., $67; Frn., $75.... 142 00
MISCELLANEOUS—Babies' Branch, Gen. 25 00

South Carolina

Ap. $35.24

KINGSTREE—St. Alban's: Gen........ 5 00
ROCK HILL—Church of Our Saviour: Gen. 4 37

TRENTON—*Church of Our Saviour:*
Gen. 12 50
UNION—*Nativity:* Gen. 13 37

Southern Ohio
Ap. $8.00 ; *Sp.* $1,018.10

CINCINNATI — *Emmanuel Church:*
Woman's Guild, Alaska............ 2 00
Wo. Aux., Sp. for St. Elizabeth's
Hospital, Building Fund, Shanghai.. 2 50
COLUMBUS—Wo. Aux., Sp. for St.
Elizabeth's Hospital, Building Fund,
Shanghai 10 60
DAYTON—*St. Margaret's:* Gen 1 00
GLENDALE—*Christ Church:* Sp. for
Rev. Mr. Reifsnider, for the hostel
for young men, Fukui, Kyoto...... 1,000 00
PIQUA—*St. James's:* Gen 2 45
SPRINGFIELD—*Christ Church:* Sp. for
rebuilding chapels, Isle of Pines,
Cuba 5 00
XENIA—*Christ Church:* Gen......... 2 55

Southern Virginia
Ap. $449.86 ; *Sp.* $238.00

AMHERST CO.—Miss S. Gay Patteson,
Gen. 5 00
APPOMATTOX CO.—*St. Paul's Church
Parish:* Dom., 50 cts.; Frn., 50 cts. 1 00
AUGUSTA CO. — *Emmanuel Church*
(Staunton) : Wo. Aux., Sp. for St.
Mary's School, Building Fund,
Shanghai 6 00
Trinity Church (Staunton) : Wo. Aux.,
Gen. 2 00
BEDFORD CO.—*St. John's* (Bedford
City) : Wo. Aux., Sp. for Building
Fund, St. Mary's Hall, Shanghai... 5 00
BUCKINGHAM CO.—*St. Peter's:* Dom.,
50 cts. ; Frn., 50 cts 1 00
CAMPBELL CO.— *Grace Memorial*
(Lynchburg) : Gen............... 55 00
St. Paul's: Gen., $5 ; First Circle, Wo.
Aux., Sp. for St. Mary's School,
Building Fund, Shanghai, $5. . . . 10 00
CHESTERFIELD CO. (Manchester)—Wo.
Aux., Sp. for St. Mary's School,
Building Fund, Shanghai.......... 2 50
DINWIDDIE CO.—*Grace* (Petersburg) :
Gen., $91.14 ; Wo. Aux., Sp. for Rev.
C. McRae, St. John's College,
Shanghai, $30 ; Second Circle, Wo.
Aux., Sp. for new building, St.
Mary's Hall, Shanghai, $2.50...... 123 64
ELIZABETH CITY CO. — *St. John's*
(Hampton) : Wo. Aux., Sp. for St.
Mary's School, Building Fund,
Shanghai 10 00
HALIFAX CO. — *Emmanuel Church*
(Houston) : $1.07 ; H. H. Edmonds,
$30, Frn 31 07
ISLE OF WIGHT CO.—*Christ Church*
(Smithfield) : Gen............... 50 00
JAMES CITY CO. (Williamsburg)—Wo.
Aux., First Circle, Sp. for St. Mary's
School, Building Fund, Shanghai.... 10 00
MECKLENBURG CO.—*St. James's* (Boyd-
ton) : Wo. Aux., Sp. for St. Mary's
School, Building Fund, Shanghai... 2 00
MONTGOMERY CO.—*Grace* (Radford) :
Sp. for Dr. Glenton, for hospital
work, Hankow................... 10 50
NANSEMOND CO.—*Lower Suffolk Par-
ish, Glebe Church:* Gen.......... 5 00
Louise McAdams Withers, Sp. for
Bishop Kinsolving, Brazil......... 2 00
NORFOLK CO.—*Christ Church* (Nor-
folk) : First Circle, Wo. Aux. (of
which Mrs. J. E. B. Stuart, $10),
Sp. for St. Mary's School, Building
Fund, Shanghai.................. 20 00
St. John's (Portsmouth) : Wo. Aux.,
Sp. for St. Mary's School, Building
Fund, Shanghai.................. 5 00
St. Luke's (Norfolk) : Gen., $153.65 ;

Wo. Aux., First Circle, Sp. for St.
Mary's School, Building Fund,
Shanghai, $5.................... 1£
St. Paul's (Norfolk) : Wo. Aux., First
Circle, $50, Second Circle, $5, Sp.
for St. Mary's School, Building
Fund, Shanghai.................. 2
St. Peter's: Wo. Aux., Sp. for St.
Mary's School, Building Fund,
Shanghai 3
St. Thomas's: Wo. Aux., Sp. for new
building, St. Mary's Hall, Shanghai.
Trinity Church (Portsmouth) : Wo.
Aux., First Circle, $5, Second Circle,
$3, Sp. for St. Mary's School, Build-
ing Fund, Shanghai...............
Miss B. M. Hudgins, S. S. class of
boys, Sp. for Rev. J. M. B. Gill,
at Yangchow, Shanghai...........
Wo. Aux., "Bishop Johns" scholar-
ship, St. Margaret's School, Tokyo.. £
NOTTAWAY CO.—*St. Luke's* (Black-
ston) : Wo. Aux., Sp. for St. Mary's
School, Building Fund, Shanghai...
PITTSYLVANIA CO. — *Epiphany* (Dan-
ville) : Wo. Aux., First Circle, $5,
Second Circle, $2, Sp. for St. Mary's
School, Building Fund, Shanghai...
PRINCE GEORGE CO. (Burrowsville)—
Wo. Aux., Sp. for St. Mary's School,
Building Fund, Shanghai..........
PULASKI CO.—*McGill Memorial* (Pu-
laski) : Wo. Aux., Sp. for St. Mary's
School, Building Fund, Shanghai...
ROCKBRIDGE CO.—R. E. Lee Memorial
(Lexington), Wo. Aux., Sp. for new
building, St. Mary's Hall, Shanghai.
ROANOKE CO.—*St. Paul's* (Salem) :
Wo. Aux., Sp. for St. Mary's School,
Building Fund, Shanghai..........
WARWICK CO.—*St. Paul's* (Newport
News) : Wo. Aux., Sp. for St. Mary's
School, Building Fund, Shanghai...
MISCELLANEOUS—Junior Aux., Sp. for
St. Mary's School, Building Fund,
Shanghai 1

Springfield
Sp. $10.00

DANVILLE—*Holy Trinity Church:* Miss
C. C. Forbes, Sp. for famine suffer-
ers, Mexico, $5 ; Sp. for Rebuilding
Fund, Isle of Pines, Cuba, $5...... 1

Tennessee
Ap. $54.10 ; *Sp.* $125.00

CHATTANOOGA—*St. Paul's:* Wo. Aux.,
"Bishop Quintard" scholarship, St.
Mary's Hall, Shanghai...........
CLARKSVILLE—*Trinity Church :*.Gen... 5
FRANKLIN—*St. Paul's:* Wo. Aux.,
"Bishop Quintard" scholarship, St.
Mary's Hall, Shanghai...........
ROSSVIEW—*Grace:* Wo. Aux., Sp. for
Miss Bull's work, Kyoto.......... 2
SEWANEE—Sp. for Tsu Property Fund,
Kyoto 10

Texas
Ap. $35.05

BELLEVILLE—*St. Mary's:* Gen........
CAMERON—*All Saints':* Gen......... ./
GALVESTON — *Trinity Church:* Wo.
Aux., for the "Gertrude Aves" schol-
arship, Hooker Memorial School,
Mexico 2
NAVASOTA—*St. Paul's:* Gen..........

Vermont
Sp. $16.11

BURLINGTON—*St. Paul's:* Sp. for Bish-
op Rowe, Alaska.................
MIDDLETOWN SPRINGS—*St. Margaret's:*
Sp. for Zangzok Station, Equipment

Fund, Shanghai................. 2 30
WHITE RIVER JUNCTION—*St. Paul's*:
Sp. for Zangzok Station, Equipment
Fund, Shanghai................. 4 75
MISCELLANEOUS—Miss E. M. Forman,
Sp. for Zangzok Station, Equipment
Fund, Shanghai................. 5 00

Virginia
Ap. $227.73; *Sp.* $95.50

ALEXANDRIA Co. — *Grace* (Alexandria): Gen.................. 11 68
CAROLINE Co. (Port Royal)—Wo. Aux.,
Miss Mann's salary, Tokyo, $1;
Miss Barber's salary, Hankow, $1. 2 00
CHARLES CITY Co.—*Westover Parish*
(Westover): (Apportionment, 1908-
09) Gen..................... 46 71
HENRICO Co. — *Emmanuel Church*
(Brook Hill): (In Memoriam), St.
John's College, Shanghai......... 25 00
"Two Virginia Churchwomen," Sp.
for St. Margaret's School, Building
Fund, Tokyo.................. 25 00
Christ Church S. S. (Richmond):
Philippines 5 45
Emmanuel Church: "A Virginia Lady,"
Sp. for Church Extension Fund,
Porto Rico.................. 10 00
Holy Trinity Church: Wo. Aux., "A
Friend," Sp. for land for St. Paul's
College, Tokyo............... 5 50
St. John's: "A Member," "Lewis W.
Burton" scholarship, St. John's
School, Cape Mount, Africa....... 40 00
St. Paul's: Brotherhood of St. Paul,
hospital at Wusih, Shanghai, $5;
Gen., $6................... 11 00
Whittle Memorial: Circle of King's
Daughters, Sp. for support of Nami
Asamo, in Mr. R. Ishii's Orphanage,
Tokyo 25 00
Miss E. M. Nolting, $25, Miss Margaret Nolting, $50, Gen....... 75 00
Mrs. Stewart M. Woodward, Sp. for
St. Margaret's School, Building
Fund, Tokyo................. 5 00
RAPPAHANNOCK Co.—*Trinity Church*
(Washington): Gen........... 10 89
MISCELLANEOUS—(In Memoriam), All
Saints' Day, 1909. Sp. for Miss
Wood's Library, Hankow......... 25 00

Washington
Ap. $276.72; *Sp.* $349.65

WASHINGTON—*Ascension* (D. C.): Wo.
Aux., Sp. for Rev. R. Browning,
Shanghai 30 50
Christ Church (Georgetown): Mrs.
L. M. Zeller, Gen............. 1 00
St. John's: Wo. Aux., Sp. for St.
Helena's, Building Fund, Boerne,
West Texas, $20; Mrs. William
Boardman, "Josephine Boardman"
scholarship, Hooker School, Mexico,
$48 .... 68 00
St. John's (Georgetown): Gen....... 175 72
St. Mark's: Sp. for Tsu Property Fund,
Kyoto 1 50
Trinity Church: "A Friend," Sp. for
Church Extension Fund, Porto Rico. 5 00
W. S. Hoge, Sp. for Church Extension Fund, Porto Rico......... 10 00
Mrs. Alfred Holmead, Sp. for Miss
Carter at St. John's-in-the-Wilderness, Alaska................ 10 00
Miss Ellen King, Mexico......... 2 00
"A Friend," rent of mission house at
Santurce, Porto Rico........... 10 00
"A Friend," Gen............... 2 00
"A Friend," Gen............... 1 00
MONTGOMERY Co. — *Christ Church*
(Rockville, Md.): Gen.......... 17 00
PRINCE GEORGE Co.—*Pinckney Memor-*

ial (Hyattsville, Md.), and *St.
Luke's* (Bladensburg, Md.): Dom.,
$6; Frn., $6................ 12 00
Wo. Aux., Sp. for Miss Langdon,
Alaska, to be used at her discretion,
$25; "A Member," Sp. for St.
Agnes's Hospital, Raleigh, North
Carolina, $25; Sp. for Brazil, $25;
Sp. for Cuba, $25; Sp. for Porto
Rico, $25; Sp. for Kyoto, $12.50;
Sp. for Tokyo, $12.50; Sp. for
repairs on House of the Holy Child,
Manila, Philippine Islands, $122.65. 272 65

Western Massachusetts
Ap. $218.47; *Sp.* $78.50

GREENFIELD—Junior Aux., Sp. for St.
Margaret's School, Tokyo, Building
Fund 4 00
LENOX—*Trinity Church*: Mrs. Anna A.
Bradford, Dom. and Frn......... 100 00
MILFORD—*Trinity Church* (Ap. 1908-
1909): Dom. and Frn.......... 8 47
NORTHAMPTON—*St. John's*: "In Memoriam," Sp. St. Margaret's School
Building Fund, Tokyo........... 5 00
SPRINGFIELD—*Christ Church*: Sp. for
St. Margaret's School, Tokyo, at the
discretion of Rev. J. H. Kobayashi,
principal 59 50
STOCKBRIDGE—*St. Paul's*: "All Saints'
Day" scholarship, St. Elizabeth's
School, South Dakota........... 60 00
WEBSTER—*Reconciliation*: Gen....... 50 00
WESTFIELD—*Atonement*: "A Friend,"
Sp. for Mexican famine sufferers... 10 00

Western Michigan
Ap. $128.29

EAST JORDAN—*Church of the Redeemer*: Gen.............. 1 05
GRAND HAVEN—*St. John's*: Gen..... 1 05
GRAND RAPIDS—*St. Mark's*: Gen..... 113 81
St. Paul's S. S.: Gen........... 8 88
MANTON—Gen. 1 50
SHERMAN—Gen. 1 00
THOMPSONVILLE—Gen. 1 00

Western New York
Ap. $294.65; *Sp.* $17.00

BATH—*St. Thomas's*: Mrs. John Davenport, Gen., $40; "A Communicant," for support of Bible-reader,
Hankow, $30................ 70 00
BUFFALO—*St. Mary's*: Mrs. Ann
Thompson, $25, Rev. G. G. Merrill,
$20, "Parishioner," $5, Gen.;
George H. Bovall, Sp. for Church
Extension Fund, Porto Rico, $2.... 52 00
St. Paul's: W. H. D. Barr, Sp. for Rev.
Dr. Pott's Building Fund, St. John's
College, Shanghai.............. 10 00
GENEVA—L. Clark, Sp. for Mexican
famine sufferers............... 5 00
OLEAN—*St. Stephen's*: Gen.......... 5 00
ROCHESTER—*St. Luke's*: Wo. Aux.,
Dom., $66.65; Colored, $3....... 69 65
WESTFIELD—*St. Peter's*: Gen........ 100 00

West Texas
Ap. $1.85

VICTORIA—*Trinity Church*: Gen...... 1 85

West Virginia
Ap. $32.94; *Sp.* $200.00

CHARLES TOWN—*St. Philip's S. S.*:
St. Paul's School, Lawrenceville,
Southern Virginia.............. 19 94
HUNTINGTON — Mrs. Margaret Lynn
Harvey, in memory of Miss Fannie
L. Thompson, Chinese Missions, $5;

Indian, $2.50; Frn., $2.50, ...   10 00
WAVERLY—*Church of the Messiah*:
Gen. 3 00
MISCELLANEOUS—Right Rev. and Mrs.
George W. Peterkin, Sp. for Bishop
Knight, Cuba, to help repair damage
to buildings on the Isle of Pines,
$100; Sp. for Bishop Thomas, Wyo-
ming, $100. ....   200 00

Missionary Districts

Alaska
Ap. $16.50
SOUTH EAST ARCHDEACONRY—Gen. ...   16 50

Arizona
Ap. $7.00
PHOENIX—*Trinity Church*: Gen 7 00

Idaho
Ap. $6.00
SHOSHONE—*Christ Church*: Gen 6 00

Nevada
Ap. $5.00
TONOPAH—*St. Mark's*: Indian 5 00

New Mexico
Ap. $30.00
EL PASO—*St. Clement's* (TEXAS): Gen.   20 00
Wo. Aux., Gen. 10 00

North Dakota
Ap. $40.60
JAMESTOWN—*Grace*: Gen 30 60
McCLUSKY—Gen. 2 00
NEW ROCKFORD—*St. Timothy's*: Gen.   8 00

Oklahoma
Ap. $10.00
MISCELLANEOUS—"A Thank-offering,"
Gen. 10 00

Olympia
Ap. $14.00; *Sp.* $5.00
MONTESANO—*St. Mark's*: "M.," Wo.
Aux., Sp. for Foreign Life Insurance
Fund 5 00
PORT TOWNSEND—*St. Paul's*: Gen. ...   14 00

Sacramento
Ap. $1.00; *Sp.* $17.35
AUBURN—*St. Luke's*: Mrs. D. W. Lu-
beck, gasoline for launch *Pelican*,
Alaska 1 00
SACRAMENTO—*St. Paul's*: Sp. for Utah.   17 35

Salina
Ap. $2.00
CONCORDIA—*Epiphany*: Gen 2 00

South Dakota
Ap. $28.92; *Sp.* $1.35
SISSETON AGENCY—*St. Mary's*: Indian.   2 25
St. John the Baptist's: Indian 3 97
St. Luke's: Indian 4 25
STANDING ROCK MISSION—*St. Eliza-
beth's*: Dom. 2 40
St. John the Baptist's: Dom. 1 25
FAIRFAX—*Trinity Church*: Sp. for

Legacies

CONN., MERIDEN—Estate of Lemuel J.
Curtis, Dom., $63.26; Indian,
$126.53; Colored, $126.53; Frn.,
$31.68 ....
EAST CAROLINA, BEAUFORT—Estate of
Rev. E. M. Forbes, Dom., $9.62;
Frn., $9.61..................... 19 23
N. Y., NEW YORK—Estate of Winfield   347 95

Tucker, to the Society...........49,111 13
W. MASS., PITTSFIELD—Estate of
Parker L. Hall, Dom., $87; Frn.,
$87 .... 174 00
NOVA SCOTIA, HALIFAX—Estate of Mrs.
Fanny Cooper Wiswell, Gen....... 300 00

Receipts for the month..........$102,082 55
Amount previously acknowledged.. 60,059 18

Total since September 1st......$162,141 73

SUMMARY OF RECEIPTS

Receipts divided according to purposes to which they are to be applied	Received during November	Amounts previously Acknowledged	Total
1. Applicable upon the appropriations of the Board.	$35,555 45	$38,091 59	$73,647 04
2. Special gifts forwarded to objects named by donors in addition to the appropriations of the Board.	16,525 34	20,826 34	37,351 68
3. Legacies for investment....................	....	....	....
4. Legacies, the disposition of which is to be determined by the Board at the end of the fiscal year.	49,952 31	1,141 25	51,093 56
5. Specific Deposit............................	49 45	....	49 45
Total...........................	$102,082 55	$60,059 18	$162,141 73

OFFERINGS TO PAY APPROPRIATIONS

Total receipts from September 1st, 1909, to December 1st, 1909, applicable upon the appropriations, divided according to the sources from which they have come, and compared with the corresponding period of the preceding year. Legacies are not included in the following items, as their disposition is not determined by the Board until the end of the fiscal year.

Source	To Dec. 1, 1909	To Dec. 1, 1908	Increase	Decrease
1. From congregations....................	$26,725 75	$23,335 45	$3,390 30	....
2. From individuals.....................	4,094 32	14,411 95	....	$10,317 63
3. From Sunday-schools..................	1,167 65	2,435 94	....	1,268 29
4. From Woman's Auxiliary..............	5,762 34	9,824 16	....	4,061 82
5. Woman's Auxiliary United Offering.......	21,000 00	9,000 00	12,000 00	....
6. From interest.......................	14,713 31	12,287 28	2,426 03	....
7. Miscellaneous items..................	183 67	1,345 12	....	1,161 45
Total	$73,647 04	$72,639 90	$1,007 14	

APPROPRIATIONS FOR THE YEAR

SEPTEMBER 1ST, 1909, TO AUGUST 31ST, 1910,

Amount Needed for the Year

1. To pay appropriations as made to date for the work at home and abroad....... $1,182,811 13
2. To replace Reserve Funds temporarily used for the current work............. 32,955 33

Total... $1,215,766 46
Total receipts to date applicable on appropriations..................... 73,647 04

Amount needed before August 31st, 1910................................. $1,142,119 42

THE

Spirit of Missions

AN ILLUSTRATED MONTHLY REVIEW
OF CHRISTIAN MISSIONS

February, 1910

CONTENTS

The Subscription Price of THE SPIRIT OF MISSIONS is ONE DOLLAR per year. Postage is prepaid in the United States, Porto Rico, the Philippines and Mexico. For other countries in the Postal Union, including Canada, twenty-four cents per year should be added.

Subscriptions are continued until ordered discontinued.

Change of Address: In all changes of address it is necessary that the old as well as the new address should be given.

How to Remit: Remittances, made payable to George Gordon King, Treasurer, should be made by draft on New York, Postal Order or Express Order. One and two cent stamps are received. To checks on local banks ten cents should be added for collection.

All Letters should be addressed to The Spirit of Missions, 281 Fourth Avenue, New York.

Published by the Domestic and Foreign Missionary Society.

President, RIGHT REVEREND DANIEL S. TUTTLE, D.D. *Secretary,* ——— ———
Treasurer, GEORGE GORDON KING.

Entered at the Post Office, in New York, as second-class matter.

Heart to Heart

An English missionary in Swatow, China, heard sounds of bitter weeping by the wayside one night. Looking for its source, he found a heathen woman bowed over a child's grave, upon which, according to the local custom, lay an overturned cradle.

A heathen baby,—that is all ;—
  And woman's lips that wildly plead ;
Poor lips that never learned to call
  On Christ, in woman's time of need!

Poor lips, that never did repeat,
  Through quiet tears, "Thy will be done !"
That never knew the story sweet
  Of Mary and the Infant Son.

An emptied cradle, and a grave—
  A little grave—cut through the sod ;
O Jesus, pitiful to save,
  Make known to her the mother's God!

O Spirit of the heavenly Love,
  Stir some dear heart at home to-day
An earnest thought to lift above
  For mother-hearts so far away.

That all may know the mercy mild
  Of Him who did the nurslings bless;
The heathen and the home-born child
  Are one in that great Tenderness

—CLARA A. LINDSAY *in Woman's Work.*

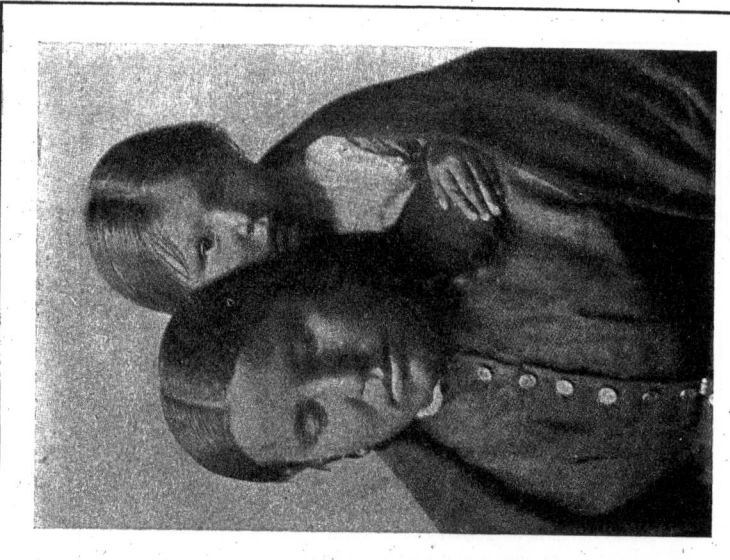

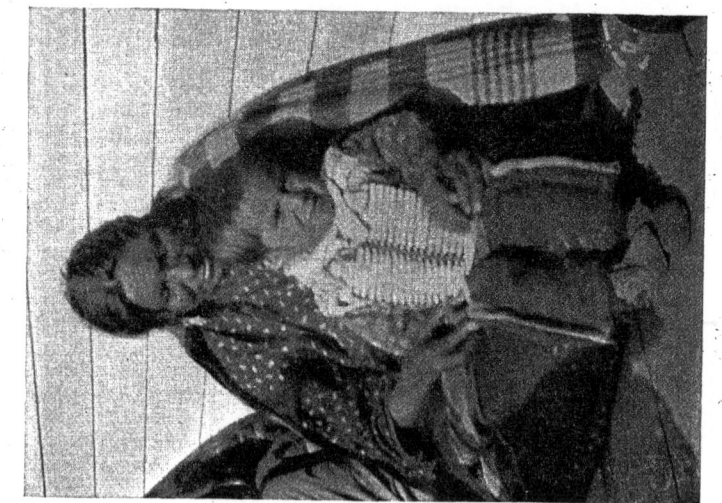

CONTRASTS IN INDIAN LIFE RESULTING FROM CREATION

THE SPIRIT OF MISSIONS

AN ILLUSTRATED MONTHLY REVIEW
OF CHRISTIAN MISSIONS

Vol. LXXV.   **February,** 1910   No. 2

TO THE YOUNGER READERS OF THE
SPIRIT OF MISSIONS

The Present Issue

PROBABLY no editor is quite capable of giving an unbiased judgment of the magazine which he produces, yet we do believe that this issue of the Children's Number compares favorably with —if it does not excel—any of our previous issues. The articles and the illustrations will speak for themselves, and we think that their variety and interesting quality will support our claim.

It will perhaps be noticed by those who are familiar with the successive Children's Numbers that one or two innovations are introduced. We give a synopsis of the last Lenten Offering; we are for the first time presenting a real story, bearing upon the Lenten Offering; we are also printing in full a debate upon missions which has been produced with great success by a club of boys; this we hope may give helpful suggestion to others who desire to interest boys in this great subject.

If the value of this number is such as to make the work of our devoted little salesmen easier, and to bring home more appealingly to the reader the realities of the mission field, the labor expended in its publication will be amply repaid.

Our Casual Readers

MANY thousands who are not usually readers of THE SPIRIT OF MISSIONS will, by the enterprise and enthusiasm of the Sunday-schools, have it brought to their attention this year, and will possess themselves of this copy. To all such we give a cordial greeting and express the hope that they may be so interested in what they find in the following pages that they will wish to follow, month by month, the record of the Church's Mission in fulfilling her Master's command, and so will desire to become regular subscribers to this magazine. A blank for the purpose of subscription will be found on page 82, and if new subscriptions are made through the Sunday-school children a liberal allowance toward their Lenten Offering is granted. May we not hope this year to retain as regular readers a large number of those who have bought this issue at the solicitation of some little friend? The inspiration and education to yourself, and the impetus to the cause of missions which your subscription would give, are far greater than you can realize. Try it for a year and see if we are not right in our statement.

(85)

THE LATE GEORGE C. THOMAS

A man who loved all his fellow-men, but most of all the little children

A Great Project

THE Sunday-school Offering has always been a wonderful and inspiring thing. Those who have watched
its growth from the very small beginning—some $7,000—to the $147,252.91
of last year, have often found it in
their hearts to wish that the older
members of the Church might be inspired with the same steady and progressive enthusiasm. This year there
is given to the Offering what we believe will be a greater and more telling
impulse. Through the suggestion of the
Rev. Dr. Duhring, special agent of the
Sunday-school Auxiliary, in conference
with other friends of our late treasurer,
it has been decided that the Sunday-
school Offering this Lent shall be made a
memorial to Mr. George C. Thomas,
whose noble work in its behalf and whose
life-long devotion to children and young
people are well-known to all who knew or
heard of him.

Dr. Duhring is so confident of an
eager and generous response from the
members of the Sunday-schools that he
says: "There will be no question about
it that the $150,000 almost reached in
1909 will be more than raised by Easter
Day, March 27th, 1910, and that we shall
present it with faith and in loving remembrance of him who originated, with
Mr. John Marston, this magnificent effort of the children of the Church to
spread the Gospel at home and abroad,
and everywhere on the face of the earth.
Indeed, with Christian enthusiasm we
believe that we can make this memorial
offering $175,000, yea, $200,000, in memory of the one who has been the greatest
Sunday-school and missionary worker
that the Church has had in the past half-
century."

He also makes these helpful suggestions toward carrying the plan into effect: "We beg most earnestly that early
preparation be made both to obtain, then
to circulate, and finally to fill, and lastly,
promptly to return, the Lenten boxes.
Not the Sunday after Ash Wednesday,

but on the one preceding, should the
boxes be given out. We have noticed
through the length and breadth of the
land how the first four days of Lent are
completely lost by the distribution of the
boxes on the First Sunday in Lent, when
they should be in the hands of our
scholars on Quinquagesima Sunday at
the very latest.

"So, if rectors, officers and teachers
will interest themselves personally in
getting the Lenten boxes at the beginning of 1910, then having them put into
form by the young people (and here is a
splendid chance for the Brotherhood of
St. Andrew, the Girls' Friendly and the
Junior Auxiliary and other societies to
have something to do), then to go still
further than that—taking the trouble, as
a large parish in New York City does
annually, to mark the name of each
scholar on each Lenten box, thus to let
them feel that their individuality is not
lost; all such preparatory work we are
sure will help to increase the interest in
and liberality of the Lenten Offering of
the Sunday-schools of the Church. We
are satisfied that several thousands of
dollars are lost annually to the Lenten
Offering just through beginning late and
neglecting to follow up with a few words
each Sunday what the boxes are to be
used for.

"Then if the rector each Sunday shall
visit his school and esteem it a privilege
to say just a few words of encouragement, letting the whole school know
from week to week some generous deeds
that have been done for the Lenten
Offering through that week, there is
nothing like this kind of promotion to
advance the gifts of our children. There
is such a thing as healthy rivalry between the classes also.

"Suppose all of us are stirred up, there
will be no question but that the $175,000
hoped for will be raised by March 27th,
Easter Day, as a worthy memorial of
George C. Thomas, the great treasurer
of the Board of Missions and match-
less leader of the children of the
Church."

NORTH DAKOTA CHILDREN EARNING THEIR EASTER OFFERING

1. Some boys who deliver the diocesan paper
2. Milking at the rate of one cent a cow
3, 6. Ten dollars earned selling ginger-cookies
4. Jack and the bean pot
5. His father pays him for keeping still, and the camera has caught him doing it. But the grin will show that he doesn't earn many pennies that way
7. She shovels snow
8. Caring for a child after school
9. Posing for his picture at the rate of five cents per pose

Twenty-five to Twenty Cents:
Atlanta, Washington, Western New York, Sacramento, Southern Florida, Newark, Springfield, Marquette, Easton, Idaho, Chicago, Ohio, Colorado, Oklahoma, Southern Ohio, Harrisburg, Tennessee, Spokane, North Carolina.

Twenty to Fifteen Cents:
Asheville, Quincy, Florida, Milwaukee, Olympia, Rhode Island, California, Western Colorado, Michigan, Michigan City, Fond du Lac, Southern Virginia, Louisiana, Nebraska, Maine.

Fifteen to Ten Cents:
Long Island, Virginia, Porto Rico.

The success of those who have attained high averages is not accidental. We have reason to know that this was accomplished by hard work; not by the generous gifts of a few, but as the result of everyone working, and doing his best.

All honor to North Dakota, Pennsylvania, Alaska, and Honolulu! Other dioceses and districts may easily take a place in the same class with these whenever they are willing to do as faithful and systematic work. It is only just to say of the two leaders—that which is doubtless true in a measure of many others which have made good records—that a large part of their success is due to the splendid work of the men in those dioceses who are the Sunday-school secretaries.

So we turn to the New Year and the new offering with the opportunity which it affords. Shall not some of us try a little harder, and so get at least above the thirty-cent class?

Two Letters

ON the two pages following we give to our young readers the encouraging messages sent to them by the Presiding Bishop of the Church, and the Treasurer of the Board of Missions, who has taken up the work which Mr. Thomas laid down. Both these men look with affection and hopefulness toward the members of our Sunday-schools as great helpers in a great work, which will this year be hallowed by being done in memory of a great man.

Dear Children of the Sunday Schools:

Last year I wrote you my thanks, my request and my greeting. I want to renew them all. My thanks were, because that since you began your Lenten offering, you have given more than two millions of dollars for Missions.

My request was that you would give $140.000.00 last year. You did it and more too. How proud I am of you! This year I want $150.000.00, in memory of Mr. Thomas, one of the greatest and best friends that American children ever had. Everybody has asked that we call this year's giving "The George C. Thomas Memorial Lenten offering." I am sure you will do your best to make it $150.000.00

My greeting is the last year's one over again. There is a spring by the side of a big rock. The sweet cool waters burst out and run away in a brooklet. A boy thinks he will put his hand or his foot over the spring and keep the waters back. He can't do it. They will bubble up and flow over and run away down the brook-bed laughing at him. In doing the Savior's work of Missions, you are like that spring. God bless you!

Daniel S. Tuttle
Presiding Bishop.

St. Louis, Mo,
Dec. 10, 1909.

Church Missions House,
281 4th Avenue, New York City.

To the Pupils in our Sunday-schools:

Three months ago I wrote a letter to the Sunday-schools, asking them to continue to work for Missions, and thereby help to tell other children about Jesus. It is easy for us to do this, surrounded as we are by those whom we love; all of whom are Christians, and all doing the same thing. But it was not so easy for those who lived at the same time as our Lord to stand up before the world and say and do what He taught them to say and do.

Those were days of great trials for Christian men, women and children. The world was hard and cruel, and it could not bear the rebukes of Jesus—so it persecuted His followers, and many were killed in most horrible ways. In Rome there was a great open theatre, the ruins of which are there to-day, where sometimes Christians were eaten alive by wild beasts, or tied to stakes and burned, because they were Christians.

One might almost think that with such treatment His followers would have been discouraged, and would no longer have stood by Him or said that they believed in Him. But was this the case? Why, no! From those days to these His Church has been growing and growing, ever getting stronger and stronger and reaching out into all the world. He told His disciples to ''preach the Gospel to every creature,'' and they immediately set about doing so. At first there were not many to do this, and the progress seemed to be slow; but bye and bye they reached out into all Europe and North Africa. As ages passed and this land of ours was discovered, the missionaries came here too, with only the thought of bringing the Gospel to other people, and with never a thought of the hardships they might have to bear. There were but few houses here in those early days and fewer stores where things could be bought. Each one had to do the best he could; oftentimes chop down a tree to make the fire with which to cook the deer he shot or the fish he caught, and by the warmth of which he slept. And yet they were always telling those they met about Jesus, and making everybody the happier for it.

The whole Church is a great Missionary Society and this magazine, as you know, tells about its work. It tells what the children of the Sunday-schools, through the Board of Missions, do for thousands of other children: here at home, in the mountains, in the valleys, among the miners, the colored children, the Indians and the Esquimaux; the Japanese and Chinese children, and ever so many more in other parts of the world.

And the best of it is that you are all helping tell this wonderful story to these other children—how that Jesus loves everybody,—and so are, in your turn, His missionaries.

GEORGE GORDON KING, Treasurer.

THE SANCTUARY OF MISSIONS

CHRIST for the world we sing!
The world to Christ we bring,
With joyful song;
The new-born souls, whose days,
Reclaimed from error's ways,
Inspired with hope and praise,
To Christ belong.
—*S. Wolcott.*

"INASMUCH as ye have done it unto one of the least of these, my brethren, ye have done it unto Me."

THANKSGIVINGS

"We thank Thee"—

For the sweet and silent years of the Holy Childhood.

For the light and gladness brought into the world by little children.

For Thy servants who, by word and good example, are protecting and guiding Thy lambs in the dark and waste places. (Pages 103 and 129.)

For the Christian nurture, Christian homes and Christian parents, which are the gifts of the Christ-Child to our nation; the strength of its life and the hope of its future.

For Thine assurance that inasmuch as we have done it unto the least of Thy little ones, we have done it unto Thee.

For the growing interest and co-operation of the children for the Church in the up-building of the world-wide Kingdom.

INTERCESSIONS

"That it may please Thee"—

To guard and protect the innocence of children, and by their example to win men and women to a worthier life. (Page 99.)

To bless family life, and direct parents in their sacred task, that Thy children may have a fear and love of Thy Holy Name.

To prosper the work of all schools, hospitals and orphanages which minister to the needs of children (especially . . . .), making them fruitful nurseries of useful and holy lives. (Pages 124, 132 and 135.)

To bless the officers, teachers and pupils of the Sunday-schools of Thy Church, giving them grace to serve Thee better and more perfectly to love Thee.

To bring to the mothers of the world the knowledge which alone can sanctify their joy and soothe their sorrow. (Page 83.)

To prosper the work begun in behalf of Thine Indian children by Thy servant, Bishop Hare. (Page 123.)

To give good success to the efforts of the Sunday-school Auxiliary in the gifts which they will make during the coming Lent in memory of Thy faithful servant. (Page 87.)

PRAYERS

FOR CHILDREN

GRANT, O Heavenly Father, that as Thy holy angels always behold Thy face in heaven, so they may evermore protect Thy little ones on earth from all danger, both of soul and body, through Jesus Christ our Lord. *Amen.*

FOR SCHOOLS

O LORD Jesus Christ, Thou Child of Bethlehem, bless, we beseech Thee, the children gathered in Christian schools; may they be truthful, pure, obedient, and ever ready to do their duty in that state of life to which Thou shalt be pleased to call them, who livest and reignest with the Father and Holy Ghost, one God, world without end. *Amen.*

FOR ORPHANAGES

FATHER of the fatherless, let the cry, we pray Thee, of the orphan and the destitute enter into Thine ears: rescue them from the perils of a sinful world and bring them to the refuge of Thy Heavenly Home, for the sake of Thy Holy Child Jesus, our only Saviour and Redeemer. *Amen.*

A FAMILY HOME

The mother and one child are within; so at least four people live in this boat

FUKAGAWA AND ITS CHILDREN

By the Reverend R. A. Walke

THE district of Fukagawa might, I suppose, be called the slummiest in the city of Tokyo. Many very poor and ignorant people live there. Several wide streets have been made, but back of these are numberless narrow lanes, running in every direction and literally swarming with men, women, and children. Children! I should think so—every size and color from the pale little one that will before many years cough away its uncomfortable existence, to the perfectly-shaped bronze youngster who daily helps his father pole, through the canals of Tokyo, a boat laden with brick or rice or lumber. This child, by the way, when at home lives, has his being, and as far as possible moves, in a very small boat the cabin of which is about six feet square

and three feet high, and his father, mother and brethren live with him. It's not so bad when the weather is good and the combination window, door and roof of the cabin can be left open, but then the weather so often isn't good!

Fukagawa hasn't a pleasant reputation sanitarily. The rats seem to generate pest germs just for spite, and small-pox once in a while appears from nowhere. But the officers are after the germs tooth and nail—or rather microscope and virus—and while they often break out, they seldom get away.

Fukagawa is, however, not entirely given over to the poor people. One of the richest men in Japan has a magnificent place right in the midst of things, and there are many other beautiful residences scattered around. But on

(93)

THE RIVER FRONT AT TSUKIJI

The little ferry-boat on which we travelled may be seen leaving the shore, just under the X marked with ink in the picture

the whole, if you leave out these, and some handsome factories recently built, it is a forlorn place.

We went exploring over there the other day. It is across the river from Tsukiji, where St. Paul's College is located. If you go up the river there is a bridge, but we took a little ferryboat—fare one-quarter of a cent.

We landed in a region chiefly occupied by fisher-folk. The canals are packed with their boats and the banks given over to the drying of nets. Rags and roughness abound, and I hoped some typical folk would come along and add a human interest to my picture. But the only attractive person that appeared was a neatly-dressed little nurse maid, holding an umbrella over herself and the baby on her back. At my request she called up two others and got them into line. She was so determined that they should look and act properly and so self-forgetful that I quite lost my heart to the little lady.

The Japanese are very fond of a sort of small shell fish—translated in my dictionary by some long impossible Latin

name. They cost about five cents a quart and many people in Fukagawa make a living by rushing out at low tide and gathering them in. The women tie a baby on the back and a towel round the head, get a basket, pull up their skirts and in they go. The experience is both pleasant and profitable. The bridge in the picture is the one we might have

"The little nursemaid to whom I lost my heart"

(94)

LOOKING ACROSS THE RIVER TO FUKAGAWA

Barefooted people may be seen in the river gathering small shellfish; while the tall chimney of the factory speaks of modern machinery—and soot!

crossed on, and the factory typical of Fukagawa.

The picture below gives an idea of the houses that line many of the canals. We

can't much blame rats that live in this neighborhood for being pestiferous! The old fellow was so busy he did not even look up, although quite a crowd gathered

We cannot blame the rats for liking such a neighborhood

THE STREET OF CHILDREN

on the little bridge to see the foreigner take a picture, and doubtless wondered he didn't go and photograph the park. Yes, Fukagawa has a lovely temple and extensive grounds around it. And that was the point for which we were aiming. But just before reaching it we wandered into a curious little street. It was very

THE BRIDGE IN THE PARK

A DOORWAY OF THE TEMPLE

Here the travellers alighted from the car on their return, and noted the god on the left of the doorway who is supposed to watch particularly over children

narrow—so narrow in fact that every one had hung the wash out on bamboo poles that reached from roof to roof across the street. You had to dodge garments as you went along. The accompanying picture gives you some idea. It shows, too, that we have hoops in Japan. The little boy on the left has not lost his arms—not he! When the Japanese get cool, they, as it were, retire within themselves and leave dangling two patriotic-looking vacant sleeves. The third little boy was much too nice looking for that street—he must have been slumming. The lady boasted one tooth.

At last we reached the park, and a beauty it is too. I only got one picture—of an old pilgrim woman returning after worshipping at the temple. She was dressed in white. Her huge pilgrim hat had fallen off onto her back, while a towel ornamented her head. She carried a long staff, and attached to her waist was a little bell which tinkled as the poor old soul hobbled along.

We took the car for home right in front of a small temple. The idol on the extreme left represents the god who watches over the children. Around his neck are several gay-colored baby bibs, put there by mothers who hope thus to persuade him to guard their little ones.

Well, what has all this to do with THE SPIRIT OF MISSIONS? Just this: right here in Fukagawa is the "Church of the True Light," the Rev. Mr. Sugiura, priest-in-charge. He is doing a fine work among just these people. No foreigner could ever do it, as he could never understand the people, nor they him. I hope, by means of the pictures and what I have to-day written, to make the Church in America understand something of the conditions in Fukagawa. Even in this dark place is the light of the Good News shining, and the people, a few at a time, are being guided by it out of the ways of ignorance and degradation into the way of purity and peace.

(97)

THE POTTERY CLASS AT BROOKS INSTITUTE, GUANTANAMO, CUBA

The teacher of the class, who also writes this letter, is seen holding a piece of pottery in her hands and giving instructions to her boy pupils

WHERE EVERY PROSPECT PLEASES

A LETTER FROM THE WEST INDIES

CALLE LAS MACEAO 31,
GUANTANAMO, CUBA

My dear Maitland:

IF I'm going to tell you about my children (I feel toward them as if they were all really mine) I must begin by curing you of what I call "tourist" opinions, that is, thinking things are just exactly as they look. For often the pretty and lovable brown-eyed Cuban children who come to us seem to be absolutely devoid of the moral sense. The innocence in which our own Anglo-Saxon childhood is nurtured is an almost unknown quantity with Cuban children after actual babyhood.

That this lack of innocence so often goes further than mere knowledge of evil is the most appalling fact that confronts us. Actual instances, that I naturally refrain from relating, would fill you with horror, and an almost panic-stricken zeal to save these sweet, tiny human beings from themselves, their degenerate inheritance, and their vitiating environment.

The poor babies! It isn't *their* fault. What can you expect them to be and think, when they are allowed to hear conversations which you and I would blush to think of? where parental discipline does not exist, yet where cruelty abounds, in a land whose morals are beyond description?

One difficulty is that everything is so outwardly civilized. If they were more savage you'd at least know how to go about teaching them. Among the better class no people could possibly be greater sticklers for appearances or would be more insulted if you intimated the existence of conditions that are notorious! Though one has reason to believe the lower classes certainly might be called in a measure uncivilized, when in neighborhoods not two blocks away from our school, children are considered over-

dressed who boast a garment. I have seen shiny little brown babies in the unique gala attire of a pair of shoes and a string of beads!

On festive occasions the old negroes, many of whom come from the Congo, dance the "Tooceeba," to the music of tom-toms, and gourd-rattles, and their own weird wailings. This relic of barbarism (and you have never seen anything so aboriginal!) is supposed to be part of their "voodoo" rites, and lasts for days at a time. A week or so ago they had a dance down by the river, a few blocks back of our house. As the weird tumult of sound came floating to us through the tropical night, it made the shivers run up my back! Such howling! Why it might have been in darkest Africa! It began at dusk Saturday and lasted till Monday noon. In a "voodoo" orgie out toward the mountains

Girls at their basket weaving

(99)

a little over a year ago these same
negroes are said to have sacrificed a
white baby—"the hornless goat"—as part
of their ritual. Some of these have been
brought to justice I believe. This is in
the midst of "civilization!" Also in the
midst of "civilization" are many people
living together, with large families
(such were our neighbors across the
street last winter)—who find a marriage
ceremony too expensive, and who are perfectly bland and flagrant about it. So
much for what we have to fight. And
the weapons? God-given enthusiasm, and
tact! *tact!* TACT!

In the Brooks School we have about
ten orphans and sixty day-pupils. It
ranks far and above any other school
here, and besides giving the children a
thorough kindergarten and grammar
school course we are teaching them many
necessary and useful things. The children who live in the house are taught
to take care of the house, and they do

Over he goes!

all except the heavy
work, which falls to the
servants. All the chil-
dren are taught sewing,
and have done some
splendid work in basket-
making. They are taught
singing by Miss Wallace,
the new missionary
teacher—who is a musi-
cian—and they love it!
To hear them singing
"Hark! the Herald
Angels Sing," with their
pretty Spanish words,
seems so odd, and sets
you thinking of the one-
ness of childhood the
world over.

I teach them drawing
and design, for which they
have considerable aptness.
Last winter they did
some very good work in
pottery decorations which
sold like "hot cakes" at
our bazaar. This offers
opportunity to improve
their taste, which is

THE DUMB-BELL DRILL

atrociously gaudy. Mr. Ackley trains the boys in drilling and gymnastics, and Mrs. Richard Brooks gives physical culture to the girls, and the teachers. This fills one of the greatest needs, as the children here are not strong, most of them paying little or no attention to the laws of health. In their homes there are anywhere from twenty-five to forty people, living in what we would consider an ordinary one-family house. They sleep at night with their rooms sealed as tightly as if the plague lay beyond. As a result there is a tremendous amount of tuberculosis.

And would you believe

A MAYPOLE DANCE

The cunning brown babies at their work

it! We have had to teach the children to play! Until they learned them at our school, such things as real, romping, outdoor games were unknown to them. As it is, the children I have noticed in the neighborhood whom we do not have in the school, seem to do nothing but hang around and make noises. A five-year-old boy who lived directly opposite the rectory last winter (who only wears clothes on Sundays, mind you! and is rarely without a cigarette in his mouth) used to spend much of his time stamping up and down the floor screaming, in "tantrums" I have never heard equalled!

There are four regular teachers — (Mr. Ackley, Mrs. Brooks and I only teaching special lines)— Miss Doolittle, the principal, and Miss Coel (two hard-working, competent women, under whom the school has weathered struggling as well as its successful years), "Doña Mercedes" Mendez, an earnest Cuban Churchwoman, who has had the training for a deaconess in the Philadelphia School, and Miss Wallace, a southern girl, whom the Board sent down this fall, and who is winning the children's hearts.

Many of the girls who were mere tots when they were taken in—wretched, starved, ignorant "reconcentrados"—have gone from us clean, intelligent, ambitious women, either to find suitable places to maintain themselves, or back among their own kinspeople to be home-builders of a higher type. "Dominica," who came to us such a wild, untamed little savage that she used to bite Miss Doolittle, and once tried to kill her with a hatchet, is now an educated, sincere Church-girl living in Santiago. The Rev. Mr. Mancebo, who is there, says that she is his staunch and faithful helper in the church and mission Sunday-school.

When some of the children first came to us, in the usual filthy condition, and were taken in to be bathed, they would fall down before Miss Doolittle and cling to her knees, begging her not to kill them. Just the other night little "Carmen" (I wish you could see her—the dearest little m i n x with yellow curls!) woke up wailing in her little bed, and begging not to be sent back home, where they beat her so! Yes, and beatings are not the worst that we save them from! With an orphan girl in Cuba the chances are nineteen to one that she will be held in a moral slavery worse than can be imagined, by whomsoever she may chance to be taken in.

If we have made it possible for these girls to live decent lives in a country where regard for women is at such a low ebb, and their chances for purity so few, to say nothing of having educated them to be intelligent and useful—if we have sent the leaven of education, orderliness, h e a l t h and the principles of right and truth with which we are striving

STANDING AT ATTENTION

imbue them into the homes of those sixty children who come to us during the day, who shall say that we are not doing the Master's work in this land of eternal summer? We calculate that it costs $150 to keep a little girl living in the school a year. So, if you know any misguided capitalists, my dear, *do* put them into communication with

Your affectionate friend,
LEONORE ACKLEY.

December 24th, 1909.

> The Brooks Institute at Guantanamo, where Mrs. Ackley teaches, is the outgrowth of a little school begun by Mrs. Brooks, an American woman, at the time when the Cubans were fighting for their independence. The thousands of orphans made by the war appealed to her sympathies, and she began the work which has grown wonderfully year by year in effectiveness and opportunity. Larger and better school buildings are greatly needed.

WHO CARES?

SOME OF OUR NEGRO MISSIONS

By Julia C. Emery

IT was just after the close of the great Civil War that the honored and beloved rector of Grace parish, Petersburg, Va., was passing down street of that old town. Noisy and dirty and neglected Negro children were playing all about, and as he went along, the black mother of one among them came up with her request: "Would he start a school, and take those children in, and teach them better things?" Dr. Gibson went to his own son, the present Bishop of Virginia, and to young Alexander Weddell, who became a beloved and now lamented priest in the diocese, and asked them to undertake this work. They opened a Sunday-school in the basement of the church, and from that small beginning have grown St. Stephen's parish with its missions and the Payne Divinity-school, which has trained so many of the Negro clergy of the Church.

Many another Negro mission, now more or less active, could trace its history back to days as far back, or even farther —to the time "before the war"—when as the writer was once told, as she visited in an old-time home and looked at the time-worn and darkened mahogany where generations of the family and their

ONE OF OUR NEGRO CLERGY WITH HIS BAND OF YOUNG CARPENTERS

guests had sat, "Yes, every night we children sat around the table here, with the little Negro children of the place, and taught them over again the lesson we had learned that day."

And years and years before that time the story has come to us from South Carolina of the S. P. G. missionaries sent from England to minister to the parishes between Georgetown and the sea, and to the Negroes on the plantation. And after the Revolution the same care was given by the resident clergy to these Negro parishioners of theirs.

But the vicissitudes of war left the once wealthy country desolate, and separated master and servant. The people who could leave went; some few lingered on the higher lands and found work for a few Negroes in their employ, and here and there at this present, in the midst of this moss-covered, live-oak country, you will find little houses with their flower gardens in front and a vegetable garden with a few fig trees, and maybe a peach tree planted here and there.

In one of these houses lives a man who for years has worked along with the rectors of All Saints' parish in caring for the numbers of Negro Churchpeople

who cling to this land, which once was filled with plenty, and even in its present condition offers to them all that they can claim for home.

Sunday after Sunday our Church leader goes out in the early morning to meet a few old communicants of the Church and to lead them in a service of prayer and praise. Many of these old people know the services of the Church by heart. The old rector, who lived in All Saints' parish for forty-five years before and after the war, had given himself faithfully to teaching them, and under his instruction they had learned not only the Church Catechism, but the Thirty-nine Articles, and had been drilled in the use of the service.

To people who live in thickly-settled neighborhoods it seems a little strange that there are no hospitals to which the sick may be sent, but that there has not been for a long time a physician within thirty miles who could come to the sick must seem incredible. Such, however, has been the case in this beautiful but deserted country. Our good leader, together with other members of the Church, makes it his business to visit the sick. If he misses any of his flock from service he inquires about them, and if he cannot learn definitely about them, he goes to see them. He has a horse and cart, and when the distance is too great for walking he rides.

One day he went to a lonely hut miles away from his home, and found one of the women very sick and all alone. She had no food nor medicine, and had no one to give her anything. So he took her in his cart, carried her to his home, and his wife and himself nursed her and shared their little store with her until she was able to get to work again. In this characteristic note to his rector he told him, in his own quaint way, the simple story of what he had done:

"Dear Rector:
"I bin to Cely house. Cely sick. Hern bin sick a week. Nobody dere and her had no medcine and noting for eat. I take Cely in my cart bring hern to we hous. My wife and we nus she and feed she.

"I would not worry you but der ain't nuting in the hous for eat now, and I hab to ask you please sir, to help we out a little bit.

"Yr. servant,
"V. B."

MEADE CHAPEL, ALEXANDRIA, VA.
The property on which this chapel stands was given for work among Negroes, and it was to its renovation that the offering at the consecration of Bishop Lloyd was devoted

GRACE CHURCH, MILLERS, VA.
An example of the small country churches by means of which the endeavor is made to spread the Church's influence among the Negroes of rural communities

So in this way the sweet life of Christ is kept before the eyes of His humble followers and the warmth of His love keeps these people pure in heart.

And as in South Carolina so in the country parts of Georgia this work goes on. Here a Negro deaconess visits among her people. She trudges miles over the sandy roads, or under the forest trees whose dropping needles make the pathway soft and sweet, or crosses on logs the swamps. She seeks the poor and sick and suffering; she encourages those more well-to-do to bring potatoes and rice and flour and meal, hominy, peas, turnips, syrup, bread, meat and fish to give to those in need; she teaches in day and Sunday-school; she helps the women clear the ground of the missionary premises, and with the children rakes and sweeps it; she decks the church for Christmas and distributes among the children the fruit from Christmas trees. She visits from mission to mission, and meets branches of the Woman's Auxiliary, and gives out mite-chests for the United Offering. All day long she works with the carpenter on the chancel of the little chapel. To know of such individual workers with the inheritance of past training or the result of the training of to-day cheers one in looking out on the

THE RISING
GENERATION

prospect of mission work among our Negro people.

It was a significant fact, and hopeful for this prospect, that at the consecration of Dr. Lloyd in Christ Church, Alexandria, the offering should have been devoted to the rebuilding of Meade Chapel in that old town. The property on which the chapel stands was bequeathed by a faithful member of Christ parish on condition that it be used for Church work among the Negroes. There a succession of students from the Theological Seminary have made their first essay at missionary service; hundreds have been instructed there; Archdeacon Pollard, of North Carolina, well-known far beyond that diocese, there received his early training. The work has known the ebbing and the flowing of the tide; with the 20th of last October we will hope that the flowing tide which then set in may bear this old work to a growing and lasting fruitfulness.

We started with Petersburg, and we will return there and end with a record of country work being done by one of the men whom its divinity-school has furnished to Virginia's Negro work.

In the county of Essex, which is the centre of a large Negro population, eight years ago a work was started. A log cabin was the place of meeting, and that in poor condition, not sufficient indeed to keep out the winter winds. Nevertheless there was warmth of heart on the part of the good man who had begun this work, and who had the love and respect of all. The first instructions were of a general character; the local prejudice among the people was bitter,

THREE LITTLE LADS AND THEIR LETTERS

THEY live away up in the north of Alaska, just inside the Arctic Circle, in a place called Allakaket, on the Koyukuk River. For two years two devoted Christian women have lived among them, and are teaching them things of which neither they nor their parents ever heard before. When it was suggested that they write something which would show their appreciation of what the Church is doing for them, the accompanying letters, couched in their own language and devised by themselves, were the result.

> I am glad Jesus was born.
> On christmas night
> jesus was born in Bethlehem, in a horse – house
> for the road house plenty
> full. jesus have no little
> bed mary make little
> bed for little jesus in
> box put plenty hay in box
>
> Oscar.

Oscar is only six years old, but can read the New Testament stories very well. He has evidently been impressed by the lovely story of the first Christmas, and here is his interpretation of it. It should be remembered that in Alaska a table is called a horse-house.

St. Johns in the. Wilderness
Allakaket
Koyukuk River
Alaska
Jan 5st 1909

My dear Mr. Wood.
I have good time at Christmas.
I hang up my stocking.
I find little fire - engine.
music gun and candy, muffer.
Toque, mittens. in my stocking
I stay at mission, and I am glad
I eat lot of hot cakes.
Oscar and I make snow house
your boy
Frank

Frank, who has recently been taken into the mission household, came them almost starved and in a thoroughly wretched condition. Small wont that he so keenly enjoyed his first Christmas, and particularly remembers h he "ate lot of hot cakes."

On the Wednesday before Christmas Son, oko and Peter go catch Christmas 🌲 and put it up in 🏠. Night time 👨‍👩‍👧‍👦 all come and fix 🌲 Christmas eve we go to 🏠 and hang up our 🧦.

Christmas Morning we go and get our 🧦. At church the 👥👥👥👥 sang.

In the afternoon everybody 🏃 races.

David

David, the artist, is ten years of age, and what he may lack in technique is made up in action. Is it not worth while for the Church to reach and train children such as these?

A TYPICAL MOUNTAIN HOME
Elevation, 11,000 feet. Seven people live in this house.

FAMINE SCENES IN CENTRAL MEXICO

By the Right Reverend Henry D. Aves, D.D.

DURING most of November and December I was in the famine-stricken district of the central *mesa,* and have travelled many miles studying the conditions, holding services at our scattered missions, and looking after the distribution of corn. I was hardly prepared for the degree of suffering I found; for the description sent me by our missionaries failed, as any verbal description must, to convey the lively impression one gets from seeing the conditions and dwelling for a time among them. Indeed, it must be difficult for the average American to imagine the cheerless, comfortless penury that characterizes the normal life of the Mexican mountaineer. There is nothing even among our poorest Negro population with which to compare it.

The typical mountain home means a stone *jacal* of one or two rooms, with dirt floor, windowless, carpetless, with neither stove nor bed. The place for resting, eating, and sleeping is the ground; and at an altitude of 8,000 to 10,000 feet it is generally cold. The daily life is reduced to its simplest terms. At nightfall when the children have brought home the little flock of goats and the poultry from the day's herding, filled the water pots from the distant stream, and ground the daily supply of corn, when the father has returned from his day's work on the neighboring *hacienda* (where he has earned two *reals*—twelve and a half cents), the supper of corn *calces,* which the mother is baking on the heap of stones, is eaten in silence, smoke and semi-darkness, bedtime has come. There is no need of light, for there is neither book nor paper in the home. Outside among the rocks and cacti (which furnishes the only fruit that grows) is the little patch, two or three acres, perhaps, of corn, for winter use. Let that little harvest come to grief, and deprive the family of the father's shilling wage, and it is plain to see what must speedily follow.

But the Mexican Indians are both stoical and proud. They are inured to

PRESIDENTE FLORES, MINE HOST FOR A NIGHT

He doubted that a bishop would come so far simply to help the starving poor.

the hard life they live; and it must be a severe strait of suffering that will compel them to complain or ask for help. Therefore, of the many evidences of destitution that I have found, none has witnessed more strongly to the common distress than the great numbers of persons asking a pittance for something to eat. And these are not the professional beggars of the highway, but people who run out from their homes to ask an alms from the passer-by.

The first car-load of corn from Houston, Tex., had reached Nopala when I arrived there; and I found that all plans for its distribution had been carefully laid. The *presidentes* (or mayors) of the twenty-five or more surrounding towns had quietly furnished lists of all the absolutely helpless destitute persons and families, and had notified them where and when they might go to get relief. As many names on these long rolls represented large families, the list looked rather formidable for our single car-load of corn. But a careful calculation had been made, based on the estimate of two-thirds of a *litro* (little more than a pint) of corn for each adult per day, and one-half a *litro* (less than a pint) for each child. By this calculation it became evident that our

carload would support 1,000 people for a month.

I shall not attempt to describe the

CORN FOR THREE

The old woman has come eighteen miles for her week's supply.

(111)

Begging their way to the mines

ninety miles to the southwest. As we were expecting another car-load of corn within a few days, we determined to carry them 140 bushels at once by means of a pack-train of burros. We started from Nopala on Wednesday and reached Tlalmimilolpan in time for service the following Sunday. Throughout the way we found the same monotonous barrenness from blight with its attendant suffering. At San Andres de Milpan, a community of 5,000 Otomis, where we spent our second night, we found the people grinding their little remnant of corn together with the cobs to make it last the longer. Our host here was the *presidente*, an intelligent and kind-hearted Indian, who was in deep distress for the suffering of his people. Our offer of corn for the most destitute was met with incredulous astonishment, and when he was told in the morning before we left that his guest in khaki was a bishop, he said, "No, that

crowds that pressed into the *patio* of the mission house on the morning of the first day of distribution. Suffice it to say that they represented the many phases of misfortune and misery with which Mexican life abounds—blind, crippled, malformed, feeble-minded, palsied, half-clad, consumptive, infirm with old age, widowed, fatherless and orphaned, with no able-bodied man among them. Many had come from far, and must have tramped a good part of the night to reach the mission house in the morning. The bales of blankets which Consul General Hanna had sent me were reserved for the very old. Without the wall of sacked corn in the background, this would have been a scene indescribably pathetic, but the looks and words of eager gratitude, together with the lively tunes a blind man *would* play for his corn, and the little helpful offices of one to another in adjusting their loads, made the picture almost happy.

An urgent appeal for help had come from Tlalmimilolpan and Mimiapan,

A blind man who would like to exchange his wares for a little corn.

WAITING FOR THE DISTRIBUTION OF THE CORN

cannot be, for bishops never go humbly. They go with eclat ("*con bomba*")! And they go always to get, never to give. If I am to believe what you say, there must be a new religion in the world, of which I have never heard." He guided us over the range, and secured a promise from our missionary to come·again and hold a service in his house.

But why are these people of the heights so very poor? I have often heard American tourists (who must see Mexico mainly through the car window) say, "How thriftless, improvident and unambitious these people must be!" And it does look like that. But when one begins to learn the true conditions and the dark logic of history that traces these people to their present helpless state; that since the Spanish conquest, which drove them from their fertile valleys, they have passed through slavery, serfdom and peonage into their present state of semi-feudalism; that they have ever been placed at the brunt of internecine wars, playing the pawn in the endless games of political contention; that they have been kept in ignorance as well as penury; that in their present semi-

feudal state they must needs "belong" more or less to the great landed estates on which they work and to which they are commonly in hopeless debt; that they have nothing with which to be "provident," no opportunity to "thrive," and no· hope to inspire "ambition"; that their only independence is the meagre and precarious foothold on life that the rocky clearing on the mountain side will afford them—when one begins to realize these facts and their dark significance, contempt must needs turn to pity.

But there is one possible door of hope for this people, the key to which is fitted to the lock—the key of education, which must open the way of opportunity. Through this doorway must come that intelligent, religious and patriotic middle class so essential to the national stability of a·self-governing people, and so necessary to its redemption from the darkness and misery of a helpless and hopeless poverty. May the love of God hold and press our hands to the key of this door, for it would seem to be the key of divine purpose for the destiny of His children.

(113)

THE LAND O

By the Reverend

YOU may think that this will be
about Japan. Perhaps you already begin to smell the cherry-
blossoms, and see the little peo-.
ple clattering about the streets on their
clogs, dressed in their flowered kimonos
and bowing their polite little bows to
those whom they meet; while Fujiyama,
the beautiful mountain, stands, as always, in the background of the picture.

In some ways I am sorry that it is not
to be Japan, and that instead you will
have to go with me to the prairie lands of
North Dakota, where the only mountain
in the picture will be Turtle Mountain,
which isn't a mountain at all, but only a
height of land that forms one of the
great watersheds, and which, though it
boasts a forest to clothe itself, does not
really grow very large trees, or very good
ones.

Here has lived for many years a little band of the Chippewa Indian tribe.
How they came to be so far from the rest
of their people is not a matter which particularly concerns this story. Their kins-
folk were in Minnesota and Canada, but
here we find them settled, some thirty
years ago, living a quiet life in a very
primitive way, trapping, hunting, and
farming a very little, far away from the
white settlements of that day, in a lonely and somewhat desolate corner of the
world.

Over in the neighboring State of Minnesota, at Faribault, there lived at that
time a man whose name was known
wherever the Indians needed a friend;
and it was to Bishop Whipple, at his
house in Faribault, that there came one
day an Indian who bore the marks of a
long journey, and who made himself
known as Rising Sun, a chief of the
Turtle Mountain Chippewas, from the
land of the Dakotas. For nearly 300
miles he had travelled to see the great
chief of the white-robed missionaries.
Through his Chippewa brethren in
White Earth he had heard something of

again he has always done—determined to have them. So the government appointed a commission of excellent men, two of them clergymen, to make a treaty with the Turtle Mountain Indians.

The performance of any public business by an Indian tribe is a matter of stately, serious, and prolonged procedure. There must be council fires, peace-pipes, and all the time-honored ritual with which these primitive people have interested their acts. So the commission—which doubtless would have been glad to get away from the Indian camp more promptly—found itself staying day after day until at last Sunday arrived.

This little party of white men, alone in the midst of heathen people, doubtless said their prayers privately, but even Dr. Knickerbacker—one of our priests and afterward Bishop of Indiana — who was a member of the party, thought it best to hold no public service. Imagine, then, his curiosity when, as he walked about the camp in company with a friend, he saw a group of Indians listening to one who was addressing them. Drawing near they heard that he was speaking in the Chippewa language, with which they were somewhat familiar, and that now and then from the people around the speaker there burst a chorus of response. As they listened the words seemed familiar, and all at once they realized that they were hearing a Christian service!

It was Rising Sun keeping his promise to the bishop. Years had passed, yet no Sunday had ever dawned but that this half-instructed Indian, in his remote wilderness, had gathered his little band around him and taught, as best he could, the truths of the Christian faith—so well that all had learned to say with him the Lord's Prayer and the Apostles' Creed.

Back to their homes, the day after this discovery, went the white commissioners, and again Rising Sun and his people were lost to view. But after twelve years more the Church at last sent a missionary bishop to North Dakota, who found this faithful man—then getting on in years—still teaching the men, women and children of his tribe. It was not always easy work; he was very much alone, for in spite of being a chief they did not all agree with him. The young men, as they

OLD RISING SUN AND HIS WIFE

Bishop Edsall and the lay-reader, Wellington Salt, in front of Rising Sun's cabin, in which service has just been held

grew up, became restless and bitter against the encroaching white man. They did not care to toil on the wilderness land about them; they had no love of hard work and wanted to make a living in some other way. They chafed as the rising tide of white men began to surround them, only waiting for a chance to seize their lands. They fell into the temptations spread for them by these same white men, and many were demoralized by liquor and disease. But all the time old Rising Sun went steadily on, preaching the gospel of peace and industry, and practising it in the fields about his cabin; sustaining, encouraging, rebuking, but most of all pleading the love of God and the saving power of the Blood of Christ. He was indeed to his people a Rising Sun of righteousness.

So you will be glad to know that after

a time he had his wish, and that teachers of Christianity for whom longed came to him and his people. I poor little log cabin has been sanctuary wherein bishops have offe: the Holy Eucharist and administered spiritual gifts of confirmation. H greatly he has appreciated his blessii is shown by these words from the di: of the Bishop of North Dakota:

"In my mail to-day there was a very touching gift of $4 for North Dakota Missions. It came from old Rising Sun, a Chippewa Indian, who lives in the Turtle Mountains. For the first time in six years he had a little money from some U. S. payment,—about $100—and he promptly devoted this much to the Church's work. Nobody who has not seen—as

Reviving in their games the memories of the old days

I have—this old man, roughly dressed, sitting in a log hut bare of furniture, or toiling in the potato patch which is his only source of income, can estimate the magnitude of his gift. Nobody who does not know—as I do—how much every Indian delights in spending on gay garments and canned foods and toys, can estimate the generosity of his gift."

The accompanying picture shows a litle group gathered about Bishop Edsall when he visited Rising Sun's cabin some years ago. The flag held by the layeader in the background is the church flag, always raised as the signal that here is to be divine service.

The long years of this old man's faithulness have not been in vain. Many a ife has been influenced for good by his uiet example, and many a dark heathen oul brought to know its Saviour through he message which this servant of Christ as delivered.

May I tell you the story of old P'te Kute, a Sioux Indian who married a Jhippewa wife and lived among that ribe in the land of Rising Sun? He was hard man through many years. Cruel, indictive, his conversion seemed hopeless; but God has many ways of bringing men to Him, and even after this man became old and blind he found the true light. As you read his story remember

that Indian cruelty has usually been the result of the white man's equal or greater cruelty, and that in every instance where Indian rights have been respected, and the proper dignity of Indian manhood and womanhood recognized, they have been friends and helpers of the white man.

Now for the story. It was told to one of our missionaries, and he gives it as far as possible in the Indian's own words:

"I am old and blind. No more is the strength of the young man in my muscles, nor the light of the sun in my eyes. And in my heart it is dark also. I have been a very bad Indian, and always hated the white man and killed him when I could. Many years ago when the Indians killed so many white men in Minnesota, I was there and helped to kill many. I did not know it was wrong. The red man kills the white man just as the white man kills the bears that come to drive him away from his land. One little woman I killed, and I know she was very good, for her face was so good, even while I killed her and her little baby.

"But now my arms are weak, nor can I any more see the daylight coming far across the prairies. And when I think of

(117)

the many bad things I have
done, it is dark in my heart also,
with a great sorrow for what I
have done.

"For three years the spirits
of those I have killed have come
to me in the dark. My eyes cannot see the men who are alive,
but those I have killed come and
wake me out of sleep, and then
I see. Most often comes the
spirit of the little white mother,
and so sadly she looks at me.

"I have been thinking of
many things in the dark, and
my heart, which has so long been
bad, is now good. I do not hate
the white man any more. I love
him now. If he should come
and take all that is in my house
I should love him still. I know
he cannot help doing as he does.
He cannot help wanting much
land, for he loves to plough it and
see the grain grow upon it, just
as the red man loves to see it
with the buffalo and the red
deer upon it. The white man
cannot help the way the Great
Spirit made him any more than
the red man can help the way
the Great Spirit made him.

"Three nights ago when the
little mother appeared to me, I
asked her how I could be for-
given for my sin in killing her,
and her baby, and so many
others. She told me to learn
about the white man's Great
Spirit, and be baptized, and the
Christ-Child King would love me
and forgive me. And now I
want you to teach me and baptize me."

The missionary baptized old P'te
Kute, and the next night he saw again
the spirit of the little white mother. The
sorrow was gone from her face, and a
sweet smile was there. She told him
she had come for the last time and would
no more trouble him, as he was her
brother, and should see her next in the
Christ-Child's Kingdom. Then she left
him. His eyes filled with tears, but his
heart was full of a great and wonderful
joy.

So again were fulfilled the words of the
prophet, "The people that walked in dark-

By the Right Reverend Nathaniel S. Thomas

Bishop Thomas's first baptism

WYOMING is the children's land. Let me begin with the babies. I am showing you, at the head of this article, a picture of the first baby I baptized in Wyoming. It happened in this way. Dean Bode and I were trying to meet an appointment in Saratoga. Our train pulled into Walcott just as the Saratoga train pulled out. We were so provoked, for we said, "Now we shall have to spend the money the children send us to do our work in hiring a conveyance to take us to Saratoga"; for we could not wait over the next day. It seemed like a sheer waste of money—and all because that Saratoga train would insist on being so true to its schedule. But we did not know, and God did, you see. For if we had caught the train we should not have had the opportunity of baptizing that beautiful baby in the far-away ranch-house between Walcott and Saratoga.

GROUP ON THE PORCH OF THE REV. SHERMAN COOLIDGE, WIND RIVER RESERVATION

(119)

This was my first Wyoming lesson on not being impatient, and it taught me the meaning of the text, "He that believeth shall not make haste." I wish the boy or girl who reads this would write me and tell me where this text is found.

You have all seen a picture of the great chief Washakie's grandson, for he occupied the cover of the Children's Number of THE SPIRIT OF MISSIONS three years ago; but possibly you have not seen the picture of the little daughter of the Rev. Sherman Coolidge, and so I am giving you a picture of a group I took upon the porch of Mr. Coolidge's bungalow on the Wind River reservation. She occupies the centre of the group, with her father on her right. Immediately above him is one of her foster sisters, and holding the papoose basket over the head of a sick Indian baby is her other foster sister.

Mrs. Coolidge, who stands at the right of the picture, is God's own blessing sent to the Indian babies of the reservation. Those she does not adopt she cares for

The girls in the shawls

in one way or another, and the Indian mothers bring their babies to her whenever they are ill. But, you are saying, I thought the babies were never ill in Wyoming. So I *did* say, but possibly sometimes they do not get the right things to eat.

Now I am going to leave the babies and show you some larger children. Here is a picture of three shawls and three children inside. Close by you see a n o t h e r picture of twenty girls and two teachers. In w h i c h group would you rather be? You see what pretty, interesting children the Indian girls are when they have some one to care for them. Children a r e h a p p y in Wyoming when people are kind to them, whether they be white or red.

If you have a map of Wyoming and will turn to it, you will see the next place where I

A GROUP OF THE INDIAN SCHOOL GIRLS

"They were not a bit afraid of me, though I came up very close"

am going to take you. It is the town of Dixon, sixty-five miles from

THE IMPROVISED MERRY-GO-ROUND

a railroad, on the Colorado border, and separated from the copper-smelting town of Encampment by the giant mountains called the Sierra Madre. It was near here that I snapped this interesting photograph, which the editor of a Wyoming paper said was the best picture of a flock of sheep he had ever seen. You see they were not a bit afraid of me, though I came up very close to them. I like to think they took me for a real shepherd.

It was in this town of Dixon that a Sunday-school superintendent — a good man who loves children—made for his scholars the unique merry-go-round which I am showing you in the accompanying picture. Do you see he has used the seat of his own wagon? I am wondering what he is doing for a seat while the children are amusing themselves. Do you suppose he has to stand up when he drives? I am also wondering whether the children think of this, and

A ride on the vigilante's pony

OUR COVER PICTURE

THE picture of the Indian mother on our cover has its own story, sadly connected with the Yukon River, which is seen in the background. The missionary at Eagle, Alaska, says:

"Mary's husband was drowned in the Yukon two years ago and she was left inconsolable. After about a year her Indian tribesmen from the Mackenzie River came to fetch her. She returned with them but only lived a few months and died a victim to consumption. No doubt grief for her husband's untimely end hastened her own."

have been thoughtful enough to thank him.

Only seven miles from Dixon is the town of Boggs. Here, as recently as only a year ago, the men of the village had to organize themselves into a committee of safety called "the Vigilantes" to secure the safety, or at least the order, of the town. The Vigilantes therefore constitute a sort of self-appointed body of policemen. You might think that they were very dreadful and sure to inspire every boy and girl with fear. Here is a picture of some of the Vigilante's children, on one of the steeds with which my friend, the doctor, is wont to race on an errand of mercy, or pursue the lawless, bad men, as the necessity may require.

Just one more picture and then I shall close. It is a picture of a happy family —just the best sort of family—for it is the picture of a sweet mother who is interested, not only in her own beautiful children, but in the children of her less fortunate neighbors. And this is the way it is in Wyoming wherever the Church is to be found.

I am already beginning to wonder what the Sunday-school Easter Offering will be, and how many pennies and nickels and dimes will find their way out to Wyoming to help the Church go to more of these children.

A WYOMING FAMILY

MISSIONARY DISTRICT
OF
SOUTH DAKOTA.

SIOUX FALLS, SOUTH DAKOTA.

Dec. 26, 1907.

My dear Mr. Wood:

I send you, in another envelope, a
Christmas card that came to me from St. Mary's
School, thinking that you can use it, either
in my article for the Children's Number, or
some other time. An inscription like this,
perhaps, might be put beneath it: Three Indian
girls of St. Mary's School. "Kind friends
send us some warm clothing: why should we feel
the cold?"

[signature]

A MESSAGE FROM BISHOP HARE

(123)

THE STORY OF A CHINESE SLAVE GIRL

By the Reverend Edmund Lee Woodward, M.D.

SOME months ago the Chinese catechist of St. James's Hospital, Anking, came to me with a blaze of indignation in his eyes. "Doctor," he said, "a little slave girl has been terribly beaten, stripped of her clothes, and thrust out into the street to die (it was mid-winter). May I bring her to the hospital?" "The sooner the better," I replied, and very shortly she was brought in—as wretched a little mite of humanity as the fiendish rage of a Chinese mistress could well make. The neighbors said that the child's screams of agony had been heard all the preceding night. Her poor body was livid with bruises and bore evidences of torture by burning and prodding with scissors— favorite methods of cruel Chinese mis-

A SLAVE GIRL IN THE HOSPITAL YARD

tresses for punishing slave girls. She had been a slave girl for only six months. She had been bought by an opium-besotted mandarin for $30 in a city not far from the great famine district of last year, which makes it probable that she was sold in order that the rest of the family might have food—a common practice.

The night after her rescue by the hospital, an elderly servant woman in the same unhappy household was treated in the same cruel way. The next morning her dead body was found floating on a pond nearby. Some said she had been beaten to death and thrown there, others that she had been driven to drown herself to end her misery.

With the tender care and good nursing in the hospital the poor slave girl soon began to grow better, and it was charming to watch her eager delight in giving a true mother's care to her obedient little slave—a fair-haired American doll-baby. It is hard to know, however, how long it will take for her half year of hideous cruelty to fade quite out of her memory. When her happy days in the children's sunny ward of the hospital were ended, she was placed in St. Agnes's School for girls. She is no longer doomed to a life worse than death, but will become a good and useful Christian woman, perhaps to do much for other poor slave girls in China. She has been baptized, and what better name could have been chosen than that given her by the godly Chinese catechist who rescued her—"Lai-An," which means in English "Peace has come."

Anking is in central China on the Yangtse River, three hundred and sixty miles from the coast. St. James's ranks with the largest and best hospitals in China and ministers each year in its wards and dispensary to TWENTY THOUSAND patients of every class. It is the only hospital in a district nearly two hundred miles square, with an estimated population of five millions. Dr. H. B. Taylor is the physician now in charge.

THE TALE OF FIVE PENNIES

By Sarah Lowrie

IVE brand new Lincoln pennies rolled on the table out of Miss
Georgiana's purse, and at a nod from her, five small hands
reached over and took possession of the shining coins. Then
the five children kneeled down and repeated after Miss
Georgiana this little prayer: "O dear Lord Jesus, as of old Thou didst
mutiply the five loaves of bread so that many men, women and children were fed, so we pray Thee multiply these pennies by Thy grace
and our endeavor that Thy Name may be glorified in many hearts.
And this we ask for love of Thee. Amen."

The five children rose from their knees and each clutching a new
penny rather solemnly, bade Miss Georgiana good-bye.

"Remember," she said, as she opened the door and let them file
out into the sunlight of the crisp winter afternoon, "remember, you
have just one week! And to make those pennies multiply into nickels
and dimes each child of you must Watch, and Work, and Pray for
missions! Now, go home and tell your mothers all about the plan.
Good-bye, and good luck to you!"

The five children, still rather solemn with the responsibility that
had just come upon them, walked very sedately down the steps to
Miss Georgiana's gate, Morton and John and little Archie first, and
the two girls, Marjorie and Katharine, last.

But at the gate the boys suddenly broke into a scurrying run, the
sight of a passing sleigh spurring them on. They knew the driver of
that sleigh and that he would not discourage a ride on his runners
along the smooth, well-packed snow of the village streets; for he was a
jolly sort of man, with room always for one more, either inside or out
of his broad old sleigh.

The little girls looked a bit scornfully after the scurrying boys, but
when the driver of the sleigh drew up and beckoned over his shoulder
for them to hurry, Miss Georgiana observed that they, too, conde-
scended to run, and in another moment the sleigh, full of laughing
children, had turned the next corner and was out of sight.

"I wonder what they will do with those pennies," Miss Georgiana
murmured to herself as she closed the door. "If each child makes as
much as five cents I shall be thankful."

*　　　*　.　　*　　　*　　　*　　　*

I wish you could have seen Miss Georgiana's happy face a week from
that afternoon, when the five children brought to her the week's earnings of the five Lincoln pennies, and she counted—not twenty-five
cents—but $1.02 as the result of their investments. I wish, too, that

you had been there to hear each child tell how he or she had set about turning those missionary pennies into nickels, and the nickels into dimes. You would have been interested to hear how by one lucky investment, the very first evening, little Archie made a whole quarter of a dollar with his bright new Lincoln cent, and how Katharine, try as she would all week, could only squeeze eleven cents out of her work with the penny; how John had bought a pen with his, and copied telephone numbers for his mother into her new desk card, and made ten cents in one evening. With that ten cents he bought some glue and some binder's-tape, and mended all the broken-backed books in use in the house—cook-books, school-books and account-books—clearing in all thirty cents by the end of the week. I think you would have been as much amused as Miss Georgiana was over Morton's investment. With his cent he purchased some cheese, and baited all the mouse-traps he could find about his own home and the houses of his relatives, and at the rate of two cents a mouse made in six nights all of sixteen cents. Perhaps of all the children Marjorie worked the hardest, for she bought a needle with her penny and darned her father's socks. She was rather a little girl, and to darn neatly took her a long, long time, so that even though she was paid five cents a sock, the twenty cents that she brought in at the end of the week meant nearly an hour each day taken from play-time.

However, even though you were not at Miss Georgiana's that afternoon, in which her Sunday-school class met to hand in the earnings of their pennies, you must by now feel nearly as interested as the children were to know how that one dollar and two cents was to be used to help forward Christ's Kingdom.

That evening Miss Georgiana made a little bag for the money and sent it to the treasurer of the Junior Auxiliary, with this note pinned to the bag: "This money was earned by five children in one week with five Lincoln pennies. It is to be used to help missions."

When the treasurer of the Junior Auxiliary opened the bag and read the note she looked very much pleased and considerably surprised. Then she placed the money in an envelope which she directed:

To George Gordon King, Treasurer,
Church Missions House, 281 Fourth Avenue, New York City.

When Mr. King opened the envelope he also was much pleased. "This will help some," said he, and he took down a great leather book and wrote $1.02 at the foot of a long column of other figures. Then he handed the money, together with other money which had come in that day, to his assistant treasurer, Mr. E. Walter Roberts. Mr. Roberts took the checks and the money and went down to the bank, where he deposited them all in one lump sum with the bankers who live all day back of gilded brass cages, for all the world like prisoners in golden jails. The bankers put the money in a dark vault and there it lay for nearly a month.

Then came a day when many wise and much-trusted men of the Church met and gravely considered what should be done with the money which had been sent in so that it might glorify God in many hearts. They were anxious that the very wisest possible use should be made of the five children's money, and of all the rest that lay waiting in the bank to be devoted to missions! So these men listened to letters from all over the world, written by missionaries who were working in China and Japan, in Brazil and the Philippines, in Porto Rico and Alaska, in Africa and the islands of the sea, and out in the Indian reservations, and near at hand in the mountains of the South.

Some of the letters came from such hot countries that the writers had to dress in white linen and be careful of sunstroke, and some came from such cold places that the writers had to wear furs, and take care not to get their noses and feet frozen. There were letters from missionary doctors whose patients lived in such damp countries that snakes crawled out from under the boards of the bed-rooms and tarantulas lurked in dark corners. There were also letters from doctors whose hospitals were in lands where no green things grow and no birds sing, and where the sand heaps up like snow about the door steps. Teachers wrote from schools where their scholars all studied out loud, like so many enormous bluebottle flies, and wore no clothes to speak of except when they went to church; while other teachers wrote about the wide padded skirts which even the boys wore, and the embroidered silk jackets and the long queues into which the scholars had to plait their hair once in so often.

Each letter asked for something. Santa Claus himself never got such a variety of requests as came in those missionary letters. One man needed a roof for his church, another an organ for his Sunday-school, another a whole saw-mill, another a boat. One desired some hymn-books and some garden-tools, another some altar furniture and church vestments. One doctor thought he could get along if he had nine more beds in his hospital, while another asked for medicine and surgical instruments. One man only asked for a wheel-chair for his hospital, but another asked for a whole children's ward. One teacher asked for pencils and paper and school-books, and another for Bibles and blackboards and chalk.

No one seemed to be needing anything for himself, but for the people about him. And each asked so eagerly and seemed so happy and cheerful in his difficult, lonely work, that the men in the Church council room, who sat all day listening to the letters, felt a great weight of care on their hearts, for they knew that there would not be enough money to go round. More than one of those eager, hopeful men would have to go without the thing he desired so greatly. You can see for yourself that even though Miss Georgiana's band had given that unexpected dollar and two cents, even though the sum total of all the Church's gifts had been many thousands of dollars, some one would have to do without his new ward, or his new roof, or even his old one mended up.

However, after the secretaries and treasurers and directors at the Missions House had Watched and Prayed and Worked quite as hard for many weeks as the five children with the five new Lincoln pennies had worked for one week, they gradually got the money all divided, so that each missionary got at least a part of what he needed. As for the one dollar and two cents, earned with the five new pennies, the last I heard of it was that:

$.01 went toward paying the salaries of the clerks who worked to distribute the missionary fund.

.01 went toward paying the freight on the goods sent to the missionaries.

.23—which was the balance of little Archie's earnings—went toward a saw-mill for the Philippines.

.11—which Katharine had worked so hard to get—helped tile the roof of a church in Porto Rico.

.30—given by John—got as far as Alaska, where it helped with an organ for a Sunday-school.

.16—which was Morton's mouse money you remember—bought some medicine which saved a child's life in a hospital in China.

.20—which Marjorie had made by darning stockings—travelled all the way to Brazil in the shape of a little New Testament, in which a little Portuguese school-girl learned to read the story of the Blessed Jesus.

You may count up those sums for yourself and see if the sum total does not come exactly to the $1.02 which the five children of Miss Georgiana's Mission Band earned in one week from the investment of their five brand new Lincoln pennies.

What was done with all the rest of the money, and what the teachers and doctors and nurses and clergymen in Japan, and China and Cuba and the South, North, East, and West were able to do because of it, does not belong to this tale, but to other, longer, ones in this same book.

I only want to caution you, in closing, that if you should happen to come across any of these five Lincoln pennies with which Miss Georgiana's band started their missionary enterprise, you would be doing the coins a real kindness if you would slip them back into the next missionary offering that passes your way. The truth is the five pennies have got so interested in missions since their first great venture into the world, that they pine to be up and at it again. Rather than risk disappointing their jolly little copper souls I fancy it would be as well to pop any Lincoln pennies which you get straight into your Lenten mite-box. Like the jolly man's sleigh, those boxes always seem to have room for one more.

A GROUP OF MOTHERS AND CHILDREN ON THE PIAZZA OF
MISS WATERMAN'S COTTAGE
One woman is offering Miss Waterman an egg

CHRISTMAS IN BONTOC AS IT
REALLY WAS

By the Reverend Walter C. Clapp

ALTHOUGH we have gotten through all the feasts of the different kinds and degrees of martyrs, and it is now the morrow of Holy Innocents', I am not quite sure that it is safe to tell you about Christmas. Only the day before yesterday, pen in hand, I was engaged in a rather peaceful retrospect, telling a friend at home that, although our enemies in the external sphere of material things were very active, yet there was great cause for thankfulness, especially, our boys had been so earnest and good about preparation for Communion, and in the many matters which were involved in getting ready for the great feast—when my ear caught an unusual tone in the babel of sounds outside, and I went to the door just in time to catch in my arms our impulsive Peter Aguilang, his bare body suffused with blood from a gash in the head, and holding in his hand a big club of wood

with which he proposed to demolish Arthur Labyang, whom he was pursuing. Now Arthur took a prize in the running races at the Sagada *fiesta,* and it may have been a saving of Peter's pride and the prevention of a feud that I happened to gather him in just then.

First, a bath all over, to find out where the blood came from; then, such a dressing and bandage as I could arrange pending Dr. Platt's professional treatment; Peter's blood-spattered "g-string" put to soak, and the boy bidden to keep quiet a bit while I finished my letter, in which I said but little more except to reaffirm my affection for the boys, notwithstanding such little side incidents. Consultation with our steady *kapatas* Jesse, and with Stanley showed that the trouble was an unaccountable outbreak, three boys being implicated—little cherubic David Fakolo being the third—and *all* to blame. Turning around, I found Arthur and

(129)

A FEW OF THE FIFTY BOYS WHO ARE NOW CARED FOR BY THE MISSION

In spite of all remonstrances the boys will assume stiff attitudes when their pictures are being taken

David waiting for me to act. It was soon over: a little sermon extempore—most of my preaching is of this sort—a simple, dispassionate putting of the case before the boys. The verdict was unanimous—there was only one thing to do, and I did it, the instrument being a leather belt. And so, because this episode was very brief, Christmas joy has been *almost* uninterrupted. One learns Malay characteristics after a while, and knows how to interpret.

I could not give you a truthful account of Christmas without telling you of this brief incidental tragedy, yet it is hardly what you expected, I fancy. Perhaps there is seldom a Christmas-tide anywhere, that some Herod does not try to get at the Holy Innocents, and the Holy Child within us—and so the incident is typical after all.

Truly, our Christmas *is* a very happy time in Bontoc. The children of the town scent its fragrance from afar. What should we be buying corn for in May and June, they say, but to pop it for their Christmas! and as they see the

big festoons of it hung for drying on wires over our heads in the crowded "back room," it awakens the frequent exclamation, "Ayaka nan piki! Kaat nan Kolismas?" ("Much the corn! How long before Christmas?")

Meantime good friends at home, who have spanned the great distance by their interest in our little people, have sent us many gifts—breadths of stout cloth for "tapises" for the girls and beautiful long strips of Turkey-red "g-strings" for the boys; and beads and whistles, and knives and combs, little looking-glasses, and a multitude of other simple articles—articles of faith to the children, for, although they have not seen them, they firmly believe that when Christmas comes these things will be forthcoming too.

As the day approaches, preparation of all sorts becomes more definite. I have already alluded to the spiritual side. A sweet and solemn thing it is to see these people, born in heathenism, with man-killing held up as admirable, and with easy standards of morals in most ways,

A group of Christian Igorot girls on the steps of Miss Whitcombe's house

thought only, "Why not? He has a simple, unformed faith in a Saviour." As a test, however, in consenting, I said he must come to church five days before his baptism. He came, and stayed too, the greater part of each day, quietly squatting, asking nothing except that we should tell him how many days it would be before the water would be put on his head, this by gesture, deprecating what we gave him from time to time. "Why, Apo, you gave me something yesterday!" or, "This is the third time you have given me something!" And so, on Christmas Eve, as a child, he knelt at the font, and although he could not see the lighted tapers, I am sure "That Light" of which St. John wrote, came to him. His presence with us has been a sort of benediction, and no trouble. The boys are very kind to Ernest Chaluyen, and carefully lead him to and from church at service time. There, and at instructions, he has been gradually learning the things which a Christian ought to know and believe to his soul's health. I have said church, but you know we haven't any church— I wish we had—only a very much patched-up and pieced-out room, with the old whitewash all scaling off. But I wonder if there is any old barn so unsightly that, with the aid of some bright pictures, and a decent white altar covering, and lights and plenty of pine boughs and trailing vines, it cannot be made to look holy and "Christmassy" for "our Lord's Nativity"? Well, ours did. The boys scaled the mountains for greens, and shinned the splintery beams of our improvised rood-screen to put them in place. They could give points to most American decorators and do the work in half the time. Festal choral Eucharists, beginning at midnight of Christmas Eve, and continuing through Innocents' Day; large congregations for us; and everyone very happy. Just before going in for the tree on the night of the Holy Innocents, we had a brief service, all in Igorot except the carols, when we sang Bishop Coxe's beautiful

"Carol, carol, Christians,"

and it was strictly true—

"Libanus and Sharon shall not greener be
Than our holy chancel, on Christ's Nativity."

Then, over three hundred gifts, with doughnuts, peanut and popcorn accompaniment, and, so far as was observed or reported, not a pouting or disgruntled child.

TWO LITTLE GIRLS OF THE ORPHANAGE

By Susan N. Pott

THE Chinese peasants are very poor. This leads to the giving away of little girl babies by their parents. Boys are always wanted, because they help to carry on the family name. Not so the girls, and sometimes in infancy they are neglected and allowed to die for want of care.

The two little girls in this picture are children at St. Mary's Orphanage. They were given to us because in each case a fortune-teller had said that bad luck would come to the families in which they were born if they were allowed to grow up in them. One is called Ping-pong, which sounds like the name of a game we play in this country. The other is called Ah-huh, which means "Blackie." This nickname was given her because her skin was so dark.

When Ping-pong was born her mother was so ill that the fortune-teller said she had brought bad luck into the family. She stated that the child was under the influence of an unlucky star, and could never be happy. All her life long she would be unfortunate, and even if she grew up and was married, she would soon become a widow. Now of course we did

AH-HUH (seated) AND PING-PONG (standing)

not believe this and were quite willing to give the little one a home—and the happiness which otherwise she could not have had.

After the children were received into the orphanage they were baptized, and we claimed for them their privilege of being God's children. So from the very beginning of their lives they will grow up as Christians.

You will want to know what they do now. They are too young to study much, but they have begun their education. Every day they study a few Chinese characters written on slips of paper, much in the same way as our children learn their letters from blocks. They hear the same beautiful stories about Jesus as American children, and are taught to pray to the Father in heaven. They are taught to sing kindergarten songs in Chinese. I am sure you would like to hear them sing, with gestures, the Chinese translation of

"Two little eyes to look to God,
Two little ears to hear His word,
Two little hands to do His work,
Two little feet to run His way,
One little tongue to sing His praise,
One little heart to love Him well."

Of course much of their time is spent in play. Whenever a guest visits the orphanage these little tots will toddle up and almost bend themselves double as they bow down and greet the stranger with the words, "May the guest enjoy peace!"

They have plenty to eat, good beds to sleep in, a sunny playground, and everything is done to make their lives bright and cheerful. Later on they will receive a good, practical education, dividing the time between their books, sewing and housekeeping.

You will also want to know what finally becomes of them. The answer is a simple one. Miss Elwin, the housemother of the orphanage, is one of the greatest matchmakers in China. With a great deal of care she seeks out for each one of the girls a good Christian husband. The second picture shows one of the orphanage girls in her bridal costume standing by the side of her husband, just after the marriage ceremony. You cannot see her face on account of the curious crown and veil she wears, and so you cannot tell how she looks. But every girl in China wants to be married and have a home of her own, and if we could get a glimpse behind the veil I

Ah-huh thinks it is time to go in

think we should find there a look of sa
isfaction and contentment.

The two little girls, Ping-pong and A
huh, will some day be brides like the gi
in the picture. How differently ever;
thing will have turned out from what tl
foolish fortune-teller said.

These two children are good exampl
of what is done for the girls of Chir
at St. Mary's Orphanage. I think ever;
one who knows at all about it will wai
to help the work, because Christ sai
"Suffer the little children to come un
Me, and forbid them not, for of such
the Kingdom of Heaven."

*In 1884 a little neglected baby
was brought to St. Mary's Hall,
Shanghai, and to save its life it
was taken into the school and cared
for. That was the beginning of the
Orphanage, which now occupies a
large and convenient building and
furnishes a home and training to
seventy of the unwelcome and
neglected little girls of China. This
work depends upon voluntary gifts,
the yearly cost of maintenance
being $2,800. Forty dollars will
care for one child.*

THE PLAYGROUND AT ST. MARY'S ORPHANAGE

-THE PRESENT TEMPORARY HOME OF HOOKER SCHOOL

THE LITTLE BROWN SISTERS OF OUR
SISTER REPUBLIC
By Mary W. Roper

ONE day last fall the Presidents of two Republics met: one was our own President Taft, and the other President Diaz, of the Republic of Mexico. Shall we take in imagination the journey that President Taft took, and see some of the little people of our sister Republic?

If we could travel down through Texas, down beyond the great mesquite and chaparral cattle-plains beyond San Antonio, and cross the picturesque stream Del Rio, we might have a picture of the two great republics. On one side are the gray-green mountains of Texas, and on the other, beyond the Rio Grande, are the dust-swept table-lands and mountains of "Old Mexico." On this side live the people of our own country, on the other are the citizens of the other republic.

If we could go across into this other land and visit some of our little sunbrown sisters, we should find their stolid peon faces, without a ripple of merriment, looking at us at every station as we travelled on the Mexican railroad. They would hold up for sale their native fruits and candies, or beg us for "un centavo," and if we gave them that penny

it would be more than one-fiftieth of their father's daily wages. Poor little brown children; life holds little for them beyond gaunt poverty and depths of ignorance. As we look out of the windows of the train we should see the flat-roofed adobe huts, but if we wanted to look into them we should have to leave the railroad and go inside the huts. There are no windows, and inside there are no books or pictures. The way these children live is quite different from our way; and yet they are our very own sisters, these little brown girls, whose backs are bending beneath the burden too early and too heavily laid upon them. Cannot you imagine them looking toward our great republic for help—looking to their sisters in this country for inspiration and education?

Twenty years ago two women went down to that sister republic to see what they could do, and there they started a school. Long ago one of the women, Mrs. Hooker, was called to her reward in that home not made by human hands. Her body lies in that foreign land, her grave surrounded by tall monuments, but none of them telling of braver deeds than the

(135)

The girls at their tasks

work she commenced. The new look of hope on many a brown girl's face is her best memorial. The friend who went with her, Miss Driggs, is still at the head of the school, which is now called after Mrs. Hooker.

Twenty years is a long time, and the childish hands that Mrs. Hooker held in hers have hardened into the self-respecting, working hands of women, but other little brown hands are in that of Miss Driggs, and other little brown faces are upturned to catch the *"Buenas Dias"* (Good morning) of their dear *"Misscita"* (little Miss).

If we might visit this school we should

A TYPICAL MEXICAN SCHOOL

A little brown sister and her two brothers

a daring deed of chivalry in old France. But what Miss Driggs of the Hooker School has done, reaches far beyond the school itself. More than one Mexican home has received its first ray of light through the little girl whom the school has trained and sent back to her *pueblo* or the *hacienda* from which she came, carrying with her the influence of the school and the message of the Church to her people. It has been worth while to bring the message of the Christ Child to these little brown sisters, and if we are quite sure that they are our true sisters, we shall see that the helping hand of our great Mother Church shall reach out to them, leading them onward and upward to perfect womanhood.

see some contrasts with the days twenty years ago. Instead of those stolid little faces we should find merry, intelligent faces to-day, and instead of little begging voices we should hear happy peals of l a u g h t e r resounding through the corridors and *patios* of the Mary Josephine Hooker School. For these little girls are being led onward and upward toward the higher and better life of good womanhood. The matted hair of the little brown sister has grown into long braids of glossy black, her crown and pride, and her daily tasks, whether of brain or hand, are performed with a sweet willingness peculiar to these gentle little folk. Instead of seeing them in their poor homes we can imagine these little girls in the Hooker School gathering in circles, as night begins to fall, for games or stories. We may listen to a thrilling tale told by a little brown girl in whose veins flows the

THE BOYS' DEBATE ABOUT MISSIONS

By Sarah Lowrie

INTRODUCTORY

PERHAPS some of you have heard about a boys' Church society that was started down in Richmond, Va., some years ago by a lady who was much interested in both boys and foreign missions. Miss Purcell is her name. She called the society the Brotherhood of St. Paul, after the greatest of all foreign missionaries, and set to work to form chapters of the Brotherhood wherever she found boys who were interested in foreign missions.

The society is a kind of boys' Junior Auxiliary, and here in Philadelphia, where four or five chapters have been formed, the Junior Auxiliary is at the head of the movement. The boys of the First and Second Chapters asked Bishop Brent, of the Philippines, to speak to them the first year, and a very large meeting, presided over by the boys themselves, was held in Witherspoon Hall.

One of the chapters held a debate on the question, "Are Foreign Missions Worth While?" the following year. The debate was arranged for them by some grown-up people, to be sure, and the arguments were all such as one would hear older folks using; but as the boys expect to grow up themselves some day they had no desire to learn childish arguments concerning so important a subject as foreign missions. Each boy, therefore, in his speech and gestures, impersonated a certain kind of friend or foe of the missionaries. There was the haphazard, ready-to-argue-at-any-time foe, the good-natured foe, the honest foe, the stingy foe, the ignorant foe, and so on. And, likewise, there was the haphazard friend, the good-natured friend, the honest friend, the generous friend and the wise friend. It may interest you to read the debate, and perhaps use it some time among the boys of your parish.

THE DEBATE

The members of the Brotherhood are seated in a semi-circle on the stage, the president occupying the central seat. The president rises and goes to the desk, or table, centre front, and, striking it with his hammer, calls the meeting to order.

PRESIDENT

Fellow-members of the Brotherhood of St. Paul, ladies and gentlemen: We meet to-night to discuss a grave subject and to answer a great question: "Are Foreign Missions Worth While?"

To-day there are many voices clamoring to be heard in the world, many hands beckoning us in as many directions. As brothers of the great Roman citizen, as true St. Paulists, we can call but one our Master and follow only where He leads. As fellow-servants with the missionary apostle, we make no question of our duty to spread the tidings of our great Lord and of His way to God among our fellow-men. The questions before us to-night are: "To whom shall we tell the Words of Jesus Christ? To all men, or to those about us? Are foreign missions worth while?" Fellow-members of the Brotherhood of St. Paul, ladies and gentlemen, the meeting is open for discussion.

The Boys' Debate about Missions 139

SECOND SPEAKER

Ladies and gentlemen: Can such a question be discussed by fellow-servants of the missionary apostle? Our Leader and St. Paul's Leader gave us our marching orders when He said: "Go ye into all the world, and make disciples of every creature." If we are true to our oaths of allegiance, we have no alternative but to obey. And what soldier worthy of the name will question his captain's orders?

THIRD SPEAKER

Mr. President, ladies and gentlemen: It must be my ungrateful task to tread on sentimentality for the sake of truth. I fear that I am but a practical person. I confess that I believe in carrying common sense into religion.

The last speaker has quoted a command of our Lord to His chosen apostles and arrogated the orders to himself. As well might a drummer boy aspire to lead the charge of the Light Brigade as for one of us to attempt to stand in the place of a St. Paul or a St. Peter. There are other words of the Great Leader's meaning for the multitudes which you and I have a right to take as our marching orders. He did command us to "Give to those that ask," but He did not say "Give to those who do not ask." On the contrary, He said: "Cast not your pearls before swine, lest they turn and rend you." And, ladies and gentlemen, that is just what, in my opinion, these good mistaken folks, the missionaries, are doing. They are casting the Pearl of the Christian religion before a lot of savage or, at best, half-civilized people, who cannot digest it any more than swine can digest pearls.

Yes, I confess to being a practical person. And when nine men out of ten that I meet in my travels have never seen any results from Church missions, and the tenth man does not like what he has happened to see, the enterprise looks a bit shady to me, not to say dark. The truth is, the missionaries simply spoil a lot of good natives for work by putting a lot of notions into their heads which they cannot understand. If you want to see the results of Western civilization in the East the *missionaries* can only show you a few poor little buildings, a school for the lower classes, and a tin church here and there; but the *traders* of the West have something to show for their money and labor. Great warehouses and harbors full of shipping and banks full of busy clerks. I did not see a Bible the whole length of Egypt, but I saw Standard Oil cans in the heart of the desert.

FOURTH SPEAKER

It is always a pleasure to deal with a practical person. I feel sure that the last speaker will be grateful to have his—ahem!—common sense strengthened upon some points about which he seems—your pardon, sir—uncommonly hazy. A traveller in Egypt who sees no Bibles, but does see Standard Oil cans, is to be pitied, but not blamed. But a man who asks the missionaries in the East for some marks of Western civilization and sees only tin churches had better consult the nearest oculist. His case is serious.

In Shanghai, China, the property of our Church alone amounts to $327,424, and in Hankow to $317,940. The hospital in Shanghai is famed the world over for its beauty and appropriateness. St. John's College buildings are valued at $51,000 and St. John's Church at $7,500. These are figures taken at random from the Church missions in one foreign country. Trinity Church in Tokyo, Japan, is valued at $15,000; at Port-au-Prince, Haiti, another Trinity Church cost $13,000. As for the results of all this expenditure, ladies and gentlemen, I fear that the nine persons to whom our traveller has alluded who saw none, and the tenth person who did not like what he saw, I fear that we cannot take their verdict very seriously in the face of the facts, verified by great public officials, and of unbiased witnesses from our own and other countries.

You saw no Bibles, sir, the length of Egypt? And yet, unless the account books of the great printing-house at Beyrout, Syria, are strangely out, Egypt and the Soudan are among their best customers for Bibles. Not one Bible, not even one for yourself! And so many Standard Oil cans!

FIFTH SPEAKER

Ladies and gentlemen: This is all very amusing, no doubt, but the last speaker has begged the question rather than dealt squarely with his facts, in my opinion. Granted that the Church has expended nearly $1,000,000 on buildings in China, how much nearer are the missionaries to the end of their labors than they were twenty years ago? Why, if in all these years that they had been at it they could have made the Christian religion as much a habit in the empire as the opium traders have made opium, I'd be silent about how much it cost us at home. If in all the years that they have been trying to work it in Africa they could have made Christianity the factor that the rum business is, I'd give the enterprise my hearty approval. If, even with their start of five hundred years, the Christian missionaries could have made as many converts as the Mohammedans, I'd—I'd give a handsome check to the Treasurer, to-morrow.

But, ladies and gentlemen, with all the money that we pour into this business of converting the heathen, $300,000 from the Men's Thank-offering and nearly $500,000 from the Church at large last year, and over $7,000,000 from American Christians all told, the world hasn't got the Christian habit one-fiftieth the degree that it has got the tea and coffee habit.

No, fellow-members! As a believer in facts, not in hopes; in results, not in dreams; and in the light of 2,000 years of cold, hard facts, it must be admitted that the foreign missions of the Church have not been a paying business.

SIXTH SPEAKER

I, too, have an interest in figures, Mr. President. It has been calculated by experts that at the lowest price for transportation and maintenance of their missionaries, it would cost the Christian Mission Boards at the rate of $2 a person to send the Gospel to every heathen yet unreached in foreign lands, there being to-day in the world something over 1,000,000,000 men, women and children who have as yet never so much as heard the name of Christ. Here, then, is a plain business proposition. In these days of advertising, when thousands of dollars are spent to prepare the minds of people for what has not yet been put on the market, calculation is the very basis of business. We are asked to spend $2,000,000,000 to carry out our Lord's command to give His Tidings to the world.

How do we meet this request? As the Standard Oil people did in their business? As the drug people do in theirs? As the liquor people do? We, as Christians of all sects, gave for foreign missions last year a little over $7,000,000. We spent on chewing-gum in this country $15,000,000, on coffee and tea $98,000,000, for tobacco we paid $270,000,000, for candy $178,000,000, while for drink we gave over $1,900,000,000. I should like the believer of cold, hard facts to ponder these.

SEVENTH SPEAKER

Mr. Chairman, Ladies and Gentlemen: To my thinking, not one of the objections raised against foreign missions to-night has touched the bull's-eye. For my part, I base my very emphatic disapproval of the Church's present course with re gard to this very matter of missionary zeal upon facts told to me by an officer high in the service of our country, who commanded part of the United States troops which were sent to China during the Boxer outbreak. He said that the missionaries gave him more trouble than all the other Americans put together. Instead of being content to avoid a place where the natives had showed clearly how greatly they hated them by burning their mission houses and churches, they insisted upon going back and beginning the thing all over again, at the risk of their lives. He said that they seemed quite indifferent to the fact that they had involved their country in a troublesome war and put many soldiers' lives in peril to defend property which did not yield the United States one cent of profit. I remember his very words on the subject: "If these missionaries want to cease to be useful citizens of the United States, if they wish to banish themselves to China or India for the sake of changing the religion of a lot of heathen who are perfectly content as they are, let them do it, I say! But when they get into trouble, and the natives rise in a body and object, and burn a few of them and drive the rest out, let them take their punishment like men, and not embroil the country that they have deliberately forsaken in a war on their account."

And, fellow-members and ladies and gentlemen, I agree with my friend, the army officer! What have these missionaries done for their country, that they should claim the protection of its army and navy? The merchants bring us trade, the sea captains carry our goods, the consuls uphold our reputation and protect our interests. What does the missionary do for his country but desert it? What have the whole breed of them done for the world that their self-chosen failures should be hailed as heroic and their deaths lauded as martyrdoms?

EIGHTH SPEAKER

You ask what missionaries have done for their country but desert it? You demand what the world owes the whole breed of them, that they should be acclaimed as heroes, and at their deaths mourned as martyrs! Surely, ladies and gentlemen, an answer springs as ready in your hearts as it does in mine. What have not the missionaries done for their country? What have they not done for the world? As explorers, as discoverers, as adventurers, as teachers, who have equalled them? Who in the dawn of America gained Canada for France, California for Spain? Who braved deserts and massacres and opened the great lakes and the great rivers, but missionaries? Who, in the nineteenth century, gained the heart of a continent for England, but Moffat and Mackay and Smith and Colenso?—all missionaries, all self-banished!

Hannington's cry, "I have purchased the road to Uganda with my life!" was the echo of a hundred brave hearts, whose gravestones to-day are their country's milestones from coast to coast of the Dark Continent they died to light.

To blot out the slave trade, to open up the untrodden continent to Christianity, David Livingston forced his way across the jungles of Africa; but in serving Christ he served England as no traveller had served her for centuries. What England thinks of her great missionary-physician she has written on his tomb in Westminster Abbey.

Fellow-members who stand with me on this great subject, I challenge you to give your testimony; I challenge you to tell of the men you know whose patriotism is represented by something more than the poll-tax—men who in giving their lives for the world have shed glory on their country.

NINTH SPEAKER

I accept the challenge joyfully. Who has not heard of Bishop Selwyn, of the Church of England, and of John Williams, the Welsh preacher, who did more in the last fifty years of the nineteenth century for the islands of the Pacific than all the navies of the world could accomplish? Cannibalism was broken up, written languages were created and civilized governments were inaugurated. Western civilization without the missionaries would have meant a traffic in rum and human beings for the islands of the Pacific from New Zealand to Japan. It was John Paton, a missionary to the New Hebrides, who, by his personal appeal to the civilized governments of the world, put a stop to the degrading trade of Western sea captains and merchants in adulterated rum that was killing off the natives of the islands by the thousands.

TENTH SPEAKER

What of Doctor Grenfell and his Labrador settlements? His country seems proud to own him.

ELEVENTH SPEAKER

What of Morrison, of China, whose dictionary revealed the hidden tongues of China and Japan to the Western World?

TWELFTH SPEAKER

What of William Carey, of India, who prevailed upon his home government, the English Crown, to put down by law the practice of burning widows and the slaughter of girl babies in its Eastern possessions; who made the first botanical garden in India and introduced the culture of grapes into Bengal? Surely he made good his right to be called an Englishman and to be defended by the army and navy of his sovereign. Surely, ladies and gentlemen, if our poorest sailor and the most careless of sightseers may claim the protection of our country's flag, surely the missionaries, who represent the best and truest of our country's ideals, may call and feel themselves—Americans!

THIRTEENTH SPEAKER

Mr. President: A word, if you please. May I be permitted to remind the audience of a man to whom his country has high cause for gratitude? I speak of Marcus Whitman, the missionary and pioneer to the great Northwest. To him we owe that Northwest. For, as you doubtless remember, ladies and gentlemen, it was this undaunted man who crossed the continent unaided and almost penniless to prove to the Congress at Washington that a wagon with wheels could be got over the Rocky Mountains, and that beyond those supposedly impassable barriers was a vast territory which was worth keeping.

FOURTEENTH SPEAKER

What do we as a country not owe to our missionaries? It was Father Marquette who acted as guide and interpreter to the discoverers of the Mississippi River. It was Junipero Serra, the Spanish monk, who planted the gardens and vineyards of California. It was Franciscan missionaries who made safe the trails of the Great Desert and opened the Southwest to the white man. It was the French missionaries to Canada who were the map-makers and the peace-makers and the guides for all who travelled by canoe and portage "from the Gulf of Saint Laurance to the camp-fires of the Illinoise."

FIFTEENTH SPEAKER

Ladies and gentlemen, what of Dr. Jeffreys? Has any man, of all our great physicians in Philadelphia, done his State and country a higher honor than that skilful, self-sacrificing doctor has in his Hospital of St. Luke, in Shanghai, China?

The Boys' Debate about Missions 143

And what of Father Damien and his life and death with the lepers of the Pacific?

Our Church in America has been tardy about seeing her duty toward foreign lands and the isles of the sea. The Christians of other names—the Methodists, Bap⁻tists, Presbyterians and Friends—have got ahead of us. But who in his right senses dares assert that Bishop Graves, of Shanghai, Bishop Kinsolving, of Brazil, or Bish⁻op Brent, of the Philippines, have proved useless citizens of the United States?

I should like to ask those individuals who call missionaries "deserters" what they themselves are doing for their country's name in the isles of the sea, in China, in South America? Nay, more. I should like to ask them what they are doing for their country's sake—at home?

Indeed, sir, I am dumfounded that such testimony should be necessary; that any one can dare to claim that the men who have started the printing presses, the industrial schools, the hospitals and the colleges of the East; who have trained the carpenters, the telegraphers and the farmers of Africa; the men who have taught the teachers, the physicians and the nurses of Japan have done nothing for their coun⁻try—but desert it.

Western civilization stripped of its missionary enterprise would, indeed, be the open sore of the world, my fellow-members. For it would mean the opium trade for China, the slave trade for Africa, the rum trade for the isles of the sea and the gun⁻powder trade to the Indians. There are many self-banished Americans scattered to the far corners of the earth to-night. The missionaries are the only representa⁻tives of our boasted civilization who are not self-banished for the sake of private gain. Our great fleet patrolling the Eastern seas was less to our credit as a civilized nation than is some lonely hospital nurse under the burning skies of Africa trying to mend by patient love the scars of a thousand hates.

Mr. President, as you know, I meant to speak against Foreign Missions: but, ladies and gentlemen, I feel as though while I'd been in swimming somebody had gone off with my clothes! The objections which I meant to put so forcibly have all been answered so convincingly that I haven't a bit of thunder left. I guess, ladies and gentlemen, that these missionary chaps are doing a great work—a great work! Of course, I've always known that the Foreign Mission Board is being better run than even the Standard Oil business. And that it makes a dollar go farther than J. D. Rockefeller has managed to yet. I have known for some time, too, that the missionaries are not spending their little salaries in riotous living. I guess they give more brain work and more heart work and more elbow work for $1.75 a day than we can get out of our carpenters at $4.50 a day. I've never heard of a mis⁻sionary striking, either. But, in spite of all this good business and successful effort, Mr. President, let's look the matter right in the face! Have we any right to spend this money and these lives for foreign missions? Should we not concentrate our efforts upon the African within our own borders? Why go to India, when we have Indians of our own? Why sail across the seas when thousands of strangers are crossing the seas to us? When the hospitals are crippled for money, and the universities are thousands of dollars in debt, what right have we to send our thanl offerings to China and Japan, and the isles of the sea? Answer me that, if yo please.

TWENTY-FIRST SPEAKER

Yes, answer that!

And I, too, have a question! I am told that it takes five years for a missionar to perfect himself in the language and to accustom himself to the habits of the pe ple in his new surroundings. I understand that he may then work for seven yea and that he sometimes works for ten years before he has made a handful of convert A score of years may pass before he can establish a church. And often a native we will in a week obliterate the work of a lifetime. Every dollar, no matter how well is spent for foreign missions, could be made to go twice as far at home; for ever heathen converted an American child could be rescued from the slums. Surely was by no chance that we nations of the West have for our inheritance the religio of Jesus Christ. We in our turn are bound to hand it down to the children (our race.

Fellow-members, are foreign missions worth while to us? Have we the rigl to take of the children's bread and give it to strangers?

TWENTY-SECOND SPEAKER (springing to his feet)

Yes, fellow-members! Yes, ladies and gentlemen! Though we know the chi dren's need, though we are frightened because of the bigness of the ungathered ha vest and the fewness of the laborers, we can yet dare take of the children's bread an give it to strangers. Remembering the last command of our Lord Jesus Christ : His apostles, we dare do nothing less. Fortifying ourselves by His last promise, v could do nothing more. "Go ye into all the world and preach the Gospel to ever creature. And lo, I am with you alway, even to the end of the world." It is indee no chance happening that we have inherited from our forefathers the religion (Christ! For 800 years, in season and out of season, through persecutions and fai ures, by torture and martyrdoms, foreign missionaries held their Master and H way before the eyes of our heathen ancestors and preached His Gospel to the dull ears.

Ladies and gentlemen, it was because the Christians of Asia, and Africa, ar Greece, and Rome sought out the haunts of savages and remembered the heathen the isles of the sea that we, the offspring of those heathen, stand to-day at the for front of the world. And does any one here believe that the Light of Life died the heart of the Egyptian, was lost by the people of Asia and flickered to a dv spark in the eyes of the men of Greece and Macedonia because they once gave their best to publish to the West the tidings of their risen Lord? It was when th ceased to care that they ceased to send. It was when they lived for themselves th they died. "He who saveth his life shall lose it; but he who loses his life for l sake shall never die."

LAST SPEAKER (the president)

Ladies and gentlemen, in bringing this debate to a close, I thank you for yo kind and intelligent attention. Although you constitute the most impartial ju that was ever impanelled, I feel sure that you need time for reflection before y give your verdict.

In dismissing you, let me suggest the following course of procedure: All the who decide that foreign missions are not worth while are requested to remit to o treasurer an offering designated for mission work in the domestic field. All prese who send no such contribution will be counted as favoring foreign missions.

The meeting is adjourned.

THE MEETING OF THE BOARD OF MISSIONS

January 11th, 1910

THE Board of Missions met at the Church Missions House on Tuesday, January 11th, the Bishop of Albany (vice-president) in the chair. The following members were present: The Bishops of Pennsylvania, West Virginia, Pittsburgh, Ohio, Massachusetts, Rhode Island, Indianapolis, Long Island and Newark; the Rev. Drs. Eccleston, Alsop, Perry, Stires, Mann, the Rev. Mr. Sedgwick and the Rev. Drs. Storrs, Smith, Page, the Rev. Mr. Miel and the Rev. Dr. Manning; Messrs. Low, Mills, Chauncey, Goodwin, Admiral Mahan and Messrs. Butler, King, Morris, Pruyn and Ryerson. Of the honorary members, the Bishop of Vermont. Representing the Missionary Departments, the Rev. Mr. Garland, Secretary of the Third, and the Rev. Wm. Meade Clark, of the same Department.

In acknowledgment of a letter from the Bishop of New Jersey, on motion of the Bishop of West Virginia, a resolution of sympathy with the former was unanimously adopted by a rising vote.

The state of the treasury was reported to be practically the same as a month ago, the contributions being about $11,000 short of last year. The receipts during December were about the same as those for the corresponding month last year. The Treasurer also reported additions to permanent funds as follows: $10,000 to the W. M. B. Reserve Deposit; $10,000 to the St. Leger Fund; bequests of $165,000 from the estate of Mr. George C. Thomas.

The Rev, William E. Gardner accepted his election by the Board as Secretary of the Department of New England. He will assume his duties on February 1st.

An appropriation of $500 was made to the Bishop of South Carolina for the immediate necessities of his work, from a gross amount previously voted for work among the Negroes.

By concurrent action of the bishop and the Board, Mr. Frank N. Fearon,

Manager of the International Banking Corporation, was appointed Treasurer of the Mission in the Canal Zone.

The Treasurer reported on behalf of the special committee appointed to consider the report of the auditors. Not only were all the accounts found correct, but the auditors took occasion to speak highly of the care with which the financial interests of the Board are safeguarded and the excellence of the office methods adopted under the supervision of the Assistant Treasurer.

A special committee on the Apportionment for the fiscal year 1910-1911 was appointed in order that they might make a careful study of all apportionment matters before September 1st. The members of the Committee are: The Right Rev. Dr. Peterkin, the Right Rev. Dr. Lines, the Rev. Dr. Mann, the Rev. Mr. Sedgwick, Mr. Morris and the officers.

Under the Woman's Auxiliary United Offering Miss Susie Campbell, at the request of the Bishop of Lexington, was appointed matron of St. John's Collegiate Institute, Corbin, Ky., vice Mrs. John S. Banks, resigned.

ANNOUNCEMENTS

Concerning the Missionaries

The Philippines

THE action of Bishop Brent in accepting the resignation of Dr. Henry Winsor, to date from November 1st, was approved by the Board of Missions at its meeting on January 11th.

Africa

MRS. NATHAN MATTHEWS and Miss Margaretta S. Ridgely, who sailed from Liverpool on November 13th, arrived at Cape Mount on December 7th.

Shanghai

THE REV. C. F. McRAE who, with his wife and little daughter, sailed from San Francisco on November 9th, arrived at Shanghai on December 3d.

Hankow

THE REV. ALFRED A. GILMAN, returning after furlough, with his wife and
child left Montclair, N. J., on January
6th, intending to stop at North Platte,
Neb., and to sail from San Francisco by
the steamer *Manchuria* on February 8th.

MISS SADA C. TOMLINSON, returning on
account of the illness of her mother,
sailed from Shanghai by the steamer
Monteagle November 24th; arrived at
Vancouver on December 15th and proceeded to her home at Nashville, Tenn.

MISSIONARY
SPEAKERS

FOR the convenience of those arranging missionary meetings,
the following list of clergy and
other missionary workers available as speakers is published:

When no address is given, requests
for the services of these speakers should
be addressed to the Corresponding Secretary, 281 Fourth Avenue, New York.

Department Secretaries

Department 1. The Rev. William E.
Gardner, 186 Upland Road, Cambridge,
Mass.

Department 2. Cared for at present
by secretaries at the Church Missions
House.

Department 3. The Rev. Thomas J.
Garland, Church House, Philadelphia.

Department 4. The Rev. R. W.
Patton, care of the Rev. C. B. Wilmer,
D.D., 412 Courtland Street, Atlanta, Ga.

Department 5. The Rev. John Henry
Hopkins, D.D., 703 Ashland Boulevard,
Chicago.

Department 6. The Rev. C. C. Rollit,
4416 Upton Avenue, South, Minneapolis,
Minn.

Department 7. The Rev. H. Percy
Silver, Box 312, Topeka, Kan.

Department 8. The Rev. L. C. Sanford, 1215 Sacramento Street, San Francisco, Cal.

THE WOMAN'S AUXILIARY

To the Board of Missions

THE BEGINNING AND PROGRESS OF WOMAN'S WORK AMONG THE DAKOTAS

By Mrs. H. Burt

(Concluded from the January number)

IN the spring of 1873 this work was given a bishop of its own, and under our dear Bishop Hare it grew apace. Before the end of his first year he had two boarding-schools in operation. St. Paul's School for boys, Yankton Agency, was the first boarding-school for either race in the territory. The other was St. Mary's at Santee Agency, already mentioned. The work was carried to Crow Creek, Lower Brulé, Cheyenne, Sisseton, and everywhere little schools were started where the children were taught to read and sew and sing. More women were needed for the work, and more came, while many, though not all, of the old ones remained. Sister Mary Graves and Miss Amelia Ives came out together in 1872, and remained for over twenty years, and many others have been faithful helpers on the same lines for long or short times. Has it paid? Has it been worth while? I wrote Miss Ives not long ago and asked her what she thought about it. From the East came her answer, and here it is. She heads it,

"STORIES ABOUT THE ENTERING WEDGE."

At one of the meetings of the Auxiliary, when the mite-boxes had been opened and the money counted, the women were asked where they would prefer to have the money used. An old woman, the widow of one of the first chiefs to embrace Christianity, and who for a long time had been a leader in the wild dances of the women, pleaded for the whites in this land, who had

had no privileges. She said, "Through the whites the light has come to us and brought us out of great darkness; and now if there are any whites sitting in darkness, the Indians should do something for them."

One day two women came to sit by the fire till the crowd at the issue house who had come to draw their rations had dispersed before they went to get their share. Sometimes on these occasions the beef would give out before all were supplied. After they had been there for some time, I asked if they were not afraid they would be too late to get any beef. One replied, "We may not get beef, but the talk of the heathen Indians is so vile, we would rather miss it than stand waiting for our turn where we are obliged to listen to it."

One of our girls, when asked before her confirmation what she asked God for in her prayers, answered shyly, "I say the little prayer you taught me long ago, 'Make me a clean heart, O God,' and then I ask, 'Make me to know, make me understand.'"

One night in one of the boarding-schools, after the children were in bed for the night, the sound of sobbing and crying came from the dormitory. The house mother went to investigate, and found one of the girls in great distress. After a little, finding that the trouble was mental, she took her to her own room, where she drew from her in broken language this story: She had, in confirmation, promised to keep God's Commandments and walk in His way; but she had forgotten and turned out of the good way and was very sorry for it. It made her sorry and made her cry. When questioned as to the immediate cause of her trouble she told, as best she could, that she had been very disrespectful to one of the teachers, and troublesome about her work. She wished to return to the right way, and was not only ready and anxious then and there to confess her sin to her Heavenly Father and ask His forgiveness, but also, as soon as she might, to express her sorrow to her teacher and promise to do better. This she did next morning without prompting.

Of one young girl after her death it was written, "She has left very beautiful words with me which I shall never forget. She looked very gentle and nice. When she was in bed she prayed often, and spoke about her faith in the Lord. Just before she died she said, 'My Lord is going to take me to His beautiful place.' "

It was my privilege to visit an old man during his last, lingering illness, who had always held aloof from the Church and from contact with its missionaries till too ill to move about. Soon he began to look for my coming. I wish you might have seen his eager, longing look, as, raising himself on his elbow, he listened with intense earnestness to the story of the Saviour. When asked once whether he remembered the story as it had been told to him from time to time he replied, "Indeed I do, and when I cannot sleep for the pain, I lie and think of what you have told me." He never asked for any bodily comforts, but soon became very anxious to be baptized, and feared it might be delayed too long. When at last the missionary thought him sufficiently instructed, his grati-

women moved out about eighteen miles from the agency. When the day for our weekly meeting came she would sew on something. This she sold, and brought the money to our treasury; and she once said to me, "I am with you in heart when it is time for the meeting, if not in body." Sometimes she even came that eighteen miles to meet with us. Finally she and a few other Christian women, who, like herself, had moved out into

that neighborhood, organized, and commenced working for a church. They at first succeeded in getting a small log building which was used for the women's meetings and for services. Later, when the bishop came, it was the eloquence of the women, emphasized by their offerings, which got the frame building. This is one instance out of many, of the women's society being the beginning and nucleus of a congregation.

WOMAN'S AUXILIARY PAPERS
NO. V. POSSIBLE MISSIONARIES
I. WHERE TO FIND THEM. II. HOW AND WHERE TO TEST AND TRAIN THEM

I. While the members of the Woman's Auxiliary have been praying since October, 1907, that the hearts of many faithful women may be turned toward the mission field, we wonder how many of these members have made earnest effort to find these young women for whom they have prayed?

We wonder how many mothers, gathering their children about them, have told them stories of the lightbearers of the past and present, of the peoples still in darkness and the shadow of death, of the new Christians who love their Christ so well that they live painfully though joyously in Him and would die for Him if need be? And how many such mothers, seeing the kindling eyes of their children, dearly loved, have thanked God, and prayed that He would put it into their hearts to serve Him in His mission field?

Or, how many of the Auxiliary members, as they have met their Sunday-school class Sunday after Sunday, their branch of the G. F. S. or of the candidates, their chapter of the Daughters of the King, the girls of the boarding-school or college in which they teach, their little band of nurses in the Guild of St. Barnabas, their missions study class, have used their opportunity to tell these same stories to them, and to ask

these young people to pray that hearts may hear and heed God's call to them for service?

And how many of the Auxiliary members, as they meet and talk and pray and influence, have come to realize more deeply than of old what the great power needed for their work, and for all work which is done with the intent of setting Christ's Kingdom forward, is? Is it more certain to them this year than last that this power is a knowledge of the One True God, Who is the reason why all missions are, a love felt in the soul for Him, a longing desire that what He has given us through His dear Son and daily increases in us through His Holy Spirit, may be known of all men? There is nothing else that makes the thing that we call missions to be indeed *worth while*.

It is this spirit of love born of a growing knowledge of God that we seek to find in our would-be missionary. Putting it together with a yearning love for one's fellows, a prime requisite of the true missionary is found.

II. A girl of such a spirit comes to us, who longs for the missionary service to which she feels she has been called. What shall we do with her? First, help her to make sure of the call. Remind her that the call to the mission field must always be subordinated to the call to do

God's will, that it must never be followed till a serene conscience and calm and settled heart give assurance that the mission field is not one's own choice, but God's chosen place for one. To begin mission work in direct opposition to parents, and when they really need their child at home, or when the Board of Missions objects, on account of ill health, will be an act which will mar the service rendered and bring its sure fruitage of remorse.

See that our girl knows how to do some one thing so well that should she stay at home she could by that means earn her own support.

Study to see that, however well trained she may be in that one thing, she will have such adaptability that she can turn from it if needed to be useful otherwise; also that trained under whatever favorable conditions, she may have grasped the capabilities of her profession so well that she can carry it out under any disadvantages.

Encourage her, whatever else she knows or lacks, to learn enough music to play the Church's chants and hymns, and to teach others to play and sing them.

Help her to realize that, however well trained at home, she enters the mission field with much to learn from experienced workers there, and that nothing in her new life will stand her in better stead—after the daily dependence upon our Lord, prayer to Him and the study of His Word and the feeding on His Sacred Food—than a stock of homely Christian virtues—humility, patience, meekness, obedience, loyalty, faithfulness, love—all of which may be brightened and cheered by that gift, natural or acquired, of a saving sense of humor.

How valuable these common graces are in the home where two or three women come together as strangers to live as sisters, in a community where non-Christians and new Christians see in the life of every Christian foreigner a book from whose pages the dullest can read the Christ who rules the every word and act of His faithful servant.

If the members of the Auxiliary think these thoughts and try to help in this work of preparation, they will see how home and social life, school, college, normal courses and those for training nurses, and physicians, as well as the training-schools for Church workers, all have their part in the testing and training that are needed.

WHERE AND HOW JUNIOR LEADERS MAY HELP TO FIND MISSIONARY CANDIDATES

THE relation which the Junior Auxiliary bears to the Church's enterprise must never be lost sight of. There is no lasting inspiration in a parish "society" called the "Junior Auxiliary." It is only as leaders look beyond parish or diocesan limits, or any limits less than world inclusive, that there comes inspiration which increases as time passes. We must still "lift up our eyes" and look out on the world. As we grow intelligent about the need and the opportunity we shall grow eager to do what we can to answer the appeal which need and opportunity make. Then we shall study the subject, and it will be easy to perceive that neither money gifts nor boxes are an adequate answer for all the demands. The call is for men and women, and if we are hearing that call we shall try to find what can be done to answer it. If, in studying the case, the realization comes to any leader that the call is a personal one, then surely she will answer it personally, answer it as did an English missionary bishop who explained that, having heard God's question, "Who will go?" he could not reply, "Here am I—send some one else!"

But to some Junior leaders the vision of the opportunity comes too late for

them to reply by personal service in the field, and to some, comes with the vision the realization that the call is not for them. Then it is for those who must stay at home to find another way of sending helpers to the front. And just here is one of the greatest opportunities before the Junior officers and Sunday-school teachers. We can turn the thoughts of those entrusted to our training toward the opportunity before the Church.

There are a few simple yet important ways of doing this. First, let us make our Junior branches and our Sunday-school classes realize this same thing—that they bear a relation to the whole. Don't let their interest rest in only the little mission to which they are sending Christmas presents, but make them see worldwide needs, and make them understand that only by live messengers can the work be done. Then let them feel the responsibility. We leaders are sometimes in danger of doing all the planning and letting the children do only the "practical work," and children are so ready to respond to responsibility if they feel it is theirs. We need not tell them it is their duty to go; let us only place before them the opportunity and ask how it is to be met, leaving them to suggest personal service. And let us stop talking about what "the Church ought to do" and make the children see that if the Church ought to do it, they as members of the Church must do their part. Let us take it for granted, too, that missionary service in the foreign field is not a preposterous idea, but a normal, natural possibility for Christian people; that it is not to be left to those whom we think of as saints, but that it may well be only a part of the obedience promised in baptism by every member of the Church. In making addresses to children, let us feel that not to touch on the possibility of service in the mission field is to leave out one of the subjects most worth while bringing to the attention of our Juniors.

Mission study classes offer an even more definite opportunity to find the possible missionary. That should be always one of the hopes and prayers of the leader, and she should see that each class realize that personal service is the best way to answer the question of how that special class can help the part of the missionary field of which it has been studying.

Junior leaders have an opportunity, and one which has not been used as much as it might to further this work of gaining volunteers. This is to be found in summer conferences like those held at Silver Bay. When, perhaps, through a study class the fitness of a certain young woman for service becomes evident, why not suggest and urge that person to go to such a conference, there to learn of the need and opportunity and possibly to hear the call?

The Junior leader cannot do a great deal of actual training of the volunteer, that must be left for colleges and deaconess' schools, but quietly, and sometimes indirectly, she can do much in the finding of the volunteer, and her first and best method will be in realizing and helping others to realize that the greatest privilege open to the Junior Auxiliary is to send out messengers to personal service in the field which is the world.

THE JANUARY CONFERENCE

THE January conference, held on Thursday, the 20th, was one of especial interest. Visitors were present from California and Shanghai, and thirty-seven officers from twelve branches—(Asheville, 1; Bethlehem, 1; Central New York, 1; Connecticut, 4; Long Island, 4; 1 Junior; Louisiana, 1; Missouri, 1; Newark, 6; 1 Junior; New Jersey, 1; New York, 13; 1 Junior; North Dakota, 1; Pennsylvania, 3.)

After brief mention of the memorial to Bishop Hare, suggested in the $50,000 endowment of All Saints' School, Sioux Falls, and of efforts being made in Pennsylvania and New York in behalf of the $200,000 called for by St. Paul's College,

Tokyo, and of Bishop Brewer's hearty
commendation of that need to his people
in Montana, the remaining time of the
conference was devoted to the subject of
the day—"Possible workers; how to find
them, how and where to test and train
them."

Mrs. Warren, president of the New
York branch, presided, and under her
guidance the conference was conducted
in such a way as to bring out many most
suggestive ideas which are earnestly commended to the prayerful thought of
officers of the Auxiliary, diocesan and
parochial, throughout the Church. Both
diocesan officers and invited speakers, experts in the work they represented, took
part in this conference: Miss Coles, who
for fifty years has conducted a Bible-class
of young women in Philadelphia; Mrs.
N. B. Potter, Secretary of the Guild of
St. Barnabas for Nurses in the Diocese
of New York; Mrs. Schulte, Chairman
of the Department of Missions of the
Girls' Friendly Society; Deaconess Mott,
of California, representing the Daughters of the King; Deaconess Goodwin,
the Student Secretary, and Deaconess
Sanford and Deaconess Knapp, of the
Church Training-schools in Philadelphia
and New York. Mrs. Roberts, treasurer
of the Pennsylvania branch, and honorary president of the Girls' Friendly Society, also spoke of the Girls' Friendly
and missions; Mrs. Wetmore, vice-president of the Asheville branch, testified to
the value of training in the mission field;
Miss Harriman, a graduate of the Philadelphia school and later at work among
the Indians in Duluth, gave some experiences of unexpected work that might
fall to the lot of a woman missionary.

The meeting closed with a statement,
by the secretary, of present needs.

SOME SOURCES OF SUPPLY

*The Guild of St. Barnabas for
Nurses:* A society started in England,
which for a time furnished all the women
nurses sent to Africa. In this country,
its associates, Churchwomen; its membership all nurses wishing to join; its
Secretary-General, Mrs. William Read

are simple mission study classes and talks on missions, and in two dioceses general missionary meetings have been held. In this way girls are trained in their duty to the Church, but I think we may not by any general appeal urge them to offer their lives to the mission field."

The Daughters of the King: "For the Spread of Christ's Kingdom Among Young Women." Works through parochial chapters, Secretary, Miss S. D. Bluxome, 281 Fourth Avenue, New York.

A number of its members have become missionaries. The salary of one in Shanghai is paid by the Order. One is now preparing to go to Alaska.

Schools and Colleges: Student Secretary, Deaconess Goodwin, 281 Fourth Avenue, New York.

A great opportunity is presented by schools and colleges. There are great numbers of these institutions. Often our Church girls form one-quarter part of the whole number of students, and the quality of these pupils is good. They are often found among the class presidents. When these girls return home the Auxiliary officers of their parishes might take pains to enlist them in Auxiliary work, as in conducting study classes after lines learned in college.

Sometimes working girls ask if they could not be used in the mission field. Is there a possibility of such being sent out in company with those intellectually equipped, that their work in the practical cares of daily life might leave others free for evangelistic and educational duties?

The Church Training-schools

Dean Knapp, 228 East 12th Street, New York

One year at least in a training home is essential for the discipline of the character. Spiritual strength is needed as well as spiritual intelligence. This development is the most important part of training.

Deaconess Sanford, 708 Spruce Street, Philadelphia.

Can we find a suggestion for providing training for a devout, practical

woman who lacks the education required for the course in our training-schools, without lowering their present standards? Why not have a recruiting centre in every diocese, where young women can be gathered, tested and trained to such a degree that they may at least be fitted for the ordinary work of the Church? At each such centre a trained worker to supervise and test applicants who may be recommended to the training-schools of greater requirements. In small towns a larger number of study classes, especially among the Juniors, to study particularly the Bible and the doctrines and history of the Church. A four days' training, possibly in connection with the Diocesan Sunday-school Association, to which the most promising students from small towns might go for lectures. The parish class, the four days' institute, the diocesan training house, serving to test, to sift and train, and to select for the higher schools those suited to take the full course of such instruction as they provide.

SOME PRESENT NEEDS

The Philippines: A deaconess for work in the barrios of Igorot villages about Baguio. Two nurses for Manila.

Honolulu: Women workers in Lahaina and Wailuku.

Kyoto: A graduate of a Church Training-school to teach vocal and instrumental music in a Church Training-school for mission workers.

Shanghai: St. Mary's Hall, two teachers, one of them for normal training; St. Luke's Hospital, a nurse.

Hankow: For St. James's Hospital, Anking, two nurses. For Wuchang, a nurse.

Tokyo: Two women for evangelistic work.

THE FEBRUARY CONFERENCE

THE February Conference of Diocesan Officers will be held at the Church Missions House on Thursday, the 17th, from 10:30 A.M. to 12 M. Subject, "Our Junior Department."

(154)

ACKNOWLEDGMENT OF OFFERINGS

Offerings are asked to sustain missions in thirty missionary districts in the United States, Africa, China, Japan, Brazil, Mexico and Cuba; also work in the Haitien Church; in forty-two dioceses, including missions to the Indians and to the Colored People; to pay the salaries of thirty-two bishops, and stipends to 2,253 missionary workers, domestic and foreign; also two general missionaries to the Swedes and two missionaries among deaf-mutes in the Middle West and the South; and to support schools, hospitals and orphanages. With all remittances the name of the Diocese and Parish should be given. Remittances, when practicable, should be by Check or Draft, and should always be made payable to the order of George Gordon King, Treasurer, and sent to him, Church Missions House, 281 Fourth Avenue, New York. Remittances in Bank Notes are not safe unless sent in Registered Letters.

The Treasurer of the Board of Missions acknowledges the receipt of the following from December 1st, 1909, to January 1st, 1910.

* Lenten and Easter Offering from the Sunday-school Auxiliary.

NOTE.—*The items in the following pages marked "Sp." are Specials which do not aid the Board in meeting its appropriations. In the heading for each Diocese the total marked "Ap." is the amount which does aid the Board of Missions in meeting its appropriations. Wherever the abbreviation "Wo. Aux." precedes the amount, the offering is through a branch of the Woman's Auxiliary.*

Home Dioceses

Alabama

Ap. $114.73; *Sp.* $91.00

AUBURN—*Holy Innocents'*: Sp. for Dr. Correll, for the Tsu Mission Fund, Kyoto	20 00	
BIRMINGHAM—*St. Mark's*: Gen	2 00	
t. *Mary's*: Wo. Aux., Sp. for Dr. Correll's work at Tsu, Kyoto	20 00	
Rev. Thomas J. Beard, Sp. for Dr. Correll's work at Tsu, Kyoto	25 00	
CARBON HILL—*St. James's*: Gen	6 00	
FLORENCE—*Trinity Church*: Gen	3 00	
GREENVILLE—*St. Thomas's*: Wo. Aux., Frn	5 00	
HUNTSVILLE—*Nativity*: Sp. for Tsu Property Fund, Kyoto	25 00	
JACKSONVILLE—*St. Luke's*: Dom	1 98	
MOBILE—*Christ Church*: Gen	83 75	
t. *John's*: Dom., $3; Mexican, $5; Brazil, $5; Sp. for Key West, Southern Florida, $1	14 00	

Albany

Ap. $183.16; *Sp.* $193.56

ALBANY—*St. Peter's*: Sp. for Bishop Brooke, Oklahoma, $70.01; Miss H. F. Miller, Gen., $4; Wo. Aux., Sp. for Bishop Brooke, Oklahoma, $25. Mrs. R. Temple, Alaska, $5; St. John's School, Cape Mount, Africa, $5	99 01	
BALLSTON SPA—*Christ Church*: Sp. for Zangzok Equipment Fund, Shanghai	10 00	
CATSKILL—*St. Luke's*: Dom	1 74	
DELHI—*St. John's*: Dom	19 50	
GLENS FALLS—*Church of the Messiah*: Gen.	27 42	
HOOSAC—*All Saints'*: Dom. and Frn., $21; Sp. for Rev. Robert Wilson, for work in Shanghai, $11.03	75 00	
SARATOGA SPRINGS — *Bethesda*: Wo. Aux., $5, S. S., $5.78, Sp. for Zang-	32 03	

zok Equipment Fund, Shanghai	10 78	
SCHENECTADY—Mrs. L. A. Chatfield, Gen.	5 00	
STOCKPORT—*St. John's*: Dom. and Frn.	10 24	
TROY—*St. Paul's*: Sp. for Rev. Mr. Wilcox, Hendersonville, Asheville...	75 00	
WARRENSBURGH—*Holy Cross*: Gen	11 00	

Arkansas

Ap. $29.00

LITTLE ROCK—*Trinity Church*: Wo. Aux., Gen	25 00	
NEWPORT—*St. Paul's*: Wo. Aux., Gen.	4 00	

Atlanta

Ap. $14.00; *Sp.* $65.70

COLUMBUS—*Trinity Church*: (Apportionment, 1908-09) Gen	14 00	
MACON—*St. Paul's*: Sp. for Dr. Correll's work, Tsu, Kyoto	55 70	
MISCELLANEOUS—Junior Aux., Sp. for "Sister Katherine" scholarship, Mrs. Brooks's School, Guantanamo, Cuba	10 00	

Bethlehem

Ap. $188.95; *Sp.* $78.50

BIRDSBORO—*St. Michael's*: Gen	36 02	
DRIFTON—*St. James's*: Wo. Aux., Sp. for St. Mary's Hall, Building Fund, Shanghai (of which Junior Aux., $10), $85; Sp. for Alaska Hospital (of which Junior Aux., $5), $15...	50 00	
DUNMORE—*St. Mark's*: Gen	7 50	
EASTON—*Trinity Church*: Sp. for Rev. I. H. Correll, Kyoto, $2.50; Wo. Aux., St. Mary's Hall Building Fund, Shanghai, $5	7 50	
GREAT BEND—*Grace*: Gen	3 75	
JONESTOWN—*St. Mark's*: Dom	5 10	
POTTSVILLE — *Trinity Church*: Wo. Aux., Sp. for Bishop Brown's Building Fund, Arkansas	1 00	

(155)

SCRANTON—*St. Luke's*: Dom., $25;
Frn., $56.03; Gen., $5; Wo. Aux.,
salary of trained nurse, St. Mary's
Hall, Shanghai, $25.............. 111 03
SOUTH BETHLEHEM — *Nativity*: Wo.
Aux., Sp. for Alaska Hospital...... 10 00
SUSQUEHANNA—*Christ Church*: Gen.... 10 35
WEST PITTSTON — *Trinity Church*:
Gen.......................... 15 20
WILKES-BARRE—*St. Stephen's*: Wood-
ward Leavenworth, Sp. for Church
Extension Fund, Porto Rico........ 10 00

California
Sp. $702.30
BERKELEY—*All Souls'*: $1.50, Mrs.
Burrows, $20, Sp. for Utah........ 21 50
St. Mark's: Sp. for Utah............ 15 50
Mrs. H. M. Sherman, Sp. for Utah. 10 00
OAKLAND—*St. John's*: Sp. for Utah.. 16 00
Trinity Church: Sp. for Utah........ 43 15
PALO ALTO—Leland Stanford, Sp. for
Utah 50 00
ROSS—*St. John's*: Wo. Aux., Sp. for
Utah 5 00
SAN FRANCISCO—*Grace*: J. T. Arundel,
Sp. for Utah.................... 50 00
St. John's: Sp. for Utah............ 12 65
Wo. Aux., M. Van Bokkelen, Sp. for
Utah 25 00
SAN JOSE—*Trinity Church*: Sp. for
Utah 14 00
SAN MATEO—*Trinity Church*: $32.50
(of which Mrs. J. Nichols, for In-
dians, $25), $30, Sp. for Utah..... 62 50
SAN RAFAEL—*St. Paul's*: $22, S. S.,
$5, Sp. for Utah................ 27 00
MISCELLANEOUS—Branch Wo. Aux., Sp.
for Mrs. Schereschewsky's Memor-
ial Station School, Shanghai....... 100 00
Wo. Aux., Sp. at Bishop Partridge's
discretion, for St. Agnes's School
Improvement, Kyoto.............. 250 00

Central New York
Ap. $635.80; *Sp.* $76.00
BINGHAMTON—*Church of the Good
Shepherd*: $7.25, Charles T. Moore
(deceased), $5, Gen.............. 12 25
Trinity Memorial: Dom............ 25 00
CAZENOVIA—*St. Peter's*: Bishop Rowe,
Alaska, $30; Bishop Kendrick, New
Mexico and Arizona, $25.......... 55 00
HOMER—*Calvary*: Gen.............. 15 00
ONONDAGA CASTLE—*Church of the
Good Shepherd*: Dom., $1; Gen., 50
cts. 1 50
ONEIDA—*St. John's*: Dom............ 7 00
SYRACUSE—*Grace*: Dom., $1; Gen.,
$6.10 .... 7 10
UTICA—*Grace*: Gen................ 165 45
WINDSOR—*Zion*: "A Friend," Gen.... 10 00
MISCELLANEOUS — Wo. Aux., Gen.,
$337.50; Sp. for Tsu Property Fund,
Kyoto, $76.................... 413 50

Chicago
Ap. $1,035.16; *Sp.* $40.00
CHICAGO—*Advent*: Gen.............. 9 27
Epiphany: Wo. Aux., Gen........... 5 00
Grace: Dom. and Frn., $64; Gen.,
$319.14; Wo. Aux., "L. H." (In-
Memoriam) scholarship, St. John's
School, Cape Mount, Africa, $40.... 423 14
Holy Cross: Dom., $2.50; Frn., $2.50. 5 00
St. Barnabas's: Gen............... 9 01
St. Chrysostom's: Gen.............. 34 75
St. Edmund's: Gen................ 5 20
St. Margaret's (Windsor Park):
$7.20, Mrs. D. J. Thompson, $1,
Gen.......................... 8 20
St. Martin's (Austin Station): Gen... 8 20
Transfiguration: Gen.............. 8 80
St. Ambrose's (Chicago Heights): Gen. 6 00

Wo. Aux., Mrs. D. B. Lyman, Sp.
for Mrs. Schereschewsky's Memorial
Station School, Shanghai.......... 25
EVANSTON—*St. Luke's*: Dom. and Frn. 85
GLENCOE—*St. Elizabeth's*: Gen...... 8
HINSDALE—*Grace*: Gen............. 22
PARK RIDGE—*St. Mary's*: Gen........ 19
WHEATON—*Trinity Church*: Alaska... 3
MISCELLANEOUS — Wo. Aux., Twenty-
fifth Anniversary Offering, Gen.,
$274.48; Babies' Branch, Sp. for
Emergency Fund, White Rocks,
Utah, $15..................... 389

Colorado
Ap. $209.00; *Sp.* $76.00
CANON CITY—*Christ Church*: Dom.
and Frn........................ 9
COLORADO SPRINGS—*Grace*: Dom. and
Frn........................... 2
St. Stephen's: Sp. for Bishop Brewster,
Western Colorado................ 76
DENVER — *Ascension Memorial*: Dom.
and Frn........................ 4
Church of Our Merciful Saviour:
Dom. and Frn.................. 33
St. Mark's: Dom. and Frn.......... 150
LAS ANIMAS—*Church of the Messiah*:
Dom. and Frn.................. 10

Connecticut
Ap. $954.78; *Sp.* $100.00
BLACK HALL—*St. Ann's*: Gen........ 17
DURHAM—*Epiphany*: Gen............ 3
EAST HADDAM—Mrs. F. C. H. Wendel,
for work in Southern Florida, $1;
Rev. F. C. H. Wendel, Gen., $1.... 2
FAIRFIELD—*St. Paul's S. S.*: For work
of Rev. Mr. Chapman, Alaska..... 5
HARTFORD—*Trinity Church*: Gen..... 53
MERIDEN—*St. Andrew's*: Dom........ 8
MIDDLETOWN — *Holy Trinity Church*:
Colored, $5; Indian, $5; Dom.,
$136.74; Gen., $47.72............ 194
St. Luke's: Gen.................. 37
MILFORD—*St. Peter's*: Gen......... 16
NEW HAVEN—*Christ Church*: Dom. and
Frn........................... 369
St. Paul's: Gen., $100; "A Friend,"
Sp. for Church Extension Fund,
Porto Rico, $10................ 110
St. James's (Westville): Gen........ 21
Ladies' Foreign Missionary Asso-
ciation, Sp. for Mann Hall Building
Fund, Shanghai................ 5
Woman's Church Missionary Asso-
ciation, Wo. Aux., Sp. for repairs,
House of the Holy Child, Manila,
Philippine Islands................ 25
NORWALK—*Grace*: Gen............. 30
RIDGEFIELD—*St. Stephen's*: Miss Eliza-
beth Lockwood, Sp. for famine suf-
ferers, Mexico.................. 5
RIVERSIDE—*St. Paul's*: "A Friend,"
Sp. for Church Extension Fund,
Porto Rico.................... 5
SALISBURY—*St. John's*: Rev. James
Starr Clark, D.D., St. Paul's Col-
lege, Tokyo, $5; St. John's College,
Shanghai, $5................... 10
WAREHOUSE POINT—*St. John's*: Dom.. 49
WEST HARTFORD—*St. James's*: Frn... 3
WINSTED—*St. James's*: Gen......... 5
MISCELLANEOUS — Offering from Con-
necticut S. S. workers, Waterbury
Convention, Gen................ 21
"A Few Children," through Mrs. D.
Parker Morgan, for work among
children in the foreign field....... 5
Litchfield Archdeaconry, Sp. for
Bishop Guerry, Charleston, South
Carolina, for "Litchfield Arch-
deaconry" scholarship............ 50

5 00
5 10
14 95

5 00

500 00

10 00

5 00

41 86

50 00

3 60
8 75

3 50
2 00

15 00
18 55

2 50
10 50
2 10
1 25
22 50

17 00

2 00

5 00

5 00

15 00

10 00

5 00

17 00

200 00

53 50

1 00

Florida

Ap. $31.50 ; *Sp.* $10.00

CEDAR KEY—*Christ Church*: Gen....	2 50
DE FUNIAK—*St. Agatha's*: Gen......	11 50
FERNANDINA—*Church of the Good Shepherd*: Gen...................	12 50
JACKSONVILLE—*St. John's*: Chapter of Daughters of the King, Gen.......	5 00
MELROSE—*Trinity Church*: Sp. for Tsu Building Fund, Kyoto..........	10 00

Fond du Lac

Ap. $13.65

JACKSONPORT—*Holy Nativity*: Gen....	5 00
ONEIDA—Junior Aux., Gen..........	1 35
RIPON—*St. Peter's*: Indian.........	7 30

Georgia

Ap. $37.22 ; *Sp.* $5.00

AMERICUS—*Calvary*: Dom,..........	14 12
AUGUSTA—*Atonement*: Wo. Aux., Sp. for Rev. E. J. Lee, St. James's Hospital, Anking, Hankow.........	5 00
BELFAST—*Mission*: Gen.............	10 00
BRUNSWICK—*St. Mark's*: Gen.......	4 75
THOMASVILLE—*Church of the Good Shepherd*: Dom.................	6 00
WAYCROSS—*Grace*: Dom............	2 35

Harrisburg

Ap. $135.34 ; *Sp.* $88.28

BEARTOWN—*Calvary*: Gen..........	8 58
BLUE RIDGE SUMMIT—*Transfiguration*: Gen.......................	50 97
CHAMBERSBURG — *T r i n i t y Church*: Junior Aux., Sp. for "Little Mary" scholarship, St. Mary's-on-the-Mountain, Sewanee, Tennessee.....	5 00
HARRISBURG—*St. Stephen's*: Gen.....	38 06
LANCASTER—*St. James's*: Sp. for Tsu Property Fund, Kyoto...........	63 25
St. John's: $15.03, S. S., $5, Sp. for Tsu Property Fund, Kyoto.........	20 03
MILTON—*Christ Church S. S.*: Gen..	9 62
MONTOURSVILLE—*Church of Our Saviour*: Gen.....................	8 67
MT. HOPE—*Hope*: Gen.............	14 02
SELIN'S GROVE—*All Saints'*: Gen....	50
STATE COLLEGE—*St. Andrew's*: Gen...	4 92

Indianapolis

Ap. $13.66

INDIANAPOLIS—*St. Alban's*: Gen......	1 15
LAWRENCEBURG—*Trinity Church*: Miss N. F. Brower, Gen..............	10 00
NEW CASTLE—*St. James's*: Gen.....	2 51

Iowa

Ap. $18.85 ; *Sp.* $2.00

DES MOINES—*St. Mark's*: Gen.......	18 35
INDEPENDENCE—*St. James's*: C. D. Jones, Sp. for Church Extension Fund, Porto Rico.................	2 00
IOWA CITY—*Trinity Church*: Wo. Aux., Gen......................	50

Kansas

Ap. $89.00

HIAWATHA—*St. John's*: Gen..........	10 00
NEWTON—*St. Matthew's*: Gen.......	9 00
TOPEKA—*Grace*: Gen...............	60 00
College Sisters of Bethany, Gen....	10 00

Kansas City

Ap. $34.52 ; *Sp.* $28.50

KANSAS CITY—*Grace Hall*: Wo. Aux., Sp. for Bishop Knight, Isle of Pines, Cuba	3 50
St. George's: Wo. Aux., Gen........	15 00
St. Mark's: Dom...................	3 22
St. Mary's: Wo. Aux., Sp. for St. Mary's-on-the-Mountain, Sewanee, Tennessee	25 00

Wo. Aux., Offering, October 28th,
1909, Gen...................... 16 80

Kentucky

Ap. $648.81; *Sp.* $50.00
HENDERSON—*St. Paul's*: Wo. Aux.,
Gen. 25 00
LOUISVILLE — *Advent*: Intermediates,
Wo. Aux., Gen.............. 18 00
Christ Church: Mrs. M. E. A. Dudley,
Sp. for Church Extension Fund,
Porto Rico, $50; Wo. Aux., Gen.,
$25 .... 75 00
St. Andrew's: Gen., $150; S. S., "St.
Andrew's S. S." scholarship, Girls'
Training Institute, Africa, $25;
"St. Andrew's S. S." scholarship,
St. John's School, Africa, $25; "W.
A. Robinson" scholarship, St. John's
University, Shanghai, $40........ 240 00
St. Paul's: Wo. Aux., Gen........... 42 50
St. Stephen's: Junior Aux., Gen..... 5 00
"Mrs. M. E. A. Dudley, John N.
Norton" scholarship, St. John's
School, Africa, $25; "Bishop Patte-
son" scholarship, Boone University,
Wuchang, $50.................. 75 00
Laymen's League................. 126 31
PADUCAH—*Grace*: Gen.............. 92 00
PEWEE—*St. James's*: Wo. Aux., Gen.. 5 00

Lexington

Ap. $14.70
COVINGTON—Miss Lizzie Wynne, Gen. 20
DANVILLE—Viola P. Cowan, Gen.... 5 00
PARIS—*St. Peter's*: Gen............ 7 50
SOMERSET—*Christ Church*: Gen...... 2 00

Long Island

Ap. $1,248.06; *Sp.* $310.00
ASTORIA—*Church of the Redeemer*:
Wo. Aux., Sp. for sewing-teacher's
salary, St. Augustine's School, Raleigh, North Carolina.............
St. George's: Wo. Aux., Sp. for sew-
ing-teacher's salary, St. Augustine's School, Raleigh, North Carolina 3 00
BELLPORT—*Christ Church*: Gen....... 5 00
BROOKLYN—*Calvary*: Wo. Aux., Sp. 10 00
for sewing-teacher's salary, St. Augustine's School, Raleigh, North
Carolina 2 00
Christ Church (Eastern District):
Wo. Aux., Sp. for sewing-teacher's
salary, St. Augustine's School, Ral-
eigh, North Carolina............ 3 00
Christ Church (Clinton Street): Wo.
Aux., Sp. for sewing-teacher's sal-
ary, St. Augustine's School, Ral-
eigh, North Carolina............ 5 00
Church of the Good Shepherd: Wo.
Aux., Sp. for sewing-teacher's sal-
ary, St. Augustine's School, Ral-
eigh, North Carolina............ 5 00
Grace (Heights): Gen., $750; Sp. for
Bishop Partridge, Kyoto, $100..... 850 00
Holy Trinity Church: Wo. Aux., Sp.
for sewing-teacher's salary, St.
Augustine's School, Raleigh, North
Carolina 5 00
Church of the Redeemer: Wo. Aux.,
Sp. for sewing-teacher's salary, St.
Augustine's School, Raleigh, North
Carolina 3 00
St. George's: Wo. Aux., Sp. for sewing-
teacher's salary, St. Augustine's
School, Raleigh, North Carolina... 2 00
St. James's: Wo. Aux., Sp. for sew-
ing-teacher's salary, St. Augustine's
School, Raleigh, North Carolina.... 4 00
St. Jude's: Wo. Aux., Sp. for sewing-
teacher's salary, St. Augustine's
School, Raleigh, North Carolina.... 2 00
St. Mary's: Wo. Aux., Sp. for sewing-

teacher's salary, St. Augustine's
School, Raleigh, North Carolina....
St. Michael's: Wo. Aux., Sp. for sew-
ing-teacher's salary, St. Augustine's
School, Raleigh, North Carolina....
St. Paul's (Flatbush): Dom., $296.51;
Gen., $163.85
St. Stephen's: Wo. Aux., Sp. for sew-
ing-teacher's salary, St. Augustine's
School, Raleigh, North Carolina....
Neville N. McElroy, Dom..........
H. E. Pierrepont, Sp. for Miss Wood,
Wuchang, Hankow ....
FAR ROCKAWAY—*St. John's*: Wo. Aux.,
Sp. for sewing-teacher's salary, St.
Augustine's School, Raleigh, North
Carolina ....
GARDEN CITY—*Cathedral of the Incar-
tion*: Wo. Aux., Sp. for sewing-
teacher's salary, St. Augustine's
School, Raleigh, North Carolina...
LAWRENCE—Mrs. Charles E. Sherman,
Sp. for Fund for St. Luke's Hospital,
Tokyo ....
MISCELLANEOUS—Wo. Aux., Sp. for
sewing-teacher's salary, St. Augus-
tine's School, Raleigh, North Caro-
lina, $4; Missionary Exhibit, Gen.,
$26.70 ....

Los Angeles

Ap. $77.20; *Sp.* $723.25
CORONADO—*Christ Church*: $48.25,
Chas. T. Hinde, $100, Wo. Aux.,
$8, Junior Aux., $1, S. S., $10, Sp.
for Utah ....
HOLYWOOD—*St. Stephen's*: Sp. for
Utah ....
LONG BEACH — *St. Luke's*: Sp. for
Utah ....
LOS ANGELES—*Christ Church*: 75 cts.,
John Harney, $100, E. K. Gif-
ford, $5, B. Breckenfeld, $10, Sp.
for Utah ....
St. John's: Dom. and Frn., $25; Sp.
for Utah (of which W. A. North-
rup, $1), $51.41...............
St. Luke's: Sp. for Utah.............
St. Matthew's: Sp. for Utah..........
St. Paul's: Mr. and Mrs. Lee, Sp. for
Utah ....
OCEAN PARK—*Church of the Good
Shepherd*: Sp. for Utah...........
PASADENA—*All Saints'*: Miss Mary
White, Sp. for Utah.............
POMONA—*St. Paul's*: Sp. for Utah,
$20; S. S., Sp. for Bishop Aves,
Mexico, for famine sufferers, $8....
REDLANDS—*Trinity Church*: Dom. and
Frn., $52.20; Sp. for Utah, $62...
RIVERSIDE—*All Saints'*: Sp. for Utah.
SAN DIEGO—*St. Paul's*: Wo. Aux.,
$3.50, Mrs. Kirby, $10, Sp. for Utah.
SANTA BARBARA—*Trinity Church*: Sp.
for Utah......................
SANTA MONICA—*St. Augustine's*: Sp.
for Utah......................
SIERRA MADRE—*Ascension*: Sp. for
Utah ....
SOUTH PASADENA—*St. James's*: Sp.
for Utah......................
MISCELLANEOUS—John Parkinson, Sp.
for Utah......................
Mrs. Macleish, Sp. for Utah.......
Margaret Middleton, Sp. for Utah..

Louisiana

Ap. $60.40; *Sp.* $29.00
ALEXANDRIA—Wo. Aux., Mrs. Evans's
salary, Alaska.................
HOUMA—*St. Matthew's*: Wo. Aux.,
Mrs. Evans's salary, Alaska.......
NAPOLEONVILLE—*Christ Church*: Wo.
Aux., support of a scholar in St.
Elizabeth's School, South Dakota,

Agnes's School, Kyoto, $50........ 108 00
9 50 Trinity Church S. S. (Towson): Sp.
 for Bishop Brent's work in the
 Philippines 6 44
 FREDERICK Co.—Catoctin Parish: Gen. 3 24
5 50 HOWARD Co.—St. John's: Frn., $20;
 30 Junior Aux., for mountain work in
10 00 Virginia, $5 .... 25 00
 MISCELLANEOUS—"Cash," Wo. Aux.,
 Sp. for Dr. Correll's Building Fund,
6 00 Tsu, Kyoto..................... 13 20

Massachusetts
4 00 Ap. $878.50; Sp. $1,746.25
12 50 Frn. ....
 ANDOVER—Christ Church: Dom. and
 Frn. 153 21
 BOSTON—Advent: W. K. Richardson,
 Sp. for Expansion Fund, St. John's
20 00 University, Shanghai, $50; Wo.
 Aux., "A Member," Sp. for Archdeacon Cornish, South Carolina, to
 buy an acre of land, $50......... 100 00
 Trinity Church: Sp. for Bishop
 Thomas, Wyoming, $390; Sp. for
16 00 Bishop Aves's famine stricken Mex-
5 00 ico (of which Miss Ethel L. Paine,
 $50), $150; "H.," Sp. for Church
 Extension Fund, Porto Rico, $5... 545 00
 E. B. Page, Sp. at discretion of
 Bishop L. H. Roots, Hankow...... 100 00
8 05 Ruth Lawrence, Bishop Brent's work,
 Philippines 25 00
1 25 BROCKTON—St. Paul's: Gen.......... 15 00
1 32 BROOKLINE—All Saints': $102, in
 memory of "W. L. B.," $1, Sp. for
 Bishop Thomas, Wyoming........ 103 00
 St. Paul's: Sp. for Archdeacon Cornish, Charleston, South Carolina,
 $25; Sp. for Bishop Thomas, Wyo-
 ming, $25...................... 50 00
10 00 CAMBRIDGE—St. Philip's: Gen....... 14 00
 CONCORD—Trinity Church: Gen...... 13 12
 DEDHAM—St. Paul's: Sp. for Bishop
5 00 Brent, Philippine Islands, $25; Sp.
100 00 for Mexican Relief Fund, $10...... 35 00
985 47 FALMOUTH—St. Barnabas's: Gen...... 8 00
 GROTON—St. John's: Gen., $100; Sp.
 for St. John's College, Shanghai,
300 00 $50 .... 150 00
 LAWRENCE—Grace: Gen............. 17 13
 LOWELL—St. Anne's: Gen........... 300 60
5 00 NEWTON—Church of the Good Shepherd (Waban): Gen............. 46 00
 Church of the Redeemer (Chestnut
32 00 Hill): Dom. and Frn........... 100 00
 St. John's (Newtonville): Gen...... 16 11
 St. Paul's (Highlands): Gen........ 45 18
3 50 Trinity Church (Centre): Mrs. Wil-
 liam Byers, Wo. Aux., Sp. for
 "Armistead Harrison" scholarship,
 St. Paul's School, Lawrenceville,
 Southern Virginia.............. 75 00
30 00 NORTH BILLERICA—St. Ann's Mission:
 Gen. 14 40
25 00 TAUNTON—St. Thomas's: Miss S. V.
 Louther, Sp. for Rev. A. A. Gilman,
10 00 Changsha, Hankow.............. 2 00
 WELLESLEY—Dana Hall, a missionary
 meeting, Frn.................. 10 75
5 00 WINCHESTER — Epiphany: Woman's
 Guild, Sp. for Archdeacon Cornish,
 Spartanburg, South Carolina....... 13 25
67 17 MISCELLANEOUS—Wo. Aux., committee
 for Mexico, Brazil, Cuba and Haiti,
 Sp. for Bishop Knight, Isle of Pines. 21 00
5 00 Wo. Aux., "A Friend of Miss
 Woods," Sp. for Boone College Library, Wuchang, Hankow......... 500 00
10 00 Wo. Aux., "A Member," $100, "A
7 20 Friend," $2, Sp. for Archdeacon
 Cornish, Charleston, South Carolina. 102 00
 Right Rev. W. Lawrence, D.D., Sp.
10 00 for Zangzok Mission Equipment
 Fund, Shanghai, $25; Sp. for Mexi-
 can Relief Fund, $25............. 50 00

Michigan

Ap. $636.02; *Sp.* $6.00

COLEMAN—*St. Andrew's*: Dom.......	1	05
DETROIT—*Grace*: Dom., $50; Frn., $50	100	00
St. Andrew's: Wo. Aux., Alaska, $15; Philippines, $3; Gen., $4; Sp. for Rev. A. W. Mann, Ohio, $2; F. E. Adams Memorial, Sp. for Good Shepherd Hospital, Fort Defiance, Arizona, $3......................	27	00
St. George's: Wo. Aux., Gen........	5	00
St. John's: Michael F. Pfau, Gen.....	2	00
St. Paul's: Gen...................	450	00
HAMBURG—*St. Stephen's*: Gen......	7	76
HILLSDALE—*St. Peter's*: Wo. Aux., Gen., $1; Sp. for Rev. H. C. Parke, Morgantown, Asheville, $1........	2	00
PONTIAC—*All Saints'*: Gen..........	18	36
ROCHESTER—*St. Philip's*: Gen.......	3	00
SAGINAW—*Calvary*: Dom. and Frn...	3	85
St. John's (West Side): Gen......	22	00

Michigan City

Ap. $21.23

FORT WAYNE—*Trinity*: Junior Aux., Gen.	16	63
KOKOMO—*St. Andrew's*: Junior Aux., Gen.	4	60

Milwaukee

Ap. $61.63

DELEVAN — *Christ Church*: Dom., $5.85; Frn., $9.23..............	15	08
KENOSHA — *St. Matthew's*: Colored work in South, $2; Gen., $38......	40	00
STAR PRAIRIE—*St. John Baptist's S. S.*: Birthday Offering day-schools in China	1	55
TOMAH—"C. W. D. V.," work among the mountaineers of the South...	5	00

Minnesota

Ap. $144.30; *Sp.* $35.10

MINNEAPOLIS—*Holy Trinity Church*: Gen.	16	30
St. John's (Linden Hills): Wo. Aux., Sp. for famine sufferers, Mexico....	5	10
St. Paul's: H. R. Lyon, $10, "A Friend," $10, Sp. for Church Extension Fund, Porto Rico...........	20	00
ST. PAUL—*Christ Church*: Gen........	3	00
W. F. Myers, Sp. for Bishop Whipple Memorial, Havana, Cuba.......	10	00
STILLWATER—*Ascension*: Gen........	125	00

Mississippi

Ap. $21.15; *Sp.* $26.55

ABERDEEN—*St. John's*: Gen........	6	50
HATTIESBURG—*Trinity Church*: Gen..	5	50
HOLLY SPRING—*Christ Church*: Wo. Aux., Rev. C. F. McRae's work, Shanghai	2	50
JACKSON—Mrs. E. L. Ragland, Gen...	1	00
MERIDIAN—*St. Paul's*: Sp. for Tsu Property Fund, Kyoto..........	26	55
SCRANTON—*St. John's*: Gen........	5	65

Missouri

Ap. $473.01; *Sp.* $56.30

KIRKWOOD—*Grace*: Sp. for Bishop Partridge's work, Kyoto..........	56	30
ST. LOUIS—*Christ Church Cathedral*: Dom.	300	00
Holy Communion: Gen..............	100	00
Holy Cross: Gen..................	5	00
St. John's: Gen..................	9	10
St. Peter's: Dom., $29.10; Frn., $29.81	58	91

Montana

Ap. $40.00

HAMILTON—*St. Paul's*: Gen........	40	00

Newark

Ap. $383.90; *Sp.* $951.18

BLOOMFIELD—*Christ Church*: Gen....	6	
EAST ORANGE—"B.," Sp. for Rev. C. E. Betticher, Fairbanks, Alaska, for the "Luke Farthing" scholarship at Neenana	100	
EDGEWATER—*Church of the Mediator S. S.*: Dom., $9.65; Frn., $9.65....	19	
GRANTWOOD—*Trinity Church S. S.*: Gen.	12	
HASBROUCK HEIGHTS—*St. John the Divine*: Sp. for the Zangzok Equipment Fund, Shanghai.............	4	
MONTCLAIR—*St. Luke's*: Sp. for plant for Changsha, Hankow...........	706	
NEWARK—*St. Paul's*: Gen...........	18	
Trinity Church: Wallace M. Scudder, Sp. for Church Extension Fund, Porto Rico......................	50	
ORANGE—*Holy Trinity Church S. S.* (West): Gen....................	32	
PATERSON—*St. Paul's*: Gen.........	7	
SOUTH ORANGE—*Holy Communion*: salary of Rev. Henry A. McNulty, Shanghai	187	
St. Andrew's: Dom., $25.51; Frn., $25.51	51	
VERNON—*St. Thomas's*: Gen.........	20	
WYOMING—Mrs. P. W. Mount, Alaska.	8	
MISCELLANEOUS—Wo. Aux., Sp. for St. John's College Expansion Fund, Shanghai, $49.54; Sp. for Rev. A. A. Gilman for Changsha plant, Shanghai, $41.54....................	91	
Collection at service of United Sunday-schools, held in St. Mark's Church, Orange, Gen.............	21	

New Hampshire

Ap. $220.18; *Sp.* $10.51

CHARLESTOWN—*St. Luke's*: Sp. for Zangzok Equipment Fund, Shanghai	3	
CONCORD—*St. Paul's*: Colored work, $6.73; Gen., $50.............	56	
St. Paul's School: Dom. and Frn...	100	
DOVER—*St. Thomas's*: Gen.........	19	
KEENE—*St. James's*: Dom. and Frn., $28.16; Sp. for Rev. R. C. Wilson, Zangzok, Shanghai, $5...........	33	
MANCHESTER—*Grace*: Sp. for Zangzok Equipment Fund, Shanghai........	2	
MISCELLANEOUS—Wo. Aux., Gen......	16	

New Jersey

Ap. $857.71; *Sp.* $19.00

ATLANTIC CITY — *Ascension*: "A Friend," Sp. for Church Extension Fund, Porto Rico.................		
BERNARDSVILLE—*St. Bernard's*: for St. Augustine's School, Raleigh, North Carolina, $55; Sp. for Boone School Teachers' Fund, Hankow, $10....	65	
BOUND BROOK—*St. Paul's*: Indian....	33	
CAMDEN—*St. Paul's*: St. John's College, Shanghai, $5; Gen., $76.90....	81	
DUNELLEN—*Holy Innocents'*: Indian..	7	
ELIZABETH—*Christ Church*: Frn.....	25	
St. John's: Gen..................	309	
Trinity Church: Gen..............	20	
FLORENCE—*St. Stephen's*: Gen......	25	
FREEHOLD—*St. Peter's*: "A Member," Wo. Aux., Sp. for St. Agnes's Hospital, Raleigh, North Carolina...	1	
LITTLE SILVER—*St. John's Chapel*: Dom.	13	
MOORESTOWN—*Trinity Church*: Dom.	35	
NEW BRUNSWICK—*Christ Church*: Wo. Aux., for St. Paul's School, Lawrenceville, Southern Virginia, $3; for St. Augustine's School, Raleigh, North Carolina, $2..............	5	
OCEAN CITY—"A Friend," Sp. for		

	Resurrection: Gen.	71 00
	St. Agnes's Chapel: Sp. for Dr. Pott's	
7 00	work, Shanghai, $40; Mrs. Vincent	
	Loeser, Sp. for St. John's Expansion	
	Fund, Shanghai, $10	50 00
	St. Andrew's (Richmond): Wo. Aux.,	
	Gen.	25 00
	St. Bartholomew's: Wo. Aux., scholar-	
20 00	ship in St. Andrew's School, Mexico,	
88 17	$250; Sp. for Rev. Mr. Matthews's	
40 00	Industrial School, Cape Mount,	
36 98	Africa, $100; St. Augustine's	
2 00	League, Sp. for Rev. Mr. Russell,	
	$50; Sp. for Rev. Mr. Hunter, St.	
60 00	Augustine's School, Raleigh, North	
	Carolina, $75; Sp. for the expenses	
	of St. Bartholomew's Day, St.	
	Agnes's Hospital, Raleigh, North	
	Carolina, $10; Sp. for Bishop	
	Gailor, Tennessee, for his Colored	
2 00	work, $150; Wo. Aux., Indian Com-	
	mission, Sp. for Miss Thackara's	
	work, Fort Defiance, Arizona, $25..	660 00
	St. George's: Woman's Branch Mis-	
27 00	sionary Society, $300; S. S., Sp. for	
	salary of Rev. Maxwell W. Rice,	
	Salt Lake City, Utah, $100	400 00
	St. James's: Wo. Aux., Sp. for Bishop	
25 00	Brown's Building Fund, Arkansas,	
1 00	$10; Afternoon S. S., Sp. for Bishop	
5 00	Brent, Philippine Islands, for Mrs.	
21 27	Hargreaves, $25	35 00
	St. Mark's: Dom., $69.90; Alaska,	
	$100; Frn., $10.	179 90
20 00	*St. Mary's* (Manhattanville): Gen. . . .	13 29
	St. Mary's (Mott Haven): Gen.	7 92
	St. Mary the Virgin: Maude A. M.	
	James, Sp. for Expansion Fund, St.	
25 00	John's University, Shanghai	1 00
218 12	*St. Matthew's:* Mrs. J. Henry Watson,	
32 80	Sp. for St. John's Expansion Fund,	
	Shanghai	25 00
	St. Paul's (Bronx): Gen.	15 00
	St. Thomas's: Wo. Aux., "M. M. Hal-	
	sted" scholarship, Hooker School,	
	Mexico, $40; work in Mexico, $30..	70 00
	Transfiguration: Mrs. Samuel Law-	
240 00	rence, Niobrara League, Sp. to en-	
	dow the "Samuel Lawrence Graduate"	
	(In Memoriam) scholarship, South	
	Dakota	1,500 00
	Trinity Church: Wo. Aux., St. Augus-	
50 00	tine's League, Sp. for St. Agnes's	
	Hospital, Raleigh, North Carolina,	
	for expenses of January 8th.	10 00
1 35	*Trinity Chapel:* Through Missionary	
	Relief Society, Mrs. Lancaster Mor-	
	gan, $5, Miss F. H. Young, $5, Frn.	10 00
	Zion and St. Timothy: "A Member,"	
	Sp. for Rev. Nathan Matthews, at	
	his discretion, for infirmary equip-	
	ment at Cape Mount, Liberia, West	
	Africa	5 00
	Mrs. R. T. Auchmuty, Domestic,	
160 00	$2,000; Colored, $1,000	3,000 00
	"A Friend," toward the deficit,	
	Gen.	3,000 00
	Miss Alice Jay, Wo. Aux., Sp. for	
110 75	Hospital of the Good Shepherd, Fort	
	Defiance, Arizona	25 00
	Miss M. G. Whitlock, Wo. Aux., Sp.	
	to endow the "Marie Antoinette	
	Whitlock" scholarship, St. Hilda's	
	School, Wuchang, Hankow.	1,000 00
	Stanley Holcomb, Molleson, Alaska.	10 00
	"A Friend," China	10 00
	"A Friend," Gen.	3 00
	OSSINING—*St. Paul's:* Wo. Aux., Frn.	4 00
	PELHAM MANOR—*Christ Church:* Wo.	
	Aux., Mrs. Munro, Sp. for Good	
	Shepherd Hospital, Fort Defiance,	
	Arizona	5 00
265 00	POUGHKEEPSIE—*Christ Church:* Gen..	30 00
	Wo. Aux., Indian	18 48
104 56	In "F's" name, Dom. and Frn.	5 00

RYE—*Christ Church:* Wo. Aux., Frn.. 100 00
SPRING VALLEY—*St. Paul's:* Alvin
  Graff, Dom. and Frn............... 10 00
STAATSBURG—*St. Margaret's:* Sp. for
  Bishop Brown, Arkansas.......... 10 00
TUXEDO—*St. Mary's:* Wo. Aux., Frn.. 12 00
YONKERS—Wm. F. Cochran and two
  sisters, Sp. for Rev. Edmund J. Lee,
  of Anking, Hankow, to complete
  Cochran Memorial Hall........... 2,000 00
  St. Augustine's League, Sp. for St.
  Paul's School, Lawrenceville, South-
  ern Virginia, $100; Sp. for St. Au-
  gustine's School, Raleigh, North
  Carolina, $120; Sp. for Rev.
  Richard Bright, Savannah, Georgia,
  $50; Sp. for Rev. P. P. Alston,
  Charlotte, North Carolina, for salary
  of teachers, $50; Sp. for a sew-
  ing-machine for St. Paul's scholar-
  ship, Lawrenceville, Southern Vir-
  ginia, $25; Sp. for St. Agnes's
  Hospital for expenses of St.
  Thomas's Day (Dec. 21), $10; Sp.
  for St. Agnes's Hospital, Raleigh,
  North Carolina, $12; from ladies of
  the Executive Committee, Sp. for
  Rev. A. T. Coombs, Hoffman Hall,
  Nashville, Tennessee, for candy for
  Christmas tree, $5.75; Niobrara
  League, "A Member," Sp. for Do-
  mestic Contingent Fund, $2; Wo.
  Aux., Foreign Committee, Frn.,
  $77.17 .... 451 92

North Carolina

Ap. $146.64; *Sp.* $70.00
JACKSON—*Church of the Saviour:* Gen. 5 00
RALEIGH—*St. Augustine's Chapel:*
  Dom., $59.39; Sp. for Rev. Dr. Cor-
  rell's work in Kyoto, $25......
  "In memory of Mrs. Brierly," Sp. 84 39
  for Miss Ridgely's Building Fund,
  Africa 25 00
SALISBURY—*St. Luke's:* Gen........ 32 25
MISCELLANEOUS—Rev. N. C. Hughes,
  Sp. for Tsu Property Fund, Kyoto.. 20 00
  "Anonymous," Gen.............. 50 00

Ohio

Ap. $125.32; *Sp.* $100.00
CLEVELAND—Samuel Mather, Sp. for
  St. John's University Expansion
  Fund, Shanghai................ 100 00
GAMBIER—*Harcourt Hall:* Dom..... 28 25
LAKEWOOD—*Ascension:* Gen.......... 17 99
NAPOLEON—*St. John's:* Gen......... 2 90
NEW PHILADELPHIA—*Trinity Church:*
  Gen. 7 18
TOLEDO—*St. Mark's:* Gen., $19; Wo.
  Aux., Oklahoma, $10............ 29 00
Trinity Church: Wo. Aux., salary Miss
  Elwin, Shanghai................ 45 00

Oregon

Ap. $16.65; *Sp.* $171.27
ASTORIA—*Grace S. S.:* Support of a
  scholar in Trinity Divinity-school,
  Tokyo 9 90
CORVALLIS—*Good Samaritan:* Sp. for
  Utah 10 90
EUGENE—*State University:* Sp. for
  Utah 20 00
GRANT'S PASS—*St. Luke's:* Dom..... 6 75
PORTLAND—*Grace Memorial:* $10; Wo.
  Aux., $22.05; Mrs. Lively, Wo.
  Aux., $5; Sp. for Utah.......... 37 05
St. Mark's: Sp. for Utah......... 29 26
*Pro-Cathedral of St. Stephen the
  Martyr:* Sp. for Bishop Spalding,
  Utah 62 86
SALEM—*St. Paul's:* Sp. for Utah.... 10 70
MISCELLANEOUS—J. L. Blaisdell, Sp.
  for Utah 1 00

Pennsylvania

Ap. $1,852.29; *Sp.* $1,247.00; *Spec. Dep.,*
$100,000.00
BRYN MAWR—*Church of the Redeemer:*
  Junior Aux., Miss Babcock's salary,
  Tokyo, $10; Miss Bull's salary,
  Kyoto, $5; Sp. for St. Paul's Col-
  lege, Tokyo, $10................ 25
  "A Friend," for support of Rev. J.
  K. Ochiai, Tokyo................ 400
GLENLOCK—*St. Paul's:* Wo. Aux., Sp.
  for Bishop Knight, Cuba, to rebuild
  chapels, Isle of Pines........... 2
ITHAN—*St. Martin's:* Dom., $2.06;
  Frn., $2.62 4
JENKINTOWN—*Church of Our Saviour:*
  "A Member," Sp. for Bishop Knight,
  Cuba, for Isle of Pines chapels.... 350
  Sp. for Tsu Property Fund, Kyoto,
  for chancel furniture............ 97
MEDIA—*Christ Church:* Wo. Aux., Sp.
  for Bishop Knight, Cuba, to rebuild
  chapels, Isle of Pines........... 5
MILL CREEK—*St. Peter's:* Sp. for Isle
  of Pines chapels, Cuba.......... 25
NORRISTOWN—*St. John's:* Dom., $10;
  Frn., $12; Gen., $106.90........ 128
PHILADELPHIA — *Advocate Memorial:*
  Gen., $32.62; Sp. for Archdeacon
  Wentworth, Lexington, $7.25....... 39
All Saints' (Lower Dublin): Wo.
  Aux., Sp. for Bishop Knight, Cuba,
  to rebuild chapels, Isle of Pines.... 5
Christ Church S. S.: For "Anne
  Flower Paul" scholarship, St. Mary's
  School, South Dakota.......... 60
Grace Church (Mount Airy): Sp. for
  Isle of Pines chapels, Cuba (of
  which for Sunday-school, $10.61,
  "W. A.," $5.11)................ 75
Holy Apostles': Junior Aux., "In Mem-
  ory of Mr. Thomas's Birthday,"
  Gen. 4
Holy Trinity Church: "A Member,"
  Sp. for plant at Changsha, Han-
  kow, $25; Miss Scholt's Bible-class,
  Sp. for St. Luke's Hospital, Ponce,
  Porto Rico, $25; St. Paul's Broth-
  erhood, Gen., $2.96; Wo. Aux., sal-
  ary of Bible reader for Training-
  school, Hankow, $60; Sp. for life
  insurance, $10; Sp. for nurse's sal-
  ary, St. Luke's Hospital, Shanghai,
  $10; Sp. for Rev. Amos Goddard's
  life insurance, Shanghai, $5....... 137
Prince of Peace Chapel S. S.: Sp. for
  Tsu Property Fund, Kyoto....... 14
Resurrection: Sp. for work of Bishop
  Johnson, South Dakota.......... 27
St. James's S. S.: Dom., $29.45; Frn.,
  $28.75 58
St. Luke's and Epiphany: "A Friend,"
  Sp. for Church Extension Fund,
  Porto Rico..................... 2
St. Mark's: Miss H. P. Lawrence, Sp.
  for Church Extension Fund, Porto
  Rico, $2; Wo. Aux., salary for Miss
  Alice F. Gates, Wuchang, Hankow,
  $97; Junior Aux., Sp. for Mrs. Res-
  tarick, for the furnishing of one of
  the rooms in the Priory School,
  Honolulu, $50.................. 149
St. Mark's (Frankford): Wo. Aux.,
  Boone College, Wuchang, Hankow.. 5
St. Martin's (Oak Lane): Dom. (of
  which Sunday-school, $8.15)....... 17
St. Paul's Memorial (Overbrook):
  Dom., $2; Sp. for Rev. J. H. Cor-
  rell's work, Kyoto, $110......... 112
St. Peter's S. S. (Germantown): "H.
  H. Houston" scholarship, S. Mary's
  School, South Dakota, $60; Bishop
  Rowe, Alaska, $20; Bishop Payne
  Divinity-school, Southern Virginia,
  $15; "St. Peter's" scholarship, Out-

Sp. for Miss Mann's work, Tokyo... 50 00
MISCELLANEOUS—Wo. Aux., Philippines,
$50; Mexico, $50; Hankow, $50;
Shanghai, $50; Sp. for Tsu Property
Fund, Kyoto, $125 .... 325 00

Quincy
Ap. $46.60
GALESBURG—*Grace*: Gen. 7 00
KNOXVILLE—*St. Mary's*: Gen......... 24 00
PEORIA—*St. Paul's*: Gen. 15 60

Rhode Island
Ap. $455.90.; *Sp.* $7.50
CROMPTON—*St. Philip's*: Gen........ 6 00
LONSDALE — *Christ Church*: Dom.,
$13.51; Gen., $80.62............. 94 13
MANVILLE—*Emmanuel Church*: Gen... 21 68
NEWPORT—*Trinity Church*: Gen...... 146 52
P R O V I D E N C E—"A Thank-offering,"
"Francis Hasseltine Chapel" schol-
arship, $50, "Pomfret" scholarship,
$70, both in St. John's University,
Shanghai 120 00
Proceeds of sale of amateur postcards,
Sp. for Miss Clara M. Carter, Alaska 7 50
WICKFORD—*St. Paul's*: Gen......... 67 57

South Carolina
Ap. $225.02; *Sp.* $91.78
AIKEN—*St. Thaddeus's*: Wo. Aux., Sp.
for Virginia mountain missions,
Standardsville, Va. 8 00
BARNWELL—*Holy Apostles'*: Mrs. Eliz-
abeth Seabrook, Frn. 5 00
BOYKIN—*Grace*: Wo. Aux., Bible-
woman, Hankow, $1.50; Sp. for
"Bishop Howe" cot, St. Mary's Or-
phanage, Shanghai, $6............ 7 50
CAMDEN—*Grace*: Wo. Aux., Gen., $10;
"N. S. Wilson" Day-school, Hankow,
$1 .... 11 00
CHARLESTON—*Grace*: Wo. Aux., Bible-
woman, Kyoto 10 00
Holy Communion: Wo. Aux., Seminole
Indians, Southern Florida, $3; Bible-
woman, Kyoto, $5; Bible-woman,
Hankow, $5; Sp. for Saluda mission,
Asheville, $2.................... 15 00
St. Luke's: Wo. Aux., Bible-woman,
Kyoto, $5; Bible-woman, Hankow, $5;
Gen., $6.42; Sp. for Miss Carter,
Alaska, $11.78 .... 28 20
St. Michael's: Gen. 62 50
Frances S. Hillyer, Sp. for Bishop
Aves for starving Mexicans 5 00
"Four Friends," Sp. for "Wilhel-
mina" scholarship, St. Mary's Or-
phanage, Shanghai 30 00
COLUMBIA—"Thanksgiving," Gen. 5 00
EASTOVER—*Zion*: Wo. Aux., "N. S.
Wilson" day-school, Hankow, $1; Sp.
for "Bishop Howe" cot, St. Mary's
Orphanage, Shanghai, $5......... 6 00
EDGEFIELD—*Trinity Church*: Wo. Aux.,
assistant for Miss McCullough, Porto
Rico, $1; "N. S. Wilson" day-school,
Hankow, $3 .... 4 00
GLEN SPRINGS—*Calvary*: Wo. Aux.,
assistant for Miss McCullough, Porto
Rico 17 50
GREENVILLE—Babies' Branch, Gen. ... 8 85
JOHN'S ISLAND—*St. John's*: Wo. Aux.,
Gen. 7 25
ORANGEBURG—*Church of the Redeemer*:
Wo. Aux., Bible-woman, Hankow,
$1.50; "N. S. Wilson" day-school,
Hankow, $2; Bible-woman, Tokyo,
$1.50; Sp. for "Bishop Howe" cot,
St. Mary's Orphanage, Shanghai, $1 6 00
SPARTANBURG — *Advent*: Wo. Aux.,
Bible-woman, Kyoto, $2; Bible-wom-
an, Hankow, $5; "N. S. Wilson"
day-school, Hankow, $5; "Margaret

C. Manning" scholarship, St. Mary's Hall, Shanghai, $25; M. E. Pinkney Fund, Bible-woman, Tokyo, $5; Sp. for "Bishop Howe" cot, St. Mary's Orphanage, Shanghai, $3; Sp. for Priory, Honolulu, $5; Sp. for Archdeacon Stuck, Alaska, $10 .... 60 00
SUMTER—*Church of the Holy Comforter*: Wo. Aux., Sp. for "Bishop Howe" cot, St. Mary's Orphanage, Shanghai 5 00
WALTERSBORO—*St. Jude's*: Gen. 15 00

Southern Ohio
Ap. $606.82; *Sp.* $55.00
CHILLICOTHE—*St. Paul's*: Wo. Aux., Sp. for Rev. McN. Du Bosé's work, Morganton, Asheville 5 00
CINCINNATI—*Advent* (Walnut Hills): Wo. Aux., Sp. for Dr. Myers, Shanghai 10 00
Church of Our Saviour: Sp. for Bishop Brooke, Oklahoma 25 00
Christ Church: Gen., $234.54; S. S., "Rev. Dr. Brooke" scholarship, St. John's University, Shanghai, $40; "Christ Church S. S." scholarship, St. John's School, Cape Mount, Africa, $25 .... 299 54
Grace (Avondale): Gen. 15 50
St. Mark's: Gen. 2 05
St. Peter's S. S.: Gen. 45 25
COLUMBUS—*Trinity Church*: Wo. Aux., Sp. for Bishop Kendrick, Arizona... 15 00
DAYTON—*Christ Church*: Gen. 174 21
GLENDALE—*Christ Church*: Dom. ... 61 83
MADISONVILLE—*Holy Trinity Church*: Gen. 4 24
MECHANICSBURG—*Church of Our Saviour*: Gen. 4 20

Southern Virginia
Ap. $455.75; *Sp.* $105.00
AUGUSTA Co. — *Emmanuel Church* (Staunton): Dom. and Frn........ 103 60
(Staunton): Stuart Hall, Missionary Society, "Patty Watkins" scholarship, Girls' Training Institute, Africa, $25; Brazil, $50; Sp. for Osuga Orphanage, Tokyo, $20; Sp. for Rev. J. C. Ambler, sewing machine for Girls' Industrial School, Tokyo, $25; Sp. for St. Margaret's School, Tokyo, $5............... 125 00
BATH Co.—*St. Luke's S. S.* (Hot Springs): Salary of Dr. Jefferys, St. Luke's Hospital, Shanghai........ 15 46
BUCKINGHAM Co.—*Emmanuel Church* (Glenmore): Dom., 60 cents; Frn., 59 cents 1 19
CAMPBELL Co.—*St. Paul's* (Lynchburg): $6, Circle of Wo. Aux., $16, Gen. 22 00
MECKLENBURG Co.—*St. Luke's*: Miss Ethel Tarry, Frn. 50 00
NORFOLK Co.—*Christ Church* (Norfolk): Gen. 178 50
St. Luke's (Norfolk): Woman's Guild, the birthday memorial gift for Miss Edmonia Lee Neilson, Gen......... 10 00
St. Paul's (Norfolk): Wo. Aux., Sp. for Rev. St. George Tucker, St. Paul's College Building Fund, Tokyo 5 00
Mrs. William C. Dickson (Norfolk), Sp. for Rev. B. L. Ancell, Yangchow, Shanghai 50 00

Springfield
Ap. $54.02; *Sp.* $5.00
ALTON—*St. Paul's*: Wo. Aux., Sp. for Miss Thackara, Arizona........... 5 00
BLOOMINGTON—*St. Matthew's*: Gen... 25 17
DANVILLE—*Holy Trinity Church*: In-

dian, $5.90; Colored, $10......... 15
EAST ST. LOUIS—*St. Paul's*: Gen..... 2
PARIS—*St. Andrew's*: Gen. 3
SALEM—*St. Thomas's*: Gen. 6

Tennessee
Ap. $133.17
BOLIVAR—*St. Katherine's School*: Junior Aux., Gen. 8
CHATTANOOGA—*Christ Church*: Wo. Aux., Gen. 10
St. Paul's: Wo. Aux. (of which Junior Aux., $5), Gen. 12
CLARKSVILLE—Wo. Aux., Gen. 7
FRANKLIN—Wo. Aux., Gen. 3
MEMPHIS—*St. Luke's*: Wo. Aux., Gen. 9
St. Mary's: Wo. Aux., Gen. 12
SEWANEE—Missionary Society, "Sewanee" scholarship, St. John's University, Shanghai, $40; Gen., $30.. 70

Texas
Ap. $159.25
HOUSTON—*Christ Church*: Wo. Aux., "Gertrude Aves" scholarship, Hooker Memorial School, Mexico.......... 60
NAVASOTA—*St. Paul's*: Gen. 5
PALESTINE—*St. Philip's*: Gen. 5
WACO—*St. Paul's*: Gen. 35
WHARTON—*St. Thomas's*: Gen. 4

Vermont
Ap. $203.06; *Sp.* $34.72
BETHEL—W. B. C. Stickney, Sp. for Zangzok Station Equipment Fund, Shanghai 5
CHESTER—*St. Luke's*: Gen. 10
CONCORD—*Mission*: Sp. for Rev. R. C. Wilson, Shanghai 2
ENOSBURG—*Christ Church*: Gen. 2
HARDWICK—*St. John the Baptist's*: Gen. 1
HYDEVILLE—*St. James's*: Gen. 2
POULTNEY—*St. John's*: Gen. 5
RANDOLPH—*Bethany*: Sp. for Zangzok Station Equipment Fund, Shanghai. 10
RICHFORD—*St. Anne's*: Gen. 11
RUTLAND — *Trinity Church*: China, $33.16; Gen., $12.11 45
ST. ALBANS—*St. Luke's S. S.*: Sp. for Bishop Restarick, Honolulu....... 15
ST. JOHNSBURY—*St. Andrew's S. S.*: Sp. for Rev. R. C. Wilson, Shanghai 2
MISCELLANEOUS—"A. H.," Gen. 125

Virginia
Ap. $554.49; *Sp.* $31.50
ALBEMARLE Co.—Isabella K. Smith (Cismont), Sp. for Mexico famine sufferers 5
ALEXANDRIA Co.—*Christ Church* (Alexandria): Dom. 34
"A Friend," Sp. for Church Extension Fund, Porto Rico 5
CLARKE Co.—*Grace* (Berryville): Wo. Aux., Sp. for Mexico famine sufferers 6
FAIRFAX Co.—*Emmanuel Church* (Theological Seminary): Fairfax Brazilian Missionary Society Brazil.... 125
GOOCHLAND Co.—*St. Mary's* (Subletts): Gen. 5
HANOVER Co. — *St. Martin's Parish* (Oliver): Dom., $4.31; Gen., $12.92 17
HENRICO Co. (Brook Hill)—In memoriam "L. W.," December 13th, Gen.. 30
Grace S. S. (Richmond): "Susie Morns" scholarship, St. Margaret's School, Tokyo 40
Holy Trinity Church (Richmond): Wo. Aux., Rev. Mr. Walke's work, Tokyo 15
St. James's (Richmond): Gen., $200; Sp. for Rev. E. J. Lee's church, Anking, Hankow, $10............. 210
J. S. Moore, Frn.................... 50

school for American boys at Baguio,
Philippine Islands................ 2 00
WORCESTER—*All Saints'*: Wo. Aux.,
Alaska Supply Fund.............. 25 00

Western Michigan
Ap. $68.50

COLDWATER—*St. Mark's*: Gen....... 60 00
GRAND RAPIDS—*St. Bede's*: Gen...... 1 50
KALAMAZOO—*Ascension*: Gen........ 1 00
MENDON—*St. Paul's*: Gen.......... 1 00
QUINCY—*St. John's*: Gen.......... 5 00

Western New York
Ap. $1,487.29; *Sp.* $170.00

BUFFALO—*St. John's*: Gen.......... 66 45
St. Mary's-on-the-Hill: Gen., $30;
Miss Hewson, Sp. for Tsu Building
Fund, Kyoto, $1; Mrs. G. G. Merrill,
Bishop Rowe's work, Alaska, $50;
Bishop Partridge's work, Kyoto,
Japan, $25..................... 106 00
Trinity Church: Gen.............. 27 44
GENEVA—*Trinity Church*: "A Friend
of the Laymen's Missionary Move-
ment," Gen., $1,000; Wo. Aux., "A
Member," Sp. for Bishop Aves for
famine sufferers, Mexico, $10...... 1,010 00
MEDINA—*St. John's*: Dom.......... 8 90
PALMYRA—"A Friend," Gen., $5; Sp.
for St. Margaret's School, Tokyo, $3 8 00
PHELPS—*St. John's S. S.*: Sp. for
Archdeacon Swan, Oklahoma...... 30 00
RIPLEY—*Trinity Church*: Gen....... 1 00
WESTFIELD—*St. Peter's*: Gen., $3.50;
"A Member of the Missionary So-
ciety," Sp. for Building Fund, St.
Margaret's School, Tokyo, $1...... 4 50
MISCELLANEOUS—Wo. Aux., Philip-
pines, $50; St. Paul's School, Law-
renceville, Southern Virginia, $50;
Cape Mount, $50; Training-school
for Bible-women, Shanghai, $50;
Sp. for Bishop Graves life insurance,
$50; Miss J. C. Smith, "Bishop
Clarkson" scholarship, Girls' Train-
ing Institute, West Africa, $25...... 275 00
Junior Aux., Alaska, $25; "Helen
M. Halsey" scholarship, Girls'
Training Institute, St. Paul's River,
West Africa.................... 45 00
Girls' Friendly Society Memorial
Fund, Sp. for House of Bethany,
Cape Mount, Africa, in recognition
of Miss Seaman's work there...... 75 00

West Texas
Ap. $12.90

CORPUS CHRISTI—*Church of the Good
Shepherd*: Gen.................. 2 40
LLANO—*Grace*: Gen.............. 5 00
SAN SABA—*St. Luke's*: Gen......... 5 50

West Virginia
Ap. $306.01

CHARLES TOWN—*Zion*: Gen......... 127 84
MOOREFIELD — *Emmanuel Church*:
Dom. and Frn................. 10 00
MORGANTOWN—*Trinity Church*: Gen.. 39 00
NEW MARTINSVILLE—*St. Ann's*: Dom. 4 00
PARKERSBURG—*Church of the Good
Shepherd*: Gen................. 50 00
RACINE—*Brookside*: Gen.......... 2 00
SPRUCE RUN—*Mission*: Gen........ 3 25
UNION—*All Saints'*: Dom.......... 5 34
WESTON—*St. Paul's*: Gen.......... 14 08
MISCELLANEOUS — Right Rev. George
W. Peterkin, D.D., "West Virginia"
scholarship, St. John's School,
Africa 50 00
Missionary League, Gen............ 50

Missionary Districts

Alaska
Ap. $18.50
ALLACHAKET — *St. John's-in-the-Wilderness*: Junior Aux., Gen 1 75
ANVIK—*Christ Church*: Wo. Aux., Gen. 1 75
MISCELLANEOUS—South Eastern Archdeaconry, Gen 15 00

Asheville
Ap. $149.06
ARDEN—*Christ Church School*: Dom., $33; Frn., $33; Gen., $34   25
BEAVER CREEK—*St. Mary's*: Dom., $33; Frn., $33; Gen., $34 ....   100 00
BILTMORE—*All Souls'*: Dom. 100 00
BREVARD—*St. Phillip's*: Indian 7 00
CASHIERS—*Church of the Good Shepherd*: Dom.   75
CHUNN'S COVE—*St. Luke's*: Dom.   50
FOSCOE—*Easter Chapel*: Dom   25
FRANKLIN—*St. Agnes's*: Gen 1 50
St. Cyprian's: Gen   50
GLEN ALPINE—*St. Paul's*: Dom 1 50
GLENDALE SPRINGS — *Holy Trinity Church*: Dom   25
GREEN RIVER—*St. Joseph's*: Dom   50
St. Andrew's: Dom.   50
GRACE—*Grace*: Gen 4 50
HICKORY—*Ascension*: Dom., $2; Frn., $2; Gen., $2 ....   6 00
HIGHLANDS—*Incarnation*: Dom. 1 50
LINCOLNTON—*St. Luke's*: Dom., $4.46; Frn., $1; Gen., $2 ....   7 46
St. Cyprian's: Dom.   50
LENOIR—*St. James's*: Dom., $2; Frn., $2; Gen., $2 ....   6 00
Chapel of Peace: Dom   25
LINCOLN CO.—*Church of Our Saviour*: Dom.   25
St. Paul's: Dom   25
St. Stephen's: Dom.   25
MORGANTON—*Grace*: Gen 1 85
St. George's: Dom.   50
St. Mary's: Gen   50
St. Michael's: Dom.   50
PRENTISS—*St. George's*: Dom., 13 cts.; Frn., 12 cts   25
RONDA—*All Saints'*: Gen.   25
SHELBY—*Church of the Redeemer*: Dom.   25
SLAGLE—*Ascension*: Dom., 13 cts.; Frn., 12 cts   25
SPRINGDALE—*St. Mark's*: Dom.   25
TODD—*St. Matthew's*: Dom., 25 cts.; Frn., 25 cts   50
VALLE CRUCIS—*Holy Cross*: Dom 1 00
WILKESBORO—*St. Paul's*: Gen.   50
YADKIN VALLEY—*Chapel of Rest*: Dom. 1 00

Eastern Oregon
Ap. $24.41
PENDLETON—*Church of the Redeemer*: Gen. 24 41

Idaho
Ap. $36.20
BONNERS FERRY—Gen. 6 00
GRANGEVILLE—*Trinity Church*: Gen...   5 50
NAMPA—*Grace*: $4, S. S.,* $15, Gen...   19 00
SANDPOINT—Gen. 5 70

Kearney
Ap. $9.35
HASTINGS—*St. Mark's*: Dom. 9 35

New Mexico
Ap. $4.35
SILVER CITY—*Church of the Good Shepherd*: Gen. 4 35

Oklahoma
Ap. $5.00
GUTHRIE—*Trinity Church*: Gen. 5 00

Olympia
Sp. $56.75
BREMERTON—*St. Paul's*: Wo. Aux., Sp. for Bishop Spalding's work, Provo, Utah ....
CHEHALIS—*Epiphany*: Wo. Aux., Sp. for Bishop Spalding's work, Provo, Utah ..
KENT—*St. James's*: Sp. for Utah....
SEATTLE—*St. Clement's*: Sp. for Utah
St. Mark's: Sp. for Bishop Spalding's work, Provo, Utah...............
TACOMA—*Holy Communion*: Sp. for Utah ....
Trinity Church: George Lawler, Sp. for Utah ....

Porto Rico
Ap. $34.55
MAYAGUEZ—*St. Andrew's*: Gen.......
PONCE—*Holy Trinity Church*: Gen...

Sacramento
Ap. $10.00; *Sp.* $34.45
CHICO—Ernest R. Armstrong, Gen....
SACRAMENTO—Union Missionary Meeting at St. Paul's Church, Sp. for Bishop Rowe, Alaska ....
WOODLAND—*St. Luke's*: $9.45, Mrs. Holt, $1.50, Sp. for Utah...........

Salina
Ap. $60.00; *Sp.* $9.07
BELOIT—*St. Paul's*: Wo. Aux., Gen. (of which Babies' Branch, $1), $6.88; Babies' Branch, Sp. for missionary font, 25 cents; Sp. for St. Mary's-on-the-Mount, Sewanee, Tennessee, 59 cents...............
BENNINGTON — *Transfiguration*: Wo. Aux., Gen. ....
FORMOSO—*Trinity Church*: Wo. Aux., Gen. (of which Babies' Branch, $3.35), $7.51; Junior Aux., Sp. for St. Mary's-on-the-Mount, Sewanee, Tennessee (of which Babies' Branch, $1), $5; Babies' Branch, Sp. for missionary font, 25 cents.........
KINGMAN—*Christ Church*: Wo. Aux., Gen. ....
MINNEAPOLIS—*St. Peter's*: Wo. Aux., Gen. ....
SALINA—*Christ Cathedral*: Gen. (of which Babies' Branch, $5.65), $15.53; Babies' Branch, Sp. for St. Mary's-on-the-Mount, Sewanee, Tennessee, $2.48; Sp. for missionary font, 50 cents ....
WAKEENY—*Heavenly Rest*: Wo. Aux., Gen. ....
MISCELLANEOUS—Wo. Aux., Gen. ....

South Dakota
Sp. $18.70
BROOKINGS—"A Friend," Sp. for sufferers in Mexico ....
SIOUX FALLS—*All Saints' School*: Sp. for sufferers in Mexico ....

Southern Florida
Sp. $40.00
OCALA—*Grace*: Sp. for Tsu Building Fund, Kyoto ....
ORLANDO—General A. B. Carey, Sp. for Bishop Whipple Memorial, Havana, Cuba ....

Spokane
Sp. $5.00
SPOKANE—*All Saints'*: Wo. Aux., "A Member," Sp. for Bishop Aves's work, Mexico ....

Philippine Islands
Ap. $45.39
MANILA—*St. Mary and St. John*: Gen.

Utah

Ap. $138.61; *Sp.* $22.70

OGDEN—*Church of the Good Shepherd*:
Sp. for Alaska 22 70
PARK CITY—*St. Luke's*: Gen........ 10 00
SALT LAKE CITY—Rowland Hall,* Gen. 123 61

Wyoming

Ap. $6.75

ENCAMPMENT—*St. James's*: Gen. ... 1 60
ROCK SPRINGS — *Holy Communion*:
Dom. 2 00
WIND RIVER—*Church of the Redeemer*:
Dom. 3 15

Foreign Missionary Districts

Ontario

Ap. $2.00

DELHI—A. W. Crysler, Sp. for Guaniguanico Chapel, Cuba 2 00

Brazil

Ap. $50.00

Wo. Aux., Africa 50 00

Haiti

Ap. $5.00

PORT-AU-PRINCE—*Holy Trinity Church*:
Children's Club, Frn............... 5 00

Miscellaneous

Interest — Dom., $1,960.38; Frn.,
$1,553.06; Gen., $3,749.88; Sp.,
$429.55; Specific Dep., $21.04..... 7,713 91

United Offering, Wo. Aux., 1907, on
account of appropriations to Septem-
ber 1st, 1910, Dom., $3,500; Frn.,
$3,500 .... 7,000 00
Through Miss Coles, Sp. for St.
Paul's College Building Fund, Tokyo 1,000 00
Guild of St. Barnabas's, Miss Bol-
ster's salary, Alaska.............. 400 00
Through Rev. E. H. Edson, Sp. for
balance of Leper Fund, Porto Rico.. 125 00
League for Eastern Oregon, Sp. for
Bishop Paddock, Eastern Oregon.. 50 00
Through Rev. A. A. Gilman, Sp.
for Changsha, Hankow 42 41
Mite-chest No. 29,405, Dom., $8.40;
Family Missionary Box No. 5,726,
Frn., $11.60 .... 20 00
A. C. Scott, Sp. for Bishop Rowe,
Alaska 5 00
Miss Gertrude Gennison, Sp. for
Zangzok Station Equipment Fund,
Shanghai 1 50

Legacies

BROOKLYN, L. I.—Estate of Harkort
Napier 100 00
OWATONNA, MINN.—Estate of James
Dean 75 00
PHILADELPHIA, PENN.—Estate of Miss
Frances J. O'Connor.............. 95 25
PRINCE GEORGE Co., WASH.—Estate of
Benjamin O. Lowndes, balance of
Thompson note, $300; Interest on
note, $61.95 .... 361 95

Receipts for the month.......... $160,628 31
Amount previously acknowledged.. 162,141 73

Total since September 1st........ $322,770 04

SUMMARY OF RECEIPTS

Receipts divided according to purposes to which they are to be applied	Received during December	Amounts previously Acknowledged	Total
1. Applicable upon the appropriations of the Board.	$ 43,468 89	$73,597 04	$117,065 93
2. Special gifts forwarded to objects named by donors in addition to the appropriations of the Board.	16,506 18	37,401 68	53,907 86
3. Legacies, the disposition of which is to be determined by the Board at the end of the fiscal year.	632 20	51,093 56	51,725 76
4. Specific Deposit.............................	100,021 04	49 45	100,070 49
Total......................	$160,628 31	$162,141 73	$322,770 04

OFFERINGS TO PAY APPROPRIATIONS

Total receipts from September 1st, 1909, to January 1st, 1910, applicable upon the appropriations, divided according to the sources from which they have come, and compared with the corresponding period of the preceding year. Legacies are not included in the following items, as their
disposition is not determined by the Board until the end of the fiscal year.

Source	To Jan. 1, 1910	To Jan. 1, 1909	Increase	Decrease
1. From congregations......................	$41,189 97	$38,786 66	$ 2,403 31	$.......
2. From individuals......................	13,224 77	21,744 80	....	8,520 03
3. From Sunday-schools..................	2,167 42	3,202 35	....	1,034 93
4. From Woman's Auxiliary..............	9,923 47	15,080 04	....	5,156 57
5. Woman's Auxiliary United Offering......	28,000 00	12,000 00	16,000 00	....
6. From Interest........................	21,976 63	18,876 61	3,100 02	....
7. Miscellaneous items..................	583 67	2,259 55	....	1,675 88
Total	$117,065 93	$111,950 01	$5,115 92	

APPROPRIATIONS FOR THE YEAR

SEPTEMBER 1st, 1909, TO AUGUST 31st, 1910,
Amount Needed for the Year

1. To pay appropriations as made to date for the work at home and abroad....... $1,188,522 50
2. To replace Reserve Funds temporarily used for the current work............. 32,955 33

Total... $1,221,477 83
Total receipts to date applicable on appropriations............. 117,065 93

Amount needed before August 31st, 1910........................... $1,104,411 90

THE

Spirit of Missions

AN ILLUSTRATED MONTHLY REVIEW
OF CHRISTIAN MISSIONS

March, 1910

CONTENTS

The Subscription Price of THE SPIRIT OF MISSIONS is ONE DOLLAR per year. Postage is prepaid in the United States, Porto Rico, the Philippines and Mexico. For other countries in the Postal Union, including Canada, twenty-four cents per year should be added.

Subscriptions are continued until ordered discontinued.

Change of Address : In all changes of address it is necessary that the old as well as the new address should be given.

How to Remit: Remittances, made payable to George Gordon King, Treasurer, should be made by draft on New York, Postal Order or Express Order. One and two cent stamps are received. To checks on local banks ten cents should be added for collection.

All Letters should be addressed to The Spirit of Missions, 281 Fourth Avenue, New York.

Published by the Domestic and Foreign Missionary Society.

President, RIGHT REVEREND DANIEL S. TUTTLE, D.D. *Secretary*, ——— ———
Treasurer, GEORGE GORDON KING.

Entered at the Post Office, in New York, as second-class matter.

THE SPIRIT OF MISSIONS is regularly on sale
In Philadelphia: By George W. Jacobs & Co., 1216 Walnut St.
In Milwaukee: By The Young Churchman Co., 412 Milwaukee St.
In Boston: By Smith & McCance, 38 Bromfield St.
In Elizabeth, N. J.: By Franklin H. Spencer, 743 Jefferson St.

ELLIOT H. THOMSON, D.D.,
ARCHDEACON OF SHANGHAI

Archdeacon Thomson is the Nestor of the China Mission, having recently completed fifty years of continuous service. For an account of the commemoration of this event see page 197

THE SPIRIT OF MISSIONS

AN ILLUSTRATED MONTHLY REVIEW
OF CHRISTIAN MISSIONS

Vol. LXXXV. **March,** 1910 No. 3

THE PROGRESS OF THE KINGDOM

ON January 31st John Marston was
called to his eternal rest and reward. Few of our readers will realize
the significance of
John Marston, this announcement.
Founder Though intimately
familiar with the
great enterprise which Mr. Marston was
instrumental in launching, they have
probably never heard of the man himself. Such is fame!

Mr. John Marston was for many years
a faithful layman of the parish of Lower
Merion, Pennsylvania. He was also a
working layman. As superintendent of
the Sunday-school he rendered efficient
and long-continued service. Back of this
service rendered to the parish there lay,
as the mainspring of his life and character, an abiding and intelligent interest
in the great Mission of the Church.
Moved by this, at the opening of Lent,
1877, he proposed to the pupils of his
school that they by their Lenten self-de-
nials should raise an offering for the
general mission work of the Church.
Eagerly they followed his lead, with the
result that at Easter time they had
gathered and were able to offer the sum
of $200—no mean offering even for these
days, and a very large one at that time.
Not long after this Mr. Marston, in con-

versation with his old-time and valued
friend, Mr. George C. Thomas, told of
the achievement of his Sunday-school.
Instantly the thought came to Mr.
Thomas's mind and sprang to his lips,
"Why not ask all the children of the
Church to join in this enterprise?" Together they considered details, and the
following Lent saw the inauguration of
the first Children's Lenten Offering,
which reached the sum of $7,000.
Thirty-one years after—in 1909—it was
$147,252.91, and the total gifts during
these years have aggregated $2,150,-
453.88. Thus did the intelligent statesmanship of these two devoted men bear
fruit for the increase of the Kingdom.

It is striking that just now as the Sunday-schools are preparing for their
thirty-second annual offering as a memorial to Mr. Thomas, there should come
the news that this man who furnished
the initial impulse of the movement and
co-operated with him in the work, has
also been called to his rest and reward.
Should we not feel then that this Lenten
Offering which is now being gathered
will be a memorial to both these good
men, who, since last Easter, have finished
their work in the Church on earth and
gone up higher?

(173)

GREAT as were the perils which St. Paul enumerates as falling to his lot while he preached the Gospel along the shores of **"In Perils in the** the Mediterranean, **Wilderness"** there are hardships endured by the devoted missionaries of to-day which deserve to rank with his.

From the shore of the Arctic Ocean comes a story of heroic perseverance and self-forgetting service which it is good for us to hear. Already something of the tale has been told, but it is from the *Dawson Daily News,* now some weeks old, that we read, in the realistic and virile phraseology of the Alaskan editor, how Bishop Stringer, of the English diocese of the Mackenzie River, and his travelling companion, the Rev. Charles F. Johnson, fought their way through a desolate waste and over the mountains of the Great Divide, in the attempt to pass from the basin of the Mackenzie River to the headwaters of the Porcupine, which empties into the Yukon. They almost reached their goal, only to be thwarted by unexpected obstacles, compelled to abandon their equipment, and driven back upon their tracks, forced to return to their starting-point with their very lives as the forfeit in case of failure.

Moccasins as Food — In one sense the experience was scarcely unique. Such things are counted as a possible part of the day's work by men like Bishop Stringer, Bishop Rowe and their missionaries. It is startling to us only because it makes us realize the possibilities which are always present. The gaunt wolf, hunger, which dogs the steps of every Arctic traveller, came into the open and showed his teeth. When they turned back on what proved to be a twenty-seven days' tramp they had food sufficient for three days. A few ptarmigan and squirrels, killed on the journey, helped to eke this out. The last few days they kept alive by eating their

The appropriations, demanded by the growing work, have doubled during the nine years. To meet these there has, of course, been increased giving. The offerings of congregations in payment on apportionment have increased 225 per cent., although they still lack $103,000 of meeting the full apportionment. Individual contributions show only a slight increase—less than 10 per cent. The Sunday-school offerings have increased 44 per cent., and the income from investments 90 per cent. The Woman's Auxiliary offerings have increased 145 per cent., or, counting the United Offering as used year by year, 195 per cent.

These figures show a great gain for the congregations, but the record of individual gifts is unsatisfactory. It would seem that those men of larger means who ought to be giving for the Church's Mission far more than it would be necessary or wise for them to give through the congregational offering, have not, during the last nine years, been making increased individual gifts. Better things are hoped as a result of the Laymen's Missionary Movement, but the definite results have not yet been felt by the Board treasury.

But the work of the women is cause for rejoicing. Their increase has been steady in its growth and magnificent in its aggregate. Had the whole Church made a like record, we should never have heard the word "deficit," and we should also be doing much good work which now goes undone.

The United Offering   There is one phase of the Auxiliary's giving upon which a further comment would be timely. It is the "United Offering." This is the special gift gathered during each triennium, in addition to all apportionments and pledges, and offered at the great Eucharistic service of the Auxiliary held at the opening of each General Convention. The growth in this offering has

been phenomenal. Beginning in 1886 in Chicago with an offering of $82.71, it reached in Richmond, three years ago, the sum of $224,251.55.

For some time this offering—or the greater part of it—has most fittingly been devoted to the training, support and care of women, at home and abroad, and it has made possible an expansion and prosecution of work by and for women which could not have been achieved in any other way. With such a fund actually in hand to cover a period of three years in advance, wise plans can be made and timely help given with definiteness and certainty. The Board has had no better or more acceptable aid than that given by the United Offering.

The growth and expansion of the work contemplated by the Offering is the most convincing proof of its value, and about this the facts ought to be known. So readily did women offer for service during the three years now drawing to a close, and so eager were the bishops to secure these helpers, that at the end of the second year after the presentation the entire sum available had been appropriated. During this fiscal year, therefore, that is, since last September—it has not been possible to place any new women workers in the field as missionaries under the United Offering. What few additional appointments were made had to be cared for from the general fund—always inadequate to the need, usually carrying a deficit; and therefore almost compelled, as a foregone conclusion, to acknowledge its inability to provide for expanding work.

This it is, then, to which we would direct the attention of the women of the Church. The next six months will decide what shall be the amount of the next United Offering. Noble as was the total of the last one, the response to its call was nobler, and the provision proved inadequate to supply the need. It seems certain that the offering of lives will be greatly increased during the coming triennium. The missionary impetus which is sweeping over the country is

awakening a sense of vocation in many
souls; and the work of our special student secretaries is contributing largely
toward the same result. If the women of
the Church desire adequately to supplement by their gifts the offering which so
many are making—and will make—of
their lives, it behooves them to work
and pray and give most earnestly for the
United Offering which is to be presented
in Cincinnati next October.

FREQUENT requests have come to us
that the "Sanctuary of Missions"
might be published separately in leaflet
form, and thus be
Prayer for   more convenient for
Missions   the use of those who
practise missionary
intercession. Desirable as it certainly is
to stimulate this practice among Church
people, a practical and efficient method
has not hitherto been proposed, and it
seemed undesirable to make the attempt
at all unless it could be done in the best
possible way.

Happily we are now relieved from the
consideration of the problem, as it has
been taken up by experts who are better
able to handle it than the staff at the
Missions House could possibly be. The
Order of the Holy Cross has undertaken
the formation of "The Church Prayer
League." It has issued a "Call to
Prayer," outlining the general plan of
the League, and proposes to publish a
quarterly leaflet containing subjects for
thanksgivings and intercessions. Its
purpose, as outlined in the preliminary
call, "will be both to rouse and inspire
the spirit of prayer, and also to suggest
definite objects for which prayer may be
offered. These objects will be connected
with the missionary work of the
Church, as it is presented in the three
numbers of THE SPIRIT OF MISSIONS immediately preceding the issue of the
quarterly, and will be arranged for daily
intercession. A list of books on prayer
will be published in each issue of the
leaflet."

We have just received the first quar-

THE SANCTUARY OF MISSIONS

SAVIOUR, sprinkle many nations;
Fruitful let Thy sorrows be;
By Thy pains and consolations
Draw the Gentiles unto Thee!

Of Thy cross the wondrous story,
Be it to the nations told;
Let them see Thee in Thy glory
And Thy mercy manifold.

"AND I, if I be lifted up from
the earth, will draw all men
unto me."

THANKSGIVINGS

"We thank Thee"—
For the growing power of the
Holy Cross, and the victory which
it promises.
For the increased gifts during the
last nine years toward the extension
of Thy Kingdom. (Page 175.)
That Thou art opening the doors
of the nations and summoning the
forces of Thy Truth to take their
part in the conquest of the world for
Thy Christ. (Page 184.)
For the good example of the life
of Thy faithful servant who, through
fifty years, has borne witness to
Thee in China. (Page 197.)
For the continued success of the
movement which is rousing the laymen to take their place in the
Church's missionary campaign.
(Page 215.)

INTERCESSIONS

"That it may please Thee"—
"That by Thy Cross and Passion
we may be brought unto the glory
of Thy Resurrection."
To teach us how by our prayers,
as well as our gifts, we may become
true helpers in the mission work of
Thy Church. (Page 176.)
To make great the gifts of Thy
servants the women of the Church,
which shall enable other women to
devote their lives to Thy service.
To bless the prayers and gifts of
Thy children who, during this holy
season, are laboring for the extension of Thy Kingdom.
To prosper the efforts of Thy servants who are conducting the mission of this Church in the Republic
of Brazil. (Page 191.)

To cheer the hearts of Thy servants who in the scattered places of
this land seek out the children of
Thy Church. (Pages 198 and 200.)
That Thy Church may realize
more fully and discharge more
faithfully her duty toward the
Negroes of our land. (Page 204.)

PRAYERS

FOR LENT

O LOVING CHRIST, Who by the
pathway of Thy Cross didst
make a way for the ransomed to
pass over the chasm of death and
enter the gateway of eternal life;
deepen in us this Lent the desire to
make all men know the wonder of
this Thy so great salvation, Who
art with the Father and the Holy
Ghost one God, world without end.
Amen.

FOR WISDOM

GRANT, O Lord, that all who
contend for the faith may
never injure it by clamor and im-
patience; but speaking Thy Truth in
love may cause it to be loved, that
men may see in it Thy goodness and
Thy beauty, through Jesus Christ
our Lord.
—*Bright (adapted).*

FOR WORK AMONG THE NEGROES

ALMIGHTY and Eternal God,
whose love and care extend
to all Thy creation; Bless, we pray
Thee, the work of the Church
among the Negro people in this our
land. Prosper every effort to supply their moral and spiritual needs.
Help them to grow in the habits of
industry, self-reliance and faithfulness. Through the power of Thy
Holy Spirit grant that they may become lovers of purity, honesty and
truthfulness. Raise up native ministers to lead them in paths of
righteousness, soberness and godliness. Send down Thy blessing
upon all bishops, clergy and teachers
working for the welfare of this
needy race; strengthen them in
every temptation; comfort them in
every discouragement. All this we
ask through Jesus Christ our Lord.
Amen.

DEACONESS CARTER AND TWO KOBUK GIRLS

THE BOYS AT ST. JOHN'S-IN-THE-
WILDERNESS

By Archdeacon Stuck

OST tourists who visit Alaska and go back to their homes and talk about it forever after, are like a man who should make a voyage from England or France across the Atlantic to Newfoundland, and then sail along the coast to Sandy Hook, and go right back to England or France and tell people that he had been to America. It would be perfectly true, but it would be only a tiny little truth. The whole great continent of America would be left out. So when a man has gone to Ketchikan, or Juneau, or Skagway, or even has done the most that ninety-nine out of an hundred visitors to Alaska do—has taken the White Pass Railway to the summit and back again—he has only wiped his feet on the mat and crossed the threshold of the outer gateway, so to speak, with all the many mansions of the vast interior unseen, unknown, unguessed-at—unless he be much more familiar with maps than most tourists seem to be.

At Ketchikan, which is the first point on the Alaskan coast which the tourist touches, it is as far to St. John's-in-the-Wilderness as it is from Sandy Hook to the Pacific Ocean. It is as far, that is, in miles, and many times farther in time, for with the exception of the little hundred-and-twenty-mile railway over the White Pass, there are no railways that will serve to quicken the journey at all. It must be made by water, by one steamboat and then another, lying over here and lying over there, with a once-a-month schedule for the last five hundred miles of the journey, and no certainty as to that within a week or two. When a man travels in the States he says: "I will be in New York on such a day and in Chicago at noon on another day, and at St. Louis at fifteen minutes past three the day after." But in the interior of

ALLAKAKET AT HIGH NOON NOVEMBER 14TH

*The sun may be seen barely above the horizon. The day will
perhaps be two hours long. The children of the mission
were crossing the frozen river and Bishop Rowe
took their photograph*

Alaska a man says: "I will get to
Tanana (or Fairbanks, or Anvik, or
wherever it is) as early in July as I
can." And if he doesn't get there till the
fifteenth or the twentieth we do not consider that he is unpunctual and make remarks about his business habits. And
we don't give him up even by the first of
August.

Every schoolboy knows that the great
river of Alaska is the Yukon, but only a
few learned geographers in the States—
or "outside" as we insiders call it—
know anything about the tributaries of
the Yukon. For this great Yukon River
has many large and fine tributaries that
drain enormous areas of country and
have native peoples living on their banks
sometimes far up to their head waters.
The mission of St. John's-in-the-Wilderness is on one of those tributaries. It
comes in from the north, and is 750
miles long, I suppose, though I do not
think that anyone has ever measured it.

It is called the Koyukuk River, with the
accent on the first syllable. Properly, it
is pronounced exactly as it is spelled, but
most white men call it Ky-uk-uk. It is
the Yukon's most important northerly
tributary.

So you come over the White Pass Railway to Whitehorse; there you take your
first steamboat and go to Dawson. At
Dawson you change and wait, and by-
and-by you get another steamer which
will take you as far as Tanana. Here
you may have to change and wait again,
and by-and-by you catch another
steamer which takes you as far as Nu-
lato. Here you may have to wait a long
time. It is not a wildly exciting place to
wait, and the mosquitoes are at least as
bad as they are anywhere else in Alaska.
In the fulness of time there comes along
a small steamboat which will take you
450 miles up the Koyukuk River to the
Allakaket, at which point is situated the
mission of St. John's-in-the-Wilderness.

The choir-boys, Deaconess Carter and Miss Heintz

If it has taken us a long time to get there, that will help to impress, upon our minds what a long way off it is. Miss Carter and Miss Heintz will welcome us, anyway, for they do not get many visitors in the course of a year. They are the only white people on the place or anywhere near the place. Ten miles away there is a white man who keeps a little trading post, but with the exception of that man the nearest white people are at Bettles, seventy-five miles away, and there is only a handful of them there. So Miss Carter and Miss Heintz are quite alone with their natives, to their entire satisfaction and delight. It means that there are no evil influences at work to counteract the good which the mission tries to do. It means that these simple, child-like people are not constantly tempted to wickedness by low-down white men. It means there is no whiskey peddled. It means everything that makes for successful work. I think if a lot of white people were to come near the mission and start a town, Miss Carter would want to gather up her natives and go off somewhere else with them.

A pretty place, the Allakaket is. The mission buildings are all of logs with the bark on. Even the window and door

frames are covered up with bark. When you look at the church you see nothing whatever but rough spruce bark, except the gilded cross on the top of the belfry, which shines and glistens all the more for the contrast. The dwelling-house is all of logs too, but the door and window frames are painted red. All around rise tall, slender spruce trees, which for eight months in the year carry a burden of snow. In front flows the Koyukuk River (when it is not frozen), and on the opposite bank comes in another river, the Alatna. To the left are high sand bluffs, always crumbling down to the water, and in the far distance there rises the Young Eagle Mountain, on the lofty summit of which the snow rests for all the year save a few weeks.

St. John's-in-the-Wilderness is the only mission in Alaska where there are two distinct and separate kinds of natives. Just above the mission is a village of Koyukuks, or Indians. Just round the bend of the river is another village, of Kobuks, or Eskimo, and the mission serves both races without distinction. But because of the two races and the two languages, it is necessary to conduct all services in English. If the service were in Indian, half the con-

THE MISSION BUILDINGS

gregation would not understand it. If the service were in Eskimo, the other half would not understand it. "So you hold service in English which none of them understand," said a man to whom I was explaining the situation. But that is not so. With great pains and care the simple unchanging parts of the service have been taught the people and explained to them. Every hymn that is sung (and they are great singers) is learned by heart, with the most constant explaining of the words by interpreters. And all the preaching and speaking to the natives is done at the mouths of two interpreters, who put it, sentence by sentence, first into Indian and then into Eskimo. A twenty-minute sermon takes an hour to deliver in that church. If some men I know were to preach in that church the folks would not get their dinner till supper-time.

I want to speak about some of the boys. Of course there are girls there too, but it is particularly about the half-dozen boys who form the vested choir that this paper is written. Four of them are Eskimo and two are Indian. The cassocks and surplices they wear are not very elaborate, for Miss Heintz made the former out of black dress lining and the latter out of cotton sheeting, I think—though it might have been gunny sacks

or anything else for that matter, for Miss Heintz has a wonderful way of making anything she pleases out of anything she has. If it is the wrong color she dyes or bleaches it until it is the right color, and if it is the utterly wrong material she pulls it all to pieces and transforms its fundamental constituents in some marvellous super-masculine way and makes it all over again until it looks like the right material. I can't explain it any better, but there are some women who have that gift, you know. Anyway, the boys look so smoothly and pronouncedly black and white when they are vested that it is difficult to get a photograph of them. They march very solemnly in procession and they lift up their voices very heartily and they pronounce very distinctly. I know a great many white choir boys who do not sing any better and who do not behave half as well. They have choir practice every day and they take the greatest interest in it, and they learn very rapidly. When I think of those little choir boys at the Allakaket, as compared with choir boys "outside" I am reminded of Kipling's "Men" that fought at Minden":

"For fatigue it was their pride,
And they would *not* be denied
To clean the cook-house floor."

(181)

A Kobuk and a Koyukuk lad

I feel disposed to hold up those little chaps, ten miles north of the Arctic Circle, in their remote and lonely mission, dressed in ragged skins and eating dried fish and glad to get it (there was great scarcity this spring) as examples to more favored youth of *esprit de corps*, and whole-souled, enthusiastic service.

Oh! they are not angels. I have my opinion of boy angels, Caucasian or Eskimo. They are very human indeed, full of fun, and up to all sorts of pranks, and bubbling over with animal spirits. If you saw them throw themselves head first from the river bank into the drifted snow beneath, if you saw them roll themselves up in balls and go head-over-heels and heels-over-head down the toboggan-slide where we haul the sleds up, if you saw them playing football for hours and hours on the frozen river with a ball made of moosehide stuffed with moose hair, you would know that they are just healthy, hearty boys. How they do love the snow! How they roll in it, and bury themselves in it, and wallow in it, and come up with the blood flushing rich beneath their dark skins! What a kind, soft, clean, dry, friendly sort of cushioning for the hard earth the snow makes for eight months of the year!

And what a pleasure it is to teach these boys! I spent six weeks there this spring, waiting for the break-up. And I did thoroughly enjoy teaching them.

KOBUK MOTHER AND CHILD (Eskimo)

boys and girls—are learning the great simple truths of Christianity. That this is God's world and not an hundred devils' world; that God is our Father and loves us; that the Lord Jesus came down from heaven to redeem us and to show us once for all how we should live; that no one, medicine man or witch or shaman, ghost or demon or familiar spirit, can hurt a hair of our heads if we put our clear trust in God and bid Satan and all his works get behind us. It makes all things take another color, it makes the whole life look different, when once these truths are taken into the heart.

More and more we are coming to realize in Alaska that the only chance the native peoples of this country have for survival in the face of the great irruption of white barbarians who have no fear of God or man before their eyes; who will trample these folk into the mire to gratify their greed; who rejoice in

teaching them wickedness and in offsetting any efforts for their elevation, is in training them betimes to resist temptation.

Here at the Allakaket the stress of the danger has not come as it has on the Yukon, but it will come by and by. The white man is increasing in numbers all over the country, is stretching out his hand little by little over all the tributary rivers. And right along with the decent, hard-working miner comes the dissolute riff-raff, the off-scouring of our civilization, lewd, drunken, foul-mouthed. Hundreds and hundreds of the Yukon Indians have fallen prey to him already. The fight on the Yukon now is to save a remnant for a new and better generation. But on the tributary streams, where as yet the influx of white men has not been great, the chances for the native are much better and brighter. It nerves one to greater efforts at the Allakaket to think that the careful instruction of one boy or one girl now may mean a whole family saved by and by. And the prayer that goes with our efforts is the prayer that they may be able to "withstand in the evil day, and having done all, to stand." As we look at it the goal of our work is nothing less than the survival of the natives of Alaska.

GEORGE, THE WATER CARRIER
In this way all the water has to be brought from a hole in the ice of the river

THE IMPENDING CONFLICT IN WESTERN ASIA

By Samuel M. Zwemer, F.R.G.S.

WHEN Mohammed taught that among the greater signs of the last days would be the rising of the sun in the West, he was a true prophet. It has risen. From the farthest western province of the Caliphate came the first proclamation of the new era and the dawn of liberty for all western Asia. We are still rubbing our eyes with wonder and amazement. More surprising and sudden than the transformation of Aladdin's lamp have been the stupendous changes wrought by the hand of God. Despotism has been displaced by constitutional government, censorship by free press, espionage by free speech, a grinding system of passports and permits by free travel and intercourse; the banishment of thousands into exile has been followed by general amnesty; instead of universal political corruption there is the proclamation of a new era of justice. The great army of spies, numbering 40,000, and costing £2,000,000 a year, has been abolished, and the peoples of Turkey and Persia, blindfolded, gagged and manacled for centuries, are almost delirious with newfound liberty. Abdul Hamid, the assassin, is a prisoner at Salonica and constitutional parliaments are sitting at Constantinople and Teheran; the Damascus railroad has reached Medina, and electric light is burning over the prophet's tomb.

Turkey, Persia and Arabia, the three great Moslem lands of the nearer East, have experienced greater industrial, intellectual, social and religious changes within the past four years than befell them in the past four centuries. This awakening of western Asia is no less a challenge than is the call of the Far East with its unprecedented opportunities. The impending struggle between the Cross and the Crescent for supremacy in western Asia is as full of grave possibilities as is the Moslem menace in Africa, while, if we consider the overwhelming influence which western Asia has always exercised throughout the Dark Continent, and its strategic position and power in the Moslem world, we cannot help feeling that here is the centre where the forces are assembling for the final conflict. Although the wisest missionaries and Christian statesmen are agreed that nothing in Turkey or Persia is yet ended or settled, something has begun in those lands which all eyes are strained to understand. The importance of the battlefield, the character of the conflict and the stupendous issues at stake may well rivet our attention.

I. The Battlefield

The countries under consideration have a total area of no less than 2,600,000 square miles, ten times the size of France, or nearly that of all the United States. Within this great area there is a total population of about 36,000,000, of whom 30,000,000 are Moslems. Persia, Turkey and Arabia have each held a place of supremacy in the history of Islam. Arabia is the cradle of its creed, Persia of its philosophy and poetry, and Turkey of its politics.

Persia, in a real sense, has for many centuries been the intellectual and religious fulcrum of Central Asia. Mother of Moslem heresies, this land has been the centre and source of authority for all Mohammedans who were not of the orthodox party. Here Aryan thought has modified the Semitic creed, and from Persia Mohammedan mysticism, poetry and philosophy have gone out on the wings of literature to the ends of the Moslem world. Hafiz, Omar Khayyan and Jélal-ud-Din the great mystic, are

international centre of Asiatic politics must be sought in the Persian Gulf. The present political condition of Arabia, therefore, deeply interests not only Great Britain and Germany, but France and Russia. Turkish rule exists in only three of the seven provinces, and British influence obtains along the entire coast of the Persian Gulf and the Indian Ocean. The Persian Gulf has become an English lake and British rule has extended far inland from Aden, while her influence is supreme in the province of Oman. The recent Turkish concession to Germany to build the Bagdad railway gave a grant in perpetuity of land twelve miles wide along the entire road, or 18,000 miles of German soil in Turkey. Then began the fight for the possession of the great highway of the nations. In this game England and Germany are the opponents; the prize for which they are playing is the commerce of all Asia; the checkerboard on which they make their moves is Mesopotamia. Within the next few years the Tigris-Euphrates basin is destined to be the scene of the greatest contest for commercial supremacy since the partition of Africa. Although checkmated by the British at Kuweit, Germany is pushing her railway, while Sir William Wilcocks, the wizard of the Nile, is working an irrigation scheme under the Young Turkish party to make 3,000,000 acres of desert soil blossom like the rose, and, in connection with this project, hopes to build a rival railway all the way from Damascus to Bagdad to be completed in two years.

Asiatic Turkey already has a total of 2,750 miles of railway. This, with splendid harbors and river navigation, makes the greater part of the empire accessible. In Persia and Arabia the hardships of travel by caravan are still many, but the fact that practically all of the great cities throughout the whole of western Asia, with the exception of Mecca, Medina, Kerbella and Meshed— closed because of religious fanaticism— are already mission stations, is full of significance. Christian missions are not

only established, but have proved their
power and influence in ever-widening
circles in every one of these centres:
Constantinople, Salonica, Adrianople,
Smyrna, Bagdad, Aleppo, Beirut,
Brussa, Kaisariyah, Mosul, Adana,
Jerusalem, Trebizond, Diarbekr, Tabriz,
Teheran, Ispahan, Kirman, Yezd, Shiraz,
Aden, Muscat and Busrah.

Within the boundaries of these five
Moslem lands, Turkey, Palestine, Syria,
Persia, Arabia, there are over 600 Protestant missionaries engaged in educational, medical and evangelistic work.
The Bible has been translated into all
the languages of western Asia, and a
large Christian literature prepared for
its polyglot people. At the Beirut Press
alone 60,000,000 pages of Christian
books were printed in a single year, and
in one month orders were on file for
100,000 copies of the Arabic Script-
ures, including eighteen cases of Bibles
sent to Shanghai for the Moslems
of China. What stronger proof can be
given of the strategic importance of
Syria in the evangelization of the Moslem world?

And who can measure the influence
and power of such great educational centres as Robert College, the Syrian Protestant College, and similar institutions
at Marsovan, Aintab, Smyrna, Tarsus,
Marash and Teheran? Robert College
has for the past forty years educated and
trained fifteen nationalities in the principles of justice and self-government and
made possible the present new era in
Turkey. "It was you Americans," said
a Turk to President Tracy, of Anatolia
College, "who, coming to Turkey, found
us in darkness and showed us the way
to the light." The American missionaries were the pioneers of modern education in every city of western Asia.
No less than forty mission hospitals and
dispensaries dot the map from Constantinople to Aden, and from Smyrna to
Kirman. Medical missions have not only
disarmed suspicion and prejudice, but
have won the life-long friendship of
thousands of the people. A single hospital in Arabia had 13,000 out-patients
last year,

change in the real character of Islam
and will fight to the end to make it the
only religion of the state.

Islam does not believe in a State
Church, as Lord Curzon has pointed out,
but in a Church State. And Lord Cromer
has shown in his *Modern Egypt* that
each of the three great defects of Islam
—the position of womanhood, its unchanging civil law, and its intolerant
spirit—is incompatible with real progress. The struggle in western Asia,
therefore, is not merely political, but industrial and social. It is a struggle between two civilizations; between the
ideals of the Moslem world and those of
Christendom.

Islam has run its roots deep for thirteen centuries into all the life of the
East. Architecture, art, music, literature—all these by their presence or by
their absence proclaim the power of Mohammed and his faith. The clash of
modern civilization against the teachings
of Islam is evident on every hand. When
it was proposed to adopt European time
for Turkey, the clerical party made such
an uproar that the President of the
Chamber was compelled to leave the
House and the motion was withdrawn.
So the days continue to begin at sunset
and watches must be reset every day because of the Koran. The new railway
to Mecca is fitted up with a chapel car in
the shape of a mosque. This car allows
pilgrims to perform their devotions during the journey and has a minaret six
feet high. Around the sides are verses
from the Koran; a chart at one end indicates the direction of prayer, and at
the other end are vessels for the ritual
ablutions. Will the orthodox Arabs consider such prayer-de-luxe in accord with
the prophet's teaching? As long as Mohammed and his teaching are the ideals
of conduct and the standard of character
there must be this clash between modern
civilization and the unchangeable standards of Arabian mediævalism. If it is
impossible to change the curriculum of
El Ashar in Cairo, will that institution
or Robert College control the thought of
western Asia?

When freedom was proclaimed in
Persia and Turkey, newspapers sprang
up like mushrooms, and nearly all of
them were advocates of liberty, equality
and freedom. In Teheran the names of
the journals themselves were indicative
of progress. The newsboys cried out
their wares and sold copies of *The Assembly, Civilization, The Cry of the
Country, The True Dawn, Progress,* and
Knowledge. The French *Revue du
Monde Musulman* published a list of no
less than 747 newspapers and magazines
which were issued in Turkey since July
24th, 1908, the birthday of liberty. The
old order of the gagged press has gone.
Censorship has ceased, but whither is the
new journalism drifting? It is very
significant that some of the leading
papers are already the mouthpieces of intolerance and show a sullen attitude toward Christianity and reform, stating
that the constitution is destructive of
the sacred law of Mohammed.

The position of womanhood will also
be determined in the coming struggle.
Some of the women themselves are asserting their rights, abolishing the use
of the veil and claiming the privileges
and honor of womanhood. There is a
demand for female education. Judge
Masim Ameen, a leading Moslem in
Cairo, recently published two books on
The Emancipation of Womanhood,
which have had a wide circulation in
western Asia. He exposes the evils of
polygamy and urges that it be prohibited
by law. "Polygamy," says he, "produces
jealousies, hatred, intrigues and crimes
innumerable. Many critics claim that
women in the harems are happy. How
do they know? Have they any statistics
of harem life?" No wonder these books
aroused a storm of opposition and bitter
reply. To prohibit polygamy by law
would be to abrogate the Koran and to
stigmatize the prophet. Civilization
alone will not end the horrors of Islam
behind the veil in Persia and Arabia.
Pierre Loti's book, *Disenchanted,* shows
that the mere civilizing of the harem
without the emancipation of womanhood
means moral suicide. Only Christ can

volt against the proclamation of religious equality. Here is the damning record: "Women were compelled to watch while their husbands and children were killed before their eyes; groups were told off and marched to some convenient place where, instead of being shot, as they entreated, they were mercilessly hacked to death—men, women and children—in order, as was said, 'not to waste powder and bullets on such swine.' Dead and wounded would then be thrown into great fires built to consume them. Mothers with newborn babes were dragged from their hiding places and life beaten out of them. The women and girls who were saved from death were reserved for a worse fate. Everywhere there was an orgy of hate and lust, with hardly a hand lifted to stay it."

Nor can we forget the missionaries, Minor Rogers and Henry Maurer, who fell in this struggle between Christian and Turk. The fury of the mob has ceased, but the character of Islam has not changed. It was not a merry Christmas in Celicia with 20,000 orphans uncared for and widows crying to God to avenge the slain. Will the New Year prove happier for them than the last? The fierceness of the persecutors in the last terrible tragedy leads one almost to hope that among them were Sauls of Tarsus who breathed threatenings and slaughter only because they themselves were already under conviction of sin and were kicking against the goads of the Christ.

There is not the least doubt that tens of thousands of Moslems in Turkey and Persia, and even in Arabia, are intellectually convinced of the truth of Christianity as against Islam. The philosophical disintegration of Islam, which began in Persia by the rise of Moslem sects, is now being hastened through newspaper discussions. There is a general unrest. There are frantic attempts to save the ship by throwing overboard much of the old cargo. The recent conferences at Mecca and Cairo, where Moslems met in council to determine the reasons for the decay of Islam, are ex-amples. Some are preaching reform, but every orthodox Moslem in Bagdad and Mecca would agree with Lord Cromer that reformed Islam is Islam no longer.

What religion will then take the place of the old traditions? What culture and civilization will be supreme in western Asia? When the shriek of the locomotive is heard at Mecca, will Arabia sleep on its patriarchal sleep, or will the nomads beat their swords into ploughshares and their spears into pruning-hooks when modern irrigation transforms the desert into a garden? Will Mohammed be the ideal of character and the Koran the standard of ethics in new Turkey and new Persia? Who is to prepare not only the teachers of to-morrow, but the statesmen to guide the ship of state over the stormy seas of racial and religious pride and selfishness?

III.   Victory

There is no question of the final issue. The struggle in western Asia and throughout the world is a struggle for the supremacy of the Christ. As a Mohammedan in Morocco expressed it: "The Koran has good advice, but when you read the New Testament a Person seems to be drawing you to Himself." Western Asia belongs not to Mohammed, but to Christ. "I, if I be lifted up." His manger and His cross stood there; His tears fell there and His blood was there spilled for these also. It was in western Asia that He said, "All authority is given unto Me," and although for thirteen centuries His royal rights have been disputed by a usurper, they have never been abrogated. He is King of kings and Lord of lords.

There is no question of the final issue, but the present time of struggle and unrest, and of a new-won liberty, is the time of times to win a speedy victory. It is now or never for a larger vision, and a bolder faith, and a pouring out of sacrifice.

In the problem of evangelizing the Moslem world, fear sees only giants, but faith sees God. "When a strong man, armed, keepeth his palace, his goods are

in peace; but when a stronger than he
shall come upon him and overcome him,
he taketh from him all his armor wherein he trusted and divideth his spoils."
The weapons of our warfare are not car-
nal, but mighty through God in this
coming conflict. Truth is our sword.
Love is our weapon. Love is strong as
death; love laughs at locksmiths, and
there are no closed doors for the Gospel
of the living Christ. It is now or never
for self-sacrificing obedience.

Thank God for the inspiration of those
pioneers who died not having received
the promise! No part of the world has a
richer heritage of predecessors. Upon
whom has their mantle fallen? "Smite
the Jordan, and it will part asunder."
Where is the Lord God of Henry Martyn
and Keith Falconer; the God of Parsons and Fiske, of Goodell and Dwight,
of Hamlin, Van Dyck and Bishop
French?

Every mission station in western
Asia calls loudly for reinforcements.
In the occupied fields there was never
such unique opportunity since the days
of the apostles; and there are glorious
impossibilities in the unoccupied fields
of western Asia for the heroes of faith.
A whole province in Persia and four
provinces in Arabia without a missionary! Twenty years ago I stood outside
the city gate at Jiddah on the road which
leads to Mecca. Over the portal was inscribed, "Ya fatah," "O Thou that open-
est." I thought then and I think now
of our Saviour Jesus Christ on whose
shoulders are the keys of the House of
David, Who openeth and no man shutteth, Who shutteth and no man openeth.
Is there no one who will place the banner of the Cross in the very centre of
Islam, and lead a forlorn hope against
Mecca?

KANSAS AFTER $1,000

THE Bishop of Kansas has put forth
a letter to the Sunday-schools of
his diocese in which he says:

"What a glorious thing if all could
make the Lent offering of the children

A BRAZILIAN SUNDAY-SCHOOL BOY

IT is hard work being a really good Sunday-school boy in Brazil. There are so many other more exciting things to fill up the Sundays, and so many people to draw one into these things.

Among other things there are sure to be horse-races, and there are always the different forms of gambling games, played by the least of the little boys and the largest of the grown-up men.

Also there are parents. Even in our own land parents do not always use every means to encourage Sunday-school attendance, but in Brazil, where many of the fathers and mothers have no knowledge of the Bible nor understanding of religious truth, they sometimes not only fail to urge their children to attend Sunday-school, but would prefer to take them to some one of the forms of recreation which fill their Sundays.

Then there are churches and priests. One would think that churches and priests would help, rather than hinder, Sunday-schools; and so they do with us, but not always so in Brazil, where many great churches are without services or worshippers, and many of the Roman Catholic clergy have, in the past, forgotten their duty to their children.

So it was not easy for the boy whom we will call Pedro to be what he became—one of the most faithful of the Sunday-school scholars in Porto Alegre. He was a bright little fellow, whose mother was not a native Brazilian, and did not speak Portuguese very well. He began coming to the school of his own accord, and after a little time his teacher visited him in his home. Finding that none of the three children had been baptized, and that they liked to attend our Sunday-school, she gained the consent of the mother and the baptism took place one morning in the presence of the school.

From that time Pedro's sense of obligation deepened, and although he lived at some distance he became one of the most regular attendants. It was beautiful to see how much the Sunday-school meant to this little lad, who had been brought up in such ignorance of sacred things. It seemed as though one could fairly see

THE SUNDAY-SCHOOLS OF PORTO ALEGRE

the grace of his baptism working in the little life, and, like many another Brazilian boy and girl, he showed a remarkable interest and steadfastness among the temptations and distractions which conspire to win them away from the influence of the Church.

It is somewhat pitiful to see how sadly these children have been deprived of the old familiar things which we have always known. Indeed they never had a real Christmas or a real Easter until the Church came to bring it. Of course there were *fiestas* on those days, but they were more like a combined picnic and vaudeville show than a festival of the dear Christ our Saviour.

So all the Sunday-schools in Porto Alegre (for you must know that they have now grown to five in number, the main school meeting on Sunday morning in the church and four others in different quarters of the city during the afternoon)—all these schools gathered at the church for their Christmas festival service. We are especially glad to make Christmas and Easter beautiful because they are connected with the life of our Lord, and in Brazil so much less is made of them than of the feasts of the Virgin Mary. He is usually spoken of as the infant Jesus or the dead Christ, not as the living Saviour and Intercessor. Ten prayers are offered to His mother where one is addressed to Him, and almost every saint in the calendar has a higher place than He in public estimation. The name of Jesus is held in so little reverence that it is often bestowed upon children, and even one of the principal streets in Porto Alegre is called the "Child-God," after Him.

So the Christmas celebration is made as beautiful and attractive as possible to the Brazilian children and for months they look forward to it with eagerness. Even the parents — Pedro's mother among them—come and enjoy hearing their children answer the questions in the Church catechism, tell the events in the life of Our Lord, and repeat in unison the Creed and the Ten Commandments. Of course there are gifts—something for every child upon the roll—for it is the day of the great Christmas Gift and we wish to make it as joyful and beautiful as we may.

Easter Day again sees the Sunday-schools gathered, this time to hear the story of the Resurrection. And thus, year by year, these dear children learn the things which make our Church life at home so beautiful and helpful.

It was not strange that little Pedro should feel the appeal which such influences as these make to a nature which is religious and affectionate. He became a model pupil, not for the sake of a good record, but because he loved the things which he learned through the Sunday-school.

Yet, of course, he was also anxious about his record. It is a rule of the school that no scholar shall be enrolled until after an attendance of three Sundays, and after enrolment, should he fail to attend for several Sundays, his name is struck off, and when he returns he is treated as a new scholar. Pedro was taken ill with typhoid fever and his first care was to send for the rector to let him know that his absence was not voluntary. As soon as he was convalescent, while still scarcely able to walk, he appeared at Sunday-school leaning on his mother. He did not rest satisfied until provided with Bible, Prayer Book and Hymnal, and is now preparing for confirmation.

In the heart of this lad there is growing up, together with the joy of his Christian faith, a great ambition and a strong desire. He does not speak of it often, and its realization is still far in the future, but he would be—oh! so glad! —if, when he has grown older, he might himself go out as a messenger of the Church of Christ to other children of Brazil. He dreams of studying for the ministry, and sees himself in the vestments of the sacred office, telling the simple and sweet story of Christ to the starved little hearts of a future generation of children.

For you see the little lad has learned already that the more we get the more we want to give, and that God sends us

blessing and truth so that we may share them with others. The Brazilian boy who, though he lived in a nominally Christian land, did not really learn about the dear Christ, felt immediately

A LITTLE BRAZILIAN

bound to let others know these beautiful truths as soon as he had learned them; and therein he is an example to us, who know these things so much better even than he.

Perhaps in the days to come some boy or girl who reads these words may be standing side by side with this little former Sunday-school scholar, telling in company with him the message of Christ to the people of Brazil, and ministering in holy things to the winsome, affectionate, spiritually-neglected children upon whom the Christian hope of the future in that great land so largely depends.

LANTERN LECTURES

WE are unable to make further engagements for lantern lectures during Lent. The demand this year has been so great that we have been compelled to disappoint many who wished to make use of this popular and effective way of informing themselves concerning the work which the Church is doing in this and other lands. Next year with increased facilities we hope to satisfy all.

HOW WOULD YOU LIKE TO BE IN THIS RING?

A KINDERGARTEN IN JAPAN

By Deaconess Ranson

"Mi yo ya juji no
Hota takaki
Kimi naru Jesu wa
Sakidateri."

THESE words ring out in high childish voices. They would not convey much meaning to a visitor fresh from America if he should come into one of our mission kindergartens some morning. But translated they would be the familiar words of a hymn dear to children in many lands:

"Onward, Christian soldiers,
Marching as to war,
With the cross of Jesus
Going on before."

For an hour before opening time little kimono-clad figures may be seen coming to the kindergarten. Japan has been called the "Land of Approximate Time," you know; and of course little children of kindergarten age cannot be expected to know just when nine o'clock comes. They step out of their wooden clogs, and up on the polished veranda, and then, going into the house, bow their heads to the soft matting-covered floor in polite greeting to the teacher.

When the bell rings all form in line, march into the circle-room and sing songs and hymns, many of the latter translations of familiar ones in America, and then kneeling down and bowing their heads the children say *"Ten ni mashi nasu, warera no Chichi yo"*—(Our Father, etc.)

Yes, these words would sound strange to an American child; but they would mean this—that little ones in Japan are being taught that they are children of the Heavenly Father, and may be soldiers of Jesus Christ.

The mission kindergarten, with its hymns, prayers and Bible stories, is just one of the means by which we try to obey our Lord's command to "Go and teach all nations," and to remember His gracious permission, "Suffer the little children to come unto Me."

See the children in the picture playing games with their new teacher, Miss Fyock, at our kindergarten in Sendai. The building has just been finished, and is next to the Training-school for Mission Women. The assistant teacher, Taguchi San, is a graduate of St. Margaret's School, Tokyo, and came to us from a government school, where she gave up a promised promotion because she wanted to do definite Christian work.

Such a house-warming as there was last October when the three buildings— the teachers' house, the training-school and the kindergarten—were opened! The mayor and governor and chief men of the city, all the Christian workers in Sendai and many other invited guests— 130 in all—were received by the teachers and students, and after being served with refreshments were shown over the buildings, which were decorated with flags, bamboo branches and flowers. Over the door of the kindergarten building was a sign-board made by the children, displaying the Japanese words "In honor of the Opening," done in purple and yellow lotuses. All the houses were greatly admired, and the members of the schools are enjoying to the utmost the happiness of finding themselves in convenient, well-equipped houses, with plenty of room to grow.

Every week a Sunday-school is held in the parish house with an enrolment of about one hundred and twenty children, but now we have opened a new one in the kindergarten building intended espe-

(195)

THE NEW HOME OF THE KINDERGARTEN

cially to reach the children who attend there every day, and their older brothers and sisters.

Once, many years ago, Christians were cruelly persecuted in Japan, and often put to death for their faith. Now there is religious freedom throughout the empire, and yet even to-day there is much ignorance and prejudice against Christianity. Several years ago some of our missionaries were trying to build up a Sunday-school in a village where there was only one Christian family. At first matters were encouraging, but after a time there was a great falling off in the attendance. The children seemed to be afraid. Finally it was discovered that the statement was being circulated that all children attending a Christian school would be *crucified* by their teachers. This rumor was probably based on the stories which had come down to the people in this country district from those days when Christians were themselves crucified.

No! there is no longer any physical persecution; no one is imprisoned or tortured or killed; yet even now it may mean sacrifice and suffering for Japanese children to be followers of our Lord. You remember that the hymn says:

"There's not a child so weak and small
    But has his little cross to take—
His little work of love and praise
    That he may do for Jesus' sake."

We have known young boys in Japan to keep on coming to the Sunday-school although it meant that their monthly averages in the public school report were constantly lowered by a spiteful teacher who hated the Christian doctrine. We have known a little, ragged, lame boy who came regularly in spite of being teased and laughed at by his playmates; which meant real persecution to a child. It is because we know that little children can love and follow the Saviour that we have in our mission not only primary and higher schools and colleges, but kindergartens as well.

¶

AT a meeting of laymen in a parish where for years no offering for general missions has been made, a committee was formed to canvass the parish. The junior warden (seventy years old) said to the speakers that he thanked them for their addresses, that he had always been opposed to missions, he did not exactly know why, but that he had had a change of heart and was willing to give his support.

ARCHDEACON THOMSON'S FIFTIETH ANNIVERSARY

By Mr. T. T. Wong

A MONTH or so before the fiftieth anniversary of Archdeacon E. H. Thomson's work in China, which took place on December 21st, 1909, several meetings were held to discuss the question of making suitable arrangements for the occasion, resulting in the formation of a committee, of which the following were members: Dr. Eli Day, Chairman; Mr. Y. T. Loh, Treasurer; Mr. P. W. Jui, Mr. M. S. Lee, Mr. T. T. Wong, Secretary.

Through this committee, and with the approval of Bishop Graves, the different congregations in the American Church mission in Kiangsu Province were invited to participate in the celebration. A number of the church members (both men and women) of the Church of Our Saviour, Hongkew, Shanghai, were asked to serve on the reception committee. It may be interesting to note that this was the first time in the history of the American Church Mission in China that the Chinese Christians took upon themselves the work of arranging a social function on such an extensive scale.

The Celebration Day

The secretaries of the Chinese Young Men's Christian Association, Shanghai, were kind enough to place the Association Building at the disposal of the management and reception committees on that day. The interior of the building was tastefully decorated with greens, flags and lanterns, with a beautifully draped arch at the entrance. By two o'clock in the afternoon the Chinese Christians from the different parts of the mission began to pour in, and at three o'clock there were over five hundred people in the Association hall, with a number of foreign friends.

The St. John's University band, which supplied the music at the different intervals, contributed much toward enlivening the occasion.

The meeting was opened with prayer by the Rev. K. C. Li. Dr. Eli Day made an address of welcome, after which the Rev. H. N. Woo, presiding at the meeting, spoke on Archdeacon Thomson's work in connection with St. Luke's Hospital, Shanghai, in the days of its inception, when the archdeacon did much toward raising money for its extension. The success of the day-schools for the poor children, and of the work among the blind in the native city of Shanghai, who were taught industrial work as the means of self-support, was mainly due to the efforts of the archdeacon in addition to his work of preaching to the people. Toward the close of the address Mr. Woo exhorted his listeners to follow the example of the venerable archdeacon.

The Rev. T. H. Tai, one of the archdeacon's old pupils, was the next speaker. In his introductory remarks he stated that the archdeacon's modesty had rendered it difficult to gather facts from which to make up an account of his life. Mr. Tai said that the Chinese Christians of the American Church Mission should feel thankful to God for sending such a man as the archdeacon to China—a true follower of Christ, and a typical Christian. In the archdeacon's work, the poor had the larger share of his sympathy and attention, for the poorer the people the greater his love for them, and but for him they would not have heard the message of Divine Love. Mr. Tai gave two main reasons why the anniversary should be celebrated: first, because his work had borne fruit, and secondly, because of his self-sacrifice for the physical, intellectual and spiritual welfare of the Chinese people.

Following the address of Mr. Tai, the Rev. H. N. Woo made a presentation address, and, on behalf of the Chinese

Christians, presented to the archdeacon a beautiful silver tea-set, the salver bearing the following inscription:

Presented to Archdeacon Thomson by Chinese members of the American Church mission, Kiangsu, as a loving token of appreciation, on the fiftieth anniversary of his faithful work in China, December 21st, 1909.

The archdeacon responded in touching terms and, disowning any credit for himself, said that whatever he might have been able to do was done through the love and mercy of God. After two short addresses by the Chinese representatives of other missions, expressing their appreciation of the archdeacon's work, the meeting was brought to- a close with the singing of a hymn specially written for the occasion, and the pronouncing of the benediction by Bishop Graves. The proceedings were followed by a largely attended reception in the beautifully decorated gymnasium of the Association, which reflected great credit on the reception committee.

The Thought of the Day

The chief thought which engaged t attention of those who took part in t celebration of Archdeacon Thomson anniversary was that they came togeth to do honor to the beloved missiona who has grown gray in the service of t mission for their welfare, and to one w does "not love in word, neither tongue; but in deed and truth." It w this love which prompted him to lea his country for China in the early da of missionary work, when travel w both difficult and perilous, and when t missionaries had so little encourageme to reward their arduous labor. It is t same love which has given him inspir tion to work for the people till it taken root in the hearts of three gene tions of Christians who have been inf enced by his example.

The enthusiasm shown by them on t occasion of his anniversary is a stro testimony to the success of his work China.

TWO INCIDENTS OF THE DOMESTIC FIEL.

A WYOMING SCHOOL MISTRESS

By Archdeacon Dray, of Wyoming

I WISH I could have taken some people who "don't believe in missions" to a little school-house I visited the other day. Having about seven or eight hours to wait at a junction where there are about thirty houses scattered around, I walked "across lots" to a little building that looked like a freight car. Entering I found a very intelligent, bright young woman who had come from an eastern city. She told me of her feelings when she first came to this sagebrush patch, but said that as she understood a friend of hers had married a missionary and had come out to the country west of her location, she thought she could stand it. She said she would have all her pupils present if

I would come back and speak to the I returned in the afternoon and fou the school assembled. There were sei pupils! After a talk, and an atten at an illustration on the blackboard school was dismissed for a while anc talked with the teacher. She was of our communion, but said she w when she could, as she did so like service. Three of her scholars (eldest eleven years old) came in de from four-and-a-half miles back in mountains. She had started a Sund school, as there was no religious serv of any kind held on Sunday. So times some missionary passing throt would hold a service on a week nic and get off by the night train; she wish this could be done regularly, h ever infrequently, so that she could the people know, "though of cour she said, "it would be expecting too m to want it on a Sunday."

As she told me how the loneliness which she had felt at first had vanished, now that she had become interested in the people and they came to her Sunday-school, I could not help feeling what a noble witness she was bearing to the better things of life in that isolated spot. Afterward as I saw the three children go off up the hills through the snow and sage-brush to their homes, four-and-a-half miles off, shouting and laughing as they huddled in a little sleigh, I reflected how relative a thing is wealth.

THE LADY WITH THE FRA-GRANT NAME

By the Right Reverend G. Mott Williams, D.D.

EVERYBODY has heard of "homestead districts," but not everyone knows all the hard work and exposure of such a district. Briefly, there is a way of getting free land from the government—free, but at a large price, for it costs hard work and a lonely residence.

Sometimes a widow with a young family files on homestead land, and tries by her own hard work and that of her young brood to make a home and a living. This was the case with a young widow and her six boys, who took up some government land near the St. Mary's River in northern Michigan. It was wet land, flat, and with a heavy soil. It had been burned over clean, and afterward covered with a thicket of second growth far thicker than the original forest, but not valuable. It made very hard land to clear; in their season the mosquitoes were awful, and it was far from a railway or town. The roads were not very bad in dry weather, but when it rained the amount of mud which could be collected on wheels or feet was beyond belief. Yet the soil was rich, so Mrs. Lavender, the lady with the fragrant name, took bravely hold of her work.

She built a house out of rough boards and tarred paper. There was one big room and a loft where the six boys slept

when they were not out in a tent after the wild hay crop, on the marshes near the river. There was a common school but no church, and Mrs. Lavender wanted a church—our Church and hers. There was some trouble over using the school-house—Roman Catholic objection —so Mrs. Lavender solved the difficulty by taking the Church to her home.

This is what happened on August 8th, 1909. It had rained the night before and the roads were very slippery, but the bishop walked from the neighboring four corners, where he had spent the night, and arrived at Mrs. Lavender's at about half-past nine o'clock. The travelling missionary came a little later with the buggy, and robe cases, books, etc. In the one room, Mrs. Lavender had pushed all the wooden chairs back against the wall, and laid boards over them to increase the seating capacity. The big table stood in the centre of the room covered with a white cloth. The dinner that the bishop was to eat was cooking on the stove—most of it from the garden at the door.

The bishop arranged his communion service on the table, and went up into the loft to put on his robes. They wanted to have everything as they had known it before they plunged into the wilderness. Not all the six boys were there, because the boy who went down to the hay marsh couldn't get across the river to them, but twenty persons in all were present. Thus the bishop preached and confirmed the lady with the fragrant name, and two of her boys and four of the neighbors, and gave them their first Communion. Then, from the table which had been an altar, Mrs. Lavender gave him his dinner, and he drove away miles and miles to another place where more homesteaders were waiting for him and his message.

But before he went, the lady with the fragrant name showed him where the church should be which she hoped to see built on her land. The name that sounds so fragrant is becoming more so through good deeds. And as the bishop went off through the mud, he knew what a text in the Acts meant, which says: "And he went on his way rejoicing."

GLENWOOD SPRINGS—THE BISHOP'S HOME

A WINTER TRIP IN WESTERN COLORADO

By the Right Reverend Benjamin Brewster

WHEN I wrote to one of our communicants at Yampa, Routt County, that I planned if possible to visit that unshepherded place on December 21st, she wrote: "You will give us the Christmas Communion, will you not? It will be the first time in nineteen years. And, for us remote ranch-folk, it seems that the Christmas feast might be anticipated by four days." So, encouraged by this, and similar words of appreciation from others in that region, I made my winter trip to the eastern part of Routt County.

About four-fifths as large as the entire state of Massachusetts, Routt County is naturally divided at present into two parts, for ecclesiastical purposes. It is almost droll to speak of the "ecclesiastical" division of this vast

county, where we have never yet had a resident clergyman, and have now only one church—and that not yet completed. The bishops, however, have held services, baptized, and confirmed at several places here for the past twenty-five years. In THE SPIRIT OF MISSIONS for December, 1908, the late Bishop Knight gave a graphic account of an exciting wagon-ride over the sage-covered *mesas* of the western part of the county, in company with the Rev. J. H. Dennis, who ministers periodically in that region and of whose work and its hopeful prospects I mean to tell at some later time. I have appointed Mr. Dennis, whose home is at Meeker in the adjoining county of Rio Blanco, archdeacon of the northwestern part of my district. He used to cover, with remarkable energy, the whole of Routt County. But th

church to us for both morning and evening services. Steamboat is a flourishing place of about twelve hundred inhabitants. Bishop Leonard wisely secured a good site for a church, centrally located; and it will be one of ˙ Archdeacon Sibbald's first aims to build here. There is a Congregational church besides the Methodist. In the absence of a church of our own both these organizations have not unnaturally received help from our communicants. But the town is growing, and the time has fully come when we should occupy this strategic point with a suitable church building. Local resources might provide perhaps one-half, but cannot avail for the whole of the necessary cost, which would be upwards of $2,000 at the lowest estimate. For the present we shall have to rent a hall or room, and even this will be difficult to secure.

We made many calls on Sunday afternoon and found several confirmation candidates. In the evening we had again a large congregation, who followed the Prayer Book service with respectful appreciation, and listened attentively to Mr. Sibbald's stirring sermon.

The next morning we went to Oak Creek, twenty miles southward, on our return trip. This is a new town, in a rich coal region, which has sprung up from nothing with the coming of the railroad in the last year and a half. Here our Church is the only religious influence, the opportunity for missionary work having been grasped by Mr. W. D. J. Harris, a lay-reader and candidate for deacon's orders, whom the late bishop, just before his last illness, sent into this region. Mr. Harris secured a lot from the town-site company upon which he has erected, largely by his own manual labor, a portion of the projected church. Here he lives in true bachelor style in the vestry room, using the future guild room for services as well as for social and educational purposes. There is no other place of recreation in the town— aside from the four saloons. A bell has been given by a friend in the neighboring town of Yampa. For several months, in the absence of other school provision, Mr. Harris has taught about twenty-five children, and has also held a night school for several foreign-born miners. While his energy in this respect has finally stirred up the local school committee to the point of providing a school building and a teacher, the solicitude which Mr. Harris showed so practically for the welfare of the children has won the loyal support of many parents. I never had a more responsive congregation than that, composed largely of men, which filled the guild room that Monday evening.

We had taken a sleighride in the afternoon out to a group of coal miners three miles away, walking back so that our willing driver (the son of a Methodist preacher) might bring in as many as possible of the miners and their families to the evening service. And they came in greater numbers than we expected, a sturdy, hard-working company, facing a temperature considerably on the wrong side of zero, to hear our message and to join in the worship of the Prayer Book—to many of them strange, but reverently enjoyed by all.

They were making ready for Christmas, and I was sorry I could not stay for the feast with them. Mr. Harris has written that two hundred and thirty people came to the Christmas Eve exercises. They must have crowded the guild room! Forty-five came out, too, next morning to church. There are no communicants besides our lay-reader as yet, although there are several confirmed persons. But all the right-minded people of the place are proud of the church (it is indeed "the Church" here; and no particularizing designation is needed in the notices posted about the town), and under the supervision of the archdeacon there may be expected a goodly accession of earnest and intelligent communicants. At any rate, the self-sacrificing work of our lay-reader has already borne fruit in righteousness, good citizenship and genuine religion among a people otherwise neglected. What could be better, under the circumstances? A comparatively

small expenditure, perhaps a thousand dollars, would complete our church building here—the first in Routt County —to be a permanent centre of light in a community which seems sure to be stable.

Yampa was our last stopping place on this trip, nine miles away on our homeward journey. This is a comparatively old town, of three or four hundred inhabitants, and is the centre of a large farming region. We celebrated the "Christmas Communion" on St. Thomas's Day, ten communicants receiving, in a private house. The "Union" church (under Congregational control) afforded a place for our evening service. Although we own a site for a church, it is not centrally located; and at present we are renting a house in the centre of the town which we call "the Parish House," and where we shall hope to minister in some degree to the social, as well as the religious, welfare of the community.

Our Christmas duties called us home after visiting these three places. But there will be work at Hayden and Craig and Hahn's Peak. Some of this territory I had visited last August and we have scattered Church people everywhere. In Grand County, Grand Lake, a popular summer resort sixteen miles from the railway, is the only place where we have a church. Along the railroad are several small but busy towns— Sulphur Springs, Troublesome, Granby, Kremmling and Fraser.

It is one of the evidences of Bishop Knight's marvellous energy that he officiated at nearly all of these places during his short episcopate, and left lists of persons whose interest was aroused. With God's blessing we shall strive to carry out his undoubted intention of giving regular ministrations in these towns. Yet one priest cannot cover this territory adequately. Could we secure the right men, and their stipends, there is room for at least two additional priests deacons. Truly the people here are "scattered abroad, as sheep having no shepherd."

CHRISTMAS IN A CHINESE HOSPITAL

By Mary V. Glenton, M.D.

WHILE our friends at home are enjoying Christmas festivities, and storing up memories that will cling through life, some of us, at the Elizabeth Bunn Memorial Hospital, in Wûchang, are trying to bring a little Christmas into the hearts of a few Chinese children who do not know what Christmas means, and who have strayed into our midst because they need our care.

Last Christmas we had six such little ones: Hsu Len Pin, who has been with us for a year and whose family—rumor has it—were all swept away in the cholera epidemic of the previous summer. His little spine is still so weak that he finds his head heavy and rests it on his hand when he walks by holding his hand under his chin. Last year he could not walk.

ONE OF DR. GLENTON'S LITTLE
PATIENTS

And there is a little beggar, or at least a little boy with hip disease, whose parents had made capital of his infirmity by having him squat on the street and beg. For about a week, while things were a little uncertain at the time of the Emperor's death, no beggars were allowed on the streets, and thus this little fellow came to us. His language was bad, very bad, but he soon forgot it. When the beggars were again allowed free play, his father came for him, but we prevailed upon him to let the little fellow stay awhile, and now this six-year-old is chubby and dimply.

On Christmas Eve a little mite of a girl was brought to us. When she was six months old she was badly scalded, and her leg was bent backward, and bound to her hip, very nearly as far down as the heel. We operated on this baby, and she is lying in the ward now with a straight leg, getting very fat. How she does scold, baby fashion with no words, when her dressing is being done. Another little fellow has a bad abscess of

the thigh, and a dear little five-year-old has a tubercular ankle. This tot resisted all advances until a few weeks ago, but now he is responsive, friendly and playful.

We sent Chen Sen home for Christmas, but as he is one of a large family, and two younger than he, he hardly received hospital care and attention, so he is at home once more with us.

Then we have a little girl who is a niece of Chang Chih Tung. She has facial eczema, and her face is bound up in a mask. She goes, with us, by the name of "Little Mollie Maguire," so much does she resemble those old-time pictures.

The happy voices and laughter of this child family have entirely replaced the moans of pain, as have the smiles and dimples the lines of suffering in their faces, and we feel that even this little has brought some Christmas joy where it was never known before.

THE ROMANCE OF THE NEGRO

By the Reverend S. H. Bishop

ONE often hears the remark, offered as an explanation of a general lack of interest on the part of our Church in missionary work among the Negroes, that the Negro is not romantic, as are the Indians, the Chinese and the Japanese, among whom the Church is laboring with so much enthusiasm and success. Perhaps from a certain point of view the Negro is not so romantic as are other peoples, but from another point of view he is not without a romance which ought to make him most attractive.

We have known the Negroes as slaves and as dependents; they have roused our sympathy as a weak and inferior people; and the nation has spent millions in treasure and much blood for the purpose of giving them freedom, as well as an immense amount of money to fit them for the use of freedom. But recent scientific investigations into the history and ethnology of the Negro peoples, ought to arouse in us some sense of the essential romance which belongs to them as to all the great stocks of mankind.

Briefly, the romantic elements belonging to the Negro are: First, he is one of the three great branches of mankind which, so far as present indications go, are likely to survive; namely: the white, the yellow, and the black. The red man and the brown man seem to be slowly perishing; but the white, the yellow, and the black men seem to be holding their own in the struggle of race. The black alone among the so-called inferior peoples have been able to stand and to increase in the presence of the stronger races. The Negroes in this land not only existed but multiplied under slavery, and are increasing in due proportion under the industrial conditions of our present life. They have withstood, and in a measure have conquered, some of the Semitic peoples. Among the Negro

tribes of northern Africa is to-day one of the strongholds of Mohammedanism, and they have effectively influenced Arabic civilization. The "call to prayer" in use throughout the Mohammedan world is the product of a Negro, and some of the prayers in extensive use among the Mohammedans are fruits of the aspiration of Negro genius.

The second element of romance belonging to the Negro is the fact, if we may trust some of the most recent scientific investigations, that he first exploited the mineral wealth of the world for artistic and commercial purposes, and that he first wove cotton and other materials into cloth. A tribe of Negroes seems to have made the beautiful cloth in which the Egyptian dead were interred, and is still making it. These facts, if they be facts, indicate that the Negro first evinced industrial ambition in the use of the products of the earth for commercial purposes.

The third element of romance in the Negro is that he has a music which is peculiarly expressive of that faith which carries a people through calamity worse than death. Every primitive music such as that of the Negro has in it the note of final despair; but the music of the Negro has the note of final hope; therefore it not only helped to carry the expatriated Negro through slavery, but has charmed the heart and uplifted the spirit of all mankind. One may add to this element of romance the fact that the Negro has a proverbial literature which in its appositeness and the fine suggestion of its literary figures compares favorably with any proverbial literature in the world—the Hebrew only excepted.

From the point of view of missions the American Negroes are peculiarly interesting. They were originally a composite people, taken from tribes some of which were not more nearly related to

no such external conversion as the driving of the Franks through the river to secure their baptism, but has meant Christian character and faith. To the credit of the Southern white people be it said that notwithstanding the curse of slavery they so thoroughly Christianized the Negro people that that people supported the South, raised the crops, and cared for the wives and children of the entire South, while to them it seemed that their white masters were fighting to retain them in slavery. The Negroes have demonstrated a Christian loyalty, gentleness, and power of forgiveness which make them one of the most splendid assets of Christianity, and surely entitle them to the profound gratitude of mankind and to continued help from all Christian people until they shall be equipped to carry on by themselves, and according to their own genius, their mission to the world.

AT WUHU

Franz E. Lund

little Church club, right in our midst, whose sole object is to extend the influence of the Church. In the absence of the clergy it chanced to be called "Endeavor Club," a descriptive name and rather characteristic of new China. Its members endeavor to accomplish their work by means of special meetings held twice a week in various parts of the city, at which they deliver addresses in turn, urging the people to amend their lives by leaving off evil habits, superstitions and all forms of idol-worship. Several men have already been brought under the influence of the Church by means of this club, and best of all it has created spiritual alertness in the members themselves.

At a series of special meetings held in St. James's Church in connection with the bishop's visit the presence of these men was felt as a new impulse in the religious life of the whole congregation.

OUR EVANGELIST FROM THE OUT-
STATION OF SAN SHANG

For five days students from our boarding-school, St. James's congregation,
and some seventy representative men
from the out-stations, filled the church
in order to receive instructions in the
Christian life and doctrine. Addresses
were delivered by the clergy and laity
on such subjects as: "The Christian
Family Life," "Bible Study," "Personal
Devotion," "Personal Work," "The Extension of God's Kingdom Within," etc.
Bishop Roots gave one lecture on "The
Native Church," three on "The Priesthood of the Laity," and one to the students on "The Value of a Christian
Education," besides preaching a sermon
on the Sunday morning. During the
meetings ten were admitted as catechumens, nine were baptized and twelve
confirmed.

Our visitors from the out-stations
were entertained in a large Chinese
guild, where the Wuhu members joined
them at meals, in turn acting as hosts,
while the bishop and the clergy mixed
freely with all, discussing various topics
and plans of progress. This way of im-

proving the occasion of the episcopal
visitation proved most stimulating, and
similar retreats are likely to become an
annual feature of the work in Wuhu.

One could not help being impressed
with two facts in particular: first, the
large number of capable men taking part
in the discussions and lecturing on practical and vital truths in a way that convinced one of their attainment of an advanced stage of spiritual education; second, the eagerness with which the average Church member hailed the idea of
responsibility and self-support. These
hopeful notes rang through all the meetings, and a practical expression of the
latter was given in the promptness with
which all expense in connection with the
retreat (about $50) was covered by self-
imposed contributions outside the ordinary collections.

Happily such signs of progress are not
confined to Wuhu; they are met with all
over China to-day. They bring to us
and, through us, to the home Church a
message of hope. As Bishop Roots re
marked the other day: "If the Church
woman who built this beautiful churcl
could see the congregation and listen t
the addresses by these laymen whos
spiritual life has been kindled in it, sh
would certainly share in our joy an
realize more fully the significant servic
she has rendered the Church of God i
this far-away station."

Were it not for such object lesso1
given by the Church at home and sin
ilar acts of love on the part of those i
the field, the people of this vast empi
could never understand the content
the Gospel of Christ.

¶

THE Bishop of Haiti, whose church
Port au Prince was recently destroy
by the great fire, writes telling of his c
sire to replace it by a fireproof buildir
He has some money for use at his d
cretion and a grant has been made by t
Government, but he will need abo
$1,000 more to complete the structure.

THE SOUTHWEST IN COUNCIL

By the Reverend F. S. White

TO the readers of this magazine, the missionary aspects of the council will doubtless prove the most interesting. We might put them under three heads: I. The territory; II. The people; III. The facts concerning the work.

The Territory

The Department of the Southwest is an empire in extent. Its more than 700,000 square miles, with a population in 1900 of nearly 12,000,000 people, has been divided by the Church into eleven dioceses, of which three are still called missionary districts, but in all of which most of the work of the Church is still missionary in character and effort.

The council of this Department met for three days in January last, under the bright skies and in the rapidly growing district of Oklahoma. Five of the eleven bishops, and about fifty accredited delegates were in attendance during those days in the well-built and attractive parish house adjoining St. Paul's Church in Oklahoma City. The city itself, rapidly growing to be a metropolis of the highest class, was a revelation to many who saw it for the first time. Less than a quarter of a century ago there was but the rolling prairie land where now are housed and hard at work some seventy thousand people, none of whom, born there, are yet old enough to vote. It is an intensely American city; there seems to be no foreign element, save the black, and they of a good class on the whole. Industry, energy, thrift and wonderful prosperity were seen on every side. What is true of the city, is true of the state, it is said; and before the council adjourned it passed a resolution to be presented to the House of Bishops next fall, asking that an additional missionary bishop be sent into this field to care for those American people to whom this American Church is as yet but a name, and a misunderstood name at that.

The People

Missouri with its metropolitical centres of St. Louis, Kansas City and St. Joseph, has the problem of helping those who are "in perils in the city"; the great sociological problems which arise where men swarm and hive, and for the most part are crushed or beaten back in the struggle for existence. The Bishop of Kansas City has as a problem the care and guidance of an entire congregation of Sicilian Roman Catholics who have lately asked him to become their chief shepherd and father in God.

Kansas, Salina and Oklahoma have the problems of the small town and the farming districts; with the task of making the Church's mission and helpfulness plain to a sturdy, independent class who have been reared in such branches of sectarian faith as to be suspicious of, if not hostile to, the teachings and practices of an historic Church. Arkansas, Louisiana and Texas have the heart-breaking task of standing with hands practically tied before the problem of ministering to the great black population within their borders. The Bishop of New Mexico and the Bishop of West Texas have not only English-speaking peoples to care for, but masses of Mexicans and some Indians, so that one priest carries with him in his work our Spanish, German, Italian and Indian versions of the Prayer Book.

These facts appeared in the reports of the bishops. The dominant note was a hopeful one. Progress in developing the work of missions was evidenced in every report. The hospital and the school, there planted, are strong agencies for good; and not only is self-help stronger, but the spirit of service for "all men everywhere" is growing stronger too.

The council was pleased to welcome, and wish "God speed" to the new Department Secretary, Mr. 'Silver, who, please God, will help the strong and weak places in this Department to rise to a still greater measure of their responsibility.

The Facts in the Case

This information came out in informal addresses and formal papers. The highest ground was reached by the Bishop of Texas, at the opening meeting of the council, in an address on "What the Church has done and is doing for the American People."

In rapid, forceful sentences he pointed out what our branch of the Church *had* done for the American people, when under the insistent leading and teaching of an English priest, the Church gave the *colonial* idea to Englishmen, and in so doing saved this country to English rather than to French or Spanish domination. The Church had further fostered the national, independent idea in the minds of the makers of the Nation. She has ever been, and still is, influential out of all proportion to her size, with the thinking people of our country. Her work to-day is the slow work of trying so to relate two paradoxical aspects of life—"an objective concreteness and a subjective spirituality"—as to make reasonable and attractive a platform on which conservatism and liberalism shall find play and power sufficient to attract and to hold the mass of the thinking religious world.

Mr. John W. Wood made the story of "The Haystack Prayer-Meeting" the germ of a clear-cut appeal to men to associate themselves with the Laymen's Missionary Movement, and produced a deep impression on the 200 guests at the men's dinner given by the parish club on the evening of the 19th.

A picturesque and helpful address was given by the Rev. J. M. Koehler, deaf-mute missionary to the mutes in this and in part of the Sixth Department. So interesting and stimulating was his story of work among the 3,000 mutes

A GRASS HOUSE IN THE GARDEN ISLAND

KAUAI, "THE GARDEN ISLAND"

By the Reverend W. S. Short

KAUAI, called the "Garden Island" of the Hawaiian group, because of its fertility, lies about ninety miles northwest from Honolulu, and is reached by regular steamers twice a week. On my first visit, after tossing all night in a small steamer, I landed at Nawiliwili about four o'clock in the morning. I was met at the small wharf by Mr. Samuel Wilcox, who married a sister of Mr. David B. Lyman, the well-known Churchman of Chicago. He took me in his automobile to his beach home, Papalinahoa. As the family was still asleep I walked up a hill near by to watch the sun rise, and there on the mount read Morning Prayer, and commended the work of the Church on this island into God's hands and asked His blessing on my undertaking.

During the days preceding Sunday I visited many of our scattered Church people. On Sunday I held service at Lihue, at which thirty-five were present. The service was held at the Union Church which is given for our use on the last Sunday of each month. On Monday I went to Kilauea, twenty-eight miles distant, and visited many families along the road. At Kilauea fifteen persons were present at the Lord's Table.

After this reconnoissance I returned to Honolulu, but shortly made a second visitation to Kauai, when I landed at Nawiliwili at 3 A.M., and took the mail wagon for Waimea, calling on Church people at the villages of Koloa, Eleele, Hanapepe and Makaweli. No arrangement for services at these places could be made on this trip, so I returned to Lihue for Sunday and on the following day held a very hearty service at Hanalei, thirty-four miles distant from Lihue.

My third visit brought me into closer touch with the life on Kauai. Landing

ONE WAY OF CARRYING BABIES

this time at Waimea, I arranged for an evening service in a public hall. Notice was given at the public school, and about fifty children, Japanese, Chinese, Korean and Hawaiian, were present, with as many more adults. It would have done any one good to hear these children sing "My Country 'Tis of Thee." The next day a fine service was held at Makaweli, with a Churchwoman presiding at the piano, and playing familiar chants and hymns. At Koloa I visited the school and several Church families.

The children in the schools on the plantations are most interesting. It was on the road near Koloa that the accompanying picture was taken of the woman carrying a baby in a basket. I wish the readers of The Spirit of Missions could have seen this cheerful Japanese mother, when in place of the smallest child she had a bundle and a stone to preserve the balance, and the other child tied on her back.

Our services at all places are helped by boys from Iolani and girls from the Priory—our schools for boys and girls in Honolulu. A Churchman at Waimea, a young Hawaiian and an old Iolani student, offered to take the offering and

made up what was lacking to pay for the hall. He also urged me to come again and to use the native church next time where there were lights and a good choir.

On the island of Kauai we have eighty communicants and many baptized members of the Church. There are difficulties in the way of building a church and of having a resident priest. The bishop considers it the best policy at present to visit the people regularly and hold services for the scattered people.

Kauai has an area of 547 square miles and a population of about 25,000 people, most of whom are Orientals.

ON THE DECK OF THE STEAMER BETWEEN HONOLULU AND KAUAI

THE DEPARTMENT SECRETARY FOR NEW ENGLAND

By the Right Reverend William Lawrence, D.D.

THE Rev. William E. Gardner, who was elected by the council of the First Department to be Department Secretary of New England, passed his boyhood in Nantucket, Mass., graduated from Brown University, and later, in 1898, from the Episcopal Theological School in Cambridge.

His first charge was a small parish in Swampscott; about ten miles from Boston. During his short rectorship there the parish developed in spiritual strength and in numbers, and gained a stronger position throughout the community.

Called to the city of Quincy, also about ten miles from Boston —a community fast increasing—he led the parish to a more active and intense life than they had ever known before. On week days,

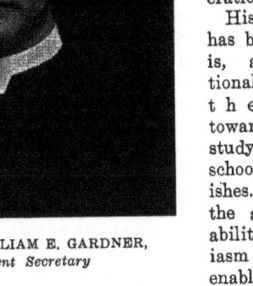

THE REV. WILLIAM E. GARDNER,
Department Secretary

at intervals, he would talk to the men of the Fall River Iron Works during their noon hour. He inaugurated a mission a few miles from the parish church. By his enthusiasm he gained the loyalty of the young. At the same time he and his wife gave themselves with great interest to the development of missionary study in the Sunday-schools of the diocese.

About two years ago he was called to succeed the late Rev. Edward Abbott at St. James's Church, Cambridge. He was just gaining a strong grasp of the work and its large opportunities when the call came to him from the Department—a call which he dared not refuse, for his life and later interests had been unconsciously fitting him for the duties of a department secretary.

He believes strongly in the invigorating force of personality, and, with this in mind, wrote a little book sketching the history of Christianity; and another called "The Winners of the World." He has also been chairman of the Sunday-school Federation.

His first interest has been, and still is, along educational lines, and the movement toward mission study in Sunday-schools and parishes. He has also the administrative ability and enthusiasm which will enable him to take hold of the other features of a secretary's work with enthusiasm and efficiency.

¶

From the Bishop of Milwaukee comes this message about the Sunday-school Missionary Day on January 16th:

WE had a splendid children's missionary rally yesterday; the church more crowded than at any time since my consecration.

A FAITHFUL COMPRADORE

THE American Church Mission in Shanghai has met with a great loss—one of its most important and valued members. How useful has been his work and how greatly he will be missed is told in the following letters:

Bishop Graves writes saying: "You will have heard of the loss we have sustained by the resignation of Mr. N. H. Ting, who has acted for so many years as the Chinese financial agent and buyer for the college—what we call, in our eastern dialect, our *compradore*. Mr. Smalley's letter is so well and truly written that there is no need for me to add anything to it further than to say that I heartily agree with him in all that he says of Mr. Ting's character, and of the loss which we have sustained. I do not think you at home can realize how rare a thing in China is an honest man, and how very much in consequence we depended upon Mr. Ting and valued his services. Dishonesty is the real thing that has to be reformed in China, and

(212)

even in Christians the old desire to make money by ways that we should call dishonorable is hard to uproot. That Mr. Ting was superior to temptations of this sort is the reason why we felt such an unfeigned respect for him."

Mr. Smalley, who is the treasurer of our American Church Mission in China, speaks more in detail of the character and services of Mr. Ting, and of the real loss which he will be to the work. He says:

"Our compradore, Mr. N. H. Ting, has been forced through ill health to resign his position. For some months past he has been ailing and last summer during the college vacation he went to Hangchow for a change, which only temporarily relieved him. Before the bishop was able to decide what should be done, Mr. Ting took the matter into his own hands and last Thursday went to the bishop and resigned of his own accord. It was a painful interview for them both. The bishop felt that there was nothing to be done but to accept the resignation. This he did with great reluctance, telling Mr. Ting that all would be done that was possible to keep him in comfort so long as he lived.

"Mr. Cooper, as Acting President of St. John's University during Dr. Pott's absence, has informed Mr. Ting that the college will continue to pay his salary for life. This decision I am sure will meet with Dr. Pott's approval and I am confident it has removed a load from off Mr. Ting's mind. It must be a great comfort to him to feel that his services have been so greatly appreciated, not only by the college authorities, but also by the bishop and the whole mission staff.

"It is over twenty years since Mr. Ting joined the college staff as compradore and became shroff for the missions. Mr. Ting came to us from the town of Kong-wan, where the mission has had a station for many years. He was a merchant there, and had long been a zealous and prominent member of the Kong-wan congregation.

"In his youth Mr. Ting most unwillingly took part in the Taiping Rebellion. He was made a prisoner by the Taipings and forced to serve in their ranks. It has often been a source of amusement to me to listen to Mr. Ting's accounts of his military career. When I asked him whether he thought he had killed or wounded any of his countrymen his action in reply was exceedingly amusing and characteristic. He would show how he held his weapon when about to discharge it, and one could readily see that his bullets must have gone soaring to the clouds rather than find a billet in a human body.

"Mr. Ting was a well-known figure in Shanghai. Hardly a day passed without his visiting one or two of the leading banks, *hongs* and stores. He was known in many of these places of business as 'St. John.' He always received kindly attention, which is a great testimonial to his character, for it is not every Chinese who is treated with politeness and respect by foreigners in Shanghai.

"That he has rendered faithful service to the mission is proved by the fact that during twenty years' tenure of his difficult office he has not once been found short in his cash. Large sums were continually passing through his hands; he was ever ready to help a new-comer to the field and has always been the medium both for the old and the new missionaries when transacting any financial matter. We shall miss his services and his genial presence in the mission office. Speaking personally, I feel I have lost one of my oldest friends."

NEWS AND NOTES

INFORMATION has reached this office from the manager of the Bureau of University Travel that there is to be a special steamer from New York on May 31st for those who wish to attend the World's Missionary Conference at Edinburgh.

¶

The following news reaches us from Cape Mount:

ON Tuesday, December 7th, Mrs. Matthews and Miss Ridgely arrived safely at Cape Mount. As the boat neared the shore the girls who had come to greet them began to sing, "God cares for every little thing." Miss Ridgely says, "I was thankful to have such a good report of them, from both Mr. Matthews and the native teachers. The new buildings are almost finished. My room was ready for me, and they had curtains at my windows. The donkey was landed safely; he seems to be a nice, gentle one, and is getting on well so far. The girls were inclined to be afraid of him at first but are getting more accustomed to him now."

ON December 16th, 1909, at the Pro-Cathedral, Shanghai, Bishop Graves advanced to the priesthood four Chinese deacons, all of whom graduated in arts at St. John's University and took their theological course in English. They have done excellent work in the diaconate and worthily won their advancement. These are among the first fruits of the newer order made possible by our fine educational equipment in Shanghai, by means of which the Chinese priest of the future may have the same educational opportunities as are available in this country.

¶

People who travel about in overheated Pullman cars find it difficult to understand the contrast represented by this brief message from one of the Alaska staff:

MRS. ROCKEFELLER, who was housekeeper at Anvik one winter, died while on the Valdez stage a week or so ago. It was 60 below those days, and despite the wolf robes she could not stand it. Mr. Betticher will bury her day after to-morrow.

This letter was recently received from a name-less friend:

MANY years ago a very dear friend left me $50 in gold to purchase a gift for myself. I never had made up my mind as to the best way to use it until the Sunday Dr. Correll preached so forcibly about his work in Japan, and the great need of giving at once to Christianize that nation; I then decided that that was my opportunity of making this gift a memorial to the donor. I felt that I ought to add to it the interest which had accumulated, or which would have accumulated if it had been placed in a bank for my own income. It was very difficult for me to find out what the accrued interest would be, but as far as I could judge, after spending much thought upon it, I decided that the interest might possibly amount to $250, making, with the $50 in gold added, $300 in all. I would like that $50, with $50 from the enclosed check, forwarded to Dr. Correll for his work in Japan; the second $100 to be used for the missions in China; the remaining $100 to be used toward the education of an Indian as a missionary to his own people in the jurisdiction of the late Bishop Hare.

¶

Archdeacon Steel writes from Cuba:

THE chapels in the Isle of Pines, at Columbia and Santa Rosalia, were destroyed in the last hurricane. With the money so generously contributed for this purpose by friends in the United States, the Rev. Mr. McCullough has already replaced one of these chapels. The former one was at Santa Rosalia but it was thought better to build the new one at Santa Fé, in the midst of a larger population. A lot was given by Mr. R. I. Wall, of the Santa Fé Land Company, in the best location in the town, and the chapel is one of which the Church need not be ashamed. It is strongly built and well braced, so that, humanly speaking, it will defy any hurricane. It was opened for services shortly after Christmas.

At Guantanamo, the splendid church,

FRUITS OF THE LAYMEN'S MISSIONARY MOVEMENT

AT the conference of Churchmen in connection with the laymen's convention in Columbia, S. C., January 17th to 19th, it was decided to endeavor to increase the offerings from Church people about 100 per cent. This would mean a total of $834. A report on February 4th says that while the canvass of Trinity congregation is not yet quite complete, $1,340 have been subscribed.

AN army officer and a Churchman who attended the convention of the Laymen's Missionary Movement in St. Louis says: "Our convention is over, and was very successful. Now the work commences. It was the greatest thing I ever saw. On Sunday evening, February 6th, a large union service for the Church congregations in St. Louis was held at the cathedral. A dozen clergy with the men of their congregations attended. The vested choir numbered over one hundred. The cathedral was packed. Rousing addresses were made by Bishop Tuttle and the Rev. H. P. Silver, the Department Secretary."

THE Nashville convention closed on January 30th. On February 2d the men of Christ Church met in one place, and the men of St. Ann's, St. Peter's and St. Stephen's in another, for congregational dinners to discuss what should be done by the men of the Nashville congregations. The Rev. Dr. Logan, rector of St. Ann's, writes:

"We cannot, just at this time, give figures and statistics, but you may rest assured Nashville will come up three times more than last year. We are at work—all at work. The convention was an undoubted success, and our people seemed more interested than any others.

"I verily believe this convention has served to wake up our people, and to open up before them a new vision. I feel that the convention has been of incalculable benefit to our churches."

In Christ Church about sixty men met to discuss the campaign, and as an earnest of what they proposed to do, they then and there subscribed $550. This is $200 more than the 700 communicants of Christ Church all together gave last year. A canvass is to be inaugurated at once.

FOLLOWING the suggestion of the Laymen's Missionary Movement Convention, the men of St. George's Church, Schenectady, to the number of 150, assembled for a parish supper on the evening of January 26th. Bishop Nelson presided, made an address and introduced the other speakers, the Rev. Dr. Taylor and Mr. John W. Wood. Dr. Taylor announced that in discussing with the vestry what St. George's ought to do in the matter of larger missionary support, it had been unanimously decided that the entire Easter offering should be given to Church extension within or without the diocese. It is proposed from the offering first to send to the General Board of Missions and to the Diocesan Board the full amounts of the respective apportionments. Whatever sum remains is to be divided equally between general and diocesan missions. By a unanimous vote the men present at the supper adopted a resolution providing for the appointment of a committee of twenty men to foster and develop the missionary enthusiasm of the men of the congregation.

BUFFALO Churchmen have been carefully following up the work of the Laymen's Missionary Movement inaugurated by the convention of last October. Conferences of laymen have been held in a number of the parishes, and a

definite canvass of some of the congregations has been made. The result is seen
in very largely increased subscriptions
and offerings. The Church of the Ascension, which last year gave less than
$100 for foreign missions, has already
secured pledges for this year of between $500 and $600, and the work is
not yet finished. St. Paul's has succeeded in securing pledges of more than
$1,500. The Movement has been carried
into some of the surrounding towns,
and great interest has been aroused in
Western New York.

ONE immediate result of the convention of the Laymen's Missionary
Movement in Hartford was a mass meeting of Churchmen in Trinity Church.
Bishop Brewster presided. Besides the
Bishop of Cuba and the Rev. Arthur M.
Sherman, of China, Mr. William R. Butler, of Mauch Chunk, Pa., and Judge
Marvin, of Hartford, made addresses.
The church, one of the largest in Hartford, was filled with men almost to the
doors. A few women sat in the side
aisles. Such a gathering in Hartford
was distinctly something new. It meant
that the committees of the different
parishes had done their work and had
visited their members individually. The
interest in the faces of the congregation
was commented upon, for the facts of
mission work are stirring. The meeting
was advertised as one to give information. That inspiration came also was a
matter of course. The singing of the
missionary hymns was, as is usual in
such gatherings, splendid to hear. Now
the parochial missionary committees are
attending to the next step—the "follow-
up work," demanding the further visiting of each man of each parish to get
him to take a hand in the work.

FROM the rector of Zion Church,
Rome, N. Y., comes this assurance:
"We are camping on the trail of the Apportionment, and for the first time in
the history of the Apportionment we are
going to raise it—thanks to the Laymen's Missionary Movement."

MEETING OF THE BOARD OF MISSIONS

February 8th, 1910

THE Board of Missions met at the Church Missions House on Tuesday, February 8th, the Bishop of Albany (vice-president) in the chair. The following members were present: The Bishops of Pittsburgh, Bethlehem, Massachusetts, Long Island, Newark and New York; the Rev. Drs. Eccleston, Vibbert, Anstice, Alsop, Perry, Stires, Smith and Manning; Messrs. Low, Mills, Chauncey, Mansfield and Admiral Mahan, Messrs. Butler, King, Morris, Ryerson and Houston; of the honorary members the Bishop of Kyoto. The Rev. Mr. Garland, secretary of the Third, and the Rev. Mr. Gardner, secretary of the Department of New England, were also present.

As usual the first business was the Treasurer's report. The decrease reported in the aggregate receipts applying on appropriations was, for the five months, $25,377. The receipts for January were smaller than those for the corresponding month last year by $14,494.

At this meeting only a few communications were received with regard to work in the domestic field and in connection with them no new action was necessary, except to approve one or two changes in appointments.

The Bishop of Asheville has informed the Church of his application to the Board for an appropriation for seven years of $15,000 per annum to enable him to carry out a well-considered plan for the mountain work in his district. The committee who had the matter in charge reported to the Board: "Your committee is impressed with the earnest effort the Bishop of Asheville is making and sympathizes deeply with his desire, but finds it impossible in the present state of the treasury, and with the already very large outstanding obligations, to increase by this sum the present appropriation."

By action of the last General Convention the Island of Guam was included within the limits of the Missionary District of the Philippines. About two years ago the American Board of Commissioners for Foreign Missions (Congregational) suggested the possibility of handing its work there to our Board, together with the title to all its property. Recently Bishop Brent visited the island and reported to the Board. He raised the definite question whether the Board would wish to take over the work on the basis of his findings. In this connection it was

"*Resolved:* That while this Board deeply appreciates the offer of the American Board of Commissioners for Foreign Missions to transfer its work in Guam, together with all its property, to this Board, and while it is highly gratified by the spirit of confidence and good will that has prompted the offer, it regrets that in view of responsibilities assumed it seems inexpedient for this Board to accept the offer at the present time."

Letters were received from the several foreign bishops. Bishop Graves reported that he had advanced four native deacons to the priesthood, men who have done good work, and are a strong addition to the force of Chinese priests. The Bishop of Tokyo reported that a fine piece of property as the new site for St. Paul's College has been secured in a desirable location on the outskirts of Tokyo. This was done under authority of ladies in Philadelphia.

The Board appropriated the sum of $600 for aid to the new boys' school, which has already been started in Cuba. It was reported that the Committee

(217)

on Audit had caused the books and accounts of the Treasurer to be examined to the first instant and had certified the same to be correct.

The appointment by the Bishop of Shanghai of Mr. Thomas Kinloch Nelson, of the Theological Seminary of Virginia, was formally approved, to take effect upon his ordination.

At the request of the Bishop of Kyoto, Mr. George M. Laning was appointed as a medical missionary to Japan, to assist his father, Dr. Henry Laning, in St. Barnabas's Hospital, Osaka, the appointment to take effect upon his graduation in medicine from the University of Michigan.

MISSIONARY SPEAKERS

FOR the convenience of those arranging missionary meetings, the following list of clergy and other missionary workers available as speakers is published:

When no address is given, requests for the services of these speakers should be addressed to the Corresponding Secretary, 281 Fourth Avenue, New York.

Department Secretaries

Department 1. The Rev. William E. Gardner, 186 Upland Road, Cambridge, Mass.

Department 2. Cared for at present by secretaries at the Church Missions House.

Department 3. The Rev. Thomas J. Garland, Church House, Philadelphia.

Department 4. The Rev. R. W. Patton, care of the Rev. C. B. Wilmer, D.D., 412 Courtland Street, Atlanta, Ga.

Department 5. The Rev. John Henry Hopkins, D.D., 703 Ashland Boulevard, Chicago.

Department 6. The Rev. C. C. Rollit, 4416 Upton Avenue, South, Minneapolis, Minn.

ANNOUNCEMENTS
CONCERNING THE MISSIONARIES

Porto Rico

THE connection of the Rev. A. S. Jukes with the mission staff in Porto Rico terminated on January 15th, 1910.

Honolulu

THE Board of Missions on February 8th approved the employment by Bishop Restarick of Miss Carrie Wheeler, who is already at work in the field.

The Philippines

THE REV. HOBART E. STUDLEY, returning after regular furlough, left Walden, N. Y., on February 11th, and, after visiting friends in the West, sailed from San Francisco by the steamer *Mongolia* on March 8th.

MISS MARGARET ROUTLEDGE, Deaconess, on regular furlough, started from Manila on January 1st; sailed by the *Chiyo Maru* from Hong Kong on January 7th; arrived at San Francisco on February 3d and proceeded to her home in Detroit.

China

SHANGHAI:

ON December 16th, in St. John's Pro-Cathedral, Shanghai, Bishop Graves advanced four deacons to the priesthood, namely: The Rev. Messrs. N. T. Ng, of Tsingpoo; Z. S. Sung, of Kiading; T. M. Tong, of Grace Church, Shanghai, and F. K. Woo, of Soochow. All graduated in arts at St. John's University and took their theological course in English. They have done good work as deacons and are a strong addition to the force of Chinese priests. The candidates were presented by the Rev. C. F. McRae; the preacher was the Rev. G. F. Mosher. Other priests attending were Archdeacon Thomson, the Rev. Messrs. H. K. Woo, T. H. Tai, K. C. Li, C. C. Woo, W. H. Standring, J. M. B. Gill, C. Y. Tong, P. N. Tsu, T. L. Dzi, and R. E. Browning. Mr. Tong will be sent to Wusih to work with Mr. Mosher. The other new priests will remain in their former positions.

AT the request of Bishop Graves the Board of Missions on February 8th approved the appointment of Mr. Thomas Kinloch Nelson, of the Theological Seminary, Virginia, the appointment to take effect upon his ordination to the diaconate.

AT the same meeting the resignation of Miss Carrie M. Palmer was accepted, to date from January 10th.

MISS ANN REBECCA TORRENCE and the Rev. William Henry Standring of Soochow were married in St. John's Pro-Cathedral, Shanghai, on February 2d.

MISS MARGARET E. BENDER, returning after furlough, left New York on February 1st and sailed from San Francisco by the steamer *Manchuria* on the 8th.

HANKOW:

THE REV. L. B. RIDGELY and wife, on furlough, sailed from Shanghai by the *Mongolia* on January 31st and, stopping over a steamer in Honolulu, arrived at San Francisco March 3d.

MISS S. H. HIGGINS, on regular furlough, sailed from Shanghai by the steamer *Manchuria* on January 4th; arrived at San Francisco on the 27th and reached her home in Philadelphia on February 7th.

Japan

TOKYO:

THE REV. JAMES CHAPPELL, wife and two children, who sailed from Yokohama on November 24th, arrived at London on January 22d.

MISS FLORA M. BRISTOWE, after spending a furlough of six months in England, returned to Japan by the N. D. L. steamer *Kleert*, which sailed from Southampton February 1st.

KYOTO:

AT the request of Bishop Partridge the Board on February 8th approved the appointment of Mr. George M. Laning as assistant to his father in St. Barnabas's Hospital, Osaka; the appointment to take effect upon his graduation in medicine from the University of Michigan.

THE REV. DR. I. H. CORRELL and wife, returning after furlough, left Philadelphia on February 5th and sailed from San Francisco by the *Chiyo Maru* on the 15th.

THE WOMAN'S AUXILIARY
To the Board of Missions

AT MATSU-YAMA, ABOVE SAKURAI

THE KYOTO CHURCH TRAINING-SCHOOL

IF we take the electric car on our arrival in Kyoto it is by a long, circuitous route that we finally reach the group of buildings of which our bishop's house is the centre. Or, we can take a jinricksha, and our jinricksha man, after making a few turns, carries us by a long, straight road to the same spot where the electric cars turn the corner by Holy Trinity Church and the High School of the City of Peace. We will not turn this corner to-day, but keep straight on, past the bishop's home with his office by its side and the Japanese guest-house beyond, and, following on the broad street bordered by the beautiful Imperial Park, come to a bit of mission property which the bishop has rented for a term of three years. This property belongs to the Do-Shi-

Sha—the Japanese mission formerly under the Congregational Board, and was used as a training-school for nurses. They were disposed to sell, and our bishop thought it wise to make the purchase, but up to the present time the necessary funds have not been forthcoming. Three years ago it would have been possible to buy this property for $10,000. Now it would cost much more, which is a sign of how ready we should be to seize our opportunities as they come. The spirit of venturing is something well worth while to have while what we call the foreign mission field so grows!

Our jinricksha turns into the driveway of this property, and brings us to the large wooden building so well arranged for the purpose to which it has

been put. It is the home for the training of women workers. Under the bishop's supervision, Miss Suthon is resident missionary in charge, and Mr.
Yamabe and Mr. Sone, two of the Japanese clergymen, are engaged in teaching.

It was on January 12th, 1909, that
Miss Suthon took the Travelling Secretary about the buildings, and again on
the 30th she visited the house. On the
ground floor are the parlor and study and
dining-room, with three bedrooms above,
while the ell stretches out, giving seventeen rooms of six mats each, for the
students. There is room for thirty of
these young women, who have their recitation room, chapel, dining, reception
and school-room on the floor below. A
little allowance is granted them, from
which they supply their fuel, food and
clothing. They do their own washing,
and pay for their cook from their allowance.

The course upon which these students
enter is one of three years, the school
year opening with September, and after
graduation they are expected to work
two years in the Church, most of these
who have graduated from the training-
schools to which this has succeeded having worked much longer. Many also
have married clergymen and catechists,
and thus are still helping in the Church's
work. Instruction is given in Old Testament history, the Epistles and Thirty-
nine Articles, the Gospel, Prayer Book
and Christian Evidences, the First
Reader in English, the hymns and chants
of the Church, the Church service. It
is planned that in the future the students who may enter the school shall be
high-school graduates, having already
some foundation in English. On Saturdays there is normal training, teaching the students how to teach Sunday-
school. They learn also how to do
Church sewing and embroidery and to
make and do up surplices, cottas, altar
linen, etc.

When the school opened Miss Suthon
was the only foreign missionary in the
house. A young Englishwoman is spend-

church I was bred for eighteen years and my late husband and my children were baptized at the same. I was therefore much pleased to work for the church. Although I am weak and cannot amount anything, I, by the help of God, taught the Sunday-school and visited the church members and the seekers of God. Notwithstanding the severe heat of last summer, I happily continued the work, as I had great interest in the work. The houses visited were pleased and the children of the Sunday-school were diligent and heard me speak with gladness. As I became sick about the middle of September I went to Avima with my younger child and got well. I desire to study hardly and work for God to the end of my life, by the help of our Lord.

By teachings of our teachers, I felt great power in my work and I thank for it. I also thank for the help of Mr. Abe.

My mother is nursing my children for me at home, and I thank to God for giving me such a good mother.

———

Niino Chiyo, Kayashima Nobu, Nitta Hide: We three have been to Wakayama. There are Nippon Kiristo and Episcopal churches in this large and beautiful city. Both churches have numerous members and notwithstanding the heat of summer, sermons for un-Christian people were sometimes held. All the Church members are very earnest and the Sunday-school children are enjoying Sunday very much. We divided about fifty children into three classes. All the children bring offerings every Sunday and the school expenses are maintained with them. Lectures on Bible are held at a Church member's on Tuesday evening, and house prayer meetings on Friday evening. More members gather in the evening of Sunday than in the morning.

We three sometimes visited Church members, and sometimes went to Wakanoura (sea shore) with Church members and prayed and sang hymns. We took children to the castle and sang and told them the tale of Christ.

Two or three days before we started for Kyoto, we visited Maeda Kogisho with the pastor. The place is three ri far from Wakayama. A beautiful meeting was held there. We thought that it was a good farm for the worker of God.

———

Yanagihara Fuku: I am sorry that I couldn't work as much as I wished. Because I was busy with housekeeping. I have been to the city of Sakai, which is my native place. I taught Sunday-school at St. Timothy Church there and played organ for the service. One day I taught the tale of Adam and Eve, and required them to tell me what you have overcome the devil next Sunday. On the next Sunday a boy of an un-Christian gentleman told me that he won the victory against devils when he was about to disobey his father's word, by recollecting the instruction of the Sunday-school. By this I felt the necessity of teaching the Gospel more deeply than before.

———

Iwasaki Ishi: I worked at my native place, Tsu, Ise, last summer vacation. I taught the youngest children of the Sunday-school. I played organ at the service of the church on Sunday and Friday evening, and taught the singing of hymns once a week. Sometimes I conducted the home prayer meeting and the fujinkwai. There was not a church but kogisho. I hear that Dr. Correll will come and live there. And I hope there shall be a splendid church. There are about seventeen Church members. Owing to the hard work of the pastor, the member is increasing. But there is no female worker. I hope you will pray to get a good worker.

———

Takenaka Chiyo, Sasaki Kumi: We went to Matsuyama. The city is surrounded with mountains and about three ri far from Sakurai station. The scenery of the place is very beautiful. We enjoyed pic-nic with the children of the Sunday-school and sang hymns. There are about twenty-six children in the Sunday-school and we both taught them. Children of the school gradually increased and they were diligent and merry and we enjoyed it very much. The member of the Church is very few; six or seven. But they are all earnest Christians.

In the evening of Tuesday and Friday we held prayer meeting at the Church member's house. We taught

hymns in the same evening and they became better singers.

We hoped to make more work for the
Church, but we couldn't. Because we
had no experience.

Kitagawa Tora, Miki Ei: We set out
for Miijazu, Tango, on the second July
last. Miijazu is a prosperous city situated near sea and mountains. The
church is on the shore and the pastor is
called Kobayashi Sonosaburo. . There
are Grecian and Congregation Churches,
Episcopal's is a *kogisho*, not a church
yet. But it has about twenty members
and over seventy Sunday-school children. Lady's meeting is held on the
second Wednesday and prayer meeting
on Friday every week, and the meeting
of Y. M. C. A. is held once a week.
Mother's meeting is held on the third
Wednesday. Many unchristian ladies
attend this meeting and pray God and
sing hymn with Christian ladies. Such
may seldom be seen. Athletic sports of
the children of the Sunday-school at
Amano-Hashidate, August 2. We
worked merrily at such a beautiful
place with thankful hearts. We hope
you will pray God that the Gospel may
be distributed even to the remote country of this country.

Okuda Yasu: I went to Koriyama,
Yamato. This is a small town and
there is a *kogisho* having about twenty
members and about sixty Sunday-school
children. The Christians are intimate
and kind mutually. Until last summer,
there was no *dendoshi* living there. But,
to their great joy, they got a good pastor
from last summer and the *kogisho* became independent. The Church members are not natives, they are teachers,
clerks of banks and officials.

Near Koriyama, there is Tatsuta village which is very famous with maples.
Here is a *kogisho* maintained by two or
three families. They are extraordinary
earnest Christians seldom seen at
cities. The Sunday-school has about
fifty children. This *kogisho* is a splendid and typical one, and it is the product
of the hard work of love of an American pastor.* To our great regret, he
has gone home last summer. I pray
that they may have a good pastor in his
stead.

---

* The Rev. Mr. Yates, of Toronto.

THE FEBRUARY CONFERENCE

THE February conference, held on Thursday, the 17th, was devoted to the Junior Department and its work. It was attended by thirty-two officers from ten dioceses, and by a visitor from the District of Kyoto. The branches represented were Bethlehem, one (Junior); Central New York, one; Connecticut, five (two Juniors); Long Island, seven (one Junior); Louisiana, one; Massachusetts, four (two Juniors); Newark, two (one Junior); New York, seven (one Junior); Pennsylvania, two (one Junior); Western Massachusetts, two.

Miss Brock, of the Pennsylvania Juniors, presided. In connection with the Secretary's report, messages of sympathy were sent to the New Jersey branch in the loss of its president, Mrs. Clark; and Mrs. McIlvaine, of the Delaware branch, disabled by accident from active work this winter. A resolution of appreciation of the work done for many years in the Junior Department was voted to Miss Jarvis, lately resigned as organizing secretary of the Connecticut Juniors.

Miss Brock opened the conference by the statement that the Junior Department was to be considered as a training-school for the Woman's Auxiliary, in work, study and prayer, and called upon Miss Alice Lindley, chairman of the New York Juniors, to introduce the first of these divisions.

Miss Lindley dwelt on the importance of interesting the Juniors in the whole rather than in any part of the work, training them from the beginning to be auxiliary to the Board of Missions.

Upon this point reports came in from the different branches: In Bethlehem it grows easier as time passes to interest the Juniors in the work as a whole, and their gifts increase. In Long Island they are making the trial, and are doing better as they grow more experienced in it. In Pennsylvania, it has proved very successful, the gifts increasing rapidly.

In Massachusetts, the effort to enlist the Juniors for general work is being tried for the first time. In New York, out of forty-seven branches, thirty-seven give outright for general missions. In Newark, the inclination is to specials, but the officers are making it their business to emphasize the general work and hope for increasing interest in it. Experiences differ in different places, one officer thinking it well to begin with specials and go on to generals, another declaring from experience that a new branch will begin with general work and do well in that. The suggestion was made not to dwell so much on the terms general missions and the Board, as to emphasize the idea of the world-wide work and opportunity.

Miss Loring, of Massachusetts, spoke of certain gifts and graces which should be developed in order to train the Juniors into useful membership in the Woman's Auxiliary. First of these she named the gift of sympathy in its highest sense, including the power to express itself, the ability to see other people's point of view, patience to persuade and the grace to forget absolutely all differences in education, social position or environment, so that those whom a leader hopes to lead and influence will regard her as a friend working with them and helping them to see the better way. Next she put enthusiasm; then loyalty to the Church and to the Auxiliary; and then the courage of their convictions. Miss Loring testified to the harmonious working of the Auxiliary and its Junior Department in the Massachusetts branch. Work there is as in a family, mother and daughter sharing the cares of the household, the daughter relieving the mother as need arises.

In connection with this bit of experience the suggestion was made that where new diocesan officers are to be chosen, if possible they should be found among the young women of the diocese.

The second subject, of training the

Junior Department through study, was dwelt upon by Miss Sturgis, of Massachusetts, who would take the Bible, and especially the courses of lessons already prepared on the Gospel according to St. Matthew, and the Acts of the Apostles, as developing the highest knowledge in the world-wide work of missions. Going on from these she recommended the study of specific facts and fields, since in order to pray definitely our Juniors must have a definite and personal knowledge.

Prayer as the training of Juniors for work in the Woman's Auxiliary was brought before the conference by Miss Hutchins, of Massachusetts, who quoted the advice of a clergyman to do away with the idea of "saying prayers." It had been suggested that a hymn should precede the prayer at the opening service of a Junior branch, and that the hymn be explained and lead up to the petitions to be offered afterwards. The need

OUR JUNIOR

IN one of his Lent Mission sermons the Bishop of London says: "I find on Boards and Committees in my diocese none but practically old men. I go to the Bishop of London's Fund Board, and I find old men sitting there who were sitting there in Bishop Jackson's time. All honor to them; but I do ask for just a few young men. When these old men die, who is going to take their places? It is the same everywhere I go in this diocese. There seem to be no young men coming to take the places of the men who have borne the heat and burden of the day. I honor them with all my soul; but why only old men?"

If this has been the experience of so persuasive a leader as is the Bishop of London, perhaps we should not be surprised if it is often the experience of veteran leaders in the Woman's Auxiliary. One such wrote a while ago, asking anxiously of the secretary, "What will become of the Woman's Auxiliary

any members of the parish best able to help them?

Thus a sub-committee on the Little Helpers of the Babies' Branch might be composed of some young mother rejoicing in her little ones, a woman whose only child has been taken from her sight, and who for that child's sake loves all children, and the teacher of the infant class; and these might enroll as helpers a company of children who would hail every baptism in the parish as an opportunity for visiting the parents of the child baptized, and explaining the purpose of the Juniors' kindergarten — the Babies' Branch.

So a Sunday-school Committee might be formed of members of the Auxiliary engaged in Sunday-school work, to cooperate with rector and superintendent in all plans for enlisting the classes in preparations for the Lent campaign, the sale of the Children's Number, the distribution of the mite-chests, the information to be given Sunday by Sunday, during Lent, the stimulating to varied effort and generous giving, the plans for making the occasion of the Easter offering one of joy and thankfulness.

The Work Committee could gather from the Sunday-school and from other members of the parish those who could meet on week-days to prepare the gifts that fill our Junior boxes.

The Study Committee might form a regular graded school, from the class where little ones recite the missionary catechism, and cut out missionary pictures and paste them in scrap-books of Africa, China, the Philippines, etc., to the normal class, where the latest methods of missionary pedagogy are taught to those who consent to practise them in teaching others.

And why should there not be a committee on the devotional life, by which Juniors should be instructed how to select readings from the Bible suited to every mission field which they may study; to find the missionary spirit which breathes in Te Deum, Litany, prayer and Psalm in our Book of Common Prayer, the meaning of hymns which testify to the love of God for man, and the love of man for God, which would show itself as His love was expressed in loving deeds to his fellow-men?

To carry on the work of the Junior Department according to such methods as these would imply on the part of the leaders of the Woman's Auxiliary a constant vigilance and an unceasing prayer for guidance. They must be always on the lookout for the person best fitted for her task. Their ranks would never be reduced to a few worn and gray-haired veterans, for they would be continually recruited—by the newcomer to the parish, whose bright face and cheery smile are a sure promise that she can win the most stubborn child; by the bride making her new home, who in her old home has been expert with the work at Christmas time; by the college girl, grown up in their midst as a Little Helper, eager Sunday-school leader, enterprising Junior, whose college training has fitted her to train others in the latest methods of missionary study.

The Juniors who have never been without the loving, helpful sympathy of their elders, who have seen again and again those elders change their plans and adopt others, even if not always quite so wise, yet which commend themselves more thoroughly to youthful enterprise and enthusiasm, will surely learn something of the sweet generosity shown before them and come to find graduation into the ranks of their long-time friends of the Woman's Auxiliary a natural and a real promotion.

¶

THE secretary of one of our oldest diocesan branches writes: "We have gained two or three new branches, but several, for different reasons, have given up working with us. We must get after these. I really do not think we pay half enough attention to these matters."

Can anyone suggest what might be done in such a case as this?

TRAINING THROUGH ORGANIZATION

STUDY classes are not the only method of training Juniors. Much can be done with their regular meetings and through the general organization of the branch. This plan has been successfully worked out in many places. The following suggestions of how to do it come from the Junior Chairman of the New York Diocese.

Try to make your branch self-governing, self-supporting, and self-propagating.

Self-governing: Never hold office yourself, but the first of each year have a formal election, first praying with the members that the right officers may be elected. After the election let the president take the chair and conduct the meetings. Very small children can be taught enough parliamentary law to run a meeting, and all children naturally love law and order when they are in authority. Let the president call all meetings to order, and read the prayers. Let the secretary call the roll and read the minutes; and the treasurer take the money, keeping an account of it and making a report at each meeting. Both the secretary's and treasurer's report should be formally approved. Give the Junior officers and members full authority. We should not like to be in a society managed by one older woman; why should the children? Let the Juniors feel it is their society, that you are only there to stand back of them. If the children come to you with a question, such a one, for instance, as what can be done when the girls do not come regularly, don't tell them what you would do, but throw the responsibility back upon them. One leader tried doing this, and the children themselves decided to have a committee known as the Membership Committee, to be appointed by the president. The chairman of this committee got from the secretary at each meeting the names of absent members, and the Membership Committee

looked up these girls, the chairman making a report at each Junior meeting about the absent members.

This committee also got new members, so that the society at once became *self-propagating*. It is well for the leader to call her Junior officers together at least once a month for a special conference, talking over the work with them, getting suggestions from them, and making suggestions to them. A whole branch can be swung in the right direction by these Juniors. Discuss with them, for instance, the question of a study class, or what can be done for an entertainment. Let all these little meetings begin with a simple prayer by the president, asking God to direct this conference. It is very beautiful to see with what quiet dignity and earnestness the children will shoulder the responsibility of their branch.

So much for self-governing, and self-propagation. Now for *self-support*. Sometimes among the very poorest this is not easy, or in some cases even possible; but when it is, it is well to have the branch take care of itself. Let the children decide whether there shall be dues. One branch decided on five cents a week from each member, and one cent for every five minutes a member was late. If the children have their own treasurer and care for the money themselves, they are only too anxious to put their branch on a sound financial basis. Sometimes in beginning work it is necessary for the branch to borrow from, perhaps, the rector's discretionary fund, but the members can understand it is only a loan and must be returned. Of course this matter of self-support involves the giving of the Apportionment by the Juniors themselves and not their elders.

THE MARCH CONFERENCE

THE Officers' Conference for March will be held on Thursday, the 17th, from 10:30 to 12, at the Church Missions House. The subject: *The Study of Missions.*

ACKNOWLEDGMENT OF OFFERINGS

Offerings are asked to sustain missions in thirty missionary districts in the United States, Africa, China, Japan, Brazil, Mexico and Cuba; also work in the Haitien Church; in forty-two dioceses, including missions to the Indians and to the Colored People; to pay the salaries of thirty-two bishops, and stipends to 2,253 missionary workers, domestic and foreign; also two general missionaries to the Swedes and two missionaries among deaf-mutes in the Middle West and the South; and to support schools, hospitals and orphanages. With all remittances the name of the Diocese and Parish should be given. Remittances, when practicable, should be by Check or Draft, and should always be made payable to the order of George Gordon King, Treasurer, and sent to him, Church Missions House, 281 Fourth Avenue, New York. Remittances in Bank Notes are not safe unless sent in Registered Letters.

The Treasurer of the Board of Missions acknowledges the receipt of the following from January 1st, to February 1st, 1910.

* Lenten and Easter Offering from the Sunday-school Auxiliary.

NOTE.—*The items in the following pages marked "Sp." are Specials which do not aid the Board in meeting its appropriations. In the heading for each Diocese the total marked "Ap." is the amount which the Board of Missions in meeting its appropriations. Wherever the abbreviation "Wo. Aux." precedes the amount, the offering is through a branch of the Woman's Auxiliary.*

Home Dioceses

Alabama

Ap. $158.54 ; *Sp.* $25.00

ANNISTON—*Grace*: Sp. for Rev. Dr. Correll's work at Tsu, Kyoto.......	25 00
CARLONVILLE—*St. Paul's*: Gen.........	22 43
FLORENCE—*Trinity Church*: Gen., $3; Junior Aux., Gen., $2.71...........	5 71
GREENSBORO—*St. Paul's*: Asheville, $20; S. S., Gen., $2.50...........	22 50
HUNTSVILLE—*Nativity*: Gen.........	46 80
MOBILE—*St. John's S. S.*: Gen........	2 50
TUSCALOOSA—*Christ Church*: Gen....	56 00
UNIONTOWN—*Holy Cross S. S.*: Gen..	2 60

Albany

Ap. $735.27 ; *Sp.* $137.50

ALBANY—*St. Andrew's*: Gen.........	50 25
St. Peter's: Frn....................	110 57
Laura Van Rensselaer, Sp. for Expansion Fund, St. John's University, Shanghai..................	10 00
AMSTERDAM—*St. Ann's*: Gen.........	42 33
BALLSTON SPA—*Christ Church*: "A Friend," Sp. for Expansion Fund, St. John's University, Shanghai....	1 00
COHOES—*St. John's*: Gen., $21.50; S. S., Sp. for Archdeacon Bryan, for St. James's West Indian Mission Chapel at Empire, Canal Zone, $10.......	31 50
COOPERSTOWN—*Church of the Holy Saviour*: Orphan House S. S., Sp. for famine sufferers in Mexico.........	4 00
COXSACKIE—*Christ Church*: Gen.....	14 55
DELHI—*St. John's*: Dom.............	1 25
FORT EDWARD—*St. James's*: Dom....	32 40
HOOSICK FALLS—*St. Mark's*: Gen....	10 00
LANSINGBURGH—*Trinity Church*: Gen..	62 00
LUZERNE—*St. Mary's*: Gen...........	25 00
MORRIS—*Zion*: Gen.................	32 20
NORFOLK—*Grace*: Gen..............	4 00
NORWOOD—*St. Philip's*: Gen., $30; Sp. for St. Paul's College, Tokyo, $1.50.	31 50

OGDENSBURG—*St. John's*: Gen........	21 00
PLATTSBURGH—*Trinity Church*: Frn...	34 35
SARATOGA SPRINGS—Mrs. Frances Bosworth (Bethesda), Sp. for Expansion Fund, St. John's University, Shanghai	50 00
SCHENECTADY—*St. George's*: Mary E. Van Nostrand, Sp. for Expansion Fund, St. John's University, Shanghai, $5; S. S., hospital work in China, for the blind, $13.75......	18 75
STILLWATER—*St. John's*: Frn.......	2 09
TICONDEROGA—*Cross*: Gen.........	25 00
TROY—*Holy Cross S. S.*: Sp. for St. Luke's Hospital, Shanghai, to be used at discretion of Dr. Jefferys..	6 00
St. Barnabas's: Dom., $2.03; Frn., $1	3 03
St. Paul's: Gen....................	200 00
MISCELLANEOUS—"Friends," Sp. for Boys' Trade School, Ichang, Hankow	50 00

Arkansas

Ap. $144.57

FORT SMITH—*St. John's S. S.*: Bishop Roots's work, Hankow...........	15 00
HELENA—*St. John's*: Gen...........	112 50
LITTLE ROCK—*Christ Church S. S.*: Hospital work in China...........	11 31
St. Margaret's S. S.*: Hospital work in China	5 26
STAFFORD—*St. Barnabas's S. S.**: Gen.	50

Atlanta

Ap. $156.04 ; *Sp.* $3.00

ATLANTA—*Incarnation*: Gen.........	1 80
St. Philip's S. S.: Gen.............	77 44
COLUMBUS—*Trinity Church*: "A Communicant," Gen...............	10 00
DECATUR—"A Friend," Gen..........	1 00
WEST POINT—*Christ Church*: Gen....	1 50
MISCELLANEOUS—Babies' Branch, "Little Helpers' " Day-school, Shanghai, $2; Angelica Church Hart Day-	

(229)

school, Wuchang, Hankow, $2;
Akita Kindergarten, Tokyo, $2;
Gen., $58.30; Sp. for missionary
font, $2; Sp. for "Little Helpers'"
cot, St. Agnes's Hospital, Raleigh,
North Carolina, $1 .... 67 30

Bethlehem
Ap. $677.95; *Sp.* $299.75

ATHENS—*Trinity Church*: Gen...... 13 00
DORRANCETON—*Grace*: Gen 6 00
DRIFTON—*St. James's*: Indian, $90.18;
Colored, $90.18................. 180 36
DUNMORE—*St. Mark's*: Wo. Aux., Gen. 1 00
HAMILTON—*St. John's*: Gen......... 2 00
LAUREL RUN—*Log Chapel*: Gen...... 6 00
PLYMOUTH—*St. Peter's*: Frn........ 6 03
POTSVILLE—*Trinity Church*: Wo. Aux.,
Sp. for Bishop Brown's Building
Fund, Arkansas.................. 67 00
READING—*Christ Church*: Gen....... 126 26
St. Barnabas's: Gen............... 35 00
St. Mary's: Wo. Aux., Sp. for Bishop
Weed, Florida................... 2 75
SAYRE—*Church of the Redeemer*:
Frn............................. 50 00
SOUTH BETHLEHEM—*Nativity*: Gen... 14 27
STROUDSBURG—*Christ Church S. S.*:
Hospital work in China.......... 2 00
WILKES-BARRE—*Calvary*: Gen....... 11 03
St. Stephen's: Wo. Aux., Gen., $25;
Sp. for scholarship at St. Paul's
School, Beaufort, East Carolina, $10. 35 00
Wo. Aux., Sp. for "Bishop Rulison
Memorial" scholarship, Alaska,
$100; support of Bible-women,
Shanghai, $50; Bishop Knight's
work, Cuba, $50; Bishop Nelson's
work, Atlanta, $50; St. Paul's In-
dian School, Lawrenceville, Southern
Virginia, $50; Sp. for Cashiers
Valley Mission, Asheville, $25; Sp.
for Miss Thackara's Hospital, Ari-
zona, $25; Sp. for Foreign Life In-
surance Fund, $50................ 400 00
MISCELLANEOUS — Scranton Archdea-
conry, Sp. for Miss Ridgeley's work,
Cape Mount, Africa.............. 20 00

California
Ap. $86.10; *Sp.* $164.75

BURLINGAME—*St. Matthew's School*:
Sp. for Catechist School, Land and
Building Fund, Shanghai......... 11 75
OAKLAND—*St. Paul's*: "A Friend," 50
cts., "F. McG.," $10, Sp. for Shang-
hai Catechist School, Land and
Building Fund................... 10 50
PALO ALTO—Mariquita C. Macondray,
Sp. for Shanghai Catechist School,
Land and Building Fund.......... 2 00
SAN FRANCISCO—*St. John's*: Gen.... 13 75
St. Luke's: Junior Aux., Rev. John W.
Nichols, Shanghai.............. 10 00
Warren D. Clark, $25, Herbert
Fryer, $25, Sp. for Shanghai Cate-
chist School, Land and Building
Fund 50 00
SAN MATEO—*Church Divinity-school*:
Missionary Society, toward salary of
Rev. J. W. Nichols, Shanghai.... 60 00
St. Matthew's: "Two Members," Sp.
for Bishop Rowe, Alaska.......... 50 00
SAN RAFAEL—*St. Paul's*: Gen....... 2 35
MISCELLANEOUS—Wo. Aux., Sp. for
Bishop Partridge, at his discretion,
Kyoto 40 50

Central New York
Ap. $1,343.61; *Sp.* $260.75

ADAMS—*Emmanuel Church*: Dom.,
$12.98; Frn., $10.61.............. 23 59
AUBURN—*St. Peter's*: Gen........... 88 63
BOONVILLE—*Trinity Church*: Dom..... 13 77
CLEVELAND—*St. James's*: Gen....... 5 50
CLINTON—*St. James's*: Gen......... 41 84

COPENHAGEN—*Grace*: (Apportionment,
1908-09) Gen....................
DEXTER—*All Saints'*: Gen...........
FORESTPORT—*Christ Church*: Dom....
HAYT'S CORNERS—*Calvary*: Dom.....
HOMER—*Calvary*: Gen...............
INTERLAKEN—*St. John's*: Dom.......
ITHACA—Professor H. N. Ogden, Sp.
for St. John's University, Expansion
Fund, Shanghai.................
LAFARGEVILLE—*St. Paul's*: Gen.....
LOWVILLE—*Trinity Church*: Gen.....
MARCELLUS—*St. John's*: Gen........
MCLEAN—*Zion*: Gen................
NEW BERLIN—*St. Andrew's*: Gen....
NORWICH—*Emmanuel Church*: Gen...
Good Shepherd: Frn.............
ONONDAGA CASTLE—*Church of the
OSWEGO—*St. Paul's*: Dom., $9.79;
Frn., $8.54; Gen., $23...........
Wo. Aux., Mrs. Clark, Sp. for Bish-
op Wells, Spokane..............
PARIS HILL—*St. Paul's*: Gen.......
PHOENIX—*St. John's*: Gen..........
SKANEATELES—*St. James's*: Dom.....
SYRACUSE—*All Saints'*: Frn........
Calvary: Gen...................
Grace: Dom., $4.70; Frn., $5; Gen.,
$2.70; S. S., support of Church hos-
pitals in China, $2..............
St. Paul's: Dom., $32.21; Frn., $33.51;
Gen., $43.18....................
Girls' Friendly Society, through
Wo. Aux., Gen...................
UTICA—*Calvary*: Frn..............
Grace: Mrs. Wolcott, Sp. for Expan-
sion Fund, St. John's University,
Shanghai ....
St. George's: Gen...............
The schools of Utica and vicinity S.
S., * Gen.......................
"Two Friends," Sp. for Expansion
Fund, St. John's University, Shang-
hai, $10; Sp. for St. Paul's College,
Tokyo, Fund, $10...............
WATERLOO—*St. Paul's S. S.*: Church
hospitals in China..............
WATERTOWN—*Trinity Church*: Gen.,
$363.54; Sp. for Bishop Brewer,
Montana, for St. Peter's Hospital,
75 cts.........................
WATERVILLE—*Grace*: Gen., $28.78;
Lucia C. Hawkins, Sp. for Expan-
sion Fund, St. John's University,
Shanghai, $10..................
WHITNEY'S POINT—*Grace*: Gen.....
WILLARD—*Christ Church*: $10, S. S.,
79 cts., Dom....................
MISCELLANEOUS—Branch Wo. Aux., Sp.
for Industrial School, Africa, $52;
Sp. for Tsu Building Fund, Kyoto,
$23............................
"From a Friend," through the bish-
op, China......................

Chicago
Ap. $747.98; *Sp.* $634.93

BERWYN—*St. Michael and All Angels'*:
"A. B.," Gen...................
CHICAGO—*Annunciation*: Gen........
Atonement: Gen.................
Calvary: Gen., $5; Sp. for Asheville,
$5.............................
Epiphany: "H. H.," Gen...........
Grace: Gen.....................
Holy Nativity (Longwood): Gen....
Incarnation: Gen...............
Incarnation (Fernwood): "O.," Gen..
St. Edmunds's: Wo. Aux., Gen......
St. Elizabeth's: Dom. and Frn......
St. James's: Sp. for Bishop Rowe,
Alaska, $103.93; Evening Guild,
South Dakota, $5; "A Member," Frn.,
$100 ....
St. John's (Irving Park): Dom. and
Frn............................
St. Paul's: Wo. Aux., Gen..........

St. Paul's (Kenwood): Wo. Aux., Sp.
for Bishop Rowe, Alaska.......... 61 00
St. Peter's: Alaska, $72.09; Sp. for
Bishop Horner, Asheville, $25; "M.,"
Gen., $5........................... 102 09
St. Philip's: Dom. and Frn.......... 5 02
St. Simon's: Dom. and Frn.......... 19 74
St. Thomas's: Gen.................. 30 00
St. Timothy's: Gen................. 8 62
Trinity Church: G. S. Blakeslee, Dom.,
$5; Frn., $5...................... 10 00
Mr. and Mrs. W. R. Stirling, Sp. for
Bishop Rowe, Alaska.............. 250 00
"L.," Sp. for Bishop Rowe, Alaska.. 25 00
GALENA—*Grace*: Alice L. Snyder's mis-
sionary box, Dom., $3.65; Frn.,
$3.65 .... 7 30
HIGHLAND PARK—*Trinity Church*: Sp.
for Bishop Rowe, Alaska.......... 165 00
HINSDALE—*Grace*: Gen.............. 1 00
LA GRANGE—*Emmanuel Church*: Dom.,
$28.62; Frn., $21.62; Gen., $31.01.. 81 25
SYCAMORE—*Waterman Hall*: Gen..... 10 00
WILMETTE—*St. Augustine's Mission*:
Dom. and Frn..................... 23 35

Colorado

Ap. $70.42; Sp. $60.00

CANON CITY—*Christ Church*: St. Eliza-
beth's, Junior Aux., Gen............ 15 00
DENVER—*St. John's*: Mrs. William E.
Lamb, Gen........................ 25 00
St. Luke's: Gen..................... 20 00
St. Mark's: Gen.................... 10 42
MISCELLANEOUS — Girls' Friendly So-
ciety, Sp. for Girls' School at Bon-
toc, Philippine Islands............. 60 00

Connecticut

Ap. $1,793.64; Sp. $956.86
Specific Deposit, $9,600.00

ANSONIA — *Christ Church*: Gen.,
$26.38; Mrs. Frinklin Farrell, Sp.
for Church Extension Fund, Porto
Rico, $75......................... 101 38
BRANFORD — *Trinity Church*: Gen.,
$68.54; S. S., hospital work, China,
$5.50 .... 74 04
BRIDGEPORT—*St. John's*: "Glover San-
ford Memorial" scholarship, St. Mar-
garet's School, Tokyo, $12.50; Gen.,
$302.29 .... 314 79
CLINTON—*Holy Advent*: Gen......... 13 25
EAST BERLIN—*St. Gabriel's Mission*:
In loving memory of Herbert E.
Smith, Gen........................ 1 00
EAST HADDAN—Mrs. F. C. H. Wendel,
for Bishop Ferguson's work, Cape
Palmas, Africa.................... 2 00
FORESTVILLE — (In Memoriam), "A.
L. T.," Gen........................ 5 00
HARTFORD—*Church of the Good Shep-
herd*: "Individuals," $4, S. S., $25,
Sp. for Rev. Dr. Pott's work in St.
John's University, Shanghai........ 29 00
St. James's: John T. Huntington, Sp.
for Church Extension Fund, Porto
Rico 5 00
St. John's: Dom................... 95 63
Trinity Church: G. Pierrepont Davis,
Dom., $100; Frn., $100; "A Friend,"
Sp. for Church Extension Fund,
Porto Rico, $10.................... 210 00
HEBRON—*St. Peter's*: Gen.......... 10 00
LITCHFIELD—*St. Michael's*: Gen...... 157 18
Mrs. G. P. Colvocoresses, Sp. for
Sagada Building Fund, Philippine
Islands 5 00
MARBLEDALE—*St. Andrew's*: "A Mem-
ber," Gen......................... 10 00
MERIDEN—*St. Andrew's*: Gen........ 78 14
NEW BRITAIN—*St. Mark's*: Dom. and
Frn. 43 04
NEW HAVEN—*Christ Church*: "Anony-
mously," Sp. for St. Paul's College,
Tokyo 25 00
St. Paul's: Sp. for Tsu Building Fund,

Kyoto, $20; "A Friend," Sp. for St.
Elizabeth's Hospital Building Fund,
Shanghai, $1...................... 21 00
Trinity Church: Gen., $161.10; S.
S., Sp. for Bishop Knight, Cuba,
toward building a chapel, $686.86.. 847 96
Mrs. T. H. Bishop, Sp. for Bishop
Brewster's work, Western Colorado.. 100 00
Woman's Church Missionary Asso-
ciation, Wo. Aux., Gen............. 6 00
NORWALK—*Grace*: Gen.............. 50 00
St. Paul's: "H. L. S.," Gen.......... 25 00
OXFORD—*St. Peter's*: Gen.......... 2 20
PINE MEADOW—*St. John's*: Gen..... 8 06
RIVERTON—*St. Paul's Mission*: Gen... 10 00
ROCKVILLE—*St. John's*: Gen........ 14 06
ROXBURY—*Christ Church*: Gen....... 10 00
SAYBROOK—*Grace Church*: Dom. and
Frn. 30 00
SHELTON—*Church of the Good Shep-
herd*: Gen........................ 9 83
STAMFORD—*St. Andrew's*: Gen...... 175 00
St. Luke's Chapel: Hospital work,
China ...,........................ 2 65
STONINGTON—*Calvary S. S.*: St. Luke's
Hospital, Shanghai................ 3 00
WATERBURY—*St. John's*: Gen....... 131 45
WESTPORT—*Memorial Church of Holy
Trinity S. S.*: St. Luke's Hospital,
Shanghai 10 00
WILLIMANTIC — *St. Paul's Mission*:
Gen. 27 00
WINDHAM—*St. Paul's*: Gen......... 9 06
WINSTED—*St. James's*: Gen......... 68 18
MISCELLANEOUS—"A Friend," for St.
Leger Fund (additional), income to
be paid during life to a named
income thereafter to be applied to
the support of two beds in such hos-
pital in Wyoming as Bishop Na-
thaniel S. Thomas or his successor
may deem best, 96 shares of American Sugar Company, preferred
stock (par value)................. 9,600 00
ANSONIA—*Christ Church S. S.*: For ⎫
children's work, China............. ⎪
Immanuel Church S. S.: For chil- ⎬ 10 60
dren's work, China................. ⎪
SEYMOUR—*Trinity Church S. S.*: For ⎪
children's work, China............. ⎭

Dallas

Ap. $420.07; Sp. $2.00

ABILENE — *Heavenly Rest*: Babies'
Branch, Sp. for missionary font.... 1 00
CORSICANA—*St. John's*: Frn., $37.50;
Babies' Branch, Gen., $1.30; Sp.
for "Little Helpers'" cot, St. Ag-
nes's Hospital, Raleigh, North Caro-
lina, $1........................... 39 80
DALLAS—*All Saints'*: Gen........... 10 00
Incarnation: Dom. and Frn......... 75 00
Chapel of St. Mary's College: S. Ss.,
Gen. 18 80
St. Matthew's Cathedral: Dom.,
$152.27; Babies' Branch, Wo. Aux.,
Gen., $3.65....................... 155 92
FORT WORTH—*St. Andrew's*: Babies'
Branch, Wo. Aux., Gen............. 1 25
Trinity Church: $50, Babies' Branch,
Wo. Aux., $2.65, Gen.............. 52 65
TEXARKANA—*St. James's*: $43.50,
Babies' Branch, Wo. Aux., $9.15,
Gen. 52 65
WICHITA FALLS—*Church of the Good
Shepherd*: Dom.................... 15 00

Delaware

Ap. $454.79; Sp. $50.00

DELAWARE CITY—*Christ Church*: Gen.. 3 00
LONG NECK—*Trinity Church*: Gen.... 5 00
MARSHALLTON—*St. Barnabas's S. S.*:
Mexico 2 20
MILFORD—*Christ Church*: Gen....... 5 48
MILLSBORO—*Trinity Church*: Gen.... 10 00
WILMINGTON—*Holy Trinity Church*

(Old Swedes') : Dom. and Frn.....   25 00
St. Andrew's: Frn., $127.30; "A Thank-offering," B i b l e-w o m e n's Training-school, Hankow, China, $10 ....   137 30
St. John's: Dom....................   20 49
Trinity Church: Dom., $209.99; Henry B. Thompson, Sp. for Expansion Fund, St. John's University, Shanghai, $50.......................   259 99
MISCELLANEOUS — Third Department service held in Trinity Church, Wilmington, Gen.................   36 33

Duluth
Ap. $113.00; *Sp.* $15.10

DULUTH—*Trinity Pro-Cathedral*: Gen.   52 50
EVELETH—*St. John's*: Gen..........   10 50
FERGUS FALLS—*St. James's*: Gen.....   28 00
GLENWOOD—*St. Paul's*: Gen., $4.50; Sp. for Rev. W. W. Steel, for work at Havana, Cuba, $10...........   14 50
MOORHEAD—*St. John's*: Sp. for St. Mary's School, Tokyo, for new building 5 10
VIRGINIA—*St. Paul's*: Dom., $2; Gen., $15.50   17 50

East Carolina
Ap. $11.62; *Sp.* $6.00

CLINTON—*St, Paul's S. S.*: Gen.....   62
ROXOBEL—*St. Mark's*: Wo. Aux., Gen. 1 00
WILMINGTON—*St. James's*: Mrs. Walter L. Parsley, Sp. for work under Bishop Horner, Asheville, $5; J. H. Hardin, Sp. for Church Extension Fund, Porto Rico, $1.............   6 00
St. John's: Junior Aux., Gen.......   10 00

Easton
Ap. $8.20; *Sp.* $2.00

CECIL Co.—*Trinity Parish* (Elkton): Gen. 5 00
QUEEN ANNE Co.—*St. Luke's* (Kennedyville): Wo. Aux., Sp. for Rev. J. Hubard Lloyd, Tokyo, Japan.....   2 00
TALBOT Co.—*All Saints' Parish*: Gen.   3 20

Florida
Ap. $4.90

DE FUNIAK SPRINGS—*St. Agatha's*: Frn. 95
MARIANNA—*St. Luke's*: Frn.........   3 95

Fond du Lac
Ap. $79.28; *Sp.* $10.00

BIG SUAMICO—*St. Paul's*: Gen.......   1 32
FOND DU LAC—*St. Paul's Cathedral*: Gen. 30 42
OSHKOSH—*Trinity Church S. S.*: Gen., $15; Sp. for St. Paul's College, Tokyo, $10................   25 00
SHEBOYGAN FALLS—*St. Peter's*: Gen...   7 54
MISCELLANEOUS — Branch Wo. Aux., Gen. 25 00

Georgia
Ap. $96.45; *Sp.* $6.00

AUGUSTA—*Church of the Good Shepherd*: Wo. Aux., Gen.............   25 00
P. H. Langdon, Sp. for Church Extension Fund, Porto Rico.........   2 00
BAINBRIDGE—*St. John's*: Dom., $2; Frn., $5 (Apportionment, 1908-09) 7 00
BRUNSWICK—*St. Mark's*: Gen.........   7 15
St. Mark's and St. Jude's S. Ss.: Gen. Junior Aux., salary of Rev. Robb White, Philippines, $3; St. Luke's Hospital, Shanghai, $3; Sp. for Holy Trinity Orphanage, Tokyo, $2; Sp. for "Sister Katharine" scholarship, Guantanamo, Cuba, $2............   8 75 / 10 00

DARIEN—*St. Cyprian's Mission*: Dom., 75 cts.; Colored, 45 cts.; Frn., 35 cts.; Gen., 30 cts................   1
HAWKINSVILLE—*St. Luke's*: Gen......   18
SANDERSVILLE—*Grace*: Dom.........
SAVANNAH—*S. S.*: Gen..............   13
THOMASVILLE—*Church of the Good Shepherd*: Frn   7

Harrisburg
Ap. $14.78; *Sp.* $25.00

COUDERSPORT — *Christ Church*: Wo. Aux., Sp. for scholarship in the Morganton Mission School, Asheville   10
HALLS—*Epiphany*: Frn...............   1
HARRISBURG—Constance Starr and Isabel Dunham Gilbert, Sp. for St. John's College, Expansion Fund, Shanghai   10
LOCK HAVEN—*St. Paul's S. S.*: Hospitals in China...............   2
PARADISE—*All Saints*: Gen., $5.31; Sp. for work in Mexico, $5........   10
YORK—George S. Schmidt, Gen.......   5

Indianapolis
Ap. $178.07; *Sp.* $50.00

INDIANAPOLIS — *Grace Pro-Cathedral*: "A Member." Gen...............   5
LAFAYETTE—*St. John's*: Gen.........   80
MUNCIE—*Grace*: Gen...............   2
TERRE HAUTE—*St. Stephen's*: Gen., $90.97; Wo. Aux., Sp. for Bishop Horner, Asheville, for a girl's scholarship, $50....................   140

Iowa
Ap. $43.40

CEDAR FALLS—*St. Luke's Parish*: Gen.   2
CEDAR RAPIDS—*Grace*: Mrs. E. C. Rock, Gen.....................   5
DUBUQUE—*St. John's*: Work of general missionary in Olympia, $15; salary of Rev. Mr. Nieh, Hanch'uan, Hankow, $5...................   20
ESTHERVILLE—*Grace*: Gen., $12.40; S. S., Gen., $4..................   16

Kansas
Ap. $370.39

ATCHISON — *Trinity Church*: Gen., $100; "Young People," hospital work in Tokyo and Kyoto, $51.26..   151
AUGUSTA — *Atonement*: "Young People," hospital work in Tokyo and Kyoto ....
BLUE RAPIDS—*St. Mark's*: "Young People," hospital work in Tokyo and Kyoto...................   6
BURLINGTON — "A Friend," Dom., $10.06; Frn., $10.63.............   20
CLAY CENTRE—*St. Paul's*: "Young People," hospital work in Tokyo and Kyoto.....................   1
EMPORIA—*St. Andrew's*: Gen........   32
FORT LEAVENWORTH—"Young People," hospital work in Tokyo and Kyoto..   11
HIAWATHA—*St. John's*: "Young People," hospital work in Tokyo and Kyoto.....................   4
HORTON—*St. Luke's*: "Young People," hospital work in Tokyo and Kyoto.....................   1
INDEPENDENCE — *Epiphany*: "Young People," hospital work in Tokyo and Kyoto...................   39
NEWTON—*St. Matthew's*: "Young People," hospital work in Tokyo and Kyoto.....................
PITTSBURG—*St. Peter's*: "Young People," hospital work in Tokyo and Kyoto.....................   5
SEDAN—*Epiphany*: "Young People," hospital work in Tokyo and Kyoto..   2

88
90 00
4 75

1 00
6 25

1 47

19 60

212 82

12 37
10 00

237 85
15 00
102 87
20 00

11 75
87 50

8 40

75 00
2 25
20 00
1 75

11 00

6 44

1 00

1 00

1 00

1 00

5 00

3 00

7 00

Fund, Porto Rico, $5; Wo. Aux., Sp. for Mrs. Schereschewsky Memorial Station School, Shanghai, $2...... 7 00
Incarnation: Miss Nannie S. Prout, Sp. for Expansion Fund, St. John's University, Shanghai, $5; through Wo. Aux., Sp. for Mrs. Schereschewsky Memorial Station School, Shanghai, $1.................... 6 00
Church of the Messiah: Wo. Aux., Sp. for Mrs. Schereschewsky Memorial Station School, Shanghai......... 1 00
Church of the Redeemer: Gen., $1; Sp. for Bishop Thomas, Wyoming, $25.61; Sp. for Salina, $26.11; Wo. Aux., Sp. for Mrs. Schereschewsky Memorial Station School, Shanghai, $2 .... 54 72
St. Ann's (Heights): William G. Low, Sp. for Expansion Fund, St. John's University, Shanghai, $1,000; ; Wo. Aux., Sp. for Mrs. Schereschewsky Memorial Station School, Shanghai, $5 .... 1,005 00
St. Clement's S. S.: Porto Rico, $1.95; Alaska, $2.40; Dom., $6.61; Japan, $3.39; Sp. for St. Andrew's School for mountain boys, Sewanee, Tennessee, $3.68.................... 18 03
St. George's S. S.: Sp. for Bishop Thomas, Wyoming, $45; Wo. Aux., Sp. for Mrs. Schereschewsky Memorial Station School, Shanghai, $1 .... 46 00
St. James's: Wo. Aux., Sp. for sewing teacher's salary, St. Augustine's School, Raleigh, North Carolina.... 2 00
St. Luke's: Mrs. W. H. Bolton, Sp. for Expansion Fund, St. John's University, Shanghai................. 2 00
St. Mark's S. S. (Adelphi Street): Sp. toward the purchase of a lamp for the mission at Cape Mount, West Africa...................... 10 00
St. Paul's: William D. Keep, Sp. for Expansion Fund, St. John's University, Shanghai, $1; Wo. Aux., Sp. for sewing teacher's salary, St. Augustine's School, Raleigh, North Carolina, $2.................... 3 00
St. Paul's (Flatbush): Wo. Aux., Sp. for sewing teacher's salary, St. Augustine's School, Raleigh, North Carolina 10 00
St. Peter's S. S.: "Lindsay Parker Graduate" scholarship, South Dakota 12 54
St. Stephen's: "A Parishioner," Sp. for Bishop Holly, Haiti, $3; Wo. Aux., Sp. for Mrs. Schereschewsky Memorial Station School, Shanghai, $1; Sp. for sewing teacher's salary, St. Augustine's School, Raleigh, North Carolina, $1.................... 5 00
Harrington Putnam, Sp. for St. John's University Expansion Fund, Shanghai 50 00
Mrs. C. L. Underhill, Dom., $2; Frn., $2......................... 4 00
"A Friend," Sp. for St. John's University Expansion Fund, Shanghai.. 1 00
BROOKLYN MANOR—*St. Matthew's*: Wo. Aux., Sp. for Mrs. Schereschewsky Memorial Station School, Shanghai. 1 00
COLLEGE POINT—*St. Paul's Chapel*: Gen. 9 21
FAR ROCKAWAY — *St. John's*: Wo. Aux., Sp. for Mrs. Schereschewsky Memorial Station School, Shanghai.... 1 00
FLUSHING—*St. George's S. S.*: Sp. for work of Rev. Mr. Gilman, Hankow, $33.05; Wo. Aux., Sp. for sewing teacher's salary, St. Augustine's School, Raleigh, North Carolina, $2; Sp. for one day's support, St. Agnes's Hospital, Raleigh, North Carolina, $10.................... 45 05
GARDEN CITY—*Incarnation Cathedral*:

Mrs. William Nicoll, Sp. for St. John's University Expansion Fund, Shanghai 5 00

GREENPORT — *Holy Trinity Church*: Sp. for work of Rev. William J. Cuthbert, Kyoto, Japan, $57.36; S. S., Sp. for one-half scholarship for Rev. J. W. Chapman, Anvik, Alaska, $25........................... 82 36

HEWLETT—*Trinity Church*: Wo. Aux., Gen. 5 00

HOLLIS—*St. Gabriel's S. S.*: Gen..... 1 00

HUNTINGTON—*St. John's*: Wo. Aux., Gen. 5 00

ISLIP—*St. Mark's*: Wo. Aux., Sp. for sewing teacher's salary, St. Augustine's School, Raleigh, North Carolina 3 00

MATTITUCK—*Church of the Redeemer*: Gen. 5 00

QUOGUE—*Church of the Atonement*: Gen. 25 00

RICHMOND HILL—*Resurrection*: Sp. for St. Paul's College, Tokyo, Japan, $14.50; "Family Missionary Box," Gen., $13.08.................... 27 58

RIVERHEAD—*Grace*: Wo. Aux., Gen... 8 00

SAG HARBOR—*Christ Church*: Dom... 8 24

ST. JAMES—*St. James's*: Gen....... 50 00

MISCELLANEOUS—Admiral A. T. Mahan, Gen. 100 00

Los Angeles

Ap. $557.55; *Sp.* $250

HOLLYWOOD—*St. Stephen's*: Dom. and Frn. 40 55

LOS ANGELES—*St. Paul's Pro-Cathedral*: Wo. Aux., Sp. for furnishings for Priory School, Honolulu..... 50 00

ORANGE—*Trinity Mission*: Gen...... 5 00

PASADENA—*All Saints'*: Dom. and Frn., $500; Sp. for Rev. F. S. Spalding, D.D., Utah, $200. .... 700 00

POMONA—*St. Paul's*: Dom. and Frn... 10 00

REDONDO—*Christ Church*: Dom., $1; Frn., $1........................... 2 00

Louisiana

Ap. $371.46; *Sp.* $15.00

LAKE CHARLES—*Church of the Good Shepherd*; Asheville, North Carolina, $1; Gen., $21.55.................... 22 55

LAUREL HILL—*St. John's*: Gen....... 4 00

LUCKNOW—Wo. Aux., Miss Suthon's salary, Kyoto, $2; Gen., $1........ 3 00

NEW ORLEANS—*Annunciation*: Wo. Aux., salary of Miss Suthon, Kyoto.. 10

Christ Church: Wo. Aux., salary of Miss Suthon, Kyoto.............. 25

Mt. Olivet S. S. (Algiers): For hospital work, China............. 6 85

St. Andrew's: Dom. and Frn....... 15 80

St. Paul's: Wo. Aux., Gen......... 10 00

Trinity Church: Gen., $269.53; S. S., $14.38; Wo. Aux., salary of Miss Suthon, Kyoto, $5............... 288 91

Charles J. Macmurdo, Sp. for Miss Gertrude Heyward, St. Margaret's School, Tokyo................... 5 00

SHREVEPORT—*St. Mark's*: Wo. Aux., Gen. 10 00

THIBODAUX—*St. John's*: Dom. and Frn. 5 00

MISCELLANEOUS—Wo. Aux., Miss Suthon's salary, Kyoto, $5; Sp. for St. Margaret's School, Tokyo, $5; Sp. for St. Paul's College, Tokyo, $5 15 00

Maine

Ap. $107.27

AUGUSTA—*St. Barnabas's Mission*: Frn. 5 00

BANGOR—*St. John's*: Gen........... 7 32

DENNISTOWN—*Emmanuel Church*; Gen. 3 00

PORTLAND—*St. Stephen's*: Dom...... 68 95

RICHMOND—*St. Matthias's Mission*: Gen. 3 00

ROCKLAND—*St. Peter's*: Gen........ 20 00

Marquette

Sp. $21.00

MARQUETTE—*St. Paul's S. S.*: Sp. for Bishop Rowe, Alaska............

Maryland

Ap. $1,875.34; *Sp.* $326.64

ANNE ARUNDEL CO.—*St. Anne's*: Wo. Aux., Mrs. Brogdan and Mrs. Pinney, Gen........................

St. Margaret's (Annapolis): Wo. Aux., Gen. ....

Christ Church (West River): Wo. Aux., Sp. for Rev. Mr. MacRae's work in Shanghai.............

BALTIMORE—*Ascension*: "Thank-offering," Gen...................

Emmanuel Church: Dom., $75; Frn., $1,275.38; St. Phoebe's Guild, Wo. Aux., Sp. for Building Fund, Tsu, Kyoto, $20................1

Grace: Wo. Aux., Sp. for Building Fund, Tsu, Kyoto..............

Memorial: Wo. Aux., woman teacher for Indians, South Dakota, $25; Sp. for Building Fund, Tsu, Kyoto, $15.

Church of the Messiah: Wo. Aux., Sp. for Building Fund, Tsu, Kyoto....

Prince of Peace (Walbrook): Wo. Aux., Sp. for Building Fund, Tsu, Kyoto ....

St. Andrew's: Dom., $40.62; Wo. Aux., Sp. for Building Fund, Tsu, Kyoto, $5 ....

St. Bartholomew's: Wo. Aux., Sp. for Building Fund, Tsu, Kyoto........

St. John's: Dom...............

St. Mary's: Frn.................

St. Paul's: Wo. Aux., Sp. for Building Fund, Tsu, Kyoto............

St. Paul's Chapel (Avalon): Sp. for Navajo Indian Hospital, Fort Defiance, Arizona...............

St. Peter's: Wo. Aux., Sp. for Building Fund, Tsu, Kyoto............

St. Stephen the Martyr: Dom., $4.13; Frn., $4.12....................

St. Thomas's (Homestead): E. A. Lycett, Frn.......................

"In Memory of Rev. William F. Gardner," Sp. for furnishing a girl's room, St. Andrew's Priory, Honolulu

"In Memorial," Dr. Woodward's work, Hankow................

Lawrence M. Miller and sisters, Sp. for "Mary Summers Miller" bed, St. Mary's Orphanage, Shanghai......

Miss Mary E. Stebbins, Sp. for St. Luke's Hospital, Ponce, Porto Rico.

"H. W. A.," Sp. for Rev. Mr. Ancell, Shanghai ....

BALTIMORE—*St. John's* (Monkton): Sp. for St. Margaret's School Building Fund, Tokyo, $5; Sp. for Rev. C. F. MacRae's work, Shanghai, $3 ....

Trinity Church S. S. (Towson): Bishop Hare's work, South Dakota......

St. Mark's-on-the-Hill (Pikesville): Wo. Aux., Sp. for Building Fund, Tsu, Kyoto ....

St. Timothy's (Catonsville): Frn., $50; Wo. Aux., Sp. for Building Fund, Tsu, Kyoto, $25................

CARROLL CO.—*Ascension* (Westminster): Dom., $3; Frn., $2........

FREDERICK CO.—*All Saints'* (Frederick): Dom., $9.41; Indian, $2.50; Colored, $3.75; Frn., $10.75; Mexico, $2.60; Brazil, $4.75; ten-cent collection through Wo. Aux., Indian, $5; Frn., $5; Mexico, $4..........

HOWARD CO.—*St. John's*: Dom., $125; Wo. Aux., Sp. for Tsu Building Fund, Kyoto, $5.................

Church of the Good Shepherd: Dom...

Trinity Church (Elkridge): Wo. Aux.,

"Paul" scholarship, Boone University, Wuchang, Hankow.......... 50 00

Massachusetts

Ap. $1,712.59; *Sp.* $269.61
ANDOVER—*Christ Church*: St. Margaret's Guild, Gen............... 50 00
AYER—*St. Andrew's*: Wo. Aux., Tanana, Alaska 5 00
ATTLEBORO—*All Saints'*: Gen........ 52 87
BARNSTABLE—*St. Mary's*: Gen....... 9 92
BOSTON—*Advent*: Gen., $27.65; Sp. for Archdeacon Cornish, Colored work, South Carolina, $41; Sp. for Father Robertson's work in Chattanooga, Tennessee, $1............... 69 65
Emmanuel Church: Wo. Aux. "A Member," Sp. for Building Fund, St. Margaret's School, Tokyo......... 5 00
Emmanuel Church (West Roxbury): Gen., $11.20; Wo. Aux., Hooker School, Mexico, $3; medical work, Tokyo, $5................... 19 20
Orient Heights Mission S. S. (East): Support of bed in the Elizabeth Bunn Hospital, Wuchang, Hankow, $11; Sp. for Bishop Thomas for his work in Wyoming, $1.72.......... 12 72
St. Mary's (Dorchester): Dom. and Frn. 50 00
St. Paul's: Wo. Aux., San Gabriel, Brazil, $10; Isle of Pines, Cuba, $10 20 00
Trinity Church: Sp. for Tsu Building Fund, Kyoto, $50; Wo. Aux., "A Member," medical work, Tokyo, $5; Sp. for Building Fund, St. Margaret's School, Tokyo, $5......... 60 00
F. W. Hunnewell, Gen........... 100 00
Mrs. Walter C. Baylies, for the "Ruth Baylies" scholarship, Girls' Orphanage, Cape Palmas, Africa... 50 00
"L.," Dorchester, for St. Margaret's School, Tokyo................. 10 00
Mrs. Herbert Beech, Sp. for Mrs. Smalley's Slave Refuge, Shanghai.. 10 00
"A Communicant," Frn........... 5 00
BROOKLINE—*Church of Our Saviour* (Longwood): Wo. Aux., Hooker School, Mexico, $10; S. S., Sp. for Church Extension Fund, Porto Rico, $18.50 .... 28 50
St. Paul's: Wo. Aux., Mrs. McCalla's salary, West Africa, $8; "A Member," Sp. for Building Fund,· St. Margaret's School, Tokyo, $1..... 9 00
CAMBRIDGE—*Christ Church*: Wo. Aux., Hooker School, Mexico, $5; Sp. for Rev. W. C. Clapp, Philippines, $5; "A Member," salary of Miss Woodruff, West Africa, $3; Sp. for Building Fund, St. Margaret's School, Tokyo, $5................... 14 00
St. James's: Gen................... 73 56
St. John's: Wo. Aux., Sp. for Rev. T. S. Tyng's life insurance, Kyoto.... 12 50
St. John's Memorial Chapel: Dom., $75.30; Gen., $25............. 100 30
St. Peter's: Asheville, $50; Gen., $80.69 .... 130 69
CONCORD—*Trinity Church*: Gen...... 20 50
COHASSET—*St. Stephen's*: Wo. Aux., medical work, Tokyo............. 10 00
DEDHAM—*St. Paul's*: Dom. and Frn., $326.94; Dom., $20; Frn., $10; S. S., Sp. for Rev. Julius Atwood, Phoenix, Arizona, $5; Sp. for Bishop Roots, Hankow, $6.33................. 368 27
FALMOUTH—*Church of the Messiah* (Wood's Hole): Dom., $31.90; Frn. (of which from "A Friend," $20), $38.36; Gen., $45.70.......... 115 96
IPSWICH—*Ascension*: Wo. Aux., Hooker School, Mexico........... 6 00
MALDEN—*St. Paul's*: Indian, $8.70; Colored, $8.70; Dom., $43.55; Frn., $58.60 .... 119 55

MANSFIELD—*St. John the Evangelist's*: Gen.......................... 13 39
MARLBORO—*Holy Trinity Church S. S.*: Sp. for the children's Christmas at Anvik, Alaska................. 4 00
MEDFORD—*Grace*: Wo. Aux., "A Member," Sp. for Building Fund, St. Margaret's School, Tokyo......... 1 00
MATTAPOISETT—*St. Philip's*: Wo. Aux., Soochow, Shanghai.............. 1 00
NEW BEDFORD—*Grace*: Dom., $215.31; for Bishop Kinsolving's work in Brazil, $50................ 265 31
NEWTON—*Church of the Messiah* (West and Auburndale): Sp. for Rev. Frederick W. Neve for Virginia mountain-folk work......... 5 00
St. Paul's (Highlands): Wo. Aux. (of which "A Member," $1), Sp. for Building Fund, St. Margaret's School, Tokyo 7 85
Fred. K. Collins, Gen.............. 6 25
NORWOOD—*Grace*: Wo. Aux., "A Member," Sp. for Building Fund, St. Margaret's School, Tokyo......... 1 00
QUINCY—*St. Chrysostom's* (Wollaston): Gen..................... 24 00
TAUNTON—*St. Thomas's*: "A Member," Sp. for Changsha plant, Hankow... 25 00
MISCELLANEOUS—Wo. Aux., "A Member," "In Memory of R. H. S.," Sp. for Archdeacon Cornish, South Carolina, to buy an acre of land....... 50 00
Wo. Aux., Normal Mission Study Class, St. Margaret's School, Tokyo, $5; Susan H. Page Bequest, salary of Rev. Nathan Matthews, West Africa, $22.50; Mrs. J. M. Hubbard, Sp. for Building Fund, St. Margaret's School, Tokyo, $5................. 32 50
Offering of Sunday-schools at a service held in the Church of the Messiah, West Newton and Auburndale, Sp. for Bishop Brent, Philippine Islands 7 71

Michigan

Ap. $1,394.73; *Sp.* $111.00
ADRIAN—*Christ Church*: Dom., $4.35; Frn., $3.65..................... 8 00
ANN ARBOR—*St. Andrew's*: Gen..... 100 00
BAY CITY—*Grace*: Gen............. 31 28
Trinity Church: Junior Aux., Sp. for Mrs. Littell, Hankow........... 5 00
BIRMINGHAM—*St. James's*: Wo. Aux., salary of Miss Bull, Kyoto, $1.50; Sp. for Mrs. Littell, Hankow, $2... 3 50
DETROIT—*Christ Church*: Gen., $511.14; Wo. Aux., salary of Miss Bull, Kyoto, $55; "J. H. Johnson" scholarship, St. John's University, Shanghai, $15; Sp. for Foreign Insurance Fund, $5; Sp. for Mrs. Littell, Hankow, $5................. 616 14
Epiphany: Junior Aux., Gen......... 5 00
Grace: Junior Aux., Gen............. 20 00
St. James's: Wo. Aux., salary of Miss Bull, Kyoto, $3; Sp. for Mrs. Littell, Hankow, $3.............. 5 00
St. John's: Wo. Aux., salary of Miss Bull, Kyoto, $50; "Harris Memorial" scholarship, St. John's University, Shanghai, $15; "J. H. Johnson" scholarship, St. Andrew's School, Mexico, $10; Africa, $10; "J. N. Blanchard" scholarship, Cuttington Collegiate and Divinity-school, West Africa, $40; Sp. for Foreign Life Insurance Fund, $5; Sp. for Mrs. Littell, Hankow, $25; Mrs. Minor, Sp. for Dr. Myers, Shanghai, $2......... 157 00
St. Joseph's: Dom. and Frn.......... 40 00
St. Paul's: Wo. Aux., "Harris Memorial" scholarship, St. John's University, Shanghai, $15; "J. H. Johnson" scholarship, St. Andrew's School, Mexico, $25; Sp. for For-

eign Life Insurance Fund, $5;
Sp. for Mrs. Littell, Hankow, $38.. | 83 00
St. Thomas's: St. Agnes's Guild, Gen. | 1 00
John W. Ashler, Gen............. | 6 00
FENTON—*St. Jude's*: Gen........... | 2 50
FLINT—*St. Paul's*: Gen............ | 102 82
HILLSDALE—*St. Peter's*: Wo. Aux., Sp.
for Mrs. Littell, Hankow.......... | 1 00
JACKSON — *St. Paul's*: (Apportion-
ment, 1908-09), Gen., $151.70; S.
S.,* Gen., $25.................... | 176 70
MIDLAND—*St. John's*: Dom., $3; Gen.,
$8.35 .... | 11 35
MONROE—*Trinity Church*: Gen....... | 10 45
PONTIAC—*All Saints'*: Gen., $35; Wo.
Aux., salary of Miss Bull, Kyoto,
$3; "Harris Memorial" scholarship,
St. John's University, Shanghai,
$3; "J. H. Johnson" scholarship,
St. Andrew's School, Mexico, $1;
Sp. for Miss Grante, Africa, $3;
Sp. for Mrs. Littell, Hankow, $2.... | 47 00
SAGINAW—*Calvary Memorial*: Gen... | 10 19
St. Paul's: Dom. and Frn.......... | 52 80
MISCELLANEOUS—"Friends," Wo. Aux.,
Sp. for Bishop Ferguson, West
Africa, for education of girls...... | 10 00

Michigan City
Ap. $8.40; *Sp.* $1.00
COLUMBIA—*Mission*: Dom. and Frn... | 8 40
HOWE—*Howe School*: Sp. for St.
Mary's Orphanage, Shanghai....... | 1 00

Milwaukee
Ap. $289.97
EAU CLAIRE—*Christ Church*: Gen.... | 10 00
KENOSHA—*St. Matthew's*: Dom....... | 21 47
MILWAUKEE—*All Saints'*: For Diocese
of Fond du Lac, $1; Associate Mis-
sion, Wuchang, Hankow, $15; Gen.,
$137.50 .... | 153 50
SPARTA—*St. John's*: "A Friend," Frn. | 5 00
MISCELLANEOUS—Wo. Aux., salary of
Miss Woods, Alaska, $50; St. Luke's
Hospital, Tokyo, $50............. | 100 00

Minnesota
Ap. $273.66; *Sp.* $37.92.
CHATFIELD—*St. Matthew's*: Dom..... | 6 35
LAKE CITY—*St. Mark's*: Gen., $40.97;
S. S., Sp. for St. Paul's College,
Tokyo, $7.92.................... | 48 89
MINNEAPOLIS—*Holy Trinity Church*:
Gen., $27; Sp. for Rev. J. P. An-
schutz, White Sulphur Springs, Mon-
tana, $5......................... | 32 00
RED WING—*Christ Church*: Gen..... | 145 00
ROCHESTER—*Calvary*: Gen.......... | 21 84
ST. PAUL — *Christ Church S. S.*:
"Alice Ives Gilman" scholarship,
Girls' Training Institute, Africa... | 17 00
St. Sigfrid's: Gen................. | 7 50
ST. PETER—*Holy Communion*: Gen... | 8 00
MISCELLANEOUS—Wo. Aux., Sp. for
Rev. Philip Anschutz, Montana,
$20; Sp. for St. Paul's College,
Building Fund, Tokyo, $5......... | 25 00

Mississippi
Ap. $280.80; *Sp.* $250.00
ABERDEEN—*St. John's*: Asheville.... | 2 50
BILOXI—*Church of the Redeemer*: Frn. | 2 15
CORINTH — *St. Paul's*: $10, S. S.,*
$4.30, Gen...................... | 14 30
GREENWOOD—*Nativity*: Sp. for Dr.
Correll's work, Tsu, Kyoto........ | 50 00
GULFPORT—*St. Peter's*: Wo. Aux.,
Gen. .... | 2 10
HERMANVILLE—*Epiphany*: Junior Aux.,
"Rev. R. W. Patton" scholarship,
St. John's University, Shanghai.... | 2 00
JACKSON—*St. Andrew's*: Gen., $240;
Sp. for Dr. Correll's new building,
Tsu, Kyoto, $100; Junior Aux.,
"Rev. Robert W. Patton" scholar-

Cuthbert's work, Kyoto............ 5 00
MORRISTOWN—*Church of the Redeemer S. S.*: St. Luke's Hospital, Shanghai 25 00
NEWARK — *Christ Church Pro-Cathedral*: Frn....................... 12 00
Grace: Missionary District of Salina.. 22 90
St. Barnabas's: Gen................ 1 00
Trinity Church: Sp. for Rev. A. A. Gilman, Changsha, Hankow, $75; Girls' Friendly Society, Sp. for salary of deacon, for Rev. S. C. Hughson, O.H.C., Sewanee, Tennessee, $10.................... 85 00
ORANGE—*Grace*: Mrs. F. E. Hagemeyer, Sp. for Expansion Fund, St. John's University, Shanghai... 25 00
St. Mark's (West): Gen., $75; Bishop Brooke's work, Oklahoma, $25.. 100 00
PASSAIC—*St. John's*: Dom.......... 32 73
RAMSEY—*St. John's Mission*: Gen.... 20 00
SHORT HILLS—*Christ Church*: William Fellowes Morgan, Sp. for equipment of one student, St. John's University, Shanghai, $200; James R. Strong, Sp. for Church Extension Fund, Porto Rico, $10........... 210 00
MISCELLANEOUS—Mrs. J. Hull Browning, Wo. Aux., Sp. for Rev. N. Matthews' Trade School, Cape Mount, West Africa.............. 100 00

New Hampshire
Ap. $141.13; *Sp.* $1.05
CHARLESTOWN—*St. Luke's*: Gen...... 15 00
DOVER—*St. Thomas's*: Gen.......... 13 83
HOPKINTON—*St. Andrew's*: Dom. and Frn............................ 25 00
KEARSARGE VILLAGE — *Grace Chapel*: Gen............................ 4 00
LANCASTER — *St. Paul's*: Missions among Indians................. 8 30
PORTSMOUTH—Rev. Alfred Langdon Elwyn, "M. M. E. Memorial" scholarship, St. Elizabeth's School, South Dakota 60 00
WOODSVILLE—*St. Luke's S. S.*: Sp. for Building Fund, St. Paul's College, Tokyo 1 05
MISCELLANEOUS—Miss Catherine Holme Balch, Dom. and Frn.......... 20 00

New Jersey
Ap. $580.55; *Sp.* $94.58
ALLENHURST — *St. Andrew's-by-the Sea*: Gen..................... 2 50
BERNARDSVILLE — *St. Bernard's*: St. Augustine's School, Raleigh, North Carolina, $50; Gen., $29.33....... 79 33
BEVERLY—*St. Stephen's*: Wo. Aux., Colored work.................. 8 00
BURLINGTON—*St. Mary's*: Wo. Aux., Colored work.................. 8 00
DELAIR—*Holy Trinity Church. S. S.*: Sp. for St. Paul's College, Building Fund, Tokyo................... 2 10
ELIZABETH — *Christ Church*: Girls' Friendly Society, Sp. for salary of deacon, for Rev. S. C. Hughson, O.H.C., Sewanee, Tennessee........ 10 00
St. John's: Dom. and Frn., $12; Woman's Foreign Aid Committee, "St. John's Foreign Aid" scholarship, St. John's School, Cape Mount, Africa, $25; Sp. for scholarship, Holy Trinity Orphanage, Tokyo, $24.... 61 00
Trinity Church: Gen., $40; S. S., hospital work, China, $10........... 50 00
FLORENCE—*St. Stephen's*: Gen....... 6 00
HELMETTA — *St. George's*: Speak Kindly Club, Sp. for Miss Farthing's work, Nenana, Alaska, $15; S. S.,* Gen., $26..................... 41 00
METUCHEN—*St. Luke's*: Gen........ 31 30
MOORESTOWN—*Trinity Church*: Frn... 50 00
NEW BRUNSWICK — *Christ Church*: Henry A. Neilson, Sp. for Church

Extension Fund, Porto Rico, $5;. S. S., Dr. Jefferys's hospital work. St. Luke's Hospital, Shanghai, to restore the sight of some Chinese child, $10.72.................. 15 72
OCEAN CITY—"A Friend," Sp. for Endowment Fund, St. Paul's College, Tokyo 5 00
PLAINFIELD—*Holy Cross*: Woman's Guild, Gen..................... 20 00
Wo. Aux., Sp. for Expansion Fund, St. John's College, Shanghai....... 21 00
RIVERTON — *Christ Church*: Dom., $125; S. S., Sp. for St. Paul's Building Fund, Tokyo, $12.48....... 137 48
ROCKY HILL—T. H. Balmer, Gen..... 2 00
SALEM—*St. John's S. S.*: Gen...... 100 00
SOMERVILLE—*St. John's*: Gen........ 34 70

New York
Ap. $3,801.41; *Sp.* $5,520.63
BEDFORD—*St. Matthew's*: Gen., $58.35; "M. F. B.," Sp. for Expansion Fund, St. John's University, Shanghai 63 35
BRONXVILLE—*Christ Church*: Sp. for St. Margaret's School, Tokyo, Japan, for Building Fund, $100; "A Member," scholarship (Divinity), Boone University, Wuchang, Hankow, $25; two beds, Elizabeth Bunn Hospital, Wuchang, Hankow, $25; Girls' School, Manila, Philippine Islands, $37.50; "A Member," Sp. for Expansion Fund, St. John's University, Shanghai, for the equipment of one student, $200......... 387 50
FISHKILL VILLAGE — *Trinity Church*: Miss Anna J. Vandervoort, Sp. for Expansion Fund, St. John's University, Shanghai.................. 10 00
FISHKILL-ON-HUDSON—Wo. Aux., Gen. 3 00
KINGSTON—*Church of the Holy Spirit*: Wo. Aux., Gen.................. 5 48
MATTEAWAN—*St. Luke's*: "C. F. C.," Gen........................... 2 40
MIDDLETOWN—*Grace*: Gen.......... 80 00
MT. VERNON—*Ascension*: Wo. Aux., Sp. for Hospital of the Good Shepherd, Fort Defiance, Arizona...... 10 00
Trinity Church: John W. Hammond, Sp. for Expansion Fund, St. John's University, Shanghai............. 3 00
NEW HAMBURG—Irving Grinnell, Sp. for St. John's University, Expansion Fund, Shanghai.............. 50 00
NEW PALTZ—*St. Andrew's*: Gen...... 6 00
NEW ROCHELLE — *Trinity Church*: Miss Agnes Lathers, $25, Mrs. S. K. Dawson, $5, Sp. for Expansion Fund, St. John's University, Shanghai; Younger Branch, Junior Aux., St. Paul's Day-offering, Sp. for St. Paul's College Building Fund, Tokyo, $1.................... 31 00
NEW YORK—*All Angels'*: Gen........ 156 14
All Souls': Wo. Aux., Sp. for Rev. Mr. Walke, Tokyo, Japan, $15; Sp. for Rev. Mr. Cuthbert, Kyoto, $15.. 30 00
Beloved Disciple: $96.18, George N. Williams, Jr., $20, St. W. O. Chrisman, United States Navy, $5, John A. Hance, $100, Miss Susie Morse, $50, Henry A. Coster, $10, Dom.; Miss Myles Standish, $50, Mrs. Myles Standish, Frn., $50.... 341 18
Calvary: Sp. for St. Luke's Hospital, Tokyo, $135; Wo. Aux., Sp. for Mrs. Schereschewsky Memorial, Station School, Shanghai, $5; Sp. for Bishop Aves's life insurance, Mexico, $129.54.................. 269 54
Christ Church: Wo. Aux., Frn., $150; Sp. for Rev. W. J. Cuthbert, Kyoto, Japan, $140; Sp. for Expansion Fund, St. John's University, Shanghai, $50; Sp. for Bishop Wells, Spokane, for support of clergy, $10;

Sp. for Rev. Mr. Spurr, Moundsville, West Virginia, Hospital for Consumptives, $125; Sp. for scholarship in kindergarten, Moundsville, West Virginia, $55; Sp. for Deaconess Carter's Hospital, Alaska, $25; Sp. for scholarship in St. Margaret's School, Boisé, Idaho, $72.50; St. Augustine's League, Sp. for Bishop Payne Divinity-school, Petersburg, Southern Virginia, toward a scholarship, $15...... **642 50**

Christ Church (New Brighton): salary of Bishop Paddock, Eastern Oregon, $817.24; Wo. Aux., Mrs. H. E. Alexander, Sp. to endow the "Mary Boorman Wheeler Alexander" scholarship, St. Hilda's School, Wuchang, Hankow, $1,000........... **1,817 24**

Church Missions House Chapel: Frn.. **56**

The Church Club of Barnard College, Sp. for Expansion Fund, St. John's University, Shanghai....... **5 00**

Epiphany: Dom., $90.05; Frn., $84.10; Gen., $410.95; Wo. Aux., Frn., $20; **605 10**

Grace: George L. Jewett, Frn., $50; L. E. Opdycke, Sp. for Church Extension Fund, Porto Rico, $10; "A Friend," Sp. for Church Extension Fund, Porto Rico, $10; Mrs. E. P. Johnson, $1, Miss Anna Murray Vail, "In Memoriam," David Olyphant Vail, $10, Sp. for Expansion Fund, St. John's College, Shanghai; Woman's Foreign Missionary Association, Sp. for Rev. Dr. Pott, St. John's College, Shanghai, $20; "Grace Church" scholarship, St. Margaret's School, Tokyo, Japan, $50; Committee on Missions to Colored People, St. Augustine's League, Sp. for the Good Samaritan Hospital, Charlotte, North Carolina, $10; Sp. for St. Augustine's Hospital, Raleigh, North Carolina, $10; Sp. for St. Augustine's School, Raleigh, North Carolina, for teacher's salary, $25; Sp. for Bishop Payne Divinity-school, Petersburg, Southern Virginia, $25........... **221 00**

Grace: Emmanuel S. S. missionary service, Sp. for Rev. Mr. Cuthbert, Kyoto, for Building Fund.......... **13 27**

Holy Apostles': Gen., $26.95; Wo. Aux., "A Member," for the "Edmund Lincoln B." scholarship, St. Mary's Hall, Shanghai, $50; for the "Cornelia Prime B." scholarship, Orphan Asylum, Cape Palmas, Africa, $50. **126 95**

Church of the Holy Communion: H. C. von Post, Sp. for Church Extension Fund, Porto Rico.......... **25 00**

Holy Faith: Wo. Aux., Frn......... **10 00**

Holyrood: St. Augustine's League, Sp. for St. Agnes's Hospital, Raleigh, North Carolina, expenses for two days **20 00**

Holy Trinity Church (East 88th Street): "Friends," Sp. for St. Paul's College, Tokyo.............. **9 00**

Incarnation: "A Member," Sp. for St. John's University, Shanghai, Expansion Fund, $50; James McLean, Sp. for Bishop Moreland, Sacramento, for work among the Indians, $100; Mr. and Mrs. G. R. Henderson, Sp. for Dr. Lee Woodward for the maintenance of the "Emily Riter Henderson Memorial" bed, St. James's Hospital, Anking, Hankow, $50; Sp. for Miss Leila Bull, Osaka, Kyoto, toward education of Mitsu Kaube, $40; Wo. Aux., "Arthur Brooks's" scholarship, St. Mary's Hall, Shanghai, $40; "A Member," St. Paul's Day Gift, Sp. for Building Fund, St. Paul's College, Tokyo, $25 **305 00**

Intercession: Miss A. D. Hopkins, Sp. for Expansion Fund, St. John's University, Shanghai, $5; Wo. Aux., Frn., $5..................... **10 00**

Chapel of the Messiah: Indian, $5.50; Gen., $2.55; S. S. children's missionary service, for China hospitals, $4.41 .... **12 46**

St. Ambrose: Gen.................. **5 00**

St. Andrew's: Mrs. E. R. Seaman, Sp. for Expansion Fund, St. John's University, Shanghai................. **1 00**

St. Andrew's (Richmond): The Misses Moore, through Wo. Aux., Frn., $5; Sp. for Rev. Dr. Pott for St. John's University, Shanghai, $50......... **55 00**

St. Agnes's Chapel: Wo. Aux., Sp. for Mrs. Schereschewsky Memorial Station School, Shanghai............. **25 00**

St. Augustine's Chapel: Missionary Guild, Dom., $33.15; Frn., $33.15.. **66 30**

St. Bartholomew's: E. P. Dutton, Sp. for Expansion Fund, St. John's University, Shanghai, $10; Wo. Aux., Sp. for Bishop Thomas, Wyoming, $125; Sp. for St. Paul's College, Tokyo, $500; St. Augustine's League, Sp. for Archdeacon Russell, Southern Virginia, $100; Sp. for Bishop Payne Divinity-school, Southern Virginia, $100; Sp. for Dr. Hayden's Hospital, North Carolina, $40; Sp. for Dr. Hunter, North Carolina, $25. **900 00**

St. George's: Sp. for fund of Rev. A. A. Gilman for Changsha, Hankow, $25; Seth Low, Sp. for Bishop Brent's Hospital, Philippine Islands, $250; Miss A. B. King $25, Helen Blagden Rich, $1, Mrs. Lockwood de Forest, $5, Sp. for Expansion Fund, St. John's University, Shanghai; Wo. Aux., Sp. for St. George's Chapel, Morganton, Asheville, $75; Sp. for Deaconess Lawrence, Dyke, Virginia, $55................ **436 00**

St. James's: Everett P. Wheeler, Sp. for St. Paul's College, Tokyo...... **20 00**

St. Margaret's: Frn., $82; S. S., Sp. for St. Paul's College, Tokyo, $14.32 .... **96 32**

St. Mark's: Gen............... **35 06**

St. Mary's (Castleton): Gen........ **150 00**

St. Martha's Chapel (Van Nest): Gen. **10 00**

St. Mary the Virgin: Sp. for Bishop White, of Michigan City, $100; Sp. for Bishop Osborne, of Springfield, $100 .... **200 00**

St. Matthew's: Wo. Aux., Sp. for St. John's College, Shanghai.......... **20 00**

St. Michael's: For the salary of Rev. A. A. Gilman, Changsha, Hankow.. **108 44**

St. Peter's (Westchester): Wo. Aux., Sp. for St. John's College, Shanghai **20 00**

St. Thomas's: "A Member," Sp. for Expansion Fund, St. John's University, Shanghai, $1; Wo. Aux., Sp. for Mrs. Schereschewsky Memorial Station School, Shanghai (of which Mrs. Combs, $10), $35.......... **36 00**

St. Thomas's Chapel: Gen......... **50 00**

Transfiguration: Miss Margaret Neilson Armstrong, $25, V. Hunter, $1, Sp. for Expansion Fund, St. John's University, Shanghai; Girls' Friendly Society, Sp. for salary of deacon for Rev. S. C. Hughson, O.H.C., St. Andrew's College, Sewanee, Tennessee, $10...................... **36 00**

Trinity Church: Mrs. George F. Bingham, Sp. for Expansion Fund, St. John's University, Shanghai....... **10 00**

Trinity Chapel: Rev. W. H. Vibbert, D.D., Dom., $50; Frn., $50; Mary W. Waldron, Sp. for Expansion Fund, St. John's University, Shanghai, $5; Missionary Relief Society, Mrs. J. B. Lawrence, $5, per Rev. Dr.

North Carolina

Ap. $306.09; Sp. $59.96

163 00	CHARLOTTE—*St. Michael and All Angels'*: Gen......................	7 00
	St. Peter's: Junior Aux., Miss Annie W. Cheshire's salary, Shanghai....	5 00
75 00	HALIFAX—*St. Mark's*: Gen..........	1 25
	HAMLET—*All Saints'*: Gen..........	10 00
1 00	JACKSON—*Church of the Saviour*: Gen., $12.15; Sp. for Bishop Horner, Asheville, for mountain missions, $10	22 15
	MAYODAN—*Church of the Messiah*: Junior Aux., Miss A. W. Cheshire's salary, Shanghai................	80
330 00	OXFORD—*St. Cyprian's*: Dom. and Frn.	2 00
	Horner Military School, Major Horner, Sp. for Tsu Building Fund, Kyoto	25 00
10 00	PITTSBORO—*St. Bartholomew's*: Gen..	15 00
300 00	RALEIGH—*Church of the Good Shepherd*: Gen......................	30 00
	St. Ambrose's: Dom................	8 00
125 00	*St. Augustine's Chapel*: Frn........	55 70
100 00	*St. Mary's School*: Sp. for St. Paul's College, Tokyo, $11.46; Junior Aux., Gen., $6; "Aldert Smedes" scholarship, St. Mary's Hall, Shanghai, $15.	32 46
100 00	Through Archdeacon N. C. Hughes, Sp. for Tsu Building Fund, Kyoto..	13 50
	RIDGEWAY—*Church of the Good Shepherd*: Gen......................	5 00
	ROCKINGHAM—*Church of the Messiah*: Gen.	1 65
160 00	ROCKY MOUNT—*Church of the Good Shepherd*: Dom. and Frn.........	60 00
	ROWAN CO.—*Christ Church*: Dom. and Frn.	2 54
50 00	SATTERWHITE—*St. Simeon's*: Dom. and Frn.	2 00
39 00	STATESVILLE—*Holy Cross*: Gen.....	1 00
10 00	TARBORO—*Calvary Parish*: Gen......	40 00
	St. Luke's Parish: Gen............	6 00
5 00	WADESBORO—*Calvary*: Dom. and Frn.	20 00

Ohio

Ap. $528.61; Sp. $483.62

5 00		
3 25	AKRON—*St. Andrew's*: Gen.........	3 00
3 00	CLEVELAND — *Incarnation*: Sp. for Bishop Rowe, Alaska.............	.17 62
2 00	*Emmanuel Church*: Wo. Aux., Alaska, $15; salary of Miss Elwin, Shanghai, $15; "Gregory T. Bedell" scholarship, St. John's University, Shanghai, $5; Fukui, Kyoto, $10........	45 00
82 00	*St. Paul's*: Wo. Aux., Alaska (of which Junior Aux., $5), $15; Sp. for Foreign Insurance Fund, $20; Mrs. Bert. Denison, Sp. for Bishop Rowe, Alaska, $2; Junior Aux., salary of Miss Elwin, Shanghai, $5;	
10 00	"Julia L. McGrew" scholarship, St.	
30 00	Hilda's School, Wuchang, Hankow, $50	92 00
	Trinity Church: Wo. Aux., Alaska (of which Mrs. E. W. Ogilby, $100)...	125 00
	Meeting at Trinity Cathedral, January 14th, 1910, Sp. for Bishop Rowe,	
85 00	Alaska	55 00
	Mrs. H. N. Osborn, Sp. for hospital	50 00
10 00	work, Alaska	14 15
	EAST LIVERPOOL—*St. Stephen's*: Gen.	1 00
	ELYRIA—*St. Andrew's S. S.*: Gen....	7 00
10 00	FOSTORIA—*Trinity Church*: Gen.....	70
	HICKSVILLE—*St. Paul's Mission*: Gen.	
	MANSFIELD—*Grace*: $12.75, S. S., $2.38, Gen...........	15 13
1 00	MOUNT GILEAD—*Transfiguration*: Gen..	1 35
1 00	OBERLIN—*Christ Church*: Gen.......	15 00
	STEUBENVILLE — *St. Stephen's*: St. Luke's Hospital, Shanghai, $12;	
25 00	Gen., $40.24; Sp. for Bishop Aves, relief of famine sufferers, Mexico, $5	57 24
	TIFFIN—*Trinity Church*: Gen........	7 09
	TOLEDO—*All Saints' Mission*: Gen....	5 28
85 00	*Trinity Church*: Gen..............	150 00

UPPER SANDUSKY—*Trinity Church*:
Gen. 3 50
WARREN—*Christ Church*: Gen....... 13 17
MISCELLANEOUS — Cleveland Convocation, Wo. Aux., Sp. for Bishop Rowe, Alaska 84 00
Wo. Aux., Sp. for Bishop Rowe, Alaska 250 00

Oregon

Ap. $121.50

ASHLAND—*Trinity Church*: Gen....... 13 35
ASTORIA—*Grace*: Dom. and Frn...... 93 00
BANDON—*St. John-by-the-Sea*: Gen... 1 65
CORVALLIS — *Church of the Good Samaritan*: Gen................... 5 00
OAKLAND—*St. Clement's*: Gen....... 3 50
WARRENTON—*St. Thomas's*: Gen..... 5 00

Pennsylvania

Ap. $7,075.62 ; *Sp.* $3,194.49

AMBLER—*Trinity Memorial*: Wo. Aux. Sp. for "Philadelphia" scholarship, St. Mary's Orphanage, Shanghai... 5 00
BRYN MAWR—*Church of the Redeemer*: Box No. 2,580, Dom., $60 ; Wo. Aux., "Richard Newton" scholarship, Cuttington College and Divinity-school, Cuttington, Africa, $5 ; "Julia C. Emery" scholarship, Orphan Asylum, Cape Palmas, Africa, $5 ; "Francesca" scholarship, Cuttington College and Divinity-school, Cuttington, Africa, $5 ; "Anna M. Stevens Memorial" scholarship, Girls' Training Institute, St. Paul's River, West Africa, $5 ; "W. Beaumont Whitney" scholarship, Havana, Cuba, $5 ; Training-school for Bible-women, Hankow, $5 ; "Pennsylvania Foreign Committee" scholarship, St. Hilda's School, Wuchang, Hankow, $5 ; Training-school, Sendai, Tokyo, $5 ; "Pennsylvania Foreign Committee" scholarship, Girls' High School, Kyoto, $5 ; "Dr. Twing Memorial" scholarship, St. John's University, Shanghai, $5 ; "Bishop Stevens" scholarship, St. John's University, Shanghai, $5 ; "Kinsolving" scholarship, Brazil, $5 ; "Pennsylvania Woman's Auxiliary" scholarship, Hooker Memorial School, Mexico, $5 ; Sp. for "Philadelphia" scholarship, St. Mary's Orphanage, Shanghai, $10 ; Sp. for Miss Ridgely for new house, Cape Mount, Africa, $5 ; Sp. for "John W. Wood" scholarship, Guantanamo, Cuba, $5 ; Sp. for Rev. Amos Goddard life insurance, Hankow, $5 ; Junior Aux., Dom., $2 ; Indian, $1 ; Colored, $2 ; Frn., $2 ; salary of Miss Wall, Tokyo, $5 ; Sp. for Archdeacon Wentworth, Lexington, $1.................... 163 00
CLIFTON HEIGHTS—*St. Stephen's*: Wo. Aux., "Pennsylvania Woman's Auxiliary" scholarship, Hooker Memorial School, Mexico, $1 ; Sp. for Bishop Knight for Guaniguanico, Cuba, $2.. 3 00
ESSINGTON—*St. John the Evangelist's*: Gen. 4 50
JENKINTON—*Church of Our Saviour*: Wo. Aux., "Kinsolving" scholarship, Brazil 5 00
"Friends," Sp. for Tsu Building Fund, Kyoto, for chancel furniture.. 27 50
LANSDOWNE—*St. John's S. S.*: Hospital work, China............... 15 00
LOWER MERION—*St. John's S. S.*: Hospital work, China............ 10 00
MEDIA—*Christ Church*: Wo. Aux., "Kinsolving" scholarship, Brazil... 5 00
NORRISTOWN—*All Saints'*: Wo. Aux., Sp. for Foreign Life Insurance..... 1 00

PAOLI—*Church of the Good Samaritan*: Frn. ....
PHILADELPHIA — *All Saints'* (Lower Dublin) : Wo. Aux., Sp. for Tsu Building Fund, Kyoto...........
Ascension: Wo. Aux., "Kinsolving" scholarship, Brazil, $4 ; Sp. for Foreign Life Insurance, $2..........
Calvary (G e r m a n t o w n) : Frn., $1,004.86 ; Wo. Aux., "Training-school, Sendai, Tokyo, $5 ; "Dr. Twing Memorial" scholarship, St. John's University, Shanghai, $5 ; Training-school for Bible-women, Hankow, $5 ; Sp. for Foreign Life Insurance, $5................. 1
Christ Church : Dom., $289.04 ; Frn., $354.14 ....
Christ Church Chapel : Wo. Aux., "Kinsolving" scholarship, Brazil...
Christ Church Hospital : Wo. Aux., "Dr. Twing Memorial" scholarship, St. John's University, Shanghai....
Covenant : Sp. for Bishop Knight, Cuba, for Isle of Pines Chapel, $23.13 ; Wo. Aux., "Kinsolving" scholarship, Brazil, $10 ; "Bishop Stevens" scholarship, St. John's University, Shanghai, $10 ; "Richard Newton" scholarship, Cuttington College and Divinity-school, Africa, $5 ; Primary Department, S. S., $5 ; Sp. for scholarship, St. Mary's Orphanage, Shanghai, $18..........
E p i p h a n y (Germantown) : Dom., $84.87 ; Wo. Aux., Sp. for "Philadelphia" scholarship, St. Mary's Orphanage, Shanghai, $5..........
Epiphany Chapel : Junior Aux., $5..
Gloria Dei (Old Swedes') *S. S.*: Sp. for Bishop Knight, Cuba, for rebuilding chapels on Isle of Pines........
Grace : Wo. Aux., "Kinsolving" scholarship, Brazil..................
Grace Chapel : Gen...............
Grace (Mount Airy) : Wo. Aux., "Kinsolving" scholarship, Brazil......
Holy Apostles' : Mrs. Mary A. Todd, Gen., $200 ; Wo. Aux., "W. Beaumont Whitney" scholarship, Havana, Cuba, $5 ; "Julia C. Emery" scholarship, Orphan Asylum, Cape Palmas, Africa, $5 ; "Richard Newton" scholarship, Cuttington College and Divinity-school, Cuttington, Africa, $5 ; Sp. for "Philadelphia" scholarship, St. Mary's Orphanage, Shanghai, $1........
Holy Trinity Church : Wo. Aux., "Dr. Twing Memorial" scholarship, St. John's University, Shanghai, $6 ; "Francesca" scholarship, Cuttington College and Divinity-school, Africa, $5 ; "Anna M. Stevens Memorial" scholarship, Girls' Training Institute, St. Paul's River, Africa, $5 ; "Foreign Committee" scholarship, St. Margaret's School, Tokyo, $5 ; Sp. for "John W. Wood" scholarship, Guantanamo, Cuba, $5 ; Missionary Bible-class, St. Andrew's Seminary, Mexico, $25 ; Sp. for Miss Bull for support of a boy in school, Osaka, Kyoto, $25 ; Junior Aux., Vacation Bible-school, Gen., $4.11 ; S. S., Sp. for Rev. P. R. Stockman, Ichang, Hankow, $10....
Incarnation : Wo. Aux., Sp. for Miss Boyd's personal work, Tokyo.......
Prince of Peace Chapel : Wo. Aux., "Pennsylvania Woman's Auxiliary" scholarship, Hooker Memorial School, Mexico, $5 ; Sp. for Foreign Life Insurance, $2..................
St. Andrew's : Frn., $39.19 ; Wo. Aux., "W. Beaumont Whitney" scholarship, Havana, Cuba, $2 ; "Pennsylvania Wo. Aux." scholarship,

Hooker Memorial School, Mexico, $10; "Richard Newton" scholarship, Cuttington College and Divinity-school, Cuttington, Africa, $5; "Francesca" scholarship, Cuttington College and Divinity-school, Cuttington, Africa, $5; "Julia C. Emery" scholarship, Orphan Asylum, Cape Palmas, Africa, $5; Hooker Memorial School, Mexico, $15 .... 81 19

St. *Andrew's* (West): Wo. Aux., Sp. for life insurance 2 00

St. *Barnabas's S. S.* (Haddington): Gen. 3 30

St. *Clement's*: Wo. Aux., Sp. for nurse's salary, St. Luke's Hospital, Shanghai 15 00

St. *James's*: Indian Hope Association, Indian, $20; "F. H. D.," Wo. Aux., Gen., $75 .... 95 00

St. *James the Less*: Gen 103 00

St. *Jude and the Nativity*: Wo. Aux., Sp. for Bishop Knight for chapel, Guaniguanico, Cuba 5 00

St. *Luke's* (Germantown): Wo. Aux. No. 1, Sp. for Bishop Knight for Guaniguanico, Cuba, $5; No. 2, "Kinsolving" scholarship, Brazil, $2 ... 7 00

St. *Luke and the Epiphany*: Wo. Aux., Sp. for Bishop Knight for chapel at Guaniguanico, Cuba 5 00

St. *Mark's*: Wo. Aux., "Kinsolving" scholarship, Brazil, $5.50; Sp. for Tsu Building Fund, Kyoto, $114 .... 119 50

St. *Martin's* (Oak Lane): Dom., $1.25; Frn., $12.86; S. S., Frn., $8.64; hospitals in China, $20 .... 42 75

St. *Martin's - in - the - Fields*: Dom., $1,336.30; Sp. for Bishop Thomas, Wyoming, $150; Sp. for Bishop Knight, Cuba, for Isle of Pines chapels, $49.89 .... 1,536 19

St. *Mary's* (West): Wo. Aux., "Foreign Committee" scholarship, St. Hilda's School, Wuchang, $5; "Bishop Whitaker" scholarship, St. John's School, Cape Mount, Africa, $10; Sp. for Miss Ridgely's new house, Cape Mount, Africa, $2 ..... 17 00

St. *Matthew's* (Francisville): Wo. Aux., Sp. for Bishop Knight for chapel, Guaniguanico, Cuba 5 00

St. *Matthias's*: Wo. Aux., Training-school for Bible-women, Hankow .. 4 00

St. *Michael's* (Germantown): Wo. Aux. (of which S. S., $10), "W. Beaumont Whitney" scholarship, Havana, Cuba 25 00

t. *Paul's* (Chestnut Hill): Frn., $700; Wo. Aux., "Foreign Committee" scholarship, St. Hilda's School, Wuchang, Hankow, $5; "Foreign Committee" scholarship, St. Margaret's School, Tokyo, $5; Training-school for Bible-women, Hankow, $5; "Dr. Twing Memorial" scholarship, St. John's University, Shanghai, $5; "Pennsylvania Woman's Auxiliary" scholarship, Hooker Memorial School, Mexico, $10; "Kinsolving" scholarship, Brazil, $5; "W. Beaumont Whitney" scholarship, Havana, Cuba, $5; Training-school, Sendai, Tokyo, $5; Sp. for Foreign Life Insurance, $5; Sp. for nurse's salary, St. Luke's Hospital, Shanghai, $5; Sp. for Rev. Amos Goddard's life insurance, $5 ..... 760 00

St. *Paul's* (Aramingo): Gen., $33.50; S. S., to restore sight of a blind child at St. Luke's Hospital, Shanghai, $10 .... 43 50

St. *Paul's Memorial* (Overbrook): Wo. Aux., 'Kinsolving" scholarship, Brazil, $10; "Foreign Committee" scholarship, St. Hilda's School, Wuchang, Hankow, $5; Training-school, Sendai, Tokyo, $5; Indian

Hope Association, Indian, $5 .... 25 00

St. *Peter's*: "A Member," salary of Rev. R. A. Walker, Tokyo, $375; Wo. Aux., "W. Beaumont Whitney" scholarship, Havana, Cuba, $5; "Anna M. Stevens Memorial" scholarship, Girls' Training Institute, St. Paul's River, Africa, $5; "Foreign Committee" scholarship, St. Margaret's School, Tokyo, $5; Sp. for Foreign Life Insurance, $2; Indian Hope Association, Indian, $10 ..... 402 00

St. *Peter's* (Germantown): Miss Greene, "Miss Greene's Bible-class" scholarship, St. John's School, Cape Mount, Africa, $25; Wo. Aux., "Anna J. Rumney" scholarship, St. Paul's College, Tokyo, $50; Sp. for Bishop Knight for Guaniguanico, Cuba, $5 .... 80 00

St. *Simeon's*: Dom., $10; Frn., $24.75; salary of Rev. Amos Goddard, Hankow, $25; Sp. for Bishop Thomas, Wyoming, $40: 99 75

St. *Stephen's*: Wo. Aux., "W. Beaumont Whitney" scholarship, Havana, Cuba, $5; Training-school, Sendai, Tokyo, $5; Training-school for Bible-women, Hankow, $5; "Bishop Stevens" scholarship, St. John's University, Shanghai, $5; "Anna M. Stevens Memorial" scholarship, Girls' Training Institute, St. Paul's River, Africa, $5; "Kinsolving" scholarship, Brazil, $5; Sp. for Bishop Knight for Guaniguanico, Cuba, $5 .... 35 00

Church of the Saviour (West): Wo. Aux., "Dr. Twing Memorial" scholarship, St. John's University, Shanghai, $5; Sp. for Foreign Life Insurance, $5; Sp. for Bishop Knight, to rebuild chapels, Cuba, $1 ... 11 00

St. *Timothy's* (Roxborough): Dom. and Frn., $49.61; S. S., hospital work, China, $15.62 .... 65 23

Transfiguration: Junior Aux., Sp. for Rev. H. H. P. Roche's work, Deland, Southern Florida 16 27

Miss Margaretta V. Whitney, $5, W. Beaumont Whitney, Jr., $5, Mrs. George M. Henderson, $5, Wo. Aux., for "W. Beaumont Whitney" scholarship, Havana, Cuba 15 00

Through Miss M. W. Schott, Wo. Aux., Hooker Memorial School, Mexico 15 00

Tuesday Missionary Bible-class, Wo. Aux. (of which "M. C.," $250), Sp. for Dr. Jefferys for furnishings for St. Luke's Hospital, Shanghai ... 500 00

Through the Tuesday Missionary Bible-class, $210, Miss Coles, $50, Sp. for Bishop Brent's work, Manila, Philippine Islands 260 00

Rosalie L. Mitchell, Mission Study Class Alumnæ, Sp. for Tsu Building Fund, Kyoto, $5; Wo. Aux., salary of Rev. Ising Toy Fang, Ichang, Hankow, $240; salary of Pao Ten En, Ichang, Hankow, $72; Sp. for Rev. D. T. Huntington, Easter present for school children, Ichang, Hankow, $25 .... 342 00

Cuban Guild, Sp. for Bishop Knight for scholarship, Divinity-school, Havana, Cuba 50 00

Dr. George Woodward, Sp. for support of St. Agnes's School, Anking, Hankow 600 00

John E. Baird, Sp. for Right Rev. N. S. Thomas, Wyoming 500 00

"R. R." (Chestnut Hill), Dom., $175; Frn., $150 .... 325 00

Cash, "A. F.," Sp. for Bishop Horner, Asheville 200 00

"B. A.," Sp. for Bishop Kinsolving, Brazil 100 00

Miss Nora Davis, Sp. for Wyoming..   100 00
Mrs. George Boker, Sp. for Bishop
Restarick's school, Honolulu.......   50 00
Thomas W. Sparks, Gen...........   15 00
Mary E. Clarkson (Germantown),
Dom. 5 00
Miss Isabel F. Jacot, Sp. for Bishop
Schereschewsky proposed Memorial
Preparatory School Fund, Shanghai.   1 00
RADNOR—*St. David's*: Dom. and Frn..   165 00
Church of the Good Shepherd (Rose-
mont): Wo. Aux., Sp. for Bishop
Knight for Guaniguanico, Cuba....   3 00
ROCKDALE—*Calvary*: Gen...........   5 89
ROCKLEDGE—*Holy Nativity*: Junior
Aux., Gen.....................   2 75
UPPER MERION—*Christ* (Swede's)
Church: Dom..................   14 10
UPPER PROVIDENCE—*St. Paul's Me-
morial* (Oaks): Wo. Aux., Sp. for
Foreign Life Insurance..........   4 00
WAYNE—*St. Mary's Memorial*: Wo.
Aux., "Foreign Committee" scholar-
ship, St. Hilda's School, Wuchang,
Hankow, $5; "Foreign Committee"
scholarship, St. Margaret's School,
Tokyo, $2.................   7 00
WEST CHESTER—*Holy Trinity Church*:
Miss Sarah H. Lindley, Sp. for hos-
pital work in Alaska, $25; Wo.
Aux., St. Andrew's Seminary, Mex-
ico, $15; "Pennsylvania Woman's
Auxiliary" scholarship, Hooker Me-
morial School, Mexico, $15; "Dr.
Twing Memorial" scholarship, St.
John's University, Shanghai, $10;
Training-school for Bible-women,
Hankow, $10; "Richard Newton"
scholarship, Cuttington College and
Divinity-school, Africa, $5; "Fran-
cesca" scholarship, Cuttington,
Africa, $5; "Julia C. Emery" schol-
arship, Orphan Asylum, Cape
Palmas, Africa, $10; "Anna M.
Stevens Memorial" scholarship, Girls'
Training Institute, St. Paul's River,
Africa, $7; Sp. for nurse's salary,
St. Luke's Hospital, Shanghai, $7;
Junior Aux., Gen., $2..........   111 00
WYNCOTE—*All Hallows'*: Wo. Aux.,
"W. Beaumont Whitney" scholar-
ship, Havana, Cuba, $5; Sp. for
"John W. Wood" scholarship,
Guantanamo, Cuba, $5; Junior Aux.,
Sp. for Rev. W. B. Thorne, Fond du
Lac, $10; Sp. for Bishop Burton,
Lexington, $50...............   70 00
MISCELLANEOUS—Branch Wo. Aux.,
Colored, $30; Diocesan Committee,
Gen., $59.50..................   89 50
Through Bishop Whitaker, Trustee,
for education in Liberia, Africa.....   500 00
Indian Hope Association, "E. M.
Graff" scholarship, St. Elizabeth's
School, South Dakota..........   60 00
Senior Members' Club, Girls'
Friendly Society, Sp. for support of
child, Girls' School, Bontoc, Philip-
pine Islands.................   50 00
Rosalie L. Mitchell, Mission Study
Class Alumnæ, "A Memorial to Bish-
op Hare," work in South Dakota...   25 00
"Cash," Sp. for Bishop Knight,
Cuba, for the Isle of Pines chapels..   4 70

Pittsburgh
Ap. $1,585.90; *Sp.* $117.05

BELLEVUE—*Epiphany*: Gen., $109.55;
S. S., Sp. for acetylene plant at St.
John's School, Cape Mount, Africa,
$5 ....   114 55
BROWNSVILLE—*Christ Church*: Dom..   15 00
Miss Mary A. Hogg, "Mary G.
Rambo" scholarship, Girls' High
School of the City of Peace, Kyoto..   50 00

ERIE—*St. Paul's*: Dom., $37.84; Frn.,
$50.76 ....
GREENVILLE—*St. Clement's S. S.*: Gen.
INDIANA—*Christ Church*: Gen......
McKEESPORT—*St. Stephen's*: Dom. and
Frn. ....
PITTSBURGH—*Ascension*: Sp. for Bish-
op Rowe's work, Alaska..........
Christ Church (Allegheny): "E. S. C.,"
Gen. ....
Church of the Redeemer: Frn.,
$4.15; S. S., Sp. toward lighting St.
John's School, Cape Mount, Africa,
$4.80 ....
St. Mary's Memorial: Gen.......
Trinity Church: Dom. and Frn......
"A Friend," Gen..............
"A Friend," Sp. for Church Exten-
sion Fund, Porto Rico..........
Miss Jane Cuddy, Sp. for Bishop
Rowe's work, Alaska..........
Mrs. James Neal, Sp. for Church Ex-
tension Fund, Porto Rico.........
TITUSVILLE—*St. James's Memorial*:
Gen. ....
MISCELLANEOUS—Branch Wo. Aux.,
Alaska, $150; South Dakota, $100;
Brazil, $150.................

Quincy
Ap. $31.62; *Sp.* $4.76

GALESBURG—*Grace S. S.*: Gen......
GRIGGSVILLE—*St. James's*: Gen......
ROCK ISLAND—*Trinity Church*: For
Orphanage, Soochow, Shanghai,
$16.10; Gen., $4...........
TISKILWA—*St. Jude's*: Gen., $6.52;
Sp. for St. Paul's College, Tokyo,
$4.76 ....

Rhode Island
Ap. $870.70; *Sp.* $659.75

APPONAUG—*St. Barnabas's S. S.*:
Gen. ....
BARRINGTON—*St. John's*: Work among
South Dakota Indians.........
BRISTOL—*St. Michael's*: Dom., $110;
Frn., $50..................
EAST GREENWICH—*St. Luke's S. S.*:
Hospitals in China...........
MANVILLE—*Emmanuel Church*: Gen..
MIDDLETOWN — *Berkeley Memorial
Chapel*: Wo. Aux., Gen.........
Holy Cross: Gen............
NEWPORT—*St. George's S. S.*: Gen...
St. John's: For Bishop McKim's
work, Tokyo...............
Trinity Church: "A Friend," Sp. for
salary of teacher, Boone College,
Wuchang, Hankow..........
Joint collection of Sunday-schools,
Gen. ....
PASCOAG—*Calvary*: Gen.........
PORTSMOUTH—*St. Mary's*: Gen.......
PROVIDENCE—*All Saints' Memorial*:
Dom. and Frn..............
Grace: Dom., $100; Frn., $100; Miss
E. M. Anthony, Sp. for St. John's
University Expansion Fund, Shang-
hai, $25..................
St. James's: "A Member," Sp. for St.
John's University Expansion Fund,
Shanghai ....
St. Stephen's: Indian Aid Depart-
ment, Wo. Aux., salary of a teacher,
St. Elizabeth's School, South Dakota
Church of the Saviour: Dom., $46.37;
Frn., $46.38...............
WAKEFIELD—*Ascension*: Gen.........
MISCELLANEOUS—Miss McVickar, Wo.
Aux., Sp. for Rev. N. Matthews for
Trade School, Cape Mount, Africa...
St. Mary's, East Providence, and St.
Mark's, Riverside, joint Sunday-
school service, Church hospitals in
China ....

10 00

5 00

1 85

2 00

1 65

2 00

University, Shanghai, $50; Colored, $200; medical supplies, Bontoc, Philippine Islands, $250; Cuba, $50; "Bishop Jaggar" scholarship, St. Mary's Hall, Shanghai, $50; "May Jaggar" scholarship, Cuttington College and Divinity-school, Cuttington, West Africa, $40; Hooker School, Mexico, $80; Brazil, $100; Industrial School, Hashimoto, Kyoto, $100; Sp. for "Ah Lam" scholarship, Priory School, Honolulu, $100; Sp. for Bishop Kendrick, Arizona, $100; Junior Aux., "Susan Randolph Lee" scholarship, Girls' High School of the City of Peace, Kyoto, $50; "Southern Ohio Junior Aux." scholarship, Girls' Training Institute, St. Paul's River, West Africa, $25; St. Paul's College, Tokyo, $25...................... 1,280 00

43 50

Southern Virginia

4 00

Ap. $327.73; *Sp.* $310.00

AMHERST CO.—*St. Mark's* (New Glascow) : Gen...................... 10 32

5 00

Emmanuel Church (Madison) : Gen... 3 00

2 00

"A Lady," Medical Missions, Frn.. 5 00

BOTETOURT CO. — *Emmanuel Church* (Eagle Rock) : Gen.............. 6 00

7 50

BRUNSWICK CO.—*St. Paul's Memorial Chapel* (Lawrenceville) : Wo. Aux., for Mrs. Moort's work, Africa..... 10 00

BUCKINGHAM CO.—*Emmanuel Church, Tillotson Parish* : Dom., $1.59; Frn., $1.59 .... 3 18

CHARLOTTE CO. — *Ascension S. S.* (Keysville) : Frn.................. 6 06

10 00

DINWIDDIE CO.—*St. John's* (Petersburg) : Brazil, $15; Gen., $17..... 32 00

20 00

JAMES CITY CO.—*Bruton Church* (Williamsburg) : Wo. Aux., Sp. for Miss Irene P. Mann, Tokyo, $10; Sp. for Rev. T. L. Sinclair, Shanghai, $15...................... 25 00

25 00

MECKLENBURG CO. — *St. James's* (Boydton) : Gen................... 35 61

1 00

St. Luke's : Dom.................... 31 31

NANSEMOND CO.—*St. Paul's* (Suffolk) : Gen...................... 50 00

2 50

3 85

NORFOLK CO.—*Christ Church Chapel S. S.* (Norfolk) : Ghent, Sp. for school at Anvik, Alaska, $30; Sp. for Mr. Osuga's Orphanage, Tokyo, $30 .... 60 00

105 71

St. Paul's, Elizabeth River Parish : Gen. 41 94

Trinity Church : Frn................. 36 79

128 42

St. Mark's S. S. (Lambert's Point) : Hospital work, China............ 1 18

POWHATAN CO.—*St. Luke's, Powhatan Parish* : Gen................. 10 00

220 00
10 00
3 50
17 47
120 99
15 45

PRINCESS ANNE CO.—*Galilee S. S.* (Virginia Beach) : Hospital work, China 76

PRINCE EDWARD CO.—*St. John's Memorial* (Farmville) : Gen.......... 7 71

7 64
33 88

ROANOKE CO.—*Christ Church* (Roanoke) : Gen., $26.87; Sp. for Dr. Correll's work, Kyoto, $25.......... 51 87

WYTHE CO.—*St. John's* : Mrs. A. A. Campbell, Gen.................. 10 00

500 00
6 00

MISCELLANEOUS—Wo. Aux., Sp. for Miss Mann's Building Fund, Tokyo.. 200 00

Springfield

Ap. $36.33

MATTOON—*Trinity Church* : Gen..... 13 90

18 03

MT. PULASKI—*St. Agnes's* : Gen..... 8 10

SPRINGFIELD—*St. Paul's* : Gen....... 14 33

Tennessee

30 00

Ap. $86.35; *Sp.* $10.06

CHATTANOOGA—*St. Paul's S. S.* : China 24 00

FAYETTEVILLE—*St. Mary Magdalene's* : Sp. for St. Paul's College, Tokyo.... 2 56

JACKSON—*St. Thomas's* : Gen........ 2 75

KNOXVILLE—*Epiphany S. S.*: Gen.... 2 10
St. John's: Junior Aux., Sp. for St.
Paul's College, Tokyo............ 5 00
MEMPHIS—*Calvary*: Wo. Aux., "Bish-
op Quintard" scholarship, St. Mary's
Hall, Shanghai.................. 5 00
MONTEAGLE—*Chapel of the Holy Com-
forter*: Gen.................... 50 00
NASHVILLE—*Christ Church*: Wo. Aux.,
"Bishop Quintard" scholarship, St.
Mary's Hall, Shanghai............ 2 50
SHERWOOD—*Epiphany S. S.*: "In Me-
moriam, Bishop Hare," Sp. for In-
dian work, South Dakota.......... 2 50

Texas
Ap. $173.25; *Sp.* $2.00

AUSTIN—*All Saints' Chapel*: Gen.... 7 00
All Saints': Thomas J. Williams, Gen.,
$1; Sp. for Asheville, $1; Sp. for
St. Saviour's Church and associate
missions, Wuchang, Hankow, $1... 3 00
CALVERT—*Epiphany*: Dom............ 4 60
GALVESTON—*Grace*: Dom. and Frn.,
$50; Gen., $27.45............... 77 45
HOUSTON—*Christ Church*: Wo. Aux.,
Gen. 40 00
R. P. Christian, Dom., $12.50; Frn.,
$12.50 .... 25 00
MARLIN—*St. John's*: Dom., $5; Frn.,
$11 .... 16 00
NAVASOTA—*St. Paul's*: Gen.......... 2 20

Vermont
Ap. $585.64; *Sp.* $12.95

ARLINGTON—*St. James's*: Gen....... 15 55
BELLOWS FALLS—*Immanuel Church*:
Gen., $11.90; Sp. for Church hos-
pital, Shanghai, $2.85........... 14 75
BENNINGTON—*St. Peter's*: Gen...... 58 87
BURLINGTON — *St. Paul's*: Dom.,
$188.60; Frn., $124.93.......... 313 53
EAST BERKSHIRE—*Calvary*: Gen...... 2 10
ENOSBURG FALLS—*St. Matthew's*: Gen. 24 65
MANCHESTER CENTRE—*Zion*: Dr. E. L.
Wyman, Dom. and Frn., $10; Sp.
for St. Luke's Hospital, Ponce, Porto
Rico, $5.10.................... 15 10
NEWPORT—*St. Mark's*: $20, S. S.,
$1.25, Gen..................... 21 25
ROYALTON—*St. Paul's*: Gen........ 5 00
RUTLAND—*Trinity Church*: Gen...... 7 00
ST. ALBANS—*St. Luke's*: Gen....... 30 05
SWANTON—*Holy Trinity Church*: Sp.
for Rev. W. C. Clapp, Philippine
Islands 5 00
VERGENNES—*St. Paul's*: Gen........ 40 00
MISCELLANEOUS—Enrolment Fund, Gen. 45 74

Virginia
Ap. $713.03; *Sp.* $116.08

ALBEMARLE Co.—*Christ Church* (Char-
lottesville): Junior Aux., Sp. for
Miss Bull, Kyoto, for support of
Tama San...................... 20 00
St. Paul's (Ivy): Gen., $10; Sp. for
St. Paul's College Building Fund,
Tokyo, $8.50; S. S., hospital work
for children, China, $13.85....... 32 35
St. John Baptist's (Ivy): Gen., $1.70;
Sp. for St. Paul's College Building
Fund, Tokyo, $2.50.............. 4 20
ALEXANDRIA Co.—*Christ Church* (Alex-
andria): Mrs. Eleanor W. Howard,
Wo. Aux., Sp. for Rev. H. St. G.
Tucker, Tokyo, $5; Sp. for Dr. A. W.
Tucker, Shanghai, $5............ 10 00
FAIRFAX Co.—*Pohick Church* (Acco-
tink): Gen..................... 5 00
Immanuel Chapel: Theological Semi-
nary, Gen...................... 50 00
FAUQUIER Co.—*Grace* (Casanova): Gen. 5 00
*Grace, Trinity Church and Whittle
Chapel, Whittle Parish* (The Plains):
Gen. 20 00

FREDERICK Co.—*Stephens City Mis-
sion*: Gen.....................
Christ Church (Winchester): Brazil,
$75; China, $25................
Miss Frances McNeece Whittle
Jones, Sp. for St. Margaret's School
Building Fund, Tokyo............
HENRICO Co.—*Emmanuel Church*
(Richmond): The Misses Stewart,
Sp. for Rev. E. J. Lee, Building
Fund, Anking, Hankow...........
Epiphany: Chapter of Brotherhood
of St. Paul, Gen................
Holy Trinity Church: Brotherhood of
St. Paul, Gen..................
Monumental: Dom., $107.60; Frn.,
$180.23; Junior Aux., "Junior B.,"
$1.70, S. S., $7.38, Sp. for Miss
Mary Packard's work, Rio Janeiro,
Brazil ....
St. Andrew's: Gen..............
St. James's: $57, Brotherhood of St.
Paul, $5, Gen.; Junior Aux., Sp. for
Miss Elizabeth Barber, Anking,
Hankow, for support of girl, St.
Agnes's School, Hankow, $20......
St. John's: Frn................
St. Paul's: Mrs. George A. Barksdale,
Sp. for St. Paul's College Building
Fund ....
KING WILLIAM Co.—*St. David's*
(Aylett): Gen...................
MATTHEWS Co.—*Kingston Parish*
(Matthews): Frn................
ORANGE Co.—*St. Thomas's* (Orange):
Wo. Aux., Sp. for Bishop C. M. Wil-
liams's church, Kyoto............
PAGE Co.—*Calvary* (Luray): Gen....
PRINCE WILLIAM Co.—*Trinity Church
S. S.* (Manassas): Gen..........
RICHMOND Co.—*St. John's* (Warsaw):
(Apportionment, 1908-09) Gen....
WESTMORELAND Co.—*St. James's*
(Montrose): $6.50, S. S., $1.56, Gen.

Washington
Ap. $473.00; *Sp.* $223.00

WASHINGTON (D. C.). — *Cathedral
School*: The Bishop Satterlee Me-
morial Association, Gen...........
Epiphany S. S.: Bishop Rowe Class,
Sp. for Bishop Rowe, Alaska......
Ascension: Wo. Aux., Sp. for Bishop
Aves, Mexico, for relief of famine
sufferers ....
Incarnation: Dom., $15; Frn., $15...
Christ Church (Georgetown): L. M.
Zeller, Gen....................
Rock Creek Parish: Mrs. Sarah M.
Day, Dom., $150; Frn., $150.....
St. John's (Georgetown): Wo. Aux.,
"Rev. George Murdoch" (In Me-
moriam) scholarship, St. Elizabeth's
School, South Dakota, $60; "Sophia
Hutchinson" scholarship, Girls' Train-
ing Institute, St. Paul's River, West
Africa, $25; Sp. for "Burnett Me-
morial" scholarship, Layton, Utah,
$40; Sp. for Rev. D. T. Hunting-
ton, work among street waifs,
Ichang, Hankow, $10.............
MONTGOMERY Co.—*St. James's* (Gar-
rett Park): Miss Elizabeth Ross,
Dom. and Frn..................
Mrs. B. H. Buckingham, Sp. for
Church Extension Fund, Porto Rico.
MISCELLANEOUS—"A Friend," Bishop
Van Buren, rent of mission house,
Santurce, Porto Rico............
Mrs. Alfred Holmead, Bishop Rowe's
work, Alaska..................
Miss Charlotte J. Dennis, Brazil....
"A Friend," Gen................
Wo. Aux., Sp. for Mrs. Wetmore for
use in Christ Church, Arden, Ashe-
ville ....

WILLIAMSTOWN—*St. John's*: Wo. Aux. Alaska Supply Fund, $4; Japanese Bible-woman, Honolulu, $2; Philippine insurance (Sagada), $2; St. Augustine's School, Raleigh, North Carolina, $2; St. Paul's School, Lawrenceville, Southern Virginia, $2; Bible-woman, Hankow, $3; Cathedral School, Havana, Cuba.... 16 00

WINCHENDON—*Emmanuel Church*: Wo. Aux., Alaska Supply Fund, $1; Japanese Bible-woman, Honolulu, $1... 2 00

WORCESTER—*All Saints'*: Gen., $200; Wo. Aux., Bible-woman, Hankow, $50; Cathedral School, Cuba, $20; "Hannah K. Tiffany" scholarship, Girls' Training Institute, St. Paul's River, West Africa, $25; "Eliza A. Vinton" scholarship, Girls' Training Institute, St. Paul's River, West Africa, $25; Sp. for Foreign Insurance Fund, $5.... 325 00

St. Mark's: Wo. Aux., Alaska Supply Fund, $6; Japanese Bible-woman, Honolulu, $4; Philippine insurance, $2; St. Augustine's School, Raleigh, North Carolina, $3; St. Paul's School, Lawrenceville, Southern Virginia, $3; Bible-woman, Hankow, $4; Cathedral School, Cuba, $2.... 24 00

Wo. Aux., "A Member," Sp. for Building Fund, St. Margaret's School, Tokyo ... 2 00

Western Michigan

Ap. $121.40; *Sp.* $50.00

ALBION—*St. James's*: Gen.... 1 00

BIG RAPIDS—*St. Andrew's*: Gen.... 4 00

GRAND HAVEN—*Ackley Hall*: Gen.... 3 25

GRAND RAPIDS—*St. Bede's Deaf-Mute Mission*: Gen.... 2 00

S. S. children of Grand Rapids, Gen. 9 51

HASTINGS—*Emmanuel Church*: Gen.. 25 00

IONIA—*St. John's*: Frn.... 28 20

KALAMAZOO—*St. Luke's*: Minnie Goodnow, Dom.... 5 00

MANISTEE—*Holy Trinity Church*: Dom. 3 50

MUSKEGON—*St. Paul's*: Junior Aux., Sp. for St. Mary's School, Sewanee, Tennessee ... 50 00

NILES—*Trinity Church*: Dom.... 40 00

Western New York

Ap. $564.35; *Sp.* $271.02

ADDISON—*Church of the Redeemer*: Dom. ... 4 60

ALBION—*Christ Church S. S.*: Toward restoring sight to a blind man at St. Luke's Hospital, Shanghai.... 3 00

AVOCA—*St. James's*: Gen.... 2 53

BATAVIA—*St. James's S. S.*: Church hospital in Wuchang, Hankow.... 5 00

BATH—*St. Thomas's*: Dom., $47; Frn., $26.75; work of Rev. Isaac Dooman, Kyoto, $2.50; "A Friend," Sp. for Expansion Fund of St. John's University, Shanghai, $1.... 77 25

BROCKPORT—*St. Luke's S. S.*: Hospital work in China.... 10 35

BUFFALO—*All Saints'*: J. B. McCall, Sp. for St. John's University, Shanghai, Expansion Fund.... 1 00

Ascension: Gen.... 48 64

St. Paul's: "Mite-chests," Dom.... 32 15

George T. Ballachey, Sp. for Bishop Rowe's work, Alaska.... 5 00

J. N. Crafts, Sp. for Bishop Rowe's work, Alaska.... 5 00

CLIFTON SPRINGS—*St. John's*: Dom... 3 80

CORNING—*Christ Church*: Gen.... 30 64

EAST RANDOLPH—*St. Paul's*: Dom... 80

ELLICOTTVILLE—*St. John's*: Dom. and Frn. ... 2 12

GENEVA—*St. Peter's*: "A Friend," Sp. for Expansion Fund, St. John's University, Shanghai.... 10 00

20 00
5 00
7 00
1 35
182 00
2 00
19 10
191 25
13 00
16 00
9 00
101 66
6 00
4 00
30 00
5 00
2 00
24 00
14 00

Trinity Church: Dom................ 213 40
"A Friend," Gen., $25; Sp. for Bishop Graves, Shanghai, $25; Sp. for Bishop Rowe, Alaska, $25; Sp. for Bishop Brewer, Montana, $25...... 100 00
L. Clark, Sp. for Expansion Fund, St. John's University, Shanghai.... 10 00
Anonymous, Sp. for Expansion Fund, St. John's University, Shanghai 1 00
Mrs. H. L. Slosson, Sp. for Bishop Graves's work in St. John's University, Shanghai................ 2 00
HORNELL—*Christ Church*: Dom., $25: Frn., $25...................... 50 00
MEDINA—*St. John's*: Frn.......... 5 50
PITTSFORD—*Christ Church*: Gen..... 1 29
RANDOLPH—*Grace*: Dom., 75 cents; Frn., $1.10................... 1 85
ROCHESTER—*Ascension*: Dom...... 2 95
Christ Church: $17.02, Mr. Williams, $5, Sp. for St. John's University Expansion Fund, Shanghai.......... 22 02
Epiphany: Dom.................. 19 16
St. Luke's: Girls' Friendly Society, Sp. for Miss Irene Mann's work, Tokyo (at her discretion)......... 10 00
St. Paul's: Miss Amelia Bissell, Sp. for St. John's University Expansion Fund, Shanghai............... 10 00
Trinity Church: Dom., $7.65; Miss E. M. Moser, Sp. for St. John's Expansion Fund, Shanghai, $5.......... 12 65
The Rochester Sunday-school Association, Gen.................. 10 67
Miss E. Clarke, Sp. for Bishop Rowe's work, Alaska.............. 100 00
"Two Friends," Sp. for St. Elizabeth's Hospital Building Fund, Shanghai 11 00
Mrs. C. R. Browne, Sp. for St. John's University Expansion Fund, Shanghai 2 00
SAVONA—*Church of the Good Shepherd*: Frn., $5; Sp. for Rev. Isaac Dooman, Kyoto, $1............. 6 00
MISCELLANEOUS—"A Friend," Gen.... 2 00

Western Texas
Ap. $26.42
ALFRED—*St. Thomas's*: Gen........ 2 50
BEEVILLE—*St. Philip's*: Gen........ 3 50
CORPUS CHRISTI—*Church of the Good Shepherd*: Gen................ 7 42
GONZALES—Mrs. M. M. Jones, Gen.... 50
SAN ANTONIO—*St. John's*: Gen...... 12 50

West Virginia
Ap. $154.20; *Sp.* $98.16
BERKELEY SPRINGS—*St. Mark's S. S.*: Sp. for St. Paul's College, Tokyo... 3 45
CHARLES TOWN—*Zion*: Mexican Aux., for "Charles E. Ambler" scholarship, Hooker School, Mexico............ 15 00
FAIRMONT — *Christ Church*: Junior Aux., Hankow, $2; "West Virginia Junior" scholarship, St. John's School, Cape Mount, West Africa, $2; Wo. Aux., Gen., $20........ 24 00
GRAPE ISLAND—Mr. R. H. Brown, China 25 00
HARPER'S FERRY—*St. John's*: Gen.... 4 00
HEDGESVILLE—*Mount Zion S. S.*: Sp. for St. Paul's College, Tokyo...... 1 01
KEARNEYSVILLE—D. W. Border and wife, Gen., 50 cents; Sp. for Rev. E. J. Lee, Hankow, for the support and education of a Chinese boy (Job), $20................... 20 50
LEWISBURG—*St. James's*: Dom...... 1 35
MARTINSBURG—*Trinity Church*: Dom., $5.50; Deaf and Dumb, $9.74; Brazil, $2.08; Cuba, $2.09; Mexico, $5.94; S. S., Sp. for Rev. H. St. George Tucker, Tokyo, $6.70...... 32 05
PARKERSBURG—*Trinity Church*: Wo.

Aux., Bequest of Mrs. Isaacs, Sp. for Elizabeth Bunn Hospital, Wuchang, Hankow, $15; Junior Aux., Hankow, $4; "West Virginia Junior" scholarship, St. John's School, Cape Mount, West Africa, $4; Sp. for Miss Barber, Anking, Hankow, $2.....
PRINCETOWN—*Heavenly Rest*: Gen....
ROMNEY—*St. Stephen's S. S.*: Gen., $3; Junior Aux., Hankow, $2; "West Virginia Junior" scholarship, St. John's School, Cape Mount, West Africa, $2...................
ST. ALBANS—*St. Mark's*: Gen........
WHEELING — *St. Matthew's*: Junior Aux., salary of Miss Dobson, Shanghai, $25; Gen., $8..............
MISCELLANEOUS—Right Rev. and Mrs. George W. Peterkin, Sp. for St. Paul's College, Tokyo............

Missionary Districts

Alaska
Ap. $63.40
FORT YUKON—*St. Stephen's Mission*: Natives, $19.75, whites, $10.50, Gen. ....
SKAGWAY—*St. Saviour's*: $14.65, S. S., $6, Gen......................
WRANGELL—*St. Philip's*: Gen........

Arizona
Ap. $5.00
FORT DEFIANCE—*Mission of the Hospital of the Good Shepherd*: Gen...

Asheville
Ap. $21.25
BREVARD—*St. Philip's*: Dom........
GASTONIA—*St. Mark's S. S.*: For hospital work, China..............
HENDERSONVILLE—*St. James's*: Dom..
SALUDA—*Transfiguration*: Gen.......

Eastern Oregon
Ap. $30.87
PENDLETON—*Church of the Redeemer S. S.*: Gen..................
THE DALLES—*St. Paul's*: Gen.......

Idaho
Ap. $18.85; *Sp.* $7.35
MOUNTAINHOME—*St. James's*: Gen....
SHOSHONE—*Christ Church*: Gen....
WALLACE—*Holy Trinity Church*: Gen., $5.40; S. S., Sp. for enlargement of St. Paul's College, Tokyo, $7.35....

Kearney
Ap. $52.36
ARAPAHOE—*St. Paul's S. S.*: Gen.....
BROWN VALLEY—*Mission*: Indian.....
GIBBON—*St. Agnes's*: Gen..........
HASTINGS—*St. Mark's*: Frn..........
LEXINGTON—*St. Peter's*: Gen........
LOUP CITY—*Mission*: Gen...........
ORD—*St. John's*: Gen...............
RED CLOUD—*Grace*: Gen...........
RIVERTON—*Mission*: Gen...........
ST. PAUL—*Holy Trinity Church*: Gen.
VALENTINE—*St. John's*: Gen........
WOOD RIVER—*St. James's*: Gen......

Nevada
Ap. $6.50
WINNEMUCCA—*St. Mary's*: Gen......

New Mexico
Ap. $35.00; *Sp.* $8.00
NEW MEXICO
CARLSBAD—*Grace*: Gen.............

<table>
<tr><td>8 0</td><td></td></tr>
<tr><td>5 0o</td><td></td></tr>
<tr><td>5 00</td><td></td></tr>
</table>

Grand River School: Frn...........   27
YANKTONNAIS MISSION—Christ Church:
   Dom. 2 67
St. John Baptist's: Dom.............   4 47
ABERDEEN—St. Mark's: Gen., $21.87;
   Sp. for St. Paul's College Fund,
   Tokyo, $1.25....................   23 12
FLANDREAU—Church of the Redeemer:
   Dom...........................   17 35
HURON—Grace S. S.: Gen., $2.50; Wo.
   Aux., Sp. for St. Paul's College Fund,
   Tokyo, $1......................   3 50
RAPID CITY—Emmanuel Mission: Gen.   30 00
SELBY—Rev. James H. George, Jr., Sp.
   for St. John's University Expansion
   Fund, Shanghai.................   5 00
SIOUX FALLS—All Saints' School: Wo.
   Aux., Sp. for St. Paul's.College Fund,
   Tokyo 3 41
Calvary: Wo. Aux., Sp. for St. Paul's
   College Fund, Tokyo..............   5 00
STURGIS—St. Thomas's: Dom. and Frn.   20 00
VOLIN—Wo. Aux., Miss West, Sp. for
   St. Paul's College Fund, Tokyo....   5 00

10 00
1 50
7 50
38 75
2 00
108 91
4 40
7 50
1 50
24 00

1 09

Southern Florida
Ap. $42.89; Sp. $4.10

LAKE WEIR—"K.," Sp. for St. Paul's
   College Fund, Tokyo..............   2 00
MISCELLANEOUS—Babies' Branch, Dom.,
   $21.45; Frn., $21.44; Sp. for missionary font, $2.10...............   44 99

5 00

2 50
2 00

Spokane
Ap. $1.00

SPOKANE—St. Matthew's: Gen.......   1 00

12 50

Philippines
Ap. $66.50

AGANA GUAN—Mission: Gen.........   15 50
BONTOC—All Saints': Gen...........   15 00
CAMP STOTSENBERG—Mission: Gen...   21 00
SAGADA—St. Mary the Virgin: Gen...   15 00

1 00
1 50

Utah
Sp. $51.84

SALT LAKE CITY—St. Paul's: Sp. for
   work of Bishop Rowe, Alaska......   20 40
St. Mark's: Sp. for Bishop Rowe,
   Alaska 31 44

11 00

30 00

Western Colorado
Ap. $49.28

GLENWOOD SPRINGS—St. Barnabas's:
   Gen. 4 50
MARBLE—St. Paul's: Gen...........   3 75
MEEKER—St. James's: Gen..........   1 28
MONTROSE—St. Paul's: Gen........   6 00
MONTROSE Co.—Mission: Gen.......   12 00
NEW CASTLE—Mission: Gen........   7 50
OAK CREEK—St. John's: Gen.......   2 25
RED CLIFF—Mission: Gen..........   3 75
STEAMBOAT SPRINGS—Mission: Gen...   3 75
YAMPA—All Saints': Gen..........   4 50

5 00
7 26
4 80

5 00

10 00
2 28

115 00

5 00

Wyoming
Ap. $14.00

DOUGLAS—Christ Church: Wo. Aux.,
   Frn. 5 00
WIND RIVER—Shoshone Indian Mis-
   sion: Dom., $5; Frn., $4.........   9 00

20 00

15 00

4 10

21 93

Foreign Missionary Districts

Africa
Ap. $117.50; Sp. $20.00

LIBERIA—Wo. Aux., "A Friend," salary of Miss Ida N. Porter, Shanghai   112 50

69 70
10 00
11 83
1 00

England

TORQUAY—Rev. and Mrs. M. Lloyd Woolsey, Sp. for Rev. Walter C. Clapp, toward maintaining his school at Bontoc, Philippine Islands, $5; Rev. Robert E. Wood's work at Wuchang, Hankow, $5.............. 10 00

China

SHANGHAI—Miss A. B. Richmond, Sp. for scholarship in Mr. Ishii's Orphanage, Tokyo............... 15 00

Miscellaneous

Ap. $23,260.60; *Sp.* $1,112.32; *Spec. Dep.* $10,021.68
Interest — Dom., $4,292.24; Frn., $3,480.42; Gen., $8,446.44; Sp., $807.82; Specific Dep., $7.07......17,033 99
United Offering, Wo. Aux., 1907, on account of appropriations to September 1st, 1910, Dom., $3,500; Frn., $3,500 .... 7,000 00
For the "W. M. B." Fund, to be used to protect the credit of the Domestic and Foreign Missionary Society under its appropriations, in accordance with the terms of agreement made between the Society and the contributor (additional).......10,000 00
Episcopal Theological School Alumni Association, Sp. for salary of Dudley Tyng, Hankow, $187.50; Sp. for salary of I. Tomita, Hankow, $50..... 237 50
League for Eastern Oregon, Sp. for Bishop Paddock, Eastern Oregon... 50 00

"K. C. B.," Gen................. 41 50
"M. T. O.," Interest........... 14 61
"Friends," Sp. for St. Elizabeth's Hospital Building Fund, Shanghai.. 10 00
Wo. Aux., Sp. for Domestic Contingent Fund.................. 4 00
"Mrs. R. B. S.," Sp. for Expansion Fund, St. John's University, Shanghai 2 00
Anonymous, Sp. for St. John's University Expansion Fund, Shanghai.. 1 00

Legacies

PA., PHILADELPHIA — Estate of George C. Thomas, $100,000, to be invested and the income to be used for the purposes of the Society; $15,000, the income to be expended or the principal used in any way which the Board of Missions may deem desirable; $50,000 to be used for the purposes of increasing the efficiency of the work done by the Society............165,000 00
MICH., DETROIT—Estate of John S. Minor, Dom., $750; Frn., $375... 1,125 00
N. Y. (Staten Island), NEW YORK (New Brighton)—Estate of Miss Mary B. W. Alexander, Frn....... 500 00
WASH., PRINCE GEORGE Co. (Bladensburg)—Estate of Benjamin O· Lowndes, Dom................. 87 91

Receipts for the month..........$268,441 38
Amount previously acknowledged... 322,722 44

Total received since Sept. 1st, 1909..$591,163 82

SUMMARY OF RECEIPTS

Receipts divided according to purposes to which they are to be applied	Received during January	Amounts previously Acknowledged	Total
1. Applicable upon the appropriations of the Board.	$ 62,204 88	$116,934 43	$179,139 31
2. Special gifts forwarded to objects named by donors in addition to the appropriations of the Board.	19,901 91	53,991 76	73,893 67
3. Legacies for investment...................	165,000 00	....	165,000 00
4. Legacies, the disposition of which is to be determined by the Board at the end of the fiscal year.	1,712 91	51,725 76	53,438 67
5. Specific Deposit........................	19,621 68	100,070 49	119,692 17
Total............................	$268,441 38	$322,722 44	$591,163 82

OFFERINGS TO PAY APPROPRIATIONS

Total receipts from September 1st, 1909, to February 1st, 1910, applicable upon the appropriations, divided according to the sources from which they have come, and compared with the corresponding period of the preceding year. Legacies are not included in the following items, as their disposition is not determined by the Board until the end of the fiscal year.

Source	To Feb. 1, 1910	To Feb. 1, 1909	Increase	Decrease
1. From congregations.....................	$ 68,702 05	$ 77,201 95	$.........	$ 8,499 9
2. From individuals.....................	17,084 06	31,980 35	....	14,896 2
3. From Sunday-schools..................	3,095 19	4,576 30	....	1,481 1
4. From Woman's Auxiliary...............	15,978 61	22,015 66	....	6,037 0
5. Woman's Auxiliary United Offering......	35,000 00	15,000 00	20,000 00	......
6. From interest.......................	38,195 73	31,482 42	6,713 31	......
7. Miscellaneous items..................	1,083 67	2,259 55	....	1,175 8
Total...........................	$179,139 31	$184,516 23		$5,376 9

APPROPRIATIONS FOR THE YEAR

SEPTEMBER 1ST, 1909, TO AUGUST 31ST, 1910,

Amount Needed for the Year

1. To pay appropriations as made to date for the work at home and abroad....... $1,197,101 5
2. To replace Reserve Funds temporarily used for the current work............. 32,955 3

Total... $1,230,056 8
Total receipts to date applicable on appropriations...................... 179,139 31

Amount needed before August 31st, 1910................................. $1,050,917 5

THE

Spirit of Missions

AN ILLUSTRATED MONTHLY REVIEW
OF CHRISTIAN MISSIONS

April, 1910

CONTENTS

The Subscription Price of THE SPIRIT OF MISSIONS is ONE DOLLAR per year. Postage is prepaid in the United States, Porto Rico, the Philippines and Mexico. For other countries in the Postal Union, including Canada, twenty-four cents per year should be added.

Subscriptions are continued until ordered discontinued.

Change of Address: In all changes of address it is necessary that the old as well as the new address should be given.

How to Remit: Remittances, made payable to George Gordon King, Treasurer, should be made by draft on New York, Postal Order or Express Order. One and two cent stamps are received. To checks on local banks ten cents should be added for collection.

All Letters should be addressed to The Spirit of Missions, 281 Fourth Avenue, New York.

Published by the Domestic and Foreign Missionary Society.

President, RIGHT REVEREND DANIEL S. TUTTLE, D.D. Secretary, ———
Treasurer, GEORGE GORDON KING.

Entered at the Post Office, in New York, as second-class matter.

THE SPIRIT OF MISSIONS is regularly on sale
In Philadelphia: By George W. Jacobs & Co., 1216 Walnut St.
In Milwaukee: By The Young Churchman Co., 412 Milwaukee St.
In Boston: By Smith & McCance, 38 Bromfield St.
In Elizabeth, N. J.: By Franklin H. Spencer, 743 Jefferson St.

(250)

An Easter Prayer

OH, let me know
  The power of Thy resurrection;
  Oh, let me show
Thy risen life in calm and clear reflection;
  Oh, let me soar
Where Thou, my Saviour Christ, art gone before;
  In mind and heart
Let me dwell always, only, where Thou art.

  Oh, let me give
Out of the gifts Thou freely givest;
  Oh, let me live
With life abundantly because Thou livest;
  Oh, make me shine
In darkest places, for Thy light is mine;
  Oh, let me be
A faithful witness for Thy truth and Thee.

  Oh, let me show
The strong reality of gospel story;
  Oh, let me go
From strength to strength, from glory unto glory;
  Oh, let me sing
For very joy, because Thou art my King;
  Oh, let me praise.
Thy love and faithfulness through all my days.

—FRANCES R. HAVERGAL.

THE RIGHT REVEREND PETER TRIMBLE ROWE, BISHOP OF ALASKA

HE SPIRIT OF MISSIONS

AN ILLUSTRATED MONTHLY REVIEW
OF CHRISTIAN MISSIONS

VOL. LXXXV.   **April,** 1910   No. 4

THE PROGRESS OF THE KINGDOM

WHAT a miracle these words wrought when they were spoken! As they sounded from the lips of the angel in the dawn of *"He Is Risen!"* the first Easter morning — falling upon incredulous ears and reaching at length the sorrowing hearts of that little company—the world which lay about them changed instantly and forever! It was indeed the "breaking of the day." Never again could things be as they had been. Toil and hardship, pain and sorrow; the cloud of a bitter disappointment, the grip of a great despair, but just now so overpowering, had vanished and left only a memory behind. Even the cross no longer meant hopeless suffering, but sublime self-sacrifice, and to its cool shadow smitten souls might creep and find their shelter. The Easter Sun had risen and at its touch life—heretofore so fragile and so disappointing—had become immortal.

Is it any wonder that after the first stunning effect of the great message they ran with eager feet to tell to others the story which could lift the cloud, and transfuse with joy the eyes that but now had brimmed with tears?

"Go Quickly, and Tell" So each new wonder in the Christian year becomes a new impulse in the Christian life. And if to us this message of the Resurrection is in any measure real and vivid—if we hear with quickened hearts the tidings, "He is risen!"—must we not also somehow find a way whereby we may go quickly and tell others the glad tidings? In spite of its noise and merrymaking, in spite of its wealth and splendor, it is a sick and sorrowing world into which comes the Easter message. Not so different after all from the broken hearts of those who crept out in the grey of the first Easter morning to weep a few hopeless tears beside the fast-sealed tomb, are the hearts of the men and women of to-day whose vision of life ends only with its Calvarys.

But we who know the rest of the story, we who by the grace of God have been brought to understand—shall anything stay our feet or silence our tongues as we hear the injunction "Go quickly, and tell that He is risen from the dead"? This is the missionary message of Easter Day, which, like every other great festival of the Church, can only be fully

understood when it is viewed in relation to the whole world. God hasten the
time when amid our Easter flowers and
our joyous carols there shall sound everywhere these final words of the angel's
message, and our gifts and prayers shall
be multiplied in order that the injunction of Easter Day may be the better
fulfilled by the Church of the risen Lord,
as she goes forth to tell the world of
"Jesus and the Resurrection!"

THE Laymen's ·Missionary Movement continues on its way, arousing and enlisting men in the cause of
world - wide evan-
gelization. The very
successful conven-
tion in New York in
January brought to-
gether a company of men which a newspaper man of long experience declared
to be the most representative gathering
of New York men ever held. Similar
reports come from the cities of the West
and South, to which the national campaign has since been extended. The attractive power of the mission of the
Christian Church has evidently been underestimated. That mission is dominat-
ing the thought and conversation of
men not only in the hundreds of meetings that are being held, but in offices,
in clubs and in home life. The missionary message and the call to service
are being delivered in the most unexpected places. Dissatisfaction with present standards of giving is being widely
expressed. Decisions to do better are being made. Well-planned efforts are under way to substitute for the more or
less haphazard method of an annual offering a careful canvass of the whole
congregation and weekly giving.* The
achievements reported elsewhere in this
issue are all typical of what is being
done in many places. The men who become advocates of the cause become also
more faithful members of the parish. In
some instances the appeal of the Lay-

The Laymen's
Missionary
Movement

* Leaflet No. 1,102, to be had from the Corresponding Secretary for the asking, contains
some suggestive information.

cities, dot the map. Hundreds of miles of rails gridiron the state. Thousands of fertile farms are sending forth their products to help feed and clothe the world. Oil wells and mines are bringing to light and use the locked up treasures of the earth. Business men are launching great projects and with fine enthusiasm plan to make Oklahoma second to no other state in the Union.

The Church in Oklahoma In the midst of all this material development the Church has been steadily bearing her witness. Twenty years ago Indian and Oklahoma territories were a western extension of the Diocese of Arkansas. Then came the opening of the region to settlement. Two young priests of the Church went into the new land among the first. In 1891 the two territories were constituted a missionary district, and early in the following year Bishop Brooke began his patient and devoted service. The communicants at that time numbered seventy-five in three congregations. There were only three clergy. The gains made since then are all the more significant when it is remembered that there has been practically no Church growth through immigration. The present population of Oklahoma has been recruited chiefly from those parts of the central West where the Church is not strong. Oklahoma is an illustration of the inevitable result of the years of indifference about Church extension in the states bordering on the Ohio and the lower Mississippi and lower Missouri Rivers. Baptists, Methodists, Campbellites have gone into Oklahoma by the thousands. In some instances they have built really imposing churches and have laid the foundations for influential educational institutions. Had the Church on the Atlantic coast seventy years ago been a little more willing to stand behind pioneers like Chase, Kemper and Freeman much Church history in this new land might be written differently. But

Bishop Brooke and his helpers have not wasted time lamenting what might have been. They have been busy dealing with present facts. They have been winning to Christian living and to fellowship in the Church some of the many who came to Oklahoma with little, if any, religious conviction or affiliation. The result is seen in a present communicant roll of nearly 2,900. The three stations have increased to seventy-seven parishes and missions. Perhaps nothing could better suggest the handicap under which this work has been done than the fact that the clergy staff of the District of Oklahoma has never exceeded twenty-five. The lay-readers number twenty-three. About two years ago a gathering of Methodists in the city of Tulsa brought together 500 clergy and "local preachers."

The Division of Oklahoma Bishop Brooke has now suggested that this district of 70,000 square miles should be divided. He desires no personal relief. He is concerned only about the needs of the people and the growth of the Church. The council of the Seventh Missionary Department has agreed unanimously that Bishop Brooke's plan is wise and statesmanlike, and has arranged to memorialize the House of Bishops at the next General Convention. The division, if made, would probably be along the north and south line formerly dividing Indian Territory from Oklahoma. Muskogee, a growing city of 30,000 people, with a self-supporting parish, would be the see city of the new district. Oklahoma City, with 50,000 people and a self-supporting parish, would remain the see city of the western district. While division means increased missionary expenditure, experience has shown that division generally means also more rapid Church growth in both parts of the divided district or diocese; in communicants, in clergy and in property. Oklahoma's strategic present and its unquestionably important future demand consideration. The achievements of Bishop Brooke's episcopate are an earnest of still greater usefulness for the Church in the years to come. This year 1910 is the year to make large plans.

New Mexico and Arizona

A similar question that might well come b e f o r e the General Convention is additional episcopal care for New Mexico and Arizona. Although they are separate districts, each with its own convocation and administrative machinery, both have been under the care of Bishop Kendrick for twenty-one years. Few people can realize the enormous extent of territory for which the Church has made him responsible. To say the combined area of the two territories is 235,-000 square miles may mean little to most readers. A study of the map will be illuminating. All of New England and New York, or all of New York and Pennsylvania could be easily included within the borders of either New Mexico or Arizona, with a few thousand square miles to spare. A straight line from the eastern border of New Mexico to the western boundary of Arizona is about as long as the line from New York City to Chicago. From north to south the distance is greater than from New York City to Richmond, Va. And lest this should not seem to be a sufficiently extended field, the Church has placed under Bishop Kendrick's care a bit of western Texas as large as Maine or South Carolina.

Bishop Kendrick's Varied Service

Over this great region Bishop Kendrick h a s been travelling diligently these many years, shepherding the people, supplying vacant congregations with services, inspiring many to live as citizens of the Kingdom. To-day he is preaching to, and confirming some of, the college men in our remarkable stu-

THE supreme purpose of the Sunday-school Lenten Offering is not the raising of money but the education of the givers. Con-

Educational Value of the Lenten Offering

spicuous as is its usefulness as an aid to the Church's Mission and notable as are the sums gathered, this feature might well be disregarded if it did not at the same time contribute toward the deeper purpose. The strongest friends and most active promoters of this offering have inevitably viewed it as a means to a much larger end—the development among the young people of the Church of a deeper sense of responsibility for, and interest in, the world-wide campaign.

The fact, therefore, that a certain Sunday-school has made a large offering is not in itself commendable, though the presumption is that where giving is generous the other elements are present. It is the superintendent who has placed the emphasis on the educational value of the effort—who has desired more than all else that his scholars should learn why and for what they are giving—who has rendered the best service to the Church.

Plans for Deepening the Impression

This has been felt so strongly that in t w o conspicuous instances a diocesan movement is under way with a view to deepening the impression made by the Lenten Offering. We naturally look to the great dioceses for leadership, and it is fitting that in this instance New York and Pennsylvania should inaugurate the movement. With the purpose of bringing the matter before the Sunday-schools in a concrete and impressive way, so that they may recognize this offering as an act of devotion, and may actually see it or its equivalent placed upon the altar, and also that they may realize the strength of a united effort and a common interest in the Church's greatest work, special services are planned, at which, in the

presence of delegates representing the Sunday-school strength of these dioceses, the presentation of their offerings shall be made.

For New York this service will be held on the afternoon of April 10th at the Church of Zion and St. Timothy, the Rev. Dr. Leighton Parks making the address and Bishop Greer presenting the offering. It is planned to have the offerings of the various schools sent promptly to the diocesan treasurer and receipts for the amounts returned, which will be deposited in the alms basin.

In Philadelphia Bishop Whitaker has named Saturday, April 23d, as the time of service, and the Church of the Holy Apostles as the place for the presentation of what will undoubtedly be the greatest diocesan offering in the entire Church. Particular interest will centre about this service in Philadelphia, in view of the fact that it is held almost to the day upon the anniversary of the death of Mr. Thomas, in loving memory of whom the children of Pennsylvania and of the entire Church are this Lent making their gifts.

These two services should go far to impress the Church with a sense of the greatness of this movement among her children, and will undoubtedly be a means of education and stimulus to those who have gathered the sums which will then be devoted to the Master's service.

MORE and more, as each triennium passes, and the General Convention assembles, does it become a missionary gathering. It is

The General Convention and Missions

not so many years ago that there was sad truth in someone's smart saying: "How hardly shall the subject of Missions enter into the General Convention!" Even so recently as the San Francisco convention of 1901, many will recall how missionary matters were shouldered out of the day and crowded into the evening sessions, when attend-

ance was small and enthusiasm lacking.
Missionary bishops whose fields of labor
and devoted service rivalled those of
Aidan and Bernard and Xaxier, and who
had come thousands of miles to tell their
story, were allowed to address for twenty
minutes a meagre gathering of politely
patient folk. But Boston, in 1904, saw
a great advance, and at the last Convention in Richmond, missions took a really
worthy place. It was found possible to
devote a large part of the choicest days
to the missionary sessions, and there was
yet time to pass more canons than the
Church had use for. Indeed it was evident, by the crowded attendance on missionary days, that the centre of interest
was swinging from matters of internal
legislation to questions of the Church's
wider mission.

It does not require the gift of second
sight to prophesy an even greater advance in Cincinnati. The impetus given
to the missionary cause, both within and
without the Church, during the last three
years would of itself assure this. The
missionary department councils, the
travels of our secretaries, the awakening
sense of responsibility evidenced in
larger gifts—not to mention the reflex
effects of the Laymen's Missionary
Movement—have stimulated interest
everywhere. It looks as though we were
really beginning to believe that the extension of the Church is the chief business of the Church.

Questions for Decision Not only is all this
true, but events are
so shaping them-
selves as to make it
seem inevitable that Cincinnati shall see
our greatest missionary convention. The
post of leadership in the missionary work
of the Church has become vacant by Dr.
Lloyd's consecration to the episcopate;
the Board of Missions has declined to fill
his place, and will refer the whole matter
to the General Convention. Together
with this there comes the suggestion that
it might be advisable to make such
changes as would allow the election of
a bishop to fill the vacant place; and on

tinued to be one. I remember when Bishop Kemper was consecrated, and that our Sunday-school teacher told all of her class to see how much we could give him. We had $10, and when the bishop came to our little country church our class was marched down to the door of the church, and our teacher said, "Bishop, these little girls want to give you this money for your Mission." I can remember how pleased he looked, although his voice trembled, and he said, "Children, this is the first money that has been given me for my work," and then he said a little prayer. I can remember this so well, and now I am an old lady of eighty-five, but I will never forget that occasion.

I have been a subscriber to The Spirit of Missions ever since and I do enjoy it so much. I hope you will not think I want to make any fuss, as we would say, for you know no more about me.

The other letter bears a well-known name and runs thus:

> Berkeley Divinity School,
> Middletown, Conn.
> January 22d, 1910.

Dear Sir:

I enclose $2 subscription to The Spirit of Missions for 1910 from my mother,

> Mrs. Henry Hart,
> Saybrook, Conn.,

and from myself at above address. Beginning in 1836 with my grandmother, our family in Saybrook has received The Spirit of Missions from the first; it was the year of my mother's marriage, and at the age of ninety-three she still receives and reads the magazine with pleasure.

> Truly yours,
> Samuel Hart.

Through what wonderful years these two readers have lived! Yet if the signs of the present may be trusted, the next seventy-five years of missionary enterprise should be equally or even more wonderful.

Now is Christ Risen from the Dead

THE SANCTUARY OF MISSIONS

'TIS the weakness in strength that I cry for! My flesh that I seek
In the Godhead! I seek and I find it.
O Saul, it shall be
A Face like my face that receives thee; a Man like to me
Thou shalt love and be loved by forever; a Hand like this hand
Shall throw open the gates of new life to thee! See the Christ stand!
—*Browning's "Saul."*

MAY He who has given us the certainty of the resurrection to countervail the awful certainty of death, help us to that preparation of heart and character which befits those who have to do with such great realities.—*Dean Church.*

THANKSGIVINGS

"Thanks be to God which giveth us the victory through our Lord Jesus Christ."

"We thank thee"—
That thou hast brought life and immortality to light through the Gospel.
For the blessings with which thou hast crowned the labors of thy servants in the district of Shanghai. (Page 264.)
For the steadfast example of thy faithful Japanese servant, Seizo Akimoto. (Page 266.)
For the ingathering of many in the fields of our own land. (Page 281.)
For the earnestness of converts to the faith in the Far North. (Page 279.)
For the completion of the school building erected in behalf of the native girls in Africa. (Page 283.)

INTERCESSIONS

"That we may know thee and the power of thy resurrection."

"That it may please thee"—

To bless the patient service of the Bishop of Alaska and those who labor in that difficult field.
To turn everywhere the feet of thy children into the way of peace. (Page 290.)
To deepen among our Christian folk both sympathy and helpfulness toward the native people of the Philippines. (Page 287.)
To bless to their spiritual upbuilding the generous gifts of the children of the Church made during the Lenten-tide just passed.
To lay strongly upon the hearts of clergy and people the responsibility and obligation that each shall share in the great work, and minister to the present need, of the Church's Mission.

PRAYER

FOR EASTER-TIDE

O GOD, the Father Almighty, who didst love the world with so great a love that thou gavest thine only-begotten Son to be sacrificed for its redemption, make us who are redeemed with His precious blood to be so fruitful in works of love that we may have our part in the first resurrection and not fear the power of the second death, through the same thy Son, Jesus Christ, our Lord.—*Mozarabic Liturgy.*

The First=Fruits of Them That Slept

THE THREE KINGS

THE FEAST OF LIGHTS

A MISSIONARY "MYSTERY"

By Susan T. Hand

AT this season when all Christian hearts are rejoicing in the Easter message of eternal life and hope, we must not forget, in ir joy, the Easter command, "Go iickly and tell His disciples that He is een from the dead." The wonderful ews was not for these alone who first ard and believed, but must.be quickly read abroad. The Church's lesson trough each one of her holy seasons in irn is the same: We must share with hers the good things that have been ade known unto us.

This truth is most emphatically im-essed upon the students and teachers ' St. Augustine's School, Raleigh, . C., at the Epiphany season, when a eautiful service, called the 'Feast of ights, is held. One can easily under-and, after seeing this service, how)werful were the impressions made pon the people by the mystery plays of

the early Church. A visitor present at the last service describes the picturesque sight substantially as follows:

Dusk was coming on as we entered the school grounds. Two long proces-sions of students were making their way to the chapel—a beautiful building of rough granite. The interior was bril-liant with lights and Christmas decora-tions. The procession was headed by the Three Wise Men, robed in rich Ori-ental costumes and bearing in their hands the gifts: gold, frankincense and myrrh. As the procession slowly moved up the aisle the lights went out and only the great Epiphany star high above the altar shone out to guide them. The burst of music from the two hundred voices was thrilling, and the organ, played by a young pupil of the school, reverberated in the darkness, reminding one of the strange, throbbing sound made on their wooden drums by the na-

A CLASSROOM SCENE IN ST. AUGUSTINE'S SCHOOL

tive Africans. The service was full choral evensong. The singing and intoning was in perfect time, and one was deeply impressed with its devotional quality. A short sermon by the principal was from the text: "And all the heathen shall praise Him." He declared that the dearest desire in the heart of a true man is to spread the Kingdom of Christ on earth, and that this is really the highest and noblest of all aspirations. The offering for foreign missions was then taken, and after the presentation of the alms each worshipper was given a wax taper. The Wise Men then lighted their tapers from a candle taken from the altar by the bishop, and they in turn lighted the hundreds of tapers held by the congregation. As the lights increased, the church grew otherwise dark, even the star itself fading slowly out. Then the procession swept out, singing the Epiphany hymn,

" As with gladness men of old,
Did the guiding star behold,"

the Wise Men leading the way out into the darkness, followed by the bishop, clergy and students.

It was strange indeed to find outside

automobiles and other worldly things, and stranger still to see, standing with quiet dignity in the Gothic archway, the Three 'Wise Men—their tapers yet aflame.

As the myriad of twinkling lights dispersed in all directions, we felt sure that each bearer must have realized the significance of what he carried and how he individually must pass on, when he leaves his school, the gifts of Christian education. Not only must he share with his own people the material blessings that he may have, but also those enduring blessings which are his as a member of Christ's Church Militant.

How conscientiously this obligation is fulfilled may be seen by the receipt from graduates of letters such as this:

"I am still teaching in the city school. Last week the children learned two beautiful Christmas hymns. For a month I have been telling them the story of the Christ Child and leading them on as far as possible to understand why we celebrate the day. We had a public programme and many of the parents were out.

"I am still fighting against the unsanitary conditions of the homes, and

PICKING COTTON
*The reason why the term is only
four months long*

the gray-haired old men and women
who have almost finished life's journey;
to the tired, troubled mother, who is
so weary and worn out with her family
cares and troubles, and to the half-
grown girls and boys who bring their
little troubles to me. It is such a help;
sometimes when I have talked and
talked and seemed to do little good, I
read from my book, or leave it with
them, and I always see a change.

"I have no special place to meet the
children. Wherever I see a crowd of
boys I go, and it is not long before I
have them interested in some story and
they will spend the whole afternoon
with me. I take them with me when I
visit the sick. It is such a good way to
have a long talk to them. They are my
friends and we work together for the
good we can do."

So do the torch-bearers carry the
beacon down the years, and by deeds of
Christian love and sanctified common-
sense kindle new light in other lives.
Surely dear Thomas à Kempis would
have wondered and rejoiced had he
known how, in the humble cabins of the
South, a negro girl would read his holy
book, and so help him to speak comfort
and counsel to the souls of these patient
black children whose race, since the day
on which unwilling Simon the Cyrenian
fared forth to Calvary, has been a bearer
of burdens for the world.

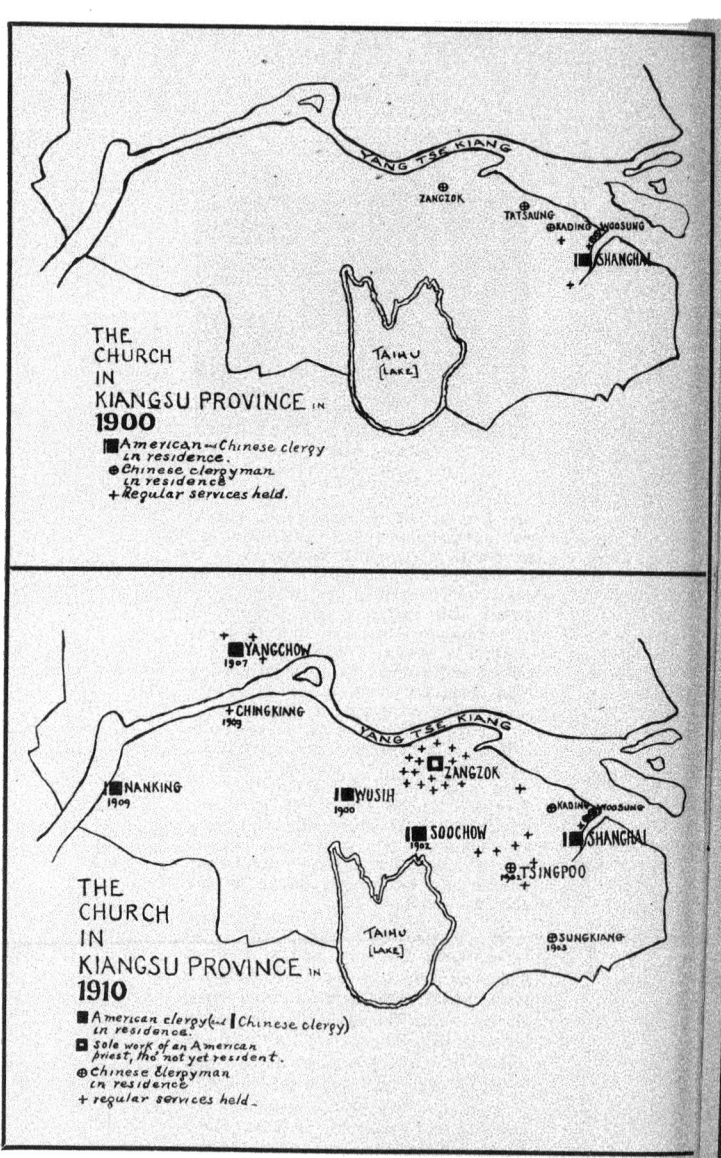

THE
CHURCH
IN
KIANGSU PROVINCE IN
1900
■ American—Chinese clergy
   in residence.
⊕ Chinese clergyman
   in residence
+ Regular services held.

ZANGZOK
TATSAUNG
⊕KADING WOOSUNG
SHANGHAI
YANG TSE KIANG
TAIHU
[LAKE]

■YANGCHOW
1907
+CHINGKIANG
1909
YANG TSE KIANG
ZANGZOK
■NANKING
1909
■WUSIH
1900
■ SOOCHOW
1902
⊕KADING WOOSUNG
SHANGHAI
TSINGPOO
THE
CHURCH
IN
KIANGSU PROVINCE IN
1910
TAIHU
[LAKE]
⊕SUNGKIANG
1903
■ American clergy (and ■ Chinese clergy)
   in residence.
□ Sole work of an American
   priest, tho not yet resident.
⊕ Chinese clergyman
   in residence
+ regular services held.

WHAT TEN YEARS HAS DONE FOR KIANGSU

TEN YEARS IN KIANGSU

THE STORY OF THE MAPS

By the Reverend John W. Nichols

THE accompanying charts ought to be gratifying to those whose prayers and gifts are continually offered for the cause of Christ in China. They represent the extension of the Church and of the worship of God which ten years' effort by the Church has accomplished in a portion of her field.

Other results—medical, educational and evangelistic—none the less real, are not here shadowed. It is attempted only to mark the centres that have been occupied, and the places about them where regular Christian worship is held. That one centre should have become six, that eight out-stations should have grown into thirty, surely will mean much to those who love "His Kingdom and the righteousness thereof."

Much that is romantic, and more that is very unromantic and prosy, has gone into the making of this ten years' record—great openings seized and lost, small starts, joyous successes, failures, daily ploddings, unexpected bursts of progress, sicknesses, deaths, strange helps, and the vigor of new lives offered—these are the invisible marks upon the map.

How shall we account for this advance in ten years when there was so little, comparatively, before? The answer, short and comprehensive, ought to ring throughout the home Church: *We have had the men.*

For fifty-odd years before 1900 there had been two, three and four American priests struggling to lead and plant the Church in Kiangsu. Sometimes there was but one to shoulder the burden. In 1900 there were six, two having just come to the work. This year there are fourteen on the bishop's staff. In 1900 there were ten Chinese clergy—mostly deacons; and seven catechists, with little or no training for their work. In 1910 there are fifteen Chinese clergy, ten of whom are priests, and sixteen catechists,

eight of whom have had two years' training for their work. With something more than a doubled American staff, then, one centre has been made six; with a not quite doubled Chinese force, the Church is working about four times the number of out-stations.

What of the next ten years? The larger half of Kiangsu to the north (it does not show on the maps) remains yet to be occupied—it is waiting for those who shall come from America to lead the advance there. With them must go Chinese clergy and catechist, without whom the foreigner can do little.

And for all our centres new Chinese heads and hands must be prepared to work out among the thousand towns and villages yet untouched. If there is achievement recorded on the map of 1910 we on the field know also, not only of work that might have been done, but of work that had to be abandoned, crosses that had to be wiped off (as around Wusih)—for lack of men to "enter into the harvest."

Are these Chinese workers forthcoming? We feel confident in saying "Yes!" We count on St. John's University to continue to send forth from its divinity-school its quota of invaluable English-trained clergy—young Chinese, of course. And we are ready to prepare more catechists and clergy in Chinese than ever before if the home Church will equip us with a place for that work. Fifty more Chinese clergy and catechists in 1920 is not too high a mark to be set before us. We have the men ready to do the training and the men ready to learn.

Look at the map once more. Each cross means a place held and worked chiefly through catechists. Does the American Church want more of these crosses around the centres? Then let the Church pray for the prospering of all plans for the increase of Chinese workers for Christ in the Province of Kiangsu of the Middle Kingdom.

SEIZO AKIMOTO

typhoid fever, and died on January 12th, 1910. At the time of his death Mr. Akimoto was about thirty-six years of age and just entering on the most successful part of his life, after several years of hard and painstaking work. He leaves a young wife and three children.

"Not only is his death a great personal loss and grief to me, but his long and intimate connection with St. Luke's made him one of the most valuable men on our staff, and it will be very difficult, if not impossible, to fill his place. Mr. Akimoto was really the first employee of the hospital. He came to me nine years ago as a clerk to assist in the little dispensary which was the beginning of our present hospital work in Tokyo. For several months we two worked together without other permanent help, and it was not until the return of Miss Araki from her training in America, in the spring of 1902, that our force was increased. Later Dr. Kubo became my assistant and it has been really through the good and faithful services of these three, Akimoto, Miss Araki and Dr. Kubo, that the success of our work has been possible. We, therefore, who knew and loved him best, feel most deeply the loss of our comrade and fellow-worker.

Mr. Akimoto was a man of great singleness of purpose, marked business capacity, and, above all else, most faithful and true to his duties and the best interests of the hospital. Through his work in the pharmacy and surgical instrument department several thousand dollars was earned each year for the support of the hospital. Under his care the development of his department has been steady, and at the time of his death every indication pointed to a greater growth in the near future.

"We extend our heartfelt sympathy to his bereaved family. He truly gave his life freely to the cause, and the good of the hospital was ever nearest his heart. His memory remains an inspiration to us and it shall be our duty to carry out his work."

D R. R. B. TEUSLER writes to tell us of a severe blow which has fallen upon St. Luke's Hospital, Tokyo, of which he is the head, in the death of Mr. S. Akimoto, the business manager and head pharmacist of the hospital. The permanent value of our work in foreign lands must always depend upon the success of our American missionaries in drawing to themselves the assistance of devoted and capable native helpers. The foreigner, as such, can never be the immediate instrument for the successful conversion of the Japanese or Chinese.

Mr. Akimoto seems to have been a conspicuous example of this faithful and effective service upon which so much depends. Dr. Teusler writes concerning him as follows:

"A letter has just been received from my associate, Dr. Kubo, bringing the sad news of the death of Mr. Akimoto. He was taken ill about December 20th with

ROMANCE AND REALITY IN ALASKA

By Bishop Rowe

AS I turn to go back to the work in the far north which the Church has committed to me, I wish to express to the many good friends throughout the Church who have helped me with their sympathy and prayers and gifts, my deep appreciation of all that they have done, and to assure them that I return greatly cheered, and determined to make more. effective than ever the work for our Master which is being carried forward in Alaska.

Also I desire to say something in a general way about that land, its promise and its needs; its vivid romance and its stern reality.

The Romance of the North

The "far north" is the centre of interest just now. After many daring attempts by heroic men for a score of years, after splendid achievements and pitiful sacrifices, a flag has been planted at the North Pole, and that flag is the Stars and Stripes. It is not strange that the world is interested. It is a wonderful achievement and we heartily applaud the persistence, endurance and bravery of the epoch-marking discoverer. No one is better able to appreciate his work than those who, living in the North, are familiar with the conditions and have some experience of the same difficulties.

But this interest in the event of such world-wide importance is in strange contrast with a work which is attended with greater benefits to humanity, though less in the public eye and esteem. For it should be remembered that during many years messengers of the Prince of Peace, the Redeemer of mankind, have lived in the North, amid the same conditions Peary faced in a dash of two years; they have met Arctic storms, crossed wastes of snow and mountains that seemed impassable, their one aim being to bring to all men the message of glad tidings, the ministry of salvation for soul and body, regardless of popular acclaim or per-

sonal profit, satisfied that they left a trail of light, hope and redemption behind them. But to this the world gives scant recognition.

Alaska has been described as "The Wonderland of the North," and it is not amiss. Poets and travellers through centuries have sung the beauties of Norse fjords and mountain glaciers and midnight sun, but the visitor to Alaska sees here wonders as grand and as majestic as any land can boast. Our people are learning this more and more. Alaska is a mighty country in the making—in the civilizing. Though the farthest outpost of civilization—the last frontier—yet by reason of the development and the increased facilities of travel, its charm as a frontier is rapidly passing. Humanizing influences are transforming its silences into throbbing life. Man is busily harnessing the forces of nature, putting in machinery to wrest from the soil its wealth, building railroads and creating settlements of life and industry where but recently the wolves howled in winter of unsatisfied hunger.

It is only eleven years ago that the great gold rush to the Klondike drew attention to Alaska—drew an army of the adventurous and the brave. Where then they faced a country seemingly impenetrable by reason of snow-covered mountains, trackless forests, mighty rivers studded with dangerous rapids and canyons, now the traveller can make the trip through Alaska, on the regular routes, with all modern conveniences, and come unexpectedly at intervals upon towns, mining settlements, canneries, isolated sawmills, roadhouses and the tent of the lone and venturesome prospector. Modern towns have sprung up, within the past eleven years, in the wilderness.

Everything in Alaska holds the interest; not only its peerless beauty, but its vast spaces, its mighty mountains and rivers, its richness, its unique conditions, its picturesque life, its tragedy and humor, lay a fascinating spell upon one.

Mining in Alaska

Mining is at present the principal industry in Alaska. It is the most attractive because it seems to be the readiest road to independence. This is a subject big enough for a volume. I must not dwell upon it. First, there are the "placer" mines. These have yielded millions—I cannot give figures—but these "placer mines" are soon exhausted. They are for the individual, and while they last they mean much in the way of population and business. It is for this reason that communities, towns, fluctuate, rise or fall. I believe that new "discoveries" will be made, of placer ground, from year to year, because Alaska is large and generally mineralized. In southern Alaska gold in quartz is found; also great deposits of coal and copper. The coal in the Matinuska, Kyak sections; the copper in the Bonanza, Nizina sections, all point to a permanent growth and development that guarantee the future prosperity of Alaska.

Fisheries

We are apt to overlook the fisheries of Alaska in our present emphasis upon its mining possibilities, and that is a serious mistake. The "fisheries" are a product equal, at least, to the mining. Last year the cannery salmon crop amounted to more than $11,000,000. This industry is operated chiefly by the Rothschilds of London and the Guggenheims of New York. For the season 4,000 Chinese and Japanese were employed, in addition to 5,000 white men. These were the "offscourings" of San Francisco, as our delegate, James W. Wickersham, states. Further he says: "Not a schoolhouse was built, nor a home established, nor a hospital helped, nor a church aided out of this great revenue obtained in Alaska." In view of this, one cannot but demand that the Government should at least compel the corporations engaged in this business to pay something for so rich a privilege, and

The Native Peoples

Up to the present time Alaska has been regarded solely as a rich place to be gleaned by corporations and adventurers. Everything is pocketed and carried out of the country, without a dollar left behind to build up either homes or communities. Even the native population, the original possessors of the country, are injured. Their abundant means of living are taken from them. They are made the playthings of a dominant people and suffer fearfully in consequence. Not only so, but officials of the government compel them to pay a tax for every tree they cut and use. Following their ancestral ways in bartering, they have been compelled, by custom officers, to pay a tax on the crude marble work which they have brought to exchange for things necessary. To my mind such impositions are an outrage, an injustice, and I do not believe that our Government would justify for a moment its officers in compelling these original possessors of the land to pay a tax on the trees they cut or on things which they brought from one side of the boundary line to the other, as all their fathers had done before them, in a country that was theirs before it became ours.

From what I have said, it can be readily seen that our mission work in Alaska is face to face with many problems, difficulties and oppositions. In the first place, adventurers, prospectors and men seeking sudden gain only, come to Alaska. On the whole they represent a high average of manhood. It would be difficult to find a better manhood anywhere. But there are exceptions. And the exceptions give us no end of trouble. They are the men who are in no fear or respect for God or man. It becomes their pastime to debauch the natives. In our efforts to defend the defenceless we, of course, arouse their anger, opposition and deadly hatred. Unhappily we have not always found much help from the officers of the government. And strange to say, even the respectable and decent people in a community are rather against us than with us in our efforts to check the deadly wrongs. No; our work is by no means easy, and our workers have to make a fight for righteousness in the face of opposition, persecution and obloquy. But it has to be made—we are set to fight for the pure life—and that should not be counted against us. And yet it sometimes is. There are smiling holiday travellers who come along and see an Indian drunk and hear from unworthy persons a tale of the abounding evils in the community, then go their way and regale their friends with a story of the "failure of missions." What do such people know of the brave fight, day in and day out, against tremendous odds, on behalf of men and women, for the pure, clean, holy life? Would they have us desert a field, just because sin and wickedness seem to reign there? From their parlor-safety positions one would think so. But we know better. We are the humble workers under one, Jesus, who will conquer sin, the world and the devil, and with Him we too shall be conquerors.

The White Population

The population in Alaska is growing, though slowly. New towns and settlements spring up within a year. It is difficult to keep up with this development, and every new place sends me a request to establish a mission. This is a compliment to our Church, but it embarrasses me. And the people are largely transients. For this reason local self-support is uncertain and one cannot bank very much upon the permanent building up of the work in any place. We are ministering to a "procession" of souls. But it is a satisfaction to learn of people who for the first time have come into touch with the Church. Their surprise and appreciation are encouraging. The Church gets close to them. And perhaps in some other place these people will give a good account of themselves.

The Work Ahead

Alaska is called "an empire in the making." The natural resources are such that eventually it is certain to have a great population. The Church is keeping up with the development that is going on, and is preparing for the future. Our first need is for a sufficient staff of workers to hold and maintain the missions already established, and to be ready to occupy new places. Then we shall need such support as will enable us to erect hospitals, reading-rooms, chapels and mission houses, as the growth of population shall demand.

It is a land of romance. The story of its early history is romantic. The life and struggle of those daring argonauts who fought their way over mountains whose tops were hidden in the clouds, who made for themselves a pathway.

through deep canyons, roaring rapids and over vast, trackless wastes, is an epic of courage and endurance. These early pioneers and pathfinders have blazed a trail which countless numbers have followed.

Alaska has a fascination which lays its strange spell upon everyone who stays for any time and seeks the secret sources of its buried wealth. More and more will it lure the brave and strong, and afford a field for the development of a manhood that cannot but enrich and ennoble our life and character as a people and a nation. More and more will it afford opportunities rare and great for man's enterprise and ambition.

FIRST CHURCH CONSECRATION IN CUBA

ENSENADA DE MORA is not the name of a town, but of an estate. In the midst of a great sugar plantation in the southeast part of Cuba, on Sunday, February 6th, there occurred the consecration of a church, erected through the generosity of a Philadelphia Churchman. This was the first use of our consecration service on the island of Cuba, and it was a great day for all concerned.

The church is in the Spanish style, beautiful and complete in every detail; and the grounds, surrounded by their iron fence and made beautiful with flowers, furnish a fine setting for this house of prayer.

The building is in the heart of a sugar estate, where, as in all such cases, there is a considerable proportion of English-speaking people—managers, engineers, overseers, and the like; all men of education and many of them Churchmen. In addition to these there are usually large numbers of Jamaica Negroes, nearly all of whom have been trained under the Church of England, and are so attached to it that they will not work where its ministrations cannot be had Although many of them cannot read they can usually follow the services an sing the hymns perfectly from memory There are also the native laborers, wh as a rule are well-disposed toward th Church, which represents to them a pur form of Christianity, which ministers f rich and poor alike. Sometimes one of these estates will have from five to te thousand of this class.

Naturally, then, this little church wi minister to a great variety and numb of people, bringing them the helps ar consolations of religion and becoming central feature of their life and wor The services will be held both in Spa ish and English.

THE MISSION HOUSE AND SOME OF ITS VISITORS

AMONG THE INDIANS OF OKLAHOMA

By Harriet M. Bedell

WE live in an Indian camp, and come in very close contact with the people. There is a Church day-school of thirty-nine pupils, ranging from five to seventeen years, and all our work goes hand in hand with work in the homes. The Indians live in *tipis*, in a most primitive way. Beds are of covered dry grass, and the cooking is done on a fire made in a hole in the ground. Around each *tipi* is a kind of stockade made of the tall weeds which grow so plentifully here. The Indians eat any kind of animal flesh, even dog, preserved by cutting very thin and hanging in the sun to dry.

Their manners, customs, language and dress are just as strange as though found in any foreign land; in fact, I sometimes wonder if I am really in our own country. Only when Uncle Sam brings my mail do I realize that I still live under the Stars and Stripes.

Among the older people many of the old-time customs still prevail, such as wailing at funerals, burying all belongings with the dead, the cries of the medicine man, calls for feasts from the hills, and the old kettle-drum ceremony, lasting all night.

Both men and women wear their hair long, in two braids over the shoulders, the men's only differing in having a third very small braid from the middle of the back of the head in memory of the old "scalp lock." The women wear a short, loose gown with flowing sleeves, belted in at the waist, with fancy metal belts or twisted colored scarfs. The men wear white man's dress, except for their moccasins of buckskin, heavily beaded in beautiful Indian designs. Many still paint their faces, and during their fes-

(271)

tive times still like to wear feathers and highly ornamented costumes. The school pupils wear clothing which we provide—when our friends help us to secure it.

The English meaning of their names is most interesting. *Wenhaya* means "Sage Woman"; *Vicrehia,* "Bird Woman"; then we have "Big Nose," "Blind Bull," "Crooked Nose," "Turkey Legs," "Short Neck," "Antelope Skin," etc. When the little children come to school I must give them names. The son of "Chicken Hawk" I call "Paul Chicken Hawk." I have "Sarah Little Man," "James Tall Meat," "Ruth Howling Crane." It is said (though I am not sure of this) that the child is named from the first thing the mother thinks about or sees after the child is born. There are a few pretty names, like "Annie Red Cloud," "Tall Chief," "White Bird," but some are very suggestive, as "Slow-as-Smoke," "Lying-on-a-Side," and "Walking Woman," etc.

It is the idea of the government and all interested in the Indians to encourage them to live on their own allotments, to have one spot which they may call home; but they will camp together in spite of all that is being done. For this reason our mission camp is approved by the government on account of the uplifting influence not only among the children but in the homes.

"What is the Church doing?" perhaps you are beginning to ask. The Church was established at Darlington by the Rev. J. W. Wicks. Its origin was as follows: In 1875, Oakerhater, a young Cheyenne leader, was sent with some seventy others to Fort San Marco, Fla. They were prisoners of war and among the worst of their tribes. They remained at the fort three years, then the older ones were allowed to return to their homes, while twenty-two young men remained in the East for education. Among these were three who had been visited during their imprisonment and taught by an earnest Churchwoman and officer of the Woman's Auxiliary of Central New York. Through her interest and efforts Oakerhater, and Oksteher,

another young Cheyenne, were placed in charge of the Rev. J. W. Wicks, who was then rector of St. Paul's Church, Paris Hill, N. Y. They were baptized and confirmed in the fall of 1880. Oksteher died soon after, but Oakerhater continued his studies until the spring of 1881, when he was ordained deacon by Bishop Huntington at Syracuse. He went immediately to his tribe, where he began work under the Rev. J. H. Wicks, who was at this time in charge. The work continued with some changes, and through the influence of Mrs. Whirlwind—an old chief's wife, who was a devout communicant of the mission—was transferred to the Whirlwind allotment, where a government day-school had been conducted, which had been closed some time, much to the disappointment of the Indians; for they love their children as well as white parents do, and it was very hard to have them taken to schools far away for five years or more. So a Church day-school was established, which was hailed with joy by the Indians, and which has continued to grow, the only drawback being the lack of funds to carry it on; but even with financial discouragements the work continues to prosper. This school and the industrial work have always been considered but means to the great end—the spreading of Christ's Kingdom. It is slow work, and often discouraging, but the Indian can accept Christ as his Saviour and still wear his hair in braids, cook his food on an open fire, and live in a *tipi.*

The Indian is thought to be unresponsive. So he is—to outsiders, but will tell one or two of my experience with him. With our Indian deacon David Oakerhater, I attended the funeral of a young Christian Indian whom I had visited while he was very sick with tuberculosis in a camp about seven mile away. After the service at the grave tried, with David's help, to comfort th parents (not Christians), saying their son was not in that hole, but tha he had gone to a beautiful place wher

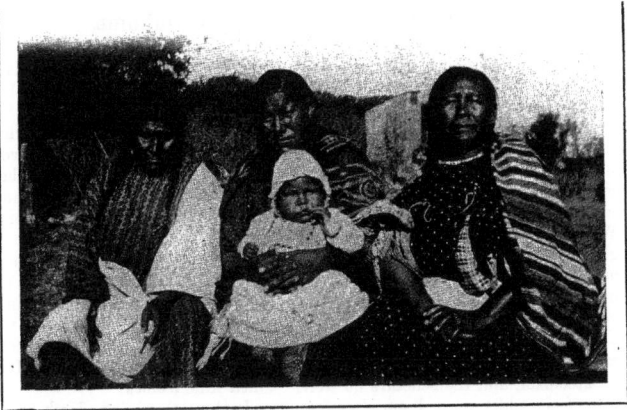

A GROUP OF THE WOMEN

Mrs. White Wolf (communicant), Mrs. Blind Bull and Mrs. Bobtail Coyote

all is peace and happiness, and where there is no sickness, and that if they would follow in his footsteps they would see him again. I apparently made no impression, and left, feeling that I had given little comfort. As the Indian never returns to live on the site where loved ones have died, these Indians came to Whirlwind. They sent for me the next morning, and through an interpreter told me how I had comforted their hearts, and that they would try to do as I said. Let us pray that they, too, may soon come into the Fold.

The other day an Indian (Robe Red Wolf) came in. I said, *"Ha na tzę̨ hu hite?"* ("What can I do for you?") He replied, "I just came in to talk." Then he said something like this: "I'm glad I'm Christian. I'm happy now different way. It's hard for Indian to be Christian, and hard to give up old ways; but when we become Christian, then we glad. I am glad missionaries are here. They teach us good way. My wife no Christian. You make her Christian." Is it worth while? Every day brings experiences similar to these.

I am often asked why, upon leaving boarding-school, the educated Indian so soon falls back into the old ways. It is quite clear to me. The girl in boarding-school learns many useful things under proper conditions and with beautiful equipments — cooking by electricity, using stationary tubs and mangles in a well-furnished laundry. She returns to her home. How different everything is! A hole in the ground instead of a stove, dried grass for beds, no chairs, no tables. How can she put into practice what she has learned? Her mother, too, is in charge of the home, and will not allow the daughter to make changes. Our own mothers would not. Then is all this education wasted? I think not. The homes of the next generation are sure to be on a higher plane.

We believe our methods are the solution of the problem. We begin with conditions as we find them, working up to higher ideals. The older schoolgirls and some of the young married women in the camp come to the mission-house each day in turn to do the work which each day brings. The boys of the mission care for the horses, help on washday, work in the garden, and learn to be useful generally. We feel quite encouraged. A few have bought stoves; some home-made tables may now be seen; beds are raised from the ground; and in many of the homes washing and bathing are regularly done.

We have short Evening Prayer every night at seven o'clock; and the pupils come as regularly as they come to school. We seldom have an absence, and so are always sure of a congregation. Many of the older Indians come too. The instruction is varied: On Monday we have the Catechism, and the scholars do well: a few of the older ones, I am sure, can say it through without a mistake; on Tuesday there is Bible drill in finding places and memorizing; Wednesday and Friday nights are specially for the older ones, though they come every night; the service is nearly all in Cheyenne, and we have a five-minute meditation. On Thursday we have Prayer Book drill in finding places and reading of rubrics. You would be pleased to see how readily even those who understand little English can find their places. On Sunday we have services both morning and evening, nearly all in Cheyenne; Sunday-school in the afternoon, and once a month a devotional meeting for the communicants. There are now twenty-five of these, and a more devout group of people it would be hard to find. A clergyman comes on a week-day to administer the Holy Communion once a month. Nearly all in the school are baptized. The older people are slow in accepting Christianity, but when they do, their faith is beautiful—so simple and trustful; I get many a lesson from them. The Indian is naturally religious, and unless the Church carries to him the true Gospel of Christ he does many strange things in the name of worship.

We have just opened a reading-room by which we hope to reach young people not in school. Though poorly equipped it has proved a success, but the room is far too small. We hope soon to have a chapel; then we can take the large room, which we are now using solely for services, for a reading-room. Some will come to the reading-room who do not now come to chapel. We have pictures for those who cannot read. Those of the life of Christ have aroused much interest, and when we told the story of each picture it was evident that some had never heard it before, though they had heard of Christianity. Quiet games are also allowed, and with very simple reading-matter, highly illustrated, we hope to have something for all who come. The room is open every night after chapel until nine o'clock.

Is it worth while? I ask again; and I say "Yes," most emphatically. But the inwrought traits of character must be considered in dealing with the Indian. With the same advantages for the same length of time, he might have stood side by side with the white man in civilization. He may not now reach the same height as his European brother, but he does approach it. Then why not help him?—for he can become a Christian long before he reaches that high plane which it has taken centuries of civilization to attain.

A little group at the pump

ST. MARY'S HOUSE

The present home of the school. The children in the picture constitute what is called the "morning school"

ST. MARY'S, MOILIILI

By Julia C. Emery

IT was on such a beautiful, bright day last April that I took the street car near Bishop Restarick's home in Honolulu, and rode out to the suburb called Moiliili. You pass the aquarium, where are the brightest colored, most fascinating of sea creatures, and by the shore along which many Hawaiians—some of the old royal race—have built their summer cottages. You see stones dug up from the beach on which human sacrifices were once offered to false gods, and banyan trees under which chiefs used to meet in council; and then you come to the hired house standing in its garden under the quiet shade of the algaroba trees, and visit the work that is helping to rear soldiers and servants of the true and gentle Christ. This is called St. Mary's Mission, and there our work has gone on since May, 1907.

The mission really began with Mrs. Folsom in charge, in what had been one of the worst opium haunts in Honolulu. But the poor, mean place had been cleaned and whitewashed, and before the change to the present place was made, so many prayers and praises had arisen there, that somehow it had taken on a homey look.

With it were associated the magic lantern exhibitions, when eager spectators thronged the room and crowded doors and windows; the Moon Feast, when people's minds were led from the moon to its Creator; Thanksgiving with its harvest hymns and games and feast; Christmas with its decorations and Christmas service; Holy Innocents' with the children's first *real* tree, who had been satisfied heretofore with branches left over from the decorations at the cathedral, tied together to make the sem-

(275)

blance of a tree. No wonder the room was crowded full again, and mothers with babies on their backs stood looking in through door and windows on the novel, pretty sight. And as they looked their children were their teachers, reciting, as had been taught to them, the story of the Annunciation and of the birth of our Blessed Lord. Again, there was the night when, through the kindness of a friend, electricity was introduced. On a Sunday evening the kerosene lights were turned out, and as all knelt in the darkness in silent prayer, the leader of the little congregation, turning on the electric light, said solemnly, "And God said, 'Let there be light, and there was light,'" thus making this gift to the mission a reminder of God's wonder-working power in the past, a symbol of the power with which He is ever working in turning darkened souls to glorious light. At another time the phonograph was the mystery, and when Mrs. Folsom started it at the back of the mission, one tiny tot wanted to see for himself where the talking and music came from; but on being lifted up to investigate seemed to get no satisfaction.

These first buildings of St. Mary's were in the midst of a fluctuating population of Japanese and Chinese, and into their homes the missionary went, in sickness ministering to them under her doctor's advice so acceptably that from camp and district generally came the verdict, "Mama's doctor and *haole* medicine too much good *kaukau*," and no matter what the trouble, they always came for "some good, kind medicine, all same like before!"

But at last the mission crowded the mission buildings beyond their utmost capacity, and it was then that the new St. Mary's was found, about ten minutes' walk away, and was rented and occupied.

But remembering the first year of the mission, it was not strange that in leaving it, Mrs. Folsom felt sad, and doubtful if it were the best thing to do. She said to herself, "How shall I know this?" when picking up a little text card, she

read, "My presence shall go with you," and felt as though an answer had been given to her questioning prayer. In the old house the school-mother lived in one little building and the school gathered in another; in the new St. Mary's all are under one roof. And the sweet influences of this new home centre in the little chapel where the children meet each morning and where Sunday night service is always held. In this new home was formerly an elaborate heathen altar with beautiful adornments, where worship had often been offered to heathen gods; now in the same room, made larger by tearing down a partition, and neatly painted and papered at the expense of the night-school, worship goes up daily to the One True God. The chapel is made beautiful by the memorials which it contains. One who was a friend to the mission from the first gave the altar in memory of his father and mother; the reredos, which he also designed, was made from *koa* wood taken from panels and doors of buildings formerly standing on the palace grounds, in which archives had been kept for many years. It is a memorial to Mrs. Mackintosh, whose memory lingers fragrant and blessed in the islands where she made her home. The cross on the altar is another memorial. The night-school men gave vases, and the Babies' Branch in Rochester the font, and with other gifts the chapel is made a beautiful place in which to draw near to the Heavenly Father.

And it was there that I first met the children of St. Mary's that April morning of last year. They had just filed in from the garden, singing as they went, for their morning prayers. Mrs. Folsom had left them for other work in Hilo, and Miss Van Deerlin was in charge, with Miss Chung, the young Chinese woman who went from Honolulu to New York, where she and Miss Van Deerlin both studied in the Training-School for Deaconesses and became fitted to do this mission work at Moiliili.

DOING THEIR BEST AT PHYSICAL CULTURE

Here are Chinese, Japanese, Portuguese and Hawaiians. The phonograph alluded to on page 276 stands on the table in the foreground

They showed their visitors over their mission home and told them of their work, of their neighbors, of the many Japanese near by, of the Portuguese just back of them, of the Chinese a little farther off; of their very small homes, some just in camps; the Japanese tidy and clean, the Portuguese untidy and dirty, with many chickens, ducks and pigs. They told how the Portuguese children love St. Mary's, and will come each morning by seven o'clock, and want no vacations. The missionaries' hardest work is to get rid of them when school hours are past. There have been as many as ninety-five of the day-school children, fifty Hawaiians, others Chinese, Japanese and Portuguese; and at night twenty-seven men and boys, Japanese, Chinese and Korean, were coming to the evening classes. The day is a busy one: :30 A.M., prayers in chapel; 7 to 9, cooking and housework; 9, short service for children; 9:15 to 12, school; 10:45 to 11, dispensary. In the afternoon come sewing-school, visiting Chinese and Japanese in their homes, dispensary, cook-

ing. From 7 to 9 is night-school, and at 9 comes a short service for the night-school men. On Sunday, Sunday-school is from 9 to 10; dispensary is from 10 to 10:30. From 7 to 8 P.M. there is reading with night-school men, and this is followed from 8 to 9 by an evening service for them, with instruction.

Thus Miss Van Deerlin and Miss Chung are kept busy from day to day. They took me through their living rooms, in which they have been able to gather only such few and simple furnishings; out on the veranda, where they often eat the simple meals which they themselves have prepared; into the room where the older children were at work with their books, and among the kindergarten children who have so few of those little tricks and toys, playing with which makes so many kindergarten children here wise about many useful things. I saw the picture-books sent by our missionary in Salt Lake to help amuse and instruct these children; I heard of the friend who sends a dollar every month to give these missionaries at St. Mary's

THE FIRST SUMMER "MORNING SCHOOL"
AT WORK ON THE PIAZZA

something to work with; I saw the little dispensary, with its slimly-equipped shelves, in which so much pain is relieved; and then I heard that the children for whom these small things are done at St. Mary's, themselves sent $17 last Easter, that missionaries as loving as Miss Van Deerlin and Miss Chung might minister to children elsewhere, who have no mission house and school and dispensary and chapel.

As I looked at these smallest children and saw how much their school-room lacked, I promised that they should have a blackboard with some colored crayons. These were soon procured and sent, and in return came to me this little note:

"St. Mary's Mission,
"Moiliili, Honolulu,
"May 3, 1909.

"My dear Miss Emery:
"We want to thank you for the nice blackboards."

This was signed by thirty-nine names. These are some of them: Lo Ah Sin, Manuel, Kanita, Man Wo Kim, Ishero, Rosie, Sizue.

Such names as these show the different races from which the children of St. Mary's come. Some of them will remain in the Hawaiian Islands, some will come to the United States, some of them will return to those distant lands in which their fathers were at home. And we who have spent a few moments where faithful friends and teachers have spent months and years may well pray that wherever, as men and women, they may go, these children may take with them a loving faith in a loving Saviour and a willing readiness to walk in His holy ways, which they learned in St. Mary's, Moiliili.

¶

A WESTERN business man, a communicant of the Church, was asked by a news agency to give his impressions of the Laymen's Movement, to be sent to a large list of daily papers. This is what he wrote: "The Laymen's Missionary Movement evidences a recognition by men of their plain, and in many cases long-neglected, duty, to 'tell it out among the heathen that the Lord is King.' It is a hopeful sign in these days of large doings in business and national affairs that men are having large visions and rising to greater activity in the business of the Church. Our aims hitherto have been altogether too small and low—we have been content with nickels where dollars would hardly suffice. We have allowed the women to man our churches and to supplement our shortcomings. The Laymen's Missionary Movement, I believe, is changing these conditions, and under God's guidance and with His blessing the change will be lasting and of ever-increasing value. Every man who can possibly attend a Laymen's Missionary Movement Convention ought to do so without fail; otherwise he will miss a rare opportunity to get information, education and inspiration that are of untold value to every one of us. The sincerity, earnestness and deep convictions of the speakers and executive officers of the Laymen's Missionary Movement and the spirit of prayer that prevails at their conventions can never be forgotten by any man who has the privilege of being present."

THE CONGREGATION AT POINT HOPE

FROM OUR "FARTHEST NORTH"

EVERYBODY has heard about Point Hope and the work there. It is our northernmost mission in Alaska, planted and ministered to through many years by Dr. Driggs. It is also the place where the bishop and the present missionary, Mr. Hoare, built a church recently, and it has probably the only whalebone-fenced cemetery in the world. As though these were not enough to distinguish it, it seems to be a place where the whole population go to church. At least the missionary, in sending a recent letter, says of the above picture that it is "a part of the congregation, September, 1909." There are some rather populous missions in this country which would consider the number in the picture rather more than a part of a congregation. Doubtless many of these people were members of those two remarkable classes, numbering eighty in all, which Bishop Rowe tells of confirming at Point Hope on his latest visitation.

Nor are these people satisfied with mere church attendance. It is evident that they are determined to have their part in the larger work of the Church. A

letter dated November 23d, 1909, which has just been received from the missionary, Mr. Hoare, covers an enclosure of $25.50, designated as follows: $15 for the apportionment; $5.50 for the Bible and Prayer Book Society; $5 for General Clergy Relief; all from the Eskimos of Point Hope. What this means among people living in such primitive fashion and so destitute of anything like ready money, it would be hard for any of our readers fully to conceive.

The missionary writes with good cheer and tells a story which is worth repeating in his own words:

"All well here, but a very backward season, open weather, much snow, southeasterly winds keeping the pack ice off the land; consequently no seals. The extraordinary absence of ducks in the fall and lack of seals now makes it rather hard for the people, who depend on their hunting, but as soon as we get the northwest wind, the pack ice will soon come in, bringing with it the bears and seals, and then there will be plenty in the land.

"Our new church is a great blessing. We can now enjoy the services in bodily comfort. Thanks to the generosity of

(279)

A GROUP OF THE SCHOOL-CHILDREN

the New York Bible Society who sent us in prayer books, hymnals and Bibles, each Eskimo who can read possesses one of each and we are now enabled to go through the *complete* service. The people manifest the greatest interest in the services and are at the church hours before the time of starting.

"The day after to-morrow (Thanksgiv-

ST. THOMAS'S CHURCH, POINT HOPE
The congregation gathering for service in the summer time

ing Day) the people will bring donations of food (rather small, I am afraid this year, on account of the scarcity of game) which will, after the service, be distributed among the deserving poor. All are looking forward toward Christmas; there is a great race this year among the school children for the 'attendance' prize. So far, out of a possible thirty-eight days' attendance, eight girls and four boys have not missed at all and many only once. This, when you consider that they have to walk over a mile each way, sometimes in fierce gales, when a man can scarcely struggle along, speaks well for the Eskimo children."

¶

A CORRECTION

AN article in last month's issue stated that the Rev. William E. Gardner, Department Secretary for New England, succeeded the Rev. Edward Abbott at St. James's, Cambridge, Mass. The Rev. Robb White succeeded Mr. Abbott, and Mr. Gardner succeeded Mr. White. The writer of the article, Bishop Lawrence, requests that we make this correction.

"The school is less than a year old and is selling the Children's Number for the first time. Twenty of the number have been baptized"

A SECOND MISSIONARY TRIP IN THE SAND HILLS OF NEBRASKA

By the Right Reverend A. R. Graves, D.D.,
Bishop of Kearney

THERE was published in THE SPIRIT OF MISSIONS (some time since) an account of my first visit to the work carried on by George G. Ware. At that visitation I confirmed twenty-five middle-aged people in a public hall in the little village of Mullen, where six months before there was hardly a single communicant of the Church. That was in May, 1909. In the following October I visited all Mr. Ware's stations and had such an experience as has rarely ever been the lot of any of our bishops since the days of Bishop Seabury.

Mr. Ware was at first a ranchman, then he became a priest of the Church. As such he planted the Church in most of the towns in the Black Hills. He became involved in trouble with the United States Government, largely through the fault of others. On this account he asked to be deposed by Bishop Hare. He is now working as a lay-reader and exhorter.

On the evening of October 16th, he met me as I alighted from the train at the little town of Seneca in the heart of the Sand Hills. The next morning, being Sunday, we drove eight miles north to a ranchman's house, where I baptized one adult and seven children. After an instruction I confirmed the mother and father of the family. We then drove on four miles further to Miller's ranch, where I baptized five adults and two children. I then gave an instruction and confirmed six adults. We took dinner there and afterward drove two miles to a sod school-house, known as Jimtown school-house, eight miles from any town. There I preached and baptized two adults and five children. After an extended instruction I confirmed fifteen and addressed them. We then drove a mile or two farther to Ricker's ranch, where we spent the night.

The next morning I baptized a child and we drove eighteen miles, against a cold wind, to the little town of Mullen on the railroad. That evening we had eighty people in the public hall, that being two-thirds of the inhabitants of the town. I baptized a school-teacher, preached, and confirmed seven adults. The next morning I confirmed one more in the hall and administered communion to twenty-four. We then held a business meeting of the congregation and decided to build a church or rectory. In the afternoon with the committee we looked at several sites for the church and decided on one which was offered as a gift.

The next morning we drove seven miles to Perkins's ranch and confirmed him and his son. After lunch we drove several miles to the L. C. Smith schoolhouse, where we had a congregation of thirty-five, which more than filled the little building. After preaching I baptized three adults and seventeen children, confirmed twelve and addressed them. We then drove some four miles to Mr. Ware's home on a ranch, where we spent the night.

The next day, October 21st, we drove to Faut's ranch, where I baptized four adults, gave an instruction and confirmed nine. After lunch there we drove to Mr. Silbaugh's house, where I baptized six children and confirmed Mrs. Silbaugh. We then returned to Mr. Ware's home, having driven twenty miles that day.

On October 22d, we drove fifteen miles to Mahaffey's ranch, and in the evening confirmed Mr. Mahaffey. There we spent the night. The next day we drove to Phillips's ranch, where I baptized two adults and two children, and confirmed Mr. and Mrs. Phillips. After lunch there we drove on to Gragg's ranch, seventeen miles in all, where we spent the night.

October 24th, being Sunday, we held service in the Eclipse school-house, where I preached to fifteen people; then returned to Gragg's ranch. In the evening I confirmed Mr. and Mrs. Gragg and their son. On Monday I was taken to Carey's ranch to rest and hunt ducks. Tuesday afternoon I returned to Eclipse post-office and held service with Mr. Ware in a private house. I gave an address, baptized six adults and two chil-

dren and confirmed seven. After another day of rest and hunting at Quinn's ranch we drove ten miles to Huffman's ranch. There I confirmed Mr. Huffman and his son. On Saturday we drove eighteen miles to Stoddard's ranch near a post-office called Lena.

On Sunday, October 31st, I made two addresses in the ranch house, baptized three adults and three children, and confirmed four. In the afternoon I preached to twenty-six in a hall at Lena, after which we drove twenty miles, facing a cold wind, to Gragg's ranch. This night, as on several other occasions, Mr. Ware slept on the floor with the carriage robes above and below him. The night before, both Mr. and Mrs. Ware slept on a load of hay in the barnyard. Mrs. Ware was with us on most of the trip and did her full share of the work in personal talks with the candidates for baptism and confirmation. The next and last day we drove twenty-eight miles to Mullen, where I again conferred with the building committee, then took the evening train toward home.

During the sixteen days we had driven over two hundred miles, held nineteen separate services—not one of them in a church building—delivered seventeen sermons or addresses, baptized seventy-two, mostly adults, and confirmed seventy-four. That made ninety-nine confirmations within six months in Mr. Ware's field, where a year before there were not half a dozen Church people and very few Christians of any kind.

¶

THE offerings of Protestant Christians throughout the world to missions in non-Christian lands have increased from $22,846,000 in 1908 to $24,613,000 in 1909. Of the total increase, over 71 per cent. came from the United States and Canada, the increase in these countries being from $10,061,000 to $11,317,000. This is more than twice the gain ever before registered in a single year from these two countries.

THE JULIA C. EMERY HALL

EWS comes from Liberia of the successful opening, on December 8th, of the new hall named after the secretary of the Woman's Auxiliary, which has been erected at Bromley on the St. Paul's River as the home of the school for girls. The occasion was unique in the history of the mission, and very interesting. There was a large concourse of people from different parts of the republic, among them the president and his cabinet, the legislators, the mayor and city officers of Monrovia, the clergy and other dignitaries. All brought congratulations and joined in expressions of appreciation for Bishop Ferguson for the notable work which he had brought to completion.

The new hall is peculiarly the product of the bishop's own efforts. "From the start," he says, "when I planned it on paper, to the finishing touch of the painter's brush, I have supervised everything pertaining to it. As you must know, we have no architects here with whom we can contract to take such a responsibility. The length across the front is 136 feet, the depth of the wings from front to back is 69 feet. It covers 8,744 square feet of land, and will furnish accommodations for 150 girls. The total cost has been in the neighborhood of $30,000."

Concerning its future the bishop says: "In the first place, we must extend its benefits as widely as possible by taking in as many girls as can be cared for. Besides those that are supported on scholarship funds—which should be confined to girls from heathenism or of civilized parentage in indigent circumstances—my plan is to admit a number of paying pupils, giving them certain special advantages as an inducement. If we make the institution what it should be there are some of the upper class who would be willing to support their daughters in it instead of sending them to Sierra Leone or elsewhere to be trained.

"As to the training to be given the girls at Bromley, it should be most practical and of the kind most needed in the country. Besides literary accomplishments—following a judiciously planned curriculum—the girls must be taught to work with their hands. They must be trained in the kitchen, the laundry, the dining-room, and every other department of household work, as well as in the school-room. They should also learn dressmaking, millinery, fancy needle-work, poultry raising and horticulture. Then, above all and underlying all, they must have a good solid, moral and religious training. In fact, we must bend all our energies to have them breathe a pure moral atmosphere."

The postmaster-general of Liberia, who was one of the guests on the day of the opening, has written most graciously

to Bishop Ferguson concerning the event. After speaking appreciatively of the building, its situation, construction and general excellence, he concludes: "I wish to congratulate you for your far-sightedness, patience and perseverance in carrying to a completion this great work. In erecting this building, as well as in your Church work generally, you have set an example which should leave its lasting mark upon the youth of the land. The giver of this splendid building will have the lasting gratitude of every girl who enjoys its advantages. I sincerely hope the work may soon be expanded into a college for girls."

THE SECRETARY OF THE SOUTHWEST
By Bishop Millspaugh

THE Rev. H. Percy Silver, who has been lately nominated by the Missionary Department of the Southwest, and has been elected by the General Board to be the Department Secretary, is eminently fitted for the work to which he has been chosen.

He graduated from the General Theological Seminary in 1894, after learning business in a book house in Philadelphia and preparation in collegiate studies. He was ordained deacon and priest by Bishop Worthington, of Nebraska, in 1894 and 1895, having come to that diocese to work in the Associate Mission at Omaha. For two years he, with two or three others, had their rooms in a common house and ate at a common table, and went as they were ordered week by week. In 1896 he took charge of the new mission of St. Andrew's, Omaha, called into being by the Associate Mission. Two years later he was called to Holy Trinity, Lincoln. In 1898 he accepted a call to the Good Shepherd, Omaha. In all these positions he was eminently a missionary as the work grew under his hand. In 1901 he

was appointed chaplain in the United States Army, where he served most faithfully for nine years, going to the Philippines twice.

The writer of this note has known the new secretary through these years, and in all the places where he has ministered, and says without hesitancy that from parishes and military posts there comes the same word of testimony as to his untiring energy, devotion to the work of the Master and the uplift of humanity. This was especially manifest when chaplain at the military prison at Fort Leavenworth, where many were baptized and confirmed, and followed by him after they had regained their liberty, in positions which he had secured by personal solicitation or by letter all over the country.

This is not intended as an encomium, but simply to let those interested know that the new Secretary of the Southwest has had a life which has prepared him for the aggressive work demanded by this hard field of eleven dioceses. He has unusual gifts as a speaker; he knows men; he is a good executive.

THE EDUCATIONAL VALUE OF THE PROBLEMS OF WORLD-WIDE CHURCH EXTENSION

By the Reverend Philip M. Rhinelander

WE must first of all have clearly in our minds what education means. It is, as we in these days have come to see, not the imparting of information but the development of life. As someone has put it, its end and aim is not "the filling of a folio," but "the training of a twig." Of course the twig in this case, being human, is a free agent. It needs to be trained, but cannot be trained unless first of all it is willing to submit itself to training. No education is at all possible unless there is co-operation between the teacher and the taught. But given co-operation, then education works for the development of life.

I might illustrate it by a trolley car. The car is cold and dark and motionless until connection is established with the current. When the current enters, instantly it does three things. It gives heat, and light, and motive power. So it is with education. If it is real, it too will give heat and light and energy. By heat I mean the kindling of the imagination. An image or picture of the knowledge to be gained, or rather of himself as the possessor of the knowledge, is held up before the pupil so as to awaken his desire and make him eager for its realization. He wants to know. And next there is light coming to the mind. Desire communicates itself to, and sets in motion the machinery of thought. How this knowledge may be gained, what it would mean when gained, how it would affect him who possesses it, what it would do for him, what powers it would give him; all these things the mind bit by bit fits in together, and so illumines and stimulates the original impulse which set it at its work. And then, lastly, comes energy, which means the actual application to the task, the actual doing of the work. The will is concentrated on acquisition. You can apply this to any special field of knowledge, to any subject taught in any school or college. Education in any special branch of learning is accomplished just in so far as the teacher has ability to impart these three things: Heat, light and energy. Now if this is the aim of education, the value of any agency for education is determined simply by its power to accomplish this result. That obviously is the best pedagogy, that is the quickest and most direct method, which most surely and speedily heats and illumines and inspires.

Turn from the general to the particular. The education we are thinking of is the education of the Christian life. We want professing Christian men and women to be educated in that which they profess, to be warmed and illumined and quickened in their faith. We want them to feel something of the fulness of the Gospel and to give themselves to it with fulness of surrender. We want to open their hearts to its glory and its beauty, to enlighten their minds with a sense of its constraining claim, to quicken their wills to a devoted surrender to its service. And, as an instrument for the accomplishment of this, there is suggested the study of the problems of world-wide Church extension. Will it do the work? That is what we are considering. Well, first of all, note that these "problems" are real, and not abstract. They are not the product of wise and learned men sitting aloof and alone among their books. They are problems which have arisen out of life, out of the heart of work. They stand for things that are really being done, or rather being attempted. They represent conditions with which living men and women find themselves confronted all the world over.

Here is the solid, solemn, impressive,
tenacious bulk of China. How is that to
be leavened by the Gospel? Here is the
alert, agile, self-confident, ambitious,
genial, resourceful Empire of Japan.
How can all its brightness and its bril-
liance be weighted and disciplined with
holiness and sacrifice? Here is the sub-
tlety of Hinduism; the childishness of
African and Bushman; the dormant
fanaticism of Islam; the new-found
liberty of Turkey: these are living opportunities, present demands, actual
problems. The Church is face to face
with them. What is to be done?

Well, I submit that he must be very
little of a man, and still less of a Christian who, if he even for a moment fairly
face these things, does not feel a thrill
stirring his slumbering imagination.
He may not have had the least "interest
in missions." He may have been continually harping on the worn-out platitudes of unbelievers. But here all over
the world are great things doing. The
Church, his Church, is launched out into
the deep, is grappling hand to hand with
these matters of extraordinary import
and extraordinary difficulty. It may all
be a mistake, it may be entirely quixotic,
but at least it is a splendid venture, this
conquest of the world. Yes, pick the man
who of all those you know has the nar-
rowest and weakest faith. Bring him
face to face with these problems of
world-wide Church extension. Will
there not come at least a flush of color to
his cheeks, at least a throb of his imagi-
native faculty, at least the suggestion of
a vision?

And then, once you have put a little
heat within, light is bound to follow. He
will do a little thinking and every
thought he thinks will be in the direction
of relating himself to and with the cam-
paigning Church. Why should he be entirely outside of it? Is he sure that he is
right in standing thus aloof? Is it the
mere silly enthusiasm of a few fanatics?
Or is it the only meaning of the Church,
the only possible demonstration of the
faith? Light in some degree will come.

SOME YOUNG PEOPLE OF *IGLESIA DE SAN LUCAS*

SOME BOYS AND·GIRLS IN THE PHILIPPINES

IN an address on the work of Christian missions, delivered by President Taft a year or two ago, he told of hearing the following sentiment sung on the streets of Manila by a gentleman who did not agree with his view of the Filipinos:

"He may be a brother of William H. Taft,
But he ain't no brother of mine!"

"This spirit," says the President, "is the one which we are altogether too likely to find among gentlemen who go to the East for the mere purpose of extending trade. They are generally quite out of sympathy with any spirit of brotherhood toward the Orientals."

However true this may be—and true it undoubtedly is concerning the attitude of the average commercial American—we see a different and a far more lovable picture when we turn to the activities of the Church among these people. There is a most interesting work carried on—under rather primitive conditions and still very much in its infancy—which gives us a pleasing glimpse of the little brown brothers and sisters, at St. Luke's Mission, Manila. The Rev. George C. Bartter, with the assistance of Deaconess Routledge, is here bringing Christian faith and fellowship into effective touch with the lives of many.

Look at the accompanying picture of

(287)

INTERIOR OF THE CHAPEL

This building serves a variety of purposes. Sliding doors shut off the chapel from the portion used for social or secular gatherings

the young people of St. Luke's Mission. What a variety they present, and how really attractive and charming many of them are! This picture was taken on Thanksgiving Day, at the close of a choral celebration of the Eucharist, at which time twenty-three of the children —doubtless those conspicuous in their white garments—had received their first Communion. Some of the girls are inmates of the Orphanage of the Holy Child, recently organized, which has its home in the settlement house near by. The priest, Mr. Bartter, may be seen standing at the left of the banner. The processional cross held by the boy at his left is one borrowed from the cathedral for use at this special service.

Attractive as are many of these children, there is a peculiar and romantic interest attaching to the little one with bushy, close-curling hair, who stands with the priest's left hand resting on her shoulder. She is a Negrita, a member of one of the wild mountain tribes, largely untouched by civilization or

Christianity, and still retaining man of their barbarous and cruel custom This poor baby was the last represent tive of her family—father, mother an brothers all having died. She was re cued by a government official just as sh was about to be offered up in sacrific according to the horrible custom of h people, who thus dispose of the last su vivor of a family, particularly if tha survivor be a child—possibly to avoi the expense and trouble of caring fo them.

The most of these neighborhood chil dren are of the respectable but poore class of Filipinos who would correspon to the artisans of our towns in thi country. According to the testimony o their teachers—and one can well believ it to be true—they are bright and at tractive little folk, and are learnin English readily and taking to America ways of living.

It is a crude place where this effect ive Christian work is being carried on The interior view which accompanie

THE GIRLS' BASKET-BALL TEAM

this article shows the wooden building which serves as chapel, etc. Not a very elaborate equipment, certainly! It was built originally for the American congregation in another part of the city, but was taken to pieces and removed when the cathedral house was ready for the American services. It is of American pine, eight years old, and cannot have very many more years of life in it. It is divided by sliding doors, the outer part being used for classes and meetings and the inner portion for a chapel.

Of course where there are children there must be amusements. Clubs of various sorts, both literary and social, have a prominent place. A mandolin club and literary society exist in the interest of the boys, while an embroidery class, under the care of Deaconess Routledge, and the delightfully American

sport of "basket-ball," engross the attention of the girls. The accompanying picture of the basket-ball team looks business-like. It would certainly be interesting to see these little brown maidens skipping about under the stress of the game. One can well believe that they would be quick and agile. The group was taken on the beautiful grounds of the settlement house, which appears in the background.

So here, as in many another place, the Church fulfils her many-sided mission in promoting the development of body, mind and spirit, and thus standing as a perpetual witness against national intolerance and racial prejudice, while she teaches by word and act the eternal truth of the words, "There is neither barbarian, Scythian, bond nor free: but Christ is all, and in all."

WAR IN AFRICA

[The letters given below were received from Bishop Ferguson on March 10th. It is hoped that his appeal may have averted a general civil war, but at the time of going to press no further definite information had been received.]

BISHOP'S HOUSE, MONROVIA, LIBERIA,
February 15th, 1910

*The Secretary, Board of Missions,
Church Missions House, New York*

MY DEAR SIR:

STARTLING news has come from Cape Palmas, that one-half of the Gedebo tribes have rebelled against the Government and war has again broken out. The trouble started in this way. There was a contention between the Cavalla tribe and the Cape Palmas tribe, with the allies of the latter, about a piece of land on the Cavalla River, which both claim. The Cavallians appealed to the Government to settle the dispute, but the others showed no disposition to yield to the local authorities. Commissioners were therefore sent down from Monrovia. Meanwhile the Cape Palmas natives began throwing up breastworks in order to protect their towns—as they said. On arrival the commissioners required them to desist from the warlike attitude which they were assuming, saying that they would then give them a hearing on the matter in dispute.

Just at that time some one clandestinely shot and killed our missionary, the Rev. B. K. Speare, at night in his own house in Harper, and one Killen (son of our catechist)—both Gedeboes —was found drowned in the river. A report went out that the said Killen had previously had some altercation with Speare and must have committed the crime and then got drowned in trying to escape. The Cape Palmas natives, however, hold the Liberians responsible for the deed. The commissioners, on the part of the Government, placarded a notice denouncing the atrocious crime and offering a reward of $100 to anyone who would give information leading to the apprehension of the guilty person or persons. The natives then wrote the president making certain demands and asking him either to appoint a new commission or to go down himself to hear and adjudge the matter. The latter sent a reply, requiring the Cape Palmas natives to demolish their barricades and that the chieftains of all the tribes concerned come to Monrovia at Government expense in order to have the matter settled. I too wrote both the heathen and the employees of the mission, urging that they yield to the requirement of the Government.

All intercourse between the people at Harper and the natives across the river had now ceased (though the letters were duly forwarded and received by them), and both sides were keeping guard at night. The Liberians also began to prepare for war, which seemed inevitable. On the night of the 11th the men on guard at Harper saw what they regarded as indications of an approach of the enemy, and fired in that direction. The natives on the other side responded, and then a general fusillade followed, which is the beginning of another war, and no one knows how it will end. At present one-half of the Gedebo tribes is with the government, viz.: Cavalla, Rocktown and Fishtown. The chief ones that are against the Liberians are living next to them—those of Cape Palmas, not many rods away, on one side, and Graway— about six miles away, on the other.

The tragic death of the Rev. B. Kedako Speare, mentioned above, is greatly regretted by the citizens of Harper as well as his own people. At the time of its occurrence he was assistant minister in St. Mark's parish. He was a fine young man and full of zeal in his work, but had met opposition from his own people. His first appointment was

(290)

War in Africa

that of assistant minister at Hoffman Station. On the death of the Rev. O. E. Shannon, I appointed him superintendent of the Graway sub-district. Last year I appointed him to work among Liberians at Harper, under the rector of St. Mark's Church, where he was made welcome and was highly respected. Just how it happened that he met such a death about three o'clock in the morning of January 20th is beyond my conception.

This trouble will interfere greatly with our work in that county. God grant that it may be brought to a speedy termination.

Yours faithfully,
S. D. FERGUSON.

P. S. For your information I enclose copies of my letters to the Cape Palmas natives.   S. D. F.

———

January 31st, 1910.
The King and Chiefs of the Nyomowe Tribe, Bigtown, Cape Palmas.

MY DEAR FRIENDS:

The letter which you sent me by Mr. Johnson (the late Bodo Ple's son), was duly received and I regret that trouble has again befallen you and especially the recent development of it, which is of a very serious nature. All of us are especially startled and grieved at the killing of the Rev. B. K. Speare and the drowning of the man who is said to have perpetrated the crime. If the latter has been falsely accused, it is to be hoped that the real criminal will be discovered and disposed of according to law. We are glad to know that the Government is putting forth efforts to find him by offering a reward for any information that may lead to his apprehension. Such a wicked person does not deserve to live on the earth.

If I were at Cape Palmas, I would come over to Bigtown and speak to you about the present trouble. As you know, I have always taken a deep interest in your welfare and you have generally listened to my advice. Though I am not

there now, I beg you to give attention to what I am writing.

The devil does not want any people to succeed and therefore he causes strife, hatred and war. He knows that war destroys people's lives, prevents them from accumulating property and advancing in civilization and Christianity; and therefore he tries to make them fight and kill each other. He does this by getting into people's hearts and filling them with hatred and a spirit of revenge. I hope you will not allow yourselves to be misled by this enemy of mankind who, as the Bible tells us, is always going about seeking whom he may devour.

God wants you to follow the right way which He has marked out for you in the Bible, and which will bring you peace, prosperity and happiness. Among other things, He requires that all subjects of a Government should submit themselves to those in authority. Let one of your civilized men read the following passages from the Bible. (Romans xiii: 1-2; I Peter ii: 13-14.) These and other passages from God's book teach that it is your duty to submit yourselves to the Government and obey its commands. If you are not satisfied with its management or with the officials who have been appointed, it is your privilege to appeal to the Legislature or the Executive Government, and it will be your duty to abide by their decision. To act otherwise and take matters into your own hands in order to redress your grievances, or to disobey the Government is rebellion; which is a great sin in the sight of God.

There is nothing to be gained by resorting to war and bloodshed. It only tends to weaken both sides and to kill our valuable men who might help to improve and build up the country. My advice to you, therefore, is to be willing to submit yourselves and to make any sacrifice rather than go into a war with the Government or any of the tribes.

I write thus to you because it is with you either to bring on a war or to make peace. From my personal knowledge the Government has no desire to go into war with you or any other tribe; but if you treat it with contempt and refuse to obey its mandates, it will be forced to resort to severe measures. Take my advice, therefore, and submit yourselves to the requirements of the Government, although you may have to make a sacrifice in doing so.

I am giving you this advice because of the interest which I have in you as well as in the interest of peace generally; and I hope I shall soon hear that the matter has been amicably settled.

Yours faithfully,

S. D. FERGUSON,
Missionary Bishop.

NEWS AND NOTES

ON Sexagesima Sunday, January 30th, the new All Saints' Church, in Guantanamo was opened for divine service by the Bishop of Cuba. The opening service was at ten o'clock in the morning. Practically all the city officials were present, in addition to a very large congregation.

The procession, entering by the western door of the church, was a very picturesque sight as it marched up the middle aisle of the building. First came the choir of little Cuban girls, which Mrs. Ackley has trained, vested in scarlet cassocks and caps and white cottas. These were followed by the senior warden, Mr. Theodore Brooks, robed in his Cambridge University gown; after him the priest-in-charge, the Rev. Charles B. Ackley, followed by the bishop. The first hymn, "Onward, Christian Soldiers," was sung in Spanish, and when the clear, sweet voices of the Cuban children rang out it was realized at once what marvellous acoustic qualities the building possessed. Morning Prayer was said in Spanish, the hymns and all the canticles being sung in the native language. The sermon was by the bishop and the celebration of the Holy Communion in English followed, the bishop being celebrant.

The congregation itself was an interesting one, for there were Spaniards and Americans, Cubans and English, Jamaica Negroes and Cuban Negroes, all gathered together in the house of God.

The architects, Messrs. Cram, Goodhue & Ferguson, are to be congratulated on the structure. As the bishop expressed it, "The chancel is simply per-

fect in lines and proportion." The nave is long and narrow, and has a high roof, which gives it a most churchly appearance. There is an easy seating capacity of more than two hundred, and a spacious choir. The walls are built of concrete pillars, with the space between filled in with cement-covered brick work. The columns are of reinforced concrete which is proof against earthquake shocks. Within, the roof is of dark native woods, and it is covered with old Spanish tiles. About the entrance are massive carvings, and elaborate decorative concrete work, after the Spanish style. Near the eastern end there is a mission bell-tower, in which is soon to be hung an old Spanish bell, the gift of Mr. Brooks, the British Vice-Consul. All of the doors, exterior and interior, are of solid mahogany.

As soon as funds may be in hand the building is to be surrounded by an iron fence. ¶

MR. WILLIAM R. STIRLING, one of the vestry of Grace Church, Chicago, and a prominent banker, attended the Detroit convention in order that he might familiarize himself with the methods and message of the Laymen's Missionary Movement. During the convention he said that nothing in his whole experience had so thoroughly aroused him to the need of the non-Christian world, and what he could do to meet it, as had the convention. He took copious notes of the addresses. On his return he dictated an admirable résumé of the convention, with frequent quotations from the striking sayings of some of the speakers. He then invited a number of his business friends, together with several clergymen of Chicago, to meet him at a luncheon. Fifty-three of them accepted the invitation and were deeply interested in Mr. Stirling's account of what he had seen and heard in Detroit. This is a novel method of propagating the L. M. M. idea, and it is a good one.

¶

THE Church of Zion and St. Timothy, New York city, has a weekly calendar distributed in the pews at the Sunday morning service. The rector has kindly assured the Corresponding Secretary that he will be glad to receive for the page of "Rector's Notes" occasional brief paragraphs telling of the Church's progress at home and abroad. How many others will make the same offer? It would be possible no doubt to prepare a mailing list of least 100 such calendars. Shall we have it?

Where no weekly calendar is published, part of the monthly music list might be set apart for missionary and other notes. The Secretary would be interested, too, in compiling a mailing list of parish papers, to each of which might go regularly a paragraph or two of fresh facts. Names and addresses should be sent on a post-card to the Corresponding Secretary, 281 Fourth Avenue, New York.

¶

THE Canadian Church has a well-organized Laymen's Missionary Movement with a layman as secretary, giving all his time to planning and holding meetings and generally furthering the work.

¶

WE are glad to be able to announce that there is now a cloth edition of "Winners of the World," which is sold at sixty cents a copy. Arrangements have also been made for selling the new edition in paper at thirty cents. In each case, add eight cents for postage. These books may be ordered from the Educational Department as heretofore.

A Massachusetts rector calls our attention to a method of missionary giving which he has introduced in his Sunday-school. It may already be familiar to many, but we give the suggestion place here.

I HAVE recently introduced into my school here a little scheme, in which, it seems to me, lie great possibilities for the development of missionary giving on the part of the children. The idea is not original with me, and yet I know of none of our schools that is using it. Briefly, it is simply this: I have a little bank, and each Sunday any child in the school who has had a birthday during the past week is asked to bring a penny for each year, and they are deposited in the box. It is a little thank-offering from each child for God's care and mercies for its life. At the end of the year the idea is to open the bank and send on its contents to the Board for its general work. My children are most enthusiastic over it, and it seems to me that the system has great potentialities for good if it might be universally adopted. St. Stephen's, Portland, Me., has followed the same plan with good results.

¶

THE REV. H. PERCY SILVER, the new Secretary of Department VII., writing of a visit to New Orleans in January, says: "From the moment I reached the city until the time of leaving there was a campaign of activity startling to contemplate. They mapped out my work and then backed me up in a magnificent way. Friday evening I met with the members of the committees from the different parishes and talked over the situation and made plans. Everybody took hold in good shape, and the rectors of the parishes agreed to stir things up. Saturday night I was the guest of honor at the annual banquet of the Church Club, where I took occasion to sound the note of 'forward march!' Every speaker fell into line and promised support. Sunday I preached to splendid congregations at three of the churches, and on Monday addressed the diocesan branch of the Woman's Auxiliary."

From Valdez, Alaska, comes this message of thanks for the blessings of a mission hospital and the service of devoted workers.

I WISH to thank the Board of Missions for the nurses sent to our Hospital of the Good Samaritan about a year ago. Enough cannot be said in praise of the conscientious work of Miss Wygant and Miss Barlowe. Thoroughly prepared by training and experience for their work, and faithfully working for the best interests of the hospital, they have proven themselves true missionaries. I had an eight weeks' siege in the hospital, and therefore speak from a personal experience. This note is a poor expression of the appreciation of the people of Valdez, but I trust it will let you know that we are grateful for the interest shown by the Board in our far-off northern country.

¶

BISHOP GRAVES, of Shanghai, replying to information sent him by one of the secretaries about the arousal of the laymen, says: "It is very cheering news that you send about the Laymen's Missionary Movement, and the figures in your letter prove pretty conclusively that it is not a movement which is to end in talk. I cannot tell you how encouraging it is to see so much new life amongst laymen in regard to foreign missions. You must remember as well as I do how when you first became secretary and I was a young and inexperienced bishop, we used to talk over this very thing and wonder what could be done to convince men that foreign missions were their duty and not something to be left to women and children. If this Laymen's Movement succeeds in implanting this idea permanently in the minds of the men of the Church, it will be one of the most important things which has happened in the Church in a long time, and I hope, too, that it will extend to men as well as to money, and be the means of providing a regular supply of the right sort of clergy as well as of laymen for teachers, doctors and other branches of missionary work."

BISHOP RICHARDSON, of Fredericton, one of the younger and most inspiring leaders of the Church in Canada, says:

"Every great call to action carries with it a solemn seat of judgment, before which those to whom the call comes will stand acquitted or condemned. Such a call has come to the Christian world in the Laymen's Missionary Movement. I believe that the Church which catches to the full the inspiration of this Movement will find her own life deepened and made more strong, as she marches on to victory in a world evangelized and brought to Christ; and I believe also that the Church which hears the call, and stands aside, will find her own certain condemnation in ultimate weakness and decay. The opportunity awaits us, and it carries with it a solemn seat of judgment."

¶

A Brazilian layman bears this testimony:

OUR Church with her sound teachings has already done a great deal to show things in their true light. I do not doubt for a moment her adaptability to our people here, an adaptability which will meet that sound thinking and that high sense, sometimes in embryo, which needs only a leader. And such leader our Church is destined to be. Those good qualities will be then developed and will produce Christian characters.

Much has been done in the past, and when we look for the great amount of work yet to be done, we have only motive of rejoicing, because we may note already the presence of that "leaven which a woman took and hid in three measures of meal."

Those who contribute to missions, at least to the mission in Brazil, may be sure that their co-operation is duly appreciated and earnestly desired, specially now, when the high ideals of our dear Church are beginning to be understood, and when they see that a true and noble patriotism finds an echo in an historical Church, that can introduce new blood in national life.

IONARY FINANCE

MR. GEORGE WHARTON PEPPER, speaking of the necessity of some better system of missionary finance than that represented by the "annual collection" says:

"Much of the trouble in which we find ourselves is due to a radical divergence between our missionary theory and our missionary practice. The theory which we emphasize is that missionary work is an essential part of Christianity, and that its support is just as much a part of the obligation of a Christian as is parochial support. Our practice, on the other hand, is to treat missionary support as a voluntary 'extra' by placing it on the same plane with a number of other worthy objects, such as the support of a diocesan hospital or the Clergy Relief Fund, or other things for which occasional offerings are taken in our parish churches. No matter how loudly we proclaim our theory, our practice will always determine the result. I believe that the fundamental reason for making a weekly offering for missions is the reason that we make weekly offerings for parochial support, and that the people will never come to look upon their responsibility in these matters as co-ordinate until something like the duplex envelope system is adopted, in which an offering for missions must be made every time an offering is made for parochial support.

MAR 20 1910   512

"As to the amount which people should be asked to give as their weekly missionary offering, I doubt the feasibility of enforcing a flat rule applicable to all sorts and conditions of people, and in all sorts and kinds of parishes. I think the thing to press for is the weekly offering and leave each parish to determine for itself how the thing shall be worked out. In my own parish (St. Mark's, Philadelphia), for example, we have adopted the duplex envelope system, and all people on the parish list are being approached by appointed persons with the request that they will pledge themselves to the stated weekly offering for missions. The three offerings for missions which we now take and shall continue to take in the course of a year will, under such a system, become the outlet for gifts by people in excess of the minimum for which they have given their weekly pledges."

FOLLOWING the notable Laymen's Missionary Movement Convention in Greensboro, N. C., a meeting of the men of the four congregations of Wilmington was held. Several brief addresses were made reviewing the situation. The rector of St. James's startled those present by saying that from one point of view the Diocese of East Carolina was giving $200 less than nothing for general missions, since, as he puts it, "our contributions from the whole diocese were about $1,300 and our appropriation from the Board of Missions $1,500." A general committee representing the four congregations was appointed with power to form sub-committees in each. So far report has been received only from St. James's, the mother parish of the city. Already more than $500 has been subscribed and the rector is confident that the gifts from St. James's alone will be at least $800 and possibly $1,000. The apportionment for the congregation is only $300, and for the entire diocese $1,000. Gifts for diocesan missions have also been stimulated and St. James's has decided on an effort to increase its gifts for work within the

diocese from $333 to $900. It is possible that as a result of this increased giving the Diocese of East Carolina may at its next council send a message to the Board of Missions that it is ready to release a part, if not the whole, of its appropriation.

LEAFLET 1102 has only four pages, but they are brimful of practical suggestions on what can be accomplished by an every-member canvass of a congregation and how to start and make the canvass. A postal to the Corresponding Secretary, 281 Fourth Avenue, New York, will bring you a copy, as well as a copy of the suggestive subscription card. Write for them to-day.

How St. Paul's parish, Concord, N. H., secured seventy-seven subscribers to THE SPIRIT OF MISSIONS:

THE parish availed itself of the offer to supply the magazine for fifty cents a year to any parish where the number of subscriptions equalled one-fifth the number of communicants. There are 384 communicants in St. Paul's parish, and it was necessary to have seventy-seven subscribers to get the magazine at this rate. The parish uses the systematic offering plan, and in the package of envelopes supplied to each communicant is one monthly envelope for all missionary apportionments and the diocesan assessment for the bishop's salary. In every case where ten cents is given each month by an individual or family, one such amount is considered a subscription to the diocesan paper. Where as much as fifty cents a month is given, the amount for one month is considered a subscription to THE SPIRIT OF MISSIONS. As more than seventy families pledge fifty cents or more a month for missionary purposes, the number of subscribers was secured in this way. In a very few instances the amount was made up from the vice-rector's fund, where a family was absolutely unable to give as much as fifty cents a month, but would appreciate the magazine.

A FAREWELL MESSAGE

THE REV. A. A. GILMAN, who during his furlough has become well known in several parts of the country, has just returned to his work in Changsha, province of Hunan, China. He sends to us a farewell message in the following words:

"Our own American Episcopal Church has had an honorable part in the awakning of China. Our school work has been second to none and our medical and evangelistic work is proceeding as rapidly as men and means are available. Our Church has undertaken to do its part in reaching the people of the five central provinces of the Yangtze River basin. In three of these provinces our work is now fairly well established.

"The Church through its Board and its bishop has sent me to Changsha, the capital city of the province of Hunan. Hunan has been the strong support of the conservative party, the dismissed leader of which lives just around the corner from our mission home. It is one of the opium-growing provinces. Here, too, the old superstitions still hold undisputed way. I am sent with orders to convert these 20,000,000 people, and I am set down in the midst of this city of 250,000 people. I am going back, full of enthusiasm through the knowledge of what others have done, full of hope as to what we shall be able to do, and, in view of the development of interest at home, confident that my work will in no wise be hampered by lack of support in any project which seems well calculated to accomplish the early evangelization of this important portion of the Chinese people.

"In our Christian warfare 'every man is expected to do his duty.' My duty has been assigned to me, and by study, preaching and social intercourse, I hope to do my best to advance our work, but if the Church desires the work to progress as rapidly as possible it will be necessary to provide for the plant and workers suggested by the bishop. This calls for the erection first of a building containing a large room for use as chapel and assembly, guest-rooms and day-school rooms. After this a second dwelling to house the clergyman and two women workers who are urgently needed to reinforce the staff.

"In order to train up native clergy and women workers of the highest grade for Hunan we should have in Changsha a boarding-school for boys and one for girls. I believe that if provision were made to accommodate forty persons in each school, they would prove very efficient for our purpose. Altogether an outlay of $30,000 is called for. The immediate contribution of $5,000 would guarantee the continuance of rapid progress and the furnishing of the whole sum within five years would insure that everything humanly possible was being done on our part to hasten the coming of Christ's Kingdom among this important section of the Chinese people."

As the result of work done during his furlough, Mr. Gilman secured $1,200. He hoped for and needed $5,000 at once and $30,000 within five years.

MEETING OF THE E

March &

THE Board of Missions met at the
Church Missions House on
Tuesday, March 8th, the Bish-
op of Albany (vice-president)
in the chair. The following members were
present: The Bishops of Pennsylvania,
Pittsburgh, Bethlehem, Ohio, Massa-
chusetts, Rhode Island, Long Island,
Newark and New York; the Rev. Drs.
Vibbert, Anstice, Alsop, Perry, Stires,
McKim, Smith, the Rev. Mr. Miel and
the Rev. Dr. Manning; Messrs. Low,
Mills, Chauncey, Goodwin, Mansfield,
Admiral Mahan and Messrs. Butler,
King, Ryerson and Houston; of the hon-
orary members: the Bishops of Alaska,
North Dakota and Porto Rico.

The resignation of the Bishop of New
Jersey was presented and read to the
Board, together with his request for its
acceptance at this time on account of his
inability longer to discharge the duties.
Whereupon the Board by a rising vote,
unanimously adopted the following
minute:

"In accepting with great reluctance
the resignation of the Bishop of New
Jersey, the Board puts on its records the
following statement:

"1. That it accepts the resignation
only under the conviction that the bishop is governed in this action, as in all
his relations to its work, by the same
conscientious sense of duty which has
governed all his relations to the Board,
namely, that he is physically disabled for
satisfactory service.

"2. That it recognizes the unsurpassed
ability and devotion of Bishop Scarborough's long and faithful service on the
Board.

"3. That in taking this action the
Board hopes to have a share in prolong-
ing the life and continuing the activity
of the bishop's work in his diocese and
for the Church at large."

The Treasurer's report was more

(298)

by secretaries at the Church Missions
House.
Department 3. The Rev. Thomas J.
Garland, Church House, Philadelphia.
Department 4. The Rev. R. W.
Patton, care of the Rev. C. B. Wilmer,
D.D., 412 Courtland Street, Atlanta, Ga.
Department 5. The Rev. John Henry
Hopkins, D.D., 703 Ashland Boulevard,
Chicago.
Department 6. The Rev. C. C. Rollit,
4416 Upton Avenue, South, Minneapolis,
Minn.
Department 7. The Rev. H. Percy
Silver, Box 312, Topeka, Kan.
Department 8. The Rev. L. C. San-
ford, 1215 Sacramento Street, San
Francisco, Cal.

China
SHANGHAI:
The Rev. F. L. H. Pott, D.D., of
Shanghai.
The Rev. John W. Nichols, of
Shanghai.
The Rev. R. C. Wilson, of Zangzok.
Dr. Angie M. Myers, of Shanghai.

HANKOW:
The Rev. Arthur M. Sherman, of
Hankow.
The Rev. L. B. Ridgely, of Wuchang.

Japan
KYOTO:
Bishop Partridge, of Kyoto.
The Rev. W. J. Cuthbert, of Kyoto.

TOKYO:
The Rev. C. H. Evans, of Tokyo.

Work Among Negroes in the South
The Rev. S. H. Bishop, Secretary of
the American Church Institute for Negroes, 500 West 122d Street, New York.
Archdeacon Russell, of St. Paul's,
Lawrenceville, Va., and the Rev. A. B.
Hunter, of St. Augustine's, Raleigh,
N. C., are always ready to take appointments, especially when a number of engagements in the same neighborhood can
be grouped.

ANNOUNCEMENTS
CONCERNING THE MISSIONARIES

Porto Rico

THE REV. F. A. WARDEN, returning after three months' leave of absence, with his wife and family sailed from New York by the steamer *Philadelphia* on March 12th, for San Juan.

AT the meeting of the Board of Missions on March 8th the transfer by Bishop Van Buren of the Rev. Leonard Read from Vieques to Ponce was approved.

The Philippines

BISHOP BRENT, coming to the Edinburgh Conference, will sail from Manila by the steamer *Goeben* about May 1st, for Naples. After the Conference he will come to the United States and the General Convention.

Africa

AT the meeting of the Board on March 8th the appointment by the Bishop of Cape Palmas of Mrs. Maria H. Williams as matron of the Girls' Training Institute at Bromley was approved, and the withdrawal of Mr. J. W. Pearson from the work at Lower Buchanan was noted.

INFORMATION has been received from Bishop Ferguson that the Rev. B. Kedako Speare was killed in his home at Harper on January 20th.

Shanghai

DR. WILLIAM H. JEFFERYS, on leave of absence because of illness, with his family sailed from Shanghai by the *Tenyo Maru* on February 7th, and, stopping over a steamer in Honolulu, reached Philadelphia on March 11th.

Tokyo

THE REV. CHARLES H. EVANS and wife, on regular furlough, left Yokohama on March 30th for England.

DR. THEODORE BLISS and wife, who sailed from San Francisco on January 7th, arrived at Tokyo on the 24th.

INFORMATION has been received from Bishop McKim that Mr. Akimoto, the thoroughly competent and reliable phar-

(300)

macist at St. Luke's Hospital, Tokyo, who also acted as steward and treasurer, died in January.

Mexico

INFORMATION has been received that the Rev. Filipe Pastrana y Castillo, Deacon, died in Mexico City on February 20th. Bishop Aves writes that he was universally loved and respected and that he was a sincere Christian and devoted servant of the Church.

¶

One of our China missionaries (an Englishwoman), on furlough in England, tells of the changes she finds there after an absence of seven years:

TIMES have changed in regard to missions, and the home churches seem thoroughly in earnest about helping. Mission study classes, meetings, etc., are the order of the day. My husband has had some really good meetings where people have afterward definitely asked what they can do to help in the great work. We still hear of the wonderful services of the Pan-Anglican Conference. Much good for missions was done then.

Our service at home has certainly filled us with hope for the future of our work. So many people are praying, working and giving as never before, and it behooves us as missionaries to see that we properly appreciate and recognize all that is being done by them. Since we were home seven years ago it seems almost impossible that such a change could have taken place. At many of the meetings where my husband has been speaking over a thousand were present, and mostly those who are already interested in missions! Then—an almost unheard of thing—the Bishop of London has given my husband a license to speak in the London churches on Sunday evening—on missions of course. I think it is wonderful in this slow old England of ours that such changes should have taken place in so short a time.

THE WOMAN'S AUXILIARY
To the Board of Missions

OUR UNITED OFFERING MISSIONARY
AND HER WORK AT PENNICK

By Deaconess Alexander

EIGHT years ago the Good Shepherd Mission School began its work among the Negro children of Pennick, Ga. It opened with twenty-four pupils; now nearly one hundred are enrolled, with a large average attendance.

The school aims to give the boys and girls higher ideals of living, and to make them good citizens, by developing their moral and Christian character, and teaching them how to do things with their hands, as well as to learn the contents of text-books. The work is growing day by day, and is now entirely too much for one person, as a teacher.

The names of 141 baptized persons, nearly all of them children, are now on the mission lists, and of these I am the sponsor for nearly every one. Of these many children, through hard struggle and prayer, five are at St. Paul's School, Lawrenceville, Va., where they pay a part of their expenses by their work.

My life in the mission is a busy one. There are times for weeks when I have not an hour to call mine. Some days, leaving home in the morning, I go to the school-house, and, after finishing the teaching for the day, I take one of the children with me for company, guide or protection, and walk nine or ten miles, visiting the people, before reaching home in the evening. It is not a strange thing for me to go on foot over bad roads and through swamps where are deep places sometimes only passable on foot logs. Many of these roads have fifty yards and more of logs. Here we will get poles about ten feet long to help us steady urselves until we get over.

Many times I find the sick person is suffering for want of attention, as much

as for the need of medicine. Then there are places where I am obliged to go a second time before I am allowed to render any service. When such persons recover the family tell what good the Church has done, and at the visitation of the bishop they will be out at service. Through these children many parents visit the church.

DEACONESS ALEXANDER
Our United Offering Missionary in Georgia

There are many children, large and small, who walk daily for miles to attend the school. They will be in time for devotions every morning. Just to hear them respond in the Litany on Wednesday and Friday mornings, and to see and hear them find and read the Psalter for the day, will bring tears to the eyes.

On Thanksgiving Day you see the children coming with their little parcels for offerings. The contents are sweet potatoes, rice, hominy, meal, flour, peas, turnips, syrup, meat, matches and bread. After the service for the day, they go away very happy, some of them waiting to help carry the offerings to the sick, aged and invalids.

Once I took a class of ten to Brunswick, fifteen miles from Pennick, to meet the bishop for confirmation, defraying the expenses of nine of the class one way, and finding a place for all to sleep that night. We walked seven miles to the next station, Sterling, in order to buy the tickets. The next morning we did

(301)

the very same thing, rode a part of the way, then got off and walked the seven miles' again. Another time when the class was smaller, I hired a wagon and took the children to Brunswick. This was before the bishop ever visited Pennick.

There are leaders and preachers in the place who tell the people of so many "evil" things: "Once in Christ you can never get out." "After going into the water and receiving immersion your soul can-

not go to hell; you will lie on your back and suffer, but to heaven you must go."

In this "Black Belt" the only light is that of the Cross. The Lord's Prayer is very seldom said, and then far from perfectly. The Apostles' Creed is not heard save in the church, and the Ten Commandments are known to be in the Bible, but we are often told the Old Testament is altogether done away with since the coming of our Lord and Saviour.

WHAT THEY CAN DO IN KENTUCKY

As a piece of Lent work in Kentucky, the united branches sent a gift of $100, and a large collection of goods, clothing and hospital supplies, valued at $1,000, to Alaska. Here is how a part of the box looked

THE SUMMER MONTHS AT FAIRBANKS

WHEN the Auxiliary branches are disbanded and their members are making holiday at seashore and mountain, the work of the missionaries in Fairbanks is heavier than ever. The few summer months are crowded with events—the coming and going of workers, the arrival of boxes and mail packages as well as letters, the hurried arrangements for the next winter's sup-

plies, and the thousand-and-one thing that depend upon navigation. All thes things, with the accumulated correspond ence of months, combine to give the mis sionaries more than they can do, and th members of the Auxiliary must mak due allowance for the over-burdene missionary, and be satisfied to fee that what they have sent is givin comfort and pleasure, even althoug they fail to be assured of this by lette

SOME OF THE TOWNS ARE VERY ISOLATED

NOTES ON A MISSIONARY JOURNEY IN IDAHO

By Mrs. James B. Funsten

JOURNEY with the bishop through Idaho proved a splendid opportunity to study the conditions of guild work in relation to our Woman's Auxiliary.

Wherever our Church services are held, there is a guild composed of a faithful little band of women who are the mainstay of the congregation, for in most cases they are practically the only workers, the men being so occupied with secular affairs that they think they have no time for Church duties. It falls to the lot of these women to sustain the work, acting in many cases as the only business committee to whom the rector (if they have one) can appeal.

My purpose was to meet these good women, to try to help and encourage them, and also to present the idea of a monthly missionary meeting, with interesting literature, preparatory to starting study classes. Some of these towns are very isolated, and we were much gratified at the reception from the Church people wherever we went. While there may be no immediate results visible, I cannot but believe that there will be an awakening that will be appreciated in the future. Everywhere we found good, strong, wide-awake citizens, and they need all the help the Church can give them in their far-away homes among the Rockies. It was a privilege to go through this country and find out how best to help the people in their varied situations. While in some cases the journey was rough, I felt well repaid in learning to know and understand better the people among whom by God's providence our lot has been cast.

IN SOME CASES THE JOURNEY WAS ROUGH

MASSACHUSETTS SETS AN EXAMPLE

Mrs. Francis C. Lowell
requests the pleasure of your company
at the Thirteenth Conference of the Parochial Officers
of the
Massachusetts Branch of the Woman's Auxiliary to the Board of Missions
on March 10th, at 2 :30 P.M.
Sewell Hall, New Century Building, 177 Huntington Avenue, Boston.
Subject—"The Responsibility of Parish Officers."
Tea at 4 o'clock.
Please reply to Mrs. F. C. Lowell, ——— St., Boston.

IN response to this invitation of our president, sent to the presidents and treasurers of the parish branches, 120 officers from sixty-two parishes met for the conference on March 10th.

We first reviewed the questions of last year, and asked the officers if anything had been done in the parishes as a result of the suggestions then made. Several had been very much interested in the plan of the "Outer Circle" reported from the parish of the Ascension, Boston, and it had been tried with great success at Newton Highlands. In pursuance of this plan a printed card was sent to every one in the parish, men, women and children, asking them to do two out of three things asked: First, read a book on a missionary subject; second, give or make two new articles of clothing; third, give ten cents to the mission circle. On the reverse side of the card was printed a prayer for all to say.

This plan was suggested in answer to the question. How to interest others in the Woman's Auxiliary? An officer from Christ Church, Cambridge, said that they had brought seventeen young girls into the mission work this winter, by inviting them to go to the rectory, talking with them about the boxes for the missionaries, and getting them interested in the sewing. As a result, these seventeen girls (about eighteen years old) were divided in committees and helped her plan and sew, each committee trying to do as well as the others. After that first meeting the girls have met Friday mornings at the parish rooms with the older women.

The Church of the Redeemer, Boston, has a visiting committee, whose members call and invite new-comers to the meetings, with twelve new members this year as a result. Several other parishes have visiting committees. It seemed to be the general opinion that an invitation to all the women of the parish to these meetings, *given from the pulpit,* had not the same effect as a personal appeal from another woman. Those who cannot attend the meetings can be associate members. Many parishes have evening meetings as well as those in the afternoon, so as to accommodate women who are busy during the day. The responsibility of the officers toward the Girls' Friendly Society in the parish was also touched upon.

Many officers asked how they should give their money—in small sums to many objects or a larger sum to one, and if it were wiser to give *undesignated,* or to some special place. It was advised to give something for the purposes of each committee, and of course it is the highest form of giving to give without designation.

The parish officers spoke up fairly well, and we think it is helpful to them to have these conferences. The diocesan officers have nothing to say, unless called upon to answer questions.

I, as diocesan secretary, suggested at the end that *my* idea of the responsibility of a parish officer is to keep the diocesan secretary informed as to changes in officers, etc., etc., and to keep an exact account of all that the parochial branches do, so that a new officer will have something to turn to.

ALICE M. MORGAN,
Secretary of the Massachusetts Branch.

THE STUDY OF MISSIONS

ONE hundred and twenty-five years ago a cobbler sat on his bench in Hackleton, his Bible daily studied by his side, his map daily scanned upon the wall. Bible and map sufficed to open his heart in love to those of whom the map vaguely told, the races of the world unknowing Christ, for whom God's Word promised a sure and certain hope.

The other day a cultivated and quick-minded high-school teacher, present at an Auxiliary meeting, confessed that she did not know who William Carey was. To read his life, which can be borrowed from the Church Missions House, might be to many a liberal education in missions.

That fascinating story suggests to us, How can we stir our people, old and young, in this missionary direction? How can we meet within the Church's borders this spirit that is awakened, missionary-wise, and give it scope?

Among many possible suggestions we indicate a few, hoping they may be studied, elaborated and acted upon where they may be found helpful.

Revivify old methods. A parish officer wrote the other day:

"Is there not some way to get the guilds or women's societies in our parishes to give at least a part of one meeting each month to the subject of missions? Our people have so little information. At a recent diocesan meeting our president was asked to explain the 'meaning' of the United Offering. Just think of it! One lady, who had received the money for the United Offering for three years, in one of the most prominent parishes, asked me to tell her what the United Offering was for, and all about it. She had 'asked' and asked'! All of this comes from the fact that there are Auxiliary meetings in a few of our parishes only. The guilds meet usually once a week throughout the winter to sew for local charities. Some three or four weeks before Christmas they begin on the Christmas boxes. Frequently these boxes are of ready-made articles, selected and packed by a committee of two or three, and sent off without consultation or knowledge of anything except the cost of the box reported at the next meeting of the guild. Could not the head of the Woman's Auxiliary ask that the guilds that contribute under the name of the Woman's Auxiliary set aside at least part of one guild day each month for the study of missions? It is true we have a mission study class, which meets four times during the year, very delightful to the few who attend. The papers are taken by the same members, I taking one and sometimes two papers each year, because no one else responds. These conditions are simply because the guilds know nothing of the mission field, and yet call themselves the Woman's Auxiliary, without knowledge making some contribution to something, somewhere. So much could be gained through regular organization. Each guild at least could set apart a portion of one day each month for missionary information. I believe such a plan would meet with much approval."

This experience certainly suggests that, after working along the same lines for many years, gathering a few women together, organizing them as a branch of the Woman's Auxiliary, getting them to meet regularly, and to work and give systematically, after putting our machine into running order—most excellent and fruitful of good results in the practical work expected year by year—we have often been unmindful of the oil which keeps the wheels in motion, of that spirit breathing within them which makes a branch of the Auxiliary not a machine so much as a living organism, a true part of, because joined in vital union with, the Body of the Lord.

If the working members of the Auxiliary are forgetting what the Woman's Auxiliary is; what are the Board of Missions and the Missionary Society; what apportionment is; what appropriations are; what are the United Offering, and

the special with which it may be their
pleasure to crown all other gifts of duty
and thanksgiving, then surely some pains
should be taken to revert to old methods,
treat the old branch as one just organized, and review before it the twice-told
tale.

A second suggestion is that we
introduce new elements. The head of a
diocesan committee has lately asked
what to do to make the meetings conducted after the same plans for many
years more interesting. Our suggestion
is to enlist the help of new young
workers, making them responsible for the
conduct of the meetings, leaving them
free to formulate and carry out their
plans as seems best to them. The officer
objected that old members of the executive body did not like to give the conduct of the meetings into other hands;
but is not this just one of those opportunities of enlisting instead of losing the
intelligent forces of the more youthful
minds, trained in school and college life,
in literary societies and study courses,
and which would find in the history, the
geography, the arithmetic, the biography,
the poetry and the romance of missions
room for every power, intellectual and
spiritual?

It is a great pleasure and encouragement to receive from branches as widespread and as diverse in strength as those
of Ohio, Dallas, Georgia, Michigan,
Hankow, Kansas City, Pennsylvania,
Central New York, Southern Ohio,
Newark, Delaware, Massachusetts, Oklahoma, Bethlehem, Florida, New Jersey,
Michigan City, New York, reports of
definite study being done. At the same
time, we cannot doubt that the difficulty
experienced in one branch is repeated in
many others: "It is hard to find leaders
in mission study. So many have to do
their own work, and are too tired. If the
women of leisure would take it up, it
would help greatly."

The women of leisure! We read in a
recent issue of a daily paper that a
woman of leisure—"a religious woman,
though not a Church member"—was
sending to seventy-five of her friends an-

invitation to meet at her house for study
of the Bible, under the instruction of a
distinguished Bible student. These
women, presumably akin in spiritual
condition to their host, responded to the
number of forty-five. And this was done
because the woman who gave the invitation felt that in these days, over full of
business and pleasure, "a more thorough
knowledge of the Bible would have a
steadying effect."

The individual effort seemed to us who
have been trained in the Church's way
an unconscious recognition on the part
of an individual of the Church's wisdom.
It suggests a return to William Carey's
method: the gathering in city after city,
and parish after parish, and mission
after mission, of "leisure women," who
shall put their Bibles and their maps together, and learn how God loved the
world, and where men still are waiting
to hear the story of that love.

And, then, the aftermath of mission
study. A young woman was asked the
other day if she had a class this winter,
and she answered, "No, I found my
teaching was getting to be cant, and this
winter I am working in a home for
crippled boys."

Does not this open up a vista before
the teachers of our study classes? They
are teaching what they think should be
done by missionaries in distant places to
win souls to Christ. Have not those missionaries a right to look back to them
and expect to see each one in her place
doing some definite work, in Sunday-
school or choir, or Girls' Friendly Society, in hospital, or home, or prison,
among rich or poor with whom she lives,
to win some ignorant or heedless or
hardened or sinful soul to His faith and
love?

Some Answers to Questions on Mission Study

I. Why have study classes for the
Juniors? (1) Study is one of the aims
of the Junior Department. (2) It is
senseless, not to say wrong, to ask people
to work for that of which they know

cese where the children have not some
kind of study.

X. How shall leaders be trained? (1)
By normal classes. (2) By summer
conferences. (3) By reading and study.

XI. What attitude toward study
shall Junior leaders take? The answer
can best be given by quoting one
Junior leader—*"Let three things be
granted at the outset: First, that
Junior Study takes all the time you can
spare and a good deal you can't spare;
secondly, that it is very difficult either
to do it as you want to or to accomplish
what you hope for; thirdly, that it is—if
not the *most* important part of the
Junior's threefold duty—at least one side
of an equilateral triangle, and absolutely
necessary, and, in spite of the first two
facts, well worth while."

THE MARCH CONFERENCE

THE conference, on Mission Study,
met on Thursday, March 17th,
Mrs. Hutchins, president of the
Long Island Branch, presiding.
The dioceses represented were: Central
New York, two; Chicago, one; Connecti-
cut, two (one Junior); Long Island, five
(one Junior); Maine, one; Newark, two;
New Jersey, one; New York, seven;
North Dakota, one; Pennsylvania, three;
Western New York, one. There were
visitors also, from Asheville, Honolulu
and the Philippines.

Miss Lindley sketched the growth of
the new methods of mission study
through the impetus given by the Student Volunteer Movement, the United
Study of Missions—a result of the Ecu-
menical Conference of 1900—the Young
People's Movement, and Silver Bay Conferences. She reported study classes
working at present in sixty-four dioceses,
and becoming all the time more and more
pedagogical, all the members doing the
work and not depending upon leaders or
papers to arouse sympathy and interest.

Miss Delafield pointed out the defects

* Quoted from a paper from Western Massachusetts, which is to be printed in THE YOUNG
CHRISTIAN SOLDIER.

and dangers arising from mission study. She said that after six years' experience, while emphasizing the necessity of such study and finding old members of the Auxiliary still ignorant of such terms as "appropriation" and "apportionment," and vague in their ideas as to the real aim of missions being less the conversion of the individual than the establishment of the great native Churches, she was sensible of the danger of members of the class feeling that they have done something when they have gone to a class. There is no use in arousing interest unless this arouses action; as definite and earnest prayer; from younger classes, the sending out of the volunteer; from classes of married women, the preparation of their own children for mission service, or the payment of substitutes for themselves in the mission field. The study work at present is much more active among Juniors and young women, but is showing its need among older women who have grown up as Christians without realizing the living Christ, and what makes the motive and reason for what we call foreign missions.

Miss Arrowsmith, of Long Island, spoke of the difficulty of organizing a diocesan normal class, where, as in her diocese, the large city lies at one end, and many parishes are remote; that it is hard to find the right person in a parish to take the course of normal study and that there is a lack of co-operation on the part of officers of the Woman's Auxiliary in helping to suggest and furnish such students.

Mrs. West reported classes held in Staten Island during the last five years, and the advantage of the study of the Bible, especially of the Gospel according to St. Matthew, as a missionary text-book. A Churchwoman on the island who had thought she did not believe in foreign missions, coming to this class, is now teaching women of her own kind to gain that new view of the subject which she has gained herself.

Miss Richards, of Newark, spoke of the study classes as opportunities to sow

ACKNOWLEDGMENT OF OFFERINGS

Offerings are asked to sustain missions in thirty missionary districts in the United States, Africa, China, Japan, Brazil, Mexico and Cuba; also work in the Haitien Church; in forty-two dioceses, including missions to the Indians and to the Colored People; to pay the salaries of thirty-two bishops, and stipends to 2,253 missionary workers, domestic and foreign; also two general missionaries to the Swedes and two missionaries among deaf-mutes in the Middle West and the South; and to support schools, hospitals and orphanages. With all remittances the name of the Diocese and Parish should be given. Remittances, when practicable, should be by Check or Draft, and should always be made payable to the order of George Gordon King, Treasurer, and sent to him, Church Missions House, 281 Fourth Avenue, New York. Remittances in Bank Notes are not safe unless sent in Registered Letters.

The Treasurer of the Board of Missions acknowledges the receipt of the following from February 1st, to March 1st, 1910.

* Lenten and Easter Offering from the Sunday-school Auxiliary.
NOTE.—The items in the following pages marked "Sp." are Specials which do not aid the Board in meeting its appropriations. In the heading for each Diocese the total marked "Ap," is the amount which does aid the Board of Missions in meeting its appropriations. Wherever the abbreviation "Wo. Aux." precedes the amount, the offering is through a branch of the Woman's Auxiliary.

Home Dioceses

Alabama

Ap. $122.70

ANNISTON—*Grace*: Gen	50 00
CAMDEN—*St. Mary's*: Gen	1 00
CARLOWVILLE—*St. Paul's*: Gen	5 90
FLORENCE—*Trinity Church*: Gen	3 00
HUNTSVILLE—*Nativity*: Gen	9 15
MONTGOMERY—*St. John's*: Gen	39 65
TUSCALOOSA—*Christ Church*: Gen	14 00

Albany

Ap. $2,370.48; *Sp.* $61.50

ALBANY—*St. Andrew's*: Gen	70 95
Kate G. Child, Gen	10 00
Dan Martin, Sp. for Bishop Rowe, Alaska	5 00
AMSTERDAM—*St. Ann's*: Gen	9 24
ATHENS—*Trinity Church*: Dom	8 55
CAMBRIDGE—*St. Luke's*: Gen	123 76
COHOES—*St. John's*: Girls' Friendly Society, Sp. for salary of deacon, for Rev. S. C. Hughson, O.H.C., Sewanee, Tennessee	10 00
GRANVILLE—Mrs. J. W. Gray, Sp. for Expansion Fund, St. John's University, Shanghai	1 00
JOHNSTOWN—*St. John's*: Miss Alice Russell, Sp. for Expansion Fund, St. John's University, Shanghai	1 00
LANSINGBURG—*Trinity Church*: Gen	21 00
OGDENSBURG—*St. John's*: Gen	12 00
SALEM—*St. Paul's*: Gen	13 25
SARATOGA SPRINGS—*Bethesda*: Dom	13 37
St. Christina School: Gen	15 00
SCHENECTADY—*Christ Church*: Gen	73 36
St. George's: Sp. for St. Paul's College, Tokyo	28 00
STAMFORD—*Grace*: Sp. for St. Paul's College, Tokyo	10 00
TROY—*St. John's*: George B. Cluett,	

Gen	2,000 00
WARRENSBURGH—*Holy Cross S. S.*: Sp. for work of Rev. Robert E. Wood, Wuchang, Hankow	6 50

Arkansas

Ap. $105.00

LITTLE ROCK—*Christ Church*: Wo. Aux., Gen	105 00

Atlanta

Ap. $10.09

TALLULAH FALLS—*St. James's*: Frn	5 00
MISCELLANEOUS—Junior Aux., Gen	5 09

Bethlehem

Ap. $741.38; *Sp.* $90.00

ALLENTOWN—*Grace*: John I. Romig, Dom. and Frn	9 00
EAST MAUCH CHUNK—*St. John's*: Gen	17 20
EASTON—Wo. Aux., Gen	5 00
DRIFTON—*St. James's*: Wo. Aux., Sp. for Dr. Correll's work, Tsu, Kyoto	50 00
DUNMORE—*St. Mark's*: Gen	1 00
GREAT BEND—*Grace*: Gen	1 00
MAHANOY CITY—*Faith Church*: Gen	4 00
MILFORD—*Church of the Good Shepherd*: Wo. Aux., Gen	5 00
POTTSVILLE—*Trinity Church*: Dom., $100; Frn., $100	200 00
READING—*Christ Church*: Wo. Aux., "Miss C. C. G.," Sp. for Bishop Restarick, Honolulu, $10; Sp. for Bishop Rowe, Alaska, $10; Sp. for Bishop Horner, Asheville, $10; Sp. for Bishop Aves, Mexico, $10	40 00
St. Mary's S. S.: Dr. Jefferys's hospital work, Shanghai	8 50
SCRANTON—*St. Luke's*: Dom	37 33

(309)

TAMAQUA—*Calvary*: Gen............. 13 35
WILKES-BARRE—*St. Stephen's*: Brazil,
$100 ; Cuba, $100 ; Frn., $225..... 425 00
MISCELLANEOUS — Archdeaconry of
Scranton, Wo. Aux., Gen.......... 15 00

California

Ap. $50.00 ; *Sp.* $730.65
BERKELEY—*St. Matthew's*: Sp. for
Shanghai Catechist School Land
and Building Fund............... 2 85
Mrs. Robinson, Sp. for Bishop Rowe,
Alaska ....,.................. 50 00
Mrs. Gray, Sp. for Bishop Rowe,
Alaska ....,.................. 50 00
Mrs. Welcher, Sp. for Bishop Rowe,
Alaska 50 00
OAKLAND—*St. Paul's*: "A Friend," 50
cts., Mr. McGee, $10, Sp. for Shang-
hai Catechist School Land and
Building Fund.................. 10 50
SAN FRANCISCO—*Grace*: Sp. for
Shanghai Catechist School Land and
Building Fund.................. 50 00
St. Luke's: Mr. and Mrs. Thomas
Archer, Sp. for Shanghai Catechist
School Land and Building Fund.... 20 00
Trinity Church; Mrs. George W.
Gibbs, Sp. for Shanghai Catechist
School Land and Building Fund... 500 00
"M.,'" Dom., $25 ; Frn., $25 ; Sp. for
Hospital of the Good Shepherd, Fort
Defiance, Arizona, $20............ 70 00
"J. A. E.," Sp. for Shanghai Cate-
chist School Land and Building
Fund 20 00
TUOLUMNE—*St. Michael's*: O. O. M.
Class, Sp. for Shanghai Catechist
School Land and Building Fund.... 1 80
MISCELLANEOUS — Missionary offering
at convention, Sp. for Shanghai
Catechist School Land and Build-
ing Fund........................ 5 50

Central New York

Ap. $1,072.51 ; *Sp.* $169.00
BINGHAMTON—*Church of the Good
Shepherd*: Gen.................. 3 10
Trinity Church: Gen.............. 25 00
CONSTABLEVILLE—*St. Paul's*: Gen.... 4 00
ELMIRA—*Trinity Church*: Georgenia
S. Edwards, Sp. for Expansion Fund,
St. John's University, Shanghai.... 1 00
JORDAN—*Christ Church*: Gen........ 17 05
MEMPHIS—*Emmanuel Church*: Gen... 8 65
ONEIDA—*St. John's*: Dom., 35 cts. ;
Frn., $2.10...................... 2 45
ONONDAGA CASTLE—*Church of the Good
Shepherd*: Gen.................. 06
OXFORD—*St. Paul's*: Frn........... 46 25
SYRACUSE—*Grace*: Gen., $2.75 ; Sp. for
St. Paul's College, Tokyo, $2.50 ;
Miss Gertrude A. L. Morecroft, Sp.
for St. John's University Expansion
Fund, Shanghai, $1.............. 6 25
St. Philip's: Gen................. 2 00
"R. F. D. No. 5," Gen.............. 94
UTICA—*Grace*: Frn., $296.38 ; Gen.,
$210.60 .... 506 98
Holy Cross Memorial: Mrs. Mary H.
Wolcott, Sp. for Expansion Fund,
St. John's University, Shanghai.... 10 00
St. Andrew's: Frn................ 16 15
St. George's: Gen................ 29 00
Trinity Church: Gen.............. 47 82
Wo. Aux., Gen., $204.78 ; Sp. for
Miss Clark, Hankow, $100 ; Second
District, Gen., $10.53 ; Sp. for Christ
School, Arden, Asheville, $50 ; Third
District, Sp. for Building Fund, In-
dustrial School, Africa, $2.50 ; Sp. for
Dr. Correll, Kyoto, $2............ 369 81
MISCELLANEOUS—Junior Aux., Gen.... 150 00

Chicago

Ap. $980.77 ; *Sp.* $75.00
ALGONQUIN—*St. John's*: Wo. Aux., Gen.
CHICAGO—*All Saints'* (Ravenswood) :
Dom. and Frn....................
All Saints' (Pullman) : Gen.........
Atonement: $58.60, Wo. Aux., $15,
Gen. ....
Christ Church (Woodlawn Park) : Gen.,
$88.20 ; S. S., work among blind
Chinese children, $2 ; Sp. for St.
Paul's College, Tokyo, $2 ; Sp. for
Porto Rico Hospital, $2...........
Grace: Wo. Aux., Sp. for Miss Mann's
mission building, Utsunomiya, Tokyo
Holy Trinity Church: Gen...........
Church of the Redeemer: Wo. Aux.,
Gen. ....
St. Ansgarius's: Gen...............
St. Barnabas's: Medical work in China
St. Joseph's (West Pullman) : Gen....
St. Luke's: Sp. for Bishop Brent's
work among the Bontoc Igorots,....
St. Mark's: Wo. Aux., Gen..........
St. Peter's: St. Monica's Guild, Gen..
St. Simon's: Alaska, $3 ; Dom. and
Frn., $27.95....................
Transfiguration: Gen...............
Trinity Church: Gen...............
Homes for Boys, Sp. for Bishop
Rowe, Alaska...................
EVANSTON—*St. Luke's*: Dom. and Frn.
GLEN ELLYN—*St. Mark's S. S.*: Gen..
HARVARD—*Christ Church*: Dom. and
Frn. ....
HIGHLAND PARK—*Trinity Church*:
$125, Wo. Aux., $2, Gen..........
LAKE FOREST—*Church of the Holy
Spirit*: Gen., $330.26 ; S. S., hospital
work in China, $10..............
MORGAN PARK—*Church of the Mediator*:
$6.80, Wo. Aux., $1, Gen..........
OAK PARK—*Grace*: Gen.............
ROCKFORD—*Emmanuel Church*: Wo.
Aux., Gen.......................
WILMETTE—*St. Augustine's*: Wo. Aux.,
Gen. ....

Colorado

Ap. $30.42
CANON CITY—Rev. G. M. I. Du Bois,
Gen. ....
DENVER—*St. Barnabas's*: Junior Aux.,
Gen. ....
PUEBLO—*Ascension S. S.**: Gen......

Connecticut

Ap. $2,296.60 ; *Sp.* $750.30
BRIDGEPORT—*Calvary*: Gen..........
St. John's: Colored paupers in the
South, $19.47 ; Gen., $41..........
CANAAN—*Christ Church*: Gen........
COLLINSVILLE—*Trinity Church*: Dom.,
10 cts. ; Frn., $2.20 ; Gen., 10 cts..
DANBURY—*St. James's*: Gen.........
DANIELSON—*St. Alban's*: Dom.......
DARIEN—*St. Luke's*: Dom..... ,....
DERBY—*St. James's*: Gen...........
EAST HADDAM—Mrs. F. C. H. Wendel,
Sp. for Bishop Horner's work, Valle
Crucis, Asheville..................
GREENWICH—*Christ Church*: Dom.,
$200 ; Frn., $25..................
HARTFORD—*St. Thomas's*: Dom., $9.06 ;
Gen., $17.68....................
Trinity Church: Dom., $25 ; Gen.,
$132.65 ....
MERIDEN—*St. Andrew's Church and
S. S.*: Sp. for Rev. William J.
Cuthbert, Kyoto..................
MIDDLETOWN—*Chapel of St. Luke's*:
Gen. ....

126 00

Duluth

Ap. $32.85 ; *Sp.* $75.00

9 50
1 00

DULUTH—*St. Paul's*: Sp. for St. Paul's
College, Tokyo.................... 75 00
Trinity Church: Wo. Aux., Gen..... 15 00

86 14

ORTONVILLE—*St. John's*: Gen......... 8 35
PINE POINT—*Breck Memorial*: Gen.. 7 50
WADENA—*St. Helen's*: Dom. and Frn. 2 00

40 43
9 72
25 46

East Carolina

Ap. $220.92 ; *Sp.* $5.00

50 00

AURORA—*Chapel of the Cross*: Gen... 10 00
BATH—*St. Thomas's*: Gen........... 5 00

8 50
10 38

BEAUFORT—*St. Paul's*: Gen......... 7 41
St. Paul's School: Wo. Aux., Gen..... 2 00
BOARDMAN—*St. Jude's*: Gen......... 6 00
COLUMBIA—*St. Andrew's*: Gen....... 2 35

46 00
50 00

ELIZABETH CITY—*Christ Church*: Gen. 15 00
GATESVILLE—*St. Mary's*: Gen........ 5 76
KINSTON—*St. Mary's*: Gen.......... 5 50

500 00

LENOIR Co.—*Holy Innocents'*: Gen... 2 25
MAXTON—*St. Matthew's*: Gen........ 2 50

4 45

MURFREESBORO—*St. Barnabas's*: Gen.. 86
NEW BERNE—*Christ Church*: Wo.
Aux., Girls' School, Honolulu, $2;
Junior Aux., Boys' School, Hankow,
$2 .... 4 00

25 00

ROPER—*St. Luke's*: Gen............ 7 73
ROXOBEL—*St. Mark's*: Gen......... 5 00

30 00

SCUPPERNONG—*St. David's*: Gen...... 5 40
TRENTON—*Grace*: Gen.............. 3 00
VANESBORO—*St. Paul's*: Frn......... 4 83

25 00

WASHINGTON—*St. Peter's*: $48.43, Wo.
Aux., $5, Gen................. 53 43
WILMINGTON—*St. James's*: Mrs. Walter L. Parsley, Sp. for Bishop
Horner's work, Black Mountain,

675 00

Asheville, $5; S. S., hospital work,
China, $15.90; Wo. Aux., Gen.,

68 55
5 83
200 00
3 52
32 00
5 00

$50 .... 70 90
WINDSOR—*St. Thomas's*: Gen........ 5 00
YEATESVILLE—*St. Matthew's*: Gen.... 2 00

Easton

Ap. $21.05

SOMERSET Co.—*Somerset Parish*: Gen. 12 28
TALBOT Co.—*Trinity Cathedral S. S.*
(Easton): Gen................. 50

100 00
14 07

WORCESTER Co.—*St. Paul's* (Berlin):
Gen. 8 27

Florida

100 00
5 00

Ap. $12.50

FERNANDINA—*Church of the Good
Shepherd*: Gen.................. 12 50

Fond du Lac

Ap. $13.33

75
3 00

SHEBOYGAN—*Grace*: Gen............. 3 33
STEVENS POINT—*Intercession*: Gen.,
$5; Knights of St. Paul, Sp. for St.

20 35

Paul's College, Tokyo, $5......... 10 00

10 00

Georgia

5 00
7 50
5 85

Ap. $113.90 ; *Sp.* $41.00

ALBANY—*Junior Aux.*, salary of Rev.
Robb White, Philippines, $3; St.
Luke's Hospital, Shanghai, $3; Sp.
for Holy Trinity Orphanage, Tokyo,
$2; Sp. for "Sister Katherine" scholarship, Cuba, $2................. 10 00
AMERICUS — *Calvary*: Frn., $12.30;
Junior Aux., salary of Rev. Robb

10 45

White, Philippines, $3; St. Luke's
Hospital, Shanghai, $3; Sp. for Holy

3 57

Trinity Orphanage, Tokyo, $2; Sp.
"Sister Katherine" scholarship,
Cuba, $2...................... 22 30

152 52

AUGUSTA—*St. Paul's*: Junior Aux.,

salary of Rev. Robb White, Philippines, $3; St. Luke's Hospital, Shanghai, $3; Sp. for Holy Trinity Orphanage, Tokyo, $2; Sp. for "Sister Katherine" scholarship, Cuba, $2 .... 10 00
BAINBRIDGE—*St. John's*: Dom., $12.50; Frn., $12.50........................... 25 00
CORDELE — *Christ Church*: Dom., $16.40; Frn.. $11.20.............. 27 60
SAVANNAH — *St. Michael's*: Junior ·Aux., salary of Rev. Robb White, $3; St. Luke's Hospital, Shanghai, $3; Sp. for Holy Trinity Orphanage, Tokyo, $2; Sp. for "Sister Katherine" scholarship, Cuba, $2........ 10 00
St. Stephen's: Gen.................. 25 00
MISCELLANEOUS — Wo. Aux., annual meeting, Sp. for Rev. R. C. Wilson, Zangzok, Shanghai................ 25 00

Harrisburg

Ap. $265.67; *Sp.* $89.00

BELLEFONTE—*St. John's S. S.*: For St. Augustine's School, Raleigh, North Carolina ....· 2 60
LANCASTER—*St. John's S. S.*: Gen., 50 cts.; Sp. for St. Paul's College, Tokyo, $5................ 5 50
LEWISTOWN—*St. Mark's*: ·Gen....... 8 00
RENOVO—*Trinity Church*: Wo. Aux., Sp. for Mrs. Charles B. Ackley, Guantanamo, Cuba................ 15 00
SHAMOKIN—*Trinity Church*: Gen...... 9 95
STEELTON—*Trinity Church S. S.*: Gen.......................... 2 75
WILLIAMSPORT — *Trinity Church*: Junior ·Aux., Gen................. 60 00
YORK—*St. John's*: Gen.............. 15 00
MISCELLANEOUS—Babies' Branch, Gen., $75; Church School among ,Indians, $25; Sp. for Miss Carter's Emergency Fund, Alaska, $10; Sp. for St. Mary's-on-the-Mountain, Sewanee, Tennessee, $30; Sp. for St. Agnes's Hospital, Raleigh, North Carolina, $5; Akita Kindergarten, Tokyo, $25; Wo. Aux., Sp. for Miss Elizabeth Newbold's organ, Tokyo, $24; Wo. Aux., Rev. Dr. Pott's work in Shanghai, $41.87................ 235 87

Indianapolis

Ap. $188.11; *Sp.* $23.12.

BEDFORD—*St. John's*: Gen.......... 28 00
EVANSVILLE—*St. Paul's*: Dom....... 51 73
GREENSBURG—*Trinity Church*: Gen... .1 60
INDIANAPOLIS — *Grace Pro-Cathedral*: Frn., $6.75; Gen., $4.25............ 11 00
St. David's: Gen.................. 21 33
St. George's: Gen.................. 16 75
United S. S. Service, Gen.......... 7 70
NEW ALBANY—*St. Paul's*: Gen...... 50 00
TERRE HAUTE—*St. Stephen's*: Sp. for St. Paul's College, Tokyo.......... 23 12

Iowa

Ap. $274.85

BURLINGTON — *Christ Church*: Wo. Aux., Miss Babcock's salary, Tokyo.. 10 00
CEDAR RAPIDS—*Grace*: Wo. Aux., Miss Babcock's salary, Tokyo, $5; Gen., $12 .... 17 00
CLINTON—*St. John's*: Gen........... 7 30
COUNCIL BLUFFS—*St. Paul's*: Wo. Aux., Miss Babcock's salary, Tokyo, $6; Gen., $10.................
DAVENPORT—*Trinity Cathedral*: Gen.. 16 00
DE MOINES—*St. Paul's*: Gen........ 48 00
DUBUQUE—*St. John's*: Bishop Keator, 12 83 Olympia, $5; salary of Rev. Mr. Nieh, Hanch'uan, Hankow, $5; Wo. Aux., Miss Babcock's salary, Tokyo,

$8 ....
HARLAN—*St. Paul's*: Wo. Aux., Miss Babcock's salary, Tokyo, $3; Gen., $3 ....
INDEPENDENCE — *St. James's*: $10.86, Wo. Aux., $5, Gen..............
Grace: Wo. Aux., Miss Babcock's salary, Tokyo..................
IOWA CITY—*Trinity Church*: Dom., $6.30; Wo. Aux., Miss Babcock's salary, Tokyo, $10; Gen., $10.....
IOWA FALLS—*St. Matthew's Missions*: Gen. ....
JEFFERSON—*St. Thomas's*: Gen.......
KEOKUK—*St. John's*: Wo. Aux., Miss Babcock's salary, Tokyo..........
LYONS—*Grace*: Wo. Aux., Miss Babcock's salary, Tokyo...........
MAPLETON—*Trinity Church*: Gen.....
MUSCATINE—*Trinity Church*: Gen....
NEWTON—*St. Stephen's*: Gen........
SIOUX CITY—*St. Thomas's*: Wo. Aux., Miss Babcock's salary, Tokyo.....:..

Kansas

Ap. $78.18

CHANUTE—*Grace*: Hospital work in Tokyo and Kyoto, $8.35; Gen., $3.50 ....
CHERRYVALE — *St. Stephen's Mission*: Gen. ....
ELGIN—*Grace*: Gen., $4.25; Young People, hospital work in Tokyo and Kyoto, 42 cts...................
EMPORIA—*St. Andrew's*: Young People, hospital work in Tokyo and Kyoto ....
GIRARD—*St John's*: Young People, hospital work in Tokyo and Kyoto....
INDEPENDENCE—*Epiphany*: Dom. and Frn., $6.10; Gen., $2.75...........
IOLA—*St. Timothy's*: Frn., $3.20; Young People, hospital work in Tokyo and Kyoto, $1.81...........
JUNCTION CITY — *Covenant*: Hospital work in Tokyo and Kyoto.........
MARYSVILLE—*St. Paul's*: Young People, hospital work in Tokyo and Kyoto ....
MANHATTAN—*St. Paul's*: Young People, hospital work in Tokyo and Kyoto ....
NEODESHA — *Grace*: Young People, hospital work in Tokyo and Kyoto..
OTTAWA—*Grace*: Young People, hospital work in Tokyo and Kyoto.....
TOPEKA—*Church of the Good Shepherd* (North): Young People, hospital work in Tokyo and Kyoto...
St. Simon's: Young People, hospital work in Tokyo and Kyoto.........
WAKEFIELD—*St. George's*: Gen.......
St. John's: Young People, hospital work in Tokyo and Kyoto.........
WAMEGO—*St. Luke's*: Young People, hospital work in Tokyo and Kyoto..
WINFIELD—*Grace*: Young People, hospital work in Tokyo and Kyoto....
WICHITA—*All Saints'*: Young People, hospital work in Tokyo and Kyoto...
WILLIAMSBURG—*St. Barnabas's*: Young People, hospital work in Tokyo and Kyoto ....

Kansas City

Ap. $69.61; *Sp.* $112.61

KANSAS CITY—*St. John's*: Mrs. A. Hockney, Sp. for Expansion Fund of St. John's· University, Shanghai....
St. Mark's: Work among Colored People, $2.87; Gen., $36.03; hospital work in China, $4.09............
St.· Paul's: Sp. for Bishop Thomas's work, Wyoming.................

Trinity Church: Gen................ 10 00
SPRINGFIELD—St. John's: "A Church-
woman," Gen..................... 4 62
WARRENSBURG—Christ Church: Gen.. 12 00

Kentucky

Ap. $540.55

BOWLING GREEN—Christ Church: Wo.
Aux., Gen...................... 12 00
LOUISVILLE—Calvary: Wo. Aux., Gen.
(of which from St. Agnes's Guild,
$12) 47 00
Christ Church Cathedral: $214.05, Wo.
Aux., $25, Gen................. 239 05
Grace: Wo. Aux., Gen............... 25 00
St. Andrew's: Gen., $150; Wo. Aux.,
salary of Mrs. Dennis, West Africa,
$50; Brazil, $12.50............. 212 50
PADUCAH—Grace: Gen.............. 5 00

Lexington

Ap. $82.00

DANVILLE—Trinity Church: Gen...... 13 00
FRANKFORT—Ascension: Gen......... 55 00
RICHMOND — Christ Church Mission:
Gen. 14 00

Long Island

Ap. $1,108.76; Sp. $514.60

ASTORIA—St. George's S. S.: St. Luke's
Hospital, Shanghai, $10; Wo. Aux.,
Sp. for Domestic Contingent Fund,
$1 .... 11 00
BRIDGEHAMPTON—St. Ann's: Gen.... 30 50
BROOKLYN — Christ Church (Bay
Ridge): Dom. and Frn., $72.20;
Junior Aux., Gen., $10.......... 82 10
Church of the Good Shepherd: Dom.
and Frn....................... 143 15
Grace (Heights): Sp. for Bishop Rowe,
Alaska, $26.60; Sp. for Bishop
Wells, Spokane, $5; Wo. Aux.,
"F. M. D. Memorial" bed, St.
James's Hospital, Anking, Hankow,
$50; Sp. for sewing-teacher's salary,
St. Augustine's School, Raleigh,
North Carolina, $25; Miss M. A.
Stevens, Sp. for Emergency Fund,
Alaska, $5..................... 111 60
Holy Apostles': Dom., $2.38; Frn.,
$3.76 .... 6 14
Incarnation: Junior Aux., Gen........ 20 00
Church of the Messiah S. S.*: Gen.. 50
St. Andrew's: Dom. and Frn......... 22 55
St. Ann's: William G. Low, Sp. for
Bishop Rowe, Alaska, $250; "A
Friend," Sp. for Church Extension
Fund, Porto Rico, $15; Wo. Aux.,
Sp. for Bishop Griswold's work in
Salina, $5; Sp. for Rev. William J.
Cuthbert's work, Kyoto, $15....... 285 00
St. Augustine's: Wo. Aux., Sp. for
Bishop Aves, Mexico, for famine suf-
ferers 1 00
St. Clement's: Dom., $11.83; Frn.,
$20.11 .... 31 94
St. John's (Fort Hamilton): Gen.... 2 55
St. Paul's (Flatbush): Frn.......... 417 03
St. Paul's: Gen.................. 25 00
St. Peter's S. S.: Boone University,
Wuchang, Hankow, $10.77; Girls'
High School, Kyoto, $10.76; Dom.,
$18.74; Frn., $18.74............. 59 01
St. Stephen's: Gen., $12.24; Wo. Aux.,
Sp. for Rev. Mr. N. Matthews's In-
dustrial School, Cape Mount, Africa,
$5 .... 17 24
Mrs. Forrest Raynor, Sp. for Expan-
sion Fund, St. John's University,
Shanghai 10 00
"A Friend," Sp. for Emergency
Fund, Alaska.................. 1 00
Mrs. E. H. Litchfield, Sp. for

Emergency Fund, Alaska.......... 50 00
Miss S. J. Breithaupt, Sp. for Ex-
pansion Fund, St. John's University,
Shanghai 5 00
FLUSHING—St. George's: Frn....... 96 70
FREEPORT—Transfiguration: Dom. and
Frn. 25 35
GARDEN CITY—Incarnation Cathedral:
"Dean Cox" (Divinity) scholarship,
Boone University, Wuchang, Han-
kow, $25; Sp. for St. John's Univer-
sity, Shanghai, $90............. 115 00
SETAUKET—Caroline Church: Frn.... 14 00
SOUTHAMPTON—St. John's: Gen..... 10 00
MISCELLANEOUS—Wo. Aux., Anniver-
sary Offering, Sp. for sewing-
teacher's salary, St. Augustine's
School, Raleigh, North Carolina.... 5 00
Girls' Friendly Society, Gen....... 25 00

Los Angeles

Ap. $741.73; Sp. $183.48

ALHAMBRA — Holy Trinity Church:
Dom. and Frn., $9.65; Sp. for Shang-
hai Catechist School Land and
Building Fund, $4.81............ 14 46
BOSTONIA—St. John's: Gen......... 2 85
CORONA—St. John Baptist's S. S.: Sp.
for Bishop Holly, Haiti........... 2 55
COVINA—Holy Trinity Church: Dom.
and Frn., $41.80; Chinese mission,
$7.46 .... 49 26
LONG BEACH—St. Luke's: Dom. and
Frn. 37 71
LOS ANGELES—St. John's: Gen...... 135 00
St. Paul's Cathedral: Gen., $257.09;
Mr. and Mrs. H. T. Lee, Sp. for
Shanghai Catechist School Land and
Building Fund, $20; S. S., Sp. for
Shanghai Catechist School Land and
Building Fund, $12.56........... 289 65
MONTECITO—All Saints': Gen........ 16 00
PASADENA—All Saints': Dom. and Frn. 50 00
POMONA—St. Paul's: Gen., $4.12; Wo.
Aux. and Young Wo. Aux., Sp. for
Shanghai Catechist School Land and
Building Fund, $15.............. 19 12
RIVERSIDE—All Saints': Wo. Aux., Sp.
for Shanghai Catechist School Land
and Building Fund, $15; Junior
Aux., Sp. for Shanghai Catechist
School Land and Building Fund, $8. 23 00
SAN DIEGO—St. Paul's: Wo. Aux., Sp.
for Shanghai Catechist School Land
and Building Fund............... 10 00
"A Friend," Sp. for Shanghai Cate-
chist School Land and Building
Fund 2 00
SAN GABRIEL—Church of Our Saviour:
Dom. and Frn.................. 5 50
SANTA BARBARA — Trinity Church:
Gen., $168; Sp. for Shanghai Cate-
chist School Land and Building
Fund, $28.55.................. 196 55
SAWTELLE—St. John's: Gen......... 1 55
MISCELLANEOUS—Wo. Aux., Sp. for
Shanghai Catechist School Land and
Building Fund.................. 65 01
"A Friend," for work in Mexico.... 5 00

Louisiana

Ap. $34.00; Sp. $2.00

NEW ORLEANS — Annunciation: Wo.
Aux., Gen., $3.75; Miss Suthon's
salary, Kyoto, $2.25............ 6 00
Christ Church: Wo. Aux., apply on
Miss Suthon's salary, Kyoto, 55 cts.;
S. S., for helping the blind in China,
$5 .... 5 55
St. John's: Wo. Aux., Gen., 25 cts.;
apply on Miss Suthon's salary,
Kyoto, 25 cts.................. 50
St. Paul's: Wo. Aux., Gen.......... 10 00

Trinity Church: Wo. Aux., apply on Miss Suthon's salary, Kyoto, $5; Miss Evans's salary, Alaska, $1; Junior Aux., apply on Miss Suthon's salary, Kyoto, $1; Sp. for St. Paul's College, Tokyo, $1; Sp. for St. Margaret's School, Tokyo, $1 .... 9 00
St. FRANCISVILLE—*Grace:* Gen. 4 95

Maine

Ap. $132.05

GARDINER—*Christ Church:* Frn. 52 05
MISCELLANEOUS—Junior Aux., Gen., $30; "Pauline Austin Osgood Memorial" scholarship, St. Hilda's School, Wuchang, $50. .... 80 00

Marquette

Ap. $6.60

MUNISING—*St. John's:* Gen. 6 60

Maryland

Ap. $1,602.08; *Sp.* $165.96

ANNE ARUNDEL —.*Christ Church* (West River): Wo. Aux., Gen. 5 00
BALTIMORE—*Ascension:* John Black, Sp. for Church Extension Fund, Porto Rico. 5 00
Christ Church: Gen. 767 00
Emmanuel Church: Wo. Aux., "A. M. Randolph Graduate" scholarship, South Dakota, $60; teacher's salary, St. Mary's School, South Dakota, $100; "Mary Randolph" scholarship, Hooker Memorial School, Mexico, $100; "Helen Whitridge" scholarship, Church Training-school, Shanghai, $50; Sp. for "J. H. Eccleston" scholarship, St. Mary's Orphanage, Shanghai, $30; Junior Aux., Sp. for "J. H. Eccleston" scholarship, St. Mary's Orphanage, Shanghai, $15. .. 355 00
Church of the Messiah: Dom. and Frn., $100; Gen., $13. .... 113 00
Prince of Peace: Brazil. 16 24
St. Andrew's: Frn., $53.76; S. S., hospital work in China, $10. ...... 63 76
St. Barnabas's and St. George's: Wo. Aux., Sp. for Hospital of the Good Shepherd, Fort Defiance, Arizona... 10 00
St. Luke's: Frn. 30 00
St. Paul's: (In Memoriam) "L. C. A.," Dom. 5 00
St. Thomas's (Homestead): Gen. 25 00
Chapel of the Guardian Angel: Dom. and Frn. 20 88
"A Friend of Missions," Sp. for St. Margaret's School, Tokyo. 25 00
"H. W. A.," Sp. for Rev. Mr. Ancell, Shanghai. .... 10· 00
BALTIMORE Co.—*St. Timothy's* (Catonsville): Wo. Aux., Gen. 29 00
Trinity Church S. S.: For the work of Bishop Rowe, Alaska, $6.05; Sp. for Rev. J. R. Ellis, Virginia, $3.67. .. 9 72
St. John's (Mount Washington): S. S. and Junior Aux., Sp. for Bishop Graves, Kearney, $10; Sp. for Bishop Rowe, Alaska, $5; Sp. for Bishop Brooks, Oklahoma, $3.35; Sp. for Bishop Griswold, Salina, $2.84; Sp. for Bishop Horner, Asheville, $4.50; Sp. for Bishop Van Buren, Porto Rico, $2.10. .... 27 29
St. Mark's-on-the-Hill (Pikesville): Dom. and Frn., $60; S. S., Dom. and Frn., $17.65. .... 77 65·
St. Matthew's S. S.: Gen. 50
St. John's, Western Run Parish (near Glyndon): Gen. 10 00
CARROLL, BALTIMORE AND HOWARD Co's.—*St. Barnabas's:* Gen. 3 00
FREDERICK Co. — *St. Paul's S. S.*

(Point of Rocks): Sp.· for Bishop Rowe, Alaska. 5 00
HARFORD Co. — *Emmanuel Church* (Bel Air): Gen. 60 00
St. Mary's (Emmorton): Gen., $40; Colored missions, $10. .... 50 00
HOWARD Co.—*St. John's* (Ellicott City): Dom. 10 00
MISCELLANEOUS—Junior Aux., Sp. for Mrs. Restarick, for furniture in dining-room, Priory School, Honolulu 35 00

Massachusetts

Ap. $13,521.02; *Sp.* $2,237.89

AMESBURY—*St. James's:* Gen. 10 00
ANDOVER—*Christ Church:* Wo. Aux., Hooker Memorial School, Mexico, $5; St. Luke's Hospital, Tokyo, $5; salary of Mrs. McCalla, West Africa, $5 .... 15 00·
AYER—*St. Andrew's:* Gen., $3.46; Wo. Aux., for Isle of Pines, Cuba, $3. ... 6 46
BEACHMONT—*St. Paul's:* Gen. 11 39
BELMONT—*All Saints':* Gen. 13 41
BOSTON—*Advent:* Miss Elizabeth Woodward, Sp. for Shanghai Catechist School Land and Building Fund, $10; L. S. Tuckerman, Sp. for Church Extension Fund, Porto Rico, $5; Wo. Aux., Sp. for Bishop Thomas, Wyoming, $100. .... 115 00
Ascension: Gen. 47 84
All Saints' (Dorchester): Gen. 250 00
Emmanuel Church: Gen., $3,098.65; Miss R. Bradley, Sp. for Expansion Fund, St. John's University, Shanghai, $5; Rear Admiral Herbert Winslow, Sp. for Expansion Fund, St. John's University, Shanghai, $20; Miss Katherine French, Sp. for Expansion Fund, St. John's University, Shanghai, $5; Miss Dorothy Fay, Sp. for Dr. Pott's work in China, $2; Wo. Aux., "A Member," Sp. for "Elizabeth" crib, St. Mary's Orphanage, Shanghai, $30. .... 3,160 65
Emmanuel Church (West Roxbury): Gen. 28 95
Church of the Good Shepherd: Gen. ... 28 00·
Church of the Holy Spirit (Mattapan): Dom., $4.69; Wo. Aux., for Isle of Pines, Cuba, $2; Wo. Aux., salary of Rev. Nathan Matthews, Africa, $2. .... 45 69
Church of the Messiah S. S.: For the "Bishop Randall" scholarship, Elizabeth's School, South Dakota. .. 60 00
Orient Heights Mission (East): Sp. for sufferers in Mexico, $28; Frn., $8.50; Dom., $4.75. .... 41 25
St. John's (Charleston): Frn. 21 36
St. John's (East): Gen. 97 11
St. John's (Jamaica Plain): Gen. 150 00
St. Margaret's S. S. (Brighton): Gen.. 13 16
St. Mark's (Dorchester): Gen. 55 50
St. Matthew's (South): Gen. 11 96
St. Paul's: "A Member," Sp. for Bishop Rowe, Alaska, $100; "A Friend," Sp. for Bishop Rowe, Alaska, $500.. 600 00
St. Stephen's: Indian, $94.90; Colored, $94.90; Sp. for St. Paul's College, Tokyo, $25.63. .... 215 43
Trinity Church: Dom., $3,044.14; Frn., $3,289.12; Sp. for St. Luke's hospital, Tokyo, $250; China, $5; Mexico, $6; Mr. Robert Treat Paine, Sp. for Bishop Brent, Philippine Islands, $100; Sp. for Bishop Cameron Mann, North Dakota, $100; Sp. for Bishop Restarick, Honolulu, $100; Sp. for Expansion Fund, St. John's University, Shanghai, $100; Wo. Aux, (of which "Mrs. H. L. J.," $5), Sp. for Bishop Rowe, Alaska, $55; Sp. for Bishop Brooks, Okla-

TAUNTON — *St. Thomas's*: Dom., $131.06; Frn., $133.31; Rev. Malcolm Taylor, Sp. for Expansion Fund, St. John's University, Shanghai, $15; "W. H. B.," Sp. for Dr. Pott, Shanghai, $25; "Mrs. W. H. B.," Sp. for Mann Memorial, Shanghai, $50 .... 354 37

WAKEFIELD—*Emmanuel Church*: Gen., $8.50; Wo. Aux., Hooker School, Mexico, $2....................... 10 50

WALTHAM—*Ascension*: Gen. 11 68

Christ Church: Gen., $40; Wo. Aux., "A Member," Sp. for insurance of Rev. T. S. Tyng, Kyoto, $2........ 42 00

WINCHESTER—*Epiphany*: Support of native clergyman, Anking, Hankow, $50; Circle City, Alaska, $50..... 100 00

MISCELLANEOUS — Branch Wo. Aux., Sp. for Miss Wheeler's salary, St. Augustine's School, Raleigh, North Carolina, $50; Sp. for salary of Miss Dickerson, St. Paul's School, Lawrenceville, Southern Virginia, $50; Colored work in Vicksburg, Mississippi, $100; Colored work in Spartanburg, South Carolina, $100; Lucy Lee Chickering Fund, San Gabriel, Brazil, $40; Mrs. C. S. Tuckerman and friends, salary of Rev. J. S. Meade, 2d, Shanghai, $400; "A Friend," St. Luke's Hospital, Tokyo, $25; "A Friend," Isle of Pines, Cuba, $5; "A Friend," Hooker School, Mexico, $10 ...... 780 00

Altar Society, Sp. for Bishop Rowe, Alaska 100 00

Michigan

Ap. $320.32; *Sp.* $58.00

ALGONAC—*St. Andrew's*: Gen........ 8 00

ANN ARBOR—*St. Andrew's S. S.*: Gen. 40

BAY CITY—*Trinity Church*: Wo. Aux., salary of Miss Bull, Kyoto, $5; "J. H. Johnson" scholarship, St. Andrew's School, Mexico, $5; Sp. for Foreign Life Insurance Fund, $5.. 15 00

BIRMINGHAM—*St. James's*: Wo. Aux., Gen., $1; Alaska, $1.50; F. E. Adams Memorial, Sp. for Good Shepherd Hospital, Fort Defiance, Arizona, $1..................... 3 50

DETROIT—*Christ Church*: Wo. Aux., Alaska, $35; F. E. Adams Memorial, Sp. for Good Shepherd Hospital, Fort Defiance, Arizona, $25; S. S., hospitals in China, $4.84......... 64 84

Grace: Wo. Aux., Gen., $15; Alaska, $10 .... 25 00

St. James's: Wo. Aux., Gen., $2; Alaska, $5; F. E. Adams Memorial, Sp. for Good Shepherd Hospital, Fort Defiance, Arizona, $1............. 8 00

St. Mary's: Dom., $34.75; Wo. Aux., Gen., $5; Philippines, 50 cts...... 40 25

St. Paul's: Wo. Aux., "Jane Stewart" scholarship, St. Mary's Hall, Shanghai 40 00

St. Stephen's: Gen. 19 41

St. Thomas's: Wo. Aux., Gen........ 4 00

Trinity Church S. S.: Jane Webers's Bible-class, Sp. for Bishop Brent, Philippine Islands................ 20 00

FLINT—*St. Paul's*: Gen., $21.50; Wo. Aux., Alaska, $15; St. Paul's School, Lawrenceville, Southern Virginia, $5..................... 41 50

HUDSON—Woman's Independent Guild, Gen. 5 00

JACKSON—*St. Paul's*: Wo. Aux., Alaska 20 00

MARINE CITY—*St. Mark's*: Dom. and Frn. 9 82

ROCHESTER—*St. Philip's*: Wo. Aux., Gen. 1 00

SAGINAW—*St. John's*: Gen., $36.60; Wo. Aux., F. E. Adams Memorial,

Sp. for Good Shepherd Hospital,
Fort Defiance, Arizona, $1......... 37 60
MISCELLANEOUS — Branch Wo. Aux.,
(In Memoriam), "H. F. C.," salary
of Miss Bull, Kyoto, $10; Sp. for
Bishop Graves, Shanghai, $5..... 15 00

Michigan City

Ap. $205.50

HOWE—*Howe School:* Dr. Sowerby's
salary, Anking, Hankow.......... 200 00
St. Mark's: Wo. Aux., Gen.......... 5 50

Milwaukee

Ap. $160.10; *Sp.* $1.00

BARABOO—*Trinity Church:* Gen..... 20 00
KENOSHA—*St. Matthew's:* Frn...... 17 33
MILWAUKEE—*St. Mark's:* Gen....... 121 65
RACINE—*Immanuel Church:* Gen..... 1 12
MISCELLANEOUS—Babies' Branch, Sp.
for missionary font.............. 1 00

Minnesota

Ap. $952.05; *Sp.* $30.00

COKATO—*St. Siegfried's:* Gen........ 1 71
JANESVILLE—*St. John's:* Gen........ 20 00
LITCHFIELD—*Emmanuel Church:* Gen. 1 30
MINNEAPOLIS—*Holy Trinity Church:*
Gen. 81 70
St. Paul's: Gen.................... 200 00
ST. PAUL—*St. Clement's:* Junior Aux.,
Mrs. Mary S. Sleppy, "Bennie G.
Sleppy" scholarship, St. John's
School, Cape Mount, Africa....... 25 00
St. John Evangelist's: Gen.......... 600 00
Junior Aux., Mrs. Mary S. Sleppy,
Sp. for Bennie G. Sleppy School,
Honolulu 25 00
STILLWATER—*Ascension:* Mr. and Mrs.
Robert Slaughter, Sp. for Church
Extension Fund, Porto Rico,....... 5 00
WASECA—*Calvary:* Gen. 12 00
MISCELLANEOUS—Gen. 10 34

Mississippi

Ap. $120.52; *Sp.* $1.20

GREENVILLE—*St. James's:* Wo. Aux.,
support of Bible-woman, Hankow... 25 00
HOLLY SPRINGS—*Christ Church:* Wo.
Aux., Alaska..................... 4 65
JACKSON—*St. Andrew's:* Wo. Aux.,
Bible-woman, China, $15; Gen., $35 50 00
MERIDIAN—*St. Paul's:* Gen.......... 27 87
SWAN LAKE—*Advent:* Frn., $1; Gen.,
$7 .... 8 00
VICKSBURG—*Christ Church:* Sp. for
St. Paul's College, Tokyo......... 1 20
WILCZINSKI—*All Saints' S. S.:* Gen.. 3 00
YAZOO CITY—*Trinity Church:* Annie
Du Buisson, gasoline, Alaska...... 2 00

Missouri

Ap. $373.50

ST. LOUIS—*All Saints':* Dom., $10;
Colored, $15; Frn., $10; Gen., $15. 50 00
St. John's: Dom. and Frn.......... 32 25
St. Peter's: Dom., $148.80; Frn.,
$126.20 .... 275 00
St. Philip's: Gen.................... 16 25

Montana

Ap. $38.85

BIG TIMBER—*St. Mark's:* Gen........ 6 05
GARDNER—*Emmanuel Church:* Gen... 4 10
HARLOWTON—*All Saints':* Gen....... 4 00
JOLIET—*Church of Our Saviour:* Gen.. 3 65
JUDITH GAP—*Epiphany:* Gen........ 4 60
PONY—*St. John's:* Gen............. 4 75
RED LODGE—*Calvary:* Gen........... 7 10
ROUNDUP—*Calvary:* Gen............ 4 60

Nebraska

Ap. $186.96; *Sp.* $17.50

ASHLAND—*St. Stephen's:* Wo. Aux.,
Dom., $3; Frn., $3................
AUBURN — *Ascension:* Gen., $10.75;
Wo. Aux., Valdez, Alaska, $5; Dom.,
$2.50; Frn., $2.50................
BEATRICE—*Christ Church:* Gen......
CENTRAL CITY—*Christ Church:* Wo.
Aux., Dom., $4; Frn., $3..........
COLUMBUS—*Grace:* Gen..............
HARVARD—*St. John's:* Gen..........
NELIGH—*St. Peter's:* Dom. and Frn...
OMAHA—*Church of the Good Shep-
herd:* Wo. Aux., Dom., $2.50; Frn.,
$2.50
St. Andrew's: Gen., $5.60; Wo. Aux.,
Frn..............................
St. Barnabas's: Wo. Aux., Dom......
St. John's: Wo. Aux., Frn..........
Trinity Church: Wo. Aux., Dom., $25;
Junior Aux., Mrs. Cameron
McRae, Shanghai, $5..............
Mrs. Stein, Wo. Aux., Sp. for Bishop
Rowe, Alaska....................
SOUTH OMAHA—*St. Martin's:* Wo.
Aux., Dom., $8.50; Frn. (of which
Junior Aux., $1), $9.50...........
TECUMSEH—*Grace:* Gen.............
MISCELLANEOUS—Junior Aux., Sp. for
Rev. Cameron McRae, Shanghai....

Newark

Ap. $1,946.14; *Sp.* $292.88

ALLENDALE—*Epiphany Mission:* Gen..
BELLEVILLE—*Christ Church:* Gen.....
BOONTON—*St. John's:* Gen..........
EAST ORANGE—*Christ Church S. S.:*
Medical work in China............
Mrs. Joseph Hunter, Dom. and Frn.
ENGLEWOOD—*St. Paul's:* James Bar-
ber, Sp. for Church Extension Fund,
Porto Rico.......................
GRANTWOOD—*Trinity Church Mission
S. S.:* Sp. for Chinese orphanage,
Shanghai
HALEDON—*St. Mary's:* Sp. for St.
Paul's College, Tokyo.............
LITTLE FALLS—*St. Agnes's S. S.:* Gen.
MILLBURN—*St. Stephen's:* Sp. for
Rev. J. W. Chapman's work, Alaska.
MONTCLAIR—*St. John's:* Gen., $89.73;
S. S., Church hospital in China,
$6.87 ....
Mrs. F. B. Carter, Sp. for Bishop
Holly, Haiti.....................
NEWARK—*St. Thomas's:* Junior Aux.,
Alaska, $10; China, $5; Gen., $5...
Trinity Church: Frn................ 1
ORANGE—*Grace:* Junior Aux., Sp. for
Bishop Rowe, Alaska.............
PASSAIC—*St. John's:* Dom., $1.50;
Frn,. $26.32.....................
PATERSON—*St. Paul's:* Charles P.
Sparkman, Sp. for Church Extension
Fund, Porto Rico.................
PHILLIPSBURG—*St. Luke's S. S.:* Chi-
nese hospital....................
RUTHERFORD—*Grace:* Sp. for St. Paul's
College, Tokyo...................
SOUTH ORANGE—*Church of the Holy
Communion:* Support of Rev. Henry
McNulty, Shanghai, $187.50; Junior
Aux., Gen., $2; Sp. for Bishop Rowe,
Alaska, $10......................
SUMMIT—*Calvary:* Gen., $190.95; Sp.
for Bishop Griswold, Salina, $55.83.
TENAFLY—*Atonement:* Junior Aux.,
Indian, $1; Sp. for Mr. Cuthbert's
work, Kyoto, $5..................
WEST HOBOKEN—*St. John's:* Alaska..
MISCELLANEOUS—"A Friend," Dom.
and Frn.........................
Offertory at meeting of Junior Aux.

122 10
1 75
14 10
100 00
30 70
6 00
6 30
25 00
10 77
49 00

10 00

20 00

9 00

5 00

27 00

11 00

21 05

1 25

80 74

80 89

5 00
10 00

92 54

5 67

52 09
28 32

10 00

205 20
175 17

PLAINFIELD—*Grace*: Wo. Aux., salary of Kimura San, Kyoto, $5; Sp. for salary of Mrs. William Holmes's lace-teacher, Santee Agency, South Dakota, $5.................. 10 00
Miss Mary W. Washington, Sp. for Rev. E. J. Lee, Anking, Hankow.. 5 00
SALEM—*St. John's*: Wo. Aux., "Bishop Odenheimer" (In Memoriam) scholarship, Trinity Divinity-school, Tokyo, $5; S. S., Sp. for St. Paul's College, Tokyo, $10.57............ 15 57
SHREWSBURY—*Christ Church*: Frn.... 32 50
SOMERVILLE—*St. John's*: Frn........ 26 45
TRENTON—*Christ Church*: Dom...... 21 00
St. Michael's: Dom., $14.75; Frn., $31.25; Gen., $14.............. 60 00
St. Paul's: Wo. Aux., Sp. for salary of Mrs. William Holmes's lace-teacher, at Santee Agency, South Dakota 2 00
VINCENTOWN—*Trinity Church*: Sp. for St. Paul's College Building Fund, Tokyo 2 45

New York

Ap. $21.993.21; *Sp.* $7,681.30

BEDFORD—"K.," Sp. for Expansion Fund, St. John's University, Shanghai 1 00
BREWSTER—*St. Andrew's*: Rev. F. Heartfield, Sp. for Bishop Rowe's work, Alaska................ 5 00
EASTCHESTER—*St. Paul's*: Sp. for Asheville 6 46
FISHKILL-ON-HUDSON — *St. Andrew's*: "A Member," Wo. Aux., "Elizabeth" scholarship, Girls' Training Institute, St. Paul's River, West Africa.. 25 00
Through Miss Seaman, Wo. Aux., Sp. for Miss Ridgely's new building, Cape Mount, West Africa, $50; Christmas Offering, Sp. for Miss Ridgely's work, Cape Mount, West Africa, $5.................... 55 00
IRVINGTON-ON-HUDSON—Wo. Aux., Sp. for Nevada.................... 100 00
MAMARONECK—*St. Thomas's S. S.*: Hospitals at Shanghai............ 8 00
MANCHESTER BRIDGE—*St. John's S. S.*; Gen...................... 3 00
MATTEAWAN—*St. Luke's*: Wo. Aux., Sp. for Bishop Thomas, Wyoming, $10; S. S., hospitals in China, $10.. 20 00
MILLBROOK—*Grace*: Gen............ 100 00
MONTICELLO—*St. John's S. S.*: Hospital work, China............... 5 00
MONTGOMERY — *St. Andrew's Chapel*: Dom. 3 20
MT. VERNON — *Ascension*: Gen., $210.46; Wo. Aux., Sp. for Hospital of the Good Shepherd, Fort Defiance, Arizona, $10............ 220 46
Trinity Church: Gen.............. 192 01
NEWBURGH — *St. George's*: Frn., $60.72; Gen., $71.76; "A Member," Wo. Aux., Sp. for Miss Ridgely's work, West Africa, $4............ 136 48
NEW ROCHELLE—*Christ Mission*: Frn.. 10 00
St. John's (Wilmot): Frn.......... 6 00
Trinity Church: Wo. Aux., Sp. for Bishop Rowe, Alaska, $3; Sp. for Expansion Fund, St. John's University, Shanghai, $3; S. S., St. Luke's Hospital, Shanghai, $10.25........ 16 25
NEW YORK—*Ascension*: Gen., $485.04; Wo. Aux., Frn., $10.............. 495 04
Ascension Memorial: Gen............ 100 00
All Angels': Gen., $448.22; Sp. for work of Bishop Thomas, Wyoming, $25; Woman's Guild, Sp. for Rev. W. J. Cuthbert's building, Kyoto, $50 .... 523 22
All Souls': Gen.................... 150 00

Beloved Disciple: Charles C. Marshall, Gen. 25 00

Calvary: Indian, $41.66; Mrs. Jacob Mersereau, $10, "A Member," $1, "A Member," $5, Sp. for Nevada; Miss I. Lawrence, Sp. for Bishop Robinson, Nevada, at his discretion, $10; "L. M.," Sp. for St. Augustine's School, Gainesville, Florida, $2; Sp. for St. Margaret's School, Tokyo, $3; "Cash," "M.," $10; Wo. Aux., $5, Sp. for Expansion Fund, St. John's University, Shanghai; Wo. Aux., support of a Bible-woman, Shanghai, $50 .... 137 66

Christ Church: Susan Sturgis Strong, Sp. for Bishop Thomas's work, Wyoming, $5; Niobrara League, Sp. for Miss Thackara's Hospital, Fort Defiance, Arizona, $35; Wo. Aux., Sp. for Rev. Mr. Spurr, West Virginia, $25; Sp. for St. James's Church, Mesilla Park, New Mexico, $26.50... 91 50

Christ Church (New Brighton, Staten Island); Wo. Aux., Frn. 12 00

Christ Church (Riverdale); Wo. Aux., Frn. 30 00

Epiphany: Dom., $92.25; Frn., $55; Gen., $94.91; Sp. for Bishop Rowe, Alaska, $25 .... 267 16

Grace: Dom., $1,367.54; Frn., $740.58; "St. Matthew's" scholarship, St. Mary's Hall, Shanghai, $50; Woman's Foreign Missionary Association, "Grace Church" scholarship, $25; "Catharine L. Wolfe Memorial" scholarship, $25, both in St. John's School, Cape Mount, West Africa; Sp. for Bishop Funsten, Idaho, $55; Mrs. Prescott Hall, Sp. for scholarship, St. Margaret's School, Boisé, Idaho, $40; "A Member," Sp. for Expansion Fund, St. John's University, Shanghai, $25; Committee on Missions to Colored People, Sp. for St. Augustine's League, Sp. for St. Augustine's School, Raleigh, North Carolina, $50; Sp. for St. Agnes's Hospital, Raleigh, North Carolina, $10; Sp. for Good Samaritan Hospital, Charlotte, North Carolina, $10; Sp. for Bishop Payne Divinity-school, Petersburg, Southern Virginia, $25; Miss Nelson, Niobrara League, "Harvey M. Nelson" scholarship, $60, "Emily Nelson" scholarship, $60, both in St. Elizabeth's School, South Dakota... 2,543 12

Grace-Emmanuel: Sp. for St. Paul's College Fund, Tokyo 1 35

Holy Apostles': Gen., $40.10; Niobrara League, "Miss Cushman and James S. Cushman" scholarship, St. Elizabeth's School, South Dakota, $60 .... 100 10

Holy Communion: Miss Henrietta M. Schwab, Wo. Aux., Sp. for Expansion Fund, St. John's University, Shanghai 10 00

Holy Trinity Church (Harlem): Sp. for Expansion Fund, St. John's University, Shanghai................. 33 33

Incarnation: Mrs. Clinton Ogilvie, Sp. for Bishop Brewster, Western Colorado, $500; Sp. for Bishop Rowe, Alaska, $250; Mrs. M. K. Bailey, $3, Uriah T. Tracy, $11, Estate of Mary H. Trotter, $50, Miss J. D. Talcott, $5, Sp. for Bishop Rowe, Alaska; John Innes Kane, $250, Miss Ethel L. McLean, $50, Mr. and Mrs. W. F. Chester, $5, "Cash," $10, Sp. for work of Bishop Rowe, Alaska; Niobrara League, Mrs. E. V. Z. Lane, "H. E. Montgomery" (Graduate) scholarship, South Dakota, $60; "Grace M. Lane" scholarship, St.

Mary's School, South Dakota, $60; Miss Alice L. Lane, "Frederick F. Johnson" (Graduate) scholarship, South Dakota, $60.................

Incarnation Chapel: $52.72, S. S., $8.09, Sp. for work of Miss Laura Bassett, Sewanee, Tennessee.......

Intercession: Sp. for Bishop Wells, for Walla Walla School, Spokane, $26; Sp. for Mrs. Wetmore, Arden, Asheville, $15; "A Member," Sp. for Bishop Rowe, Alaska, $25.........

St. Agnes's Chapel: Sp. for Bishop Robinson's work, Nevada, $18; Miss J. S. Kirby, Sp. for Bishop Rowe, Alaska, $100; Wo. Aux., Frn., $60..

St. Andrew's: Miss Mabel D. Burnham, Sp. for Expansion Fund, St. John's University, Shanghai, $1; Mrs. E. S. Baker, Sp. for Expansion Fund, St. John's University, Shanghai, $10..

St. Ann's Church for Deaf-mutes: Wo. Aux., "Ephphatha" scholarship, St. John's School, Africa.............

St. Bartholomew's: Wo. Aux., Sp. for Dr. Pott's Expansion Fund, Shanghai ....

St. Chrysostom's Chapel: Miss Esther A. Rolph, Sp. for Bishop Thomas's Hospital, Wyoming, $1; Sp. for Expansion Fund, St. John's University, Shanghai, $1; Babies' Branch, Gen., $5; Sp. for missionary font, $1; Sp. for "Little Helpers'" cot, $5; Sp. for St. Agnes's Hospital, Raleigh, North Carolina, $1.35.................

St. George's: Sp. for Indian work, Oneida, Fond du Lac, $5, The Misses Reynolds, $5, "A Friend," $2, Sp. for Expansion Fund, St. John's University, Shanghai; Woman's Branch, Missionary Society, support of bed in St. James's Hospital, Anking, Hankow, $50; "Mary Emma Leavitt" scholarship, Girls' Training Institute, Africa, $25; Sp. for Expansion Fund, St. John's University, Shanghai, $480; St. Augustine's League, Sp. for St. Paul's School, Lawrenceville, Southern Virginia, $25; Wo. Aux., Sp. for Bishop Thomas, Wyoming, $15............

St. James's: Dom. and Frn., $1,273.33; Miss E. H. Belloni, Sp. for Expansion Fund, St. John's University, Shanghai, $1; Wo. Aux., Easter School, Baguio, Philippine Islands, $400; Frn., $100; Sp. for Archdeacon Spurr, West Virginia, $25; Missionary Guild, Wo. Aux., Sp. for Miss A. E. Wright, Mito, Tokyo, for organ, $12.50; S. S., two patients in hospital, China, $20....

St. John the Evangelist's: Gen......

St. Luke's: $199.57, S. S., $18.26, Gen. ....

St. Mark's Chapel: Dom., $20; S. S., Gen., $15.22.....................

St. Mark's: Frn., $71.91; Gen., $16.63; S. S., Indian, $9.59...............

St. Mary's (Lawrence Street): Girls' Friendly Society, Sp. for Girls' School, Bontoc, Philippine Islands..

St. Mary's (Mott Haven): Gen., $2.05; S. S., "Stephen Wheatley Moore" scholarship, "St. Mary's, Mott Haven" scholarship, both in Boys' School, Soochow, Shanghai, $25.92..

St. Mary-the-Virgin: Sp. for Bishop Webb, Milwaukee...............

St. Matthew's: Wo. Aux., Sp. for Rev. Dr. Correll, Kyoto...............

St. Michael's: For Rev. Mr. Gilman's salary, Changsha, Hankow, $580.35; Sp. for Bishop Rowe's work, Alaska (of which from Ida Lathers, $25), $26 ....

St. Paul's (Edgewater, Staten Island) : St. Augustine's League, Sp. for St. Paul's Hospital, Lawrenceville, Southern Virginia, for furnishings 5 00
St. Peter's (Westchester) : Dom., $73.18 ; Gen., $55 ; Niobrara League, Sp. for Miss Thackara's work among Navajo Indians, Arizona, $25 ; Wo. Aux., "Keble" scholarship, St. Mary's Hall, Shanghai, $45........ 198 18
St. Simeon's : Deaconess Mabel W. Nicholas, Sp. for Expansion Fund, St. John's University, Shanghai.... 5 00
St. Thomas's : Dom., $2,254.29 ; Frn., $8,500 ; Wo. Aux., "William L. Morgan Memorial" scholarship, St. John's University, Shanghai, $100 ; St. Margaret's School, for "St. Thomas's" scholarship, Tokyo, $40 ; Sp. for Bishop Thomas's Hospital, Wyoming, $4 ; "Members," Sp. for Bishop Rowe, Alaska, $235 ; St. Augustine's League, Sp. for scholarship, St. Paul's School, Lawrenceville, Southern Virginia, $25 ; Sp. for St. Mary-the-Virgin's School, Nashville, Tennessee, $40 ; Sp. for "Langford Memorial" scholarship, Bishop Payne Divinity-school, Petersburg, Southern Virginia, $25 ; Sp. for "Langford Memorial" scholarship, Petersburg, Southern Virginia, $10..11,233 29
St. Thomas's Chapel : Wo. Aux., Gen.. 100 00
Transfiguration : Mrs. L. Williams, Niobrara League, "George L. Williams" scholarship, St. Elizabeth's School, South Dakota, $60 ; St. Augustine's League (In Memoriam), "J. K. W.", Sp. for St. Mary-the-Virgin's School, Nashville, Tennessee, $25 .... 85 00
Trinity Parish : Sp. for work of Rev. William J. Cuthbert, Kyoto....... 15 00
Trinity Chapel : Dom., $25 ; Missionary Relief Society, Mrs. H. P. Bartlett, Frn., $2 ; Missionary Relief Society, Sp. for St. John's University Expansion Fund, Shanghai (of which Miss Elizabeth Cotheal, $5, Mrs. J. B. Lawrence, $10), $40.......... 67 00
Zion and St. Timothy's : Gen., $2,330 ; Mrs. Samuel A. Blatchford, Wo. Aux., native church work, Mexico, $10 ; Mrs. Hooker Memorial School, Mexico, $5.25 ; Niobrara League, "C. C. Tiffany" (Graduate) scholarship, South Dakota, $60 ; St. Augustine's League, Sp. for St. Agnes's Hospital, Raleigh, North Carolina, $10 ; Missionary Chapter, Sp. for scholarship, St. Paul's School, Lawrenceville, Southern Virginia, $25 ; Sp. for St. Augustine's School, Raleigh, North Carolina, $25...... 2,465 25
Mrs. James Herman Aldrich, Wo. Aux., Frn....................... 10 00
Miss E. Cotheal, Niobrara League, "Cotheal Memorial" scholarship, St. Mary's School, South Dakota.... 60 00
Miss Mary E. Robert, Dom., $30 ; Frn., $30......................... 60 00
"Anonymous," Gen................. 5 00
Mrs. J. Hull Browning, $500, Lily M. Buxton, $1, Mrs. Cornelia A. Benjamin, $500, Miss I. Benjamin, $50, Kingsland Adams Haskell Coffyn, $1, Mrs. Samuel Lawrence, $100, Miss P. C. Swords, $25, Miss E. A. Thorn, $25, Sp. for Bishop Rowe, Alaska 1,202 00
Mrs. W. Irving Clark, $10, Mrs. John H. Stevens, $5, Mrs. R. T. Auchmuty, $500, Sp. for Nevada... 515 00
Miss Georgine H. Thomas, Sp. for Church Extension Fund, Porto Rico. 325 00
S. F. Zabriskie, Sp. for St. John's-

in-the-Wilderness, Alaska.......... 100 00
Mrs. Mary C. Scrymser, $1,000, Miss Mary E. Thomas, $10, Miss E. R. Delafield, $10, H. C. Van Post, $50, Mrs. Francis McNeil Bacon, Jr., $5, Selden S. Brown, $5, Miss Isabella Lawrence, $10, "A Friend," $25, Sp. for St. John's University, Shanghai 1,115 00
Mrs. G. R. Henderson, Sp. for brass tablet for "Emily Riter Henderson Memorial" bed, children's ward, St. James's Hospital, Anking, Hankow.. 12 00
Ossining—St. Paul's : Mrs. Edward N. Strong, $50, Miss Evelina K. Strong, $50, Sp. for Bishop Rowe, Alaska, at his discretion ; Mrs. Edward N. Strong, industrial work, Cape Mount, West Africa, "In Memory of Edward N. Strong," $25............. 125 00
Pelham Manor—Christ Church : Wo. Aux., Frn........................ 2 00
Pine Plains—Regeneration : Gen..... 5 00
Poughkeepsie—Christ Church : Gen. 30 00
Rye—Christ Church : Wo. Aux., Sp. for Hospital of the Good Shepherd, Fort Defiance, Arizona........... 25 00
Scarsdale—St. James the Less : Mrs. A. B. Crane, Sp. for Expansion Fund, St. John's University, Shanghai 5 00
Somers—St. Luke's S. S. : Sp. for Expansion Fund, St. John's University, Shanghai............... 2 50
Staatsburg — St. Margaret's : Wo. Aux., Sp. for Bishop Horner's work among poor whites, Asheville, $10 ; Sp. for Hospital of the Good Shepherd, Fort Defiance, Arizona, $10 ; Sp. for Bishop Rowe's work, Alaska, $10 .... 30 00
Tarrytown—Christ Church : work of Bishop Spalding, Utah, $58.25 ; Wo. Aux., Sp. for Hospital of the Good Shepherd, Fort Defiance, Arizona, $20.50 .... 78 75
Tuxedo Park—St. Mary's : Wo. Aux., Sp. for Mrs. Wetmore's work, Christ School, Arden, Asheville, $330 ; Sp. for rebuilding chapel, Isle of Pines, Cuba, $25..................... 355 00
Wappinger's Falls—Zion : Mrs. Temple Bowdoin, Sp. for Expansion Fund, St. John's University, Shanghai 100 00
Yonkers—St. Andrew's : Gen., $100.80 ; Wo. Aux., Frn., $10.............. 110 80
St. John's : Wo. Aux., Frn., $13 ; Gen., 80 cts.................... 13 80
Mrs. A. V. W. Jackson, Gen......... 1 00
Miscellaneous — St. Augustine's League, Sp. for St. Paul's School, Lawrenceville, Southern Virginia, $100 ; Sp. for St. Augustine's School, Raleigh, North Carolina, $100 ; Sp. for Rev. R. Bright, Savannah, Georgia, $50 ; Sp. for Rev. P. P. Alston, Charlotte, North Carolina, $50 ; Sp. for Meade Chapel Building Fund, Virginia, $50....... 350 00
Sunday-school rally, held in Zion and St. Timothy's Church, Gen.... 17 11

North Carolina

Ap. $445.09 ; Sp. $51.02
Advance—Ascension : Wo. Aux., salary of Miss Annie Cheshire, Shanghai, $1 ; salary of Miss Babcock, Tokyo, $1 ; Miss Elizabeth Cheshire's work, St. Hilda's School, Wuchang, Hankow, $1 ; Gen., $1...... 4 00
Ansonville—All Souls' : Dom. and Frn. 10 00
Bristow—St. Mark's : Dom. and Frn. 4 00
Charlotte—Church of the Holy Com-

forter : Gen 20 00
St. Peter's : Wo. Aux., Miss Hicks's
work, Philippines, $5; Frn., $1.... 6 00
DURHAM—*St. Philip's* : Gen.......... 16 00
GASTON—*St. Luke's* : Gen........... 4 73
GREENSBORO — *St. Andrew's* : Gen.,
$24.16; Wo. Aux., Frn., $3.95; sal-
ary of Miss Babcock, Tokyo, $3;
Sp. at Rev. Mr. Ancell's disposal,
Shanghai, $5; "Thank-offering," Sp.
for Miss Annie Cheshire, Shanghai,
to use in aid to the sick, $5....... 41 11
St. Barnabas's : Wo. Aux., Sp. for
Bishop Gray, Southern Florida.... 2 00
HENDERSON — *Holy Innocents'* : Wo.
Aux., Alaska................... 5 00
HILLSBOBO—*St. Matthew's* : Wo. Aux.,
Alaska, $2.83; Miss Hicks's work,
Philippines, $2; salary of Miss
Cheshire, Shanghai, $15; Gen., $2;
Sp. for "Bishop Cheshire" scholar-
ship, Holy Trinity Orphanage,
Tokyo, $1.50; Sp. for "Lindsay Pat-
ton" scholarship, at Bishop McKim's
disposal, Tokyo, 84 cts............ 24 17
IREDELL CO.—*St. James's* : Dom. and
Frn. 3 00
JACKSON—*Church of the Saviour* :
Gen. 3 00
LITTLETON—*St. Alban's* : Gen., $16.34;
S. S., hospital work in China, $2.10. 18 44
LOUISBURG—*St. Matthias's* : Gen..... 2 00
MIDDLEBURG — *Heavenly Rest* : Wo.
Aux., Alaska, $1; Miss Hicks's work,
Philippines, $1; salary of Miss An-
nie Cheshire, Shanghai, $2; Sp. for
"Bishop Cheshire" scholarship, Holy
Trinity Orphanage, Tokyo, $1...... 5 00
NOISE—*St. Philip's* : Gen........... 1 00
OXFORD—*St. Stephen's* : Gen........ 50 00
RALEIGH—*Christ Church* : Gen....... 81 75
Church of the Good Shepherd : Wo.
Aux., Miss Elizabeth Cheshire's
work, St. Hilda's School, Wuchang,
Hankow 5 00
St. Mary's School : Gen., $8.50; Sp.
for St. Paul's College, Tokyo,
$4.68; Wo. Aux., "Aldert Smedes"
scholarship, St. Mary's Hall, Shang-
hai, $6.20..................... 19 38
St. Saviour's : Wo. Aux., salary of
Annie Cheshire, Shanghai......... 5 00
ROCKINGHAM—*Church of the Messiah* :
Dom. and Frn................. 5 00
SCOTLAND NECK — *Trinity Church* :
Asheville, $8.89; Wo. Aux., Alaska,
$1; salary of Miss Babcock, Tokyo,
$1; Frn., 98 cts.; Sp. for Bishop
Gray, Southern Florida, $1........ 12 87
SMITHFIELD — *Transfiguration* : Wo.
Aux., salary of Miss Annie Ches-
hire, Shanghai.................. 5 00
TARBORO—*Calvary* : Gen., $25; Wo.
Aux., Alaska, $5; Frn., $2.65; Sp.
for Bishop Gray, Southern Florida,
$5 .... 37 65
WADESBORO—*Calvary* : Wo. Aux., Frn. 3 35
WARREN CO.—*St. Luke's* (Near Ridge-
way) · Gen..................... 2 00
WARRENTON—*All Saints'* : Gen........ 4 00
Emmanuel Church : Bishop Horner's
work, Asheville, $2; Gen., $14.16.. 16 16
WELDON—*Grace* : Wo. Aux., salary of
Miss Annie Cheshire, Shanghai, $3;
Gen., $2; Miss Elizabeth Cheshire's
work, St. Hilda's School, Hankow, $2 7 00
WILSON—*St. Mark's* : Gen........... 4 00
WINSTON—*St. Paul's* : Gen.......... 40 00
WOODLEAF—*St. Andrew's* : Dom. and
Frn. 3 50
MISCELLANEOUS—The Convocation of
Charlotte, Sp. for Building Fund,
Tsu, Kyoto.................... 25 00

Ohio

Ap. $639.51; *Sp.* $138.91

AKRON—*Church of Our Saviour* : Gen. 21 85
ASHTABULA—*Old St. Peter's* : Gen... 10 10
BELLEFONTAINE—*Holy Trinity Church* :
Gen. 2 10
CLEVELAND — *Emmanuel Church* : Sp.
for Bishop Rowe, Alaska, $68.50;
Wo. Aux., Daughters, Alaska, $5;
Oklahoma, $10; Fukui, Kyoto, $5;
salary of Miss Elwin, Shanghai,
$20; Gen., $5.................. 113 50
Grace : Dom., $17.28; Frn., $17.27... 34 55
St. John's : Wo. Aux., Alaska (of
which Mrs. Lascelles $5), $10;
Mrs. Lascelles, for "Ohio" scholarship,
St. Elizabeth's School, South Dakota,
$5; "Gregory T. Bedell" scholar-
ship, $5; "Julia Bedell" scholarship,
$5; St. John's University, Shang-
hai, Mrs. C. D. Rhodes, in memory
of Stewart Rhodes, Sp. for Foreign
Life Insurance Fund, $14......... 39 00
St. Paul's : Wo. Aux., Sacramento,
$25; "Gregory T. Bedell" scholar-
ship, St. John's University, Shang-
hai, $15; Gen., $10.............. 50 00
COSHOCTON—*Trinity Church* : Frn.... 2 25
CUYAHOGA FALLS—*St. John's* : Gen.. 43 10
HUDSON—*Christ Church* : Gen....... 19 40
HURON—*Christ Church* : Gen....... 2 00
LAKEWOOD—*Ascension* : $30.68, S. S.,
$20.78, Sp. for Bishop Rowe, Alaska. 51 44
MARYSVILLE—*St. Mary's* : Gen...... 2 10
MONROEVILLE—*Zion Parish* : Frn..... 16 78
NILES—*St. Luke's* : Gen........... 2 45
OBERLIN—*Christ Church* : Gen....... 5 00
PAINESVILLE — *St. James's* : Gen.,
$241.87; Wo. Aux., Oklahoma, $5;
Sacramento, $5; Fukui, Kyoto, $5;
salary of Miss Elwin, Shanghai,
$10; "Julia Bedell" scholarship,
St. John's University, Shanghai, $5. 271 87
PENINSULA—*Bronson Memorial* : Gen.. 4 25
RAVENNA—*Grace* : Gen............. 8 98
SHELBY—*St. Mark's* : Gen.......... 10 00
TOLEDO—*All Saints'* : Wo. Aux., Gen.. 2 00
Grace : "C· F. P.," Gen.......... 5 00
St. Andrew's : Gen.............. 8 70
St. Mark's : Junior Aux., Alaska, $10;
Sp. for Rev. Walter Clapp, Philip-
pines, $5..................... 15 00
Trinity Church : Wo. Aux., Alaska,
$15; "Gregory T. Bedell" scholar-
ship, St. John's University, Shang-
hai, $10..................... 25 00
UPPER SANDUSKY — *Trinity Church* :
Wo. Aux., Gen................. 4 19
WELLSVILLE—*Ascension* : Gen........ 6 65
YOUNGSTOWN — *St. John's* : Woman's
Society, Gen................... 1 19

Oregon

Ap. $175.05

CORVALLIS—*Good Samaritan* : Gen.... 31 55
PORTLAND—*Trinity Church* : Gen..... 130 00
ROSEBURG—*St. George's* : Gen....... 18 50

Pennsylvania

Ap. $17,577.08; *Sp.* $3,934.94·

ANDALUSIA—*Chapel of the Redeemer* :
Sp. for Rev. W. W. Steel, Cuba, $9;
Gen., $1.58................... 10 58
BRISTOL—*St. Paul's* : Gen.......... 13 27
BRYN MAWR—*Church of the Redeemer* :
Through Wo. Aux., Sp. for Miss
Wood for library, Wuchang, Han-
kow, $5; Sp. for Building Fund, St.
Elizabeth's Hospital, Shanghai, $10;
"Pennsylvania Wo. Aux." scholar-
ship, Hooker Memorial School, Mex-
ico, $5; Junior Aux., Kyoto, $25... 45 00
OGONTZ—*St. Paul's* : Through Wo.

kota, $60; Dom., $4,010.79; Frn.,
$5,163.20; Wo. Aux., "W. Beaumont
Whitney" scholarship, Cuba, $5;
"Foreign Committee" scholarship,
St. Hilda's School, Wuchang, Han-
kow, $7; "Anna M. Stevens Me-
morial" scholarship, Girls' Training
Institute, St. Paul's River, Africa,
$1; "Kinsolving" scholarship, Bra-
zil, $6; Sp. for Miss Wood for li-
brary, Wuchang, Hankow, $5; Sp.
for Building Fund, St. Elizabeth's
Hospital, Shanghai, $10; Sp. for
"Philadelphia" scholarship, St.
Mary's Orphanage, Shanghai, $3;
Sp. for Bishop Knight for Divinity-
school, Cuba, $25.................. 9,295 99
Old St. Paul's: Gen................ 10 00
Resurrection: Gen................... 77 86
St. Andrew's (West): Wo. Aux., Sp.
for Foreign Life Insurance Fund...   1 00
St. Andrew's (Eighth and Spruce):
Indian Hope Association, Indian....   5 00
St. Clement's: Dom., $5; China, $10;
Gen., $55; Sp. for Bishop Horner,
Asheville, $75; Sp. for Bishop
Weller, Fond du Lac, $7; Sp. for
Bishop White, Michigan City, $10;
Sp. for Bishop Griswold, Salina,
$162.50; Sp. for St. Andrew's
School, Sewanee, Tennessee, $5;
Girls' Friendly Society, Sp. for Rev.
S. C. Hughson, salary of deacon,
Sewanee, Tennessee, $2........... 331 50
St. James's: Dom., $792.49; Frn.,
$680.57; Gen., $508.82; Colored,
$180; Indian, $139; Sp. for Dr.
Pott's work, St. John's University,
Shanghai, $15..................... 2,315 88
St. James's (Kingsessing): Through
Wo. Aux., Sp. for Foreign Life In-
surance Fund....................   2 00
St. Jude and the Nativity: Sp. for
Bishop Rowe, Alaska.............   100 00
St. Luke and Epiphany: Wo. Aux.,
"Kinsolving" scholarship, Brazil,
$10; "Bishop Stevens" scholarship,
St. John's University, Shanghai,
$10; Training-school for Bible-
women, Hankow, $10; "W. B. Whit-
ney" scholarship, Havana, Cuba,
$10; Sp. for St. Elizabeth's Hos-
pital, Shanghai, $5; Sp. for Foreign
Life Insurance Fund, $10........   55 00
St. Luke's (Germantown): Frn.,
$174.90; Wo. Aux., "W. B. Whit-
ney" scholarship, Havana, Cuba, $5;
Sp. for Foreign Life Insurance
Fund, $10; Sp. for Miss Wood for li-
brary, Wuchang, Hankow, $2; Girls'
Friendly Society, Sp. for Bishop
Rowe, Alaska, $2.................   193 90
St. Luke's (Kensington): Elizabeth
Turner Bible-class, Gen...........   5 00
St. Mark's: "A Parishioner," Sp. for
Bishop Rowe, Alaska.............   500 00
St. Mark's (Frankford): Gen., $125;
Sp. for Rev. Dr. Correll's work,
Kyoto, $25.......................   150 00
St. Martin's (Oak Lane): Indian,
$8.30; S. S., Indian, $7.58; Sp. for
Building Fund, St. Paul's University,
Tokyo, $8.69.....................   24 57
St. Martin-in-the-Fields (Wissahickon):
Brazil, $150; Frn., $1,383.50; Sam-
uel Porcher, Sp. for Church Exten-
sion Fund, Porto Rico, $3; Wo.
Aux., Gen., $4.65; Sp. for Miss
Wood for library, Wuchang, Han-
kow, $5; Sp. for Building Fund, St.
Elizabeth's Hospital, Shanghai, $5;
Indian Hope Association, Indian, $5. 1,556 15
St. Mary's (Hamilton Village): Dom.·
$11; Frn., $11...................   22 00
St. Mary's (West): Wo. Aux., Sp. for

nurse's salary, St. Luke's Hospital, Shanghai 5 00
St. Matthew's: Sp. for Bishop Thomas, Wyoming, $25; Wo. Aux., Sp. for nurse's salary, St. Luke's Hospital, Shanghai, $5; Sp. for Miss Wood for library, Wuchang, Hankow, $6.... 36 00
St. Matthias's: Wo. Aux., for "Dr. Twing Memorial" scholarship, St. John's University, Shanghai, $2; Junior Aux. Branch No. 1, $7.50, Branch No. 2, $7.50, Gen.......... 17 00
St. Michael's (Germantown): Wo. Aux., "Kinsolving" scholarship, Brazil, $5; Sp. for Miss Wood for library, Wuchang, Hankow, $10; Junior Aux., Sp. for Building Fund, St. Margaret's School, Tokyo, $1... 16 00
St. Paul's (Chestnut Hill): Wo. Aux., "W. Beaumont Whitney" scholarship, Cuba, $15; "Julia C. Emery" scholarship, Orphan Asylum, Cape Palmas, Africa, $3; "Francesca" scholarship, Cuttington Collegiate and Divinity-school, Africa, $2; "Bishop Stevens" scholarship, St. John's University, Shanghai, $5; "Foreign Committee" scholarship, Girls' High School, Kyoto, $5; Sp. for Miss Wood for library, Wuchang, Hankow, $5; Sp. for "John W. Wood" scholarship, Cuba, $10..... 45 00
St. Paul's S. S. (Overbrook): Hospital in China, $50; Alaska, $50; "A Friend," for education of an Indian, South Dakota, $100; China, $100; Sp. for Dr. Correll's work, Kyoto, $100; Wo. Aux., "Foreign Committee" scholarship, St. Hilda's School, Wuchang, Hankow, $3; Training-school, Sendai, China, $3; Sp. for Foreign Life Insurance Fund, $5; Sp. for Building Fund, St. Elizabeth's Hospital, Shanghai, $5; Sp. for Miss Wood for library, Wuchang, Hankow, $6................... 422 00
St. Peter's: Frn., $845.83; Indian Hope Association, Indian, $20...... 865 83
St. Philip's (West): Wo. Aux., Sp. for Rev. Amos Goddard's life insurance, Hankow, $5; Sp. for Miss Wood for library, Wuchang, Hankow, $2..... 7 00
St. Stephen's: Frn., $130.95; St. Paul's School, Lawrenceville, Southern Virginia, $53.91; Wo. Aux., Sp. for Building Fund, St. Elizabeth's Hospital, Shanghai, $5; Sp. for Miss Wood for library, Wuchang, Hankow, $5...................... 194 86
Church of the Saviour: Frn., $648.08; Wo. Aux., Training-school for Bible-women, Hankow, $5; Training-school, Sendai, Tokyo, $5; Sp. for Foreign Life Insurance Fund, $5 .... 663 08
Zion: Gen., $10; Dom. and Frn., $27.54.......................... 37 54
"Two Friends," Sp. for Bishop Rowe, Alaska 1,000 00
John E. Baird, Sp. for Bishop Rowe, Alaska, $500; Sp. for Bishop Restarick, Honolulu, $250; Sp. for Bishop Funsten, Idaho, $250...... 1,000 00
H. W. Potts, "In Memory of Mrs. Annie Potts," Gen............... 150 00
Miss C. C. Biddle, Frn........... 100 00
B. Frank Clapp, Sp. for Bishop Rowe, Alaska................... 100 00
Mrs. W. D. Windsor, Sp. for St. Luke's Memorial Hospital, Ponce, Porto Rico................... 20 00
"A Friend," Gen................ 10 00
Joseph E. J. McGee, Gen......... 1 00
Wo. Aux., Tuesday Missionary Bible-class, Gen., $120; Sp. for Bishop Brent, Philippines, $75; Sp. for Bishop Spalding, Utah, $150....... 345 00

RADNOR—St. Martin's: Wo. Aux., "Kinsolving" scholarship, Brazil, $4; Sp. for Miss Neely, Mayebashi, Tokyo, $10; Sp. for Foreign Life Insurance, $5; Sp. for Rev. W. W. Steele, Cuba, $2...............
WAYNE—St. Mary's Memorial: Frn., $78.39; Wo. Aux., "Pennsylvania Wo. Aux." scholarship, Hooker Memorial School, Mexico, $5; S. S. "T. K. Conrad Memorial" scholarship, Trinity Divinity-school, Tokyo, $70; Junior Aux., Gen., $25; Sp. for Building Fund, St. Paul's College, Tokyo, $20.50; Indian Hope Association, Indian, $5.......
WEST CHESTER—Holy Trinity Church: Wo. Aux., Sp. for Miss Wood for library, Wuchang, Hankow.........
MISCELLANEOUS—"A Friend," China, $1.50; Indian education, South Dakota, $1.50; Sp. at discretion of Dr. Correll, Kyoto, $1.50.........
Wo. Aux., Sp. for Miss Wood for library, Wuchang, Hankow, $25; "E. S.," "Kinsolving" scholarship, Brazil, $10; Training-school, Sendai, Tokyo, $10; Training-school, Hankow, $5; Cuban Guild, Sp. for Bishop Knight Divinity-school, Cuba, $17....................
Junior Aux., Misses Brock and Welsh, Gen., $10; Mrs. Parker S. Williams, Sp. for Archdeacon Atwood, St. Luke's Sanitarium, Phoenix, Arizona, $25..............

Pittsburgh

Ap. $1,011.29; *Sp.* $348.74

BELLEVUE—Epiphany: Gen...........
BROWNSVILLE—Christ Church: Frn., $15; Sp. for St. Paul's College, Tokyo, $5.....................
FREEPORT—Trinity Church S. S.: Sp. for St. John's School, Cape Mount, Africa ....
GREENVILLE—St. Clement's: Gen.....
JOHNSONBURG—St. Martin's: Frn....
KITTANNING—St. Paul's: Dom. and Frn.........................
NORTH GIRARD—Grace: Gen.........
PITTSBURGH—Ascension S. S.: Sp. for light, St. John's School, Cape Mount, Africa ....
Calvary: Bishop Rowe, Alaska......
Christ Church (Alleghany): Alaska, $6; Frn., $21.04...............
Emmanuel Church (Alleghany): Frn.
St. Andrew's: Sp. for Bishop Rowe, Alaska ....
Trinity Church: Sp. for Bishop Rowe, Alaska ....
RIDGWAY—Grace S. S.: Sp. for lamps for St. John's School, Cape Mount, Africa ....
SEWICKLEY—St. Stephen's: Gen.....
TARENTUM—St. Barnabas's S. S.: Sp. to aid in installing acetylene gas plant, St. John's School, Cape Mount, Africa..................

Quincy

Ap. $60.29

GALESBURG—Grace: Gen............
GALVA—Holy Communion: Gen.......
KEWANEE—St. John's: Gen.........
PEORIA—St. Paul's: Gen...........

Rhode Island

Ap. $2,737.34; *Sp.* $485.30

ASHTON—St. John's Chapel: Gen.....
BRISTOL—St. Michael's S. S.: "St. Michael's" (Graduate) scholarship, South Dakota..................

Trinity Church: Dom............... 15 00
GREENVILLE—St. Thomas's: Gen..... 21 50
LONSDALE—Christ Church: Frn...... 88 24
MIDDLETOWN—Holy Cross: Gen...... 6 09
NEWPORT—Emmanuel Church: Gen.. 71 33
Trinity Church: Gen............... 108 74
PORTSMOUTH—St. Mary's: Gen...... 4 11
PROVIDENCE — All Saints' Memorial:
  Sp. for Bishop Rowe, Alaska....... 120 30
Grace: Wo. Aux., St. Augustine's
  School, Raleigh, North Carolina... 25 00
St. James's S. S.: Hospital work,
  China 12 50
St. John's: Dom., $349.04; Frn.,
  $396.38; Gen., $253; Sp. for Bish-
  op Rowe, Alaska, $10; S. S., hos-
  pital work, China, $2.50........... 1,010 92
St. Stephen's: Dom., $593; Indian,
  $45.25; Frn., $382.85; Gen., $27.65;
  Mr. and Mrs. R. H. S. Goddard, $30,
  Miss Mary Grinell, $20, Miss Mary
  L. Austin, $5, Sp. for Expansion
  Fund, St. John's University, Shang-
  hai 1,103 75
"A Friend," Sp. for Bishop Rowe,
  Alaska 250 00
E. R. Gardiner, Sp. for Bishop Rowe,
  Alaska 50 00
WICKFORD—St. Paul's: Frn......... 65 16
MISCELLANEOUS—Rt. Rev. W. N. Mc-
  Vickar, D.D., St. Paul's School, Law-
  renceville, Southern Virginia...... 100 00
Miss E. C. McVickar, St. Augus-
  tine's School, Raleigh, North Caro-
  lina 100 00

South Carolina

Ap. $343.97; *Sp.* $89.49

BARNWELL—Holy Apostles': Gen..... 6 11
BEAUFORT—St. Helena's. Wo. Aux.,
  Gen............................. 10 00
BRADFORD SPRINGS—St. Philip's: Gen. 5 00
CAMDEN—Grace: Wo. Aux., Sp. for
  "Bishop Howe" cot, St. Mary's Or-
  phanage, Shanghai, $2; Bible-wom-
  an, Kyoto, $5; Bible-woman, Han-
  kow, $5......................... 12 00
CHARLESTON—Grace: Juniors, Bishop
  Capers Day-school, Wuchang, Han-
  kow 4 00
Holy Communion: Wo. Aux., Sp. for
  "Bishop Rowe" scholarship, Anvik,
  Alaska 10 00
St. Luke's: Wo. Aux. (of which Junior
  Aux., $5), Gen., $12.31; Sp. for
  Miss Carter, Alaska, $5.05........ 17 36
St. Paul's: Gen.................... 9 80
Branch Wo. Aux., Gen............. 4 80
CHERAW—St. David's: Wo. Aux., as-
  sistant for Miss McCullough, Porto
  Rico, $3; Bible-women, Kyoto, $2;
  N. S. Wilson Day-school, Hankow,
  $2; Sp. for "Bishop Howe" cot, St.
  Mary's Orphanage, Shanghai, $10.. 17 00
COLUMBIA—Trinity Church: Wo. Aux.,
  Bible-woman, Kyoto, $5; Bible-
  woman, Hankow, $5; Sp. for
  "Bishop Howe" cot, St. Mary's
  Orphanage, Shanghai, $5.......... 15 00
EDISTO ISLAND—Trinity Church: Wo.
  Aux., Gen....................... 15 25
EXCHANGE—Mrs. W. E. Fripp, Gen.. 10 00
FLORENCE—St. John's: Asheville..... 4 60
JOHN'S ISLAND—St. John's: Wo. Aux.,
  Bible-woman, Hankow, $5; Gen.,
  $20 .... 25 00
LAURENS—"E. B. S.," Gen.......... 8 00
PINOPOLIS—Babies' Branch, Gen..... 4 60
SPARTANBURG—Advent: (of which Wo.
  Aux, $30), Gen., $133.50; Sp. for
  Zang Zok Station Equipment Fund,
  Shanghai, $47.44................. 180 94
Mrs. John B. Cleveland, Sp. for
  Zang Zok Station Equipment Fund,
  Shanghai 10 00

SUMMERVILLE—St. Paul's: Dom., $30;
  Frn., $30....................... 60 00
WREN—"Our Mite-chest," Dom. and
  Frn. 4 00

Southern Ohio

Ap. $260.05; *Sp.* $110.00

CINCINNATI — Emmanuel Church:
  Woman's Guild, work in Alaska.... 3 35
Grace (Avondale): Gen........... 92 10
Hyde Park Mission: Gen.......... 7 00
St. Paul's Cathedral; Gen......... 119 21
DAYTON—Christ Church: Wo. Aux.,
  St. Agnes's Guild, Sp. for Dr.
  Angie Myers's work, St. Elizabeth's
  Hospital, Shanghai............... 10 00
MARIETTA—St. Luke's: Gen......... 24 64
ZANESVILLE—St. James's: Gen...... 13 75
MISCELLANEOUS — Branch Wo. Aux.,
  Sp. for Bishop Brooke, Oklahoma.. 100 00

Southern Virginia

Ap. $355.95; *Sp.* $337.45

BUCKINGHAM Co.—Emmanuel Parish:
  Dom., 60 cts.; Frn., 59 cts........ 1 19
CAMPBELL Co.—Church of the Good
  Shepherd (Lynchburg): Sp. for St.
  Paul's College, Tokyo............. 5 00
Grace Memorial (Lynchburg): Gen.. 50 00
Grace S. S. (Lynchburg): Hospital
  work in China, $3.25; Sp. for St.
  Paul's College, Tokyo, $9.......... 12 25
Grace (Mount Athos): Dom., 50 cts.;
  Frn., 50 cts..................... 1 00
DINWIDDIE Co.—St. John's (Peters-
  burg): Frn...................... 26 75
St. Paul's: Gen., $200; Sp. for St.
  Paul's College, Tokyo, $287.45..... 487 45
ELIZABETH CITY Co.—Chapel of the
  Centurion S. S.* (Fort Monroe):
  Gen. 18 11
St. John's (Hampton): Gen........ 25 15
NORFOLK Co.—St. John's (Ports-
  mouth): Gen., $5.50; Second Circle,
  Wo. Aux., Sp. for personal work of
  Rev. Mr. Gill, Yang Chow, Shang-
  hai, $6......................... 11 50
St. Paul's (Norfolk): Second Circle,
  Wo. Aux., Sp. for support of a
  child, in Mr. Ishii's Orphanage,
  Tokyo 5 00
Miss Hoggard (Norfolk), Sp. for
  Bishop Rowe, Alaska............. 25 00
WARWICK Co.—St. Paul's (Newport
  News): Frn..................... 25 00

Springfield

Ap. $145.39

ALTON—St. Paul's: Gen............ 39 11
CARROLLTON—Trinity Church: Gen... 3 15
CHESTERFIELD—St. Peter's: Gen..... 14 40
DANVILLE—Holy Trinity Church: Gen. 10 00
EDWARDSVILLE—St. Andrew's: Gen... 4 60
GRANITE CITY — St. Bartholomew's:
  Gen. 7 90
JERSEYVILLE—Holy Cross: Gen...... 4 50
MATTOON—Trinity Church: Gen..... 1 00
SPRINGFIELD—St. Paul's: $49.71, Wo.
  Aux., $10, S. S., $1.02, Gen....... 60 73

Tennessee

Ap. $266.71

BOLIVAR—St. Katherine's School: Wo.
  Aux., Gen...................... 2 75
CHATTANOOGA — Christ Church: Wo.
  Aux........................... 10 00
St. Paul's: Gen.................. 26 23
KNOXVILLE—Epiphany: $22.60, Wo.
  Aux., $5, Gen................... 27 60
St. John's S. S.: Hospital work in
  China 10 00

MEMPHIS—*Calvary*: Wo. Aux., Gen.. 40 00
Grace: Wo. Aux., Gen.............. 12 50
St. Luke's: Wo. Aux., Gen.......... 9 38
St. Mary's Cathedral: Wo. Aux., Gen.. 12 50
NASHVILLE—*Advent*: Wo. Aux. "Bishop Quintard" scholarship, St. Mary's Hall, Shanghai..................... 50
Christ Church: Wo. Aux. (of which Junior Aux., $12.50), Gen........ 25 00
St. Peter's: Gen.................... 5 00
ST. ELMO—*Thankful Memorial*: Wo. Aux., Gen....................... 2 50
SEWANEE—*Otey Memorial*: Gen...... 25 00
Branch Wo. Aux., "Bishop Quintard" scholarship, St. Mary's Hall, Shanghai, $1.25 ; Gen., $5........ 6 25
Missionary Society, pledge for year 1908-09, Gen................... 20 00
SOUTH PITTSBURG—*Christ Church*: $10, Wo. Aux., $10, Gen........ 20 00
TRACY CITY—*Christ Church*: Wo. Aux., Gen...................... 1 50
MISCELLANEOUS — Fairmont School, Junior Aux., Gen............... 10 00

Texas

Ap. $166.23

ANGLETON—*Church of the Holy Comforter*: Junior Aux., Gen.......... 8 00
AUSTIN—*St. David's*: $13.82, Altar Society, $26.25, Gen.............. 40 07
GALVESTON — *Trinity Church*: Wo. Aux., Gen....................... 18 00
GROESBECK—*Trinity Church*: Gen... 3 30
MATAGORDA—*Christ Church*: Gen.... 4 25
SAN AUGUSTINE—*Christ Church*: Gen. 16 00
TEMPLE—*Christ Church*: Gen........ 23 36
MISCELLANEOUS—Junior Aux., "Bishop Kinsolving" scholarship, St. Mary's Hall, Shanghai, $30.25 ; "Bishop Aves" scholarship, Hooker Memorial School, Mexico, $23.............. 53 25

Vermont

Ap. $90.79 ; *Sp.* $121.25

BURLINGTON—*St. Paul's*: Henry Wells, Sp. for Church Extension Fund, Porto Rico..................... 10 00
CANAAN—*St. Paul's*: Gen........... 3 00
MIDDLETOWN SPRINGS—*St. Margaret's*: Gen. 5 00
NORTHFIELD—*St. Mary's*: China..... 2 60
NORWICH—*St. Barnabas's*: Gen..... 3 00
RANDOLPH CENTRE—*Grace*: Gen...... 2 75
RUTLAND—*Trinity Church*: Sp. for St. Paul's College, Tokyo............. 6 25
ST. ALBANS—*St. Luke's*: Frn., $3.44 ; "A Communicant," Gen., $25 ; S. S., Sp. for Bishop Kinsolving, Brazil, $15 ; Sp. for Bishop Griswold, Salina, $15...................... 58 44
WINDSOR—*St. Paul's*: Gen., $22 ; Wo. Aux., Bible-woman, China, $24..... 46 00
MISCELLANEOUS—Branch Wo. Aux., Sp. for Rev. R. C. Wilson's work, Shanghai 75 00

Virginia

Ap. $1,230.11 ; *Sp.* $575.63

ALBEMARLE Co.—*Emmanuel Church, Greenwood Parish*: Gen., $10 ; Sp. for St. Paul's College, Tokyo, $109.25 .... 119 25
Grace (Campbell) : Gen............. 5 89
(Cismont)—"A Friend," for Rev. H. St. George Tucker's work, Tokyo.. 10 00
ALEXANDRIA Co. — *Grace* (Alexandria) : Gen....................... 17 50
St. Paul's: Alaska, $4.94 ; Indian, $5.82 ; Africa, $3.04 ; Frn., $6.05 ; Gen., $73.52.................... 93 37
CAROLINE Co. — *St. Peter's* (Port Royal) : Wo. Aux., Sp. for insurance

of Rev. W. C. Brown, Brazil....... 1 00
FAIRFAX Co.—*Church of the Holy Comforter, McGill Parish* : Gen.... 16 00
Zion Church, Truro Parish : Gen..... 17 00
St. Timothy's (Herndon) : Miss Edith Fitzhugh, Gen.................. 1 00
FAUQUIER Co. (Marshall)—Mrs. J. M. Rainey, Sp. for "Mary Fitzhugh" scholarship in Mr. Ishii's orphanage, Tokyo 22 00
Trinity Church, Meade Parish : Gen... 3 00
GREENE Co.—*Whittle Memorial and Missions* : Gen.................. 17 64
HENRICO Co.—*Emmanuel Church* (Richmond) : Frn., $400 ; Brotherhood of St. Paul, for St. Paul's College, Tokyo, $10 ; Junior Aux., for St. James's Hospital, Anking, work, Tokyo, $5................ 420 00
Epiphany (Richmond) : Brotherhood of St. Paul, Sp. for Rev. R. A. Walke, Tokyo 2 00
Grace (Richmond) : "Jeannie Alston" scholarship, $60, "Little Anna" scholarship, $60, both in St. Mary's School, South Dakota ; Anking hospital, Hankow, $240 ; Brazil, $160.. 400 00
Holy Trinity Church (Richmond) : Brotherhood of St. Paul, $11, John Gordon Meyers, through Brotherhood of St. Paul, $1.25, Sp. for Rev. R. A. Walke, Tokyo ; Brotherhood of St. Paul, Sp. for feed for Bishop Rowe's dogs, Alaska, $10........ 22 25
Monumental (Richmond) : Brotherhood of St. Paul, Gen., $5 ; Sp. for Rev. R. A. Walke, Tokyo (of which S. S., $5.67), $7.67................ 12 67
St. James's (Richmond) : Wo. Aux.,. Sp. for Dr. Brown for Peterkin Library, Brazil.................. 25 00
St. John's (Richmond) : Dom., $20 ; Frn., $40..................... 60 00
Weddell Memorial S. S. (Richmond) : Sp. for one light for St. John's School, Cape Mount, Africa....... 10 55
(Richmond)—Brotherhood of St. Paul, Sp. for Rev. R. A. Walke, Tokyo.... 10 91
(Richmond)—"One Interested," for St. Paul's College, Tokyo........... 20 00
PRINCE WILLIAM Co.—*Trinity Church* (Manassas) and *St. Ann's* (Nokesville) : Frn...................... 19 68
SPOTTSYLVANIA Co. — *St. George's* (Fredericksburg) : Gen.......... 114 03
St. George's Chapel : "A Family," Sp. for St. Paul's College, Tokyo...... 15 00
MISCELLANEOUS—Branch Wo. Aux., Sp. for St. Paul's College, Tokyo, $200 ; Junior Aux., Sp. for Rev. R. A. Walke, for St. Paul's College, Tokyo, $100 ; Sp. for work of Rev. E. J. Lee, Anking, Hankow, $50... 350 00

Washington

Ap. $3,843.06 ; *Sp.* $22.00

WASHINGTON (D. C.) — *Ascension* : Dom. and Frn................... 100 00
Christ Church (Georgetown) : Gen.... 90 00
Epiphany : Dom., $800 ; Frn., $1,200 ; S. S., hospital work, China, $15.45.. 2,015 45
Grace S. S. (Georgetown) : Hospital work, China.................... 23 05
Grace : S. B. Taylor, Sp. for Church Extension Fund, Porto Rico........ 2 00
St. Andrew's : Gen............... 242 00
St. George's Mission : Gen.......... 9 00
St. John's : Frn................... 21 46
St. Margaret's : Gen.............. 1,000 00
St. Mark's S. S. : Hospital work, China 14 10
St. Thomas's : Mrs. A. S. Worthington, Sp. for Church Extension Fund, Porto Rico..................... 5 00
Rock Creek Parish : Gen........... 300 00

scholarship, Utah, $40; Wo. Aux., Japanese Bible-woman, Honolulu, $15; Alaska Supply Fund, $18; Philippine insurance, $3; St. Augustine's School, Raleigh, North Carolina, $8.50; St. Paul's School, Lawrenceville, Southern Virginia, $8.50; Bible-woman, Hankow, $15; Cathedral School, Havana, Cuba, $3; Sp. for Building Fund, St. Margaret's School. Tokyo, $40.60............ 211 60

WARE—*Trinity Church*: Gen., $63; Wo. Aux., Cathedral School, Havana, Cuba, $5................ 68 00

WILLIAMSTOWN—*St. John's*: Wo. Aux., Sp. for Building Fund, St. Margaret's School, Tokyo............ 10 00

Mrs. C. N. Mason, Sp. for equipment for two students of St. John's University, Shanghai............... 400 00

C. L. Maxcy, Sp. for Expansion Fund, St. John's University, Shanghai 5 00

WORCESTER—*All Saints'*: Sp. for Bishop Rowe, Alaska............... 200 00

St. George's Chapel: St. Margaret's Guild, St. Luke's Hospital, Shanghai 5 00

St. John's: Wo. Aux., Alaska Supply Fund, $5; Bible-woman, Hankow, $5 10 00

St. Matthew's: Wo. Aux., Bible-woman, Hankow, $5; Cathedral School, Havana, Cuba, $3; Japanese Bible-woman, Honolulu, $8; Alaska Supply Fund, $8; St. Augustine's School, Raleigh, North Carolina, $4; St. Paul's School, Lawrenceville, Southern Virginia, $4............ 32 00

St. Luke's S. S.: Sp. for St. Paul's College, Tokyo................... 10 00

United S. S.'s of Worcester, Sp. for Bishop Rowe, Alaska............ 36 48

Western Michigan

Ap. $202.80; Sp. $53.00

ALLEGAN—*Church of the Good Shepherd*: Gen., $31.80; Wo. Aux., "Bishop Gillespie" scholarship, St. Margaret's School, Tokyo, $5; "Bishop McCormick" scholarship, St. Mary's School, South Dakota, $10 .... 46 80

BATTLE CREEK—*St. Thomas's*: Sp. for St. Paul's College, Tokyo......... 3 00

ELK RAPIDS—*St. Paul's*: Gen........ 3 07

GRAND RAPIDS—*St. Mark's Pro-Cathedral*: Wo. Aux., "Bishop Gillespie" scholarship, St. Margaret's School, Tokyo, $20; Sp. for Bishop Rowe's Hospital, Circle City, Alaska, $10; Mrs. L. Boltwood, Sp. for "C. C. Comstock" bed, St. Matthew's Hospital, Fairbanks. Alaska, $40; Junior Aux., "Guy Van Gorder Thompson" scholarship, St. John's School, Cape Mount, West Africa, $25 .... 95 90

HASTINGS—*Emmanuel Church*: Wo. Aux., "Bishop McCormick" scholarship, St. Mary's School, South Dakota, $5; "Sarah K. Bancroft" gift, St. Hilda's School, Wuchang, Hankow, $5.................... 10 00

MARSHALL—*Trinity Church*: Wo. Aux., "Sarah K. Bancroft" gift, St. Hilda's School, Wuchang, Hankow........ 5 00

NILES—*Trinity Church S. S.*: Gen.... 1 00

PETOSKEY—*Emmanuel Church*: Wo. Aux., "Sarah K. Bancroft" gift, St. Hilda's School, Wuchang, Hankow.. 5 00

Miss Lucy B. Rice, Gen.......... 10 00

STURGIS—Rev. J. E. Walton, Dom., $25; Frn., $25................. 50 00

MISCELLANEOUS—Offering at Council of Fifth Department, Wo. Aux., Gen. 26 93

Western New York

Ap. $1,943.05; Sp. $4,680.12

ALBION—Mrs. S. J. Allen, Sp. for Alaska	1 00	
BATAVIA—"A Friend," Sp. for Rev. R. E. Wood, Wuchang, Hankow....	5 00	
BELFAST—Grace: Gen..............	72	
BUFFALO—Ascension: Frn., $20; Gen., $42.72; Sp. for Bishop Rowe, Alaska, $10	72 72	
Grace: Dom. and Frn..............	85 00	
St. John's: Gen....................	136 40	
St. Mary's-on-the-Hill: Sp. for Bishop Rowe, Alaska (of which Mrs. Sarah E. Smith, $50; George H. Boxall, $4; Wo. Aux., $10; In Memoriam, $5)	166 06	
St. Simon's: Frn...................	25 00	
Trinity Church: Sp. for Bishop Rowe, Alaska	417 31	
E. L. Allen, Sp. for Bishop Rowe, Alaska	1 00	
W. E. Townsend, Sp. for Bishop Rowe, Alaska....................	1 00	
George T. Ballachey, Sp. for Bishop Rowe, Alaska...................	5 00	
Mrs. John D. Larkin, Sp. for Bishop Rowe, Alaska...................	100 00	
Buffalo Section, Wo. Aux., Sp. for Bishop Rowe's hospital, Ketchikan, Alaska	124 00	
Mass Meeting of the S. S.'s, Sp. for Bishop Rowe, Alaska............	51 57	
CANASERAGA—Trinity Church: Frn....	8 00	
CLIFTON SPRINGS—St. John's: Frn....	5 85	
CORNING—Christ Church: Gen........	13 85	
EAST RANDOLPH—St. Paul's: Frn....	2 28	
GENEVA—Trinity Church: Dom., $46.25; Sp. for St. Paul's College, Tokyo, $55.05; "A Friend," Sp. for St. John's University Expansion Fund, Shanghai, $5...................	106 30	
HOLLEY—St. Paul's: Gen............	6 50	
HONEOYE FALLS—St. John's: Dom., $4.10; Frn., $8.12..............	12 22	
LOCKPORT—Grace: Miss C. D. Douglas, Sp. for Expansion Fund, St. John's University, Shanghai..............	2 00	
OLEAN—St. Stephen's: Dom..........	19 19	
RANDOLPH—Grace: G. F. Mussey, Sp. for Expansion Fund, St. John's University, Shanghai...............	2 00	
ROCHESTER—Christ Church: Mrs. J. F. Alden, Sp. for Expansion Fund, St. John's University: Frn.........	5 00	
Epiphany: Frn.....................	33 00	
St. Luke's: Frn., $42.06; Sp. for Bishop Rowe, Alaska, $72.63; Minnie A. Bellows, Sp. for Rev. C. E. Betticher, Jr., Fairbanks, Alaska, $5; Wo. Aux., Gen., $59; S. S., St. Elizabeth's School, South Dakota, $33.34; Boone University, Wuchang, Hankow, $33.33; St. Mary's Hall, Shanghai, $33.33..............	278 71	
St. Paul's: Philippines, $307.11; Miss Carter's salary, Alaska, $600; Sp. for Rev. Dr. Pott, St. John's University, Shanghai, $147; Sp. for work of Rev. Dr. Correll, Kyoto, $200; Sp. for Bishop Payne Divinity-school, Southern Virginia, $100; Sp. for St. Paul's College, Tokyo, $16.20; Sp. for Bishop Rowe, Alaska, $113.30; "A Member," Sp. for building hospital ward for women and children at Wusih, Shanghai ("Caroline M. Watson Memorial"), $3,000.............	4,483 61	
St. Thomas's: Frn..................	4 10	
WATKINS—St. James's: Dom., $10.29; Frn., $13.54...................	23 83	
MISCELLANEOUS — Branch Wo. Aux., Philippines, $100; St. Paul's School, Lawrenceville, Southern Virginia, $25; Church Training-school for		

Bible-women, Shanghai, $25; Lawrenceville, Southern Virginia, $50; Cape Mount, West Africa, $50; Yangchow, Shanghai, $50; Windsor Day-school, Wusih, Shanghai, $50; Sp. for Bishop Wells, Spokane, $50. ... 400 00
"S.," Sp. for Expansion Fund, St. John's University, Shanghai....... 25 00

West Texas

Ap. $25.45; Sp. $7.00

GOLIAD—St. Stephen's: Gen..........	8 00	
GONZALES—Church of the Messiah: Gen.	1 95	
KENDALL CO.—St. Helena's S. S.: Sp. for Miss Farthing, Alaska, for her use as she thinks best..........	13 00	
KERRVILLE—Junior Aux., Sp. for St. Luke's Hospital, Ponce, Porto Rico..	4 00	
LAREDO—Christ Church: Gen........	10 00	
SAN ANTONIO—St. Philip's: Gen.....	5 50	

West Virginia

Ap. $191.87; Sp. $5.00

BLUEFIELD—Christ Church: Sp. for work of Rev. J. M. B. Gill, Shanghai	5 00	
CHARLESTON—St. Matthew's: "In Memoriam," Gen...................	2 00	
FAIRMONT—Christ Church: Wo. Aux., Gen.	16 00	
FORT SPRING—Church of the Holy Comforter: Frn.................	1 00	
NEW MARTINSVILLE—St. Ann's: Colored, $5.35; Frn., $7.36; Gen., $1.22	13 93	
PARKERSBURG—Church of the Good Shepherd: Dom., $6; Frn., $1.20; Gen., $5.50; work among Colored people, $6.50...................	138 00	
RONCEVERTE—Incarnation: Gen......	1 35	
SISTERSVILLE—St. Paul's: Honolulu, $1.60; Philippines, $1.61; Gen., $2.07	5 28	
UNION—All Saints': Gen., $2.43; Frn., $3.97; Colored, $2.35; Brazil, $1.06; Cuba, $1.05; S. S., Mexico, $1.73; Porto Rico, $1.72..............	14 31	

Missionary Districts

Alaska

Ap. $133.70

DOUGLAS—St. Luke's: Gen..........	9 00	
EAGLE—St. Paul's: Gen............	7 50	
KETCHIKAN—St. John's: Gen........	10 00	
POINT HOPE—St. Thomas's: Gen.....	15 00	
TANANA—St. James's: Gen..........	53 60	
Church of Our Saviour: Gen........	17 25	
VALDEZ—Epiphany: Gen............	6 35	
MISCELLANEOUS — Archdeaconry of Southeast, Gen..................	15 00	

Arizona

Ap. $15.40

PHOENIX—Trinity Church: Dom., $8; Frn., $7.40................... 15 40

Asheville

Ap. $34.12

ARDEN—Christ Church: Frn., $2.55; Gen., 25 cts....................	2 80	
BREVARD—St. Philip's: Frn.........	11 06	
CHUNN'S COVE—St. Luke's: Frn., 50 cts.; Gen., $1...............	1 50	
FRANKLIN—St. Cyprian's: Gen......	50	
GASTONIA—St. Mark's: Dom........	25	
GRACE—Gen. Dom., $1.30; Frn., $1.25; Gen., $1.95..............	4 50	
GREEN RIVER—St. Joseph's: Frn.....	50	
St. Andrew's: Frn.................	50	

4 51	
1 50	
50	
1 00	
50	
25	
2 00	
1 00	
25	
1 00	
2 00	
182 45	
30 00	
20 00	
10 00	
2 00	
12 00	
2 00	
68 15	
8 55	
50	
1 70	
15 60	
14 05	
5 00	
15 00	
10 00	
5 00	
10 00	
10 00	
10 50	
10 00	
15 00	
5 00	
5 00	
10 00	
70 00	
6 50	
5 00	
22 00	
25 07	
1 50	
2 25	
4 30	
1 50	
2 00	
5 00	
4 00	
4 85	

Oklahoma
Ap. $112.58

BARTLESVILLE—*St. Luke's*: Gen...... 10 00
CHECOTAH—*St. Mary's*: Gen......... 2 25
FAY—*St. Luke's Indian Mission*: Gen.. 4 00
GUTHRIE—*Trinity Church*: Gen...... 5 36
OAK LODGE—*St. John's*: Gen........ 75
OKLAHOMA CITY—*St. Paul's Cathdral*:
Gen. 42 00
PURCELL—*St. James's*: Gen......... 2 00
MISCELLANEOUS—"Thankful," Frn.... 5 00
Gen. 41 22

Sacramento
Ap. $101.65

BENICIA—*St. Paul's*: Gen............ 2 50
GRASS VALLEY—*Emmanuel Church*:
Gen. 6 85
MARYSVILLE—*St. John's*: Gen....... 5 95
NEVADA CITY—*Trinity Church*: Gen.. 5 30
OAK PARK—*Christ Church*: Gen..... 25
PETALUMA—*St. John's*: Gen......... 55 80
SACRAMENTO—*St. Paul's*: Gen...... 25 00

South Dakota
Ap. $67.24; *Sp.* $7.00

CHAMBERLAIN—*Christ Church*: Gen... 2 60
FORT PIERRE—*St. Peter's Mission*:
Gen. 3 46
GROTON—Wo. Aux., Sp. for St. Paul's
College Fund, Tokyo.............. 2 00
HILL CITY—Episcopal Guild, work in
South Dakota................... 5 00
LEMMON—Gen. 4 50
SELBY—*Christ Church*: Gen........ 1 75
SISSETON AGENCY—*St. James's*: Frn.. 6 07
St. John Baptist's: Frn............. 3 44
St. Luke's: Frn.................... 5 02
St. Mary's: Frn.................... 4 60
STANDING ROCK MISSION—*St. Eliza-
beth's*: Babies' Branch, Indian work,
South Dakota, $4; Akita Kindergar-
ten, Tokyo, $5; medical work among
children, Africa, $3.27; Gen., $3;
Sp. for "Little Helpers'" cot, St.
Agnes's Hospital, Raleigh, North
Carolina, $5.................... 20 27
YANKTON MISSION—*Church of the
Holy Name* (Choteau Creek): Wo.
Aux., Gen...................... 13 00
St. Philip's (White Swan): Wo. Aux.,
Gen. 2 53

Southern Florida
Ap. $40.00; *Sp.* $100.00

LAKELAND—*All Saints*: "Albert and
Rhett" scholarship, St. Hilda's
School, Wuchang, Hankow........ 25 00
MAITLAND—Mrs. Henry B. Whipple,
Sp. for Bishop Whipple Memorial,
Havana, Cuba.................... 100 00
OCALA—*Grace*: "A Member," Frn. and
Dom. 15 00

Spokane
Ap. $2.50

MABTON—*Mission*: Gen............. 2 50

The Philippines
Ap. $202.08

MANILA—*Cathedral of St. Mary and
St. John*: Gen.................. 152 08
MISCELLANEOUS—Wo. Aux., Gen..... 50 00

Utah
Ap. $30.26

EUREKA—*St. Andrew's*: Gen........ 2 50
FORT DUCHESNE—Gen.............. 1 35
LOGAN—*St. John's*: Gen........... 7 08
MYTON—Gen. 1 00
SALT LAKE CITY—*St. Paul's*: Gen.... 10 00
THEODORE—*St. Paul's*: Gen........ 68
VERNAL—*St. Paul's*: Gen.......... 2 65
MISCELLANEOUS—Gen. 5 00

Western Colorado
Ap. $31.50

DURANGO—*St. Mark's*: Gen.........	26	25
MANCOS—*St. Paul's*: Gen..........	1	50
RICO—Gen.	3	75

Wyoming
Ap. $40.91

BAGGS—*St. Luke's*: Wo. Aux., Gen....	2	50
CHEYENNE—*St. Mark's*: Wo. Aux., Frn.	5	00
LANDER—*Trinity Church*: Gen.......	1	05
RAWLINS—*St. Thomas's*: Wo. Aux., Frn.	10	00
SARATOGA—*St. Barnabas's*: Wo. Aux., Gen.	5	00
SHERIDAN—*St. Peter's*: Wo. Aux., Gen.	5	00
SUNDANCE—*Church of the Good Shepherd*: Frn..................	4	36
WIND RIVER—*Church of the Redeemer*: Frn.	8	00

Foreign Missionary Districts
Ap. $232.67 ; *Sp.* $5.00

Brazil

RIO GRANDE AND SAN JOSÉ DEL NORTE— S. S.: Japan....................	41	99

Cuba

CHAPARRA—Miss A. M. Reed, Sp. for work in Mayaguez, Porto Rico......	5	00

France

NICE—*Church of the Holy Spirit*: Gen.	41	35
PARIS—*American Church of the Holy Trinity*: Frn·················	149	33

Miscellaneous

Interest — Dom., $1,717.23; Frn., $529.42; Gen., $67.03; Sp., $340.11; Specific Dep., $1,116.39...........	3,770	
United Offering of Wo. Aux., on account of appropriation to September 1st, 1910, Dom., $3,500; Frn., $3,500	7,000	
League for Eastern Oregon, Sp. for Bishop Paddock, Eastern Oregon...	50	
Through Bishop Courtney, Sp. for Manila Cathedral site, Philippine Islands	67	
"J. E.," for Indian missions, Alaska.	1	

Legacies

CONN., HARTFORD—Estate of Mrs. Lucretia Terry..................	96	
CONN., NEW HAVEN—Estate of Mrs. Lucy H. Boardman, Dom........	5,000	
N. H., PORTSMOUTH—Estate of Rev. Henry E. Hovey...............	1,000	
N. Y., DOVER PLAINS—Estate of Rev. William R. Harris..............	20	
VA., CULPEPER CO., RAPIDAN—Estate of Margaret W. Crenshaw........	200	
W. N. Y., BUFFALO—Estate of Mrs. Harriet L. Smith, Dom., $1,536.11; Frn., $1,536.11..................	3,072	
Receipts for the month..........	$134,28	3
Amount previously acknowledged..	591,16	2
Total received from Sept. 1st, 1909	$725,45	5

SUMMARY OF RECEIPTS

Receipts divided according to purposes to which they are to be applied	Received during February	Amount previously Acknowledged	Tot
1. Applicable upon the appropriations of the Board.	$ 97,611 09	$179,170 26	$276,81 35
2. Special gifts forwarded to objects named by donors in addition to the appropriations of the Board.	26,142 19	73,862 72	100,00 91
3. Legacies for investment................	....	165,000 00	165,00 00
4. Legacies, the disposition of which is to be determined by the Board at the end of the fiscal year.	9,388 22	53,438 67	62,82 89
5. Specific Deposit.......................	1,116 43	119,692 17	120,80 60
Total...................	$134,287 93	$591,163 82	$725,48 75

Total receipts from September 1st, 1909, to March 1st, 1910, applicable upon the appropriations, divided according to the sources from which they have come, and compared with the corresponding period of the preceding year. Legacies are not included in the following items, as their disposition is not determined by the Board until the end of the fiscal year.

OFFERINGS TO PAY APPROPRIATIONS

Source	To March 1, 1910	To March 1, 1909	Increase	Dec	
1. From congregations.......................	$145,819 12	$135,095 43	$10,723 69	$...	..
2. From individuals....................	20,687 62	35,252 75	....	14,5	13
3. From Sunday-schools...................	4,019 41	5,368 04	....	1,3	63
4. From Woman's Auxiliary...............	22,941 12	27,769 48	....	4,8	36
5. Woman's Auxiliary United Offering........	40,000 00	20,000 00	22,000 00	....	..
6. From interest........................	40,509 41	37,301 21	3,208 20	...	..
7. Miscellaneous items.....................	834 67	2,337 69	....	1,5	02
Total....................	$276,811 35	$263,124 60	$13,686 75		

APPROPRIATIONS FOR THE YEAR

SEPTEMBER 1ST, 1909, TO AUGUST 31ST, 1910
Amount Needed for the Year

1. To pay appropriations as made to date for the work at home and abroad......	$1,202,6	59
2. To replace Reserve Funds temporarily used for the current work............	32,5	83
Total...	$1,235,9	
Total receipts to date applicable on appropriations......................	276,3	
Amount needed before August 31st, 1910.................................	$ 959,	57

THE

Spirit of Missions

AN ILLUSTRATED MONTHLY REVIEW
OF CHRISTIAN MISSIONS

May, 1910

CONTENTS

The Subscription Price of THE SPIRIT OF MISSIONS is ONE DOLLAR per year. Postage is prepaid in the United States, Porto Rico, the Philippines and Mexico. For other countries in the Postal Union, including Canada, twenty-four cents per year should be added.

Subscriptions are continued until ordered discontinued.

Change of Address: In all changes of address it is necessary that the old as well as the new address should be given.

How to Remit: Remittances, made payable to George Gordon King, Treasurer, should be made by draft on New York, Postal Order or Express Order. One and two cent stamps are received. To checks on local banks ten cents should be added for collection.

All Letters should be addressed to The Spirit of Missions, 281 Fourth Avenue, New York.

Published by the Domestic and Foreign Missionary Society.

President, RIGHT REVEREND DANIEL S. TUTTLE, D.D. *Secretary*, ————
Treasurer, GEORGE GORDON KING.

Entered at the Post Office, in New York, as second-class matter.

GOLDEN HILL PARK, YANGGLOW.

HE SPIRIT OF MISSIONS

AN ILLUSTRATED MONTHLY REVIEW
OF CHRISTIAN MISSIONS

VOL. LXXXV.   **May, 1910**   No. 5

THE PROGRESS OF THE KINGDOM

ONE item in the business transacted by the Board at its last meeting will be of unusual and widespread interest. It is that the Right Rev. Arthur Selden Lloyd, D.D., Bishop Coadjutor of Virginia, was unanimously elected to fill the place made vacant by the resignation of Bishop Scarborough.

Dr. Lloyd Returns to the Board

How much this means, not only to those hosts of friends to whom Dr. Lloyd has endeared himself in the Missions House and elsewhere, but also to the successful carrying on of the Church's mission, must be evident to all who have knowledge of these matters. One great regret which was felt in losing Dr. Lloyd from the General Secretaryship arose from the fact that both by temperament and experience he was peculiarly fitted to render large service in guiding the action of the Church's executive in mission work. His circuit of the world and visitation of the mission field had of course added to and intensified his capabilities in this direction. To lose his presence from the councils of the Board was a loss indeed. This in a measure is made good to us by his election and appointment upon the Advisory Committee. With satisfaction we add that Bishop Lloyd has accepted this election and will immediately take a share in the work where he is so peculiarly qualified to serve the Church.

AGAIN our mission work has suffered through one of those sudden outbreaks which have more than once marked our experience in China. As our readers already know through the daily press, on April 15th our mission in Changsha—the last of four to suffer thus—was totally destroyed, and Rev. and Mrs. A. A. Gilman, our foreign workers there, together with all the other missionaries, were obliged to leave the city. The destruction of property seems to have been complete. The medical and educational work conducted by Yale University and some other missionary centres have suffered more seriously than we in that they had larger and more complete missionary plants. Ours, while excellent so far as the real estate was concerned, was really disgraceful in the matter of buildings, the work being carried on in two native houses.

Destruction at Changsha

The Rev. Mr. Gilman, who had but just returned to Changsha from his furlough in this country, has been earnestly petitioning for $30,000 with which to carry' out a complete programme for equipment and enlargement at Changsha. This amount would not all be needed at once, but should be contributed in such a way that the means for taking the successive steps planned might be assured. When leaving this country, Mr. Gilman felt that for the proper equipment of the mission there should be an immediate gift of $5,000 and an additional $5,000 each year f·r the next five years, making $30,000 in all. How much more will be needed to make good the loss suffered by this misfortune we cannot at this time state, but the personal loss to Mr. and Mrs. Gilman is complete. Everything they had was destroyed. It is matter for thankfulness that no foreigner suffered physical injury and all the missionaries are being comfortably cared for in Hankow.

L

The Underlying Cause

We used to speak of these sudden outbreaks as "unaccountable and fanatical," but as time goes on and foreigners come better to understand the native point of view, it is not so strange that a starving populace, suffering—or imagining that they suffer—from the misgovernment and extortion of high-placed officials, should make its protest in deeds of violence. In few, if any, instances of such uprisings has the underlying motive been a bitter opposition to Christianity. More frequently it has been some such cause as in the present case, where it is reported that corrupt officials have cornered the rice market and so brought the people face to face with starvation.

In other words, the chief causes have been almost always social and political, but rarely religious. The property of the foreigner, and particularly that of the missionary, has been first attacked because it afforded the safest and most effective means of calling public attention to conditions and of creating difficulty for the officials against whom the mob was angered. The local officials are.

held responsible by the central government for any disturbance in their district, and failure to suppress an uprising is always punished by degradation from office. Probably missionary property would be less carefully guarded than that of the government, and its destruction would inevitably and immediately embroil China with foreign governments who are bound to protect the lives and property of their citizens. We urge, therefore, that this matter be not misunderstood, and that "no man's heart fail him" because of this. It is cause for regret that the poor fellows in China should have tried to relieve their hunger-pangs by burning down missionary property, and that they will probably suffer bitterly at the hands of an exasperated government. Undoubtedly steps will be taken to prevent the repetition of the affair, which, in a place so recently opened to Christianizing influences as Changsha, is not without precedent.

We do not for a moment suppose that this riot is the prelude of an uprising like the Boxer outbreak of 1900. That was rendered possible by the fact that many officials of the government sympathized with the aims of the Boxers. No earnest attempt was made to oppose the spread of the outrages until too late. The humiliation which China suffered on that occasion has not been forgotten, and wherever local disturbances occur at the present time the government is most prompt in suppressing them and cashiering the officials in whose district they take place. It is certain that in this matter there is no connivance on the part of the government with the lawless element in China.

What Will We Do About It?

It is to be regretted that mission work must receive a check by the destruction of the plants where it was carried on but that the Christian bodies who have put their hands to the plough in Changsha will redouble their efforts and reinforce their staff we do not doubt. In every like instance good has come out of the temporary evil, and those who in

Easter Feast large amounts of missionary money are received, in addition to
the sums designated for the Children's
Lenten Offering. Therefore the figures
of one year against another may not in
this instance be a fair basis for deduction. Nevertheless, there is little question that the treasury is beginning to
feel some of the good results flowing
from the Laymen's Missionary Movement, and that there is every reason to
believe that the present hopeful condition will continue, with the possible
meeting of the Church's obligations. We
say "*possible* meeting," because only by
the most faithful and systematic effort
on the part of each diocese and parish to
discharge that portion of the obligation
resting upon it, will such a result be
reached. It is as yet not a time for congratulation, but for an earnest girding
up of the loins in the hope of running
the race well to the end.

INEVITABLY, those who form the
outposts of that army which is
moving forward to conquer the world for
Christ will always
Church Unity feel most keenly the
in China difficulties and discouragements aris-
ing from a divided Christendom. Face
to face with the entrenched religions
and philosophies of ancient peoples in
alien lands, they yearn for the com-
panionship and support of their fellow-
Christians. By the very nature of
things these men, even more than others,
are moved to echo our Lord's Prayer
"that they all may be one."

Nor is it for themselves alone, or
chiefly, that they feel this need. They
realize how hard—indeed how impossible—it is to explain to their converts
the reasons for those divisions which
have rent the Church. In so many instances these have ceased to be living
issues that we sometimes find difficulty
in explaining them to ourselves. Unquestionably, a divided Christianity is at
a great disadvantage in its effort to make
our Lord known to the world.

Because of this the longing for unity seems to be deepest and strongest in the mission fields. Missionaries are everywhere pondering and debating it more and more earnestly. They cannot give up the effort, or rest content with things as they are. They cannot wish to perpetuate in other lands the divisions which we find so unfortunate in our own. Particularly is this true in China and Japan, where the forces are so few, the struggle so fierce and the promise of victory so splendid.

Recent Utterances Concerning Unity
In this issue we print an article on Church Unity, by the Bishop of Shanghai. It appeared, in company with others bearing upon the same subject, in *The Chinese Recorder and Missionary Journal* for February. One reading this symposium of articles is impressed by two facts: first, that there is a deepening sense of the vital need of unity, and, secondly, that there is on all sides a franker recognition of its real difficulties. Both these are hopeful signs. The time when denominational diversity was championed as a desirable thing has long passed; and with it is also passing the disposition to say in offhand fashion that we have unity enough already, being virtually at one in all essential teachings and purposes. It is a deeper, more serious, and, may we say, an honester purpose that lies behind these later utterances. There is no display of merely oratorical good-will. The writers do not confine themselves to general expressions indicating the desirability of Church unity. They strive earnestly to go to the root of the matter and demonstrate both the need of its attainment and the exceeding difficulty of the problem.

So far as the Chinese Christian is concerned, one article, written by a Chinese pastor, sets forth his position. The writer asserts—what must be readily recognized—that the questions which

have divided the Christian Church and have given titles to several denominations are of little or no interest to the Chinese Christians, who belong to these different denominations because they were so led to Christianity, but have inherited none of the traditions, and in most cases do not share the temperament which brought these sects into being. As the editor of *The Recorder* succinctly remarks: "To begin our work in China with the presumption that we are facing denominational instincts among the Chinese is wrong in point of fact. The Chinese churches are denominational only so far as the foreign missionaries have made them so."

Then, too, there is the point of view of the missionary sent out by his denominational board, but compelled, as he would not be in this country, to give a reason for the creed which he teaches and the particular doctrine for which his people stand. This is well voiced by another writer, a clergyman under the London Missionary Society, who calls attention to the significant fact that unity is not likely to come by a process of mutual surrender, but by an emphasis upon vital truths. "As students of philosophy," he says, "we have early to learn that truth is not found in a compromise between two apparently opposite statements, but rather in a deeper unity that can hold the apparent opposites together; and it may be that as students of ecclesiastical systems we are to find the one true Body of Christ is an organism more complex than can be fully represented by any one Christian organization." It is this writer who, with keen analysis and broad sympathy, goes on to speak of the more intimate bearings of the question. From his discussion of the matter we cannot refrain from making the following quotation:

"While, however, we loyally guard those principles for which God has made us severally responsible, let us see to it that we are not wasting time and energy in guarding that which is no longer a living issue. And let us not impose

He rejoiced in the work of the Evangelical Alliance, he labored for the Central China Religious Tract Society, he
was the friend of every undenominational and interdenominational effort,
yet the Church that he labored to build
up was on Methodist lines, and the sum
total of the best work of his life was all
bound up with the Methodism that was
so dear to him. And I think we all loved
him the more for it. Then again we
had Bishop Ingle, A man of more massive sincerity I never knew, and his influence on the Central China Mission
was strong and deep. Alike in the common worship in Kuling and in our
monthly prayer-meetings at Hankow, he
loved to join. He deeply valued the
prayer of the united Christian body and
desired both to join in those prayers and
to receive the benefit that he realized resulted from them. He looked sympathetically upon the whole work, and I
believe as truly loved as he was beloved
by every member of the Central China
missionary community. Yet Bishop
Ingle was an Anglican through and
through, and could not have done his
best work on any other than Anglican
lines. May I refer for a moment to the
beloved leader for fifty years or more of
our London Mission, Griffith John? It
was his joy to be of assistance to any
mission. In the earliest days at Hankow he started the English liturgical
service, which he gladly handed over to
an Episcopal clergyman as soon as the
community was able to arrange for his
support. He rejoiced to transfer his first
convert at Hankow to the Wesleyan
Mission to be trained as an evangelist
when the Wesleyan Mission was started
in Hankow, and this man, Mr. Chu, was
subsequently ordained as the first Methodist pastor in Hankow. Yet it is absolutely certain that Griffith John could
not have done his life work on either
Anglican or Methodist lines. He felt at
home in the somewhat modified Congre-
gationalism that is typical of the work
of the London Missionary Society, and I
do not think he could have done equally
good work under any other system."

Surely we are coming upon better and more hopeful days for the cause of Christian unity when Christian men can so frankly recognize the great good which God has accomplished through the instrumentality of organizations and methods different from their own, and we may feel thankful that Bishop Graves, in the article which will be found elsewhere in this issue, has, with his usual wisdom and sanity, spoken in behalf of the Anglican Communion, voicing at the same time her sympathy toward all those who love and labor for the extension of Christ's Kingdom, and her unchanging loyalty toward the truth which she has received and of which she is made the trustee—not for her own aggrandizement but for the benefit of the whole world.

M R. WILLIAM T. ELLIS, the Philadelphia journalist and a Presbyterian, who recently spent a year looking

An Opinion upon St. John's University

"into the entire missionary enterprise, both as a principle and in practical operation," says in a letter to a friend in this country:

"St. John's University, Shanghai, is unquestionably the greatest educational institution in China. I have talked over the subject with many men of many denominations, and they all concede this. It has stood for the highest ideals of culture and of Christianity. The thoroughness of its work and the excellence of its standing have commanded the allegiance of the very best class of Chinese in the empire. Doubtless you know something about the standing its graduates have attained in the universities of America, when they have come here, for postgraduate work. There is really little I can say about the university, except in sheer eulogy, and that might sound fulsome. I have been chagrined to find many Episcopalians on this side of the water who did not know of this immense work which their Church is doing on the other side of the world. It seems to me that if St. John's were the property of

my Church, I would do a deal of bragging about it—in fact, I have bragged not a little about it as it is. You cannot make too strong a plea for the university, nor too strong a presentation of the character of its faculty, and of the work which it does."

The Rev. Dr. Pott, president of St. John's University, has been in this country during the winter, speaking on behalf of the Expansion Fund. This is to be used in paying for additional property and in erecting new buildings for the preparatory department. Of the $65,000 about $15,000 has been given. It is imperative that the remaining $50,000 should be secured without delay. Unfortunately the accommodations at St. John's have never been abreast of the need. Although Mann Hall, the newest building, is barely more than completed, more students are seeking admission than can be received. Bishop Graves, writing just after the China new year entrance examinations says: "It is evident that the plan of doubling the capacity of the present buildings to provide for 750 instead of 375 students is wise and timely. There is no institution of higher learning in this country where an investment of $65,000, or of twice that amount, will provide so much enlargement. There is no point in the whole mission field where the expenditure of $65,000 will exert greater influence for the world's present and future good than right at St. John's, Shanghai. That $50,000 still needed should be forthcoming without delay."

¶

I N the weekly Church journals announcement has already been made of the Conference for Church Work to be held at Cambridge, Mass., July 9th-24th, 1910. An excellent and helpful programme has already been decided upon and will be published in our next issue. At this time we can only briefly call attention to the conference and commend the purpose for which it stands.

THE SANCTUARY OF MISSIONS

O SPIRIT of the living God,
 In all thy plenitude of
 grace,
Where'er the foot of man hath trod,
' Descend on our apostate race.

Convert the nations! far and nigh
 The triumphs of the cross record;
The Name of Jesus glorify,
Till every people call Him Lord.
—*James Montgomery.*

INTERCESSIONS

"May it please thee"—
 To bless and reward all those
who carry thy word to the Indian
tribes of this land, and to raise up
for them helpers from among thy
people. (Pages 340 and 371.)
 To forgive those who in their ignorance count themselves as the
enemies of thy Gospel, to protect
them against the consequences of
their own mistaken acts, and to turn
their hearts at length toward thee.
(Page 334.)
 To comfort with a sense of thy
presence and to support with thy
power thy messengers in the lonely
outposts of heathen lands. (Page
354.)
 To send forth laborers into thy
harvest and especially to call by thy
Spirit those helpers who are at this
• time critically needed to carry forward thy great work.
 To bring good out of the present
evil and crown with completer success our mission work in Changsha.
(Page 333.)
 To guide and direct to thy honor
and glory the impulse which is moving the Christian laymen of this
land.
 To prosper the efforts of those
who seek to bring to the students of
Japan the treasures of wisdom and
knowledge which are hidden in
Christ Jesus.

THANKSGIVINGS

"We thank thee"—
 That now as on the day of Pente-
cost the Gospel which thou hast
committed to thy Church has power
over the lives and hearts of men.
 For the deliverance of thy servants our missionaries in Changsha
who have been "in perils among the
heathen."
 For the awakening desire throughout the Church to have a share in
sending thy message abroad. (Page
335.)
 For every impulse which draws
the hearts of Christians closer together in the hope of final unity in
thee. (Page 359.)
 That those who stand nearest to
the great problems of our Mission
are also those who have cheerful
courage and a good hope. (Page
348.)
 That in the habitations of cruelty
there shines the purifying light of
thy Gospel, before which old shapes
of foulness disappear. (Page 357.)

PRAYER

FOR THE UNITY OF THE SPIRIT

O GREAT Lord of the Harvest,
 send forth, we beseech
thee, laborers into the harvest of
the world, that the grain which is
even now ripe may not fall and
perish through our neglect. Pour
forth thy sanctifying Spirit on our
fellow-Christians, and thy converting grace on the heathen. Raise up,
we beseech thee, a devout ministry
among the native believers, that all
thy people being knit together in
one body in love, thy Holy Church
may grow up into the measure of
the stature of the fulness of Christ,
through Him Who died and rose
again for us all, the same Jesus
Christ our Lord. *Amen.*

¶ Persons wishing to join the "Church Prayer League" of intercession
for missions should address the Rev. Harvey Officer, O.H.C., Holy Cross,
West Park, Ulster County, N. Y.

THROUGH BAXTER PASS
Up its winding line crawls the little narrow-gauge train

A MEDICAL MISSIONARY IN UTAH

By Mary Latimer James, M.D.

PROBABLY few persons living in the East realize that there are places in the United States as remote from the railroad as the Uintah Indian Reservation of northeastern Utah. This tract of land is about the size of the State of Connecticut. Though consisting chiefly of cobblestones and sage-brush desert, it is the home of about 1,100 Indians and more than twice as many white settlers, the latter being largely Mormons. Even this desert affords pasturage for innumerable sheep and cattle. The Church supports three missionaries to work on this reservation, the Rev. M. J. Hersey at Randlett, and Miss Camfield and myself at Whiterocks. At the latter settlement there are also four other workers, selected by Bishop Spalding, but holding government positions in the Indian School.

The trip to the reservation offers more novelty than most journeys now possible in this country. One leaves the main railway at Mack, Colorado, to take the

little narrow-gauge train over Baxt[Pass to Dragon, Utah, a mining can fifty-four miles northwest of Mack. Tl pass is about 8,000 feet above sea lev and commands a wonderful view of t surrounding mountains. It is frequer ly blocked during the winter months, that mail and all traffic are held up f a few days or a week or more, at a tin Dragon is situated in a deep valley, wi the mountains rising abruptly on sides. Yet, beneath the bleak sides these mountains are rich mines of g sonite, a mineral peculiar to this s tion of the country. It is used in t manufacture of paints, varnishes a imitation rubber.

From Dragon a stage line runs Fort Duchesne, a distance of sevel miles. Snow, floods, or dust, at the c ferent seasons of the year, make wonder which is the least objectiona time for the trip. For most of the v the road winds through the "bad lan[so-called because at present irrigat[

(340)

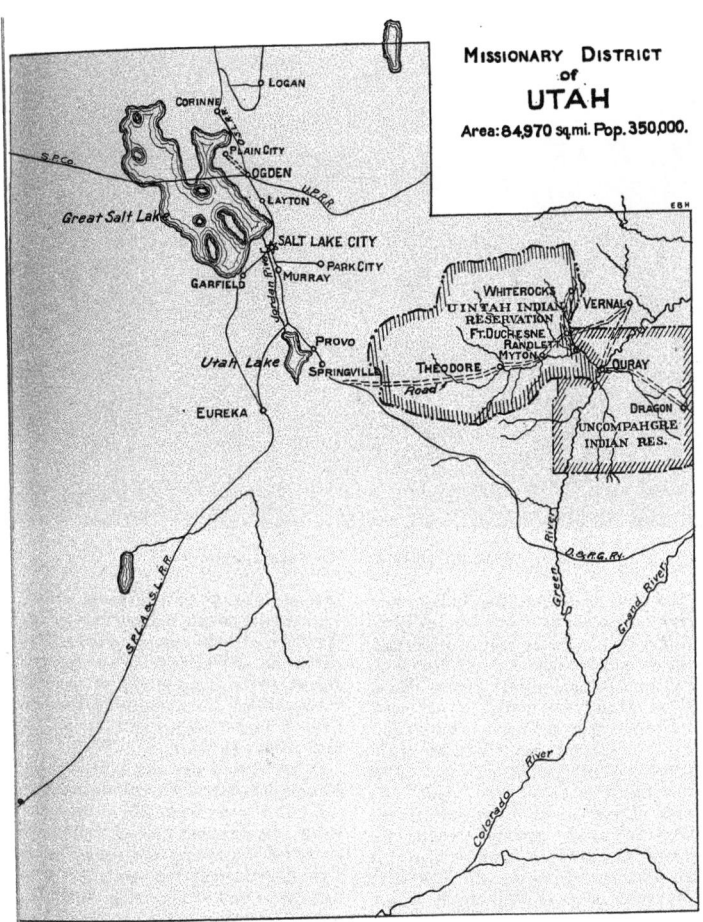

MISSIONARY DISTRICT
of
UTAH
Area: 84,970 sq.mi. Pop. 350,000.

ems impossible. Though rocks, sage-
rush and prairie dogs in most places
e the only product of the country, the
der inhabitants of the reservation al-
ays resent any insinuation on the fer-
lity of the land. They vehemently de-
are that the soil is good, and all it
eds is water. I am of the opinion that
e Sahara Desert would have been re-
aimed long ago had Americans in-
bited Africa.

The scenery is varied by deep canyons,
steep sandstone cliffs, sandy mountain
slopes, and broad expanses of plain, with
wonderfully tinted sand-formations in
the distance. Occasionally one comes to
a river, bordered by a fringe of stunted
trees.

Nineteen miles south of Fort Duchesne
the traveller crosses Green River, by ice,
or rowboat, or cable-ferry, according to
the time of year. On the northern bank

STAGING THROUGH THE "BAD LANDS"

of the river is Ouray, the Indian sub-
agency, a cluster of a few log buildings
and one or two frame houses. Another
fourteen miles brings one to Randlett,
with its chapel and missionary residence.
Several other frame buildings are scattered over this extensive "town-site."
Here one begins to see cultivated fields,
watered, of course, by ditches. Fort
Duchesne is reached that night. Its
square of wooden buildings encloses an
attractive "parade ground" where the
industry of man has made a grove of
trees grow out of the desert. The drive
of fourteen miles to Whiterocks, which

one can take the next morning with th
mail carrier, seems a small matter afte
the journey of the preceding day. White
rocks, the seat of the Indian agency, i
almost at the extreme end of the rese
vation, about ten miles from the beat
tiful Uintah Mountains. It is 6,00
feet above sea level. .

In the agency live about seventy whi
persons, almost all Government emplo
ees. At the northern end of the villag
is the Government School, with abo
seventy-five boarding and six day pupi
Two stores supply the wants of the se
tlement as well as is possible so far fro

FORT DUCHESNE
A little island of fertility in the midst of the desert

THE STORE AT WHITEROCKS, UTAH

A characteristic scene. Observe the stolid-looking customers and the disconsoate dogs

he railroad. Freight is most uncertain, that there may be a famine of almost nything at any time. For instance, om October to January, the village was ithout kerosene oil a large part of the me.

Although the climate is dry and invigorating, there is a great deal of illness on the reservation, due to the diet nd unhygienic manner of living. Most the people are very poor and live in nts or tiny log cabins. Coal and wood are both so expensive that they economize fuel by barring out all the fresh air possible. Also the clothing is frequently insufficient, especially for a region where the thermometer hovers around zero during the winter, often falling far below that. Beef, potatoes, apples and canned goods are almost the only food obtainable except in summer and early fall. The people are able to raise some vegetables and fruit, but few of them have yet constructed cellars in

A SAGEBRUSH RANCH

INDIANS READY FOR A DANCE

which to store these for the winter. Herds of cattle belonging to the Indians wander over the plains and mountains, but milk is extremely scarce because the cows are not milked. Eggs are almost unknown articles in winter. The food brought into the country is naturally very high. In fact, prices of most things on the reservation almost rival Alaskan prices.

Under such circumstances it is very hard to combat illness, for practically everything suitable for a patient's diet is unobtainable. Also it is impossible to give proper attention to all the sick people, for they are scattered over such a vast area. Could those needing most attention be gathered in a hospital, and could this hospital keep its own cows and chickens, and raise and store its own vegetables, a far greater amount could be done with the same expenditure of labor. Not only would we hope to help those already ill, but also to prevent disease by teaching the people, through object lessons, how to meet the requirements of hygiene. By a hospital, too, we would hope to get closer to the people than we are able to do at present, and to teach them more of the love of Christ, which is, of course, the primary object of all our

work. There is no hospital on the reservation, or, in fact, within miles of it, except the army hospital, which can take in civilians only occasionally in case of emergency.

Some medical work can, of course, be carried on even in the camps and cabins, but one is thwarted at every turn by ignorance and superstition. The Indians are not inclined to take one's medicine if they are very sick, because they doubt its efficiency. If they do take it and begin to get better they think there is no need of continuing the treatment, hence relapses are frequent, especially in chronic cases. On the other hand, if they notice no improvement after one or two doses they are inclined to give up the trial. Others, having been cured of one trouble by a certain medicine, declare it "heap good" and want the same thing every time. Another of their peculiarities is that they resent examinations of any part of the body other than that affected. For example, for indigestion, headache, etc., they object to an examination of the tongue or pulse, and for pneumonia or bronchitis they sometimes refuse to let their temperature be taken anywhere but in the armpit. Except in the case of babies, it is generally impossible to per

turned, a few days later, she was walking around!

One conspicuously successful case does a great deal toward winning the confidence of the Indians. Of course, overcoming their superstition and ignorance is a matter of years, but the work among them is not without hope.

Our desire is to erect a hospital in the near future—this summer, if possible. For this purpose we need at least $6,000, as building materials are very expensive so far from the railroad. The little mission building at Whiterocks, which has long been used for hospital purposes, is entirely inadequate for extension of the work such as we hope for under a medical missionary. Besides this, located as it is, at almost the extreme northern end of the reservation, it is not central enough to reach the scattered population of Indians and white settlers. The people realize the need of a hospital so strongly that we are likely to have little difficulty in getting land given to us wherever we want to build, so long as we do not choose a location owned by the Government. Already we have had more than one offer of land.

A TYPICAL PATIENT

IN THE COURTYARD OF THE NEW ST. AGNES'S SCHOOL
The pupils are out on the lawn engaged in washing their clothes

ANKING AFTER A YEAR

By the Reverend Edmund J. Lee

TO the returning resident of Anking the improvements during the past year are everywhere apparent. The principal thoroughfares have been newly paved, and rickshaws now ply over them, contesting successfully the monopoly formerly held by the sedan chair. Policemen in foreign-style uniforms stand at the corners. Many of the important buildings of the city are lighted with electricity, and electric street lamps, it is said, are soon to follow. A number of pretentious, if not imposing foreign-style buildings have been built within the year. In short, everything indicated that the wonderful movement of modern progress in China was being felt here with full force.

On entering our mission compound the material changes there burst suddenly upon us. Luxuriant grass covered our erstwhile barren lawn; vines, now flaming red and wonderful, made the bare new walls look picturesque. Flowers and shrubs were everywhere, making our compound look a little paradise here in the midst of the heathen city. Over

between the hospital and our residence one could see piles of brick and lumber marking the place where stood the house of Mr. Nien, which was our Naboth's Vineyard when I left for America last year. Over to the right the new St. Agnes's School showed above its surrounding wall; while far to the back of our splendid fifteen-acre compound we could see the new St. Paul's School, the building up to the second story, and next to it the teachers' houses, already completed, with the school chapel, also under construction, farther to the right. We wish contributors to the Anking Fund to realize that their investments are not being laid up in a napkin, and that no time is being lost in making them productive.

St. Paul's School itself was still in its unsatisfactory quarters on the old compound, pending the completion of the new buildings. It is doing as well as it can under this handicap. St. Agnes' School for girls, while still small, is growing and healthy. Its attractive quarters leave nothing to be desired in

(346)

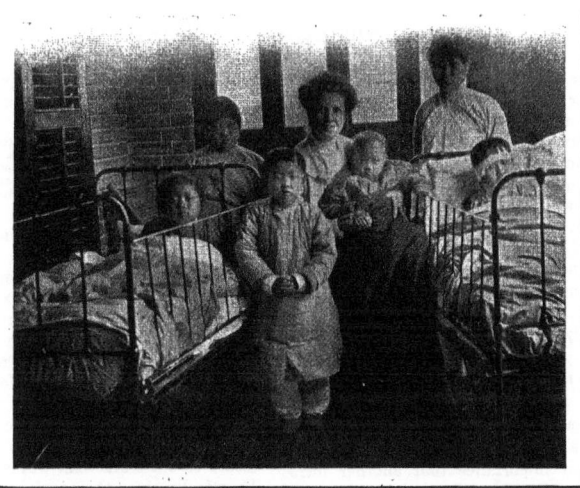

Miss Barber on the veranda surrounded by some of the child patients

he material line. The children seem
nthusiastic both at work and play. As
hey pass my study to prayers every day,
notice that all the faces are bright and
miling, including that of the sweet-
aced little teacher, who walks with con-
ious pride behind. St. Francis once
aid that a cheerful face was the sign of
good conscience and a great defence
gainst the devil. At any rate, we think
hat in our schools it may be taken as an
ndication that things are going well.
t. Agnes's School is at present under
he direction of Miss Elizabeth Barber,
ho was obliged to add this to her other
uties when Mrs. McCarthy left on fur-
ugh last summer. This makes it im-
ossible for her to give much time to her
egular evangelistic work among the
omen, a work for which one worker
iving all her time is utterly inadequate.
can be seen how urgent is the need
r another woman worker to be added
our staff.

St. James's Hospital we found in ex-
llent condition so far as its reputation
d the character of its work is con-
rned. A staff of competent nurses has
en trained, and the work is being kept
up to the high standard of efficiency
with which the hospital began its career
in its new quarters. Its reputation has
been steadily growing, and difficulty is
experienced in holding down the work
within limits where it can be properly
handled. Dr. Taylor told me recently
that he had done more than fifty operations under anesthesia during the past
month; that every bed in the hospital
was filled, and that he had a waiting
list of patients eager to come in. Out-
calls to wealthy and official families have
become so numerous as to be a severe
drain on the time of the physician in
charge; these are at times to the yamens
of the highest officials. Shortly after
my arrival I noticed one afternoon an
imposing sedan-chair carried by four
bearers and followed by a military escort
approaching the hospital. It proved to
contain two little maidens of about five
years each, one being the grand-daughter of the great governor of the province
himself, who was sending her to the
hospital for treatment.

The trouble with the hospital lies in
the inadequacy of the present staff to
meet the demands made on them for the

(347)

proper running of the institution. Dr. Taylor, who is the only foreign physician, is beginning to break down under the strain of work and responsibility, and unless relief comes soon it is merely a question of time when it will be necessary for him to stop work altogether. This will simply mean the closing of the hospital.

In addition there is also urgent need for another trained nurse to be added to the hospital staff. The two nurses already here have both done splendid work and are exceptionally efficient. Even they, however, are unable fully to meet the strenuous demands of the hospital work. The furlough of one is due next summer, and it is of the greatest importance that another nurse be in the field at that time to take her place.

The evangelistic work in Anking has been to a large extent lying fallow during the last year, so far as human agencies are concerned. We have had no resident foreign clergyman and the native priest is a semi-invalid and unable to undertake much work. The result has been no great numerical progress, though I think that even in this line the year has marked advance. At any rate, we think the prospects excellent for the future and are setting ourselves to work with energy and hope to realize them.

Since the above article was written the even foreboded therein has come to pass. Dr. Taylo has been compelled, as a result of overstrair to leave his work and take a year's furlougl En route to this country, he writes from th steamer as follows:

"Our hospital is the only one in quit a large city on the Yangtse River an for several hundred miles round abou We treat about 18,000 to 20,000 patien a year and the work is growing tr mendously. In addition we have ha two foreign-trained nurses, who und me had charge of the schools for men ar women nurses. These nurses are need now in mission hospitals all over Chin and in time to come will be more ne essary to our work than Chinese doctor Practically since the opening of the n hospital I have had the burden of tl work, and you can well imagine that has proved too much for me. I will n attempt to reopen without a colleagu and if possible he should leave at on so as to get in almost a year on langua study before I return. I can assure a doctor who wants to put his life whe it will count for the most helpfuln that he can get supreme satisfaction China. It is the greatest place for w in the world, and if I had ten lives put every one in China."

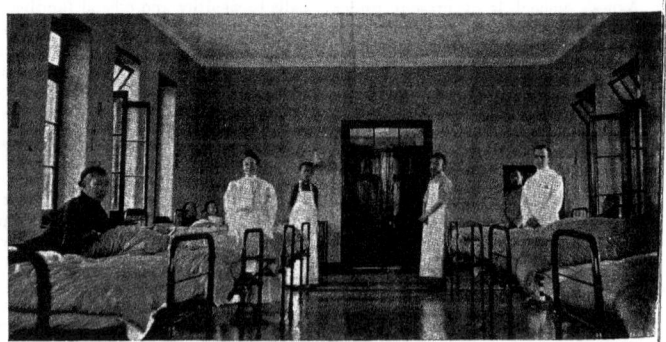

IN THE MEDICAL WARD

A STUDENTS' CHURCH FOR STUDENTS IN JAPAN

By the Reverend J. A. Welbourn

ON Advent Sunday, November 28th, 1909, Bishop McKim consecrated St. Timothy's Church, which is to become a centre for the work in Hongo, the northernmost district of Tokyo. The congregation dates back to 1903, when I first came to live in Hongo. The Rev. Barnabas T. Sakai had just started a dormitory for university students, and I came to work with him. Some work here, begun years before, had been abandoned, so we had to begin at the beginning. For some years one room of my Japanese house was fitted up as a chapel, and for the last year or two we have rented a small house in the neighborhood. This served for the Christians, and we have gradually gathered a congregation of the members of our Church in this district. It was, however, of no use at all as a means of aggressive evangelization; for this a church was absolutely necessary.

Several years ago a strong committee was formed in the United States through which an appeal was issued to college men and students for this church in one of the great student districts of Tokyo. Several thousand dollars was

(349)

received—Yale and the University of Pennsylvania each giving $1,000, and lesser contributions were given in the names of Columbia, Harvard, Johns Hopkins, Kenyon, University of Virginia, University of Texas, and the following schools: Groton, Hoosac, Howe, Pomfret, Shattuck, Yeates and Hannah More Academy. In addition to this a grant of $6,000 was received from the Men's Thank-offering, which with general gifts made the church possible. The plans for the church were kindly given by Mr. Julian Le Roy White, of Baltimore, and were those made for St. Stephen's church, Baltimore, by Mr. Vaughan.

As the map shows, the church is excellently situated; indeed, it is on one of the very few sites that now are suitable for a church without being too near that of some other Christian body St. Timothy's is on a street much frequented and yet not noisy, facing the grounds of the Government college, so that it is seen a block off as one approaches from the south. It is in the centre of Hongo and toward the north is a growing residential section, while just opposite is a group of boarding-houses in which live several hundred students.

Each district of Tokyo has its own characteristics. Nihonbashi and Kyobashi (in the latter are Trinity Cathedral and our Church schools) are the great mercantile districts; in Hongo and Fukagawa, across the river, are the factories and the homes of the working classes; Akasaka, Azabu and Kojimachi are the fashionable residence quarters Kanda has miles of shops and also numberless schools, with more students in than any other ward of the city, nearly 20,000, while Hongo with its 143,000 people has, besides the mansions of a few great noblemen, the houses of people of moderate means, and especially noted for being the seat of the Imperial University, the head the Government educational system, with 4,000 students, and has also a Government college with 1,000 more. Certainly more than 15,0 students live in Hong 600 of whom are in the college dormitory just across from our church.

Such is our field—from very poor or very rich, but a district which is perhaps the greatest intellectual centre in the empire Surely it has been well put a church worthy its cause in such

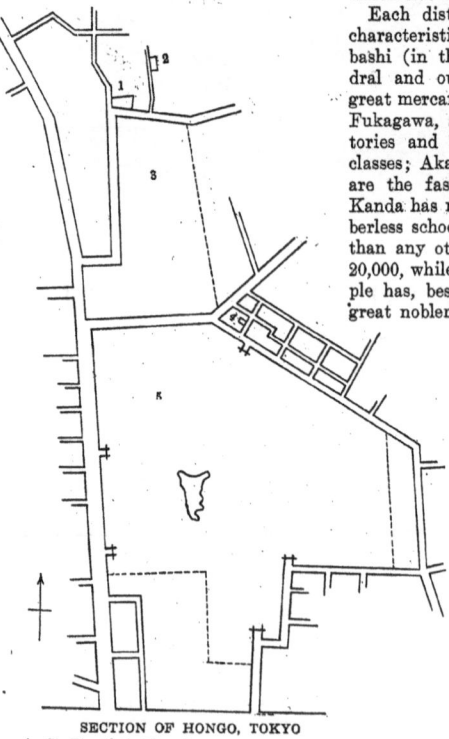

SECTION OF HONGO, TOKYO

1 St. Timothy's Church
2 Doshikwai, boarding-house for University students
3 Government College
4 House of Rev. J. A. Welbourn
5 Imperial University

GOVERNMENT COLLEGE GROUNDS—OPPOSITE THE CHURCH

important place and undoubtedly a great work lies before it. At the fiftieth anniversary evangelistic meetings and at other special times we had fine congregations made up of both students and townspeople. Mr. Yamagata and Mr. Kobayashi, who are good preachers, come on certain Sunday evenings, and we shall have special preaching meetings from time to time. One young man, who said he had never been to a church before St. Timothy's was built, has just been admitted catechumen, and Mr. Nuki, the catechist, is instructing some half-dozen other enquirers who will, we trust, be the first-fruits of the new church.

Quite apart from the students, how-

GATEWAY OF IMPERIAL UNIVERSITY

ever, the Church has in one way certainly begun its work among the children. We have a Sunday-school with an attendance of sixty to seventy every Sunday—even after Christmas! It is taught by the catechist and three young students, and, as I play the organ, it is run, at present at any rate, entirely by men. That is not saying that a woman would not be a help, but we have no Bible-woman as yet and no one among our few Christian women who could teach in it.

The Sunday-school is enough to rejoice one's heart and if once you heard the children sing, learning a new hymn in two or three trials, you would never say, as people have said, that the Japanese have no liking or gift for music.

At Christmas time these children, more than half of whom only came to Sunday-school in October, surprised me by what they could do. The Japanese are exceedingly clever at anything of this kind and the children told the Christmas story in many forms—as a recitation, a reading from the Bible, a composition, or really as if telling a story. The big ones and the little tots sang carols, and three little girls had a dialogue made up of texts from the Bible about the love of God, ending by all bowing with the words "God is Love," which sounded very sweetly in the Japanese. Last of all there came in a group of children with lanterns, each showing how he gave forth his light in the world.

It was our first Christmas in the new church, and surely no church could begin its work more appropriately than by telling to some of God's little ones of His love in the sending to them of His Son.

The chancel is furnished by memorials, many given by New York laymen. Tablets commemorating the gifts of the various schools and colleges are to be placed in the church.

THE SECRETARY OF THE SOUTHWEST

UNDER the above title a brief sketch appeared in our last issue, which should have been illustrated by the accompanying picture. As it arrived too late we print it here, in order that our Church-folk generally may become better acquainted with the Rev. Mr. Silver, who has begun under such favorable conditions his promising work as secretary of the Seventh Department, including the dioceses and missionary districts of Missouri, Kansas City, Kansas, Salina, Oklahoma and Indian Territory, Arkansas, New Mexico, Dallas, West Texas, Texas and Louisiana.

It should be explained that Mr. Silver here appears in his uniform as a chaplain in the United States Army, which position he resigned to accept the secretaryship.

THE YANGCHOW SCHOOL

FORWARD IN NORTH KIANGSU

By Bishop Graves and Mr. Ancell

Two years ago the new mission in North Kiangsu was inaugurated by means of a gift from the Men's Thank-offering. The pioneers were the Rev. B. L. Ancell, who had successfully carried through a similar mission in Soochow six years before, and the Rev. T. L. Sinclair, who had but recently come to China. These notes record some of the progress made.

A GOOD house has been secured in the city of Yangchow, the central station of the mission, and more than a thousand services and meetings have been held in it. Many trips have been made to the country round about. A flourishing school has been established. The Rev. J. M. B. Gill and three Chinese catechists have joined the staff. A large plot of ground has been purchased. Some prejudice has been broken down, and some friends have been made.

Regular work has been begun in the great city of Nanking. This puts our mission in the capitals of each of the five provinces in which we work—Kiangsi, Kiangsu, Anhui, Hupeh, Hunan.

The city of Taichow has been made the objective of an effort at extension. Two travelling catechists were sent on a prospective tour, taking with them Mr. Ho, a faithful old Christian who has been a teacher in our mission in Soochow. Mr. Ho is to settle in Taichow, opening a small school if it seems well, but primarily to make friends and "talk the doctrine." He is a devout man, and willingly gives up the much easier work in the school in Soochow, saying that he is glad of the opportunity to go off to Taichow, and it may be "eat a little bitterness" for the sake of the Saviour who suffered for him. It will be a hard and lonely life, and Mr. Ancell asks the prayers of friends for this old man, off among unsympathetic strangers, for the sake of the Gospel. The catechists will visit him regularly, and Mr. Sinclair will also go frequently. Indeed, he has already made acquaintance with the place, and may spend a good deal of his time there.

The Yangchow school has been a decided success. Beginning with just two pupils, there were thirteen before the first half-session closed. The new term began with twenty-five enrolled. The growth will be steady. The income for the last term has been about $350, which would be enough to pay all expenses, were it not for the necessity of providing furniture, which costs more in Yangchow than in Soochow.

One of the teachers in the school at Yangchow is a young man named Fang, one of Mr. Ancell's first pupils in Soochow, who later went to St. John's College for three years. He does not need to work, as he has money, but he accompanied Mr. Ancell to Yangchow more for friendship's sake than for any other reason, and he has proven highly efficient. Mr. Ancell is making an effort to secure a succession of competent teachers, no easy thing, by assisting through St. John's some boys who will repay the loan by teaching in the mission at a low salary.

A man whom Mr. Ancell calls "my right hand," started out as our gateman in Soochow nearly seven years ago, and is now sexton, school steward and cook, and general utility man of the highest value. "He came up with me from Soochow," says Mr. Ancell. "Indeed, I find him almost indispensable. He seems one of those choice souls naturally Christian. He was baptized about five years ago, and has been very faithful. His real piety shows in many ways. For instance, last Christmas he came and handed me a dollar, saying that all he had came from God, and that he wanted to make this special acknowledgment. This, too, when he makes his regular of-

fering at every communion, though h was getting only $7 Mexican (about $ gold) a month, and has a wife and tw children to support. I wish all who rea this would ask themselves whether th Chinese are capable of becoming gener ous Christians. At the beginning of thi term, I raised the salaries of the teacher a little, and also raised his wages to $8 month. At the first communion afte that, he made an offering of $1! Hov many Christians of long standing hav that much gratitude or faith?"

Speaking of the work of the cate chists, Mr. Ancell says: "One remain here in Yangchow, and two of them travel out into the country, making trip each week, but getting back here fo Saturday and Sunday. For their use we hire a boat by the month. Throug their labors we are becoming known, an the way is opening up for the extension of our influence. They sell a surpris ingly large number of tracts and Gospels, whose use, let us hope, will open the minds and hearts of the readers And so our work goes on, something being done all the time, showing indeed little enough of tangible result, but be ing as seed sown, which will bring harvest in God's own good time."

Bishop Graves calls for reinforce ments for North Kiangsu. He says:

"During the time that our men hav been at Yangchow they have made con siderable progress. The land has bee bought. A plain and substantial hous for them to live in, situated on this land is almost finished and we are going o with another building which will serv for a school as soon as the house is com pleted. There are already several wh are to be admitted as catechumens. Th baptized Christians connected with ou work are sixteen at Yangchow and nin at Nanking; and the communicants ar twelve at Yangchow, and seven at Nan king, making nineteen. These, o course, are not, excepting one or tw cases, the results of the work that ha been done there, but Christians residen as at Nanking, or connected with ou work as in Yangchow, still they mak

terview with me urged very strongly that
we should take up this particular side
of the work in Nanking, which it seemed
to him that other missions were not doing. Mr. Ancell has gone into the matter thoroughly and is of the opinion that
this course would be wise. It would be
necessary that the man to go to Nanking should be a man of very good ability and thorough education—the best
kind of a man that we could secure."

¶

HAS any reader of THE SPIRIT OF
MISSIONS a copy of the following
numbers with which he would be willing
to part: January, 1896, and October,
1902?
    They are needed to complete a file at
the Cathedral Library in Washington.

¶

TWO new churches, made possible by
the Men's Thank-offering, have just
been opened for use in the Diocese of
Oklahoma, one at Enid and the other at
Shawnee. It is hoped that another may
be built at Guthrie by the same means
during this summer. The Men's Thank-
offering has also helped largely in the
building of a church and rectory at Bartlesville and a rectory at Tulsa, and has
provided some important repairs on the
hospital at McAlester, as well as the
purchase of ground and the moving of
a church at Norman, the seat of the
State University. It would seem that
Bishop Brooke has made most excellent
use of the modest sum assigned him
from the Thank-offering.
    At Norman, the place last named, the
bishop has purchased property to establish a Church hall for girls who are attending the university. A part of the
expense comes from the legacy of Miss
Mary Rhinelander King, but about
$4,000 remains to be provided. Such an
institution is greatly needed and is along
the line of the latest and most approved
methods of religious work in connection
with colleges.

A TYPICAL BONTOK·HEAD-HUNTER

This is Makalan, commonly known as Tommy, who became a constabulary soldier

Note that the shield is cut in such a way that when held before the naked body the two projections at the bottom cover the thighs and the three points at the top protect most of the head without obstructing the vision

WARRIORS ON THE MARCH

These are the Talubing men returning to town with weapons after giving notice to the governor

HEAD-HUNTING IN BONTOK

By the Reverend Walter C. Clapp

POSSIBLY you may have paid your ten cents at some fair or "midway" summer resort in your region, to go in and see the people whom the hoarse-voiced "barker" outside with the megaphone described as "the dog-eating, head-hunting Igorots of the mountains of Northern Luzon!"—and were then rather disappointed to see a smiling, good-natured group of people. Well, the barker was right. These people do take heads, and every little while something occurs to remind us of the fact. Only the other morning, as I was returning to my house after the early Eucharist, I was told that old Isaac was dead. Now Isaac Wai-wai was, for an Igorot, a very old man, father of one of our Christian women. She had persuaded him to become a Christian a year or so ago; and at that time, from living in a distant town, Talubing, he came here to live with his daughter. I remember distinctly how earnestly he affirmed his purpose to be a good Christian when the baptismal service was explained to him. I always had a special affection for the emaciated old man as he tottered along the way, and I used often to call to him as he passed, and give him, for his comfort, perhaps a leaf or two of tobacco, or a box of matches.

So, when I heard that old Isaac was dead, I went around to the house, and I found that in the night, while the daughter was away in another town, a man or men had entered the window beneath which the old man was sleeping on the floor, and with a "head-axe" had made a terrible gash on one side of the neck and a savage cut on the back of the scalp and had run off, leaving the old man to die. My desire and efforts to arrange for and to accomplish Christian burial were unavailing. Already the news had reached Talubing, and soon long files of grim warriors from that town, each armed with spear and shield and axe, crossed the river and passed in ominous silence and dignity up to the governor's office to give notice that, unless the doer of this deed to their fellow-townsman were found and punished within three days, they would take vengeance on Bontok. Meantime relatives of old Isaac had tied the poor mangled, bleeding body to a pole, and, amid much wailing and lamentation, were taking it back to Talubing.

The people of Bontok are apprehen-

A DEMONSTRATION IN FORCE

The Talubing men in front of the governor's office, giving notice of intention to fight Bontok

sive of trouble, and probably some of them deserve to have it. Our boys huddle together in groups indoors and talk in whispers. The public ways are deserted and dogs are let loose. Not long ago a man from the neighboring town of Tukukan was enticed under promise of feasting, waylaid and murdered. Four young men were found to have been implicated in the crime, one of them one of our earliest house-boys, whose picture has appeared in THE SPIRIT OF MISSIONS. Three of these are now in Bilibid Prison, Manila, and two of them are there awaiting execution for this deed. Talubing people say that Bontok is now taking revenge, by the killing of Isaac, for testimony which they were obliged to bear in that case. And all this murderous business to appease the "anito" or evil spirits, to satisfy old women's dreams, to fulfil the demands of "religion"!

This is the third day. Precautions have been taken, additional constabulary support summoned, and I daresay nothing will happen to-day, even if Talubing tries to keep its word. But the determination of revenge cannot be openly suppressed, and it is reasonable to expect that sooner or later the tally of "heads" will be made up by some deed of

violence. Let us pray that God may enable us to implant a true faith in Him among these people that shall be as strong as is now their ingrained superstition!

———

LATER: Two youths, one of them a brother of one of our Christian girls living in Samoki, just across the river from Bontok, have been taken and have confessed the crime. There are rumors that, long ago, Isaac was guilty of killing members of their family; of this I do not know; times are changing and a message of peace and good-will has reached this mountain valley. A Talubing man was taken in the act of trying to spear a Samoki woman working in her rice-paddy, a distance from her village. There was great excitement in town. Men left their work and, seizing their weapons, rushed breathless across the river and out on the trail. But the governor was prompt, and matters quieted down. To-day there has been much dancing and feasting at the home of the murderers, and the sound of the "kangsas" (gongs)—the same that you heard at some "White City" perhaps—has floated constantly across the water, and to-night there are many more lights than usual in Samoki.

THE PROBLEM OF CHURCH UNITY
IN CHINA

By the Right Reverend F. R. Graves, D.D.,

Bishop of Shanghai

THE subject of church unity is one which is beset by so many prejudices and beclouded by so many controversies that it is extremely difficult to write about it so as to be clearly understood and yet to avoid wounding feelings which are associated with the most sacred convictions which men hold. I ↄ not pretend that I can treat of it adequately, nor to offer any final solution. ndeed I am so strongly impressed by these considerations that I should never ave offered to write of my own motion and if I had not been assured that it might ↄ of some use. Controversy is idle and harmful and something for which there is ↄ space in the face of our pressing work in the mission field. And yet it is useless ↄ say anything unless it has a direct bearing on what may be done to bring about ion. Nothing is to be gained by repeating platitudes and vague expressions of ur mutual oneness and the Christian love we bear one another. The fact is that e are outwardly divided, sometimes openly antagonistic, and what we have to find it is the way in which division may be done away. It is of no use repeating ırases about unity while we refuse to take thought and exert ourselves to attain . It is true we may never be able to solve the problem, but we can at least do a ttle to make its conditions plainer and to clear away some preliminary obstacles. f course in the brief compass of this paper all one can hope to do is to state what the present position of things and indicate some directions in which our efforts e likely to bear fruit.

There was a time, not so long ago, when church unity was but the pious as- ration of a few. Men were contented with separation and competition, and viewed e spectacle of the divisions of Christianity without realizing the evil and sin of em and without being stirred to bring them to an end. Happily, at the present me, the evils of division are acknowledged and deplored and men have gone back r inspiration to the prayer of our Lord that all may be one. Of course there has ways been a large amount of unity of heart amongst those who held so much in mmon, but the necessity for translating that disposition into practical terms, for hibiting outwardly the unity we feel inwardly, is only just beginning to come me to the mass of Christians.

If we are to describe the state of things in China to-day it will be something e this: Christian missions from all the great countries of the world are working re, each on its own lines and each perpetuating its own ecclesiastical character. here is the great mass of the Roman Catholics separated from the Protestant urches by what appears to be an impassable gulf; the Greek Church, a small mis- ɔn, but the representative of a vast body of Christians in Europe and western ia, which is separated from Roman Catholics and Protestants alike; the Prot- tant missions sent out by the Churches which arose at the time of the Reformation have sprung from those bodies since; and the Anglican Communion, which is storically Catholic and at the same time reformed. All these bodies are separate d not in communion with one another.

From this state of division all sorts of evils have arisen, rivalry and competition, needless reduplication of churches and institutions, jealousy and misunderstanding, and as the gross result of all a divided witness for Christ and a weakened influence for Christian life and morality in the face of the heathen world. One knows that these evils are tempered by the exercise of common sense and Christian feeling, but they exist nevertheless.

Now we feel these evils more acutely in the mission field because we see so clearly the necessity of this united witness, and we are likewise inclined to seek for more of union, for we are driven here to deal with essentials and to disregard matters of secondary importance, and are drawn closer together by a sense of a common cause and common effort no less than by the pressure of surrounding heathenism. It is well recognized in the home lands that, in this matter of unity, missions must furnish, if not the solution, certainly the impulse to grapple with the problem and the spirit of love and sacrifice in which it must be solved. Thus in a sermon preached in Westminster Abbey on St. Andrew's Day (November 30th), at the consecration of two bishops for Japan and of the bishop of the new see of Kwangsi and Hunan, the Dean of Westminster spoke as follows:

"If the Church of England is set, as we believe, in the middle place, holding tenaciously to the immemorial creeds and customs of the Catholic past, and yet claiming and appropriating the fresh light and new lessons that come with the progressive ripening of the human mind; if our position in God's time may prove to be a mediating one in the western world, then you may face your problems with an eager hope. Nay, more—and I say it advisedly—it probably rests with you and your brethren in these two great mission fields to take steps in advance toward the Christian unity of the future which seem wholly impracticable to our stereotyped divisions at home. The imperative requirements of native converts, the necessity of shaping truly native churches, the brotherliness of missionaries who are serving the same Master with the same spirit under the same difficulties, the repeated suggestions of combined effort in regard to medicine and higher education—all these things force the pace and offer an opportunity to a Christian statesmanship."

Surely if the Churches which sent us out are looking to their missions to contribute their part to bring in this great consummation, we in the field must not be found wanting nor disappoint so great a hope.

And now to turn to what has been done and to what remains to be accomplished. It is unquestionable that the Shanghai Centenary Conference did a great deal to promote the spirit of unity and set in motion influences that have been felt at home. Out of it have sprung many experiments in practical co-operation, as in medical and educational work, which appear to be working successfully.

The conference tried to attain its broad and high conception of unity by two paths. It appointed a Committee on Federation and a Committee on Church Union. The first committee has succeeded, to a certain extent, in federating missions in different parts of China by a system of representation. It is probably too soon to say what the result will be. For myself it has seemed to me that it was an attempt to accomplish by the creation of a machinery of representative councils, provincial and so on, a union which could have no real basis, which was, so to speak, in the nature of a truce and not of a peace. If one is impatient of delay and eager for visible results, federation promises a short road to the desired end, but it ignores differences which must ultimately assert themselves. Behind any such expedient always lies the greater and more difficult question of church unity, the real and vital question which we must answer soon or late, and all attempts to put it aside and accept some substitute are sure to fail. I believe that the longer and more difficult ath through the work of the Committee on Church Union is the safer and surer. It is well at this point to ask ourselves what we mean when we speak of church nity in China. Are not most missionaries thinking of a union of Protestant missions? As one reads much that is written on the subject this seems to be the underlying assumption. It was not ignored in the conference, however, that we have to ice a far larger and graver question. Unless church union can embrace all Christians in China, Catholic and Protestant, the problem will be nearly as far from olution as ever. One sees sometimes an uncharitable map which professes to be a iap of the world's religions, with black for the heathen, dark gray for the Catholics and white for the Protestants. That is an image of which we have to rid our iinds. We have to remember that Christianity is a greater thing than Protestantm and to widen our minds and hearts to entertain the conception of a unity which iall embrace all. We have to confess that the practical difficulties are at present isurmountable. But yet we must recall our minds to the fact that church unity, ith the majority of Christians left out, would be no solution of the problem. the difficulties are insurmountable now they may not be so forever. What we ive to see to is that in our efforts at partial reunion we do not erect additional irriers against the larger unity for which we hope and pray.

From these general considerations let us turn to consider how things stand in lation to church unity between the various missions in China. Though we can ankfully say that there is a real desire for unity we must frankly confess that the forts of the Committee on Church Union have had little or no visible result. The me is true of the Committee on Unity appointed in 1907 by the Conference of the iglican Communion. That committee addressed a brotherly letter to all missionies, but in the three years that have intervened no response has been received. ie fact that these two committees which exist for the promotion of church unity ceive no response sufficiently indicates that the time is not ripe for any movement that direction. But it would ill become us to cease our efforts. We can all do a eat deal by preparing the way for such a movement in the future.

1. By prayer for the unity of the Church.

2. By such mutual co-operation as is possible on common ground and for mmon objects.

3. By informal meetings where such explanations of our respective positions ght be made as would clear away the misunderstandings which now obscure the ie issues.

4. By putting practices which are of secondary importance and mere theologi-opinions into a subordinate place and concentrating attention upon the essenls in doctrine and practice. In this way documents like the XXXIX Articles the Westminster Confession would take their proper place as subordinate to the tement of belief in the facts of Christianity as contained, for instance, in the cene and Apostles' Creeds. Men can never unite on the ground of theological nion, but there is no reason why they should not unite upon a confession of belief the great facts which are the foundation of Christianity.

5. We must learn to know that union will have to take place by inclusion and by exclusion. That it will never be reached, that is, by stripping away all to ich anyone may have an objection, but by recognizing that each is to contribute best he has to the final result.

6. We must keep the ideal before us, distant as its realization may seem to and learn to prepare for it by greater personal devotion. It is only as each one us is united to God by union with His Son that we can ever hope to overcome many obstacles that divide us and attain to union in the one Body, the reunited irch of Christ.

EDINBURGH FROM CALTON HILL

THE WORLD MISSIONARY CONFERENCE
By Seth Low, LL.D.

THE World Missionary Conference, to meet in Edinburgh on
June 14th next, is an event
of supreme significance. The
Conference will consist of 1,000 delegates, representing officially, I believe,
substantially every Protestant Church in
Christendom. The German, the Dutch,
the Moravian, the Scandinavian, the
Swiss and the French Protestant
Churches, so far as they maintain foreign missions, will be represented there,
as well as the English and the American Churches.

Many who attend will wish that our
Roman Catholic brethren and our
brethren of the Eastern Church might
also have been present; but, just as it
stands, the Conference raises the momentous question, whether the centrif-
ugal forces of Christianity, which have
been operating for centuries, have not
at length spent their strength; and
whether, in the happy years to come, the
centripetal forces in Christianity that
make for unity are not going to predomi-
nate. All history presents no such effort
since the divisions of early days, on the

part of the many churches of many nations to get together on any subject. It
is not the least significant thing about
it all, that the august cause which is animating this unique movement toward
unity in action is the cause of Christian
missions. It is as though the churches
that have been conducting foreign missions had suddenly cried out with St.
Paul, "Is Christ divided?" And as if
each church had said to itself, "The
churches may be divided, but Christ is
not! Therefore, despite our divisions,
let us come together to learn from one
another how best to carry Christ to the
non-Christian world." So much for the
spiritual significance of this inspiring
gathering.

The Conference itself had its initiative in the Fourteenth Conference of the
Foreign Missions Boards of the United
States and Canada, an organization in
which the Domestic and Foreign Missionary Society of our own Church is
officially represented. Bishop Whitaker
was in attendance at the Conference of
these Foreign Missionary Boards at the
meeting when the movement for the

(362)

investigation, and to co-ordinate missionary experience from all parts of the world. In seriously undertaking this task the World Missionary Conference of 1910 will be distinguished from all previous missionary conferences, while the thoroughly representative character which is already assured to it fits it for making a unique contribution to the advancement of the Kingdom of God." The document then adds: "The Conference is one of Missionary Societies and Committees convened to consider missionary plans and methods. It is therefore not a gathering that is in any way constituted for the discussion of matters of doctrine or ecclesiastical polity, which at present separate Christians from one another. Accordingly it has been clearly laid down that all such matters regarding which the co-operating Churches or Societies differ among themselves shall be excluded from the purview of the Conference."

The writer has been a member of Commission VII on the "Relation of Missions to Governments," of which the Right Honorable Lord Balfour, of Burleigh, is the chairman, and of which the writer has been the vice-chairman for America. His American colleagues have been: The Rev. Thomas S. Barbour, D.D., Corresponding Secretary of the Foreign Department of the American Baptist Missionary Union; the Honorable R. L. Borden, Leader of the Conservative Party in the Canadian Parliament; the Honorable John W. Foster, LL.D., Ex-Secretary of State; Professor Rufus E. Jones, of Haverford College; the Rt. Rev. William Lawrence, D.D., Bishop of Massachusetts; Rear-Admiral Alfred T. Mahan, U. S. Navy.

The study into the relations of Missions to Governments made by this Commission has been most thorough; and their report, when printed, will make a volume that is likely to be of great value to all mission boards and to missionaries in the field. It will consist of two parts: Part I., dealing with actual conditions as found in different parts of the foreign mission field; and Part II., which endeavors to formulate principles that appear to the Commission as those which should govern the relations of missions to governments, in the different countries in which foreign missions are maintained. Stated baldly, the relation of missions to governments seems an unattractive and perhaps an unimportant theme; but when one considers the questions that it raises, one perceives that the theme is of vital importance, as well as of intense human interest. Such questions are, for instance: What should be the attitude of missionaries in regard to compensation for the destruction of property or for the loss of life? What should be the attitude of missionaries toward the extra-territorial system, as found in China, for example, where different nations have the right to maintain, within certain limits, their own courts? What should be the attitude of missionaries toward Christian converts who get into trouble?

The advantage of having such questions as these studied out with care, and in the light of the experience of all the Protestant missions of the whole world, can readily be understood. Similar light will no doubt be thrown on all the other subjects to be considered by the Conference, by the Commissions to which they have been committed. We are justified in hoping, therefore, that this great Edinburgh gathering will be a milestone in the history of missionary enterprise, which shall not so much mark the length of the road which has been already travelled, as indicate the starting point for new and larger advances of Christian missions in non-Christian lands.

His imagination, and his spiritual vision also, must be small indeed, who is not inspired by the thought that cooperation of this kind by the representatives of many churches is, so far as it goes, practical unity; and he will be a believer of little faith indeed, who as he contemplates this sublime spectacle of divided brethren gathering together in unity in the cause of missions, does not thank God, and take courage to believe more unshakenly than ever in the Divine ideal of a unity that some day shall go further still, until at last it unites Christian men of every name in the complete unity for which our Lord and Master so earnestly prayed.

DELEGATES TO THE WORLD MISSIONARY CONFERENCE

THE delegates appointed by the Board of Missions to represent this Church to the World Missionary Conference, to be held in Edinburgh, June 14th-23d, are:

At Assembly Hall

CHICAGO:	Right Rev. C. P. Anderson, D.D.
CONNECTICUT:	Rev. W. P. Ladd.
HANKOW:	Right Rev. L. H. Roots, D.D.
HONOLULU:	Right Rev. H. B. Restarick, D.D.
LONG ISLAND:	Rev. Reese F. Alsop, D.D.
	Mr. William G. Low.
MARYLAND:	Rev. J. H. Eccleston, D.D.
MASSACHUSETTS:	Right Rev. Wm. Lawrence, D.D.
NEWARK:	Rev. Charles T. Walkley.
NEW YORK:	Rev. J. C. Roper, D.D.
	Mr. John W. Wood.
	Mr. William Jay Schieffelin.
	Miss Julia C. Emery.
NEVADA:	Right Rev. H. D. Robinson, D.D.
PHILIPPINES:	Right Rev. Chas. H. Brent, D.D.
PENNSYLVANIA:	Rev. J. deW. Perry, D.D.
	Rev. H. L. Duhring, D.D.
RHODE ISLAND:	Rev. Robert B. Parker.
SHANGHAI:	Rev. F. L. H. Pott, D.D.
TOKYO:	Right Rev. John McKim, D.D.
	Rev. C. H. Evans.
WESTERN N. Y.:	Rev. Charles H Smith, D.D.

At Synod Hall

MASSACHUSETTS:	Rev. Sherrard Billings.
	Mr. Douglas T. Davidson.
	Mrs. William Lawrence.
LONG ISLAND:	Mr. Silas McBee.
NEBRASKA:	Mr. John E. Smith.
NEW YORK:	Mrs. Seth Low.
PENNSYLVANIA:	Mrs. J. deW. Perry.
	Mr. Charles E. Beury.
	Dr. J. Nicholas Mitchell.
	Mrs. J. Nicholas Mitchell.
	Mrs. John Markoe.
	Miss Lucy B. Duhring.
RHODE ISLAND:	Rev. Richard E. Graham.
	Mrs. Richard E. Graham.
SO. VIRGINIA:	Rev. W. E. Rollins.
	Mrs. W. E. Rollins.
VIRGINIA:	Mr. Lawrence R. Lee.
BETHLEHEM:	Rev. G. H. Sterling.
	Mrs. Sterling.
HONOLULU:	Mr. James Wakefield.
MILWAUKEE:	Miss Pearl Howard Campbell

next class. The following are some of
the results of our canvass:

1. Marked increase in the attendance
at the Sunday services, to say nothing
of the enthusiasm.

2. To my surprise, they seem to
think I have been making—what they
call—a sacrifice. Hence they are going
to start out to raise my salary. What
is the use trying to quench the smoking
flax!

3. They have discovered that the interior of our chapel-church needs decorating. A committee was appointed to-
night to get "bids" and report at the
next meeting.

4. They are going to finance a parish
paper, and I am to edit it.

5. Already some are talking of building our new church. Up to the present
a chapel has been sufficient, seating 225·

6. And I am assured more is to follow. One of our women said: "Most
movements seem to 'spring up,' this
movement seems to have 'come down.'"
One is reminded of the Kentucky hill
man who had no breeching on his har-
ness because he said he would not have
a horse who could not keep ahead of the
buggy going down hill. That is the condition here. One must throw aside the
barrier that has so easily upset one, and
run, or else be run over.

¶

AT the Laymen's Missionary Movement Conference in Portland,
Oregon, Churchmen decided to double
offerings for the foreign field.

¶

CEYLON is in line with a Laymen's
Missionary Movement. On Octo-
ber 14th, 1909, just as the national series
of conventions in this country was about
to begin, a public meeting was held in
Colombo to enlist the energies of native
Christian laymen. The purposes of the

gathering were outlined in this unanimously adopted resolution:

That in view of the large number of districts and villages in this island that are still un-evangelized, and recognizing the fact that the laymen of all Churches are equally responsible with the ordained ministers to pray and work for the coming of the Kingdom of God on earth, and that every Christian should recognize the world as his field and, to the full measure of his ability, work for its evangelization, the time has come, in the opinion of this meeting, when a forward movement should be made on the part of the lay members of the Christian Churches of Ceylon with a view to enlisting the intelligent and practical interest of others in the evangelization of this island.

¶

AN American layman (a Presbyterian), and a Canadian layman (a Baptist), have, under the inspiration of the Laymen's Missionary Movement, announced their intention of not adding another dollar to their accumulated wealth. They will give all they earn and all their invested capital earnings above living expenses to missions and other forms of Christian work.

¶

THE FOUR SQUARE LEAGUE

NEARLY every convention in the national campaign of the Laymen's Missionary Movement has made some special contribution to the development of better plans for extending the Kingdom. One of the most practical and suggestive of these is that proposed at St. Louis, under the name of "The Four Square League." At one of the sessions a speaker called attention to the fact that our Lord's programme for wit-

ness-bearing was a four-sided one, with equal emphasis on Jerusalem, Judea, Samaria and the uttermost part of the earth. But this fourth side of the quadrilateral, it was pointed out, had not been sufficiently regarded or provided for by Christian people. *Men and Missions* thus describes the working out of the plan:

"Putting the two ideas together, a number of men met after the concluding session of the convention on Sunday afternoon, and, as the result of much conference, decided that they would associate in a league those who felt moved (1) to give annually in at least four figures ($1,000 or more); (2) who would endeavor to induce three others to join them in the pledge, thus making of themselves four; (3) who would work to lead the whole Church to give at least fourfold its present offering of service and of substance to foreign missions; and (4) who would promote the idea of each congregation increasing its foreign missionary contributions to at least one-fourth of the total giving to Christian work.

"There was no thought of an added Church organization, or of anything mechanical in the proposition. It was simply an expression of a belief that a considerable number of men throughout the country, and possibly the world, might be led to relate themselves to a voluntary league, having its central idea in these terms of four; a movement among men who are able to lead by example in the stimulation of large gifts from those who are financially able, by the grace of God, to give in a large way for the financing of His Kingdom.

"There was much prayer, and a deep spiritual power in the informal conference. One man was led to make himself a member of the league, and also to enroll his fifteen-year-old son as a member. Another man enrolled his name who said he had never before given a thousand cents to foreign missions, bu desired to crystallize into action the impulses that had been aroused in his own heart by the convention."

CONFERENCE OF TOKYO MISSIONARY DISTRICT

BISHOP McKIM invited each foreign worker in his large district to meet him in conference on Wednesday, Thursday and Friday, January 26th-28th. The wives of the married missionaries were included in the invitation, and the result was a large and most helpful gathering. Thirty-nine of those who are carrying on the Church's work in the district of Tokyo were present, only five being prevented from attending, while the four remaining absentees were those on furlough in the United States. The bishop in his opening address commented upon the excellent advance made during the year, speaking in most appreciative terms of the generous effort being made by the Church at home in behalf of St. Paul's College.

Those who have known of the long connection of the late Rev. E. R. Woodman with the Japan Mission will be gratified to learn that the following resolution proposed by the Rev. C. F. Sweet was unanimously carried:

"In view of the long service of the late Rev. Edmund Radcliffe Woodman in the mission, it is evidently fit that some memorial of his ministry should be placed in the cathedral in lasting token of his devotion, therefore, be it .

"Resolved: That a Committee of Five be appointed (the bishop being one) to arrange for such suitable memorial in the cathedral, the expense to be met by voluntary subscription."

The bishop appointed the Rev. Messrs. Sweet and Cooke with Miss Mann and Miss Neely to serve with him on this committee.

The following resolution, proposed by Mr. Cooke and seconded by Mr. Evans, was carried:

"Resolved: That it is the opinion of this conference that neither in the value of their work nor in the expense of living is there sufficient difference between the unmarried women and the unmarried men of the Tokyo District to justify the present inequality in their salaries."

After Mr. Madeley had read his thoughtful and suggestive paper on "The Deepening of the Spiritual Life of the Missionary," a resolution was proposed and carried, to the effect that the bishop be respectfully recommended to draw up a quarterly intercession paper embodying the chief needs of the work of each mission centre, to be distributed among the members of the mission.

Mr. Ambler's paper on the Catechetical School was admirable, going to the root of the question as to how we can best improve the catechetical school and make it more effective in evangelistic work. As a result of the report of the committee appointed to consider this subject, resolutions were passed covering the following: (1) Requirements for admission to be raised. (2) The course of instruction to extend over four years, the first to be probationary. (3) Revision of the curriculum.

Miss Heywood's paper on "The Future of St. Margaret's School" aroused great interest. The history of the school since its foundation in 1873 was briefly sketched; its very real influence upon Japanese women and girls was shown by the remarkable proportion of its graduates who are Christians, and the large number who, as wives of Japanese clergymen or catechists, or as Bible-women or kindergartners, are giving the greatest assistance to the Church. Finally the dire needs of the school for a new recitation-hall were shown and the following resolutions carried:

"Resolved: That the giving up or the crippling of the work at St. Margaret's School would be not only a loss to the general work among women in the City of Tokyo, but also a definite and serious loss to the work being done among women and children in the whole Tokyo District.

"Resolved: That an appeal be made from this conference of the missionaries of the Tokyo district to the Church

at home for the $25,000 required to put
up a new recitation building in accordance with the demands of the Japanese
Board of Education."

Both Mr. Evans and Mr. Tucker, in
their addresses on the future policy of
the mission—whether it should be one
of intention or extension—agreed it was
better with the limited number of
workers in this large district to build up
the work by strengthening our present
stations rather than by opening new stations.

The conference had been so helpful to
all, and its meetings marked by such
earnestness of purpose and keen interest
in the problems of the mission that a
proposal "that the bishop be requested
to assemble the mission in annual conference (during the latter part of January if possible), and to provide in connection therewith a Quiet Day" was
carried without a dissenting voice.

CUBAN NOTES

ON Sunday, March 6th, the
bishop opened the new chapel
at Santa Fe, on the Isle of
Pines, with a celebration
of the Holy Communion, followed later
by baptism, matins and confirmation,
at which four persons were confirmed.
The congregation overtaxed the seating capacity of the building. This
chapel is the first to be rebuilt of those
which were ruined by the hurricane. It
is a handsome structure, most substantially constructed, storm-proof, and by
far the most attractive of all the public
buildings on the island. As soon as possible, other buildings will be erected at
Columbia and McKinley, made possible
by the contributions from friends in the
United States in response to the recent
appeals made in this connection.

Owing to the very rapid extension of
the work in Cuba it has become necessary to redistrict the provincial system
of the island. Originally the archdeacon of Havana made visitations over

OUR LETTER BOX

Intimate and Informal Messages from the Field

AFLOAT AND ASHORE
(Mostly the Latter!)

The Rev. Mr. Newton, who is supported in the Alaska field as the special missionary of Calvary Church, New York, sends a communication to the parish paper, from which we quote the following:

YOU will be interested in hearing of my annual pilgrimage to Katalla, which I made last summer. This is the one thing which introduces aught of hardship into my life, and while the discomforts are not pleasant, yet I would not forego them for the sweets of variety and experience which they introduce. I was away from Valdez three Sundays in making the trip. I went first to Cordova, hoping soon to find a launch going across the flats, but just missed one, so I had the Sunday in Cordova. The end of the week a launch wished to go, but the weather was stormy. We did venture on Sunday afternoon, and went so far as Cape Whitshed, where we go from Prince William Sound out on the open ocean. It was so rough that we turned back to Cordova. Monday we had better luck, but on the Copper River Flats we stuck in the mud as usual, and the Tuesday morning tide was not high enough to float us, and we remained stuck for nineteen hours. Fortunately we had an empty scow alongside, which we boarded for exercise, and to play quoits, with railroad spikes for quoits. We got into Katalla at 11 P.M. Tuesday night, and I held service on Wednesday, not knowing how soon I might get away. As it happened the launch did not leave until the following Tuesday, which gave me a Sunday there, for which I was thankful. I held two services, and catechised the Sunday-school, which showed evidence of having done a good year's work. It is always a pleasure to hold services in Katalla, the people are so appreciative, and turn out in large numbers. It is inspiring to see the patience and courage of these people, who are waiting for Congress to settle the coal land legislation, so that the wonderful mines of the district may be worked. The Coast Survey has disclosed a better harbor in Controller Bay, which has always been the great desideratum for Katalla, and the people are all very happy.

We left Tuesday afternoon, and had to turn up Martin River to Camp 7 to get part of an oil well which had to go to Cordova for repairs. In coming down the river where it empties on to the flats, with no buoys to mark the channel, the night being dark and foggy so that no landmarks might be seen, we ran on to high ground at flood of the highest tide of the month. When morning dawned we were perched on a hill, with the river channel some forty feet away. There would be no tide high enough to float us for thirty days. There was no help for it, so our "able seaman" walked back to Camp 7, and brought men and spades in a row-boat and they dug a channel on the starboard side (we were listed to port), three feet or more deep the length of the boat and to the river.

There was aboard a Mr. McLean, of Wilkes-Barre, a lawyer. He and I were playing cooks, as the engineer had been on a spree and was left in Katalla, while the captain did his duty and the cook was pilot. When the boat slid down into the channel, and flopped violently to starboard, Mr. McLean was in the kitchen, and received "a shower" of dishes from the pan, and a pot of hot coffee down his leg. When the tide came in, by dint of an anchor cast at stern, and the windlass, pike poles, and the propeller, with some running forward and back, we got away into the channel. So we sailed until the next ebb left us

THE RECTORY AT VALDEZ

"We have passed the thirty-foot limit in snowfall and it has drifted as never before"

his coat. He was doubtful, evidently
sizing up the place in relation to his
tastes. Soon he drifted on to the piano
stool and strummed a bit. Then he took
a Morris chair and a magazine. Later
Mr. Ziegler got him to the pool table,
and the coat came off and he spent the
evening. He might easily have spent
the evening at the saloons, and with half
a chance have been drunk by that time.
The Red Dragon is one against twenty
odd saloons, but at least it offers shelter
for those who have the better tastes and
inclinations, and you will find anywhere
from ten to fifty men in it all the time.
The men appreciate it, and they showed
their appreciation by taking up a subscription at one of the largest camps and
sending in $130 for its maintenance.

Valdez is the old settled town, with
more homes and more people than the
others, but they, with their brighter
prospects and hopes, say, "It has seen its
best days"; but time will tell. In November we had the fiercest winds I have
experienced, and our snow came late, but
we have lots of it. Over twenty feet have
fallen and we've had wind and drifting
so that we can scarce see from the rectory windows. Personally I love the
snow and revel in the winter weather. It
is not cold except when the wind blows.

The work here is like church work in
any small town, though seemingly more
important as frontier foundation work.
I trust that the future may prove its
value.
                    EDWARD PEARSONS NEWTON.

.

Our missionary to the Indians on the Cannon
Ball Reservation, North Dakota, writing
March 16th, says:

PLEASE excuse pencil. Ink frozen.
Shall get more. Have just returned from Fort Berthold; walked 130
miles; roads awful. The work there is
strengthening.

The husband of Bessie Black Wood-
pecker (a heathen woman recently confirmed) was buried two weeks ago. He
refused Christianity until the very last,
then sent for me, and I went on foot in
the storm twenty-eight miles to baptize

him. Came back by the same conveyance. Have walked about 700 miles this
winter.

Lent here is such a success as any
church might greatly desire. The Indian wants a good stiff Lent—even if he
kicks about it, still he wants it. Are
we not all built that way? There have
been meetings with Litany, singing,
Morning or Evening Prayer (with
neighbors invited in) in nearly every Indian home. There will have been in all
before Lent closes. I have not been present at half of these—indeed I could not
be—but they have been a great success.
These meetings are often held in three
or four places at the same time. Indians, though easily discouraged, are
naturally religious.

·Joe Two Bear started a rebellion at
Red Hail at the beginning of Lent, carrying some families with him, but all
are in line again and Joe is pulling as a
bucking horse always does when he
really starts, and I am glad to let him
go ahead. I used to think a "kicker"
would not be a safe leader, but have had
to revise my early ideas about almost
everything.

* *

A letter from Wakamatsu, Japan, says:

THOUGH the winter has not been
as cold as usual, it has been quite
cold enough to cause much suffering in
a place where there is so much poverty
as there is in Wakamatsu, and I
long to go about with pockets full
of money, distributing bags of rice
and charcoal and other things where
they are most needed. People may
talk of "pauperizing" and all that.
It sounds very well, but there is a
good deal to be said on the other side
from the point of view of the "Sermon on the Mount." And what about a
poor old woman over seventy who lives
all alone in a wretched little hut and
winds thread for a living, who works
bravely and does all she can and yet
whom I found one bitter day without
any fuel in the house and the wind
blowing her old newspaper-covered doors

and windows to tatters? It makes m
feel like a wicked Dives rolling in th
lap of luxury to have a fire and a be
and enough to eat when you see thes
people. There are a man and his wif
and child not ten minutes' walk fron
here whom I found nearly starving. H
is a gardener, but who calls a gardene
to work when everything is deep in
snow? And so he got sick from lack o
food; the doctor—our Christian docto
—said that was all that ailed him. H
had not a quilt under him, as they usual
ly have, but slept on the mats, with on
quilt over. Nearly all the people her
look poor. In a place like this it is lik
a dream to shut one's eyes and imagin
a life like that in New York; the con
trast is so intense it seems strange tha
both places should be in the same world

* *

ON THE TRAIL TO AND FROM ALLAKAKET

Archdeacon Stuck, writing of his journey t
and from our lonely mission at Allakaket
gives a few vivid pen and camera pictures o
travelling in the Far North.

WE reached St. John's-in-the-Wilder
ness safely on December 14th, nine
teen days out of Fort Yukon. Da
after day we travelled at 45 t
50 below zero; one night we pitche
our tent on the bank of the Chandala
River at 59 degrees, with the steam fro
the overflow water condensing on ever
thing around us. When these shallo
rivers freeze solid on the riffles, th
water backs up until it has power
break through the superincumbent ic
and then we have the familiar and mo
unpleasant phenomenon of "overflow."

From the Chandalar to the Koyuk
we had no trail and the "strong cold"
as the natives call it—continued, so
hired a Kobuk hunter whom we e
countered to accompany us to Coldfo
The long, steady cold weather was tryi
to man and beast and rather "took
out" of me, but I much prefer to cr
that wild, open region in the still cold
50 degrees below zero than in the stor
of wind and snow which I have e

Washday at Allakaket

washes them. Tuesday is ironing day;
Wednesday is mending day; Thursday
is Junior Auxiliary day, and Friday is
bath day. I made two flash-light photographs—one of wash-day, and one of
bath day, with the younger boys each
seated in his proper tub. They are not
what you would call pictorial, but I
think they are decidedly interesting.

Regular training like this is doing a
great deal for the children and is big
with fair promise. It does my heart
good that it has been possible to undertake it. I rejoice in the spreading influence and usefulness of this mission.
I glory in the work that it has already
done. Miss Carter and I went over the
vital statistics of the past two years and
a half, and we found that twenty-three
babies had been born at and around the
mission in that time, of whom all but
one are living and thriving to-day—and
that one was overlaid by its mother and
thus died a violent death. I do not
think it is any exaggeration to say, in
view of all experience with native children, that had not the mission been here,
with Miss Carter's skill and devotion,
many of those children would have suc-

"Each seated in his proper tub"

cumbed to the ignorant neglect of their
parents—perhaps half of them.

So to that extent, certainly, here at
the Allakaket we are fulfilling what I
believe to be our prime mission—the
saving alive God's Indians in Alaska.
More and more of the people are coming
and building around the mission—
like birds flying to the shelter of a stout
tree and making their nests in the
branches—and for the most part they
are a docile people, willing to be taught,
indeed eager to learn. And my heart
goes out in gratitude to God that here
at the Allakaket we are free from the
hateful drawback of intoxicating liquor.

I am writing this last from Tanana,
after the hardest and slowest trip that I

Lunch on the trail at 50° below

have made since I came to Alaska. Fifteen
days making the 120 miles from
Allakaket; breaking trail through three
feet of new snow; lying up two days in a
dog-kennel of a hut, with no door and
no window, so that we had to take part
of our precious bedding to hang in the
door-opening, with the thermometer at
70 degrees below zero; forcing the passage
of the Melozitna-Tozitna divide in
a howling blizzard, dead ahead; short of
dog-feed, short of grub—I am just in
from it, dead tired. Yet when I read
Miss Wood's letter telling me that Bishop
Stringer, of the British Yukon diocese,
came into Fort Yukon from
Herschel Island a week after I left there,
with one native and a pack on his back,
having lost his way and having subsisted
for twenty days on rations for three,

In response to the resolution of the Board of Missions, passed at its December meeting, congratulating both Archdeacon Thomson and the Church upon the completion of his fifty years of service in China, the archdeacon has sent the following reply. It is characteristic of the man, and will give both friends and strangers a glimpse of the simple sincerity and unselfish devotion which have marked throughout his sojourn in China as a herald of his Master's Kingdom.

My dear Brethren:

I FEEL a deep sense of my inability to express in words my reply to your exceedingly kind resolution of December 16th, congratuating me on the fiftieth anniversary of my arrival in China.

It was with me a simple case of one trying to do his duty. After I felt my call to the Holy Ministry of the Church, the call to a mission came, and I went. That was all. There was no sense of self-sacrifice, but to meet each duty as that for which I came. My longing desire was to do better work, and go right on to bring the men and women of China to know Christ our Lord as their Saviour and Redeemer—that was all. I would be glad to begin again for another fifty years, by which time China will have been brought to Christ in a very great measure, I am sure.

I thank each one of you for your kind words and kind deeds to me and mine in the past, for the Board has always been very kind to us.

If I have done anything worthy of your approval or congratulation, it was Christ our gracious Lord using His servant; and to the Lord, and to Him only, be all the honor and the praise. The failures and the shortcomings were mine. To Him be the thanks, that He has used me in some little measure to be a fellow-worker with you all.

It is truly a great and a glorious enterprise you have in hand—the bringing this immense and wonderful people into the Kingdom of God and His Christ. With my daily prayer that the blessing of God may rest upon you all, spirit, soul and body, in your labors for His glory through His Church, with my true thanks, I remain as ever, in love and sincerity, Yours,

ELLIOT H. THOMSON.

ANNOUNCEMENTS
CONCERNING THE MISSIONARIES

Alaska

AT the meeting on April 12th, at the request of Bishop Rowe, the Board of Missions accepted the resignation of the Rev. Thomas Jenkins from the work at Skagway, to date from April 1st, and the resignation of Miss Isabel M. Emberley, as superintendent of St. Matthew's Hospital, Fairbanks, at the end of her furlough, August 31st, 1910.

Porto Rico

AT the meeting on April 12th the Board rescinded its action of October 12 appointing the Rev. G. H. Moscoso, of Washington, D. C., as a missionary to San Juan.

Hankow

AT the request of Bishop Roots, the Board of Missions on April 12th approved the appointment of Mr. Robert A. Goodwin, Jr., of the Theological Seminary of Virginia; the appointment to take effect upon his ordination to the diaconate.

AT the same meeting, at the request of the bishop, Miss Sarah Elizabeth Hopwood, of St. Paul's Church, New Haven, was appointed as a missionary worker under the Woman's Auxiliary United Offering; the appointment to take effect upon her graduation from the Church Training and Deaconess House, Philadelphia, Pa.

J. H. SOWERBY, M.D., having resigned from the Hankow District, sailed from Shanghai by the steamship *Monteagle* on February 26th.

Harry B. Taylor, m.d., on regular furlough, left Shanghai February 19th *via* the Suez Canal. He intends to remain in England until August and take a course in the London School of Tropical Medicine. He will come to the United States later.

Tokyo

The Rev. Roger A. Walke was married to Miss Emeline Agnew Condict in Trinity Church, Newark, N. J., on April 20th. On his return to duty, with his wife, he sailed from New York by the steamer *Minneapolis* on April 23d for England.

Kyoto

The Rev. Dr. I. H. Correll and wife, who sailed from San Francisco on February 15th, arrived at Osaka on March 8th and proceeded to their station at Tsu.

The Rev. William J. Cuthbert, returning after regular furlough, left New York on April 15th, and, with his wife, is to sail from San Francisco by the *Chiyo Maru* on May 3d.

Brazil

The Rev. Guido Zumbuhl, after six months' leave of absence in England, was purposing to sail for Brazil on March 24th.

MISSIONARY SPEAKERS

FOR the convenience of those arranging missionary meetings, the following list of clergy and other missionary workers available as speakers is published:

When no address is given, requests for the services of these speakers should be addressed to the Corresponding Secretary, 281 Fourth Avenue, New York.

Department Secretaries

Department 1. The Rev. William E. Gardner, 186 Upland Road, Cambridge, Mass.

larged by the addition of Mr. Arthur Ryerson.

A letter was submitted from the Bishop of New Jersey expressing his gratitude to the Board of Missions for "its kind and generous estimate of my long service," and, later in the meeting, Bishop Lloyd was elected to fill the vacancy caused by Bishop Scarborough's resignation, and was appointed on the Advisory Committee.

An appropriation of $200 was made from the income of the Anna Mary Minturn Fund as the last payment on the erection of a church at Kennewick, Washington, and another of $200 to assist in building a church at Steamboat Springs, Western Colorado.

From the income of the Elizabeth S. Fowler Fund an appropriation was made for the education of daughters of deceased missionaries.

At the request of the Bishop of Oklahoma, Miss Hunter was appointed under the Woman's Auxiliary United Offering from her date of graduation in the place of Deaconess White, retired; at the request of the Bishop of Utah, Miss Alice Newitt in place of Deaconess Knepper, resigned. Permission was given to use $200 released by reason of a resignation to supplement the stipend of Deaconess Sands at Graniteville, S. C. From general funds, Miss Cornelia B. Edwards was appointed as a missionary at Vernal, Utah, from March 1st.

Letters were received from all the foreign bishops, submitting their estimates for the next fiscal year, which were laid over for action at the May meeting with all the other appropriations.

The Standing Committee on Audit and Finance reported that "the accounts of the Treasurer for the lapsed portion of the fiscal year up to April 1st had been duly audited and the certificate of the Auditing Committee attached to the report."

Training-school for Mission Women, Sendai, Tokyo District, Japan. Built with the $10,000 appropriation made from the United Offering of 1907

A corner in the balcony; students being trained by United Offering Missionaries from West Virginia, Tokyo, Pennsylvania and Connecticut

THE WOMAN'S AUXILIARY
To the Board of Missions

St. Margaret's School, Tokyo, graduating class of 1909 with United Offering Missionary from Western Massachusetts. Most of the students in Sendai Training-school are graduates of St. Margaret's

THE CHURCH TRAINING-SCHOOL, SENDAI, TOKYO DISTRICT
By Bessie McKim

OUR prosperity has hindered our writing, for our work seems to grow up suddenly without our having to go out and find it. This is mostly due to the fact that our house, the school and the kindergarten are such attractive buildings, and, besides these, our gate and front fence excite a great deal of admiration, for they are the handsomest in the neighborhood.

One day in October a young high-school girl who lives across the street came to call on me and ask me to teach her English. I told her to come on the following Tuesday afternoon and we

Learning to sew in Asheville District under a Texas United Offering Deaconess

would begin the lessons. The next Tuesday she came, and so did Miss Abé, with four other girls. The class has grown steadily since then, and now eleven girls come every Tuesday afternoon. Four of them began to attend church regularly without any suggestions from me, and some of the others have come occasionally.

A little while before Christmas, when I was calling on a woman who is not a Christian, but whose husband is a member of the Church, she said she thought it was a great pity that they lived so far away that her little boy could never go to Sunday-school. "Aren't there any other Sunday-schools near you?" I asked. "No, there is one a little nearer than the Church Sunday-school, but *Tosli Chan* is so small he can't walk so far." "Perhaps some day we can start a Sunday-school in the neighborhood," I said. "Are there many children?"

"What are you asking? Why, the noise is something terrible. Just in these two houses there are twelve children, and there are at least thirty on this side of the block alone. I could get you as many more as you could stand. It would be a fine thing to have a Sunday-school for them."

"Would you be willing to lend us a room if we should start one?" "Of course, you can have all I've got, if you'll only come," she said earnestly.

As there were already three Sunday-schools on Sunday, and none of the teachers could be spared, I arranged to have a Saturday afternoon school, which has a regular attendance of thirty children, mostly boys.

Besides the Church Sunday-school, which has an average attendance of about sixty, there are two Sunday-schools in the kindergarten building, Miss Fyock's kindergarten Sunday-school in the morning, and an afternoon Sunday-school of thirty-nine girls and one boy. These Sunday-schools not only give the young women in the training-school the necessary experience in teaching, but greatly increase the opportunities for missionary work by making it possible for us to call on and keep in touch with the parents and elder

The Cooking-school at St. Elizabeth's, Honolulu, with the United Offering Deaconess from Western New York

Another Western New York United Offering Missionary visiting the Utah Indians in their camp

brothers and sisters of the children. It is this calling, and also the visiting connected with Miss Fyock's kindergarten, that keeps the inmates of the school so busy. It makes us feel that we are really progressing and helping to widen the Church's influence. In making these calls the girls often gain good friends who come to the school to see them. At such times the pretty rooms in the school building are ideal places for entertaining friends.

If the kind friends who gave to the United Offering could come and visit us and see how much our present quarters help us in our work, they would not only receive a most grateful welcome, but would know that they have every reason to feel proud of their gift.

OUR UNITED OFFER-ING MISSIONARIES

IN the March SPIRIT OF MISSIONS an editorial drew attention to the next Triennial United Offering of the Woman's Auxiliary.

This offering is to be made in Cincinnati on the sixth day of next October, and its purpose is the same as that of the offering made in Richmond in 1907. Of

A Manila waif waiting outside the House of the Holy Child for our United Offering Missionaries from Michigan and Massachusetts to take her in

(381)

Our New York doctor and Pennsylvania nurse in the children's ward of the Elizabeth Bunn Memorial Hospital, Wuchang, Hankow District, China

the offering of 1910, $15,000 will be used for needed building in the mission field, and the remainder for the training, sending and support of women missionaries, and for caring for those disabled in the service. The $214,251.55 devoted to these latter purposes in 1907 has provided for a long list of workers in the past two and a half years.

At the present time 150 persons are being supported on what remains of this amount. Of these 150, fifty-three are at work in the foreign and ninety-four in the domestic field, two are retired missionaries, one foreign and one domestic, and one is in training for mission service.

Of the workers at home and abroad, fifty-four are teachers, five are doctors, eighteen nurses; eleven are employed in industrial, and nine in institutional work, while fifty are engaged more exclusively in evangelistic effort. With this, however, the greater number of the

women workers are also more or less concerned.

These 150 United Offering missionaries come from fifty or more of our dioceses and missionary districts, as widely separated as Marquette and Louisiana, Eastern Oregon and Texas, Los Angeles and West Virginia; there are fifteen deaconesses among them, of whom three are graduates of the Philadelphia and nine of the New York School, and there are two Sisters of the Sisterhood of the Holy Nativity.

In this number of THE SPIRIT OF MISSIONS we are giving a series of scenes which we hope will bring our United Offering missionaries and their work vividly before the minds of our readers, and enlist their hearts in behalf of those all too few who make our advance guard. Perhaps some others of our younger women, seeing the places in which and the people among whom they move, will be prompted to join their ranks.

A Chicago United Offering Missionary with her Alaska children at Nenana

WANTED—SENTRIES FOR THE OUTPOSTS

ONE Sunday afternoon a few years ago, in a village of Central China, some young Chinese women were sitting together in a small room. A strange new person had come to that village the day before with her husband. While the man talked to men, this foreign woman was telling a story to the women who had never heard it before: it was the story of One Who loved everyone and wanted everyone to know and love Him. Only one of the Chinese women listened and understood; she came up to the foreigner and asked her to stay on in the village. "Only tell us more," she said. "You will teach me, and then you and I will tell the other women in this village and the other villages beyond." But the foreigner answered, "I cannot stay. My work is in the capital of this province, the great city miles from here. There are too few of us even there; no one can be spared to come and help you. I would send you a book to teach you

A doctor from Maine with the baby from the Little Helpers' Cot, on the porch of St. Agnes's Hospital, Raleigh

*Their Chicago teacher taking the Hooker Orphanage girls
to chapel, in Mexico*

more, but you cannot read." And the next day the two foreigners went away together. The Chinese woman was left alone with the secret of life and peace in a village where many women and girls were unhappy.

Two years later, the same stranger came again, and the first person to greet her was the eager friend who had wanted her to stay. "I have told others all I know," she said, "and now we would like to know more. Send us now a teacher." Again the foreign woman must answer, "There is no one to send." Is the Chinese woman still waiting for the teacher who does not come?

Such an outpost as that little town cannot be occupied until there are reinforcements for the main stations. When a missionary bishop sends word to the Board of Missions that he needs eight women for eight definite positions, he does not mean that eight are all he could use, but after careful consideration he knows that eight are immediately necessary. As soon as they are provided, as many more will be needed to meet opportunities he sees all about him in the work. But the Board

has only a few volunteers ready to go, and cannot send him more than two new workers. Six positions remain vacant. Meanwhile the bishop receives from those among whom he works an appeal for more helpers, and he, too, must answer, "There is no one to send."

The plans for Church extension are on a large scale. Leaders are training leaders for the future. Men who have vision see that a school established now in a certain centre will send its influence far out beyond that one town. The boys' school and the girls' school must each have two teachers. A hospital in that town needs a doctor and two nurses; it is perhaps the only hospital within a radius of a hundred miles; unless the station is in a large city, then a clergyman and parish helper may complete the staff. A similar staff is needed in a dozen places where work has not yet been opened. When a worker lays down the tools, as in the case of the young teacher in Africa, who died so soon after reaching her post, some one is needed at once to fill the gap. Four nurses for the Philippines and six for China, eight teachers for China, and

A room in which United Offering Missionaries in Asheville, Tokyo, Los Angeles, Spokane, Oregon, Kyoto, Duluth, Hankow and Cape Palmas have been trained

ght for Japan, and parish helpers r each district are some of the immediate needs in the distant fields. ne teacher writes, "We appeal to e young women of the Church at me, because they must realize it is t fair that the freedom and happiness ought to women by the teachings of esus Christ should be confined to the men of the western world." The orkers on the field to-day are calling ck to those at home, "Say not ye, ere are yet four months, and then meth harvest? Behold, I say unto u, lift up your eyes and look on the lds, for they are white already to rvest."

Surely we must answer, "The harvest uly is great, but the labourers are few." e "pray therefore the Lord of the harst, that He would send forth labourers to His harvest." And there are in ission study classes, among leaders

and among older Juniors, those who will have the privilege of answering the call from the field for reinforcements.

Our United Offering doctors from New York and Minnesota, with a Connecticut missionary whom the Daughters of the King support, on the steps of the Ladies' House, Sinza, Shanghai, looking for reinforcements.

(385)

ACKNOWLEDGMENT OF OFFERINGS

Offerings are asked to sustain missions in thirty missionary districts in the United States, Africa, China, Japan, Brazil, Mexico and Cuba; also work in the Haitien Church; in forty-two dioceses, including missions to the Indians and to the Colored People; to pay the salaries of thirty-two bishops, and stipends to 2,253 missionary workers, domestic and foreign; also two general missionaries to the Swedes and two missionaries among deaf-mutes in the Middle West and the South; and to support schools, hospitals and orphanages. With all remittances the name of the Diocese and Parish should be given. Remittances, when practicable, should be by Check or Draft, and should always be made payable to the order of George Gordon King, Treasurer, and sent to him, Church Missions House, 281 Fourth Avenue, New York. Remittances in Bank Notes are not safe unless sent in Registered Letters.

The Treasurer of the Board of Missions acknowledges the receipt of the following from March 1st to April 1st, 1910.

* Lenten and Easter Offering from the Sunday-school Auxiliary.

NOTE.—*The items in the following pages marked "Sp." are Specials which do not aid the Board in meeting its appropriations. In the heading for each Diocese the total marked "Ap." is the amount which does aid the Board of Missions in meeting its appropriations. Wherever the abbreviation "Wo. Aux." precedes the amount, the offering is through a branch of the Woman's Auxiliary.*

Home Dioceses

Alabama

Ap. $730.99; *Sp.* $10.00

NISTON—*Grace*: Gen.	13 00
BMINGHAM—*St. Mary's*: Gen.	92 77
LIGEE—*St. Mark's*: Dom. and Frn.	10 00
SLEY—*St. John's*: Dom. and Frn.	35 00
FALA—*St. James's S. S.*: Gen.	6 00
TAW—*St. Stephen's*: $35.14, S. S.,* $35, Gen.; Sp. for Dr. Burke, Alaska, for invalid children, $10.	80 14
UNSDALE—*St. Michael's*: Gen.	20 00
ORENCE—*Trinity Church*: Gen.	3 00
DSDEN—*Church of the Holy Comforter*: $20, S. S.,* $14.37, Gen.	34 37
EENSBORO—*St. Paul's S. S.*: Gen.	10 00
EENVILLE—*St. Thomas's S. S.*: Gen.	53 63
RLEY—Gen.	2 00
NTSVILLE—*Nativity*: Gen.	102 80
VINGSTON—*St. James's*: Dom. and Frn.	15 00
BILE—*St. John's*: Dom., $10; China, $5; Brazil, $5; Japan Training-school, $5.	25 00
NTGOMERY—*Church of the Holy Comforter*: $100, S. S.,* $25, Gen.	125 00
MEIGS—*Grace*: Gen.	10 00
W DECATUR—*St. John's*: $45, Apportionment, 1908-09, $15, Gen.	60 00
RDUB HILL—*St. James's S. S.*: Gen.	10 06
BFFIELD—*Grace S. S.*: Gen.	5 22
OTTSBORO—*St. Luke's*: Gen.	1 00
LLADEGA—*St. Peter's*: Gen.	7 50
SCUMBIA—*St. John's S. S.*: Gen.	19 50

Albany

Ap. $1,173.20; *Sp.* $86.46

BANY—*All Saints'*: Gen. $294.85; "Friends," St. John's University, Expansion Fund, Shanghai, $15.50, Mrs. G. P. Wilson, Sp. for Brazil, Theological books.	310 35
	10 00
ASHLAND—*Trinity Church*: Gen.	16 00
BALLSTON SPA—*Christ Church*: Gen.	2 21
CAIRO—*Calvary*: $21, S. S.,* Sp. for Rutherford Associate Mission, Asheville, $5.	26 00
CAMBRIDGE—*St. Luke's*: Gen.	10 51
CANTON—*Grace S. S.*: Gen.	31 44
COLTON—*Zion*: Dom., $4.95; Miss Elizabeth Clarkson, St. John's University, Shanghai, $100; S. S.,* Dom., $18.45.	123 40
COOPERSTOWN—*Orphan House of the Holy Saviour S. S.*: Gen.	33 04
COXSACKIE—*Christ Church*: Gen.	9 80
DELHI—*St. John's*: Frn., $42.76; Wo. Aux., Sp. for Bishop Horner's mountain work, Asheville, $10; Sp. for Bishop Griswold, Salina, $4.11; S. S.,* Gen., $35.31.	92 18
FAIRFIELD—*Trinity Church*: Frn.	25
GOUVERNEUR — *Trinity Church*: Miss Grace H. Coslin, Sp. for Expansion Fund, St. John's University, Shanghai	1 00
GRANVILLE — *Trinity Church*: Dom., $4.80; Frn., $4.80; S. S.,* Dom., $7; Frn., $7.	23 60
KINDERHOOK—*St Paul's*: Wo. Aux., Sp. for St. John's University, Shanghai, $4.25; Sp. for St. Margaret's School, Tokyo, $2.75; Sp. for St. Mary's Hall, Shanghai, $2.75.	9 75
LAKE GEORGE—*St. James's S. S.*: Gen.	16 00
MECHANICVILLE—*St. Luke's*: Wo. Aux., Sp. for Rev. R. C. Wilson's work, Shanghai	3 10
MIDDLEVILLE—*Memorial*: Frn., $11.75, S. S.,* $5, Gen.	16 75
OGDENSBURG—*St. John's*: Indian.	23 00
PHILMONT—*St. Mark's*: Gen.	5 00
SALEM—*St. Paul's*: Wo. Aux., Sp. for Bishop Kendrick, Arizona, $1; Sp. for St. Luke's Hospital, Tokyo, $2.	3 00
SCHUYLERVILLE—*St. Stephen's S. S.*: Gen.	11 33

SOUTH CAIRO—"A Friend," Frn., $25; Sp. for Expansion Fund, St. John's University, Shanghai, $10......... 35 00
SPRINGFIELD CENTRE — St. Mary's: Gen. 162 74
STOTTVILLE—St. Barnabas's S. S.*: Gen. 26 48
TROY—Holy Cross: In memoriam "A. J. S.," Gen.................... 100 00
St. Barnabas's: Dom., $8.22, Frn., $17.72, S. S.,* $33.03, Gen....... 58 97
St. Paul's: Sp. for Mrs. T. C. Wetmore, Christ Church School, Arden, Asheville 15 00
WALTON—Christ Church S. S.*: Gen.. 43 15
WARRENSBURGH—Holy Cross S. S.*: Gen. 40 61

Arkansas
Ap. $193.93

CAMDEN—St. John's: Wo. Aux., Gen.. 17 00
FORREST CITY—Church of the Good Shepherd: Wo. Aux., Gen 5 00
HELENA — St. John's: Wo. Aux., "Helena" scholarship, St. Hilda's School, Wuchang, Hankow......... 50 00
"A Friend," Porto Rico........... 7 50
LITTLE ROCK—Christ Church: Frn., $23.43; Gen., $75................. 98 43
St. Margaret's: Gen................. 6 00
NEWPORT—St. Paul's: Gen............ 10 00

Atlanta
Ap. $131.83; *Sp.* $100.00

ATHENS—Emmanuel Church: Brazil, $3; Dom. and Frn. (of which "Thank Easter Offering," $5), $62.03 .... 65 03
Incarnation: Gen.................. 16 20
ATLANTA—St. Luke's: Sp. for Dr. Correll, Kyoto 100 00
GRIFFIN—St. George's S. S.*: Gen... 10 60
ROME—St. Peter's: Gen............. 40 00

Bethlehem
Ap. $1,402.82; *Sp.* $87.47

BETHLEHEM—Mrs. Joseph W. Richards, Sp. for Expansion Fund, St. John's University, Shanghai............. 1 00
CANTON—St. James's S. S.*: Dom... 1 50
CARBONDALE—Trinity Church: Wo. Aux., Gen....................... 10 00
DUNMORE—St. Mark's: Gen......... 7 50
EAST MAUCH CHUNK—St. John's: St. Agnes's Guild, Sp. for St. Mary's-on-the-Mountain, Sewanee, Tennessee 25 00
EASTON—Trinity Church S. S.*: Dom. and Frn.................... 52 61
GREAT BEND—Grace: Gen......... 8 00
HAZLETON—St. Peter's: Gen., $52.80; Junior Aux., Sp. for work of Rev. W. B. Thorn, Oneida, Fond du Lac, $5 .... 57 80
JONESTOWN—St. Mark's: Gen....... 10 00
MAHANOY CITY—Faith Church: Gen.. 16 00
MILFORD—Church of the Good Shepherd: Dom., $36.15; Frn., $7.71.. 43 86
PLYMOUTH—St. Peter's: Gen......... 29 68
POTTSVILLE—Trinity Church: Mrs. G. R. Kaercher, Sp. for Alaskan Hospital Fund.................... 10 00
SAYRE—Church of the Redeemer: Frn. 52 52
SCRANTON—Church of the Good Shepherd: Dom., $11.01; Frn., $100.... 111 01
St. David's: Gen., $6.77; Sp. for St. Paul's College, Tokyo, $3......... 9 77
St. Luke's: Dom., $20; Frn., $360; Gen., $2.47; Sp. for St. Paul's College, Tokyo, $8.47............... 390 94
SOUTH BETHLEHEM—Nativity Cathedral: Gen., $38.10; John L. Meigs, Sp. for St. John's College Expansion Fund, Shanghai, $25........... 63 10
SPRINGFIELD—Mrs. H. M. H. Root,

Porto Rico......................
WHITE HAVEN—St. Paul's: Gen......
WILKES-BARRE—Calvary S. S.: Gen..
St. Stephen's: Dom., $530; Junior Aux., Sp. for scholarship, St. Paul's School, Beaufort, East Carolina, $10 ....

California
Ap. $214.77; *Sp.* $295.07

ALAMEDA—Christ Church: Sp. for Shanghai Catechist School, Land and Building Fund................
BERKELEY—St. Mark's: Gen.........
BURLINGAME — St. Matthew's School: Gen. ....
FRESNO—St. James's: Gen..........
HANSFORD—Church of the Saviour: Gen. ....
MILL VALLEY—Church of Our Saviour: Ladies' Guild, Sp. for Shanghai Catechist School, Land and Building Fund ....
MODESTO—St. Paul's: Sp. for Rev. J. W. Nichols's School, Shanghai.....
MONTEREY—St. James's: Gen........
OAKLAND—St. Paul's: Miss Mary K. Robertson, Sp. for Shanghai Catechist School Fund...........
ROSS—St. John's: Natalie Coffin, Sp. for Shanghai Catechist School, Land and Building Fund...........
SAN FRANCISCO—St. John's: Gen.....
St. Luke's: $29.50, S. S.,* 50 cts. Gen.; A. N. Drown, Sp. for Shanghai Catechist School Fund, $25...
Trinity Church: Mrs. Huntsman, $5, Mrs. H. Babcock, $50, Mrs. W. B. Bourn, $100, Sp. for Shanghai Catechist School Fund.............
Wo. Aux., "A Diocesan Officer," Gen. ....
SANGER—Gen. ....
SAN JOSE—Trinity Church: St. Paul's School, Lawrenceville, Southern Virginia, $5; Sp. for Rev. J. W. Nichols's School, Shanghai, $20....
SAN RAFAEL—St. Paul's: Gen........
STOCKTON—St. Paul's: Wo. Aux., Sp. for Anvik Mission, Alaska, $10; S. S.,* Gen., $3................
VISALIA—St. Paul's: Gen...........
MISCELLANEOUS—Offering at convention, Sp. for Shanghai Catechist School Fund..................

Central New York
Ap. $721.30; *Sp.* $182.20

AUGUSTA—St. Andrew's: Gen........
AURORA—St. Paul's: Gen...........
BAINBRIDGE—St. Peter's: Sp. for St. Paul's College, Tokyo.............
CAZENOVIA—St. Peter's: King's Daughters, Sp. for Rev. John S. Moody, Hickory, Asheville................
CLAYTON—Christ Church: $17.26, "H. X.," $5.50, "T. I.," $1, S. S,* $7.14, Gen. ....
CLINTON—St James's: Gen..........
HARPURSVILLE—St. Luke's: $8, S. S.,* $7.70, Gen...................
KINGS FERRY—Sarah A. Goodyear, Gen. ....
LACONA—Miss L. Wadsworth, Indian.
LAFARGEVILLE—St. Paul's: Gen......
MANLIUS—Christ Church: $50, S. S.,* $9.56, Gen.....................
ONONDAGA CASTLE—Church of the Good Shepherd: $1.31, S. S.,* $13.19, Gen...................
ORISKANY FALLS—Church of the Good Shepherd: $13, S. S.,* $4, Gen....
OXFORD—St. Paul's: Colored.........
PULASKI—St. James's S. S.*: Gen...

130 00	
9 16	
2 00	

Connecticut

Ap. $6,841.61; *Sp.* $1,276.85

BANTAM—"C. H. B.," Frn...........	5 00
BETHLEHEM—*Christ Church*: Gen....	25 00
Miss Emeline Doolittle, Gen.......	1 00
BRIDGEPORT—*St. John's*: Dom. and	
Frn., $293.76, S. S.,* 50 cts., Gen..	294 26

53 17	St. Luke's: Gen.................... 8 00
101 11	Trinity Church: Bishop Kinsolving,
	Brazil, $1; Gen., $307.48.......... 308 48
	BROOKLYN—*Trinity Church*: Gen..... 5 00
	CHESHIRE—*St. Peter's*: Gen........ 80 00
69 57	CLINTON—*Holy Advent*: $7.35, S. S.,*
	50 cts., Gen.................... 7 85
	DARIEN—*St. Luke's* Gen............. 100 00
	EAST HADDAM—Mrs. F. C. H. Wendel,
	Bishop Graves's work in Shanghai,
	$1; Rev. Dr. F. C. H. Wendel, Bish-
	op Partridge's work, Kyoto, $1.50;
61 99	Sp. for Rev. W. J. Cuthbert's work
	at St. Mary's, Kyoto, $1.50....... 4 00
	EAST HARTFORD—*St. John's*: Gen.... 60 00
	GLASTONBURY—*St. James's*: Gen..... 35 00
150 00	GREENWICH — *Christ Church*: "A
9 32	Friend," Sp. for Brazil, theological
	books 20 00
	HARTFORD — *Christ Church*: Dom.,
25 00	$300; Frn., $200; Gen., $100...... 600 00
	St. John's: Gen.................. 50 00
	St. Monica's: Gen................. 6 30
	St. Thomas's: Gen................. 30 00
	Trinity Church: Dom., $117.33; Arch-
	deacon Joyner, North Carolina, $5;
1 00	Frn., $117.32; Bishop Van Buren,
	Porto Rico, $5; "A Member," Gen.,
53 00	$2,000; Sp. for Rev. J. S. Russell,
	St. Paul's School, Lawrenceville,
	Southern Virginia, $250; Sp. for
203 30	Rev. A. B. Hunter, St. Augustine's
	School, Raleigh, North Carolina,
297 17	$250; Sp. for Bishop Brooke, All
67 56	Saints' Hospital, South McAlester,
	Oklahoma, $75; Sp. for Bishop
80 91	Rowe, Alaska, $100; Sp. for memor-
20 00	ial to Bishop Hare, South Dakota,
	$25; Sp. for Rev. D. T. Huntington,
1 00	Ichang, Hankow, $250; Sp. for
	Boone College Library, Wuchang,
1 00	Hankow, $50; "A Friend," Sp. for
	Bishop L. H. Wells, Spokane, Wash-
29 00	ington, $3.................... 3,247 65
30 00	Rev. I. T. Beckwith, D.D., Gen...... 20 00
	LITCHFIELD—*St. Michael's*: "A Mem-
40 00	ber," Wo. Aux., Gen............. 5 00
15 00	LONG HILL—*Grace*: Gen............. 40 00
	MIDDLE HADDAM—*Christ Church*: Rev.
5 00	W. P. Waterbury, Sp. for salary
1 00	of Mr. Howard Richards, Jr., Boone
	College, Wuchang, Hankow......... 20 00
	MILFORD—*St. Peter's*: Frn., $5; Gen.,
15 00	$25.85; Junior Aux., Sp. for Expan-
15 00	sion Fund, St. John's University,
2 35	Shanghai, $7.75................. 38 60
	NEW HAVEN—*Christ Church*: Gen.,
40 00	$99.77; Sp. for Bishop Rowe, Alaska,
	$6; "A Member," Sp. for Bishop
2 00	Rowe's work, Alaska, $5; Daughters
17 75	of the King, Sp. for Rev. Mr. Cuth-
	bert, Kyoto, $3.................. 113 77
	Epiphany: Gen................... 22 00
48 80	St. James's (Fair Haven): Gen...... 109 44
10 00	St. Paul's: Gen.................. 333 60
237 00	St. Thomas's: Gen................ 415 59
	NEWINGTON—*Grace*: Gen............ 11 00
	NEW MILFORD—*St. John's*: $50, Chap-
	ter No. 17, Brotherhood of St. Paul,
	$5, Gen........................ 55 00
	NORWALK—*St. Paul's*: $151.64, "E.
	L. S.," $15, Gen................. 166 64
	NORWICH—*Christ Church*: Gen., $360;
	Sp. for Bishop Johnson, South Da-
	kota, $20.60 .... 380 60
40 00	Trinity Church: Gen............. 1 00
1 12	PLAINVILLE—*Church of Our Saviour*:
100 00	Gen. 13 00

POMFRET—Pomfret School: Expenses of running Pelican, Alaska, $100; Gen., $60 .... 160 00
RIDGEFIELD—St. Stephen's: Gen 200 00
ROXBURY—Christ Church: Gen 27 12
SANDY HOOK—St. John's: Gen 42 00
SOUTH LYME—St. Michael's: Gen.... 2 00
SOUTH MANCHESTER—St. Mary's: Frn. 73 68
SOUTHPORT—Trinity Church: Dom., $10.16; Frn., $11.70; Dom. and Frn., $50.15 .... 72 01
STAFFORD SPRINGS—Grace: Gen 15 00
STAMFORD—St. Andrew's: Gen 283 08
St. John's: Sp. for Irvin H. Correll, Kyoto, $25; "A Member," Sp. for Bishop Rowe, Alaska, $100; Wilson L. Baldwin, Sp. for Expansion Fund, St. John's University, Shanghai, $5; Miss Elizabeth M. Brown, Sp. for salary of Mr. Howard Richards, Jr., Boone College, Wuchang, Hankow, $10; S. S.,* Gen., 50 cts 140 50
THOMASTON—Trinity Church: Gen.. 73 15
THOMPSONVILLE—St. Andrew's: Gen.. 33 54
TORRINGTON—Trinity Church: Gen 135 16
WASHINGTON—St. John's: Gen 8 03
WATERBURY—St. John's: Gen 54 54
WATERVILLE—St. Paul's: Gen 12 43
WILTON—St. Matthew's: Gen 12 00
YANTIC—Grace: $74.44, S. S.,* $17, Gen 91 44
MISCELLANEOUS—St. Leger Fund, "A Friend," Sp. at discretion of Miss Bessie Mead, Tokyo, for the education of a young girl 50 00

Dallas
Ap. $163.73; Sp. $6.75
ABILENE—Heavenly Rest: Gen 6 50
AMARILLO—St. Andrew's: Wo. Aux., $10, S. S.,* 50 cts., Gen 10 50
DALLAS—All Saints': Gen 10 00
FORT WORTH—St. Andrew's: Dom. and Frn., $71.25; Wo. Aux., Gen., $30.. 101 25
Trinity Church S. S.: Sp. for St. John's University, Shanghai 6 75
HAMILTON—St. Mary's: Gen 4 50
TEXARKANA—St. James's: Gen 21 00
MISCELLANEOUS — Wo. Aux., Alaska, $2.50; Mexico, $2.50; Gen., $5 .... 10 00

Delaware
Ap. $352.64
BRIDGEVILLE—St. Mary's: Gen 5 00
CAMDEN—St. Paul's: Gen 20 00
CLAYTON—Trinity Church: Gen 10 00
DOVER—Christ Church: $22.35, S. S.,* $22.95, Gen 45 30
GEORGETOWN—St. Paul's: Frn 12 56
MIDDLETOWN—St. Anne's: Gen 3 55
WILMINGTON—Immanuel Church: Frn. 73 29
St. Andrew's: Frn 10 00
Trinity Church: Frn 172 94

Duluth
Ap. $215.40
DULUTH—St. Paul's S. S.*: Gen 165 00
WILLOW RIVER—St. Jude's S. S.*: Gen 50 40

East Carolina
Ap. $403.33; Sp. $68.17
AVOCA—Holy Innocents': Gen 5 00
AYDEN—St. James's S. S.*: Gen 7 50
COLUMBIA—St. Andrew's: Gen 62
EDENTON—St. Paul's: M. Wakely, Sp. for Church Extension Fund, Porto Rico 10 00
ELIZABETH CITY—Christ Church: Wo. Aux., Sp. for St. Paul's College, Tokyo 11 92
FAYETTEVILLE—St. John's: Gen 16 27
KINSTON—St. Mary's S. S.*: Asheville,

$5.92; Gen., $30 .... 35 9
MURFREESBORO—St. Barnabas's: Gen.. 2
SCUPPERNONG—St. David's: Gen.. 2
SNOW HILL—St. Barnabas's: $10, S. S.,* $7.45, Gen 17
TRENTON—Grace: Gen 1
WILMINGTON—St. James's: Sp. for Asheville 5
St. John's: Gen 50
St. Paul's: Miss E. Watson, Dom.. 5
"E. C., In Memory of Mrs. A. A. Watson," St. Margaret's School, Tokyo 158
"A Friend," Sp. for care of one child at St. Mary's Orphanage, Shanghai, $40; expenses of one pupil for one year at Church Training-school for Women, Shanghai, $50.. 90
Julia N. Parsley, Sp. for Bishop Horner's work, Asheville 1
WINDSOR—St. Thomas's: Gen 5
WOODVILLE—Grace: Gen ....
MISCELLANEOUS—Junior Aux., Gen.... 45

Easton
Ap. $57.72
KENT Co.—Shrewsbury (Kennedyville): $12.50, S. S.,* $27, Gen.... 39
QUEEN ANNE's Co. (Centreville): "Two Friends," Gen 10
SOMERSET Co.—St. Mark's S. S.* (Kingston): Dom., $1.73; Frn., $1.73 3
WORCESTER Co.—St. Paul's-by-the-Sea (Ocean City): $1.26, S. S.,* $3.50, Gen 4

Florida
Ap. $84.81
CEDAR KEY—Christ Church: Gen 4
FORT GEORGE—St. George's: Gen 7
JACKSONVILLE—Church of the Good Shepherd S. S.*: Gen 69
WEWAHITCHKA—St. John's: Gen 4

Fond du Lac
Ap. $186.40; Sp. $13.00
APPLETON—All Saints': St. Peter's Hospital, Wuchang, Hankow 2
FOND DU LAC—St. Paul's: Dom 82
GREEN BAY—Church of the Blessed Sacrament S. S.*: Gen 1
OSHKOSH—Trinity Church S. S.*: Gen. 100
SHEBOYGAN FALLS—St. Peter's: Sp. for operating table, St. Peter's Hospital, Wuchang, Hankow 13

Georgia
Ap. $147.49
AUGUSTA—St. Andrew's S. S.*: Gen.. 2
DUBLIN—Christ Church: $5, S. S.,* $2.52, Gen 7
FITZGERALD—St. Matthew's S. S.*: Dom 6
HAWKINSVILLE—St. Luke's: $6.10, S. S.,* $7.75, Gen 13
ST. MARY'S—Church of Our Saviour S. S.*: Gen. (of which for Apportionment, 1909, $2.25) 7
SAVANNAH—Christ Church: Wo. Aux., "Bishop Elliott" scholarship, Boone University, Wuchang, Hankow, $40; "Isabel C. Habersham" scholarship, St. Mary's Hall, Shanghai, $40 80
THOMASVILLE—St. Thomas's S. S.*: Gen 30

Harrisburg
Ap. $854.48
BEDFORD—St. James's: $13.68, S. S.,* $4.66, Gen 18
EVERETT—Christ Church: $7.98, S. S.,*

12 98
29 37

5 00
25 90

87 82
216 50
34 00
25 00
12 13
19 49

2 50

335 45
30 00

4 64
14 14
7 26
1 00
10 00
3 40

32 22

10 00
15 00
4 50
129 07
2 85

20 00
10 52
3 95
33 72
21 76

10 00
1 80
41 65
6 64

39 60
3 20
39 76

5 00
3 80
5 00
2 00
10 72
9 00
3 90
166 52

60 00

45 00
100 00

40 00
10 00

Gen.	12 52
MARSHALL—*Trinity Church S. S.**:	
Gen.	20 00
SPRINGFIELD—*Christ Church S. S.**:	
Gen.	16 57

Kentucky
Ap. $276.12

GLASGOW—Harry G. Whitney, Gen...	1 00
GUTHRIE—Kate O. Smith,* Gen......	47
HENDERSON—*St. Clement's*: Gen....	3 00
St. Paul's: Dom....................	35 00
LOUISVILLE—*Christ Cathedral*: Wo. Aux. (of which Junior Aux., $27.50), Gen.....................	100 50
St. Mark's (Crescent Hill): Wo. Aux., $15, Boys' Branch, Junior Aux., $2, Gen.	17 00
OWENSBORO—*Trinity Church*: Gen....	35 00
PADUCAH—*Grace*: Gen...............	73 40
UNIONTOWN—*St. John's S. S.**: Gen..	10 75

Lexington
Ap. $68.25

CORBIN—*St. John's*: Gen.............	5 00
COVINGTON—*St. Stephen's Mission*: Gen.	5 00
Trinity Church: Gen...............	43 75
HARRODSBURG—*St. Philip's S. S.**: Gen.	3 00
LEXINGTON—*St. Andrew's*: Gen......	2 25
NICHOLASVILLE—*All Saints'*: Gen.....	1 75
PARIS—*St. Peter's*: Gen.............	7 50

Long Island
Ap. $5,922.87; *Sp.* $1,971.35

ASTORIA—*St. George's*: Gen.........	60 00
BELLPORT—*Christ Church*: $10, S. S.,* $3.54, Gen....................	13 54
BRIDGEHAMPTON—*St. Ann's*: $11.50, S. S.,* 50 cts., Gen..............	12 00
BROOKLYN—*Ascension*: Wo. Aux., Sp. for sewing-teacher's salary, St. Augustine's School, Raleigh, North Carolina	1 00
Christ Church (Clinton Street): Dom., $137; China, $5; Frn., $30; Africa, $15; Japan, $18; Brazil, $524.25; Gen., $514.96; Sp. for Rev. J. L. Taylor, Newberne, East Carolina, $20; Wo. Aux., Sp. for sewing-teacher's salary, St. Augustine's School, Raleigh, North Carolina, $2.	1,266 21
Church of St. Mark (Eastern Parkway): Miss Hubbard's Sunday-school class, Sp. for Bishop Rowe, Alaska	2 00
Church of St. Matthew: Dom., $178.62; Frn., $178.63........	357 25
Grace (Heights): Sp. for Bishop Rowe, Alaska, $1,100; Sp. for Bishop Graves, Kearney, $200; Sp. for Bishop Wells, Spokane, $100; Sp. for Bishop Gailor, Tennessee, for Colored work, $100; Sp. for Bishop Cheshire, North Carolina, for Colored work, $100; Sp. for Bishop Restarick, Honolulu, $50; Sp. for Bishop Johnston, West Texas, for Colored work, $50; Sp. for Bishop Funsten, for St. Margaret's School, Boisé, Idaho, $50............	1,750 00
Holy Trinity Church: Wo. Aux., Sp. for sewing-teacher's salary, St. Augustine's School, Raleigh, North Carolina	5 00
Incarnation: Gen..................	136 88
Church of the Redeemer: Gen., $7.82; Sp. for Bishop Rowe, Alaska, $50; Wo. Aux., Sp. for Building Fund, St. John's University, Shanghai, $5.	62 82
St. Andrew's S. S.: Dom. and Frn....	10 18
St. Ann's: China, $5; Japan, $5; Africa, $5; Brazil, $4; Mexico, $4;	

Cuba, $4; Haiti, $3; Frn.,
$2,883.76; Sp. for Rev. Mr. Hunt-
ington for Beggar School, Ichang,
Hankow, $20; Wo. Aux., Rev. H.
St. George Tucker's work, Tokyo,
$10; Sp. for Rev. Dr. Pott's Build-
ing Fund, St. John's University,
Shanghai, $10; Sp. for sewing-
teacher's salary, St. Augustine's
School, Raleigh, North Carolina, $2. 2,905 76
St. Augustine's: Wo. Aux., Sp. for
sewing-teacher's salary, St. Augus-
tine's School, Raleigh, North Caro-
lina 2 00
St. George's: Wo. Aux., Sp. for sew-
ing-teacher's salary, St. Augustine's
School, Raleigh, North Carolina.... 3 00
St. Mark's (Adelphi Street): Wo. Aux.,
Sp. for sewing-teacher's salary, St.
Augustine's School, Raleigh, North
Carolina 1 00
St. Martin's: Gen. 25 00
St. Michael's (High Street): Gen..... 85 66
St. Paul's (Flatbush): Gen. (of which
S. S.,* $249.20), $254.20; Sp. for
American Church Institute for
Negroes, $25..................... 279 20
St. Philip's Chapel S. S.*: Gen...... 10 00
Transfiguration: Gen.................. 8 00
Mrs. Margaret T. Clark, Gen...... 1 00
Bequest of Mrs. Helen D. Par-
tridge, Sp. for Bishop Rowe, Alaska 19 35
M. L. Lockwood, Sp. for Brazil,
theological books.................. 5 00
FLUSHING—St. George's: Dom., $3.50;
Frn., $1.05; Wo. Aux., Sp. for
sewing-teacher's salary, St. Augus-
tine's School, Raleigh, North Caro-
lina, $1; S. S.,* Gen., $119.34.... 124 89
FREEPORT—Transfiguration: Frn...... 1 32
GARDEN CITY—Cathedral of the Incar-
nation: Gen........................ 450 00
GREAT NECK—All Saints' S. S.:
Church hospital in China........ 4 00
GREAT RIVER—Emmanuel S. S.*: Gen. 12 00
HUNTINGTON—St. John's S. S.*: Gen. 50
JAMAICA—Grace: Gen.................. 20 30
LAUREL HILL—St. Mary's Chapel S. S.*:
Dom. and Frn...................... 20 00
MANHASSET—Christ Church S. S.*:
Gen. 15 51
MASSAPEQUA—Grace S. S.*: Gen...... 16 85
MERRICK—Church of the Redeemer
S. S.*: Gen......................... 1 50
RICHMOND HILL—Resurrection: Dom.. 100 00
RIVERHEAD—Grace S. S.*: Frn....... 6 50
ROSLYN—Trinity Church: Wo. Aux.,
Sp. for sewing-teacher's salary, St.
Augustine's School, Raleigh, North
Carolina 5 00
STONY BROOK—St. James's: Gen..... 51 00
MISCELLANEOUS—The Church Club,
Sp. for Expansion Fund, St. John's
University, Shanghai.............. 25 00
Rev. William T. Holden, Sp. for
Expansion Fund, St. John's Univer-
sity, Shanghai.................... 10 00
Wo. Aux., Anniversary Offering, Sp.
for sewing-teacher's salary, St.
Augustine's School, Raleigh, North
Carolina 8 00

Los Angeles

Ap. $169.21; Sp. $31.75

LONG BEACH—St. Luke's: Sp. for
Land and Building Fund of Shang-
hai Catechist School............... 10 15
LOS ANGELES—Epiphany: Wo. Aux.,
Sp. for Rev. J. W. Nichols, Shang-
hai 7 00
St. John's: Wo. Aux., Mrs. M. E.
Cowles, Sp. for Priory School, Hono-
lulu, $1; Sp. for St. Mary's-on-the-
Mount, Sewanee, Tennessee, $1.... 2 00
Mary C. Dunlap, "In Memory of

Bishop Dunlap," Gen............. 7 00
REDLANDS—Trinity Church: Dom. and
Frn., $91.21; Sp. for St. Paul's Col-
lege Fund, Tokyo, $7.75........... 98 96
SAN BERNARDINO—St. John's; Wo.
Aux., Sp. for Rev. J. W. Nichols,
Shanghai 4 85
SAN DIEGO—All Saints': Gen........ 10 00
St. Paul's: Gen.................... 46 80
SAN PEDRO—St. Peter's Mission: Gen.. 14 20

Louisiana

Ap. $549.76

COVINGTON—Christ Church: Dom. and
Frn................................ 11 70
LAKE CHARLES—Church of the Good
Shepherd: Junior Aux., Gen...... 11 28
LAKE PROVIDENCE—Grace: Gen..... 2 70
MANSFIELD—Christ Memorial Church:
Gen............................... 10 00
NEW IBERIA—Epiphany: Frn., $5;
Gen., $22......................... 27 00
NEW ORLEANS—Grace: Frn.......... 115 00
St. Andrew's: Dom. and Frn....... 14 50
St. George's: Dom. and Frn., $17.58;
Gen., $90......................... 107 58
St. Luke's: Gen................... 20 00
St. Paul's: Gen................... 215 00
Mrs. Elizabeth A. T. Harris, Frn... 10 00
RAYVILLE—St. David's: Gen......... 5 00

Maine

Ap. $173.70

CALAIS—St. Anne's: Gen............
S. S.,* Dom., $2.50; Frn., $2.50.... 15 00
CAMDEN—St. Thomas's: Dom. and Frn. 25 00
NEWCASTLE—St. Andrew's: Gen...... 2 00
NORWAY—Christ Church: Gen........ 5 00
PORTLAND—St. Stephen's: Frn....... 17 95
Trinity Chapel S. S.* (Woodford):
Gen............................... 50
PRESQUE ISLE—St. John's: Frn...... 6 00
RICHMOND—St. Matthew's Mission:
Gen............................... 1 75
ROCKLAND—St. Peter's S. S.*: Gen... 50
MISCELLANEOUS—Wo. Aux., Gen..... 100 00

Marquette

Ap. $165.72

BIG BAY—"A Baptismal Offering,"
Gen............................... 1 00
CRYSTAL FALLS—St. Mark's S. S.*:
Frn............................... 19 77
CURTIS—Gen........................ 3 57
DONALDSON—All Saints': Gen....... 8(
FAIRVIEW—St. Matthias's: Gen..... 2 3:
KELDON—Gen....................... 4(
KENNEDY'S—Gen.................... 4 8:
MARQUETTE—St. Paul's: $32.15, S. S.*
$30, Gen.......................... 62 1:
NEWBURY—All Saints': Gen......... 3 6(
ONTONAGON—Ascension S. S.*: Gen. 4 0(
RED JACKET—Christ Church S. S.*:
Gen............................... 27 8(
ROBER—Gen........................ 2 3:
RUDYARD—Gen...................... 2 1(
SPENCER—St. Barnabas's: Gen...... 1 0(
ST. IGNACE—Church of the Good Shep-
herd: Gen........................ 11 0'
VULCAN—Bethany S. S.*: Gen....... 2 0'
MISCELLANEOUS—Bishop G. Mott Wil-
liams, Gen........................ 20 0'

Maryland

Ap. $1,480.07; Sp. $1,052.43

ANNE ARUNDEL CO.—St. Anne's (Annapolis): Surgeon and Mrs. L. N.
Carpenter, $5, "A Friend," $5, Sp.
for Expansion Fund, St. John's University, Shanghai; Wo. Aux., Sp. for
famine sufferers, Mexico, $5...... 15 0
All Saints' (Annapolis Junction): Wo.

2 00	Sp. for Asheville.................	5 00
	Mt. Calvary: Gen...................	13 40
	HOWARD AND ANNE ARUNDEL Co's.—	
	Christ Church (Guilford): Gen....	25 50
182 54	WASHINGTON Co.—*St. John's* (Hagerstown): Wo. Aux., St. Luke's Hospital, Tokyo, $5; Sp. for Tsu Building Fund, Kyoto, $5; S. S., Young Ladies' Bible-class Society, St. Margaret's School, Tokyo, $15.50..	
50		
406 00		25 50
231 64	*St. Paul's* (Sharpsburg): $8.50, S. S.,* $7.18, Gen...............	15 68
88 78	*St. Anne's* (Smithburg): Dom. and Frn., $2.85; Sp. for St. Paul's College Building Fund, Tokyo, $2.25..	5 10
105 75	MISCELLANEOUS—Wo. Aux., expenses of St. Margaret's School, Tokyo.....	61 00
32 51		
	Junior Aux., Sp. for Bishop Rowe, Alaska	20 00
110 00		

Massachusetts

11 00	*Ap.* $5,531.20; *Sp.* $1,701.50	
	ANDOVER — *Christ Church*: Gen., $51.02; Wo. Aux., salary of missionary, Logan, Utah, $5..............	56 02
	BEACHMONT—*St. Paul's S. S.**: Gen..	1 25
8 98	BOSTON—*Ascension*: Gen............	10 05
5 00	*Emmanuel Church*: Gen., $500.98; Sp. for Bishop Rowe, Alaska, $5; Sp. for St. John's College Expansion Fund, Shanghai, $337.12; Wo. Aux., "Sarah F. Hoyt" scholarship, Orphan Asylum, Cape Palmas, West Africa, $50; Sp. for insurance, Bishop Ferguson, West Africa, $50; Sp. for insurance, Dr. Henry Laning, Kyoto, $50; Sp. for insurance, Rev. G. F. Mosher, Shanghai, $50; "A Member," Sp. for Rev. F. E. Lund, Wuhu, Hankow, $100; "A Member," Sp. for Rev. W. J. Cuthbert, Kyoto, $25; "A Member," Sp. for W. S. Claiborne's work, Tennessee, $25; Sp. for Rev. E. N. Joyner's work, Asheville, $5.......................	
5 00		
250 00		
250 00		
5 00		
10 00		
20 00		
200 00		1,198 10
50	*Emmanuel Church* (West Roxbury): Gen., $22.10; Wo. Aux., salary of missionary, Logan, Utah, $10......	32 10
22 36	*Church of the Holy Spirit* (Mattapan): Frn., $72.80; Wo. Aux., salary of missionary, Logan, Utah, $4.......	76 80
64 84		
3 00		
59 26	*Church of the Redeemer* (South Boston): Gen., $32.30; Wo. Aux., salary of missionary, Logan, Utah, $1; Soochow Mission, Shanghai, $1.50..	34 80
5 00		
	St. James's: Wo. Aux., salary of missionary, Logan, Utah, $5; salary of Rev. Nathan Matthews, Africa, $5; Sp. for Rev. W. J. Cuthbert, Kyoto, $50	60 00
30 00		
	St. John's (Jamaica Plain): Sp. for Bishop Wells, Spokane...........	17 00
25 00	*St. Mark's* (Dorchester): Gen........	10 00
	St. Mary's: Gen., $125; S. S.,* Gen., 50 cts.........................	125 50
5 00	*St. Paul's*: Dom., $325; Frn., $75; Gen., $1,597.36; Wo. Aux., salary of missionary, Logan, Utah, $10; "A Member," Sp. for "Christina" crib, St. Mary's Orphanage, Shanghai, $30.....................	2,037 36
4 48		
3 26	*St. Stephen's*: "A Parishioner," work of Bishop Funsten, Idaho..........	1 00
23 50	*Trinity Church*: Sp. for Bishop Rowe, Alaska, $463.35; Sp. for Bishop Griswold, Salina, $47; Sp. for St. Paul's College, Tokyo, $2; William O. Kellen, Sp. for Church Extension Fund, Porto Rico, $25; Wo. Aux., Sp. for St. Paul's College, Tokyo, $25; salary of Miss Wall, Tokyo, $50; salary of missionary, Logan, Utah, $384.84; salary of Rev. Nathan Matthews, West Africa, $100; Sp. for Life Insurance, Rev. T. S. Tyng, Kyoto, $3; "Frances A. Caryl	
3 80		
5 00		
10 00		
6 62		
127 00		
23 00		

Memorial" scholarship, Girls' Training Institute, St. Paul's River, West Africa, $25; S. S.,* Gen., 50 cts 1,125 69
Mrs. Thayer, Sp. for Alaska........ 200 00
"A Friend," Sp. for St. John's University Expansion Fund, Shanghai.. 1 00
BRIDGEWATER—*Trinity Church*: Gen.. 3 40
BROCKTON—*St. Paul's*: Gen......... 31 90
BROOKLINE—*All Saints'*: Sp. for Bishop Thomas, Wyoming, $7; Sp. for Bishop Griswold, Salina, $32.86. 39 86
Church of Our Saviour: Dom., $183.55; Wo. Aux., salary of missionary at Logan, Utah, $5; salary of Rev. Nathan Matthews, Africa, $1...... 189 55
St. Paul's: Wo. Aux., salary of missionary, Logan, Utah.............. 5 00
CAMBRIDGE—*St. James's*: Gen., $13.39; Wo. Aux., Soochow Mission, Shanghai, $20...................... 33 39
COHASSET—*St. Stephen's*: Wo. Aux., salary of missionary, Logan, Utah.. 5 00
DEDHAM—*St. Paul's*: Wo. Aux., salary of missionary, Logan, Utah..... 5 00
FALL RIVER—*Ascension*: Dom., $100; Frn., $100.................... 200 00
St. Mark's: Gen................... 65 18
FALMOUTH—*Church of the Messiah* (Wood's Hole): Indian, $11.90; missions to Colored people, $17.91; S. S. Infants' class, Sp. for children of Nenana, Alaska, $8.17.......... 37 98
St. Barnabas's: Gen............... 7 90
FRAMINGHAM — *St. Andrew's*: Wo. Aux., salary of missionary at Logan, Utah 1 00
GROTON—*Boys of Groton School*, Sp. for Alaska.................... 82 50
St. Andrew's: Gen............... 8 60
HAVERHILL—*St. John the Evangelist's*: Gen......................... 16 88
Trinity Church: Wo. Aux., salary of Mrs. McCalla, Africa............ 5 00
HINGHAM—*St. John's*: Wo. Aux., St. Luke's Hospital, Tokyo......... 1 00
LAWRENCE—*Grace*: Gen........... 306 67
St. Augustine's: Gen............. 60 49
LYNN—*St. Stephen's*: Gen......... 114 67
MALDEN—*St. Luke's*: Gen......... 19 69
MANSFIELD—*St. John Evangelist's*: Wo. Aux., salary of missionary at Logan, Utah 5 16
MARBLEHEAD—*St. Michael's*: Wo. Aux., "Penny Savings," salary of Mrs. McCalla, West Africa............... 5 00
MAYNARD—*St. George's S. S.**: Gen.. 50
MELROSE—*Trinity Church*: Wo. Aux., salary of missionary at Logan, Utah, $1; St. Luke's Hospital, Tokyo, $2...................... 3 00
NEW BEDFORD—*Grace*: Gen., $193.36; Wo. Aux., salary of missionary at Logan, Utah, $15; St. Luke's Hospital, Tokyo, $10; "A Member," Sp. for Archdeacon Spurr, West Virginia, $25.................... 243 36
NEWTON—*Church of the Redeemer* (Chestnut Hill): Wo. Aux., salary of missionary at Logan, Utah, $10; Soochow, Shanghai, $5; Sp. for insurance of Rev. T. S. Tyng, Kyoto, $5 .... 20 00
St. Paul's (Highlands): Wo. Aux., salary of missionary at Logan, Utah, $2; salary of Mrs. McCalla, Africa, $2 .... 4 00
St. Mary's (Lower Falls): Wo. Aux., salary of missionary at Logan, Utah, $2; salary of Rev. Nathan Matthews, Africa, $2................... 4 00
Trinity Church (Centre): Gen., $25.61; Wo. Aux., salary of missionary at Logan, Utah, $10; salary of Mrs. McCalla, Africa, $5....... 40 61
NORTH ANDOVER—*St. Paul's*: Wo. Aux., salary of missionary at Logan,

Utah ....
NORTH ATTLEBOROUGH—*Grace*: Gen...
NORWOOD—*Grace*: Gen., $6.13; Sp. for St. Paul's College, Tokyo, 50 cts...
PEABODY—*St. Paul's*: Gen., $16.54; Frn., $6....................
PLYMOUTH—*Christ Church*: Gen....
ROCKPORT—*St. Mary's Mission*: Gen..
SALEM—*Grace*: Gen............
SOUTHBOROUGH—*St. Mark's*: Gen....
SWANSEA—*Christ Church*: Wo. Aux., "Easter Offering," Sp. for Bishop Rowe, Alaska................
TAUNTON—*St. Thomas's*: Dom., $1.35; Colored, $108.59; Frn., $11.05; Gen., $104.28................
WAKEFIELD—*Emmanuel Church*: Wo. Aux., salary of missionary at Logan, Utah, $2; salary of Rev. Nathan Matthews, West Africa, $2......
WELLESLEY—*St. Andrew's*: Wo. Aux., Soochow Mission, Shanghai........
QUINCY—*St. Chrysostom's* (Wollaston): Gen......................
MISCELLANEOUS—Wo. Aux., Gen., $38.37; "A Memorial to Mrs. Charlotte F. Wilson," support of Bible-woman, China, $43; "In Memory of R. H. S.," Sp. for small organ for Ota, Tokyo, $25..............

Michigan

Ap. $1,268.80; Sp. $280.34

ANN ARBOR—*St. Andrew's*: Gen., $100; Wo. Aux., salary of Miss Bull, Kyoto, $10; "Harris Memorial" scholarship, St. John's University, Shanghai, $2.50; Sp. for Foreign Insurance Fund, $2................
BAY CITY—*Trinity Church*: Dom....
DETROIT—*Christ Church*: Sp. for Bishop Rowe's work, Alaska, $61.84; Mr. and Mrs. W. H. Hinckle, Sp. for Alaska, $50................
Church of the Messiah: Wo. Aux., salary of Miss Bull, Kyoto, $3; Sp. for Foreign Insurance Fund, $5; Sp. for Mrs. Littell, Hankow, $5......
St. Andrew's: Salary of Miss Bull, Kyoto, $3; "Harris Memorial" scholarship, St. John's University, Shanghai, $3; Sp. for Foreign Insurance Fund, $3; Sp. for Mrs. Littell, Hankow, $2; Sp. for Bishop McKim, Tokyo, $5................
St. James's: Wo. Aux., salary of Miss Bull, Kyoto, $10; Sp. for Foreign Insurance Fund, $2; Sp. for Mrs. Littell, Hankow, $2..........
St. John's: Gen., $845; "H. L.," Sp. for Bishop Horner, Asheville, $5...
St. Joseph's: Wo. Aux., salary of Miss Bull, Kyoto, $2; "Harris Memorial" scholarship, St. John's University, Shanghai, $3; "J. H. Johnson" scholarship, St. Andrew's School, Mexico, $5; Sp. for Foreign Insurance Fund, $2; Sp. for Mrs. Littell, Hankow, $3................
St. Matthew's: Wo. Aux., salary of Miss Bull, Kyoto, $2.50; "Harris Memorial" scholarship, St. John's University, Shanghai, $2.50........
St. Peter's: Wo. Aux., salary of Miss Bull, Kyoto, $2; Sp. for Mrs. Littell, Hankow, $2................
St. Philip's: Wo. Aux., Sp. for Mrs. Littell, Hankow................
St. Stephen's: Wo. Aux., salary of Miss Bull, Kyoto, $1; S. S.," Miss A. K. Molle's class, Sp. for St. Mary's Orphanage, Shanghai, $3..........
Trinity Church: Wo. Aux., salary of Miss Bull, Kyoto, $1; Sp. for Foreign Insurance Fund, $1; S. S.,* Sp.

70 00	MINNEAPOLIS—*All Saints' S. S.*: Sp. for St. Paul's College, Tokyo...... 5 00
21 00	OWATONNA—*St. Paul's*: Dom. and Frn., $53.05; Sp. for St. Paul's College, Tokyo, $1............... 54 05
30 00	RUSHFORD—*Emmanuel Church S. S.*;
10 00	Sp. for St. Paul's College, Tokyo..... 1 37
	ST. CHARLES—*Trinity Church*: Dom.
1 00	and Frn................... 3 00
50 00	ST. PAUL—*Christ Church and S. S.*: Gen., $20; Sp. for St. Paul's Col-
3 00	lege, Tokyo, $7.................. 27 00
	Epiphany: Gen................... 12 00
	St. John Evangelist's: Sp. for St. Paul's College, Tokyo, $12.93; Sp. for Bishop Brewster, Western Col- orado, $100; Sp. for Catechist's School, Shanghai, $50; S. S., Sp. for St. Paul's College, Tokyo,
19 50	$12.20 .... 175 13
1 00	*St. Matthew's*: Sp. for St. Paul's Col-
8 92	lege, Tokyo.................. 1 05
	"A Friend," Philippine Islands.... 54
	SLAYTON—*St. Barnabas's S. S.*: Gen. 1 71
	WABASHA—*Grace S. S.*: Gen........ 9 50
8 00	WATERVILLE—*St. Andrew's S. S.*:
3 93	Gen. 6 50

Mississippi

Ap. $350.54; *Sp.* $52.00

5 89	ABERDEEN—*St. John's S. S.*: Gen.... 4 12
5 89	BILOXI—*Church of the Redeemer*: Wo. Aux., Gen................... 4 50
93 47	CANTON—*Grace*: Wo. Aux., Gen..... 7 00
2 26	GREENVILLE—*St. James's*: Gen...... 21 56
10 00	GREENWOOD—*Nativity*: Wo. Aux., Gen. 10 00
8 23	JACKSON—*St. Andrew's*: Wo. Aux., Sp. for Foreign Life Insurance Fund, $50; Junior Aux., Gen., $16.64; S. S.,* Frn., $126.79............ 193 43
	St. Colomb's S. S.: Frn............ 14 87
5 00	LEXINGTON—*St. Mary's*: Wo. Aux., Gen. 5 50
	MERIDIAN—*St. Paul's*: Gen........ 57 85
	OCEAN SPRING—*St. John's*: Gen.... 4 65
	SCRANTON—*St. John's*: $4.16, S. S.,* $3.09, Gen.; Junior Aux., "Rev.
9 28	John's Patton" scholarship, St.
15 00	John's University, Shanghai, $2.40.. 9 65
4 43	SUMMIT—*Christ Church S. S.*: Gen.. 12 00
5 62	VICKSBURG—*All Saints' College*: Gen.,
15 96	$2.50; Junior Aux., "Rev. Robt. W. Patton" scholarship, St. John's Uni- versity, Shanghai, $2.50.......... 5 00
2 50	*St. Mary's S. S.*: Dom............. 10 00
1 00	WEST POINT—*Incarnation*: $19.11,
17 00	Wo. Aux., $3, Gen............... 22 11
	WINONA—*Immanuel Church*; Junior
44 05	Aux., "Rev. Robert W. Patton" schol-
34 50	arship, St. John's University,
10 35	Shanghai, $2; Gen., $2.......... 4 00
373 84	WOODVILLE—*St. Paul's*: Junior Aux.,
4 91	"Rev. Robert W. Patton" schol-
1 80	ship, St. John's University, Shang- hai 80
	YAZOO CITY—*Trinity Church*: Wo.
10 25	Aux., Gen................... 5 50
24 03	COMO and SARDIS—Babies' Branch, Gen., $8; Sp. for font, $2........ 10 00

Missouri

Ap. $1,703.10

100 00	COLUMBIA—*Calvary S. S.*: Gen...... 39 23
	FERGUSON—*St. Stephen's*: Gen....... 28 50
	MEXICO—*St. Paul's*: Gen........... 5 05
13 30	ST. LOUIS—*Christ Church Cathedral*: Dom., $55.59; Middle West Deaf-
4 15	Mutes, $34; Colored, $217.91; Frn.,
5 75	$182.50 .... 490 00
3 00	*Church of the Holy Communion*: Gen.. 157 29
	Hosmer Hall S. S.: Rev. Mr. Clapp,
12 14	Bontoc, Philippine Islands, $7.50;
14 75	Rev. Mr. Stanton, Sagada, Philippine
7 00	Islands, $7.50................ 15 00
10 00	*St. Alban's*: Gen................. 10 00
50	*St. John's*: Gen................. 2 00
12 00	*St. Peter's*: Dom., $44; Frn.,

$163.28; S. S.,* Dom., $120.22;
Frn., $120.23................... 447 73
VALLEY PARK—S. S.*: Gen.......... 8 30
MISCELLANEOUS—Right Rev. Daniel S.
Tuttle, D.D., Gen................ 500 00

Nebraska
Ap. $64.26

AUBURN—*Ascension S. S.*:* Gen...... 10 31
BEATRICE—*Christ Church*: Dom. and
Frn. 2 60
BLAIR—*St. Mary's*: Gen............ 15 00
CENTRAL CITY—*Christ Church*: Gen.. 3 05
CREIGHTON—*St. Mark's*: Dom. and
Frn. 5 25
NELIGH—*St. Peter's S. S.*:* Gen.... 10 00
OMAHA—*Church of the Good Shepherd*: Dom. and Frn., $17.05;
S. S.,* Gen., $1.............. 18 05

Newark
Ap. $2,519.63; *Sp.* $230.00

BAYONNE—*St. John's S. S.*:* Gen.... 8 69
CHATHAM—*St. Paul's S. S.*: Gen..... 3 73
CLIFTON—*St. Peter's*: Gen......... 2 16
EAST ORANGE—*Christ Church*: $198.77,
S. S.,* 50 cts., Gen............ 199 27
St. Agnes's: Gen................. 20 00
St. Paul's: Gen.................. 61 66
ENGLEWOOD—*St. Paul's*: Wo. Aux., Sp.
for Building Fund, St. Margaret's
School, Tokyo, $5; Junior Aux.,
Gen., $40.................... 45 00
GRANTWOOD—*Trinity Church S. S.*:
Gen. 7 03
HOBOKEN—*St. Paul's*: Gen......... 110 07
JERSEY CITY—*St. Paul's S. S.*:* Gen.. 50
MADISON—*Grace S. S.*: Gen......... 7 45
MAPLEWOOD—*St. George's*: Gen...... 50 00
MONTCLAIR—*St. James's S. S.* (Upper): Sp. for Bishop Rowe, Alaska. 10 00
St. Luke's: "Mary L. Carter" scholarship, Orphan Asylum, Cape Palmas,
$50; Frn., $350; Cuba, $37.70;
Brazil, $37.71................. 475 41
NEWARK—*St. Barnabas's*: Gen...... 24 00
St. Paul's: Gen.................. 52 15
ORANGE—*Grace*: $1,150, S. S.,* Miss
Richard's class, 50 cts., Gen.; Sp.
for Bishop Rowe, Alaska, $15..... 1,165 50
RUTHERFORD—*Grace*: Gen.......... 100 00
SUMMIT—*Calvary*: Gen., $162.01;
S. S., for Chinese hospital work,
$10 .... 172 01
SHORT HILLS—*Christ Church*: Mr.
Morgan, Sp. for St. Mary's Church,
Kyoto, Japan................. 200 00
VERNON—*St. Thomas's*: Gen........ 5 00
WASHINGTON—*St. Peter's S. S.*:* Gen.
(Apportionment, 1909)......... 5 00
MISCELLANEOUS—Juniors, "Grace
Lindley" scholarship, St. John's
School, Cape Mount............ 25 00

New Hampshire
Ap. $437.25

ASHLAND—*St. Mark's*: $13.75, S. S.,*
$19.38, Gen.................. 33 13
CONCORD—*St. Paul's*: Gen......... 50 00
DANBURY—*Church of the Holy Spirit*:
Children's,* Gen............... 2 50
DOVER—*St. Thomas's*: Gen......... 11 97
DREWSVILLE—*St. Peter's*: Gen...... 1 00
EXETER—*Christ Church*: Gen....... 26 08
GROVETON—*St. Mark's*: $5, S. S.,*
$11.40, Gen.................. 16 40
HANOVER—*St. Thomas's S. S.*:* Gen.. 9 17
KEARSARGE VILLAGE—*Grace Chapel*:
Gen. 16 62
KEENE—*St. James's*: Rev. E. A.
Renouf, D.D., Colored.......... 60 00
LINCOLN AND WOODSTOCK—*Church of
the Messiah Mission*: Children's,*
Gen. 2 50
LITTLETON—*All Saints'*: Gen........ 3 20

MANCHESTER—*Grace*: Alaska, $23.45;
Gen., $102.69................ 126
NORTH CONWAY—*Christ Church*: Gen. 1
NORTH HAVERHILL—*Trinity Church*:
Gen. 2
TILTON—*Trinity Church*: Gen....... 20
WALPOLE—*St. John's*: Gen......... 10
MISCELLANEOUS—Wo. Aux., Gen.... 45

New Jersey
Ap. $695.90; *Sp.* $131.73

BERNARDSVILLE—*St. Bernard's*: Miss
Kathleen L. Goold, Sp. for St. John's
University, Shanghai........... 5
BEVERLY—*St. Stephen's*: Dom. and
Frn. 41
BOUND BROOK—*St. Paul's*: Dom., 35
cts.; Frn., $51.40............. 51
CAMDEN—*St. Paul's*: Gen.......... 104
DUNELLEN—*Holy Innocents'*: Frn.... 10
ELIZABETH — *Christ Church*: Frn.,
$37.98; Gen., $20............. 57
St. John's S. S.: "Rev. S. A. Clark
Memorial" scholarship, St. Margaret's School, Tokyo.......... 40
Trinity Church: Wo. Aux., salary of
Kimura San, Kyoto, $10; "Emma
Williamson Memorial" bed, St.
James's Hospital, Anking, Hankow,
$5; St. Paul's School, Lawrenceville,
Southern Virginia, $5; Sp. for Mrs.
Wetmore's work, Arden, Asheville,
$10 30
HADDONFIELD—*Grace*: Gen......... 80
HAMMONTON—*St. Mark's*: Gen...... 19
LAKEWOOD—*All Saints'*: Gen....... 170
LAMBERTVILLE — *St. Andrew's*: Wo.
Aux., "Olga Randolph White" scholarship, St. Mary's Hall, Shanghai,
$25; Sp. for St. Agnes's Hospital,
Building Fund, Raleigh, North Carolina, $4.................... 29
LITTLE SILVER—*St. John's Chapel*:
Gen. 26
MANTUA—*St. Barnabas's*: Gen...... 2
MEDFORD—*St. Peter's S. S.*:* Gen.... 2
MOORESTOWN — *Trinity Church*: Wo.
Aux., salary of Kimura San, Kyoto,
$5; "Bishop Odenheimer" (In
Memoriam) scholarship, Trinity
Divinity-school, Tokyo, $7; Colored,
$30; Indian, $25.41; S. S.,* for hospital work in China, $131........ 193
NEW BRUNSWICK — *Christ Church*:
Western Colorado, $10; Dom., $1.25;
Colored, 30 cts.; Frn., $108.20;
Brazil, $26; Gen., $1; Wo. Aux., St.
Margaret's School, Tokyo, $10..... 156
St. John the Evangelist's: Gen., $2;
Sp. for Rev. Mr. Warden, San Juan,
Porto Rico, for education of native
minister, $50; Sp. for Chapel of the
Annunciation, $10; Wo. Aux. (In
Memoriam), Sp. for Christ School,
Arden, Asheville, $10........... 72
PEMBERTON—*Grace*: Sp. for St. Paul's
College, Tokyo............... 2
PLAINFIELD—*Grace S. S.*:* Frn...... 104
St. Stephen's: Gen.............. 5
Rev. W. H. Neilson, Gen......... 200
POINT PLEASANT—*St. Mary's-by-the-
Sea*: Gen., $1.56; S. S.,* Dom., $4;
Frn., $3; Gen., $4.70.......... 13
RAHWAY—*Church of the Holy Comforter*: Dom. and Frn........... 9
St. Paul's: Gen................. 15
RIVERTON—*Christ Church*: Wo. Aux.,
"Bishop Odenheimer" scholarship,
Trinity Divinity-school, Tokyo, $23;
Chinese Bible-woman, $2......... 25
SALEM—*St. John's*: Frn., $59.92; Wo.
Aux., Sp. toward scholarship in
Bishop Payne Divinity-school, Southern Virginia, $3............. 62
SEWAREN—*St. John's S. S.*:* Gen.... 6
SHREWSBURY — *Christ Church*: Gen.,

95 18

5 00

104 18
21 37

garet's School, Tokyo Building Fund, $1; St. Augustine's League, Sp. for Archdeacon Russell, Lawrenceville, Southern Virginia, $10; Sp. for St. Paul's School, Lawrenceville, Southern Virginia, $25; Sp. for St. Augustine's School, Raleigh, North Carolina, $25............. 141 31

Christ Church: Gen., $1,303.53; Sp. for Archdeacon Spurr, West Virginia, $10; Sp. for Bishop Wells's Clergy Fund, Spokane, $5......... 1,318 53

4 00
46 25
5 00

Christ Church (New Brighton, Staten Island): Wo. Aux., Sp. for St. John's University, Shanghai.............. 50 00

10 00

Epiphany: Dom., $3; Frn., $54.75; Gen., $115; Wo. Aux., "Edward L. Atkinson Memorial" scholarship, Boone University, Wuchang, Hankow, $50; St. Martha's Guild, kindergarten at Wakamatsu, Tokyo, $10 .... 232 75

1 00
45 85

94 64

5 00

8 50

1 00

Grace: Dom., $2,000; Colored, $291.07; "M. E. L.," Gen., $100; Committee on Missions to Colored People, St. Augustine's League, Sp. for St. Agnes's Hospital, Raleigh, North Carolina, $10; Sp. for Good Samaritan Hospital, Charlotte, North Carolina, $10; Sp. for Rev. J. W. Mundy, St. Clement's Mission, Henderson, Kentucky, for Building Fund, $65; Niobrara League, salary of teacher at Rosebud Agency, South Dakota, $420 "Alonzo Potter" (Graduate) scholarship, $70; Women's Foreign Missionary Association, Hooker School, Mexico, $50; Sp. for Dr. Laning's Bible-women, Osaka, Kyoto, $72; Sp. for Mrs. Auer, Africa, $50; Sp. for Bishop McKim's insurance, Tokyo, $50......... 3,188 07

10 00

Grace-Emmanuel Church: Gen....... 12 20

Heavenly Rest: Mrs. G. F. Cornell, $25, Mr. Augustus L. Clarkson, $400, Gen.; Women's Foreign Missionary Association, Sp. for work in Mexico, $24.95; St. Augustine's League, Sp. for St. Paul's School, Lawrenceville, Southern Virginia, $24.95.... 474 90

135 58

6 59
4 83
50
30 46
5 00

Holy Apostles': Gen., $176.40; Niobrara League, "J. P. Lindley" scholarship, St. Mary's School, South Dakota, $60; "R. C. Rogers" scholarship, St. Mary's School, South Dakota, $60....................... 296 40

Holy Faith: Gen.................... 29 50

25 42

Holy Trinity Church: Brazil,, $15; Gen., $1,392; Sp. for Zangzok Equipment Fund, Shanghai, $10; St. Augustine's League, Sp. for Meade Chapel, Alexandria, Virginia, $10. 1,427 00

2 00

Holy Trinity Church (East 88th Street): Wo. Aux., Frn............ 10 00

21 25

86 51
1 00

264 43

6 94

252 86

50

83 20

Incarnation: Dom., $6,726; Frn., $4,407; Gen., $263.95; James McLean, Sp. for Rev. W. J. Cuthbert, Tokyo, $200; St. Augustine's League, Sp. for Mrs. A. B. Hunter, St. Agnes's Hospital, Raleigh, North Carolina, $20; Wo. Aux., St. Augustine's League, Mrs. J. H. Haskill and Mrs. J. H. Preston, Sp. for "Arthur Brooks" scholarship, in Bishop Payne Divinity-school, Petersburg, Southern Virginia, in memory of Mrs. J. L. Riker, $150; Niobrara League, "Rev. William M. Grosvenor" (Graduate) scholarship, South Dakota, $60; S. S., Junior Aux., Sp. for "Langford Memorial" scholarship, Alaska, $5; Sp. for "Rev. Arthur Brooks" scholarship, St. Augustine's School, Raleigh, North Carolina, $50........11,881 95

Intercession: Dom., $35.07; Frn., $42.23; Wo. Aux., Sp. for Expansion Fund, St. John's University, Shang-

hai, $10 .... 87 30
Resurrection: Gen. 71 00
St. Agnes's: Gen., $5,011.66; Sp. for
Bishop Rowe, Alaska, $10; Wo. Aux.,
Sp. for Bishop Rowe, Alaska, $41;
"Two Members," Sp. for St. Paul's
College Building Fund, Tokyo, $5.. 5,067 66
St. Ann's (Morrisania): Niobrara
League, Sp. for Miss Thackara's
work, Fort Defiance, Arizona........ 25 00
St. Augustine's: Dom., $35.35; Frn.,
$36.17 .... 71 52
St. Barnabas's House S. S.: Frn..... 1 50
St. Bartholomew's: Dom., $4,000;
Frn., $4,000; Wo. Aux., Frn., $84;
Elizabeth Bunn Hospital, Wuchang,
Hankow, $150; Sp. for Bishop Brent,
Porto Rico, $100; Sp. for Bishop
Rowe, Alaska, $100; Niobrara
League, "Compo" scholarship, St.
Mary's School, South Dakota, $30.. 8,464 00
St. Cornelius's S. S.*: Gen......... 35 56
St. Chrysostom's: Through Wo. Aux.,
Sp. for Domestic Contingent Fund.. 90 00
St. George's: Frn., $1,693.01; Gen.,
$3,500; Mr. James T. Gardner, Sp.
for St. John's College, Shanghai,
$50; S. S., Gen., $600............. 5,843 01
St. James's: "A Member," Sp. for
Bishop Rowe, Alaska, $5; Wo. Aux.,
Sp. for Mrs. Wetmore, Asheville,
$134.60; Sp. for Rev. R. N. Wilcox,
Hendersonville, Asheville, $30..... 169 60
St. James's (Fordham): Gen........ 18 31
St. John's (Clifton, Staten Island):
Sp. for Bishop Rowe, Alaska....... 8 00
St. Luke's: Gen................... 116 41
St. Luke's Chapel: $105, S. S.,*
$51.53; Gen....................... 156 53
St. Mark's: Frn., $159.21; Gen.,
$112.06 .... 271 27
St. Matthew's: Wo. Aux., Frn., $7;
St. Augustine's League, Sp. for
Bishop Payne Divinity-school,
Petersburg, Southern Virginia, $10.. 17 00
St. Michael's: Dom., $1; salary of
Rev. Mr. Gilman, Changsha, Han-
kow, $201.40; Wo. Aux., Frn., $30;
St. Augustine's League, Sp. for
Bishop Payne Divinity-school, Peters-
burg, Southern Virginia, $18; Sp.
for Rev. W. J. Morton, Alexandria,
Virginia, $18...................... 268 40
St. Paul's: Gen................... 6 00
St. Peter's: Gen.................. 223 65
St. Peter's (West Chester): Frn.,
$14.12; Gen., $63.62.............. 77 74
St. Philip's: Through Wo. Aux., Sp.
for work of Rev. George E. Bene-
dict, Haiti......................... 10 00
St. Simeon's: Junior Aux., Gen.... 5 00
St. Thomas's: Dom., $1,980; Sp. for
St. Mary's Church, Kyoto, $100;
Sp. for Bishop Rowe's work, Alaska,
$3; Sp. for Rev. Mr. Cuthbert,
St. Mary's Church Building Fund,
Kyoto, $150; Rev. E. M. Stires, D.D.,
Sp. for Brazil theological books,
$25; Wo. Aux., "St. Thomas's"
scholarship, St. John's University,
Shanghai, $70; Niobrara League,
"Rev. Dr. J. W. Brown" scholar-
ship, St. Elizabeth's School, South
Dakota, $60; Sp. for "St. Thomas's"
scholarship, Shoshone, Wyoming,
$40 .... 2,428 00
St. Thomas's Chapel: Gen......... 50 00
Transfiguration: Niobrara League,
Choteau Creek, South Dakota, $100;
St. Augustine's League, Sp. for
Bishop Meade Memorial Chapel,
Virginia, $15...................... 115 00
Trinity Church: St. Augustine's
League, Sp. for support of a schol-
arship in Bishop Payne Divinity-
school, in memory of Dr. Dix,
Petersburg, Southern Virginia, $150;

Sp. for support for one day at St.
Agnes's Hospital, Raleigh, North
Carolina, $10.....................
Trinity Chapel: Gen., $25; Missionary
Relief Society, Miss F. H. Youngs,
Sp. for Expansion Fund, St. John's
University, Shanghai, $5; Niobrara
League, Miss P. C. Swords, "James
R. Swords" scholarship, St. Mary's
School, South Dakota, $60.........
Zion and St. Timothy's: Niobrara
League, "G. J. Greer" scholarship,
St. Mary's School, South Dakota,
$60; St. Augustine's League, Sp. for
Bishop Gailor, Tennessee, $25; Mis-
sionary League, Mrs. John A. Gaine,
$1, Miss Adele Low, $3, work in
Mexico ....
Wo. Aux., United Branches on Staten
Island, Sp. for Bishop Rowe, Alaska.
Wo. Aux., Mrs. H. Fairfax, Frn.,
$5; Emma H. Delafield, Sp. for fuel
for the mission at Point Hope,
Alaska, $25; Priscilla and Eleanor
Lockwood, Sp. for Widely Loving
Society, Kyoto, $22; Niobrara
League, Miss Jane E. Schmelzel,
"Schmelzel Memorial" (Graduate)
scholarship, South Dakota, $60....
Girls' Friendly Society (Bronx), Sp.
for Girls' School, Bontoc, Philippine
Islands, for maintenance of child..
Henry Lewis Morris, $25, Samuel
Thorne, Jr., $25, Andrew C. Za-
briskie, $10, Frederick E. Hyde, $10,
Miss Elizabeth H. Wisner, $10, Wil-
liam Alexander Smith, $5, Sp. for
Brazil theological books...........
Samuel Thorne, Jr., Sp. for Boone
College, Wuchang, Hankow.......
James J. Goodwin, Sp. for Bishop
Kinsolving, Brazil.................
Miss Ida Benjamin, $125, Mrs.
Clarkson, $100, Sp. for Bishop
Rowe, Alaska.....................
"A Friend," Sp. for Church Exten-
sion Fund, Porto Rico.............
Francis L. Stetson, Sp. for Rev. W.
J. Cuthbert, Kyoto................
Rev. I. H. Watson, Sp. for Shanghai
Catechist School, Land and Build-
ing Fund.........................
Robert M. Thompson, Sp. for Ex-
pansion Fund, St. John's University,
Shanghai ....
Mrs. L. E. Opdyke's S. S. Class, Sp.
for Deaconess K. E. Phelps, Wu-
chang, Hankow, for the support of
"Silver Lotus"....................
"Cash," Gen. ....
Miss A. A. Osborne (Staten Island),
in memory of Alice Amanda Bedell,
Dom..............................
E. C. Bogert, Sp. for "Olivia Hawks
Bogert" scholarship, Idaho, $40;
Sp. for "Rev. Francis Hawks" schol-
arship, Idaho, $25.................
Miss Mary E. Cox, Dom., $25; Frn.,
$25 ....
Mrs. E. Mabel Clark, Sp. for Miss
Ethel W. Wheeler, Wuchang, Han-
kow ....
Miss A. J. Boyle, Gen.............
"I. A. V. N.," Dom................
Mrs. S. Reville, Frn...............
"A Friend," Dom. and Frn........
OSSINING—*St. Paul's*: Junior Aux.,
Gen..............................
Trinity Church: Junior Aux., Gen....
PELHAM—*Church of the Redeemer*:
Frn., $2; Sp. for a donkey at Cape
Mount, Africa, $1.................
PELHAM MANOR—*Christ Church*: Miss
Fanny Schuyler, St. James's Hos-
pital, Anking, Hankow............
Wo. Aux. (of which Miss Schuyler,

LOUISBURG—*St. Paul's*: Frn., $21.03;
S. S.,* Gen., $5................. 26 03
MADISON—*St. John's*: Gen., $10.74;
Sp. for St. Paul's College Building
Fund, 45 cts.................. 11 19
MAYODAN — *Church of the Messiah*:
Gen., $25.31; Sp. for St. Paul's Col-
lege Building Fund, $6.60.......... 31 91
Junior Aux., Miss Elizabeth T. Ches-
hire's salary, Hankow.............. 80
PITTSBORO—*St. Bartholomew's*: $10.96,
S. S.,* $17.14, Gen............. 28 10
RALEIGH—*Christ Church*: $250, S. S.,*
$99.20, Gen.................. 349 20
St. Mary's School: $28.42, S. S.,* $81,
Gen. 109 42
RIDGEWAY—*Church of the Good Shep-
herd*: Gen.................... 2 00
ROWAN CO.—*Christ Church*: Frn..... 2 18
SCOTLAND NECK — *Trinity Church*:
Frn., $8.23; Gen., $6.20.......... 14 43
SPEED—*St. Mary's S. S.**: Gen....... 21 58
STATESVILLE—*Trinity Church*: Dom.
and Frn., $17.30; S. S.,* Gen., $2.. 19 30
STOKES CO.—*Knowlhurst Chapel*: Gen. 1 22
STONEVILLE—*Emmanuel Church*: Gen. 1 00
TARBORO—*Calvary*: $25, S. S.,* 50 cts.,
Gen. 25 50
TILLEY—*Mission*: Gen............. 1 00
WADESBORO — Bishop Gray, Branch
Junior Aux., Gen................ 1 00
WALNUT COVE—*Christ Church*: Gen... 5 16
MISCELLANEOUS—Convocation of Char-
lotte, Sp. work of Rev. I. H. Correll,
Tsu, Kyoto................... 25 00
Babies' Branch, Gen., $7; Sp. for
"Bishop Atkinson" cot, Holy Trinity
Orphanage, Tokyo, $16; Sp. for mis-
sionary font, $1................ 24 00

Ohio

Ap. $2,048.57; *Sp.* $50.00

AKRON—*Grace*: Deaf-Mute Mission,
Gen. 1 00
CANTON—*Epiphany*: Gen........... 1 00
*St. Paul's S. S.**: Gen............ 50
CLEVELAND—*All Saints'*: Gen....... 10 00
Grace: Wo. Aux., salary of Miss Elwin,
Shanghai 10 00
St. John's: Gen., $20.53; Wo. Aux.,
Philippines, $5; Alaska, $5; salary
of Miss Elwin, Shanghai, $5........ 35 53
St. Luke's: Gen............... 64 28
St. Paul's: Wo. Aux., "Ohio" scholar-
ship, St. Elizabeth's School, South
Dakota, $5; salary of Miss Elwin,
Shanghai (of which from Miss Ella
T. Wright, $10), $135; C. F.
Schweinfurth, Sp. for "Mary Ella
Schweinfurth Memorial" bed, St.
Matthew's Hospital, Fairbanks,
Alaska, $50.................. 190 00
Trinity Cathedral: Dom., $2.45; Col-
ored, 85 cts.; Frn., $1,356.96...... 1,360 26
CUYAHOGA FALLS—*St. John's*: Col-
ored, $7.67; Wo. Aux., "Ohio" schol-
arship, St. Elizabeth's School, South
Dakota, $4; salary of Miss Elwin,
Shanghai, $6................. 17 67
DENNISON—*St. Barnabas's S. S.**: Gen. 4 75
EAST PLYMOUTH—*St. Matthew's S.
S.**: Gen................... 50
FREMONT—*St. Paul's*: $31.75, S. S.,*
$1, Gen.................... 32 75
GAMBIER—*Bedell Mission*: Wo. Aux.,
"Julia Bedell" scholarship, St.
John's University, Shanghai........ 5 00
Harcourt Parish: Wo. Aux., "Julia Be-
dell" scholarship, St. John's Univer-
sity, Shanghai, $5; salary of Miss
Elwin, Shanghai, $5............. 10 00
GENEVA—*Christ Church*: Wo. Aux.,
Oklahoma, $5; Sacramento, $5...... 10 00
MEDINA—*St. Paul's*: Junior Aux., sal-
ary of Miss Elwin, Shanghai....... 3 00
MT. VERNON — *St. Paul's*: Dom.,
$73.50; Frn., $73.50............ 147 00

NEW PHILADELPHIA—*Trinity Church*
  S. S.:* Gen......................... 3 80
NORWALK—*St. Paul's*: Frn., $50; Wo.
  Aux., "Julia Bedell" scholarship, St.
  John's University, Shanghai, $10;
  salary of Miss Elwin, Shanghai, $5. 65 00
OBERLIN—*Christ Church*: $10, S. S.,*
  $14, Gen......................... 24 00
PAINESVILLE—*St. James's S. S.*:*
  Gen................................. 50
SANDUSKY — *Calvary*: Junior Aux.,
  Sacramento 3 00
Grace: Work of Rev. W. C. Clapp,
  Philippine Islands, $6.46; Gen.,
  $22.23 .... 28 69
STEUBENVILLE—*St. Paul's*: $26.34, Wo.
  Aux., $8, Gen.; Wo. Aux., salary of
  Miss Elwin, Shanghai, $5.......... 39 34
TOLEDO—*Trinity Church*: Wo. Aux.,
  Oklahoma, $10; Junior Aux., Alaska,
  $5 .... 15 00
WARREN—*Christ Church*: Wo. Aux.,
  Oklahoma, $5; salary of Miss Elwin,
  Shanghai, $10..................... 15 00
YOUNGSTOWN — *Emmanuel Church*:
  Deaf-Mute Mission, Gen........... 1 00

Oregon

Ap. $235.25

COQUILLE—*St. James's*: Gen......... 4 00
CORVALLIS—*Good Samaritan S. S.*:*
  Gen.............................. 1 50
GARDNER—*St. Mary-the-Virgin's*: Gen. 3 50
GRANT'S PASS—*St. Luke's*: Gen...... 15 75
MARSHFIELD—*Emmanuel Church*: Gen. 20 00
PORTLAND—*All Saints*: Gen......... 17 00
Trinity Church: Gen............... 173 50

Pennsylvania

Ap. $12,265.19; *Sp.* $4,317.39

ANDALUSIA—*Church of the Redeemer*:
  Junior Aux., Gen................. 25 00
ARDMORE—*St. Mary's*: Sp. for Nevada. 36 00
BALA—*St. Asaph's*: Wo. Aux., "Kin-
  solving" scholarship, Brazil, $5; Sp.
  for St. Elizabeth's Hospital Build-
  ing Fund, Shanghai, $5; Sp. for For-
  eign Life Insurance Fund, $3...... 18 00
BRISTOL—*St. James's*: Sp. for Nevada. 11 25
BRYN MAWR—*Church of the Redeemer*:
  Frn., $361.40; Miss Eleanor De
  Graff Cuyler, $100, James Rawl,
  $25, Mrs. C. W. Harnor, $25, Sp. for
  Nevada; Wo. Aux., "Kinsolving"
  scholarship, Brazil, $10; Junior
  Aux., Sp. for Archdeacon Spurr,
  West Virginia, $25; Sp. for Dr.
  Myers, Shanghai, $5............... 551 40
CHELTENHAM — *St. Paul's (Ogontz)*:
  Frn. 32 45
CHESTER—*St. Paul's*: Frn.......... 106 33
CLIFTON HEIGHTS—*St. Stephen's*: Gen. 20 00
CONSHOHOCKEN—*Calvary*: Indian Hope
  Association, Indian, $11; Wo. Aux.,
  "Kinsolving" scholarship, Brazil, $4 15 00
GWYNEDD—*Katherine D. Hover*, Sp.
  for Rev. Yoshimichi Suguira, Tokyo 5 00
HATBORO—Mrs. M. J. Hyndman,
  Children's Lenten Offering, Gen.... 1 00
KENNETT SQUARE—*Advent*: Wo. Aux.,
  Frn. 7 60
LANSDOWNE — *St. John the Evan-
  gelist's*: Gen., $85.76; Wo. Aux.,
  "Kinsolving" scholarship, Brazil,
  $5 .... 90 76
OGONTZ—L. E. C. Barney, Sp. for Bra-
  zil theological books.............. 5 00
PAOLI—*Good Samaritan*: Dom. and Frn 2 00
PHILADELPHIA—*Advocate Memorial*:
  Gen., $68.90; Sp. for Archdeacon
  Wentworth, Lexington, $3; Sp. for
  Alaska Emergency Fund (of which
  Mrs. Martha S. Stevenson, $10),
  $70.37 .... 142 27
All Saints: Junior Aux., Gen........ 3 00
Annunciation: Dom................. 17 64
Ascension: Wo. Aux., Sp. for Foreign

Life Insurance Fund...............
Atonement Memorial: Wo. Aux., "Kin-
  solving" scholarship, Brazil.......
Calvary (Germantown): St. Mary's
  School, South Dakota, for children's
  work, $30; Sp. St. Paul's College,
  Tokyo, $50; Wo. Aux., "Francesca"
  scholarship, Cuttington Collegiate
  and Divinity-school, Africa, $5;
  "Foreign Committee" scholarship,
  St. Margaret's School, Tokyo, $5...
Christ Church: Colored...........
Christ Church Chapel: Wo. Aux.,
  "Kinsolving" scholarship, Brazil...
Christ Church Hospital Chapel: Gen..
Christ Church (Germantown): Wo.
  Aux., Sp. for Building Fund, St.
  Elizabeth's Hospital, Shanghai, $3;
  S. S.,* Sp. for Bishop Robinson, for
  his work in Nevada, $20..........
Covenant: Wo. Aux., "Bishop Stevens"
  scholarship, St. John's University,
  Shanghai ....
Crucifixion: Sp. for Nevada........
Emmanuel Church (Holmesburg):
  Gen..............................
Church of the Good Shepherd (Ken-
  sington): Gen., 50 cts.; Sp. for
  Nevada, $11......................
Grace: "A Parishioner," $10, Mis-
  sionary Society, $10, Sp. for Nevada;
  Wo. Aux., "Kinsolving" scholarship,
  Brazil, $5.50.....................
Grace (Mt. Airy): Wo. Aux., "Kin-
  solving" scholarship, Brazil, $5;
  S. S., "Rev. S. C. Hill" scholarship,
  St. John's School, Africa, $25;
  "Bishop Stevens" scholarship,
  Hooker Memorial School, Mexico,
  $10 ....
Holy Apostles': Dom. and Frn.
  $2,600.66; Mrs. Mary A. Todd, Gen.
  (of which S. S.,* 50 cts.), $200.50.
Holy Innocents' (Tacony): Dom. and
  Frn., $35.60; Sp. for Bishop Harz's
  memorial, South Dakota, $4; S. S.,*
  Gen., 50 cts.....................
Holy Trinity Church: Dom., $700;
  Frn., $700; Theodore H. Morris,
  $25, Mrs. P. Blakiston, $10, Miss
  Mary Blakiston, $10, "Cash," $1,
  Harry C. Hart, $1, Walter Freeman,
  $5, Miss Corinne Freeman; $5, Sp.
  for Nevada; Indian Hope Associa-
  tion, St. Mary's School, South Da-
  kota, $60; Indian missions, $150;
  Wo. Aux., "Kinsolving" scholarship,
  Brazil, $10; Sp. for Foreign Life In-
  surance Fund, $5; Junior Aux., Sp.
  for Building Fund, St. Paul's Col-
  lege, Tokyo, $5.55................
Holy Trinity Memorial Chapel: Wo.
  Aux., " Kinsolving " scholarship,
  Brazil ....
Incarnation: Gen., $58.87; Income
  from the Bequest of Mary E.
  Stockton, Dom. and Frn., $81.....
Church of the Mediator: Dom. and
  Frn. ....
Prince of Peace Chapel: Gen.,
  $33.48; Wo. Aux., "Kinsolving"
  scholarship, Brazil, $5...........
Resurrection: Indian Hope Association,
  Indian, $2; Wo. Aux., Sp. for For-
  eign Life Insurance Fund, $2......
St. Andrew's: Dom., .$85; W. W.
  Strand, $5; J. H. Higgins, $1; Sp.
  for Nevada.......................
St. Andrew's (West): Indian Hope As-
  sociation, Indian, $10; Wo. Aux.,
  "Kinsolving" scholarship, Brazil, $5
St. Clement's: Wo. Aux., Sp. for Miss
  Wood, for library, Wuchang, Han-
  kow ....
St. George's (West): Gen...........
St. James's: Miss Darrach, Sp. for
  Bishop Rowe, Alaska, $50; Indian
  Hope Association, "J. B. G.,"

St. Peter's: Dom., $1,361.06; Mrs. James Large, $15, Mrs. A. J. Dallas Dixon, $10, Sp. for Nevada.. 1,386 06

St. Peter's (Germantown): $11.15, Edith H. Gregory, $5, Martha M. Greene, $40, Edw. A. Groves, $25, Mrs. C. N. Barrett, $1, W. F. Kurtz, $8, Sp. for Nevada............... 90 15

St. Philip's: Gen., $123.39; Sp. for Nevada, $35.25; Wo. Aux., Sp. for "John W. Wood" scholarship, Guantanamo, Cuba, $5................ 163 64

St. Simon's: Dom. and Frn.......... 2 40

St. Stephen's: Wo. Aux., "Pennsylvania Wo. Aux." scholarship, Hooker Memorial School, Mexico, $5; "Foreign Committee" scholarship, St. Margaret's School, Tokyo, $5; Sp. for Foreign Life Insurance Fund, $5; Sp. for Rev. Amos Goddard's life insurance, Hankow, $5; Sp. for nurse's salary, St. Luke's Hospital, Shanghai, $5; Sp. for Dr. Glenton, for Elizabeth Bunn Memorial Hospital, Wuchang, Hankow, $25 .... 50 00

St. Timothy's (Roxborough): Dom. and Frn., $29.75; Church hospital, China, $3.85; Sp. for St. Paul's College, Tokyo, $17.52; Wo. Aux., "Dr. Twing Memorial" scholarship, St. John's University, Shanghai, $10; "Bishop Stevens" scholarship, St. John's University, Shanghai, $10; Sp. for Building Fund, St. Elizabeth's Hospital, Shanghai, $8; Sp. for Foreign Life Insurance Fund, $5; S. S.,* Gen., 50 cts.......... 84 62

Church of the Saviour: Indian, $21.64; Brazil, $9.70; Mexico, $15.05; Wo. Aux., "Julia C. Emery" scholarship, Girls' School, Cape Palmas, Africa, $5; "Kinsolving" scholarship, Brazil, $9.05; "W. Beaumont Whitney" scholarship, Havana, Cuba, $5; "Pennsylvania Wo. Aux." scholarship, Hooker Memorial School, Mexico, $5; "Francesca" scholarship, Cuttington Collegiate and Divinity-school, Africa, $5; "Foreign Committee" scholarship, St. Margaret's School, Tokyo, $5; Sp. for Archdeacon Steel, Cuba, $1; Sp. for nurse's salary, St. Luke's Hospital, Shanghai, $5........... 86 44

"Some Friends of Bishop Brent," salary of a medical missionary, Philippine Islands................ 900 00

Brinton Wetherell, Shanghai....... 10 00

Mrs. W. L. Elkins, $25, T. Broom Belfield, $100, Miss E. H. Brown, $5.20, "M. C. M.," $5, Gen........ 135 20

"S. C.," $100, Charlotte C. Buckley, $25, The Misses Taylor, $10, "Friends," $5.52, "B. B.," $5.25, Esther S. Zebley, $5, Mrs. H. B. Gill, $2, Mrs. J. H. Metzger, $1, Sp. for Bishop Rowe, Alaska.......... 153 77

Arthur E. Newbold, $1,000, R. Winder Johnson, $50, Mrs. Samuel Chew, $10, Mrs. A. J. Cassatt, $100, Sp. for Nevada.................. 1,160 00

John E. Baird, Sp. for work of Bishop Robinson, Nevada............. 250 00

Miss Maria Blanchard, $15, Allen Childs, $10, Mrs. W. Beaumont Whitney, $5, Sp. for Brazil theological books...................... 30 00

R. B. Sterling, Sp. for Church Extension Fund, Porto Rico.......... 10 00

Through the Tuesday Missionary Bible-class, Sp. for Bishop Brent's work, Manila, Philippine Islands... 100 00

Mrs. Charles H. Graff, "Charles H. Graff" scholarship, Cuttington Collegiate and Divinity-school, Africa,

$40; Sp. for "Nella R. Gilder" scholarship, Alaska, $40..................   80 00
Miss E. W. Vaux, Sp. for Miss Irene P. Mann's life insurance, Tokyo....   52 78
Wo. Aux.,* Sp. for Bishop Rowe, Alaska 125 00
Wo. Aux., Rosalie L. Mitchell, Missionary Study Class Alumnæ, profits on sale of Missionary Calendar, native worker, Tsu, Kyoto, $50; native worker, Africa, $50; native worker, Cuba, $50; native worker, Mexico, $50; native worker, Brazil, $50; native worker, Haiti, $25; collected by Mrs. J. Nicholas Mitchell (of which Mrs. Deming, $10, Miss Huber, $10, Mrs. J. L. Ketterlinus, $10, Miss Pechin, $5, extra profits on 1909 Calendar, $10), Sp. for Miss Wood's library, Wuchang, Hankow, $45; Miss Bangs, "W. Beaumont Whitney" scholarship, Havana, Cuba, $10..............   330 00
Domestic Committee, Wo. Aux., Sp. for Nevada......................   50 00
POTTSTOWN—Christ Church: Gen....   7 00
RADNOR—St. David's: Gen 107 50
MISCELLANEOUS—Wo. Aux. Convocation of Chester collection of midLent Missionary Meeting, Japan, $5.50; Alaska, $5.75..............   11 25
Domestic Committee Missionary Study Class Alumnæ, profits from Church Missionary Calendar, Wo. Aux., salary of Domestic missionary bishop, $50; work among Mormons, $50; work among mountaineers, Asheville, $50; native work in Philippine Islands, $50; native work, Honolulu, $50; native work, Alaska, $50; work in Porto Rico, $25....   325 00
Domestic Committee, Wo. Aux., hospital work, Alaska, $10; Sp. for Bishop Rowe, Alaska, $25; Sp. for Rev. C. E. Betticher, Alaska, $5....   40 00
Wo. Aux., Miss Peterson, Sp. for Foreign Life Insurance Fund, $2; Mrs. Walter W. Pharo, Sp. for "Helen Lloyd Pharo" scholarship, St. Mary's Orphanage, Shanghai, $50 ....   52 00

Pittsburgh

Ap. $594.92; Sp. $315.00

BUTLER—St. Peter's: Dom..........   20 75
CRAFTON—Nativity: Gen............   12 66
EMPORIUM—Emmanuel Church: Gen..   17 64
GREENSBURG—Christ Church: Gen....   126 70
JEANNETTE—Advent: Gen...........   8 26
KITTANNING—St. Paul's S. S.*: Gen..   50
OSCEOLA MILLS—St. Lawrence's: Gen.   1 00
PITTSBURGH—Calvary S. S.: "Calvary" scholarship, St. Mary's School, South Dakota, $60; "Calvary S. S." scholarship, St. John's University, Shanghai, $40..................   100 00
St. Andrew's: Sp. for Bishop Thomas, Wyoming, $100; Sp. for Bishop Funsten, Idaho, $100; Mrs. F. S. Bissell, Sp. for Bishop Rowe, for his work in Alaska, $100......   300 00
St. Peter's: Gen.................   275 00
Mrs. Ormsby Phillips, Sp. for Brazil theological books 15 00
ST. MARY'S—St. Agnes's: Frn.......   5 65
TITUSVILLE—St. James's: Gen.......   20 00
WASHINGTON—Trinity Church: Gen..   6 76

Rhode Island

Ap. $1,146.57; Sp. $100.00

BARRINGTON—St. John's S. S.*: Gen..   17 44
St. Matthew's (West): Gen........   4 56
CRANSTON—St. Bartholomew's: Gen..   12 84
EAST GREENWICH—St. Luke's: Gen..   145 83
EAST PROVIDENCE—St. Mary's (Apportionment, 1908-09): Gen.......   22 72

MANTON—St. Peter's: Gen..........   32 00
MIDDLETOWN—St. George's School*: "From Ten Boys," Gen............   11 54
St. Columba's Berkeley Memorial Chapel: Frn...................   64 37
NEWPORT—Emmanuel Church: Gen..   29 13
Trinity Church: $25, S. S.,* $1.25, Gen...........................   26 25
St. George's School: Sp. for St. John's University Expansion Fund, Shanghai 100 00
PAWTUCKET—Church of the Good Shepherd: Dom. and Frn.........   43 76
St. Paul's: Gen..................   200 00
PORTSMOUTH—St. Paul's: Dom. and Frn............................   14 00
PROVIDENCE—Calvary: Gen........   51 00
Christ Church: Dom. and Frn......   15 12
Epiphany: Gen...................   103 00
Church of the Messiah: Gen.......   114 89
St. Stephen's: Gen...............   36 50
St. Thomas's: Dom...............   15 00
WAKEFIELD—Ascension: Gen.......   17 00
WESTERLY—Christ Church: $19.75, S. S.,* $75.13, Gen.............   94 88
WICKFORD—St. Paul's: Frn., $4.90; Gen., $39.84..................   44 74
MISCELLANEOUS—Rhode Island Branch, Wo. Aux., Alaska...............   28 00
Rhode Island Branch, Wo. Aux.,
Bishop Restarick's work, Honolulu.   2 00

South Carolina

Ap. $430.99

BARNWELL—Holy Apostles': Gen.....   8 89
CAMDEN—Grace S. S.*: Gen........   51 00
CHARLESTON—Holy Communion: Gen.   75 00
St. Michael's: Gen...............   62 50
"A Friend," Alaska..............   2 50
CHERAW—St. David's: Frn..........   35 00
COLUMBIA—Trinity Church: Gen.....   55 40
Trinity Chapel S. S.* (Olympia Mills): Gen...........................   26 06
GREENVILLE—St. Andrew's S. S.*: Gen............................   4 10
LAURENS—Epiphany: Wo. Aux., $24, S. S.,* $25.68, Gen............   49 68
"E. B. S.," Gen.................   4 00
SOCIETY HILL—Trinity Church: Gen..   7 50
SUMMERTON—St. Matthias's: Gen....   10 00
SUMTER—Church of the Holy Comforter S. S.*: Gen..............   25 86
WINNSBORO—St. John's: Gen.......   13 50

Southern Ohio

Ap. $885.58; Sp. $310.00

CINCINNATI — Christ Church: Gen., $472.34; Mrs. A. Howard Hinkle, Sp. for Church Extension Fund, Porto Rico, $25.................   497 34
Church of Our Saviour: Gen., $30.50; "A Friend," Frn., $1; Girls' Friendly Society, Sp. for salary of deacon, for Rev. S. C. Hughson, Sewanee, Tennessee, $10.................   41 50
COLLEGE HILL—Grace S. S.*: Dom. and Frn......................   5 50
COLUMBUS—St. Paul's S. S.*: Gen...   4 00
DAYTON—St. Margaret's Mission S. S.*: Gen......................   50
GLENDALE—Christ Church: Rev. C. K. Benedict, Sp. for Church Extension Fund, Porto Rico..............   200 00
Bethany Home: Children's*, Gen....   46 00
GREENVILLE—St. Paul's: Gen.......   29 00
HILLSBORO—St. Mary's S. S.*: Gen..   14 11
LANCASTER—St. John's: $14.50, S. S.,* $7.54, Gen................   22 04
LONDON—Trinity Church: $5.50, S. S.,* $4.21, Gen...............   9 71
MARIETTA—St. Luke's: Gen........   132 36
MIDDLETOWN—Ascension S. S.*: Gen.   5 00
NEWARK—Trinity Church: "S. B.," Gen............................   5 00
PORTSMOUTH—All Saints': Gen......   18 52
MISCELLANEOUS — Southern Ohio

40 00	CARROLLTON—*Trinity Church*: Gen... 2 60
	DANVILLE—*Holy Trinity Church*: Sp. for St. Paul's College, Tokyo...... 3 75
	JERSEYVILLE—*Holy Cross*: Gen...... 2 70
	MATTOON—*Trinity Church S. S.**: Gen. 13 75
	SPRINGFIELD—*St. John's*: Dom., $2; Frn., $3...... 5 00
125 00	*St. Luke's*: Gen...... 5 40
	St. Paul's: $20.26, Wo. Aux., $10, Gen. 30 26

Tennessee

Ap. $183.68 ; *Sp.* $55.00

13 00	ATHENS—*St. Paul's*: $4, S. S.,* $8, Gen. 12 00
26 39	BUNTYN—*St. John's*: Gen...... 3 50
4 37	CHATTANOOGA—*St. Paul's*; Wo. Aux., "Bishop Quintard" scholarship, St. Mary's Hall, Shanghai...... 2 50
	COALMONT—*St. Alban's S. S.**: Gen.. 2 05
	COWAN—*St. Agnes's*: Gen...... 2 50
12 50	JUMP OFF—*Church of Our Saviour*: Gen. 2 50
	LOST COVE—*St. James's*: Gen...... 2 50
6 00	MEMPHIS—*Calvary*: Gen...... 100 00
5 00	*Emmanuel Church*: Wo. Aux., Bishop Ferguson's work, Africa...... 5 00
10 00	*Church of the Good Shepherd*: Gen.... 25 00
	Grace: Wo. Aux., Sp. for Rev. I. H.
3 14	Correll's work, Kyoto...... 10 00
	NASHVILLE—*Christ Church*: Wo. Aux., "Bishop Quintard" scholarship, St.
10 70	Mary's Hall, Shanghai...... 2 50
20 27	ROARK'S COVE—*Calvary*: Gen...... 2 50
	RUGBY—*Christ Church S. S.**: Gen.. 6 13
22 16	SEWANEE—*St. Paul's-on-the-Mountain*: Gen...... 2 50
56 00	*University of the South, University Chapel*: Sp. for St. John's College,
12 00	Shanghai 45 00
	SHERWOOD—*Epiphany*: Gen...... 2 50
	WINCHESTER—*Trinity Church*: Gen... 10 00

Texas

Ap. $762.60 ; *Sp.* $21.70

15 00	
10 00	AUSTIN—*All Saints'*: "A Member," $1; Bishop Horner's work, Asheville, $1; Bishop Brent's work, Philippines, $1...... 2 00
20 71	BEAUMONT—*St. Mark's*: Dom...... 25 00
	CALVERT—*Epiphany*: Frn...... 5 85
	HEMPSTEAD—*St. Bartholomew's*: Gen.. 35 25
	HOUSTON—*Christ Church*: $467, Wo.
249 18	Aux., $30, Gen...... 497 00
103 25	*Trinity Church*: $140, Wo. Aux., $33, Gen. 173 00
	NAVASOTA—*St. Paul's*: Sp. for Asheville 21 70
10 00	TYLER—*Christ Church*: Wo. Aux., Gen. 25 00

Vermont

Ap. $308.71 ; *Sp.* $25.05

30 00	
6 00	BELLOWS FALLS—*Immanuel Church S. S.**: Gen...... 18 55
6 00	BENNINGTON—*St. Peter's*: Gen...... 30 00
26 05	BRATTLEBORO—*St. Michael's*: $45, S. S.,* 50 cts., Gen...... 45 50
16 23	BURLINGTON—*St. Paul's*: Sp. for St. Paul's College, Tokyo...... 25 05
	ENOSBURG FALLS—*St. Matthew's S. S.**: Gen...... 41 52
154 09	ENOSBURG—*Christ Church S. S.**: Gen. 1 51
12 69	ISLAND POND—*Christ Church S. S.**: Gen. 9 59
15 00	MANCHESTER CENTRE—*Zion*: Gen..... 18 93
2 36	MONTGOMERY — *St. Bartholomew's*: Gen. 5 00
5 00	POULTNEY—*St. John's*: Gen...... 35 29
	RUTLAND—*Trinity Church*: Gen...... 9 50
	SHELBURNE—*Trinity Church*: Dom... 62 50
4 50	SHERBOURNE—*Church of Our Saviour*: Gen. 3 00
3 60	SWANTON — *Holy Trinity Church*:

Dom., $8.96; Frn., $8............ 16 96
WINDSOR—*St. Paul's S. S.**: Gen..... 10 86

Virginia

Ap. $1,483.17; *Sp.* $289.80
ALBEMARLE Co.—*St. George's* (Crofut): Sp. for St. Paul's College, Tokyo 1 89
ALEXANDRIA Co.—Mrs. Charlotte C. Berryman (Alexandria), Sp. for tablet in St. James's Hospital, Hankow, $10; Sp. for Chinese inscription on the "John Berryman, M.D., Memorial" bed tablet, St. James's Hospital, Hankow, $2.............. 12 00
CLARKE Co.—*Christ Chapel S. S.** (Wickliffe): Gen................ 16 10
Grace (Berryville): Gen........... 72 05
CULPEPER Co.—*All Saints' S. S.** (Mitchell's): Gen.............. 1 00
ESSEX Co.—*St. Anne's:* Gen...... 3 59
FAIRFAX Co.—*Church of the Holy Comforter* (Fairfax): Frn., $3.50; S. S.,* Gen., $1.75............ 5 25
Zion: Frn., $8; Gen. (of which S. S.,* $2.50), $7.50 .... 15 50
FAUQUIER Co.—*Grace, Trinity Church and Whittle Chapel, Whittle Parish* (The Plains): Gen.......... 25 00
FREDERICK Co.—*Christ Church* (Winchester): "Edward McG. Tidball" scholarship, Boone University, Wuchang, Hankow, $50; Gen., $55... 105 00
GLOUCESTER Co. —*Abingdon Parish* (Gloucester): Dom., $1; Frn., $3.60 4 60
Ware Parish (Gloucester): Gen...... 13 90
Abingdon and Ware Parishes: "Friends," Sp. for Rev. J. L. Sinclair, Yangchow, Shanghai........ 17 00
HANOVER Co.—*Immanuel Church S. S.** (Old Church): Sp. for Lydia Hospital, Ragged Mountain Mission, under Rev. F. Neve, Virginia, $6.55; Sp. for Miss Lucy Carter, White Rocks, Utah, $6.60.............. 13 15
HENRICO Co.—*Church of the Holy Comforter S. S.** (Richmond): Frn.... 31 86
Holy Trinity Church (Richmond): Gen............................ 360 00
Monumental (Richmond): Wo. Aux., Sp. for Holy Trinity Orphanage, Tokyo 20 00
St. James's (Richmond): Gen., $150; Sp. for Building Fund, St. Paul's College, Tokyo, $50............ 200 00
St. John's S. S.* (Richmond): Gen... 50
St. Mark's (Richmond): Gen....... 66 00
St. Paul's (Richmond): Dom., $255; Frn., $255; Wo. Aux., Sp. for Rev. H. St. G. Tucker, to be used for the interior furnishing of All Saints' Church, Tokyo, $41.25........... 551 25
LOUDOUN Co.—*Church of Our Redeemer* (Aldie): Gen.......... 33 00
NEW KENT Co.—*St. Peter's S. S.** (Tunstall): Gen............... 3 76
ORANGE Co.—*Christ Church* (Gordonsville): Dom. and Frn........... 11 19
RICHMOND Co.—*Emmanuel Church:* Gen............................ 7 10
St. John's (Warsaw): Sp. for Rev. J. M. B. Gill, Shanghai, at his discretion 25 00
ROCKINGHAM Co.—*Emmanuel Church:* Gen............................ 19 45
Grace Memorial, Trinity Mission, St. Stephen's, Rocky Bar Mission, Lynnwood Parish: Gen.............. 4 32
WESTMORELAND Co.—*Washington Parish:* Dom. and Frn., $24; Sp. for St. Paul's College, Tokyo, $9.51.... 33 51
MISCELLANEOUS—Wo. Aux., Sp. for Bishop Rowe, Alaska............ 100 00

Washington

Ap. $1,796.33; *Sp.* $620.90
DISTRICT OF COLUMBIA—*Ascension:*

Gen., $178.57; Wo. Aux., "A Member," Sp. for Miss Woods, Alaska, $5 ....
Ascension S. S.* (Colored mission): Gen..........
All Saints' (Chevy Chase) Gen......
Christ Church (Georgetown): Gen., $80; Wo. Aux., salaries of missionaries in the field, $25; L. M. Zeller, Gen., $2...................
Epiphany: Sp. for Bishop Rowe, Alaska, $92.25; Sp. for Dr. Correll, Kyoto, $5................
Grace S. S.*: (Georgetown): Gen....
Nativity: Dom., $17.24; Frn., $28.52.
St. Agnes's: Gen...............
St. John's: Dom. and Frn., $1,200; Wo. Aux., Sp. for Miss Thackara, Hospital of the Good Shepherd, Fort Defiance, Arizona, fund for laundry and bathroom, $12............ 1
St. John's (Georgetown): Wo. Aux., "William Murdoch" scholarship, St. Margaret's School, Tokyo, $50; Sp. for Dr. Correll's work, Tsu, Kyoto, $10; Sp. for Bishop Brent, Philippine Islands, $5; Sp. for "Beverly Murray" scholarship, St. Paul's School, Lawrenceville, Southern Virginia, $25..............
St. Mark's: Wo. Aux., Sp. for Bishop Rowe, Alaska..........
St. Thomas's: Sp. for Bishop Rowe, Alaska, $100; Miss Ellen King, Sp. for Church Extension Fund, Porto Rico, $25................
National Cathedral School (Mt. St. Alban): Missionary Society, Sp. for Bishop Rowe, Alaska, for a dog; Miss Ellen King, Sp. for Bishop Rowe, Alaska, for crosses........
Henry L. Bryan, Sp. for Bishop Rowe, Alaska................
"A Friend," Sp. for Bishop Rowe, Alaska............
"A Friend," rent of mission house at Santurce, Porto Rico.......
"E. L. H.," Gen............
"A Friend," Sp. for Bishop Rowe, Alaska ....
Gunston Hall, through Junior Aux., Sp. for Miss Alice M. Clark's work, Hankow, China, $35; Sp. for St. Margaret's School Building Fund, Tokyo, $10.............
MONTGOMERY Co.—*Christ Church* (Rockville): Gen., $20; Junior Aux., Sp. for Ragged Mountain work under Rev. Mr. Neve, Virginia, $25 ....
St. Peter's: Brazil...........
St. Peter's and Christ Church S. S.* (Poolesville): Gen...............
PRINCE GEORGE Co.—*St. Hilda's S. S.** (Berwyn): Gen...............
MISCELLANEOUS—Wo. Aux., Sp. for Bishop Rowe, Alaska, $50.65; Sp. for St. John's University Expansion Fund, Shanghai, $20...........

Western Massachusetts

Ap. $1,434.43; *Sp.* $424.75
ADAMS—*St. Mark's:* Gen............
AMHERST—*Grace:* Frn.............
CHERRY VALLEY—*St. Thomas's:* Wo. Aux., Sp. for Foreign Insurance Fund ....
FITCHBURG—*Christ Church:* Gen......
GREAT BARRINGTON—*St. James's:* Wo. Aux., St. Paul's School, Lawrenceville, Southern Virginia, $1.50; St. Augustine's School, Raleigh, North Carolina, $1.50.............
GREENFIELD—*St. James's:* Wo. Aux., St. Paul's School, Lawrenceville, Southern Virginia, $7.50; Sp. for

	ELK RAPIDS—*St. Paul's S. S.**: Dom.	10 95
66 00	GRAND HAVEN—*Akeley Institute*: Gen.	2 14
	GRAND RAPIDS—*Grace*: Gen.........	5 00
	St. Mark's: Dom. and Frn..........	114 66
	PENTWATER—*St. James's*: Gen......	87
	THREE RIVERS—*Trinity Church*: Gen.	1 69
18 15	TRAVERSE CITY—*S. S.**: Gen........	50

Western New York
Ap. $1,638.87; *Sp.* $152.28

1 00		
125 00	BATH—*St. Thomas's*: Frn., $5.75; Wo. Aux., Mission Study Class, Asheville, $4....................	9 75
2 00		
5 40	BUFFALO—*St. James's*: Dom., $59.41; Frn., $53.16: "Buffalo Church-	
1 00	man," Sp. for Expansion Fund, St. John's University, Shanghai, $20...	132 57
	Trinity Church: Dom., $490; Frn., $260	750 00
	Mrs. W. H. Walker, Jr., Sp. for St. Luke's Memorial Hospital, Ponce, Porto Rico.....................	5 00
97 25	CANASERAGA—*Trinity Church S. S.**: Gen.	
244 80	GENESEO—*St. Michael's*: Gen......	16 50
	GENEVA—*Trinity Church*: Wo. Aux.,	82 00
60 00	Sp. for Valle Crucis, Asheville,	
30 10	$2.75; "V. M. H.," Sp. for Building Fund, St. Margaret's School, Tokyo,	
50	$5	7 75
	"T. S.," Dom....................	100 00
	LOCKPORT—*All Saints'*: Wo. Aux., Sp. for Expansion Fund, St. John's University, Shanghai.................	2 50
109 00	MOUNT MORRIS—*St. John's*: Gen.....	10 84
	NEWARK—*St. Mark's*: Gen..........	9 00
21 25	NIAGARA FALLS—*St. Peter's*: Gen....	228 93
	NORTH TONAWANDA—*St. Mark's*: Frn.	12 40
4 50	OAKFIELD—*St. Michael's*: Dom., $12; Frn., $12; Gen., $12; S. S.,* Gen., $15	51 00
3 75	PALMYRA — *Zion*: $30.87, S. S.,* $18.01, Gen.....................	48 88
5 50	PHELPS—*St. John's*: Frn...........	2 00
	ROCHESTER—*St. Luke's*: $30.65, "Elizabeth," $25, Gen.; St. Paul's College, Tokyo, $3.85...................	59 50
157 00	Wo. Aux., Mission Study Class, Sp. for Rev. Murray Bartlett, Porto Rico	6 50
13 50	Miss P. S. Elly, Sp. for Building Fund, St. John's University, Shanghai	1 00
1 00	SODUS—*St. John's S. S.**: Gen......	50
23 05	MISCELLANEOUS—Wo. Aux., Windsor Memorial Day-school, Wusih, Shang-	
35 00	hai, $50; Church Training-school for Bible-women, Shanghai, $10; Yangchow, Shanghai, $20; Gen., $65; Sp. for Miss Thackara, Arizona, $15	160 00
13 00	Babies' Branch, "Mothers," "In memory of some 20 little helpers," Sp. for comfort of sick Chinese children, California..................	94 53

West Texas
Ap. $271.75; *Sp.* $25.00

331 78	CORPUS CHRISTI—*Church of the Good Shepherd*: Gen., $5.45; Wo. Aux.,	
175 00	Sp. for Belen, New Mexico, $1;	
10 00	George C. Thomas Memorial, Gen., $2.50	8 95
	FORT McKAVETT—*St. James's*: Gen..	3 50
25 00	Mission: Junior Aux., Gen..........	3 00
	JUNCTION—*Trinity Church*: Gen.....	3 50
10 00	LAREDO—*Christ Church*: Gen.....	18 00
	MENARDVILLE—*Calvary*: Gen........	5 00
	SAN ANTONIO—*St. Mark's*: Gen.....	100 00
	St. Mary's Hall: Branch Wo. Aux., Gen.	
	St. Paul's: Junior Branch, Wo. Aux., gasolene for *Pelican*, Alaska, 80 cts.; Sp. for Bishop Aves, Mexico,	5 50
25 00	$8; S. S.,* Gen. $1..............	9 80
12 00	(Lancel Heights), Branch Wo. Aux.,	

Gen., $5; Sp. for Tsu Property
Fund, $5...................... 10 00
Bishop Johnson, Branch Wo. Aux.,
Sp. for Rev. Mr. Wentworth, Lex-
ington 5 00
Roberta Johnson, Branch Wo. Aux.,
Gen., $32; Sp. for Rev. Hunter
Lewis, Mesilla Park, New Mexico,
$6 .... 38 00
W. R. Richardson, Branch Wo. Aux.,
Gen. 10 00
W. D. Christian, Gen. 5 00
SONORA—St. John's: Gen........... 3 50
VICTORIA—Trinity Church: Wo. Aux.,
Gen. 18 00
MISCELLANEOUS—Wo. Aux., China
Bible-women 50 00

West Virginia

Ap. $233.77; Sp. $59.20

BERKELEY SPRINGS—St. Mark's: Gen.. 5 00
BLUEFIELD—Christ Church: Gen..... 13 00
CHARLESTOWN—Zion: Junior Aux., Sp.
for Building Fund, St. Margaret's
School, Tokyo................... 25 00
GRAFTON—St. Matthias's: Colored, $1;
Cuba, 50 cts.; Brazil, 50 cts...... 2 00
HANSFORD—Church of the Good Shep-
herd S. S.*: Sp. for Miss E. P.
Barbour, Anking, Hankow...... 9 20
HUNTINGTON—Trinity Church: Dom.,
$12.50; Frn., $68.80............ 81 30
LEWISBURG—St. James's: Dom...... 1 50
MARTINSBURG—Trinity Church: Gen.,
$26.82; Junior Aux., "West Virginia
Junior" scholarship, St. John's
School, Cape Mount, Africa, $2;
Hankow, $2; S. S.,* Gen., $50.... 80 82
MOOREFIELD—Emmanuel Church: Gen. 4 53
MOUNDSVILLE—Trinity Church: Junior
Aux., "West Virginia Junior" schol-
arship, St. John's School, Cape
Mount, Africa, $2; Hankow, $2.... 4 00
NEW MARTINSVILLE—St. Ann's:
"E. H. T.," Brazil, $1.76; Sp. for
Rev. W. M. M. Thomas, Rio Grande
do Sul, for his own use, $25...... 26 76
RONCEVERTE — Incarnation S. S.*:
Gen. 10 33
WELLSBURG—Christ Church S. S.*:
Gen. 8 08
WHEELING—St. Andrew's: Gen....... 17 00
St. Matthew's: Junior Aux., "West
Virginia Junior" scholarship, St.
John's School, Cape Mount, West
Africa, $2; Hankow, $2; S. S.,*
Gen., 50 cts................... 4 50

Missionary Districts

Alaska

Ap. $248.30

ALLAKAKET—St. John's-in-the-Wilder-
ness: Gen..................... 142 00
FAIRBANKS—St. Matthew's: Gen..... 89 50
JUNEAU—Trinity Church: Gen...... 11 55
SEWARD—St. Peter's: Gen.......... 5 25

Arizona

Ap. $80.25

NOGALES—St. Andrew's: Gen........ 25 00
PHOENIX — Trinity Church: Frn.,
$5.25; Wo. Aux., Gen., $10........ 15 25
TOMBSTONE—St. Paul's: Gen........ 5 00
TUCSON—Grace: Gen............... 35 00

Asheville

Ap. $172.39; Sp. $1.00

BALSAM—Church of the Holy Com-
munion: Frn................... 10 25
BELL—Trinity Church: Dom......... 22
BILTMORE—All Souls': Frn.......... 50 00

BREVARD—St. Philip's: Gen........
BLOWING ROCK—Church of the Holy
Spirit: Dom., $1; Frn., $1; Gen.,
$1
BOONE—St. Luke's: Dom., 25 cts.;
Frn., 25 cts..................
CANTON—St. Andrew's: Frn........
CULLOWHEE—St. David's: Frn......
FRANKLIN—St. Agnes's: Dom., 50
cts.; Frn., 50 cts.; Gen., 50 cts....
LENOIR—St. James's: Dom., $2; Frn.,
$2; Gen., $2; C. B. Harrison, Sp.
for Church Extension Fund, Porto
Rico, $1......................
Chapel of Peace: Frn............
Alice S. Carsson, $2, "In Loving
Memory of Annie J. Carsson," St.
James's Hospital, Anking, Hankow.
MARION—St. John's: Dom., 75 cts.;
Frn., 75 cts...................
MICADALE—St. Mary's: Frn........
MORGANTON — Grace: Dom., $3.75;
Frn., $3.75; Gen., $3.75........
Church of the Good Shepherd: Dom.,
50 cts.; Frn., 50 cts............
St. George's: Frn..............
St. Margaret's: Dom., 66 cts.; Frn.,
67 cts.; Gen., 67 cts...........
St. Michael's: Frn.............
St. Stephen's: Dom., 66 cts.; Frn.,
67 cts.; Gen., 67 cts...........
OLD FORT—St. Gabriel's: Gen.....
SHELBY—Church of the Redeemer:
Frn. ....
ST. JUDE—St. John the Baptist's: Dom.,
25 cts.; Frn., 25 cts...........
SYLVA—St. John's: Frn..........
TRYON—Holy Cross: Gen.........
WAYNESVILLE—St. Michael's: Frn....
YADKIN VALLEY—Chapel of Rest: Frn..

Idaho

Ap. $4.75

MULLAN—St. Andrew's: Gen........

Kearney

Ap. $188.60

ATKINSON—Gen..................
ARAPAHOE—St. Paul's: Gen........
BENKELMAN—Gen................
BLOOMINGTON—St. Mary's: Gen.....
CODY—Gen.....................
CULBERTSON—Annunciation: Gen. ...
EWING—Trinity Church: Gen......
GRAND ISLAND—St. Stephen's: Gen...
HAIGLER—St. Philip's: Gen.......
HASTINGS—St. Mark's: Frn., $1.30;
Gen., $7.77..................
INDIANOLA—Gen................
KILGORE—Gen..................
LEXINGTON—St. Peter's: Junior Aux.,
Gen. ....
McCOOK—St. Alban's: $21.60, S. S.,
43 cts., Gen..................
MULLEN—St. Joseph's: Gen........
NAPONEE—Gen..................
ORLEANS—Gen..................
SHATTON—Gen..................
TRENTON—Gen..................

Nevada

Ap. $5.00

ELY—St. Bartholomew's: Gen......

New Mexico

Ap. $38.00

DEMING—St. Luke's: Gen..........
GALLUP—Church of the Holy Spirit:
Gen. ....
HILLSBORO—Christ Church: Gen.....
MISCELLANEOUS — Branch Wo. Aux.,
Gen. ....

	St. Barnabas's: Dom.	88
	St. James's: Dom.	70
2 00	*St. John's*: Dom., $4.22; Frn., $3.36..	7 58
	St. Luke's: Dom., $1.93; Frn., $2....	3 93
19 10	*St. Mary's*: Dom., $6.78; Frn., $6.46.	13 24
	St. Paul's: Dom., 10 cts.; Frn., 10 cts.	20
	St. Stephen's: Dom., $2.98; Frn., $3.75	6 73
	St. Thomas's: Dom., $3.50; Frn., 75 cts.	4 25
6 90	PINE RIDGE—*Advent*: Frn............	1 25
4 10	*Christ Church*: Frn.................	76
4 00	*Grace*: Frn.	16
9 00	*Epiphany*: Frn.	1 40
3 85	*Holy Cross*: Frn.	70
4 05	*Church of the Messiah*: Frn.........	45
2 20	*St. Alban's*: Frn..................	25
6 66	*St. Julia's*: Frn..................	65
5 15	*St. Luke's*: Frn.	29 00
1 35	*St. Mark's*: Frn.	56
2 25	*St. Mary's*: Frn..................	68
2 25	*St. Mary's* (Sand Hill): Frn........	85
58 00	*St. Peter's*: Frn..................	1 58
	St. Paul's: Frn...................	3 45
	St. Philip's: Frn.................	75
	St. Thomas's: Frn.................	1 39
68	SISSETON AGENCY—*St. James's*: Dom..	2 19
10 00	*St. John the Baptist*: Dom..........	2 71
1 10	*St. Mary's*: Dom..................	10 85
2 80		
5 60		
2 40	**Southern Florida**	
	Ap. $157.03	
6 00	APOPKA—*Church of the Holy Spirit*:	
5 75	Gen.	2 00
5 60	AUBURNDALE—*St. Alban's*: Frn.......	5 00
2 27	BRAIDENTOWN—*Christ Church*: Gen..	20 00
5 60	BROOKSVILLE—*St. John's*: Gen.......	1 00
	BUENA VISTA—*Holy Cross*: Gen.....	2 00
	DANIA—*St. John's*: Gen.............	2 00
	ENTERPRISE—*All Saints'*: Gen......	2 00
117 12	FORT MYERS—*St. Luke's*: Gen.......	5 00
	KISSIMMEE—*St. John's*: Gen........	2 00
50	LEESBURG—*St. James's*: Gen........	12 00
	MAITLAND—*Church of the Good Shepherd*: Gen.	25 00
30 00	MIAMI—*Trinity Church*: Gen........	25 00
	PALM BEACH—*Bethesda-by-the-Sea S. S.,** Gen.	24 03
2 50	NARCOOSSEE—*St. Peter's*: Gen.......	4 00
	SUMTERVILLE—*Mission*: Gen.	1 00
50 00	TAMPA—*House of Prayer*: Gen.......	10 00
	St. James's: Gen.................	8 00
	WINTER PARK—*All Saints'*: Gen.....	2 00
	ZELLWOOD—*St. James's*: Gen........	5 00
	Spokane	
	Ap. $13.00	
5 00	SUNNYSIDE—*Trinity Church*: Gen....	10 00
	WENATCHEE—Miss Orillia A. Kean, Gen.	3 00
	The Philippines	
4 44	*Ap.* $8.00	
	MANILA — *St. Stephen's* (Chinese): Gen.	8 00
2 65	**Utah**	
4 40	*Ap.* $17.34	
11 38	OGDEN—*Church of the Good Shepherd S. S.*: Gen.	3 34
1 00	SALT LAKE CITY—*St. Mark's Cathedral*: Kindergarten Class, Babies'	
30 00	Branch, Sp. for Bishop Spalding's	
2 50	work, Utah, $5.60; Bishop Spalding's	
15 50	work among the Indians, Utah, $1.40	7 00
66 40	*St. Paul's*: Gen..................	10 00
7 50		
12 00	**Wyoming**	
25 00	*Ap.* $142.60	
	CHEYENNE — *St. Mark's*: Gen. (of	
13 46	which Wo. Aux., $5; $105; Frn.,	
3 90	$25	130 00
	HANNA—Gen.	1 25
9 48	LANDER—*Trinity Church*: Gen.......	10 00
5 16	MILFORD—Gen.	1 35

Foreign Missionary Districts

Brazil

Ap. $119.09

SAO JOSE DEL NORTE—*Resurrection*:
Gen. (of which S. S., 42 cts.)...... 2 41
RIO GRANDE—*Church of the Saviour*:
Gen. (of which S. S., $12.35)...... 39 02
JAGUARAO—*Christ Chapel*: Gen....... 10 99
PELOTAS—*Church of the Redeemer*:
Gen. 7 26
SANTA HELENA—*Redemption*: Gen.... 1 86
BAGE—*Church of the Crucified*: Gen.. 10 83
RIO DE JANEIRO—*Church of the Re-
deemer*: Gen. 16 84
PORTO ALEGRE—*Trinity Church*: Gen. 8 67
SANTA RITA—*Calvary*: Gen.......... 1 88
SAO LEOPOLDO—*Church of the Mes-
siah*: Gen. 2 90
SANTA MARIA—*Church of the Mediator*:
Gen. 9 30
PINHAL—*Mission*: Gen. 3 85
IJUHY—*Mission*: Gen. 3 78

Miscellaneous

Ap. $12,061.98; *Sp.* $1,045.61
Interest — Dom., $2,666.33; Frn.,
$1,074.79; Gen., $616.91; Sp.,
$953.86; Specific Deposit, $26.67... 5,338 56
United Offering of Wo. Aux., on
account of appropriations to September 1st, 1910, Dom., $3,500;
Frn., $3,500 .... 7,000 00

In memory of a sainted mother, Sp.
for Bishop Rowe, Alaska......... 5
An aunt and godson, Sp. for Bishop
Rowe, Alaska 5
Gen. 5
Passengers on "S. S. Philadelphia,"
Sp. for Church Extension Fund,
Porto Rico 6
In loving memory of Mary Hazlett
Abbott, Sp. for Bishop Rowe,
Alaska 10
"A Friend," Gen. 11
Through *The Churchman*, Sp. for
Rev. Mr. Gilman, Hankow........ 15
League for Eastern Oregon, Sp. for
Bishop Paddock, Eastern Oregon... 50
Daughters of the King, for Miss
Annette B. Richmond's salary,
Shanghai 187

Legacies

PENN., PHILADELPHIA—Estate of Miss
Mary Lewis, to the Society........10,000
CONN., NEW HAVEN—Estate of Mrs.
Lucy H. Boardman, Dom......... 2,075
W. N. Y., BUFFALO—Estate of Mrs.
Charles H. Smith, Dom., $194.11;
Frn., $194.10 388
Estate of Mrs. Charles H. Smith,
Dom., $150; Frn., $150.......... 300

Receipts for the month.......... $157,020
Amount previously acknowledged... 725,451

Total received from Sept. 1st, 1909. $882,472

SUMMARY OF RECEIPTS

Receipts divided according to purposes to which they are to be applied	Received during March	Amounts previously Acknowledged	Total
1. Applicable upon the appropriations of the Board.	$124,116 57	$276,811 35	$400,927 2
2. Special gifts forwarded to objects named by donors in addition to the appropriations of the Board.	20,113 95	100,004 91	120,118 6
3. Legacies for investment.	......	165,000 00	165,000 0
4. Legacies, the disposition of which is to be determined by the Board at the end of the fiscal year.	12,763 21	62,826 89	75,590 0
5. Specific Deposit.	26 67	120,808 60	120,835 7
Total.	$157,020 40	$725,451 75	$882,472 5

Total receipts from September 1st, 1909, to April 1st, 1910, applicable upon the appropriations, divided according to the sources from which they have come, and compared with the corresponding period of the preceding year. Legacies are not included in the following items, as their disposition is not determined by the Board until the end of the fiscal year.

OFFERINGS TO PAY APPROPRIATIONS

Source	To April 1, 1910	To April 1, 1909	Increase	Decr.
1. From congregations.	$240,090 05	$203,295 63	$36,794 42	$....
2. From individuals.	26,587 81	40,301 85	.....	13,71 4
3. From Sunday-schools.	9,616 09	5,986 13	3,629 96	....
4. From Woman's Auxiliary.	29,744 36	36,376 77	.....	6,63 1
5. Woman's Auxiliary United Offering.	49,000 00	25,000 00	24,000 00	....
6. From interest.	44,867 44	40,974 82	3,892 62	....
7. Miscellaneous items.	1,022 17	2,337 69	.....	1,31 2
Total.	$400,927 92	$354,272 89	$46,655 03	

APPROPRIATIONS FOR THE YEAR

SEPTEMBER 1ST, 1909, TO AUGUST 31ST, 1910

Amount Needed for the Year

1. To pay appropriations as made to date for the work at home and abroad..... $1,206,45 7
2. To replace Reserve Funds temporarily used for the current work............ 32,95 3

Total... $1,239,41 0
Total receipts to date applicable on appropriations...................... 400,92 2

Amount needed before August 31st, 1910.............................. $ 838,48 8

THE

Spirit of Missions

AN ILLUSTRATED MONTHLY REVIEW
OF CHRISTIAN MISSIONS

June, 1910

CONTENTS

The Subscription Price of THE SPIRIT OF MISSIONS is ONE DOLLAR per year. stage is prepaid in the United States, Porto Rico, the Philippines and Mexico. For other countries i t Postal Union, including Canada, twenty-four cents per year should be added.
Subscriptions are continued until ordered discontinued.
Change of Address: In all changes of address it is necessary that the old as well as the new ress should be given.
How to Remit: Remittances, made payable to George Gordon King, Treasurer, should be ne by draft on New York, Postal Order or Express Order. One and two cent stamps are re- c ed. To checks on local banks ten cents should be added for collection.
All Letters should be addressed to **The Spirit of Missions, 281 Fourth Avenue, New York.**

Published by the Domestic and Foreign Missionary Society.

President, RIGHT REVEREND DANIEL S. TUTTLE, D.D. *Secretary*, ——
Treasurer, GEORGE GORDON KING.

Entered at the Post Office, in New York, as second-class matter.

TH SPIRIT OF MISSIONS is regularly on sale
In Philadelphia: By George W. Jacobs & Co., 1216 Walnut St.
In Milwaukee: By The Young Churchman Co., 412 Milwaukee St.
In Boston: By Smith & McCance, 38 Bromfield St.
In Elizabeth, N. J.: By Franklin H. Spencer, 743 Jefferson St.

THE SPIRIT OF MISSIONS

AN ILLUSTRATED MONTHLY REVIEW
OF CHRISTIAN MISSIONS

Vol. LXXV.   **June,** 1910   No. 6

THE PROGRESS OF THE KINGDOM

The Children's Lenten Offering

IT is as yet impossible to form any adequate judgment concerning the Children's Lenten Offering for the current year. Up to the time of writing the sums received by the treasury were not quite equal to those for a like period last year, but it is doubtful whether this furnishes a sufficient basis for deduction as to the final result. At any rate, it seems certain that the children have again done wonderfully well, even though they may not have reached the goal of $150,000 toward which they have been striving in recent years. When more accurate details are at hand we shall have something to say on the general features of this effort, which has already brought more than $100,000 into the treasury since Easter.

The State of the Treasury

SO far as an opinion can at this time be formed the state of the treasury is scarcely satisfactory. The report presented at the May meeting of the Board shows, up to May 1st, an increase over last year of $35,000. This is encouraging—provided it continues. It should be remembered that an extraordinary effort was made last summer, and an amount far above the average was received. This, and much more, must be done this year if we are to close without a deficit. Even if the apportionment is met in all cases, without large additional gifts, there is likely to be a deficit. Let every diocese and every congregation bear in mind that if it neglects to do its part, it is failing the Church in her great need, and that there is left to her only the forlorn hope that some one more loyal and more generous may volunteer to make good the dereliction of the unwilling and the apathetic.

The Men's Missionary Congress

WAS that friend over-enthusiastic who declared that the Men's Missionary Congress in Chicago embodied the greatest religious movement of modern times? We can only say that none who took part in it would be prepared to dispute his statement, and a large number would echo it.

It certainly looked like something akin to the millennium when 3,000 men, some of whom had come hundreds of miles, and each of whom had paid $5 for the privilege, met day after day to hear the story of world-wide missions

(413)

told by representatives from the battle-line. *Men, remember!* all of them! Not a half-dozen bonnets in the Auditorium theatre, where, three times a day, for two or three hours at a sitting, the great audience listened with deepening interest and growing enthusiasm.

Yet enthusiasm, in the ordinary sense of the word, was not the conspicuous note. It was rather a deep, serious, self-controlled purpose; a desire and determination to know the facts and face the issues involved in the proposal to evangelize the world. And the facts were plentifully supplied. The speeches, as a whole, could not be called great. A few were conceived in rhetoric and brought forth in oratory, but for these the audience did not greatly care. Yet the strong and simple statements of men who *knew* met with instant and inspiring response. Indeed, the greatest thing about the Congress was the Congress itself. Unanimity, sincerity and serious purpose pervaded it like an atmosphere. Most of the speakers were at the close of a long campaign through the West. Few reached the highest forensic mark of which they are capable, and some had lost much of their force and brilliancy; but never did they produce better results. Those who had real things to say met with a real response.

To summarize the proceedings in our limited space would be impossible. Those who wish an outline of the thirty or forty speeches delivered must turn to the weekly Church journals. It is for us to speak rather of this Congress as marking an epoch in the progress of the Kingdom. Its power was tremendous, and its results must be far-reaching. Never again, we believe, can the attitude of Christian men be as it has been toward the Church's world-wide mission. The leaven has been introduced into the measures of meal, and by the grace of God it will do its work.

The Church's Part

In this good work our own Church took no inconspicuous part. Proportionately the attendance of Churchmen

was very large, and they were from among our best and strongest. It was the best sort of loyalty to the Church which took them there—a loyalty to Christ and His Kingdom. And we venture to say that all were surprised to find how little, after all, there was to fear in the way of complication or compromise, and how great was the profit to be gained from this participation in a common cause.

In the "Message to the Men of the Church," which appears in the following pages, the Church participants in the Congress voice their convictions, summarizing results and outlining an adequate policy for the Church.

And now the real test comes. "The end of the campaign is the beginning of the work." How far will the Church respond to the call and rise to the opportunity? It behooves us who believe in Christ's purpose for the world to redouble our prayers that the men of His Church "may both perceive and know what things they ought to do, and also may have grace and power faithfully to fulfil the same."

L AST winter there appeared in the Church press a suggestive letter from the Bishop of the Philippine Islands entitled "An Apportionment of Men." I called attention to

Men for the Battle

the need for a more systematic, definite and statesmanlike method of procuring volunteers for missions in the foreign field. It set forth the fact that all apportionment plans, however effective, which stop short at procuring money for the work, can have only a partial and secondary value, unless, together with these, some plan is devised by which there may be an adequate and steady flow of reinforcements toward the front of the Church's battle-line.

Out of what bitter experience, struggle and disappointment the bishop wrote—with what memories of opportunities not seized, of victories delayed and advantages surrendered, while the general of the Church's forces sent his ringing call for help, which nó one answered—only he can know. But that he spoke whereof he knew, and that he voiced the heartfelt wish of every other missionary bishop, is abundantly evident.

An Answer to the Call
Partly, no doubt, in response to t h i s summons, and partly, it may be, as a result of that great awakening to the importance of the missionary cause which is sweeping over the Church, there has been put .forth by certain of our seminary students a most interesting and timely statement. It is entitled: "A plan for concerted action between the missionary societies in the seminaries of the Church for providing clergy for the foreign fields on a scale adequate to the present needs."
After reciting the needs of the mission fields and the crisis they are facing, the statement goes on to say:

> The time seems to have come for concerted action on the part of the students at the seminaries. To this end, the following plan, by which each seminary of the Church may assume a definite share of responsibility in providing the necessary men, seems to present decided advantages.
> The urgent appeals for recruits from the bishops in all the missions abroad, received and correlated at the office of the Board of Missions, indicate that within the next ten years the Church should send at least 250 ordained men to the fields abroad for which she has assumed definite responsibility. Only so can the vacancies which will inevitably occur be filled, and some adequate provision be made for the extension of the work.
> In the following table will be seen the names of the Church seminaries with the approximate number of their students and the number of men that each should furnish if this standard is to be reached. Because of the varying strength of the classes

from year to year the student generation, or three years, has been taken as a fairer unit of responsibility by which to be guided. The analysis is therefore made upon a three-year basis rather than upon a one-year basis.

List of Seminaries	Number of Students	Proportionate for 10 Years	Missionaries for 3 Years
General	100	60	18
Virginia	45	30	9
Cambridge	34	22	7
Philadelphia	31	20	6
Seabury	25	12	3
Nashotah	22	12	3
Berkeley	9	6	2
Western	16	8	2
Sewanee	7	3	1
Bexley Hall	15	6	2
San Mateo	15	6	2
	319	185	55

It will be seen that this provides fot 185 out of 250 which the Church should send within the next ten years. The responsibility for supplying the remaining 65 may rightly devolve upon the younger parish clergy, who have hitherto provided a number of candidates for the mission field each year.

Is such a plan capable of being carried out, or are its formulators seeking an impossible ideal? Five years ago one might have classed this as an "iridescent dream," but now none of us is prepared to say what God may not do with a Church alive to His call and empowered by the Spirit to proclaim worthily and effectively the Gospel of His Son. At any rate it is cause for encouragement that the young men whom the Church is rearing for her ministry can seriously propound such a plan—that these, who alone can do the work and answer the call, believe that "there is now an unprecedented opportunity to begin a movement which may profoundly change the whole missionary situation at home and abroad."

This last phrase is a significant one. It points to the fact that in advocating a plan for recruiting the Church's staff

abroad there is no intention of ignoring the needs at home. Indeed, those
who put forth the statement go on to
say—what we believe is profoundly true
—that "just as gifts of money for the
work abroad stimulate and increase gifts
for the work at home, so the offering of
lives for the work abroad will increase
the number of volunteers for definite
missionary service at home."

When such a spirit shall animate the
Church—when she shall see her opportunity and frankly accept Christ's challenge of service—she will have begun to
come everywhere into her own.

What of the Layman? But even if this plan
should be carried
out in its fulness
there is yet more
which must be done. Modern missions
are not of or for the clergy only; lay
men and women are needed in equal or
larger proportions. The work is manifold, and calls for manifold gifts. The
physicians, the teachers, the nurses—
what of them? May we not hope and
pray that among them some like effort
may develop for securing an adequate
supply? In our schools and colleges and
universities, among our Sunday-schools
and guilds and parish workers, are the
men and women who must do this work,
if it is done at all. Might not parishes
or dioceses take a voluntary share in
finding them? Many are coming, but
many more are needed, and nothing
would so awaken the life, and stimulate
the zeal, and increase the knowledge of
parish or diocese as conscientious and
systematic effort to send forth, from
among the children of its own household, men and women who shall help
to reap those fields which "are white already to harvest."

THE American nation stands in a
unique relation toward the Liberian Republic. Indirectly at least, we
brought it into
The Liberian Situation being. The work of
the early coloniza-
tion societies was
fostered and encouraged by our Govern-

.That t h i s great
Measures   wrong may not be
Proposed   done—that the ex-
. periment station in
Negro self-government which this nation has planted may not disappear from
the map, is the earnest desire of the
Commissioners, the Secretary of State
and the President himself. These are
the recommendations made with a view
to improving the present situation:

(1) That the United States
extend its aid to Liberia in the
prompt settlement of pending
boundary disputes.

(2) That the United States
enable Liberia to refund its debt
by assuming as a guarantee for
the payment of obligations under
such arrangement the control
and collection of the Liberian
customs.

(3) That the United States
lend its assistance to the Liberian Government in the reform of
its internal finances.

(4) That the United States
lend its aid to Liberia in organizing and drilling an adequate
constabulary or frontier police
force.

(5) That the United States establish and maintain a research
station in Liberia.

(6) That the United States reopen the question of establishing a naval coaling station in
Liberia.

Now it only remains for Congress to
act. It is almost inconceivable that it
should do other than approve the plans
proposed; but great possibilities of surprise are latent in Congress, and the
friends of Liberia cannot but be concerned as to the outcome.

The relation of our
Our Mission   Church to Liberia
in Liberia   is singularly like
that of the Nation.
From the beginning we have been concerned for and have borne a part in the
enterprise. Indeed, it was with the pur-

pose of undertaking work in Liberia
that the Domestic and Foreign Missionary Society was formed. To no part of
the world-field has more faithful fostering care been given, and nowhere else do
so many of our American missionaries
sleep in foreign graves.

We thank God for the work He
has permitted us to do in Liberia.
The peace, order and Christian habits
of the Liberian population as a whole, to
which the Commission bears cordial witness, are in some considerable measure
due to the labor and sacrifice of the
American Episcopal Church.

BISHOP ANDERSON'S address on
"The Will of Christ for the
World," delivered at the opening of the

"Prophets of Unity" Laymen's Missionary Congress, was
something m o r e
than a t e l l i n g
speech. It was a noble and timely utterance, breathing robust manhood and
fearless sincerity, and the great audience
heard in it the voice of a prophet.

We may be profoundly thankful that
it was given to a leader of the Church
to sound the keynote of the great Congress, and to do it so wonderfully. The
speaker faced his task with courage and
enthusiasm. He did not avoid nor evade
the conclusions to which his subject led
him. He addressed himself to the difficult and delicate question which lay
back of the whole matter, and he treated
it so courageously and so Christianly
as to win the admiration and approval
of the most varied and composite body
of Christian men who ever met to face a
serious task in common. "Let us," he
said, "be prophets of unity," and admirably he led the way. This was an
achievement well worth while, and it not
only did much toward creating the atmosphere which made the Congress so
marked a success, but it also gave to hundreds of our fellow-Christians a new
conception of the Church's attitude
toward them and their purposes. We
are glad to be able to publish in the fol-

To the Men of the Church

This message was sent out by the members of the Churchmen's
Conference, National Missionary Congress, held in Chicago,
May 3-6, 1910

An Acknowledgment

The Churchmen assembled in Chicago for their conference in
connection with the National Missionary Congress record their
gratitude for the work of the pioneers who laid the foundations
for a Christian civilization in the Mississippi Valley. This
frontier trading-post of seventy-five years ago now numbers its
Christian congregations by the hundred and their influence is
felt in every quarter of the world. There could be no better
illustration of the value and results of such home missionary effort as that of pioneers like Bishop Chase, Bishop Kemper, and
many others whose names are less well known to us.

We are thankful, too, that together with this work at home,
the Church, even in that early day, sent self-sacrificing men and
women to carry her message to Asia and Africa. These and
others have labored, and we have entered into their labors.

We recognize that we face to-day a world-wide opportunity
and responsibility which call for new and better methods and for
earnest devotion to the Church's Mission.

An Affirmation

We affirm that upon every Churchman rests the responsibility
for:

1. The "Local Parish"—which includes his own congregation
and the community in which he lives.

2. The "Diocesan Parish"—which includes those parts of his
diocese where the Church is unknown or weak, and where help
is needed to establish it strongly.

3. The "National Parish"—which includes that part of our

own country beyond the borders of his diocese where the Church as a whole is carrying on mission work.

4. The "World Parish"—which includes the non-Christian world, and especially those fields to which this Church has sent her representatives.

We believe that the gifts of Churchmen for the work in the diocesan, the national and the world parishes ought at least to equal the gifts for the support of the local parish.

An Adequate Policy

In order that the Church may discharge her responsibility to the whole world there should be created in every congregation some simple and adequate organization such as a representative and active missionary committee.

We advocate the use of every effective means for the dissemination of missionary information, especially frequent missionary sermons, the systematic study of missions, the reading of THE SPIRIT OF MISSIONS, and missionary education in the Sunday-school.

We would remind Churchmen everywhere of the vital importance of creating in their own homes a missionary atmosphere, and a love, especially on the part of the young people of the home, for the Church's Mission. There is no more effective way of insuring an adequate supply of volunteers for missionary service.

We recognize that our growing and successful work should be strongly supported. We cannot believe that the present ratio of giving—$800,000 for both home and foreign work from 900,000 communicants—fairly represents the ability of the Church, particularly when we remember that one-third of this total is the gift of the Woman's Auxiliary and the Sunday-schools.

The occasional missionary offering has proved manifestly inadequate, because—as is indicated by inquiry in many directions—it secures gifts from not more than one-fifth of the members of the average congregation, and even to these it does not teach the principle of proportionate and systematic giving.

We favor, therefore, the weekly missionary offering as being more scriptural, more effective and of greater educational value.

We believe that the time has come for the general adoption of the plan of an "every member" canvass of the congregation for definite personal subscriptions to our Mission Work.

Such a canvass gives to the congregation a new vision of the Mission of the Church. It brings out latent energies by giving the people some really large thing to do. It deepens the spiritual life of those engaged in the work. It puts those opposed to missions on the defensive. It increases interest in and contributions to the work at home. It gives courage and confidence to the clergy at home and the missionaries in the field by making them feel that they have the men of the Church behind them.

The Duty of Prayer

We should guard against the mistake of supposing that we can discharge our duty to the Church's Mission by our money and our work alone. It must have our constant and intelligent prayer as well.

We recommend therefore:

1. The practice of mid-day prayer for the extension of the Kingdom.

2. The use of the Sanctuary of Missions which appears in the monthly issues of THE SPIRIT OF MISSIONS.

3. That Churchmen enroll as members of the Church Prayer League and make use of its quarterly intercession paper.

4. The use of carefully planned intercession services for the extension of Christ's Kingdom, and particularly that at every celebration of the Holy Communion some prayer for missions be used. Thus our obedience to our Lord's command, "Do this in remembrance of Me," is linked with the recognition of our duty to discharge His final commission to His Church: "Make disciples of all the nations."

A Declaration

We rejoice that several thousand Churchmen, led by their bishops and clergy, have shared the stimulus of the national campaign of the Laymen's Missionary Movement, and because of this have expressed their intention to increase the missionary offerings of their several congregations from $333,466 given during the last fiscal year to $640,662 for the coming year.

We call upon the men who have taken part in these conferences to put into operation at once concerted plans for realizing their expressed intention.

For ourselves, recognizing the importance of converting our resolutions into action, we assure the Board of Missions that we will personally endeavor to carry out in our own congregations the suggestions outlined in this policy.

THE SANCTUARY OF MISSIONS

"IF I have eaten my morsel
   alone,"
The Patriarch spoke in scorn.
What would he think of the Church
   were he shown
Heathendom huge, forlorn,
Godless, Christless, with soul unfed,
While the Church's ailment is full-
   ness of bread,
Eating her morsel alone?

"I am debtor alike to the Jew and
   the Greek,"
The mighty Apostle cried,
Traversing continents, souls to seek,
For the love of the Crucified.
Centuries, centuries, since have
   sped,
Millions are famishing—we have
   bread—
Yet we eat our morsel alone.

Ever from those who have largest
   dower
Will Heaven require the more.
Ours is affluence, knowledge, power,
   Ocean from shore to shore;
And East and West in our ears
   have said,
"Give us, O give us this living
   Bread"—
Yet we eat our morsel alone.

"Freely ye have received, so give,"
   He bade Who hath given us all.
How shall the soul in us longer
   live
Deaf to their starving call
For whom the Blood of the Lord
   was shed,
And His Body broken to give them
   bread,
If we eat our morsel alone?
     —*Archbishop Alexander.*

INTERCESSIONS

"That it may please Thee"—
That we may better understand
and set forward the will of Christ
for the world. (Page 423.)
To give us wisdom and earnestness that we may rightly discharge
our duty to the black people of this
land. (Page 437.)
To bring to better knowledge and
worthier life those who but dimly
understand the power of God unto
salvation. (Page 431.)

To direct and bless all Christian
conferences for the extension of thy
Kingdom, particularly the World
Missionary Congress at Edinburgh
and the Conference for Church
Work at Cambridge. (Page 447.)
To move the hearts of students
and young people that they may
more freely offer themselves to "go
up to the help of the Lord against
the mighty." (Page 414.)
That the men of the Church may
hear and respond to the call of their
representatives. (Page 419.)

THANKSGIVINGS

"We thank Thee"—
For the worthy part which the
Church has taken in awakening the
Christian men of this country to
their missionary responsibility and
opportunity.
For the persevering faithfulness
shown by the poor and the untaught
to whom thy truth has been revealed. (Page 435.)
For the quality of the native
clergy who are being brought into
the ministry of thy Church in
China. (Page 412.)
For the noble way in which our
schools in China and Japan are fulfilling the purpose for which they
were established. (Pages 429-441.)
For the presence and influence of
thy Church in our institutions of
learning. (Page 453.)

PRAYER

FOR FULLER CONSECRATION,

O LOVING FATHER of all
   men, Who in the life of thy
dear Son hast revealed thy desire
that none should perish but that all
should come to the knowledge of
thee; Accomplish in us thy good purpose for ourselves and for our fellow-men. Suffer us not to withhold
love and life only to lose them; but
teach us how we, by giving them in
thy service, may keep them unto
life eternal. And bring us, with all
thy children, home at length to our
Father's house, for the sake of our
Elder Brother and only Saviour,
thy Son, Jesus Christ our Lord.
Amen.

THE WILL OF CHRIST FOR THE WORLD

By the Right Reverend Charles P. Anderson, D.D., Bishop of Chicago

This speech was the opening word of the National Missionary Congress in Chicago, and no utterance during the sessions produced a more profound impression

HAVE made a considerable number of missionary addresses of late, both in connection with the Church which I have the privilege of representing, as well as with the Chicago Convention of the Laymen's Missionary Movement. I almost feel as if I were obtruding myself in appearing upon the platform once ore. I have been asked, however, to make the opening address at this National ongress and I esteem it a great privilege and honor to do so.

The subject which has been assigned to me is "The Will of Christ for the World." It is a subject which one ought to approach on one's knees. It is an awful sponsibility to undertake to interpret the mind of Christ for the world. ortunately, we are not left to our own resources; we do not have to guess at it. e do not have to depend on any mental process of ratiocination. It does not have be evolved out of our inner consciousness. We have only to listen to the Divine, ithoritative voice, and then interpret that voice in the language of practical edience.

I shall venture to interpret the will of Christ for the world, so far as the pur-ses of this gathering are concerned, in two words: They are Universality and nity—the universality of the religion of Jesus Christ, the unity of the Christian hurch. I take it that there are no two things that stand out more prominently in o pages of the New Testament than these. First, that the religion of Christ is for e whole world; and secondly, that there is to be oneness on the part of the disciples Christ, in order that the whole world may know and believe.

I.

First: Universality. I do not have to argue it in this gathering. It is an iom. It is a postulate. It is the very central belief of our religion. Christ is the on of God. "God has made of one blood all nations of men to dwell on the face of e whole earth." Whatsoever God purposes through Christ for any part of the orld, He purposes for all parts of the world. Christ belongs to no nation, but to l nations; to no race, but to all races; to no age, but to all ages. He is not simply man, but Man, universal Man; not a god, but God incarnate for all humanity. od of God, Light of light, . . . who for us men and for our salvation . . . as made Man." And if we come away from the somewhat stiff statements of theo-gical language to the mellower language of the New Testament, we find that every ge is full of the same idea. "God so loved the world"—not a portion of it, but e whole world—"that He gave His only begotten Son." "Come unto me, all ye at labour and are heavy laden." "Go into all the world and preach the Gospel to l nations, baptizing them in the name of the Father, and of the Son, and of the oly Ghost." Men sometimes speak of "Christ and other Masters." Christ alone Master, and all others are brethren. Christ has no competitors. Christ has no vals. "There is none other name given under Heaven whereby man can be saved it in the name of Jesus Christ." "In the name of Jesus, every knee shall bow."

This does not involve that you and I deny that the non-Christian ethnic faiths the world have any ethical or moral value. We rejoice when we find that they ave. God hath not left Himself without witnesses. In every nation the people ve some idea of God, some consciousness of right and wrong, some glimmering of

(423)

424   The Will of Christ for the World

immortality. In some cases these exist in a very rude and crude form, and lead·
all kinds of fantastic cruelties in the name of religion. In some cases they exist
a more developed form. That is our starting point. The Christian missionaries, li
Christ, came not to destroy but to fulfil. We hold that Christ is the logical a
inevitable outcome of all religions. As St. Augustine said, men are natural
Christians. We hold that there are in every man certain instincts and intuitio
and endowments which, if given a proper environment and proper cultivation, w
inevitably lead up to his being a Christian man. "If ye believe in God, belie
also in Me."

We do not seek to destroy the good that people already have; but to lead the
from what they have to what they have not. "Whom ye ignorantly worship, Hi
declare we unto you." The goal of the Christian religion is Christ. It is not
question of whether there are good things in their sacred books, or whether th
have some virtues,_or whether they or we have an open Bible, or whether a Chur
organization exists. The great question is, Have they, have we, Christ? That
the goal. "He that hath the Son hath life, and he that hath not the Son of G
hath not life." "I am come that ye might have life, and that ye might have it mo
abundantly." I am thankful that we do not have to argue this proposition in tl
presence. It is of the very essence of the Gospel of Christ that it is an univers
Gospel.

But the universality of the Christian Religion not only rests upon our clai
for Christ, but also upon the fact that it has demonstrated its fitness to be the u
versal religion and its power to be the universal religion. Just think of a f(
broad facts. Christianity was born in the world at a time when there were ma
ancient civilizations. Egypt had seen great days; Babylon had been mighty; Gree
had reached a high pinnacle of fame; Rome had seen some proud and imperi
times; China had at that time an ancient civilization. Those civilizations h
failed to save them. And Christianity, in less than two thousand years, practisi
upon decadent civilizations, or upon barbarous conditions, has in a short space
time brought those nations in which it has operated away ahead of all the ancie
civilizations. It is indubitably true that the Christian religion injects certain in
tinguishable elements into human society, with the consequence that the Christi
nations make much more progress in all the higher things of life than all the otl
nations of the world.

Let us take a brief but striking illustration; let us contrast Christianity wi
Mohammedanism. Freeman says in his book upon the Saracens that "Mohamn
danism has consecrated despotism; has consecrated polygamy; has consecrat
slavery." Now, contrast the influence of Christianity with that. Is it not true tl
Christianity has consecrated liberty, not despotism? It has consecrated monogan
not polygamy; it has abolished slavery. Christianity at an early date touched tl
ancient civilization of Greece. It was at a decadent period. Her art and l
architecture had not saved her. Her poets and her orators, her philosophers and l
statesmen had not saved her. Bear in mind that Christianity overtook that civili:
tion at a time when it was doomed to absolute destruction. What saved it fr
destruction? What preserved the national life in spite of most appalling calamiti(
What saved that little country of Greece from Ottoman tyranny, from the Mosl(
scimitar, from external disaster, from her own internal corruption? Why,
we can believe such thoughtful students as Freeman and Finley and Stanley, no
ing else preserved the continuity of that country than the introduction into it of t
Christian religion. Go into that country to-day, and though you may find ma
things that are not admirable, though you may find that they are very short
having attained anything like the highest standard of Christian life, neverthele

if you pick out the strong things, the enduring things, the things that have saved them, they have been the things that were not born within themselves, but the things which Christianity contributed to them. That religion brought to them it a perilous time certain principles that appealed to them—the eternity of God, the brotherhood of man through Jesus Christ—and though their armies might be destroyed, though terrible calamities might ensue, they imbibed those Christian principles which have held that nation together.

Come over to the civilization of the Latin races. Bear in mind that we are contrasting the effects of religion in a civilization that was decadent, at a time of political weakness, with other religions at the height of civilization and at the height of political power. It is not putting our religion to a proper advantage, and yet it can stand the test. Compare the great men, the ideals, the poets of the Latin races after Christianity was introduced, with the ideals and the poets and the great men of the Roman Empire prior to the time of the birth of Christ or the missionary labors of St. Paul. Compare, if you will, a Virgil with a Dante. Does not Dante have something grander and sublimer; did he not have visions which the great poet Virgil never saw, because he had never heard of Christ? Compare St. Augustine with Marcus Aurelius. We do not care to minimize the virtues of Marcus Aurelius; but is it not true that Augustine penetrated down deeper, that he reached up higher, that he saw things that Marcus Aurelius never saw? Compare such a man as St. Francis d'Assisi with a Seneca or an Epictetus. Think of the great Latin doctors that have made their contributions to Christian literature. Think of their great saints, men and women. Think of their great hymns. Think of their great prayers. Is there anything in the ancient Roman world, with all its might and power and organization, that ever produced such types of men as Christianity produced?

Take our own civilization. Christianity overtook us at a time when our forefathers were rude barbarians. Where did we get our ideas of God, our ideas of truth, of honor, of purity, of charity, of home, of wife, of child, of mother? You say they came as the result of civilization. What is civilization but the humanization of men, but where did the humanizing power come from? They are nothing more nor less than the direct contribution of the religion of Jesus Christ to the humanity that we share.

Yes, the greatest power in the world has been the power of Christ. His work is not yet completed, but it is working toward completeness. He has given birth to spiritual kingdoms. He has laid the corner-stone of our highest civilization. He has revivified old, dead maxims into living realities. He has scattered the face of the earth with principles that were based upon the eternal love of the Eternal Father. He has been the preacher of liberty, fraternity and equality. He has abolished slavery from our midst. He has inspired our best literature. He has founded institutions of learning. He has been giving new conceptions of sin, new ideas of duty, and new hopes of immortality. He has been consecrating childhood, He has been dignifying womanhood, He has been sanctifying our homes, He has been helping the poor, He has been delivering people from the oppressor, He has been lifting people by the thousands, one by one, one by one, out of the dunghill of their sins and causing them to throw themselves upon the all-redeeming love of the Saviour of the World. Notwithstanding the faults that can be found in the administration of the Christian Church, notwithstanding the weaknesses that can be found there, the most magnificent, the most pervasive, the greatest power in the direction of all that is highest in human life has been Christ and the Christian Church.

Every altar that is erected is consecrated to the truth that sets men free. Every

tower that is built rests upon the Eternal Rock of Ages. Every spire points men
the highest things, to their future home, and Heaven and God. Obliterate Chri
tianity out of the world, strike it out of our literature, burn up your Bibles, thrott
the choirs, hush up the preacher's voice, break down the altars, take away the
things, and there is no archangel that would be sufficiently eloquent to depict t
horribleness and the vastness of the catastrophe that would ensue. In spite of o
faults we can sing the old psalm: "Oh, that men would therefore praise the Lord f
His goodness, and declare the wonders that He doeth for the children of men."

So I say that we start out in this conference first with the conviction that Chri
is universal; that the Christian religion is to be universal; that it has the power
being universal, and that it is the most potential thing for righteousness that t
world has ever seen. That is the first part of our programme.

II.

And now Unity. Of course, unity is not uniformity. Unity is not unanimit
of opinion. Unity is not platform agreement. Unity is not a federation of sep
rated churches; nor is it organic separation and rivalry. Unity is that oneness
the visible body of Christ that makes men know and believe. This, of course, is n
the time or the place to discuss unity as a platform. It is not the time or t
place to say a single word of a controversial character. Neither is it the time or t
place for any of us to say foolish things for the sake of saying perhaps the popul
things; but I, for one, cannot discuss the subject, "What Is the Will of Christ for t
World?" without touching unity. And you and I cannot consider the most state
manlike, the most economic, the most efficient methods of missionary administratio
without considering unity.

It is well for us to remember that the greatest triumphs that the Christia
Church has ever won were in the days when the Church was one. It is well for
to remember that the greatest triumphs that Christianity has ever won were wo
shall I say, before the Thirty-nine Articles were written, or the Westminster Co
fession, or the Augsburg Confession? And the greatest triumphs that Christianit
is going to win will be the triumphs of a united Christian discipleship.

Let me take you to a little town not very far from Chicago. It has but 1,3(
population—men, women and children. It has nine churches. Some of these ni
churches are being supported by contributions from Home Mission Boards. The
are 55 per cent. of the men of that town that do not belong to any of the nine. B
why? Because they are so feeble, necessarily so feeble when they divide 1,300 sou
up among nine of them—they are all necessarily so feeble as not to be commandir
exponents of the Christian religion in the town in which they exist. Does t
number of religions increase the amount of religion? Is there not a danger th
these labels become libels on true Christianity?

Let me take you to another town, not so very far from Chicago. It is a larg
town. It has thirty-two churches in it—thirty-two separate organizations, I a
told. Some of these churches are in need of support from the Home Missiona
Board, when anything like Christian statesmanship would strengthen the Chur
in that town and make it a great contributory force to spreading the Gosp
throughout the world. I believe that we are wasting more money through ove
lapping, through dove-tailing, through rivalries, than would evangelize a whole ra
in a single generation. Is it wise? Is it statesmanlike? Is it Christian?

I would be the very last person to put forward the economic argument as or
of the first arguments on behalf of Christian Unity. Better have 500 churche
each one with its own truths and its own spiritual convictions, than one unite
Church at the sacrifice of a single truth or of a single spiritual reality. Bett
waste $1,000,000 than to sacrifice a spiritual experience or a precious truth. But

ecessary either to waste money on the one hand or to sacrifice convictions on other?

I am quite sure that many of us have been approaching the subject wrong-end t. We have been asking, What can we give up in the interests of unity? That is ot the question. It is not what we can give up, but What can we give? You have right to give up—no right to give up anything that you have had that ever has n of value, that is of value, or that is likely to be of value. You have no right to e up anything that has ever received the Divine sanction and the Divine ap- val. It is not what we can give up, but what we can give. I have a horror of t kind of unity that would be based on a sort of residuum. I am not attracted by ty on the basis of an irreducible minimum. I do not want to belong to a Church minimums. I want to belong to a Church of maximums—maximum beliefs, ximum duties, maximum sacrifices. The Church of minimums is incapable of ducing martyrdoms.

There *are* things that we can give up, but nobody is asking anybody to give up thing that is of value. We can give up pride; we can give up our ecclesiastical ceit; we can give up our denominational jealousies; we can give up our inherited judices; and perhaps, by the grace of God, we can give up some of our ignorance.

I lay this down, brethren, as a proposition that has already demonstrated itself: rist-like Christians cannot stay apart. Take this Laymen's Missionary Move- nt. To me the most significant thing about it is this: That, as I see it, all kinds Christians—Roman Christians if they would, Oriental Christians, Anglican ristians, Protestant Christians of every name can, without a single scruple of science, come and take their part and their portion in this great enterprise.

Why? It is because we all have the same central unity up to this point. We all lieve in Christ. We believe that the world is for Him, and we believe that He has ne to have the whole world. Glory be to God! that at the end of 2,000 years, spite of bitter controversies and interminable logomachies and almost bloody re- ious warfare, Christians throughout the whole world can get together on that plat- m—Christ for the world and the world for Christ. There is more unity than we nk. The things that separate Christians are inconsequential in comparison with se that separate Christians from non-Christians. "He that hath the Son hath , and he that hath not the Son of God hath not life."

III.

Well, that is our programme: The universality of the Christian religion and ultimate unity of the Church of Christ. Isn't it a big enough programme? Is world big enough for you? Is Christ attractive enough for you?

"Ashamed of Jesus, can it be,
A mortal man ashamed of Thee?"

t us rigidly and loyally adhere to that programme in spite of the worldliness of Church, in spite of the unbelief of our Christian membership, in spite of our d love and our painless sacrifices, in spite of the absolutely unchristian talk that hear from the pews that they do not believe in missions, in spite of everything, us not pull down the flag one inch. Christ is for the whole world and the whole rld for Christ. And as a means to that end let us all be prophets of unity, priests unity, apostles of unity. We can do that much, at any rate. We can say of unity we say of universality: We can if we will; *We can and we will.*

May I conclude by throwing these thoughts into the most efficient language ich I know how to employ, the language of prayer: O God, Who hast made of one od all nations of men for to dwell on the face of the whole earth, and hast sent Thy

Son, Jesus Christ, to preach peace to them that are afar off and to them that
nigh, grant that all men everywhere may seek after Thee and find Thee. B
the nations into Thy Fold, and add the heathen to Thine inheritance. And we
Thee shortly to accomplish the number of Thine elect, and to hasten Thy King
Give us grace seriously to lay to heart the great dangers that we are in by our
happy divisions. Take away from us all pride, envy, jealousy, hatred and
.charitableness, and anything that hinders godly union and concord; that as the
but one Lord, one faith, one baptism, one God and Father of us all, so we may b
of one heart and of one soul, united in one holy bond of truth and peace, of f
and charity, and may with one mind and one mouth glorify Thee, the only
through Jesus Christ our Lord.

May our *lex credendi* always be our *lex orandi!*

DEFINITE RESULTS

People often ask for individual instances of the changes brought about by mission
work. Here are a few from the Anvik mission, Alaska:

ISAAC FISHER came one day to Mr. Chapman, to ask if any one might read the Bible, for some taught that only priests might read it. It came out, further, that "Little Doctor" (a shaman in the village) had been asking questions on faith and doctrine, of Isaac. Mr. Chapman told Isaac where, in the Bible, answers to such questions were found, and on more than one Sunday afternoon Isaac took his Bible to the village to read to Little Doctor, and others.

TWELVE or thirteen years ago, when two young white men, friends of the mission, were traders at the trading-post, a half mile from the mission, they sent a young native man, one of Mr. Chapman's first pupils, into the Innoko country to trade for skins. They entrusted him with goods for trading, and made him their agent in that section. Edwin could speak English, read and write, and keep accounts enough to show his dealings with the natives.

ONE Sunday at the afternoon service when Mr. Chapman began to read the second lesson, one of the village boys recognized it as one of the Gospels appointed for a certain day. He immediately found the place in his Prayer Book and followed. As the minister read

on, more than was to be found at place, the boy recognized another "pel for the Day" and found the again in his Prayer Book to fol Whether the young Indian was "verted" or not, he certainly showed training and intelligence in the us his Prayer Book, to compare well any white child.

WHEN the girls of the school ried, Miss Sabine visited t day after day in their own homes, carried them advanced Readers, Testaments, so that they should not back into ignorance; and with pat labor learned the native language that she might tell the Bible storie the older women who could not s English. Nearly every one of the you generation in the village underst English, and some on the Chageluk Most of them could read a simple t

AS Mr. Chapman says, the Christia of these people may be of a order, but some of it is genuine gro and growing toward the Light. It i much better than their own old supe tion. Even if the webs of supersti are clinging to them, they are reac toward better things, and struggling the Right, even in the face of f temptation from bad white men.

THE PENALTY OF SUCCESS

By the Reverend S. H. Littell

"WHAT are we going to do with an institution like this?" The Chinese teacher l o o k e d per-ked. "We planned a building large ugh to allow growth for some years," continued, "counting on a normal in-crease; we occupied the new building only in January of last year, and here we are, full to overflowing already!"

And what he said is true. In the days when the Catechetical School could only receive twelve men at a time, it seemed like a great venture of faith to erect a building accommodating fifty students, but in our second year in the new school, we have accepted fifty-five, the extra ones being willing to sleep in the attic, which we are dividing off into compart-ments for them. New men always enter on trial for a month, and I have not thought that all the successful candidates at the recent entrance ex-amination will be allowed to remain, for we drop men every year, for one cause or another. Still, we are full of thankful-ness for the unexpected development of the school, and shall try our best to meet the extra demands of our teaching forces. The many friends of All Saints' will help, I am sure, with their prayers, all we ask for such help in this responsible work of training Chinese mission-aries.

The men now in train-ing come from six of China's eighteen prov-inces: Hupeh, Hunan, Kiangsi, Anhui, Kiangsu and Chili, and represent five of our ten Angli-can dioceses: Hankow,

Shanghai and North China. By classes they number: 9 seniors, 11 middlers, 22 juniors, five in the preparatory class (with two to come), and a review class of six old catechists. These latter have been out at work for ten years or more, and we have brought them back for one or two terms to renew and refresh them spiritually and mentally, as they seemed to have "run dry," and to have fallen behind the standards required of pres-ent-day catechists.

A Chinese priest, a catechist and an-other teacher give all their time to the institution, but the school is worthy of the entire time of an American mission-ary as well.

THE CATECHIST SCHOOL IN HANKOW

(429)

A CARNIVAL SCENE IN CUBA

SHOOTING JUDAS IN CUBA

By the Venerable W. W. Steel

CUBA is a country of most curious contrasts. Were one wandering in the heart of Africa he would not be surprised to see children without clothing playing under the trees, but it is a great surprise to see them here, not only in the country round about the palm shacks but in the villages under acetylene lights, and even here in Havana, one of the great capitals of the world, under the arc lights of the well-paved, clean streets. It is curious also to see the great *carretas*, or ox carts, with wheels about seven feet in diameter, drawn by two, four or six oxen, with the yokes on their horns, laden with three or four tons of sugar cane, trying to dodge the automobiles along the country roads.

Here in the city there are splendid houses built of concrete or cement, or stone, beautifully tinted without, with marble staircases and polished tile floors within, and on all sides the marks of a great civilized city; yet in the middle of a square of good dwelling-houses one will encounter just such a sight as he might come upon in an African jungle—a negro band with several instruments of music, accompanied by a cocoanut grater scraped by a knitting needle, or possibly by the head bones of a horse, taken to rattle the loose teeth in it, while the negroes are all singing and shouting, leaping and dancing, with all the antics and gestures of the wildest savages.

On Easter Eve I saw a curious sight at Ocean Beach, which I am sure will be of some interest to the readers of THE SPIRIT OF MISSIONS. I went out there Maundy-Thursday for the Good Friday and Easter services. On arriving I found that a large number of Cubans had come to the Beach, bringing in their *carretas* their families and a portion of their household goods, and had camped in some of the vacant houses for the purpose of enjoying the Holy Week holidays!

Now among the many curious things of this curious land is the fact that Lent has none of the features of a fasting season. It is anticipated with the greatest pleasure. The carnival with which it begins continues through Mid-Lent Sunday, and this is the gayest time of all the year. There is a slight intermission of the frolics—but not of the Sunday night dances—between Mid-Lent Sunday and the beginning of Holy Week, and then, in the country, and oftentimes in the city, all the men cease work and gather in the fondas—the eating and drinking places, where they sing and shout, play checkers or cards, eating a great deal but drinking very little, and never to excess; whatever faults a Cuban may have he never drinks to intoxication.

So on my arrival at the Beach I found all the neighborhood filled with Cubans and their families, all chattering like magpies, and wandering about among the trees, making a general frolic of it. When I went into the room in the hotel for the Good Friday night service (I had held the morning service at Guaniguanico, thirteen miles distant), I was surprised to find the back part of the room filled with Cuban men. They were not as quiet as I could have wished, but they were very respectful, and while they were talking, it was in a low voice.

I was told as I entered that they would expect me to preach a Spanish sermon for them. And so I did. I read in English the second lesson for the morning, instead of the first for the night; and then I read it over again in Spanish as the second lesson. Then I preached the sermon in English, following it by one in Spanish. Immediately before the English sermon I spoke to the Cubans, saying that I would talk to them after I had delivered the other sermon, and as I addressed them they all rose to their feet and listened most respectfully to the announcement. During the English sermon many of them left the room, but waited quietly in the next room until I began the Spanish sermon, when they all returned and would have remained standing had I not given them permission to sit. Most of them could not read their own language, and as I told them the story of the Cross, the tears flowed down their cheeks. It is more than possible that some of them had never heard the account of the Crucifixion before, and that the others had only heard it long ago, when possibly they were living in one of the pueblos where there might have been a priest.

The next day, Easter Eve, I noted that all the people were very busy, running about and collecting sticks and dried grass, which they brought to one place; they then proceeded to make what we would call a "scare-crow"—the figure of a man dressed in rags with a horrid representation of a face and a thatch of palm leaves for a hat. By a rope of dried grass passed about the neck they hung this to a post on the seashore. Then they each got two sticks of dry wood and all took their places on one side of the figure. There they were—men, women and little children; the men bare-footed, wearing only a shirt, a pair of trousers and straw hats with the brims frayed by way of ornament; the women a little better clad, but most of the children just as they were born, or some of the boys with only a pair of trousers. For a little time they stood in silence, which was broken only by the slight rattle of the machetes, or broad swords which every gaujiro (countryman) in Cuba wears. They were watching the sun, awaiting a certain hour of the day, which I soon found to be eleven o'clock. Almost on the moment one of them fired a gun at the figure, which was followed by several more, and then a blaze was kindled at the feet which soon spread upward; then suddenly there was a great explosion, for the figure had been filled with powder. As soon as this occurred, all the men drew their machetes and rushed at the fragments, cutting and slashing them with the greatest vigor, and when this had ended they all began to strike their two sticks together, making a great clatter.

I asked what this latter might mean and they told me that they were "Rattling the bones of Judas"! I found also that they performed this ceremony just at eleven, because that is the hour at which in the churches the Alleluia is sung on Easter Eve. The remainder of the day they spend in innocent amusements, bathing in the sea, and playing checkers and such like, and on the afternoon of Easter Day they all loaded their carretas and began their homeward journey.

Cuba is surely a very curious country. We are trying to bring this poor people to a knowledge of better things!

HANKOW IN CONFERENCE

THE second annual conference of the Hankow district met in the see city February 22nd-27th. Thirty clergymen and an equal number of lay delegates were present, as shown in the above picture.

The bishop in his opening address reviewed the development of the Church during the two years since the last conference:

In the Church outside of the district he spoke of the organization of two new Anglican dioceses, making ten in all; of the work of the Opium Commission; of the prospect of a great university in Hankow or Wuchang, manned and supported by the universities of England, and of the conference of all the Anglican dioceses held in Shanghai last year to determine the organization of a united Church for China. Within the district he mentioned the ordination of seven deacons, the first class to be graduated from our Divinity-school, the incorporation of Boone University; the new library at Boone; the new Catechetical School in Hankow; the receiving of the Lutheran Church and congregation in Hankow; the organization of a Girls' School Teachers' Institute; the station class in Hankow for the training of country women; the addition of land and buildings in places too numerous to mention, and the organization of a Japanese congregation in Hankow with a Japanese graduate from the Cambridge Theological School in charge.

His statistics for the past year were as follows: Catechumens, 1,339; baptisms, 685; confirmations, 250; day-schools, 50, with 1,394 pupils; boarding-schools, 16, with 804 pupils; total contributions from the Chinese, $4,852.40, this exclusive of school and hospital fees. Perhaps the most interesting item was that there are now 108 students in our different schools for the training of workers preparing to enter some department of our mission work.

The work accomplished by the conference may be summarized as follows: (1) The constitution and canons for the Synod of the United Anglican Church in China were approved, together with the proposed name, *Chung Wha Sheng Kung Whei*—the Holy Catholic Church of China. (2) A constitution and canons for the district were perfected and adopted, subject to the approval of the coming General Convention. In these canons it is provided that no congregation which does not give at least one-fifth of its annual expenses can vote in the synod. (3) A Board of Education for the district was organized to improve methods and co-ordinate courses in the mission schools. (4) The most conspicuous forward movement was the organization of a district missionary society—or rather, following the example of the American Church, the declaration that the Church itself is the missionary society of which all the baptized are members. The conference was made a Board of Missions, and officers of such Board were elected, who will constitute the executive committee between sessions and administer its affairs. This executive committee have chosen as the first field for operations the prefecture of *Si-nan Fu*, in the extreme west of the

district. It is a country of great natural beauty, but the people are indolent and unprogressive, probably because sodden with opium.

In addition to the business of the conference there were social and religious features of considerable interest, among them the daily Chinese luncheon, at which both native and foreign delegates were the guests of the bishop, and the reception of the Boone Alumni Association. On St. Matthias's Day, being the anniversary of the consecration of Bishop Ingle, special services were held at his grave, when appropriate hymns were sung and thanks given for those "who having finished their course in faith, do now rest from their labors." The closing service of the conference was held on Sunday, the 27th, in St. Paul's Cathedral. All the clergy were in the chancel and a great congregation crowded the church. Stirring addresses were made on missionary themes and the offering was for the work of the new missionary society.

A NATIVE MISSION IN MEXICO
By the Reverend Samuel Salinas

The following simple narrative of the struggles and growth of a native Mexican mission gains an additional significance from the fact that it was written in English by the Rev. Samuel Salinas, one of the most efficient of our native Mexican clergy. It will be remembered that Bishop Aves voiced in these pages his high appreciation of the services Mr. Salinas has rendered among the famine-stricken people under his charge.

SEVENTEEN years ago, when only a lay-reader, I first knew Calvary Mission, Huminí, Hgo. In that time the services were held in a room, 8x10 feet, which belonged to Mr. Vicente Frujillo, one of the oldest and most faithful members of our Church here. It was not only small but uncomfortable. The congregation naturally wished another place, and a new building was bought, which in comparison with the first was much better, though it measured only 9x15 feet, so the crowded condition continued.

In the year 1898—I was then a priest —a portion of the congregations of

Hidalgo were under my care, among them, Huminí. In those days the Right Rev. John Mills Kendrick, Bishop of New Mexico and Arizona, made his official visitation to that place. On the 8th of July, this venerable bishop with the episcopal vicar, the late beloved Rev. Henry Forrester, visited Huminí. There were confirmation and Holy Communion.

The bishop could see the urgent necessity of enlarging the little chapel, which could not contain the congregation. It was so crowded that it was literally impossible to move, and as the room had only a small door it was so dark that

WHERE BISHOP KENDRICK HELD SERVICES AT HUMINI

s difficult to read the service, and bedes the ceiling was so low that we could
most touch the roof with our heads.
le bishop, knowing the intention to enge the building, became interested and
ldly offered to assist in carrying out
ie plans. Although the people were so
or it was decided not only to enlarge
chapel, but to build a new one capa

ble of holding the congregation. Bishop
Kendrick's gift was the basis for the
new building, which was begun a few
days after his memorable visitation.

How great difficulties and struggles to
get what was necessary in money, work
and material!

The chapel was very humble, but it
cost $200, which for rich people would

THE NEW SCHOOL AND CHAPEL

A GROUP OF THE SCHOOL CHILDREN

have been nothing, but was an immense sum for people who earn only twelve cents daily; however, there was a firm purpose, and the construction progressed little by little. It was very impressive to see the boys and girls and women carrying the stones for the church, and the men of the congregation giving weekly one day's work as their part. A year and a half afterward we had the pleasure to see the chapel finished. On Friday, December 22d, 1899, the episcopal vicar, assisted by the priest-in-charge, held, amidst great joy, the opening service in the new chapel, built to the honor and glory of our heavenly Father. This building was a great stimulus to the people. The little congregation grew and filled the new chapel.

Needs of different kinds were also be-fore the Church; particularly the work of education. There were many children without any instruction at all; they cried for intellectual food. Plans were made to erect a school-room. We had confidence in God that He would pro-vide the necessary means for the build-ing and that He would open the way to get a teacher.

Three years ago we began the school-room with gifts from some friends and fortnightly contributions of the faithf parishioners. Bishop Aves became i terested and sent us a good gift, and few months after notified us that he h gotten an appropriation from the Boa of Missions to pay the teacher. T school was opened in January, 1908 (this month begins here the school yea under the care of the Misses Bustamar graduates of Hooker School.

We have now more than forty pupi and the room begins to be inadequate f the present needs. The congregati has also grown and the chapel mention above is not now large enough for the But fortunately, during the last offici visitation of the Bishop of Mexico, M and Miss Aves, it was resolved to e large the chapel and the school-roo Mrs. Aves promised to help us in th good work and so we began immediate the enlarging of the building. Wi such a great help we are now nearing t end, and we hope that in a few days will have realized our purpose and the will be room enough for the congreg tion and the school.

Shall we have need in the future enlarge the room more and more? Th is my earnest desire; and, God willin I believe it will come to pass.

THE NEGRO AND THE CHURCH

By the Reverend Samuel H. Bishop

HE relation of the Church to the Negro people in this land has been determined by somewhat peculiar conditions, differing arkedly from those determining the re- tion of other Christian bodies to that ople. The first Negroes were landed this country in Virginia, and were ught in large numbers by members of e Church of England in that colony. At first very little attention was paid their spiritual welfare, as they were t supposed to have souls to be saved, at best, souls only partially developed. hen, however, it became evident to the ners of the slaves that they had moral ponsibility for their Christian train- g, the masters and mistresses began to in some measure to fulfil that re- onsibility. These masters or the mis- sses gathered the slaves about the ntation house, sometimes in chapels vided for that purpose, and instructed m in the simple duties of Christianity l in those beliefs by which Christian- is first apprehended. Then the min- r of the parish, when opportunity of- ed, continued this instruction, and en- vored to prepare the slaves for tism.

In 1724 the Rev. William Beach re- ted, in response to an inquiry from Bishop of London, that he had in- ucted and baptized during the fifteen rs previous over two hundred Negroes, rring that the owners of slaves were erally careful to bring them to tism. There are no records which determine accurately the ownership the slaves as between Church people others, but in other colonies aside n Virginia a much larger proportion them was owned by members of the er Christian bodies than in Virginia. some recent statistics as to owner- p of the slaves show that a very small portion of the white people through-

out the South owned more than one or two slaves; and it is reasonable to infer that not only in Virginia, where the Church was by law established, but in the other colonies where the Church quite generally constituted the religious con- nection of the aristocracy, a large propor- tion, perhaps the majority, of the slaves were for the first one hundred or one hundred and fifty years owned by men and women who had a more or less direct relationship to the Church. In colonies such as North Carolina, where the Eng- lish and the Church contingency were less numerous, slave-holders were less numerous, and the democratic ideal was more powerful. Under the leadership of Oglethorpe, Georgia for nineteen years resisted slavery; and perhaps partly by reason of the doctrines of Wesley and Whitfield (though these men recognized slavery as a fact), for a number of years after the regime of Oglethorpe had ended, relatively few slaves were owned in Georgia. The first strongholds of slavery were Virginia and South Caro- lina, where also the aristocratic element and the Church were the strongest.

This condition of things, continuing for about a century and a half, resulted in the nominal control by the Church of a considerable proportion of the Negro slave population; but by the beginning of the third quarter of the eighteenth century slave ownership, though never involving more than a small minority of the white population, had spread. A larger proportion of non-Church people bought and owned slaves, and then the Negroes themselves came into contact with other forms of Christian belief and practice. Before the last quarter of the eighteenth century independent Baptist and Methodist churches were formed and grew rapidly. At that time they were, of course, not permitted to govern them- selves as they are now, but they were

probably given a larger measure of responsibility for the conduct of their own
religious affairs than they were in the
Church.

In 1859 there were recorded 468,000
Negro members of the various churches
in the South, of which it is fair to assume that at least 50,000 and perhaps
75,000 to 100,000 were connected directly or indirectly with the Church. This
connection, however, if we have not over-
estimated the numbers, must have been
of a somewhat adventitious sort, and in-
hered rather in the slave connection than
in the free and spontaneous choice of the
Negroes themselves. At any rate, after
the war the number began rapidly to drop.
The reasons for this are partly to the
credit and partly to the discredit of the
Church—to its credit by virtue of the
fact that the Church alone refused to
disavow her responsibility for the Christian culture and life of the Negroes and
to detach them from herself to a separate
communion; to the discredit of the
Church by virtue of the fact that,
through whatever causes, the Church
made the Negroes uncomfortable and
evinced a decided inertia and indifference to their religious condition.

The fundamental reasons for the condition of the Church to-day among the
Negroes are: First, the reaction both by
the whites (who in *antebellum* days were
the so-called poor whites, but are now the
ruling classes) and by the Negroes
against the Church as a symbol of the
hated aristocratic regime; secondly, the
fact that the detachment of the Negroes
from the other Christian bodies and their
segregation in independent communions
of their own has given to them a measure
of politico-ecclesiastical initiative and responsibility which our Church has denied
to them. The ecclesiastical and religious
field is the only one in which the Negro
is free. He suffers from economic hos-
tility and from political and social restraint and limitation; and he therefore
seeks freedom and responsibility and
privilege in that field in which they are
open to him.

The Church, however, has not refused

the practical work of life. They are
mostly industrial schools, but with such
a measure of academic training as in-
sures thoughtfulness, pleasure, intelligence, together with such moral and religious training as strengthens character.
This we believe to be the first and
strategic task of our Church.

But there is another work of a more
distinctly evangelistic character. The
condition of the labor market in the
South and the migratory habit of the
Negroes are continuously severing
church connection and bringing together
large numbers of men into lumber and
mining camps; and here the archidiaconal organization of our Church is of
special value. Our schools supplement
the archidiaconal missionary work by
training boys and girls as preachers and
teachers for communities where there is
little church privilege; and the bishops
and archdeacons are ascertaining critical
places, planting missions, and placing
men who preach and teach and minister
to the religious needs of the people.
Our western missionary bishops tell us
of the pathetic cry of places for Church
services and men. And the same plea
comes from many a group of Negroes in
the South. Though the Church is small
in numbers she does a great work in
leavening the segregated life of the Negroes, and wherever she is represented
the moral and religious tone of the community is helped and uplifted.

Without discourtesy to the other
Christian bodies it is fair to say that
our Church is serving the practical and
daily needs of Negro life through her
parochial, industrial and normal schools
with peculiar and distinguishing success;
and through her reverent forms and
ethical standards is inspiring and building steady, upright character and citizenship in a way which is exemplary, and
serviceable to all other forms of religious
activity. Our clergy are taught the
practical implication of religion in industry, self-control, purity and honesty;
to avoid an excitement which terminates
in noise and money-lifting, and to cultivate in themselves and in their people

the virtues which make for citizenship, social and moral uplift, and strong individual character.

Among the many activities of the Church on behalf of Negro youth, perhaps none is more significant than its two hospitals, one at Raleigh, N. C., the largest and best-equipped hospital for colored people south of Washington, and the other at Charlotte, N. C. In connection with St. Agnes's Hospital and St. Augustine's School at Raleigh, there is a training-school for nurses which has a three years' course, instruction being given by the resident superintendent and Raleigh physicians, with opportunity for hospital practice in St. Agnes's Hospital. This provides for colored girls a professional opportunity, the only one open to colored women in the South, aside from teaching, and one which is of great service not only to individual girls but to the racial life of the Negro people. It means self-respect and ambition, not only personal but racial; and is an opportunity for the exercise of a most valuable aptitude or talent in human service.

There are two facts respecting the work of the Church among the Negroes in the South which are of much interest and encouragement, and which together involve great promise for our work. The first is the increasing interest of southern white people in work for the Negroes, illustrated not only by their willingness to tax themselves for Negro education, but also by their increasing disposition to give active personal service in that cause. There are two white archdeacons who are earnest and devoted workers, and who are giving ample evidence of the white man's real power to serve the Negro. The bishops also are manifesting a deep desire for the religious and moral welfare of the Negroes, and are giving much thought and energy to their Negro work. Bishop Guerry, of South Carolina, has a system of sixteen parochial schools of great value, which are serving not only the religious but also the moral uplift of the people. He is securing white teachers who are giving

tute for Negroes. Discipline, self-control and high ideals are the notes of the whole life at St. Augustine's.

St. Augustine's School and the Bishop Payne Divinity-school have graduated over 50 per cent. of our Negro clergy, and they are almost to a man living the life which the Master commanded and giving intelligent and faithful service to God and their kind. The Conference of Negro Workers, held annually, is a most interesting assemblage of clergy and laity—all deeply concerned with the problems of the Kingdom of God. May God grant that our dear Church shall see her opportunity and provide the material means by which the love of our Lord Jesus Christ may be made the all-controlling motive of this people, to whom we as Americans and as Churchmen owe much, and whose need of our best is great.

'S COLLEGE, TOKYO

St. George Tucker

sions. The good record of these graduates is the basis of our present prosperity, and the proof of their interest in the school and of its influence over them is found in the fact that quite a large proportion of the new students who come to us are relations or connections of our alumni.

Nearly 25 per cent. of this year's graduating class are Christians, and judging from our past experience it is safe to predict that within five years another 25 per cent. will receive baptism. Six of them are candidates for the ministry. In this way St. Paul's helps to extend the influence of Christianity among those who are destined to be future leaders of thought and action in this country, and also plays an important part in supplying the Church with well-trained and competent workers.

It is worth noting that these results
are obtained by a system of purely voluntary religious instruction. Our own
experience is that this is in the long
run more effective than the compulsory
method of teaching Christianity, and
certainly it is more in accord with the
best Japanese educational ideals.

The middle school student is an exceedingly interesting and attractive
youth. He comes up from the primary
school at the age of thirteen or fourteen,
with a goodly store of the *Yamato-
damashii*, *i.e.*, "the Spirit of Japan."
The five years he spends in the middle
school are very critical ones in shaping
his character, for he is now brought into
direct contact with what we may call
"the Spirit of the Modern World." The
importance of healthy moral and spiritual influences at this period is self-evi-
dent, for there is danger that in the
process of adjustment and amalgamation
of the old and the new he will be left
without any sufficient moral ideals. It
is just here that we feel that a school
with a strong Christian atmosphere can
render great service.

One sometimes meets with queer problems in dealing with these young Christian Samurai. Recently I received a
letter from a student telling me of his
determination to become a Christian, in
which he stated that in order to emphasize his resolution to fight against
temptation and build up a true character he had decided to cut off one of his
fingers. He was so much in earnest
about this that one of the teachers had
to argue with him until three o'clock in
the morning before he could be prevailed upon to adopt some other method
of proving the sincerity of his purpose.
But the *Yamato-damashii*, though at
times it manifests itself in ways that
seem rather fanciful to us of the West,
forms, with its high ideals and intense
earnestness, a splendid foundation for
Christian faith.

The session just ended established a
new record in point of attendance with
a total enrolment of 723 in the various

tion of the electric belt line. In the immediate neighborhood are the new Peers' School and a normal school, which is an indication of the suitableness of the locality for educational purposes. The new Sei Ko Kwai Theological College has bought land just across the road from our property. This will ensure a measure of co-operation between the two institutions that will mean much for the future of our work. The land cost $50,000. Of this we were able to pay in cash only $6,000, and as we have to pay interest on the amount still due it is to be hoped that it may be raised as soon as possible. Yet it was economical to buy when we did, even if we do have to pay interest on the balance due, for the development of car-lines in the neighborhood of Tokyo makes it certain that there will be a great rise in land prices within a few years. Indeed, this has already taken place in the case of the land we were looking at last year; the price practically doubled within six months.

But apart from the financial side of the question, St. Paul's is in urgent need of a new plant. As I have explained above, without it further growth is impossible. If, however, we can put up proper buildings on this splendid piece of ground already purchased, I feel sure that we shall have laid the foundation of a strong Christian college. We have already made a good beginning here in Tsukiji. We have a faculty, a good curriculum, a nucleus of earnest, hardworking students, and a constantly increasing reputation. All that we now need is room for expansion.

¶

SUMMER conferences under the charge of the Young People's Missionary Movement will be held at Lake Geneva, Wis., July 1st-10th; Cascade, Colo., August 3d-12th; Asheville, N. C., July 1st-10th; Silver Bay, N. Y., July 22d-31st. The number of young Church people attending has been increasing year by year.

A NEW CHURCH FOR CUBA

O N Thursday, April 21st, the Bishop of Cuba laid the corner-stone of the chapel to be known as La Trinidad (Trinity Chapel), Macagua, Province of Matanzas. On arrival at Macagua the bishop and clergy were met at the station by Mr. Ledo, the missionary-in-charge of the work, with the members of the Sunday-school and the choir, and large numbers

The bishop laying the stone

of the congregation, the procession passing through the streets of the pueblo amid the ringing of bells and the firing of rockets, to the old chapel where the clergy and choir vested.

Thence the procession, with banners

flying, again passed through the streets to the building site, accompanied by the whizz of fire-works, bell-ringing and hymn-singing.

In accordance with local custom a broad ribbon was tied about the stone, and the ends were held by the "Padrino" (god-father), and the "madrina" (god-mother).

The first services at Macagua were held in 1907 by the Rev. Mr. Diaz, who went there from Matanzas, a distance of about 125 miles. It was at first a work among the farmers, attracting very large congregations, chiefly of men, some of them coming from a distance of nine or ten miles. The visitation of the bishop, made on May 27th, 1907, was the first official visit of any bishop to Macagua. At this time thirty-one persons were presented for confirmation.

In 1909 the Rev. Sergio Ledo, appointed in charge, transferred the mission to the pueblo itself, where a temporary chapel was fitted up in a private house in which Mr. Ledo took up his residence, being the first clergyman of any sort to live among this people. From the very beginning the work has grown apace, and the list of communicants now numbers about one hundred.

The funds for the construction of this beautiful chapel have been most generously contributed by the Sunday-school of Trinity Church, New Haven, Conn.

CLERGY MAKING THE CIRCUIT OF THE WALLS

A GLIMPSE OF THE SAGEBRUSH LAND

AN ARCHDEACON IN NORTHWESTERN COLORADO

The following is from the pen of a thirteen-year-old boy and will therefore have a peculiar interest. It is also true that the missionary district of Western Colorado is oné which, through the late Bishop Knight, has been brought particularly and appealingly to the notice of the Church

AT the recent convention of the clergy of Western Colorado, the Rev. J. H. Dennis was appointed archdeacon of the ınties of Rio Blanc and Routt. All gained by this advancement was thé ttering title of "venerable," there be-ʒ no assistants over whom he could ʒrt authority. On his solitary jour-ʒs he meets with experiences, however, ıt in some part repay his labor. ·

The country through which he travels most lonely and desolate. Many of ʒ families to which he carries the rd of God seem merely to exist. The ʒt plains he traverses in Routt County ʒ destitute of any kind of vegetation ʒe cactus and sage-brush. In the ɲmer these deserts quiver with heat, ɫ no shade or water can be found for les; in the winter the snow reaches a ʒat depth, and the thermometer often ɔps below zero. Through all these dis-ɲfᵉrts does Mr. Dennis travel, some-

A recent confirmation candidate

THE BISHOP AND THE ARCHDEACON *EN ROUTE*

times to administer the Sacrament to a dozen souls.

The lack of railroads hinders his work, as stages are the only available means of travel. These are often most uncomfortable, the roads are usually rough, and the other occupants often obnoxious.

He also suffers from the contempt and disregard of any authority so common in wild and undisciplined countries such as this, but the ever-increasing list of communicants greatly encourages him to continue his praiseworthy work.

At Maybell, one of his chief missio[...] the only other minister of any name w[...] visited this place through the year w[...] the Congregationalist. After Mr. D[...] nis had held services here several tim[...] those who had attended the services [...] pressed their pleasure at "having a r[...] church here now."

Down the White River near Utah[...] another mission which Mr. Dennis h[...] lately opened. Some of the children[...] this district have never seen a Bi[...] and the school-teacher was the only p[...] son who had ever before seen a pri[...]

Sagebrush and sand

The result of irrigation

of he Church. Mr. Dennis hopes, from
the hospitable reception given him in
the region, to have a flourishing mission there in the near future.

the church attendance at Meeker, in
proportion to the number of communicants, is good. On every hand Mr. Dennis receives hearty support, and as the
town grows we look forward to a proportionate growth in the Church here.

profanity is a prevalent vice amongst
the ranchers and cowpunchers, sometimes even affecting women. One evening as Mr. Dennis and the bishop
were travelling through Routt County,
they saw a lantern tossing to and fro
a short distance from them; inquiring of
its bearer the distance to the nearest
ranch, they received the astonishing reply in a woman's voice, "Who the devil
are you, and where in hell are you go-
in."

Mr. Dennis could have the help of
assistants in the missionary labor, more
attention could be given to the various

ST. JAMES'S CHURCH, MEEKER

missions scattered throughout this district, and the Church would grow accordingly.

CONFERENCE FOR CHURCH WORK
CAMBRIDGE, MASS., JULY 9TH-24TH, 1910

THE Summer Conference of last
year demonstrated that the
Theological School at Cambridge is a delightful and
practical place for a Church Conference.
A beautiful chapel with refectory, dormitory and lecture rooms near by, furnish the requisite plant. The school library, the historic common, Harvard
University, and old Christ Church, with
its memories of Revolutionary days, give
an environment that is stimulating.
These reasons and many others led
those who desire to see the Summer Conference a permanent feature of the
Church's life to select Cambridge for
the Conference of 1910.

Time

The dates are July 9th-24th. As these
days follow immediately the annual
convention of the National Educational

Association, it is hoped that many
teachers who are Churchmen and
Churchwomen will remain for the Conference in Cambridge after the Convention in Boston. The Conference lasts two
weeks, but as the work of each week is
a unit, one can profitably attend the first
or second week only, if it be incon-
venient to attend both.

Personnel

The personnel of the teaching staff of
the Conference offers an unusual opportunity. To be able to live and work for
one or two weeks with some of those who
are leading in Church movements of the
day is to gain power for greater consecration and more intelligent and
efficient service. Professor Philip M.
Rhinelander, the chairman of the Committee of the Conference, besides teaching a course on "The Nations in the

THE SEMINARY CHAPEL

Kingdom," will welcome consultation. Assistant Secretary, the Rev. H. L. Burleson; Secretary of the First Department, the Rev. Wm. E. Gardner; Miss Julia C. Emery, Secretary of the Woman's Auxiliary, and Deaconess Knapp, of the New York Training-

school, will attend and conduct cou es and will welcome conference. he Bible Study periods will be condu d by Professor Max Kellner, D.D., d the Rev. Harvey Officer, O.H.C. he noon hours, when the entire confer ce will meet for inspiration, will be o upied by Dean Hart with "Studies in he Prayer Book," and Bishop Kinsmar f Delaware, on "Principles of Angli nism." The courses in Mission Study d in the various forms of Church ck will all be conducted by a numbe f men and women of experience who ve already made definite contribution to the development of the Church's lif A portion of each afternoon and eve g will be devoted to the discussior f definite problems in Church life, and e explanation of definite methods in Church work, so that each membe f the Conference will find his partic ar interest emphasized, and may also e the opportunity to gain breadth of vi n by seeing the fields of work in w h others are interested. A complete ogramme showing all the periods and bjects may be obtained by addressing e secretary.

Purpose

A careful perusal of the progra e will reveal the purpose of the Cor rence. It is planned "for the instruc n

THE REFECTORY AND LIBRARY

d training of men and women in the
irit and method of Church work at
me and abroad." It will be satisfied
th no smaller intention than that of
king each Churchman feel his re-
nsibility for the "Local Parish," the
iocesan Parish," the "National Par-
" and the "World Parish."

Who Should Attend?

The following should attend the Con-
ence: rectors and church officers;
cers and members of Woman's Aux-
ries; leaders of the Junior Aux-
ries; Sunday-school superintendents,
chers and officers, and workers in all
various Church organizations;
urch men and women who "do not
kow how," but who want to serve.

Social and Recreation

he latter part of each afternoon is
l free for recreation. From Cam-
b ge interesting roads radiate in all
d ctions, furnishing opportunity for
w ks, drives and trolley rides. Two
m utes' walk from the school is the
C rles River, with its Parkway, canoe
a boating privileges. Boston Harbor,

the various libraries and museums, and
the vast wealth of historic haunts furnish a variety of interests suited to all
tastes.

The committee-in-charge of the con-
ference consists of the Bishop of Massa-
chusetts, *ex-officio;* the Rev. Philip M.
Rhinelander, chairman; Miss E. H.
Houghton, secretary; Mr. Eugene M.
Camp, treasurer; the Rev. Drs. Samuel
Hart, Max Kellner and J. G. H. Barry;
the Revs. Philip Cook and Samuel R.
Colladay; Messrs. Burton Mansfield,
Thomas Nelson Page, Robert H. Gardi-
ner, George Wharton Pepper and John
Ely; Mrs. R. W. Woodward and the
Misses Marian DeC. Ward, J. F. Bum-
stead, A. W. Fisher and M. E. Thomas.

Registration, etc.

A registration fee of $5 will be
charged to meet the various expenses of
the Conference.

Board at the School Refectory will be
$7 per week. Lodgings can be secured
for $2 per week and upward.

Applications for registration and all
communications should be addressed to
Miss E. H. Houghton, Secretary, 58
Garden Street, Cambridge.

A GLIMPSE OF THE CLOISTERS

THE RICE RIOTS IN CHANGSHA

It will be remembered that the Rev. Mr. Gilman and his wife, our missionaries at Changsha, were in the storm centre of the recent uprising in the province of Hunan. Following is the first authoritative letter from Mr. Gilman received at headquarters since those occurrences:

Hankow, April 18th, 1910

MRS. GILMAN and I returned to Changsha just in time to have a most thrilling experience. We arrived on the twelfth of March and found the work in a most flourishing condition. The love of our workers was shown in the way that they had cared for our house, and especially for our garden. The schools were opened just after our arrival. The boarding-school was filled to its capacity of twenty-five boys, all of small size, such as I have been working for. We had twenty-one girls and nineteen boys in the day-schools. The day scholars are from the neighborhood and there was an evident growth of confidence in our work. The principal of the High School, the highest institution of learning in Hunan, called and begged me to help them by teaching two days a week.

This was the outlook for our mission work. But the general outlook was quite different. All winter there have been large numbers of famine refugees, who have depended upon the officials and missionaries for food. The depreciation of the currency has lowered the purchasing value of the cash, so that in all trades there is a demand for more pay. The lowest classes suffer the most, and find it most difficult to demand more pay. As the winter wore on the price of rice advanced, as usual, and where in normal years a pint would sell for thirty cash the price advanced to seventy cash. This meant starvation to the lower classes. According to Confucius, the first duty of an official is to feed his people, and following the law of the land the people demanded that the governor bring down the price of rice. This is

often done by the officials. The governor, however, seemed stubborn, and irritated the people to the point that on Wednesday night, April 13th, an immense mob demanded an immediate response from the governor. Soldiers tried to disperse the mob. Infuriated, they rushed through the streets and shortly after midnight attacked the Post-Office, the Government Bank, and the Wesleyan Mission, which are all near together on the west side of the city. About the same time rioters attacked the Norwegian and China Inland Missions in the south part of the city. The members of these three missions had to flee for their lives, but fortunately all escaped without a single scratch. It would seem that not even was a missile hurled at them.

On Wednesday afternoon Mrs. Gilman and I attended the union Chinese prayer-meeting, which was held outside the south gate, walking there and back — a distance altogether of about six miles. We passed right by the Norwegian Mission and through the governor's house, and all the way heard not one word of reviling or ill will. About nine o'clock my servant reported to me that there was a row at the governor's, which is situated very near us. I was very much alarmed, but went to bed as usual. At two in the morning Mr. Huang came to tell me that the Wesleyan Mission had been raided and shortly afterward we heard of the trouble at the Norwegian Mission. I prepared my fire hose and planned measures of escape, while Mrs. Gilman packed three bags with essentials. About four o'clock two soldiers appeared, who said that forty were coming to protect us, but they never came. However, neither did the rioters. Daylight came

(450)

shortly afterward a mob entered our place and smashed and looted generally. But until now none of our mission buildings have been destroyed.

All of our workers and their families, who were natives of Hupeh, were brought with us on the boat to Hankow. There is a strong feeling against the natives of Hupeh, because the foreign houses have mostly been built by their labor. A short time ago the Hunanese carpenters and masons appealed to the governor to expel the Hupeh contractors. This, of course, he was unable to do, and this had a considerable part to play in the burning of buildings.

Much property has been destroyed, both foreign and Chinese, but strangely enough, so far, I have heard of no American property which has been burned.

I shall write again as soon as more definite news comes. I fear that there are so many complications that a speedy settlement is not to be expected.

CONCERNING BACK NUMBERS

ON behalf of the Cathedral Library in Washington we would thank those who sent the back numbers of THE SPIRIT OF MISSIONS asked for in our May issue.

A correspondent in Buffalo, N. Y., now writes: "I need the following copies to complete my file—the only one in the city to which a large study class has access. I will be glad to pay for them: 1843: August, December; 1845: January, February, September, November, December; 1846: March, June, July, August, October, November, December; 1848: September; 1849: December; 1850: June, September, November, December; 1851: January, February, March, June, July, August, September, October, November, December; 1856: October; 1868: April. Address Mrs. A. F. Holloway, 492 Porter Avenue, Buffalo, N. Y."

OUR LETTER BOX
Intimate and Informal Messages from the Field

Our missionary among the Indians in Oklahoma tells of some interesting experiences:

THE last few weeks have been busy ones, there being much sickness in our camp and also in the neighboring camps. In Big Horse Camp an Indian is dying with tuberculosis. I try to drive over after school about twice a week. There is little to do for him except to furnish something nourishing and perhaps relieve the hard breathing and lower temperature. He knows he cannot live and realizes what death means to the Christian.

A few weeks ago there was a strange Indian at the service. He had come about thirty miles with a sick child for me to care for, and begged me to make her well. She had the same dreadful disease, and I knew she could live but a few days. It was hard to tell him, but I did it as carefully as I could, explaining that the life of his little one was in God's hands, and that I would do what I could. The child died yesterday, and when the family went away they gave me a pair of moccasins that had belonged to the child and said what a comfort I had been to them. They said: "We will think of what you said. Maybe some day we will be Christians."

Sometimes funny things happen. Last Sunday during service I saw an old Indian at the door and went to ask him in. It seems that I had met him in American Horse Camp last summer. He was then very demonstrative, telling me how pleased he was that I was their friend, and that I would teach them the "Jesus Road." David, our deacon, told him at that time, my Indian name, *Vicsehin* (Bird Woman) and he promised to visit us sometime. As I opened the door, he shouted in a loud voice, "How! Vicsehin! Epiva!" (good)— tapping me on the chest. I shook hands and led him in, quieted the children— and the old ones too—and we went on with the service.

The homes of Sunmaker and Bobtail Coyot[e]

The bishop visited us in January a[nd] confirmed two—an Indian woman a[nd] one of my older school girls. Anoth[er] woman was baptized two weeks ago. S[he] will be confirmed when the bishop com[es] again. The receiving of the Christi[an] name is interesting to them. M[rs.] Chicken Hawk is now Sarah, and M[rs.] Antelope Skin's name is Mary. M[rs.] Chicken Hawk's own name is "Worki[ng] woman." Among their own people they [re]tain their maiden names after marria[ge].

It is not easy for the older ones to become Christians. They must give [up] many of the old-time customs and [it] often means isolation for them, as th[ere] are many Indian festivities into wh[ich] they cannot enter.

There are so many opportunities [in] the Church here. We try to meet [as] many as we can, but we do need [a] clergyman who is a leader and wh[ose] wife is a practical housekeeper. The [se]

The teacher and two of her pupils

A young Churchwoman, studying at the University of Chicago, writing to one of the student secretaries, says:

THE first Church service ever held at the university was held this morning in Mandel Hall, with about thirty present. I wish you might have been there and hope that next fall when you come you can stay over Sunday, because the service is to be permanent. It was a service of which we all have a right to feel very proud. We have a beautiful altar, well-appointed and everything 'of the very finest. Mr. Merrill, a priest of the Church, teaching in the Latin department, was the celebrant, and is a splendid man. Everyone present was impressed by his earnestness and sincerity and I am sure as time goes on we shall have all the Church people in the university present, beside many of their friends.

Nearly everything has been given us, and what is borrowed we hope to return very soon, for we have practically no expenses and can use the offerings to buy what else we need. I am going to suggest that we give a part of them to missions, so that in some other school or college, either in this country or abroad, the students may have the privilege of Church services.

Isn't it splendid to think that every Sunday from now on there will be a service in a university building carried on by university students and teachers with the entire approval of the university authorities? This last is the best of all.

***

A NEW CHURCH IN YAMAGATA

The Rev. W. H. Smart, who has just accomplished the building of his third church in Japan, tells the following story:

IN August, 1907, I was sent by the bishop to open up work in the large province of Yamagata, where we had no mission stations, and, so far as we then knew, no Christians. There are 2,000,000 people in this province, and they are the most conservative in holding fast to the old religion of Japan. It is only within a few years that a line of railway

The site of the church and its builder

has run through this mountainous district. The City of Yamagata contains 50,000 people.

There are scores of Buddhist temples and Shinto shrines—in fact, it may be said that at least one-tenth of the city is taken up with temples and temple grounds. I found on opening a preaching place that there were in the city three Christians belonging to the Church. One man was a doctor, baptized fifteen years ago by the late Archdeacon Shaw, of Tokyo, and he soon brought his family for baptism.

I did not come quite alone, for during the famine in Northern Japan some five years ago, I adopted fifteen poor orphan boys. On arriving here I had just a baker's dozen—thirteen—with two Christian servants. We made a little Christian community and had regular services, hoisting a huge flag up on Sundays and Holy Days.

Pushing on single-handed against anti-Christian forces has been up-hill work, but not without some good results. God has sent His Holy Spirit to help us and during the two and a half years of the mission twenty-three have been baptized and two confirmed, while there are yet others who, I hope, will be baptized soon.

When we had a few Christians I was anxious to build a church. The bishop gave us the ground, but said that I should have to build the church with-

D NOTES

The bishop of one western diocese writes apropos of the work he is doing to have every congregation give its share of the apportionment for diocesan missions and for general missions:

A FEW months ago a committee in one mission said to me, "Bishop, if you are short of funds, why don't you go East and coal up, and come out here and help us? Bishop —— used to do this. He did not expect us to pay street assessments, insurance, improvements, or full salary of minister." Their attitude—and it is the stand taken by most places—seemed hopeless. I dealt with it patiently, but firmly, suggesting that if they did not awake to their responsibilities I might be forced to sell the property. Now, within a year, they have changed, and pay $35 into our "family fund," *i.e.*, diocesan missions, have a settled rector, and within a year or so will be a self-supporting parish.

¶

BISHOP KNIGHT has recently visited the missions under the care of the Rev. C. E. Snavely, whose home station is La Gloria. This is almost entirely an American colony on the north coast. Here during the past six months Bishop Knight has confirmed twenty-two. As there were only seventeen communicants in the congregation when Mr. Snavely took charge in the autumn of 1909, the growth is notable, more than doubling the membership of the mission. Bishop Knight says: "The classes were thoroughly prepared. Quite a number of others gave in their names for the next class, some of whom spoke to me. At Camaguey, too, the work is taking on new life, and I had the largest congregation that I ever had there for a week night. At Bartle everything is smooth, and while there were only two confirmed, it is the beginning, and if he holds his own as he has been doing, there will be quite a class for the next visitation."

¶

IF one of our readers has a second-hand typewriter, or would be willing to buy a new one for the use of one of our missionaries in Japan, the Editor would be glad to hear from him or her.

BISHOP BRENT, who recently returned to the Philippines from a visit to Guam, has since made a visitation to the southern part of his district, touching at Zamboanga, Cebu, Iloilo, and other important towns. He spent March largely among the mountain missions in the Sagada and Bontok districts. During April he will be in Manila. Early in May he expects to sail for Europe to attend the World's Missionary Conference in Edinburgh in accordance with his appointment by the Board of Missions as a delegate. Between May 1st and July 1st, letters on any necessary business should be addressed to him in care of Church House, London, England.

¶

This news comes from Mississippi:

THE Woman's Auxiliary of St. Andrew's, Jackson, took as its Lenten work the making of a canvass of the women of the parish. Nearly $800 for missions by pledges on a weekly basis was raised. The Brotherhood visited the men and the total amount pledged for the year is about $2,100.

¶

THE Bishop of Shanghai writes that three doctors are needed—one for Wusih, one to open work at Zangzok, and the third to be ready to supply the place of men going on furlough or falling sick. At least one doctor should always be in training.

¶

BISHOP McKIM writes of the great necessity for a fund of $25,000 to bring the St. Margaret's School plant up to the standard of equivalent required by the Japanese authorities with regard to buildings, and adds: "That we may not be put to shame by refusal of Government recognition, please save us and the Church at home from this humiliation."

MEETING OF THE BOARD OF MISSIONS
May 10th, 1910

THE Board of Missions met at the Church Missions House on Tuesday, May 10th, the Bishop of Albany (vice-president) in the chair. The following members were present: The Bishops of West Virginia, Pittsburgh, Ohio, Massachusetts, Indianapolis, Long Island and Newark; the Rev. Drs. Vibbert, Anstice, Alsop, Stires, McKim, Parks, Mann, Storrs, Smith, the Rev. Mr. Miel and the Rev. Mr. Manning; Messrs. Low, Mills, Goodwin, Mansfield, Admiral Mahan, and Messrs. King, Morris and Ryerson.

The Treasurer reported that receipts for the month of April were $15,000 larger than in 1909, and the total increase applying on appropriations to May 1st was $37,000.

The Sunday-school Lenten offering for the six weeks after Easter, from 769 Sunday-schools, was $95,967.05, an average of $34.65 per school. During the same length of time last year there was received from 2,632 Sunday-schools $6,963.67, an average of $36.84 per school.

In accordance with the action of the last General Convention the Treasurer of the Society was instructed to seek the opinion of the Counsel as to the effect which would be produced by changing the corporate name by dropping from the title the words "Domestic and Foreign." The Counsel reported that the change of name would in no way affect present titles to property or future bequests already written in the present corporate name.

The most important business to come before the meeting was the making of appropriations for the fiscal year 1910-[?]. The appropriations proposed were adopted, making in the aggregate $1,252,520.97, as against the appropria-

tions of $1,142,519.46 made a year ago at a similar date.

The Order of the Day was the report of the Special Committee of the Board of Missions on Specials and Special Appeals, which, with action thereupon, is to be issued to the Church in pamphlet form.

Announcement having been made that May 10th was the eightieth anniversary of the birth of the Bishop of Pennsylvania, and he being absent in attendance upon his diocesan convention, it was "Resolved: That the secretary of the meeting be instructed to send to the Bishop of Pennsylvania the greetings of the Board and its good wishes for the future."

The Diocese of New Hampshire has voluntarily relinquished $600 of its annual grant. This relinquishment was accepted by the Board with cordial thanks.

A question which has been before the Board for several months with regard to approval of the division of the Missionary District of Hankow recurring, it was "Resolved: That the letters of the Bishop of Hankow and the Council of Advice, and the whole question raised by them with regard to the division of the Missionary District of Hankow, be referred to the House of Bishops without recommendation on the part of the Board."

By the sale of house and lot, 15 Bancho, the Bishop of Tokyo, by the approval of the Board, is able to provide St. Margaret's School with necessary buildings and a house is also to be erected in a convenient neighborhood for Dr. Theodore Bliss. It should be stated though that only about one-half of the money needed for the required extension and improvements of St. Margaret's

School was realized by the sale of the property mentioned.

The report of the Apportionment Committee for the next fiscal year was adopted. The Apportionment was made on the same basis as heretofore, with an increase to meet the growth of the work of about $75,000.

The Treasurer was requested in his triennial address to the General Convention to rehearse the problems and difficulties encountered in working the apportionment plan and to ask for the appointment of a committee, whose membership shall be apart from that of the Board of Missions, to confer with the Apportionment Committee of the Board and report back to a later joint session of the two Houses.

The Office Committee was given power and instructed to erect in the Church Missions House a suitable tablet to the memory of Mr. George C. Thomas, our late Treasurer.

ANNOUNCEMENTS

Concerning the Missionaries

Alaska

AT the meeting of the Board on May 10th, at the request of the Bishop of Alaska, the Rev. Louis H. Buisch, of St. Paul's Cathedral, Buffalo, was appointed as missionary to Fairbanks.

MISS MABEL H. PICK was appointed under the Woman's Auxiliary United Offering as missionary teacher at Wrangell, to fill a vacancy. Miss Pick was set apart as a Deaconess by Bishop Rowe in the Chapel of the Good Shepherd, Berkeley, Cal., on May 20th.

Porto Rico

AT the same meeting, at the request of Bishop Van Buren, Miss Iva Mary Woodruff, of St. James's Parish, Long Branch, was appointed as missionary teacher at Mayaguez.

The Philippines

THE REV. HOBART E. STUDLEY, who sailed from San Francisco on March 8th, arrived at Manila on April 2d.

JUNIOR ROOMS IN PHILADELPHIA

THE WOMAN'S AUXILIARY
To the Board of Missions

AUXILIARY QUILTS IN SOUTH DAKOTA
One means of increasing the United Offering

PLANS FOR THE UNITED OFFERING

South Dakota: Niobrara Deanery

The Secretary writes:

I HAVE received from Miss Emery some very interesting leaflets about the United Offering. She says we may have more, as many as we need, for distribution.

We may well be thankful when we read of the great good which has been accomplished by the United Offering; and I wish that our women, who have been giving of their money toward it for many years, could all know of the good it has done.

So I want to ask the wives of our Niobrara priests to help place these leaflets in the hands of the English-reading women and those who have someone to translate them for them.

I have asked Miss Emery to send a set to each of you. Will you please examine them and let me know as soon as convenient which ones you would like to have sent to you and how many?

Pittsburgh

"We have appointed a committee of five to work up the United Offering in this diocese. We are planning to send a typewritten letter, explaining briefly the progress made, particularly in our own diocese, to each clergyman. Accompanying this will be a personal note from the committee (these are to be divided among the five members) asking the co-operation of the clergyman. Also a copy of each leaflet will be mailed him for his inspection, and a return postal card on which he is asked to indicate the number of any particular leaflet or leaflets he may think would interest the women of his parish. Of course this may be turned over by the clergyman to the collector of the offering to attend to, but we are going first to get the attention of the rector, feeling he will be more interested, and take a pride in it, and naturally the women will fall in line then.

"This is our plan, and we expect this mail to go out this month—March."

United .Offering Treasurer. This committee will send out a letter to the branches to stir them to greater activity, and also will invite certain ladies who speak well to visit among the branches. We hope to raise $3,000 between May and September, in addition to what the branches ordinarily raise. And we hope to make the United Offering meeting in May a splendid one.

THE WOMAN'S AUXILIARY IN MEXICO

AT last we feel that the Woman's Auxiliary has really come to stay with us. We have branches at San Pedro Martir, Xochitenco, Jojutla, Cuernavaca. These are native branches. Our only English-speaking one is in Christ Church, Mexico City. It will not bring much money into the treasury this year, as we thought best to urge only the putting of the pennies in the little blue box, until September. They will make furnishings for the altars and vestments for our clergy.

I am very thankful, for my greatest desire has been that we might have a good working Woman's Auxiliary in Mexico.

We held our first annual meeting, Thursday, March 31st. As reports had to be in both languages, the Deaconess and I were a little fearful. Mrs. Garius, a member of San Pedro, translated for us, so we did very well.

A corporate communion was held in San Pedro church at ten; the business meeting was opened by the Rev. Mr. Melendez, with our Auxiliary prayers in Spanish. In the afternoon we held a missionary meeting. It was opened by the bishop. An address to the native women by Archdeacon Limric was followed by short addresses by the Rev. Allan L. Burleson, A. H. Mellen and Eugene F. Bigler.

It means much hard work and earnest prayer, but my fellow-officers are faithful and earnest. You must not forget us in your prayers, for we need them.

A JUNIOR OFFICE

By Sarah Coleman Brock

IN May, 1906, the Junior leaders in Pennsylvania felt it was absolutely necessary for the diocesan branch of the Junior Auxiliary to have a permanent home, so the officers set themselves to find one. The most appropriate place was, of course, in the Church House, the centre of all diocesan activities. Through the generosity of ten members of the Woman's Auxiliary, who pledged themselves to contribute toward the expense annually, they were able to rent an office, which has been the headquarters of the Juniors ever since.

Here are kept the maps, collections of curios, and the lantern and sets of slides. Here are also reference libraries for the mission study courses, and scrap-books on the work in the different countries in the mission field, all of which are for the use of the Juniors, Woman's and Sunday-school Auxiliaries in the diocese. A supply of all the pamphlets published at the Church Missions House is also kept on hand.

The Junior Office is open from 10 to 12:30 A.M. daily, except on Saturdays; during which hours one of the diocesan officers is always present. On the first Saturday of each month a conference of the leaders of the parish branches is held at 10:30 A.M., followed by a half-hour of intercessions for missions at 11:30, to which all visitors are cordially welcomed.

The normal mission study classes for Junior leaders are also held in the Junior office; and its walls are decorated with charts and maps, the work of the Junior branches whose leaders have benefited by these classes.

It is hard to estimate what this office has meant to the Junior work in Pennsylvania. Through it, the leaders have come into much closer touch with each other and with the diocesan officers; and throughout the whole work there is a new strength and spirit of oneness, with a resulting growth in prayer and gifts.

Headquarters:—

From October 4th to 25th the Woman's Auxiliary, with its Junior Department, will have its headquarters in the Music Hall, in a wing of the same building in which General Convention will meet. Here will be found a registry, information bureau, post-office, rest rooms; the Junior Department will display their exhibit, and missionary literature will be shown. Here, also, it is expected that on week-day mornings informal conferences will be held, closing with noonday prayers and missionary addresses. In the late afternoon the Southern Ohio parishes will invite their guests to tea.

The members of the Auxiliary are asked at once to suggest to the Secretary of the Auxiliary the subjects most important and helpful to consider in the morning conferences.

Mission Study —

The first hour of the morning—9 to 10:15—Normal Classes for the study of Missions are to be held in St. Paul's Cathedral Parish House.

Notices:—

Detailed notices will be sent in due season to all desiring them. Please inquire of the Secretary of the Woman's Auxiliary.

For information about the Study Classes, the Junior Exhibit and other Junior plans, address Miss Lindley,

Church Missions House, 281 Fourth Avenue, New York.

TO DIOCESAN OFFICERS

THE October Conference of Diocesan Officers will be held on the afternoon of Wednesday, October 5th, at the Headquarters of the Woman's Auxiliary in Cincinnati.

An adjourned session will follow this Conference at a time then voted upon.

All diocesan officers, of both the Woman's Auxiliary and the Junior Department, who expect to attend are asked to notify the Secretary of the Woman's Auxiliary at the earliest opportunity.

UNITED OFFERING MISSIONARIES IN PORTO RICO AND CUBA

I. MAYAGUEZ, PORTO RICO

THESE are some of the things I have tried to accomplish: That the children should learn to come to school at the appointed time, with some effort toward accuracy, show some regard for truth, and develop some degree of school spirit. Rudimentary work, you perceive, but we are still in the stump-digging stage in the cultivation of this field. They have made progress. Their work can be assigned with a reasonable certainty that it will be done to the best of their ability. Truth is not their strong point, yet there are some who will now own to a fault though they know punishment will follow the confession. I do not dare to remit the punishment, lest they should learn to tell the truth for their own advantage.

A little brown girl, sitting on my balcony, was telling me the Spanish names of the stars. A little later, while others were talking, I heard her murmuring to herself in Spanish, "The heavens declare the glory of God and the firmament showeth His handiwork." Mr. Bland had given a beautiful and clear exposition of the nineteenth psalm some nights before, and this little heart had heard and heeded.

Our numbers seem small by the hundreds of the other schools, but I think they are enough to make for righteousness. Our enrolment is 150, but the largest attendance has been 125, in the alluring weeks of middle December. Our average is between 95 and 110.

My associates are real helps in the school. I am sorry not to have had time to give them some training in pedagogy. They take readily any hints in that line, but my own two class-rooms have left me no time for the training of the teachers. One of them, however, has succeeded in managing some boys who were supposed to be unmanageable. The other helps me in the sewing-class, which we began in January. As we have no special teacher for sewing, we had to wait until the c[...] work was well under way before beg[...] ning the sewing-class. The children [...] very fond of sewing, and would like [...] give more time to that than to stu[...]. Few of them can do plain sewing, thou[...] some can make lace. They have li[...] useful knowledge.

There are many joys in this wo[...]. Besides the incommunicable joy of [...] teacher, there is the delight of seeing [...] Church strike her roots downward, [...] seeing these pliant natures lend the[...] selves to her influence, of seeing th[...] love and loyalty to her growing.

II. GUANABACOA, CUBA

Our school is situated in one of t[...] oldest cities of Cuba. The building its[...] is the old home of a wealthy family, w[...] large rooms, marble floors, barred w[...] dows, and a beautiful garden of tropi[...] plants where the children play.

We have over twenty regular pup[...] with a kindergarten and advanc[...] course. As there are many famil[...] made destitute by the wars, we also h[...] some free pupils. The children ha[...] studies in both Spanish and English a[...] make rapid progress, as the Cuban ch[...] dren are naturally intelligent. The k[...] dergarten work is especially interesti[...] for them, as it is so entirely differe[...] from what they have in any of th[...] Spanish schools.

At our entertainments, or "fiestricta[...] the children all give recitations a[...] sing, and the tiniest tot of the sch[...] leads the march afterwards. Their re[...] tations and songs are really remarkab[...] considering the length of time th[...] have studied English. Of course th[...] have an accent, and our Americ[...] boys and girls would laugh over th[...] rendition of "Twinkle, twinkle, lit[...] star," and "The pretty moon," but th[...] readily catch the idea of the picturesq[...] and beautiful, and like our Americ[...] verses.

ACKNOWLEDGMENT OF OFFERINGS

Offerings are asked to sustain missions in thirty missionary districts in the United States, Africa, China, Japan, Brazil, Mexico and Cuba; also work in the Haitien Church; in forty-two dioceses, including missions to the Indians and to the Colored People; to pay the salaries of thirty-two bishops, and stipends to 2,253 missionary workers, domestic and foreign; also two general missionaries to the Swedes and two missionaries among deaf-mutes in the Middle West and the South; and to support schools, hospitals and orphanages.

With all remittances the name of the Diocese and Parish should be given. Remittances, when practicable, should be by Check or Draft, and should always be made payable to the order of George Gordon King, Treasurer, and sent to him, Church Missions House, 281 Fourth Avenue, New York. Remittances in Bank Notes are not safe unless sent in Registered Letters.

The Treasurer of the Board of Missions acknowledges the receipt of the following from April 1st to May 1st, 1910.

* Lenten and Easter Offering from the Sunday-school Auxiliary.

NOTE.—*The items in the following pages marked "Sp." are Specials which do not aid the* Board *in meeting its appropriations. In the heading for each Diocese the total marked "Ap." is the* amount *which does aid the Board of Missions in meeting its appropriations. Wherever the abbreviation* "Wo. Aux." *precedes the amount, the offering is through a branch of the Woman's Auxiliary.*

Home Dioceses

Alabama

Ap. $1,036.78

ANNISTON—*Grace S. S.**: Gen	33	93
St. Michael and All Angels' S. S.*: Gen.	23	00
AUBURN—*Holy Innocents'*: Gen	20	00
AVONDALE—*Christ Church S. S.**: Gen.	30	00
BESSEMER—*Trinity Church*: Gen. (of which S. S.,* $5)	32	00
BIRMINGHAM—*All Saints' Mission S.*: Gen.	26	22
St. Mark's: Gen. (of which S. S.,* $3)	11	00
St. Mary's S. S.*: Gen.	100	00
BRICTON—*Mission S. S.**: Gen	5	00
BRIGEE—*St. Mark's*: Gen	5	00
CLOWVILLE—*St. Paul's*: Gen. (of which S. S.,* $30.93)	32	13
DECATUR—*St. Paul's S. S.**: Dom.	3	50
DEMOPOLIS—*Trinity Church*: Gen. (of which S. S.,* $25)	125	00
FINSDALE—*St. Michael's S. S.**: Gen.	11	35
FLORENCE—*Trinity Church*: Gen. (of which S. S.,* $34.20)	37	20
GAINESVILLE—*St. Alban's*: Gen	3	00
HUNTSVILLE—*Nativity S. S.**: Gen	84	97
JACKSONVILLE—*St. Luke's S. S.**: Dom. and Frn	2	50
LANDESBORO—*St. Paul's*: Gen	10	00
MARLENE—*All Saints' S. S.**: Gen	25	71
MOBILE—*St. John's*: Dom., $5.50; Cuba, $12.50; S. S.,* Gen., $20	38	00
MONTEVALLO—*St. Andrew's S. S.*: Gen.	8	19
DECATUR—*St. John's S. S.**: Gen.	28	27
OPELIKA—*Emmanuel Church*: Gen	10	00
PRATTVILLE—*St. Mark's S. S.**: Gen.	10	25
SELMA—*St. Paul's S. S.**: Gen	40	90
SPRING HILL—*St. Paul's S. S.**: Gen.	11	02
TALLADEGA—*St. Peter's*: Gen. (of which S. S.,* $25)	32	50
TROY—*St. Mark's S. S.**: Gen	12	55

TUSCALOOSA—*Christ Church*: Gen. (of which S. S.,* $115.59)	170	59
TUSCUMBIA—*St. John's*: Gen	15	00
UNION SPRINGS—*Trinity Church S. S.**: Dom. and Frn	8	00
WOODLAWN—*Grace*: Gen.: Dom., $5; Frn., $5; Gen., $20	30	00

Albany

Ap. $4,820.61; Sp. $76.00

ALBANY—*All Saints' Cathedral*: St. Luke's Hospital, Tokyo, $5; Gen., $107.75; Wo. Aux., salary of Bishop Aves, Mexico, $50; salary of Bishop Knight, Cuba, $20; Seminole Indians, Southern Florida, $20; white work, Alaska, $15; native work, Philippines, $40	257	75
Holy Innocents': For "De Witt" (In Memoriam) scholarship, St. Elizabeth's Indian School, South Dakota, $60; Wo. Aux., native work, Alaska, $2; native work, Philippines, $2; salary of Bishop Aves, Mexico, $2; salary of Bishop Knight, Cuba, $2	68	00
*St. Andrew's S. S.**: Gen	35	00
St. Paul's: Gen., $450; Wo. Aux., white work, Alaska, $12; native work, Philippines, $10; Seminole Indians, Southern Florida, $9; salary of Bishop Aves, Mexico, $12; salary of Bishop Knight, Cuba, $12; Sp. for "J. Livingston Reese" room, St. Peter's Hospital, Helena, Montana, $25	530	00
St. Peter's: Wo. Aux., "Bishop Doane" (Graduate) scholarship, South Dakota, $60; white work, Alaska, $25; native work, Philippines, $25; Seminole Indians, Southern Florida, $20; salary of Bishop Aves, Mexico, $25; salary of Bishop Knight, Cuba, $20.	175	00
Trinity Church: Wo. Aux., Seminole Indians, Southern Florida, $1; white work, Alaska, $2; salary of Bishop		

Aves, Mexico, $1; salary of Bishop Knight, Cuba, $1................ 5 00

Miss Kate Child, Sp. for Shanghai Catechist School, Loan and Building Fund 5 00

AMSTERDAM—*St. Ann's*: Gen., $179.68; Wo. Aux., white work, Alaska (of which Junior Aux., $4), $9; native work, Philippine Islands (of which Junior Aux., $4), $9; Seminole Indians, Southern Florida (of which Juniors, $4), $9; salary of Bishop Aves, Mexico, $5; salary of Bishop Knight, Cuba, $5.............. 216 68

ASHLAND—*Trinity Church*: Wo. Aux., white work, Alaska, $3; salary of Bishop Aves, Mexico, $3; S. S.,* Gen., $9.45.................... 15 45

ATHENS—*Trinity Church*: Wo. Aux., white work, Alaska, $1; native work, Philippine Islands, $1............ 2 00

AUSABLE FORKS—*St. James's S. S.*: Gen. 5 74

BALLSTON SPA—*Christ Church S. S.*: Dom., $17.42; Frn., $8.71........ 26 13

BLOOMINGDALE—*Church of the Redeemer S. S.*: Gen. 3 00

BLOOMVILLE—*St. Paul's S. S.*: Gen. 2 26

BOLTON—*St. Sacrament's*: Gen. (of which S. S.,* $7.82)........... 60 00

BRUSHTON—*St. Peter's S. S.*: Dom.. 13 15

BURNT HILLS—*Calvary*: Frn., $19.72; Wo. Aux., white work, Alaska, $3; native work, Philippine Islands, $3; Seminole Indians, Southern Florida, $3; salary of Bishop Aves, Mexico, $4; salary of Bishop Knight, Cuba, $4 .... 36 72

CAMBRIDGE—*St. Luke's*: Gen., Wo. Aux., $17; S. S.,* $18.50.......... 35 50

CATSKILL—*St. Luke's*: Gen. (of which S. S.,* $42)................... 142 00

CHAMPLAIN—*St. John's*: Wo. Aux., white work, Alaska, $1; native work, Philippine Islands, $1; Seminole Indians, Southern Florida, $1; salary of Bishop Aves, Mexico, $1; salary of Bishop Knight, Cuba, $1; S. S.,* Gen., $17.25................... 22 25

CHARLTON—*St. Paul's*: Wo. Aux., Seminole Indians, Southern Florida, $1; white work, Alaska, $1; native work, Philippine Islands, $1.50; salary of Bishop Aves, Mexico, $1; salary of Bishop Knight, Cuba, $1.. 5 50

CHERRY VALLEY—*Grace*: Wo. Aux., Seminole Indians, Southern Florida, $1; white work, Alaska, $1; native work, Philippine Islands, $2; salary of Bishop Aves, Mexico, $2; salary of Bishop Knight, Cuba, $2.. 8 00

CLAVERACK—*Trinity Church*: Gen.... 2 67

COHOES—*St. John's*: Gen. (of which S. S.,* $32.77, Wo. Aux., $10), $60.26; Wo. Aux., native work, Philippine Islands (of which Junior Aux., $2), $8; Seminole Indians, Southern Florida, $1; salary of Bishop Aves, Mexico (of which Junior Aux., $1), $1); salary of Bishop Knight, Cuba (of which Junior Aux., $1), $4.............. 76 26

COBLESKILL—*Grace*: Dom. and Frn... 1 48

COOPERSTOWN—*Christ Church*: Wo. Aux., Seminole Indians, Southern Florida, $5; white work, Alaska, $5; native work, Philippine Islands, $8; salary of Bishop Aves, Mexico, $8; salary of Bishop Knight, Cuba, $8.. 34 00

COPAKE IRON WORKS—*St. John's*: Gen. 5 00

DELHI—*St. John's*: Wo. Aux., Seminole Indians, Southern Florida, $5; white work, Alaska, $6; native work, Philippine Islands, $5; salary of

Bishop Aves, Mexico, $5; salary of Bishop Knight, Cuba, $5; Junior Aux., Gen., $48................

DELANSON—*St. Peter's S. S.*: Gen..

DUANESBURGH—*Christ Church*; Gen. (of which S. S.,* $10.76).......

EAST LINE—*St. John's S. S.*: Gen.

EAST SPRINGFIELD—*St. Paul's*: Wo. Aux., Seminole Indians, Southern Florida, $1; white work, Alaska, $2; native work, Philippine Islands, $1; salary of Bishop Aves, Mexico, $1; salary of Bishop Knight, Cuba, $1..

ESSEX—*St. John's*: Wo. Aux., Gen...

FONDA—*Zion*: Wo. Aux., white work, Alaska ....

FORT COVINGTON—*St. Paul's S. S.*: Gen. ....

FORT EDWARD—*St. James's*: Wo. Aux., native work, Philippine Islands, $2; salary of Bishop Aves, Mexico, $2; salary of Bishop Knight, Cuba, $2..

FRANKLIN—*St. Paul's*: Gen..........

GILBERTSVILLE—*Christ Church*: Gen. (of which S. S.,* $9.12), $43.86; Wo. Aux., Seminole Indians, Southern Florida, $2.50; white work, Alaska, $2; native work, Philippine Islands, $2; salary of Bishop Aves, Mexico, $5....................

GILBOA—*Mission*: Gen.............

GLEN'S FALLS—*Church of the Messiah*: Gen. (of which S. S.,* $56.37), $106.37; Wo. Aux., white work, Alaska, $5; native work, Philippine Islands, $5; Seminole Indians, Southern Florida, $5; salary of Bishop Aves, Mexico, $5; salary of Bishop Knight, Cuba, $5...........

GLOVERSVILLE — *Christ Church*; Wo. Aux., Seminole Indians, Southern Florida, $2; white work, Alaska, $2; native work, Philippine Islands, $2; salary of Bishop Aves, Mexico, $3; salary of Bishop Knight, Cuba, $2 ....

GOUVERNEUR—*Trinity Church S. S.*: Dom., $8.16; Frn., $8.16..........

GRANVILLE—*Trinity Church*: Wo. Aux., Gen., $5; Junior Aux., white work, Alaska, $1; Seminole Indians, Southern Florida, $1..........

GREEN ISLAND—*St. Mark's*: Dom. and Frn. ....

GREENVILLE—*Christ Church S. S.*: Frn. ....

GRIFFIN CORNERS—*Emmanuel Church*: Gen. ....

HERKIMER—*Christ Church S. S.*: Gen.

HOBART—*St. Peter's S. S.*: "Birthday Offering," Gen., $4.64; S. S.,* Gen., $8.43....................

HOGANSBURG—*St. James's S. S.*: Gen.

HOOSAC—*All Saints'*: Wo. Aux., Seminole Indians, Southern Florida, $2; Junior Aux., Gen., $5..........

HOOSICK FALLS—*St. Mark's*: Wo. Aux., Gen.....................

HUDSON—*All Saints'*: Gen. (of which S. S.,* $9.75)..................

Christ Church: Wo. Aux., Seminole Indians, Southern Florida, $2.50; white work, Alaska, $30; native work, Philippine Islands, $2.50; salary of Bishop Aves, Mexico, $5; salary of Bishop Knight, Cuba, $5...

HUDSON FALLS—*Zion*: Dom., $39.26; Gen. (of which S. S.,* $28), $48.01; (Wo. Aux., Seminole Indians, Southern Florida, $1; white work, Alaska, $2; native work, Philippine Islands, $2; salary of Bishop Aves, Mexico, $2; salary of Bishop Knight, Cuba, $2....................

ILION—*St. Augustine's*: Wo. Aux.,

44 00
59 00
17 90
14 94
15 74
52 73
10 00
1 00
100 00
8 30
15 00
49 83
67 51
15 00
3 20
3 05
19 14
4 00
20 36
23 00
41 75
47 00
102 32
3 55

Gen., $52.................... 63 00
Church of the Messiah S. S.*; Gen... 10 00
RENSSELAERVILLE — *Trinity Church*:
  Wo. Aux., Gen.................... 10 00
RICHFIELD—*St. Luke's*: Gen. (of which
  S. S.,* $2.30).................... 14 30
RICHFIELD SPRINGS—*St. John's*: Wo.
  Aux., Seminole Indians, Southern
  Florida, $1; white work, Alaska,
  $1; S. S.,* Gen., $8.90.......... 10 90
ROUND LAKE—*All Saints'*: Wo. Aux.,
  white work, Alaska, $1; native work,
  Philippine Islands, $1............ 2 00
SARANAC LAKE—*St. Luke's S. S.**:
  Gen. 25 33
SARATOGA SPRINGS — Bethesda: Wo.
  Aux., Seminole Indians, Southern
  Florida, $8; white work, Alaska,
  $8; native work, Philippine Islands,
  $8; salary of Bishop Aves, Mexico,
  $8; salary of Bishop Knight, Cuba,
  $8 .... 40 00
St. Christina's S. S.*: Gen......... 60 51
SCHENECTADY — *Christ Church*: Wo.
  Aux., Seminole Indians, Southern
  Florida, $1; white work, Alaska,
  $1; native work, Philippine Islands,
  $1 .... 3 00
St. Andrew's: $7.65, S. S.,* $12.76.. 20 41
St. Agnes's S. S.*: Gen............ 2 31
St. George's: Dom. and Frn. $473.75;
  S. S.,* Gen., $233.45; Wo. Aux.,
  white work, Alaska, $10; native
  work, Philippine Islands, $10;
  Seminole Indians, Southern Florida,
  $5; salary of Bishop Aves, Mexico,
  $6; salary of Bishop Knight, Cuba,
  $5 .... 742 20
St. Paul's: $10, S. S.,* $1.94, Gen... 11 94
SHARON SPRINGS — *Trinity Church*:
  Dom. and Frn.................... 16 53
SPRINGFIELD CENTRE—*St. Mary's*: Wo.
  Aux., Seminole Indians, Southern
  Florida, $3; white work, Alaska, $3;
  native work, Philippine Islands, $3;
  salary of Bishop Aves, Mexico, $4;
  salary of Bishop Knight, Cuba, $3.. 16 00
STAMFORD—*Grace*: Gen. (of which S.
  S.,* $10.83).................... 82 30
STOCKPORT—*St. John the Evangelist's
  S. S.**: Gen.................... 20 75
UNADILLA—*St. Matthew's S. S.**: Gen. 13 61
TICONDEROGA—*Chapel of the Cross S.
  S.**: Gen...................... 25 00
TROY—*Ascension*: Wo. Aux., Seminole
  Indians, Southern Florida, $4; white
  work, Alaska, $4; native work,
  Philippine Islands, $9; salary of
  Bishop Aves, Mexico, $9; salary of
  Bishop Knight, Cuba, $9; Gen. (of
  which Junior Aux., $11), $16..... 51 00
Holy Cross: Gen. (of which In
  Memoriam, "H. J. S.," $11, S. S.*
  $40), $51; Wo. Aux., Seminole In-
  dians, Southern Florida (of which
  Junior Aux., $3.50), $8.50; white
  work, Alaska (of which Junior Aux.,
  $5), $10; native work, Philippine
  Islands (of which Junior Aux., $5),
  $14; salary of Bishop Aves, Mexico
  (of which Junior Aux., $5.50),
  $13.50; salary of Bishop Knight,
  Cuba (of which Junior Aux., $5),
  $13; Babies' Branch, Sp. for mis-
  sionary font, $3; Gen., $10........ 123 00
St. John's: Wo. Aux., Seminole In-
  dians, Southern Florida (of which
  Junior Aux., $5), $30; white work,
  Alaska, $25; native work, Philip-
  pine Islands (of which from Minis-
  ters' Aid, $5), $15; salary of Bish-
  op Aves, Mexico, $10; salary of
  Bishop Knight, Cuba, $10; Mothers,
  Gen., $20.75; Daughters of St.
  John, Sp. for Bishop Horner, Ashe-

ville, $25.............................. 135 75
St. Paul's: Wo. Aux., Seminole Indians, Southern Florida, $5; white work, Alaska, $10; native work, Philippine Islands, $5; salary of Bishop Aves, Mexico, $10; salary of Bishop Knight, Cuba, $10; Junior Aux., Sp. for Miss Cody, Alaska, $8; S. S.,* Gen., $40............. 88 00
Mrs. Edward W. Babcock, for St. Elizabeth's Hospital, Shanghai..... 12 00
VALLEY FALLS—Trinity Church: Wo. Aux., Gen......................... 25 00
WALTON—Christ Church: Wo. Aux., Seminole Indians, Southern Florida, $10; white work, Alaska, $20; native work, Philippine Islands, $10; salary of Bishop Aves, Mexico, $7; salary of Bishop Knight, Cuba, $7. 54 00
WATERFORD—Grace: Dom., $7; Frn., $7.10 .... 14 10
WATERVLIET — Trinity Church: Wo. Aux., Seminole Indians, Southern Florida, $1; white work, Alaska, $2; native work, Philippine Islands, $2; salary of Bishop Aves, Mexico, $4.50; salary of Bishop Knight, Cuba, $4.50................... 14 00
WHITEHALL—Trinity Church S. S.*: Dom. and Frn.................... 21 15

Arkansas

Ap. $647.93; Sp. $6.03

BATESVILLE — St. Paul's: Frn., $16.80; Gen. (of which Wo. Aux., $15, S. S.,* $30), $45............ 61 80
CAMDEN—St. John's: Junior Aux., St. Hilda's School, Wuchang, Hankow, $5; S. S.,* Gen., $43.25.......... 48 25
EUREKA SPRINGS—Miss Nellie Perkins, Sp. for Mr. Winthrop Peabody, Tanana, Alaska.................... 3 00
FORREST CITY—Church of the Good Shepherd S. S.*: Gen............... 17 43
FORT SMITH—Church of the Messiah S. S.*: Gen....................... 2 78
St. John's S. S.*: Gen........... 50 00
HELENA—St. John's S. S.*: Gen.... 156 15
HOT SPRINGS—St. Luke's: Gen. (of which Wo. Aux., $15, S. S.,* $53.42) 68 42
LITTLE ROCK—Christ Church: Frn., $7.15; Gen., $70; S. S., Sp. for Bishop Roots's work, Hankow, $3.03; S. S.,* Gen., $50.............. 130 18
St. Margaret's S. S.*: Gen........... 8 00
St. Paul's S. S.*: Frn............ 15 00
MARIANNA—St. Andrew's S. S.*: Gen. 12 45
NEWPORT—St. Paul's S. S.*: Gen.. 21 42
VAN BUREN—Trinity Church: Gen. (of which Wo. Aux., $10, S. S.,* $33.82). 43 82
WASHINGTON—"Two Families,"* Gen.. 15 26

Atlanta

Ap. $811.18; Sp. $15.00

ATHENS—Emmanuel Church S. S.*: Gen. 51 37
ATLANTA—All Saints' S. S.*: Gen.... 90 13
Incarnation S. S.*: Gen............ 19 35
St. Andrew's S. S.*: Gen.......... 18 37
St. Luke's: Gen., $200; Wo. Aux., Sp. for Rev. W. Sakabara, Tokyo, $15.. 215 00
St. Paul's S. S.*: Gen............ 14 00
CEDARTOWN—St. James's: Dom. and Frn., $25; S. S.,* Gen., $9.35..... 34 35
COLUMBUS — St. Mary-the-Virgin's: Dom., $3; Frn., $2.25; Gen., $25... 30 25
Trinity Church: Gen. (of which S. S.,* $107.57)................... 178 42
LA GRANGE—St. Mark's: Gen........ 8 00
MACON—Christ Church S. S.*: Gen.. 86 00
MARIETTA—St. James's S. S.*: Gen.. 34 98
MT. AIRY—Calvary: Gen........... 3 00

MILLEDGEVILLE—St. Stephen's S. S.*: Gen. ....
TOCCOA—St. Matthias's: Gen.........
WEST POINT—Christ Church: Gen....

Bethlehem

Ap. $4,127.03; Sp. $210.00

ALDEN—St. Andrew's: Dom., $3; Frn., $7.50; S. S.,* Gen., $10.11...
ALLENTOWN—Grace S. S.*: Gen......
Church of the Mediator S. S.*: Gen.
ASHLAND—St. John's S. S.*: Gen....
ASHLEY—St. John's: Gen...........
ATHENS—Trinity Church: Gen. (of which Wo. Aux., $10, S. S.,* $7.85)
BANGOR—Leonard Hall Mission S. S.*: Gen...............................
BETHLEHEM—Trinity Church: Gen. (of which S. S.,* $15.58)............
BIRDSBORO—St. Michael's S. S.*: Gen.
CARBONDALE—Trinity Church S. S.*: Gen. ....
CATASAUQUA—St. Stephen's S. S.*: Gen. ....
DORRANCETOWN—Grace: Wo. Aux.. Sp. for Rev. N. Joyner, Pine Ridge, South Dakota, $5; S. S.,* Dom., $67.96 ....
DRIFTON—St. James's: Dom., $59.83; Wo. Aux., Sp. for Mrs. W. H. Marston Fitzgerald, Georgia, for St. Matthew's Guild, $1; S. S.,* Gen., $151.03; for scholarship (In Memoriam), Rev. J. P. Bixton, Boone University, Wuchang, Hankow, $50...
DUNMORE—St. Mark's S. S.*: Gen...
EAST MAUCH CHUNK—St. John's: Gen. (of which S. S.,* $62.23).....
EMMAUS—St. Margaret's S. S.*: Gen..
FISHBACH—St. John's S. S.*: Gen..
FOREST CITY—Christ Church: Gen. (of which S. S.,* $4.05)..........
FORESTVILLE—St. Stephen's S. S.*: Gen. ....
FRACKVILLE—Christ Church: Gen....
GREAT BEND—Grace S. S.*: Gen.....
HACKELBERNIE—S. S.*: Gen........
HAZLETON—St. Peter's S. S.*: Gen..
HELLERTOWN—St. George's S. S.*: Gen. ....
HONESDALE—Grace: Gen., $25.13; S. S.,* Gen., $17.75; for "Mrs. Sophie C. Memner" (In Memoriam) scholarship, St. John's University, Shanghai, $50......................
JERMYN—St. James's: Wo. Aux., Gen., $1; Sp. for Valle Crucis Mission, Asheville, $1; S. S.,* Gen., $13.50..
JONESTOWN—St. Mark's: Frn.......
LEBANON—St. Luke's S. S.*: Gen....
LEHIGHTON—All Saints' S. S.*: Gen..
MAHANOY CITY—Faith S. S.*: Gen...
MAUCH CHUNK—St. Mark's: Gen. (of which S. S.,* $135.89), $525.59; Dom., $6.53; Indian, $7.47; Colored, $7.52; Frn., $8.80............
MECHANICSVILLE—St. Paul's S. S.*: Gen. ....
MILFORD—Church of the Good Shepherd S. S.*: Gen...............
MINERSVILLE—St. Paul's: Gen. (of which S. S.,* $12.09)............
MONTROSE—St. Paul's: Wo. Aux., $1, S. S.,* $56.55; Gen.............
NANTICOKE—St. George's S. S.*: Gen.
NAZARETH—St. Paul's: Gen........
OLIVER'S MILLS—Log Chapel S. S.*: Dom. ....
OLYPHANT—St. George's: Gen. (of which S. S.,* $26)..............
PACKERTON—S. S.*: Gen..........
PALMERTON—St. John's S. S.*: For Bishop Spalding's work in Utah....
PECKVILLE—St. Paul's S. S.*: Gen....

HAYWARD—*Trinity Church S. S.**: Gen.		5 30
HOLLISTER—*St. Luke's S. S.**: Gen...		1 10
KING CITY—*St. Mark's S. S.**: Gen...		5 00
LIVERMORE—*Grace*: Gen. (of which
  S. S.,* $4.46)....................		14 21
LODI—*St. John's*: Frn., $2; Gen. (of
  which S. S.,* $6.66), $16.41.......		18 41
MADERA—*Trinity Church S. S.**: Gen..		1 50
MONTEREY—*St. James's*: Gen. (of
  which S. S.,* $5)................		10 50
OAKDALE—*St. Michael's*: $1.70, S. S.,*
  $9.28, Gen....................		10 98
REEDLEY—*Church of the Good Shep-
  herd S. S.**: Gen..............		28 71
RICHMOND—*Trinity Church S. S.**
  Gen.		7 73
ROSS—*St. John's S. S.**: Gen......		16 55
SAN ARDO—*St. Matthew's S. S.**:
  Gen.		1 40
SAN FRANCISCO—*Advent*: Wo. Aux.,
  Gen.		3 00
*All Saints' S. S.**: Gen............		1 25
Grace: Salary of Rev. J. W. Nichols,
  Shanghai, $50; Gen. (of which
  S. S.,* $47.53), $335.53...........		385 53
*Holy Innocents' S. S.**: Gen.........		14 75
*Incarnation S. S.**: Frn.............		8 80
*St. James's S. S.**: Gen.............		5 00
St. John's: Gen...................		6 00
*St. Luke's S. S.**: Gen.............		55 62
*Trinity Church S. S.**: Sp. for Rev.
  J. W. Nichols, Soochow, Shanghai...		60 00
SAN LUIS OBISPO—*St. Stephen's*: Gen.
  (of which S. S.,* $14.65)..........		34 20
Trinity Church: Gen..............		16 20
SAN JOSÉ—*Christ Church*: Gen.......		302 00
SAN MATEO—*Grace*: Gen..............		4 70
Lemita Chapel: Gen................		4 70
St. Matthew's: Gen...............		385 00
SAN MIGUEL—*St. John's S. S.**: Gen..		2 90
SANTA CLARA—*Church of the Holy
  Saviour S. S.**: Frn...............		6 76
SANTA CRUZ—*Calvary S. S.**: Gen....		7 10
SAUSALITO—*Christ Church*: Gen., $25;
  Sp. for Catechist School Land Build-
  ing Fund, Shanghai, $2.50; S. S.,*
  Gen., $18.15...................		45 65
SELMA—*St. Luke's S. S.**: Gen......		3 00
SONORA—*St. James's*: Gen. (of which
  S. S.,* $20)....................		33 00
STOCKTON—*St. John's*: Gen..........		167 50
TUOLUMNE—*St. Michael's S. S.**: Frn.		12 88
TULARE CITY—*St. John's S. S.**: Gen..		3 90
VISALIA—*St. Paul's S. S.**: Gen......		4 00
WATSONVILLE—*All Saints'*: Gen......		20 00

Central New York

Ap. $2,986.81; *Sp.* $296.15

AFTON—*St. Ann's S. S.**: Gen.......		5 27
AUBURN—*St. John's S. S.**:........		13 80
St. Peter's: Frn., $102.40; S. S.,*
  Gen., $146.11...................		248 51
AURORA—*St. Paul's S. S.**: Dom......		16 24
BAINBRIDGE—*St. Peter's S. S.**: Gen..		12 25
BALDWINSVILLE—*Grace S. S.**: Sp. for
  Rev. W. J. Cuthbert's use in build-
  ing St. Mary's Church, Kyoto......		7 00
BIG FLATS—*St. John's*: Gen. (of which
  S. S.,* $6.25)..................		9 79
BINGHAMTON—*Christ Church*: Dom.,
  $35.20; Indian, $10.27; Colored,
  $2.07; Frn., $29.38; Gen., $27.80..		104 72
Trinity Memorial Church: Colored,
  $6.82; S. S.,* Gen., $76..........		82 82
BOONVILLE—*Trinity Church S. S.**:
  Gen.		7 85
BROOKFIELD—*St. Timothy's S. S.**:
  Gen.		2 39
CAMDEN—*Trinity Church S. S.**: Gen.		3 00
CANASTOTA—*Trinity Church*: Gen.....		2 56
CANDOR—*St. Mark's S. S.**: Dom.....		3 00
CAPE VINCENT—*St. John's*; Gen......		20 00
CARTHAGE—*Grace S. S.**: Dom., $3.50;
  Gen., $3.50....................		7 00

CAZENOVIA—*St. Peter's S. S.**: Gen... 7 41
CHADWICKS—*St. George's S. S.**: Gen. 8 00
CHITTENANGO—*St. Paul's*: Gen........ 4 32
CLARK'S MILLS—*St. Mark's S. S.**:
  Gen. 21 00
COPENHAGEN—*Grace S. S.**: Gen.... 7 25
DEXTER—*All Saints' S. S.**: Gen..... 2 00
EARLVILLE—*Grace*: Gen............. 12 00
ELMIRA—*Grace S. S.**: Sp. for St.
  Mary's, Kyoto, Japan.............. 26 15
ENDICOTT—*St. Paul's S. S.**: Gen.... 1 00
FAYETTEVILLE—*Trinity Church*: For
  support of two Christian schools,
  China (of which S. S.,* $18.51).... 120 42
FORESTPORT—*Christ Church S. S.**:
  Gen. 4 03
GREENE—*Zion S. S.**: Gen.,......... 80 00
HAMILTON—*St. Thomas's*: Gen. (of
  which S. S.,* $18.02)............. 45 07
HATT'S CORNERS—*Calvary*: Gen. (of
  which S. S.,* $1.63)............. 5 38
HOLLAND PATENT—*St. Paul's S. S.**:
  Gen. 2 80
HOMER—*Calvary S. S.**: Gen.......... 15 50
HORSEHEADS—*St. Matthew's*: Gen. (of
  which S. S.,* $4.92)............. 9 52
INTERLAKEN—*St. John's*: Gen. (of
  which S. S.,* 80 cts.)............ 10 13
ITHACA—*St. John's*: Gen.......:..... 300 00
JORDAN—*Christ Church*: Gen. (of
  which S. S.,* $14.46)............ 19 58
KENDAIA—*St. Andrew's S. S.**: Gen.. 1 38
LA FARGEVILLE—*St. Paul's S. S.**:
  Gen. 5 00
LOWVILLE—*Trinity Church S. S.**:
  Gen. 5 00
MARCELLUS—*St. John's S. S.**: Gen.. 27 81
MANLIUS—*St. John's Boys S. S.**: Gen. 25 00
McDONOUGH—*Calvary S. S.**: Gen..:. 6 66
McLEAN—*Zion*: Gen............. 5 00
MILLPORT—*St. Mark's*: Dom. and Frn.
  (of which S. S.,* $3.18).......... 9 24
MEMPHIS—*Emmanuel Church S. S.**:
  Gen. 1 38
MORAVIA—*St. Matthew's*: Gen. (of
  which S. S.,* $2.83)............. 42 83
NEW BERLIN—*St. Andrew's*: Gen..... 93 00
NEW HARTFORD—*St. Stephen's*: Gen.
  (of which S. S.,* $14)............ 35 04
ONONDAGA—*Church of the Good Shep-
herd*: Indian (of which S. S.,*
  95 cts.)......................... 1 50
OWEGO—*St. Paul's*: Dom. (of which
  "A Member," $25), $37; "A Mem-
ber," Frn., $25; Gen. (of which
  S. S.,* $26.10), $47.10............ 109 10
OXFORD—*St. Paul's*: Gen. (of which
  S. S.,* $80.35)................... 146 60
PARIS HILL—*St. Paul's S. S.**: Gen.. 1 00
PHOENIX—*St. John's S. S.**: Gen..... 4 86
PORT LEYDEN—*St. Mark's S. S.**: Gen. 5 20
REDWOOD—*St. Peter's*: Gen. (of which
  S. S.,* $14)..................... 35 00
ROME—*Zion*: Gen. (of which S. S.*
  $45.20).......................... 100 92
ROMULUS—*St. Stephen's S. S.**: Gen. 5 25
SHERBURNE—*Christ Church*: Gen. (of
  which S. S.,* $39.58)............. 109 58
SKANEATELES—*St. James's*: Wo. Aux.,
  Sp. for St. John's University Expan-
sion Fund, Shanghai, $2; S. S.,*
  Gen., $35......................... 37 00
SMITHBORO—*Emmanuel Church S. S.**:
  Gen. 1 00
SYRACUSE—*All Saints**: Indian, $11.80;
  Gen., $11.30...................... 23 10
Calvary S. S.*: Gen............. 18 91
Grace: Dom., 65 cts.; Frn., 85 cts.;
  Gen., $6.10....................... 7 66
St. Paul's S. S.*: Gen............ 87 76
  "Josephine, Eleanor and Douglas,"
  S. S.,* Gen....................... 2 34
THERESA—*St. James's*: Gen......... 15 00
TRUMANSBURG—*Epiphany S. S.**: Gen. 2 20
UTICA—*Calvary S. S.**: Gen......... 85 00
Holy Cross S. S.*: Gen............ 56 03
St. Andrew's: Dom., $5; Frn., $8.30;

Gen. (of which S. S.,* $22.50),
  $46.50
St. George's: Gen. (of which S. S.,
  $21.48)
Trinity Church: Gen.
WATERTOWN—*St. Paul's*: Wo. Aux.,
  Sp. for Bishop Rowe, Alaska........
Trinity Church S. S.*: "Bishop Brewer
  Graduate" scholarship, South Da-
kota, $60; "Bishop Huntington"
  scholarship, Girls' Training Insti-
tute, Africa, $25; "Rev. Dr. Olin
  Memorial" scholarship, St. John's
  University, Shanghai, $70; "W. H.
  Moore" scholarship, St. Margaret's
  School, Tokyo, $50...............
WATERVILLE—*Grace S. S.**: Gen....
WHITNEY'S POINT—*Grace*: Gen.....
WILLARD—*Christ Church*: Gen. (of
  S. S.,* $11.08)..................
WINDSOR—*Zion S. S.**: Gen........
MISCELLANEOUS — Branch Wo. Aux.,
  Third District, Rev. Mr. Gilman's
  work in Changsha, Hankow, $50;
  Sp. for Building Fund of the In-
dustrial School, Cape Mount, Africa,
  $1 ....
  Fifth District, Wo. Aux., Gen......
  Branch Wo. Aux., Fourth District,
  for "Frederic Dan Huntington"
  scholarship, Cuttington Collegiate
  and Divinity-school, Africa, $50;
  Gen., $137.50....................
  Branch Wo. Aux., Sp. for Rev. Dr.
  Correll, Kyoto, $100; Second Dis-
trict, Sp. for Chinese baby, Sophie,
  St. Mary's Orphanage, Shanghai,
  $30; Third District, Sp. for Chi-
nese baby, Sylvia, St. Mary's Orphanage, Shanghai, $30...........

Chicago

Ap. $4,592.72; Sp. $31.59

BATAVIA—*Calvary S. S.**: Gen......
BELVIDERE—*Trinity Church S. S.**:
  Gen., $26.25; Branch Wo. Aux., Sp.
  for Dr. Myers, Shanghai, $6.59....
BERWYN—*St. Michael and All Angels'
  S. S.**: Gen.....................
CHICAGO—*All Angels** (Deaf-mutes):
  Gen...........................
Advent: Gen., $38.33; S. S.,* Frn.,
  $4.26
All Saints' S. S.* (Pullman): Dom...
Annunciation S. S.*: Gen.........
Ascension: Dom., $10.25; Frn., $10...
Atonement: Wo. Aux., Sp. for Rev. R.
  W. Andrews, Tokyo...............
Christ Church: Wo. Aux., Gen......
Epiphany: Wo. Aux., "Bishop Theodore
  N. Morrison" scholarship, Girls'
  Training Institute, West Africa,
  $25; S. S.,* Gen., $21.04.........
Church of the Good Shepherd: Gen....
Grace: Gen. (of which Wo. Aux.,
  $150), $168.67; Dom. and Frn.,
  $28.70
Holy Trinity Church: Frn...........
Church of Our Saviour: Colored,
  $6.39; Gen. (of which S. S.,*
  $52.57), $56.92..................
Church of the Redeemer: Dom.,
  $144.95; Frn., $149.35; Gen. (of
  which S. S.,* $78.25, Wo. Aux., $9),
  $87.25
St. Alban's (Norwood Park): Gen. (of
  which S. S.,* $3.50).............
St. Barnabas's S. S.*: Gen........
St. Bartholomew's: Wo. Aux., Gen...
St. Chrysostom's: Frn., $52.27; Wo.
  Aux., Gen., $2...................
St. Edmund's S. S.*: Gen.........
St. Elizabeth's S. S.* (Chicago Lawn):
  Dom. and Frn...................
St. James's: Wo. Aux., Gen., $20;
  "Julia Newbold Vibbert" scholarship,

Seymour (of which S. S.,* $8.89),
Gen. 13 89
COLORADO CITY—*Church of the Good
Shepherd S. S.**: Gen.............. 6 50
COLORADO SPRINGS—*St. Stephen's S.
S.**: Gen 60 21
COMO—*St. Mary's S. S.**: Gen........ 2 50
CRIPPLE CREEK—*St. Andrew's S. S.**:
Gen. 12 45
DENVER—*Ascension Memorial S. S.**:
Gen. 3 00
St. Barnabas's: Frn................. 20 13
St. John's Cathedral: Gen.......... 403 00
St. Mark's: St. Agnes's Branch, Junior
Aux., Gen......................... 10 00
St. Paul's S. S.**: Gen.............. 5 00
St. Peter's S. S.**: Gen............. 10 00
Trinity Memorial: Dom. and Frn..... 34 31
EVERGREEN—*Transfiguration S. S.**:
Gen. 12 25
FLORENCE—*St. Alban's S. S.**: Dom.
and Frn........................... 5 50
FORT COLLINS—*St. Luke's S. S.**: Gen. 42 00
FORT LUPTON—*St. Andrew's S. S.**:
Gen. 2 13
FORT MORGAN—*St. Paul's S. S.**: Gen. 8 63
GEORGETOWN—*Grace S. S.**: Gen..... 3 01
GREELEY—*Trinity Church S. S.**: Gen. 10 00
HUGO—*St. Michael's S. S.**: Gen..... 3 45
LAS ANIMAS—*Church of the Messiah
S. S.**: Gen...................... 3 32
LITTLETON—*St. Paul's S. S.**: Gen... 6 00
LONGMONT—*St. Stephen's S. S.**: Gen. 11 86
MANITOU—*St. Andrew's S. S.**: Dom.. 5 00
PUEBLO—*Ascension S. S.**: Gen...... 10 00
St. James's S. S.**: Sp. for St. Paul's
College Building Fund, Tokyo, $1;
Sp. for Rev. J. A. Staunton, Juniors'
work in Sagada, Philippine Islands,
$6.35 .... 7 35

Connecticut

Ap. $5,568.69; *Sp.* $1,130.85

ANSONIA—*Christ Church*: Gen....... 180 00
BANTAM—*St. Paul's*: Gen........... 8 38
BETHEL—*St. Thomas's*: $45.44, "A
Friend of Missions," $10, Gen...... 55 44
BRANFORD—*Trinity Church*: Gen.... 37 56
BRIDGEPORT—*Nativity S. S.**: Gen.... 2 15
St. George's S. S.**: Gen............ 13 00
St. John's: "Glover, Sanford Memor-
ial" scholarship, St. Margaret's
School, Tokyo..................... 12 50
St. Luke's: $17, S. S.,* $20.89, Gen.. 37 89
BRISTOL—*Trinity Church*: Dom. and
Frn............................... 60 00
BROAD BROOK—*Grace S. S.**: Gen.... 14 00
BROOKFIELD—*St. Paul's*: Gen....... 37 69
CHESHIRE—*St. Peter's*: Gen......... 11 00
CHESTER—*St. Luke's Mission S. S.**:
Gen. 4 42
COLCHESTER—*Calvary*: Gen.......... 20 00
DANBURY—*St. James's*: $211, Parish
House Chapter, $21, Gen.......... 282 00
DANIELSON—*St. Alban's S. S.**: Gen.. 11 50
DARIEN—*St. Luke's*: Gen........... 20 00
DERBY—*St. James's*: Gen........... 176 17
EAST HADDAM—Mrs. F. C. H. Wendel,
Bishop Restarick's work, Honolulu,
$1; Sp. for Priory School, Honolulu,
$1; Rev. Dr. F. C. H. Wendel, Bish-
op Restarick's work, Honolulu, $1. 3 00
EAST HARTFORD—*St. John's*: Sp. for
Dr. Mary V. Glenton's hospital work,
Wuchang, Hankow, $10; Sp. for
Miss Elizabeth Woods's library work,
Wuchang, Hankow, $10; Sp. for
Mrs. Roots's work for women at
Hankow, $34.60................... 54 60
EAST NORWALK—*Christ Church*: Gen.,
$6.74; S. S.,* Frn., $8.36......... 15 10
FAIRFIELD—*St. Paul's*: Gen........ 29 40
GALES FERRY—Mrs. H. S. Bisbing, Sp.
for St. John's-in-the-Wilderness, Al-
lakaket, Alaska................... 4 00
GREENWICH — *Christ Church*: Dom.,

$600; Frn., $175................   775 00
Chapel Rosemary Hall: Gen..........   42 00
HARTFORD — *Christ Church:* Dom.,
$115.24; Frn., $291.73; Gen.,
$23.09; Mrs. G. W. Russell, $100,
Miss A. Tuttle, $5, Mrs. Johnson, $5,
Miss A. Williams, $25, Sp. for
Shanghai Catechist School Land and
Building Fund..................   565 06
Church of the Good Shepherd: Gen.
(of which "A Member," $10), $510;
"A. S. S. Class," Sp. for work of
Mrs. Roots, Hankow, $26..........   536 00
Grace Chapel: Dom. and Frn........   25 00
St. Monica's Mission: Gen..........   3 80
St. Thomas's: Gen..................   1 52
Trinity Church: Gen................   139 75
IVORYTON—*All Saints' S. S.*:* Gen....   20 00
KILLINGWORTH — *Emmanuel Church:*
$4, S. S.,* $3, Gen..............   7 00
LIME ROCK—*Trinity Church:* Gen....   123 04
MARBLEDALE—*St. Andrew's:* Gen.....   39 12
MERIDEN—*St. Andrew's:* Frn., $16.50;
Gen., $421.42..................   437 92
MIDDLE HADDAM—*Christ Church S.
S.*:* Gen.....................   2 50
St. John's Chapel: $2, S. S.,* $7.06,
Gen. 9 06
MIDDLETOWN — *Berkeley Divinity-
school:* Sp. for Shanghai Catechist
School Land and Building Fund....   5 00
Holy Trinity Church: Colored, $36.30;
Dom., $5.50; Frn., $14.76; Gen.,
$12.94 ....   69 50
MILFORD—*St. Peter's:* Gen..........   4 00
MILTON—*Trinity Church:* Gen........   20 56
MONROE—*St. Peter's:* Dom...........   4 48
NEW HAVEN—*Christ Church:* Sp. for
St. Mary's Building Fund, Kyoto...   28 25
Grace: $19.81, S. S.,* $25.70, Gen....   45 51
St. Paul's: Gen., $101; Sp. for Rev.
Irvin H. Correll, Kyoto, $5; Paro-
chial School, Sp. for St. Mary's,
Kyoto, $15...................   121 00
Trinity Church: Sp. for St. Mary's
Building Fund, Kyoto............   12 00
Branch Wo. Aux., Sp. for St. Mary's
Building Fund, Kyoto............   9 00
Mrs. Bishop, $50, Mrs. White, $10,
Sp. for St. Mary's Building Fund,
Kyoto 60 00
S. A. Eddy, Sp. for Church Exten-
sion Fund, Porto Rico...........   5 00
NEW LONDON—*St. James's:* Gen.,
$219.75; Wo. Aux., Sp. for Bishop
Partridge's work, Kyoto, $50......   269 75
NEWTOWN—*Trinity Church:* Frn.....   42 02
NICHOLS—*Trinity Church S. S.*:* Gen.   9 17
NORTH GUILFORD—*St. John's:* Dom.
and Frn......................   5 00
NORTH HAVEN—*St. John's:* Gen.....   179 69
OAKVILLE—*All Saints':* Gen.........   42 44
PINE MEADOW—*St. John's:* Dom. and
Frn. 85 00
PLAINVILLE—*Church of Our Saviour:*
Gen. 12 00
PLYMOUTH—*St. Peter's:* Gen........   23 17
PONSETT—*St. James's:* Gen..........   3 00
PUTNAM—*St. Philip's S. S.*:* Gen....   7 00
REDDING—*Christ Church S. S.*:* Gen..   10 72
SALISBURY—*St. John's:* Gen.........   158 82
SEYMOUR—*Trinity Church:* $22.80, S.
S.,* $18.19, Gen...............   40 99
SHELTON—*Church of the Good Shep-
herd:* Gen....................   116 47
SOUTH MANCHESTER—*St. Mary's:* Gen.   50 00
SOUTH NORWALK — *Trinity Church:*
$19.35, S. S.,* $55.85, Gen......   75 20
STAFFORD SPRINGS—*Grace:* Gen.....   43 00
STAMFORD—*St. John's:* Gen., $150;
Sp. for Bishop Brent, Philippine
Islands, $25; Sp. for Bishop Rowe,
Alaska, $71; Sp. for Miss Mead,
Tokyo, $25...................   271 00
Miss E. J. Mead, Sp. for books for
library, Wuchang, Hankow........   50 00

STONINGTON—*Calvary:* $19, S. S.,*
$25.30, Gen...................
TARIFFVILLE—*Trinity Church S. S.*:*
Gen. ....
TERRYVILLE—"A mite to aid the cause
of Christ," Gen................
WASHINGTON—*St. John's:* Gen.......
WATERBURY—*St. John's:* Frn.......
WATERTOWN—*Christ Church:* Gen....
WEST HARTFORD—Miss Edith Beach,
Sp. for Shanghai Catechist School
Land and Building Fund..........
WEST HAVEN—*Christ Church:* Gen...
WESTON—*Emmanuel Church S. S.*:*
Gen. ....
WETHERSFIELD—*Trinity Church:* Gen..
WILLIMANTIC—*St. Paul's:* $13.46, S.
S.,* $8.60, Gen................
WILTON—*St. Matthew's:* Gen.......
WINDHAM—*St. Paul's:* $1.55, S. S.,*
$5.20, Gen....................
WINDSOR—*Grace:* Frn..............
YALESVILLE—*St. John the Evangel-
ist's S. S.*:* Indian, South Dakota..
MISCELLANEOUS—"A Friend," from St.
Leger Fund, Sp. for Bishop Thomas's
Hospital, Wyoming..............
Archdeaconry of New Haven, Junior
Aux., Sp. for St. Elizabeth's Build-
ing Fund, Shanghai..............

Dallas

Ap. $868.14; Sp. $16.15

ABILENE—*Heavenly Rest S. S.*:* Gen.
AMARILLO—*St. Andrew's S. S.*:* Gen..
BAIRD—*Holy Cross S. S.*:* Gen......
BIG SPRING—*St. Mary's S. S.*:* Gen..
BONHAM—*Trinity Church:* Gen., $20;
S. S.,* St. James's Hospital, An-
king, Hankow, $40.............
BROWNWOOD—*St. John's S. S.*:* Gen..
CLARENDON—*St. John the Baptist's:*
$14.56, S. S.,* $18.20, Gen......
COLORADO—*All Saints' S. S.*:* Gen..
CORSICANA—*St. John's S. S.*:* Dom.
DALLAS—*Incarnation S. S.*:* Gen....
St. Matthew's Cathedral: $50, S. S.,*
$200, Gen....................
DENISON—*St. Luke's S. S.*:* Gen.
(1909-1910) ....
FORNEY—*Holy Trinity Church S. S.*:*
Sp. for Archdeacon Stuck's work,
Alaska, $4.69; Gen., $4.69.......
FORT WORTH—*St. Andrew's:* Young
Wo. Aux., Gen., $10; S. S.,* Sp. for
St. Paul's College, Tokyo, $11.46...
GRAHAM—*Church of the Holy Spirit:*
Gen. ....
GREENVILLE—*St. Paul's S. S.*:* Dom.,
$3.50; Frn., $3.65..............
HAMILTON—*St. Mary's S. S.*:* Gen..
McKINNEY—*St. Peter's S. S.*:* Gen...
MINERAL WELLS—*Church of the Good
Shepherd S. S.*:* Gen...........
PARIS—*Holy Cross S. S.*:* Gen......
SHERMAN—*St. Stephen's:* $25.66, S.
S.,* $28.84, Gen...............
TEXARKANA—*St. James's:* Junior Aux.,
$5, S. S.,* $37.22, Gen.........
WICHITA FALLS—*Church of the Good
Shepherd S. S.*:* Gen...........

Delaware

Ap. $625.12

BRANDYWINE HUNDRED—*Grace:* Gen..
CHRISTIANA HUNDRED—*Christ Church:*
Wo. Aux., $10, S. S.,* $31.31, Gen..
CLAYMONT—*Ascension:* Gen........
CLAYTON—*Trinity Church S. S.*:* Gen..
DELAWARE CITY—*Christ Church:* Wo.
Aux., Gen....................
GEORGETOWN—*St. Paul's S. S.*:* Gen..
INDIAN RIVER—*St. George's:* Gen.....
LEWES—*St. Peter's:* Dom. and Frn...

23 64
65 52
14 66
11 51
19 21
26 20
65 00
2 60
25 00
77 00
110 00
4 00
50 00
8 59
2 21
7 00
17 35
12 17
22 14
80 00
22 75
8 25
19 25
47 89
50 00
4 05
20 00
15 77
7 00
24 00
8 72
59 01
10 00
3 36
6 00
1 67
1 00
8 40
12 00
2 94
28 35
3 50
15 00
3 10
22 50
5 00
17 12
50 76
1 65
6 02

BONNERTON—*St. John's*: $6, S. S.,* $12.58, Gen. 18 58
CAMDEN—*St. Joseph's S. S.*: Gen. 1 60
CLINTON—*St. Paul's*: Gen. 15 00
COLUMBIA—*St. Andrew's S. S.*: Gen. 5 00
CRESWELL—*St. David's*: Wo. Aux., Gen. 1 00
EDENTON—*St. Paul's*: Gen. (of which Junior Aux., $7.29, S. S.,* $71.87), $129.16; Sp. for Asheville, $9.23... 138 39
St. John the Evangelist's: $5, S. S.,* $3.77, Gen. 8 77
EDWARD—*Church of the Redeemer*: Gen. 5 00
ELIZABETH CITY—*Christ Church*: $35, S. S.,* $122, Gen. 157 00
FARMVILLE—*Emmanuel Church S. S.*: Dom. 10 00
FAYETTEVILLE — *St. John's*: Gen., $77.73; Wo. Aux., Sp. for St. Paul's College, Tokyo, $5. .... 82 73
St. Joseph's: Gen., $13.30; Sp. for St. Paul's College, Tokyo, 45 cts... 13 75
GATESVILLE—*St. Mary's*: Junior Aux., $1.44, S. S.,* $3.78, Gen. 5 22
GOLDSBORO—*St. Stephen's*: $25, Wo. Aux., $5, Gen. 30 00
GREENVILLE—*St. Andrew's*: Gen...... 2 42
St. Paul's: $20, S. S.,* $38.65, Gen.. 58 65
HAMILTON—*St. Martin's*: $10, S. S.,* $20, Gen. 30 00
HERTFORD — *Holy Trinity Church*: Gen., $25; S. S.,* Gen., $28; Sp. for Bishop Horner, Asheville, $28...... 81 00
HOPE MILLS—*Christ Church*: Gen.... 5 00
JESSAMA—*Zion*: Gen. 19 28
St. Mary's: Gen. 4 00
KINSTON—*St. Augustine's S. S.*: Gen. 14 50
LAKE WACCAMAW—*S. S.*: Gen....... 1 00
LENOIR Co.—*Holy Innocents'*: $4.20, S. S.,* $8, Gen................. 12 20
NEW BERNE—*Christ Church*: $100, Wo. Aux., $5, S. S.,* $76.60, Gen.. 181 60
St. Cyprian's: $7.50, S. S.,* $5, Gen. 12 50
PITT Co.—*St. John's*: Gen.......... 20 00
PLYMOUTH—*Grace*: $10, Wo. Aux., $1, S. S.,* $25, Gen. 36 00
ROPER—*St. Luke's*: $3, S. S.,* $11, Gen. 14 00
ROXOBEL—*St. Mark's*: Junior Aux., $2.50, S. S.,* $7.60, Gen........... 10 10
SCUPPERNONG—*St. David's*: $3.40, S. S.,* $12.07, Gen. 15 47
SOUTHPORT—*St. Philip's S. S.*: Gen. 2 30
SUNBURY—*St. Peter's S. S.*: Gen.... 2 00
TRENTON—*Grace S. S.*: Gen........ 1 34
VANCEBORO—*St. Paul's*: Gen....... 5 00
WASHINGTON — *St. Peter's*: $147.68, Wo. Aux., $2, S. S.,* $180, Gen.... 329 68
St. Paul's: Gen................... 4 10
Union S. S.: Gen. 1 83
WILLIAMSTON — *Advent*: Deaf and Dumb, $1.50; Gen. (of which Wo. Aux., $5, S. S.,* $63.61), $83.13... 84 63
St. Andrew's S. S.: China.......... 5 30
WILMINGTON—*Church of the Good Shepherd*: Wo. Aux., Seminole Indians, Southern Florida, $1; St. Paul's College, Tokyo, $2; Gen., $5. 8 00
St. James's: Gen. (of which Guild, $25, Wo. Aux., $75.10, S. S.,* $359.87), $734.97; Sp. for Asheville, 25 cts.; Mrs. Walter L. Passley, Indian, $5; Gen., $5................. 745 22
St. John's: Wo. Aux., $10, S. S.* $40, Gen. 50 00
St. Paul's: $25, S. S.,* $10.66, Gen.. 35 66
"A Friend," Gen.................. 60
WINDSOR—*St. Thomas's S. S.*: Gen.. 29 34
WINTERVILLE—*St. Luke's*: Wo. Aux., Sp. for St. Paul's College, Tokyo, $2; S. S.,* Gen., $30.60.............. 32 60
WINTON—*St. John's*: Wo. Aux., $2, S. S.,* $1, Gen................... 3 00
WOODVILLE—*Grace S. S.*: Gen..... 10 00
YEATESVILLE—*St. Matthew's S. S.*: Gen. 2 02

Easton

Ap. $526.29

CAROLINE Co.—*Christ Church S. S.**
(Denton) : Gen.................. 7 36
Holy Trinity Church S. S.* (Greens-
boro) : Gen.................. 17 00
DORCHESTER Co.—*Christ Church
S. S.** (Cambridge) : Gen........ 32 58
KENT Co.—*Emmanuel Church S. S.**
(Chestertown) : Gen........... 20 19
St. Clement's (Massey) : $9.65, S. S.,*
$14.65, Gen................. 24 30
Holy Cross (Millington) : $13.62, S. S.,*
$8.02, Gen................. 21 64
(Shrewsbury) — Branch Wo. Aux.,
Alaska 50 00
QUEEN ANNE Co.—*St. Luke's Parish*
(Church Hill) : Gen.......... 35 50
St. Paul's Parish (Centreville) : Gen.. 57 35
Wye Parish S. S.* (Queenstown) :
Gen. 20 69
SOMERSET Co.—*St. Andrew's S. S.**
(Princess Anne) : Gen.......... 43 17
St. Bartholomew's Parish (Crisfield) :
Gen. 12 50
St. Stephen's (Upper Fairmount) ⎰
St. Mark's (Kingston) ⎱ Gen.. 3 64
St. Mark's S. S.* : Gen. (additional).. 27
TALBOT Co.—*Christ Church S. S.**
(Easton) : Day-school, Shasi, Han-
kow, $20 ; Gen., $75.64........ 95 64
All Faith's Chapel S. S.* (Tunis) :
Gen. 6 67
Good Shepherd Chapel S. S.* (Cor-
dova) : Gen................ 4 83
All Saints' S. S.* (Near Easton) ∹ Gen. 17 34
Holy Trinity Church S. S.* (Oxford) :
Gen. 25 00
WICOMICO Co.—*St. Peter's S. S.** : Gen. 26 02
WORCESTER Co.—*Holy Cross Chapel
S. S.** (Stockton) : Dom.......... 4 60

Florida

Ap. $217.53 ; *Sp.* $16.53

APALACHICOLA—*Trinity Church S. S.** :
Gen. 25 00
FERNANDINA—*St. Peter's S. S.** : Gen.. 20 36
GAINESVILLE — *Holy Trinity Church
S. S.** : Gen................ 25 93
JACKSONVILLE—*St. Stephen's S. S.** :
Gen. 7 05
MONTICELLO—*Christ Church* : Gen..... 10 00
PALATKA—*St. Mary's S. S.** : Gen..... 1 00
PENSACOLA—*St. Katherine's S. S.** :
Gen. 10 00
ST. AUGUSTINE—*Trinity Church* : Gen.,
$110 ; S. S.,* Sp. for Rev. C. M.
Sturges, Cuba, $16.53.......... 126 53
ST. NICHOLAS—*Emmanuel Church S.
S.** ; Gen................. 3 19
WARRINGTON—*St. John's* : Gen........ 5 00

Fond du Lac

Ap. $305.79

ALGOMA—*St. Agnes's S. S.** : Gen.... 4 50
ANTIGO—*St. Ambrose's S. S.** : Gen.. 5 25
ASHLAND—*St. Andrew's S. S.** : Gen.. 12 63
BIG SUAMICO—*St. Paul's S. S.** : Gen.. 3 33
FOND DU LAC—*St. Michael's S. S.**
(North) : Gen................ 10 60
St. Paul's : Gen.............. 53 09
GREEN BAY—*Christ Church S. S.** :
Dom. 33 00
JACKSONPORT—*Holy Trinity Church
S. S.** : Gen................ 4 32
MANITOWOC—*St. James's* : Dom., $15 ;
S. S.,* Gen., $10............ 25 00
MARSHFIELD—*St. Alban's S. S.** : Gen.. 10 85
MEDFORD—*St. Mary's* : Gen......... 6 00
MOSINEE—*St. James's S. S.** : Gen.... 4 11
ONEIDA—*Hobart* : $32, S. S.* $3, Gen.. 35 00
OSHKOSH—*Christ Church S. S.** :
Dom., $2 ; Frn., $2........... 4 00
PLYMOUTH—*St. Paul's S. S.** : Gen... 6 21

SHEBOYGAN FALLS—*St. Peter's* : $23.51,
S. S., $18.37, Gen............
WAUPACA—*St. Mark's S. S.** : Gen....
WAUPUN—*Trinity Church S. S.** :
Gen. ....
WESTBORO—*St. Philip's* : Gen........
MISCELLANEOUS—Wo. Aux., Gen......

Georgia

Ap. $449.90 ; *Sp.* $33.10

ALBANY—*St. John's S. S.** : Gen......
AMERICUS—*Calvary S. S.** : Gen.....
AUGUSTA—*Atonement* : $75, S. S.,*
$35, Gen..................
Church of the Good Shepherd S. S.* :
Gen. ....
St. Paul's : Dom., $50 ; Frn., $50....
Wo. Aux., Sp. for premium on life
insurance of Dr. Boone........
BRUNSWICK—*St. Mark's S. S.** : Gen..
CORDELE—*Christ Church S. S.** : Frn..
DOUGLAS—*St. Andrew's S. S.** : Gen..
PENNICK—*Church of the Good Shep-
herd* : $2, S. S.,* $5, Gen......
SAVANNAH—*St. Andrew's S. S.** Gen..
St. Stephen's S. S.* : Gen.........
THOMASVILLE—*Church of the Good
Shepherd* : $6, S. S.,* $6, Gen....
St. Thomas's : Junior Aux., Rev.
Robb White's salary, Baguio, Phil-
ippine Islands, $3 ; St. Luke's Hos-
pital, Shanghai, $3 ; Sp. for "Sister
Katherine" scholarship, Guantanamo,
Cuba, $2 ; Sp. for Holy Trinity Or-
phanage, Tokyo, $2 ; Sp. for Rev.
Robert Wilson, Shanghai, $4.......

Harrisburg

Ap. $1,373.34 ; *Sp.* $38.15

BELLEFONTE—*St. John's* : Dom.......
BERWICK—*Christ Church* : Gen.......
BLOOMSBURG—*St. Paul's S. S.** : Gen..
BROOKLAND—*All Saint's* : $24.07, S. S.,
96 cts., Gen................
CARLISLE—*St. John's* : Gen..........
CENTRALIA — *Holy Trinity Church* :
Gen. ....
CHURCHTOWN—*Bangor* : Gen.........
COUDERSPORT—*Christ Church S. S.** :
Gen. ....
DANVILLE—*Christ Memorial Church* :
Gen. ....
GALETON—*Church of the Good Shep-
herd S. S.** : Gen............
LANCASTER—*St. James's* : Dom. and
Frn., $10.57 ; Wo. Aux., Sp. toward
Miss Elizabeth Newbold's organ,
Tokyo, $2 ; S. S.,* Gen., $281.93....
St. John's : Junior Aux., Sp. for St.
Paul's College, Tokyo, $2 ; Sp. for
"Little Mary" scholarship, St.
Mary's - on - the-Mountain, Sewanee,
Tennessee, $2 ; S. S.,* Gen., $128.87.
LOCK HAVEN—*St. Paul's* : Gen. (of
which S. S.,* $12.78), $57.79 ; Sp.
for St. Paul's College, Tokyo,
$4.15
LYKENS—*Christ Church* : Gen.......
MILTON—*Christ Church* : Gen........
MONTOURSVILLE—*Church of Our Saviour
S. S.** : Gen................
MOUNT CARMEL—*St. Stephen's* : Dom.,
$28.07 ; S. S.,* Gen., $5.37......
MUNCY—*St. James's* : Frn., $7.75 ;
S. S.,* Gen., $10.20..........
NEWPORT—*Nativity* : Sp. for Bishop of
Asheville
PHILIPSBURG—*St. Paul's* : $35, S. S.,*
$25.94, Gen................
SELINGSGROVE—*All Saints' S. S.** :
Gen. ....
SHAMOKIN—*Trinity Church* : $8.04,
S. S.,* $55.49, Gen...........
SHIPPENSBURG—*St. Andrew's* : $9.85,
S. S.,* $1, Gen...............

	GLENWOOD—*St. John's S. S.**: Gen... 2 00
6 10	HARLAN—*St. Paul's S. S.**: Gen...... 20 00
	INDEPENDENCE—*St. James's*: $11.10, S.
1 00	S.,* $32.30, Gen............... 43 40
	IOWA CITY—*Trinity Church*: Wo. Aux.,
20 00	Gen., 50 cts.; S. S.,* Sp. for Bishop
	Brown's Building Fund, Arkansas,
17 02	$5; Dom., $14.98; Frn., $14.97.... 35 45
7 46	IOWA FALLS—*St. Matthew's S. S.**:
	Gen. 3 25
17 25	KEOKUK—*St. John's S. S.**: Gen..... 24 93
	LE MARS—*St. George's S. S.**: Gen... 2 88
	MOOAR—*St. Andrew's S. S.**: Gen.... 6 94
	MT. PLEASANT—*St. Michael's*: $2.75,
	S. S.,* $14.47, Gen............. 17 22.
14 00	MUSCATINE—*Trinity Church S. S.**:
21 04	Gen. 11 07
	NEWTON—*St. Stephen's*: Gen....... 2 95
	OTTUMWA—*Trinity Church*: Gen..... 184 20
10 00	POPEJOY—*Loving Service Society S.
	S.**: Gen................... 3 00
230 00	SIOUX CITY—*St. Thomas's*: Dom., $75;
	S. S.,* Dom. and Frn., $45........ 120 00
	SPENCER—*St. Stephen's S. S.**: Gen.. 6 43
	WATERLOO — *Christ Church*: $20.02,
5 30	S. S.,* $29, Gen............... 49 02

Kansas
Ap. $615.24

8 85	S.*: Gen....................
3 10	ARKANSAS CITY—*Trinity Church S.
6 33	S.*: Gen.................... 9 00
55 00	ATCHISON—*Trinity Church S. S.**: Gen 223 27
22 70	BLUE RAPIDS—*St. Mark's*: $5.25, S.
	S.,* $9.60, Gen............... 14 85
48 15	BURLINGTON—*Ascension S. S.**: Gen... 8 00
9 56	CLAY CENTRE—*St. Paul's S. S.**: Gen. 9 00
21 00	COFFEYVILLE—*St. Paul's*: "Young Peo-
	ple," hospital work, Tokyo and
28 14	Kyoto, $2.90; Gen., $8.......... 10 90
	DWIGHT—*St. Paul's*: $3, S. S.,* $1.25,
	Gen. 4 25
83 11	ELGIN—*Grace*: 75 cts., S. S.,* $1.67,
	Gen. 2 42
45 97	FORT LEAVENWORTH—Children's,* Gen. 23 17
18 28	GALENA—*St. Mary's S. S.**: Gen...... 3 65
4 10	GIRARD—*St. John's S. S.**: Gen...... 14 78
32 29	HIAWATHA—*St. John's S. S.**: Gen... 50 00
	HOLTON—*St. Thomas's S. S.**: Gen... 2 85
	IRVING—*Trinity Church*: $6.25, S. S.,*
70 91	$4, Gen..................... 10 25
	IOLA—*St. Timothy's S. S.**: Gen..... 3 00
6 30	JUNCTION CITY—*Covenant S. S.**:
1 20	Dom. 7 00
	KANSAS CITY—*St. Peter's S. S.**: Gen. 6 00
10 00	LAWRENCE—*Trinity Church S. S.**:
36 00	Gen. 10 71
	MANHATTAN—*St. Paul's S. S.**: Gen.. 9 00
	NEWTON—*St. Matthew's S. S.**: Gen.. 22 00
1 67	OLATHE—*Emmanuel Church S. S.**:
2 47	Gen. 5 00
	PITTSBURG—*St. Peter's S. S.**: Gen... 12 17
33 50	TOPEKA—*Calvary S. S.**: Gen....... 2 00
6 70	*Church of the Good Shepherd S. S.**:
	Gen. 1 00
69 00	*Grace S. S.*: South Dakota.......... 4 50
2 10	*St. Simon's S. S.**: Gen.......... 2 43
	WAKEFIELD—*St. George's S. S.**: Gen. 9 01
77 25	*St. John's S. 'S.**: Gen............ 5 85
7 50	WAMEGO—*St. Luke's S. S.**: Gen..... 8 65
	WETMORE—*S. S.**: Gen............ 9 00
50 52	WICHITA—*All Saints' S. S.* (West):
23 82	Gen. 2 22
	St. John's S. S.*: Gen.......... 92 50
20 00	*St. Stephen's S. S.**: Gen......... 5 00
	WILLIAMSBURG—*St. Barnabas's S. S.**:
18 55	Gen. 5 00
5 00	WINFIELD—*Grace S. S.**: Gen........ 8 61

Kansas City
Ap. $592.01; *Sp.* $6.71

2 74	BOONVILLE—*Christ Church S. S.**:
	Gen. 10 00
	CARTHAGE—*Grace*: Gen............ 2 00
11 50	CAMERON—*St. John's S. S.**: Gen.... 14 86

INDEPENDENCE—*Trinity Church S. S.**:
Gen. 10 50
KANSAS CITY—*Grace*: Wo. Aux., Gen. 2 00
Grace Hall: Wo. Aux., Indian, $2;
Colored, $2; Sp. for Miss Ridgely's
house, Cape Mount, Africa, $2; Sp.
for Bishop Holly, Haiti, for flood
sufferers, $3...................... 9 00
*St. Augustine's S. S.**: Gen.......... 5 50
St. John's: $40, Junior Aux., $2, S.
S.,* $28, Gen..................... 70 00
St. Mark's: Indian, $2.78; Wo. Aux.,
Gen., $2......................... 4 78
St. Mary's: Wo. Aux., Gen........... 10 00
St. Paul's: Wo. Aux., Gen........... 4 00
Trinity Church: Wo. Aux., $2, S. S.,*
$50, Gen......................... 52 00
LEBANON—*Trinity Church*: Gen...... 15 00
LEXINGTON—*Christ Church S. S.**:
Infant Class, Sp. for St. John's-in-
the-Wilderness, Alaska............ 1 71
MONETT—*St. Stephen's S. S.*: Dom.
and Frn.......................... 2 13
NEVADA—*All Saints' S. S.**: Gen..... 14 61
SEDALIA—*Calvary S. S.**: Gen....... 30 16
SPRINGFIELD—*St. John's S. S.**: Gen.. 19 36
ST. JOSEPH—*Christ Church*: $225, S.
S.,* $74.32, Gen.................. 299 32
St. Matthias's: Gen................. 5 00
*St. Paul's S. S.**: Gen.............. 12 29
WEST PLAINS—*All Saints'*: Junior
Aux., Gen........................ 5 00

Kentucky

Ap. $1,773.88

ANCHORAGE—*St. Luke's*: Through Wo.
Aux., $12, S. S.,* $1.45, Gen..... 13 45
BOWLING GREEN—*Christ Church*: $36,
S. S.,* $31.14, Gen............... 67 14
COLUMBUS—*Christ Church S. S.**:
Gen. 3 72
ELIZABETHTOWN—*Christ Church*: $6,
S. S.,* $16.65, Gen............... 22 65
FULTON—*Trinity Church*: Gen....... 11 00
HENDERSON—*St. Paul's S. S.**; Gen.. 88 50
HICKMAN — *St. Paul's*: Wo. Aux.,
Alaska, $5, S. S.,* $17.32, Gen.... 22 32
HOPKINSVILLE—*Grace*: Wo. Aux., Gen.,
$10; S. S.,* Dom. and Frn., $20.... 30 00
LOUISVILLE—*Advent*: Gen........... 120 00
*All Saints' S. S.**: Dom. and Frn.... 14 00
All Souls': Deaf-Mutes, Gen........ 1 00
Calvary: Gen., $600; S. S.,* Frn.,
$10; "A. B. W. Allen" scholarship,
St. Margaret's School, Tokyo, $40;
"Thomas E. Locke, Jr.," scholar-
ship, St. John's School, Africa, $25;
"Richard L. McCready" scholarship,
Girls' Training Institute, Africa,
$25 .... 700 00
Christ Church: Colored, $12.25; Frn.,
$5; Gen., $40..................... 57 25
Epiphany: Gen.................... 20 75
*Church of Our Merciful Saviour S. S.**:
Gen. 15 00
St. Andrew's: W. A. Robinson, Frn.,
$100; through Wo. Aux., Brazil,
$12.50; S. S.,* Dom., $75; Frn.,
$75 .... 262 50
*St. George's S. S.**: Gen............ 11 00
St. Mark's: Frn., $51.50; Junior Aux.,
Gen., $6; S. S.,* $43.20, Frn...... 100 70
St. Paul's: Charles H. Pettet, "W. F.
Pettet" scholarship, St. John's
School, West Africa, $25; Junior
Aux., Gen., $15................... 40 00
*St. Peter's S. S.**: Gen............. 10 00
St. Thomas's: $57.13, S. S.,* $9.96,
Gen. 67 09
LYNDON—*St. Thomas's*: $5.75, S. S.,*
$13, Frn......................... 18 75
OWENSBORO—*Trinity Church S. S.**:
Gen. 7 00
PADUCAH—*Grace*: Gen.............. 19 60

PEWEE VALLEY—*St. James's*: $10, S.
S.,* $14.15, Gen.................. 10 50
RUSSELLVILLE—*Trinity Church*: $15,
S. S.,* $6.31, Gen................ 2 00
SHELBYVILLE—*St. James's S. S.**: Gen.

Lexington

Ap. $738.18; *Sp.* $5.50

ASHLAND—*Calvary S. S.**: Dom., $8;
Frn., $8.........................
CORBIN—*St. John's S. S.**: Gen......
COVINGTON—*Trinity Church*: $72.74,
S. S.,* $25, Gen..................
CYNTHIANA—*Advent*: Gen..........
DANVILLE—*Trinity Church*: $12.50, S.
S.,* $8.20, Gen..................
FORT THOMAS—*St. Andrew's S. S.**:
Gen. ....
FRANKFORT — *Ascension*: Frn., $50;
Wo. Aux., Sp. for St. Margaret's
School, Tokyo, $5.50; S. S.,* Gen.,
$104 ....
HARRODSBURG—*St. Philip's*: Gen.....
LEXINGTON—*Christ Church*: $137.50,
S. S.,* $157.82, Gen..............
MT. OLIVET—Osborne Children,* Gen..
MAYSVILLE—*Nativity S. S.**: Gen....
NEWPORT—*St. Paul's*: Gen..........
VERSAILLES—*St. John's S. S.**: Gen...

Long Island

Ap. $5,642.20; *Sp.* $1,821.38

ASTORIA—*Church of the Redeemer*:
Gen. (of which S. S.,* $100). $165;
through Wo. Aux., Nevada, $2.....
St. George's: Gen. (of which S. S.,*
$42.09), $77.40; through Wo. Aux.,
Sp. for Bishop Rowe's work, Alaska,
$2 ....
BABYLON—*Christ Church S. S.**: Gen..
BAY SHORE—*St. Peter's S. S.**: Gen..
BRENTWOOD—*Christ Church S. S.**:
Gen. ....
BROOKLYN—*Calvary*: Wo. Aux., Sp.
for Bishop Rowe, Alaska..........
Christ Church (Bay Ridge): Wo. Aux.,
Sp. for Bishop Rowe, Alaska, $5;
S. S.,* $95.25....................
Christ Church (Clinton Street): Wo.
Aux., Bishop Payne Divinity-school,
Southern Virginia, $1; Sp. for St.
Paul's School, Lawrenceville, South-
ern Virginia, $2; Sp. for Bishop
Rowe, Alaska, $12; S. S.,* Gen.,
25 cts...........................
Christ Church (Bedford Avenue): Wo.
Aux., Sp. for St. Paul's School, Law-
renceville, Southern Virginia......
Church of the Good Shepherd: Wo.
Aux., Bishop Payne Divinity-school,
Southern Virginia, $2; Nevada, $6;
Idaho, $3; Sp. for St. Paul's School,
Lawrenceville, Southern Virginia,
$5; Sp. for Rev. Mr. Claiborne's
work, Sewanee, Tennesee, $6; Sp.
for Bishop Rowe, Alaska, $5; Sp. for
Domestic Contingent Fund, $1.....
Grace (Eastern District): Wo. Aux.,
Sp. for sewing teacher's salary, St.
Augustine's School, Raleigh, North
Carolina, $1; Sp. for St. Paul's
School, Lawrenceville, Southern Vir-
ginia, $2.........................
Grace (Heights): Dom., $335; Frn.,
$185; Wo. Aux., Nevada, $5; Idaho,
$5; Gen., $1,352.62; Sp. for Rev. Mr.
Claiborne, Sewanee, Tennessee, $5;
Sp. for Bishop Brent, Philippine Isl-
ands, $50; Sp. for Bishop Paddock,
East Oregon, $25; Sp. for Bishop
Graves, Kearney, $25; Sp. for Bish-
op Rowe, Alaska, $136; Sp. for
Bishop Wells, Spokane, $150; Sp. for

Rowe's white work, Alaska, $5; S. S.,* Gen., $58.60................. 63 60

St. *Matthew's*: Wo. Aux., Sp. for Bishop Rowe's white work, Alaska, $11; S. S.,* Dom., $23.79; Frn., $23.79; Gen., 50 cts..................... 59 08

St. *Mary's*: Dom. and Frn., $19.71; Wo. Aux., Sp. for Bishop Rowe's white work, Alaska, $2............ 21 71

St. *Michael's*: Wo. Aux., Nevada, $1; Sp. for St. Paul's School, Lawrenceville, Southern Virginia, $1; Sp. for Rev. Mr. Claiborne, Sewanee, Tennessee, $2................... 4 00

St. *Paul's* (Flatbush): Wo. Aux., Sp. for St. Paul's School, Lawrenceville, Southern Virginia, $6.42; Sp. for Bishop Rowe's white work, Alaska, $5; Sp. for sewing teacher's salary, St. Augustine's School, Raleigh, North Carolina, $3; Junior Aux., Gen., $20; S. S.,* Gen., $78.18..... 112 60

St. *Peter's S. S.**: Sp. for Bishop Paddock's work, Eastern Oregon, $50; Sp. for Archdeacon Wentworth's work among the mountaineers of Lexington, $100................. 150 00

St. *Philip's*: Wo. Aux., Sp. for St. Paul's School, Lawrenceville, Southern Virginia..................... 2 00

St. *Philip's* (Dyker Heights): Wo. Aux., Bishop Payne Divinity-school, Southern Virginia, $1; Sp. for St. Paul's School, Lawrenceville, Southern Virginia, $2; Sp. for sewing teacher's salary, St. Augustine's School, Raleigh, North Carolina, $2. 5 00

St. *Stephen's*: Gen................... 22 91

Mr. and Mrs. William G. Low, Sp. for St. Mary's Building Fund, Kyoto. 500 00

Wo. Aux., "A Thank-offering," Sp. for Dr. Pott, Shanghai............ 5 00

BROOKLYN MANOR — St. *Matthew's*: Mountaineer's Mission, Tennessee, $5; Gen. (of which S. S.,* $19.67), $24.91 .... 29 91

CENTRAL ISLIP—*Church of the Messiah S. S.**: Gen.................... 8 00

CENTRE MORICHES—St. *John's S. S.**: Gen. 4 25

COLLEGE POINT—St. *Paul's S. S.**: Gen. 29 95

CORONA—*Grace S. S.**: Gen........ 13 64

CREEDMOOR—St. *Andrew's*: $4.50, S. S.,* $11.35, Gen.............. 15 85

EAST HAMPTON—St. *Luke's*: Dom., $28.15; Frn., $77.21; Wo. Aux., "share" in St. Mary's Hall, Shanghai, $50; S. S.,* Gen., $22.58......... 177 94

EAST HAUPPAUGE—St. *Boniface's S. S.**: Gen....................... 3 90

ELMHURST—St. *James's*: Wo. Aux., Bishop Payne Divinity-school, Southern Virginia..................... 5 00

FAR ROCKAWAY—St. *John's*: Wo. Aux., Sp. for Bishop Rowe's white work, Alaska 5 00

FLUSHING — St. *George's*: Colored, $5.45; Wo. Aux., Nevada, $2; Utah, $2; Bishop Payne Divinity-school, Southern Virginia, $2; Sp. for St. Paul's School, Lawrenceville, Southern Virginia, $2; Sp. for Rev. Mr. Claiborne, Sewanee, Tennessee, $2; S. S.,* Gen., $2.13............ 17 58

St. *John's*: $25, S. S.,* $24.21, Gen.. 49 21

GARDEN CITY—*Incarnation S. S.**: Gen. 25 71

GLENDALE—*Annunciation*: $10.23, S. S.,* $3.75, Gen.................. 13 98

GREAT NECK—*All Saints'*: Wo. Aux., Sp. for sewing teacher's salary, St. Augustine's School, Raleigh, North Carolina, $4; S. S.,* Gen., $70.53.. 74 53

HEMPSTEAD—St. *George's*: Wo. Aux., sewing teacher's salary, St. Augus-

tine's School, Raleigh, North Carolina, $1; Sp. for St. Paul's School, Lawrenceville, Southern Virginia, $1 .... 2 00
St. John's S. S.*: Gen.............. 9 50
HEWLETT—Trinity Church S. S.*: Gen. 20 00
HICKSVILLE—Holy Trinity Church S. S.*: Dom. and Frn.............. 8 04
HOLLIS—St. Gabriel's S. S.*: Gen.... 9 65
HUNTINGTON—St. John's: $47.33, S. S.,* $26.61, Gen................ 73 94
Miss Cornelia Prime, Sp. for Miss Thackara, Hospital of the Good Shepherd, Fort Defiance, Arizona.. 50 00
LONG ISLAND CITY—St. John's S. S.*: Gen. 7 00
MERRICK—Church of the Redeemer: Frn. (of which S. S.,* 16 cts.), $1.41; Gen., $1.................... 2 41
NORTH BABYLON—St. Elizabeth's S. S.*: Gen 13 32
NORTHPORT—Trinity Church: Rev. W. H. Morrison, "Little Girl Memorial Offering," for education of a child in the Southland, $5; S. S.,* Dom., $68.13 .... 73 13
OYSTER BAY—Christ Church: Gen. (of which S. S.,* $24.24), $48.15; S. S.,* Dom., $8.16................ 56 31
QUEENS—St. Joseph's S. S.*: Dom., $5.29; Frn., $5.29.............. 10 58
RICHMOND HILL—Resurrection: Wo. Aux., Bishop Payne Divinity-school, Southern Virginia, $1; Sp. for St. Paul's School, Lawrenceville, Southern Virginia, $2; Sp. for sewing teacher's salary, St. Augustine's School, Raleigh, North Carolina, $2; S. S.,* Gen., $41.50........... 46 50
ROCKVILLE CENTRE—Ascension: Wo. Aux., Sp. for sewing teacher's salary, St. Augustine's School, Raleigh, North Carolina, $1; Sp. for St. Paul's School, Lawrenceville, Southern Virginia, $1; S. S.,* Gen., $18.75 .... 20 75
ROSLYN—Trinity Church S. S.*: Gen.. 20 00
SAG HARBOR — Christ Church: Wo. Aux., Sp. for St. Paul's School, Lawrenceville, Southern Virginia, $3; S. S.,* Gen., $13.............. 16 00
SETAUKET—"Caroline," S. S., Dom., $10; Frn., $10................ 20 00
SHELTER ISLAND—St. Mary's S. S.*: Medical Missions, China, $10; Gen., $15.65; Sp. toward new rectory, Gooding, Idaho, $10............ 35 65
ST. JAMES—St. James's S. S.*: Gen.. 40 00
STONY BROOK—St. James's S. S.*: Gen. 10 00
ST. JOHNLAND—Testimony of Jesus: $32.12, S. S.,* $70, Gen......... 102 12
WOODSIDE—St. Paul's S. S.*: Gen.. 5 00
YAPHANK—St. Andrew's S. S.*: Gen.. 3 00
MISCELLANEOUS—Wo. Aux., Miss Leverich, "Anna M. Leverich" scholarship, St. Mary's Hall, Shanghai, Babies' Branch, Gen., $100; Sp. for mission font, $1; Sp. for Bishop Rowe's white work, Alaska, $25; Sp. for seats for St. Stephen's Mission, Fort Yukon, Alaska, $10; Sp. for St. Agnes's Hospital, Raleigh, North Carolina, $2.................... 40 00
.... 138 00

Los Angeles

Ap. $1,990.08; *Sp.* $125.00

ALHAMBRA—Holy Trinity Church S. S.*: Gen......................... 10 95
BOSTONIA—St. John's S. S.*: Gen.... 2 45
CORONA—St. John Baptist's: "Two Individuals," $4, S. S.,* $20.17, Gen. 24 17
CORONADO—Christ Church S. S.*:

Boone University, Hankow, $50; Dom. and Frn., $100............
ESCONDIDO—Trinity Mission S. S.*: Gen. ....
GLENDALE—St. Mark's S. S.*: Gen..
HEMET—Church of the Good Shepherd: $14, S. S.,* $1, Gen............
LONG BEACH—St. Luke's S. S.*: Gen..
LOS ANGELES—All Saints' S. S.* (Highland Park): Gen............
Ascension S. S.*: Gen.............
Epiphany S. S.*: Gen.............
St. James's S. S.*: Gen..........
St. John's: Dom., $20; China, $40; Gen., $140.45; S. S.,* Gen., $373.98.
St. Mark's S. S.*: Gen............
St. Matthias's: Dom. and Frn., $35.50; S. S.,* Gen., $25...........
St. Paul's Pro-Cathedral S. S.*: Gen.. $35, Gen..........................
MONTECITO—All Saints': $16, S. S.,* $35, Gen.........................
NATIONAL CITY—St. Matthew's S. S.*: Gen. ....
OCEAN PARK—Church of the Good Shepherd: Gen., $10; S. S.,* Dom., $6.50; Frn., $6.25............
ORANGE—Trinity Church S. S..
OXNARD—All Saints' Mission S. S.*: Gen. ....
OCEANSIDE—Grace Mission S. S.*: Gen.
PASADENA—All Saints': Wo. Aux., Sp. for Rev. J. W. Nichols, Shanghai..
REDLANDS—Trinity Church: Dom. and Frn., $20; S. S.,* Gen., $77.19....
RIVERSIDE—All Saints': Gen.........
SAN DIEGO—All Saints' S. S.*: Gen..
St. Paul's: Bishop Spalding's work, Utah, $11; Sp. for work in China carried on by the Rev. Mr. Nichols, Shanghai, $5; S. S.,* Gen., $80.10.
SAN JACINTO—St. Paul's Mission: Dom. and Frn................
SAN GABRIEL—Church of Our Saviour S. S.*: Gen.....................
SAN PEDRO—St. Peter's: $2, S. S.,* $10.68, Gen....................
SANTA BARBARA—Trinity Church S. S.*: Gen.........................
SANTA MONICA — St. Augustine's-by-the-Sea: Dom. and Frn..........
SIERRA MADRE—Ascension S. S.*: Gen.
TERMINAL—St. Michael and All Angels' S. S.*: Gen.....................
UPLAND—St. Mark's S. S.*: Gen.....
WHITTIER—St. Matthias's S. S.*: Dom., $30; Frn., $15.15..........
MISCELLANEOUS—"Go Quickly," Gen.; Wo. Aux., Bishop Funsten's work, Idaho, $30; Bishop Spalding's work, Utah, $25; Bishop Kendrick's work, Arizona, $30; Bishop Brewster's work, Western Colorado, $25; Bishop Robinson's work, Nevada, $20; Bishop Restarick's work, Honolulu, $20; Bishop Aves's work, Mexico, $20; "George F. Bugbee" scholarship, Girls' Training Institute, Paul's River, West Africa, $40; "Lawrence B. Ridgley" scholarship, Boone University, Wuchang, Hankow, $50; Gen., $50; Sp. for Mrs. L. B. Ridgley, Hankow, $25........

Louisiana

Ap. $957.80; *Sp.* $56.90

ALEXANDRIA—Christ Church S. S.*: Gen. ....
BATON ROUGE—St. James's S. S.*: Gen. ....
CHENEYVILLE—Mrs. Wiatte Marshall, Gen. ....
CROWLEY—Trinity Church S. S.*: Gen.
DONALDSONVILLE—Ascension S. S.*: Gen. ....
FRANKLIN—St. Mary's: Wo. Aux.,

Maine

Ap. $474.20

22 57	AUGUSTA—*St. Barnabas's*: $7, S. S.,* $2, Gen....................	9 00
6 10	*St. Mark's S. S.* *: Gen.............	13 65
10 78	BANGOR—*St. John's*: $13.70, "A Member," $5, Gen....................	18 70
	BAR HARBOR—*St. Saviour*: $36.88, S. S.,* $50....................	86 88
	Young's District S. S.,* Gen......	2 98
	BROWNVILLE JUNCTION—*St. John's S. S.* *: Gen....................	7 86
36 81	BRUNSWICK—*St. Paul's S. S.* *: Gen..	11 58
	CALAIS—*St. Anne's S. S.* *: Dom., $1;	
10 00	Frn., $1....................	2 00
	CAMDEN—*St. Thomas's S. S.* *: Gen...	14 19
6 82	CARIBOU—*St. Luke's S. S.* *: Gen.....	1 00
4 66	FORT FAIRFIELD—*St. Paul's S. S.* *:	
4 00	Gen.	15 30
16 70	GARDINER—*Christ Church*: Work among the Colored people, $55.90; S. S.,* Gen., $17.84....................	73 74
	HOULTON—*Church of the Good Shepherd*: $25, S. S.,* $5, Gen........	30 00
8 25	HULL'S COVE—*Church of Our Father S. S.* *: Gen....................	6 63
3 00	LIMESTONE—*Advent*: Gen............	1 85
	LISBON FALLS—*St. Matthew's S. S.* *:	
4 00	Gen.	2 50
20 00	LONG COVE—*St. George's*: Frn., $3; S. S.,* Gen., $1.23............	4 23
6 60	MADISON—*St. Margaret's S. S.* *: Gen.	3 22
16 00	NORTH EAST HARBOR—*St. Mary's-by-the-Sea S. S.* *: Gen..............	9 35
	PITTSTON—*St. Andrew's*: Gen.......	5 00
22 25	PORTLAND—*St. Stephen's S. S.* *: Frn., $50; Gen., $20....................	70 00
12 40	*Trinity Church S. S.* (Woodford): Gen.	18 63
10 70	PRESQUE ISLE—*St. John's*: $15.15, Junior Aux., $1.72, S. S.,* $4.03, Gen.	20 90
	RUMFORD—*St. Barnabas's*: Gen.....	3 00
47 70	SACO—*Trinity Church S. S.* *: Gen.....	14 01
	SEAL HARBOR—*St. Jude's S. S.* *: Gen.	3 00
	WISCASSET—*St. Philip's S. S.* *: Gen..	19 00
	Trinity Church S. S. *: Gen..........	6 00

Marquette

Ap. $218.73; *Sp.* $7.50

52 80		
52 11	CHOCOLAY—*St. James-the-Less*: Gen..	1 50
22 50	CRYSTAL FALLS—*St. Mark's*: Gen....	5 70
50	DOLLAR BAY—*St. Luke's*: Gen.......	3 05
	ESCANABA—*St. Stephen's*: Dom......	50 32
	GREENLAND—*St. John's*: Gen........	2 61
5 80	HOUGHTON—*Trinity Church*: Dom., $2.25; Frn., $3.81; Gen., $32.92...	38 98
	IRON MOUNTAIN—*Holy Trinity Church*:	
8 25	Gen.	4 08
	IRONWOOD — *Transfiguration*: Dom., $6.15; Gen., $8.60..............	14 75
	ISHPEMING—*Grace*: Gen.............	7 75
	MANISTIQUE—*St. Alban's*: Gen.......	7 44
	MUNISING—*St. John's*: Gen..........	21 07
	NEGAUNEE—*St. John's*: Gen.........	35 00
	NEWBURY—*All Saints'*: Gen........	7 85
415 34	ROCKLAND—*St. Thomas's*: Gen......	2 65
14 40	ST. IGNACE—*Church of the Good Shepherd*: Gen....................	3 00
	SAULT STE MARIE—*St. James's*: Gen..	7 87
8 00	VULCAN—*Bethany*: Gen.............	5 11
	WINONA—*Winona Mission*: "A Member," Sp. for St. Margaret's School, Tokyo, $3.75; Sp. for Archdeacon Stuck, Alaska, $3.75..............	7 50
4 00		
5 00		

Maryland

Ap. $4,481.13; *Sp.* $480.24

39 81		
7 00	ALLEGHANY Co. — *Emmanuel Deaf-Mute Mission* (Cumberland): Gen...	2 50
	St. George's S. S. * (Mt. Savage): Gen.	39 46
29 32	*St. James's S. S.* * (Westernport):	
9 92	Gen.	18 58

St. John's (Frostburg): Gen........ 76 50
St. Peter's S. S.* (Lonaconing): Frn.. 6 44
ANNE ARUNDEL CO.—St. Andrew's Mission S. S.* (Davidsonville): Gen... 5 72
All Saints' Chapel S. S.* (Annapolis Junction): Gen.................. 5 93
Christ Church (West River): Brazil, $5.50; Mexico, $5.50; Cuba, $5.50; Gen. (of which Lenten Offering, including St. John's and St. Luke's, $24.58), $145.................. 161 50
St. John's: Gen.................. 3 00
St. Anne's (Annapolis): Wo. Aux., Dom., $5; Gen., $20; S. S.,* Gen., $53.................. 78 00
St. Margaret's: $2, S. S.,* $15.53, Dom. and Frn.................. 17 53
BALTIMORE CITY—All Saints' S. S.*: Gen.................. 47 39
Christ Church: Wo. Aux., salary of teacher, St. Mary's School, South Dakota, $50; S. S.,* Gen., $100.... 150 00
Christ Church Chapel S. S.*: Gen.... 21 50
Church of the Holy Comforter S. S.*: Gen.................. 9 16
Church of the Messiah: "Lina Burt" scholarship, St. John's School, Cape Mount, Africa, $25; S. S.,* Gen., $25.................. 50 00
Church of Our Saviour S. S.*: Gen... 30 00
Emmanuel Church. S. S.: St. Luke's Hospital, Shanghai, $10; S. S.,* Gen., $71.89.................. 81 89
Grace: Wo. Aux., Miss A. R. Clarke, "Martha E. Clarke Memorial" scholarship, St. Mary's Hall, Shanghai.. 50 00
Grace (Deaf-Mute): Gen.................. 15 00
Holy Evangelists' S. S.*: Gen....... 6 00
Memorial S. S.*: Sp. for Miss Ridgely, House of Bethany Mission, Cape Mount, Africa.................. 25 00
Mt. Calvary: Sp. for Bishop Osborne, Springfield, $113.41; Sp. for Rev. J. A. Staunton, Sagada, Philippine Islands, $113.41; Wo. Aux., Sp. for Tsu Building Fund, Kyoto, $10.... 236 82
Prince of Peace: $22.11, Wo. Aux., $30, Brazil.................. 52 11
Redemption: Gen.................. 17 35
St. Andrew's S. S.* (Hamilton): Gen.. 1 40
St. Andrew's S. S.*: Gen.................. 20 00
St. Bartholomew's S. S.*: Gen....... 41 65
St. John's S. S.* (Waverly): Gen.... 54 44
St. Luke's: Dom. and Frn.................. 98 00
St. Margaret's S. S.*: Gen.................. 29 00
St. Mary's (Hampden): Frn., $5; S. S.,* Gen., $11.................. 16 00
St. Michael and All Angels' S. S.*: Gen.................. 126 54
St. Paul's Chapel S. S.*: Dom., $37.50; Frn., $37.50.................. 75 00
St. Paul's: Gen.................. 1,020 00
St. Peter's: Bishop Rowe's work, Alaska.................. 97 08
St. Barnabas's and St. George's S. Ss.*: Gen.................. 22 62
St. Philip's: Gen.................. 10 00
St. Stephen's S. S.*: Dom., $2.50; Frn., $2.50.................. 5 00
Missionary Box No. 5,726, Frn..... 4 90
Mite Chest No. 29,405, Dom.... 3 50
"Retired Clergyman," Gen........ 5 00
Miss Emma Knapp, Wo. Aux., Sp. for Holy Trinity Orphanage, Tokyo. 25 00
"H. W. A.," Sp. for Rev. Mr. Ancell, Shanghai.................. 10 00
BALTIMORE CO.—All Saints': $35.45, S. S.,* $16.18, Gen.................. 51 63
Epiphany (Govans): Gen.................. 25 00
Chapel of the Good Shepherd (Sherwood): Sp. for St. Paul's College Fund, Tokyo, $5; S. S.,* Gen., $37.12.................. 42 12
Chapel of the Holy Comforter S. S.* (Lutherville): Gen.................. 10 37
Church of the Redeemer: Dom. and Frn.................. 255 81

Grace Chapel (Mt. Winans): Gen.... 5
(Reisterstown)—Hannah More Academy, Sp. for Bishop Horner, Asheville.................. 5
St. David's (Roland Park): Gen..... 31
St. James's (Monkton): Gen., $13; Sp. for Rev. C. F. McRae's work in Shanghai, $5; S. S.,* Gen., $8.... 26
St. John's (Mt. Washington): Dom., $16.15; Gen., $10; Wo. Aux., Sp. for Bishop Rowe, Alaska, $5; Sp. for Bishop Horner, Asheville, $5; Sp. for Bishop Brooke, Oklahoma, $2; Sp. for Bishop Kinsolving, Brazil, $2.................. 40
Mission S. S.* (Fuland): Gen....... 2
St. Luke's S. S.* (Harrisonville): Gen. 2
St. John's S. S.* (Glyndon): Gen.... 4
St. Mark's S. S.* (Pikesville): Gen... 27
St. Matthew's (Sparrow's Point): $50, S. S.,* $12, Gen.................. 62
St. Thomas's S. S.* (Owing Mills): Dom.................. 14
St. Timothy's (Catonsville): Wo. Aux., Sp. for St. Margaret's School Building Fund, Tokyo, $100.32; S. S.,* Gen., $73.79.................. 174
Sherwood (Cockeysville): Frn., $7.66; S. S.,* Gen., $25.53.................. 33
Transfiguration (West Arlington): Alaska, $13.43; Hankow, $13.42; S. S.,* Alaska, $16.63; Hankow, $16.................. 59
Trinity Church (Long Green): $44, S. S.,* $10.43, Gen.................. 54
Trinity Church (Towson): Gen., $100; Sp. for St. Paul's College, Tokyo (of which Wo. Aux., $5), $19.10; S. S.,* Gen., $34.35.................. 153
(Kingsville)—Mr. Edward J. Bell,* Gen.................. 1
CALVERT CO.—Christ Church (Port Republic): $31.21, S. S.,* $14.92, Gen.................. 46
St. Paul's (Prince Frederick): $20.73, S. S.,* $10.55, Gen.................. 31
St. Peter's (Solomons): $2.68, S. S.,* $2.39, Gen.................. 5
Middleham: $2.95, S. S.,* $8.65, Gen. 11
Hungerford Creek*: Gen.................. 1
FREDERICK CO.—All Saints' (Frederick): Gen., $33.76; Wo. Aux. "Five-Cent" collection, Indian, $3; Frn., $6; Mexican, $5; S. S.,* Dom., $53.25; Frn., $53.25.................. 154
Grace Chapel S. S.* (Brunswick): Gen.................. 41
St. Luke's Chapel S. S.* (Brownsville): Gen.................. 12
St. Mark's S. S.* (Petersville): Gen.. 7
St. Luke's (Adamstown): $13, S. S.,* $3.27, Gen.................. 16
St. Paul's Chapel (Point of Rocks): $12.75, S. S.,* $70, Gen.................. 82
St. Stephen's S. S.* (Thurmont): Gen. 10
FREDERICK AND WASHINGTON COS.—St. Mark's (Brunswick): Gen., $106.81; Sp. for Rev. J. M. B. Gill, Yanchow, Shanghai, to be used for the purchase of a motor boat for aid in visiting, $25; Sp. to be used for repairs to chapel in Isle of Pines, Cuba, or toward the erection of a new chapel, $10.................. 141
GARRETT CO.—St. Matthew's S. S.* (Oakland): Dom. and Frn.................. 3
HARFORD CO.—Deer Creek (Darlington): $25.50, S. S.* (of which Grace Memorial S. S., $8.67, Ascension Chapel, $2.79), $11.46, Gen.................. 36
Emmanuel Church (Bel Air): Gen... 42
St. George's (Perryman): $17.93, S. S.,* $12.51, Gen.................. 30
HOWARD CO.—Grace S. S.* (Elkridge): Gen.................. 27
St. Alban's S. S.* (Alberton): Dom.· $5.78; Frn., $5.78.................. 11

"Training-school for Catechists," Shanghai 100 00
(Jamaica Plains)—"E. J. B.," Sp. for Training-schools for Catechists, Shanghai 10 00
BROCKTON—*St. Paul's*: Gen.......... 22 65
BROOKLINE—*All Saints'*: Wo. Aux., salary of Rev. Nathan Matthews, Africa, $25; salary of Miss Woodruff, Africa, $2; Sp. for life insurance of Rev. T. S. Tyng, Kyoto, $3; Sp. for furnishing Mrs. Moort's school, Africa, $15; Sp. for St. Paul's College, Tokyo, $3; Sp. for Building Fund, St. Margaret's School, Tokyo, $2................ 50 00
Church of Our Saviour: Wo. Aux., Sp. for insurance dues of Mr. Bedinger, Tokyo.................. 50 00
St. Paul's: Dom., $200.05; Frn., $190.18; Wo. Aux., Hooker Memorial School, Mexico, $5; San Gabriel, Brazil, $5; Isle of Pines, Cuba, $5...................... 405 23
"A Friend," Sp. for Bishop Rowe's work in Alaska, $25; Sp. for Bishop Hare Memorial Fund, South Dakota, $10 .... 35 00
CAMBRIDGE—*Christ Church*: Dom., $223.50; Frn., $57.35; Wo. Aux., Isle of Pines, Cuba, $12; Sp. for Rev. J. A. Holly, Haiti, $5; Sp. for insurance of Rev. T. S. Tyng, Kyoto, $14 .... 311 85
St. James's: Gen., $15.95; "Mission Study Class in China," Sp. for Bishop Roots's work, Hankow, to be used at his discretion, $15; Sp. for Mr. Nichols's School for Catechists, Shanghai, $5................... 35 95
St. John's Memorial Chapel: Frn., $9.67; Mrs. Alex. V. Hallin, Gen., $15; Dakota League, "George Zabriskie Gray" (Graduate) scholarship, South Dakota, $60................ 84 67
St. Philip's: Gen., $7.67; Wo. Aux., Sp. for life insurance of Rev. T. S. Tyng, Kyoto, $6.25................ 13 92
CANTON—*Trinity Church*: Gen....... 7 00
CHELMSFORD—*All Saints' S. S.**: Gen. 50
CHELSEA—*St. Luke's*: Wo. Aux., Isle of Pines, Cuba.................... 2 00
CONCORD—*Trinity Church*: Dom. and Frn. 20 50
DANVERS—*Calvary*: Gen............ 30 00
DEDHAM—*Church of the Good Shepherd*: Dom. and Frn............. 70 00
FALL RIVER—*Ascension*: Wo. Aux., San Gabriel's, Brazil, $5; Hooker Memorial School, Mexico, $5; Haiti, $5; Missionary Society, Sp. for Rev. B. M. Spurr's work, Moundsville, West Virginia, $5.......... 20 00
FOXBORO—*St. Mark's*: Gen......... 11 00
GROTON AND AYER—*St. Andrew's*: Gen. 25 92
The Groton Missionary Society, Sp. for Thayer Addison, St. John's University, Shanghai, China.......... 20 00
Groton School—Endicott Peabody, Sp. Training-school for Catechists...... 25 00
GROVELAND—*St. James's*: Gen....... 3 60
HAVERHILL — *Trinity Church*: Wo. Aux., Hooker Memorial School, Mexico 1 00
HINGHAM — *St. John's*: Wo. Aux., Hooker Memorial School, Mexico... 1 00
HOPKINTON—*St. Paul's*: Gen......... 19 12
HYDE PARK—*Christ Church*: Dom. and Frn., $158.86; Sp. for Rev. A. A. Clattenburg, North Dakota, $58.71; S. S.,* Sp. for Rev. W. J. Cuthbert, Japan, $10; Sp. for Bishop Rowe, Alaska, $10; Sp. for Bishop Wells, Spokane, $10.................... 247 57

LYNN—*St. Stephen's*: Sp. for St. Mary's Building Fund, Tokyo...... 20 00
MARBLEHEAD — *St. Michael's*: Wo. Aux., "Penny Savings" for Isle of Pines, Cuba..................... 5 00
MEDFIELD—*Advent*: Gen............. 15 63
MEDFORD—*Grace*: Gen............. 41 27
MELROSE—*Trinity Church*: Wo. Aux., Hooker Memorial School, Mexico.... 2 00
NEW BEDFORD—*Grace*: Wo. Aux., San Gabriel's, Brazil, $10; S. S.,* Dom., $50; Frn., $75; work of Rev. W. J. Cuthbert, Kyoto, Japan, $50....... 185 00
St. Martin's—Gen................. 50 00
NEWBURYPORT—*St. Paul's*: Dom. and Frn., $123.74; Girls' Friendly Society, Sp. for Bishop Rowe, Alaska, $18 .... 141 74
"Cash," Sp. for St. Mary's Building Fund, Tokyo..................... 50 00
NEWTON—*Grace*: Wo. Aux., Hooker Memorial School, Mexico, $10; salary of Mrs. McCalla, Africa, $10; Soochow, Shanghai, $5; St. Luke's Hospital, Tokyo, $5.............. 30 00
Church of the Redeemer (Chestnut Falls): Wo. Aux., Hooker Memorial School, Mexico................. 10 00
St. Mary's (Lower Falls): Wo. Aux., Hooker Memorial School, Mexico.... 4 00
St. Paul's (Highlands): Gen., $17.60; Wo. Aux., Hooker Memorial School, Mexico, $2.................... 19 60
Trinity Church (Centre): Gen., $112.60; Wo. Aux., Hooker Memorial School, Mexico, $8............... 120 60
PEABODY—*St. Paul's*: Gen........... 40 18
PLYMOUTH—*Christ Church*: Gen..... 47 00
QUINCY—*St. Chrysostom's* (Wollaston): Wo. Aux., Hooker Memorial School, Mexico 2 00
READING — Rev. and Mrs. George Walker, Gen.................... 5 00
ROXBURY—*St. John's*: For Bishop Horner, Asheville, $217; Girls' Friendly Society, Sp. for Dr. Jeffreys's work, Shanghai, $8.50...... 225 50
SALEM—*St. Peter's Church and S. S.*: Sp. for St. Paul's Building Fund, Kyoto, $65; Wo. Aux., salary of Mrs. McCalla, West Africa, $15.......... 80 00
SOUTHBOROUGH—*St. Mark's*: Wo. Aux., San Gabriel's, Brazil.............. 3 00
Fay School—For the many expenses of the *Pelican*, Alaska............ 100 00
St. Mark's School: For the many expenses of the *Pelican*, Alaska, $100; Gordon Hamersley, Sp. for St. John's University Expansion Fund, Shanghai, $50....................... 150 00
SWAMPSCOTT—*Holy Name*: Sp. for Bishop Wells's school for boys, Spokane 25 00
SWANSEA—*Christ Church*: Gen....... 29 40
WALPOLE — *Epiphany*: $21.63, Wo. Aux., $6, Gen.................... 27 63
WATERTOWN—*Church of the Good Shepherd*: Gen.................. 52 62
WELLESLEY—*St. Andrew's*: Wo. Aux., Hooker Memorial School, Mexico... 5 00
WHITMAN—*All Saints' S. S.*: For work in China.............. 10 00
WINCHESTER—*Epiphany*: Gen........ 100 00
WINTHROP—*St. John's*: Gen........ 7 35
MISCELLANEOUS—"S.," Gen.......... 1,000 00
Wo. Aux., "Friends," Sp. for insurance dues of Rev. A. A. Gilman, Hankow, $3.50; Sp. for Christmas gifts for Gates's School, Shanghai, $9,40; "A Friend," Hooker Memorial School, Mexico, $1.......... 13 90
Wo. Aux., Colored Committee, Sp. for salary of Miss Whalen, St. Augustine's School, Raleigh, North Carolina, $25; Sp. for salary of

Miss Dickerson, St. Paul's School, Lawrenceville, Southern Virginia, $25 ....
Dakota League, Miss S. E. Whittemore, "Loving Mothers" scholarship, St. Mary's School, South Dakota....

Michigan

Ap. $2,128.88; *Sp.* $178.23

ALGONAC—*St. Andrew's S. S.*: Gen..
ALMA—*St. John's*: Wo. Aux., $4, S. S.,* $18.80, Gen. . . . .
ALPENA—*Trinity Church*: Gen.......
ANN ARBOR—*St. Andrew's*: Wo. Aux., Gen., $20; Sp. for F. E. Adams Memorial, Fort Defiance, $2.50; Sp. for Point Hope, Alaska, $10; Sp. for Archdeacon Neve for mountain child, Virginia, $10; S. S.,* Gen., $58.55 ....
AU SABLE—*St. John's S. S.*: Gen....
BAD AXE—*St. Paul's S. S.*: Gen.....
BAY CITY—*St. John's Mission*: Gen...
Trinity Church: Wo. Aux., Gen., $20; Sp. for Tanana, Alaska, $5; Sp. for Bishop Nelson, Atlanta, $12; Junior Aux., Gen., $5; S. S.,* Gen., $65...
BIRMINGHAM—*St. James's S. S.*: Gen. ....
BROOKLYN—*All Saints' S. S.*: Gen..
CARO—*Trinity Church*: $15.36, S. S.* $16, for Asheville..............
CLINTON—*St. John's S. S.*: Gen.....
DEARBORN—*Christ Church*: Dom. and Frn., $12.11; S. S.,* Gen., $4.85....
DETROIT—*Christ Church*: Wo. Aux., Philippines, $25; St. Augustine's School, Raleigh, North Carolina, $20; S. S.,* Gen., $122.15......
Epiphany: Junior Aux., Sp. for Miss Routledge, Manila, Philippine Islands
Grace: Dom., $102.86; Frn., $102.86; Wo. Aux., Gen., $10; Sp. for American Church Institute for Negroes, $1
Church of the Messiah: Junior Aux., Alaska, $10; Gen., $4; Sp. for Archdeacon Russell, Lawrenceville, Southern Virginia, $3; Sp. for Miss Routledge, Manila, Philippine Islands, $10; Sp. for Mrs. Littell, Hankow,
St. John's: Wo. Aux., Arizona, $75; Alaska, $50; St. Paul's School, Lawrenceville, Southern Virginia, $25; St. Augustine's School, Raleigh, North Carolina, $25; Philippines, $25; Gen., $55; Sp. for F. E. Adams Memorial, Fort Defiance, Arizona, $5; Sp. for St. Agnes's Hospital, North Carolina, $5; Sp. for Rev. H. C. Parke, Jr., Waynesville, Asheville, $5; Sp. for Rev. A. W. Mann, $4; Junior Aux., Mrs. Best, Gen., $1............
St. Joseph's: Wo. Aux., Alaska, $5; St Paul's, Lawrenceville, Southern Virginia, $3; St. Augustine's School, North Carolina, $3; Philippines, $5; Sp. for F. E. Adams Memorial, Fort Defiance, Arizona, $3; Sp. for Miss Routledge, Philippines, $4; S. S.,* Gen., $104.57..............
St. Mark's S. S.: Gen.............
St. Matthew's: Wo. Aux., St. Paul's School, Lawrenceville, Southern Virginia, $2.50; St. Augustine's School, Raleigh, North Carolina, $2.50; Junior Aux., Sp. for Miss Routledge, Manila, Philippine Islands, $3; Sp for Mr. Littell, Hankow, $3........
St. Matthias's: Gen., $60; Wo. Aux., Gen., $4; St. Paul's School, Lawrenceville, Southern Virginia, $4;

Rev. H. C. Parke, Jr.'s, work in
Waynesville, Asheville............ 20 00
ST. JOHNS—*St. John's*: Gen......... 47 15
SANDUSKY—*St. John's S. S.**: Gen... 7 31
TRENTON—*St. Thomas's S. S.**: Gen.. 24 74
VASSAR—*St. John's*: $1, S. S.,* $1.37,
Asheville 2 37
WAYNE—*St. John's Mission*: Gen..... 98
WYANDOTTE—*St. Stephen's*: Wo. Aux.,
$5, S. S.,* $15.50, Gen............ 20 50
YPSILANTI—*St. Luke's S. S.**: Gen... 22 50
MISCELLANEOUS—Junior Aux., Gen.... 2 50

Michigan City

Ap. $361.46

BRISTOL—*St. John's S. S.**: Gen..... 10 06
COLUMBIA CITY—Wo. Aux., Gen...... 1 00
ELKHART—*St. John's*: Wo. Aux., Gen. 5 00
FORT WAYNE—*Trinity Church S. S.**:
Gen............................. 24 13
GARY—*Christ Church S. S.**: Gen.... 11 80
GAS CITY—*St. Paul's*: $14.70, S. S.,*
$13.70, Gen.................... 28 40
HAMMOND—*St. Paul's S. S.**: Gen.... 34 41
HOWE—*St. Mark's*: $20.58, St. James's
Chapel, Howe School, $44.10, S. S.,*
$39.83, Gen.................... 104 51
KENDALLVILLE—*Trinity Church*: Gen.. 10 00
MARION—*Gethsemane*: Frn., $16.70;
S. S.,* Gen., $31.95............. 48 65
MICHIGAN CITY — *Trinity Cathedral*:
$63, S. S.,* $2.50, Gen........... 65 50
PERU—*Trinity Church S. S.**: Gen... 18 00

Milwaukee

Ap. $984.39

BARRON—*St. Mark's S. S.**: Gen...... 5 00
BELOIT—*St. Paul's*: $12.40, "Two
Communicants," $10, Gen......... 22 40
BURLINGTON—*Church of St. John the
Divine*: Gen., $5; S. S.,* Frn., $6.24 11 24
CHIPPEWA FALLS—*Christ Church S.
S.**: Gen...................... 18 90
COLUMBUS—*St. Paul's S. S.**: Gen.... 21 09
DELTON—*Holy Cross*: $2, S. S.,* $2.83,
Gen........................... 4 83
EAU CLAIRE—*Christ Church S. S.**:
Gen........................... 35 07
JANESVILLE — *Trinity Church*: $6.60,
S. S.,* $5.25, Gen.............. 11 85
JEFFERSON—*St. Mary's*: $2.70, S. S.,*
$6.30, Gen..................... 9 00
KENOSHA—*St Matthew's S. S.**: Gen.. 62 65
KILBOURN—*St. Paul's*: $3, S. S.,* 60
cts., Gen...................... 3⁴ 30
LA CROSSE—*Christ Church*: Gen..... 8 36
LAKE GENEVA—*Holy Communion S.
S.**: Gen...................... 10 71
MADISON—*Grace*: Gen.............. 12 00
MELVILLE SETTLEMENT—*St. Simeon's
S. S.**: Gen................... 5 12
MILWAUKEE — *St. James's Bible
School**: Frn.................. 70 00
St. John's S. S.*: Dom., $20; Frn.,
$20 .... 40 00
St. Mark's S. S.*: Gen.......... 27 12
St. Paul's: Frn., $96.90; S. S.,* Gen.,
$81.06 .... 177 96
St. Paul's Mission House: $13, S. S.,*
$20, Gen...................... 33 00
St. Stephen's S. S.*: Gen........ 10 75
MINERAL POINT—*Trinity Church*: Gen. 14 50
MONROE—*Holy Trinity Church*: Gen.. 2 00
OCONOMOWOC—*Zion*: Gen.......... 13 01
OKAUCHEE—*St. Chad's S. S.**: Gen... 2 00
RACINE—*Immanuel Church S. S.**:
Gen........................... 7 17
St. Luke's S. S.*: Gen.......... 25 16
St. Stephen's S. S.*: Gen........ 15 20
SHELL LAKE—*St. Stephen's S. S.**:
Gen........................... 12 00
SOUTH MILWAUKEE—*St. Mark's S. S.**:
Gen........................... 7 00

STAR PRAIRIE—*St. John the Baptist's
  S. S.**: Gen..................... 9 00
SUPERIOR—*Church of the Redeemer S.
  S.**: Gen........................ 18 15
  *St. Aidan's S. S.**: Gen......... 1 50
  *St. Alban's S. S.**: Dom......... 14 43
SUSSEX—*St. Alban's*: Gen., $25; S.
  S.,* Frn., $10................... 35 00
TURTLE LAKE—*St. Philip's S. S.**:
  Gen............................. 1 00
WATERTOWN—*St. Paul's S. S.**: For
  work in Alaska.................. 18 76
WAUKESHA—*St. Matthias's S. S.**:
  For work under Rev. C. W. Peabody,
  Tanana, Alaska................. 11 73
Trinity Church: $6.08, S. S.,* $20.05,
  Gen............................ 26 13
MISCELLANEOUS—Wo Aux., St. Paul's
  School, Lawrenceville, Southern Vir-
  ginia, $50; Cuba, $50; Elizabeth
  Bunn Memorial Hospital, Wuchang,
  Hankow, $50................... 150 00

Minnesota

Ap. $1,823.79; *Sp.* $81.80

ALBERT LEA—*Christ Church S. S.**:
  Gen............................ 28 25
ANOKA—*Trinity Church S. S.**: Gen.. 6 57
APPLETON—*Gethsemane S. S.**: Dom.. 10 40
AUSTIN—*Christ Church S. S.**: Gen.. 35 32
BASSWOOD GROVE—*St. Mary's S. S.**:
  Gen............................ 8 56
BECKER—*Trinity Church S. S.**: Frn. 3 00
BELLE CREEK—*St. Paul's S. S.**: Gen. 8 54
BENSON—*Christ Church S. S.**: Gen.. 5 00
BIRCH COULEE—*St. Cornelius's S. S.**:
  Gen............................ 44 57
CALEDONIA—*Trinity Church S. S.**:
  Gen............................ 2 00
CANNON FALLS—*Church of the Re-
  deemer S. S.**: Gen............. 8 00
CHATFIELD—*St. Matthew's*: Gen..... 2 90
CORDOVA—*Christ Church*: Gen...... 4 00
FARIBAULT — *Shattuck School*: $100,
  St. James's S. S.,* $54.45, Gen.... 154 45
  Seabury Divinity-school: Sp. for Bish-
  op Horner's work among mountain
  whites, Asheville............... 25 00
FAIRMONT—*St. Martin's S. S.**: Gen. 50 72
FARMINGTON—*Advent S. S.**: Gen.... 2 50
FRIDLEY—*Holy Trinity Church*: $5, S.
  S.,* $12.25, Gen................ 17 25
GOOD THUNDER—*St. Luke's S. S.**:
  Gen............................ 3 57
HASTINGS—*St. Luke's*: Gen......... 10 00
HENDERSON—*St. Jude's S. S.**: Gen.. 6 15
HUTCHINSON—*St. John's S. S.**: Frn. 3 90
LAKE CITY—*St. Mark's*: Gen. (of
  which S. S.,* $36.39), $70.42; Sp.
  for St. Paul's College, Tokyo, 35 cts. 70 77
LE SUEUR—*St. Paul's S. S.**: Gen.... 26 15
LITCHFIELD — *Emmanuel Church S.
  S.*; Gen....................... 4 50
*Trinity Church S. S.**: Gen......... 13 47
LUVERNE—*Holy Trinity Church S. S.**:
  Gen............................ 5 80
MINNEAPOLIS — *Gethsemane S. S.**:
  Gen., $106.65; Sp. for Rev. J. P.
  Anschutz, Montana, $25......... 131 65
*Holy Trinity Church S. S.**: Gen.... 80 01
*St. Mark's S. S.**: Gen.............. 112 50
*St. Mary's S. S.**: Gen............. 6 57
St. Matthew's: Gen................ 15 00
*Shepherd's Fold S. S.**: Gen........ 5 00
*Wells Memorial S. S.**: Gen......... 10 00
MONTEVIDEO—*Grace S. S.**: Gen..... 2 80
MORTON—*Ascension S. S.**: Gen..... 90
NEW ULM—*St. Peter's S. S.**: Gen... 9 00
OWATONNA—*St. Paul's S. S.**: Gen... 17 37
PINE ISLAND—*Grace Church*: $10, S.
  S.,* $10, Gen................... 20 00
RED WING—*Christ Church*: Dom.,
  $57.10: Sp. for Bishop Brewster,

11 75	Holy Innocents' S. S.*: Gen......... 25 55
	Church of the Redeemer S. S.*: Frn. 79 47
	St. Augustine's S. S.*: Gen........ 43 49
3 00	St. George's: Sp. for Rev. Dr. I. H.
	Correll, Kyoto................. 5 00
	St. James's S. S.*: Gen........... 35 50
	St. Matthew's: $10, S. S.,* $17.25,
6 00	Gen.......................... 27 25
1 00	St. Paul's S. S.*: Gen............ 9 65
	St. Peter's: Dom. (of which S. S.,*
	$14.02), $91.47; Frn. (of which S.
	S.,* $14.02), $215.43......... 306 90
	St. Philip's: Dom. and Frn., $48.75;
13 50	S. S.,* Gen., $39.25.......... 88 00
	St. Thomas's: Gen............... 6 00
35 00	Bishop Robertson Hall S. S.*: Gen... 14 02
8 20	St. Timothy's S. S.*: Gen......... 4 00
	Through Sister Martha, Sp. for Mrs.
3 40	S. H. Littell, Hankow......... 55 00
5 00	SULLIVAN—St. John's: Gen......... 2 60
2 00	MISCELLANEOUS—Wo. Aux., "Carroll
	M. Davis" scholarship, Boone Uni-
49 00	versity, Wuchang, $50; Sp. for
	"Bishop Tuttle" scholarship, Anvik,
	Alaska, $100.................. 150 00
	"Friends," Gen................. 105 00
104 50	**Montana**
	Ap. $1,232.61
	BIG TIMBER—St. Mark's: Gen....... 19 00
	BILLINGS—St. Luke's: Gen......... 100 00
184 44	BOULDER—St. Thomas's: Gen....... 26 40
20 00	BRIDGER—Church of the Good Shep-
	herd: Gen.................... 5 00
11 24	BUTTE—St. Andrew's: Gen......... 13 90
	St. John's: Gen.................. 295 35
5 35	St. Paul's: Gen.................. 25 00
	COLUMBUS—St. Paul's: Gen....... 6 00
88 60	DARBY—St. Thomas's: Gen......... 5 00
	DEER LODGE—St. James's: Gen...... 35 85
4 00	DILLON—St. James's: Frn......... 189 00
	DORSEY—Church of the Good Shep-
10 58	herd: Gen.................... 5 00
38 35	ELECTRIC—St. Clement's: Gen....... 5 00
18 04	FORT BENTON—St. Paul's: Gen....... 40 00
	FRIDLEY—St. John's: Gen.......... 10 00
	GARDINER—Emmanuel Church: Gen... 6 00
	GRANITE—St. Peter's: Gen......... 5 00
	HARLOWTON—All Saints': Gen....... 7 00
10 00	HARVE—St. Mark's: Gen.......... 33 71
3 25	HEDGESVILLE—Advent: Gen.......... 3 00
79	JOLIET—Church of Our Saviour: Gen. 1 35
16 00	JUDITH GAP—Epiphany: Gen........ 5 00
29 58	KLEIN—St. David's: Gen.......... 5 00
	LAVINA—Ascension: Gen........... 5 00
45 22	LIVINGSTON—St. Andrew's: Gen...... 57 50
4 72	MADISON VALLEY — Trinity Church:
10 26	Gen......................... 40 00
104 67	MARTINSDALE—Trinity Church: Gen.. 12 00
6 10	MILES CITY—Emmanuel Church: Gen. 75 00
7 00	PHILIPSBURG—St. Andrew's: Gen..... 30 00
	PONY—St. John's: Gen............ 21 15
65 00	RED LODGE—Calvary: Gen......... 42 90
	ROSEBUD—Mission: Gen........... 10 00
	ROUNDUP—Calvary: Gen.......... 10 00
6 00	SHERIDAN—Christ Church: Gen...... 25 00
30 00	TWIN BRIDGE—St. Jude's: Gen...... 5 00
	TWODOT—St. Matthew's: Gen........ 13 00
6 80	WHITEHALL—St. Mark's: Gen....... 5 00
2 50	WHITE SULPHUR SPRINGS — Grace:
8 00	Gen.......................... 35 00
42 57	**Nebraska**
	Ap. $524.41
5 10	ASHLAND—St. Stephen's: $5, S. S.,*
	$11.85, Gen.................. 16 85
11 00	AURORA—St. Mary's S. S.*: Gen..... 4 00
20 35	BANCROFT—Atonement: $1.30, S. S.*
50 20	$2.66, Gen................... 3 96
8 25	BLAIR—St. Mary's S. S.*: Gen..... 17 50
30 32	COLUMBUS—Grace S. S.*: Gen...... 23 77
	CREIGHTON—St. Mark's S. S.*: Gen... 5 66
18 00	DECATUR—Incarnation: $1.50, S. S.*
82 82	$2.31, Gen................... 3 81
50 55	

FALLS CITY—*St. Thomas's S. S.**:
Gen. 5 72
FAIRBURY—*Emmanuel Church S. S.**:
Dom. 4 32
LINCOLN—*Holy Trinity Church*: Dom.
and Frn., $144.99; S. S.,* Frn.,
$19.24 .... 164 23
St. Luke's: $3.40, S. S.,* $5, Gen.... 8 40
NEBRASKA CITY—*St. Mary's*: $44.88,
S. S.,* $6.36, Gen............... 51 24
NIOBRARA—*St. Paul's S. S.**: Dom.... 4 00
OMAHA—*Church of the Good Shepherd
S. S.**: Gen.................... 25 02
St. Andrew's S. S.*: Dom. and Frn... 39 09
St. Matthias's: Dom. and Frn........ 30 00
PLATTSMOUTH—*St. Luke's*: Dom. and
Frn., $27.17; S. S.,* Gen., $14.93.. 42 10
SCHUYLER—*Holy Trinity Church S.
S.**: Gen....................... 10 00
SOUTH OMAHA—*St. Clement's S. S.**:
Gen. 5 30
St. Edward's S. S.*: Gen............ 1 88
St. Martin's: Dom. and Frn., $10;
Gen. (of which S. S.,* $7.56),
$11.66 .... 21 66
TEKAMAH—*Holy Cross S. S.**: Gen... 2 95
TOBIAS—*St. Andrew's S. S.**: Gen.... 4 34
TRYON—*S. S.**: Gen................. 13 00
WYMORE—*St. Luke's S. S.**: Gen..... 15 61

Newark

Ap. $5,116.60; *Sp.* $697.00

ALLENDALE—*Epiphany S. S.**: Gen.... 10 00
BAYONNE—*Calvary*: Gen.............. 11 30
Trinity Church: Gen................. 10 00
BELLEVILLE—*Christ Church*: Gen.... 29 38
BELVIDERE—*Zion*: (of which S. S.,*
$2.42) Gen...................... 5 87
BLOOMFIELD—*Ascension S. S.**: Gen.. 35 30
Christ Church (Glen Ridge): Dom.,
$120.74; S. S.,* Gen., $200.21...... 320 95
BOONTON—*St. John's*: Gen.......... 48 35
CHATHAM—*St. Paul's*: Gen.......... 7 03
CLIFTON—*St. Peter's S. S.**: Gen..... 14 44
COYTESVILLE—*St. Stephen's S. S.**:
Gen. 4 63
DELAWANNA—*St. Stephen's S. S.**: Gen. 3 11
EAST ORANGE—*Christ Church*: For
mission at Zangzok, Shanghai,
$13.76; Gen., $114.84; Junior Aux.,
work among mountain whites, $50.. 178 60
St. Agnes's S. S.*: Gen............. 17 75
EDGEWATER—*Church of the Mediator
S. S.**: Gen.................... 24 57
ENGLEWOOD—*St. Paul's*: (of which S.
S.,* $81.64) Gen................ 210 34
ESSEX FELLS—*St. Peter's*: (of which
S. S.,* $42.85) Gen............. 149 85
GRAND VIEW—*Grace S. S.**: Gen.,
$13.03; Wo. Aux., Gen., $9; Sp. for
donkey, for Cape Mount, Africa, $1.. 23 03
GRANTWOOD—*Trinity Church*: Gen... 24 21
HACKENSACK—*Christ Church*: Dom.,
$5.20; Frn., $5.20; Gen., $124.69;
S. S.,* Gen., $139.48............ 274 57
HAMBURG—*Church of the Good Shepherd*: Gen...................... 20 00
HARRISON — *Christ Church*: Dom.,
$72.05; S. S.,* Gen., $15.10....... 87 15
HASBROUCK HEIGHTS — *St. John-the-Divine S. S.**: Gen............... 23 82
HOBOKEN—*Holy Innocents'*: Sp. for St.
Mary's Building Fund, Kyoto....... 30 00
HOBOKEN—*St. Bartholomew's Chapel
S. S.**: Gen.................... 7 30
HOPE—*St. Luke's*: Gen.............. 5 50
JERSEY CITY—*Grace* (Greenville): Gen. 10 00
Grace (Van Vorst): Gen. (of which
S. S.,* $29.14)................. 129 14
St. John's S. S.: Sp. for St. Mary's
Building Fund, Kyoto............ 50 00
St. Mark's S. S.*: Frn............. 35 00
St. Paul's S. S.*: Gen............. 54 65
St. Stephen's: Gen. (of which S. S.,*
$86.81) 121 81

	Hankow, $5; Sp. for Archdeacon	
5 00	Wentworth's work, Lexington, $5..	17 00
	St. Augustine's S. S.*: Gen...........	10 00
	St. James's S. S.*: Gen.............	25 00
	BERLIN—*Church of the Good Shep-*	
100 00	*herd S. S.**: Gen..................	2 00
	BERNARDSVILLE—*St. Bernard's*: Dom.,	
	$54.60; Colored, $5.55; Gen.,	
	$122.41; Wo. Aux., salary of Mrs.	
	Sung, Soochow, Shanghai, $40.....	222 56
	St. John's Chapel: Colored, $3.50; Gen.,	
	$62.64	66 14
	BEVERLY—*St. Stephen's S. S.**: Gen...	32 86
	BOUND BROOK—*St. Paul's S. S.**: Gen.,	
	$36.01; Wo. Aux., St. Paul's School,	
	Lawrenceville, Southern Virginia,	
	$6; salary of Kimura San, Kyoto, $5	47 01
	BRIDGETON—*St. Andrew's*: Dom. and	
	Frn., $100; S. S.,* Gen., $52.62....	152 62
	CAMDEN—*Church of Our Saviour S.*	
	S.*: Sp. for use of St. Andrew's	
	School, Sewanee, Tennessee........	20 00
	St. Augustine's: Gen. (of which S. S.,*	
	$9.25)	17 25
	St. Paul's: Wo. Aux., salary of Kimura	
	San, Kyoto, $5; Cape Mount, Africa,	
	$5; Chinese Bible-woman, $16; "Dr.	
	T. S. Tidball" scholarship, Brazil,	
	$30; Sp. for "Dr. J. F. Garrison"	
	scholarship, Colored School, Colum-	
445 00	bia, South Carolina, $25; Gen., $2..	83 00
	St. Stephen's; Gen.................	25 00
	St. Wilfrid's S. S.*: Gen...........	16 29
	CAPE MAY—*Advent S. S.**: Gen.......	3 00
	CHEESEQUAKE—*Church of Our Saviour*:	
	Gen. (of which S. S.,* $12.47).....	84 67
57	CHEWS—*St. John's S. S.**: Gen......	5 00
	CLARKSBORO—*St. Peter's*: Gen. (of	
13 57	which S. S.,* $12)...............	37 00
139 95	CLEMENTON—*St. Mary's S. S.**: Gen..	2 00
193 00	CRANFORD—*Trinity Church S. S.**:	
	Gen., $39.61; Wo. Aux., Sp. for	
	Archdeacon Wentworth's work, Lex-	
20 00	ington, $5....................	44 61
	CROSSWICKS—*Grace*: Gen..........	19 00
4 02	DELAIR—*Holy Trinity Church*: Gen.	
6 50	(of which S. S.,* $11.92).........	21 92
	DOROTHY—*Holy Nativity*: Gen.......	1 87
18 81	DUNELLEN—*Holy Innocents' S. S.**:	
10 13	Gen.	20 00
4 50	ELIZABETH—*Christ Church*; Wo. Aux.,	
	Colored, $14.87; salary of Kimura	
31 28	San, Kyoto, $8; "Emma Williamson"	
	Memorial" bed, St. James's Hospital,	
79 57	Anking, $2; Sp. for Archdeacon	
2 00	Wentworth's work among the moun-	
	taineers, Lexington, $3; Dom., $1;	
5 85	S. S.,* $53.38..................	82 25
	St. John's: Gen., $74.68; Frn., $31.39;	
13 36	Rev. O. A. Glazebrook, D.D., Sp. for	
	Brazil theological books, $5; Wo.	
57 00	Aux., Sp. for Archdeacon Went-	
7 31	worth's work, Lexington, $5; Sp.	
20 49	for Christ School, Arden, Asheville,	
7 50	$5; St. Paul's School, Lawrenceville,	
	Southern Virginia, $5; salary of	
	Kimura San, Kyoto (of which "A	
	Member," $20), $25; Woman's	
	Foreign Aid, Sp. for Bishop Holly,	
	toward rebuilding church, Haiti, $15	166 07
	Trinity Church: Gen. (of which S. S.,*	
18 00	$103.26)	133 26
	FAIR HAVEN—*Church of the Holy Com-*	
	munion S. S.*: Gen..............	8 64
	FAIRVIEW—*Trinity Church*: Gen. (of	
	which S. S., $8), $15.50; Wo. Aux.,	
	St. Paul's School, Lawrenceville,	
	Southern Virginia, $1; salary of	
	Kimura San, Kyoto, $1.50........	18 00
	FLORENCE—*St. Stephen's*: Gen. (of	
	which S. S.,* $39.09), $55.17; St.	
	Ann's Guild, "A Member," St. Paul's	
76 68	School, Lawrenceville, Southern Vir-	
	ginia, $5; Bishop Payne Divinity-	
	school, Petersburg, Southern Vir-	

ginia, $5; Wo. Aux., salary of Kimura San, Kyoto, $2; "Bishop Odenheimer" scholarship, Trinity Divinity-school, Tokyo, $2; Chinese Bible-woman, $2.................. 71 17

FORT HANCOCK—Mrs. J. V. White, Sp. for St. Elizabeth's Hospital, Shanghai 5 00

FREEHOLD—*St. Peter's*: Gen. (of which S. S.,* .$30).................... 50 00

GLASSBORO—*St. Thomas's S.*, *S.*: Gen. 6 00

GLOUCESTER—*Ascension*: Gen. (of which S. S.,* $5)................... 17 00

HADDONFIELD—*Grace*: Sp. for St. Paul's College Fund, Tokyo, $3; Wo. Aux., Sp. for Archdeacon Wentworth's work, Lexington, $4; Rev. J. A. Staunton's work, Philippines, $1; salary of Kimura San, Kyoto, $1 9 00

HAMMONTON—*St. Mark's S. S.*: Gen.. 6 36

HIGHLANDS—*St. Andrew's S. S.*: Gen. 11 97

LAKEWOOD—*All Saints' Memorial S. S.*: Gen..................... 150 02

LAMBERTVILLE—*St. Andrew's S. S.*: Gen., $37.41; Wo. Aux., Sp. for Archdeacon Wentworth's work, Lexington, $1...................... 38 41

LINDEN—*Grace S. S.*: Gen........ 12 51

LITTLE SILVER—*St. John's Chapel S. S.*: Gen..................... 13 66

LONG BRANCH—*St. James's*: Asheville, $25; China, $36.91; S. S.,* Gen., $35 .... 96 91

MANTUA—*St. Barnabas' S. S.*: Gen., $1.59; Wo. Aux., St. Paul's School, Lawrenceville, Southern Virginia, $1.50; St. Augustine's School, Raleigh, North Carolina, $1........ 4 09

MERCHANTVILLE—*Grace S. S.*: Gen., $58.14; Wo. Aux., Gen., $5.66; salary of Kimura San, Kyoto, $5..... 68 80

METUCHEN—*St. Luke's*: Gen. (of which S. S.,* $24.62); $38 27; Wo. Aux., Sp. for Rev. Mr. Cuthbert, Kyoto, $17.87; Sp. for Archdeacon Wentworth's work, Lexington, $1....... 57 14

MIDDLETOWN—*Christ Church*: Gen. (of which S. S.,* $6.10).......... 31 10

MOORESTOWN—*Trinity Church*: Wo. Aux., Sp. for Colored work in school. Columbia, South Carolina, $5; Sp. for scholarship in Bishop Payne Divinity-school, Southern Virginia, $3 .... 8 00

MT. HOLLY—*St. Andrew's*: Gen. (of which S. S.,* $112.22), $149.57; Wo. Aux., Colored, $5; salary of Kimura San, Kyoto, $8; "Emma Williamson Memorial" bed, St. James's Hospital, Anking, $2....... 164 57

NAVESINK—*All Saints' Memorial S. S.*: Gen..................... 28 57

NEW BRUNSWICK — *Christ Church*: Cuba, $24.56; S. S.,* Gen., $124; Wo. Aux., Sp. for Archdeacon Wentworth's work, Lexington, $2; Bishop Restarick's work, Honolulu, $2; Miss Ridgely's work, Cape Mount, $5; Girls' Friendly Society, St. Augustine's School, Raleigh, North Carolina, $2................... 159 56

St. John's: Wo. Aux., St. Paul's School, Lawrenceville, Southern Virginia 5 00

St. John the Evangelist's: Gen. (of which S. S.,* $125), $138.70; Wo. Aux., Sp. for Christ School, Arden, Asheville, $13.................. 151 70

In Memoriam, McKee Swift and A. Hortense Swift, Easter, 1896 and 1898, Gen..................... 50 00

OCEAN CITY—"A Friend," Sp. for the new building, St. Paul's College, Tokyo.. 5 00

PERTH AMBOY—*St. Peter's*: Gen. (of

which S. S.,* $31.58), $241.58; Wo. Aux., Sp. for St. Agnes's Hospital Building Fund, Raleigh, North Carolina, $2; Bishop Payne Divinity-school, Petersburg, Virginia, $2; salary of Kimura San, Kyoto, $5; "Emma Williamson Memorial" bed, St. James's Hospital, Anking, Hankow, $2....................

PISCATAWAY—*St. James's*: Gen. (of which S. S.,* $26.02).............

PLAINFIELD—*Grace*: Dom. and Frn., $1,200; Wo. Aux. Systematic Fund, Colored; $15; Frn., $15........... 1,

St. Stephen's S. S.: Gen...........

PRINCETON—*Trinity Church*: Dom., $237.15; Frn., $123.85; Indian, $18.41; Sp. for St. John's College, Shanghai, $1; Sp. for St. Paul's College, Tokyo, $21.50; Sp. for All Saints' Church, Sioux Falls, South Dakota, $5; Wo. Aux., "Emma Williamson Memorial" bed, St. James's Hospital, Anking, $2...........

RAHWAY—*St. Paul's*: B. C. Mead, Gen. (of which S. S.,* $25), $30; Wo. Aux., Colored, $5; Sp. for Mrs. Wetmore's school, Asheville, $1; Sp. for Archdeacon Wentworth's work, Lexington, $1; Sp. for Holy Trinity Orphanage, Tokyo, $5.............

RED BANK—*Trinity Church*: Wo. Aux., Colored, $5; salary of Kimura San, Kyoto, $5...................

RIVERTON—*Christ Church*: Frn., $50; Gen., $50; Wo. Aux., Bishop Payne Divinity-school, Petersburg, Southern Virginia, $10; Sp. for Good Samaritan Hospital, Charlotte, North Carolina, $2.50; S. S.,* Gen., $130.17...

ROCKY HILL—*Trinity Church S. S.*: Sp. for Archdeacon Spurr, West Virginia, $5; Sp. for Rev. M. S. Taylor, Yadkin Valley, Colwell County, Asheville, $5; Sp. for Rev. A. M. Sherman, Hankow, $3; In Memoriam, Daniel C. Faulk, Gen., $5.. Sarah V. Balmer, Gen...........

ROSELLE—*St. Luke's S. S.*: "De La Rue Home" scholarship, St.. Margaret's School, Tokyo..........

RUMSON — *St. George's-by-the-River*: Gen. (of which S. S.,* $40)........

SCOTCH PLAINS—*All Saints' S. S.*: Gen. ....

SHREWSBURY—*Christ Church*: Gen. (of which S. S.,* $31), $42; Wo. Aux., Colored, $2; Frn., $2; salary of Kimura San, Kyoto, $1.............

SOMERVILLE—*St. John's S. S.*: Gen..

SOUTH AMBOY—*Christ Church*: Dom., $6.05; Frn., 50 cts.; Gen., $65.12; Wo. Aux., salary of Kimura San, Kyoto, $4.26; "Emma Williamson Memorial" bed, St. James's Hospital, Anking, Hankow, $2; Dom., $6.26; Colored, $6.26...................

Christ Church S. S.: $86.20; Doane Memorial S. S.*: $11.89; Chapel of the Good Shepherd, $5.57; for Boone University, Wuchang, $50; for St. Mary's School, Shanghai, $50; Sp. for St. Mary's Orphanage, Shanghai, $3.66

SOUTH VINELAND— *Christ Church S. S.*: Gen. ....

SPOTTSWOOD—*St. Peter's S. S.*: Gen.

SPRING LAKE—"In Memory of G. A. S." Gen. ....

SWEDESBORO—*Trinity Church S S.*: Sp. for the Building Fund of school in Porto Rico under Rev. Mr. Worden ....

TRENTON—*All Saints'*: Gen. (of which S. S.,* $60.69)..................

for Rev. John S. Moody, Hickory,
Asheville, $25....................... 226 33
MARLBORO—*Christ Church S. S.*:
Gen. 5 10
MATTEAWAN—*St. Luke's S. S.*: Gen.. 85 00
MIDDLETOWN—*Grace S. S.*: Gen..... 42 48
MILLBROOK—*Grace S. S.*: Gen...... 40 00
MOHEGAN—*St. Mary's S. S.*: Gen.... 1 00
MONROE—*Grace*: Gen.............. 7 00
MONTGOMERY — *St. Andrew's Chapel
S. S.*: Gen..................... 90
MONTICELLO—*St. John's S. S.*: Gen., 20 00
MONTROSE—*Divine Love S. S.*: Gen.. 6 63
MOUNT VERNON—*Ascension*: Wo. Aux.,
Sp. for the Hospital of the Good
Shepherd, Fort Defiance, Arizona,
$20; S. S.* Gen., $212.86....... 232 86
Trinity Church: Junior Aux., $10, S.
S.,* $93.03, Gen................ 103 03
NEWBURGH—*St. George's*: Junior Aux.,
Gen. 15 00
St. Paul's S. S.: Gen............. 10 00
NEW CITY—*St. John's S. S.*: Gen..... 5 39
NEW ROCHELLE—*Trinity Church*: Wo.
Aux., Sp. for Rev. Mr. Nichols for
Training-school for Catechists,
Shanghai, $7.25; St. Augustine's
League, Sp. for St. Agnes's Hospital,
Raleigh, North Carolina, $10; Junior
Aux., for travelling expenses of
Archdeacon Stuck, $30............ 47 25
NEW YORK—*All Angels'*: Gen........ 133 94
All Saints' S. S.: Gen............. 19 67
Ascension: Sp. for St. Mary's Build-
ing Fund, Kyoto, $50; S. S.,* Gen.,
$86.57 .... 136 57
Ascension Memorial: Wo. Aux., Sp.
for Mrs. Wetmore, Asheville...... 50 00
Ascension (West New Brighton): Wo.
Aux., Sp. for Rev. Dr. Pott, Shang-
hai, $42.56; Girls' Friendly Society,
Sp. for Archdeacon Spurr for
schools in West Virginia, $12.50... 55 06
Atonement (Bronx): Gen. (of which
S. S.,* $15).................... 25 00
Beloved Disciple: $25.65, S. S.,*
$69.33, Gen.................... 94 98
Calvary: Gen., $1,594.59; Wo. Aux.,
Frn., $50; Junior Aux., $10, S. S.*
$67.47, Gen....................1,722 06
Christ Church: Wo. Aux., Frn., $1.50;
S. S.,* Bontok Mission, Philippine
Islands, $20; Gen., $40.......... 61 50
Christ Church (New Brighton): Wo.
Aux., Sp. for Mrs. Wetmore's medical
missionary, Asheville, $5; Sp. for
Bishop Robinson, Nevada (of which,
"In Memory of A. B. C.," $50),
$92.56; Sp. for Mrs. Wetmore, Ashe-
ville, $113; Junior Aux., $15, S.
S.,* $123, Gen.................. 348 56
Epiphany: Brotherhood of St. Andrew,
Gen., $15; Girls' Branch Junior
Aux., Gen., $15; St. Augustine's
League, Sp. for scholarship at St.
Mary's School, Nashville, Tennessee,
$25; S. S.,* Dom., $75; Frn., $100. 230 00
Grace: Indian, $307.43; Frn., $731.03;
Mrs. C. H. Coster, $25, W. Brenton
Welling, $25, Frn.; Woman's For-
eign Missionary Association, "Bishop
H. C. Potter" scholarship, Girls'
High School, Kyoto, $50; Elizabeth
Bunn Memorial, Wuchang, Hankow,
$50; Mexico, $100; Frn., $100; Sp.
for Dr. Pott, Shanghai, $200; "A
Member," Sp. for Rev. R. C. Wilson,
Zangzok, Shanghai, $30; through St.
Augustine's League Committee on
Missions for Colored People, Sp. for
one day, August 6th, at St. Agnes's
Hospital, Raleigh, North Carolina,
"In Memory of Dr. Huntington,"
$250; Sp. for St. Agnes's Hospital,
Raleigh, North Carolina, $10; Sp.

for Good Samaritan Hospital, Charlotte, North Carolina, $10; Sp. for the "Edward Delafield" scholarship, St. Paul's School, Lawrenceville, Southern Virginia, $25............ 1,913 46
Grace S. S.* (West Farms): Gen.... 15 00
Grace Emmanuel S. S.*: Gen........ 10 00
Heavenly Rest: Gen., $1,683.66; Woman's Foreign Missionary Association, "Loving Hand" scholarship, St. John's University, Shanghai, $50; "Parker Morgan" scholarship, Girls' Training Institute, Africa, $40; "Howland" scholarship, $50, "Pure in Heart Memorial" scholarship, $50, "Anna" scholarship, $50, Girls' High School, Kyoto; S. S.,* Gen., $33.72.................... 1,957 38
Holy Apostles': Gen., $67.85; Woman's Missionary Association, Sp. for Foreign Life Insurance Fund, $5; Sp. for Rev. Mr. Cuthbert's work, Kyoto, $51.65 .... 124 50
Church of the Holy Communion: Wo. Aux., Frn., $25; Junior Aux., Sp. for "Langford" scholarship, Alaska, $5; S. S.,* Gen., $12.20........... 42 20
Holy Cross: Frn................. 6 00
Holyrood: Gen., $42; S. S.,* Dom., $60; Frn., $23.27............... 125 27
Holy Trinity (Harlem): Colored, $19.82; Sp. for St. Mary's Building Fund, Kyoto, $21; S. S.,* Gen., $783.50 .... 824 32
Incarnation: Sp. for Rev. W. J. Cuthbert, for a church in Kyoto, $200; Wo. Aux., Frn., $155; Sp. for St. John's Industrial School, Cape Mount, Africa, $10; Sp. for Expansion Fund, St. John's University, Shanghai, $50; Sp. for St. Mary's Building Fund, Kyoto, $100; the Montgomery Memorial Society, for Mrs. Hooker's School for Girls in Mexico, $254; Sp. for translating, publishing, Spanish Church literature, $30; "A Member," through Niobrara League, Sp. for Bishop Hare Memorial, All Saints' School, South Dakota, $5; St. Augustine's League, Sp. for St. Agnes's Hospital, North Carolina, $105; S. S., for the "Montgomery" scholarship, St. John's University, Shanghai, $40... 949 00
Incarnation Chapel: $170.61, S. S.,* $180.30, Gen..................... 350 91
Intercession: Woman's Missionary Society, Sp. for Dr. Myers, for hospital work, Shanghai, $20; S. S.,* Gen., $160.25 .... 180 25
Church of the Mediator: Colored, $24.41; S. S.,* Gen., $31.39....... 55 80
Church of the Mediator (Kingsbridge): Gen., $8; Sp. for St. Paul's College, Tokyo, $2.43; Wo. Aux., Sp. for Bishop Thomas, Wyoming, $20; Sp. for Rev. G. P. Mayo, Virginia, $20.. 45 43
Messiah Chapel S. S.*: Gen.......... 38 88
Church of the Redeemer: Gen........ 43 61
San Salvatore S. S.*: Gen.......... 10 63
St. Agnes's Chapel: Wo. Aux., Sp. for Zangzok Station Equipment Fund, Shanghai 15 00
St. Andrew's: Gen., $571.40; Mrs. P. J. L. Searing, Wo. Aux., Sp. for Hospital of the Good Shepherd, Fort Defiance, Arizona, $20; S. S.,* Gen., $41.27 .... 632 67
St. Andrew's (Richmond): Mrs. J. McE. Ames, Wo. Aux., $25, S. S.,* $45, Gen. 70 00
St. Ann's S. S.* (Morrisania): Gen.. 191 00
St. Augustine's S. S.*: Gen........ 75 00
St. Bartholomew's: Dom., $2,000; Frn., $2,000; Wo. Aux., Sp. for Domestic Contingent Fund, $25; Junior Aux., Gen., $55; Alaska, $175; Philippine Islands, $175; S. S.,* Sp. for Rev. Dr. Pott, Shanghai, $235.. 4,665
St. Bartholomew's Swedish S. S.* (Bronx): Sp. for Rev. Dr. Pott, Shanghai 30
St. Chrysostom's Chapel: Frn., $23.61; Wo. Aux., Sp..for St. Mary's, Kyoto, $6; S. S.,* Gen., $22.03........... 51
St. Clement's: For Rev. R. C. Wilson's work in Zangzok, Shanghai, $27.13; S. S.,* Gen., $25.................. 52
St. Esprit's S. S.*: Gen........... 25
St. Faith's: Missionary Society of the New York Training-school for Deaconesses, Alaska, $8; Sp. for Dr. Brown, Brazil, for purchase of books for students, $10; Sp. for Deaconess Routledge's work, Philippines, $4; Gen., $1; Sp. for Deaconess Patterson, Oklahoma, $5.50; Sp. for Miss Van Deerlin, St. Mary's House, Molili, Honolulu, $14.25; Sp. for Deaconess Affleck, Mexico, $7; Sp. for Miss Virginia Mitchell, Glendale Springs, Asheville, $7.50.......... 57
St. George's: Wo. Aux., Sp. for Bishop Graves's Clergy Fund, Kearney, $100; Sp. for Bishop Funsten's Clergy Fund, Idaho, $100; Sp. for Archdeacon Spurr, West Virginia, $50; Sp. for Charlotte Lowery School, Moundsville, West Virginia, $25; Sp. for scholarship, Bishop Garrett's School, Dallas, $75; Missionary Society, Frn., $100; Sp. for St. John's University, Shanghai, $520; St. Augustine's League, Sp. for St. Paul's School, Lawrenceville, Southern Virginia, $50; Girls' Friendly Society, Sp. for Girls' School, Bontok, Philippine Islands, $20 1,040
St. James's: Sp. for St. Mary's Building Fund, Kyoto, $50; Wo. Aux., Frn., $25; Sp. for St. Mary's Church, Kyoto, $545; Sp. for Bishop Brown's Building Fund, Arkansas, $50; Sp. for Archdeacon Spurr, West Virginia, $25; Sp. for Bishop Nichols, San Francisco Sunshine Fund, California, $2.50; Domestic Committee, Wo. Aux., Sp. for Rev. Mr. Mayo, Virginia, $25; Girls' Friendly Society, Sp. for Girls' School, Baguio, Philippine Islands, $50; S. S.,* Gen., $320.35.................... 1,092
St. James's (Fordham): Gen......... 180
St. John's (Clifton): Wo. Aux., Sp. for Bishop Rowe, Alaska.............. 42
St. Luke's: Colored................. 20
St. Luke's S. S.* (Rossville): Gen.... 5
St. Margaret's S. S.*: Dom.......... 73
St. Mark's: $39.27, S. S.,* $76.68, Gen. 115
St. Mary's S. S.* (Castleton): Gen... 42
St. Mary's S. S.* (Manhattanville): Gen. 50
St. Mary's S. S.* (Mott Haven): For the "Stephen Wheatly Moore and St. Mary's, Mott Haven" scholarships, Boys' School, Soochow, $24.08; Gen., $10.25 34
St. Mary-the-Virgin S. S.*: Gen...... 10
St. Matthew's: Gen., $10.75; Wo. Aux., "E. S. D. B.," Sp. for "Constance" scholaship, St. Mary's Orphanage, Shanghai, $30; St. Augustine's League, Sp. for St. Christopher's ward, St. Agnes's Hospital, Raleigh, North Carolina, $10; Mr. Smith, St. Augustine's League, Sp. for St. James's Mission, Lunenburg, Southern Virginia, $5; S. S.,* Gen., $85.. 1,205

Mrs. E. A. Hoffman, Sp. for Zang-
zok Station Equipment Fund, Shang-
hai 100 00
R. F. Cutting, $100, Mrs. Scrymser,
$100, Miss Blanche Potter, $50,
Bishop Greer, $100, "A Friend,"
$10, "A Friend," $250, "A Friend,"
$150, Sp. for St. Mary's Building
Fund, Kyoto...................... 760 00
"A Friend," Colored, $50; Sp. for
Bishop Hare Memorial, South Da-
kota, $50........................ 100 00
Wo. Aux., former members of the
Central Committee, for the "Mrs.
John H. Clark" scholarship, Hooker
School, Mexico................... 80 00
"Eight men of the G. T. S.," Sp. for
Catechist School, Shanghai........ 50 00
William Alexander Smith, Sp. for
St. John's University Expansion
Fund, Shanghai................... 50 00
The United Monthly Missionary
meetings of the Staten Island
branches of the Wo. Aux., Sp. for
Bishop F. F. Johnson, South Da-
kota, $42.56; "A Member, Wo. Aux.,
Sp. for Shanghai and Catechist's
School, Land and Building Fund,
$100 .... 142 56
"I. B.," Sp. for Bishop Rowe, Alaska,
for Thermos bottles, for four mis-
sionaries in Alaska.............. 35 47
Joseph W. Cushman, Sp. for St.
John's University Expansion Fund,
Shanghai 25 00
Miss Mary F. Ogden, Gen.......... 25 00
Sarah W. Swords, Sp. for Miss Ethel
J. Wheeler, Boone College, Wu-
chang, Hankow, for Miss Byerley's
Industrial School, Wuchang, Han-
kow 25 00
Miss E. S. Johnson, Sp. for Bishop
Rowe, Alaska..................... 15 10
Mrs. Mary E. Watson, Wo. Aux.,
Sp. for Rev. Nathan Matthews, Cape
Mount, for Industrial School, Af-
rica, $5; contents of a red mite-
box, Africa, $5.................. 10 00
"A Friend," Sp. for Expansion Fund,
St. John's University, Shanghai.... 6 00
Mrs. N. E. Baylies, Wo. Aux., Sp.
for Hospital of the Good Shepherd,
Fort Defiance, Arizona........... 5 00
Emily S. Walker, Gen............. 5 00
Isabel F. Jacot, Sp. for Alaskan
Hospital Fund................... 1 00
NORTH SALEM—*St. James's*: $31.74,
S. S.,* $17.46, Gen.............. 49 20
NYACK—*Grace*: Junior Aux., $15, S.
S.,* $32.86, Gen................ 47 86
OSSINING—*All Saints' S. S.** (Briar
Cliff) : Gen.................... 23 12
Grace Hall: $16.25, S. S.,* $6, Gen.. 22 25
PEARL RIVER—*St. Stephen's S. S.**:
Gen. 88
PEEKSKILL—*St. Peter's S. S.**: Dom.. 90 50
PELHAM—*Church of the Redeemer*:
Wo. Aux., Sp. for Hospital of the
Good Shepherd, Fort Defiance, Ari-
zona, $15; S. S.,* Gen., $9.05..... 24 05
PELHAM MANOR—*Christ Church S. S.**:
Gen. 21 75
PINE PLAINS—*Regeneration S. S.**:
Gen. 2 36
PLEASANTVILLE—*St. John's S. S.**:
Gen. 27 08
PORT JERVIS—*Grace S. S.**: Dom.,
$1.50 ; Frn., $1.50.............. 3 00
POUGHKEEPSIE—*Christ Church*: Gen.,
$30; Sp. for Dr. Pott, St. John's
College, Shanghai, $1............ 31 00
St. Faith's School: Junior Aux., Gen.. 5 00
St. Paul's: Colored, $27.29; Gen.,
$10.67; Sp. for St. John's Univer-
sity Expansion Fund, Shanghai,
$18.25 .... 56 21

RHINEBECK—*Church of the Messiah S.
S.*: Gen........................ 30 17
RIVERDALE—*Christ Church*: Wo. Aux.,
Sp. for Bishop Rowe, Alaska....... 35 00
RYE—*Christ Church*: Wo. Aux., for
the "W. W. Kirkby" scholarship,
St. John's School, East . Mount,
Africa 25 00
SCARBOROUGH—*St. Mary's*: Dom., $90;
S. S.,* Gen., $12.25............. 102 25
SOMERS—*St. Luke's*: $12.29, S. S.,*
$2.71, Gen...................... 15 00
SPARKILL—*Christ Church S. S.*: Gen. 1 95
SPRING VALLEY—*St. Paul's S. S.*:
Gen. 3 50
STAATSBURG—*St. Margaret's*; $68, S.
S.,* $31.50, Gen................. 99 50
STONE RIDGE AND HIGH FALLS—*St.
Peter's and St. John's S. S.*: Gen. 37 40
SUFFERN—*Christ Church*: $9.12, S.
S.,* $20, Gen.................... 29 12
TARRYTOWN—*Christ Church S. S.*:
Sp. for Mrs. Wetmore, Christ School,
Arden, Asheville................. 39 55
St. Mark's S. S. (North) Gen...... 12 00
TIVOLI—*St. Paul's*: Gen....,....... 83 87
TUCKAHOE—*St. John's S.*: Gen... 18 92
TUXEDO—*St. Mary's S. S.*: For the
"Tuxedo" scholarship, St. Eliza-
beth's School, South Dakota....... 60 00
Junior Aux., Gen................. 75 00
WEST PARK—*Ascension S. S.*: Gen.. 13 02
WEST POINT—United States Military
Academy, Gen., $27.12; Sp. for
Bishop Knight, Cuba, $25; Sp. for
Catechists' School at Shanghai, $25. 77 12
YONKERS—*Advent Chapel S. S.*: Gen. 19 27
St. John's: Junior Aux., Gen., $400;
Sp. for the "William S. Langford"
scholarship, Alaska, $25; Sp. for
Archdeacon Spurr, West Virginia,
$25 .... 450 00
St. Paul's S. S.: Gen............. 60 00
Thomas Ewing, Jr., Sp. for St.
John's University Expansion Fund,
Shanghai 100 00
MISCELLANEOUS—Domestic Committee,
Wo. Aux., Dom.................. 1,150 00
St. Augustine's League, Sp. for St.
Paul's School, Lawrenceville, South-
ern Virginia, $100; Sp. for St. Au-
gustine's School, Raleigh, North
Carolina, $100; Sp. for Rev. Rich-
ard Bright, Savannah, Georgia, $50;
Sp. for Rev. P. P. Alston, Charlotte,
North Carolina, $50............. 300 00
United Monthly Missionary meetings
of the Staten Island branches of the
Wo. Aux., Sp. for Rev. R. A. Walk-
er's work, Tokyo................ 42 56
Archdeaconry of Orange, Wo. Aux.,
for the "Mrs. J. J. Mitchell Memor-
ial" scholarship, Girls' High School,
Kyoto 40 00
Estate of Dr. Andrew H. Smith, for
the "Sophia Davison" scholarship,
St. John's School, Cape Mount, West
Africa 25 00
Girls' Friendly Society,· Sp. for St.
Elizabeth's Building Fund, Shanghai. 32 00

North Carolina

Ap. $1,654.77; *Sp.* $192.58

ANSONVILLE—*All Souls' S. S.*: Dom. 3 71
BATTLEBORO—*St. John's*: $4.50, S.
S.,* $5, Gen.................... 9 50
BURLINGTON — *St. Athanasius's*: Wo.
Aux., salary of Miss Annie Cheshire,
Shanghai, $3, S. S.,* $10, Gen..... 13 00
CHAPEL HILL—*Chapel of the Cross*:
Dom. and Frn., $14.18; Gen., $52.80. 66 98
CHARLOTTE—*St. Martin's Chapel*: Gen. 7 30
St. Mary-the-Virgin: Indians in South-
ern Florida, $2.16; Dom., 94 cts.;

Frn., $7.45; Sp. for St. Paul's Col-
lege, Tokyo, Japan, $3.41; Junior
Aux., St. Augustine's School, Ral-
eigh, North Carolina, $1.50; Miss
Cheshire's salary, Shanghai, $3.97;
Sp. for Mrs. N. P. Jeffroy's School,
Beaufort, East Carolina, $1.90; S.
S.,* Gen., $11................... 32
St. Peter's: Wo. Aux., salary of Miss
Annie Cheshire, Shanghai, $25; sal-
ary of Miss Babcock, Tokyo, $5;
Frn., $210; Gen., $10; Sp. for "Bish-
op Cheshire" scholarship, Holy Trin-
ity Orphanage, Tokyo, $10........ 260
COOLEEMEE—*Church of the Good Shep-
herd*: Wo. Aux., Alaska, 25 cts.; sal-
ary of Miss Annie Cheshire, Shang-
hai, $1.25; salary of Miss Babcock,
Tokyo, 25 cts.; Miss E. T. Ches-
hire's work, Hankow, $1.25; Sp. for
Bishop Gray, Southern Florida, 50
cts.; Sp. for "Bishop Cheshire"
scholarship, Holy Trinity Orphanage,
Tokyo, 50 cts.; Sp. for Bishop Mc-
Kim, Tokyo, for "Lindsay Patton"
scholarship, 50 cts............... 4
DUKE—*St. Stephen's*: Gen., $5; Wo.
Aux., Alaska, $1; salary of Miss
Annie Cheshire, Shanghai, $1; Sp.
·for ."Bishop Cheshire" scholarship,
Holy Trinity Orphanage, Tokyo, $1. 8
DURHAM—*St. Philip's*: Gen., $79; Wo.
Aux., Dom., $8; Sp. for Bishop Gray,
Southern Florida, $3............. 90
St. Philip's Deaf-Mute Mission S. S.:
Gen. .... ·8
St. Philip's Mission S. S. (East Dur-
ham): Gen...................... 10
ENFIELD—*Advent*: Wo. Aux., Sp. for
Bishop Gray, Southern Florida, $5;
S. S.,* Gen., $29.16.............. 34
GREENSBORO—*Church of the Redeemer
S. S.*: Gen...................... 3
St. Andrew's: Wo. Aux., Miss Hicks's
work, Philippines, $1; salary of Miss
Annie Cheshire, Shanghai, $5; Miss
E. T. Cheshire's work, Hankow, $5;
Gen., $5; Sp. for Bishop Gray,
Southern Florida, $2; S. S.,* Gen.,
$16.13 34
St. Barnabas's: Wo. Aux., Miss Hicks's
work, Philippines, $3; Frn., $2.50;
salary of Miss Annie Cheshire,
Shanghai, $5; Miss E. T. Cheshire's
work, Hankow, $5; Gen., $1; Sp. for
"Bishop Cheshire" scholarship, Holy
Trinity Orphanage, Tokyo, $4; Sp.
for Bishop McKim, for "Lindsay
Patton" scholarship, Tokyo, $3; S.
S.,* Gen., $15................... 38
HALIFAX—*St. Mark's*: Wo. Aux., sal-
ary of Miss Annie Cheshire, Shang-
hai, $1; Miss E. T. Cheshire's work,
Hankow, $1; Junior Aux., Gen.,
$1.15 3
HENDERSON — *Holy Innocents'*: Wo.
Aux., Frn., 78 cts.; salary of Miss
Annie Cheshire, Shanghai, $5; Miss
E. T. Cheshire's work, Hankow, $5;
Gen., $5; Sp. for Bishop Gray,
Southern Florida, $5............. 20
HIGH POINT—*St. Mary's S. S.*: Gen. 5
HILLSBORO—*St. Matthew's*: Gen., 50
cts.; Wo. Aux., Frn., $2.75; salary
of Miss Annie Cheshire, Shanghai,
$15; Sp. for Bishop McKim, for
"Lindsay Patton" scholarship, Tokyo,
67 cts.; Junior Aux., St. Augustine's
School, Raleigh, North Carolina, $1;
Sp. for Holy Trinity Orphanage,
Tokyo, $5; Gen., $5; S. S.,* Gen.,
$44.45 123
JACKSON—*Church of the Saviour*: Wo.
Aux., salary of Miss Babcock, Tokyo,
$2; Gen. (of which Junior Aux., $1).

(of which S. S.,* $21.05), $31.05;
Sp. for Holy Trinity Orphanage,
7 00 Tokyo, $5; St. Augustine's School,
5 00 S. S.,* Gen., $42.01.............. 78 06
50 *St. Mary's School*: Gen., $7.91; Wo.
Aux., $5; Junior Aux., $15; "Aldert
Smedes" scholarship, St. Mary's
Hall, Shanghai.................. 27 91
17 19 *St. Saviour's*: Gen., $14; Wo. Aux.,
salary of Miss Annie Cheshire,
17 20 Shanghai, $5.................. 19 00
19 75 RIDGEWAY—*Church of the Good Shepherd*: Wo. Aux., salary of Miss Annie
16 32 Cheshire, Shanghai, $1; Miss E. T.
Cheshire's work, Hankow, $1; salary
of Miss Babcock, Tokyo, 25 cts.;
Gen., 25 cts.; Sp. for "Bishop
Cheshire" scholarship, Holy Trinity
12 00 Orphanage, Tokyo, 25 cts.; Sp. for
7 00 Bishop McKim for "Lindsay Patton"
1 00 scholarship, Tokyo, 25 cts.; Sp. for
Bishop Gray, Southern Florida, 25
cts.; Junior Aux., Sp. for Holy
Trinity Orphanage, Tokyo, $1...... 4 25
*St. Luke's S. S.**: Gen.............. 2 31
5 00 ROCKINGHAM—*Church of the Messiah
S. S.**: Gen..................... 3 15
2 00 ROCKY MOUNT—*Church of the Good
Shepherd*: Wo. Aux., Alaska, $5;
$36.53; Gen. (of which S. S.,* $31.53),
salary of Miss Babcock,
4 72 Tokyo, $5; salary of Miss Annie
• Cheshire, Shanghai, $10; Sp. for
Bishop Gray, Southern Florida,
$2.50; Sp. for "Bishop Cheshire"
scholarship, Holy Trinity Orphanage,
Tokyo, $5; Sp. for Cathedral School
for girls, Havana, Cuba, $5........ 69 03
15 81 SALISBURY—*St. Luke's*: Wo. Aux., salary of Miss Babcock, Tokyo, $2;
1 00 Gen. (of which S. S.,* $15.18),
$20.18; Sp. for "Bishop Cheshire"
1 84 scholarship, Holy Trinity Orphan-
1 00 age, Tokyo, $2.................. 24 18
SCOTLAND NECK—*Trinity Church*: Wo.
1 48 Aux., salary of Miss Annie Cheshire,
Shanghai, $1; Miss E. T. Cheshire's
work. Hankow, $1; salary of Miss
Babcock, Tokyo, $1; Gen., $1; Sp.
for "Bishop Cheshire" scholarship,
Holy Trinity Orphanage, Tokyo, $1;
Junior Aux., St. Augustine's School,
Raleigh, North Carolina, $1; Sp. for
Holy Trinity Orphanage, Tokyo, $1. 7 00
SOUTHERN PINES—*Emmanuel Church*:
Frn., $5; Gen., $11.80; Sp. for St.
Paul's College Building Fund,
28 50 Tokyo, 50 cts.; S. S.,* Gen., $7.62.. 24 92
SPRAY—*St. Luke's Chapel*: Gen...... 12 16
2 00 STATESVILLE—*Trinity Church S. S.**:
Gen. 59
STONEVILLE—*Emmanuel Church*: Wo.
Aux., Alaska, 25 cts.; salary of Miss
Annie Cheshire, Shanghai, 25 cts.;
Miss E. T. Cheshire's work, Hankow,
25 cts.; Miss Hicks's work, Philip-
pines, 15 cts.; Gen., 50 cts.; Sp. for
"Bishop Cheshire" scholarship, Holy
Trinity Orphanage, Tokyo, 10 cts... 1 50
77 80 TARBORO—*Calvary*: $50, S.S.,* $107.50,
Wo. Aux., $10, Gen.; Wo. Aux., sal-
ary of Miss Annie Cheshire, Shang-
hai, $2.35; salary of Miss Babcock,
Tokyo, $5; Sp. for "Bishop Cheshire"
scholarship, Holy Trinity Orphanage,
Tokyo, $5; Junior Aux., Alaska, $1;
St. Mary's Hall, Shanghai, $3; Sp.
for Easter School, Baguio, Philippines, $6....................... 189 85
St. Luke's: Wo. Aux., Sp. for Bishop
Ferguson, West Africa............ 2 00
TROUTMAN'S—*St. James's S. S.**: Gen. 1 64
127 38 WADESBORO — *Calvary*: Wo. Aux.,
3 00 Alaska, $1; Sp. for Bishop Gray,
Southern Florida, $1.25; Sp. for St.

Mary's Orphanage, Shanghai, $3;
S. S.,* Gen., $6.72................. 11 97
WARRENTON—*All Saints'*: Wo. Aux.,
Gen. 2 00
Emmanuel Church: Wo. Aux., Gen.
(of which S. S.,* $34.17), $37.17;
Alaska, $2; salary of Miss Annie
Cheshire, Shanghai, $1; Miss E, T.
Cheshire's work, Hankow, $1..... 41 17
WELDON—*Grace S. S.**: Gen......... 22 50
WEST DURHAM—*St. Joseph's*: Gen.... 5 00
WILSON—*St. Timothy's*: Wo. Aux.,
Wo. Aux., salary of Miss Annie
Cheshire, Shanghai, $5; Sp. for
"Bishop Cheshire" scholarship, Holy
Trinity Orphanage, Tokyo, $2.50;
Junior Aux., $1, S. S.,* $32.31, Gen. 40 81
WINSTON—*St. Paul's*: Wo. Aux., Gen.
(of which S. S.,* $18.96),
Alaska, $1; salary of Miss Annie
Cheshire, Shanghai, $5; salary of
Miss Babcock, Tokyo, $3.......... 32 96
WINSTON-SALEM—*Mission S. S.**: Gen. 5 32
WOODLEAF—*St. George's Chapel S. S.**:
Gen. 50
MISCELLANEOUS—Convocation of Char-
lotte, North Carolina, Sp. for work
under Rev. Dr. Correll, Tsu, Kyoto.. 25 00
Convocation of Raleigh, North Caro-
lina, Sp. for work under Rev. Dr.
Correll, Tsu, Kyoto................. 41 50

Ohio

Ap. $2,566.34; *Sp.* $18.61

AKRON—*Church of Our Saviour*: Gen.
(of which S. S.,* $20)............ 28 15
St. Paul's: Gen., $150; Daughters of
the Church, Sp. for Dr. A. M.
Myers's hospital, Shanghai, $5..... 155 00
ASHTABULA—*St. Peter's*: Wo. Aux.,
salary of Miss Elwin, Shanghai.... 5 00
BUCYRUS—*St. John's*: Gen........... 5 00
CARDINGTON—*Church of the Good Shep-
herd*: Gen............................ 1 09
CLEVELAND—*All Saints'*: Gen........ 3 21
*Christ Church S. S.**: Gen.......... 10 00
Emmanuel Church: Gen............ 175 08
Grace (South): Gen................. 15 13
*Incarnation S. S.**: Gen............ 20 00
St. Luke's: Babies' Branch, Gen..... 1 05
St. Mark's: Gen..................... 8 62
St. Paul's: Dom. and Frn., $800; Wo.
Aux., Brooks Society, $10, St. Moni-
ca's Society, $5, Sacramento;
"Ohio," scholarship, St. Elizabeth's
School, South Dakota (of which St.
Monica's Society, $5), $25; salary of
Miss Elwin, Shanghai (of which St.
Monica's Society, $5), $20; Alaska,
$10; Kearney, $10; The Philippines,
$10; Fukui, Kyoto, $10; Cape
Palmas, Africa, $10; "Julia Bedell"
scholarship, $10, "G. T. Bedell"
scholarship, $5, St. John's Univer-
sity, Shanghai, S. S.,* Gen., $70... 995 00
Trinity Cathedral S. S.: Sp. for Bishop
Rowe, Alaska, $8.61; Wo. Aux., Mrs.
Leonard, Alaska, $100; salary of
Miss Elwin, Shanghai, $50; Gen.,
$100; Mrs. C. P. Ranney, Alaska,
$25; salary of Miss Elwin, Shanghai,
$5; Junior Aux., salary of Miss
Elwin, Shanghai, $10; Sp. for Row-
land Hall, Utah, $5; Gen., $5...... 308 61
S. S.,* Gen........................... 1 00
DEFIANCE—*Grace S. S.**: Gen....... 8 02
DENNISON—*St. Barnabas's*: Gen..... 12 00
FREMONT—*St. Paul's S. S.**: Gen.... 13 54
GALION—*Grace*; Gen................ 12 00
GAMBIER — *Bedell Memorial Chapel,
Harcourt Parish*: Gen............. 2 78
Harcourt Parish: St. Margaret's
School, Tokyo, $2; Dom. and Frn.,
$29.53 .... 31 53

GENEVA—*Christ Church*: Gen.......
HURON—*Christ Church*: Wo. Aux.,
"Julia Bedell" scholarship, St.
John's University, Shanghai, $10;
salary of Miss Elwin, Shanghai, $5.
KENTON—*St. Paul's*: Gen...........
KINGSVILLE—Mrs. Warren H. Roberts,
Gen. ....
LAKEWOOD—*St. Peter's*: Gen.......
LISBON—*Trinity Church*: Gen.......
LORAIN—*Church of the Redeemer*:
Gen. ....
MARION—*St. Paul's S. S.**: Gen.....
MEDINA—*St. Paul's*: Gen...........
MT. VERNON—*St. Paul's*: Dom., $9;
Frn., $9..............................
NORWALK—*St. Paul's*: Juniors, salary
of Miss Elwin, Shanghai, $2; Gen.,
$1 ....
OBERLIN—*Christ Church*: Wo. Aux.,
salary of Miss Elwin, Shanghai....
PAINESVILLE — *St. James's*: Juniors,
Alaska, $5; Oklahoma, $5; Gen., $5.
PENINSULA — *Bronson Memorial
Church S. S.**: Gen.................
SANDUSKY—*Calvary*: Juniors, Okla-
homa, $5; salary of Miss Elwin,
Shanghai, $5; Fukui, Kyoto, $2....
Grace: Juniors, Philippines.........
"In loving memory of one gone be-
fore," Gen............................
SHELBY—*St. Mark's Mission S. S.**:
Gen. ....
TIFFIN—*Trinity Church*: Gen.......
TOLEDO—*Grace*: Gen...............
St. Andrew's: Church Extension, $1.30;
Juniors, Gen., $1....................
St. John's: Wo. Aux., salary of Miss
Elwin, Shanghai......................
St. Mark's: Gen. (of which Wo. Aux.,
$5), $157.58; Wo. Aux., Alaska, $10
Trinity Church: Gen., $210; Juniors,
"Ohio" scholarship, St. Elizabeth's
School, South Dakota, $1; Fukui,
Kyoto, $5............................
WARREN—*Christ Church*: Gen.......
YOUNGSTOWN—*St. John's*: Frn., $7;
Gen., $50.54.........................
MISCELLANEOUS—"Friends," Gen.....

Oregon

Ap. $756.37

ALBANY—*St. Peter's*: Gen..........
ASHLAND—*Trinity Church*: Gen. (of
which S. S.,* $17.80)..............
ASTORIA—*Grace*: Junior Aux., support
of scholar, Trinity Divinity-school,
Tokyo, $3.30; S. S.,* Gen., $57.30..
*Holy Innocents' S. S.**: Gen........
BANDON—*St. John's S. S.**: Gen.....
CARLTON—Gen........................
COQUILLE—*St. James's S. S.**: Gen..
CORVALLIS—*Good Samaritan S. S.**:
Gen. ....
COTTAGE GROVE—Gen................
DAYTON—Gen.........................
EUGENE—Mrs. W. J. Beeve, Gen.....
GRANT'S PASS—*St. Luke's S. S.**:
Frn. ....
HAMMOND—*St. John's*: Gen........
MARSHFIELD—*Emmanuel Church*: $15,
S. S.,* $9.02, Gen...................
MEDFORD—*St. Mark's*: $23.50, S. S.,*
$11.25, Gen..........................
MILWAUKEE—*St. John's S. S.**: Gen..
PORTLAND—*Church of the Good Shep-
herd S. S.**: Gen...................
Grace: Gen..........................
St. Andrew's (Portsmouth): $7.50, S.
S.,* $16, Gen........................
St. David's: Gen....................
St. Helen's Hall: Gen..............
St. Matthew's: Gen. (of which S. S.,*
$16.20) ....

141 67	
72 00	
2 00	
30 17	
2 56	
56 75	
5 00	
7 00	
25 00	
170 77	
20 00	
135 73	
586 83	
5 50	
19 47	
44 28	
325 50	
991 80	
23 36	
21 00	
700 00	
32 73	
381 73	
85 00	
47 00	
21 84	
32 35	
59 00	
10 71	
25 00	

JENKINTOWN—*Church of Our Saviour S.S.**: Gen. 330 90

Hattie C. Crawfurd, Sp. for Nevada. 20 00

KELTON—*St. John's S. S.**: Gen. 14 66

LANSDALE — *Holy Trinity C h u r c h*: $6.75, S. S.,* $55.58, Gen. 62 33

LANSDOWNE—*St. John's S. S.**: Gen... 240 00

LOWER MERION—*St. John's S. S.**: Gen. 164 43

McKINLEY—*St. Andrew's Chapel S. S.**: Gen..................... 15 00

MEDIA—*Christ Church*: Indian Hope Association, "Indian Hope" scholarship, St. Mary's School, South Dakota, $2; Wo.. Aux., "Kinsolving" scholarship, Brazil, $5; "Elsie Gertrude Arnold" scholarship, Girls' School, St. Paul's River, Cape Palmas, Africa, $25............. 32 00

MILL CREEK—*St. Joseph's Chapel S. S.**: Gen. 34 09

MORTON—*Atonement S. S.**: Gen..... 24 31

NEWTOWN—*St. Luke's S. S.**: Gen... 31 00

NORRISTOWN—*All Saints'*: Gen. (of which S. S.,* $91.77) $147.62; S. S.,* Sp. for Bishop Rowe, Alaska, $25; Sp. for Bishop Robinson, Nevada, $25; Sp. for Rev. P. P. Alston, Charlotte, North Carolina, $15; Sp. for Bishop Kinsolving, Brazil, $25; Sp. for Rev. A. A. Gilman, Hankow, $12.............. 249 62

*Holy Trinity Chapel S. S.**: Gen...... 18 57

*St. John's S. S.**: Gen.............. 60 00

NORTH WALES—*Church of the Good Shepherd S. S.**: Gen. 20 00

NORWOOD—*St. Stephen's*: Junior Aux., $15, S. S.,* $30.22, Gen. 45 22

OAKBOURNE — *Pennsylvania Epileptic Hospital S. S.**: Gen............. 10 00

PAOLI—*Good Samaritan*: Wo. Aux., Sp. for nurse's salary, St. Luke's Hospital, Shanghai, $4; S. S.,* Gen., $103.25 .... 107 25

PARKESBURG—*Ascension S. S.**: Gen.. 10 00

PHILADELPHIA — *Advocate Memorial*: Wo. Aux., Sp. for Land and Building Fund, Catechists' School, Shanghai, $5; Sp. for Hooker Memorial School, Mexico, $5; S. S.,* Gen., $400..... 410 00

All Saints' (Lower Dublin): Wo. Aux., Sp. for Elizabeth Bunn Memorial Hospital, Wuchang, Hankow, $5; S. S.,* Gen., $30.16................ 35 16

All Saints' (Moyamensing): $35, S. S.,* $265, Gen. 300 00

All Souls' (Deaf): Gen........... 12 50

*Annunciation S. S.**: Gen........... 6 00

Ascension: Gen., $15.40; Wo. Aux., Sp. for Foreign Life Insurance Fund, $5; S. S.,* Sp. for Rev. W. C. Clapp, Bontok, Philippine Islands, $47.11.. 67 51

*Atonement Memorial S. S.** (West): Gen. 160 64

*Beloved Disciple S. S.**: Gen......... 5 00

Calvary (Germantown): Dom., $300; "Calvary" scholarship, St. Mary's School, Rosebud Agency, South Dakota, $60; Sp. for St. Paul's College, Tokyo, $35; Indian Hope Association, Indian, $15; "Indian Hope" scholarship, St. Mary's School, South Dakota, $11; Wo. Aux., Sp. for Foreign Life Insurance Fund, $10; S. S.,* Gen., $401................ 832 00

*Christ Church S. S.**: Gen., $115.41; "Louis C. Washburn" scholarship, St. John's School, Africa, $25...... 140 41

*Christ Church S. S.** (Germantown): Gen. 126 95

*Christ Church S. S.** (Franklinville): Gen. 100 40

Christ Church Chapel: Sp. for Nevada, $6; Wo. Aux., Sp. for "R. J. Smith Memorial" scholarship, St. Mary's

Orphanage, Shanghai, $30.......... 36 00
Church of the Good Shepherd S. S.*
(Kensington) : Gen................ 60 00
Church of the Mediator : Dom. and
. Frn., $11.30 ; Indian Hope Associa-
tion, "Indian Hope" scholarship, St.
Mary's School, South Dakota, $1;
S. S.,* Gen., $234.23.............. 246 53
Church of the Messiah S. S.* (Port
Richmond) : Gen................ 21 00
Church of the Redeemer : Junior
Aux., Indian Hope Association, "In-
dian Hope" scholarship, St. Mary's
School, South Dakota, $1; S. S.,*
Gen., $37.25.................... 38 25
Church of the Saviour : Indian Hope
Association, "Indian Hope" scholar-
ship, St. Mary's School, South Da-
kota, $2 ; S. S.* "Church of the Sa-
viour" (Graduate) scholarship, South
Dakota, $60 ; scholarship, Hooker
Memorial School, Mexico, $60 ; "Wil-
liam W. Farr Memorial" scholar-
ship, St. John's School, Africa, $25 ;
Gen., $905.................... 1,052 00
Covenant : Wo. Aux., Bible-woman,
Hankow 25 00
Crucifixion S. S.* : Gen.............. 41 07
Emmanuel Church (Holmesburg) : In-
dian Hope Association, Indian, $17 ;
S. S.,* Gen., $83 54.............. 100 54
Epiphany (Mt. Airy) : Dom., $4.98;
Sp. for Nevada, $28.93 ; S. S.,*
Gen., $112.78................... 146 69
Epiphany S. S.* (Sherwood) : Gen.... 220 49
Epiphany Chapel S. S.* : Gen........ 132 18
Gloria Dei : "A Vestryman," Sp. for
Nevada, $5 ; S. S.,* Sp. for Rev. C.
E. Betticher, Alaska, $250 ; Sp. for
Rev. G. Hammarsköld, Yonkers,
N. Y., $100 ; Sp. for Rev. E. N.
Joyner, Biltmore, Asheville, $100 ;
Sp. for Bishop Kendrick, Arizona,
$100; Sp. for Rev. J. S. Russell,
Lawrenceville, Southern Virginia,
$100 ; Sp. for Bishop Thomas, Wy-
oming, $100 ; Sp. for Bishop Rob-
inson, Nevada, $100 ; Sp. for Rev.
P. C. Daito, Tokyo, $200 ; Sp. for
Rev. W. H. Standring, Soochow Or-
phanage, Shanghai, $100 ; Gen.,
$1,089.61 .... 2,244 61
Grace : Dom.................... 50 27
Grace S. S.* (Mt. Airy) : Gen........ 195 61
George L. Harrison Memorial Home
for Incurables' S. S.* : Work among
the mountaineers of North and
South Carolina.................. 2 25
Holy Apostles' : Indian Hope Association, Indian, $10 ; "Indian Hope"
scholarship, St. Mary's School,
South Dakota, $3 ; S. S. and Bible-
class, Sp. for work of Bishop Rowe,
Alaska, $25 ; Sp. for work of Bishop
Thomas, Wyoming (of which for
carriage furnishings, $5), $10 ; Sp.
for Bishop Wells, Spokane, "In Me-
moriam, Annie Louise Warwick,"
$20 ; Sp. for Bishop Spalding for
hospital, Utah, $20.60 ; S. S.,* St.
Paul's, Lawrenceville, Southern Vir-
ginia, $500 ; St. Augustine's School,
Raleigh, North Carolina, $500 ; sup-
port of Rev. W. H. Fenton Smith,
Hilo, Honolulu, $300 ; salary of Rev.
J. Roberts, Wind River Indian
Agency, Wyoming, $1,000 ; salary of
Rev. A. R. Hoare, Alaska, $1,500 ;
salary of Rev. H. A. Dobbins, Ashe-
ville, $400 ; toward expenses of St.
James's Hospital, Anking, Hankow,
$1,000 ; St. Ann's Industrial School,
Nara, Kyoto, $300 ; salary of Rev.
William Watson, St. Andrew's Semi-
nary Guadalajara, Mexico, $850 ;
Gen., $19.62.................... 6,458 22

Holy Communion Memorial Chapel
S. S.* : Gen....................
Holy Comforter Memorial S. S.* : Gen.
Holy Innocents' (Tacony) : Sp. for
Bishop Hare Memorial, South Da-
kota, $1 ; S. S.,* Gen., $50.73......
Holy Trinity Church : Dom., $200 ;
Frn., $200 ; Brazil, $200 ; Sp. for
Nevada, $200 ; John Bohlen Fund,
for St. John's College, Shanghai,
$600 ; Wo. Aux., Training-school
for Bible-women, Hankow, $25 ;
Training-school, Sendai, Tokyo, $25 ;
Sp. for St. Mary's Building Fund,
Kyoto, $85 ; Junior Aux., $25, S.
S.* (of which Colored S. S., $75),
$287.78, Gen....................1
Holy Trinity Church Memorial Chapel :
Indian Hope Association, "Indian
Hope" scholarship, St. Mary's School,
South Dakota, $2 ; S. S.,* Sp. for
work of St. James's School, Ichang,
Hankow, under Rev. D. T. Hunting-
ton, $97.36....................
Home for Consumptives' S. S.* (Chest-
nut Hill) : Gen..................
Home of the Merciful Saviour S. S.* :
Boys' school in China, $50 ; Africa,
$25 ; Sp. for work of Miss Sabine,
Alaska, $25 ; Sp. for Dr. Correll's
work, Tsu, Kyoto, $65.74..........
Incarnation : Sp. for Bishop Robinson's
work, Nevada, $78.16 ; S. S.,* Gen.,
$550 ....
L'Emmanuello Church S. S.* : Gen....
Prince of Peace Chapel : Indian Hope
Association, "Indian Hope" scholar-
ship, St. Mary's School, South Da-
kota, $1 ; Wo. Aux., Sp. for Land
and Building Fund, Catechists'
School, Shanghai, $5 ; S. S.,* Gen.,
$511.40 ....
Redemption : Gen., $15 ; S. S.,* St.
Luke's Hospital, Shanghai, $12 ;
Gen., $108.96..................
Resurrection S. S.* : Gen...........
St. Agnes's Hospital S. S.* : Gen.,
$34.50 ; Sp. for St. Agnes's Hospital,
Raleigh, North Carolina, $10.......
St. Alban's (Roxborough) : Wo. Aux.,
Sp. for Foreign Life Insurance
Fund, $2.50 ; S. S.,* Gen., $20.....
St. Alban's (Olney) : Sp. for Asheville,
$10 ; S. S.,* Gen., $18.55.........
St. Ambrose's S. S.* : Gen..........
St. Andrew's : "A Parishioner," Frn.,
$6 ; S. S.,* Sp. for work of Bishop
Robinson, Nevada, $200 ; Sp. for
work of Rev. C. E. Betticher,
Alaska, $50...................
St. Andrew's (West) : Indian Hope As-
sociation, "Indian Hope" scholar-
ship, St. Mary's School, South Da-
kota, $5 ; S. S.,* Gen., $105.......
St. Anna's S. S.* (West) : Gen.......
St. Barnabas's (Kensington) : $31.30,
S. S.,* $25, Gen................
St. Barnabas's S. S.* (Germantown) :
Gen. ....
St. Bartholomew's S. S.* : Gen......
St. Clement's : Bishop Griswold's sal-
ary, Salina, $224 ; salary of Rev.
R. E. Wood, Wuchang, Hankow,
$224 ; Sp. for Oneida Indians, Fond
du Lac, $4.63 ; Sp. for Rev. R. E.
Wood, Wuchang, Hankow, for pur-
chase of land, $100 ; Sp. for Nevada,
$158 ; S. S.* Sp. for Christ School,
Arden, Asheville, $60.19..........
St. David's S. S.* (Manayunk) : Gen..
St. George's S. S.* (Richmond) : Gen.
St. George's S. S.* (Venango) : Gen...
St. James's : Mrs. Samuel Dickson, $5,
for Land and Building Fund, Cate-
chists' School, Shanghai, $25 ; Indian
Hope Association, Indian, $30 ; Wo.

St. *Nathaniel's S. S.* *: Gen......... 35 00

St. *Paul's* (Aramingo): Gen., $25; Wo. Aux. "Kinsolving" scholarship, Brazil, $5; S. S.,* Gen., $100......... 130 00

St. *Paul's* (Chestnut Hill): Indian Hope Association, "J. Andrews Havens" (Graduate) scholarship, South Dakota, $60; Indian, $5; Wo. Aux., Sp. for Hooker Memorial School, Mexico, $22.............. 87 00

St. *Paul's* (Overbrook): Indian Hope Association, "Indian Hope" scholarship, St. Mary's School, South Dakota, $5; Wo. Aux., "Bishop Stevens" scholarship, St. John's University, Shanghai, $2; Sp. for Foreign Life Insurance Fund, $10; S. S., Gen., $135.13.............. 152 13

St. *Paul's Memorial* (Fifteenth and Porter Streets): Miss A. R. Sturgis,* $5.25, S. S.,* $265 88, Gen........ 271 13

St. *Peter's*: Dom., $5; Wo. Aux., Sp. for Land and Building Fund, Catechists' School, Shanghai, $22; S. S.,* Gen., $227.18..................... 254 18

St. *Peter's* (Germantown): Dom., $385.70; Frn., $937.58; Wo. Aux., Sp. for evangelist's salary, St. Luke's Hospital. Shanghai, $75; Sp. for Land and Building Fund. Catechists' School, Shanghai, $10....... 1,408 28

St. *Philip's* (West): Wo. Aux., Gen... 30 00

St. *Saviour's S. S.* *: Gen............ 8 19

St. *Simeon's S. S.* *: Salary of Rev. A. Goddard, Hankow, $150; Gen., $215.42 .... 365 42

St. *Simon the Cyrenian's S. S.* *: Gen.. 128 18

St. *Stephen's*: Sp. for Bishop Robinson, Nevada, $58; E. E. Holman, $10, Catharine M. Shipley, $5, Sp. for Dr. Pott's work, St John's University. Shanghai; Wo. Aux., "Dr. Twing Memorial" scholarship, St. John's University. Shanghai, $5; "W. Beaumont Whitney" scholarship, Cuba, $5; "Kinsolving" scholarship, Brazil, $7; Sp. for Foreign Life Insurance Fund, $5........... 95 00

St. *Stephen's S. S.* * (Bridesburg): Gen. 30 00

St. *Timothy's S. S.* * (Roxborough): Gen., $178.19; Sp. for Bishop Spalding. Utah, $100; Sp. for Bishop Brewster, Western Colorado, $50; Sp. for Bishop Roots, Hankow, $100; Sp. for Bishop Graves, Shanghai, $50 478 19

St. *Timothy's Chapel S. S.* *: Gen..... 30 00

St. *Titus's S. S.* *: Gen.................. 5 00

Trinity Church *S. S.* * (Oxford): Gen. 70 00

Trinity Church *S. S.* * (Germantown): Gen. 45 00

Trinity Chapel *S. S.* * (Crescentville): Gen. 69 37

Zion *S. S.* *: Gen.................... 293 06

Diocesan Library *S. S.,* * Gen...... 5 25

Mrs. S. K. Boyer, $5, "M.," $50 Gen. 55 00

Estate of George C. Thomas. Sp. for reading-room, Fairbanks, Alaska.... 500 00

Mrs. Edith Boker, Sp. for Bishop Rowe's Rebuilding Fund, Alaska.... 100 00

Through Walter Stokes. $100, E. Lowber Stokes, $100, Eckley B. Coxe, Jr., $100, George H. Frazier, $25, Sp. for Bishop Robinson's work, Nevada 325 00

W. W. Frazier, $500, S. F. Houston, $50, Sp. for Nevada.......... 550 00

T. Broom Belfield, Sp. for Bishop Restarick, Honolulu, for Rectory and Organ Fund. Church of the Holy Apostles, Hilo..................... 50 00

Through "F E. McI.," Sp. for Rev. J. W. Nichols, for a catechist's house, Shanghai.................. 60 00

Tuesday Missionary Bible-class, Sp. for Bishop Restarick, Honolulu, for Priory School, $50; through Wo.

Aux., Sp. for Foreign Life Insurance **Fund, $10** 60 00
PHOENIXVILLE—*St. Peter's*: Wo. Aux., Frn., $5; S. S.,* Gen., $66.89 ...... 71 89
POTTSTOWN—*Christ Church S. S.**: Gen. 125 00
QUAKERTOWN—*Emmanuel Church S. S.**: Sp. for work of Rev. Mr. Betticher, Alaska 31 00
RADNOR—*St. Martin's*: Dom., $10; Frn., $10; Indian Hope Association, Indian, $4 .... 24 00
RIDLEY PARK—*Christ Church S. S.**: Gen. 65 00
ROCKDALE—*Calvary S. S.**: Gen. 114 69
ROSEMONT—*Church of the Good Shepherd*: Wo. Aux., Sp. for Foreign Life Insurance Fund 2 00
ROYERSFORD—*Epiphany S. S.**: Gen.. 20 00
UPPER MERION—*Christ Church S. S.**: Gen. 77 75
UPPER PROVIDENCE—*St. Paul's Memorial S. S.**: Gen. 46 00
VALLEY FORGE—*Washington Memorial Chapel*: $5, S. S.,* $40, Gen. 45 00
WARWICK—*St. Mary's S. S.**: Gen..: 16 21
WAWA—*Chapel of the Holy Angels' S. S.**: Gen. 6 85
WAYNE—*St. Mary's Memorial*: Sp. for Dr. Correll's Building Fund, Kyoto, $40; Indian Hope Association, "Indian Hope" scholarship, St. Mary's School, South Dakota, $5; Indian, $5; Wo. Aux., "Foreign Committee" scholarship, St. Margaret's School, Tokyo, $3; "Pennsylvania Wo. Aux." scholarship, Hooker Memorial School, Mexico, $5 .... 58 00
WESTCHESTER—*Holy Trinity Church*: Indian Hope Association, Indian, $25; Wo. Aux., Brazil $12; "Kinsolving" scholarship, Brazil, $18; S. S., Sp. for Bishop Thomas, Wyoming, $45.49; S. S.,* Gen., $124.20 .... 224 69
Hugh P. Brinton, Jr.,* Gen. 2 00
WEST END—*St. George's S. S.**: Sp. for St. Paul's, Edneyville, Asheville 27 50
WEST WHITELAND—*St. Paul's* (Glen Lock): Indian Hope Association, "Indian Hope" scholarship, St. Mary's School, South Dakota, $2; S. S.,* Gen., $7 .... 9 00
WHITEMARSH—*St. Thomas's*: "X. Y. Z.," $25, S. S.,* $50, Gen. 75 00
WILLOW GROVE—*St. Anne's S. S.**: Gen. 59 00
WYNCOTE—*All Hallows'*: Wo. Aux., Sp. for Foreign Life Insurance Fund, $1; S. S.,* Gen., $82.90 ..... 83 90
YARDLEY—*St. Andrew's S. S.**: Gen.. 26 50
MISCELLANEOUS—Domestic Committee, Dom., $15; Alaska hospital work, $20; Sp. for Bishop Rowe, Alaska, $12 .... 47 00
Rosalie L. Mitchell, Mission Study Class, Wo. Aux., salary of Colored evangelist 50 00
Junior Aux., Sp. for Training-school for Catechists, Shanghai ... 10 00
"Y. Z.," Gen. 200 00
Mrs. D. K. Rodman, $100, Miss Mary Coles, $50, Mrs. J. H. Hutchinson, $25, Sp. for Land and Building Fund, Catechists' School, Shanghai 175 00
P. E. Sexton Association S. S.,* Gen. 5 00
Home Department Class of Mrs. E. A. Beaumont, S. S.,* Gen. 3 00
Home Department Class of Miss H. W. Williams, S. S.,* Gen. 55 32
"A Former S. S. Worker,"* Gen. 3 00
Home Department Class of Miss Reynolds, S. S.,* Gen. 12 00
Offering at meeting of Sunday-school

Institute, January 17th, 1910,* Gen. Offerings at meeting of S. S. Aux., April 23d,* Gen. ....

Pittsburgh

Ap. $811.73; *Sp.* $100.00

BEAVER—Josephine Stengel, 33 cts., Freda Stengel, 33 cts., Bettie Barrett, 55 cts., Morgan Barrett, 56 cts., Jack Sparhawk, $1.25, George Sparhawk, $1.31, S. S.,* Gen.......
BEAVER FALLS—*St. Mary's*: Gen.......
BROWNSVILLE—*Christ Church*: Work among the Colored. ....
Miss Mary A. Hogg, Sp. for Brazil theological books..................
BUTLER—*St. Peter's*: Dom. and Frn..
CRAFTON—*Nativity*: Gen ....
EMPORIUM—*Emmanuel Church*: Gen..
FAIRVIEW—*St. Paul's*: Gen............
FOXBURG—*Memorial Church of Our Father*: Church Guild, Sp. for Mrs. Littell, Hankow, for "Sarah Lindley Fox" scholarship ....
FREEPORT—*Trinity Church*: Gen .....
GEORGETOWN—*St. Luke's*: Gen.......
JOHNSONBURG—*St. Martin's*: Gen....
LATROBE—*St. Luke's*: Dom. and Frn..
McKEESPORT—*St. Stephen's*: Dom. and Frn.......................
MERCER—*St. Edmond's*: Gen..........
MT. JEWETT—*St. Margaret's*: Dom. and Frn.......................
NEW KENSINGTON—*St. Andrew's S. S.**: Gen.......................
PITTSBURG—*Christ Church*: $5, "E. S. C.," $100, Gen.......................
St. Luke's: Indian, $10; Colored, $10; Deaf-mutes, $4; Frn., $4...........
St. Mark's: Gen.......................
St. Peter's S. S.*: Gen...............
Mrs. A. V. Holmes, Sp. for Church Extension Fund, Porto Rico.......
RIDGWAY—*Grace*: Dom. and Frn., $70; S. S.,* Gen., $51.05...........
SMETHPORT—*St. Luke's*: Gen..........
WASHINGTON—*Trinity Church*: Gen..
MISCELLANEOUS—Wo. Aux., Southern Florida, $100; Porto Rico, $50; Cape Mount, West Africa, $50; Japan, $50; Sp. for Dr. Correll, Tsu, Kyoto, $55.......................

Quincy

Ap. $615.96

FARMINGTON—*Calvary*: Gen.........
GALESBURG—*St. John's*: Gen. (of which S. S.,* $7.15)..............
GRIGGSVILLE—*St. James's*: Gen. (of which S. S.,* $5)..............
KNOXVILLE—*St. Mary's*: "Bertha Leffingwell" scholarship, St. Mary's Hall, Shanghai, $50; Gen., $16....
MOLINE—*Christ Church*: Gen........
PEORIA—*St. Paul's*: Gen...........
PITTSFIELD—*St. Stephen's*: Gen. (of which S. S.,* $2.50)...........
PRE-EMPTION—*St. John's S. S.**: Gen.
QUINCY—*Church of the Good Shepherd S. S.**: Gen...............
St. John's Cathedral: Gen. (of which S. S.,* $25.10)..............
ROCK ISLAND—*Trinity Church*: Gen. (of which S. S.,* $60)..............
WARSAW—*St. Paul's S. S.**: Gen....
MISCELLANEOUS—Gen.................

Rhode Island

Ap. $2,096.44; *Sp.* $100.00

ASHTON—*St. John's Chapel*: Gen......
BARRINGTON—*St. John's*: Dom., $10; Frn., $10; Gen., $15..............
CROMPTON—*St. Philip's*: Gen........

	woman, Hankow, $2; Sp. for "Bish-	
48 61	op Howe" cot, St. Mary's Orphanage,	
60 00	Shanghai, $1; Junior Aux., Gen.,	
57 62	$4; Bishop Capers Day-school, Han-	
	kow, $2..................	66 00
28 13	CHARLESTON—*Calvary S. S.**: Gen...	7 40
	Christ Church: Gen...............	12 50
	*Holy Communion S. S.**: Gen., $42;	
	Wo. Aux., M. E. Pinkney Fund, for	
33 95	Bible-woman, Tokyo, $1; N. S.	
	Wilson Day-school, Hankow, $1....	44 00
6 96	*Grace*: Gen., $150; Wo. Aux., assist-	
	ant for Miss McCollough, Porto Rico,	
	$2; M. E. Pinkney Fund for Bible-	
159 27	woman, Tokyo, $3..............	155 00
25 00	*St. John's Chapel*: Gen. (of which	
39 12	S. S.,* $25.67)...............	45 67
	*St. Luke's S. S.**: Gen., $53.84; Wo.	
	Aux., N. S. Wilson Day-school, Han-	
10 00	kow, $10; Gen., $26.32; Miss Car-	
22 00	ter's work, Alaska, $33.17; Junior	
	Aux., Gen., $2; Babies' Branch,	
15 52	Gen., $2.03..................	127 88
6 06	*St. Michael's S. S.**: Gen............	64 20
	CHERAW—*St. David's*: Gen..........	17 85
40 00	CLEMSON COLLEGE—*Holy Trinity	
	Church S. S.**: Gen............	6 16
	COLUMBIA—*Church of the Good Shep-	
100 00	herd*: Gen. (of which S. S.,*	
	$29.36), $45.26; Wo. Aux., Bible-	
45 31	woman, Kyoto, $5; N. S. Wilson	
	Day-school, Hankow, $2..........	52 26
140 00	*St. Andrew's S. S.**: Gen............	3 17
47 96	*St. Timothy's S. S.**: Gen...........	10 13
17 00	*Trinity Church S. S.*: "To restore the	
	sight of a blind man," $10.32; Gen.,*	
	$178.16; Babies' Branch, Gen., $12	200 38
41 79	Mrs. B. F. Gee, Gen.............	4 00
125 00	CONGAREE—*St. John's S. S.**: Gen....	2 42
150 00	DARLINGTON — *St. Matthew's*: Gen.,	
	$44.30; Junior Aux., Gen., $5;	
25 00	Bishop Capers Day-school, Hankow,	
35 10	$5	54 30
	EASTOVER—*Zion S. S.**: Gen., $13.46;	
100 00	Wo. Aux., Sp. for St. Andrew's	
	School, Tennessee, $3.90; Junior	
16 19	Aux., Gen., $2..................	19 36
10 00	EDGEFIELD—*Trinity Church*: Gen. (of	
1 00	which S. S.,* $2.61)	5 74
	EDISTO, ROCKVILLE AND WARDMALAW—	
439 13	Babies' Branch, Gen.............	4 85
	ENTERPRISE—Mrs. M. C. LaRoche, Sp.	
	for Brazil theological books........	5 00
	EUTAWVILLE—*Epiphany*: Gen........	15 00
	FORT MOTTE—*St. Matthew's*: Gen....	3 50
	GLENN SPRINGS—*Calvary S. S.**: Gen.	8 25
	GRAHAMVILLE — *Holy Trinity Church*:	
	$8.18, S. S.,* $7, Wo. Aux.,	
230 00	$16; Mrs. Bell, M. E. Pinkney	
	Fund for Bible-woman, Tokyo, $2..	33 18
	GREENVILLE—*Christ Church S. S.**:	
	Wyoming, $16.13; Kyoto, $15.90;	
	Tokyo, $13.62; Cuba, $10.67; Porto	
	Rico, $9.17; South Dakota, $8.27;	
2 12	Mexico, $10.69; Sacramento, $5;	
	Alaska, $5.52; Western Colorado,	
	$5.40; Honolulu, $5.01............	105 38
	*St. James's S. S.**: Dom., $2.85; Gen.,	
	$2	4 85
48 00	Senior Aux., Bible-woman, Kyoto,	
	$5; Sp. for "Bishop Howe" cot,	
3 10	Shanghai, $3..................	8 00
25 42	GREENWOOD—*Resurrection*: Gen. (of	
	which S. S.,* $6.64)	9 89
	HAGOOD—*Ascension*: Frn., $7.50; S.	
5 60	S.,* Gen., $8.92; Wo. Aux., Bible-	
	woman, Hankow, $1; N. S. Wilson	
90 17	Day-school, Hankow, $2; Gen., $1.75	21 17
	LAURENS—*Epiphany*: Wo. Aux., Gen..	13 55
13 15	"E. B. S.," Gen.................	4 00
10 29	MARION—*Advent S. S.**: Gen........	10 00
	McPHERSONVILLE—*Sheldon*: Gen. (of	
11 43	which S. S.,* $7)................	14 18
	MT. PLEASANT—*Christ Church S. S.**:	
	Gen.	17 40
	*St. Andrew's Chapel S. S.**: Gen.....	7 35

NORTH AUGUSTA—*Epiphany*: Sp. for Mrs. Potwine's Organ Fund, Honolulu 5 00
ORANGEBURG—*Church of the Redeemer S. S.*: Gen...................... 8 15
PENDLETON—*St. Paul's S. S.*: Dom.. 7 32
PINOPOLIS—Babies' Branch, Gen..... 12 01
PLANTERSVILLE—*P r i n c e Frederick*: Gen., $1.30; Wo. Aux., N. S. Wilson Day-school, Hankow, $1; Bible-woman, Kyoto, $2; M. E. Pinkney Fund for Bible-woman, Tokyo, $1; Bible-woman, Hankow, $3; Sp. for "Bishop Howe" cot, St. Mary's Orphanage, Shanghai, $3.......... 11 30
RIDGEWAY—*St. Stephen's*: Gen...... 12 50
RION—"A Little Girl,"* Gen......... 5 00
ROCK HILL—*Church of Our Saviour S. S.*: Sp. for Asheville, $6.41; Wo. Aux., Sp. for "Bishop Howe" cot, St. Mary's Orphanage, Shanghai, $5; N. S. Wilson Day-school, Hankow, $2; for assistant to Miss McCollough, Porto Rico, $3; Junior Aux., Bible-woman, Kyoto, $2.......... 18 41
SENECA—*Ascension S. S.*: Gen..... 2 11
SPARTANBURG—*Advent*: Brazil, $65; Philippines, $65; China, $50; C. F. McRae's mission work, Shanghai, $15; Sp. for Bishop Horner's work, Asheville, $120.................. 315 00
STATEBURG—*Holy Cross*: Wo. Aux., Gen. 4 00
SUMMERVILLE—*Epiphany S. S.*: Gen. 7 40
St. Barnabas's S. S.: Gen.......... 5 76
St. Paul's: Gen., $2; S. S.,* Dom., $12.50; Frn., $13.10; Junior Aux., Bishop Capers Day-school, Hankow, $5 .... 32 60
UNION—*Nativity S. S.*: Gen........ 11 00
WACCAMAW—*All Saints'*: Gen....... 4 55
WAVERLY MILLS—*All Saints' S. S.*: Gen. 6 00
WATERBORO—*St. Jude's S. S.*: Gen.. 15 00
WILLINGTON — *St. Stephen's*: Children,* Gen................... 3 83
WINNSBORO—*St. John's*: Gen. (of which S. S.,* $11)............... 16 00
YORKVILLE—*Church of the Good Shepherd S. S.*: Gen................ 17 17

Southern Ohio

Ap. $1,622.35; *Sp.* $57.42

ADDYSTON — *St. Andrew's Mission S. S.*: Gen........................ 10 50
BELLAIRE—*Trinity Mission*: Gen..... 15 00
CHILLICOTHE—*St. Mark's*: Gen. (of which S. S.,* $1.28)............. 9 28
St. Paul's: Gen. (of which S. S.* $7.50) 37 50
CINCINNATI—*Advent S. S.*: Gen., $72.65; Wo. Aux., Gen., $5........ 77 65
Calvary (Clifton): Frn., $50; Colored, $40; S. S.,* Gen., $114.16; Wo. Aux., Sp. for house for resident physician, Ponce, Porto Rico, $10... 214 16
Christ Church: Wo. Aux., Josephine Lytte Foster Memorial for support of Bible-woman, Shanghai........... 50 00
Emmanuel Church S. S.: Gen...... 12 42
Epiphany (Walnut Hills): Gen. (of which S. S.,* $41.05)............. 86 83
St. John's S. S.: Gen............ 7 00
St. Paul's Cathedral S. S.: Gen..... 52 66
St. Philip's: Gen. (of which S. S.,* $11.68) 38 78
COLUMBUS—*Church of the Good Shepherd S. S.*: Gen............... 25 00
Trinity Church: Gen. (of which S. S.,* $17.36), $167.36; Girls' Friendly Society, Sp. for salary of missionary curate for Rev. S. C. Hughson, Sewanee, Tennessee, $5.75........ 173 11
DAYTON—*Christ Church*: Gen., $213.99;

9 00
7 65
19 00
29 65
12 27
6 25
43 25
3 00
52 67
46 23
3 82
3 00
13 84
1 00
65 00
3 00
4 36
6 25
63 54
8 75
13 33
5 55
38 00
28 00
10 00
2 80
6 00
32 13
9 47
2 98
54
50
24 55
5 28
36 11
63 67
2 47
5 00
3 03
2 18

Stras Memorial S. S.* (Tazewell): Gen. ... 3 80
WARWICK Co.—St. Paul's S. S.* (Newport News): Gen., $15; Wo. Aux., Alaska, $10 ... 25 00
WASHINGTON Co.—St. Paul's S. S.,* Preston Parish: Gen. ... 17 00
WISE Co.—Christ Church S. S.* (Big Stone Gap): Gen ... 3 52
Intermont Parish: Gen ... 10 00

Springfield

Ap. $1,052.34; Sp. $30.00

CAIRO—St. Mary's: Wo. Aux., Gen ... 15 00
CARROLLTON—Trinity Church S. S.*: Gen. ... 10 42
CENTRALIA—St. John's S. S.*: Gen ... 8 25
COLLINSVILLE—Christ Church S. S.*: Gen. ... 7 07
CHESTERFIELD—St. Peter's S. S.*: Gen. ... 10 85
DANVILLE—Holy Trinity Church S. S.*: Gen. ... 51 23
St. Mark's S. S.*: Gen ... 5 71
DECATUR—St. John's S. S.*: Gen ... 87 72
EAST ST. LOUIS—St. Paul's S. S.*: Gen. ... 6 83
EDWARDSVILLE—St. Andrew's S. S.*: Gen. ... 11 70
GRANITE CITY—St. Bartholomew's S. S.*: Gen ... 13 35
LINCOLN—Trinity Church S. S.*: Gen. ... 8 50
MOUND CITY—St. Peter's S. S.*: Gen. ... 10 96
PEKIN—St. Paul's S. S.*: Gen ... 7 00
SPRINGFIELD—St. Luke's S. S.*: Gen. ... 6 50
St. Paul's S. S.*: Gen ... 21 58

Tennessee

Ap. $1,052.34; Sp. $30.00

ARLINGTON—Holy Innocents' S. S.*: Gen. ... 1 60
BOLIVAR — St. Katherine's School: Junior Aux., Gen ... 12 00
St. Philip's S. S.*: Gen ... 3 60
BROWNSVILLE—Christ Church: Gen. (of which Wo. Aux., $8) ... 11 70
CHATTANOOGA—Christ Church S. S.*: Gen. ... 9 95
St. Paul's: (of which Wo. Aux., $7.50) Gen. ... 57 50
Thankful Memorial Church: Sp. for Zangzok Equipment Fund, Shanghai. ... 5 00
CLARKSVILLE — Trinity Church: For Mexico, $5; Gen. (of which S. S.,* $48.25), $50 ... 55 00
Wo. Aux., Gen ... 7 50
CLEVELAND—St. Luke's S. S.*: Gen ... 30 00
COLLIERVILLE—St. Andrew's: (of which Children,* $8) Gen ... 13 00
COLUMBIA—Church of the Holy Comforter: (of which S. S.,* $3.10) Gen. ... 4 20
COVINGTON—St. Matthew's S. S.*: Gen. ... 2 10
ETOWAH—Holy Cross S. S.*: Gen ... 3 09
FAYETTEVILLE—St. Mary's: (of which S. S.,* $11.02) Gen ... 16 52
HARRIMAN—St. Andrew's S. S.*: Gen. ... 3 02
JACKSON—St. Thomas's S. S.*: Gen. ... 13 02
JOHNSON CITY—St. John's: (of which S. S.,* $5) Gen ... 10 00
KNOXVILLE—Epiphany S. S.*: Gen ... 19 69
St. John's S. S.*: $53.03, Junior Aux., $5, Gen ... 58 03
MASON—St. Paul's S. S.*: Gen ... 5 00
Trinity Church: (of which S. S.,* $7, Wo. Aux., $5) Gen ... 19 85
MEMPHIS—Calvary: (of which S. S.,* $28.91) Gen ... 44 81
Emmanuel Church S. S.*: $9.95, Wo. Aux., $5, Gen ... 14 95
Church of the Good Shepherd S. S.*: Gen., $12.50; Wo. Aux., for "Bishop Quintard" scholarship, St. Mary's Hall, Shanghai, $1; Gen., $10 ... 23 50

Grace: Dom. and Frn., $100; S. S.,*
$80, Wo. Aux., $12.50, Gen........ 192 50
Holy Trinity Church: (of which S. S.,*
$32.40, Wo. Aux., $5) Gen........ 57 40
St. Andrew's Mission S. S.: * Gen..... 1 62
St. Luke's: Wo. Aux., $9.38, S. S.,*
$10, Gen........................... 19 38
St. Mary's Cathedral S. S.: * $80, Wo.
Aux., $12.50, Gen.................. 92 50
NASHVILLE—*Advent S. S.*: * Gen.,
$7.50; Wo. Aux., for "Bishop Quin-
tard" scholarship, St. Mary's Hall,
Shanghai, 50 cts.; Gen., $6........ 14 00
Christ Church S. S.: * $93.32, Wo.
Aux., $12.50, Junior Aux., $10, Gen. 115 82
Holy Trinity Church S. S.: * Gen.... 2 00
St. Ann's: Wo. Aux., Gen., $15; for
"Bishop Quintard" scholarship, St.
Mary's Hall, Shanghai, $5.......... 20 00
St. Mary's S. S.: * Gen............. 1 05
St. Peter's S. S.: * $17.60, Wo. Aux.,
$6, Gen............................ 23 60
St. Stephen's: (of which Wo. Aux., $5)
Gen............................... 7 25
ROSSVIEW—*Grace*: Wo. Aux., Sp. for
Miss Bull's work, Kyoto........... 25 00
ST. ELMO—*Thankful Memorial S. S.*: *
Gen............................... 14 11
SEWANEE—Wo. Aux., Gen., $5; for
"Bishop Quintard" scholarship, St.
Mary's Hall, Shanghai, $1.25...... 6 25
SHERWOOD—*Epiphany S. S.*: * Alaska,
$2.50; China, $2.50; Philippines,
$2.50; Mexico, $2.50; Gen., $3.93.. 13 93
SOMERVILLE—*St. Thomas's S. S.*: *
Gen............................... 5 29
SPRING HILL—*Grace S. S.*: * Gen..... 4 55
TRACY CITY—Wo. Aux., Gen.......... 1 50
TULLAHOMA—*St. Barnabas's S. S.*: *
$10.11, Wo. Aux., $3.90, Gen...... 14 01
WEST NASHVILLE—*St. Andrew's S.
S.*: * Gen......................... 5 95

Texas

Ap. $886.47; *Sp.* $28.00

ALVIN—*Grace S. S.*: * Gen........... 9 50
ANGLETON—*Church of the Holy Com-
forter*: (of which S. S.,* $19.25)
Gen............................... 38 25
AUSTIN—*All Saints' Chapel*: Gen.... 29 50
St. David's: Gen., $2.50; S. S.,* Sp.
for Bishop Rowe, Alaska, $10; Sp.
for Bishop Aves, Mexico, $10...... 22 50
BAY CITY—*St. Mark's S. S.*: * Gen... 10 00
BEAUMONT—*St. Mark's*: (of which S.
S.,* $55) Gen...................... 96 90
BELLVILLE—*St. Mary's S. S.*: * Gen... 16 48
BELTON—*St. Luke's*: Gen............ 10 80
BRAZONIA—*St. John's Mission S. S.*: *
Gen............................... 4 79
BRENHAM—*St. Peter's S. S.*: * Gen... 12 63
BRYAN—*St. Andrew's*: (of which S.
S.,* $25.20) Gen................... 42 30
CAMERON—*All Saints'*: (of which S.
S.,* $10.43) Gen................... 18 13
COLUMBUS—*St. John's*: (of which S.
S.,* $16.35) Gen................... 18 35
DICKINSON—*Holy Trinity Church S.
S.*: * Sp. for Bishop Aves, Mexico,
for Indian Mission at Humini...... 8 00
EAGLE LAKE—*Christ Church*: Gen. (of
which S. S.,* $20.82)............... 48 82
GALVESTON—*St. Augustine's S. S.*: *
Gen............................... 5 40
HEARNE—*St. Philip's S. S.*: * Gen.... 5 60
HEMPSTEAD—*St. Bartholomew's*: For
Alaska............................ 4 00
HOUSTON—*St. Mary's S. S.*: * Gen.... 13 85
Trinity Church; Gen............... 100 00
JACKSONVILLE — *Trinity Mission S.
S.*: * Gen......................... 3 00
LONGVIEW—*Trinity Mission S. S.*: *
Dom. and Frn...................... 5 80
MARSHALL—*Trinity Church*: Gen.... 38 10

MATAGORDA—*Christ Church*: (of which
S. S.,* $18.40) Gen................
NAVASOTA—*St. Paul's S. S.*: * Gen....
PALESTINE—*St. Philip's*: Gen........
PORT ARTHUR—*Christ Church Mission
S. S.*: * Gen.......................
RICHMOND—*Calvary*: Gen...........
ROCKDALE—*St. Thomas's Mission S.
S.*: Gen...........................
SAN AUGUSTINE—*Christ Church S.
S.*: * Gen.........................
TAYLOR—*St. James's S. S.*: * Gen....
TEMPLE—*Christ Church S. S.*: * Gen..
TYLER—*Christ Church*: (of which S.
S.,* $15.53) Gen...................
WACO—*St. Paul's S. S.*: * Gen., $79.31;
Wo. Aux., for the "Frank Page"
scholarship, St. Hilda's School. Wu-
chang, Hankow, $50; Gen., $25.....
WHARTON—*St. Thomas's Mission*: (of
which S. S.,* $17.40) Gen..........

Vermont

Ap. $967.79

ALBURGH—*St. Luke's*: Colored, $1.45;
Gen., $10.25.......................
ARLINGTON—*St. James's S. S.*: * Gen..
BARRE—*Church of the Good Shepherd
S. S.*: * Gen.......................
St. John the Baptist's S. S.: * Gen...
BENNINGTON—*St. Peter's S. S.*: * Gen.
BETHEL—*Christ Church*: (of which S.
S.,* $4) Gen.......................
BRANDON—*St. Thomas's S. S.*: * Gen..
BRATTLEBORO—*St. Michael's S. S.*: *
Gen...............................
BURLINGTON—*St. Paul's*: Dom., $3;
Frn., $263.29......................
CANAAN—*St. Paul's S. S.*: * Gen.....
EAST BERKSHIRE—*Calvary S. S.*: *
Gen...............................
EAST FAIRFIELD—*St. Barnabas's S.
S.*: * Gen.........................
EAST GEORGIA—*Emmanuel Church*: (of
which S. S.,* $1.92) Gen...........
ENOSBURG—*Christ Church S. S.*: *
Gen. (additional).................
ENOSBURG FALLS — *St. Matthew's*:
Colored, $5.76; Gen. (of which S.
S.,* $1.05), $10.65................
FAIR HAVEN—*St. Luke's*: (of which
S. S.,* $7.21) Gen.................
FORESTDALE—*Grace S. S.*: * Gen.....
GUILFORD—*Christ Church*: Gen.....
HARDWICK—*St. John the Baptist's*:
Gen...............................
HIGHGATE—*St. John's*: (of which S.
S.,* $2.79) Gen....................
HYDEVILLE—*St. James's*: (of which
S. S.,* $3.76) Gen.................
ISLAND POND—*Christ Church*: Gen....
LYNDONVILLE—*St. Peter's S. S.*: * Gen.
MANCHESTER CENTRE—*Zion*: (of which
S. S.,* $13.59) Gen................
MIDDLEBURY—*St. Stephen's*: Gen....
MIDDLETOWN SPRINGS—*St. Margaret's
S. S.*: * Gen.......................
MILTON—*Trinity*: (of which
S. S.,* $5.08) Gen.................
MONTGOMERY — *St. Bartholomew's S.
S.*: * Gen.........................
MONTPELIER — *Christ Church*: (of
which S. S.,* $33.58) Gen..........
NEWPORT—*St. Mark's S. S.*: * For
China.............................
NORTHFIELD—*St. Mary's*: (of which S.
S.,* $9.30) Gen....................
RANDOLPH—*St. John's*: Gen.........
RANDOLPH CENTRE—*Grace*: Gen......
RICHFORD—*St. Ann's*: Gen..........
RUTLAND—*Trinity Church S. S.*: * Gen.
ST. ALBANS—*St. Luke's*: Frn., $7.68;
Gen., $37..........................
SHELBURNE — *Trinity Church*: Frn.,
$62.50; S. S.,* Gen., $9.29........

Hill) : $397.33, S. S.,* $58.79, Gen. ;
Wo. Aux., Philippines, $10 ; China,
$10 ; Japan, $10 ; Sp. for Rev. E. J.
Lee's School, Hankow, $5 ; Sp. for
Rev. Mr. Snavely's work among
lepers, Porto Rico, $2.............. 493 12
*Epiphany S. S.** (Richmond) : Gen... 14 50
Grace (Richmond) : Wo. Aux., Gen.,
$75.75 ; Sp. for Bishop Hare Memor-
ial Fund, South Dakota, $30.25 ;
Sp. for work in the mountains of
Virginia, $2 ; Brazil, $2 ; S. S.,*
Dom. and Frn., $23.10............ 133 10
Church of the Good Shepherd (Rich-
mond) : Frn...................... 1 88
Holy Trinity Church (Richmond) :
Gen. 100 00
Monumental (Richmond) : Dom.,
$119.78 ; Brazil, $100 ; St. John's
University, Shanghai, $25 ; Gen.,
$66.37 ; Wo. Aux., Gen., $11 ; S. S.,*
Dom. and Frn., $47.69 ; S. S. Sp.
for Widely Loving Society, Osaka,
Kyoto, $18...................... 387 84
St. James's (Richmond) : Dom. and
Frn., $700 ; Sp. for Rev. E. J. Lee,
Lee Chapel, Anking, Hankow, $250. 950 00
St. John's (Richmond) : Dom., $60 ;
Frn., $165 ; S. S.,* Dom. and Frn.,
$37.78 ; "Solomon Memorial" schol-
arship, St. John's School, Africa,
$25 ; Sp. for "Mary Goodwin Memor-
ial" scholarship, Holy Trinity Or-
phanage, Tokyo, $30 ; Junior Aux.,
Rev. Roger A. Walker's work, St.
Paul's College, Tokyo, $6.......... 323 78
*St. Luke's S. S.** (Richmond) : Gen.. 3 36
St. Paul's (Richmond) : Dom.,
$444.65 ; Frn., $409.66 ; Sp. for St.
Paul's College, Tokyo, $200 ; Wo.
Aux., Brazil, $60................. 1,114 31
*St. Thomas's S. S.** (Richmond, Ginter
Park) : Gen..................... 9 91
Richmond Junior Auxiliaries (Rich-
mond), St. James's Hospital, An-
king, Hankow................... 50 00
KING WILLIAM CO.—*St. David's S. S.**
(Aylett) : Frn.................. 16 00
LANCASTER CO.—*Grace, Christ Church
Parish* : $16, *Trinity Church*, $2.57,
Gen. 18 57
LOUDOUN CO.—*Church of Our Saviour,
John's Parish* : Gen.............. 15 00
*St. James's S. S.** (Leesburg) : "Mat-
thew Harrison" scholarship, Boone
University, Wuchang, Hankow...... 50 00
*St. Paul's S. S.** (Hamilton) : Gen... 6 93
LOUISA CO.—*Incarnation S. S.** (Min-
eral City) : Dom. and Frn........ 18 16
MATTHEWS CO. — *Kingston Parish* :
Gen., $25 ; Sp. for St. Paul's Col-
lege, Tokyo, $5 ; Sp. for Bishop
Horner's mountain work, Asheville,
$5 ; Rev. Giles B. Cooke, "Mrs. C.
W. Bragg" scholarship, St. John's
School, Africa, $25.............. 60 00
Christ Church S. S., Kingston Par-
ish* : Gen....................... 89
St. John's S. S., Kingston Parish* :
Gen. 4 97
Trinity Church S. S., Kingston Par-
ish* : Gen....................... 42
NORTHUMBERLAND CO.—*St. Stephen's,
St. Stephen's Parish* : $13.87, Lower
St. Stephen's Mission, $6.87, Gen... 20 74
Wicomico Parish (Wicomico) : Frn.. 6 98
ORANGE CO.—*Epiphany S. S.** (Somer-
set) : Gen...................... 1 25
*Church of the Holy Comforter S. S.**
(Madison Mills) : Gen............ 2 00
*St. Thomas's S. S.** (Orange) : Gen... 10 00
PAGE CO.—*Calvary S. S.** (Shenan-
doah) : Gen..................... 1 57
Luray S. S., Luray Parish*, $5.25,
Ingham S. S.,* 33 cts., Gen........ 5 58
PRINCE WILLIAM CO.—*Old Quantico*

Church, Deltingen Parish: $8, Dumfries S. S.,* $2, Gen.............. 10 00
Trinity Church (Manassas): Frn., $22.45; S. S.,* Gen., $5.13........ 27 58
RAPPAHANNOCK Co.—E m m a n u e l Church, Bloomfield Parish: $3.20, St. Paul's, $8.46, Dom.; Trinity Church, Frn., $16.88.............. 28 54
RICHMOND Co.—North Farnham Parish S. S.*: Gen...................... 4 65
St. John's, Lunenburg Parish: Gen.. 19 91
ROCKINGHAM Co.—Emmanuel Church S. S.* (Harrisonburg): Dom. and Frn. 6 07
SPOTSYLVANIA Co.—St. George's S. S.* (Fredericksburg): Frn............ 43 00
WESTMORELAND Co.—Washington Parish (Colonial Beach): Sp. for St. Paul's College, Tokyo.............. 1 95
St. James's S. S.* (Montrose): Gen.. 8 75
St. Peter's, Washington Parish: Frn.. 3 52
MISCELLANEOUS — Virginia Branch Junior Aux., Gen................ 29 50

Washington

Ap. $3,297.09; *Sp.* $355.73

WASHINGTON—Ascension: $50, S. S.,* $116.57, Gen................... 166 57
Calvary: $7.16, S. S.,* $3.29, Gen.... 10 45
Christ Church (Georgetown): $105, S. S.,* $100, Gen................... 205 00
Christ Church: Gen., $91.96; S. S.,* Dom., $33.35; Frn., $33.35....... 158 66
Esther Memorial S. S.*: Gen........ 8 86
Emmanuel Church S. S.*: Gen...... 72 68
Church of the Good Shepherd: Junior Aux., Sp. for Alaska, $5; Sp. for Settlement House, Manila, Philippine Islands, $3................... 8 00
Incarnation: "A Member," Sp. for Miss Thackara's work, Fort Defiance, Arizona 10 00
St. Agnes's Chapel: Gen........... 3 00
St. Alban's S. S.*: Frn............ 74 15
St. Barnabas's Deaf-Mute Mission: Gen. 7 09
St. Barnabas's S. S.* (Langdon): Gen. 8 25
St. George's Mission (Tenally Town): $2, S. S.,* $9, Gen............ 11 00
St. James's: Alaska, $10; Frn., $1; Gen., $46.20; Sp. for St. Paul's College, Tokyo, $3; Sp. for St. John's University, Shanghai, $3.80...... 64 00
St. John's (Georgetown): Frn., $108 30; Wo. Aux., Brazil, $5; S. S.,* Gen., $147......*........ 260 30
St. Luke's: Dom................ 25 00
St. Mark's: Dom., $75.33; Frn., $75.14; Hawaii, $1.80; Colored, 65 cts.; Indian, 10 cts.............. 153 02
All Saints' (Chevy Chase): Wo. Aux., Rev. W. C. Brown, Brazil........ 30 00
St. Michael and All Angels': Dom. and Frn., 1909-1910.............. 60 65
St. Paul's: Wo. Aux., Sp. for St. Peter's-on-the-Mountain, Virginia, $5; Sp. for Mrs. Sharpe, Edneyville, Asheville, $8; Sp. for Miss Thackara, hospital window, Arizona, $5 .... 18 00
St. Thomas's Parish: Dom. and Frn., $1,000; "A Member," Sp. for Miss Thackara's work, Arizona, $50...... 1,050 00
Trinity Church: $116.36, Wo. Aux., $5, Gen.; Sp. for Rev. G. P. Mayo, Dyke, Virginia, $33.............. 154 36
Trinity Church (Tacoma Park): Wo. Aux., Gen................... 2 00
Rock Creek Parish S. S's.*: Gen...... 125 00
"A Friend," rent of mission home, Santurce, Porto Rico, $10; Sp. for Bishop Van Buren's use at his discretion, Porto Rico, $5.......... 15 00
Mrs. Mary E. Boggs, Sp. for Right

Rev. H. D. Aves, D.D., famine sufferers, Mexico..................
Wo. Aux., Bishop Rowe's companion, Alaska, $169.50; "Catharine E. Jones" scholarship, St. Mary's Hall, Shanghai, $40; Sp. for Miss Higgins, Hankow, $10.90; Sp. for Mission Study Class, for Rev. F. L. H. Pott, D.D., St. John's College, Shanghai, $143....................
CHARLES Co.—Oldfields School: Junior Aux., $25; "Two Pupils," $32; Sp. for Building Fund, for St. Margaret's School, Tokyo..........
MONTGOMERY Co.—Prince George Parish: Gen..................
Christ Church (Rockville): Work among mountain whites in Virginia or North Carolina, $5; Sp. for Mrs. Wetmore's work, Asheville, $5; Frn., $50; Wo. Aux., $18.40; S. S.,* Frn., $37.04..............
Ascension (Gaithersburg): Frn., $20; Wo. Aux., Gen., $5; S. S.,* Frn., $7.30 ....
St. John's S. S.* (Bethesda): Gen....
Grace (Silver Spring): Gen., $17.50; Wo. Aux., Dom., $5; Frn., $7.85...
PRINCE GEORGE Co.—Holy Trinity Church S. S.* (Mitchellville): Gen..
King George Parish: Frn............
St. Matthew's Parish: Dom. and Frn..
Pinkney Memorial Church S. S.* (Hyattsville): Brazil............
St. Luke's S. S.* (Bladensburg): Brazil ....
Epiphany (Forestville): Dom., $15; Frn., $5...................
St. Philip's S. S.* (Laurel): Frn.....
PRINCE GEORGE AND CHARLES Co's.— Christ Church: Gen...............
St. John's Chapel: Gen............
St. MARY'S Co.—All Faith's Parish (Mechanicsville): Dom. and Frn...
St. Mary's Parish S. S.*: Dom. and Frn.........................
All Saints' (Oakley): Dom., $5; Frn., $5; S. S.,* Gen., $5.50........
MISCELLANEOUS — Washington Junior Aux., Gen., $51.58; Sp. for scholarship in Rev. Mr. Lund's School, Wuhu, Hankow, $25............

Western Massachusetts

Ap. $3,077.14; *Sp.* $119.20

ADAMS—St. Mark's S. S.*: Gen......
AMHERST—Grace S. S.*: Education of Liberian child, Africa............
ASHFIELD—St. John's: $4, S. S.,* $5.43, Gen..................
ATHOL—St. John's S. S.*: Dom., $8; Frn., $8...................
BLACKINTON—St. Andrew's Mission S. S.*: Gen....................
CHICOPEE—Grace S. S.*: Gen......
CLINTON—Church of the Good Shepherd: Wo. Aux. Alaska Supply Fund, $5; Philippine insurance, $5.
EASTHAMPTON—St. Philip's S. S.*: Gen.........................
GARDNER—St. Paul's S. S.*: Gen......
GREAT BARRINGTON—St. James's S. S.*: Gen., $24.05; Wo. Aux., Alaska Supply Fund, $3; Japanese Biblewoman, Honolulu, $3............
GREENFIELD—St. James's: Gen., $50; Wo. Aux., Sp. for Building Fund, St. Margaret's School, Tokyo, $2.85; Sp. for Rev, F. B. Wentworth, Lexington, $1...............
LEE—St. George's S. S.*: Gen.......
Church of the Good Shepherd S. S.* (South): Gen................
LENOX—Trinity Church S. S.*: Gen..

BIG RAPIDS—*St. Andrew's*: $6, W. J.
Sloss, $2, S. S.,* $14, Gen....... 22 00
CHARLEVOIX—*Christ Church S. S.*:*
Dom. 8 14
COLDWATER—*St. Mark's S. S.*:* Dom.,
$13.60 ; Frn., $13.60 ; Junior Aux.,
Gen., $2....................... 29 20
GRAND HAVEN—*Akeley Hall*: Junior
Aux., " J. W. Bancroft" scholarship,
St. Hilda's School, Wuchang, Han-
kow 40 00
St. John's S. S.:* Gen.............. 18 18
GRAND LEDGE—*Trinity Mission S. S.*:*
Gen. 11 35
GRAND RAPIDS—*Grace*: Gen., $82.34 ;
Wo. Aux., "Bishop McCormick"
scholarship, St. Mary's School, South
Dakota, $10 ; "Sarah K. Bancroft"
gift, St. Hilda's School, Wuchang,
Hankow, $5 ; Colored Salary Fund,
$10 ; S. S.,* Frn., $150 ; Sp. for
the "Julia" cot, St. Mary's Orphan-
age, Shanghai, $5 ; Sp. for Bishop
Horner, Asheville, $5............ 267 34
St. Mark's: $20.30, S. S.,* $95.26,
Gen. ; Wo. Aux., "Dr. Cuming" schol-
arship (of which "Industrial Band,"
$5), $18, "Ellen E. Robinson" schol-
arship, $17, both in St. Elizabeth's
School, South Dakota ; S. S., Sp. for
"Julia" cot, St. Mary's Orphanage,
Shanghai, $5..................... 155 56
St. Paul's Memorial S. S.:* Gen..... 7 16
HOMER—*Christ Church S. S.*:* Dom.
and Frn........................ 4 25
KALAMAZOO—*St. Luke's*: Wo. Aux.,
"Bishop McCormick" scholarship, St.
Mary's School, South Dakota, $10 ;
"Ellen E. Robinson" scholarship, St.
Elizabeth's School, South Dakota,
$20 ; "Sarah K. Bancroft" gift, St.
Hilda's School, Wuchang, Hankow,
$15 ; Colored Salary Fund, $25.... 70 00
MUSKEGON—*St. Paul's*: Wo. Aux.,
"Bishop McCormick" scholarship, St.
Mary's School, South Dakota, $10 ;
"Sarah K. Bancroft" gift, St. Hilda's
School, Wuchang, Hankow, $5 ; Col-
ored Salary Fund, $10 ; S. S.,*
Frn., $53.39.................... 78 39
NILES—*Trinity Church*: Gen., $5 ; S.
S., Sp. for "Julia" cot, St. Mary's
Orphanage, Shanghai, $5.......... 10 00
PETOSKEY—*Emmanuel Church S. S.*:*
Gen. 12 90
STURGIS—*St. John's S. S.*:* Gen..... 21 00
TRAVERSE CITY—*Grace*: $5, S. S.,*
$19.17, Gen.................... 24 17

Western New York

Ap. $4,108.10 ; *Sp.* $4,845.64

ADDISON—*Church of the Redeemer S.
S.*:* Gen....................... 2 60
ALFRED—*S. S.*:* Gen.............. 3 92
ANGELICA—*St. Paul's S. S.*:* Gen.... 6 30
AVON—*Zion S. S.*:* Gen........... 3 20
BATAVIA—*St. James's*: Dom., $52.82 ;
Frn., $4.05 ; Gen., $17.37 ; S. S.*
Sp for Rev. Robert E. Wood, for his
work, Wuchang, Hankow, $37..... 111 24
BATH—*St. Thomas's*: Gen........... 6 05
BELMONT—*St. Philip's*: $18.90, S. S.,
$4.37, Gen.................... 23 27
BOLIVAR—*Church of Our Saviour*:
$2.06, S. S.,* 50 cts., Gen......... 2 56
BRANCHPORT—*St. Luke's S. S.*; Gen.. 8 00
BUFFALO — *Ascension*: Frn., $7.50 ;
Gen., $74.89................... 82 39
Church of the Good Shepherd: Dom.
and Frn....................... 54 00
Epiphany S. S.:* Gen............. 2 87
Grace: Dom. and Frn., $100 ; S. S.,*
Gen., $72.98.................. 172 98
St. John's: Gen.................. 56 30

St. Paul's: Dom. and Frn. (of which
 S. S.,* $91.55), $608.86; Gen.,
 $847.82 .... 1,456 68
*St. Stephen's S. S.**: Gen. 5 50
*Trinity Church S. S.**: Gen. 136 34
CANANDAIGUA—*St. John's S. S.**: Gen. 23 00
CATHARINE—*St. John's*: $25.76, S. S.,*
 $9.72, Gen. 35 48
CLIFTON SPRINGS—*St. John's S. S.**
 Gen. 3 68
CORFU—*St. Luke's S. S.**: Gen. 1 70
CORNING—*Christ Church*: $26.04; S.
 S.,* $20, Gen. 46 04
CUBA—*Christ Church S. S.**: Gen. 13 56
DARIEN CENTRE—*St. Paul's Mission
 S. S.**: Gen. 2 90
DEFEW—*St. Andrew's Mission S. S.**:
 $17.05, "Birthday Bank," $3.95,
 Gen. 21 00
DUNDEE—*Mission S. S.**: Gen. 4 06
ELLICOTTVILLE—*St. John's*: $20, S.
 S.,* $5, Gen. 25 00
FRANKLINVILLE—*St. Barnabas's S. S.**:
 Gen. 1 15
GENESEO—*St. Michael's*: Gen. 78 00
GENEVA—*St. Peter's*: Gen. 285 19
*Trinity Church S. S.**: Gen. 124 67
*St. Andrew's Chapel S. S.** (East):
 Gen. 12 93
HIMROD—*St. Paul's S. S.**: Gen. 3 69
HOLLEY—*St. Paul's S. S.**: Gen. 7 14
HONEOYE FALLS—*St. John's S. S.**:
 Gen. 3 70
HORNELL—*Christ Church S. S.**: Dom.,
 $7.50; Frn., $7.50; Gen., $10 .... 25 00
LE ROY—*St. Mark's S. S.**: Gen. 16 00
LOCKPORT—*All Saints' Chapel S. S.**:
 Gen. 10 00
*Christ Church S. S.**: Gen. 10 00
Grace: Gen., $238.38; Sp. for St.
 Paul's College Fund, Tokyo, $2.85;
 S. S.,* Gen., $90 .... 331 23
LYONS—*Grace*: $25, S. S.,* $12.86,
 Gen. 37 86
MEDINA—*St. John's*: $4, S. S.,* $18.03,
 Gen. 22 03
MT. MORRIS—*St. John's*: $4, S. S.,*
 $17.01, Gen. 21 01
NEWARK—*St. Mark's S. S.**: Gen. 16 62
NIAGARA FALLS—*St. Ambrose's*: Dom.
 and Frn., $1.91; S. S.,* Gen., $3.94. 5 85
NORTH TONAWANDA—*St. Mark's*:
 $26.32, S. S.,* $29.25, Gen. 55 57
OLEAN—*St. Stephen's*: (of which Wo.
 Aux., $25) Dom., $26; Frn., $34.91. 50 91
ORCHARD PARK—*St. Mark's Mission*:
 $5.48, S. S.,* $3.55, Gen. 9 03
PERRY—*Holy Apostles' S. S.**: Gen... 1 35
PITTSFORD—*Christ Church*: Dom.,
 $68.93; S. S.,* Dom., $9.30; Frn.,
 $10; Gen. (additional), 70 cts. ... 88 93
ROCHESTER—*Ascension*: Frn. 4 80
Christ Church: Dom., $100; Frn.,
 $100; S. S.,* Gen., $40; James M.
 Hawley, Sp. for Bishop Rowe,
 Alaska, $5 .... 245 00
*St. Andrew's S. S.**: Gen. 20 39
St. Luke's: Gen., $19.92; Wo. Aux.,
 Indian, $40.25; Frn., 75 cts. 60 92
St. Paul's: Sp. for Arthur Yates Me-
 morial Hospital, Alaska, $4,000; Sp.
 for Bishop Rowe, Alaska, $401.93;
 Sp. for scholarship, Bishop Payne
 Divinity-school, Petersburg, South-
 ern Virginia, $143.86; Mrs. G. A.
 Hollister, Sp. for Rev. Murray Bart-
 lett's special use, Manila, Philippine
 Islands, $200 .... 4,745 79
Trinity Church: Gen. 25 00
ROLAND—*Church of Our Saviour S.
 S.**: Gen. 2 63
SALAMANCA—*St. Mary's S. S.**: Gen.. 19 11
SAVONA—"Three Children,"* Gen. 38
SILVER CREEK—*St. Alban's S. S.**:
 Gen. 7 15

SINCLAIRVILLE—*All Saints' S. S.**:
 Gen. ....
SODUS—*St. John's S. S.**: Gen. .....
SPRINGVILLE—*St. Paul's S. S.**: Gen..
STAFFORD—*St. Paul's S. S.**: Gen....
WARSAW—*Trinity Church S. S.**: Gen.
WELLVILLE—*St. John's S. S.**: Gen...
MISCELLANEOUS—Wo. Aux., Yangchow,
 Shanghai, $30 ; "J. G. Webster"
 scholarship, St. Hilda's School, Wu-
 chang, Hankow, $50; Gen., $130;
 Sp. for Bishop Wells, Spokane, $50;
 Sp. for Miss Thackara, Arizona, $5..

West Texas

Ap. $1,039.53; *Sp.* $76.00

BEEVILLE—*St. Philip's S. S.**: Gen....
KENDALL CO.—*St. Helena's Parish*:
 Gen. ....
BRACKETTVILLE—*St. Andrew's S. S.**:
 Gen. ....
BROWNSVILLE—*Advent*: $27.50, S. S.,*
 $22.84, Gen. ....
CORPUS CHRISTI—*Church of the Good
 Shepherd*: Gen., $3.40; Wo. Aux.,
 Sp. for Rev. T. M. Tummon for
 building church at Fitzgerald,
 Georgia $1; S. S.,* Gen., $42.20....
EAGLE PASS—*Church of the Redeemer
 S. S.**: Gen. ....
EDNA—*Trinity Church*: Gen. ....
GANADA—*St. Andrew's*: Gen. ....
GOLIAD—*St. Stephen's S. S.**: Gen...
GONZALES—*Church of the Messiah S.
 S.**: Gen. ....
HALLETTSVILLE—*St. James's S. S.**:
 Gen. ....
KERRVILLE—*St. Peter's*: Frn., $4;
 Gen. (of which S. S.,* $43.50), $98
 Frn. ....
LAGUNA—"Two Boys,"* Dom. and
 Frn. ....
LAREDO—*Christ Church S. S.**: Gen..
LLANO—*Grace S. S.**: Dom. ....
LOCKHART—*Emmanuel Church S. S.**:
 Gen. ....
LONG MOTT—Gen. ....
LULING—*Annunciation S. S.**: Gen...
MONTELL—*Ascension*: $3, S. S.,* $5,
 Gen. ....
MORRIS RANCH—Gen. ....
PEARSALL—*Trinity Church S. S.**: Gen.
PORT LAVACA—*Grace*: $15, S. S.,*
 $12.94, Gen. ....
ROCKPORT—*St. Peter's S. S.**: Bishop
 Kinsolving's work, Brazil. ....
SAN ANTONIO—*St. John's*: $15.70, S.
 S.,* $10, Frn. ....
St. Luke's: $15, S. S.,* $15.92, Gen..
St. Mark's: $186.70, S. S.,* $14.65,
 Gen. ....
St. Paul's: $100, S. S.,* $37, Gen.....
 Rev. and Mrs. J. T. Hutcheson, Gen.
 Wo. Aux., Mrs. J. L. Patton, Sp. for
 Rev. St. George Tucker, Wilson Me-
 morial, St. Paul's College, Tokyo...
SAN MARCOS—*St. Mark's S. S.**: Gen.
SAN SABA—*St. Luke's S. S.**: Gen....
SEGUIN—*St. Andrew's S. S.**: Gen....
SISTERDALE—*St. Helena's Mission S.
 S.**: Gen ....
UVALDE—*St. Philip's*: $10.90, S. S.,*
 $10.15, Gen. ....
VICTORIA—*Trinity Church*: $23.15, S.
 S.,* $38.41, Gen. ....

West Virginia

Ap. $1,419.91; *Sp.* $40.00

ALDERSON—*Church of the Messiah*:
 Gen. ....
BEALE—*Bruce Chapel S. S.**: Gen....
BERKELEY SPRINGS—*St. Mark's S. S.**:
 Gen. ....
BLUEFIELDS — *Christ Church*: Gen.,

25 00
1 50

167 75

131 58

15 00
5 00

34 04
10 00
12 40
8 54
9 61

10 00
2 00
10 70

10 82

12 54
30 00

36 00

19 50

33 00

10 00

4 83

21 19

15 10
58 27

28 42

5 00

4 00

70 51

15 00

10 00
3 06
2 32
19 44
3 45

15 48

5 21
7 16
5 00

20 00

32 24

WAKE FOREST—Mrs. V. P. Zimmerman, Dom. and Frn., $2; S. S.,* Gen., $8.75...... 10 75

WESTON—*St. Paul's*: Wo. Aux., Gen., $10; S. S.,* Porto Rico, $1.21; Mexico, $1.21; Gen., $40.09........ 52 51

WHEELING—*St. John's S. S.* (Leatherwood): Gen................ 5 34
St. Matthew's: $350, S. S.,* $74.70, Gen. 424 70

Missionary Districts

Alaska

Ap. $340.53; *Sp.* $25.00

ANVIK—*Christ Church Mission*: Gen.. 13 81
EAGLE—*St. Paul's*: Gen............ 10 00
FORT YUKON—*St. Stephen's*: Wo. Aux., $10, Junior Aux., $5, Gen........ 15 00
JUNEAU—*Trinity Church*: Gen........ 12 20
KETCHIKAN—*St. John's Mission*: $100, S. S.,* $14, Gen........... 114 00
SKAGWAY—*St. Saviour's*: $5, S. S.,* $7.75, Gen............... 12 75
VALDEZ—*Epiphany*: $118.90, S. S.,* $26.27, Gen.; S. S., Sp. for Fort Yukon, Alaska, $25........... 170 17
ELLAMAR—*Mission S. S.*: Gen...... 3 10
MISCELLANEOUS — Southeast Archdeaconry, Gen.............. 14 50

Arizona

Ap. $363.96

BISBEE—*St. John's*: Bishop Kendrick's salary, New Mexico and Arizona, $8.70; Wo. Aux., $5, S. S.,* $8.67, Gen................... 22 37
DOUGLAS—*St. Stephen's*: $35, Wo. Aux., $5, S. S.,* $31.20, Gen....... 71 20
GLOBE—*St. John's*: $11.60, Wo. Aux., $5, S. S.,* $20.75, Gen......... 37 35
MESA—*St. Mark's Mission*: Gen...... 5 15
NOGALES—*St. Andrew's*: Wo. Aux., $5, S. S.,* $16.89, Gen........... 21 89
PHOENIX — *Trinity Church*: Bishop Kendrick's salary, New Mexico and Arizona, $16; Frn. (of which Wo. Aux., $6, S. S.,* $35), $46; Gen., $14.90 .... 76 90
PRESCOTT—*St. Luke's*: $65, Wo. Aux., $5, S. S.,* $43, Gen........... 113 00
TEMPLE—*St. James's Mission*: Gen.... 4 00
TOMBSTONE—*St. Paul's*: Bishop Kendrick's salary, New Mexico and Arizona 7 00
WINSLOW—*St. Paul's*: Gen.......... 5 10

Asheville

Ap. $717.59

BALSAM—*Church of the Holy Communion*: Dom., $16.29; S. S.,* Gen., $82.50 .... 98 79
BELL HAW CREEK—*Trinity Church S. S.*: Gen................... 3 03
BILTMORE—*All Souls'*: $25, S. S.,* $100, Gen................... 125 00
BLACK MOUNTAIN—*St. James's S. S.*: Gen. 1 00
BREVARD—*St. Philip's*: Dom., 25 cts.; Frn., 25 cts.; Gen. (of which S. S.,* $16.66), $26.66............ 27 16
CANTON—*St. Andrew's*: Dom., $8.07; S. S.,* Gen., $36................ 44 07
CASHIER'S VALLEY—*Church of the Good Shepherd*: Frn............ 75
CHUNN'S COVE—*St. Luke's S. S.*: Gen. 6 00
CULLOWHEE—*St. David's*: Dom., $18.39; S. S.,* Gen., $18.44........... 36 83
FLETCHER—*Calvary*: Dom., $5; Frn., $5; Gen., $5; S. S.,* Gen., $1.67.... 16 67
FRANKLIN—*St. Agnes's S. S.*: Gen... 10 00

St. Cyprian's S. S.*: Gen..... 5 52
GRACE—Grace: Gen.............. 5 00
HICKORY—Ascension: Dom., $4; Frn., $4; Gen., $4; S. S.,* Gen., $10.... 22 00
HOT SPRINGS—St. John's: Dom., $2; Frn., $2; Gen., $3.............. 7 00
LENOIR—St. James's S. S.*: Gen..... 8 78
LINCOLNTON—St. Luke's: 4 cts., S. S.,* $4.72, Dom................. 4 76
St. Cyprian's S. S.*: Dom.......... 4 36
MICADALE—St. Mary's: Dom., $9.09; S. S.,* Gen., $79.25............ 88 34
MORGANTON — Grace: Dom., $3.96; Frn., $3.97; Gen., $3.97; S. S.,* $6.37 18 27
Church of the Good Shepherd S. S.*: Gen. 6 45
St. George's S. S.*: Gen.......... 1 50
St. Margaret's S. S.*: Gen........ 6 92
St. Mary's S. S.*: Gen............ 9 64
St. Stephen's S. S.*: Gen......... 1 36
MURPHY—Church of the Messiah S. S.*: Gen. 3 50
NONAH—St. John's S. S.*: Gen...... 6 00
OLD FORT—St. Gabriel's S. S.*: Gen.. 1 32
PRENTISS—St. George's S. S.*: Gen.. 4 61
RONDA—All Saints' S. S.*: Gen..... 8 00
RUTHERFORDTON—St. Francis S. S.*: Gen. 20 27
SALUDA—Transfiguration S. S.*: Gen. 5 00
SHELBY—Church of the Redeemer S. S.*: Gen. 6 10
SYLVA—St. John's: Dom., $8.32; S. S.,* Gen., $7.92.............. 16 24
TYRON—Holy Cross: Dom., $4.50; Frn., $4.50; Gen., $4.50; S. S.,* $20.44 33 94
VALLE CRUCIS—Holy Cross S. S.*: Gen. 25 76
WAYNESVILLE — St. Michael's: Dom., $8.43; S. S.,* Gen., $11.33........ 19 76
YADKIN—Chapel of Rest: Dom........ 7 89

Eastern Oregon
Ap. $258.58

BAKER CITY—St. Stephen's: $36, S. S., $12.02, Gen.................. 48 02
COVE—Ascension S. S.*: Gen........ 3 15
ECHO—Gen. 1 85
HOOD RIVER—St. Mark's S. S.*: Gen.. 2 62
LA GRANDE—St. Peter's: $39.50, S. S.,* $20.40, Gen.............. 59 90
PENDLETON—Church of the Redeemer: Gen., $59.09; S. S.,* Dom. and Frn., $80.10 139 19
THE DALLES—St. Paul's: Gen........ 3 85

Honolulu
Ap. $9.85

HONOLULU—St. Clement's S. S.*: Gen. 9 85

Idaho
Ap. $536.45

BLACKFOOT—St. Paul's S. S.*: Dom.. 10 13
BOISE—Christ Church: $10, S. S.,* $35, Gen. 45 00
St. Michael's Cathedral: $150, S. S.,* $98.65, Gen................ 248 65
CALDWELL—St. David's: Gen......... 10 00
COEUR D'ALENE—St. Luke's: $5.50, S. S.,* $10.63, Gen............. 16 13
DU BOIS—All Saints' S. S.*: Dom.... 5 00
GRANGEVILLE—Trinity Church S. S.*: Gen. 6 10
NAMPA—Grace: Gen................ 20 00
POCATELLO—Trinity Church S. S.*: Gen. 7 14
ROSS FORK—Church of the Good Shepherd: $17.80, S. S.,* $8.77, Babies' Branch, $1.55, Gen.............. 28 12
SALMON—Church of the Redeemer S. S.*: Gen. 31 00
SHOSHONE—Christ Church: Dom. and

Frn., $7.25; S. S.,* Gen., $22.04.. 29
WALLACE—Holy Trinity Church: Frn., $3.30, S. S.,* $34.09, Gen......... 37
WARDNER—St. Peter's: Dom......... 13
WEISER—St. Luke's: $15, S. S.,* $14.50, Gen.................. 29

Kearney
Ap. $310.81

AINSWORTH—Guild, Gen............. 20
ALLIANCE—St. Matthew's: Gen....... 17
ARAPAHOE—St. Paul's S. S.*: Gen... 12
BAYARD—St. Margaret's: Gen........
BASSETT—Ladies' Guild, Gen........ 10
BENKLEMAN—S. S.*: Gen...........
BRIDGEPORT—Church of the Good Shepherd: Gen. 4
BROKEN BOW—St. John's S. S.*: Gen.. 11
CALLAWAY—Holy Trinity Church: $10, S. S.,* $6.09, Gen............. 16
CULBERTSON—Annunciation: $2, S. S.,* 43 cts., Gen................ 2
DONALD—St. Andrew's S. S.*: Gen... 2
ECLIPSE—S. S.*: Gen............. 1
FRANKLIN—Calvary Mission: Gen..... 4
GERING—St. Timothy's: Gen......... 2
GRAND ISLAND—St. Stephen's S. S.*: Gen. 14
HASTINGS—St. Mark's S. S.*: Gen.... 36
HAIGLER—St. Philip's S. S.*: Gen.... 1
HOOKER Co.—Centre School House S. S.*: Gen. 1
IMPERIAL—S. S.*: Gen............ 1
INDIANOLA—S. S.*: Gen........... 3
JIMTOWN—Mission S. S.*: Gen...... 1
KEARNEY—St. Luke's: Gen.......... 35
LENA—Trinity Church S. S.*: Gen... 1
McCOOK—Grace: Gen..............
St. Alban's S. S.*: Gen.......... 12
MINATARE—Gen. 1
LEXINGTON—St. Peter's S. S.*: Gen.. 16
MULLEN—St. Joseph's S. S.*: Gen.... 4
OCONTO—St. Mark's: Gen.......... 2
OGALALLA—St. Paul's Mission: Gen... 10
O'NEILL—St. Paul's S. S.*: Gen..... 1
SCOTT'S BLUFFS—Mission: Gen....... 1
SIDNEY—Christ Church S. S.*: Gen... 19
St. PAUL'S—Holy Trinity Church S. S.*: Gen. 8
STRATTON—Mission S. S.*: Gen..... 3
TRENTON—S. S.*: Gen............ 3
VALENTINE—St. John's: $3, S. S.,* $23.50, Gen.................. 26

Nevada
Ap. $437.32

BATTLE MOUNTAIN—St. Andrew's S. S.*: Gen. 26
CARSON CITY—St. Peter's: $60, S. S.,* $40, Gen.................. 100
CLOVER VALLEY—St. Luke's S. S.*: Gen. 16
ELKO—St. Paul's S. S.*: Gen...... 55
ELY—St. Bartholomew's: $10, S. S.,* $42, Gen.................. 52
EUREKA—St. James's S. S.*: Dom.... 16
RENO—Trinity Church: $64.50, S. S.,* $87.32, Gen................. 151
SPARKS—St. Paul's: $10, S. S.,* $10, Gen. 20

New Mexico
Ap. $234.37

ALAMOGORDO—St. John's S. S.*: Gen.. 5
ALBUQUERQUE—St. John's S. S.*: Gen. 22
BELEN—St. Philip's: $5, S. S.,* $1.81, Gen. 6
DEMING—St. Luke's S. S.*: Gen..... 20
MESILLA PARK—St. James's S. S.*: Gen. 25
ROSWELL—St. Andrew's: $25, S. S.,* $12.30, Gen.................. 37

5 00	WAGONER—*St. James's*: $5, S. S.,* $2.70, Gen......................	7 70
53 04	WOODWARD—*St. John's*: $7, S. S.,* $1.50, Gen......................	8 50
54 18	MISCELLANEOUS — Wo. Aux., "Tithe," Sp. for Holy Trinity Orphanage,,	
5 00	Tokyo	4 00

Olympia

Ap. $610.04 ; *Sp.* $39.00

3 00	ANACORTES—*Christ Church*: Gen.....	1 25
	AUBURN—*St. Matthew's*: $7.50, S. S.,*	
10 48	$10.12, Gen......................	17 62
2 00	BREMERTON—*St. Paul's*: $5, S. S.,*	
4 50	$6.70, Gen......................	11 70
15 10	CENTRALIA—*St. John's S. S.*: Gen...	2 10
50	CHEHALIS—*Epiphany S. S.*: Gen.....	31 63
2 50	EVERETT—*Trinity Church S. S.*:	
50	Gen.	16 10
12 00	HOQUIAM—*Trinity Church S. S.*: Gen...	15 79
85 00	KENT—*St. James's S. S.*: Gen.......	35 00
3 00	OLYMPIA—*St. John's*: $20, S. S.,* $22,	
4 00	Gen.	42 00
	PORT TOWNSEND—*St. Paul's S. S.*:	
15 00	Gen............................	12 00
17 00	PUYALLUP—*Christ Church S. S.*:	
2 00	Dom. and Frn....................	2 78
2 25	SEATTLE—*All Saints'*: Gen., $5.60; S.	
18 00	S.,* Alaska, $30.80..............	36 40
2 00	*St. Clement's*: $16, S. S.,* $19, Gen..	35 00
5 00	*St. Mark's*: Wo. Aux., Sp. for memor-	
20 00	ial to P. E. Hyland, St. John's-in-	
8 13	the-Wilderness, Alaska, $10; S. S.,*	
5 00	Dom., $75.60; Frn., $75.60; Gen.,	
5 00	$8.71	169 91
25 00	*St. Stephen's S. S.*: Dom..........	2 55
	Trinity Church: Gen., $14.51; Wo.	
	Aux., Sp. for one-half pledge, for	
	fitting up room in St. Andrew's	
	Priory, Honolulu, $25; S. S.,* Gen.,	
	$41.65	81 16
8 93	SNOHOMISH—*St. John's S. S.*: Gen...	7 50
7 25	SUMAS—*St. George's S. S.*: Gen.....	5 85
4 00	TACOMA—*Grace*: $3.05, S. S.,* $3.50,	
	Gen.	6 55
23 20	*Holy Communion S. S.*: Gen.........	10 00
	St. Andrew's S. S.: Gen............	17 54
13 05	*St. John's*: Gen...................	5 60
	St. Luke's S. S.: (of which Annie	
10 00	Wright Seminary,* $8.46) Gen....	30 83
	St. Peter's S. S.: Gen.............	9 10
22 48	*Trinity Church*: Wo. Aux., Sp. for	
2 20	Bishop Spalding, Utah...........	4 00
5 82	Matthew Miller* (South), Gen.....	50
4 75	VANCOUVER—*St. Luke's S. S.*: Gen..	38 58

Porto Rico

Ap. $26.48

18 68		
13 30	PONCE—*Holy Trinity Church*: Gen...	16 48
	VIEQUES—*S. S.*: Gen...............	10 00
3 70		
4 46		

Sacramento

Ap. $478.11

12 00		
6 45	ARCATA—*St. John's S. S.*: Gen......	22 00
15 00	BENICIA—*St. Paul's*: Gen............	5 00
	CHICO—*St. John's*: Gen.............	20 25
98 97	CLOVERDALE—*Church of the Good*	
3 05	*Shepherd*: $16.20, S. S.,* $2.72,	
6 40	Gen.	18 92
2 70	COLUSA—*St. Stephen's*: Gen.........	40
4 76	EUREKA—*Christ Church*: $96.20, S.	
3 66	S.,* $50, Gen...................	146 20
1 75	FORT BRAGG—*St. Michael and All*	
2 15	*Angels' S. S.*: Gen..............	10 11
	GRASS VALLEY — *Emmanuel Church*:	
1 50	$40, S. S.,* $12, Gen............	52 00
6 91	LOOMIS—*All Saints'*: $5.60, S. S.,*	
	$2.50, Gen.....................	8 10
3 72	MARYSVILLE—*St. John's S. S.*: Gen..	4 62
	NAPA—*St. Mary's*: $4.36, S. S.,*	
5 00	$17.75, Gen....................	22 11
	NEVADA—*Trinity Church*: Gen.......	11 95
62 90	OAK PARK—*Christ Church*: Gen.....	7 85
3 05	PETALUMA—*St. John's S. S.*: Gen...	16 00

SACRAMENTO—*St. Paul's*: Gen........ 57 25
SUISUN—*Grace*: $16.20, S. S.,* $39.74,
　Gen. ..,................. 55 94
WILLOWS—*Holy Trinity Church*: Gen.. 2 70
WOODLAWN—*St. Luke's S. S.**: Gen.. 16 71

Salina

Ap. $560.31; *Sp.* $75.00

BELLEVILLLE—*St. James's*: Gen...... 5 00
BELOIT—*St. Paul's*: Gen.... 35 00
BROOKVILLE—*Mission S. S.**: Gen.... 87
CONCORDIA—*Epiphany*: Gen.......... 26 00
DODGE CITY—*St. Cornelius's*: $17.50,
　S. S.,* $11.78, Gen............. 29 28
ELLSWORTH—*Holy Apostles'*: $36.36,
　S.S.,* $27.50, Gen............. 63 86
FORMOSO—*Trinity Church S. S.**: Gen. 8 26
GOODLAND—*St. Paul's*: $15, S. S.,*
　$13.24, Gen................. 28 24
HAYS—*Mission*: Gen.............. 10 00
HUTCHINSON—*Grace*: Gen........... 55 00
KINGMAN—*Christ Church*: $14, S. S.,*
　$10.24, Gen................. 24 24
MEADE—*Mission*: Gen............. 5 00
MINNEAPOLIS—*St. Peter's*: $36.20, S.
　S.,* $33.62, Gen............. 69 82
NORTON—*Mission*: $5.25, S. S.,* $3.75,
　Gen..................... 9 00
OBERLIN—*Holy Trinity Church*: $6,
　S. S.,* $5, Gen............. 11 00
SALINA — *Christ Cathedral*: Alaska,
　$10; Gen. (of which S. S.,* $25),
　$116.97; Sp. for Rev. W. J. Cuth-
　bert's church building, Kyoto, $75,
　St. John's Military School: St. John's
　School scholarship; St. John's Uni-
　versity, Shanghai............... 201 97
WAKEENEY—*Heavenly Rest*: Gen.... 42 77
　10 00

South Dakota

Ap. $1,268.05

BELLE FOURCHE—*St. James's*: Gen... 5 00
BRISTOL—*St. John's S. S.**: Dom.,
　$8.40; Frn., $8.40............. 16 80
CHAMBERLAIN—*Christ Church S. S.**:
　Gen..................... 16 56
DELL RAPIDS—*Living Water*: $15, S.
　S.,* $15.37, Gen............. 30 37
DE SMET—*St. Stephen's S. S.**: Gen.. 10 15
FLANDREAU—*Church of the Redeemer*:
　Wo. Aux., Gen., $5; S. S.,* Dom.,
　$23; Frn., $10; Gen., $10...... 48 00
PORT PIERRE—*St. Peter's*: $2.57, S.
　S.,* $4.25, Gen............. 6 82
GETTYSBURG—*Christ Church S. S.**:
　Dom...................... 1 58
HOT SPRINGS—*St. Luke's S. S.**: Gen. 32 66
HOWARD—*Trinity Church*: $20, S. S.,*
　$25, Gen................. 45 00
HURON—*Grace S. S.**: Gen......... 24 25
MADISON—*Grace*: $20, S. S.,* $3, Gen. 23 00
MILBANK—*Christ Church S. S.**: Dom.,
　$18.88; Frn., $9.44........... 28 32
MITCHELL—*St. Mary's S. S.**: Gen.. 16 00
PIERRE—*Trinity Church S. S.**: Gen.. 33 10
REDFIELD—*St. George's S. S.**: Dom.,
　$5.43; Frn., $6............. 11 43
SISSETON—*Gethsemane S. S.**: Dom.,
　$5.52; Frn., $2.75........... 8 27
SIOUX FALLS—*All Saints' S. S.**: Bish-
　op Rowe's work, Alaska, $50; sup-
　port of Bible-woman, Shanghai, $50;
　Gen., $31.60............... 131 60
Calvary: $4.17, S. S.,* $43.51, Gen.. 47 68
SPEARFISH—*All Angels'*: Gen., $13; S.
　S.,* Dom., $25.35........... 38 35
SPRINGFIELD—*Ascension S. S.**: Gen. 50 03
STURGIS—*St. Thomas's*: Wo. Aux., Gen. 5 00
WATERTOWN—*Trinity Church S. S.**:
　Gen..................... 100 00
YANKTON—*Christ Church S. S.**: Gen. 20 10
CHEYENNE RIVER RESERVATION — *As-
　cension*: Colored............... 1 13

Calvary: Colored...............
Emmanuel Church: Colored......... 2
St. Andrew's: Colored............ 1
St. Barnabas's: Colored.............
St. James's: Colored.............
St. John's: Colored............. 7
St. Luke's: Colored.............
St. Mark's: Colored.............
St. Mary's: Colored............. 1
St. Paul's: Colored.............
St. Stephen's: Colored.............
St. Thomas's: Colored............. 1
PINE RIDGE—*Christ Church Station*:
　Gen.....................
Epiphany Station: Gen.............
Grace: Gen................. 2
Holy Cross: Gen............. 1
Church of the Messiah: Gen...... 1
St. Alban's: Gen.............
St. James's: Gen.............
St. John's Station: Gen.........
St. Julia's: Gen............. 1
St. Luke's: Gen............. 1
St. Mark's: Gen.............
St. Mary's: Gen.............
St. Mary's (Sand Hills): Gen...... 2
St. Matthew's Station: Gen...... 1
St. Paul's: Gen............. 2
St. Peter's: Gen............. 1
St. Philip's: Gen.............
St. Thomas's: Gen............. 2
SISSETON MISSION—*St. James's*: $3.05,
　Babies' Branch, $2.28, S. S.,* $9.90,
　Gen..................... 15
St. John the Baptist's: $1.16, Babies'
　Branch, $4.71, S. S.,* $13.75, Gen.. 19
St. Luke's: $6.70, S. S.,* $5.34, Gen.. 12
St. Mary's: $11, Babies' Branch, $3.15,
　S. S.,* $7.36, Gen........... 21
STANDING ROCK MISSION—*Grand River
　School*: Frn.................
Church of the Good Shepherd: Dom.,
　$2; Frn., $2.67............. 4
St. Elizabeth's: Dom., $33.50; Frn.,
　$37.33................... 70
St. John the Baptist's: Dom., $15.50;
　Frn., $16.50............... 32
St. Thomas's: Dom., $3.50; Frn.,
　$4.14................... 7
YANKTON MISSION—*Holy Fellowship*:
　$196, S. S.,* $22.16, Gen........ 218
Holy Name Chapel: $35, S. S.,* $10,
　Gen..................... 45
St. Philip's: $25, S. S.,* $5, Gen...... 30

Southern Florida

Ap. $471.55

APOPKA—*Church of the Holy Spirit*:
　Gen..................... 2
AUBURNDALE—*St. Alban's*: Gen...... 2
AVON PARK—*Church of the Redeemer*:
　$5, S. S.,* $5.20, Gen......... 10
BROOKSVILLE—*St. John's S. S.**: Gen. 10
DELAND—*St. Barnabas's*: Gen...... 25
FORT PIERCE—*St. Andrew's*: $12, S.
　S.,* $21.43, Gen............. 33
FORT MYERS—*St. Luke's*: Gen...... 5
　Children's, $4............. 4
JUPITER—*St. Martin's*: Gen...... 12
KEY WEST—*St. Alban's S. S.**: Gen.. 5
*St. Paul's S. S.**: Gen............. 73
*St. Peter's S. S.**: Gen............. 20
LAKELAND—*All Saints' S. S.**: Gen.. 15
LONGWOOD—*Christ Church*: Gen..... 5
OCALA—*Grace S. S.**: Gen......... 36
ORANGE CITY—*St. Timothy's*: Gen.. 5
ORLANDO—*St. John Baptist's S. S.**:
　Gen..................... 9
St. Luke's: Gen............. 37
ORMOND—*St. James's*: $10, S. S.,*
　$5.07, Gen................. 15
PALM BEACH—*Bethesda-by-the-Sea*:
　Gen..................... 50
PLANT CITY—*St. Peter's S. S.**: Gen.. 5

	EVANSTON—*St. Paul's S. S.**: Gen.... 26 00
20 64	FORT WASHAKIE—*Mission S. S.**: Gen. 6 00
	GLEN ROCK—*Christ Church*: Gen.... 7 30
5 00	GREEN RIVER—*St. John's*: $5, S. S.,*
10 00	$10.20, Gen.................... 15 20
20 00	HUDSON—*St. Matthew's S. S.**: Gen... 3 25
	LANDER — *Trinity Church*: $30.15,
3 75	S.,* $19.29, Gen................. 49 44
	LARAMIE — *St. Matthew's Cathedral*:
24 00	$48.36, Wo. Aux., $10, S. S.,* $27.66,
2 00	Gen. 86 02
5 00	ROCK SPRINGS—*Church of the Holy Communion*: $18, S. S.,* $17.20,
	Gen. 35 20
	SARATOGA—*St. Barnabas's S. S.**: Gen. 6 10
	SHERIDAN—*St. Peter's S. S.**: Gen.... 23 53
2 31	SUNDANCE—*Church of the Good Shepherd*: Frn..................... 1 80
60 00	WIND RIVER—*Church of the Redeemer S. S.*: Gen., $9.38; Indian S. S.,*
108 70	Dom., $81.60................... 90 98
1 00	*Shoshone Mission*: $2.50, S. S.,*
	$10.25, Gen.................... 12 75
5 00	
39 75	## Foreign Missionary Districts
15 50	
7 50	*Ap.* $244.28
33 00	
16 35	### Africa
8 09	
5 00	LIBERIA—"A Friend," Wo. Aux., salary of Miss Ida N. Porter, Shanghai. 112 50
24 59	
4 50	### Cuba
	HAVANA—*Holy Trinity Church S. S.**:
	Gen. 50 08
	*Peñalver Station S. S.**: Gen.......... 1 20
22 92	LA GLORIA—*Holy Trinity Church S. S.**: Dom., $5; Frn., $5........... 10 00
5 57	MACAGUA—*S. S.**: Gen............... 4 25
	MATANZAS—*Fieles á Jesus S. S.**: Gen. 2 20
13 20	
9 38	
42 26	### France
21 60	NICE—*Church of the Holy Spirit*: Rev. George Stanley Fiske, Frn........ 4 80
4 00	
43 56	### Germany
	DRESDEN—*St. John's*: Gen........... 50 00
6 00	### Mexico
22 93	MONTEREY—*St. Paul's*: Frn.......... 4 00
12 57	SAN LUIS POTOSI—*Grace S. S.**: Gen.. 5 25
10 00	
	## Miscellaneous
24 50	
5 15	*Ap.* $10,521.68; *Sp.* $3.487.24; *Specifio Deposit,* $7.07
5 00	
7 60	Interest — Dom., $1,671.20; Frn., $819.55; Dom. and Frn., $518.01;
62 31	Gen., $325.42; Specials, $2,218.14;
4 58	M. T. O., $7.07.................. 5,559 39
	United Offering, Wo. Aux., 1907, on
10 33	account of appropriations to September 1st, 1910, Dom., $3,500; Frn.,
3 41	$3,500 .... 7,000 00
	Alumni Association, Cambridge Episcopal Theological School, Sp. for
3 40	salary of S. T. Tomita, Hankow,
2 00	$100; Sp. for salary of Rev. Dudley
6 38	Tyng, Hankow, $487.50........... 587 50
	"Two Friends," Sp. for St. John's University Expansion Fund, Shanghai 550 00
4 63	Daughters of the King, salary of
20 00	Miss A. B. Richmond, Shanghai..... 187 50

"Friends." Sp. for St. Mary's Build-
ing Fund, Kyoto.................... 80 75
Sp. for Foreign Fund for John J.
Gravatt, Jr., for publication of mis-
sion pamphlets.................... 39 85
"Friends." Sp. for St. Elizabeth's
Building Fund, Shanghai.......... 6 00
"A Friend," Sp. for the purchase of
land and the erection of a Training-
school for Catechists, Shanghai..... 5 00

Legacies

ILL., CHICAGO—Estate of Mrs. Mary R.
Gordon, St. Paul's School, Lawrence-
ville, Southern Virginia............. 357 16
L. I., FLUSHING—Estate of Mrs. Frances
Seton Potter, to the Board for Dom.
and Frn. Missions................ 5,000 00
PENN., PHILADELPHIA—Estate of Miss
Rebecca Coxe, to the Society....... 5,000 00

W. N. Y., BUFFALO—Estate of Miss
Susan E. Kimberly, to the Society.. 1,0 0
W. N. Y., BUFFALO—Estate of Mrs.
Charles H. Smith, Dom., $500 ; Frn.,
$500 .... 1,0 0

Receipts for the month.......... $239, 8
Amount previously
acknowledged $882,472 15
Less amount received
from Massachusetts,
Andover, Christ
Church, general
missions and ac-
knowledged in
the May SPIRIT
OF MISSIONS, now
said to apply on
apportionment for
1910-11 .... 51 02
—————— 882,4 1
- $1,121,8 0

SUMMARY OF RECEIPTS

Receipts divided according to purposes to which they are to be applied	Received during April	Amounts previously Acknowledged	T
1. Applicable upon the appropriations of the Board.	$194,334 09	$400,839 44	$595,1 5
2. Special gifts forwarded to objects named by donors in addition to the appropriations of the Board:	31,947 57	120,156 32	152,1 8
3. Legacies for investment.....................	....	165,000 00	165,0 0
4. Legacies, the disposition of which is to be determined by the Board at the end of the fiscal year	12,857 16	75,590 10	88,4 2
5. Specific Deposit............................	7 07	120,835 27	120,8 3
Total	$239,145 89	$882,421 13	$1,121,5 0

Total receipts from September 1st, 1909, to May 1st, 1910, applicable upon the appr ria-
tions, divided according to the sources from which they have come, and compared with th or-
responding period of the preceding year. Legacies are not included in the following items, a eir
disposition is not determined by the Board until the end of the fiscal year.

OFFERINGS TO PAY APPROPRIATIONS

Source	To May 1, 1910	To May 1, 1909	Increase	Dec se
1. From congregations....................	$327,079 04	$272,756 88	$54,322 16	$.... ..
2. From individuals.....................	30,537 71	44,252 15	....	13,7 44
3. From Sunday-schools.................	86,727 50	44,168 38	42,559 12	... ..
4. From Woman's Auxiliary...............	45,417 99	47,613 85	....	2,1 86
5. From interest.......................	48,201 62	43,524 96	4,676 66	... ..
6. Miscellaneous items..................	1,209 67	2,551 19	....	1,3 52
Total.....................	$539,173 53	$454,867 41	*$84,306 12	... ..
Woman's Auxiliary United Offering........	56,000 00	30,000 00	26,000 00	... ..
Total........................	$595,173 53	$484,867 41	$110,306 12	... ..

* As Easter fell two weeks earlier this year, we have had that much more time in which receive Sunday-school Lenten offerings, so an adjustment for this must be made. Aside from St ay-
school offerings there is an increase to May 1st of $41,747. The Sunday-school offerings to Ma st,
as compared with the same number of days after Easter last year, show a decrease of $6,8 90.
We may, therefore say the net increase in offerings to May 1st is $34,904.10. A month a the
increase was $22,655.03.

APPROPRIATIONS FOR THE YEAR

SEPTEMBER 1ST, 1909, TO AUGUST 31ST, 1910
Amount Needed for the Year

1. To pay appropriations as made to date for the work at home and abroad........ $1,211,7 84
2. To replace Reserve Funds temporarily used for the current work............. 32,9 33

Total.. $1,244,7 17
Total receipts to date applicable on appropriations.......................... 595,1 53

Amount needed before August 31st, 1910...................................... $ 649,5 64

THE
Spirit of Missions

AN ILLUSTRATED MONTHLY REVIEW
OF CHRISTIAN MISSIONS

July, 1910

CONTENTS

The Subscription Price of THE SPIRIT OF MISSIONS is ONE DOLLAR per year. Postage is prepaid in the United States, Porto Rico, The Philippines and Mexico. For other countries in the Postal Union, including Canada, twenty-four cents per year should be added.

Subscriptions are continued until ordered discontinued.

Change of Address: In all changes of address it is necessary that the old as well as the new address should be given.

How to Remit: Remittances, made payable to George Gordon King, Treasurer, should be made by draft on New York, Postal Order or Express Order. One and two cent stamps are received. To checks on local banks ten cents should be added for collection.

All Letters should be addressed to The Spirit of Missions, 281 Fourth Avenue, New York.

Published by the Domestic and Foreign Missionary Society.
President, RIGHT REVEREND DANIEL S. TUTTLE, D.D.   Secretary, ——— ———
Treasurer, GEORGE GORDON KING.
Entered at the Post Office, in New York, as second-class matter.

THE SPIRIT OF MISSIONS is regularly on sale
In Philadelphia: By George W. Jacobs & Co., 1216 Walnut St.
In Milwaukee: By The Young Churchman Co., 412 Milwaukee St.
In Boston: By Smith & McCance, 38 Bromfield St.
In Elizabeth, N. J.: By Franklin H. Spencer, 743 Jefferson St.

AN OREGON FOREST

HE SPIRIT OF MISSIONS

AN ILLUSTRATED MONTHLY REVIEW
OF CHRISTIAN MISSIONS

OL. LXXV.   July, 1910   No. 7

THE PROGRESS OF THE KINGDOM

A New Declaration of Independence

T seems not unfitting that in our July number we announce a new declaration of independence. Not as though the old one was not sufficient for American uses; but as a result of the spirit which it has developed in the American people there are, om time to time, new ones of a different character put forth.

The latest comes from the Pacific ast, and the District of Olympia is s author. For many years this district s been under the fostering care of the oard of Missions. So rapid has been e development of the splendid coast untry that it was practically impossible to keep pace with the opportunities fered to the Church. In the attempt to so the district has had to postpone the atification of its ambition to become a ocese. Some have asked why Olympia, th its three great cities and its comparatively small extent of territory, has t already swung into the line of merican dioceses, but those who know e problems which were there being cononted know also the answer to this estion. Now, however, Olympia has ade its declaration of independence. s last convention unanimously voted to raise from various sources the necessary endowment and to apply at the coming General Convention for admission as a diocese. Bishop Keator, who was the prime mover in the matter, is to be congratulated on the statesmanlike energy with which he has handled the situation and brought about the result. Though the total amount necessary is not yet raised, those who know the district feel assured that within a few weeks it will be in hand, and already, by anticipation, we welcome Olympia among the dioceses of the American Church.

The Critical Summer Season

THE Treasurer's message to the Board of Missions when it met on June 14th, for its last session until next fall, showed an increase in contributions up to June 1st of $43,000 over last year. Last month the increase stood at $35,000. There has therefore been an improvement of $8,000 during the month. Were our obligations identical with those of last year this information would be most encouraging, but since they are more than $100,000 greater, the relative increase shown only marks the need for further improvement.

The summer season is always the critical time in the missionary treasury. Parishes or individuals who have forgotten or neglected to make their gifts for missions earlier in the year are likely to keep on forgetting. Congregations are growing small and rectors consider it not worth while to announce missionary offerings, while it is too rarely the case that summer residents worshipping elsewhere than in their own churches recognize any obligation toward the missionary work of the Church. Might not readers of THE SPIRIT OF MISSIONS who are away for the whole or a part of the summer bear in mind the critical situation of the missionary treasury, and try to bring it about that in the church where they worship a special opportunity shall be given to contribute, and that at least some portion of the amount expended in summer outings and recreation be dedicated to the furtherance of the task which our Lord has set before His Church?

Though the record of giving in most instances is better than ever before, it must, in these next three or four months, be even more improved if the Church is to show a clean balance sheet when the General Convention meets.

T HE organization which was begun by the passing of the missionary canon three years ago in Richmond will be completed before the next General Convention meets in Cincinnati. T h e various departments have availed themselves of the permission given in that Canon, perfected department organization and elected their several secretaries. Department II—embracing New York and New Jersey—at its meeting last fall in Syracuse, chose the Rev. John R. Harding, D.D., the rector of Trinity Church, Utica, for nomination to the Board of Missions as its Department Secretary. Unfortunately, at that time Dr. Harding felt that he could not take up the work, and his name did not come before the Board.

Our New Department Secretary

The Second Department has, therefore, during the past year, been the only one which had not its own secretary. So far as they could do so, the secretaries on the staff at the Missions House have tried to supply the deficiency, but in view of the admirable results being obtained in other departments, where efficient and energetic secretaries are at work, it seemed unfortunate that a more aggressive campaign could not be carried on in so important a part of the Church as that embraced in Department II.

It was therefore with pleasure that the Board heard at its last meeting the announcement that Dr. Harding had reconsidered the matter, and felt that he could now take the work proffered. He was immediately elected, and expects to assume his duties on September 1st.

It is no doubt somewhat early to draw conclusions as to the value of the Missionary Departments and the work of the department secretaries. In many instances the organization has been too recent and the term of the secretary's service too brief to justify generalization, but it ought to be said that the effect thus far upon the Church has been most stimulating, and that the work goes on with every promise of success.

W ITH the September number of THE SPIRIT OF MISSIONS a new department will be opened. Each month a few pages will be devoted to the subject of "Missions in the Sunday-school." This department will aim to meet the needs of the Sunday-school teacher who desires to supplement regular work by a limited amount of missionary instruction.

Missions in the Sunday-school

In each issue will be presented material of a definite sort for a monthly lesson on missions. References will be made to books, pictures and maps, so that any teacher who takes the task seriously can have a sufficient amount of material to give valuable and effective instruction.

Beside the lesson there will be short

sands of really devout Christian folk utterly ignored and perhaps altogether condemned the missionary enterprise, have passed away—we believe, forever. While the average layman is probably not to-day fully prepared to admit that the cause of missions is the cause of Christ, and that in such a matter there is only one place for the loyal follower of Christ to stand, yet we believe that he, more than ever before, feels a responsibility for definitely making up his mind and convincing himself as to the point of view which he ought to adopt. In other words, he really wants to know whether the missionary business is worth while, and his conscience—at least that one which he carries with him to church on Sundays—is slightly uneasy so long as he remains undecided.

How Are Men to Know? But it must be frankly recognized that not many opportunities for deciding such a question with any real knowledge of the facts present themselves to the average business man. He does not give much time to reading the Church papers, he takes no missionary magazine, and whatever information he does get on the subject will probably be from the secular papers and periodicals. Perhaps his rector preaches an occasional missionary sermon, or gets someone else to do so, but the layman is probably elsewhere when the sermon is preached. How, then, is he really to settle this question except in the negative?

Of course the easiest thing is to decide offhand and without a hearing that the whole missionary propaganda is preposterous. But somehow it has linked itself in his religious consciousness with certain definite words of the Master which echo there in spite of him, and though claiming to have convinced himself that missions are anathema, he remains at bottom unconvinced. For such a man, who really wants to know—or feels that he ought to try to know—the facts, the article entitled, "Are Foreign Missions

a Failure?" which appears elsewhere in
this issue, furnishes a distinct opportunity. Here are certain categorical answers to definite and fundamental questions concerning the missionary enterprise which were asked in public print
by a man who "did not believe in missions." We must probably assume that
they expressed his thought upon the matter, and what he thought others may be
thinking. These questions are answered
by a man who *knows*—a layman and
business man to whom the reality and
urgency of the missionary enterprise became so absolutely vital, that after
thorough investigation he gave to it his
life and fortune. He has staked these
upon the accuracy and truth of his judgment. Such a man as George Sherwood
Eddy, who backs his convictions with all
that he has and is, deserves to be heard
with consideration when he tells his
story.

AS a result of many months of consideration, involving the work of
two or three different committees, the
Board at its May
A Policy on   meeting adopted
Specials   certain regulations
concerning appeals
for special gifts, the substance of which
was that missionaries, either domestic or
foreign, whose salaries are in whole or
in part paid by appropriations of the
Board, "shall not make any *general* appeal for special gifts without having first
obtained the permission of the Bishop
and the Board, in consultation with
whom all such special funds secured
shall be expended."

This action was taken, not with the
purpose of discouraging "specials," but
because it was felt that the interest of
all parties concerned would be better
safeguarded by the adoption of some
settled policy. While it may seem to
prevent individual initiative on the part
of the missionaries, it does so only to
the extent of bringing in the other two
parties who have a real interest in the
matter, and in case of agreement securing to the enterprise their backing and

people. We have heard of bishops of this American Church who have laid down the proposition—we do not dare to characterize it—that the Church ought to abandon the foreign field, turn her work there over to the English Church societies, if they would take it, and confine her missionary work to the limits of the United States.

The Nation Must Be Fully Represented Abroad

Not so this young naval officer. As a man in the service of the nation he, perhaps, recognizes that the relations of this Christian land to the non-Christian people of the East must not be confined to diplomacy and trade, as some contend. If our ambassadors and consuls are to be sent to them, if our merchants are to establish branch houses in eastern cities, or otherwise carry on trade in distant markets, if our naval vessels are to visit eastern waters and their officers to pay their respects to the rulers and naval authorities of other lands, so, too, the nation must be represented abroad by those who go to teach the Christian Gospel, through chapel, school and hospital. Indeed, this last must be done whether the others are done or not, because the teaching of these missionary representatives has to do with the fundamental facts and necessities of human life, while trade, diplomacy and war are simply the things of a day.

Whether or not this young Churchman has had opportunity to see the work of foreign missions at first hand, we do not know; but when he does, his devotion will doubtless be made all the deeper; his conviction of the void in non-Christian life and of the sufficiency of the Christian Gospel to fill it, all the stronger. Some day he may return from the Far East to bear his testimony, as an eye witness, to the necessity and success of Christian missions, as such Churchmen and naval officers as Admiral Alfred T. Mahan and Admiral Charles H. Stockton have already done.

THE SANCTUARY OF MISSIONS

O SUN of righteousness, thy
    healing give,
That all the earth may look to thee
    and live;
That all the peoples, gathered here,
    may know
The health and peace that from thy
    presence flow.

Grant us the fruitage of the heaven-
    ly birth,
Thy Kingdom come, thy will be
    done on earth;
O'er mighty river and from sea to
    sea,
Let all be one in loyalty to thee.
              —*Bartlett.*

THANKSGIVINGS

"We thank thee"—

For the good land and the glorious Christian heritage which thou
hast given to our fathers and to us.

For the ringing witness to the
truth of thy promise borne by those
who in heathen lands have seen thy
Word become "the power of God
unto salvation." (Page 523.)

For the deliverance granted to
our Christian brethren at Aomori in
the hour of their peril. (Page 543.)

For the manifestation by converts
in heathen lands of a desire to become in their turn the instruments
for proclaiming thy Gospel. (Page
531.)

For the good service which in the
Name and after the manner of her
Lord, the Church is doing for the
people of Mexico. (Page 532.)

For the awakening desire to give
to the young a better knowledge
and a greater inspiration, that they
may worthily set forward the progress of thy Kingdom. (Page 518.)

INTERCESSIONS

"May it please thee"—

To strengthen our hands for the
extension of the Kingdom of thy
Son in this land where thou hast
placed us.

To remember for good all those
"who go down to the sea in ships
and occupy their business in great
waters," guiding them to the sure
haven of trust and faith in thee.
(Page 535.)

To move the hearts of thy people
that they may generously support
thy Church's Mission, and especially
that in this present summer they
may not miss the privilege of being
workers together with thee. (Page
517.)

To cheer and encourage all the
lonely and scattered children of thy
Church, granting them a sense of
oneness in Christ and the privilege
of service to him. (Page 547.)

To bless the ministry of those
who in acts of loving service carry
the message of the Great Physician
to those who are sick in body or
in soul. (Page 548.)

PRAYERS

FOR GENEROUS GIVING TO
MISSIONS

O HEAVENLY FATHER, who
    openest thy hand and fillest
all things living with plenteousness;
We glorify thy holy Name for thy
loving care of us, thine unworthy
children. May a grateful sense of
thy mercy and pity move us to love
thee truly, and to offer generously
for the service of thy Kingdom
the earthly treasures which thou
hast committed to our hands;
through Jesus Christ our Lord.
Amen.

FOR MISSIONS IN THE
UNITED STATES

O GOD, we pray for thy bless-
    ing upon all the people of
this land. May those who have
gathered within our borders from
the four quarters of the earth acknowledge thee as their Ruler and
Guide, and learn to speak, as with
one tongue, of thy glory and salvation. Bless those who labor here
for the upbuilding of thy Kingdom,
that in the spirit of love they may
lead many who are in darkness and
error to thy truth and light. And
grant, O Lord, that enlightenment
and virtue, piety and peace may prevail among us, and that through us
thy light may be dispersed to those
who are far off. Through Jesus
Christ our Lord. *Amen.*

ARE MISSIONS A FAILURE?

By George Sherwood Eddy

The interest aroused by the Laymen's Missionary Movement has focussed attention in an unusual way on the foreign missionary enterprise. This has naturally resulted in bringing out expressions hostile as well as friendly. A few magazines and newspapers have published critical or condemnatory articles. As an answer to all such, we reprint this article, which appeared in "World's Events," a monthly paper published in Chicago. More effective than any words which could be written by a representative of the mission boards are these statements of a man who holds no office, draws no salary, but has invested his life in the great campaign, and speaks concerning that which he has seen.

I HAVE been asked by the editor of *World's Events* to answer certain specific questions relative to misapprehensions or recent mis-statements with regard to the foreign missionary enterprise. I am a layman and business man and speak from that point of view. I have been working at my own expense in India, as a missionary, for thirteen years. I have received no salary during that time and have devoted one-half of my income to paying my household and travelling expenses and the other half to the mission work itself. My work among the students of the Orient has taken me throughout the colleges and mission stations of India, Burma and Ceylon, as well as to China and Japan in the Far East, and to Egypt and Palestine in the Levant. I have thus had an opportunity from a somewhat disinterested point of view to gain a wide survey of the work of missions and a general estimate of their results. I will try to answer as briefly as possible the questions of the editor, which follow:

1. *Is it true that "it takes a dollar to send a dollar" or that "only one dollar in twelve actually touches the spot"? Are mission funds administered in an unbusinesslike fashion?*

The actual cost of administration of most mission boards varies from 3 to 10 per cent., including women's boards. One is as low as 3¾ per cent.; two of the largest and most efficient boards have reduced the cost of administration to 5 and 6 cents on the dollar. Thus, of every dollar given to missions, from 90 to 95 cents actually goes into the work. The remaining 5 or 10 cents is spent in efficient administration and in the cultivation of the field and its base of supplies by a system of education which develops increased giving as well as efficiency. How many of our large business concerns can reduce the cost of administration to less than 5 or 10 per cent.? These mission boards have on them business men and able financiers; their accounts are audited, their expenditures scrutinized and their methods improved by the best talent of leading business men.

And how is the more than 90 per cent. that reaches the field expended? In the field where I am working, $3 a month will support a native teacher; $12 a year will educate a boy in boarding-school; $20 builds a school or church, and $30 to $50 supports a native worker for a year. Four years' education of a boy in an expensive college in this country would cost, perhaps, $4,000. That sum will run an entire college in the East for a year, with, perhaps, several hundred native Chris-

tian students and as many non-Christians—a college which is a centre of light
influence in a large district numbering several million inhabitants, and which
mighty force for the uplift of the community. The accounts of every missio₁
on the field are strictly audited, and the expenditures of each mission are submi
to the home boards, where they can be inspected by any business man. For my
mission station last year, for instance, the board appropriated about $1,300. V
this sum I was expected to pay 30 native workers, to run 1 boarding-school, 15 ·
schools, 30 congregations struggling toward self-support, and to carry on evangel
work among 150,000 non-Christians. A little calculation will show how m
room there was for "missionary waste" or extravagance upon such a budget. I k
of few missionaries to-day who are receiving enough money from their board
carry on their work.

2. *In the hundred years of modern missions, have the results been as great
as gratifying as the Church had a right to expect? What are these results?*

A few facts may indicate in part some of the results achieved:
A hundred years ago there were less than 100 missionaries in the field; to
there are about 22,000. A century ago the Bible was translated into only sixty
languages; within the century it has been translated into over 500 languages
made accessible to more than 800,000,000 of the human race, with its mighty m
and educational uplift. A hundred years ago there were no medical missionaries
more than two-thirds of the world was without any adequate medical knowle
to-day there are several hundred medical missionaries treating annually
3,000,000 patients. A century ago there was a little handful of mission schools
day there are more than 29,000 mission schools and colleges, educating a million
a half students and pupils in the great strategic centres of the Orient. A hun
years ago a few thousand dollars were given annually to foreign missions; to-
missionary contributions amount to about $25,000,000 annually, while a
$5,000,000 is given by foreign converts.*

It took nearly a century to win the first million Protestant Christians;
second million were won within twelve years; it is taking less than six years to
the third million. During 1909, on foreign mission fields, we gained 2,600 comm
cants every week and over 10,000 Christian adherents, or a total of 581,000 new
herents. There are to-day in the world 4,866,661 Protestant Christian adherent
mission fields. Sixty years ago there was not a professing Protestant Christia
Japan, not one in Korea, less than fifty in the Chinese Empire and a few thous
in India. To-day there is a Protestant community of 70,000 adherents in Ja
200,000 in Korea, nearly half a million in China, and a million souls in Ind
India, with one possible exception, is the hardest mission field in the world,
even India is becoming, slowly but surely, Christian. The government census
the tale. During the last ten years, while the population increased 2½ per c
Protestant native Christians increased more than 62½ per cent. While the Hi
lost a fraction of 1 per cent., and while the Parsees gained 4 per cent., the Je
per cent., the Mohammedans 8 per cent., Protestant Indian Christians increased ₁
than 62½ per cent. In China the Protestant community has increased about
per cent. every seven years. The Boxer uprising tried to wipe out Christianity
the Church has gained more converts in the eight years since the Boxer upri
than in the first eighty years of missions in China. In Korea, a nation is ₁

* For fuller statistics, see the "Missionary Review of the World," January, 1910.

† NOTE.—It is always difficult to secure accurate figures concerning the work of the R
Catholic and Greek Catholic Churches. Mr. Eddy has therefore omitted the Christian convel
these bodies from the statistics given above. Were they added the total in each case wou
increased greatly and in some cases would be doubled.—EDITOR.

orn in a day." Twenty-five years ago there was not a Christian in the country. Twenty years ago, seven men met behind closed doors to take the communion of the Lord's Supper. To-day, with over 200,000 Protestant adherents, they have gained an average of one convert an hour, night and day, during the twenty-five years that the missionaries have been in Korea. Increasing now at the rate of about per cent. a year, if the present rate of increase should continue, Korea would be a Christian country within thirty years, to be followed later by the Philippines, Japan, China and India. Sixty years ago in the islands of the South Sea, young girls were fed and fattened like cattle to be eaten by cannibals. To-day, they have their schools and colleges, their hospitals and institutions, and are advancing in a moral, Christian civilization. As Charles Darwin wrote, "The march of improvement consequent on the introduction of Christianity throughout the South Sea, probably stands by itself in the records of history." If space permitted, pages could be given to describing transformed communities that I have seen in India and other lands.

3. Is it true that the converts are "rice Christians" and that Christianity has had "absolutely nothing to do with the moral and intellectual development of Japan"—of China, Korea and India?

As for "rice Christians," every convert that has come out within my memory, in my own station, has been persecuted by his caste, even where he came from the lowest class. There are 50,000,000 outcasts at the doors of the church in India who have been ground into dust, counted lower than the dogs, "as the filth of the world and the offscouring of all things." Before Christianity came, they could not afford to eat rice; their only meat, in some sections of India, was the carrion, or dead cattle that died of disease; they were not allowed to hold land, to get an education or to enter the temples of Hinduism. In India we have never, within my knowledge, given a penny nor any worldly help to induce any man to become a Christian. It is true that the Christians are living generally upon a higher plane than the heathen about them, but they get no "rice" save what they earn by hard work or as the result of their education. By Christian education whole communities are being uplifted socially and physically.

Christianity has had much to do with the moral and intellectual development of India, China, Japan and other lands. The present unrest in India is chiefly the result of Western education and the conflict of the new Christian civilization with the old. Outside the Christian Church and largely as the direct or indirect result of Christian missions there is in India to-day a new ideal of life. The changeless life of contemplation is giving place to an ideal of progress, activity, self-realization and self-government. A new patriotism and a new national consciousness are sweeping over the people. There is a new demand for reform; concubinage, polygamy, the Nautch and other abuses are being condemned. Suttee, or the burning of widows, has been abolished, the murderous Thugs suppressed, infanticide prohibited, human sacrifices forbidden, obscenity in religion condemned. The age of actual marriage, which was formerly ten years, has been raised; there is a new attitude toward woman, a new condemnation of caste, and a hundred reforms, led both by Christians and Hindus, as the result of Christian missions. As Lord Lawrence, India's great viceroy, said, "Notwithstanding all that the English have done to benefit that country, the missionaries have done more than all other agencies combined." Before me as I write are the words of Lord Napier, the Earl of Northbrook, Sir Charles Aitchison, Sir Bartle Frere, Sir Mackworth Young and a long line of the rulers of India, not to mention the writings of Indian editors and educated Hindus, who could be quoted.

In China, also, there is a new passion for reform. The prohibition of foot id-
ing, the abolition of the opium traffic, the sentiment against slavery and polyg ny,
and other reforms, were all begun by Christian teaching and agitation. In J: in.
Christianity has spread chiefly among the Samurai and upper classes. Chris ns
occupy by far a larger percentage, in proportion to their numbers, of positio in
the legislative assemblies and government posts than members of any other reli n.
I have before me quotations from addresses of leading Japanese statesmen as t he
influence of Christianity upon Japan and as to the need and value of the Chri an
religion in that land. Three thousand foreigners have been laboring for more an
forty years in Japan for her welfare; a large percentage of them have been Chri an
men with Christian ideals who have achieved Christian results, not only in c ect
conversions, but in shaping the ideals and leavening the life of the nation. he
Christians are among the leading patriots of Japan and I could fill the entire ue
of this magazine with stories of converts whom I have personally known fron he
higher classes in India, China and Japan. The editor of a Japan daily wi s:
"Looking over Japan, our 40,000,000 have a higher standard of morality than ey
have ever known, and when we inquire the cause of this great moral advanc we
can find it in nothing less than the religion of Jesus." Marquis Ito wrote: "Ja l's
progress and development are chiefly due to the influence of missionaries ex ed
in right directions when Japan was studying the outer world." Count Okuma, fo er
prime minister, says: "The efforts which Christians are making to supply t he
country a high standard of conduct are welcomed by all right-thinking people. . .
The noble life which it (the Bible) holds up to admiration is something at
will never be out of date, however much the world may progress. Live and p ch
this life and you will supply to the nation just what it needs at this juncture."

4. *Is it true that missionary effort to-day is merely a side line to busi s?
Do "foreign missions seem now to be based on business rather than Christianit ?*

It is, emphatically, untrue. I have pointed out in several conventions o he
Laymen's Movement that our foreign trade was inevitably increased by fo gn
missions, and that in an amount far in excess of the entire cost of foreign is-
sions. But it has always been stated that any gain in trade was a mere by-pr ct
of the enterprise. The real result which we have sought and obtained has be in
changed character and in the education of the nations. It is true that our de
with China is nearly fifty millions of dollars, with India over seventy mil s,
and with Japan nearly one hundred millions annually.* A considerable propo on
of this trade has been developed by Christian missions. This has been inevi le,
but it was not the motive or main result of the enterprise. It is with no thc ht
of selfish commercial gain that business men in America are contributing to is-
sions to-day. The single motive of their benevolence is Christian philanth y.
But though those who give, and those who go as missionaries, have sought no in,
the fact remains that the nation has gained commercially as the indirect resu of
their altruistic sacrifice. As Hon. T. R. Jernegan, Consul-General of the U ed
States at Shanghai, said, "Missionary work has accomplished advantages to de
which the present awakening of China will soon evidence to be of great prac al
value. . . . The ensign of commerce follows close in the wake of the bann of
the Cross, and he that would strike down the hand that carries the latter in es
the interests of the former." Colonel Charles Denby, for thirteen years U ed
States Minister to China, wrote: "The manufacturing and commercial inte sts
in the United States, even though indifferent or directly hostile to the *direct*

---

* See World Almana, page 249: Imports, $28,798,723; $63,907,896 and $70,392,722
Exports, $19,420,024 · $10,255,630 and $26,691,613, for China, India and Japan, respectively

ose of the missionary enterprise, could well afford to bear the entire cost of all American missionary effort in China for the sake of the large increase in trade which results from such effort."

5. *What is the Laymen's Movement? What is its basis of appeal? Is it fooling all these business men, or is their endorsement so generally given an indication that it is sound?*

The Laymen's Movement, organized about four years ago in this country, represents the spontaneous effort of the Christian business men of the country to give the blessings of the Christian Gospel and of Christian civilization to the world in our day. All over the country business men are using their business talents in the administration of the great missionary enterprise. It does not profess to believe that all the world will be converted in one day, but it holds the conviction that it is our duty to share with our fellow-men the blessings that we have received from our Christian civilization, and to give every man a chance. It is meeting with unprecedented success. The laymen are not being fooled, for they are conducting the movement themselves. They are giving their own money, their own time and energy to the solution of the great problem of the world's need. It is Christian, it is humanitarian, it is businesslike, and it is succeeding.

6. *Are foreign missions "a mania for saving worlds which belongs to the Middle Ages"?*

Let us clearly recognize the basis and authority for this great enterprise. It is not the dream of a few modern optimists, but the central command of Christ's message. All human advancement depends upon passing on the blessings that we have received. Almost every advantage that we possess, as Benjamin Kidd has pointed out, is the result of our Christian civilization—our liberty, our free institutions, our education, our moral attainments, all are surely the result of the Christian civilization that we received from the East, brought to us through foreign missions. If the men who sacrificed their lives, and those who gave of their substance to send the Christian Gospel to our savage ancestors in Europe had not believed in foreign missions, where would we be to-day? We may believe in missions, or we may not, but if we choose to be against the missionary movement, let us realize at least what we are doing; let us recognize Whom it is we are opposing and Whose authority we challenge; let us admit that we begrudge the blessings that we have received to those of the other half of the human race who are still in darkness.

Half the world to-day has not heard of Christ. Broadly speaking, that is the half that is ignorant; for half our fellow-men to-day cannot read or write in any language; and they are without any adequate medical knowledge. Half the world is poor. We have what they need; they lack just that which has uplifted us. It is estimated that to give a chance to every man in the world, to furnish the number of missionaries that would be needed to adequately give the Christian message to the other half of the world, would cost but 5 cents a week from every Christian. It is true that we have needs at home, but we have men enough and money enough for both. As with the individual, no nation liveth to itself alone. We shall save America by saving the world. We shall be blessed in giving; we shall grow strong with generous impulses, with strenuous endeavor, with noble sacrifice. We believe in missions because we believe in God. Naturally, one who does not believe in the Founder of missions will not believe in their results. If Christ is nothing to us, we will believe Him to be superfluous to other men. What He is to us, we will want Him to be to the world. If we fairly interpret missions in the spirit of their Founder, in their purpose, in their methods and results, we will, I think, agree that missions are not a failure.

A MIGHTY SENTINEL

*Here it has stood for ages, guarding the far reaches of the Columbia River and look
out over the great stretches of Oregon plain and mountain*

OREGON AND ITS PROBLEM

If you were an Easterner visiting for the first time the Middle West, and should hear some resident of that section tell you that he was going to "The Coast," you would doubtless picture him as appearing shortly in Boston or New York. But beyond the Mississippi there is only one "Coast," and it is not on the Atlantic. "The Coast" means Oregon, Washington or California. Toward that coast thousands of eyes are looking and thousands of feet are marching—an increasing army, year by year. Those who a decade ago went to what was then the West, in search of home and fortune, are now seeking a farther West; and though they may tarry in their journey, for many of them the march will not be finally stopped except by the waves of the Pacific.

Here, then, is one of the Church's problems which our bishops in those far western states must face and solve. It is with this thought in his heart that Bishop Scadding of Oregon writes:

RECENTLY I made an extended visitation of the missions in the coast counties in southern Oregon. The ... ry is difficult of access, for no rail ... has yet been built across the coast ... of mountains, and travelling must ... ne by stage over winding trails, or ... the beach at low tide, or by boat ... e many beautiful rivers. Although ... a "diocese," Oregon is practically ... ng more than a vast missionary ... ct, twice the size of the Diocese ... hio. It is both undermanned and ... -equipped for the problems before ... Church. Thousands of home- ... rs are settling in southern Oregon. ... are stalwart, sturdy citizens—not ... ement which forms the "tenement ... em" of large Eastern cities, but a ... y agricultural and commercial ele- ... They need the preaching of the ... l and pastoral care quite as much ... merican residents in the foreign ... In my judgment, this can best be ... at present on the scriptural and ... lic plan of an associate mission. ... s plan, as it is being carried on ... ere, has for its object the develop- ... of the spiritual life of the clergy ... ited prayer and study; encourage- ... and cheer by association in work; ... ny with efficiency of service in the ... by encouraging self-help and rous- ... he people to feel their own re- ... bility, which is in the end the as- ... ce of growth and development.

I often speak of my associate mission clergy as a "flying squadron." Last summer they were sent into the coast counties under Archdeacon Horsfall to minister to the many missions where services had been carried on only intermittently, resulting in loss of children to the Church and prestige in the community. The Rev. F. B. Bartlett began at the California line and worked north, visiting every rancher in any way connected with the Church, and holding services wherever groups could be gathered. The Rev. H. R. Talbot and two young laymen went in by stage from Drain, and ministered to the missions on their way south. They met at Ban-

The bishop and his "flying squadron".

(529)

ST. MARY'S CHURCH, GARDINER

don, and were joined by Archdeacon Horsfall and a theological student from the General Seminary. They lived in my bungalow on Bandon Beach, and did their own cooking and housekeeping. From this associate mission centre they conducted regular services Sundays and week-days at Bandon, Coquille, Empire, Gardiner, Marshfield, North Bend, and at "St. Peter's-in-the-Rock," an improvised chapel in a large cave on the shore about two miles from Bandon, and close to the bungalow. An early celebration of the Holy Communion was held here on Thursday and Sunday mornings, and at one time ten were present. Later in the season, ac-

St. Peter's-in-the-Rock

companied by Mrs. Scadding, I [ne] down by steamer, and we took up [ur] headquarters in the bungalow, and [he] work of the clergy was followed u [by] the bishop's official visitation for [n-] firmations.

The bungalow, which I expect to [ke] headquarters for missionary work [ry] summer, is a small cabin built of r [gh] lumber, containing a large, open [re-] place, with three small rooms [ilt] around it. The furniture is strong [nd] serviceable and was nearly all mac [by] the clergy and the young laymen [th] them. The site is one of the most [ic-] turesque in Oregon. The cabin is [ilt] half-way down the cliff, and is [ut] fifty feet from the sea at high tide [In] front is a hard sand beach, and on e [er] side large and beautiful rocks reac [ar] out to sea. This is a beautiful as w [as] strategic point for a "prophet's cham [r."]

Fifty miles north, reached onl [by] stage driving on the beach at low [le,] is St. Mary's Church, Gardiner, [ch] has service only three times a year. [ut] the loyal and faithful communi [ts] have not lost heart, and have just [ilt] an attractive church upon the hill. [he] estimate was $800, but, alas! it [st] $1,000. The parishioners raised th [es-] timated cost, and the bishop has [m-] l to try to raise dollar for dollar, if y will pay off the balance. This they undertaking with zeal, for they are py in the thought that through the l⟨⟩ of the associate mission clergy, A⟨⟩hdeacon Horsfall can arrange many n⟨⟩e services.

⟨⟩he policy in Oregon is not to see

how widely funds can be scattered, or how many men can be appointed, but rather to put men who know how to bring things to pass, in fields where something can be brought to pass. It is estimated that under the associate mission plan $25 will keep a mission station open one month.

A CHINESE LAYMEN'S MISSIONARY MOVEMENT

By Bishop Graves

BOUT four years ago a society known as the Men's Auxiliary was organized in the District of Shanghai. Its object is to b⟨⟩ the laymen in all our various sta⟨⟩tions together, to raise money for Church w⟨⟩k and to rouse the men to do work f⟨⟩ the Church among non-Christian C⟨⟩nese. Interest in the enterprise has g⟨⟩dually grown, and one station after an⟨⟩ther has established branches. At the pr⟨⟩ent time every station has a branch e⟨⟩pt Yangchow, where there are not as⟨⟩yet Christians enough to constitute on⟨⟩

⟨⟩he Chinese laymen have year by y⟨⟩ shown greater capacity for conduct⟨⟩ing the affairs of the society. It is very m⟨⟩h their own, for by the Constitution th⟨⟩foreign missionaries are not eligible to⟨⟩hold office in it. Up to this year I h⟨⟩e myself presided at the meetings in o⟨⟩r to insure that the society should h⟨⟩e every encouragement and also st⟨⟩t on reasonable lines. Last year the ab⟨⟩ity of the members to manage their ow⟨⟩ affairs without any help beyond oc⟨⟩ca⟨⟩onal advice from the foreigners was q⟨⟩e evident, so I wrote to the com⟨⟩⟨⟩ee suggesting that at the meeting th⟨⟩ year their own president should pre⟨⟩si⟨⟩ and the business be entirely in their ha⟨⟩ls. This plan was followed at the m⟨⟩ting recently held, and was ab⟨⟩dantly successful.

⟨⟩here was a service of Holy Com⟨⟩m⟨⟩ion in the morning. The preacher w⟨⟩ the Reverend C. C. Li, of St.

Peter's, Sinza. The church was well filled, and there were 120 communicants. The business session began at two o'clock in the afternoon. By invitation I opened it with prayer and a short address of welcome. It was most interesting after that to see how the business was conducted. Dr. Eli Day, of St. Luke's Hospital, was in the chair. The treasurer reported that they had on hand $680 from the collections of last year and this year. This money they proposed to use to start a new station with a catechist from our school. The secretary reported that there are now thirteen branches at the various stations and that there were 142 representatives present. Short reports were made by the secretaries of the various branches, and then followed a discussion as to the location of the proposed new station. Changchow—a large and important city on the Shanghai-Nanking Railway—was finally decided upon.

Throughout the business was conducted with as much smoothness and as careful regard for parliamentary procedure as in any such assembly in the United States. The actual results achieved in the way of raising money and of conducting work at the different stations are, considering the size of the Church here, by no means inconsiderable, but it is in the promise of the ability to manage business on a large scale and to do it in a business-like way that the chief interest of the experiment consists.

LIGHTS AND SHADOWS IN MEXICO

By Bishop Aves

This private letter to a personal friend was not written for publication, but it contains matter so interesting and vivid that the Editor has requested permission to print it.

FOR a long time I have been wishing for a clear moment in which to write to you, but somehow I continue to poke along like a sandwich man between the things I want to do and the things I ought to do but have not. However, I'm going to follow for a few minutes the suggestion of the front placard and try to forget for the time the pressing announcement of the one behind; for I want to tell you of many things about the work, some of which are making me happy and some of which are keeping me very humble. Altogether, however, as I look back over my extended trips among the congregations—each with its own little hopes, plans and problems—the field looks brighter than ever before, notwithstanding the great dark spot of suffering from famine (which still continues) in the midland mountain districts. However, with the generous supply of corn and blankets furnished by the "home folks," and from our American congregations here, we have been able to take off the mortal edge of suffering from thousands

The wild cactus or tuna

of helpless beings, and are doing so s[ ]. And with the help rendered there come the blessed sense of gratitude t[ ] the Church, by its presence and spirit ministry to a few, has had the oppo[ ]. nity to help so many. Distribution is being made from four points at the of a pint of corn a day for each per[ ]. There is no fruit in the country (exc[ ] that of the wild cactus, the tuna, wh[ ] comes in August) and the only gr[ ] thing to eat is the leaf of the cactu boiled. But the rains will come in J[ ] and the garden stuff will follow in a weeks; and the annual corn harvest (D. V.) come in November and cember.

But I am trying to get nearer to root of the evil. Extreme poverty chronic. The foothold on life is too certain. To give some of the destit[ ] girls and women—mostly widows w[ ] children—a chance for a little self-h[ ], I am establishing at Nopala, Hidalg[ ] House of Industry. I have rente[ ] commodious house (at $5 a mon[ ] which I shall furnish with sewing chines. With these and a stock of terial (which I can get at nearly cos[ ] an English mill here), the women wil[ ] taught to make cheap garments for market, and so earn a few centavos themselves. I have already three ing machines in place and hope to b[ ] seventeen more by fall. I had hope might use the little amount gi[ ] for relief for the purchase of n sewing machines, but Mr. Sal[ ] writes me that the distress is dri[ ] the people in from great distan[ ], some coming over a hundred m[ ], that he cannot send them away em[ ], and will soon need more corn he is to relieve these growing cro of far-off people. I shall, therefore, what money remains—something $200—for more corn.

But over against this dark spot of

but as "Catholics — American, not
Roman." To give you an idea of the
degree of infamy that attaches to the
term "Protestant" in the minds of our
own people here, I must refer to another
dark spot, though a very small one. A
few weeks ago while in Guadalajara I
was told of the shameful persecution
which three maiden ladies belonging to
the higher class, members of our
congregation, had suffered at the hands
of Roman Catholics. The Rev. William
Watson, in charge of our native work in
Guadalajara, took me to call on these
three sisters. The eldest showed me how
all the windows had been broken out by
stones; that it was impossible to retain
a servant; and that the produce from
their gardens, the source of their support, was boycotted. "But," she said,
"I went to complain to the bishop, and
when at last they admitted me, I told
him how we had been treated by his people. Then one of the priests standing
near said, 'This woman, your worship,
is a Protestant.'" *"Me!"* she cried, *"Me*
he called *a Protestant!* O my God!
That was the worst of all—to be called
a Protestant!" Then, after hiding her
tears with her hands for a moment, she
raised her right hand and said, "But I
called God to witness that I am no
Protestant, but as good a Catholic as
they, though not of Rome."

It is difficult to realize the ignominy
attached to the word Protestant in
Mexico. The popular conception of its
meaning is an infidel who is in league
with Satan—the enemy of Christ and
His Church. However we may cherish
the name for its historic meaning, the
moral propriety of identifying the native of this country with it under its
popular meaning, and with the consequent hatred and persecution it engen-
ders, is a subject for serious consideration. For Mexico, at least, the name
Protestant should, I am persuaded, be
eliminated from the title page of the
Spanish version of the Book of Common Prayer. For forty years these native Church people have repudiated it,

declaring themselves "Catholic, but not
Roman; Evangelical, but not Protestant." Now, by canon law, they must
use the Book of Common Prayer, which
declares by its title that it and they are
"Protestant!" It is hardly fair.

Marked advances have been made
along all lines the past year, as shown
by our statistics. The women of our
Auxiliary have come into helpful, co-
operative touch with our native women
in many places, organizing them and

"La Señora" (Mrs. Aves) in the saddle

teaching them how to do things that
help. And the earnest zeal with which
the native women have responded is
most encouraging. Mrs. Aves has made
many visits with me in the native field,
where the saddle work is least, giving
instructions, organizing them, and planning definite work. Good fruit will
come from this.

In the English-speaking field we are
also moving ahead. The new church and
parish house at Chihuahua, with a fine
east window in memory of the late Rev.
Henry Forrester, have been completed—
though there is still a small debt. Land
and a small sum of money have been
given at San Luis Potosi. At Guadalajara a good piece of property has been
donated for a church. Here also land
has been given for a Church hospital
and sanitarium, and the foreign colony

ALL WE HAD IN MAY, 1906

"THEY THAT GO DOWN TO THE SEA IN SHIPS"

By the Reverend Frank Stone,
Chaplain of the Seamen's Institute, San Francisco

"THERE are no American seamen!" Such is the burden of many an article in the popular press; but when I turn to the official statistics of the Bureau of Navigation I find that there are American seamen—over 180,000 of them—serving in American ships alone. What is the Church doing for them? And what for those tens of thousands of seamen of other nationalities who constantly throng our seaports? Those of our readers who reside in New York, Boston or Philadelphia know the splendid work being done there by our Church —now how in spite of many difficulties

Chaplain Mansfield in New York banks nearly $250,000 a year of sailors' earnings, an eloquent testimony as to the immense number of men who attend his institutes.

Those who reside on the Pacific Coast know how this work among seamen was first started in 1893 by the generous aid of the Church of England "Missions to Seamen" Society, which has in seventeen years sent out eleven English clergy and $52,000 hard cash to the bishops of the Eighth Department to enable them to cope with this great problem. Our Church is under a deep obligation to this venerable British society for its

INTERIOR OF SAN FRANCISCO SEAMEN'S INSTITUTE

munificence—unexampled since we became a separate nation and an independent Church.

SEAMEN'S CHURCH INSTITUTE,
PORT COSTA, CAL.

Do you know what it feels li[ ] t "come in from the sea"? You have [ ]e at sea five months, let us say from [ ]v York to San Frar [ ]sc around the Horn; you [ ]av known what it was to [ ]av everything flooded in [ ]the "foc's'le," fourteen [ ]ys, perhaps, without a [ ]lry moment; the tedium ([ ]al- ways seeing the same [ ]ces and hearing the same v [ ]es, the unchanging circle ([ ]sea and sky, the absenc [ ]of literature and the ge [ ]ral air of boredom. But a [ ]ast you "tie up" alongsid [ ]the wharf; a few dollars a [ ]in your pocket, the whole [ ]ity before you! Yes; but [ ]t a door open to you exce[ ] [ ]he door of the saloon o [ ]he houses on the "Ba [ ]ry Coast." But stay! Th [ ] is one other door open; fl [ ]ed by six saloons, with t [ ] four saloons in the op[ ] block, stands the Sea [ ] Church Institute—a dio [ ] property w o r t h $7 [ ] erected since the grea[ ] aster of 1906.

Let us enter; it is typical of the others in other ports. The main hall will seat 200 men, and is supplied with newspapers in eight languages, games, billiards and music. There is a writing desk with the injunction to "Write home, and do it now!" paper, envelopes, pen and ink being provided. The assistant manager receives and sends out about 700 such letters a year; he has banked $5,000 of sailor's pay since the earthquake; he gives any man who wants it as much reading matter as he can carry to his ship. Our baggage room is crowded with sailor's chests and bags, our bedrooms well patronized, but above all our record of attendance at Church is most encouraging, over 8,000 men having attended during the past year.

The Institute is as free as a saloon, without any restraints, but with a good moral and spiritual tone. Concerts and stereopticon lectures are given regularly by uptown friends, the hospitals regularly visited by the staff, and incoming deep-water ships met.

The Church has flourishing institutes at San Francisco, Port Costa, Tacoma and Honolulu—all in the Eighth Department—but we want to see these institutes in every port. On the Pacific Coast several new ports are opening up, and the Church is alive to its responsibilities, but before another step forward is taken we must have a closer organization between existing institutes. For this reason the General Convention of 1907 recognized the Church's obligation in this respect and founded the Seamen's Church Institute of America, to unite all those institutes at present existing, and to provide that all future work in this connection be undertaken under the guidance of the Board of Missions.

The great, vital necessity at present is for an organizing secretary. Other Christians are busy in this matter, and it behooves the Church to bestir herself. We want $2,000 a year for five years to enable us to put a secretary in the field who shall visit every port in the States and stir up Church people to do their duty. We say that "the men don't come to Church," but the history of the Seamen's Church Institutes has shown that men do come to Church, if the Church first goes out and seeks the men.

THE LAST PORT
"Peter Iredale" wrecked at Astoria

WHY MORE FOREIGN MISSIONARIES FOR JAPAN?

By the Reverend H. St. George Tucker

THE Japan mission needs more ordained men and needs them at once. On this point all who are acquainted with the present situation, both Japanese and foreigners, are agreed. Even those who some years ago were inclined to doubt the wisdom of sending out more missionaries are now earnestly pleading for an increased supply of foreign helpers. This does not indicate a step backward, or any lessening of the spirit of independence on the part of Japanese Christians, but only a deeper appreciation of the magnitude of the task before us, and a realization born of experience that, even in what may be called the second stage of the work of building up the Church in Japan, the foreign missionary's aid is not only valuable but essential.

The reason why ordained men from abroad are needed in Japan is twofold: First, the work for which a foreigner is peculiarly qualified is not yet completed; Second, the supply of Japanese ordained men is insufficient to maintain even the work in which they are more efficient than foreigners.

Despite the many disadvantages under which a foreigner labors in Japan, as, for example, imperfect knowledge of the language and inability to enter intimately into the life of the people, there are certain phases of the work for which he is perhaps better qualified than any but exceptional Japanese. He has a positive grasp of the truths of Christianity, to which it is difficult for those to attain to whom the faith is not an inheritance. He has behind him the long centuries of Christian traditions. The Church for him means not only the brave little band of Christians in Japan, but the great Church of the home land, with its history of past triumphs and its consciousness of present strength. In pioneer evangelistic work in remote dis-

tricts these things give him a certain advantage even over his Japanese brother, who may be in other respects better qualified and more efficient. Again, his very ignorance of the language and separation from the life of the community protect him from the disheartening influences of an indifferent or hostile social environment.

But apart from these considerations, the supply of Japanese clergy is insufficient to carry on the work already begun, to say nothing of expansion. At present there are in this diocese only three Japanese priests outside of Tokyo. To man the stations already established we should have at least twenty. Even were there no further expansion it would be a long time before we could obtain this number of men; but surely we expect the work to grow, and growth means a demand for more workers. The yearly additions to our Japanese staff will for some time to come do no more than meet the increasing demand. In other words, to supply the exigencies of country work already begun we need seventeen foreign priests. At present we have seven. This estimate does not take into consideration large and important districts in which as yet our Church has no work at all. Were we to consider only the needs of these as yet unevangelized communities there would be ample opportunity for an almost unlimited number of missionaries. A foreigner, however, is of little use without a Japanese assistant, and the supply of catechists is limited. Furthermore, as our aim is to build up a self-supporting native Church, we must devote ourselves to the strengthening of centres already established rather than to indefinite expansion. Therefore, perhaps five additional men would suffice for the present for what may be called new work. Later on, as the Japanese begin to take over the churches already organized, foreign

main church, but there is a constant migration to them of Christians from the larger cities.

The progress of the work in Japan is greatly hampered by the fact that we have not a force large enough to do these two things—develop the centres and still maintain the out-stations. Both are essential to real growth and real advance toward the ideal of a self-supporting, independent Japanese Church. If anyone will take the trouble to examine the statistics of the Japan mission for the last ten years he will find that while there has been a steady increase in the total number of communicants in the district, yet there has been but little growth in the central country churches themselves. But the *sine qua non* of an independent Japanese Church is a network of independent congregations in the important towns throughout the country. Were the number of communicants ten times what it is, if they are simply scattered about in little non-self-supporting mission stations, we should be no nearer independence than at present. The lack of continuous growth in the central points is therefore a very serious phenomenon and calls for explanation.

One explanation of this is obvious. *The reinforcement of the mission staff has not kept pace with the natural development of the work.* In 1898 the bishop of this district, realizing that the time was ripe for the development of the country work, sent home a stirring appeal for men. There was a splendid response and within two years seven men were added to his staff. He was consequently encouraged to put into practice his plan of occupying the strategic points throughout the district. In some of these, indeed, work was already being carried on, so that within a few years he was enabled, with the help of the new men, to establish central stations in nearly all the provinces north of Tokyo. But the success of this policy of expansion was clearly dependent upon the constant reinforcement of his staff. In the beginning the men were sent out

singly, for one priest was sufficient so
long as the work was to a large extent
confined to the one central station. For
the first few years these stations made
steady progress, but with the natural and
necessary development of out-stations, a
large part of the missionary's time was
drawn away from the central church.
This was the point at which a second
man became necessary, but unfortunately it was just at this point that men were
not forthcoming. To carry out the
policy inaugurated in 1898 we should
have had on an average two new men
every year. But instead of this only
two ordained men have come to us during the period from 1900 to 1910.
Furthermore, during this period we have
lost four men from the country work.
The result is that we have only ten men
(including three Japanese priests) to
carry on a work for which twenty-two
are absolutely essential.

This statement of our needs does not,
however, give any ground for pessimism
in regard to the work in Japan. It is no
confession of failure. On the contrary,
it means that during the past ten years
a firm basis has been laid for a magnificent forward movement. The preliminary task of occupying the territory has
been accomplished. The seeds of future
churches have been planted in important
points. But already the time has come
when we must give our attention to the
development of these churches into full-
grown, self-nourishing organisms. In
some of them, indeed, this work should
have been begun several years ago. But
the loss caused by this delay, while unfortunate, is not irreparable. Speaking
generally, the critical point has only just
been reached. But it *has* been reached,
and from now on we must have more
men or the work will stand still. Give
us these men—that is, give us the means
of maintaining the progress already begun—and we believe that we can promise the realization of the vision that
first brought us to Japan—an independent Nippon Sei Ko Kwai.

But our appeal for men is based not
only upon the fact that without them the

A NAVAL OFFICER'S WITNESS TO CHRISTIAN MISSIONS

By Rear-Admiral Charles H. Stockton, U. S. N. (Retired)

I AM sorry to hear that some naval officers are quoted as being unfriendly to foreign missions at the present day. My experience, especially with Chinese and Japanese missions, formed upon two cruises in eastern waters, is entirely to the contrary.

At one time it used to be said with relation to the East that there were no Sundays east of Singapore. Treaty port opinion and treaty port life in the East at that time were not unnaturally opposed to missionaries and all that they represented in behalf of the Chinese especially, and the Christianity they sought to convey to them. Results in the early days were meagre in the eastern countries. It was truly the seed-time of the Church. Now any one who has visited China, Japan or Korea with clear vision must know that the harvest time has set in, and with no greater success to any missionaries than those from own country.

I remember when a lad reading the first address that I had ever met with from a layman in advocacy of missions. It was delivered by Rear Admiral (then Commodore) S. F. Du Pont at the session of the General Convention of the Church at Richmond, Va., in 1859. Commodore Du Pont had recently returned from a cruise in the East and spoke with a personal knowledge of the facts. The navy had at that time no officer who stood higher as an officer of high standards than Du Pont.

At the present time there is no officer in our navy with greater and more world-wide reputation than Rear Admiral A. T. Mahan. His services in behalf of foreign missions as a leading member of the General Board of Missions and in connection with the Laymen's Mission-ary Movement, are too well known to the Church at large to call for more than mention on my part. He, too, by cruises in the East, has seen the missionary at work in the eastern field.

I know of other officers of the service who have testified to the same effect, not only in public by addresses, but privately by contributions and memorials made while on the spot, or from knowledge guided by observation while there.

My own experience, about which I can speak more freely, was gathered on two cruises in the East during which I made frequent visits to missions of our own and other churches in China, Japan and Korea, making myself to an extent an unofficial inspector in many directions. I doubt whether any officers in the navy have of late years availed themselves of the opportunities to do so to a greater extent than myself.

While in command of the *Yorktown* I went up the Yangtze as far as Hankow and had not only the opportunity of seeing what had been done in Hankow under Bishop Ingle but also the Boone School and its surrounding mission buildings, then under the direction of the present Bishop Roots.

My second cruise, in command of the *Kentucky*, was limited to the larger ports and the establishments thereabouts, but I renewed my acquaintanceship at the mission houses at Jessfield near Shanghai and St. John's College, Shanghai, whose efficient work has evoked admiration from English visitors like Lord William Cecil, none too eager to express admiration for purely American educational establishments.

It was then also that I saw more of the mission work of Tokyo and its vicinity and the hospital in Tsukiji. In

China the mission hospital stands for more good than in Japan. Japan has adopted the modern system of medicine and surgery. China as a whole and the Chinese as a mass cling to the grotesque curing art of the past. St. Luke's Hospital in Shanghai does noble work which is appealing to the Chinese of all classes who contribute toward its up-keep. I am under the impression also that the contributions toward the enlargement and expansion of that hospital from one of the physicians attached to it and his family, equal, if they do not exceed, the total amount given by some of our own dioceses to the cause of foreign missions in the past year.

The day of spectacular heroism has gone by in most, if not all, of our treaty ports of China, Japan and Korea. In most of the ports the missionaries enjoy the benefit of cheap labor and a silver currency to the effect that they can be housed and live on equal terms with European clerks and foremen. In the interior of China, and so far as travelling evangelists are concerned, this case does not prevail, and hardships are largely habitual matters with them as pioneers in the work.

I find myself singularly in accord with a recent writer in the London *Spectator* with respect to these men and their services to civilization and Christianity, when he says that nine out of ten, even of those who write comparatively intelligent books about China, at most deal with the missionary in the treaty ports and leave out of account the missionary pioneer in the interior, though he belongs to a class at once more numerous and more important.

Without missionary spirit a Church lacks life and progress, and I believe that this spirit should not be confined to the limitations of parish, diocese, section or country. All of these have their demands and all their needs, and any discrimination as to race, color, or region is to my mind so much of a failure in Christian duty.

THE PRESIDENT'S OPINION

PRESIDENT TAFT, speaking recently at a meeting in New York commemorating the diamond jubilee of Methodist mission work in Africa, defined a mission station as "a nucleus and an epitome of the civilization that is expected to widen out in that neighborhood." Continuing, Mr. Taft said: "I have heard missions criticised. I have heard men say that they would not contribute to foreign missions at all; that we have wicked people enough at home, and we might just as well leave the foreign natives and savages to pursue their own happy lives in the forests, and look after our own who need a great deal of ministration.

"I have come to regard that as narrow-minded, like the case of a man who does not understand the things that God has provided for the elevation of the human race.

"The missionaries in China, the missionaries in Africa, are the forerunners of our civilization, and without them we would have no hope of conquering the love and the admiration and the respect of the millions of people that we hope to bring under the influence of the Christian civilization.

"Those who go for mercantile purposes into those distant lands, I am sorry to say, are quicker to catch the savage tendencies than the savages are to catch from them the best of our Christian civilization, and if they had to depend, for their belief in the good that is to come to them from embracing Christianity and accepting the civilization that we offer them, upon that which they learned from the adventurers that go far into the interior to buy things from them at a price much below what ought to be paid, we should never succeed at all. I say that with all the sense of moderation that I know I ought to have in dealing with countries so far from here, and in saying things that cannot be contradicted."

SOME OF THE CHRISTIANS AT AOMORI

They are gathered in front of the building "which Bishop McKim and Dr. Lloyd both hoped would burn"—but which of course didn't!

THE BURNING OF AOMORI, JAPAN

ON Tuesday, May 3d, within four hours' time, practically the entire old city of Aomori disappeared before the resistless advance of a great conflagration. About 300 buildings were destroyed and nine-tenths of the inhabitants made homeless. The loss is estimated at 3,000,000 *yen.* Our mission there, established in 1893, is under the charge of the Rev. J. C. Ambler, who lives in Hirosaki. Our resident woman worker, Miss Flora M. Ristowe, tells of her experience:

"The fire started at Yamata and then caught the big temple. A fierce wind drove on the flames, which soon burned our church, and also every mission church or preaching place in Aomori. Just before the fire reached our house it turned to the north and for the time we were safe. I felt happy, and went to see how some of our Christians and native workers were getting on. As I reached them the second temple caught. I found them in a terrible state, getting ready to flee and not knowing where to go. Returning home, I found that the fire was sweeping down on us from two directions. The people who had been helping us were gone, and the sparks were falling in showers upon our roof with no one to sweep them off or pour on water, though a neighbor had already swept the sparks from our out-house. If the fire crossed the street we could not be saved; so we decided to go over into the burned section and wait our fate. We got our things out and put them where the church had stood. As it was five hours since it burned, the

(543)

place had pretty well cooled before we put our belongings there. Until seven P.M. we were not out of danger. We got some food at ten and kept watch all night because there was still so much débris burning, and all night and to-day "go-downs" have been bursting into flame. We are all quite safe now, have plenty of food, and have got our belongings back into the house. There are terrible tales of distress, and, I fear, a great loss of life."

Miss Wall, our woman worker at Hirosaki, who the morning after the fire accompanied Mr. Ambler to Aomori, gives more details about the suffering and loss of life:

"Aomori is practically a waste. The fire burned in three directions, leaving the railway station and a strip of buildings, but swallowing up practically everything else. We were glad to find that though the combined church and parish house is gone, Miss Bristowe's house was saved, as was also the house in which the sewing-school was held— the one which Bishop McKim and Dr. Lloyd both hoped would burn. So close did the fire come to Miss Bristowe's dwelling that part of the fence at the back was at one time in flames and the house so filled with smoke that they could distinguish nothing. We found her very thankful for the Providence which had spared her home. Though we asked her to return with us, she felt her place was there and was already planning to shelter children whose parents were lost in the fire."

Our church was a two-storied building, used also as a parish house and the home of the kindergarten.

In addition to these two communications the following letter has been received from Bishop McKim:

"All the Christians except two were 'burned out,' and the distress among the 35,000 sufferers is pitiable; it is a great mercy that summer instead of winter is approaching. What would those houseless and starving multitudes have done

ment according to actual needs. That in a nutshell is the situation at Tsu.

¶

Translation of an editorial from the *Shun Pao*, a daily Chinese-controlled paper in Shanghai, in its issue about April 18th:

THE mandarins do not fear the people at all. The people fear the mandarins most of all. That which the mandarins most fear is that there should be any disturbance of the Christians. The one thing that the people can do to frighten the mandarins is to disturb the Church. For these reasons, no matter in what place a riot may start up, the people are certain first of all to vent their spite by disturbing the Christians and the Church. It is not that the people necessarily have any grudge against the Church, but they thoroughly hate the mandarins. Therefore they use this method of showing their hatred. When the riots are over and peace restored then the mandarins use this destruction of the churches to frighten the people (or to oppress them). The ignorance of the people, after all, is not equal to the wisdom of the mandarins. Therefore the people suffer.

¶

ON Friday, May 20th, at the Chapel of the Good Shepherd, West Berkeley, Cal., Miss Mabel Howard Pick was set apart as a deaconess by Bishop Rowe of Alaska. In the chancel with the bishop were the clergy of St. Mark's parish, Berkeley, and Dean Gresham, of Grace Cathedral, San Francisco. The bishop preached the sermon and the candidate was presented by the Rev. William Higgs, vicar of the Good Shepherd, under whom Miss Pick has been at work while connected with the deaconess school in Berkeley, from which she has just graduated. Deaconess Pick was appointed by the Board of Missions on May 10th, to work in the district of Alaska, and will sail for Wrangell in about a month.

Writing of the first service held in the new chapel at the University of the South, the chaplain, the Rev. Arthur R. Gray, says:

I HEREWITH enclose a check for $45. It represents the first offering taken in the new university chapel. After waiting many years for a chapel, and sometimes despairing whether we ever should have one, at last our dream is realized. It seemed most fitting that the offering made at the first celebration of the Holy Communion held in this chapel should be sent to St. John's College, Shanghai. I hope that in the future we shall not only be able to realize that there should be a more vital connection between Sewanee and St. John's, but that we may also be able to send men to help carry on the work.

¶

ST. JOHN'S UNIVERSITY, Shanghai, has been significantly placed by the Joint Board of Examiners of the Scottish Universities on a par with the English Universities. The Joint Board has provided that examinations in the arts' curriculum of St. John's, taken and passed by the graduates of that university, shall exempt them from corresponding preliminary examinations of the Joint Board of Scottish Examiners.

¶

A SUMMER school for Sunday-school teachers of the Diocese of Pennsylvania will be held at Pocono Pines, Pa., August 21st to 27th. Among those who will conduct courses on Bible study, missions in the Sunday-school, the Prayer Book, etc., are the Rev. L. N. Caley, the Rev. W. E. Gardner, Secretary for the Department of New England, the Rev. T. J. Garland, Secretary for the Third Department, and the Rev. W. Herbert Burk. Bishop Darlington will hold the services on August 21st. Further particulars may be had by applying to the Rev. H. L. Duhring, D.D., 225 South Third Street, Philadelphia.

THE Diocese of Quincy has t... viable record of being the fi... the Fifth Department to comple... apportionment, which it did by... 1st. Last year also this was th... diocese in its department to comple... minimum sum asked by the Boar... this year the amount has been... much earlier, thus setting a com... able example of promptness in pa...

¶

AT a recent visit by the Bish... Western Colorado to Our... that district, both the Roman Ca... and the Presbyterian churches o... their services on Sunday evening. ... Presbyterian minister read the less... the Church service, the Roman Ca... choir led the singing, and Bishop I... ter preached on "Christian Unity...

¶

THE Brotherhood of St. A... will hold its twenty-fifth a... convention in Nashville, Tenn., S... ber 28th to October 2d, 1910. Th... sions will be held in the ch... of the House of Representativ... the State Capitol. It is ex... that from 1,500 to 2,000 del... and visitors will be in attendance... doubt many men of international ... nence will visit the Brotherhood... vention on their way to the G... Convention at Cincinnati, which... venes immediately after the f... meeting.

¶

AN interesting pamphlet sets for... work done at St. Luke's ... Phœnix, Arizona. It was design... the treatment of tuberculosis and... the exception of the Oakes Ho... Denver is the only institution ... kind under the control of the C... Archdeacon Atwood has oversight ... work, which is growing—though ... proportion to the increasing de... Last year sixty persons were cared ...

OUR LETTER BOX
Intimate and Informal Messages from the Field

A clergyman in a Middle Western diocese writes to a friend, who had recently told the members of the congregation of the success-ful work of his men in securing larger gifts for the Church's Mission:

I OUGHT to thank you again for your goodness in coming out for that night. Our canvass proceeds encouragingly. We have already pledges exceeding all apportionments. Eighty people have subscribed $641 for missions. Many more are yet to be heard from. I am now working for $1,000. In addition we are planning to spend about $4,000 on our property this year (debt and improvements). Moreover, the vestry materially increased my salary last night. Simply proofs that unselfishness pays selfishly."

Last year the same congregation, with more than 300 communicants, made an offering of $10.15 for general missions.

¶

The writer from whose letter the following is taken is an earnest young Colored man, a school teacher, who for love of the Church and without compensation is trying to do what he can in that destitute part of Oklahoma where lies his work places him.

NONE but those actually engaged in the Vineyard of our Master, and working for the spread of His Kingdom can fully appreciate THE SPIRIT OF MISSIONS. Sent by some kind friend it reaches me when discouragement seems to press me close; it cheers me in lonely hours and keeps me in touch with the Church. To-day I am forty-five miles from the nearest church and the cost of attendance is prohibitive. I walk five miles and board the train for Ft. Smith, Arkansas. I reach the latter place at midnight and stay until morning. It means ten miles' walk, $1.80 railroad fare and forty hours time, besides board and lodging.

But I have at my side my Bible, and Prayer Book. These are my constant companions. As I follow the trails through primeval forests I read and study the best way to introduce the Church to these people. It is almost un-known here. One otherwise intelligent old man, who laughed on for half an hour when I told that I was a member of the Episcopal Church, said: "Who ever heard of such a Church?"

There are three classes of people here —white, red, and colored. I work among the colored, but I have been able to teach some of the Church doctrines to all classes.

The colored children may be divided into two classes—those with land and those without land. All children of mixed colored and Indian blood, and children descended from former slaves of Indians, have land which was allotted by the Government. The amount varies from 40 to 360 acres. After it was al-lotted, on some land oil was found. Thus one child may have eighty acres of good farming land worth $1,600, and another have the same amount, but oil is found on the second and the owner gets a royalty. In one case I know a boy who draws $100 a week royalty while his brother gets nothing in this way.

Then come the children without land —mostly immigrants from other States, or those who are not counted with the Indians, or the large number who have been "juggled" out of their land with-out any return. Here you find abject poverty. How the Church could change the lives of these people! Many are dis-satisfied with present conditions, and for them the Church would fill the "long felt want."

I only wanted to tell you why THE SPIRIT OF MISSIONS was so doubly dear to me, so far from services and in a re-ligious desert, as far as the Church is concerned.

LEND A HAND

PEOPLE as a rule are glad of the
opportunity to help a worthy
cause, provided it does not involve
too much expenditure of time and
labor.   This doubtless is the secret
of the success recorded below, and
is, we may hope, the promise of a still
larger success. We are sure that any of
our readers who can do so will be glad
to lend a hånd to the good work being
done in the Tanana Valley by Mr. Betticher and those associated with him.
There is no better in the entire district
of Alaska.

ST. MATTHEW'S MISSION,
FAIRBANKS, ALASKA

For the four years last past, St. Matthew's Hospital, Fairbanks, Alaska, has
benefited from the sale of fancy and useful articles.   These articles have been
contributed by friends in various parts
of the States and the members of the
local guild have arranged and sold them.
It now happens, owing to new missions,
wider extent of work and other reasons,
that about the only outside source of income that the hospital can count on is
the Fair.   The last year has been the
busiest in the history of the hospital,
and more than ever before it is filling a
distinct need in the life of the Church
and the people in the far North.

We herewith make our formal appeal
to Church people everywhere to aid in
this work by contributing articles suitable for a Fair. In a peculiar way St.
Matthew's has demonstrated the possibility of a large work being accomplished
through the small efforts of many.   The
previous Fairs have been a burden to
none and the results have been splendid,
and have gone more than half way in
making the work possible.   The amounts
cleared were: 1906, $1,618.75; 1907,
$2,043.50; 1908, $1,455, making a total
of $5,117.25, and in 1909 over $2,200
were cleared.   Can we not make this
year's Fair the best of all?

We appeal for all sorts of articles,

GROUP ON STEPS OF THE HOSPITAL

Thomas Atkinson at left of door; little Jim on the lowest step; one of the oldest men on the reservation at extreme right of picture. The head-bandage does not indicate headache; it is only a Navajo hat!

k, crossed the *arroyo*, and drove up in front of the hospital. Miss Thackara gave us a hearty welcome, while her red children stood by, interested spectators. What it meant to her to see friends from the East will be appreciated by one who remembers the necessary isolation attending her fourteen years of patient, faithful, loving service among the sick Indians.

First came the tour of the buildings, including the stable. On the left of the little entrance hall was the small reception room, behind this the women's ward. At the right of the entrance hall was the tiny dining room used by Miss Thackara. Adjoining this was the little kitchen and Indians' dining-room, pantry, etc. There were four rooms on the second floor, one of which was used as a children's ward. A detached building consisting of three small rooms was the men's ward. There was also a specially constructed small building for tuberculous patients. In the centre of the building on the main floor was the operating room, with *one window* and the sides dark.

In our hospitals in the East a surgeon is considered great if he operates successfully with the best equipment and all modern conveniences, while here, with no electric light, not even gas, Dr. Wigglesworth had just performed an operation for appendicitis, and I saw the man, who was then convalescent! But an even greater marvel is the woman with the courage to run a hospital for the Indians without a bath-room! and no modern conveniences. There is a well at some distance from the house, but the water is so strong of alkali that it can be tasted in tea. Fortunately a kind friend has come to the rescue, and nearly enough is in hand to bring the spring water over from the Fort. The pipes for this will be laid as soon as the weather permits.

Miss Thackara's great desire is to have a native Catechist established there who will reach the souls of the Indians, but I fear I should reverse the old proverb and put cleanliness first. I would like to see a new operating-room and the old one turned into a much-needed bath-room.

We finally reached the beautiful new

THE HAYSTACKS

A striking group of red sandstone rocks found on the way from the station to the hospital

Approaching the cliff-dwelling known as the "White House" in the cañon of Chelly. The house is seventy-five feet above the ruins below, and of the thirteen cliff-dwellings seen, it was the most striking. Approach without ladders was impossible

chapel. On the corner-stone was w
ten: "The Chapel of the Good Sheph,
to the Glory of God and in Loving M
ory of Cornelia Jay."

It seems eminently fitting that
many friends throughout the coun
who knew of her years of devotion to
cause of the Indians and to Foreign M
sions should have created this endur
monument to her memory. The cha
is complete and all paid for, incl
ing the windows, which are of stai
glass. The furniture has also b
given by friends. The building is
grey stone, quarried within half a n
under the direct supervision of M
Thackara, to whose forceful energy
constant vigilance is due the per
chapel it now appears. The Indians
much impressed and come from gr
distances to see it. The white man
font is their especial admiration. T
go up and touch it wonderingly, say
they "never saw stone like that befo

The morning following our arriva
was asked to be down to prayers at se
o'clock. "The Indians expected
Each one was formally introduced as
appeared: Denatchely, Huskyda
Henry Whipple, Thomas Atkinson—
the way down to the cook's baby g
Adelchee. Little Jim, with his croo
spine, won my heart and sympathy fr

rst. His little face was bright and
igent, yet with such a wistful and
tic expression of endurance.

er prayers we saw them all at
fast, which consisted of oatmeal,
read (never butter) and coffee. In-
g the help there were twenty-seven.
are coming to the hospital as they
le to break away from their super-
s, and the awful domination of the
icine men."

necessity a nomadic tribe, the
vajos do not live—they exist. Their
an fires are to be seen all over the
es and they drive their flocks wher-
ve the best grazing and water are to be
ou. There can be no better air in
he orld, yet their manner of life is the
au of so much tuberculosis and other
lis ees among them. From the hot,
ind interior of the "hogan" they
me re into the zero cold atmosphere,
nd o amount of added clothing would
re nt the shock caused by the contrast.
gn ance of sanitary laws (which, how-
ve if they understood, they could not
oll because of the scarcity of water—
he rst element required for their observance), is also a factor conducive to
the prevalence of disease.

In a trip of four days to the Cañon de
Chelly I experienced this lack of water,
since when I have had more charity for
the "dirty" Indian.

It is a sad, sad moment for a sick Indian when once his friends determine
that he will not live. He is carried out
of the hogan and deposited on the
ground, in a protected place if there
happen to be one, and there left alone to
die. If allowed to die in the hogan the
rest of the family would leave it at once,
in possession of the *Chindee* (devil),
which they fear and always associate
with death.

The Hospital of the Good Shepherd
has given "sanctuary" to many such, and
with care they may be nursed back to
health, or at least those last moments
soothed by the "cup of cold water." And
"Whosoever shall give to drink unto one
of these little ones, a cup of cold water,
in the name of a disciple, verily I say
unto you, he shall in no wise lose his
reward."

—J. M. H.

nearer view of the White House and the ruins below. The walls are built of gray stone,
ortared together. From the depth of the cañon below it looks like a miniature dwelling,
but an ordinary person can stand upright in the rooms, now roofless

GRATITUDE FO

THE following preamble and resolutions were presented to the Bishop of Mexico by a representative gathering of natives in that section where he and those whose interest, he had aroused did so much to alleviate suffering and ward off death in the recent famine. We have been asked to give them as wide a publicity as possible in order that all who assisted in this good work, may be reached by these words of thanks:

WHEREAS, On account of the heavy frosts in the Central Table Land, in the last part of last September, the crops were completely destroyed and a great number of laborers were ruined:

WHEREAS, In consequence of the great loss there has been an extreme lack of absolutely necessary grain, which has reached such exorbitant prices as to be absolutely out of the reach of the poverty-stricken, who have suffered unspeakably:

WHEREAS, When the Right Rev. H. D. Aves, Bishop of Mexico, was informed of the privation of the poor in this region, he tried, with paternal solicitude, in every possible way, to relieve that distress, and obtained enough money from our brethren of the American Church to buy several carloads of corn, which is now being distributed weekly from the parish house of this place, and

WHEREAS, In this beneficent work the said bishop has been efficiently helped, in the United States, by the Rev. Peter G. Sears, and the congregation of Christ Church, Houston, Tex.; and, in Mexico, by the American Consul-General, Mr. Philip C. Hanna, and by Mr. E. N. Brown, President of the National Railway of Mexico, and

WHEREAS, There is a debt of gratitude which we owe to the above-named persons, therefore, in

THE LITERATURE OF MISSIONS

The Religion of the Chinese, by J. J. M. Degroot, Ph.D. The Macmillan Company.

THE study of the religion of the Chinese is of interest not only to missionaries at work in the field, but to all who are anxious understand the religious ideas of the non-Christian world. As Professor Degroot says in his introduction: "A proper understanding of the religions of East Asia in general requires in the first place an understanding of the religion of China."

The question is often asked, "What is the religion of the Chinese?" It is not easy to give a brief reply. In China we find a somewhat complex religious problem. In the first place, this is the primitive religion—that which Confucius in his writings sought to conserve; but in addition we have Buddhism, which came into China from India about the year A.D., and Taoism, the cult which has grown out of the philosophical teaching of Laotse, a contemporary of Confucius. There has been a fusion of the three to form the popular religion of China.

Much has been written on the subject. Legge's scholarly work has enabled us to understand Confucianism. Edkins and Beal have expounded Chinese Buddhism. Several translations have been made of the Taoist classic, the Tao-Teh King. Dr. Degroot is now engaged in writing his monumental work on "The Religious System of China," of which Volumes I—III have already been published. When completed this will be the most thorough and exhaustive study of the religion of China which has thus far appeared. In the meantime he has given us in the present volume, consisting of a course of lectures delivered at Hartford Theological Seminary, an excellent short handbook on the religion of China.

Any one desirous of getting a lucid and concise statement of the religious ideas of a people who form three-fourths of the world's population will be well repaid by a study of the book. The first part is devoted to an account of China's religion proper, as distinguished from Buddhism, which is of foreign introduction. The former, he tells us, is "a spontaneous product, spontaneously developed in the course of time."

Dr. Degroot finds that animism is the very core of the religion of China, "based upon an implicit belief in the animation of the universe, and of every being and thing which exists in it."

To quote his own words: "The universe is full of two souls or breaths, called *Yang* and *Yin,* the former representing light, warmth, productivity and life, also the heavens from which all these good things emanate; and the *Yin* being associated with darkness, cold, death, and the earth. The *Yang* is subdivided into an indefinite number of good souls or spirits, called *Shen,* and the *Yin* into evil spirits, called *Kwei.*"

The belief in evil spirits, or *Kwei,* leads to Polydemonism, and the belief in good spirits, or *Shen,* to Polytheism.

As a consequence of Polydemonism he points out that China groups her religious acts around the ghosts and spirits, with the object of averting their wrath. "No people in this world ever was more enslaved to fear of spectres than the Chinese; no people, therefore, has excelled the Chinese in inventing means to render them harmless."

In Polytheism—the existence of the *Shen*—we find two classes of gods: (1) the gods of nature, Heaven and Earth, the Sun and Moon, and the spirits in the hills, streams and trees; and (2) the gods embodied in men. Each man has a *Shen,* and in a sense is a god. When he dies his *Shen* still exists. Hence we can understand ancestral worship. It consists in offering sacrifices to the *Shen* of the departed.

In discussing the question as to whether ancestral worship is idolatrous, Dr. Degroot is very emphatic. He says: "Ancestral worship answers exactly to idolatry and fetichism, it being addressed to tablets, deemed just as well as images of gods to be inhabited by the souls of those whom they represent."

In the chapter on Confucianism, we learn that the classics handed down for so many years have exercised a great conservative influence. They have perpetuated the orthodox interpretation of the religious ideas of China, and helped to petrify the religious traditions and customs. In commenting upon the worship offered by the Emperor of China to "Imperial Heaven" or "The Supreme Emperor" (*Shang Ti*), Dr. Degroot gives what appears to us to be the true explanation. It is not, as some suppose, a vestige of an original monotheism, but "Imperial Heaven-Supreme Emperor" is worshipped "as the oldest, the original procreator" of the long-line of earthly emperors. When missionaries use *Shang Ti* as the translation of the name of God, its connotation to the Chinese mind is very different from the Christian idea of God.

Concerning the conversion of China to Christianity, the author well says: "China's conversion will require no less than a complete revolution in her culture, knowledge, and mode of thought. In this connection we might note that the present intellectual awakening in China, and the adoption of a western system of education is full of hope for the cause of missions.

In the chapter on Taoism Dr. Degroot points out its affinity with many of the primitive religious ideas of China. As it exists at the present day it is a cult for the exorcism of demons, and for propitiating the gods. Its ritual is highly developed, and was created to a great extent in imitation of Buddhism.

The philosophy of Laotse himself was

THE CHURCH MISSIONARY CALENDAR ,FOR 1911

UNDER the´ supervision of Mrs. J.
Nicholas Mitchell, Educational
Secretary for. Pennsylvania, the Church
Missionary Calendar has become a recognized feature in our missionary work.
It has given to a large number of people
the opportunity of making to some
friend a gift which might be at the same
time a token of friendship and an inspiration to larger missionary knowledge and interest. The net proceeds of
the sale of this calendar will be donated
to work under the Board of Missions.
Last year these amounted to $740. It
will be ready for sale by September 1st.
Enclosed in a box the price is 50 cents.
Postage paid. Orders may be sent to
Mrs. Mitchell at the Church House,
Twelfth and Walnut Streets, Philadelphia, or to the Corresponding Secretary,
281 Fourth Avenue, New York.

¶

A correspondent in a distant diocese writes:

I have for several years been a subscriber to THE SPIRIT OF MISSIONS
and it is indeed a welcome visitor to our
home, and has been´ of especial benefit
in our immediate family, its influence
being a great help to me in my effort to
bring my own father into the Church before his death. So you may well realize
I would not be without it.

¶

YALE has a Bible study group of
fifteen Chinese students and another of about ten Japanese. Time was
when a class for Bible study in an
American college would have been made
the target of endless ridicule, while even
the most ardent Christian people hardly
dreamed of the coming of a time when
Christian men from the great empires
of the Orient would be studying the
Bible in racial groups. Nor did they
dream of seeing, as they might see at
Yale to-day, more than twenty groups
of men studying missions.

MEETING OF THE BOARD OF MISSIONS

June 14th, 1910

THE Board of Missions met at the Church Missions House, on Tuesday, June 14th, the Bishop of Pittsburgh in the chair. The following members were present: The Bishops of Pennsylvania, Bethlehem, Newark, New York, and the Bishop Coadjutor of Virginia; the Rev. Drs. Anstice and Parks, the Rev. Mr. Sedgwick and the Rev. Dr. Storrs; Messrs. Mills, Chauncey, Butler, King, Pepper, Pruyn and Ryerson. Of the honorary members, the Bishops of Olympia and Kyoto.

The Treasurer reported that there was a further gain in contributions of $43,000 over June 1st of last year. The Lenten offering to June 11th, from 3,774 Sunday-schools, was $128,704.13, an average of $34.10 per school. During the same period last year $133,072.28 were received from 3,679 Sunday-schools, an average of $36.17 per school.

The Treasurer submitted a communication from the Bishop of Maine relinquishing further appropriation to his diocese from this Board after September 1st next. Whereupon these resolutions were adopted:

"*Resolved:* That the grateful thanks of the Board of Missions be extended to the Right Rev. Robert Codman, D.D., and to the Diocese of Maine for their recent action."

"That the Board highly appreciates the action of the Diocese of Maine, as communicated by its bishop, in relinquishing all assistance, and congratulates them upon the progress which this step indicates, especially in view of the fact that the Diocese of Maine pays its full missionary apportionment."

The Rev. John R. Harding, D.D., of Utica, N. Y., who last autumn as nominated as Secretary of the Se d Department, communicated his ac t- ance of the nomination; whereupo he was elected and the necessary appro a- tions made.

Letters were submitted from a l ge number of domestic bishops with re rd to matters connected with their a o- priations and the appointment of s- sionaries.

At the request of Bishop Rowe, he Rev. George Edward Renison, latel f San Francisco, was appointed to ce charge of the work at Juneau.

Appropriations were made for N o work for the next fiscal year from e amount set apart for the purpose at e last meeting, and permission was g n to the committee to suggest such n i- fications at the next meeting as they y find to be necessary. In connection h this the following resolution s adopted:

"That notice be given to the bis s whose work among the Negroes is a d by this Board, that with the fiscal r beginning September 1st, 1911, a - priations to dioceses and districts r evangelistic work (or for other than t of schools) will not be made in exce f $2 for each dollar raised for said k within the diocese or district."

An extra appropriation of $180 s made under recommendation of a sp l committee to the Church in Hait o cover, with the appropriation made t month, the needs of Bishop Holly a - pressed in his estimate.

The Standing Committee on Audi - ported that they had caused the b s and accounts of the Treasurer to be - amined to the first instant and had tified the same to be correct.

(556)

ANNOUNCEMENTS

CONCERNING THE MISSIONARIES

Alaska

the meeting of the Board on June
the appointment by Bishop Rowe
he Rev. George Edward Renison as
missionary at Juneau was formally ap-
ed.

Porto Rico

the same meeting, at the request
ishop Van Buren, Miss Una F. Dudley of St. James's parish, Long Branch,
N.J., was appointed as a missionary
nu e in St. Luke's Hospital, Ponce.

Honolulu

the request of Bishop Restarick
the Board, at its meeting on June 14th,
ap inted Miss Sarah Jane Simpson, of
Sp ane, as a missionary teacher in
Ho olulu.

RS. LOUISE F. FOLSOM, returning to
du after furlough, left Rochester April
6th and, after visiting friends in the
W t, sailed from San Francisco by the
ste mer *Lurline* on June 1st.

The Philippines

the request of Bishop Brent, at the
ing on June 14th, Miss Lillian M.
n, of New York, was appointed a
ionary nurse in the University Hos-
pit, Manila, in the room of Miss
F se, resigned. Miss Owen left New
Y k on June 21st, and sailed from San
Fr cisco by the steamer *Siberia* on the
28

HE REV. JOHN A. STAUNTON, JR., be-
in a deputy to the General Convention
fr the missionary district of the
Ph ppines and, at the request of Bishop Brent, anticipating his furlough a
fe weeks, with his wife sailed from
M ila June 2d by way of the Suez
Ca l.

MRS. HOBART E. STUDLEY, returning to
Manila with her two children, left New
York June 8th and sailed from Seattle
by the steamer *Minnesota* on the 20th.

Africa

THE REV. GARRETSON W. GIBSON, D.D.,
for many years a missionary of the
Board and sometime President of the
Republic of Liberia, died at Monrovia
on April 26th in the seventy-eighth
year of his age. He was ordained by
Bishop Payne on January 15th, 1854.

THE appointment by the Bishop of
Cape Palmas of the Rev. Robert Z.
Johnstone, a West Indian and a recent
graduate of the Philadelphia Divinity
School, was approved by the Board on
June 14th; it being understood that he
would spend six months in the United
States, awaiting Priest's Orders, before
proceeding to Africa.

THE resignation of Miss Ruth Margaret Dodge as an assistant at the Girls'
Training Institute, Bromley, was accepted, to date from May 1st.

Hankow

THE REV. EDMUND LEE WOODWARD,
M.D., who received a special leave of absence two years ago in order to take a
course at the Theological Seminary,
Virginia, was advanced to the priesthood
on June 17th and was married on the
22d to Miss Frances P. Gibson, daughter
of the Bishop of Virginia. They sailed
from New York by the steamer *Minne-
tonka* on June 25th. After spending the
summer in England and Switzerland
they will sail from Naples by the steamer
Prinz Eitel Friedrich on August 26th
for Shanghai.

MISS EMILY L. RIDGELY, Deaconess,
was appointed as a missionary to Han-

(557)

kow at the instance of Bishop Roots, on June 14th. She will proceed to the field with her brother later in the summer.

MISS RUTH KENT, whose appointment was announced last month, has been compelled to decline acceptance of it on account of family reasons which have recently developed.

THE REV. AMOS GODDARD, wife and two children, on regular furlough, sailed from Shanghai by the steamer *Delhi* on May 10th for London.

Shanghai

DR. HENRY W. BOONE, having received orders from his doctor to return to the United States for one year, with his wife and daughter Frances sailed from Shanghai by the *Chiyo·Maru* June 14th, which is due to arrive at San Francisco on July 8th.

MR. HAROLD B. BARTON, who was appointed May 10th, sailed for Shanghai *via* Europe on June 23d.

Tokyo

MISS LISA LOVELL, who was appointed as a missionary on December 10th, 1889, but who, because of illness, was obliged to retire on August 31st, 1906, died at Worthing, Sussex, England, on June 7th.

Mexico

THE resignation of Miss Mary W. Roper as teacher in the Mary Josephine Hooker Memorial School, Mexico City, was accepted by the Board, to take effect on August 31st.

MISSIONARY SPEAKERS

FOR the convenience of those arranging missionary meetings, the following list of clergy and other missionary workers available as speakers is published:

When no address is given, requests for the services of these speakers should be addressed to the Corresponding Secretary, 281 Fourth Avenue, New York.

Department Secretaries

Department 1. The Rev. William Gardner, 186 Upland Road, Cambri Mass.

Department 2. The Rev. John Harding, D.D., 44 Broad Str Utica, N. Y.

Department 3. The Rev. Thomas Garland, Church House, Philadelphi

Department 4. The Rev. R. Patton, care of the Rev. C. B. Wiln D.D., 412 Courtland Street, Atlanta,

Department 5. The Rev. John He Hopkins, D.D., 703 Ashland Bouleve Chicago.

Department 6. The Rev. C. C. Roll 4400 Washburn Avenue, South, M neapolis, Minn.

Department 7. The Rev. H. Pe Silver, Box 312, Topeka, Kan.

Department 8. The Rev. L. C. S. ford, 1215 Sacramento Street, 8 Francisco, Cal.

China

SHANGHAI:
The Rev. F. L. H. Pott, D.D., Shanghai.
The Rev. R. C. Wilson, of Zangzok

HANKOW:
The Rev. Arthur M. Sherman, Hankow.
The Rev. L. B. Ridgely, of Wucha

Japan

KYOTO:
Bishop Partridge, of Kyoto.

Work Among Negroes in the Sout

The Rev. S. H. Bishop, Secretary the American Church Institute for I groes, 500 West 122d Street, New Yo

Archdeacon Russell, of St. Pau Lawrenceville, Va., and the Rev. A. Hunter, of St. Augustine's, Ralei N. C., are always ready to take appoi ments, especially when a number of gagements in the same neighborhood be grouped.

THE WOMAN'S AUXILIARY

To the Board of Missions

IN THE GARDEN OF THE HOUSE OF THE HOLY CHILD

THE HOUSE OF THE HOLY CHILD, MANILA

By Frances W. Sibley

[Miss Sibley, the Michigan diocesan president of the Girls' Friendly Society, went out to Manila last winter, giving her services for a year during Deaconess Routledge's furlough at home. Bishop Brent says: "I wish her example might be followed, and that we could get more volunteers to give a year or so in the mission field."]

THE House of the Holy Child is situated in the native part of Manila and is surrounded by *nipa*, or grass, huts, built on stilts to keep them out of the water in the rainy season. They would not look very home-like or comfortable to American eyes, but the thick thatched roof of grass keeps the sun and the rain off very well and they are the coolest kind of house, which is a great consideration in this country. In the midst of such huts these stands our own abode, an old Spanish house built of stone and covered with lovely flowering vines, and with large shaded grounds where the children play. On one side of the *salon*, or living room, are the rooms for the ladies in charge, and on the other side live our little orphans, where we can see and hear them singing and playing. They have a dormitory in which each little girl has her own bed, except that four or five weak children sleep outdoors on a veranda. These little beds are covered with mosquito bar under which each child crawls at night, as into a cage. There is a dining-room like an enclosed porch, with a similar room for lessons. Downstairs is a small chapel where, after the half-past six o'clock breakfast, the day begins with prayers at seven. These are said in the Tagalog dialect, but the hymns are sung in English, which the children are learning. After prayers they have industrial work, making beds,

(559)

sweeping, washing dishes, washing and ironing their own clothes, which the older ones make for themselves. From nine to twelve is school. As the children are of different ages and speak several different dialects, this is rather a problem, but all are learning English. None of them are strong enough to be sent to the public school, and this is the best if not the easiest way to educate them. Part of their time is taken up with kindergarten games, and their voices sound very sweet as they sing their little songs. Lessons over, the family gathers again in the chapel, for noon intercessions for missions. The children are most reverent, with attentive little brown faces and folded hands. Directly after prayers comes dinner, and then everybody goes to bed to take a *siesta*. The long continued heat makes this necessary. The afternoon is taken up with baths, play for the little ones, and two hours' sewing for the older ones in the embroidery school in the guild room in connection with our little parish church, St. Luke's.

To me, coming as a stranger six weeks ago, this seems the most homelike and wholesome and natural way of taking care of little girls that I have ever seen. While in a way it makes the work more difficult, having the girls of such various ages, still it has distinct advantages. Each of the older ones is put in charge of a younger one, whom she bathes, dresses and looks after generally, as an older sister would. The larger girls take a commendable pride in their little charges, and we hope the experience may develop some of them into gentle, trustworthy nurses for children. Here is no suggestion of an institution. The children are devoted to the housemother, who takes the place of mother, teacher and playmate, and her sympathy and wise and gentle discipline cannot fail to have a lasting effect on their characters. It is hard to believe that the whole undertaking was started only seven months ago—it has so much the *home* atmosphere. I wish you could look in any evening at seven o'clock, when,

der the laws of the Philippine Islands, and papers have to be signed to that effect.

It is a temptation to me to make this account still longer and to tell something of Deaconess Routledge's especial work in her school for embroidery for the native girls of the neighborhood—which we hope will give them a trade that will keep them out of the cigarette factories —her needlework exchange, to help the desperately poor native women, and her clubs and classes for boys and girls, which have had a remarkably steadying and refining influence on them. She is at present in America on her furlough, and it is to try to carry on at least a part of her work in her absence that I am here, at the bishop's invitation, spending a most interesting year at the Settlement House. For these efforts toward social uplift we have absolutely no appropriation from the Board, and the deaconess has, I know, spent many anxious and wearing hours, trying to devise plans to make the two ends meet— her resources being the scanty proceeds from her Exchange and now and again a very welcome "special" from home.

REE MONTHS

Church, Cincinnati. So many worshippers are apt to gather on this occasion, that the church may be more than filled, and to accommodate those who shall be disappointed, it is expected that St. Paul's Church will be opened for the Service of Holy Communion, to begin a quarter of an hour later. Thus those who cannot attend at Christ Church may go from there to St. Paul's. The Music Hall will accommodate so large a number that we hope no one may be disappointed in gaining admittance there in the afternoon.

We are sure that in all branches of the Auxiliary earnest efforts are being made in these remaining months to increase the amount of the United Offering; and we hope that the apportionment of the Woman's Auxiliary is also remembered, and that, in branches where the sum suggested has not yet been given, an earnest endeavor is now being made to complete or surpass the amount. These summer months are the time to make known these objects of our interest to our friends and to the new acquaintances whom we may meet in our jour-

neyings and visits. Are they not also the time when we may remember in our prayers those who in their work for Christ and the upbuilding of His Church have so little holiday, and may that needed reinforcements may so be sent to strengthen the posts when the working force is now so small?

THE UNITED OFFERING IN TEXAS

[A paper prepared by Mrs. F. W. Catterall, Custodian of the United Offering, in the Texas Branch of the Woman's Auxiliary.]

IN 1904 the United Offering from the Diocese of Texas was $246.68. In 1907, it was $561.61. The entire United Offering was $224,251.55. The United Offering is completed every three years, and the next one will be presented at Cincinnati in October of 1910. We have now in the bank $502.08, and there is one more collection before October.

How much are we going to send from the diocese of Texas? Let us try to make a larger offering than ever before, for the United Offering follows this rule: As the work grows, so shall the offering grow. We have only the summer months in which to work for this United Offering, and it is an accepted fact that the summer time is not our working time. That rule may apply to some departments of Church work, but this is different. This work we may carry with us when we go away, and we may also enjoy its privileges among the restful pleasures of a summer at home. So I am going to ask you to take with you some of the little blue boxes and some of the leaflets, and use all diligence and zeal to bring this work to the knowledge and understanding of every Churchwoman in your parish or mission.

Now, because there are so many departments of the Auxiliary work, and because this one is so entirely independent and distinct from all other departments, I shall ask you to let me explain exactly what is the United Offering, who gives it, and for what it is given.

In the first place, what is the United Offering? The United Offering is a Thank-offering. It is placed on the altar at the Triennial Service of Thanksgiving, at the time when the Woman's Auxiliary has its Triennial meeting, and also at the time and place where the Church holds its General Convention. It is the national Thank-offering of our women. It is the expression of our gratitude for the Christian privileges which we enjoy; and while it expresses our thankfulness, it also kindles our thankfulness. Who that has ever been present at one of these services and joined in the hymn of praise which goes up with the presentation of the offering, but has thrilled with the joy of giving thanks? Who can contemplate with indifference the gift of $220,000, almost a quarter of a million, laid on the Altar of God by the women of the Church, and remember that with that gift, and because of that gift, more than 160 women have been able to give themselves to missionary work?

Who gives the United Offering? It is given by the women and girls of the American Church and its missions, not Auxiliary members only, but all women. It excuses no one from any other oblation, and it entails no other obligation, except that, to our united gifts there shall be added our united and earnest prayers that God will put it into the hearts of many faithful women to give themselves to the work of the Master in the mission field. The United Offering

sionaries, in kindergartens, schools and hospitals, are also helping to assimilate the vast hordes of immigrants—one of the most serious problems of our Republic.

Others of these women, United Offering missionaries, are in Alaska. Some are in Honolulu, in Porto Rico, in the Philippines. If you do not realize the good they are doing, if you do not know the wonderful results of missionary labors, take down your file of SPIRIT OF MISSIONS. Read the articles written by our Travelling Secretary, by Archdeacon Stuck and Bishop Rowe, by Bishop Kinsolving of Brazil, by Bishop Aves of Mexico, and many others. Travellers, writers, students, agree that the age is ripe for missionary work. The bars are down, the gates are open. Everywhere ignorance is looking toward the light.

In the foreign field, supported by the United Offering, are nurses, teachers, mission workers; a little band carrying in their hands the torch of civilization, the balm of healing, the Message of Salvation. Comparatively, there are not many who hear the call and who are willing to go. There are not many who have the faith and courage and happy optimism. One woman, when reminded of the discouragements and delays of foreign mission work, answered: "Yes; but one of these girls in the mission school may be the mother of a Moses who will lead his people out of bondage." The girls are, indeed, the hope of the Woman's Auxiliary; the future mothers and teachers in heathen countries, and also the future workers in our own country.

To the Junior Auxiliary, in particular, comes the call for more volunteers. They have not yet assumed the obligations of maturity, and they have the courage and enthusiasm of youth. We believe there are many members of the Junior Auxiliary who are unconsciously fitting themselves to become missionaries; there are many who long to do the work, and there are many already pledged. The January SPIRIT OF MISSIONS tells us that "Only once before, in a single calendar year, have so many recruits been added to the staff of our distant missions. The Church is giving more largely of its best life." Theirs to sow the seed and wait for the glorious harvest. Theirs to lift the standard and sound the pibroch that will raise the mighty army, and our share is to furnish the "sinews of war."

Let us see that no woman is kept from the "firing line" by the lack of mon[...] And so we come back again to th[...]be-ginning. Will you take the little [...]ue boxes and the leaflets, and ask [...]ur friends and Churchwomen to ex[...]ess their thankfulness in this manner?

"THE WHOLE LINE STEPPED FORWARD"

By Grace Hutchins

A N Eton boy stood in the aisle of the crowded parish church and listened to the Bishop of New Zealand. He wrote home that evening that the bishop had talked of going out to found a Church in the islands of the Pacific Ocean, and of meeting danger and difficulty there with trust in God. "Then, when he had finished, I think I never heard anything like the sensation, a kind of feeling that if it had not been on so sacred a spot, all would have exclaimed, 'God bless him.' "[1]

The boy was John Coleridge Patteson. He went back to the cricket field and lived the natural life of a boy at Eton. But in the background of his mind there was always the wish to go out with the Bishop of New Zealand, and work among the people of the islands. Twelve years afterward his purpose was carried out, and he left England, not to return again. It was as Missionary Bishop of Melanesia that he gave his life for the islanders whom he loved.

In Patteson's case, the call to missionary service was the natural result of his life at home and his training at school and college. He had given himself, all that he had and all that he was, to the One who wished to use him, and after that consecration of himself, the geographical location of his service was of secondary importance. He knew that all Christians should be missionaries, the sent ones of the King; "and not our fields, but our faithfulness matters."[2]

With a missionary vision and a mi[...]on-ary purpose dominating his life at [...]ne he waited only for the definite [...]rd which came to him, as it does to [...]ny people, through some one already o[...]the field, to tell him where his place [...]was to be.

There would be less confusion i[...]our minds about the terms "foreign mi[...]on-ary" and "missionary call," if we [...]on-stantly realized that we are all [...]der marching orders. Not only our [...]g's command, but our own consciousn[...] of privilege constitutes our responsi[...]ity If we take our stand by Christ ar[...]tr[...] to "view the world of men from thi[...]igh vantage ground,"[3] we cannot but [...]are Christ's vision; and "he who [...]re Christ's vision, shares His w[...]k." Those of us who are already en[...]ted through mission study classes, Aux[...]ar Junior work, or any service i[...]th Church at home, are as truly m[...]on aries as those at the front, provid[...]w have the Church's vision. "Thoug[...]t i possible that anyone may be called [...]g it is certain that all are called to [...]e." If we have given our very selves a[...]le the One who can fulfil all our nee[...]ak possession of our lives, then th[...]nl point to be determined is the place [...]er we are to serve. He will show [...]th corner of the field, whether at h[...]e o abroad, where we shall be of most [...]e t Him, because we have not chosen [...]Hi but He has chosen us. With a r[...]iz[...] tion of His power to meet every [...]ma need, and of His expectation th[...] al

---

[1] "Life of John Coleridge Patteson," C. M. Yonge.
[2] "From Far Formosa," Mackay.

[3] "Adventure for God," Brent.

Any one of us, knowing the character of the work waiting to be done, would say at once, "I am not fitted to go." We may have heard the call from within, we may recognize the need and the call from the field, and yet hesitate to offer ourselves. There must be also the call from the Church through her authorized agency before we know that our place of service ought to be on some mission field. The question of our fitness must finally be determined by those who know what are the requirements. We may find out through waiting alone upon God whether or not our way seems to lead. toward the place of greatest need and highest privilege. The next step is then to apply for appointment, and let others decide the result.

The time will come, if we are faithful, when many more Juniors will not only support the work from the home base, but will go out themselves in the vanguard. There are those now who would willingly go if they only knew that they were called. Many would gladly be like the Scots Guards that day at Windsor, when the colonel described the proposed Ashinta Expedition and its difficulties. He ended by saying, "I will turn my back for a moment. Any man who will volunteer to go on the expedition may step forward out of the line." He turned his back, and when he looked again, all were standing apparently as before. The colonel's eyes flashed with indignation, "What, the Scots Guards, and no volunteers!" A sergeant saluted. "Colonel," he said, "the whole line stepped forward."

A PICNIC MEETING

IN Western New York the Auxiliary officers of a certain district held a picnic meeting at the lakeshore home of one of their number. The day was occupied with discussion of Auxiliary matters, and was found to be both interesting and helpful, and from the little gathering came the contribution of $5.25 toward general missions to help the Board in its time of summer need.

NOTES FROM AUX

Encouraging Words from Kansas City

LAST October when discussing the matter of the apportionment assigned to the Kansas City branch, we found so few who really understood it that the President appointed me to visit every parish branch to give instruction upon this matter. I have just finished my visits and feel sure they have been of service. I found such a lack of knowledge. At each visit I explained the apportionment and said that the money for General Missions, or the designated sums which apply on our apportionment, should be paid first and promptly. I tried to discourage specials; but it is so hard to do this when these needs are so forcibly put. However, we are growing, though slowly. Our annual meeting last week was such a success—the best we have ever had, and I have missed only one meeting, either annual or quarterly, in the twenty years of our existence. We started a new scholarship. Two places were brought forward prominently—the Philippines and the work at Corbin, Ky. When asked if gifts for the latter would aid the Board, and it was thought not, the work in the Philippines was selected, but the plea for Corbin was so good that when the amount of pledges was counted there was enough for both.

Our Juniors took everything by storm. Two years ago last April our leader had never heard of a Junior Auxiliary, and we had never had a leader. She has never met anyone in charge of Junior work, but on Junior day the room was packed, even the window-sills were filled and the hall also, and then people went away. The Juniors have not given up one penny of their gift for General Missions, while struggling at the same time to secure a Mexican Scholarship, and beside that they have voted aid toward the Board's appropriations for educational work in Mexico. I think our Juniors are starting out right, and that they will not have to unlearn things. In them so much of our hope lies.

ACKNOWLEDGMENT OF OFFERINGS

Offerings are asked to sustain missions in thirty missionary districts in the United States, Africa, China, Japan, Brazil, Mexico and Cuba; also work in the Haitien Church; in forty-two dioceses, including missions to the Indians and to the Colored People; to pay the salaries of thirty-two bishops, and stipends to 2,253 missionary workers, domestic and foreign; also two general missionaries to the Swedes and two missionaries among deaf-mutes in the Middle West and the South; and to support schools, hospitals and orphanages. With all remittances the name of the Diocese and Parish should be given. Remittances, when practicable, should be by Check or Draft, and should always be made payable to the order of George Gordon King, Treasurer, and sent to him, Church Missions House, 281 Fourth Avenue, New York. Remittances in Bank Notes are not safe unless sent in Registered Letters.

The Treasurer of the Board of Missions acknowledges the receipt of the following from May 1st to June 1st, 1910.

* Lenten and Easter Offering from the Sunday-school Auxiliary.

NOTE.—The items in the following pages marked "Sp." are Specials which do not aid the Board in meeting its appropriations. In the heading for each Diocese the total marked "Ap." is the amount which does aid the Board of Missions in meeting its appropriations. Wherever the abbreviation "Wo. Aux." precedes the amount, the offering is through a branch of the Woman's Auxiliary.

Home Dioceses

Alabama

Ap. $1,112.81

BIRMINGHAM—*Advent* : Gen.	335	00
St. Andrew's : Gen.	79	96
Trinity Church S. S.* : Gen.	1	91
CARLEN—*St. Mary's* : Dom., $5; S.		
S. Gen., $2.47	7	47
CITRONELLE—*St. Thomas's* : Dom.	4	70
ENSLEY—*St. John's S. S.** : Gen.	8	20
LIVINGSTON—*St. James's* : Indian, $1;		
Dh., $2; Frn., $2	5	00
MARION—*St. Wilfred's S. S.** : Gen.	1	70
MOBILE—*Christ Church* : Gen.	24	22
OAKVILLE—*Mission* : Gen.	3	00
SHEFFIELD—*Grace* : Gen.	20	40
MISCELLANEOUS—Branch Wo. Aux.,		
support of bed, St. James's Hospital,		
Anking, Hankow, $50; Gen., $490.80	540	80
Branch Junior Aux., Gen.	55	45
Ladies' Branch, Gen.	25	00

Albany

Ap. $1,741.47; *Sp.* $148.00

ALBANY—*All Saints' Cathedral* : St.		
Luke's Hospital, Tokyo, $5; St.		
John's University, Shanghai, $16;		
Gen., $311.68; Dan Mather, Sp. for		
Expansion Fund, St. John's Univer-		
sity, Shanghai, $1	333	68
St. Paul's S. S.* : Gen.	280	17
Jno A. Dix, Gen.	5	00
ATHENS—*Trinity Church S. S.** : Gen.	27	00
CHATHAM—*St. Paul's S. S.** : Gen.	10	00
CHATHAM—*St. Luke's* : Gen.	4	90
COHOES—*Zion Memorial* : Dom., $1.92;		
Sp. for Bishop Spalding, Utah, $80.	81	92
COOPERSTOWN—*Christ Church* : Frn.	112	13
CUTCHIN—*Church of the Good Shepherd*		
S. S.** : Gen.		50
DELHI—*St. John's* : Wo. Aux., Gen.	18	52
DUANESBURG — *Christ Church* : Wo.		
Aux., Sp. for Alaska	12	00
FORT EDWARD—*St. James's S. S.** :		
Gen.	9	66

FORT PLAIN—*Holy Cross S. S.** ; Frn.	4	21
GLENS FALLS—*Church of the Messiah* :		
$50, S. S.,* $1.68, Gen.	51	68
HOOSAC—"M. N.," for work of Rev.		
Mr. Clapp, Bontok, Philippines.	5	00
HOOSICK FALLS—*St. Mark's S. S.** :		
Sp. for Rev. L. Kroll, Honolulu.	25	00
HUDSON—*Christ Church S. S.** : Salary		
of Rev. Lloyd Benson, care of Bishop		
Griswold, Salina.	50	00
ILION—*St. Augustine's* : Gen.	50	00
MECHANICSVILLE—*St. Luke's S. S.** :		
Gen.	12	14
MOHAWK—*Grace S. S.** : Gen.	5	00
MORRIS—*Zion and the Mission of New*		
Lisbon : Gen.	21	00
PALENVILLE—*Gloria Dei S. S.** : Gen.	9	34
POTSDAM—*Trinity Church* : Frn., $9.50;		
Miss Elizabeth Clarkson, St. John's		
University, Shanghai, $100; "T.		
Streatfield Clarkson" (In Memoriam)		
scholarship, St. John's University,		
Shanghai, $100; Miss Lavinia Clark-		
son, "Lavinia Clarkson" scholarship,		
Boone University, Wuchang, Hankow,		
$40	249	50
SARATOGA SPRINGS—*Bethesda* : Dom.	46	79
SCHENECTADY—*Christ Church S. S.** :		
Gen.	53	50
St. George's : St. Mary's Guild, Sp. for		
Dr. Pott's work in Shanghai, $25 ;		
Junior Aux., Gen., $25 ; Babies'		
Branch, Sp. for missionary font, $5 ;		
Akita Kindergarten, Tokyo, $16.64.	71	64
SIDNEY—*St. Paul's S. S.** : Gen.	6	94
STILLWATER — *St. John's* : Colored,		
$3.44; Frn., 75 cts.	4	19
TROY—*St. Barnabas's* : Dom., $5.81;		
S. S., Gen. $2.25	8	06
St. Paul's : Gen.	300	00
WALTON—*Christ Church* ; Frn.	20	00

Arkansas

Ap. $84.23; *Sp.* $46.00

CAMDEN—*St. John's* : Babies' Branch,		
$1.54, S. S.,* $2.20, Gen.	3	74
FOREMAN—*St. Barnabas's S. S.** : Gen.	1	00
HELENA—*St. John's* : Wo. Aux., Gen.	9	00

JONESBORO—*St. Mark's*: Wo. Aux.,
Gen. 10 00
LITTLE ROCK—*Christ Church*: Babies'
Branch, Gen., $7.58; Sp. for mis-
sionary font, $1.................. 8 58
St. Mark's S. S.*: Gen.............. 2 00
St. Paul's: Wo. Aux., Sp. for support
of boy at Soochow, Shanghai....... 45 00
Trinity Cathedral: Babies' Branch,
Gen. 88
MARIANNA—*St. Andrew's*: Wo. Aux.,
Gen. 7 75
NEWPORT—*St. Paul's*: Wo. Aux., Gen. 11 00
PINE BLUFF—*Trinity Church*: Wo.
Aux., Gen....................... 25 00
SILOAM SPRINGS—*Grace S. S.**: Gen.. 2 97
WINSLOW—*St. Stephen's S. S.**: Gen.. 3 81

Atlanta

Ap. $414.37; *Sp.* $25.00

ATHENS—*Emmanuel Church S. S.**:
Gen. 3 20
ATLANTA—*Epiphany S. S.**: Gen..... 50 00
Holy Innocents': Gen............... 1 50
Incarnation: Gen.................. 2 00
St. Luke's: Frn.................. 50 00
S. S. Rally, Gen.................. 11 48
"A Friend," Gen................... 5 00
COLUMBUS—*Trinity Church*: $40, Wo.
Aux., $18.75, Gen............... 58 75
ELBERTON—*Holy Apostles' S. S.**: Gen. 5 00
GAINESVILLE—*Grace S. S.**: Gen..... 8 71
MACON—*St. Paul's*: Dom. (of which S.
S.,* $44.63), $71.89; Frn. (of which
S. S.,* $44.62), $89.49; Sp. for
Dr. Correll's work, Tsu, Kyoto (of
which S. S.,* $6, Junior Aux., $4,
Juniors, $5), $25................ 186 38
MOUNT AIRY—*Calvary S. S.**: Gen.... 2 00
TOCCOA—*St. Matthias's S. S.**: Gen... 2 35
MISCELLANEOUS—Junior Aux., Chinese
Day-schools, Hankow, $18; Gen.,
$35 .... 53 00

Bethlehem

Ap. $761.67; *Sp.* $256.00

DRIFTON—*St. James's*: Wo. Aux. (of
which Junior Aux., $5), St. Paul's
School, Lawrenceville, Southern Vir-
ginia, $30; S. S.,* Infant Depart-
ment, "The Drifton" scholarship, St.
Mary's School, South Dakota, $60.. 90 00
DUNMORE—*St. Mark's*: Wo. Aux., Sp.
for St. Mary's-in-the-Mountains,
Sewanee, Tennessee.............. 5 00
GREAT BEND—*Grace*: Gen............ 7 50
HAZELTON—*St. Peter's*: Junior Aux.,
Sp. for St. Margaret's School, Tokyo,
$5; Sp. for Bishop Hare's Memorial
Fund, South Dakota, $5; Sp. for
Miss Thackara's work, Arizona, $5;
Sp. for Rev. Mr. Gilman, Changsha,
Hankow (personal use), $5....... 20 00
LANSFORD—*Trinity Church*: Gen..... 26 50
LEBANON—*St. Luke's*: Gen.......... 121 40
MILFORD—*Church of the Good Shep-
herd*: Wo. Aux., Sp. for Bishop Van
Buren, Porto Rico............... 10 00
MONTROSE—*St. Paul's*: Colored, $1;
Indian, $2; Dom., $53; Frn., $44.. 100 00
NEW MILFORD—*St. Mark's*: Gen...... 6 10
POTTSVILLE—*Trinity Church*: Frances
Koercher, Sp. for Alaskan Hospital
Fund 10 00
READING—*Christ Church*: Wo. Aux.,
Sp. for St. Agnes's Hospital, Raleigh,
North Carolina, $25; Young Wom-
en's Branch, Sp. for "Valle Crucis"
scholarship, Asheville, $10...... 35 00
St. Barnabas's: Gen., $32.25; Wo.
Aux., Sp. for Rev. Mr. Betticher,
Jr., Fairbanks, Alaska, for door
and window, $10................. 42 25
St. Mary's: Gen.................. 36 00
SCRANTON—*St. Luke's*: Wo. Aux., Gen.,

	GREIG—*Trinity Chapel S. S.**: Gen....	1 00
	†GUILFORD.	
	HOLLAND PATENT—O. Kingman, Sp. for	
95	St. John's College, Shanghai........	1 00
30	JAMESVILLE—*St. Mark's*: Dom., $2.54;	
	Frn., $1.50......................	4 04
00	KIDDERS—Wo. Aux., Sp. for Rev. J. A.	
	Staunton, Jr., Sagada, Philippine	
	Islands	4 15
23	MARCELLUS—*St. John's*: Gen.........	18 12
	NORWICH—*Emmanuel Church*: Gen....	98 66
00	ONEIDA—*St. John's*: Dom., 75 cts.;	
	Frn., 50 cts.; Gen. (of which S. S.*	
01	$35.66), $38.12.................	39 37
45	ONONDAGA CASTLE—*Church of the Good*	
25	*Shepherd*: Colored..............	20
00	OSWEGO—*Evangelist's*: (of which S.	
	S.,* $19.50) Gen.................	26 75
	St. John's Chapel S. S.*: Gen........	2 90
00	PIERREPONT MANOR—*Zion S. S.**: Gen.	1 54
	PULASKI—*St. James's*: Dom., $4.81;	
	Frn., $6.78.....................	11 59
00	ROMULUS—*St. Stephen's*: Frn........	2 00
75	SKANEATELES—*St. James's*: Frn......	18 83
93	SYRACUSE—*All Saints' S. S.**: Gen....	48 70
	Grace: Frn., $1.25; Gen. (of which S.	
00	S.,* $32.79)....................	35 04
	St. Mark's S. S.*: Gen., $75; S. S.,	
	Sp. for St. Paul's College, Tokyo,	
	$8.26	83 26
81	*St. Paul's*: Dom., $104.01; Gen.,	
	$28.37; Sp. for Catechist Building	
	Fund, Kyoto, $10.47..............	142 85
	St. Philip's: Gen...................	1 00
01	*Church of the Saviour*: Gen..........	44 20
	Trinity Church: Dom., $1; Frn., $1;	
	Gen. (of which S. S.,* $4.23),	
	$61.89	63 89
	THERESA—*St. James's*: Gen..........	20 66
	TRENTON—*St. Andrew's S. S.**: Gen...	1 70
	UNION SPRINGS—*Grace*: Gen..........	1 50
	UTICA—*Calvary*: Gen...............	23 49
	Grace S. S.*: Dom., $37.88; Frn.,	
	$75.75	113 63
	Trinity Church: Gen...............	66 30
	WATERTOWN—*St. Paul's*: Gen. (of	
	which S. S.,* $33)...............	89 03
45	*Trinity Church*: Colored, 25 cts.; Gen.,	
	$93.03; Sp. for St. Peter's Hospital,	
	Montana, $513.08; Sp. for Bishop	
	Rowe, Alaska (of which Wo. Aux.,	
	$65), $238.01...................	844 37
	WATERVILLE — *Grace*: Gen., $100.49;	
	Sp. for Dr. Taylor's Hospital, Anking,	
00	Hankow, $15.10.................	115 59
	WAVERLY—*Grace*: Gen...............	7 25
	WHITESBORO—*St. John's*: (of which	
	S. S.,* $6.50) Gen..............	31 50
73	MISCELLANEOUS — Wo. Aux., Fourth	
85	District, Sp. for St. John's College,	
	Shanghai, $2; Second District, Sp.	
50	for hospital, Sagada, Philippine	
	Islands, $34.28..................	36 28
48	Junior Aux., Sp. for St. Agnes's Hos-	
04	pital, Raleigh, North Carolina......	60 00
27	**Chicago**	
00		
00	*Ap.* $1,802.33; *Sp.* $124.90	
	AURORA—*Trinity Church*: Dom. and	
82	Frn.	119 22
55	BATAVIA—*Calvary*: Gen..............	9 00
	CHICAGO—*Advent*: Gen..............	3 54
75	*All Saints' S. S.**: Gen.............	20 00
	Epiphany: Day-school for Boys at	
02	Ichang, Hankow.................	5 05
	Immanuel Church (Swedish): Gen....	11 28
70	*Incarnation S. S.**: Gen............	9 27
00	*St. Alban's*: Dom., $8.42; Frn., $8.42;	
25	S. S.,* Sp. for Bishop Horner, Ashe-	
00	ville, $24.90....................	41 74

† $120.42 credited in the June SPIRIT OF
MISSIONS to Fayetteville, Trinity Church, should
have read, Guilford, Christ Church, $101.91, S.
S.,* $18.51, General Missions.

St. Barnabas's: Gen. (of which S. S.,*
$6.69) 22 52
St. Bartholomew's S. S.: Dom., $40;
Frn., $42.23 .... 82 23
St. John the Evangelist's: Gen 50 00
St. Luke's S. S.: Gen 10 80
St. Mark's: Gen 35 69
St. Paul's: Gen 48 80
St. Paul's-by-the-Lake S. S.: Dom.
and Frn 60 33
St. Peter and Paul Cathedral: Dom.,
and Frn 25 00
St. Peter's S. S.: Support of Rev. Lelo
Ying Tsung, Hankow, $180; support
of Rev. J. H. Kobayashi, Tokyo,
$120; Sp. for Bishop Brewster,
Western Colorado, $100 .... 400 00
Western Theological Seminary, Bish-
op Anderson's Missionary Society,
Gen. 25 06
EVANSTON—*St. Luke's*: Dom. and
Frn. 7 82
GLEN ELLYN—*St. Mark's*: Gen 6 00
HIGHLAND PARK—*Trinity Church*: Gen. 35 00
HINSDALE—*Grace S. S.*: Gen 42 52
JOLIET—*Christ Church*: Gen 43 88
LA GRANGE—*Emmanuel Church*: Dom.,
$11.50; Frn., $12.50; Gen., $57.25 . . 81 25
MAYWOOD — *Holy Communion*: Dom.
and Frn., $4.88; S. S.,* Gen., $14.91. 19 79
MOMENCE—*Church of the Good Shep-
herd*: Gen. (of which S. S.,* $15.50),
$33.85; Mrs. E. D. Cone, support of
Bible-woman, Hankow, $50 .... 83 85
OTTAWA—*Christ Church*: Gen 9 65
ROCKFORD — *Emmanuel Church*: Gen.
(of which S. S.,* $20) 30 00
STERLING—*Grace*: Frn. 7 50
STREATOR—*Christ Church S. S.*: Gen. 5 44
WAUKEGAN—*Christ Church*: Gen. 10 00
WINNETKA—*Christ Church*: Gen. 565 00

Colorado

Ap. $1,308.47; *Sp.* $44.50
ADAMS CITY—*St. Stephen's Mission S.
S.*: Gen 7 45
BYERS—*Ascension*: Gen. 3 00
COLORADO CITY—*Church of the Good
Shepherd*: Gen 4 20
COLORADO SPRINGS — *St. Stephen's*:
Dom. and Frn., $139.80; Sp. for
Bishop Rowe, Alaska, $25; Sp. for
St. Paul's College, Tokyo, $19.50 ... 184 30
COMO—*St. Mary's*: Gen 5 00
CREEDE—*St. Augustine's*: Gen 1 00
CRESTINE—Gen. 25
DENVER—*Epiphany*: Gen 2 25
DENVER—*All Saints' S. S.*: $15,
Junior Aux., $2, Gen 17 00
Emmanuel Church S. S.: Gen 11 00
St. Barnabas's S. S.: Gen 93 25
St. John's Cathedral: Dom., $146;
Frn., $117; S. S.,* Gen., $149.26 . . . 412 26
St. Luke's S. S.: Gen 10 62
St. Mark's: Gen 350 00
St. Stephen's S. S.: Gen 17 25
FLORENCE—*St. Alban's*: Gen 1 00
FORT COLLINS—*St. Luke's*: Gen 94 00
FORT LUPTON—*St. Andrew's*: Gen.... 4 65
FORT MORGAN—*St. Paul's*: Gen 10 00
GAROS—*St. Alban's*: Gen 4 00
GOLDEN—*Calvary S. S.*: Gen 4 39
HUGO—*St. Michael's*: Gen 15 00
IDAHO SPRINGS—*Calvary*: Gen 10 00
LEADVILLE—*St. George's*: Gen 8 00
LONGMONT—*St. Stephen's*: Gen 5 00
MONTE VISTA—*St. Stephen's*: Gen.... 3 05
PUEBLO—*St. James's*: Gen 3 00
SAGUACHE—*Incarnation*: Gen 1 00
STERLING—*All Saints'*: Gen 6 50
TRINIDAD—*Trinity Church S. S.*: Gen. 44 55
VILLA GROVE—*St. James's*: Gen 30
WALSENBURG—*St. Peter's*: Gen 13 50
WEST CLIFF—*St. Luke's*: Gen 6 20

Connecticut

Ap. $8,163.44; *Sp.* $172.55
ANSONIA—*Christ Church*: Gen ......
Immanuel Church: Gen ....
BANTAM—*St. Paul's S. S.*: Dom.,
$4.14; Frn., $4 ....
BETHEL—*St. Thomas's S. S.*: Gen ...
BETHLEHEM—*Christ Church*: Gen. (of
which S. S.,* $8.40) ....
BLACK HALL—*Guild Room*: Gen .....
BRANFORD—*Trinity Church S. S.*:
Gen. ....
BRIDGEPORT—*St. John's S. S.*: Gen ..
Trinity Church S. S.: Gen ....
BRIDGEWATER—*St. Mark's S. S.*: Gen.
BRISTOL—*Trinity Church*: Dom. and
Frn., $15; S. S.,* Gen., $37.19 . . . .
BROOKLYN—*Trinity Church S. S.*:
Gen. ....
CANAAN—*Christ Church S. S.*: Gen...
CHESHIRE—*St. Peter's S. S.*: Gen ...
CLINTON—*Holy Advent S. S.*: Gen...
COLLINSVILLE—*Trinity Church*: Frn.,
20 cts.; Gen., $2.10; S. S., Gen.,
$8.50 ....
DANBURY—*St. James's*: Gen. (of which
S. S.,* $100) ....
DARIEN—*St. Luke's S. S.*: Gen ......
DERBY—*St. James's S. S.*: Gen ......
DURHAM—*Epiphany S. S.*: Gen ......
EAST HADDAM—*St. Stephen's S. S.*:
Gen. ....
Grace Chapel S. S. (Hadlyme): Gen..
Mrs. F. C. H. Wendell, Sp. for Miss
Thackara's work, Fort Defiance, Ari-
zona, $1; Rev. Dr. F. C. H. Wendell,
for Bishop Johnson's work in South
Dakota, $2 ....
EAST HAMPTON—*St. John's*: Gen ....
EAST HARTFORD—*St. John's*: Sp. for
Mrs. Roots's work for women at
Hankow, $3; S. S.,* Gen., $9.30 ....
EAST HAVEN—*Christ Church*: Gen ...
FAIRFIELD—*St. Paul's S. S.*: Gen ...
FARMINGTON—*St. James's*: Gen. (of
which S. S.,* $7) ....
FORESTVILLE—*St. John's S. S.*: Gen..
GLASTONBURY—*St. James's S. S.*:
Gen. ....
GREENWICH—*Christ Church S. S.*:
Gen. ....
GUILFORD—*Christ Church*: Gen. (of
which S. S.,* $40.46) ....
HAMDEN—*Grace*: Gen ....
HARTFORD—*Church of the Good Shep-
herd S. S.*: Gen ....
Grace Chapel S. S. (Parkville): Gen.
St. James's: Gen. (of which S. S.,*
$17.43) ....
St. John's: Gen. (of which S. S.,*
$90.90) ....
St. Thomas's: Gen. (of which S. S.,*
$40.79) ....
Trinity Church: For Rev. Dr. Hunt-
ington's work, Hankow, $5; Gen.
(of which S. S.,* $561.51), $689.51.
HEBRON—*St. Peter's S. S.*: Gen .....
HUNTINGTON—*St. Paul's S. S.*: Gen..
IVORYTON—*All Saints'*: Gen ....
JEWETT CITY—*Mission*: Gen ....
KENT—*St. Andrew's*: China, $20;
Gen. (of which S. S.,* $14.35),
$39.53 ....
LIME ROCK—*Trinity Church S. S.*:
Gen. ....
LITCHFIELD—*St. Michael's S. S.*:
Gen. ....
LONG HILL—*Grace S. S.*: Gen ......
MARBLEDALE—*St. Andrew's S. S.*:
Gen. ....
MERIDEN—*St. Andrew's S. S.*: Gen ...
All Saints' S. S.: Gen ....
MIDDLEFIELD—*St. Paul's S. S.*: Gen..
MIDDLETOWN — *Christ Church*: Gen.,
$25; S. S.,* Dom., $3.71; Frn.,
$7.47; Gen., $20.44 ....

knowledgments 571

10 00
18 00
14 00
7 15
75 90

277 06
34 80
21 74
104 00
30 00
35 00

27 55
58 05
30 00
20 00

260 88
28 50

1,038 44
17 17

282 61

25 00

240 35

30 67
12 00

7 37

45 06

3 00
52 00
38 66
66 66

130 00

16 25

88 00

10 63
11 48

23 26
13 68
32 80

.2 00

12 56

11 00
54 57

43 37

28 59

20 85
16 00
40 00
20 00

68 00
23 21

17 68

18 00

SOUTHPORT—*Trinity Church S. S.**:
Gen. 52 50
SPRINGDALE — *Emmanuel Church S.
S.**: Gen..................... 6 80
STAFFORD SPRINGS—*Grace*: $23, S. S.*
$38, Gen..................... 61 00
STAMFORD—*St. Andrew's S. S.**: Gen. 60 00
*St. John's S. S.**: Gen............... 190 20
*St. Luke's Chapel S. S.**: Gen....... 29 87
STONINGTON—*Calvary*: Gen.......... 60 00
TASHUA—*Christ Church S. S.**: Gen.. 7 66
THOMASTON — *Trinity Church*: Gen.
$10; Sp. for Bishop Horner, Ashe-
ville, $20; S. S.,* Gen., $32.28..... 62 28
TORRINGTON—*Trinity Church S. S.**:
Gen. 61 78
WALLINGFORD—*St. Paul's S. S.**: Gen. 38 87
WAREHOUSE POINT—*St. John's S. S.**:
Gen. 44 42
WATERBURY—*St. John's*: $165.29; S.
S.,* $650.19, Gen................. 815 48
Trinity Church: Gen. (of which S. S.*
$75), $363.20; S. S.,* Sp. for Bish-
op Wells, Spokane, $25............ 388 20
WATERTOWN—*All Saints' Chapel* (Oak-
ville): S. S.,* Gen................ 10 00
Christ Church: $90, S. S.,* $69.33,
Gen. 159 33
WATERVILLE—*St. Paul's S. S.**: Frn.. 7 07
WEST HARTFORD—*St. James's*: Gen.. 4 70
WEST HAVEN—*Christ Church S. S.**:
Gen. 52 72
WESTPORT—*Christ Church S. S.**:
Gen. 32 59
Holy Trinity Church: For St. Paul's
School, Southern Virginia, $25; Gen.
(of which S. S.,* $50), $95; Mrs.
John B. Morris, Gen., $20......... 140 00
WETHERSFIELD — *Trinity Church S.
S.**: Gen..................... 19 20
WINDSOR—Rev. W. H. Dean, Sp. for
Catechist School Land and Building
Fund, Shanghai................. 5 00
WINSTED—*St. James's S. S.**: Gen... 40 35
YALESVILLE—*St. John's*: Gen........ 15 75
MISCELLANEOUS—Babies' Branch. Gay-
lord Hart Mitchell Memorial Kinder-
garten, Tokyo, $5; Angelica Church
Hart Day-school, Wuchang, Hankow,
$5; "Little Helpers'" Day-school,
Shanghai, $5; Gen., $50; Sp. for
mission, White Rocks, Utah, $5;
Sp. for missionary font, $1........ 71 00

Dallas

Ap. $319.95

AMARILLO—*St. Andrew's*: Wo. Aux.,
Gen. 10 00
COMANCHE—*St. Matthew's S. S.**:
Gen. 15 17
CORSICANA—*St. John's*: Wo. Aux., Gen. 10 00
DALLAS—*Incarnation*: Wo. Aux., Gen. 20 00
St. Matthew's: Wo. Aux., Dom., $25;
Asheville, $5; Porto Rico, $5; Frn.,
$25; Brazil, $5; Cuba, $5; Mexico,
$5; Hooker Memorial School, Mexico,
$20; Junior Aux., Gen., $5....... 100 00
Trinity Church: Wo. Aux., Alaska, $5;
Mexico, $5; S. S.,* Gen., $73...... 83 00
FORT WORTH—*St. Andrew's*: Wo. Aux.,
Frn. 20 00
HILLSBORO—*St. Mary's S. S.**: Gen.. 8 28
MINERAL WELLS—*Church of the Good
Shepherd*: Wo. Aux., Gen......... 5 00
PARIS—*Holy Cross*: Wo. Aux., Dom.,
$5; Frn., $5................... 10 00
TERRELL—*Church of the Good Shep-
herd*: Wo. Aux., Gen............. 15 00
TEXARKANA—*St. James's*: Gen....... 23 50

Delaware

Ap. $523.65; *Sp.* $95.00

CHRISTIANA HUNDRED—*Christ Church*:
Wo. Aux., Point Hope, $5; Sp. for
Rev. D..T. Huntington, Hankow, $5;

Sp. for Foreign Life Insurance Fund,
$5 .... 15 00
CLAYMONT—*Ascension S. S.**: Gen.... 11 87
DELAWARE CITY—*Christ Church S.
S.**: Gen...................... 5 72
DOVER—*Christ Church*: Wo. AUX.,
Point Hope, Alaska, $5; Hooker
School, Mexico, $5; Gen., $15..... 25 00
GEORGETOWN—*St. Paul's S. S.**: Gen. 71
MARSHALLTON—*St. Barnabas's*: Gen.. 10 00
St. Barnabas's (Marshallton): Wo.⎫
  Aux., Point Hope, Alaska, $5....⎪
St. James's (Newport): Sp. for Rev.⎬ 10 00
  D. T. Huntington, Hankow, $2 .⎪
St. James's (Stanton): Sp. for For-⎭
  eign Life Insurance Fund, $3..⎰
MIDDLETOWN—*St. Anne's*: Gen., $5.35;
  Wo. Aux., Point Hope, Alaska, $5;
  Sp. for Rev. D. T. Huntington, Han-
  kow, $5; Sp. for Foreign Life In-
  surance Fund, $5................ 20 35
NEWARK—*St. Thomas's*: Wo. Aux.,
  Point Hope, Alaska............... 5 00
NEW CASTLE—*Immanuel Church*: Wo.
  Aux., Point Hope, Alaska, $5; Sp.
  for Foreign Life Insurance Fund,
  $5 .... 10 00
SEAFORD—*St. Luke's*: $15, Wo. Aux.,
  $1, Gen.......................... 16 00
SMYRNA—*St. Peter's*: Wo. Aux., Sp.
  for Bishop Aves, Mexico, for house,
  $1; Sp. for Rev. D. T. Huntington,
  Hankow, $1; Sp. for Foreign Life
  Insurance Fund, $5; S. S.,* Gen.,
  $12 .... 19 00
WILMINGTON—*Holy Trinity Church*:
  Wo. Aux., Gen., $2; Sp. for Rev. D.
  T. Huntington, Hankow, $3........ 5 00
St. Andrew's: Wo. Aux., Point Hope,
  Alaska, $5; Sp. for Rev. D. T. Hunt-
  ington, Hankow, $10; Sp. for For-
  eign Life Insurance Fund, $5...... 20 00
St. John's: Dom., $280; Wo. Aux.,
  Point Hope, Alaska, $5; Gen., $10;
  Sp. for Rev. S. H. Littell, Hankow,
  $15; Sp. for Foreign Life Insurance
  Fund, $5........................ 315 00
Trinity Church: Wo. Aux., Point Hope,
  Alaska, $10; Sp. for Rev. D. T.
  Huntington, Hankow, $5; Sp. for
  Foreign Life Insurance Fund, $5;
  S. S.,* Gen., $100............... 120 00
MISCELLANEOUS—Wo. Aux., Sp. for
  Bishop Aves, Mexico, for house.... 10 00

Duluth

Ap. $259.72

BRAINERD—*St. Paul's*: $19, S. S.,*
  $14.57, Gen...................... 33 57
BRECKENRIDGE — *St. Paul's S. S.**:
  Dom. and Frn.................... 2 50
BROWN VALLEY—*St. Luke's*: Gen.... 2 80
DULUTH—*Park Point Mission S. S.**:
  Gen. 10 00
St. Paul's: Wo. Aux., Gen........... 43 21
EVELETH—*St. John's*: Gen.......... 13 02
FERGUS FALLS—*St. James's S. S.**:
  Gen. 73 11
GRAND RAPIDS — *Holy Communion*:
  Gen. 10 00
MELROSE—*Trinity Church S. S.**:
  Gen. 9 06
ONIGUM—*St. John's S. S.**: Gen..... 5 00
ROYALTON—*Grace*: $12.25, S. S.,* $7,
  Gen. 19 25
TWIN LAKES — *Samuel Memorial S.
  S.**: Gen. — 8 90
VIRGINIA—*St. Paul's*: Gen.......... 27 00
WADENA—*St. Helen's*: Dom.......... 2 30

East Carolina

Ap. $313.23; *Sp.* $47.88

BATH—*St. Thomas's*: Wo. Aux., Gen. 1 00
BELHAVEN—*St. Mary's*: Gen......... 1 00
COLUMBIA—*St. Agnes's Guild*: Wo.
  Aux., Gen....................... 1 00

Georgia

Ap. $1,224.65 ; *Sp.* $79.00

16 80	ALBANY—*St. Paul's*: Wo. Aux., Gen..	3 15
	AMERICUS—*Calvary*: Dom...........	15 46
	AUGUSTA—*Christ Church S. S.* * : Gen.	29 00
12 05	*Epiphany* (North) : Gen............	3 27
1 37	*St. Paul's S. S.* * : Gen.............	100 00
	BAINBRIDGE—*St. John's S. S.* * : Frn...	7 50
1 00	CORDELE—*Christ Church* : Gen......	7 50
2 97	DARIEN—*St. Andrew's* : Wo. Aux., Gen.	6 00
	Junior Aux., Rev. Robb White's sal-	
15 00	ary, Philippine Islands, $3; St.	
	Luke's Hospital, Shanghai, $3; Sp.	
22 39	for "Sister Katherine" scholarship,	
	Guantanamo, Cuba, $2; Sp. for Holy	
	Trinity Orphanage, Tokyo, $2......	10 00
	FREDERICA—*Christ Church S. S.* * :	
25 97	Gen.	50 00
	SAVANNAH—*Christ Church* : $574.41,	
69 80	S. S.,* $152.24, Gen.; Sp. for An-	
10 55	vik, Alaska, $75................	801 65
1 25	*St. John's* : Wo. Aux., salary of Miss	
	Sabine, Alaska, $25; S. S.,* Gen.,	
	$122.82	147 82
	St. Paul's : Wo. Aux., Gen...........	10 30
	THOMASVILLE—*St. Thomas's* : Junior	
41 80	Aux., Gen.....................	7 00
11 00	MISCELLANEOUS—Wo. Aux., Japanese	
	Bible-woman, Tokyo, $55; "Bishop	
50	Nelson" scholarship, St. Hilda's	
	School, Wuchang, Hankow, $50.....	105 00
13 81		

Harrisburg

Ap. $661.14 ; *Sp.* $69.00

75 00	ALTOONA—*St. Luke's* : Gen...........	75 00
5 25	BELLEFONTE—*St. John's* : Gen........	27 14
25 12	BLOSSBURG—*St. Luke's S. S.* * : Gen..	13 00
30 42	CAMP HILL—*Mount Calvary* : Gen....	4 16
2 00	CARLISLE—*St. John's* : Wo. Aux., Sp.	
4 00	for Bishop Horner's work, Valle	
9 90	Crucis, Asheville, $5; Sp. for Bishop	
12 85	Brown's work, Arkansas, $1; S. S.,*	
10 50	Gen., $12.....................	18 00
	COLE'S CREEK—*St. Gabriel's S. S.* * :	
33 05	Gen.	1 60
11 00	COUDERSPORT—*Christ Church* : Gen....	10 00
5 00	DANVILLE—*Christ Church* : Frn.......	12 00
5 85	HARRISBURG — *St. Stephen's* : Junior	
7 80	Aux., Sp. for Bishop Rowe, Alaska,	
20 00	$5; Sp. for St. John's-in-the-Wilder-	
5 00	ness, Alaska, $3; Sp. for Deaconess	
	Carter's work, Alaska, $5; Sp. for	
31 55	Good Samaritan Hospital, Valdez,	
13 55	Asheville, $3; Sp. for "Little Mary"	
17 04	scholarship, St. Mary's School,	
	Sewanee, Tennessee, $10.........	31 00
4 88	HUNTINGDON—*St. John's S. S.* * : Gen..	15 00
	LANCASTER—*St. John's* : Wo. Aux., Sp.	
7 03	for Miss Elizabeth Newbold, Tokyo,	
3 00	for her personal use, $10; Sp. for	
6 50	W. B. Thorn, for Oneida Indians,	
	Fond du Lac, $5................	15 00
	LOCK HAVEN—*St. Paul's S. S.* * : Gen..	1 65
	MANHEIM—*St. Paul's S. S.* * : Gen....	6 00
	MECHANICSBURG—*St. Luke's* : Gen....	15 00
	MILTON—*Christ Church S. S.* * : Gen..	14 42
9 38	NORTHUMBERLAND—*St. Mark's* : Gen.	
4 60	(of which S. S.,* $3.29)...........	5 17
4 75	RIVERSIDE—*Grace S. S.* * : Gen...:...	60
	SHAMOKIN—*Trinity Church S. S.* * :	
5 00	Gen.	4 06
	WILLIAMSPORT—*All Saints'* : Gen.....	8 50
1 50	*Christ Church S. S.* * : Gen...........	165 84
11 77	*St. John's S. S.* * : Gen..............	10 00
7 62	YORK—*Holy Cross* : Junior Aux., Sp.	
	for "Little Mary" scholarship, St.	
	Mary's School, Sewanee, Tennessee..	4 00
58 23	MISCELLANEOUS—Wo. Aux., for Rev.	
	A. M. Sherman's work in Hankow,	
25 55	$50; St. Mary's School, Rosebud,	
11 00	South Dakota, $50; St. Augustine's	
	School, Raleigh, North Carolina,	
2 73	$50; Brazilian Missions, $50; Gen.,	
6 00	$50	250 00

Junior Aux., Sp. for "Little Mary"
scholarship, St. Mary's School,
Sewanee, Tennessee............... 13 00
"Anonymous," Gen............... 10 00

Indianapolis

Ap. $511.28 ; *Sp.* $0.25

ANDERSON—*Trinity Church* : Gen. (of
which S. S.,* $5)............... 16 25
EVANSVILLE—*Holy Innocents'* : Gen... 5 20
INDIANAPOLIS — *Christ Church* : Gen.
(of which S. S.,* $27.96)........ 77 96
*Grace S. S.** : Gen.............. 16 00
St. Alban's : Gen................ 1 15
St. David's : Gen............... 10 00
St. Paul's : Gen. (of which Wo. Aux.,
$10 ; S. S.,* $25.68)............ 208 44
JEFFERSONVILLE—*St. Paul's* : Gen.... 3 40
LAWRENCEBURG — *Trinity Church S.
S.** : Gen...................... 3 48
MUNCIE—*Grace S. S.** : Gen........ 25 00
NEW ALBANY—*St. Paul's* : Wo. Aux.,
Gen. 5 75
NEW HARMONY—*St. Stephen's* : Gen.,
$20 ; S. S.,* Dom., $5.88 ; Frn.,
$2.94 .... 28 82
RICHMOND—*St. Paul's* : Sp. for St.
Paul's College, Tokyo, 25 cts. ; S.
S.,* Gen., $16.62............... 16 87
TERRE HAUTE — *St. Stephen's* : Wo.
Aux., Gen...................... 17 78
VINCENNES—*St. James's* : Gen. (of
which S. S.,* $16).............. 26 00
MISCELLANEOUS—Mass meeting of S.
S. children, held in Indianapolis,
Gen. 3 62
Junior Aux., Gen. (of which from
Babies' Branch, $25)............ 45 81

Iowa

Ap. $379.35 ; *Sp.* $48.00

BOONE—*Grace* : Gen.............. 10 20
BURLINGTON — *Christ Church* : Wo.
Aux., Gen., $10 ; China, $5 ; Babies'
Branch, Gen., $2.63............. 17 63
CEDAR FALLS—*St. Luke's* : Wo. Aux.,
Gen............................ 1 00
CEDAR RAPIDS—*Grace* : Gen. (of which
Junior Aux., $1.25)............. 11 25
CHARITON—*St. Andrew's S. S.** : Gen.,
$11.38 ; Wo. Aux., salary of Miss
Babcock, Tokyo, $5 ; Gen., $5 ;
Junior Aux., Sp. for Deaconess
Drant's work among Chinese at San
Francisco, $5................... 26 38
CHARLES CITY—*Grace* : Wo. Aux., sal-
ary of Miss Babcock, Tokyo, $2 ;
Sp. for Bishop Rowe, Alaska, $2 ; S.
S.,* Gen., $5................... 9 00
COUNCIL BLUFFS—*St. Paul's* : Wo.
Aux., Sp. for Bishop Rowe, Alaska. 10 00
DAVENPORT — *Trinity Cathedral* : Wo.
Aux., salary of Miss Babcock, Tokyo,
$20 ; Gen., $20 ; China, $5 ; Sp. for
Bishop Rowe, Alaska, $5 ; Sp. for
Bishop Brooke, Oklahoma, $5...... 55 00
DES MOINES—*St. Mark's* : Wo. Aux.,
salary of Miss Babcock, Tokyo.... 5 00
St. Paul's : Wo. Aux., Gen. (of which
S. S.,* $3.36), $8.36 ; salary of Miss
Babcock, Tokyo, $22.35.......... 30 71
DUBUQUE—*St. John's* : Mrs. W. J.
Reeves, $1.50, Wo. Aux , $5, Gen... 6 50
EMMETTSBURG—*Trinity Church* : Wo.
Aux., salary of Miss Babcock, Tokyo,
$8 ; Gen., $8.85................ 16 85
FORT DODGE—*St. Mark's* : Wo. Aux.,
salary of Miss Babcock, Tokyo, $5 ;
Gen., $5....................... 10 00
HARLAN—*St. Paul's* : Babies' Branch,
Gen. 54
INDEPENDENCE — *St. James's* : Babies'
Branch, Gen.................... 2 63
IOWA CITY—*Trinity Church* : Gen..... 7 65

42 00
1 00
4 80
5 00
48 00
5 00
75 00

17 50
1 60

11 00
15 74
20 00
2 50
20 00

18 00

20 25
2 00

2 50

25 00

12 48
4 60
50 00
43 63

85 00
7 50
7 50
4 12
1 00
70 00
2 00
42 50

3 52

18 00

10 00

2 00

6 00

2 00

scholarship, St. John's University, Shanghai 2 00

Christ Church (Bay Ridge): Wo. Aux., "Charlotte Annan" scholarship, Hooker School, Mexico........... 1 00

Christ Church (Bedford Avenue): Wo. Aux., "Long Island" scholarship, St. John's University, Shanghai, $2; support of bed, St. James's Hospital, Anking, Hankow, $3; Idaho, $5; Sp. for Bishop Rowe's white work, Alaska, $5.................. 15 00

Christ Church (Clinton Street): Wo. Aux., "Long Island" scholarship, St. John's University, Shanghai, $2; "Mary E. Peck" scholarship, Church Training-school, Shanghai, $3; Oklahoma, $5; Idaho, $5; S. S.,* Gen., $52.11..................... 67 11

Church of the Good Shepherd: Wo. Aux., "Long Island" scholarship, St. John's University, Shanghai, $2; support of bed, St. James's Hospital, Anking, Hankow, $2; "Mary E. Peck" scholarship, Church Training-school, Shanghai, $2; "Charlotte Annan" scholarship, Hooker School, Mexico, $5; Junior Aux., Gen., $2.. 13 00

Grace (Eastern District): Wo. Aux., "Charlotte Annan" scholarship, Hooker School, Mexico, $1; Idaho, $7 .... 8 00

Grace (Heights): Wo. Aux., "Long Island" scholarship, St. John's University, Shanghai, $5; support of bed, St. James's Hospital, Anking, Hankow, $2; "Mary E. Peck" scholarship, Church Training-school, Shanghai, $6; "Charlotte Annan" scholarship, Hooker School, Mexico, $5; Sp. for St. Michael's School, Charlotte, North Carolina, $100; S. S.,* Gen. $61.89................. 179 89

Holy Cross: Gen..................... 35 00

Church of the Holy Spirit: Wo. Aux., support of bed, St. James's Hospital, Anking, Hankow, $2; Sp. for Bishop Rowe's white work, Alaska, $1 .... 3 00

Church of the Holy Trinity: Dom. and Frn., $1,001.88; Sp. for American Church Institute for Negroes, $200; Wo. Aux., "Long Island" scholarship, St. John's University, Shanghai, $8; Idaho, $5; Nevada, $7; Philippines, $5; Sp. for St. John's University Expansion Fund, Shanghai, $10; Sp. for Rev. W. S. Claiborne's work, Sewanee, Tennessee, $15; S. S.,* Gen., $39.12...... 1,291 00

Incarnation: Gen., $20; Wo. Aux., support of bed, St. James's Hospital, Anking, Hankow, $3; "Mary E. Peck" scholarship, Church Training-school, Shanghai, $2; "Charlotte Annan" scholarship, Hooker Memorial School, Mexico, $5; Sp. for Rev. W. S. Claiborne, Sewanee, Tennessee, $10....................... 40 00

Church of the Redeemer: Gen., $82.70; Wo. Aux., "Long Island" scholarship, St. John's University, Shanghai, $2; support of bed, St. James's Hospital, Anking, Hankow, $2; "Mary E. Peck" scholarship, Church Training-school, Shanghai, $2; "Charlotte Annan" scholarship, Hooker Memorial School, Mexico, $2; Idaho, $3.................. 93 70

Church of the Messiah: Gen. (of which S. S.,* $41).............. 118 50

St. Ann's: Dom., $2,560.81; Arizona, $30; Bishop Thomas's work, Wyoming, $70; Wo. Aux., "Long Island" scholarship, St. John's University, Shanghai, $2; support of bed, St.

James's Hospital, Anking, Hankow, $2; "Mary E. Peck" scholarship, Church Training-school, Shanghai, $2; "Charlotte Annan" scholarship, Hooker Memorial School, Mexico, $4; Oklahoma, $4; Junior Aux., Gen., $10...................... 2,704 81

St. Augustine's: Wo. Aux., Oklahoma.. 2 00

St. Bartholomew's: Wo. Aux., "Long Island" scholarship, St. John's University, Shanghai, $6; "Charlotte Annan" scholarship, Hooker Memorial School, Mexico, $1......... 7 00

St. Gabriel's S. S.*: Gen............ 14 05

St. George's: Sp. for use of Rev. Theodore Andrews, of Franklin, Asheville, $50; Wo. Aux., "Mary E. Peck" scholarship, Church Training-school, Shanghai, $4; "Charlotte Annan" scholarship, Hooker Memorial School, Mexico, $2; Brazil, $2 .... 58 00

St. James's: Wo. Aux., "Mary E. Peck" scholarship, Church Training-school, Shanghai, $6; "Charlotte Annan" scholarship, Hooker Memorial School, Mexico, $3; Nevada, $7 .... 16 00

St. Jude's: Wo. Aux., support of bed, St. James's Hospital, Anking, Hankow, $2; "Charlotte Annan" scholarship, Hooker Memorial School, Mexico, $2; Idaho, $2............... 6 00

St. Luke's: Dom., $128.39; Frn., $157.90; Wo. Aux., support of bed, St. James's Hospital, Anking, Hankow, $5; Sp. for Rev. W. S. Claiborne's work, Sewanee, Tennessee, $20 .... 311 29

St. Lydia's: Wo. Aux., Sp. for Bishop Rowe's white work, Alaska........ 1 00

St. Mark's (Adelphi Street): Dom. and Frn., $100; S. S.,* Gen., $8.87. 108 87

St. Mark's (Eastern Parkway): Wo. Aux., "Long Island" scholarship, St. John's University, Shanghai, $1; support of bed, St. James's Hospital, Anking, Hankow, $1; Oklahoma, $5; Sp. for Rev. W. J. Cuthbert's work, Kyoto, $1.50.................... 8 50

St. Martin's: Wo. Aux., Gen......... 7 27

St. Mary's: Wo. Aux., "Mary E. Peck" scholarship, Church Training-school, Shanghai, $2; "Charlotte Annan" scholarship, Hooker Memorial School, Mexico, $2; Oklahoma, $3.. 7 00

Church of St. Matthew: Gen., $73.28; Wo. Aux., "Mary E. Peck" scholarship, Church Training-school, Shanghai, $5; Idaho, $5; Junior Aux., Gen., $5........................ 88 28

St. Michael's: Wo. Aux., support of bed, St. James's Hospital, Anking, Hankow, $2; "Charlotte Annan" scholarship, Hooker Memorial School, Mexico, $2..................... 4 00

St. Paul's: Wo. Aux., Sp. for Bishop Rowe's white work, Alaska, $3; S. S.,* Gen., $50.................... 53 00

St. Paul's (Flatbush): Dom., $3; Frn., $3; Wo. Aux., "Mary E. Peck" scholarship, Church Training-school, Shanghai, $5; "Charlotte Annan" scholarship, Hooker Memorial School, Mexico, $5; Oklahoma, $6; Philippines, $18.38; Junior Aux., Gen., $25; S. S.,* Gen., $2.20.................... 67 58

St. Philip's: Wo. Aux., Sp. for Bishop Rowe's white work, Alaska........ 1 00

St. Philip's S. S.* (Dyker Heights): Dom. and Frn................... 18 83

St. Stephen's: Wo. Aux., "Mary E. Peck" scholarship, Church Training-school, Shanghai, $3; Philippines, $3 .... 6 00

Transfiguration: Mrs. S. E. Coxe, Sp. for Bishop Brown's Building Fund, Arkansas, $1; S. S.,* Sp. for Bishop Brooke, Oklahoma, at his discretion, $10; Sp. for educational work under Bishop Woodcock, Kentucky, $10; Sp. at discretion of Bishop Aves, Mexico, $10................ "I. H. N.," Sp. for Rev. R. C. Wilson's work in Zangzok, Shanghai....

BROOKLYN MANOR—St. Matthew's: Wo. Aux., Sp. for Bishop Rowe's white work, Alaska....................

COLLEGE POINT—St. Paul's: Gen.....

DOUGLASTON—Zion S. S.*: Gen......

ELMHURST—St. James's: Wo. Aux., "Long Island" scholarship, St. John's University, Shanghai, $2; "Charlotte Annan" scholarship, Hooker Memorial School, Mexico, $5; Idaho, $8..................

FARMINGDALE—St. Thomas's S. S.*: Gen.

FAR ROCKAWAY—St. John's: Wo. Aux., "Charlotte Annan" scholarship, Hooker Memorial School, Mexico, $1; Idaho, $8.................

FLUSHING—St. George's: Wo. Aux., "Long Island" scholarship, St. John's University, Shanghai, $2; support of bed, St. James's Hospital, Anking, Hankow, $2; "Mary E. Peck" scholarship, Church Training-school, Shanghai, $2; "Charlotte Annan" scholarship, Hooker Memorial School, Mexico, $2; Sp. for Bishop Rowe's white work, Alaska, $1; Sp. for Rev. W. S. Claiborne's work, Sewanee, Tennessee, $4...................

GARDEN CITY—Incarnation Cathedral: "Dean Cox Memorial" scholarship, Boone University, Wuchang, Hankow, $50; Wo. Aux., St. James's Hospital, Anking, Hankow, $5; "Charlotte Annan" scholarship, Hooker Memorial School, Mexico, $10; Nevada, $10...........

GLEN COVE—St. Paul's: Wo. Aux., "Long Island" scholarship, St. John's University, Shanghai, $2; S. S.,* Gen., $41.50....................

GREAT NECK—All Saints': Dom. $200; Indian, $50; Colored, $50; Frn., $50; Gen., $54.61; Sp. for St. Paul's College, Tokyo, $23; Wo. Aux., Nevada, $15; S. S., work in South Dakota, $8.78; Sp. for Bishop Gray, Southern Florida, $7.91; Sp. for Bishop Aves, Mexico, $4.68; Sp. for Bishop Graves, Kearney, $9.07; Sp. for Bishop Wells, Spokane, Utah, $5.65; Sp. for Bishop Spalding, Utah, $8.58; Sp. for Bishop Morrison, Duluth, $4.33; Sp. for Bishop Funsten, Idaho, $8.07; Sp. for Bishop Brooke, Oklahoma, $3.96; Sp. for Bishop Rowe, Alaska, $4.99; Sp. for Bishop Graves, Shanghai, $4.08; Sp. for Bishop Moreland, Sacramento, $2.79; Sp. for Bishop Keator, Olympia, $4.02; Sp. for Bishop Van Buren, Porto Rico, $7.34......

GREAT RIVER—Emmanuel Church: Wo. Aux., Idaho....................

GREENPORT—Holy Trinity Church S. S.*: Gen.......................

HEMPSTEAD—St. George's: Wo. Aux, support of bed, St. James's Hospital, Anking, Hankow, $2; Oklahoma, $2; S. S.,* Gen., $72.52...............

HUNTINGTON—St. John's: Wo. Aux., "Long Island" scholarship, St. John's University, Shanghai.............

ISLIP—St. Mark's: Wo. Aux., support of bed, St. James's Hospital, Anking, Hankow, $3; Philippines, $2......

OCEANSIDE—*Grace*: Dom. and Frn.... 13 00
ONTARIO—*Christ Church S. S.**: Sp.
for Rev. Mr. Hughson, St. Andrew's,

43 50   Sewanee, Tennessee............. 11 00
PASADENA—*All Saints' S. S.**: Gen.. 142 46
5 27   POMONA—*St. Paul's*: Dom. and Frn.,
$89.32; S. S.,* Gen., $67.10; S. S.,
Sp. for Bishop Horner, Asheville,
1 00 $5; Sp. for St. Paul's College Fund,
Tokyo, $5....................... 166 42
REDLANDS—*Trinity Church*: Dom. and
4 00   Frn. 31 55
RIVERSIDE—*All Saints' S. S.**: Gen... 32 99
SAN BERNARDINO—*St. John's S. S.**:
28 44   Gen. 13 00
SAN DIEGO—*St. James's S. S.**: Gen.. 7 00
SAN PEDRO—*St. Peter's S. S.**: Gen.. 50
1 00   SANTA ANA—*Church of the Messiah*:
$71, S. S.,* $19.53, Gen......... 19 53
SAWTELLE—*St. John's*: Dom. and
10 00   Frn. 7 16
SIERRA MADRE—*Ascension*: Dom. and
Frn. 20 00
SOUTH PASADENA—*St. James's*: $31.66,
4 00   S. S.,* $38, Gen.............. 69 66
5 00   TERMINAL — *St. Michael and All
Angels'*: Colored............... 50
VENTURA—*St. Paul's*: Dom. and Frn.. 7 05
WHITTIER—*St. Matthias's*: Dom. and
3 00   Frn. 12 00
MISCELLANEOUS — Through Bishop
Johnson, Dom. and Frn.......... 100 00
Wo. Aux., missions in China, $15;
5 00   "Bishop Johnson" scholarship, St.
Mary's Hall, Shanghai, $50; Babies'
6 80   Branch, Alaska, $15; St. Luke's
75 00   Hospital, Shanghai, $10; St. Mary's
Hall, Shanghai, $10; South Da-
kota, $10; North Dakota, $10;
1 00   Oklahoma, $10; Orphanage, Cape
Palmas, $10; Gaylord Hart Mitchell
Memorial Kindergarten, Tokyo, $15;
Sp. for St. John's Orphanage,
Kyoto, $10; Sp. for "Little Help-
ers'" cot, St. Agnes's Hospital, Ral-
40 00   eigh, North Carolina, $10; Sp. for
Bishop Spalding, White Rocks Emergency Fund, Utah, $10........... 185 00

Louisiana

Ap. $144.47; *Sp.* $5.00

25 45
8 70   LAKE CHARLES—*Church of the Good
Shepherd S. S.**: Gen............. 19 22
NEW ORLEANS—*Annunciation*: Gen.,
43 42 $50; Wo. Aux., Mrs. Evans's salary,
Alaska, 60 cts.; Miss Suthon's sal-
33 57   ary, Kyoto, 45 cts.............. 51 05
Christ Church: Gen., $43.80; Wo.
10 00   Aux., Miss Suthon's salary, Kyoto,
36 00   40 cts......................... 44 20
St. Anna's: Wo. Aux., Miss Suthon's
salary, Kyoto.................... 1 00
5 00   *St. George's*: Wo. Aux., Mrs. Evans's
salary, Alaska, 25 cts.; Miss
1 00   Suthon's salary, Kyoto, 25 cts.;
Junior Aux., Sp. for Rev. A. DeR.
19 00   Meares, Biltmore, Asheville, for the
building of a church at Black Moun-
64 50   tain, Asheville, $5.............. 5 50
2 44   *St. Luke's S. S.**: Gen............. 7 50
59 42   *St. Paul's*: Wo. Aux., Mrs. Evans's
3 90   salary, Alaska, $4; Miss Suthon's
14 30   salary, Kyoto, $7................ 11 00
51 44   *Trinity Church*: Wo. Aux., Mrs.
500 00   Evans's salary, Alaska, $1; Miss
3 64   Suthon's salary, Kyoto, $5........ 6 00
27 00   Miss Wilson, Gen................ 2 00
SLAUGHTER—Mrs. C. S. Mills, Gen... 2 00

Maine

Ap. $262.12

ASHLAND—*Emmanuel Church*: Gen... 15 00
222 91   AUBURN—*St. Michael's*: $5, S. S.,* $4,
9 73   Gen. 9 00
2 00   BANGOR—*St. John's S. S.**: Gen..... 24 92

CARIBOU—*St. Luke's*: Gen.......... 5 00
DEXTER—*Church of the Messiah S. S.*: Gen............... 2 51
FORT FAIRFIELD—*St. Paul's S. S.*: Gen....................... 1 00
HALLOWELL—*St. Matthew's*: Gen.... 8 00
LEWISTON—*Trinity Church S. S.*: Gen....................... 25 00
MILLINOCKET—*St. Andrew's S. S.*: Gen....................... 8 14
NEWCASTLE—*St. Andrew's S. S.*: Gen. 1 00
PRESQUE ISLE—*St. John's*: Frn...... 9 00
ROCKLAND—*St. Peter's S. S.*: Dom., $3.63; Frn., $3.63.............. 7 26
RUMFORD—*St. Barnabas's S. S.*: Gen. 2 40
SANFORD—*St. George's*: $10, S. S.,* $12.50, Gen.................. 22 50
WATERVILLE—*St. Mark's S. S.*: Gen.. 16 39
MISCELLANEOUS—Wo. Aux., St. John's College, Shanghai, $20; Gen., $80.. 100 00
Junior Aux., Dom................ 10 00

Marquette
Ap. $59.98

ESCANABA—*St. Stephen's*: Dom..... 9 10
ISHPEMING—*Grace*: Gen.......... 44 02
MANISTIQUE—*St. Alban's*: Gen...... 4 36
NORWAY—*St. Mary's*: Gen.......... 2 50

Maryland
Ap. $2,285.54; *Sp.* $246.60

ALLEGHENY CO. — *Emmanuel Church S. S.** (Cumberland): Gen......... 56 96
ANNE ARUNDEL CO.—*St. Anne's* (Annapolis): Indian, $10; Gen., $50; Wo. Aux., Gen., $40........... 100 00
BALTIMORE—*Advent S. S.*: Gen.... 80 00
Ascension: "Thank-offering," Sp. for St. Paul's College Fund, Tokyo, $6; S. S.,* Gen., $325.17; Wo. Aux., Gen., $40; Sp. for "Baltimore" scholarship, Tortella Hall, Alaska, $20 .... 391 17
Christ Church: Gen., $110; Frn., $5; Girls' Friendly Society, Sp. for Rev. Mr. Mayo's work, Charlottesville, Virginia, $5.10.............. 120 10
*Christ Church Chapel S. S.**: Gen.... 40 00
Emmanuel Church: Chinese S. S.,* support of a Bible-reader in China, $50; Wo. Aux., Sp. for St. Mary's-on-the-Mountain, Sewanee, Tennessee, $15............... 65 00
Grace: Wo. Aux., Gen., $19.50; Sp. for Boone Library, Wuchang, Hankow, $5 .... 24 50
Memorial: Gen., $150; Wo. Aux., Gen., $5; Junior Aux., "William M. Dame" scholarship, St. Mary's School, South Dakota, $60; Sp. for Bishop Rowe, Alaska, $5.......... 220 00
Church of the Messiah: Dom. and Frn., $100; Wo. Aux., Frn., $29... 129 00
Mount Calvary: Wo. Aux., Gen...... 10 00
Church of Our Saviour: Gen........ 8 08
St. Andrew's: Wo. Aux., Indian work, Idaho 5 00
St. Barnabas's and St. George's: Dom. and Frn., $114; Wo. Aux., Sp. for Tsu Building Fund, Kyoto, $1; memorial to Mrs. Frank West, Sp. at Bishop Rowe's discretion, $30... 145 00
St. David's (Roland Park): Wo. Aux., Sp. for Archdeacon Wentworth, Lexington 1 00
St. James's: Junior Aux., Sp. for Bishop Rowe, Alaska................ 2 00
St. Luke's: Wo. Aux., Gen.......... 20 00
St. Mary's (Roland Avenue): Wo. Aux., Gen.................. 6 70
St. Michael and All Angels: Wo. Aux., Gen........................... 25 00
St. Paul's: Wo. Aux., $30, S. S.,* $110, Gen.................. 140 00
St. Paul's Chapel and Guild House:

"Mothers' Union" scholarship, St Hilda's School, Wuchang, Hankow,.
St. Peter's: Junior Aux., Sp. for Bish op Rowe, Alaska...............
"M. L. E. K." Gen...............
"H. W. A.," Sp. for Rev. Mr. Ancell Shanghai ....
BALTIMORE CO.—*Epiphany* (Govans) Wo. Aux., $15, S. S.,* $71, Gen...
Church of the Holy Comforter S. S. (Lutherville): Rev. J. G. Meem
Pelotas, Brazil...............
*Incarnation S. S.** (St. Helena): Gen
*St. John's S. S.** (Mount Washington) Gen. ....
St. Mark's-on-the-Hill (Pikesville) Wo. Aux., Sp. for mission at Birc Coolee, Minnesota............
St. Timothy's (Catonsville): Frn....
Trinity Church (Towson): Wo. Aux Frn. ....
Mrs. John Duer (Roslyn), Sp. fo St. Mary's Orphanage, Shanghai...
CALVERT CO. — *Middleham Chape* (Solomons): Gen.............
*Hungerford Creek S. S.** (Solomons) Gen. ....
FREDERICK CO.—*All Saints'* (Fred erick): Wo. Aux., Indian, $3.75 Mexico, $5; Frn., $5.25.....
FREDERICK AND CARROLL CO'S.—*S Paul's, Linganore Parish* (M Airy): Gen..................
HARFORD CO.—*Emmanuel Church S.** (Bel Air): Gen...........
Grace (Hickory): $2, S. S.,* $2. Ge
St. Mary's (Emmorton): Gen.......
*St. David's S. S.** (Creswell): Gen..
HOWARD CO.—*Grace* (Elkridge): Frn
*Mount Calvary S. S.** (Highland) Gen. ....
St. John's (Ellicott City): Gen.....
St. John's Mission (Ellicott City) Gen. ....
WASHINGTON CO.—*St. John's* (Hager town): Wo. Aux., Sp. for St. Ma garet's School, Tokyo, $20; Sp. f Rev. George P. Mayo's work, Indu trial School, Blue Ridge Mountain Virginia, $20.50; S. S.,* "Franc Howell Kennedy" scholarship, Hilda's School, Wuchang, Hanko $50; Gen., $123.14; Sp. for fi scholarships in schools, Blue Rid Mountains, West Virginia, $25..
MISCELLANEOUS—Junior Aux., Indi teacher's salary.............
Babies' Branch, Akita Kindergart Tokyo, $13; Sp. for Miss Ridgel Mission, Cape Mount, Africa, $2 Sp. for school at Anvik, Alaska, $2 Sp. for children's ward, St. Agne Hospital, Raleigh, North Caroli $15 ....

Massachusetts
Ap. $9,413.64; *Sp.* $708.2

AMESBURY—*St. James's S. S.*: Ge
ANDOVER—*Christ Church*: Junior Au Indian Missions, South Dakota, $1 Gen., $22; S. S.,* "Andover" sch arship, Boone University, Wucha Hankow, $23.66................
ARLINGTON—*St. John's*: Wo. Aux., ary of missionary, Logan, Ut $2.50; Hooker School, Mexico, $ S. S.,* Gen., $26.14.........
ATTLEBORO—*All Saints' S. S.*: Gen
AYER—*St. Andrew's S. S.*: Gen...
St. Andrew's (Forge Village): S. S
Gen. ....
BELMONT—*All Saints' S. S.*: Gen..
BEVERLY—*St. Peter's S. S.*: (of whi * $34.10) Gen................
BEVERLY FARMS—*St. John's S. S* (of which * $9) Gen...........

work, Alaska, $150; Wo. Aux., salary of Rev. Nathan Matthews, Africa, $5; S. S.,* Gen., $46.97.... 478 72
Trinity Church: Wo. Aux., salary of missionary, Logan, Utah, $10.15; Western Colorado, $86; Nevada, $86; St. Luke's Hospital, Tokyo, $100; salary of Rev. N. Matthews, West Africa, $50; Soochow, Shanghai, $10; Sp. for Rev. A. A. Gilman, Hankow (of which $25 for personal use), $30; Sp. for Rev. T. S. Tyng, insurance dues, $3.50; salary of Miss Woodruff, Africa, $5; "A Member," "Cora Lyman" scholarship, St. Mary's School, South Dakota, $60; "A Member," "Henry Herbert Smythe" scholarship, St. Mary's School, South Dakota, $60; Junior Aux., Gen. (of which "A Member," $20), $91.62; Sp. for Bishop Thomas, Wyoming, $10 .... 602 27
United Offering, Central Branch, S. S. Union in Trinity Church, May 1st, 1910, Colored mission in Africa. 54 36
(Dorchester)—Rev. George L. Paine, Gen. 500 00
BEACHMONT—*St. Paul's:* Gen........ 9 50
BRAINTREE—*Emmanuel Church:* Junior Aux., China, $2; S. S.,* Gen., $9... 11 00
BRIDGEWATER—*Trinity Church S. S.*:* Gen. 15 50
BROCKTON—*St. Paul's:* Gen........ 35 00
BROOKLINE—*All Saints':* Gen., $723.88; Wo. Aux., St. Luke's Hospital, Tokyo, $15; Soochow, Shanghai, $10; salary of Mrs. McCalla, Africa, $1; salary of Miss Woodruff, Africa, $8; Sp. for Rev. A. A. Gilman, Hankow, $2; Sp. for insurance, Rev. T. S. Tyng, Kyoto, 75 cts.; Sp. for St. Luke's Hospital, Ponce, Porto Rico, $10; Sp. for Christ School, Arden, Asheville, $10; Junior Aux., Alaska, $5; Liberia, Africa, $5; Gen., $30; S. S.,* Gen., $75................. 895 63
Church of Our Saviour: Wo. Aux., Sp. for Rev. R. H. McGinnis, Kyoto, $5; Junior Aux., "A Member," Sp. for Rev. W. S. Claiborne's work, Sewanee, Tennessee, $1............ 6 00
St. Paul's: Gen. (of which Junior Aux., $11, S. S.,* $105.34)........ 116 34
CAMBRIDGE—*Ascension* (East): Gen.. 25 00
Christ Church: Dom., $16; Wo. Aux., salary of missionary, Logan, Utah, $8.35; Sp. for Rev. R. C. Wilson, Zangzok, Shanghai, $5; S. S.,* Gen., $67.51 .... 96 86
Episcopal Theological School: St. John's Society, Sp. for Rev. Dudley Tyng for purchase of books, Boone College, Wuchang, Hankow, $50; Sp. for Rev. Remsen Brinckerhoff Ogilby, Philippine Islands, $36.34... 86 34
St. James's: Gen., $19.90; Wo. Aux., salary of missionary, Logan, Utah, $10; Western Colorado, $5; Nevada, $5; Hooker Memorial School, Mexico, $5; San Gabriel, Brazil, $5; Isle of Pines, Cuba, $5; Haiti, $5.. 59 90
St. John's: Wo. Aux., salary of Miss Woodruff, Africa, $30; "Sarah F. Hoyt" scholarship, St. Mary's Hall, Shanghai, $50; S. S.,* Gen., $170 .... 250 00
St. Peter's S. S.:* Gen.......... 39 74
St. Philip's: Junior Aux., Gen., $5; S. S.,* Gen., $19.48............ 24 48
CANTON—*Trinity Church S. S.*:* Gen.. 18 90
CHELMSFORD—*All Saints' S. S.*:* Gen. 3 12
CHELSEA—*St. Luke's:* Wo. Aux., "A Member," salary of Miss Woodruff, Africa, $2; S. S.,* Gen., $13.02.... 15 02
COHASSET—*St. Stephen's S. S.*:* Gen.. 47 63

Left column figures:
142 75
147 15
48 27
390 71
49 39
50 19
144 22
72 51
36 70
31 39
51 14
20 37
15 00
100 00
50 00
62 82
1 00
101 26
28 23
128 64
155 00
35 44
32 20
78 88
38 00

CONCORD — *Trinity Church*: Junior
Aux., Gen., $8; S. S.,* Gen., $24...   32 00
DANVERS—*Calvary*: Wo. Aux., Sp. for
Rev. W. J. Cuthbert, Kyoto, $8.65;
S. S.,* Gen., $40..............   48 65
DEDHAM—*Church of the Good Shep-
herd*: Wo. Aux., Sp. for Trade
School, Cape Mount, Africa, $2; S.
S.,* Gen., $61.09..............   63 09
*St. Paul's S. S.**: Gen..............   77 68
DODGEVILLE—*St. Andrew's S. S.**:
Gen. 15 00
DUXBURY—*St. John's S. S.**: Gen.....   2 78
EVERETT—*Grace*: Sp. for St. Paul's
College, Tokyo, $1; S. S.,* Gen.,
$22.30 ....   23 30
FALL RIVER—*Ascension*: Wo. Aux.,
salary of missionary, Logan, Utah,
$15; salary of Miss McCalla, Africa,
$15; S. S.,* Dom., $35; "Ascension
S. S." scholarship, Cape Palmas Or-
phan Asylum, Africa, $50.........   115 00
*St. James's S. S.**: Gen............   68 74
St. John's: Junior Aux., Gen........   15 00
*St. Stephen's S. S.**: Gen., $9.40; Sp.
for Bishop Roots, Hankow, China, $10   19 40
FALMOUTH—*Church of the Messiah S.
S.**: Gen......................   23 00
St. Barnabas's: Gen..............   3 20
FOXBOROUGH—*St. Mark's S. S.**: Gen.   7 00
FRAMINGHAM—*St. Andrew's S. S.**
(South): Gen...................   14 38
*St. John's S. S.**: Gen.............   5 00
FRANKLIN—*St. John's*: Gen.........   10 00
GLOUCESTER—*St. John's S. S.**: Gen.   50 00
GROTON—*St. Andrew's S. S.** (Shir-
ley): Gen......................   10 00
*Groton School, St. John's Chapel S.
S.**: Gen......................   225 77
HANOVER—*St. Andrew's S. S.**: Gen..   75 04
HAVERHILL—*St. John the Evangelist's
S. S.**: Gen...................   9 40
Trinity Church: Wo. Aux., salary of
missionary, Logan, Utah.........   1 00
HINGHAM—*St. John's*: Wo. Aux., sal-
ary of missionary, Logan, Utah, $1;
S. S.,* Gen., $82.89............   83 89
HOPKINTON—*St. Paul's S. S.**: Gen..   5 86
HUDSON—*St. Luke's*: Junior Aux.,
Dom., $2; S. S.,* Gen., $7.50......   9 50
HYDE PARK—*Christ Church S. S.**:
Gen. 30 00
IPSWICH—*Ascension S. S.* (of which
*$71), Gen....................   73 40
LAWRENCE—*Grace S. S.**: Gen.......   81 42
*St. John's S. S.**: Gen.............   5 00
LINCOLN—*St. Anne's S. S.**: Gen....   9 77
LOWELL—*St. Anne's S. S.**: "St.
Anne's" scholarship, St. Margaret's
School, Tokyo, $40; Gen., $15......   55 00
LYNN—*Incarnation*: Frn...........   25 00
St. Stephen's: Gen., $42.44; Wo. Aux.,
salary of missionary, Logan, Utah,
$10; Hooker Memorial School, Mex-
ico, $10; Missionary Club, Sp. for
Rev. Mr. Gilman, Changsha, Han-
kow, $5; S. S.,* Gen., $140.......   207 44
MALDEN—*St. Luke's S. S.** (Linden):
Gen. 37 44
St. Paul's: For Bishop Roots's work,
Hankow, $4.14; S. S.,* Gen., $40...   44 14
MARBLEHEAD—*St. Michael's*: Wo. Aux.,
salary of missionary, Logan, Utah..   5 00
MARLBOROUGH—*Holy Trinity Church*:
Gen., $10; "Candidates G. F. S.,"
China, $1; S. S.,* Gen., $30......   41 00
MEDFORD—*Grace S. S.**: Gen........   34 02
MELROSE — *Trinity Church*: Junior
Aux., Gen.....................   3 00
MIDDLEBOROUGH — *Church of Our
Saviour*: Bishop Graves's work in
Shanghai, connected with G. C.
Thomas Memorial...............   9 17
MILLIS—*St. Paul's*: Gen...........   2 00
MILTON — *Church of Our Saviour*
(East): Gen., $4.62; S. S.,* Gen.,
$34.44 ....   39 06

250 00	St. *Matthias's*; Wo. Aux., Sp. for Holy Trinity Orphanage, Tokyo......... 10 00
	St. *Paul's*: Dom. and Frn., $272.06; S. S.,* Gen., $110............... 382 06
	St. *Peter's* S. S.*: Gen............. 25 67
15 54	St. *Philip's*: Wo. Aux., Gen......... 2 00
	St. *Stephen's*: Wo. Aux., salary of
33 00	Miss Bull, Kyoto, $1; F. E. Adams
21 05	Memorial, Sp. for Hospital of the
5 00	Good Shepherd, Fort Defiance, Arizona, $1......................... 2 00
64 83	Trinity *Church*: Wo. Aux., Sp. for Rev.
53 74	H. C. Parke, Asheville (of which
25 00	Mrs. Mercier, $5, Mrs. Baker, $5). 10 00
	DEXTER—St. *James's*: Gen.......... 6 05
18 66	DRYDEN—St. *John's*: Gen....... 1 00
	FLINT—St. *Paul's*: Gen., $16; Wo. Aux., salary of Miss Bull, Kyoto, $10; "Harris Memorial" scholarship, St. John's University, Shanghai, $10; Sp. for Mrs. Littell, Hankow, $5; Sp. for Foreign Insurance Fund, $5...................... 46 00
	GREENFIELD—St. *Paul's*: Gen........ 3 92
	GROSSE ILE—St. *James's*: Wo. Aux.,
282 00	Alaska, $5; St. Augustine's School, Raleigh, North Carolina, $5....... 10 00
	HENRIETTA—Christ *Church*: Wo. Aux.,
36 07	Alaska, $2; salary of Miss Bull, Kyoto, $1; Africa, $1; Sp. for Porto Rico, $2.................. 6 00
	LANSING—St. *Paul's*: Wo. Aux., Alaska, $3; St. Augustine's School, Raleigh, North Carolina, $3; St. Paul's School, Lawrenceville, Southern Virginia, $3; Gen., $2; Sp. for Dr. Myers, Shanghai, $2............. 13 00
	MACKINAC ISLAND—Trinity *Church*:
53 00	Wo. Aux., Alaska, $2; salary of
2 25	Miss Bull, Kyoto, $2............. 4 00
	MT. CLEMENS—Grace: Wo. Aux., Gen. 5 00
5 00	OWASSO—Christ *Church*: Wo. Aux.,
1 00	Alaska, $5; Gen. (of which "Personal," $5), $10; Sp. for Mrs. Littell, Hankow, $5; "A Friend," sal-
1 00	ary of Miss Bull, Kyoto, $2; "Harris Memorial" scholarship, St. John's University, Shanghai, $2; Sp. for Foreign Insurance Fund, $1; S. S.,* Gen., $5.............. 30 00
	PORT HURON—Grace: Gen., $22.63;
43 00	Wo. Aux., Alaska, $5; Gen., $5; S. S.,* Gen., $33.93................. 66 56
	St. *Paul's*: Wo. Aux., Sp. for Mrs. Littell, Hankow.................. 2 00
	ROCHESTER—St. *Philip's* S. S.*: Gen.. 7 53
	SAGINAW—St. *John's*: Wo. Aux., Sp. for Mrs. Littell, Hankow, $1; Sp. for
16 00	Foreign Insurance Fund, $1; S. S.,* Gen., $75...................... 77 00
	St. *Paul's*: Dom. and Frn........... 35 00
26 57	ST. JOHNS—St. *John's*: Wo. Aux., $10, S. S.,* $15.94, Gen............. 25 94
	WEST BRANCH—Trinity *Church*: Gen.. 23 00
	MISCELLANEOUS—Branch Wo. Aux.,
24 00	"J. H. Johnson" scholarship, St. An-
2 00	drew's School, Mexico (of which collection of Quiet Morning, $18.10, St. Matthew's Day, $5.40), $23.50; Sp.
	for Bishop Rowe, Alaska, $42.10;
8 00	"A Friend," "Harris Memorial"
16 50	scholarship, St. John's University, Shanghai, $3; salary of Miss Bull,
47 31	Kyoto (of which "A Friend," $2, collection, St. Matthew's Day, 13 cts.), $2.13.................... 70 73

Michigan City

Ap. $49.02; Sp. $4.50

	GARRETT—Emmanuel *Church*: Gen. (of
40 55	which S. S.,* $2.80).............. 5 00
	HOWE—St. *Mark's* S. S.*: Gen....... 2 76
	KENDALLVILLE—Trinity *Church*: Gen.. 3 20
	LOGANSPORT—Trinity *Church* S. S.*:
10 50	Gen. 13 50

MARION—*Gethsemane*: Wo. Aux., Gen. 5 00
MICHIGAN CITY—*Trinity Church*: Gen.
of which Junior Aux., $3) 14 56
MISHAWAKA—*St. Paul's*: Gen........ 5 00
MISCELLANEOUS—Branch Wo. Aux.,
Sp. for Deaconess' Routledge's work,
Manila, Philippine Islands 4 50

Milwaukee

Ap. $504.08 ; *Sp.* $100.60

ASHIPPUN—*St. Paul's* : Gen.......... 5 00
BARABOO—*Trinity Church S. S.**: Gen. 26 30
COLUMBUS—*St. Paul's*: Gen........ 5 50
CORLISS—*St. Paul's S. S.** : Dom.... 6 54
EVANSVILLE—*St. John's S. S.** : Gen.. 7 50
GENOA JUNCTION—*Holy Cross Mission*:
Sp. for Rev. R. E. Wood, Wuchang.
Hankow 1 00
HARTLAND—*Grace*: Gen.............. 8 16
HAYWARD—*Ascension S. S.**: Gen.... 4 00
KILBOURNE—*St. Paul's S. S.**: Frn... 6 00
LA CROSSE—*Christ Church S. S.**: For
Dr. MacWillie's work, Hankow, $50;
Gen., $20.50 .... 70 50
*St. Peter's S. S.** (North): Gen...... 5 00
MADISON—*Grace S. S.**: Gen........ 33 00
MANSTON—*St. John's S. S.**: Gen.... 6 00
MAZOMANIE—*St. Luke's*: Gen. (of
which S. S.,* $3.47) 6 47
MENOMONIE—*Grace S. S.**: Gen...... 9 30
MILWAUKEE — *All Saints' Cathedral*:
Gen. (of which S. S.,* $95.61).... 197 11
St. Andrew's: Gen.................. 6 85
St. Mark's (South): Gen............ 5 00
St. Paul's: Gen, (of which Junior Aux.,
$20), $52.40; Junior Aux., Sp. for
Rev. Mr. Littell's work, Hankow,
$50 .... 102 40
St. Stephen's: Gen................. 10 75
PLATTSVILLE—*Trinity Church*: Gen... 6 40
PORTAGE—*St. John's S. S.**: Frn.... 21 30
TOMAH—*St. Mary's S. S.**: Gen...... 5 00

Minnesota

Ap. $1,346.68 ; *Sp.* $137.71

APPLETON—*Gethsemane*: Gen........ 20 00
CHATFIELD—*St. Matthew's S. S.**:
Frn., children's work, China, $1.03;
Gen., $5.02 .... 6 05
EXCELSIOR—*Trinity Chapel*: Gen..... 6 00
FARIBAULT—*St. Mary's Hall*: Gen.,
$50; through Junior Aux., "Cornelia
Whipple" scholarship, St. Mary's
Hall, Shanghai, $50; Darlington
Missionary Society, Sp. for Japanese
orphanage, Mr. Ishii, Tokyo, $25;
S. S.,* Sp for Bishop Van Buren,
Porto Rico, $100 .... 225 00
GOOSE CREEK—*Mission*: Sp. for St.
Paul's College, Tokyo............. 1 21
HASTINGS—*St. Luke's S. S.**: Gen... 25 36
MANKATO—*St. John's*: $12, S. S.,* $26,
Gen. 38 00
MINNEAPOLIS—*All Saints' S. S.**: Gen. 123 39
*Grace S. S.**: Gen................. 9 65
*St. John the Baptist's S. S.**: Salary
of Bishop Van Buren, Porto Rico,
$62.49; Gen., $25.01.............. 87 50
*St. Paul's S. S.**: Gen............. 428 99
*St. Thomas's S. S.**: Gen........... 4 72
PIPESTONE—*St. Paul's*: Gen......... 10 00
RUSH CITY—*Grace*: Sp. for St. Paul's
College, Tokyo.................... 1 50
ST. JAMES—*Calvary Mission*: $5.70,
S. S.,* $7.58, Gen................. 13 28
ST. PAUL—*Christ Church*: Gen....... 5 50
*Church of the Good Shepherd S. S.**:
Gen. 6 62
*Epiphany S. S.**: Sp. for Bishop Van
Buren Fund, Porto Rico........... 1 00
*Lilydale Mission S. S.**: Gen....... 11 32
*Resurrection Chapel S. S.**: Gen.... 20
*St. John the Evangelist's S. S.**: Gen. 370 00
*St. Matthew's S. S.** (St. Anthony
Park): Gen........................ 17 00

*St. Paul's S. S.**: Gen.............
*St. Philip's S. S.**: Gen.. ..●.......
SLAYTON—*St. Barnabas's*: Gen.......
STILLWATER—*Ascension S. S.**: Gen..
MISCELLANEOUS—Wo. Aux., part of
offering at Semi-Annual Meeting,
Sp. for Deaconess Routledge, Phil-
ippines ....

Mississippi

Ap. $249.64

BOVINA—*St. Alban's*: Dom., $10; Gen.,
$6.50 ; Wo. Aux., Gen., $2.50......
GREENVILLE—*St. James's*: Wo. Aux.,
Gen. ....
HOLLANDALE—*St. Thomas's*: Wo. Aux.,
Gen. ....
HOLLY SPRINGS—*Christ Church*: Wo.
Aux., Gen. ....
MAYERSVILLE—*Holy Cross*: Gen......
MERIDIAN—*St. Paul's*: Wo. Aux., $22,
S. S.,* $36.46, Gen................
NATCHEZ—*Trinity Church*: Wo. Aux.,
Gen., $15 ; S. S.,* Frn., $31.98....
OXFORD—*St. Peter's S. S.**: Gen.....
RIPLEY—Wo. Aux., Mr. J. M. Cole,
Gen. ....
VICKSBURG—*Christ Church S. S.**:
Gen. ....
WATER VALLEY—*Nativity*: Gen.......
YAZOO CITY—*Trinity Church*: Wo.
Aux., Gen. ....
MISCELLANEOUS—Wo. Aux., Gen......

Missouri

Ap. $1,517.89 ; *Sp.* $80.00

CANTON—*St. Peter's*: Gen...........
CAPE GIRARDEAU—*Christ Church S.
S.**: Gen. ....
COLUMBIA—*Calvary*: Dom., $40; Frn.,
$5 ....
DE SOTO—*Trinity Church*: Gen......
FERGUSON—*St. Stephen's*: Gen., $36;
Mrs. January, Junior Aux., Sp. for
scholarship, Morganton, Asheville,
$10 ....
HANNIBAL—*Trinity Church*: Gen.....
JACKSON—*Church of the Redeemer S.
S.**: Gen. ....
JEFFERSON—*Grace*: Gen............
KIRKSVILLE—*Trinity Church S. S.**:
Gen. ....
KIRKWOOD—*Grace*: Dom., $25 ; Frn.,
$125; Sp. for Rev. H. Lewis's
Chapel Building Fund, Las Crucis,
New Mexico, $10..................
MACON—*St. James's S. S.**: Gen.....
MEXICO—*St. Paul's S. S.**: Gen.....
OVERLAND PARK—*St. Paul's S. S.**:
Gen. ....
PALMYRA—*St. Paul's S. S.**: Gen....
POPLAR BLUFF—*Holy Cross*: Gen....
PRAIRIEVILLE—*St. John's*: Gen......
ST. LOUIS—*Christ Church Cathedral
S. S.**: Gen. ....
*Epiphany S. S.**: Gen.............
Holy Innocents': Gen.............
*St. Alban's S. S.**: Gen..........
*St. Andrew's S. S.**: Gen.........
*St. George's S. S.**: Gen., $165.33 ; S.
S. Primary Department, Sp. for
Bishop Rowe for Lizzie J. Woods,
for education of child in Alaska, $50.
Gen., $38.88.....................
St. James's Memorial: Gen........
St. Mary's: $15, S. S.,* $8.78, Gen...
St. Timothy's: Gen...............
"A Friend," Sp. for Bishop Whipple
Memorial, Havana, Cuba..........
MISCELLANEOUS—Wo. Aux., for native
Japanese Bible-woman, $101; for
Indian work at Birch Coulee. "In
Memory of Bishop Gilbert," $53;
Gen., $38.88.....................
Junior Aux., for Annie E. Lewis
Fund, work among Southern moun-

TOBIAS—*St. Andrew's*: Dom......... 2 25
MISCELLANEOUS—Junior Aux., "Adelaide Williams" scholarship, Girls' School, Cape Palmas, Africa....... 47 50
Babies' Branch, Akita Kindergarten, Tokyo, $8; Gen., $9.71........... 17 71
Offering taken at the Council, Dom.. 14 65

Newark
Ap. $4,336.69; *Sp.* $708.78

ARLINGTON — *Trinity Church*: Dom. and Frn...................... 65 00
BAYONNE—*Trinity Church*: Wo. Aux., Mexico, $15; Jnuior Aux., Gen., $2; S. S.,* F. R. Cuttington Collegiate and Divinity-school, Africa, $75; Gen., $102.80.............. 194 80
BELLEVILLE—*Christ Church*: Junior Aux., Gen................. 10 00
BLOOMFIELD—*Ascension*: Gen........ 15 00
Christ Church: Miss Brooks's Sunday-school Class,* Sp. for Miss Farthing, Tortella Hall, Nenana, Alaska 2 00
BOONTON—*St. John's*: Philippines.... 10 00
CHATHAM—*St. Paul's S. S.**: Gen.... 18 38
EAST ORANGE—*Grace*: Wo. Aux., "A Member," Sp. for Zangzok Station Equipment Fund, Shanghai......... 1 00
St. Paul's: Junior Aux., "Sarah Lord Payson" scholarship, St. John's School, Cape Mount, Africa........ 25 00
EDGEWATER—*Church of the Mediator*: Gen. 75 00
ENGLEWOOD — *St. Paul's*: $150.14, Senior Branch Junior Aux., $12.50, Gen. 162 64
FORT LEE—*Church of the Good Shepherd*: $25, S. S.,* $15.42, Gen.... 40 42
GARFIELD—*Holy Innocents' S. S.**: Gen. 5 42
HALEDON—*St. Mary's*: $2, S. S.,* $34.48, Gen.................. 36 48
HAMBURG—*Church of the Good Shepherd*: $20, S. S.,* $10, Gen........ 30 00
HAWTHORNE—*St. Clement's*: Gen..... 2 50
HOBOKEN—*St. Paul's S. S.**: Gen.... 100 00
Trinity Church: $142.19, S. S.,* $123.33, Gen.................. 265 52
IRVINGTON—*Trinity Church S. S.**: Gen. 25 00
JERSEY CITY—*Holy Cross*: $29.16, S. S.,* $22, Gen................. 51 16
St. John's: Gen.................. 100 00
MAPLEWOOD — *St. George's*: Junior Aux., Gen.................. 5 00
MENDHAM—*St. Mark's S. S.**: Gen.... 5 00
MILLBURN—*St. Stephen's S. S.**: Gen.. 32 71
MONTCLAIR—*St. John's*: Brazil, $2.33; Cuba, $2.33; Gen., $8.42.......... 13 08
St. Luke's: Gen., $31.84; Mrs. Fanny L. Carter, Sp. for Mrs. A. A. Gilman for Changsha Christians, Hankow, $50; S. S.,* Dom., $112.61; "St. Luke's" scholarship, St. Mary's School, South Dakota, $60; Frn., $112.61; Junior Aux., Gen., $12.39.. 379 45
MORRISTOWN — *Church of the Redeemer*: Junior Aux., Gen......... 1 00
St. Peter's: Junior Aux., Alaska..... 24 62
NEWARK—*Christ Church*: Junior Aux., Gen. 1 00
*Grace S. S.**: Bishop Brent's work, Bontok, Philippine Islands, $28.43; Rev. R. E. Wood, Wuchang, Hankow, $28.43 .... 56 86
House of Prayer: Dom. and Frn...... 12 05
*St. Andrew's S. S.**: Sp. for Bishop Horner's Industrial School, Asheville 32 52
*St. James's S. S.**: Missionary Society, Sp. for Bishop Rowe, "Tommy of Anvik," $20; Sp. for Rev. Mr. Bartter, St. Luke's Mission, Manila, Philippine Islands, $10; Sp. for Miss Byerly, Wuchang, Hankow,

$15; Sp. for Bishop Williams's Purse, Nebraska, $15; Sp. for Miss Elizabeth T. Upton, Tokyo, $15....   75 00
St. John's S. S.*: North Dakota, $10; Dom., $20....................   30 00
Transfiguration S. S.*: Dom........   13 40
Trinity Church: Sp. for Archdeacon Spurr, Moundsville, West Virginia. $125; Junior Aux., Gen., $5......   130 00
NEWTON—*Christ Church S. S.**: Gen.   32 20
NORDHOFF—*St. John's*: Gen.........   10 00
NUTLEY—*Grace*: Junior Aux., Gen...   2 67
ORANGE—*All Saints'*: Altar Guild, support of Rev. Henry A. McNulty, Shanghai, $35; S. S.,* Gen., $20.50.   55 50
Epiphany: Junior Aux., Sp. for Miss Ridgely's school, Cape Mount, Africa, $25; S. S.,* Gen., $16.55.......   41 55
Grace S. S.*: Gen..............   196 00
PASSAIC—*St. John's S. S.**: Gen....   68 55
PATERSON—*St. Paul's*: Girls' Friendly Society, Sp. for salary of deacon for Rev. S. C. Hughson, O.H.C., St. Andrew's School, Sewanee, Tennessee..   10 00
Trinity Church S. S.*: Dom., $26.25; Frn., $26.25....................   52 50
POMPTON LAKE—*Christ Church S. S.**: Gen......................   5 00
RAMSAY—*St. John's*: Gen...........   30 00
RIDGEWOOD — *Christ Church*: Dom., $300; Frn., $100; S. S.,* Gen., $67.77..........................   467 77
SHORT HILLS—*Christ Church*: Sp. for Archdeacon Neve's Industrial School, Blue Ridge District, Virginia   20 00
SOUTH ORANGE—*Church of the Holy Communion*: Rev. Henry McNulty, Shanghai, $187.50; S. S.,* Gen., $63.23 ....   250 73
St. Andrew's S. S.*: Sp. for Rev. D. T. Huntington, Ichang, Hankow.   129 25
SUMMIT — *Calvary S. S.**: Gen., $122.98; Sp. for Rev. Andrew T. Sharp, Havana, Cuba, $16.50; Sp. for Miss Upton, Tokyo, $16.50.....   155 98
TENAFLY — *Atonement*: Junior Aux., Gen. 10 00
WASHINGTON—*St. Peter's S. S.**: Gen.   2 00
MISCELLANEOUS—"A Friend," Gen....   50 00
Wo. Aux., Indian, $100; Southern Florida, $100; "Bishop Lines" scholarship, St. Elizabeth's School, South Dakota, $60; "Mary M. Lines" scholarship, St. Mary's School, Rosebud, South Dakota, $60; Manila hospital, Philippine Islands, $10; Sagada mission, $10; Colored, $201.50; "Hope" scholarship, $25, "Cornelia W. Bigelow" scholarship, $25, at Girls' Training Institute, St. Paul's River, Africa; Africa, $100; "Anna E. Niles" scholarship, St. Hilda's School, Wuchang, Hankow, $50; "Julia Starkey" scholarship, Mexico, $80; Mexico, $128; Cuba, $101; Brazil, $50; Sp. for Fort Defiance, Arizona, $100; Sp. for "Carrie Boylan" scholarship, Shoshone Mission, Wyoming, $40; Sp. for "Alice Broome" scholarship, Rowland Hall, Salt Lake, Utah, $50; Sp. for Bishop Van Buren, Porto Rico, $15..............   1,305 50
Junior Aux,. "Newark" scholarship, St. Elizabeth's School, South Dakota, $60; Gen., $17.25; "Rethmore" scholarship, Girls' Training Institute, St. Paul's River, Africa, $25......   102 25
Wo. Aux., Sp. for Shanghai Catechist School Land and Building Fund 1 00

New Hampshire

Ap. $489.86; *Sp.* $94.05

BERLIN—*St. Barnabas's S. S.**: Gen...   38 00
CHARLESTOWN—*St. Luke's S. S.**: Gen. 9 00

CLAREMONT—*Trinity Church*: $75, S. S.,* $21.65....................
CONCORD—*St. Mary's School*: Junior Aux., Sp. for St. Mary's-on-the-Mountain, Sewanee, Tennessee.....
St. Paul's: Junior Aux., Gen.......
EXETER—*Christ Church S. S.**: Gen..
FRANKLIN—*St. Jude's S. S.**: Gen....
KEENE—*St. James's*: Mrs. O. G. Dort, Sp. for Rev. S. H. Littell, Hankow..
LISBON—*Epiphany*: $2, S. S.,* $6.76, Gen. ....
LITTLETON—*All Saints'*: $28.07, S. S.,,* $10.93, Gen..............
MANCHESTER—*Grace S. S.**: Wuchang, Hankow, $50; Gen., $57.73......
St. Andrew's: $10.43, S. S.,* $33.66, Gen. ....
NASHUA—*Church of the Good Shepherd S. S.**: Gen................
NEWPORT—*Epiphany S. S.**: Gen....
TILTON—*Trinity Church S. S.**: Gen..
WOODSVILLE—*St. Luke's*: Gen.......
MISCELLANEOUS—Wo. Aux., Sp. for Foreign Insurance Fund..........

New Jersey

Ap. $1,735.94; *Sp.* $71.00

ALLENTOWN—*Christ Church*: $5, S. S.,* $17, Gen..................
ASBURY PARK—*St. Augustine's S. S.**: Gen. ....
"A Friend," Gen................
ATLANTIC CITY—*Ascension*: $5, S. S.,* $82, Gen..................
BERNARDSVILLE—*St. Bernard's*: Gen..
BORDENTOWN—*Christ Church*: $60, S. S.,* $25.47, Gen...............
BURLINGTON—*St. Mary's*: Gen.,......
CAMDEN—*St. Barnabas's*: Dom.......
St. John's: $26.17, S. S.,* $13.83, Gen. ....
St. Paul's: Wo. Aux., S. S.,* $278.58, Gen...................
COLLINGSWOOD—*Holy Trinity Church S. S.**: Gen...................
CRANFORD—*Trinity Church*: Wo. Aux., Sp. for Holy Trinity Orphanage, Tokyo ....
CROSSWICKS—*Grace S. S.**: Gen.....
DOROTHY—*Holy Nativity S. S.**: Gen.
ELIZABETH—*Christ Church*: Dom.....
Grace: Gen...................
St. John's: Mrs. T. Johnson's Circle, Wo. Aux., Sp. for Christ School, Arden, Asheville; $10; Wo. Aux., "A Member," Sp. for Bishop Partridge, Kyoto, $25..........
Trinity Church: Mrs. Darrach's Circle, Wo. Aux., Sp. for Christ School, Arden; Asheville..........
GLADSTONE—*St. Luke's*: Gen........
LOWER PENN'S NECK—*St. George's S. S.**: Gen...................
MANTUA—*St. Barnabas's*: Wo. Aux., salary of Kimura San, Kyoto, $1; Sp. for Archdeacon Wentworth's work among mountaineers, Lexington, $1:50; Sp. for Bishop Partridge's work, Kyoto, $1.50........
MAPLE SHADE—*St. John's*: Dom......
MIDDLETOWN — *Christ Church*: Wo. Aux., Gen....................
MOUNT HOLLY—*St. Andrew's*: Dom...
MULLICA HILL—*St. Stephen's S. S.**: Gen. ....
NETHERWOOD—*St. Stephen's*: Gen....
NEW BRUNSWICK—*Christ Church*: Indians, $31.03; Cuba, $1..........
St. John Evangelist's: Wo. Aux., salary of Kimura San, Kyoto, $5; Sp. for Miss Ridgely's work, Africa, $10
OCEAN CITY—"A Friend," Sp. for St. Paul's College, Tokyo..........
PAULSBORO—*St. James's S. S.**: Gen..
PLAINFIELD — *Holy Cross S. S.** (North): Gen...................

Ascension: Wo. Aux., Dom., $10 ; Frn.,
$356 ; Mrs. William Floyd, $10,
110 36   Mrs. James A. Wright, $5, Wo. Aux.,
        Sp. for St. Elizabeth's Hospital,
4 96   Shanghai ; St. Augustine's League,
17 60   Sp. for St. Agnes's Hospital, Raleigh,
100 00   North Carolina, $50 ....   431 00
4 00   *Beloved Disciple:* $23.75, S. S.* (addi-
        tional), 50 cts., Gen. 24 25
2 00   *Calvary:* Girls' Friendly Society: Sp.
        for Girls' School, Bontok, Philippine
10 00   Islands, $10 ; Sp. for Dr. Myers,
43 55   Shanghai, $10 ....   20 00
6 75   *Christ Church* (New Brighton): Sal-
        ary of Bishop Paddock, Eastern Ore-
        gon 93 76
        Church Missions House Chapel: Gen...   85
        Grace: Dom., $250 ; Frn., $200 ; Gen.,
4 00 $1,890.84 ; Mrs. Morton L. Fearey,
150 00 Gen., $10 Indian Committee,
50 00   "Alonzo Potter" (Graduate) schol-
        arship, South Dakota, $30 ; Commit-
        tee on Missions to Colored People,
        St. Augustine's League, Sp. for St.
        Agnes's Hospital, Raleigh, North
115 00 Carolina, $10 ; Sp. for Hospital of
        the Good Samaritan, Charlotte,
        North Carolina, $10 ; Miss Nelson,
        Niobrara League, "Wm. Reed Hunt-
        ington" scholarship, St. Elizabeth's
        School, South Dakota, $60 ; Mrs.
2 25   W. M. Kingsland, Niobrara League,
        "Cornelius Kingsland Memorial"
        (Graduate) scholarship, South Da-
10 00   kota, $60 ; Grace Chantry S. S.,
        "Grace Chantry" scholarship, St.
        Elizabeth's School, South Dakota
22 61   (of which *$31.47), $60 .... 2,580 84
        Grace Chapel, Italian Congregation:
        Frn., $5 ; Junior Aux., Gen., $15...   20 00
        Heavenly Rest: Wo. Aux., St. James's
        Hospital, Anking, Hankow, $40 ; The
10 00   Misses Strong, Sp. for scholarship
10 00   for Elijah Whitehurst, St. Paul's
        School, Beaufort, East Carolina, $10   50 00
        Church of the Holy Communion: Gen.,
14 30 $1,077.23 ; Sp. for Church of the
        Holy Communion, Tacoma, Olympia,
7 17 $100 ; Sp. for Bishop Brewer, Mon-
        tana, $50 .... 1,227 23
16 10   *Holy Faith* (Bronx): Sp. for Zang-
10 00   zok Station Equipment Fund, Shang-
        hai, $2 ; Junior Aux., Gen., $5......   7 00
45 00   *Holyrood:* Wo. Aux., Frn. 5 00
        Incarnation: Mrs. Clinton Ogilvie, Sp.
7 78   for Bishop Thomas, Wyoming, for
72 00   clergy conferences, $450 ; Sp. for
500 00 Bishop Brewster, Western Colorado,
1 59   for clergy conferences, $135 ; Wo.
1 84   Aux., Mrs. Hooker's Memorial
        School, Mexico (of which Montgom-
        ery Memorial Society, $30), $33 ;
        Niobrara League, "Rev. Arthur
        Brooks" scholarship, St. Elizabeth's
        School, South Dakota, $60 ; S. S.,
50 00   Gen. (of which *$39.35), $64.35...   742 35
5 00   *Incarnation Chapel:* Junior Aux.,
        Gen., $17.60 ; Junior Boys' Club,
        Sp. for Miss Bassett's work, Sewanee,
        Tennessee, $6.79 ....   24 39
        Church of the Mediator S. S.: Gen...   2 16
        Church of the Messiah Chapel: Rev.
325 63 Mr. Gilman's work, Hankow, $4.10 ;
        Junior Aux., $16, Girls' Friendly So-
14 50   ciety, $8.91, Primary Department S.
        S. Birthday Bank, $3.42, Gen......   32 43
        St. Agnes's Chapel: Niobrara League,
        "Rev. E. A. Bradley" scholarship,
        $60, "St. Agnes" scholarship, $60,
        both in St. Mary's School, South Da-
        kota ; Girls' Friendly Society, Sp.
140 20 for Girls' School, Bontok, Philippine
        Islands, $10 ....   130 00
7 41   *St. Ambrose's S. S.*: Gen 2 60
        St. Andrew's (Richmond): Wo. Aux.,
        Gen., $42.56 ; Sp. for Miss Farthing,
10 00   Alaska, $15 ; S. S.,* Gen., $60.....   117 56

St. *Ann's* (Morrisania): Gen......... 393 00
St. *Ann's for Deaf-Mutes*: Gen....... 21 00
St. *Augustine's Chapel*: Gen......... 5 00
St. *Bartholomew's*: "Hilda Elizabeth Potter" scholarship, St. Hilda's School, Wuchang, $50; Sp. for Bishop Rowe's work, Alaska, $6,534; Sp. for Bishop Thomas, Wyoming, $25; Sp. for St. John's University, Shanghai (of which Expansion Fund, $750), $1,265; Sp. for Dr. Pott, Shanghai, $100; Sp. for St. Paul's College, Tokyo, $250; Niobrara League, salary of teacher, South Dakota, $500; "Campe" scholarship, St. Mary's School, South Dakota, $30 .... 8,754 00
St. *Bartholomew's Parish House S. S.*: "David H. Greer" scholarship, St. Elizabeth's School, South Dakota... 60 00
St. *Chrysostom's Chapel*: $37.57, Junior Aux., $8.12, S. S.* (additional), $1.05, Gen.; Associate Branch, Wo. Aux., Sp. for Rev. R. C. Wilson's work, Zangzok, Shanghai, $5.18................. 51 92
St. *Cornelius the Centurion* (Governor's Island): Gen............. 50 00
St. *David's S. S.*: Sp. for Bishop Holly, Haiti, $10; Sp. for Bishop Ferguson, Africa, $10............ 20 00
St. *George's*: Missionary Society, Wo. Aux., St. John's School, Cape Mount, Africa, $5; Sp. for Rev. A. A. Gilman's insurance, Hankow, $4; Niobrara League, "St. George's" scholarship, St. Mary's School, South Dakota, $60; Sp. for "Sherman Coolidge" scholarship, Idaho, $40; Sp. for St. John's Church, Ketchikan, Alaska, $250; Sp. for Bishop Funsten's Indian work, Idaho, $50; Girls' Friendly Society, Sp. for Dr. Myers, Shanghai, $5................. 414 00
St. *James's*: Junior Aux., Bishop Rowe's work, Alaska, $75; children's work, Philippine Islands, $62.50; St. Elizabeth's School, South Dakota, $60; work among poor whites, Sewanee, Tennessee, $25; St. Paul's School, Lawrenceville, Southern Virginia, $22.52; "Rev. E. Walpole Warren" scholarship, St. John's School, Cape Mount, Africa, $25; child's bed, Elizabeth Bunn Memorial Hospital, Wuchang, Hankow, $30; Kawagoe Kindergarten, Tokyo, $25; scholarship, St. Hilda's School, Wuchang, Hankow, $50; St. James's Hospital, Anking, Hankow, $25; support of boys' school, Soochow, Shanghai, $50; St. Agnes's School, Kyoto, $25.35; Gen., $45; Sp. for Mrs. Wetmore, Arden, Asheville, $100; Sp. for St. Agnes's Hospital, Raleigh, North Carolina, $25; Sp. for St. Margaret's School, Boisé, $25; Sp. for St. Paul's College, Tokyo, $25; Girls' Friendly Society, Sp. for Dr. Myers, Shanghai, $2.08. 697 45
St. *John's* (Clifton): Wo. Aux., Sp. for Mrs. Wetmore for Christ School, Arden, Asheville, $55; Junior Aux., Gen., $25.................... 80 00
St. *John Evangelist's*: Girls' Friendly Society, Sp. for Dr. Myers, Shanghai 5 25
St. *Luke's* (Convent Avenue): Gen., $25.95; Wo. Aux., Frn., $5........ 30 95
St. *Luke's Chapel*: Gen............. 75 00
St. *Margaret's*: Junior Aux., Gen., $5; S. S.* (additional), Dom., $1.07.... 6 07
St. *Mark's*: Gen., $25.77; S. S., Indian, $9.70.................... 35 47
St. *Mary's* (Manhattanville): Wo. Aux., Sp. for Bishop Paddock, Eastern Oregon................. 5 00

St. *Mary's* (West New Brighton): Wo. Aux., Frn....................
St. *Matthew's*: St. Hilda Chapter, Sp. for Miss Knight's work, Echo, Eastern Oregon..................
St. *Michael's*: Rev. Mr. Gilman's salary, Changsha, Hankow, $41.45; Wo. Aux., Sp. for Bishop Thomas, Wyoming, for work at Lander, $4.55; Sp. for Rev. Mr. Gilman, Changsha, Hankow, $20; St. Augustine's League, Sp. for St. Agnes's Hospital, Raleigh, North Carolina, $4; S. S. Sheltering Arms, "James Cook Richmond" scholarship, St. John's School, Africa, $25.........
St. *Peter's*: Gen.
St. *Peter's S. S.** (Westchester): Colored, $15.50; Dom., $25; Frn., $25.
St. *Stephen's*: Gen..............
St. *Thomas's*: Sp. for St. John's University Building Fund, Shanghai, $200; Sp. for Rev. Mr. Nichols for school for training native workers, Shanghai, $105; Wo. Aux., Sp. for Rev. G. P. Mayo, for school at Lost Mountain, Virginia, $185; to defray expenses of educating Miss Kaul Umezawa, Tokyo, $200; Sp. for Dr. Angie M. Myers for St. Elizabeth's Hospital, Shanghai, $100; Sp. for Bishop Aves's work, Mexico, $90; "M. M. Halsted" scholarship, Hooker Memorial School, Mexico, $40; Miss Anna B. Halsted, Wo. Aux., Mexico, $30; St. Augustine's League, Sp. for Bishop Payne Divinity-school, Southern Virginia (of which scholarship, $150), $190; Junior Aux., Gen., $25; Girls' Friendly Society, Sp. for Dr. Myers, Shanghai, $5; S. S. "Ernest M. Stires" scholarship, Boone University, Wuchang, Hankow, $50....... 1
Trinity Church: Gen., $2,500; Wo. Aux., Sp. for Dr. Pott, St. John's University, Shanghai, $5; S. S.,* Gen., $50.................... 2
Trinity Chapel: Missionary Relief Society, Wo. Aux. (of which Mrs. S. Edward Nash, $10, Miss C. W. Crane, $1), Frn., $11; St. Augustine's League, Sp. for Dr. Hunter, St. Augustine's School, Raleigh, North Carolina, $32.01...........
Zion and St. Timothy's: Missionary Chapter, Niobrara League, Sp. for window in Cornelia Jay Memorial, Fort Defiance, Arizona, $35; Niobrara League, "Henry Lubeck" scholarship, St. Elizabeth's School, South Dakota, $60; Junior Aux., Gen., $5.37
Niobrara League, teachers, workers and catechists, South Dakota, $400; Sp. for Miss Dickson, South Dakota, $5; Sp. for Indian school, Anvik, Alaska, $15.50..............
Mrs. George Cabot Ward, Wo. Aux., Sp. for Rev. F. E. Lund, Wuhu, Hankow ....
Miss Elizabeth A. Hyde, "Arthur Brooks" scholarship, Brazil......
Mr. and Mrs. G. Zabriskie, Wo. Aux. (In Memoriam), Sp. for Bishop Aves, Mexico, for House of Industry, Nopala ....
Lenten Indian League, Niobrara League, "Lenten League" (Graduate) scholarship, South Dakota, $60; "Charlotte Augusta Astor" scholarship, St. Elizabeth's School, South Dakota, $60; catechist, St. James's Chapel, South Dakota, $75.........
"T. and T.," work in Africa (among cannibals, if possible)............

100 00	Blessed are the Pure in Heart," support of Bible-woman, Training-school, Kyoto..................... 60 00
31 05	Branch Junior Aux., Sp. for "Langford" scholarship, Alaska......... 65 00
36 25	Babies' Branch, Akita Kindergarten, Tokyo, $10 ; Angelica Church Hart Day-school, Wuchang, Hankow, $20 ;
25 00	Gen., $377.31; Sp. for St. Agnes's
25 00	Hospital, Raleigh, North Carolina,
25 00	$5 ; Sp. for missionary font, $1.... 413 31

North Carolina

15 00	
	Ap. $147.71 ; Sp. $30.25
1 00	CHAPEL HILL—Chapel of the Cross: Sp. for Dr. Correll's work, Tsu, Kyoto 10 00
	Rev. N. S. Hughes, Sp. for Dr. Correll for his work, Tsu, Kyoto...... 10 00
14 00	CHARLOTTE—Church of the Holy Comforter: Wo. Aux., Sp. for Bishop Aves, Mexico, for famine relief.... 4 25
	DURHAM—St. Philip's S. S.* : Gen.... 28 00
37 00	GASTON—St. Luke's S. S.* : Gen........ 1 43
	GREENSBORO—St. Andrew's : Gen..... 15 00
	MAYODAN—Church of the Messiah S. S.* : Gen........................ 25 00
161 19	PITTSBORO—St. James's S. S.* : Gen... 6 17
15 00	RALEIGH—Christ Church: Gen....... 20 40
	St. Ambrose's S. S.* : Gen.......... 11 28
	ROWAN CITY—Christ Church: Wo.
15 00	Aux., Sp. for Bishop McKim, Tokyo. 1 00
	SPRAY—St. Luke's: Gen............ 6 30
5 00	STONEVILLE—Emmanuel Church S. S.* :
31 00	Gen. 1 42
30 00	STOVALL—St. Peter's: Dom. and Frn.. 5 00
92 11	TARBORO—St. Luke's S. S.* : Gen..... 26 00
	WALNUT COVE—Christ Church S. S.* : Gen. 1 71
130 00	MISCELLANEOUS—Through Rev. N. C. Hughes, Sp. for Dr. Correll for Tsu
19 32	Building Fund, Kyoto............ 5 00

Ohio

1 09	
10 00	Ap. $2,821.96 ; Sp. $1,311.00
	AKRON—St. Andrew's S. S.* : Gen.... 3 10
	St. Paul's: Frn., $42.26 ; Gen. (of
70 00	which S. S.,* $29.17), $89.57 ; Wo. Aux., salary of Miss Elwin, Shanghai (of which Junior Aux., $15),
45 68	$40 ; "Julia Bedell" scholarship, $10 ;
50 00	John's University, Shanghai, $10... 181 83
7 00	BELLEFONTAINE—Holy Trinity Church S. S.* : Gen.................... 3 17
	BELLEVUE—St. Paul's: Wo. Aux., salary of Miss Elwin, Shanghai, $4 ;
500 00	S. S.,* Gen., $22.17............ 26 17
	BOARDMAN—St. James's S. S.* : Gen.. 7 06
24 00	CANTON—St. Paul's: Gen. (of which
70 00	S. S.,* $11).................... 24 25
	CLEVELAND—All Saints': Wo. Aux.,
70 82	Alaska 10 00
	Atonement S. S.* : Gen............ 3 03
	Christ Church: Wo. Aux., Alaska..... 5 00
398 27	Emmanuel Church: Junior Aux., Gen., $10 ; St. Margaret's Guild, Day-school, Hanch'uan, Hankow, $3.56 ; S. S.,* Gen., $168.78............. 182 34
	Church of the Good Shepherd S. S.* : Gen. 13 46
	Grace S. S.* : Gen................ 40 84
261 88	Grace (South): Wo. Aux., salary of Miss Elwin, Shanghai, $5 ; S. S.,*
65 91	Gen., $8.50.................... 13 50
	Church of the Holy Spirit S. S.* : Gen. 11 51
	St. John's S. S.* : Gen............. 45 00
	St. Luke's: Wo. Aux., salary of Miss Elwin, Shanghai, $3 ; "Ohio" scholarship, St. Elizabeth's School, South Dakota, $3 ; S. S.,* Gen., $28...... 34 00
	St. Mark's S. S.* : Gen............. 6 33
	St. Mary's: Work in China, $5 ; Gen. (of which S. S.,* $6.63), $39.63.... 44 63
650 00	St. Paul's: Wo. Aux., Mrs. L. Z. Norton, Alaska, $25 ; Mr. C. F. Schwein-

furth, Sp. for endowment of the "Mary Ella Schweinfurth Memorial" bed in a Church hospital, Alaska, $1,300 .... 1,325 00

St. Philip's: Wo. Aux., salary of Miss Elwin, Shanghai, $5; S. S.,* Gen., $4.41 .... 9 41

Trinity Church: Wo. Aux., Gen. (of which St. Monica's Society, $2, Miss K. Mather, Daughters of the Church, $100), $102; salary of Miss Elwin, Shanghai (of which Daughters of the Church, $50, Mrs. Benton, $5, Mrs. E. S. Isom, $5), $135; "Gregory T. Bedell" scholarship (of which from Daughters of the Church, $5), $18, "Julia Bedell" scholarship, $5, both in St. John's University, Shanghai; Oklahoma (of which from Daughters of the Church, $25, Miss Mather, $25), $75; Sacramento (of which Daughters of the Church, $25), $50; "Daughters of the Church Ohio" scholarship, St. Elizabeth's School, South Dakota, $10; Alaska (of which Miss Mather, $100, Mrs. Benton, $5, Mrs. Isom, $5), $115; Sp. for Foreign Insurance Fund, $10; Junior Aux., Day-school, Hanch'uan, Hankow, $5; S. S.,* Gen., $110.13 .. 635 13

CONNEAUT—St. Paul's: Gen. (of which S. S.,* $5) 10 00

COSHOCTON — Trinity Church: Wo. Aux., Gen. (of which S. S.,* $3.18) . 4 18

CUYAHOGA FALLS—St. John's S. S.*: Gen. 21 18

DEFIANCE—Grace: Wo. Aux., "Mrs. Clapp Memorial" bed, St. Elizabeth's Hospital, Shanghai 5 00

EAST LIVERPOOL—St. Stephen's S. S.*: Gen. 55 08

ELYRIA—St. Andrew's: Wo. Aux., salary of Miss Elwin, Shanghai (of which from Junior Aux., $3), $5; Junior Aux., Gen., $2 .... 7 00

FINDLAY—Trinity Church S. S.*: Gen. 10 04

FOSTORIA—Trinity Church S. S.*: Gen. 11 00

FREMONT—St. Paul's: Gen. 98 25

GALION—Grace S. S.*: Gen. 12 00

GAMBIER — Harcourt Parish: Frn., $32.32; Dom. and Frn., $12.90; Junior Aux., Day-school, Hanch'uan, $1; S. S.,* Gen., $41.90; "Rev. Alfred Blake, D.D.," scholarship, St. Mary's Hall, Shanghai, $40 ...... 128 12

HUDSON—Christ Church S. S.*: Gen. 9 05

HURON—Christ Church S. S.*: Gen... 4 20

KENT—Christ Church S. S.*: Gen.... 3 00

LAKEWOOD — Ascension: Wo. Aux., Alaska, $5; salary of Miss Elwin, Shanghai, $5 .... 10 00

St Peter's S. S.*: Gen. 7 50

LIMA—Christ Church S. S.*: Gen.... 12 40

LORAIN—Church of the Redeemer S. S.*: Gen. 6 00

St. David's: Gen. 15 48

LYME—Trinity Church: Gen 5 00

MANSFIELD—Grace: Gen. (of which S. S.,* $16.57), $30.87; for the work of Rev. C. Reifsnider, Fukui, Kyoto, $6.90 .... 37 77

MASSILLON—St. Timothy's: Wo. Aux., salary of Miss Elwin, Shanghai, $10; S. S.,* Gen., $43.69 .... 53 69

MEDINA—St. Paul's S. S.*: Gen...... 15 02

MONROEVILLE—Zion: Wo. Aux., "Julia Bedell" scholarship, St. John's University, Shanghai, $5; S. S.,* Gen., $25 .... 30 00

MOUNT VERNON—St. Paul's: Wo. Aux., salary of Miss Elwin, Shanghai, $7; "Gregory T. Bedell" scholarship, St. John's University, Shanghai, $25; Sp. for Foreign Insurance Fund, $1; S. S.,* Gen., $33 .... 51 00

NAVARRE—Frank E. Shilling, Gen....

NORWALK—St. Paul's S. S.*: Gen.... 3

PAINESVILLE—St. James's: Wo. Aux., Alaska, $10; salary of Miss Elwin, Shanghai (of which from Junior Aux., $5), $15; Junior Aux., Day-school, Hanch'uan, Hankow, $5; S. S.,* Gen., $81.40................ 11

PENINSULA—Bethel: Wo. Aux., salary of Miss Elwin, Shanghai.........

PERRY—St. Anne's: Wo. Aux., Alaska, $3; Oklahoma, $3................

PORT CLINTON—St. Thomas's: Wo. Aux., Alaska, $2; S. S.,* Gen., $7.05

RAVENNA—Grace S. S.*: Gen........

SALEM—Church of Our Saviour S. S.*: Gen. ....

SANDUSKY—Grace: Gen. (of which S. S.,* $28.56) 12

STEUBENVILLE — St. Paul's S. S.*: Gen. 3

St. Stephen's: Wo. Aux., salary of Miss Elwin, Shanghai, $5; S. S.,* Gen., $42 4

TIFFIN—Trinity Church S. S.*: Gen.. 1

TOLEDO—All Saints' S. S.*: Gen......

Calvary S. S.*: Gen...............

Grace S. S.*: Gen.................

St. John's Evangelist: Wo. Aux., "Mrs. Clapp Memorial" bed, St. Elizabeth's Hospital, Shanghai, $5; S. S.,* Gen.,

St. Mark's: Gen. (of which S. S.,* $35), $39.25; Wo. Aux., "Mrs. Clapp Memorial" bed, St. Elizabeth's Hospital, Shanghai, $5; Gen., $5........ 4

St. Paul's S. S.*: Gen..............

St. Thomas's: Gen................

Trinity Church: Wo. Aux., "Ohio" scholarship, St. Elizabeth's School, South Dakota, $2; "Mrs. Clapp Memorial" bed, St. Elizabeth's Hospital, Shanghai, $29; Cuba, $25; Junior Aux., salary of Miss Elwin, Shanghai, $5; Oklahoma, $5; S. S.,* Gen., $125 18

Toledo Convocation, Wo. Aux., Gen., $5.19; "Gregory T. Bedell" scholarship, St. John's University, Shanghai, $2; "Mrs. Clapp Memorial" bed, St. Elizabeth's Hospital, Shanghai, $6 ....

S. S. Rally collection,* Gen.........

WARREN—Christ Church S. S.*: Gen..

WELLSVILLE—Ascension S. S.*: Gen..

YOUNGSTOWN—St. John's S. S.*: Gen. 1

MISCELLANEOUS—Junior Aux., Day-school, Hanch'uan, Hankow, $35.44; Gen., $14.56.....................

Oregon

Ap. $456.98; Sp. $15.00

ASTORIA—Grace: Wo. Aux., Gen., $10; Junior Aux., support of scholar, Trinity Divinity-school, Tokyo, $3.78

EUGENE—St. Mary's: Gen............

NEWPORT—St. Stephen's S. S.*: Gen..

OREGON CITY—St. Paul's S. S.*: Gen..

PORTLAND—St. David's: Wo. Aux., $12, S. S.,* $202.54, Gen......... 2

St. John's (Sellwood): Wo. Aux., $2.50, S. S.,* $8.50, Gen........

St. Mark's: $21.95, Wo. Aux., $12, Gen. ....

St. Matthew's S. S.*: Gen..........

St. Stephen's: Wo.· Aux., Gen........

Trinity Church S. S.*: Gen.......... 1

G. Frank Shelby, Sp. for St. John's University, Shanghai.............

SALEM—St. Paul's: Wo. Aux., Gen., $10; Sp. for scholarship, St. Paul's School, Beaufort, East Carolina, $10

TOLEDO—St. John's S. S.*: Gen......

YAQUINA—Mission S. S.*: Gen.......

School, Sp. for St. Agnes's Hospital, Raleigh, North Carolina, $10 ...... 247 17
Holy Trinity Memorial Chapel: Wo. Aux., Sp. for Hooker Memorial School, Mexico 5 00
House of Prayer (Branchtown) : Gen.. Children of Home of the Holy Child, Sp. for Rev. D. T. Huntington's orphanage, Ichang, Hankow 25 00
Prince of Peace Chapel : Wo. Aux., Sp. for building St. Elizabeth's Hospital, Shanghai, $5 ; J. Nicholas Mitchell's Men's Bible-class, support of native priest, Hankow, $25 ; S. S., Gen., $11.95 ; Sp. for Bishop Robinson, Nevada, $11.66 ; Sp. for Bishop McKim, Tokyo, $12.18 ; Sp. for Bishop Aves, Mexico, $12 .... 77 79
St. Andrew's (West) : Wo. Aux., Sp. for Hooker Memorial School, Mexico 10 00
St. Andrew's (Eighth and Spruce Streets) : Wo. Aux., Cuba 15 00
St. Anna's : Sp. for Rev. J. W. Nichols, Shanghai, $16.65 ; Wo. Aux., Miss Higgins's work, Hankow, $3 ; Sp. for Rev. R. C. Wilson, Zangzok, Shanghai, $1 .... 20 65
St. Clement's : Sp. for Bishop Robinson, Nevada 15 00
St. George's (Richmond) : Juniors, Gen. 5 00
St. James's (Kingsessing) : Wo. Aux., Frn. 1 00
St. Luke's (Germantown) : Wo. Aux., St. Andrew's Seminary, Mexico 10 00
St. Luke's (Bustleton) : Gen 33 50
St. Mark's : "A Parishioner," Sp. for building house for Mr. and Mrs. Staunton, Philippines, $200 ; Wo. Aux., Miss Gates's salary, St. Margaret's School, Wuchang, Hankow, $100 ; Sp. for Miss Ridgely, House of Bethany, Cape Mount, Africa, $100 ; Junior Aux., Gen., $15 ..... 415 00
St. Mark's (Frankford) : Wo. Aux., Frn. 4 00
St. Martin-in-the-Fields, St. Martin's : Frn., $25 ; Gen., $42.37 .... 67 37
St. Matthew's : Junior Aux., Gen 12 00
St. Mary's (West) : St. Agnes's Guild, Alaska, $5 ; Juniors, Gen., $2.25 .. 7 25
St. Matthias's : Wo. Aux., Sp. for building St. Elizabeth's Hospital, Shanghai, $18 ; Sp. for St. Luke's Hospital, Shanghai, $4 .... 22 00
St. Michael's (Germantown) : Juniors, Gen. 25 00
St. Nathaniel's : Gen., $10 ; Wo. Aux., Japan, $3 .... 13 00
St. Paul's Memorial (Fifteenth and Porter Streets) : Gen 53 77
St. Paul's Memorial (Overbrook) : Dom., $1 ; Indian, 75 cts.; Gen., $135.20 ; Wo. Aux., Frn., $10 ; Sp. for land and building, Catechists' School, Shanghai, $9.59 ; Indian Hope Association, Indian, $3.75 .... 160 29
St. Paul's (Chestnut Hill) : Wo. Aux., Frn., $20 ; Juniors, Philippines, $25 ; Nevada, $5 ; Gen., $26 ...... 76 00
St. Peter's : Indian Hope Association, Indian, $3 ; Juniors, Gen., $25 .... 28 00
St. Peter's (Germantown) : Wo. Aux., Sp. for St. Elizabeth's Memorial Hospital, Shanghai 10 00
St. Philip's (West) : Juniors, Gen 10 00
St. Stephen's : Dom., $211.23 ; "A Friend," Sp. for Expansion Fund, St. John's University, Shanghai, $1 ; Wo. Aux., Frn., $10 ; Sp. for Hooker Memorial School, Mexico, $10 ; Sp. for Rev. G. E. M. Benedict, Haiti, $2 ; Sp. for Rev. R. G. Wilson, for Zangzok, Shanghai, $2 .... 236 23
St. Thomas's : Juniors, Gen 2 00
St. Timothy's (Roxboro) : Wo. Aux., Frn., $5, Juniors, $10, Gen 15 00

00
00
14
00
00
00
50
60
00
00
00
50
00.
00
00
00
00
19
50
00
00
00
59
00
00
00
00
00
00

Church of the Saviour: Wo. Aux.,
Frn., $5; Indian Hope Association.
"William B. Bodine" scholarship, St.
Elizabeth's School, South Dakota,
$60 .... 65 00
Transfiguration (West): Gen., $25;
Juniors, St. Augustine's School, Ral-
eigh, North Carolina, $5.......... 30 00
"A. H. M.," Sp. for Church work,
Mexico 500 00
J. T. Lee, Sp. for Shanghai Catechist
School, Land and Building Fund... 50 00
Miss Mary C. Yarrow, Frn........ 35 00
"A Friend," Sp. for Church Exten-
sion Fund, Porto Rico............ 10 00
J. E. J. McGee* (Roxborough), Gen. 1 50
RADNOR—*St. David's*: Gen.......... 149 00
St. Martin's: Indian Hope Association,
Indian 5 00
WAYNE—*St. Mary's Memorial*: Dom.,
$66.65; Wo. Aux., Frn., $5; Juniors,
Gen., $10........................ 81 65
WEST CHESTER—*Holy Trinity Church*:
Sarah H. Lindley, in loving memory,
hospital bed in St. James's Hospital,
Anking, Hankow................... 50 00
WEST WHITELAND—*St. Paul's*: Gen.... 7 25
WHITEMARSH—*St. Thomas's*: Dom.... 105 00
WYNCOTE—*All Hallows'*: Juniors, Sp.
for Mrs. Wetmore, Christ School,
Arden, Asheville.................. 10 00
MISCELLANEOUS—"Y. Z.," Gen........ 100 00
Offering at opening of convention,
Gen. 78 99
R. L. Mitchell, Mission Study Class
Alumnæ, Indian Hope Association,
proceeds of Church Missionary Cal-
endars, toward salary of native
Indian worker.................... 50 00
Foreign Committee, Wo. Aux., Sp.
for Christmas gifts, for Africa..... 12 00
Diocesan Committee, Wo. Aux., Gen. 12 00
Wo. Aux., Sp. for Rev. C. E. M.
Bénedict, Aux Cayes, Haiti, $28;
"Members of R. L. M." Mission
Study Class Alumnæ, Sp. for Hot
Water Fund, St. Elizabeth's Hos-
pital, Shanghai, $30; Cuban Guild,
Sp. for "John P. Rhoads" scholar-
ship, Divinity-school, Havana, Cuba,
$83 .... 141 00
Juniors, Miss Margaret Morris, Gen. 5 00

Pittsburgh

Ap. $3,824.48; *Sp.* $28.00

AMBRIDGE—*St. Matthias's S. S.**: Gen. 4 05
ASHCROFT—*Church of the Good Shep-
herd S. S.**: Gen................. 24 52
BARNESBORO—*St. Thomas's*: Gen. (of
which S. S.* $10.10)............. 17 10
BEAVER FALLS—*St. Mary's S. S.**: Gen. 16 31
BELLEVUE—*Epiphany S. S.**: Gen.... 72 87
BLAIRSVILLE—*St. Peter's S. S.**: Gen. 5 18
BRADDOCK—*St. Mary's S. S.**: Gen... 4 40
BRADFORD—*Ascension S. S.**: Gen.. 48 79
BROOKVILLE—*Holy Trinity Church S.
S.**: Gen........................ 12 85
BROWNSVILLE—*Christ Church S. S.**:
Gen. 36 00
BUTLER—*St. Peter's*: $7, S. S.,*
$15.77, Gen...................... 22 77
CANONSBURG—*St. Thomas's S. S.**:
Gen. 3 10
CARNEGIE—*Atonement S. S.**: Gen... 5 00
CHARLEROI—*St. Mary's S. S.**: Gen... 7 70
CLAIRTON — *Transfiguration S. S.**:
Gen. 2 25
CLEARFIELD—*St. Andrew's S. S.**: Gen. 10 00
CONNEAUTVILLE — *Trinity Church S.
S.**: Gen........................ 3 25
CORAOPOLIS—*St. John's S. S.**: Gen.. 2 62
CRAFTON—*Nativity S. S.**: Gen....... 25 00
DECATUR—*St. Saviour's S. S.**: Gen.. 10 50
DU BOIS—*Church of Our Saviour S.
S.**: Gen........................ 60 00

knowledgments

591

17 50	CRANSTON—*St. Bartholomew's S. S.**:
7 60	Gen. 10 00
	CROMPTON—*St. Philip's S. S.**: Gen.. 57 00
40 12	EAST PROVIDENCE—*St. Mary's S. S.**:
5 00	Gen. 21 42
106 13	EDGEWOOD — *Transfiguration S. S.**:
1 68	Gen. 20 00
37 50	LONSDALE—*Christ Church S. S.**:
	Dom., $75; Frn., $58.43.......... 133 43
4 23	MANTON—*St. Peter's S. S.**: Gen..... 17 82
11 57	MANVILLE—*Emmanuel Church S. S.**:
	Gen. 30 01
7 50	MIDDLETOWN—*Holy Cross*: Gen...... 4 56
14 00	NEWPORT—*Emmanuel Church S. S.**:
	Gen. 50 65
17 05	*St. George's S. S.**: Gen............ 25 00
	Trinity Church: Gen., $61.66; "A
5 00	Friend," Sp. for salary of Mr. Kemp,
	Boone College, Wuchang, Hankow,
245 00	$431.25 .... 492 91
43 14	PASCOAG—*Calvary Church S. S.**: Gen. 18 60
	PAWTUCKET—*Advent S. S.**: Gen.... 13 35
5 75	*Church of the Good Shepherd*: Gen... 16 16
17 26	*St. Luke's*: $7, S. S.,* $7, Gen....... 14 00
	St. Paul's S. S.*: Gen............. 41 19
8 90	*Trinity Church*: Gen., $75; Junior
56 00	Aux., Alaska, $5; China, $5;
2 75	S. S.,* Frn., $15............... 100 00
13 10	PAWTUXET—*Trinity Church S. S.**:
15 02	Gen. 20 00
	PHENIX—*St. Andrew's S. S.**: Gen.... 27 60
71 22	PHILIPSDALE—*St. David's S. S.**: Gen. 2 25
75 00	PONTIAC—*All Saints' S. S.**: Gen..... 15 50
	PORTSMOUTH—*St. Mary's*: Gen...... 2 76
100 00	*St. Paul's S. S.**: Dom. and Frn..... 16 71
	PROVIDENCE — *All Saints' Memorial*:
9 34	"Bishop Henshaw Memorial" schol-
	arship, St. John's University, Shang-
10 00	hai, $70; Dom. and Frn., $40; S.
	S.,* Gen., $164................ 274 00
9 17	*Calvary S. S.**: Frn................ 50 30
4 25	*Christ Church S. S.**: Gen.......... 39 30
	Fruit Hill S. S.*: Gen............. 9 80
15 50	*Grace*: $500; Junior Aux., $5; S. S.,*
	$327.86 .... 832 86
10 00	*Church of the Messiah*: Gen......... 62 40
	St. Andrew's: Junior Aux., Indian,
17 50	$1.50; China, $1............... 2 50
	St. Ansgarius's S. S.*: Gen......... 21 50
	St. James's: Gen., $120; S. S.,* Dom.,
	$50; Frn., $50................ 220 00
165 00	*St. John's S. S.**: Gen............. 150 00
50 00	*St. Stephen's S. S.**: Gen.......... 188 16
	Miss E. C. McVickar, Sp. for a
	boy's support in school, Nenana,
13 00	Alaska, $100; Sp. toward comple-
	tion of library, Boone School, Wu-
	chang, Hankow, $100........... 200 00
	RIVERSIDE—*St. Mark's S. S.**: Gen... 12 20
	THORNTON—*Holy Nativity*: Gen...... 15 00
	TIVERTON—*Holy Trinity Church S.
8 32	S.**: Gen...................... 5 75
10 00	WICKFORD—*St. Paul's S. S.**: Gen... 11 25
51 00	MISCELLANEOUS—Wo. Aux., support of
5 30	a bed, Elizabeth Bunn Hospital, Wu-
57 35	chang, Hankow, $30; "Harriet H.
	Gilpin Memorial" scholarship, Eliza
39 00	F. Drury Station, Africa, $25;
	"Emily Waterman" scholarship,
	Girls' Training Institute, St. Paul's
	River, Africa, $25; "Carrington"
	(In Memoriam) scholarship, St.
	John's School, Cape Mount, Africa,
6 00	$25.......................... 105 00
10 00	Babies' Branch, Akita Kindergarten,
7 86	Tokyo, $5; Gen., $19; Sp. for mis-
	sionary font, $1.................. 25 00

South Carolina

Ap. $923.04; *Sp.* $37.50

38 00	AIKEN—*St. Thaddeus's*: Junior Aux.,
30 00	Gen. 10 00
17 24	ANDERSON—*Grace*: Wo. Aux., salary
	of assistant for Miss McCullough,
54 00	Porto Rico..................... 3 00

BEAUFORT—*St. Helena's* : Junior Aux.,
Gen. 10 00
BENNETTSVILLE—*St. Paul's* : Wo. Aux.,
Gen. 10 00
BOYKIN—*Grace* : Wo. Aux., Gen..... 5 00
CAMDEN—*Grace* : Wo. Aux. (Section
B.), Sp. for Asheville............ 2 00
CHARLESTON—*Grace* : Wo. Aux., N. S.
Wilson Day-school, Hankow, $10 ;
Gen. (of which Junior Aux., $4,
Babies' Branch, $10, S. S.,* $53.87),
$78.62 .... 88 62
Holy Communion : Wo. Aux., Gen..... 13 55
Porter Military Academy, $2, S.
S.,* $5.19, Gen.................... 7 19
St. John's : Wo. Aux., Gen........... 6 00
St. John's Chapel : Junior Aux., Gen.. 5 00
St. Luke's : Gen., $75 ; Wo. Aux., Sp.
for mission at Highlands, Asheville,
$5 .... 80 00
*St. Mark's S. S.** : Work in South Caro-
lina 30 00
St. Michael's : Junior Aux., Gen...... 2 00
St. Paul's : Wo. Aux., Gen. (of which
Junior Aux., $2, Babies' Branch,
$1.53), $13.53 ; M. E. Pinkney Fund
for Bible-woman, Tokyo, $5........ 18 53
St. Philip's : Wo. Aux., Gen., $3.75 ;
Junior Aux., Bishop Capers Day-
school, Hankow, $15 ; N. S. Wilson
Day-school, Hankow, $1........... 19 75
CHESTER—*St. Mark's* : Gen........... 5 00
CLEMSON COLLEGE — *Holy Trinity
Church* : Gen., $12.70 ; Junior Aux.,
salary of assistant for Miss McCul-
lough, Porto Rico, $1............. 13 70
COLUMBIA—*Church of the Good Shep-
herd* : Wo. Aux., Bible-woman, Han-
kow, $5 ; salary of assistant for Miss
McCullough, Porto Rico, $2 ; Junior
Aux., Bishop Capers Day-school,
Hankow, $10 ; Gen. (of which
Babies' Branch, 50 cts.), $9.20.... 26 20
Trinity Church : Gen., $169.60 ; Wo.
Aux., salary of assistant for Miss
McCullough, Porto Rico, $5 ; N. S.
Wilson Day-school, Hankow, $5 ;
M. E. Pinkney Fund for Bible-
woman, Tokyo, $5................. 184 60
CONGAREE—*St. John's* : Gen........... 7 50
DARLINGTON—*St. Matthew's S. S.** :
Gen. 21 44
EASTOVER—*Zion* : Gen., $12.50 ; Wo.
Aux., salary of assistant for Miss
McCullough, Porto Rico $1 ; Sp. for
mission at Highlands, Asheville, $2. 15 50
EDGEFIELD—*Trinity Church* : Wo. Aux.,
Gen., $3.50 ; Sp. for mission at High-
lands, Asheville, $5............... 8 50
FLORENCE—*St. John's* : Wo. Aux., N. S.
Wilson Day-school, Hankow, $1 ; Sp.
for "Bishop Howe' cot, St. Mary's
Orphanage, Shanghai, $5 ; M. E.
Pinkney Fund for Bible-woman,
Tokyo, $1......................... 7 00
GRANITEVILLE—*St. Paul's* : Gen....... 11 27
GREENVILLE—*Christ Church* : Babies'
Branch, Gen...................... 6 00
GREENWOOD—*Resurrection* : Wo. Aux.,
Bible-woman, Kyoto, $1.50 ; salary
of assistant for Miss McCullough,
Porto Rico, $2 ; Gen., $1 ; Sp. for
"Bishop Howe" cot, St. Mary's Or-
phanage, Shanghai, $1............ 5 50
HARTSVILLE — *St. Bartholomew'- S.
S.** : Gen........................ 1 64
JAMES ISLAND—*St. James's* : Wo. Aux.,
N. S. Wilson Day-school, Hankow,
$2 ; Bible-woman, Kyoto, $5 ; Sp. for
"Bishop Howe" cot, St. Mary's Or-
phanage, Shanghai, $3............ 10 00
JOHNS ISLAND—*St. John's* : Wo. Aux.,
Sp. for mission at Highlands, Ashe-
ville 5 00
LAURENS—*Epiphany* : Babies' Branch,
Gen. 2 25

"E. B. S.," Gen.....................
ORANGEBURG—*Church of the Redeemer*
M. E. Pinkney Fund for Bible-
woman, Tokyo, $2 ; Wo. Aux., Sp. for
"Bishop Howe" cot, St. Mary's Or-
phanage, Shanghai, $3.............
PENDLETON—*St. Paul's* : Gen., $7.50 ;
Wo. Aux., salary of assistant for
Miss McCullough, Porto Rico, $5....
PLANTERSVILLE—*Prince Frederick* : Wo.
Aux., Gen........................
RIDGE SPRING—*Grace* : Babies' Branch,
50 cts., S. S.,* $2.24, Gen.........
ROCK HILL—*Church of Our Saviour* :
Wo. Aux., Gen. (of which Junior
Aux., $2), $12 ; Sp. for mission at
Highlands, Asheville, $2..........
SENECA—*Ascension* : Gen..............
SPARTANBURG — *Advent* : Wo. Aux.,
Bishop Horner's work, Asheville,
$25 ; Sp. for mission at Highlands,
Asheville, $2.50 ; Sp. for Rectory
Building Fund, Lamar, Kansas City,
$2 ; Junior Aux., Gen. (of which
Babies' Branch, $11.56, S. S.,*
$151.66), $154.22 ; Bishop Capers
Day-school, Hankow, $5...........
SUMMERVILLE—*St. Paul's* : Wo. Aux.,
$10, Junior Aux., $10, Babies'
Branch, $2.05, Gen...............
SUMTER—*Church of the Holy Com-
forter* : $9.62, Babies' Branch, $1.40,
Gen. ....
WINNSBORO—*St. John's* : Babies'
Branch, Gen......................
MISCELLANEOUS — Branch Wo. Aux.,
$15.60, Junior Aux., $24.54, Gen....

Southern Ohio

Ap. $1,079.54 ; *Sp.* $368.45

CARTHAGE—*St. Peter's* : Gen.........
CINCINNATI—*Advent* : Dom., $21.35 ;
Frn., $14.46 ; Gen. (of which Wo.
Aux., $2), $280.77................
Calvary (Clifton) : Wo. Aux., Sp. for
Rev. W. B. Thorne, Oneida, Fond du
Lac ....
Christ Church : Sp. for Bishop Ken-
drick, Arizona, $10 ; Wo. Aux., $5,
S. S.,* $91.79, Gen...............
Grace : $26.50, S. S.,* $35.07, Gen....
*Church of the Redeemer S. S.** (Hyde
Park) : Gen......................
*St. Andrew's S. S.** : Gen...........
St. John's : Gen..................
*St. Luke's S. S.** : Gen...........
St. Paul's Cathedral : Gen., $88.84 ; Sp.
for Bishop Rowe, Alaska, $2......
Mrs. G. H. Thomas, Sp. for Church
Extension Fund, Porto Rico.......
COLUMBUS—*St. John's Chapel S. S.** :
Gen., $12 ; Sp. for Bishop Roots,
Hankow, $1.45....................
St. Paul's : Gen..................
St. Philip's : Gen................
DAYTON—*Christ Church S. S.** : Gen..
St. Andrew's : Gen...............
*St. Margaret's S. S.** : Dom. and Frn..
DELAWARE—*St. Peter's* : Wo. Aux., Gen.
GALENA—*Church of Our Saviour* : Wo.
Aux., Sp. for Bishop Rowe's hospital
work, Ketchikan, Alaska..........
GLENDALE—*Christ Church* : Wo. Aux.,
"Charlotte Proctor Memorial" bed,
St. James's Hospital, Anking, Han-
kow ....
HAMILTON—*Trinity Church S. S.** :
Gen. ....
LONDON—*Trinity Church S. S.** : Gen..
MADISONVILLE—*Holy Trinity Church* :
Gen. ....
NORWOOD—*Church of the Good Shep-
herd* : Gen......................
OAKLEY—*St. Mark's S. S.** : Gen......
PIQUA—*St. James's* : Wo. Aux., $10.

NANSEMOND Co.—*Glebe Church S. S.** (Driver): Gen... 1 07
NELSON Co.—*Christ Church*: Brotherhood of St. Paul, for feeding one of Bishop Rowe's dogs, Alaska, $5; Frn., $1... 6 00
NORFOLK Co.—*Christ Church* (Norfolk): Gen. (of which S. S.,* $85.21), $536.71; S. S.,* Indian, $15; Alaska, $10... 561 71
*Emmanuel Church S. S.** (Norfolk): Gen. ... 7 50
St. Luke's (Norfolk): Bishop Payne Divinity-school, Southern Virginia, $5; Gen. (of which S. S.,* $235.26), $361.01... 366 01
*St. Mark's S. S.** (Lambert's Point): Gen. ... 5 03
*All Saints' S. S.** (Portsmouth): Gen.. 8 76
*Trinity Church. S. S.** (Portsmouth): Gen. ... 19 50
NOTTOWAY Co.—*St. Luke's* (Blackstone): Wo. Aux., Sp. for Bishop Ferguson, Cape Palmas, Liberia, Africa ... 5 00
PITTSYLVANIA Co.—*Chatham Episcopal Institute S. S. ** (Chatham): Gen.. 15 51
Emmanuel Church (Chatham): Gen. (of which S. S.,* $2.78), $29.78; Sp. for deaf and dumb work under Rev. Mr. Whildin, Baltimore, Md., $4.17 ... 33 95
St. Luke's (Chatham): Gen... 2 00
Epiphany (Danville): Junior Aux., Mary Page Dame Memorial, St. James's Hospital, Anking, Hankow, $50; S. S.,* Gen., $42.50... 92 50
Grace, Banister Parish: Dom. and Frn. ... 1 77
Trinity Church (Elba): Gen... 2 00
PRINCESS ANNE Co.—*Emmanuel Church* (Kempsville): $10, S. S.,* $5, Gen... 15 00
*Galilee S. S.** (Virginia Beach): Gen.. 2 62
*East Lynnhaven Parish S. S.**: Gen... 2 00
PRINCE GEORGE Co.—*Brandon* (Burrowsville): Wo. Aux., Sp. for work of Rev. J. C. Ambler, Tokyo, at his discretion ... 5 00
Brandon Church and Belle Harrison Memorial Chapel (Burrowsville): Gen. ... 23 25
Ritchie Memorial (Claremont): Gen... 5 83
Grace (Calvin Point): Gen... 5 00
ROANOKE Co.—*Christ Church* (Roanoke): Wo. Aux., Sp. for Holy Trinity Orphanage, Tokyo... 15 00
St. John's (Roanoke): Sp. for St. Paul's College Fund, Tokyo, $7; S. S.,* Gen., $35... 42 00
ROCKBRIDGE Co.—*St. John's S. S.** (Glasgow): Gen... 4 00
TAZEWELL Co.—*St. Mary's S. S.** (Graham): Gen... 3 09
Stras Memorial (Tazewell): Gen... 15 00
WARWICK Co.—*St. Paul's* (Newport News): Dom... 25 00
WYTHE Co.—*St. John's S. S.** (Wytheville): Gen., $35; Sp. for a Chinese child, Dowchaw Tsung, St. Mary's Hall, Shanghai, $15... 50 00
MISCELLANEOUS—"Friends," Sp. for medical expenses of Student Volunteer missionary... 30 00
Wo. Aux., Rev. H. St. George Tucker's salary, Tokyo... 850 00
Wo. Aux., salary of Miss Sabine, Alaska, $50; salary of Miss Mann, Tokyo, $100; Brazil, $25... 175 00

Springfield

Ap. $261.56; *Sp.* $10.25

ALTON—*St. Paul's*: Wo. Aux., $15, "A Member," $25, Gen.; Girls' Friendly Society, Sp. for salary of missionary

---

Left-margin amounts column:

20 00
29 14
31 41
9 26
28 12
28 60
6 86
4 75
25 48
53 86
16 00
8 21
9 74
20 00
2 00
2 62
50
117 44
57
11 89
7 02
5 50
48 80
10 00
207 16
15 00
472 37
4 00
25 00
145 65
39 37
10 75
3 00
17 80
2 00
30 15

curates for Rev. S. C. Hughson,
o.h.c., St. Andrew's School, Sewanee,
Tennessee, $10.25; S. S.,* Gen.,
$58.54 .... 108 79
Trinity Chapel S. S.*: Gen.......... 14 04
BLOOMINGTON—St. Matthew's: Gen.... 29 53
CARBONDALE—St. Andrew's: Gen...... 4 80
CHESTER—St. Mark's: Gen.......... 4 50
COLLINSVILLE—Christ Church: Gen... 7 80
DANVILLE—Holy Trinity Church: Frn. 11 60
DECATUR—St. John's: Gen........... 31 20
McLEANSBORO—St. James's: Gen...... 2 30
MOUND CITY—St. Peter's: Gen....... 1 50
PEKIN—St. Paul's: Gen............. 12 00
SPRINGFIELD — Christ Church: Wo.
  Aux., $10, S. S.,* $25, Gen........ 35 00
St. John's S. S.*: Gen............. 2 75
WAVERLY—Christ Church; Gen...... 6 00

Tennessee
Ap. $720.39; *Sp.* $111.00

BOLIVAR—St. Philip's: Gen.......... 2 50
CHATTANOOGA—Christ Church: Wo.
  Aux., Gen........................ 5 00
St. Paul's: Wo. Aux., "Bishop Quin-
  tard" scholarship, St. Mary's Hall,
  Shanghai, $2.50; Gen. (of which S.
  S.,* $79.83), $87.33............... 89 83
CLEVELAND—St. Luke's: Wo. Aux.,
  "Bishop Quintard" scholarship, St.
  Mary's Hall, Shanghai............. 2 00
FRANKLIN—St. Paul's S. S.*: Gen.... 4 30
GREENVILLE—St. James's S. S.*: Gen.. 1 50
JACKSON—St. Luke's: Wo. Aux., Gen.
  (of which Junior Aux., $2)......... 24 00
KNOXVILLE—St. John's: $27, S. S.,*
  $50, Gen.; Wo. Aux., woman's work,
  Japan, $50........................ 127 00
MEMPHIS—Calvary: Junior Aux., Gen. 5 00
Church of the Good Shepherd: Wo.
  Aux., Gen........................ 10 00
Emmanuel Church: Wo. Aux., West
  Africa 5 00
Grace: Junior Aux., Gen............. 5 00
St. Luke's: Wo. Aux., Gen.......... 10 00
St. Mary's Cathedral: $69.65, Junior
  Aux., $5, Gen..................... 74 65
MONTEAGLE—Fairmount School: Porto
  Rico 3 93
NASHVILLE—Advent: Junior Aux., Gen. 3 00
Christ Church: Gen. (of which Wo.
  Aux., $17.50), $192.35; Wo. Aux.,
  Sp. for "Bishop Quintard" scholar-
  ship, St Mary's Hall, Shanghai, $2.50 194 85
Holy Trinity Church: Gen.......... 5 00
St. Andrew's (West): $2.75, Junior
  Aux., $1.25, Gen.................. 4 00
St. Anne's: Junior Aux., Gen....... 2 50
St. Peter's: $5, Junior Aux., $1.60,
  Gen.............................. 6 60
St. Stephen's: Junior Aux., Gen.... 2 00
SEWANEE—St. Paul's-on-the-Mount S.
  S.*: Gen.......................... 13 48
Otey Memorial S. S.*: Gen.......... 19 75
TRACY CITY—Christ Church S. S.*:
  Gen.............................. 9 50
MISCELLANEOUS—Right Rev. Thomas
  F. Gailor, d.d., Sp. for Dr. Correll's
  Tsu Building Fund, Kyoto......... 100 00
Babies' Branch, Akita Kindergarten,
  Tokyo, $15; Little Helpers' Day-
  school, Shanghai, $5; Gen., $70;
  Sp. for "Little Helpers'" cot, St.
  Agnes's Hospital, Raleigh, North
  Carolina, $5; Sp. for Bishop Spald-
  ing Emergency Fund, White Rocks,
  Utah, $5; Sp. for missionary font, $1 101 00

Texas
Ap. $904.70; *Sp.* $317.66

AUSTIN—All Saints': "Communicant,"
  work of Rev. W. H. Smart, Yamagata Shi, Tokyo, $1; Gen., $1;
  Wo. Aux., Gen., $15; Babies'

Branch, Gaylord Hart Mitchell Kin-
  dergarten, Akita, Tokyo, $8; Dom.
  and Frn., $33; S. S.,* Gen., $57....
St. David's: Wo. Aux., Gen........
BEAUMONT—St. Mark's: Wo. Aux.,
  Gen..............................
COLUMBUS—St. John's: Gen.........
DICKINSON—Holy Trinity Church: Gen.
EAGLE LAKE—Christ Church: Gen....
GALVESTON — Trinity Church: Frn.,
  $87.70; Wo. Aux., Gen., $15; S. S.,*
  Sp. for Bishop Aves, Mexico, $317.66
HEARNE—St. Philip's: Gen..........
HOUSTON — Christ Church: Colored,
  $20; S. S.,* Gen., $293.77........
MARLIN—St. John's S. S.*: Gen.....
MARSHALL—Trinity Church: Wo. Aux.,
  $19.25, S. S.,* $26, Gen.........
NACOGDOCHES — Christ Church: Wo.
  Aux., Gen........................
TEMPLE—Christ Church: Wo. Aux.,
  Gen..............................
WACO—St. Paul's: Frn.............
MISCELLANEOUS—Junior Aux., Alaska,
  $25; "Bishop Aves" scholarship,
  Hooker Memorial School, Mexico,
  $37; "Bishop Kinsolving" scholar-
  ship, St. Mary's Hall, Shanghai,
  $19.75; Gen., $49.48.............

Vermont
Ap. $439.75; *Sp.* $125.00

BENNINGTON—St. Peter's: Gen......
BURLINGTON — St. Paul's: Colored,
  $17.97; Bontok, Philippine Islands,
  $9; Tokyo, $1.75; S. S.,* Gen.,
  $128.93; Sp. for Rev. W. C. Clapp,
  Bontok, Philippine Islands, $25....
EAST FAIRFIELD—Mission: Gen......
ENOSBURG—Christ Church: Gen......
HARDWICK—St. John Baptist's: Gen..
MIDDLEBURY—St. Stephen's: Gen....
NORTH TROY—St. Augustine's: Gen...
POULTNEY—St. John's S. S.*: Gen....
ROYALTON—St. Paul's: Gen.........
ST. ALBANS—St. S. S.*: Gen......
ST. JOHNSBURY—St. Andrew's S. S.*:
  Gen..............................
SHELDON—Grace: Gen..............
SHERBURNE—Church of Our Saviour S.
  S.*: Gen.........................
WOODSTOCK—St. James's: Gen......
MISCELLANEOUS—"A Vermont Church-
  woman," Gen.....................
Windsor District, Wo. Aux., Bible-
  woman, China.....................
Wo. Aux., Sp. for St. Augustine's
  School, Raleigh, North Carolina....

Virginia
Ap. $1,395.26; *Sp.* $273.55

ALBEMARLE Co.—Christ Church (Char-
  lottesville): Gen., $181; Wo. Aux.,
  Brazil, $50.......................
Chapel of the Good Shepherd S. S.*:
  Gen..............................
St. Luke's Chapel, St. Anne's Parish:
  Gen..............................
ALEXANDRIA Co.—Chapel of the Good
  Shepherd (Alexandria): Gen., $4.62;
  S. S.,* $2.48; Sp. for work
  under Bishop Ferguson, $5.16......
St. Paul's (Alexandria): Junior Aux.,
  Sp. for Dr. E. L. Woodward for his
  hospital, Hankow, $10; Sp. for Mrs.
  Ackley, Guantanamo, for work
  among Cubans, $5.................
CAROLINE Co.—St. Peter's (Port Royal):
  Wo. Aux., Alaska, $1; Babies' Branch,
  Sp. for Mr. Neve's work in Vir-
  ginia, $1.........................
Grace: Gen.......................
CULPEPER Co.—St. Paul's, Ridley Par-
  ish: Gen.........................

20 00
125 00
20 00
3 75
4 44
6 15
17 16
4 65
67
10,00
146 91
15 00
2 00
132 92
5 18
325 07
131 00
120 00
40 87
35 00
5 00
4 65
7 57
20 00
23 00
3 20
17 04
17 95
4 10
1 14
2 53
16 51
4 68

WESTMORELAND Co. (Colonial Beach)—
Wo. Aux., Sp. for Rev. R. A. Walke,
Tokyo, $1; Sp. for St. Paul's College,
Tokyo, $1.................... 2 00
St. Paul's Chapel, Montrose Parish:
Gen. 2 50
MISCELLANEOUS—"Friends," Sp. for
medical expenses of a Student Volun-
teer missionary.................. 10 00
Junior Aux., Gen., $121.49; Sp. for
Rev. R. A. Walke, Tokyo, $8.24; Sp.
for Rev. E. J. Lee, Hankow, $4.50.. 134 23

Washington

Ap. $1,199.95; Sp. $66.60

WASHINGTON—Ascension: "A Mem-
ber," Sp. for Shanghai Catechist
School, Land and Building Fund.... 1 00
Advent: Gen..................... 17 70
Brookland Parish: Gen........... 40 00
All Saints' S. S.,* Chevy Chase Parish:
(of which *$35.95) Brazil, $25;
Dom., $25; Frn., $25.............. 75 00
Epiphany Parish Morning and After-
noon S. Ss.: Alaska, $54.22; Sp. for
Bishop Rowe's work, Alaska, $5;
Gen.,* $209.83 .... 269 05
Epiphany Chapel S. S.*: Gen........ 111 67
Grace S. S.* (Georgetown): Gen. (ad-
ditional) 2 00
St. Agnes's Chapel: Gen. (of which S.
S.,* $8.44)..................... 28 44
St. John's (Georgetown): "A Member,"
Sp. for Shanghai Catechist School,
Land and Building Fund........... 10 00
St. John's: Dom. and Frn........... 127 39
St. Paul's: Gen., $300; Sp. for Colored
work, St. Paul's School, Lawrence-
ville, Southern Virginia, $5; Sp. for
Bishop Rowe, Alaska, $5; Sp. for
St. Paul's College, Tokyo, 50 cts.... 310 50
Trinity Church S. S.,* Takoma Par-
ish: Gen....................... 25 00
Trinity Church S. S.*: Gen., $75;
"Trinity" scholarship, St. Hilda's
School, Wuchang, $50 .... 125 00
Mrs. L. M. Zeller, Gen............. 1 00
Mrs. Alfred Holmead, Sp. for Priory
School, Honolulu, $5; Sp. for slave
refuge for girls, Shanghai, $5...... 10 00
Mrs. Browning, Sp. for Shanghai
Catechist School, Land and Build-
ing Fund...................... 1 00
MONTGOMERY Co.—Chapel of the Re-
deemer (Glen Echo): Gen......... 1 35
Christ Church (Kensington): Gen. (of
which S. S.,* $6.80)............. 14 80
Christ Church S. S.* (Rockville) Gen. 1 00
PRINCE GEORGE Co.—King George Par-
ish: Dom...................... 3 00
St. Simon's Chapel S. S.* (Croom):
Gen........................... 5 00
Zion Parish: Gen................. 51 51
ST. MARY'S Co.—All Saints' (Oakley):
Dom., $3.30; S. S.* (additional),
Gen., $2.74.................... 6 04
MISCELLANEOUS—Wo. Aux., Sp. for
Rev. J. W. Nichols, Shanghai, $10;
Sp. for Miss S. H. Higgins, Hankow,
toward support of a bed for one year
in her hospital, $19.10........... 29 10

Western Massachusetts

Ap. $1,051.14; Sp. $42.00

CLINTON—Church of the Good Shep-
herd: Gen...................... 24 51
DALTON—Grace: Dom., $6; Frn., $6;
Wo. Aux., Alaska Supply Fund, 40
cts.; Sp. for Foreign Insurance
Fund, $3; S. S.,* Dom., $5.73; Frn.,
$5.72 .... 26 85
FITCHBURG — Christ Church: Junior
Aux., medical work, Cape Mount,
$10; S. S.,* Gen., $105.......... 115 00
GARDNER—St. Paul's: Junior Aux.,

China, $1; medical work, Cape
Mount, Africa, 75 cts............ 1 75
GREENFIELD—*St. James's*: Junior Aux.,
Gen., $15; medical work, Cape
Mount, $10................... 25 00
LANESBORO—*St. Luke's*: Dom., $5.50;
Frn., $5.50; S. S.,* Dom., $4.57;
Frn., $4.57.................. 20 14
LEE—*St. George's*: Wo. Aux., Sp. for
Foreign Insurance Fund.......... 1 50
MILFORD — *Trinity Church*: Dom.,
$19.10; Wo. Aux., St. Paul's School,
Lawrenceville, Southern Virginia,
49 cts.; Alaska Supply Fund, $1;
Japanese Bible-women, Honolulu,
$1; Sp. for Foreign Insurance Fund,
$1 .... 22 59
MILLVILLE—*St. John's*: Wo. Aux., Jap-
anese Bible-women, Honolulu...... 1 00
MONSON PALMER—Wo. Aux., Sp. for
Building Fund, St. Margaret's
School, Tokyo................. 50
NORTH ADAMS—*St. John's*: Wo. Aux.,
Sp. for Mrs. Hunter, St. Augustine's
School, Raleigh, North Carolina.... 10 00
NORTHAMPTON—*St. John's*: Wo. Aux.,
Japanese Bible-woman, Honolulu,
$2; Philippine insurance, $2; Sp. for
Building Fund, St. Margaret's School,
Tokyo, $10.................. 14 00
OXFORD—*Grace*: Wo. Aux., Alaska
Supply Fund 50
SOUTHBRIDGE—*Holy Trinity Church*:
Wo. Aux., Japanese Bible-woman,
Honolulu, $5; Sp. for Foreign Insur-
ance Fund, $2................ 7 00
SPRINGFIELD—*All Saints'*: Junior Aux.,
for medical work, Cape Mount..... 2 00
Christ Church: Gen., $11.75; Junior
Aux., medical work, Cape Mount,
$20 .... 31 75
St. Peter's: Wo. Aux., Japanese Bible-
woman, Honolulu, $5; Junior Aux.,
Sp. for St. Margaret's School, Tokyo,
$2 .... 7 00
WARE—*Trinity Church*: Junior Aux.,
medical work, Cape Mount........ 75
WEBSTER—*Reconciliation*: Junior Aux.,
medical work, Cape Mount........ 85
WESTBORO—*St. Stephen's*: Wo. Aux.,
Japanese Bible-woman, Honolulu... 5 00
WESTFIELD—*Atonement*: Junior Aux.,
Dom., $1; Gen., $2............. 3 00
WILLIAMSTOWN — *St. John's*: Junior
Aux., Dom., $1; Indian, $1; Col-
ored, $1; Gen., $2............. 5 00
WORCESTER — *All Saints'*: Indian,
$26.18; Frn., $146.67; Gen.,
$127.15; Sp. for Rev. R. C. Wilson,
Shanghai, for travelling expenses,
$8; Junior Aux., medical work,
Cape Mount, $18; S. S.,* Gen.,
$115.11 .... 441 11
St. John's: Junior Aux., Indian, $2.50;
Colored, $2.50; medical work, Cape
Mount, $20; Gen., $10; Sp. for St.
Margaret's School, Tokyo, $4; S. S.,*
Gen., $44.................... 83 00
St. Luke's: Junior Aux., medical work,
Cape Mount, $8.50; S. S.,* Gen.,
$28.84 .... 37 34
St. Mark's: Gen., $200; Junior Aux.,
medical work, Cape Mount, $1.50... 201 50
Junior Aux., Junior Rally, Miss Em-
berley's work, Alaska............ 4 50

Western Michigan
Ap. $187.62; *Sp.* $1.00

ALLEGAN — *Church of the Good
Shepherd*: Gen.................. 10 00
BENTON HARBOR—*Holy Trinity Church*:
Gen. 1 00
BIG RAPIDS—*St. Andrew's*: Gen...... 18 25
CHARLEVOIX—*Christ Church*: Gen., $1;
Junior Aux. Gen., $3............. 4 00

	Honolulu, $1.02 ; Philippines, $1.02 ;
	Porto Rico, $1.01................ 21 95
95 00	MOOREFIELD—*Emmanuel Church*: Lay-
	men's Missionary Movement, Frn... 2 72
	MORGANTOWN—*Trinity Church*; Junior
	Aux., "West Virginia Junior" schol-
	arship, St. John's School, Cape
1 75	Mount, $2 ; Hankow, $2.......... 4 00
	NEW MARTINSVILLE—*St. Ann's*: Gen.. 9 89
24 80	POINT PLEASANT—*Christ Church*: Gen. 42 00
	PRINCETON—*Heavenly Rest*: Frn..... 3 50
2 00	ROMNEY—*St. Stephen's*: Frn......... 3 62
80	RONCEVERTE—*Incarnation*: Dom., $2.79 ;
	Frn., $4.29 .... 7 08
4 00	SHEPHERDSTOWN — *Trinity Church*:
	Dom. and Frn................ 30 51
21 35	TAVERNERSVILLE—*Grace Chapel*: Gen.. 5 00
	WESTON—*St. Paul's*: "A Society of
10 40	Small Girls," Sp. for St. Mary's Or-
	phanage, Shanghai, $15.36 ; S. S.*
11 75	(additional), Gen., $2.50........ 17 86
8 00	WHEELING — *St. Andrew's*: Rector's
	Guild, Sp. for St. Paul's College,
15 50	Tokyo 4 00
	*St. Luke's S. S.**: Gen............. 120 00
159 56	WHITE SULPHUR—*St. Thomas's*: Lay-
8 00	men's Missionary Movement, Frn... 1 50
6 54	WILLIAMSTOWN—*Christ Church*: Gen. 8 10
2 25	
5 00	

Missionary Districts

Alaska

Ap. $478.48 ; *Sp.* $44.00

	ALLACHAKAT — *St. John's-in-the-Wil-*
	derness: Wo. Aux., Deaconess Car-
15 00	ter, Gen., $15 ; S. S.,* Gen., $15.... 30 00
17 50	ANVIK—*Christ Church*: Sp. for Bish-
	op Rowe, Alaska, $44 ; S. S.,* Gen.,
9 00	$7.37 .... 51 37
	CHENA—*St. Barnabas's Mission*: Gen.. 9 75
	CIRCLE—*Heavenly Rest*: Gen......... 8 25
	FAIRBANKS—*St. Matthew's S. S.**:
	Gen. 353 11
	FORT YUKON—*St. Stephen's S. S.**:
46 00	Gen. 16 00
4 00	NENANA—*St. Mark's Mission*: Gen.... 10 00
	POINT HOPE—*St. Thomas's*: Gen..... 10 00
	SKAGWAY—*St. Saviour's*: Gen....... 16 00
	WRANGELL—*St. Philip's* (of which S.
4 00	S.,* $15) Gen.................. 18 00
2 82	

Arizona

Ap. $38.15

19 54	GLOBE—*St. John's*: Gen............ 13 40
	PHOENIX—*Trinity Church*: Indian, $5 ;
20 00	Frn., $5...................... 10 00
9 73	YUMA—*St. Paul's*: (of which S. S.,*
	$4.75) Gen.................... 14 75

Asheville

Ap. $658.26 ; *Sp.* $181.90

	ARDEN—*Christ Church*: Dom., $1 ;
	Gen., $1 ; S. S.,* Gen., $3......... 5 00
122 39	ASHEVILLE—*Trinity Church*: Dom.,
	$48.33 ; Frn., $48.33 ; Gen., $48.34 ;
25 00	Wo. Aux., for "Jarvis Buxton" schol-
4 25	arship, St. John's University, Shang-
	hai, $40 ; S. S.,* Gen., $91.87.... 276 87
3 50	BEAVER CREEK—*St. Mary's*: Dom.,
8 25	79 cts. ; Frn., 79 cts. ; Gen., 77 cts. ;
	S. S.,* Gen., 91 cts.............. 3 26
74 76	BESSEMER CITY—*St. Andrew's*: Dom.,
4 31	25 cts. ; Frn., 25 cts............ 50
	BILTMORE—*All Souls'*: Gen.......... 100 00
	FOSCOE—*Easter Chapel*: Frn....... 40
4 00	GASTONIA—*St. Mark's*: Dom., 33 cts. ;
	Frn., 33 cts. ; Gen., 34 cts........ 1 00
	GLENDALE SPRINGS — *Holy Trinity*
2 08	*Church*: Dom., 28 cts. ; Frn., 53
	cts. ; Gen., 53 cts.............. 1 34
	GLEN ALPINE—*St. Paul's*: Frn, 50
	cts. ; Gen., $2 ; S. S.,* Gen., $9.06.. 11 56

GRACE—*Grace S. S.**: Gen........... 17 10
HICKORY—*Ascension*: Dom., $2; Frn.,
$2; Gen., $2..................... 6 00
HIGHLANDS — *Incarnation*: Dom.,
$1.50; Frn., $1.50.............. 3 00
MARION—*St. John's*: Dom., 25 cts.;
Frn., 25 cts.; Gen., $1; S. S.,* Gen.,
$2.75 .... 4 25
MORGANTON—*St. George's*: Gen...... 1 00
St. Mary's: Gen...................... 50
St. Michael's: Gen.................. 1 00
NONAH—*St. John's*: Gen.............. 50
RUTHERFORDTON—*St. Francis's*: Dom.,
$1; Frn., $1; Gen., $1.............. 3 00
St. Luke's: Gen.................... 50
SALUDA—*Transfiguration*: Dom., $1.50;
Frn., $1.50; Gen., 50 cts.......... 3 50
TODD—*St. Matthew's*: Dom., 41 cts.;
Frn., 42 cts.; Gen., 67 cts.; S. S.,*
Gen., $1.98...................... 3 48
TRYON—*Holy Cross*: Dom., $1.50;
Frn., $1.50; Gen., $1.50........... 4 50
MISCELLANEOUS — Wo. Aux., Gen.,
$210; Sp. for Bishop Robinson's
work, Nevada, $105.15; Sp. for St.
Anne's Embroidery School, Kana-
zawa, Kyoto, $76.75.............. 391 90

Eastern Oregon
Ap. $132.05

BAKER CITY—*St. Stephen's*: Junior
Aux., $3.28, Babies' Branch, $3,
Gen.............................. 6 28
CANYON CITY—*St. Thomas's S. S.**:
Gen.............................. 13 00
ENTERPRISE—*S. S.**: Gen............ 3 00
FREEWATER—Wo. Aux., Gen........... 1 25
HEPPNER—*All Saints*: Gen. (of which
S. S.,* $5)...................... 8 55
MONUMENT—*S. S.**: Gen............ 4 40
PENDLETON—*Church of the Redeemer*:
Wo. Aux., Gen................... 11 50
THE DALLES—*St. Paul's*: Gen., $9.50;
Wo. Aux., Gen., $10.12; S. S.,*
China, $64.45................... 84 07

Honolulu
Ap. $678.78; *Sp.* $23.00

HILO—*Holy Apostles'*: Gen. (of which
S. S.,* $21.80).................. 26 80
HONOLULU—*Holy Trinity Church S.
S.**: Gen....................... 12 30
St. Andrew's Cathedral: Sp. for St.
Pau. s College, Tokyo, $3; S. S.,*
Gen., $150.89.................... 153 89
*St. Andrew's (Native) S. S.**: Gen... 19 45
*St. Andrew's Priory S. S.**: Gen...... 52 22
St. Elizabeth's: Gen. (of which S. S.,*
$100.90) 110 90
St. Peter's: Sp. for Elizabeth Bunn
Memorial Hospital, Hankow, $20;
for support of a bed in Elizabeth
Bunn Memorial Hospital, Hankow,
$20; "E. M. S.," for bed in Eliza-
beth Bunn Memorial Hospital, Han-
kow, $20; S. S.,* Gen., $92.40
(Kipahulu)—S. S.**: Gen......... 152 40
*Iolani College S. S.**: Gen........... 9 45
KOHALA—*St. Augustine's*: Gen. (of
which S. S.,* $20.33)............ 10 96
LAHAINA—*Holy Innocents*: Gen. (of
which S. S.,* $25)............... 42 28
MOILILI—*St. Mary's*: Gen. (of which
S. S.,* $30.55).................. 34 00
MAKAPALA—*St. Paul's S. S.**: Gen... 32 55
PAAUILO AND LAUPAHOEHO—Gen...... 6 50
WAILUKU—*Church of the Good Shep-
herd S. S.**: Gen................ 3 50
                                    34 58

Idaho
Ap. $88.88; *Sp.* $20.00

BOISE—*Grace Mission*: Church Guild,
Sp. for St. Paul's College, Tokyo... 20 00
*St. Michael's Cathedral S. S.**: Gen... 5 37

HAILEY—*Emmanuel Church*: Gen. (of
which S. S.,* $24)
MURRAY—*St. Thomas's*: Dom.........
PAYETTE—*St. James's*: Gen..........
TWIN FALLS—*Ascension*: Gen. (of
which S. S.,* $3)................
WALLACE—*Holy Trinity Church S. S.**:
Frn. ....

Kearney
Ap. $162.83; *Sp.* $8.25

CHADRON—*Grace S. S.**: Gen........
FARNAM—Gen. (of which S. S.,* $7.81)
FORT ROBINSON—*Post S. S.**: Gen...
HASTINGS—*St, Mark's*: Junior Aux.,
Sp. for St. Paul's College, Tokyo,
$8.25; S. S.,* Gen., 91 cts.......
HOLDREGE—*St. Elizabeth's*: Gen. (of
which S. S.,* $2.80).............
LEXINGTON—*St. Peter's*: Gen........
NORTH PLATTE—*Church of Our Sa-
viour*: Gen. (of which S. S.,* $76.61)
PALISADE—Children,* Gen...........

Nevada
Ap. $20.00

LAS VEGAS—*Christ Church*: Gen.....

New Mexico
Ap. $102.02

ALAMOGORDO—*St. John's*: Gen.......
CARLSBAD—*Grace S. S.**: Gen.......
CLOVIS—*St. James's*: Gen..........
EAST LAS VEGAS—*St. Paul's S. S.**:
Gen............................
FARMINGTON—*St. John's S. S.**: Gen.
LA MESA—Wo. Aux., Gen............
TUCUMCARI—*St. Michael's*: $5, S. S.,*
$3.70, Gen.....................

North Dakota
Ap. $1,036.08

BISMARCK—*St. George's S. S.**: Gen..
BYRON—*Mission S. S.**: Gen.......
CANNON BALL—*Mission S. S.**: Gen..
CARRINGTON—*Mission S. S.**: Gen...
CASSELTON—*St. Stephen's S. S.**: Gen.
DEVIL'S LAKE—*Advent S. S.**: Gen...
DICKEY—*St. John's S. S.**: Gen....
DICKINSON—*St. John's S. S.**: Gen...
DRAYTON—*Mission S. S.**: Gen......
ESMOND—*Mission S. S.**: Gen......
FARGO—*Gethsemane Cathedral S. S.**:
Gen............................
FORMAN—*Mission S. S.**: Gen......
FESSENDEN—*Mission S. S.**: Gen....
FULLERTON—*Mission S. S.**: Gen....
GRAFTON—*St. James's S. S.**: Gen...
GRAND FORKS—*St. Paul's S. S.**: Gen.
HAMPDEN—*Mission S. S.**: Gen.....
HARVEY—*Mission S. S.**: Gen......
HEATON—*Mission S. S.**: Gen......
JAMESTOWN—*Grace S. S.**: Gen.....
KENMARE—*Mission S. S.**: Gen.....
KULU—*Mission S. S.**: Gen........
LAKOTA—*Church of the Good Shepherd
S. S.**: Gen....................
LARIMORE—*St. John's S. S.**: Gen...
LA MOURE—*Mission S. S.**: Gen....
LAWTON—*Mission S. S.**: Gen......
LISBON—*Trinity Church S. S.**: Gen..
MANDAN—*Christ Church S. S.**: Gen.
McCLUSKY—*Mission S. S.**: Gen....
MILNOR—*Mission S. S.**: Gen......
MINNEWAUKON—*Grace S. S.**: Gen...
MINOT—*All Saints' S. S.**: Gen.....
MONANGO—*Mission S. S.**: Gen.....
NEW ROCKFORD—*St. Timothy's S. S.**:
Gen............................
PARK RIVER—*St. Peter's S. S.**: Gen..
PEMBINA—*Grace S. S.**: Gen.......
RED HAIL—*St. Gabriel's S. S.**: Gen..
ROLLA—*St. John's S. S.**: Gen......

Salina
Ap. $109.55

BELOIT—*St. Paul's*: Wo. Aux., Gen. (of which Babies' Branch, $4.05)......	11 49
BENNINGTON — *Transfiguration*: Wo. Aux., Gen......................	3 12
BROOKVILLE—Gen.	1 00
CAWKER CITY—*St. Mary the Virgin*: Gen.	17 51
FORMOSA—*Trinity Church*: Gen. (of which Babies' Branch, $3.64)......	7 80
FREEPORT—*Trinity Church*: Gen......	5 00
GREAT BEND—*St. John's*: $4.40, S. S.,* $5.83, Gen...................	10 23
HARPER—*St. James's S. S.*: Dom...	2 00
KINGMAN—*Christ Church*: Gen. (of which Wo. Aux., $5.72)..........	18 48
LARNED—*Bethany*: $2.19, S. S.,* $1.58, Gen.	3 77
LYONS—*Mission*: $5.08, S. S.,* $1.31, Gen.	6 39
MINNEAPOLIS—*St. Peter's*: Wo. Aux., Gen.	6 76
SALINA—*Christ Cathedral*: Gen. (of which Wo. Aux., $9.92)...........	10 92
WAKEENEY—*Heavenly Rest*: Wo. Aux., Gen.	5 24

South Dakota
Ap. $432.88

CHEYENNE AGENCY—*Ascension S. S.*: Gen.	7 51
Calvary S. S.: Gen.............	1 89
St. Andrew's S. S.: Gen...........	9 45
St. Barnabas' S. S.: Gen..........	2 90
St. James's S. S.: Gen............	2 40
St. John's S. S.: Gen.............	7 78
St. Luke's S. S.: Gen............	5 50
St. Mark's S. S.: Gen............	5 27
St. Mary's S. S.: Gen............	6 49
St. Stephen's S. S.: Gen.........	3 51
MILBANK—*Christ Church*: Wo. Aux., Gen.	5 03
WILMOT—*Trinity Mission*: Gen.......	5 00
PINE RIDGE AGENCY—*Christ Church Station S. S.*: Gen...............	63
Grace Chapel S. S.: Gen.........	7 03
St. Mary's Chapel S. S. (Sand Hills): Gen.	6 73
St. Mary's Chapel S. S. (Grass Creek): Gen....................	3 75
St. Julia's Chapel S. S.: Gen......	3 02
St. Paul's Chapel S. S.: Gen........	4 97
St. Philip's Chapel S. S.: Gen.......	3 47
St. Thomas's Chapel S. S.: Gen.....	7 68
St. Matthew's Station S. S.: Gen.....	4 76
St. Mark's Chapel S. S.: Gen......	5 75
Chapel of the Messiah S. S.: Gen....	6 11
St. Alban's Chapel S. S.: Gen......	4 95
St. John's Station S. S.: Gen.......	2 75
St. Jude's S. S.: Gen............	1 45
St. Luke's Chapel S. S.: Gen.......	2 13
St. Peter's Chapel S. S.: Gen.......	4 87
St. James's Chapel S. S.: Gen......	2 00
Holy Cross Chapel S. S.: Gen.....	16 51
Advent Station S. S.: Gen..........	5 71
Epiphany Station S. S.: Gen........	25
Inestimable Gift Church (Corn Creek District): Dom., $5; Frn., $7; China, $5; S. S.,* Gen., $10.......	27 00
St. Barnabas's (Corn Creek District): Dom., $1.50; Frn., $2; China, $4; S. S.,* Gen., $3................	10 50
Church of the Mediator (Corn Creek District): Dom., $1; Frn., $2; China, $3; S. S.,* Gen., $4........	10 00
Gethsemane (Corn Creek District): Dom., $3; Frn., $4.50; China, $5; S. S.,* Gen., $5...........	17 50
Trinity Church Station (Corn Creek District): Dom., $1; Frn., $1.50; China, $2; S. S.,* Gen., $2.50......	7 00
Faith Station (Corn Creek District): Dom., $2; Frn., $2; China, $4; S. S.,* Gen., $4.................	12 00

Hope Station (Corn Creek District):
Dom., $1; Frn., $2; S. S.,* Gen., $3. ... 6 00
ROSEBUD MISSION—*Church of Jesus S.
S.*: Gen. ... 2 90
Calvary Chapel S. S.: Gen. ... 11 50
St. Peter's Chapel S. S.: Gen. ... 1 42
Grace Station S. S.: Gen. ... 1 22
Holy Innocents' Chapel S. S.: Gen. ... 8 21
Epiphany Chapel S. S.: Gen. ... 1 58
Ephphatha Chapel; *St. Mary's School
S. S.*: Gen. ... 25 67
Trinity Chapel S. S.: Gen. ... 16 26
St. George's Chapel S. S.: Gen. ... 1 44
Chapel of the Mediator S. S.: Gen... 23 10
Other Stations, S. S's.: Gen. ... 9 02
STANDING ROCK MISSION—*Church of
the Good Shepherd*: Frn. ... 2 00
Grand River School: Dom., $1; Frn.,
$2 ... 3 00
St. Elizabeth's: Frn. ... 2 00
St. John the Baptist's Chapel: Frn... 2 00
St. Thomas's: Frn ... 05
YANKTONNAIS MISSION—*Christ Church*:
Frn., $4.55; Wo. Aux., mite-boxes,
$2.80, S. S.,* $40.84, Gen. ... 48 19
St. John the Baptist's: Frn., $3.80;
S. S.,* Gen., $9.52. ... 13 32
All Saints' S. S.: Gen. ... 1 86
St. Peter's: Wo. Aux., mite-boxes,
$1.83, S. S.,* $7.40, Gen. ... 9 23
Ascension: 60 cts., S. S.,* $1.06, Gen... 1 66

Southern Florida

Ap. $482.74

BARTOW—*Holy Trinity Church*: Gen... 5 00
BUENA VISTA—*Holy Cross S. S.*:
Dom., $2.50; Frn., $2.50. ... 5 00
COCOANUT GROVE — *Christ Church*:
Gen. ... 1 00
DAYTONA—*St. Mary's*: $30, S. S.,* $20,
Gen. ... 50 00
ENTERPRISE—*All Saints' S. S.*: Gen... 20 20
DANIA—*St. John's S. S.*: Gen. ... 1 00
EUSTIS—*St. Thomas's*; Gen. ... 6 00
JUPITER—*St. Martin's S. S.*: Gen. ... 15 00
KEY WEST—*Holy Innocents'*: $10, S.
S.,* $32.95, Gen. ... 42 95
LAKELAND—*All Saints'*: Gen. ... 12 00
LEESBURG—*St. James's Mission S. S.*:
Gen. ... 5 61
LONGWOOD—*Christ Church S. S.*:
Gen. ... 9 00
NEW SMYRNA—*Grace*: Gen. ... 10 00
OCALA—*Grace*: Gen. ... 2 00
ORLANDO—*St. Luke's S. S.*: Gen. ... 40 94
PORT ORANGE—*Grace*: Gen. ... 5 00
REDLANDS—*Grace S. S.*: Gen. ... 3 37
SANFORD—*Holy Cross*: $20, S. S.,*
$37.67, Gen. ... 57 67
ST. PETERSBURG—*St. Peter's*: Gen... 20 00
WEST PALM BEACH — *Holy Trinity
Church*: $29, S. S.,* $52, Gen. ... 81 00
MISCELLANEOUS—Branch Wo. Aux.,
Gen. (of which "In Memory of
"Mrs. Mary P. Dawson," $5) ... 90 00

Spokane

Ap. $143.16; *Sp.* $30.00

DAYTON—*Grace S. S.*: Gen. ... 2 23
HILLYARD—*Epiphany*: Gen. ... 16 25
PALOUSE—*Holy Trinity Church*: Dom.
and Frn. ... 10 00
SPOKANE—*All Saints' Cathedral S. S.*:
Gen. ... 51 24
Brunot Hall: Junior Aux., George C.
Thomas Memorial, Gen., $25; Sp. for
Miss Bull for "Brunot Hall" schol-
arship, Kyoto, $30 ... 55 00
St. David's: Gen. ... 7 50
St. James's S. S.: Gen. ... 7 18
St. Peter's: Gen. ... 7 50
St. Thomas's Mission S. S.: Gen. ... 1 76
STARBUCK—*Trinity Church S. S.*:
Gen. ... 3 00

SUNNYSIDE—*Trinity Church*: Frn. ...
ZILLAH—*Christ Church*: Gen. ...

The Philippines

Ap. $138.38

MANILA—*St. Mary's and St. John's S.
S.*: Gen. ...
BAGUIO—*Resurrection*: Gen. ...
ZAMBOANGA—*Holy Trinity Church*:
Gen. ...

Utah

Ap. $253.78; *Sp.* $10.00

GARFIELD—Sp. for reconstruction of
Mr. Gilman's work, Changsha, Han-
kow ...
LOGAN—*St. John's S. S.*: Gen. ...
OGDEN—*Church of the Good Shepherd*:
$8.20, S. S.,* $36.73, Gen. ...
SALT LAKE CITY—*St. Mark's Cathe-
dral*: Gen. ...
St. Mark's Hospital: Gen. ...
St. Paul's: Gen. ...
St. Peter's: Gen. ...
Rowland Hall: $12.50, S. S.,* $78.35,
Gen. ...

Western Colorado

Ap. $51.48

DURANGO—*St. Paul's S. S.*: Gen. ...
HOTCHKISS—*St. George's S. S.*: Gen.
FRUITA—*Mission*: Gen. ...
MACK—*Mission*: Gen. ...
MANCOS—*St. Paul's*: $2.25, S. S.,*
$4.60, Gen. ...
OAK CREEK—*S. S.*: Gen. ...
PAGOSA SPRINGS—*Mission*: Gen. ...
PITKIN—*St. Bartholomew's*: Gen. ...
RICO—*Mission S. S.*: Gen. ...
TELLURIDE—*St. Michael's*: Gen. ...

Wyoming

Ap. $253.70

BAGGS—*St. Luke's*: Gen. ...
BUFFALO—*St. Luke's*: Gen. ...
CHEYENNE—*St. Mark's S. S.*: Gen...
CODY—*Christ Church*: Gen. ...
DIXON—*St. Paul's*: Gen. ...
DOUGLAS—*Christ Church*: Gen. ...
EVANSTON—*St. Paul's S. S.*: Gen. ...
LARAMIE—*St. Matthew's Cathedral S.
S.*: Gen. ...
LUSK—*St. George's*: Gen. ...
NEWCASTLE — *Christ Church*: "The
Ladies' Guild," Gen. ...
SHERIDAN—*St. Peter's*: Gen. ...
WIND RIVER—*Boarding-school S. S.*:
Gen. ...

Foreign Missionary Dist

Ap. $121.12

Africa

LIBERIA—*Kroo Chapel S. S.*: Gen. ...
St. Peter's (Caldwell): $7, S. S.,*
$4.50, Gen. ...
St. John's (Lower Buchanan): Gen. ...

China

HANKOW—*St. John the Evangelist's S.
S.*: Gen. ...
SHANGHAI—Gen. ...

Cuba

CARDENAS—*San Francisco*: Gen. ...
GUANABACOA—*S. S.*: Gen. ...

France

PARIS—*St. Luke's S. S.*: Gen. ...

Miscellaneous

$15,478.30 ; Sp. $1,369.17 ; Specific
Deposit, $50.58

— Dom., $3,581.36 ; Frn.,
4.64 ; Dom. and Frn., $1,881.24 ;
$802.56 ; Sp., $1,065.59 ; Spe-
Deposit, $50.58............... 9,565 97
d Offering, Wo. Aux., on ac-
of appropriations to Septem-
st, 1910, Dom., $3,500 ; Frn.,
0 .... 7,000 00
eds of sale of copies of "Mis-
ry Litany of the American
r League," for China........ 1 00
riend," Sp. for Bishop Gibson
Archdeacon Neve, mountain
Virginia................... 175 00
e of Eastern Oregon, Sp. for
p Paddock, Eastern Oregon... 100 00
hters of the late Cortlandt
tarr," for the "Cortlandt W.
scholarship, St. John's Uni-
ry, Shanghai............... 25 00
gh Angie Myers, M.D., Sp. for
ment of St. Elizabeth's Hos-
Shanghai.................. 25 00
"J. I. H.," "W. H. M. H." and

"G. L. M. H.," Sp. for St. Mary's,
Moiliili, Honolulu................ 3 58
Anonymous, Gen................. 2 50

Legacies

PENN., PHILADELPHIA—Estate of David
Roberts, Dom................. 47 50
W. N. Y., BUFFALO—Estate of Mrs.
Charles H. Smith, Dom., $400.60 ;
Frn., $400.60................... 801 20

Receipts for the month........ $148,883 30
Amount previously
acknowledged $1,121,354 84
Less amount from
O h i o, Youngs-
town, St. John's,
Woman's Society,
general missions
acknowledged in
April SPIRIT OF
MISSIONS, n o w
said to be for
Educational Sec-
retary supplies... 1 19
———————— 1,121,353 65

Total since September 1st.......$1,270,236 95

SUMMARY OF RECEIPTS

Receipts divided according to purposes to which they are to be applied	Received during May	Amounts previously Acknowledged	Total
Applicable upon the appropriations of the Board.	$120,824 44	$594,885 74	$715,710 18
Special gifts forwarded to objects named by donors in addition to the appropriations of the Board.	27,159 58	152,178 31	179,337 89
Legacies for investment......................	....	165,000 00	165,000 00
Legacies, the disposition of which is to be determined by the Board at the end of the fiscal year	848 70	88,447 26	89,295 96
Specific Deposit...........................	50 58	120,842 84	120,892 92
Total	$148,883 30	$1,121,353 65	$1,270,236 95

Total receipts from September 1st, 1909, to June 1st, 1910, applicable upon the appropria-
ons, divided according to the sources from which they have come, and compared with the cor-
sponding period of the preceding year. Legacies are not included in the following items, as their
sposion is not determined by the Board until the end of the fiscal year.

OFFERINGS TO PAY APPROPRIATIONS

Source	To June 1, 1910	To June 1, 1909	Increase	Decrease
From congregations.....................	$372,962 16	$312,215 63	$60,746 53	$.......
From individuals......................	32,764 68	50,274 38	....	17,509 70
From Sunday-schools...................	125,207 32	109,062 78	16,144 54	....
From Woman's Auxiliary.................	63,913 93	65,473 65	....	1,559 72
From interest.........................	56,651 42	52,114 78	4,536 64	....
Miscellaneous items....................	1,210 67	4,356 05	....	3,145 38
Total........................	$652,710 18	$593,497 27	*$59,212 91	
Woman's Auxiliary United Offering........	63,000 00	35,000 00	28,000 00	....
Total........................	$715,710 18	$628,497 27	$87,212 91	....

*s Easter fell two weeks earlier this year, we have had that much more time in which to re-
ve nday-school Lenten offerings, so an adjustment for this must be made. Aside from Sunday-
ool ferings there is an increase to June 1st of $43,068.87. The Sunday-school offerings to June
, a compared with the same number of days after Easter last year, show a decrease of $364.
e m, therefore, say the net increase in offerings to June 1st is $43,432.37. A month ago the
rea was $34,904.10.

APPROPRIATIONS FOR THE YEAR

SEPTEMBER 1ST, 1909, TO AUGUST 31ST, 1910
Amount Needed for the Year

To y appropriations as made to date for the work at home and abroad........ $1,214,632 07
To place Reserve Funds temporarily used for the current work.......... . 32,955 33

Total $1,247,587 40
Total receipts to date applicable on appropriations............................. 715,710 18

nount needed before August 31st, 1910.................................. $ 649,536 64

ST. PAUL'S COLLEGE, TOKYO, FUND

To June 1st, 1910

Last December, a committee was appointed in Philadelphia by the 「r
Committee of the Woman's Auxiliary (but without any official connection 、l
Woman's Auxiliary) for the purpose of raising funds to purchase land ar (
buildings thereon, for St. Paul's College, Tokyo. This committee was comp e
the following persons: Miss Fanny Brock, Miss Mary Blakiston, Mrs. A. J).
Dixon, Miss Anne Hubbard, Mrs. John Markoe, Mrs. Charles R. Pancoa
Walter E. Penrose, Mrs. Geo. Wharton Pepper, Miss Randolph, Mrs. W. W. r.
Miss Coles, and Mrs. Geo. F. Knorr, ex-officio. This committee was orgar e
electing Miss Coles, Chairman; Mrs. W. W. Arnett, Secretary, and M S
Houston was asked to be treasurer of the committee.

In the following six months, this committee has succeeded in raising
which, added to the funds given to the Board of Missions for the same purp (
in many instances so given through the efforts of this committee) is sufficien o
for the land, fourteen acres, purchased on the outskirts of Tokyo by Bishop c
for St. Paul's College. It is earnestly hoped that the members of the Pr s
Episcopal Church will, at an early date, insure the usefulness of this pur s
donating a sufficient sum to erect the necessary buildings.

An inspection of the accompanying list of donors shows that those oc
which are not considered financially strong are, in many cases, better rep e
by contributions than some of the more wealthy dioceses. The Treasurer's st en
is submitted herewith.

S. F. HOUSTON, TREASURER, ST. PAUL'S COLLEGE, TOKYO, COMMITTEE.

To contributions received as per acompanying list.................... $31,869 52	
To loans 5,000 00	
	$ 86
By amounts forwarded to Treasurer of the Board of Missions:	
December 3d, 1909..................... $ 1,000 00	
February 14th, 1910..................... 9,250 00	
April 18th, 1910..................... 12,500 00	
June 1st, 1910..................... 14,616 22	
$37,366.22	
By special contributions for expenses of committee (not forwarded) 510 00	
Balance, June 1st, 1910.................................. 3 30	
	$ 86

Diocese of Alabama

Demopolis, Trinity Church	$12 10	
Gadsden, Church of the Holy Comforter......	3 25	
		$ 15 35

Missionary District of Alaska

Tanana Valley Mission.........	53 50

Diocese of Albany

Cohoes, St. John's......	21 50	
Cooperstown, Christ Church	7 10	
Johnstown, St. John's Sunday-school	3 36	
Little Falls, St. Agnes's Ministering Guild.....	1 00	
Middleville, Memorial...	2 90	
Troy, Holy Cross, Mrs. E. W. Babcock.......	10 00	
		45 86

Missionary District of Arizona

Globe, St. John's..............	1 50

Diocese of Arkansas

Camden, St. John's.....	17 50	
Helena, St. John's, Mrs. J. B. Pillow..........	16 00	
Little Rock, Christ Church Woman's Auxiliary....	5 00	
Van Buren, Trinity Church	1 00	
		39 50

Missionary District of Asheville

Hendersonville, St. James's......	1

Diocese of Bethlehem

Woman's Auxiliary of Diocese	10 00	
Mrs. B. H. Buckingham.	250 00	
Miss Freeman...........	250 00	
Drifton, Mrs. Chas. B. Coxe	250 00	
Drifton, Mrs. Eckley B. Coxe	500 00	
Lebanon, Mrs. Horace Brock	500 00	
Lebanon, St. Luke's.....	5 05	
Montrose, St. Paul's.....	11 05	
Reading, St. Mary's.....	2 00	
Reading, St. Mary's Sunday-school, Class No. 11	3 00	
Scranton, Church of the Good Shepherd, Mrs. J. B. Dimick........	10 00	
		,7

Diocese of California

Palo Alto, All Saints'...	4 25	
San Francisco, Japanese Mission	4 40	
San Francisco, Mrs. L. P. Monteagle	100 00	
		1

	Fort Thomas, St. Andrew's	2 00
	Lexington, Christ Church	24 90
	Lexington, Christ Church, Woman's Auxiliary...	10 00
	Middlesborough, St. Mary's	10 75
		63 65

169 10 | **Diocese of Long Island** | |
	Lynbrook, Christ Church.	4 20
	St. James, St. James's...	15 00
		19 20

| **Diocese of Los Angeles** | |
| Alhambra, Holy Trinity Church .... | 1 25 |
123 13 | Covina, Holy Trinity Church .... | 1 50 |
Los Angeles, St. Matthias's	6 35
Pasadena, All Saints' Woman's Auxiliary...	10 00
	19 10

Diocese of Maine	
Bar Harbor, St. Saviour.	8 20
Camden, St. Thomas's...	5 00
Gardiner, Robert H. Gardiner	25 00
	38 20

115 72 | **Diocese of Maryland**... 1,769 86 | |
| Anne Arundel Co., St. Margaret's .... | 2 55 |
Oregon | Baltimore City, the Rev. J. S. B. Hodges...... | 5 00 |
20 00 | Baltimore City, the Rev. E. L. Kemp......... | 5 00 |
West Arlington, Transfiguration	7 55
Howard and Anne Arundel Cos., Trinity Parish	12 00
Washington Co., St. John's Parish	19 00
6 61 | | 1,820 96 |

Diocese of Massachusetts	
Anonymous, through the Rev. Roger A. Walke.	1,040 00
Andover, Christ Church Sunday-school	15 00
11 00	Boston, Miss L. C. Sturgis	10 00
Boston, Mrs. John Thorndike	10 00
Boston, Emmanuel Church	35 00
Boston, the Rev. G. L. Paine	250 00
Boston, Miss Ethel L. Paine	500 00
24 27	Cambridge, St. Peter's Sunday-school	2 77
Concord, Trinity Church Sunday-school	11 80
Falmouth, Church of the Messiah Sunday-school.	6 00
8 15	Marblehead, the Rev. Henry L. Foote......	2 00
Milton, Church of Our Saviour Sunday-school.	5 55
1 25	Newton (Lower Falls), St. Mary's..........	27 88
Quincy, the Rev. A. E. Clattenberg	5 00
Wellesley, St. Andrew's..	6 00
9 65 | | 1,927 00 |

2 0) | **Diocese of Michigan** | |
Detroit, the Rev. W. S. Sayres, D.D..........	1 00
Detroit, St. John's......	68 16
	69 16

Diocese of Milwaukee

Kenosha, St. Matthew's, Woman's Auxiliary...	18 75	
Wauwatosa, T r i n i t y Church	1 18	
Wauwatosa, the Rev. C. E. Jones..........	2 00	21 93

Diocese of Minnesota

Caledonia, Trinity Church	1 50	
Cannon Falls, the Rev. T. G. Crump........	2 50	
Minneapolis, Gethsemane.	21 63	
Minneapolis, St. John Baptist's	7 76	
Redwood Falls, Church of the Holy Communion..	5 90	
St. Paul, Church of the Good Shepherd.......	10 00	
Stillwater, A s c e n s i o n Church and Sunday- school	25 00	74 29

Diocese of Mississippi

Aberdeen, St. John's.....	2 00	
Hattiesburg, T r i n i t y Church	4 00	6 00

Diocese of Missouri

Miss S. B. Cable........	25 00	
The Right Rev. Daniel S. Tuttle, D.D........	100 00	
St. Louis, Church of the Redeemer	10 00	
St. Louis, St. George's..	50 00	185 00

Diocese of Montana

Anaconda, St. Mark's...	33 25	
Big Timber, St. Mark's..	3 44	
Billings, St. Luke's......	3 58	
Bozeman, St. James's...	1 75	
Butte, St. John's.......	25 60	
Deer Lodge, St. James's.	4 00	
Dillon, St. James's.....	40 00	
Helena, St. Peter's.....	40 00	
Kalispell, Christ Church.	10 00	
Livingston, St. Andrew's.	12 50	
Sheridan, the Rev. J. W. Heyward	3 00	165 12

Missionary District of Nevada

Reno, Trinity Church, the Rev. Samuel Unsworth.............		5 00

Diocese of Newark

Hackensack, Christ Church	32 45	
Monclair, Mrs. R. E. Durham	1 00	
Montclair, the Rev. C. M. Roome	5 00	
Newark, St. Alban's....	20 50	58 95

Diocese of New Hampshire

Concord, St. Paul's.....	30 51	
"Friends in Hanover"...	40 00	70 51

Diocese of New Jersey

Asbury Park, Trinity Church	3 00
Bernardsville, St. Ber- nard's	10 00
Bound Brook, St. Paul's.	16 65
Camden, St. John's.....	7 00
C h e w's Landing, St. John's, Miss Mont- gomery	5 00
Dunellen, Holy Innocents'	4 65
Elizabeth, Christ Church, Miss Melville........	25 00

Elizabeth, Trinity Church	5 00	
Highlands, St. Andrew's.	2 94	
Lambertville, St. Andrew's	15 10	
Lambertville, St. Andrew's Sunday-school	4 14	
Merchanville, Grace.....	5 71	
Moorestown, T r i n i t y Church	21 50	
Navesink, All Saints' Me- morial	12 83	
Navesink, All Saints' Me- morial, the Rev. John C. Lord.............	10 00	
New Brunswick, Christ Church Woman's Aux- iliary	12 75	
New Brunswick, St. John the Evangelist's......	9 50	
Plainfield, Grace........	3 25	
Plainfield, Guild of the Heavenly Rest.......	2 00	
Rocky Hill, Trinity Church	2 00	
Somerville, St. John's...	34 46	
Trenton, Christ Church..	11 00	
Trenton, Grace.........	6 34	229

Missionary District of New Mexico

Deming, St. Luke's......	3 00	
Farmington, St. John's..	6 40	
Mesilla Park, St. James's	9 18	
San Marcial, C h r i s t Church	5 00	
Sante Fé, Holy Faith...	3 00	
Silver City, Church of the Good Shepherd....	5 00	31

Diocese of New York

Anonymous	5 00	
Baylies, Mrs. N. E......	100 00	
Browning, Mrs. J. Hull..	100 00	
Cole, the Rev. Lawrence T.	10 00	
Davis, Miss H. A.......	25 00	
General Seminary......	100 00	
Hadden, Mrs. H. F.....	50 00	
Hoe, Mrs. Richard March	57 50	
Holbrooke, Mr. George O.	10 00	
King, Mr. George Gordon	100 00	
Mathews, Mrs. R. I.....	10 00	
Morgan, J. P., Jr........	100 00	
Paris, Mrs. F. U........	25 00	
Stokes, Mrs. Anson Phelps	50 00	
Van Ingen, Mrs. E. H...	50 00	
Ward, Mrs. George Cabot	200 00	
Warren, Mrs. E. Walpole	1,000 00	
Highland, Holy Trinity Church	2 50	
Mamaroneck, the Rev. D. A. Bonar............	1 00	
New Paltz, St. Andrew's.	2 50	
New York, St. Alban's...	1 10	
New York, Holy Trinity Church, St. James's Parish, the Rev. J. V. Chalmers	5 00	
New York, St. Mary's...	5 00	
New York, T r i n i t y C h u r c h, Four Com- municants of........	15 00	
New York, St. Luke's Chapel	5 00	
Nyack, the Rev. Frank- lin Babbitt..........	7 25	2,03

Diocese of North Carolina

Raleigh, St. Augustine's........		2

Missionary District of North Dakota

Dickinson, St. John's....	3 55
Jamestown, Grace.......	2 25
Lakota, Church of the Good Shepherd.......	3 40

	Paul, Miss M. W	200 00
	Pharo, Mrs. Walter W..	2 00
	Porter, Miss C. J	3 00
	Randolph, Miss Anna (for expenses)	100 00
32 00	Riley, Mr. and Mrs. L. A.	200 00
	Robbins, Mr. and Mrs. George S.	200 00
	Siter, Miss Charlotte	20 00
2 95	Smith, Miss S. R	200 00
	Tatham, Mrs	1 00
	Thomas, Dr. and Mrs. Charles Herman	50 00
	Thomas, Mrs. George C., Jr.	10 00
	Thomas, Walter H	10 00
	Tuesday Missionary Bible-class	1,000 00
	Whelan, Charles S	10 00
	Whelan, Miss Emily	25 00
	Wister, Mrs. Jones	2 00
	Witherspoon Hall collection	245 90
	Woman's Auxiliary, Foreign Committee (for expenses)	20 00
	Woman's Auxiliary of St. Peter's House	10 00
	Wood, Miss Juliana	40 00
	Yarnall, Mrs. Charlton	50 00
	Andalusia, Church of the Redeemer	7 33
	Andalusia, Church of the Redeemer, Junior Auxiliary	20 00
	Cheltenham, St. Paul's	72 73
	Cheltenham, St. Paul's Sunday-school	13 33
	Chester, St. Luke's	1 00
	Chester, St. Paul's	10 05
	Jenkintown, Church of Our Saviour	75 75
	Lower Merion, Church of the Redeemer, Woman's Auxiliary	15 00
	Norristown, All Saints', Woman's Auxiliary	18 00
	Norristown, St. John's, Woman's Auxiliary	10 00
	Paoli, Good Samaritan	5 00
	Philadelphia, Advocate	30 53
	Philadelphia, All Saints', Lower Dublin	28 88
	Philadelphia, All Saints', Lower Dublin, Woman's Auxiliary	17 00
	Philadelphia, All Souls'	3 66
	Philadelphia, Calvary, Germantown, Woman's Auxiliary	35 00
	Philadelphia, Christ Church, Second and Market	24 92
	Philadelphia, Christ Church Sunday-school, Franklinville	15 00
	Philadelphia, Covenant, Woman's Auxiliary	100 00
	Philadelphia, Epiphany, Germantown	8 41
	Philadelphia, Grace, Woman's Auxiliary, Mt. Airy	60 00
	Philadelphia, Holy Apostles' Sunday-school	50 00
	Philadelphia, Holy Communion Chapel	5 00
	Philadelphia, Holy Trinity Church	617 99
	Philadelphia, Holy Trinity Church, Missionary Bible-class	25 00
	Philadelphia, Prince of Peace Chapel, Woman's Auxiliary	7 50

Philadelphia, St. Andrew's, Woman's Auxiliary, Eighth and Spruce	6 00
Philadelphia, St. Andrew's, West Philadelphia	5 00
Philadelphia, St. Anna's.	1 00
Philadelphia, St. Clement's	142 00
Philadelphia, St. George's, Richmond	3 00
Philadelphia, St. James's, Twenty-second a n d Walnut	35 00
Philadelphia, St. James's, Twenty-second a n d Walnut, Woman's Auxiliary	38 50
Philadelphia, St. Luke's, Germantown	100 00
Philadelphia, St. Luke's, Woman's Auxiliary....	11 45
Philadelphia, St. Mark's, Sixteenth and Locust.	5 00
Philadelphia, St. Mark's, Sixteenth and Locust, Woman's Auxiliary....	43 00
Philadelphia, St. Mark's, Sixteenth and Locust, a member of........	500 00
Philadelphia, St. Martin's-in-the-Fields ...	1,154 63
Philadelphia, St. Martin's-in-the-Fields Sunday-school	13 54
Philadelphia, St. Mary's, Woman's Auxiliary...	7 00
Philadelphia, St. Matthew's, Francisville...	30 34
P h i l a d e l p h i a, St. Michael's, Woman's Auxiliary, Germantown	15 00
P h i l a d e l p h i a, St. Michael's, Miss E. H. Brown............	5 00
Philadelphia, St. Paul's, Chestnut Hill........	1,130 00
Philadelphia, St. Paul's Memorial, Overbrook..	25 42
Philadelphia, St. Paul's Memorial, Woman's Auxiliary	25 00
Philadelphia, St. Peter's, Third and Pine.......	621 70
Philadelphia, St. Peter's, Third and Pine, a member of..........	1,000 00
Philadelphia, St. Peter's, Third and Pine, Junior Auxiliary	40 00
Philadelphia, St. Peter's, Germantown	636 27
Philadelphia, St. Peter's, Germantown, Y o u n g Women's Chapter.....	5 00
Philadelphia, St. Peter's, Germantown, Woman's Auxiliary	10 00
Philadelphia, St. Stephen's, Tenth above Chestnut	54 10
Philadelphia, St. Stephen's, Tenth above Chestnut, W o m a n ' s Auxiliary	2 00
Philadelphia, Church of the Saviour, Miss E. Blakiston	500 00
Philadelphia, Church of the Saviour, Miss M. J. Blakiston	500 00
Philadelphia, Church of the Saviour, Woman's Auxiliary	10 00

	Halifax Co., Randolph Parish, Trinity Church	16 00
	Henry Co., Henry Parish, Christ Church........	5 75
	James City Co., Bruton Parish	34 10
146 20	Mecklenburg Co.:	
	St. James's Parish, St. James's	32 50
	St. James's Parish, St. Paul's Sunday-school	3 00
	Montgomery Co.:	
	Montgomery Parish, Christ Church......	20 25
	Radford Parish, Grace.	28 34
	Nansemond Co.:	
	Upper Suffolk Parish, St. Paul's.........	51 35
	Lower Suffolk Parish, Glebe Church......	2 50
	Nelson Co., Nelson Parish	11 00
	Norfolk Co.:	
	Elizabeth River Parish, Christ Church.....	79 25
	Elizabeth River Parish, St. Mark's........	77
	Elizabeth River Parish, St. Paul's.........	125 41
	Elizabeth River Parish, St. Peter's........	10 00
	Elizabeth River Parish, Ascension	4 50
	St. Bride's Parish, St. Paul's	5 00
	St. Bride's Parish, St. Thomas's	35 16
	Nottoway Co.:	
	Nottoway Parish.....	9 89
	Nottoway Parish, St. Luke's	11 00
	Pittsylvania Co.:	
	Banister Parish, Emmanuel Church Sunday-school	5 00
	Banister Parish, Trinity Church........	1 63
	Camden Parish, Epiphany	39 17
	Princess Anne Co.:	
	East Lynnhaven Parish	5 00
	East Lynnhaven Parish, Galilee........	76
	Lynnhaven Parish, Emmanuel Church.....	30 00
	Prince Edward Co., Wilmer Parish, Johns Memorial	12 00
	Prince George and Surrey Co's.:	
	Martin's Brandon and Southwark Parishes, Ritchie Memorial...	3 75
	Martin's Brandon and Southwark Parishes, Brandon	5 00
	Martin's Brandon and Southwark Parishes, Grace	1 25
	Pulaski Co., Pulaski Parish, Christ Church and Sunday-school	15 00
	Roanoke Co., Salem Parish, St. Paul's........	16 15
	Rockbridge Co.:	
	Latimer Parish, R. E. Lee Memorial......	37 75
	Natural Bridge Parish, Christ Church........	1 20
	Natural Bridge Parish, St. John's.........	3 35
	Warwick Co.:	
	Warwick Parish, St. Paul's	5 59
	Warwick Parish, St.	

Paul's, the Rev. C.
S. Harrison........ 5 00
Washington   Co.,   St.
Paul's, Saltville...... 11 53
Wise Co., Intermont Par-
ish, Christ Church.... 59 00
Wythe Co., Wythe Parish,
St. John's........... 34 85
York Co., Mr. J. W.
Clements, Yorktown... 10 00
———————— 1,427 51

Diocese of Springfield

Lincoln, Trinity Church.. 1 50
Mattoon, the Rev. A.
Goodger 50
Carrolton, Trinity Church 25
———————— 2 25

Diocese of Vermont

The Right Rev. A. C. A.
Hall, D.D............ 20 00
Bellows Falls, Immanuel
Church 5 00
Brandon, St. Thomas's.. 6 10
Forrestdale, Grace...... 1 82
Shelburne, T r i n i t y
Church 2 60
St. Albans, St. Luke's... 3 10
———————— 38 62

Diocese of Virginia

Anonymous, through the
Rev. Roger A. Walke.. 60 00
Eagle, Wm. Stuart, Min-
eral 10 00
Goodwin, Miss Mary F.,
Fairfax 2 00
Goodwin, Miss Marie Lee,
Fairfax 2 00
Goodwin, the Rev. E. L.,
Fairfax 6 00
Stringfellow, Miss M. Y.,
Richmond 1 00
Williams, John S., Rich-
mond 25 00
Albemarle Co., Freder-
icksville Parish, St.
Luke's Chapel........ 2 75
Clarke Co., Wickliffe
Parish, Wickliffe.... 11 40
Culpeper Co., Slaughter
Parish, All Saints'.... 7 00
Fairfax Co. :
F a i r f a x Parish,
Chapel of Theological
Seminary 46 53
F a i r f a x Parish,
St. John's Chapel... 4 16
F a i r f a x Parish,
Sharon Chapel..... 1 02
F a i r f a x Parish,
Church of the Holy
Spirit Chapel....... 5 00
F a i r f a x Parish,
St. Paul's Chapel,
Lencolina 2 00
F a i r f a x Parish,
Christ Chapel...... 3 30
F a i r f a x Parish,
Glen Carlyn Miss... 5 02
F a i r f a x Parish,
Church of the Good
Shepherd Chapel... 2 47
F a i r f a x Parish,
St. Paul's, Bailey's.. 5 50
F a i r f a x Parish,
Students' Missionary
Society 25 00
Fauquier Co., Whittle
Parish, Grace and
Trinity Churches...... 15 00
Goochland Co., St.
James's, N o r t h a m

THE

Spirit of Missions

AN ILLUSTRATED MONTHLY REVIEW
OF CHRISTIAN MISSIONS

August, 1910

CONTENTS

The Subscription Price of THE SPIRIT OF MISSIONS is ONE DOLLAR per year.
stage is prepaid in the United States, Porto Rico, The Philippines and Mexico. For other countries
the Postal Union, including Canada, twenty-four cents per year should be added.
Subscriptions are continued until ordered discontinued.
Change of Address: In all changes of address it is necessary that the old as well as the new
dress should be given.
How to Remit: Remittances, made payable to George Gordon King, Treasurer, should be made
draft on New York, Postal Order or Express Order. One and two cent stamps are received. To
ecks on local banks ten cents should be added for collection.
All Letters should be addressed to The Spirit of Missions, 281 Fourth Avenue, New York.

Published by the Domestic and Foreign Missionary Society.
President, RIGHT REVEREND DANIEL S TUTTLE, D.D.   Secretary, —— ——
Treasurer, GEORGE GORDON KING.
Entered at the Post Office, in New York, as second-class matter.

Lord Balfour, of Burleigh, President, is in the Chair. On his right side Sir Andrew Fraser. On his left, next

[E SPIRIT OF MISSIONS

AN ILLUSTRATED MONTHLY REVIEW
OF CHRISTIAN MISSIONS

LXXV.   **August,** 1910   No. 8

THE PROGRESS OF THE KINGDOM

report, however graphic or detailed, could do full justice to the

The Spirit of the World Conference

Missionary Conference. The Conference was notable for what it was rather than for what was said or done. Two great notes dominated the gathering. On the one hand there was the intense desire to make our Lord known to all men. To this end the Conference carefully reviewed the non-Christian world, noting occupied fields, measuring the strength of the opposing and favoring forces and including sympathetically the deepest need of human life—its need for God. It considered how missionaries might be prepared the better for their exacting task, how education might be more effectively used as an ally in bringing the world to our Lord and how the Christian forces at home might be thoroughly organized and more courageously led for world conquest. On the other hand, there was the almost equally intense desire to draw nearer to fellow-Christians in order that all followers of the one Lord may in fact be one; that through unbroken witness the world may know and believe in the Christ. To this end the Conference considered what might be done to promote co-operation

and unity, not only in the mission field, but particularly among home Christians. If the things that divide Christ's followers in Christian lands can be surmounted, conditions in the mission field will speedily adjust themselves. The passing of denominationalism is one of the present facts of the mission field. Newly won Christians in every land refuse to be interested in the intricacies of denominational controversy. Confessions of faith which date mainly from the sixteenth century are frankly laid aside. The aim everywhere is not to reproduce loyalty to a denomination at home, but to promote the growth of a Christianity which shall be really indigenous to the land where it has been planted. The spirit of missions and the spirit of unity—really two expressions of one exalted purpose—these were the motives that dominated the Conference. This is the fact stated in one form or another by those who have kindly contributed their impressions to this number of The Spirit of Missions.

The Catholic Basis of the Conference

A successful effort was made to eliminate from the name and the character of the Conference every suggestion of division or sec-

tarianism. With rare statesmanship, the
international committee that laid the
original plans aimed to make it a "world
conference" in fact. It was not a conference of foreign missionaries and
members of the home constituency alone,
for it included Chinese, Japanese, Indians, Africans and others. It was not
a conference of the English-speaking
world, for a large section of the floor
was occupied by delegates from the missionary societies of Germany and Holland, France and Belgium, Norway,
Sweden and Finland. Unfortunately,
the Conference was not as representative ecclesiastically as it was representative geographically and racially. Two
great communions were unrepresented,
in spite of the hope that the adoption of
a truly catholic title and basis for the
Conference might result in securing the
co-operation of all of Christendom. A
complete representation of the Anglican
communion was insured by the decision
last April of the Society for the
Propagation of the Gospel to rescind its
former adverse action with regard to
sending delegates. The S. P. G. representatives from the home land as well
as from the mission field made valuable
contributions. The presence of both
archbishops of the Church of England,
and especially Archbishop Davidson,
whose sympathetic attitude and strong
words did much to interpret the Church
of England to members of the various
Protestant communions, the active part
taken on some of the commissions by
men like Bishop Talbot, of Southwark;
Bishop Gore, of Birmingham; Bishop
Montgomery, of the S. P. G.; the Dean
of Westminster, Father Frere, of the
Community of the Resurrection; Father
Kelly, of the Society of the Sacred Mission; the Rev. J. P. Maud, Vicar of
Bristol; the Rev. J. O. F. Murray, Mas-
ter of Selwyn College, Cambridge, and
Mr. Eugene Stock proved most valu-
able. On behalf of the American Church
similar service was rendered by Bishop
Doane, of Albany; Bishop Lawrence, of
Massachusetts; Mr. Seth Low, Admiral
Mahan, Mr. Silas McBee, Mr. George W.
Pepper and Mr. John W. Wood.

A Case in Point

A recent trip by Bishop Graves in northwest Nebraska, while not altogether typical, gives an insight into conditions that still have to be faced in parts of the West. An all-day railroad journey carried the bishop from his home in Kearney to a district without railroads, where for more than two weeks he was constantly driving from one hamlet to another, or from ranch to ranch, frequently sleeping at night on the open prairie. Every day had its round of duties. Now he is on a journey to some lonely ranch house to minister to a sick man. Again he is driving fifteen or twenty miles for a service in a schoolhouse. Here the farmers and their families gather from miles around. The bishop holds service and preaches, and then, in the fashion of long ago, there is a picnic lunch. Early in the afternoon a second service is held before the people start on the homeward drive. To baptize a child, or confirm four or five people, the bishop may drive twenty or twenty-five miles. We find him entering, too, into the social life of the farmers, so that in fact he becomes the chief shepherd of those scattered but needy people, who, in their farming life, are rendering a service to our city-dwelling populations too often quite unrealized.

The Record of a Fortnight

At the end of a fortnight of such work Bishop Graves found that he had driven 259 miles, held thirty-four services, delivered twenty sermons or addresses, baptized sixty-nine, confirmed fifty-nine and administered the Holy Communion to ninety-seven people. The heaviest day's work involved twenty-seven miles in the wagon, with six services and five sermons or addresses. Not a single service during the fortnight was held in a church. And all this in one man's parish. Work such as this must command the admiration and support of all good citizens, for it means ministering to the springs of national life. Certainly the Church should be profoundly grateful that in spite of slender and often uncertain stipends, and in spite of heart-breaking difficulties, she can command the services of men like Bishop Graves and scores of others, who in obscure places, with none of the stimulus of romance or novelty, and too often with no recognition, are steadily doing their work.

JULY is being devoted, in the missionary calendar, to summer conferences. Last month several hundred leaders gathered under the auspices of the Young People's Missionary movement to prepare themselves the better to organize and lead the young people of their several communions. They received instruction in the methods of conducting mission study classes, of organizing missionary institutes and of making more effective the missionary machinery already existing in the average congregation. The Conference for Church Work, formerly held under the management of the Seabury Society, has passed into the control of a committee headed by the Rev. Professor Rhinelander and including Mr. Burton Mansfield and Mr. George Wharton Pepper, of the Board of Missions. It is now generally known as the "Cambridge Conference" and its session this year, held in the buildings of the Episcopal Theological School at Cambridge, was thoroughly useful. In addition to Bible study and lectures on the Prayer Book and the "Principles of Anglicanism," it offered courses for the study of missions in China, in our own West, in Latin America and in India. Particularly effective was the course on domestic missions conducted by the Rev. H. L. Burleson, Assistant Secretary of the Board of Missions. Other helpers from the Church Missions House staff were Miss Julia C. Emery, Deaconess Goodwin, Miss M. G. Lindley and Mr. John W. Wood. Much practical help on

Summer Conferences

Hankow

The Rev. and Mrs. L. B. Ridgely.
*The Rev. and Mrs. Frederick G. Deis.
The Rev. Dr. and *Mrs. E. L. Woodward.
*The Rev. R. A. Goodwin, Jr.
Dr. and Mrs. John MacWillie.
Mr. and Mrs. William McCarthy.
*Deaconess Emily L. Ridgely.
Miss S. H. Higgins.
*Miss Sarah E. Hopwood.

Porto Rico

*Miss Iva Mary Woodruff.

Shanghai

The Rev. F. L. Hawks Pott, D.D.
The Rev. and Mrs. R. C. Wilson.
*The Rev. T. K. Nelson.
*Dr. Frances F. Cattell.
*The Rev. H. S. Osburn.
*Mr. and Mrs. Tracy R. Kelley.
*Mr. Harold B. Barton.
Dr. Angie M. Myers.

The Philippines

*Miss Lillian M. Owen.

Tokyo

The Rev. and Mrs. James Chappell.
Dr. and Mrs. R. B. Teusler.
The Rev. and *Mrs. Roger A. Walke.

Unfortunately, not all members of this goodly company will be present at the service. Some have already started on their journey. We ask that these out-going missionaries, and the work to which they are going, may be remembered by the readers of THE SPIRIT OF · MISSIONS on August 10th and throughout the coming year.

¶

THROUGH an error in proof-reading in the May number Bishop Graves, of Shanghai, was credited with certain statements concerning St. John's University, which were really an editorial comment on the necessity for equipping St. John's with a new building.

THE SANCTUARY OF MISSIONS

WHAT shall I render unto the Lord for all His benefits toward me?
I will take the cup of salvation and call upon the name of the Lord.

THE WORK OF INTERCESSION

I FEEL sure that, as long as we look on prayer chiefly as the means of maintaining our own Christian life, we shall not know fully what it is meant to be. But when we learn to regard it as the highest part of the work entrusted to us, the root and strength of all other work, we shall see that there is nothing that we so need to study and practise as the art of praying aright. . . . It is only when the Church gives herself up to this holy work of intercession that we can expect the power of Christ to manifest itself in her behalf. . . . With disciples full of faith in Himself, and bold in prayer to ask great things, Christ can conquer the world. "Lord, teach us to pray."—*Andrew Murray.*

THANKSGIVINGS

"We thank Thee"—

For the life and work of Thy servant, William Neilson McVickar. (Page 619.)

For the success of the World Missionary Conference and for the spirit of unity manifested throughout its sessions. (Page 613.)

For the vigorous work being done by laymen in Chicago on behalf of the Church's Mission. (Page 670.)

For the privilege given to Thy servants of erecting the first Christian Library in China. (Page 672.)

INTERCESSIONS

"That it may please Thee"—

To give to all who attended the World Missionary Conference the grace to work patiently and faithfully to carry into effect the things then shown to them.

To bless and prosper the Christian communities throughout the world, that there may be manifested in the native Christians everywhere the fruits of the Spirit, that ignorance and superstition may be banished, that home life may be ennobled and that in all things Thy Name may be exalted and Thy wondrous works declared.

To grant to all the outgoing missionaries the assurance of Thy presence in their journeys and Thy enabling power for their work. (Page 617.)

To make all members of the Church duly sensible of the need of the scattered communities in our own land, that life and money may be offered in more abundant measure for the furtherance of the Church's work.

To lead Thy people everywhere to put aside mere opinion and preference that they may attain to the unity which is agreeable to Thy will.

PRAYERS

FOR GRACE TO DO GOD'S WILL

ALMIGHTY GOD, who through Thine only begotten Son, Jesus Christ, hast overcome death and opened unto us the gate of everlasting life; we humbly beseech Thee that as by Thy special grace preventing us Thou dost put into our minds good desires, so by Thy continual help we may bring the same to good effect; through Jesus Christ our Lord, who liveth and reigneth with Thee and the Holy Ghost, ever one God, world without end.

FOR THE MISSION AT HOME

BLESS, we beseech Thee, O Lord, this our land, and grant that Thy Church may ever be diligent in the endeavor to leaven the life of the Nation with Christian truth. Make us quick to see the spiritual needs of the growing communities and wealths of the great West (especially ——), and may more laborers offer for this service. To all the home missionary clergy grant wisdom in difficulty, help in trouble, the sense of Thy presence in loneliness and, if it be Thy will, visible success after labor, that Thy Name may be glorified, through Jesus Christ our Lord. *Amen.*

WILLIAM NEILSON McVICKAR,
BISHOP AND DOCTOR

WITH his splendid powers still undimmed, leaving behind him the record of a life filled full with loving service to the Church and to humanity, on June 28th Bishop McVickar was summoned to rest from the work which God had given him.

The third Bishop of Rhode Island was an impressive figure and a real power in the American Church. What he did in parish and diocese, as priest and citizen, other pens will set forth in other places. It is for us to speak of his long, wise and patient service to the Church's Mission.

A man of large mould, both in body and mind, but most of all of large heart and even larger faith, it was inevitable that Bishop McVickar should be, first of all things, a missionary. As such the Church early recognized him and summoned him to

become her counsellor as a member of the Board of Missions. For thirty-three years—twenty-one as priest and twelve as bishop—he served faithfully.

Never was he discouraged nor faltering. His was a faith and a vision which could not believe in the possibility of failure or defeat, and in every great advance he was a leader. As chairman for nine years of the Committee on China and Japan, he championed the work of those fields with sane enthusiasm and indomitable purpose, and elsewhere on the Church's battle-line he stood always for re-enforcement and advance. Those who attended the session of the General Convention of 1895, at Minneapolis, will recall how earnestly, in the face of much halting timidity, he advocated the giving of a bishop to Alaska. To him it was in some measure due that the American Church has been able to write into her history the story of Bishop Rowe.

Nor was it in public place or official relations only that Bishop McVickar's loyalty to the missionary work of the Church was made evident. A generous giver himself, he inspired generosity in others, and led his people to know and desire the joy of sharing in the campaign which is to win the world for Christ.

Far out on the firing-line, men who perhaps have never seen him, but have been cheered by the aid of the bishop and his people, will feel, when they hear of his going from us, that they have lost a valued friend.

The Standing Committee of Rhode Island has voiced the conviction of the whole diocese in saying:

"Called from a wide and conspicuous field of parochial experience to the exalted station of the episcopate, Dr. McVickar was amply and eminently prepared to maintain the work and traditions of one of the oldest dioceses of the American Church. . . . The episcopate, which now appears to have ended so abruptly, has already had its harvests, and will yet yield others as the fruit of his patient serving. The people of Rhode Island, of all sorts and conditions, of all creeds and of none, have seen a vision of the Good Shepherd reflected in Bishop McVickar, and the effects of that vision will be realized for many years to come."

The Scott monument in the foreground, the Castle at the left, the spire of St. Mary's Cathedral in the distance

MISSIONARY
RENCE

e 14th-23d, 1910

THE CONFERENCE

in Synod Hall. Here, likewise, about 1,200 representatives selected by the mission boards and about 1,000 others gathered day after day to hear addresses by the missionaries and other students of missions. At night a third meeting place, the Old Tolbooth Church, was pressed into service to accommodate the thousands of people desiring to share in the Conference, but who were not fortunate enough to have tickets for either Assembly Hall or Synod Hall.

These eight main themes were selected for the consideration of the Conference, one being assigned to each week-day of its session:

I. Carrying the Gospel to all the non-Christian World.

II. The Church in the Mission Field.

III. Education in Relation to the Christianization of National Life.

IV. The Missionary Message in Relation to Non-Christian Religions.

V. The Preparation of Missionaries.

VI. The Home Base of Missions.

VII. Missions and Governments.

VIII. Co-operation and the Promotion of Unity.

Each subject was assigned to a representative international commission which, about two years ago, began gathering information on its subject from missionaries and from home experts.

ST. MARY'S CATHEDRAL, EDINBURGH

*A daily celebration of the Holy Communion made it possible for some of the delegates to
each day at the Lord's Table*

*In the cathedral, on June 24th, the day after the Conference adjourned, the Rev. G. H
Walpole, D.D., was consecrated Bishop of Edinburgh*

The result was a great volume of correspondence containing information of the utmost value. In each case this correspondence was carefully digested by the members of the Commission and made the basis of the report to the Conference. These reports, supplied in proof form to all the official delegates before the Conference assembled, will make a missionary library of eight volumes, ranging from about 150 to 450 pages each.

On the morning of each day the chairman of one of the Commissions presented the report and made an explanatory address. The subject was then thrown open to discussion by the delegates, no one being allowed to speak more than seven minutes, and no member of the Commission being allowed to take part in the debate. At the close of the afternoon's session, the chairman or vice-chairman endeavored to summarize the discussion and give a final message from the Commission.

In the following pages an attempt has been made to bring out some of the salient points in the report of each Commission and in the discussion of it. No report is given of the parallel meetings in Synod Hall, or of the evening meetings in Assembly Hall. The former dealt with the same material as that discussed by the official Conference, and the latter were devoted to addresses of a general character.

II. THE SETTING OF THE CONFERENCE

By Miss Julia C. Emery

THE Edinburgh Conference was too big and too serious a thing to be treated lightly by those whose most earnest prayer is that in His own good time, through the united efforts of His people, Christ may establish His Kingdom throughout the world. But there are some memories connected with those ten days, other than the actual work of the conference, which those privileged to be a delegates will be as little likely to forget.

We went with a dutiful eagerness to our task, determined not to be beguiled the Castle or Holyrood, or by the alluring shops of Princes Street, by the light of Arthur's Seat or Calton Hill. But the most urgent suggestions of the Business Committee that nothing should draw us from the absorbing work for which we had come together could not prevent Edinburgh from assuming her most enchanting air, making every morning climb up the Mound and every pause within the quadrangle of Assembly Hall, looking up at the cross-tipped spire of Old Tolbooth Church, a daily joy.

Nor could the Committee go so far as to hinder the hospitality which brought thousands of guests, the night before the opening day, to receive the welcome of the Lord Provost of the city. As we slowly made our way in the great procession, where were seen not a dozen familiar faces, came the first realization of being a part of a world-wide gathering of pilgrims from all lands, whom one common purpose had brought to the good old town.

And on the next afternoon the Business Committee again was lenient, allowing us to see the University of Edinburgh honor men chosen from various lands, among them five of our own Americans.

When the Conference had once opened it would have been difficult indeed to have kept enthusiastic delegates away. The blue ticket procured on arrival was jealously guarded, for, unless shown at

THE KESWICK HIGH (or ...)

...The members of the Conference passed through the gateway between the two central towers into a large quadrangle and so into the admirable

ry time of entrance, the delegates ld not be admitted. The choice of a d seat being made, that seat was se-ed by prompt arrival and diligent at-dance, and visiting missionaries in crowded galleries would curtail cheon and hasten back to get some ce of vantage long before the opening the session.

Each noon and again at night, as the thern twilight lingered, a strange ht was seen. Coming down the steep ps from the hall to the quadrangle ow would be a mixed assembly: an glican bishop and a delegate from Society of Friends; a Scotch Pres-erian and a Swiss pastor; a Japanese ined in the Congregational system a brother of a religious order in lia; an English sister, training young men for mission work, and a thodist of like experience from our Middle West. Here, too, might be the Primus of the Scottish Episco-Church and the Secretary of the erican Methodist Board of Missions, the venerable Principal Whyte, of e St. George's, sturdiest of Presbyte-s and most lovable of men, in ear-t conversation with Father Kelly, ctor of the Society of the Sacred

Mission. And all met at the feet of John Knox, whose statue made for friends separated in the hall a convenient rendezvous.

What that grim old divine would have thought of such a gathering we can hardly fancy; but the sight of this wonderful company might well assure its members that God's world does move, that His Kingdom shall come, and some day the knowledge of Himself cover the earth as the waters cover the sea.

And these words as to the setting of the Conference would be incomplete if we forgot to add the crowning beauty of the following day, when the consecration of Dr. Walpole in St. Mary's Cathedral gave some of us that opportunity for worship and thanksgiving which the leaders of the Conference had told us we should offer to God for His great goodness. To American Churchmen this service had a special significance, in that the man chosen to be Bishop of Edinburgh had given years to the training of men for our ministry, and that among the hands laid upon his head in consecration—thereby giving to Scotland the same blessing she once gave to us—were those of our Bishops of the Philippines and Hankow.

II. THE BEGINNING OF THE CONFERENCE

THE delegates met for a preliminary business session on the afternoon of June 14th, with Lord Balfour, of Burleigh, president of the Conference, in the ir. After the opening devotions, the ting proceeded at once to effect the ssary organization for the conduct he sessions. A Business Committee appointed with the understanding it should guide the proceedings of Conference and that no vote should aken by the whole body unless the iness Committee by a majority of at t two-thirds so recommended. It

was decided that during the reception and discussion of the reports of commissions, the Conference should sit as a committee under the chairmanship of Mr. John R. Mott. Mr. J. H. Oldham, who, as secretary of the executive committee, has rendered such invaluable service in preparing for the Conference, was elected the secretary, with the Rev. J. H. Ritson, of England, and Mr. N. W. Rowell, of Canada, as recording clerks. After the adoption of simple rules for the guidance of the debates the Conference adjourned to attend the session of the Senate of the University of

dinburgh, where honorary degrees were
nferred upon a number of dis-
nguished delegates, including the Rev.
, L. Hawks Pott, D.D., president of St.
ohn's University, Shanghai, who re-
eived the degree of Doctor of Divinity,
he Archbishop of Canterbury, and Mr.
eth Low of New York, who received
he degree of Doctor of Laws.

The formal opening of the Conference
as held Tuesday evening. After the
nging of the "Old Hundredth," the
ev. Principal Whyte, pastor of Free St.
eorge's, Edinburgh, offered prayer, ex-
ressing the gratitude of the members of
he Conference for the rich inheritance
f Christian life, thought and devotion
erived from the early mediæval saints
 well as from the reformers and Chris-
an leaders of a later day. Lord Bal-
our, who was in the chair, then read a
essage from King George V., in
hich his Majesty expressed deep inter-
st in the Conference, his gratification at
he spirit of fraternity that had brought
 together, his recognition of the su-
reme importance of missionary work,
nd his satisfaction that the Conference
et in one of the capitals of the United
ingdom.

Lord Balfour delivered the opening
residential address, voicing the two
eelings dominant in the minds of all—
rst, "profound sorrow that our dif-
erences should make necessary so many
ifferent organizations," and, secondly,
thankfulness that if we are separated
 some respects we are drawn together
ow as perhaps we have never before
een drawn together in the prosecution
f the great enterprise in which we are
l interested." After outlining some of
e complicated questions with which
e missionary enterprise has to deal,
e president introduced the Archbishop
 Canterbury.

Dr. Davidson made what was general-
 regarded as one of the most remark-
le speeches of the Conference, coming,

as it did, from the recognized leader of
the Church of England. His first words,
"Fellow-workers in the Church Militant,
the Society of Christ on earth," created
a bond of sympathy between him and
the varied audience to which he spoke
that was only strengthened by what followed. Speaking of the importance of
the Conference, he declared that if men
be weighed rather than counted the assembly before him had no parallel in
history. As it was unique in character,
so he trusted that it might be unique in
fruit. Speaking as one who necessarily
held a position of central responsibility
in the religious life of England, he said
that one result of his frequent intercourse with missionaries was the deepening conviction that what matters most,
what ought to loom largest in the life of
the Church, is the directly missionary
work. The place of missions in the life
of the Church must be the central place
and none other. "Secure for that
thought its true place, in our plans, our
policy, our prayers, and then—why then,
the issue is His, not ours. But it may
well be that if that come true there be
some standing here to-night who shall
not taste of death till they see here on
earth, in a way we know not how, 'the
Kingdom of God come with power.'"

The last address was given by Mr.
Robert E. Speer, of New York, on
"Christ the Leader of the Missionary
Work of the Church." With frequent
reference to the lives of great missionaries, he illustrated the fact, the meaning and the method of Christ's leadership, which involves for Christian people
a world vision and a world purpose.

Archbishop Davidson led the large audience in the Lord's Prayer, at the end
giving his benediction. It is well within the truth to say that never before has
an Archbishop of Canterbury blessed
such a gathering as that which had
met in the Scotch capital that June
evening.

IV. THE CONFERENCE DISCUSSIONS

COMMISSION I.

Carrying the Gospel to All the Non-Christian Worl

June 15th

The Report

WEDNESDAY morning the Conference settled down to its work in earnest. The first commission report to be considered was naturally that outlining the present situation in the mission field and emphasizing the necessity for a speedy carrying of the Gospel to the whole non-Christian world. In the preliminary chapter the Commission pointed out the present unique opportunity and urgency for an aggressive policy. The non-Christian religions are losing their hold on certain classes. In some parts of the world they are attempting to adapt themselves to modern conditions, and are manifesting increased activity, enterprise and aggressiveness. Western civilization is spreading its corrupting influence in non-Christian lands. Non-Christian nations are in a plastic condition. There is a growing spirit of nationalism, as well as a rising spiritual tide in every mission field.

Then the Commission proceeded to an exhaustive survey of the non-Christian world. Country after country was taken up. The geographical, social and political facts about it were stated; its population and the characteristics of its people were described; forces at work and their location were enumerated; the achievements of the past were set forth; the difficulties of the present were frankly faced, and the work remaining to be done was pointed out, followed by a statement of the forces and equipment needed for the accomplishment of the task.

Mr. John R. Mott, in introducing the

report, stated that among the in res sions which the Commission had gat re as the result of its study, were t se 1. The Church has been commiss ne to undertake a vast and difficult sk 2. The time is at hand when the ris tian Church must stir itself as nev be fore in countries where it is alrea a work, for there is no warrant any er in Scripture for a merely supe ia proclamation of the Gospel. 3. h time has come for the Church to te unoccupied fields; if not now, when 4 If the needs of the world are to b ne there must be united planning and rk Effective co-operation would be eq t a doubling of the present force. 5. h state of the Church at home is one th most serious obstacles to its pr es abroad, for, after all, missions s pl mean the projection of the home C rc into the mission field. Attentio wa called to some fields, such as na Equatorial Africa and the Mohamr la world generally, as fields already ar tially occupied, but in which all ris tian forces should centre attentio an effort. Others, like Korea and J an may be left for the reinforced eff o the agencies now at work. The ur cu pied fields, especially those of C ra and Western Asia and the parts of ica where the Mohammedan menace is os grave, have a claim of peculiar v gh and urgency.

The report of the Commission wa accompanied by a valuable stati ica atlas, including, in addition to car ll prepared maps, the latest figures itl regard to the present missionary ce and achievements.

the other hand, there is a growing tendency to recognize the social character of the Kingdom of God, with the consequent necessity for effort to Christianize not only individuals, but families and nations. As one of the continental delegates, speaking particularly of the work in Africa, pointed out, the individual wants to be a good member of his family, of his tribe, of his state. At present it is impossible in many instances to be this and at the same time a good Christian, because family, tribe and state are ruled by non-Christian practices. Hence arises the importance of evangelizing not only the individual, but the whole community. Be indulgent, the speaker pleaded, of the failings of converts. Build for them the golden bridge from the old life to the new which we, as heirs of many Christian centuries, have found already constructed for us. The general sentiment of the Conference seemed to be expressed by Mrs. Carus-Wilson in the sentence, "We must seek to change 'heathendom' into 'Christendom.'"

Another vital question is whether it is wiser statesmanship to concentrate effort on fields already occupied, or to reach out into fields at present unoccupied. One worker among Mohammedans advocated the policy of concentration save where Islam is advancing. There effective expansion must be the policy in order to check Islamic progress. On the other hand, it was urged that the greatest argument for entering a field was not the apparent opportunity of success, but the destitution of the field. God so loved the world, not of opportunity, but of need. Our Lord's command is universal. His glory is at stake in unoccupied fields. Though unoccupied by the forces of righteousness they are occupied by the forces of sin. One missionary told of having seen a Mohammedan stable in a building that was once a Christian cathedral. Moreover, in some of the unoccupied fields there are races and classes of the highest strategic influence.

THE RIGHT REV. WILLIAM LAWRENCE, D.D.,   THE MOST REV. RANDALL T. DAVIDSON, D.,
Bishop of Massachusetts and Chairman of the   *Archbishop of Canterbury*
House of Bishops of the American Church

Photo—Chickering   Photo—Elliott & Fry

THE MOST REV. COSMO GORDON LANG, D.D.,   THE MOST REV. JOHN FORBES ROBBERDS
Archbishop of York   *Bishop of Brechin and Primus of the Sco-*
                            Episcopal Church

Photo—Russell & Sons   Photo—Elliott & Fry

COMMISSION II.

The Church in the Mission Field

June 16th

MANY people still think that the missionary enterprise can be defined simply as "an effort to make converts to Christian-
y." From their point of view, when a onvert" is "made"· the missionary's sk and anxiety, so far as that particu-r individual is concerned, are at an end. fact, they have only begun. In many ission fields the all-important question no longer how missionaries from west-n lands can win converts to Christian ith and life, but how the growing "na-/e Church" can be organized, disci-ned, strengthened and equipped so at it may worthily express the Chris-n ideal and enter upon the great task bringing all the people of the land to obedience to our Lord.

The Report

All this was admirably brought out the report of Commission II. on he Church in the Mission Field." nong other things, the report dealt th the progress made in build-g up self-supporting, self-propagat-g and self-governing Christian com-nities; the instruction and prepara-n given to inquirers before baptism d confirmation; the exercise of cipline in cases where the young ristian disciple falls back into ctices inconsistent with Christian fession; the attitude to be taken ard questions affecting social as well religious life, such as polygamy, ed marriages, ancestor worship, the ervance of the Lord's day; and the ining of native Christian workers. The chairman of the Commission, Rev. Dr. J. Campbell Gibson, who rendered such signal service to the gress of Christianity in China, de-

clared in his introductory address that "the Church in the Mission Field" exists as a fact. Every human soul separated from non-Christian systems is a living organism and inevitably associates it-self with other similar living organisms. Thus "the Church in the Mission Field" represents the drawing together of spiritual life. This fact, so far from lessening the responsibility of home Christians, increases it. More leaders and better trained leaders are needed to guide this developing life aright.

The Discussion

The discussion of the report by the house centred first upon the "Constitu-tion and Organization of the Church." The Rev. Dr. Brown, of New York, secretary of the Presbyterian Board, de-precated the policy of too much control by the white man, and especially by the distant mission board at home. The task of ruling the native Church was naturally a congenial one for the for-eigner, but he must learn to take his place as an ally. This view was heartily approved by missionaries from India, Japan and China, who felt that the young Christian communities in these lands must be encouraged to develop on distinctly national lines. Bishop Honda, from Japan, was especially em-phatic in declaring that in this age of nationalism the Christian Church should express the national spirit of each land. Otherwise a weak-kneed band of Chris-tians will be produced. But the ideal of a national Church does not do away with the necessity for the sending of mis-sionaries from the West. On the con-trary, many more are needed. All de-pends, however, upon their ability to un-derstand and adjust themselves to the growing national spirit. While sympathizing fully with national aspirations an English Congregational missionary pointed out the danger of an unregulated nationalism leading to a Far Eastern Church separated from the Catholic Church of Christendom.

At this point Bishop Gore, of Birmingham, won the good will of the Conference by remarking that he had been told at the time of his consecration that "it was his function as a bishop to make himself disagreeable at public meetings." So he would speak plainly. The more true it is that the people of the West should do everything possible to foster the independent and indigenous character of "the Church in the Mission Field," the more important it is that they should keep in mind the fundamental truths belonging not to India, China or Japan, but to the Christian Church everywhere. Students of history must have noticed the rapidity and facility with which churches in the early Christian centuries became indigenous. There were no marked differences among them. All stood for a definite creed, the Bible and duly-constituted sacraments. Of late years there had been an unprecedented breaking down of denominational standards and barriers. No catholic-minded Christian would desire to denominationalize the young "Church in the Mission Field," but there was needed a frank statement as to what constitutes the Church. Protestantism shows a tendency to drift in this respect. Men no longer cherish some of the old assertions. What is to be substituted for them? No religious system can hope to stand without undergoing the painful process of defining its principles. To shirk this responsibility is to shirk something essential to continuous life. Continuous life depends on continuous principles. The Conference recognized instantly the vital truth of Bishop

COMMISSION III.

ducation in Relation to the Christianizing of National Life

June 17th

ONE of the first needs of a new Christian community in a non-Christian land is education. To be a really efficient community, to contribute toward e uplift of the whole national life, it ust be an educated community. It is t always possible to secure this education apart from the Christian Church because, in the majority of non-Christian nds, there is still no system, either of blic or private education, worthy the me. Even in lands like Japan, whose stem of public instruction rivals that the West in its thoroughness and comehensiveness, the pervading non-Christn atmosphere naturally develops a nstant downward pull upon the moral ndards of Christians and non-Christ ns alike. In other lands, such for innce as Egypt, where a system of inuction has been developed under the ministration of an imposed governnt, the spirit of the schools is almost tirely Islamic. Not only is it necess ry to give the Christian disciples edution; it is even more necessary to delop in every mission land an inenous Church with strong native ders. This can only be done as the ristian Church makes education in its adest aspects one of the fundamental tures of its missionary policy.

The Report

What has already been done in this ection? What needs to be done? at are the principles that should guide Christian churches of the West in ir educational efforts? To the task of wering such questions as these Comssion III. addressed itself. To it had n entrusted the great subject of ducation in Relation to the Christianng of National Life." It is not too ch to say that its report was a docu- ment of immense and permanent value. When published in book form it will make a volume of at least 450 pages. The report first reviewed the state of missionary education in all the great fields. It then turned to the consideration of special questions, such as how to relate Christian truth to indigenous thought and feeling; industrial training; the training of teachers; and the production of a literature by native authors. Each section of the report was followed by specific conclusions and recommendations based upon actual experience in the field. Any attempt to transplant the "form" or "type" of Christianity prevalent in the lands from which the missionaries come into that to which they go was distinctly deprecated. As a safeguard against this the Commission recommended that emphasis upon distinctive views of any one branch of the Christian Church should be avoided when not imperatively demanded by fidelity to vital truth. The Commission was convinced that however far the development of government education may go, higher education under missionary control should never be abandoned. Christian colleges are needed in all the great strategic centres. In some instances not only colleges, but Christian universities are an imperative need. This is especially true of China and Japan, but an effort should be made to develop such institutions as a result of united rather than denominational enterprise.

While one of the most important aims of Christian education is the planting and development of an indigenous Church, with its own leaders, the Commission pointed out that a great work is to be done in equipping men and women, whether Christian disciples or not, for positions of usefulness in their home

THE RIGHT REV. CHARLES P. ANDERSON, D.D.,
Bishop of Chicago
Photo—Gibson, Sykes & Fowler

THE RIGHT REV. EDWA
Bishop of S
Photo—Russell & Sons

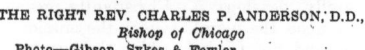

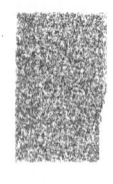

THE RIGHT REV. ROWLAND ELLIS, D.D.,
Bishop of Aberdeen and Orkney
Photo—Moffatt

THE RIGHT REV. HANDL
Bishop of D
Photo—Elliott & Fry

Four Distinguished Members of the Episcopate at Edin

munities. There is a possibility of nging a Christian community by giving education in a form which is suited only for the training of mission nts.

The necessity for adequately staffing missionary institutions as an essential condition of success was strongly emphasized the report. In too many instances men of great ability and absolute devotion are being sacrificed and their work is being made ineffective because they are expected to maintain educational institutions with an utterly insufficient staff and equipment. With full recognition of the wide aims of Christian education, including even "the philanthropic desire to promote the general welfare of the people," the Commission stressed the importance of making the missionary aim predominant. There should be no satisfaction in a school that is successfully serving certain social ends in a community if it fails not only to seek but to secure the conversion to God of a considerable proportion of those whom it teaches.

The Discussion

The Right Rev. Dr. Gore, Bishop of Birmingham, chairman of the Commission, introduced the report in an effective speech. The Commission, he assured the Conference, had done its best not to be original. The report had really been written by the more than 200 correspondents of the Commission in the mission field. No missionary was a member of the Commission. All comment and criticism, therefore, expressed the thought of missionaries themselves. For himself he thought it "shocking" that so many teachers and pastors in the mission field had been trained in the use of denominational symbols current in the West. Documents like the Thirty-Nine Articles and the Westminister Confession were so full of controversy and, in view of their origin, so necessarily partial in statement, that they could not be regarded as belonging to the universal substance of the Christian faith. Among the considerations he suggested were,

Have native helpers always been put in positions of sufficient responsibility in educational work? Has a sufficiently careful study of native literature been made to determine what elements can be used in the Christian propaganda?

The report of the Commission having been so largely the work of missionaries themselves, the discussion of it was in some particulars not quite as fresh and vigorous as the discussion of the preceding days. Emphasis was laid upon the importance of making missionary education frankly Christian. Its primary purpose is not simply to make individual Christians, but to develop a Christian community and to make that community more efficient in its elevating influence. The Rev. Dr. Pott, president of St. John's University, Shanghai, urged courage and determination in giving to the Chinese Empire the thoroughly trained leaders she needs. He was fully in accord with the report in believing that the aim of education is not only evangelistic, edificatory and leavening, but must be even more general. The Christian college, especially in China, must be prepared to extend the hand of help in every phase of Chinese life. Given help of this definite, yet comprehensive, character, China would develop into one of the greatest nations of the world; but to do this a much higher standard of efficiency must be sought and secured. Better material equipment must be provided, better trained educationalists must be drafted into the service. To his mind a scheme of Christian education adequate to the needs of the non-Christian world might well include schools of engineering, law and political science, no less than schools of theology and medicine. Dr. Duncan Main, a Church Missionary Society physician in China, strongly emphasized the need for medical education. The physical miseries of China, with 400,000,000 of people and a handful of trained doctors, are beyond belief. The West must give of her best men. Training counts in the field quite as much as at home. No men are wanted whose ability is limited to administering patent pills and other like remedies. China needs the best surgeons and diagnosticians in the world. Bishop Roots urged that in the consideration of advanced education the needs of the children should not be forgotten. Not only universities, but primary schools, literally thousands of them, are needed. Dr. Ibuka, of Japan, while recognizing the good work done by Christian schools, was of the opinion that they are no longer adequate to meet the demands. Give us in Japan, he urged, a Christian university. His plea was warmly seconded by Dr. Gulick, who claimed that there was no danger of injuring indigenous churches by providing them with educational institutions. A Christian university in Japan, equipped at a cost of $1,000,000, would accomplish five times as much as a similar institution in the United States or Great Britain. Professor Sadler, of the University of Manchester, a member of the Commission, in summing up the discussion acknowledged his indebtedness as an educator to what he had learned from missionaries. He believed that education and science generally had much to learn from the mission field.

COMMISSION IV.

The Missionary Message in Relation to Non-Christian Religions

June 18th

QUITE naturally the average observer of missionary work fails to take into account some of the most important conditions under which it must be done. Its effectiveness involves much more than the selection of missionary workers, the establishment of missionary institutions, and the learning of a difficult language. One of the most important elements of success is the ability to reach the heart of a non-Christian religion, ascertain how and why it grips its followers, and what it contains that will help to the understanding of the Christian religion. This means a study in comparative religions and in what might be called "missionary psychology." For truth is conveyed not simply by words, but by planting ideas in the minds of individuals and communities. For these reasons the subject intrusted to Commission IV., "The Missionary Message in Relation to the Non-Christian Religions," was one of the most important practical bearing. It was also one of the most difficult and complex subjects coming to the attention of the Conference. Most people realize that it is not possible to say that any non-Christian religious system is altogether bad. The more widely the missionary enterprise has been projected, the more intimately its representatives have come into contact with non-Christian life, the more clear has it become that there are some elements of goodness in almost every religion that claims the allegiance of men.

The Report

To an extent even greater than was the case with the report of the Commission on Education, the report of Commission IV. was written by the missionaries themselves. It is therefore all the more significant that the Commission should have been able to report a substantial agreement that the true method of approach is that of knowledge and charity combined with a seeking for the noblest elements in the non-Christian religion in order that they may be used as steps to higher things. The investigation of the Commission was conducted with rare skill and insight and its report will be

number of sick people does not decrease; the same number of people die,"
is the lament of another. Chinese expressed dissatisfaction because their religions do not help men to get rid of sin
or give moral and spiritual strength for
a better life. "Confucianism," said one
Chinese, "only teaches men how to talk
about duty; Christianity teaches them
how to do it." Japan's dissatisfaction
is expressed in similar terms. There is
general agreement that there is a lack
of spiritual power. As Japan mounts
higher in the scale of intelligence and
civilization, there is a growing recognition of the unscientific character and
the incomplete moral teaching of the
native religions. Greater dissatisfaction
is being directed against Buddhism than
any other form of belief. This seems to
be inevitable when it is remembered that
Buddhism is essentially pessimistic, while
the Japanese are to a greater extent
probably than any other nation of the
world to-day optimistic.

The low moral standards of Islam are
causing many thoughtful people to become dissatisfied with Mohammedanism
as an ideal of character. As one Moslem put it, "Wherever Christianity
goes, there goes civilization, but there
is darkness where Mohammedanism
prevails." There seems to be less expressed dissatisfaction with Hinduism
among the people of India than is the
case in any other great field. The Christian disciples are drawn more by the
positive and attractive character of
Christianity. After they become Christians their dissatisfaction with what formerly satisfied them is intensified. In
India, as elsewhere, and especially among
the student class, some dissatisfaction
is expressed because of the failure of
Hinduism to give effective help in the
effort to reach a higher moral standard.
Then such dissatisfaction as there is
seems to be largely with the practical result of Hinduism rather than with its
doctrine and teaching or its demand
upon the intellect.

After the report had been introduced
with a brief address by the chairman,

MR. WM. JAY SCHIEFFELIN,
President of the American Church Missionary Society

THE REV. REESE F. ALSOP, D.D.,
of the Board of Missions of the American C
Photo—Moffatt

MR. EUGENE STOCK,
Formerly Editorial Secretary of the English Church Missionary Society
Photo—Debenham & Gould

SIR JOHN KENNAWAY,
President of the English Church Missi Society
Photo—Elliott & Fry

Home Leaders of the Church's Mission

Christians in the face of death. He believed that a distinction should be made between the Hinduism of the report and the Hinduism of daily life.

To the Chinese the doctrine of the Fatherhood of God seems to make a strong appeal. Unlike Hindus, Chinese find no difficulty in the idea of an atonement, but like the Hindus they are deeply impressed by the sympathy and kindness embodied in Christianity as shown in our Lord's earthly life. The Rev. Dr. Gibson disagreed with the suggestion of the report that the Chinese are deficient in a sense of sin. He had found them deeply impressed by the fact of God's willingness to forgive. One difficulty seemed to be that there is no word in Chinese synonymous with the English word "sin." To the Chinese mind what we call sin generally conveys the idea of criminality. A congregation of English-speaking Christians would readily assent to the proposition that they were all miserable sinners, when they would wrathfully resent the suggestion that they were all vicious criminals. The worship of Shang-ti by the Chinese Emperor, Dr. Gibson believed to be the nearest Chinese approach to the worship of God. Such worship is no longer permitted to the common people. The missionary may reasonably therefore tell the Chinese that he has come to preach the God their fathers knew and worshipped, a God who encourages the approach to the highest by the lowliest. Shang-ti has been displaced in the minds of the people by Buddha and Confucius. The greatest hindrances in China are not Buddhism or Taoism, because they hold men by fear, but Confucianism, because that inculcates the idea of man's self-sufficiency.

From a Korean missionary came the suggestion that one of the obstacles to the progress of Christianity in the Orient is what seems to the native mind its inability to solve the emerging social problems of the East. Another pointed out that it is a significant fact that the excellence of non-Christian religions has been discovered and proclaimed by the

Christian mind, not by the heathen mind.

President Harada, of Japan, declared that the aspect of the Gospel which made the strongest appeal to his people was the love of God. Many Japanese Christians called St. John iii. 16 the Fujiyama of the New Testament—the "peerless peak" of truth and hope. During the last half-century since the preaching of the Christian message in Japan, the two words whose significance had been most changed are *"Kami"*— meaning God, and *"Ai"*—love. The character of Japanese Christians, their courage, manliness, serenity, self-sacrifice, make a strong appeal to the best element in non-Christian Japanese life. Japan's greatest difficulty seems to be in the region of theology and doctrine. "Deal with the Japanese sympathetically," Dr. Harada pleaded. "Emphasize those features of the Christian message which they can at the present time most readily understand."

One missionary had found very few educated Japanese who were devotees of the old faiths, though many of the principles of Buddhism and Shintoism form the unconscious background of their lives. He had found hindrances to the spread of Christianity in its supposed conflict with the spirit of nationalism and loyalty to the Empero., in its supposed inability to give a scientific explanation of the world and its processes, in its supposed impractical character, and in the supposed necessity of subscribing to elaborate statements of faith.

The venerable Dr. Chatterji told how he had been led from Hinduism to the Christian faith, and asked that missionaries who were dealing with Hindus should first of all acknowledge fully what good there is in Hinduism, and should deal fully and sympathetically with the intellectual as well as the social difficulties of the Hindu inquirer.

One of the most suggestive contributions to the discussion, so far as it bore on India, was made by Brother Western, of the Brotherhood of the Imitation,

traversing Mohammedan prejudices. So
serious is the situation that the Commission expressed the opinion "that
in E.,ypt, the Sudan, and Northern
Nigeria, the restrictions deliberately laid
upon Christian mission work and the
deference paid to Islam are excessive,
and that a respectful remonstrance
should be made to the British Government on the subject."

On the vexed question of indemnities
the Commission was of the opinion that
the propriety of accepting indemnity
was in large degree a question as to the
stage of advancement reached by the
people by whom the wrong to the mission has been committed. On the one
hand, it seems unwise to insist upon the
payment of indemnities, and the Commission thought that good might result
if missionary boards would adopt the
practice of returning indemnities where
they do not represent the genuinely free
action of the authorities, supported in a
reasonable degree by public sentiment.
It recognized, however, that leniency in
this particular might be followed by results damaging to the interests of
others.

Native Christians, the Commission
declared, ought not to be subjected to
legal disabilities because of their Christian profession. Enlightened nations
may well unite in making freedom of
action with regard to religion the birthright of every man. It seems reasonable
to ask of Christian governments that
they should use their good offices with
those of other nations for the free admission and exercise of missionary endeavor wherever such admission is not
now granted. For governments to undertake to allot spheres of missionary influence seemed to the Commission unwise, save with the concurrence of the

THE RIGHT REV. CHARLES H. BRENT, D.D.,
Bishop of the Philippine Islands

THE RIGHT REV. CHARLES GORE
Bishop of Birmingham

THE RIGHT REV. LOGAN H. ROOTS, D.D.,
Bishop of Hankow

THE RIGHT REV. JOHN WORDSWOR
Bishop of Salisbury
Photo—Russell & Sons

Leaders at the Front and at Home

ernment in view of the more stable conditions which they produce. One British officer in Africa was quoted as having said that it is only Moslems who cause trouble.

The attitude of the British Government in the Sudan was made the subject of pointed criticism. Friday, for instance, is being observed as the Sabbath in deference to the preference of Mohammedans. Christian officials fall in with this practice and native Christians are denied their Sunday privileges. Worse still, the college erected at Khartum as a memorial of General Charles Gordon is being given a distinctly Mohammedan tone. On the question of the relation of a missionary to officials from his own country, a Norwegian worker in Madagascar spoke words which Lord Balfour described as the quintessence of common sense. "Don't complain to the consul about trifling things, or you dissipate your influence. Then when something really important comes up you will not have that influence to call upon. Any missionary who can work only with the support of his consul had better pack up and go home."

Bishop Brent urged a suspension of judgment on the British Government for its connection with the opium traffic in China. It is a situation of immense perplexity, not merely a question of revenue. He felt sure that the government was sincere in its desire to find a way out. His words as an American were in strange contrast to the vigorous criticism of Dr. Harford, an Englishman, who assailed the British Government for permitting the liquor traffic in West Africa. After the situation in the Congo had been reviewed, Lord Balfour, in closing the discussion, paid a tribute to the influence of missionary work in assisting governments in the effective administration of foreign dependencies. Trade may provide revenue, but trade does not produce sympathy and pity. If a government desires to elevate the people of a dependent state, it is to the ideal of the missionary that it must turn.

COMMISSION VIII.

Co-operation and the Promotion of Unity

June 21st

THROUGHOUT the mission field there is a desire for unity. A divided Christianity cannot hope to be a completely victorious Christianity. The desire for unity is manifested not only among missionaries, but in some fields to an even greater extent among the native Christians. Bishop Roots, of Hankow, has put the matter none too strongly in saying: "If the missionaries cannot supply this demand for leadership in the practical development of Christian unity among the Chinese Christians, that leadership will undoubtedly arise outside the ranks of the missionaries, and perhaps even outside of the ranks of the duly authorized ministers of the Christian Church in China."

The Report

The subject intrusted to Commission VIII., "Co-operation and the Promotion of Unity," is, therefore, one of the most strategic importance. Although the last of the commissions numerically, it was thought best not to delay the consideration of the report until the last day of the session. Plans for ecclesiastical reunion were entirely outside the function of the Commission. Its report was confined to a careful statement of the facts relating to movements for co-operation and unity in the mission field. These statements included no reference to the co-operation with Roman Catholics, for the Roman Communion had manifested no willingness to share in the Conference. The Commission was able to report, however, that in many mission fields personal relations with Roman Catholics are often of a friendly character.

Under the general heading of "Comity," the Commission first considered those aspects of the subject relative to co-operation of a negative rather than of a positive kind, such as the methods for preventing overlap, church discipline and the transfer of native workers and Christians, a common standard of salaries, etc. Next the Commission considered conference on the mission field as one of the earliest expressions of the spirit of co-operation among the perplexing and often baffling questions that arise. They represent fellowship in counsel and are for the most part of an entirely practical character. The Commission highly commended them. "Missionary workers who have once been drawn together," it said, "are not readily sundered, and the sphere of co-operation widens with experience." A chapter on "Joint Action" showed missionary forces going a step further along the line of co-operation and working unitedly on such common tasks as Bible translation and distribution, the production of Christian literature, the founding and maintenance of mission publishing agencies. While such ventures are not by any means free from difficulties, their results more than justify the efforts made.

Co-operation in education, the Commission felt, was an insistent need, and urged new endeavors on this line, in view especially of the result of such an effort as the Shantung Christian University in North China, where American Presbyterians and English Baptists have united, while the Church of England mission is represented informally on the faculty and some of its students are in the college. Joint language schools for the training of new missionaries seem to offer an opportunity for co-operation. A valuable section of the report described the steps already taken by separate denominations within a single communion to maintain united work on the mission field. All the Methodist Christian in

must be a confident and kindly approach
to the Roman Church. In order that
this might be brought about, he laid
down these principles. Treat Roman
Catholics as true and sincere Christians.
Always preach constructive, not destructive truth. Be sure you have an
intelligent understanding of Roman
methods before talking in public about
them. Don't frame an indictment
against a whole church. If fighting ever
becomes necessary, fight fairly, as Christian gentlemen.

A Baptist missionary from India told
of the better understanding that had
grown up between the members of his
mission and of the Cambridge Mission
in Delhi, urging that the first bit of co-
operative work that came in sight should
be undertaken; the next will soon
appear.

The Bishop of Southwark, speaking
with fine spirit and entire frankness,
urged that all Christians should strive
to be loyal to the fact of such unity as
does already exist, confident that the
Spirit of God will lead on to what is
fuller and greater. He claimed unity
with the Roman and Greek Communions
no less than with Protestant Christians,
but in both cases it is a sadly broken
unity. At least we may say we are
united in one faith, though woefully divided in religious belief, instancing what
he meant by reference to the Anglican
position with regard to the sacraments,
the ministry and the Church as a visible
organism. Unity is to be won by giving
rather than by giving up. It will never
be reached by slenderness, but rather
fulness. The Conference, he believed,
was creating an atmosphere in which it
would be possible for God to fuse differences.

Bishop Montgomery, Secretary of the
Society for the Propagation of the Gospel, humorously described himself as one
of a small band of lions in a den of
Daniels, and announced that he proposed to do a little roaring. Although
he spoke frankly, what he said was in
such good spirit that the Conference applauded heartily. Undenominational-

THE REV. H. H. KELLY,

Director of the Society of the Sacred Mission

THE REV. J. DeWOLF PERRY, D.D.,

of the Board of Missions of the American Church

after the World Missionary Conference is over, and may be referred to it.

"(3)   To consider when a further World Missionary Conference is desirable, and to make the initial preparations.

"(4)   To devise plans for maintaining the intercourse which the World Missionary Conference has stimulated between different bodies of workers, *e.g.*, by literature or by a system of correspondence and mutual report, or the like.

"(5)   To place its services at the disposal of the Home Boards in any steps which they may be led to take (in accordance with the recommendation of more than one Commission) toward closer mutual counsel and practical cooperation.

"(6) To confer with the Societies and Boards as to the best method of working toward the formation of such a permanent   International   Missionary Committee as is suggested by the Commissions of the Conference and by various missionary bodies apart from the Conference.*

"(7)   And to take such steps as may seem desirable to carry out, by the formation of Special Committees or otherwise, any practical suggestions made in the Reports of the Commissions.

"II.   That the work of the Continuation Committee be subject to the proviso stated in the following paragraph from the Report of Commission VIII.:

" 'If the formation of such an International Committee is accomplished, the Continuation Committee of the World Missionary Conference should be authorized to transfer to it, wholly or in part, the task which it has itself re-

---

* The principles on which the Commission are agreed constructive work could be built are stated in their report as follows:
(*a*) It should from the beginning be precluded from handling matters which are concerned with the doctrinal or ecclesiastical differences of the various denominations.
(*b*) This being assured, it would be desirable that it should be as widely representative as possible.
(*c*) Yet it should be a purely consultative and advisory association, exercising no authority but such as would accrue to it through the intrinsic value of the services that it may be able to render.

ceived from the Conference; but if an.
International Committee be not formed,
the Continuation Committee should,
either wholly or in part, carry on the
work allotted to it.'

"III. That the Continuation Committee shall consist of thirty-five members of the World Missionary Conference, distributed as follows:—ten from
North America; ten from the Continent
of Europe; ten from the United Kingdom; and one each from Australasia,
China, Japan, India and Africa respectively.

"IV. That the Business Committee of
this Conference be instructed to nominate the members of this Continuation
Committee."

Everyone felt the moment to be one of
great significance. There was something akin to an awed silence as the
chairman put the question. Twelve hundred delegates on the floor shouted back
"aye." When the "noes" were called for,
once again the silence seemed vibrant.
Then, realizing that the most critical
point in the entire Conference had been
passed and that a notable forward step
had been taken, the delegates on the
floor and the missionaries and visitors
in the crowded galleries rose by common
impulse and twenty-two hundred voices
joined in "Praise God, from Whom all
blessings flow!" The names of the
"Continuation Committee," appointed
at a later session, in accordance with the
resolution, are as follows:

The Membership of the Con-
tinuation Committee

From Great Britain: Mrs. Creighton,
Sir Andrew Fraser, Dr. H. T. Hodgkin,
G. W. Macalpine, Esq., the Rev. J. N.
Ogilvie, the Rev. J. H. Ritson, the Rev.
George Robson, D.D., the Right Rev. the
Bishop of Southwark, Dr. Eugene Stock,
the Rev. R. Wardlaw Thompson, D.D.

From North America: The Rev. T. S.
Barbour, D.D., the Rev. James L. Barton,
D.D., the Rev. Arthur J. Brown, D.D.,
President Goucher, the Rev. Bishop
Lambuth, Mr. Silas McBee, Mr. John

ivity always exercises on the individual." "Are not these elements," he
asked, "more than sufficient to constitute
common ground for agreement and to
afford a sound basis for further discussion tending to promote a union of all
believers in Christ?"

After the Bishop of Gippsland had
told of the apparently successful efforts
of Anglicans and Presbyterians to work
out a common basis of agreement in
Australasia, a meeting notable not only
in the Edinburgh Conference, but in the
history of Christendom, came to an end.

COMMISSION V.

The Preparation of Missionaries

June 22d

IN the last analysis the missionary
enterprise is largely a question of
men and women. Without the
army in the field no amount of
home organization would be effective.
Without efficient and well-trained missionaries there can be little advance. It
speaks volumes for the spirit and quality
of the missionary force that such notable
results have been achieved as were reported to the Edinburgh Conference, but
is always possible to secure higher
standards of ability and training. This
was the conviction with which Commission V. approached its task of investi-
gating and reporting upon "The Preparation of Missionaries."

The Report

After a rapid survey of the modern
situation in the mission field, the Commission reviewed the facts concerning
the present preparation of missionaries.
It found everywhere a high, indeed an
ideal, standard of physical, social, intellectual and spiritual qualifications.
While most of the boards adhere to such
standards as rigidly as possible, they are
not able to reach their ideals in every
individual missionary. The requirements in some respects, the Commission
reported, were so high as to seem almost
prohibitive, and there was a gratifying
desire to obtain the best, even though it
is often necessary to be satisfied with
good.

The Commission went at great length
into methods of selecting and training
missionaries, dealing in turn with gen-

eral, theological and professional preparation, whether educational or medical.
It outlined certain principles which in
its judgment were fundamental and indicated how these principles might be applied to the training of the various
classes of workers. Missionaries themselves are fully awake to the necessity
for thorough training. Some suggested
a central union training college at home
for the preparation of missionaries;
others, no less convinced of the need for
such an institution, thought that each
great field should have such a common
training-school and that the special
preparation of the missionaries should
be given in the field. The Commission
urged strongly upon missionaries the
need for continuing the habit of study in
the midst of their exacting work. Nowhere else in the world are the possibilities for mental stagnation and spiritual
degeneration so great. In closing the report the Commission expressed the
opinion that if missionaries are to be
prepared adequately, the standard of the
home ministry must be raised. It therefore suggested a careful inquiry regarding the intelligence of the home church
itself, and the methods of training its
ministry.

The Introduction

The Rev. W. D. MacKenzie, D.D.,
President of Hartford Theological Seminary, introduced the report as chairman of the Commission. The frankest
critics, he said, of missionary preparation and attainment were the mission-

aries themselves and the mission boards.
He believed it quite possible for a ministry to acquit itself creditably in
America or Europe, but, with the same
measure of preparation, to fail miser-
ably in China or Japan or India. The
unprepared missionary is likely to take
the line of least resistance, as evidenced
by the failure of some missionaries in
fields with a considerable, though not
exclusively Mohammedan population, to
endeavor to reach Mohammedans because they felt themselves unfitted for
the task. Too many men who have had
no training in pedagogy are being
pressed into educational work, often
against their own best judgment. He
urged that whenever it became necessary
to draft into a position of responsibility
in the educational work one who had no
previous training, he should be sent
home for at least a year's special course.
Language study Dr. MacKenzie felt was
in some instances also a weak point.
There were many fine linguists in the
missionary body, and the whole standard
of attainment is undoubtedly high, but
it could be improved. Most of the language teachers supplied to the missionary on the field are untrained. They are
unable to give the missionary any adequate introduction to the language.
Again the period of study is too often
interrupted because of the necessities of
the work. The Commission was convinced that it is better to allow a mission
station to lie fallow for two years while
a man is acquiring the language than to
cripple a wise man for forty years by
overloading him with responsibility before he has the language.

The Discussion

Mrs. Creighton, speaking also on behalf of the Commission, felt that one reason for insufficient training is that the
destination of the missionary is rarely
determined early enough to make possible preparation especially adapted to
the field to which he is going. A board
of missionary study would be useful in
this connection. It could recommend to
missionary societies and expectant mis-

ticised the mission boards for their ~~liquated~~ methods for providing for ~~guage~~ study. He had talked about ~~matter~~ until he was weary. He ~~uld~~ have in China at least six union ~~ools~~ for the training of new mission- ~~es~~ in China's various dialects.

~~n~~ closing the discussion Dr. Mac-

Kenzie pointed out that the qualities called for by the missionaries themselves meant a finely-balanced personality. This does not necessarily mean an over-abundance of geniuses. It is perfectly true that average men and women are needed, but they should have their powers developed to the highest point.

COMMISSION VI.

The Home Base of Missions

June 23d

The Report

THE Conference reserved for its last day the consideration of how to secure adequate support for the missionary enter-~~prise~~. It is evident that without a home ~~base~~ there can be no permanent mis-~~sionary~~ work. After dealing with what it ~~called~~ "the spiritual resources of the ~~Church~~," the Commission turned its at-~~tention~~ to "the promotion of missionary ~~intelligence~~" through church services, ~~congregational~~ activities, and the work ~~of~~ mission boards. Emphasis was laid ~~upon~~ the desirability of using news-~~papers~~ and other general periodicals, as ~~well~~ as the religious press and mission-~~ary~~ magazines, for the purpose of dis-~~seminating~~ information. The report ~~showed~~ that most boards are fully alive ~~to~~ the value of a literature bureau, ~~though~~ not all may produce effective ~~results~~ or use them with the best judg-~~ment~~. With the millions of copies of ~~pamphlets~~ and missionary magazines ~~circulated~~ every year, it would seem ~~that~~ the excuse, "lack of knowledge," so ~~frequently~~ offered for indifference to the ~~missionary~~ enterprise, is not well ~~grounded~~. Mission study classes, mis-~~sionary~~ curricula in educational institu-~~tions~~, conferences, institutes, exhibits ~~and~~ similar methods, were all treated in ~~the~~ report. It emphasized especially the ~~value~~ of visits by members and officers ~~of~~ mission boards to the mission fields

as a means of insuring more intelligent and adequate administration. Methods of enlisting missionaries were outlined. The necessity for home leadership, first on the part of the ordained ministers, and then by laymen and women, was strongly emphasized.

Under the general heading, "Problems of Administration," the Commission dealt with the "deficits." A great variety of opinion was reported, ranging on the one hand from the statement, "Deficits are unavoidable and must ever follow devotion and daring," to the practice of one board which collects money a year in advance, banks it, and bases its appropriations for the following year upon the amount of money thus collected. Fortunately such a conservative method is exceptional. Every board reported its vigorous effort to keep expenditure as far as possible within the probable limits of income. It was evident that nearly all are basing their missionary activities not upon the needs of the field, but upon the amount which their various constituencies are likely to give. They have practically ceased, the Commission said, "to ask the Lord to lead into the fields He would have them win for Him, but they rather inquire of the home constituency how much it plans to give during the year."

A suggestive section of the report dealt with the reflex influence of the missionary enterprise upon the home church. The Commission strongly rec-

THE RIGHT REV. E. GRAHAM INGHAM, D.D.,
*Home Organization Secretary of the Church
Missionary Society*
Photo—Haines

THE RIGHT REV. H. H. MONTGOMERY,
*Secretary of the Society for the Propaga(
of the Gospel*
Photo—Russell & Sons

THE REV. CHARLES H. ROBINSON, D.D.,
*Editorial Secretary of the Society for the
Propagation of the Gospel*
Photo—Watson

HERBERT LANKESTER, M.D.,
Lay Secretary of the Church Missionary Sc
Photo—Haines

English Missionary Secretaries

When the Conference turned to a consideration of how to secure an adequate offering of lives for missionary service, the Rev. Tissington Tatlow, of the British Student Volunteer Union, lamented the unwillingness of parents to have their children offer for the field. He could unfold many an astounding tale of the obstacles thrown in the way of sons and daughters by home leaders of the enterprise. The pull of the Church at home is against the offering of lives for missionary service. Some, while ready to make the sacrifices involved in a missionary vocation, find it difficult to subscribe unequivocally to all dogmatic statements of belief required by some mission boards. For a missionary society to show signs of retrenchment or unwillingness to increase its staff inevitably results in lessening the number of volunteers.

Mr. J. Campbell White was sure that laymen of strength and influence can be led to devote their time and effort to systematic missionary support if the thing to be done is clearly and definitely put before them, if the mission boards will propose to undertake not a part of the work, but all that ought to be done, and if men are asked to give their whole ability and not only their money.

The Rev. J. P. Maud, vicar of Bristol, and one of the vice-chairmen of the Commission, closed the discussion. What is needed is the bringing of a new spirit into the same old activities. The clergy especially, he felt, must be men of a new spirit. Let all go back home with a determination, not only to pray more, but to pray with new intelligence, purpose and definiteness. The reports of the Commissions would be valuable for this use. Let all go back to work, and especially to do more by personal contact with others to lead them to take their share in the enterprise. Let all go back to hope as never before. The front and the rear of the Lord's army have met and been bound together in a comradeship that can never be broken. The Lord Himself is standing in our midst, and that vision is the basis for our hope.

V. SOME IMPRESSIONS OF THE CONFERENCE

UNITY THE DOMINANT NOTE

By the Right Reverend William Lawrence, D. D.,
Bishop of Massachusetts

EVERY member of the Conference came away from it full of hope and confidence. There was a true ring to all the talk, a reality to every part of the discussion—from beginning to end frankness and love dominated the assembly.

To jot down impressions as they came to me there I put, first, a sense of humiliation and exhilaration: Humiliation that I should be in such noble company as many of these missionaries were: men that had hazarded their lives for Christ; exhilaration that the Christian Church has such men and women, and that these at Edinburgh were only representatives of an army of such heroes of every nation and clime.

My second impression was that these people, experts in the work, were conscious that a new and greater day for missions is already here. Missions do not consist of groups of natives about isolated missionaries. Missions are now a great force, including great institutions, demanding able administration and strong co-operation. Missions are not only converting thousands upon thousands of people to Christ, but are leavening great peoples, and changing their conditions, and lifting individuals. Missions are a power, a beneficent power, which all governments should reckon upon. Moreover, the time is soon coming when national Churches must be recognized among people of the East. It was significant that all speakers were united in ceasing to talk of "native Christians." Said a missionary who sat beside me, "I haven't used the word 'native' of converts for years—we are American Christians; others are Indian Christians, Chinese Christians, Japanese Christians—and they will have an Indian, a Chinese, a Japanese Church." "Teach these Christians to carry Christ to their own people," was the cry, and let the foreign missionary gradually continue his work to teaching the teachers, and in time retire altogether.

My third impression was not only of the devotion and fine spirit but of the intelligence, tact and judgment of the missionaries as represented at Edinburgh. How I wished, time and again, that those men and women who, knowing almost nothing of missions, carp at them, could have been at the conference and gained their knowledge at first hand. Of course there are tactless missionaries and mediocre men, but I know of no body of men who on the whole show such good sense, fine spirit and patience.

Another impression was that behind all work and talk was the spirit of prayer. Each morning session began with fifteen minutes of devotion. Besides, the best half hour of the day, between eleven and twelve, was given to devotion. It was, I believe, a unique experience in the history of the Church —1,200 delegates from all over the world, from Christian bodies of almost every name, men of many races all joining together in prayer and praise; and no one asked or cared to know what denomination the leader belonged to. He might be a Baptist, a Presbyterian, a cassocked priest of the Church of England or a Methodist; all joined in that greatest of all forces for Christian unity, prayer and praise.

Hence the dominant note of the con-rence gradually became stronger and tronger—the note of unity. Not that hen should think alike, or compromise heir differences, or conceal them, but hat deeper than all these was the love f God in Christ by which all Christians re bound together in spiritual unity.

Hence there could be said with truth what was told me two hours ago, a week after the Conference, by an English bishop: "The Conference has given an illustration of the true spirit of Christian unity which is unique, at least in the history of the Church of England."

THE RECONCILING POWER OF THE EDINBURGH CONFERENCE

By Bishop Montgomery,

Secretary of the Society for the Propagation of the Gospel

UPON the whole, I think the Edinburgh Conference has been one of the most remarkable experiences of my life. or the first time one became conscious an extent never quite so definite before, that we were in the presence of a iristian force, greater perhaps than y other in the world—greater, in my timation, even than Rome, and much rer in its aims, without any secondary tives. It was a great joy also to meet e leaders of these societies, many of om were such noble-minded men of h calibre intellectually. The thing ich was the least familiar to us High urchmen was, of course, the extempre prayer. At the same time, some of se who prayed showed that they re approximating much more to what may call the Catholic spirit in all blic prayers.

Personally, there is hardly anything should have deplored more than the sence of English High Churchmen m that Conference. Speaking quite mbly but honestly, I think we had a ssage to give that Conference, which alone could give, because we were pared to give it sanely and lovingly, h all respect for those who had shown ry spiritual gift and all the fruits of Spirit, but who were not in comnion with us. Again, I do not think could have put our own case—a case important and vital for the future of

Christianity—more plainly and thoroughly than we did before them. The leaders, of course, welcomed every utterance as being the honest conviction of Anglican Churchmen, and therefore worthy of full respect. Naturally, again, the rank and file to a certain extent were made unhappy, and I could not help feeling that they showed great forbearance. I should say that we were just about as much as they could stand.

One of the happiest memories of that fortnight has been the extraordinarily affectionate spirit in which we were welcomed by many of the leaders. The day is coming when great races in Asia will be asking this great Protestant force, more than any other body, how to create national churches. I cannot help feeling that when that day has come, our advice will be of inestimable importance to the future of Christianity, but we cannot expect that advice to be asked unless we show cordial respect for the work of these great Protestant societies. Our value in regard to them cannot be reckoned so far as bulk is concerned, more than a pinch of salt in a great mass. Numerically we are nowhere, but as a link between Protestant Christianity and Catholic Christianity, it would seem to be impossible to over-rate the importance of our task, since we are chiefly Catholic and only Protestant in parts, or as a detail.

Events move quickly in these days,

and it is impossible to forecast what may
happen ten years hence. I confess I
should like to live to see the enormous
advance in unity made in ten years'
time, but I have no fear whatever that
the Catholic position will have been
weakened. On the contrary, I believe it
will have been enormously strengthened,
and in this I cannot but feel that we
shall have played a very important part.
Of course, it is impossible to over-rate
the value of the words of Bishop Brent
in this aspect of the question. We have
to work for the true unity of all Christian people, ignoring none. Our present
duty is one the gravity of which it is

quite impossible to overestimate—
show to Protestant Christianity
spirit in which differences can e
when they are conscientious differen
the spirit of a truly courteous, lov
Catholic Christianity which minim
no differences but speaks the truth,
in hate and spite and contempt, but
love—which certainly does not dism
this magnificent Christian force with
words "heretics" and "schismatics."
duty is to win their respect and love
cultivating personal intimacies and t
to make it reasonable that they sho
turn to us for counsel in the day of t
perplexity.

SOME PRACTICAL ASPECTS OF THE CONFERENCE

By Eugene Stock,

Sometime Editorial Secretary of the Church Missionary Society

I HAVE already written a few lines
to *The Churchman,* giving my
general impressions of the Edinburgh Conference; but I reserved
for THE SPIRIT OF MISSIONS a brief comment on its practical bearing upon the
missionary enterprise.

The principal value of the Conference
in this respect lies in the remarkable reports presented by the Eight Commissions of Inquiry. No such contribution
to missionary literature has ever before
been given to Christendom. They do
not profess to be complete. They explicitly suggest further inquiries, which
are to be undertaken by the Continuation Committee. But even as they
stand, they are a mine of information,
and their conclusions—in some cases
called "findings," are for the most part
marked by a sagacious judgment which
was not always manifest in the Conference debates upon them, good as these
were upon the whole. On the Unevangelized World, on Native Churches, on
Education, on Non-Christian Religions,
on Missions and Governments, on Co-
operation and Unity, on the Preparation of Missionaries, and on the Home

Base of Missions, excellent spee
were made, but the Commission re
were of more permanent value.

No mission board or society
afford in the future to come to impor
decisions without first seeing how
these reports throw light on the
tions to be decided; and this means
no board or society can rightly d
gard the methods and work of
boards or societies. The direct re
of the Conference in this matter o
to be quickly manifest. Board A
Society B. may be quite sure tha
own method, say of fostering the n
Church, or of training missionarie
of local administration, is really
best; but, if so, that is all the more
son for letting others have the b
of its experience. It will be a
disappointment if much more frank
frequent interchange of views
experiences is not secured for
future.

In one important respect the Co
ence was defective. In the presen
vanced state of many missions the
cipal questions of practical policy
ecclesiastical; that is to say, the

ncerned with the life and organization the infant Church, which is the fruit the missionary work. But such questions were necessarily excluded from the rview of a conference of diverse ristian communions. All the greater ason for the different missions of one mmunion, as for example those of the nglican Communion, abandoning the st policy of isolation and taking council together. The S. P. G. and C. M. S., r instance, should be in more frequent mmunication with each other, and th of them with the Board of Missions

of the American Church. And even in not a few questions of the kind referred to, the methods of Presbyterian and other non-Anglican missions are quite worth our careful study. So also the methods of Roman missions, which inevitably had no place at Edinburgh. We can all learn from one another without in the least compromising our respective principles.

These are only general and pretty obvious remarks. I must not occupy space by referring to particular problems. *Domine dirige nos!*

HE NATIVE CHURCHES AND THE NEED FOR UNITY

By the Reverend Reese F. Alsop, D. D.,

Member of the Board of Missions of the American Episcopal Church

THE World Missionary Conference at Edinburgh has come and gone, leaving in the minds of all who attended it memories iich will be slow to fade. There was uch about it which appealed to the iagination. From every quarter of the rld men came from far-away mission lds to attend its sessions. Europe, ia, Africa, America, Australasia, sent ch its contingent. The number of the mes together was twelve hundred— elve hundred official delegates and as iny more Synod Hall delegates. Day day three great assembly rooms were irly filled, often thronged, morning, ternoon and evening. As one thinks such numbers, such enthusiasm, such stained prayer, his thoughts go back that upper room in Jerusalem with one hundred and twenty. That room came the power house whence light d heat have streamed down through centuries. Why should not this er gathering, calling with a mighty ice upon the same God, depending on the same Spirit, be in its turn an ch-making body? That early assembly went forth to create in three hundred ars a Christendom. Who shall dare to iit the result when ten times one hun-

dred and twenty, dowered with the same Spirit, move upon the world?

As one attended the sessions he could hardly fail to be struck with the thoroughness of the preparations which had been made. The eight commissions, each with its distinct subject, had been at work nearly two years. They had corresponded with every part of the missionary field, and from the gathered experience and thought of men from all over the world had compiled their reports. The reports therefore had the authority of practical workers as well as that of the expert who compiled them. One day was given to the reception, exposition and discussion of each of these extended reports. Speeches, except in case of those speaking for the Commission, were limited to seven minutes and always more wished to speak than time would allow.

Two days stand out in the memory of the writer: The day given to the discussion of the rights and duties and powers of the native churches and that given to the subject of unity and co-operation.

From all parts of the field, from foreign workers and those who had been gathered in, came with one voice the opinion, rather the conviction, that the

MR. SETH LOW

COLONEL ROBERT WILLIAMS, M.P.,
*Treasurer of the English Church Missionary
Society*
Photo—Russell & Sons

Distinguished Lay Members o

nction of the foreign missionary is lly provisional and temporary. He es and works that the time may come en he will be no longer needed. A ined, competent native ministry is r the goal toward which he presses th all his might. To that end he aches and teaches and educates. Yea, that he lives. I must decrease, but y—these men and women whom we winning for the Master and training be worthy members of His Church— st increase. To them just as soon as y can take it up we are ready to pass r the work. Gladly will we efface selves that they may be the teachers converters and saviours of their own ple. For only so we are sure can ole nations be won. China must be n by the Chinese; Japan by the Japse, India by Indians. The consent this proposition was unanimous.

Perhaps the most momentous of all days of the Conference was that deed to the discussion of Christian nity, unity and even union. The one ught was, If we are really to conquer world for the Master we must somey get together. While such vast parts the field are as yet unworked, there uld be no intrusion, no overlapping, interference with other men's work. t there be no strife, I pray thee, been thy herdmen and mine"—so said raham to Lot and divided with him

the land. So be it still. Choice, delimitation, courtesy, mutual helpfulness, brotherly kindness, these be the marks of missionary activity. Let the aim be not to project denominational differences but to make Christians. Let the heathen say, as they said centuries ago, "See how these Christians love one another."

Nor did such a hope for the Church's work through the world seem in the atmosphere of the Conference an impossible one. We forgot for a time our differences in the things that unite us— love to God, loyalty to the Master, zeal for the coming of the Kingdom. We got our feet upon the foundations. Not one unbrotherly word was spoken. Envying, rivalries seemed to melt away. All phases of Churchmanship, of denominationalism were there, but in all and through all there was just one thought, one feeling—Let us stand together for the conquering of the world. One is our Master and all we are brethren. That prayer of our Lord, so sternly rebuking our unhappy divisions— "That they may all be one, as Thou Father art in Me and I in Thee, that they may be one in us, that the world may know that Thou hast sent Me"—that prayer seemed to brood upon our deliberations, and lo! to many a soul came the vision of a united church and a world won to know, to love, to obey the Lord Jesus Christ.

A GATHERING UNIQUE IN HISTORY

By Seth Low

THE World Missionary Conference at Edinburgh was called by the Archbishop of Canterbury a gathering unique i history, and his prayer for it was that t results of it for good might be as que as the gathering itself.

he gathering was unique in at least t respects. There were men there could tell us at first hand about the

Protestant missions conducted by France, Switzerland, Germany, Holland, Denmark, Norway, Sweden and Finland, as well as men who could tell us about such missions conducted by Great Britain and America. In no other gathering of the reformed churches has such a world-wide study of missions been possible. The Conference was even more wonderfully unique, in

that it embraced in its membership
official delegates, not only from the
great missionary societies of the Church
of England and the Board of Missions
of our own Church, but also from substantially all the missionary societies of
the Protestant world.

Nothing has ever before brought together, in an official capacity, men representing churches of such diverse opinions as to church government, to say
nothing of differences in doctrine, and it
is full of significance that the cause
which produced this unique gathering
was the cause of Christian missions.

Eight reports were submitted to the
Conference, dealing with different aspects of the missionary problem, all of
which reports had been the subject of
study for eighteen months by commissions that in their make-up were fairly
representative of the Conference itself.
It is noteworthy that every one of these
reports was unanimous. Such a careful
world-wide study of missionary work is
itself a new thing. The result of it was
to present to the Conference a view of
missions as a whole which has never been
had before. Several impressions resulted from this presentation which may
be clearly stated.

First: Protestant missions as a whole
have passed the day of small things. In
all of the great mission fields, such as
India, China and Japan, and in not a
few of the smaller ones, there are now
many native congregations which are
ministered to by 'Christian men of their
own race and which are entirely self-
supporting.

Second: Such independent and self-
supporting congregations are so numerous that Protestant missions are now
face to face with the problem of organizing an indigenous Church in the mission field.

Third: Foreign missionaries and the
converts all want to establish one Christian Church in each country, so as not
to afflict these countries with a divided
Christianity. The Conference at Edinburgh itself is an evidence of the

unity among the churches conduct-
missions is to be brought about the
ference did not consider; except that
the was, I think, a very unanimous
response to the statement made by Bishop Gore of the Anglican Church that any
union of Christendom must be inclusive and not exclusive. The dominating
message, therefore, to the churches, from
the World Missionary Conference at
Edinburgh, is to work together and to
get together. Any church failing to lend
itself to such a course must recognize
that it is hindering the cause of Christ
in the mission field, and that it may, by
its policy of isolation, make it impossible
successfully to carry the Gospel of Christ
to mankind.

WHAT A MISSIONARY THINKS OF IT

By the Reverend F. L. Hawks Pott, D. D.,
President of St. John's University, Shanghai

AMONG the official delegates were
many missionaries from the
field. It is natural to ask what
was the chief impression carried away by them from the notable
gathering at Edinburgh.

Speaking as one of them it seems to
me that it can all be summed up in the
word encouragement.

In the first place, we realized as never
before that the Church of Christ is being
aroused to a sense of its great mission
to the whole world. The Archbishop of
Canterbury gave powerful expression to
this thought in the opening address on
"The Central Place of Missions in the
Life of the Church."

In some ways the Conference at Edinburgh might be compared to the Council of Clermont. The enthusiasm for a
far nobler holy war spread from member
to member, and it was as if a great voice
went up from the assemblage, crying
with earnest determination "God wills
it."

To the missionaries in their loneliness waging their conflict against what
at times appears to be overwhelming
odds there will come fresh courage, because they know the Christian Church
is in earnest in carrying out the great
enterprise of winning the world to
Christ.

Then, again, we derived encouragement
from the evidence afforded by the Conference that the missionary campaign
was to be carried on according to scientific methods. To underestimate the
strength of the enemy, as has often been
pointed out, is the surest way to court
disaster. The immensity of the task
and its tremendous difficulties were
faced squarely and honestly. It was
seen to be an undertaking requiring the
highest wisdom and most vigorous energy. It seemed as if the death knell
has sounded to that way of presenting
missions which makes the cause appear
like the wild fad of deluded enthusiasts.

The presentation of a report on the
relation of Christianity to non-Christian
religions was an event of unique significance, because it showed so clearly
the growth of an irenic spirit in the
place of one that was iconoclastic. The
Church, mindful of the words of the
Lord, goes to fulfil and not to destroy.

Once more, the missionary could not
but be encouraged when he listened to
addresses delivered by Chinese, Japanese, Korean, Indian and African delegates. A vision dawned of the not distant day when the religion of Christ
would become indigenous in the non-
Christian world. Leadership in the
Church of the lands represented by these
delegates will more and more be exercised by those who are native to the
soil. The sagacious utterances of these
men manifested the great latent power

for leadership existing in members of the Christian Church on the mission field.

Lastly there came a great sense of encouragement from the manifestation of the growth of the spirit of unity. It is striking to think that the Conference was held in Scotland, a land so troubled by religious strife in the past, and where the Christian forces are still so sadly disunited. Throughout the sessions little was said to emphasize dissension, much was said to mark the desire for unity. The organic unity of Christ's Church is still an impracticable ideal. The healing of the divisions is still far off, but certainly there is great encour-agement in the fact that there is a m[...]vellous growth of the spirit of unity, b[...] that is the absolutely preliminary es[...]-tial to union.

Speaking of the crusades, Bis[...] Creighton says, "The outburst of [...]-sading zeal united Christendom in c[...]-mon action, in which the unity of [...]e Church, which had before been a [...]-ception of the mind, became a rea[...]y, and Europe seemed one vast army u[...]er the leadership of the Pope." So als[...]lo missions make for unity.

The great desire to work in harm[...]y, to co-operate with one another, to m[...]i-fest the unity of the spirit are the d[...]p-est cause for encouragement.

THE OBLIGATION TO UNITE AND TO PROTEST

By the Reverend Samuel Bickersteth, D.D.,
Vicar of Leeds

THE Conference c e r t a i n l y achieved one result, it dealt a deathblow to the misuse of the term "the native Church." I trust that it has also, consciously or un-consciously, done something to bring into fuller and more frequent use an-other term, "the Holy Catholic Church."

On the last morning Commission VI. recommended us to discuss "How to present the world-wide problem to the *imagination* of the Church, so that it shall become an impelling and dominat-ing motive in all its life."* If this is to be done we must lead the Church to fix its mind on a world-wide idea. Nothing smaller will fit the needs of the case. A world-wide problem needs a world-wide solution. "Give me a great idea," said R. W. Emerson, "and I will feed upon it." But that which feeds the mind fills it, and in time fires the imagination.

But who has ever had a greater idea than that proclaimed by the Risen

* The suggestion is that the imagination of the Church, not of the world, must first be impressed.

Christ, when He designed to be [...]he Head, not of a local Church, how[...]er orthodox, nor of a national Chu[...]h, however ancient, nor of the Churc[...]n earth even if it was world-wide, bu[...]of the whole Church in Heaven and [...]n earth? for

"In concert with the holy dead
The warrior Church rejoiceth."

If the Church, however, is fully to [...]r-render to Christ's great idea, it [...]st learn to use the phrase in which [...]at idea is enshrined in the Creed, "[...]ly Catholic Church," holy because al[...]its members are called to be saints, [...]nd Catholic, which (be it remembe[...]l), means proportionate as well as univ[...]al.

The Conference, I believe, has em[...]a-sized to what we in the Church Mil[...]nt are committed, when we surrend[...] to Christ's great idea.

(1) To unity, because who can [...]bt that a subtle and spiritual unity al[...]dy binds together those who have been [...]p-tized by one Spirit into one Body! [...]ch union existing between them, thei[...] di-

ons are not only waste of power, but
.., are also woeful schisms.

2) To be protestants, for how can the
Church be holy, unless she ceaselessly
protests against sin in others, and still
more in herself? And how can the
Church be proportionate as well as universal, unless in her apprehension of the
Faith, as well as in its propagation
among others, she protests with increasing discernment against what is out of
proportion in others, and still more in
herself? In architecture what is out of
proportion may be useful, but it is always ugly, and we, who are called 'to
worship in the beauty of holiness, can
never do so until our worship is the interpretation of the perfect symmetry of
the Catholic Faith. Of the two things,
symmetry is harder than saintliness. It
is hard for a sinner to become a saint,
but it is still harder for a saint to become symmetrical, with all his angles
and awkward corners smoothed down.

How then did the Conference help to
the ultimate goal of the Church? I answer by what I may call its "parable of
the badges."* Our Lord loved to teach
by parables, and we are indebted to the

Business Committee for the idea of the
badges, the meaning of which I understood to be as follows: "Reveal yourself,
recognize others. In this assembly to be
anonymous is to be uninteresting, and to
be undenominational is to be obscurant-
ist. Therefore, let us know who you
are, and go about among others, labelled,
not libelled, by the name by which you
are prepared to stand."

Did not the badges carry us one step
further than this? They became an opportunity of revealing not only ourselves, but the Christ in us, and of helping us to recognize not only others, but
the Christ in others. During the singing
of the hymns, or when the "Our Father"
was said, with a voice like the sound of
many waters, then the Christ in us went
out to meet the Christ in others, hands
clasped hands, hearts were fused in one
fellowship, and at such a moment the
Holy Catholic Church was felt to be a
reality.

Starting then from the first germ of
its reality in Baptism, there will follow
on the growth of a unity, which will
eventually be the fulfilment of Christ's
great idea. The question is sometimes
asked, "Shall we recognize one another
in eternity?" The Conference, to my
mind, raised a previous question by saying, "Shall we begin to recognize each
other here and now?" Such recognition
has done infinite good to those who took
part in it.

---

*Notice to Delegates: Blank cardboard
badges will be provided for each delegate, who
is asked to write his name legibly upon the
badge, and wear it during the time of the Conference. It is thought that this arrangement
will enable delegates to get to know one another more easily. Badges may be obtained
from the Enquiry Office.

A NEW ERA

By the Reverend J. De Wolf Perry, D.D.,
Member of the Board of Missions of the American Episcopal Church

THE Conference deeply impressed
me as marking a new era in
missionary work and enterprise. Witnesses from all parts
of the world agreed in testifying that
all peoples which are not yet Christianized are feeling and expressing unsatisfied desires that can be adequately and

permanently filled by the Christian religion, and by that alone. Opportunities
for making the whole world Christian
are now offered, and for the first time
are thrown wide open, and must be used
promptly or they will be lost. Simul-
taneous with these opportunities is an
awakening, and an appreciation of oppor-

tunity and obligation, and a sense of human brotherhood, as indicated in "The Laymen's Missionary Movement," and in women's aggressive work.

The weakness and wastefulness of a divided church are felt and acknowledged. Co-operation and unity, specially in missionary work, are not only desired and attempted, but in a measure already practised, as appears, for instance, in distribution of fields for work in order to avoid overlapping and consequent waste.

This gathering from all the world and from many churches showed that Christians of various denominations can plan and work together, without either emphasizing their differences or surrendering their convictions, in a spirit of inclusiveness and comprehensiveness, laying emphasis on essentials in which they agree. This "unity of the spirit in the bond of peace" was manifestly due to, and was devoutly ascribed to the presence of Christ in the Spirit. It was evident that He had called and caused t[s] Conference to meet at this critical ti[e] in the history of His Church, and t[t] He was personally present both in [e] hearts of the delegates and in the C[.] ference as a body, prompting and gu[-] ing its purposes and plans, fulfilling [s] promise, and with impartiality best[-] ing blessing upon all who seek and [y] to serve Him.

The Conference gave encouragem[t] and assurance to united prayer, [d] furnished evidence that God is answ[-] use, "Thy kingdom come, Thy will [e] done on earth." It testified that [s] Kingdom is extending as never bef[o], is influencing nations as well as in[-] viduals, and will make "the kingdoms[f] the world the Kingdom of our Lord [d] of His Christ" if His people cheerf[y] accept and thankfully appreciate [e] privilege of being "workers toget[r] with God."

THE CHALLENGE TO LOFTIER HEIGHTS OF SERVI[E]

By the Reverend J. P. Maud,
Vicar of Bristol

IT is no easy task to record impressions of what must undoubtedly be held the greatest of all missionary conferences. But the outstanding impression I take to be the fact that such a gathering has been possible. It must remain a striking object lesson that 1,200 delegates, representing all churches and societies, with the exception of the Roman Catholic and Orthodox Eastern Churches, did assemble to confer how best to conduct the world-wide enterprise of Christian missions.

It is a wonderful thing that in this old country, where religious differences have been so marked, the Archbishops of Canterbury and York, the Moderator of the General Assembly of the Church of Scotland, Anglican bishops, Moravian bishops, the president of the Bap[t] Union, Congregationalists, Methodist[-] in fact men who were representative[f] every hue of ecclesiastical color, sho[d] have met, not only in peace and frien[-] ness for common counsel, but that t[y] should have done so without it being [-] pected that any one should surren[r] the least or minimize the greatest of [s] convictions. There was throughout the [n] days of the Conference perfect frien[-] ness and cordiality, but withal absol[e] frankness and openness. It has b[n] successfully proved that there are [o] insuperable barriers to the frier[y] meeting of Christians, widely and [-] parently hopelessly separated on m[y] matters of vital principle. The exp[-] ence is new, at least in this old coun[.] What has made it possible? Men[n]

the Conference. When delegates such as those were sent—men in the front rank in the professional, commercial and financial world—it is not surprising that they should make an impression so striking and arresting. It cannot fail to impress the apathetic laymen on their side of the Atlantic that the missionary enterprise in the New World has not only succeeded in enlisting the best men in the country but in calling out everything that is best in them.

With such conspicuous examples in view it will no longer be possible to describe the enterprise as only "worthy of women and children," except as a barefaced confession of man's unpardonable failure to play a man's game in life.

While the Conference was being forced to the conclusion that the methods of co-operation must be substituted for those of competition; while it counted up all the obstacles which such a policy must encounter, it was possible to point to real achievement along a line which can no longer be termed experimental. The answer was the Laymen's Missionary Movement. One clear message came to the men on this side from the laymen in the United States and Canada, and it was this: *God always intended the missionary enterprise to be a man's movement.*

The message comes from those who have already made it such, and have proved how fruitful such co-operation can be. A lead has been given from America not only in the conduct of such a conference as that just held at Edinburgh, but in supplying a practical scheme and the working results of an experience which is capable of worldwide application. This has been a contribution which we may dare to hope will be of permanent value, and which, we may even venture to prophesy, will cause the Edinburgh Conference to be known as the inauguration of a new era in the greatest enterprise entrusted by God to man.

A NEVADA MINING TOWN CELEBRATING A HOLIDAY

A LAYMAN'S VIEW OF WESTERN
MINING CAMPS

I DOUBT if any desert in the whole world could outdo Death Valley, Panamint Valley and parts of the Mojave and Great Amagosa Desert in point of general wretchedness. Terrific heat, lack of water, no shade, great scarcity of wood, broiling winds and whirling clouds of sand make life at times almost unbearable. One has to foot it around in the desert for about six months or a year to appreciate it fully. I did not realize how bad it was till I got out to San Francisco and noted the difference between nice fresh oysters and fish and a steady ménu of bacon and beans and "sough-dough" bread.

The average miner never saves his money anyway, but in a decent community he may try to live decently. When his general style of living is a continual roughing it, his one idea seems to be to have such a good time (?) on pay day as will compensate for the rest of the month.

Most mining camps are more or less on the "Bowery" order. The number of saloons is something to wonder at. Big gambling establishments with games running right through the twenty-four hours are wide open on the ground floor of the main street of the town. Dance halls, race track pool rooms, "variety" shows, concert halls and brothels are everywhere. Of course there are men who are always looking for this sort of thing, and they find it, too, wherever they are—that is, in towns of sufficient size. The point is that in the average mining camp it is all so obvious that you can't overlook it if you want to.

Any number of men frequent saloons and gambling halls there, not only because the other fellows do, but because there is no other place to go evenings. After the day's work is over you have the choice of a solitary evening in your hut trying to read by sputtering candle light, or join the crowd. I have spent a good many evenings playing "high five" or "seven-up" on a cracker box in an eight by ten adobe cabin with a crowd of prospectors and miners. It did not amuse me very much, but they were a steady, quiet sort, and did not care much for knocking around town, so they would come to the cabin after supper and smoke and tell yarns or play cards. Some sort of a men's club or reading-room would be a good thing in every one of those camps. The trouble is there is no such thing as Sunday, the day of rest, in any western camp that I have been in. Work at the mines and mills goes on day and night all the year round, and most of the stores and offices and all the saloons, etc., are open Sundays.

A DIOCESAN EXPERIMENT

By the Reverend Joseph N. Blanchard, D.D.,
Rector of Grace Church, Madison, N. J.

GROWING out of a plan outlined in a paper which was read last fall by the writer before the clergy of the Archdeaconry of Newark, an interesting experiment, under the direction of a committee appointed by Bishop Lines, has, during the last few months, been in operation in the diocese. The plan proposed and successfully carried out was that of conducting in a number of centres, which should reach as many parishes and missions as possible, a series of informal missionary meetings. These were held in the evening, and wherever possible in the parish house, and were limited in almost all cases to men. Addresses were made upon the three kinds of mission work—diocesan, domestic and foreign, and an opportunity given at the close for questions and discussion. There was no service and no collection. Through the cordial co-operation of the clergy and many of the laity, the men of the various congregations were personally invited and the response was encouraging.

Owing to the position of Newark it was possible to secure an unusual number of speakers from the Missions House, New York. The secretaries filled several appointments and the Rev. Dr. Pott and other missionaries on furlough also spoke in several places on foreign missions. A number of the clergy and laity of the diocese also gave their help. Between February 11th and May 22d thirty-seven conferences were held, covering 115 parishes and missions. The aggregate attendance was about 1,545 men, and the average attendance was over 41.

It is perhaps too early to form an estimate of results, but at least these meetings have done much to unite different parts of the diocese in the recognition of a common work, and the missionary cause, presented in a direct way, by men to men, for the purpose of education and not exhortation, has made a strong appeal. The questions and discussions which marked several of the after-meetings were the best proof of the value of these conferences.

It may not, perhaps, be a direct result of these meetings, but it is due to their effect upon the men of one parish that, in response to the earnest and forceful plea of their rector, returning from the National Congress of the Laymen's Missionary Movement at Chicago, that parish has undertaken to support a missionary in Japan at a cost of $1,650, their apportionment being but $1,000. Another benefit is that there has been placed before the men of the different parishes the imperative need of systematic giving for all kinds of missions. The canvass of the men before the meetings has suggested a similar canvass afterward to make the result permanent.

This statement of what has thus been done in the diocese of Newark in presenting to its men the differing forms of mission work is made in the hope that something of the sort may be undertaken elsewhere. Those who are disposed to follow this suggestion should be encouraged by this testimony of one who is most intimate with the Newark campaign and its results: "It has brought to our laity and clergy a new sense of the privilege we all share in the spread of the Master's Kingdom beyond our own borders; it has given us a vision of our immediate duty which we cannot lose."

OUR LETTER BOX

Intimate and Informal Messages from the Field

A priest on the western boundary of Montana writes:

THE lack of the ministrations of the Church and the many opportunities for reaching people with the Church's message come home to us very often in these sparsely-settled regions of the West. In many parts of this vast region people are living and children are growing up, who see and hear almost as little of Christ and His Church as they would in a heathen land. From one year's end to another they have no opportunity to attend a religious service of any kind, and probably seldom hear Christ's name spoken, except in blasphemy.

Not long ago I held a service in a small mining camp, and at its close one man came to me expressing his hope that I would come again, and saying that it was the first time he had heard a sermon in thirty years. Another said it was the first time he had been to church in twenty-two years, and the sad thing is that the children, many of whom could be easily reached and won for Christ, are being neglected.

Some time ago I married one of my communicants to a man who has a country store in a small railway hamlet in Idaho, not far from the top of the continental divide. She wrote urging me to come down and give them an Easter service, as I was their nearest clergyman, and only eighty miles away. I suggested that she would better come up to Dillon for Easter, as the place was in another diocese and out of my field. But she insisted on my coming, and obtained permission from Bishop Funsten. So I went down on Easter Monday. On Tuesday morning we had the Communion in her parlor, with nine or ten to partake, and I baptized seven persons and preached to a very attentive congregation on "The Church and the Sacraments." In the evening we had service in the little stone schoolhouse, which loving hands had cleaned and decor[ed] with flowers. There were about sev[enty-]five people in the congregation and [th]ey seemed deeply interested. First I h[ad] a short illustrated sermon for the chil[dre]n, and then for the older ones I spok[e of] Christ and the Resurrection. The [peo]ple had prepared music and I do [n]ot know when I have enjoyed a se[rvi]ce more, or had a more attentive cor[gr]egation.

As a result one woman and her [son] are to be confirmed when Bishop [Fun]sten goes there next week. An[d] a charming young man, an Austrian, [a]nd a Roman Catholic, has come into [o]ur branch of the Holy Catholic Church, [a]nd is coming to the rectory a week fro[m to-]day to begin preparation for the m[in]is-try, to which he feels that he has [de]-cided vocation. I believe he will [ma]ke a most useful man.

It is a sad pity that the Church [has] not the men and the means to carr[y the] glad tidings into these remote [a]nd scattered places in our own land.

* *
*

A correspondent tells of the visit of [Bish]op Horner to one of our little mountain mi[ss]ons in North Carolina, which is under the c[ha]rge of the Rev. McNeely Du Bose, of [Mor]ganton:

WE drove out to find the little c[ha]pel overflowing with a reverent [co]n-gregation of uplifted mountain peop[le,] all eager to hear the "living words" [th]at fell from the bishop's lips. Th[ou]gh every woman seemed to have a bab[y] on her lap, the solemn silence was not i[nt]er-rupted during the beautiful confirm[ati]on service, which followed the baptism [of a] whole family of five children. [Af]ter-ward the father and mother, tog[eth]er with eighteen other persons, men [a]nd women, boys and girls, knelt rever[en]tly to receive the Holy Spirit in the so[le]mn rite of confirmation.

A picture came to me of that [sa]me spot some ten years ago, when ma[ny] of

tribution of some $30. The cheerfulness with which this was given made it doubly encouraging. In this connection I may say that several natives have made contributions for this purpose, of from twenty-five cents to two dollars. A contribution of a dollar was made by the medicine man.

On December 6th I started with Isaac Fisher, and two white neighbors who were going upon business of their own, to visit the new mining camps which lie in the heart of the wilderness, ninety miles east of Anvik. I was glad of the company of agreeable companions and experienced "mushers." We were obliged to follow a sled trail ten days old, as none of us knew the location of the mines, except that the general direction was pointed out to us by the natives. We lost this trail at times, which occasioned so much delay that we were nine days in reaching our destination. I was greatly interested in what I saw, and in the people whom I met in these camps, but there was nothing there to warrant the extravagant reports. which, as we have since learned, were sent out and published in the United States. There was no gold dust whatever in circulation, as there would have been in a successful mining camp, and the absence of a saloon in the village at the mouth of the creek spoke eloquently of the little hope that any one could have had of reaping a golden harvest where there was no gold.

Moreover, the fifteen hundred or more miners in the district were beginning to move out, preferring to bear the ills that they had in Fairbanks rather than to remain and meet with others that they knew not of.

We attempted to return by the same way that we came, but heavy snowstorms made progress so slow that provisions became short, and we were obliged to make a long detour of some two hundred miles to the northwest and southwest, in order to keep within reach of provisions for ourselves and our dogs. We finally reached home on January 2d. We had been gone twenty-eight days, of which all but three had been spent in actual travel. We had slept in a tent or in the open twenty-one nights. It was a disagreeable trip. The days were the shortest of the year, storms were frequent and progress slow, and three times the temperature fell to forty degrees below zero or lower, only to be followed in a few hours by a rise of temperature, bringing snow and rain.

We found our friends at Anvik anxious about us, and our welcome home fully compensated for the tedium of the trip. The Christmas tree had been kept for my return.

HOW CHICAGO LAY
FOR THE CHU

HERE are some instances of larger giving resulting from the Chicago convention of the Laymen's Missionary Movement last April:

* *

THE rector of Emmanuel Parish, La Grange, under whose leadership an every member canvass was organized after the Chicago Convention early in May, says that already more than $1,850 has been pledged for all missionary purposes, diocesan and general, although the canvass is not yet complete. At the same time last year, under the old methods, only about $750 were in sight.

* *

AT a dinner given to the men of St. Simon's parish, the "Every Member Canvass" was inaugurated with every prospect of an advance of at least 60 per cent. over the amount given for missions last year.

* *

THE parish of the Redeemer was one of the first churches to have a supper for its men. A committee was appointed and has been at work since, canvassing every member for pledges for missions with satisfactory results.

A MEXICAN OX CART

By the Reverend A. H. Mellen

HE City of Mexico thrills with its many lines of electric cars; horses and wagons clatter upon its pavemen.s, and the siren-whistle of the latest style motor car adds to the bustle and the noise. But in more remote parts of the country there are scenes like the above. The lines of faithful donkeys or mules carry packs over many a mountain trail to mining camp and distant village; the patient oxen are often loaded down with fire-wood, or with saddle and human cargo; and the old-fashioned Spanish carts are everywhere.

The yoke does not rest upon the necks of the oxen, but is bound firmly to the horns by rope or leathern thong. The wheel of the cart is made in five pieces, as you may see by a look at the picture. The centre piece must be originally as thick as the hub, then cut down by hand work and the hole made for the axle; next you see the two pieces so cut as to complete the circle, and these are held in position by two small, straight sticks mortised all the way through the great

blocks forming the central portion of the wheel.

But if you look on the cart you will see something quite different—an altar, a prayer desk and a lectern. These will be carried into the door plainly seen, for this cart is standing in front of the house at Rincon Antonio where regular services are held. This furniture, made of cedar and paid for by the congregation, will not be the only set to find its way into the bare halls at different places on the Isthmus of Tehuantepec.

¶

THE Training-school for Deaconesses in the Diocese of California in Berkeley has issued its announcement for its fourth year, which begins the first Tuesday in September. The Board of Managers, with the bishop at its head, and the faculty, are a guarantee for the character of the school. For further information application may be made to Deaconess Anita Hodgkin, 2539 Durant Avenue, Berkeley, Cal.

THE NEW LIBRARY AT BOONE UNIVERSITY, WUCHANG, THE ONLY ONE OF ITS KIND IN THE CHINESE EMPIRE

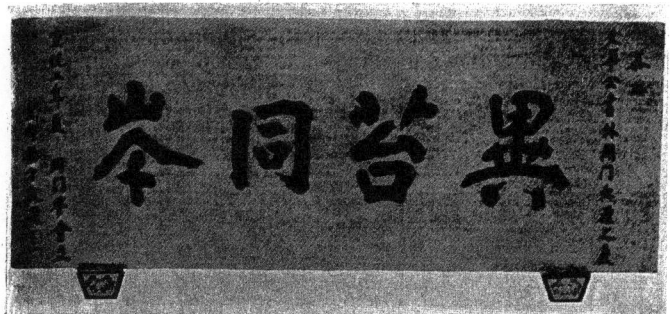

THE TABLET PRESENTED BY THE ALUMNI ASSOCIATION
THE ORIGINAL IS SEVERAL FEET LONG. THE CHARACTERS EXPRESS A SENTIMENT
WHICH MAY BE RENDERED INTO ENGLISH:

Varied are the mosses on the mountain peak;
Here the books are many for those who wisdom seek

BOONE UNIVERSITY LIBRARY
A STEP FORWARD

By Edward M. Merrins, M.D.

WITH a fine library within easy reach of almost everyone, it is difficult for people in the United States to realize that in the whole of China, among a people devoted to learning and very anxious at the present time to acquire a knowledge of western civilization, there are only three native libraries open to the public. Even these are so small and seldom heard of, that few people are aware of their existence. Hence the great and widespread interest which has been taken in the founding of Boone University Library, the latest enterprise of the Hankow Mission, as its benefits are intended not only for the 420 students connected with the university, but also for the large number of educated young men in the three cities of Wuchang, Hankow, and Hanyang, and the surrounding district.

The institution owes its existence to the energy and devotion of Miss Elizabeth Wood, the librarian. With the hearty support of Bishop Roots and of Dr. Jackson, the President of the University, and the approval of the Board of Missions, she appealed to the Church at home for money to purchase land, to erect the building and to provide books. About $14,000 was given. The contract to build was awarded in the spring of 1909, and the foundation stone was declared by Bishop Roots to have been well and truly laid on June 2d of the same year. An interesting description of the ceremony appeared in THE SPIRIT OF MISSIONS for October, 1909.

After many trials—for Chinese contractors, unlike those of whom Emerson sang, never build better than they know, and it required incessant vigilance to prevent bad work and the substitution of poor material—the library is now practically finished. As the accompanying photographs show, the architectural style is Grecian. Around the building in the

frieze are the following inscriptions in Chinese, the characters being carved on granite and covered with gold:

"In whom (Christ) are all the treasures of wisdom and knowledge hidden."—*Colossians* ii. v. 3.

"I looked up to them (the Master's doctrines) and they seemed to become more high; I tried to penetrate them, and they seemed to become more firm."

"He enlarged my mind with learning, and taught me the restraints of propriety."—*Confucian Analects*.

The interior of the building, with its happy combination of Chinese and foreign art, makes a most pleasing impression. The pillars of teak-wood brought from Singapore (this wood being very resistant to the attacks of white ants), divide the main floor into alcoves. The pillars are massive, as they support the floor above, where there is an auditorium seating 650. Provision for this valuable addition to the library was made by Miss Olivia E. Phelps Stokes, in memory of her sister, Miss Caroline Phelps Stokes, who died little more than a year ago. Altogether, the building is the largest and most beautiful of its kind in China.

The day selected for the opening of the library was May 16th, 1910. On the preceding evening, the alumni of Boone University held a reception in honor of the event, which was well attended by both foreigners and Chinese. During the course of the entertainment, the Rev. James Tsang, the president of the Alumni Association, presented a handsome Chinese tablet to the library. The inscription,

"*ib t'ai t'ung ts'en,*"

with its implications, may be translated:

"*Varied are the mosses on the mountain peak,*
Here the books are many for those who wisdom seek."

Among the other gifts to the library

were two pairs of scrolls from the teachers of the college; a dragon flag from the Useful Knowledge Society; and a history of the library in Chinese, by members of the Young Men's Christian Association.

Early the next morning there was a celebration of the Holy Communion, special prayers being offered for God's blessing on the library, and on all its benefactors.

In the afternoon, favored by beautiful weather, a large and picturesque assembly met in the auditorium for the opening ceremonies. On the platform were Bishop Roots and Dr. Jackson, flanked by the Chinese visitors in their official costumes with the insignia of their rank or scholarship. One old gentleman, whose flowing white hair and beard gave him a most venerable appearance, wrote the inscription for the outside of the building. He is said to be one of the finest caligraphers in China. The viceroy, unable to be present because of illness, sent in his stead a mandarin holding the high offices of Commissioner of Education and president of the Provincial Legislature, who came with a retinue of twenty-one under-officials and servants. Several foreign clergy, and the lay members of the faculty, were also on the platform. In the body of the hall were Bishop Bannister, of the provincial diocese of Hunan, and several English clergy, representatives of other missions, ladies and gentlemen from Hankow and elsewhere not connected with missions, but interested in their progress, and the 420 students of Boone. The college brass band was also there under the leadership of Professor Kemp, and the Glee Club, with its conductor, Dr. Samuel Ohio. The selections of music rendered by them added much to the pleasure of the occasion.

After Bishop Roots had dedicated the library to the glory of God and the welfare of the Chinese, he made an address explaining all that the Church hoped to accomplish by its means, and then spoke

benefit of the strangers present, urged
the students, while they were acquiring
foreign learning, not to neglect the study
of their own literature, and pointed out
that as so much had been done for the
library by a lady, it behooved them as
belonging to the sturdier sex to work for
it with like spirit and energy, so as to ensure its future prosperity.

After the bishop had pronounced the
benediction, refreshments were served to
the visitors, and the gathering dispersed.
It was generally agreed that a most important and far-reaching work had
been fittingly inaugurated.

Not much more need be said on the
advantages of the library to the Chinese,
except that in addition to its moral, intellectual and political value, it will be
most useful to the Church for the social and religious work it will enable
us to accomplish. Not that an aggressive attack will at once be made on all
non-Christians who enter its doors. The
influence will be more indirect. By the
reading of books morally and spiritually
helpful, and by pleasant contact with
Christian students, prejudice will be
gradually disarmed, and then those who
are far off may be brought nigh, and induced to consider favorably the claims
of the Lord Jesus Christ.

In the description of the internal arrangements of the library one point has
been omitted. It has room for 50,000
volumes, and this is none too many for
the one public library for three cities
with over one million inhabitants. At
present there are only 5,000 books. The
empty shelves are pleading mutely to be
filled. Money will enable us to buy the
books we know are required, but if
friends at home will overhaul their libraries and send us the books they can
spare, we shall be most thankful, and
all will be well used. To give another
version of the inscription of our library
tablet once more:

"Varied are the mosses on the moun-
tain peak,
Many books are needed for those
who knowledge seek.

THE CONVOCATION
OF CUBA

THE meeting of the Convocation of the Missionary District of Cuba, on June 8th, was one which breathed a spirit ·of great hope and encouragement. In presenting his report of work for the year the bishop showed 454 persons confirmed —167 in Cuba, 222 in the Canal Zone and sixty-five for the Bishop of New York. He had travelled 25,000 miles and written 2,000 letters. The communicants now number nearly 1,500, and Sunday-school pupils over 1,000. In fourteen parish schools nearly 500 pupils are enrolled. There are now twelve churches and four parish buildings; there is also a theological seminary. Twenty-one clergy care for forty missions. Five years ago there was but one priest and one deacon at work in the field.

That the district is thoroughly alive, and studying the problem of its own needs· with confident hope of continued and important progress, was evidenced throughout the proceedings. Among other actions taken were the following resolutions:

(1) That it be made known to the General Convention that the Convocation of the Church in the Missionary. District of Cuba believes that the truth of Catholicism, which is a Christian heritage, demands that the word "Protestant" be not used in the name of the Church in Cuba, nor in any kind of official literature of the Church used in Cuba.

(2) Whereas the development of the Church in this land has rendered her present title misleading and inadequate: *Resolved:* That this Convocation desires to place itself on record as favoring such legislation as will lead to the adoption of a legal title for our Church that will adequately set forth her claims to be a true branch of the Holy Catholic Church.

The Convocation also asked for a new, revised and corrected edition of the Book of Common Prayer in Spanish.

THE ANNUAL CONVOCATION OF THE DISTRICT OF PORTO RICO

OUR MISSION IN PORTO RICO

By the Right Reverend James H. Van Buren, D.D.

BRIEFLY, the situation in Porto Rico to-day is this—the work has outgrown the workers. To equalize the terms is to solve the problem. And there are two ways in which this may be done; either by reducing the work or by augmenting the workers. The former of these two methods would be dishonorable, for it would mean neglect of as fair an opportunity as ever was presented. The latter alone is worthy of consideration.

The Church's mission in Porto Rico must have reinforcements! A bishop and three clergy—with half a dozen native catechists, cannot cope with nineteen mission stations in a land where the means of travel are so inadequate. We must have more clergy, and we must have them soon. Already six missions have stood without services of any sort for more than a year. Two clergy are caring for six places, with three native catechists to assist them. Another, with three native helpers, is charged with eleven places; and six places are waiting.

Last winter one of our clergy came north in need of a vacation. The bishop took charge of his duties for three months and found himself with four Christmas festivals on his hands. Had it not been for the splendid work of the teachers and of the native catechists, by whose united efforts the contents of the many generous missionary boxes were distributed, the bishop would have come out of such a cyclonic Christmas-tide a wreck.

But there is such energy and harmony in action, such devotion, among the faithful little band! "Diminutive but determined," we have much to keep us in cheer and in courage. We make no complaint, we ask no easier lot. All we ask is that more clergy will come, more of the ministers and stewards of the mysteries of God to help us break the bread of life among these hungry souls; more fishers of men to help us, for the net is breaking.

Of those who are with us, whether clergy, teachers or lay helpers, no praise is too great. Give us ten more clergy

as devoted as these, and we will make
Porto Rico ring with the triumphs of the
Cross! Give us five, give us three, and
see what our advance will be.

If the clergy in the home land possessed the same missionary spirit as the
laity who have so generously responded
to my appeals for money, my appeal for
men would not be in vain! And if the
clergy could but visit our missions they
would be astonished at the triumphs our
little band has won. Porto Rico makes
no apology for meagre results. It is the
Church in the home land, that should
apologize for neglect of such a harvest
field.

In 1901, there were three missions—
at Ponce, Vieques and San Juan—each
with its priest, its congregation and Sunday-school.

There are now nineteen missions, nine
Sunday-schools, four day-schools, four
branches of the Woman's Auxiliary. We
own four churches, one hospital, two rec-
tories, two schoolhouses, one bishop's
residence and one large lot adjoining the
church in Ponce, all free of debt.

The clergy list has grown from three
to seven, but through removals has
dropped back to three again. There are
six lay-readers, four native catechists

(two of whom are studying for Holy
Orders), eleven day-school teachers,
twenty-four Sunday-school teachers, two
parish helpers, one medical director and
fifteen nurses.

In 1901 the Church property amounted
to $6,000; it is now valued at $153,8[ ],
of which there has come from Me[ ]s
Thank-offering $7,000, from Women's
United Offering of 1901, $2,500, and
$2,000 from the Ponce people for the
hospital. I have raised the balance,
$142,381, by special appeals, beside some
$10,000 for first two years' expenses of
St. Luke's Hospital. We have 4[ ]
communicants, 852 Sunday-school pupils,
406 day-school pupils.

In the Memorial Hospital of St. Luke
the Beloved Physician, during the first
two years and four months, we had 8[ ]
patients. One-half of these were treated
free of charge.

Porto Rico asks for men of courage
and endurance, of sound mind and
scholarly training, wise men and godly.
They need not be versed in Spanish
first, for such as these will learn it when
they have to; and what Porto Rico
needs is a stronger impression of all that
is best and manliest in American Christian life!

A PORTO RICAN BRANCH OF THE WOMAN'S AUXILIARY

! Department 3. The Rev. Thomas J. Garland, Church House, Philadelphia.

Department 4. The Rev. R. W. Patton, care of the Rev. C. B. Wilmer, D.D., 412 Courtland Street, Atlanta, Ga.

Department 5. The Rev. John Henry Hopkins, D.D., 703 Ashland Boulevard, Chicago.

Department 6. The Rev. C. C. Rollitt, 4400 Washburn Avenue, South, Minneapolis, Minn.

Department 7. The Rev. H. Percy Silver, Box 312, Topeka, Kan.

Department 8. The Rev. L. C. Sanford, 1215 Sacramento Street, San Francisco, Cal.

China

SHANGHAI:

The Rev. R. C. Wilson, of Zangzok.

HANKOW:
Bishop Roots.
The Rev. Arthur M. Sherman, of Hankow.

Cuba
Bishop Knight.

Japan
KYOTO:
Bishop Partridge, of Kyoto.

Porto Rico
Bishop Van Buren.

Work Among Negroes in the South

The Rev. S. H. Bishop, Secretary of the American Church Institute for Negroes, 500 West 122d Street, New York. Archdeacon Russell, of St. Paul's, Lawrenceville, Va., and the Rev. A. B. Hunter, of St. Augustine's, Raleigh, N. C., are always ready to take appointments, especially when a number of engagements in the same neighborhood can be grouped.

ANNOUNCEMENTS

CONCERNING THE MISSIONARIES

Alaska

THE REV. L. H. Buisch, who was appointed May 10th, with his wife left Buffalo July 27th, intending to sail from Seattle by the steamer *Jefferson* on August 10th, *en route* to Fairbanks.

THE REV. George E. Renison, who was appointed June 14th, with his family left San Francisco July 25th, and sailed from Seattle for Juneau.

MISS MABEL H. PICK, deaconess, who was appointed May 10th, sailed from San Francisco for Seattle by the steamer *Umatilla* on July 26th, and for Wrangell by the steamer *Cottage City* on August 1st.

Brazil

BISHOP KINSOLVING, coming to attend the General Convention, with his wife, expects to reach New York about August 4th.

Hankow

BISHOP ROOTS, coming to attend the General Convention, left Hankow May 20th; sailed from Southampton by the steamer *Majestic* on July 6th and arrived at New York on the 14th.

THE REV. and Mrs. L. B. Ridgely, returning after furlough, left New York July 15th and, after visiting friends in the West, are to sail from Vancouver by the steamer *Empress of Japan*, September 7th.

DR. HARRY B. TAYLOR, coming to the United States for the remainder of his furlough, sailed from Southampton with Bishop Roots.

DR. MARY V. GLENTON, on regular furlough, left Shanghai by the steamer *Manchuria* on June 8th, arrived at San Francisco on July 2d, and proceeded to Austin, Ill.

Kyoto

GEORGE M. LANING, who was graduated in medicine from the University of Michigan on June 26th, was married to Miss Beatrice Goodhew on the 30th. Dr. and Mrs. Laning left Ann Arbor July 2d, and sailed from San Francisco by the *Chiyo Maru* on the 19th, for Kobe.

Shanghai

MR. N. H. TING, who for many years was the Chinese financial agent and buyer for St. John's University, died on May 13th. The services at his funeral were held on the 16th.

THE REV. G. F. Mosher, on regular furlough, with his wife and son, sailed from Shanghai by the steamer *Manchuria* on June 8th, arrived at San Francisco July 2d and reached Trenton, N. J., on the 22d.

MISS MARY A. HILL, on regular furlough, sailed from Shanghai by the steamer *Empress of Japan* on June 7th, arrived at Vancouver on the 26th and reached her home, Montreal, N. C., on July 2d.

Tokyo

THE REV. Charles H. Evans and wife, coming to the United States for the remainder of their furlough, expect to sail from Liverpool by the steamer *Corsican* on August 11th for Montreal and proceed to St. Paul, Minn.

THE REPORT OF THE EDINBURGH CONFERENCE

THE report of the Edinburgh Conference will be published in the volumes early in September. A volume will be devoted to the report of each Commission and to the discussion upon it. The ninth volume will contain the addresses made at the evening meetings and other general matter. These nine volumes will constitute a missionary library of unique interest and value. Nothing like them has ever before been offered.

Until August 31st the price of the nine volumes will be $4, delivered anywhere in North America. Remittances in New York funds should be made to Mr. V. Henry Grant, 156 Fifth Avenue, New York.

THE WOMAN'S AUXILIARY
To the Board of Missions

A MISSION HOSPITAL IN SYRIA

MISSION FIELDS OF THE MEDITERRANEAN

By Mrs. Thomas Roberts

TO go over missionary ground twice, in 1900 and 1910, carried with it an interest not to be found in every-day travel of the ordinary sight-seeing kind. Missionaries themselves are hospitable beyond bounds, and their cordiality conveys genuine comfort to the tourist in a strange land. It was so thrilling, in this instance, to hear practically the same story of the blood-curdling experiences of the revolution and counter-revolution of 1908, in such centres as Constantinople and Smyrna, from the lips of men and women who went through those heroic experiences, and to witness their gratitude for the partial lifting of the Islamic veil of darkness from womanhood.

The whole of Syria is full of missionary zeal, an oasis in the midst of Mohammedanism, a mission field covering all educational needs, primary, advanced and normal. In the day-schools, in ad-

dition to Bible and other religious training, all elementary branches of American common schools are taught; on Sunday these schools become Sunday-schools, and each pupil is a messenger to bring parents and friends to the services. Adult visitors delight in listening to Scripture teaching, singing of hymns by the children, and preaching, and all creeds are represented. There are native Christian teachers, not only in Syria, but in Palestine, Egypt, along the Mediterranean coast and the interior, graduates of the Beyrout and Constantinople colleges.

The Syrian Protestant College at Beyrout is a direct outgrowth of missions, but has for years been independent of any missionary society. With its campus of forty acres and fourteen stately buildings standing out in bold relief, in full view from the harbor, the picture forms a beacon light of missionary progress. The students are Roman, Greek,

(683)

Armenian, Coptic, Protestant, and
Druses, Jews and Moslems. Among the
last prominent Islam families are represented. Graduates take rank in professions and commercial life the world
over. The graduates in medicine and
pharmacy are to be found throughout
the empire. An imperial commission is
sent annually by the Sultan from Constantinople to examine these students,
and rarely does one fail to pass, although
the ordeal is severe. All patients, however, are not yet converted to the newer
medical *régime,* for a sign we saw in
passing a prominent drug store in Cairo
read as follows: *"Pharmacie Nouvelle et
Esculapius"* (Pharmacy Modern and
Esculapius).

Haifa for many years has been blessed
with a medical mission hospital, under
the auspices of the S. P. C. K. Sufferers from desolate regions of Asia, far
beyond the Jordan, take refuge in its
wards, and the influence resulting is
widespread. There has been a gradual
abatement of prejudice because of the
increase of Turkish patients; and the
recent successful issue of a serious operation on the chief sheik of the Mosque
has done much toward altogether breaking down the wall. Moslem officials now
take decided interest in the hospital.
There are said to be ten times as many
Turks treated now as heretofore, and
Russian Jews, Greeks and Bedouins, as
well as Syrians, are among the patients.
The Bedouins, being accustomed to sleeping in open air on the ground, object
strenuously to bedsteads, and prefer to
lie *under* instead of on them. The
spring mattress is another terror, because it will not keep still! The hospital and church in one enclosure are
beautifully situated at the base of Mt.
Carmel, the Bay of Acre in front, with
the coast mountains in full view.

"Let us not be weary in well-doing" is
the thought on visiting the Tabeetha
Mission at Jaffa, established fifty-two
years ago by a Scotch lady of means,
Miss Walker-Arnott, who gave herself
and her income to the uplift of her sex
there. The field was of her own choos-

around English governesses, stenog-
raphers, trained nurses, interpreters,
etc., employed in Mohammedan offices
and families, show abundant evidence of
growing and strengthening through the
ten years between our visits. There are
Girls' Friendly branches in Smyrna and
Bournabat, fifteen miles away, both in
fine condition, not only progressing in-
ternally, but reaching out and helping
others. The associates of the Girls'
Friendly Society belong to the Anglican
Church or one of its branches; the members are of any creed or none, and many
a young English wage-earner, perforce
under the ungodly atmosphere of Mohammedanism, is cheered, protected and
uplifted by her Girls' Friendly Society
affiliations. The Girls' Friendly Society is always a centre of light in these
dark environments. The secretary of the
Smyrna Girls' Friendly Society is the
head of the London work for Jewish
women there, and seldom has a life been
more signally blessed in results than has
been hers.

Work for Jews throughout Asia
Minor, Syria, Palestine and Egypt shows
encouraging and deepening results.
Doors are opening wide for Christianity
to enter. Jews are working up their
own schools, and are *eager* to send their
children to mission schools. "The London Society for Promoting Christianity
among the Jews" is doing noble duty.
In Smyrna, especially, numbers are
higher than ever before in the girls'
school, and there is a large waiting list
of those who cannot be admitted, for
want of room. About half of these children are in Sunday-school; industrial
teaching is making mothers glad not
only that it promotes self-helpfulness,
but because, after leaving school, their
daughters can eke out the meagre family support. Many missionaries laboring
among Moslems make time to pray and
work more or less among the Jews. The
Church Missionary Society throughout
its widely extended mission fields is
noted in the East in this respect.

The learned Jew, when Christianized,
is master of the situation in argument

with the Mohammedan on the weaker points of the Koran; and English theologians, making this feature a special study, claim that the Christianizing of Jews of the Moslem dominions is the strongest influence that can be brought to bear on the evangelization of Islam. The stream of general education is gradually being diverted from Jewish to Christian channels. The Christianizing of the intelligent Jew is taking on peculiar significance. American and English missionaries agree that every centre of evangelical Hebrews becomes a light to a wide region in the Mohammedan empire where now the Gospel is practically excluded."

Whilst in Cairo the new girls' college was dedicated with appropriate ceremonies, in which Mr. Roosevelt took a prominent part. The institution was originally the Esbekieh American Mission Girls' School, which outgrew its former quarters, so great was the demand for liberal education of Egyptian girls of high rank, daughters of beys and pashas. Their new building, although open only two months, had already 137 girls in attendance.

Many Moslem girls are educated in the higher schools; they join in the worship of the one God and strive to be good and do good. There are Moslem patients of all degrees in the Cairo hospitals, who listen gladly and read the Christian literature given to them.

The attitude of Egyptians is strikingly changed. In Cairo and up the Nile American schools are demanded for their children by men of every rank. Syria has inoculated Egypt. Even old El-Azhar is struggling with a movement for a broader curriculum.

The automobile at the base of Cheops, and in Jerusalem, the ban removed from use of electricity, the change in marriage contracts, the freedom of religious usage and argument, the open doors of mosques and government schools, the interest in female education—all point to the "daybreak" that is coming everywhere.

FOUR YEARS IN THE ELIZABETH BUNN MEMORIAL HOSPITAL, WUCHANG

By Susan H. Higgins

IN thinking of the past four years in our hospital for women and children in Wuchang, the three movings stand out most strongly, as disagreeable things are apt to do; yet not wholly for that reason, but because that first move from the main compound was a most important step in the hospital's career, and the first break in the compound family.

For nearly two years after Dr. Glenton returned after furlough, taking me out as her nurse, the hospital remained in the compound, with Boone University, St. Peter's Hospital for Men and St. Hilda's School for Girls. With these thriving institutions the compound was growing more and more overcrowded, and our little hospital more and more shut in by the schools and hospitals for men and boys, so that the timid Chinese women would not come to us. Of these first two years—from 1905 to 1907—spent on the compound, there is little for me to say, for a newcomer in China does little but study the language for that length of time. One day, however, in 1907, Dr. Glenton and I were together at a patient's house—a big, roomy, official's home—when the idea occurred to us that we might rent such a house and move our hospital to a more advantageous site. I say "our idea" advisedly, for it came to us both at the same instant. Our "ideas" are always carefully labelled, but neither of us can claim this most brilliant of all ideas, exclusively! After some discussion of pros and cons, we were given permission to look for a house, and a dreary house-hunting time followed. Desirable houses at low rentals were not plentiful, and the one we took was pretty bad, but the best we could do—a semi-foreign structure, the foreign part of which was built by a Chinese carpenter who evidently had never seen a foreign house.

In this house, in a populous part of the city, a long way from the compound, the little Elizabeth Bunn Hospital took a new lease of life. With all its inconveniences and flimsy walls the place had sunshine, and the wards were bright and pleasant. We had twenty-two or three beds here, instead of the eleven beds we had on the compound, and in six months we were turning away patients; our dispensaries were large, and I wish the doctors and nurses at home could see the room where we worked. The consulting, dispensing and redressings had to be done in this one room, and we had to pay our nextdoor neighbor a dollar a month not to block up, by building, the only window that gave us any light.

The class of nurses, now senior pupils was started in this building. There can be no greater contrast than that between those timid, ignorant girls as they came to us there, and the self-reliant, helpful nurses they now are. Their development has been wonderful. This is a part of hospital work which counts for a great deal, this opening a way of helpfulness and self-support to Chinese women who ordinarily have no aim in life beyond dress and gossip. Our girls are all Christians whose kindness and unselfishness win many patients.

As we outgrew this place, Bishop Roots gave us permission to go to a larger house, still in the same neighborhood. This move was well indeed, for the old place was blown down less than two days after we left, and we could hardly have escaped some serious injury.

Our second house was an improvement on the first, accommodating thirty-two patients, and we had a few feet of courtyard where we could exercise without going out on the Chinese street; but the whole place was wretchedly damp, and w

A GROUP OF CHILD PATIENTS

pital; a large bright room in the centre of the building, with twelve little chairs and low tables for meals. It is a favorite resting place for us all, and many of our visitors ask to be taken in to see the babies, who are always quite ready to sing or play or talk.

HOSPITAL FINANCES

The Board of Missions appropriates $750 toward the work of the hospital, in addition to the salaries of the doctor and head nurse. This appropriation was made when the hospital was a small eleven-bed building. There are now forty beds, with all the extra expenses of the larger place; there are eleven servants, against five of former years; there is a class of nurses who must be clothed and fed and receive a small monthly pittance; there is a regular laundry man for the washing, which an *amah* used to do. Oil and fuel cost more; bandage cloth and cotton used in the large daily dispensary are expensive; there is the telephone, and these are only some of the extras. We need about twice as much as we get, and that will be allowing only twelve and a half cents gold a day to each of the forty beds. If we had this, it would cover everything, food, medicine, redressing materials, etc. Bishop Roots is asking for an appropriation of $1,200 this year. Out-calls will supply deficiencies and help equip the operating rooms. There is little chance to operate because there are so few instruments. Nor is there as much good pay out-practice as was looked for. The hard times in the past year have extended to the upper classes, and people who ordinarily would pay $5 Mexican ($2.50) for a visit now come to the hospital for the small fee at the gate. It is impossible to grow without increasing the expense.

THE NURSE'S WAIL

At the present the first of every month is a nightmare, trying to condense bills amounting to $150 in gold to within the monthly $62.50 check. This is the only part of the work in China which I mind!

THE UNITED OFFERING FROM TH[E] STANDPOINT OF A PARISH TREASURER IN MAINE

ONLY two short months are left before the last contributions must be made toward the United Offering of 1910. This offering will be given in Cincinnati, on the eighth day of next October, on the big gold alms basin presented to the Church of America by the Church of England. Any woman who has been a United Offering treasurer will appreciate with what anxiety this last collection is prayed for, thought over and worked for!

As the treasurer looks back it seems a very short time since, directly after the triennial in Richmond, the new blue boxes and leaflets were received for 1910, and the names of all baptized women in the parish gone over and over and over again, for fear some one might be left out. And then the visits that were paid, armed with blue boxes and leaflets, the letters that were written to women who had left the home parish and knew nothing of the United Offering, giving them the privilege of contributing through the blue boxes with the name of the home church written across the top. And as those first six months passed, how the list was pondered over and studied, and new names added, as women were found by the treasurer and others interested in the work. There were discouraging days, many disappointments often one after the other, but as the three years draw to a close, the treasurer seems to see only the blessings, which shine out like beacons to cheer and encourage all work in the Master's service.

And after each collection, the treasurer remembers how she wondered just what it represented besides dollars and cents, what self-sacrifice, real interest and thankful love for God and man.

And now, as the last collection approaches, every treasurer must ask herself, with deep concern, how many of her contributors really feel the desire, th[e] necessity of telling some other wom[an] of passing on the story of the [Un]ite[d] Offering, until every baptized wom[a]n i[n] the Church shall know and have a [s]har[e] in it. For, after all, while the [o]ne is important, the chief thing is to [sp]rea[d] the news. For nearly three years [m]an[y] of us have been praying that Go[d] wil[l] put it into the hearts of more and [m]ore women to offer themselves for His s[er]vice in the mission field; and if He a[ns]wers our prayers, we must be ready t[o] help the Board of Missions to send thes[e] new recruits, and that means that our U[n]ited Offering in Cincinnati in 1910 m[us]t be very much larger than that ma[de] in Richmond in 1907.

What are we doing about this [—]you and I?

Are we giving a mite, saying, "[I] can do nothing more," without realizin[g t]hat "*I can't*" is a lie on the lips that [r]peat "I believe in the Holy Ghost"? O[r] are we giving more than ever as our [sh]are, giving what we really can afford to [gi]ve? Are we each one of us seeking out [ev]ery woman in our parish, urging her to [sh]are in this? Are we looking for the [sc]attered Churchwomen in our diocese[s,]the Churchwomen who come by the [th]ou-sands every summer to our diocese[, the] women who are away from home? [A]re we really trying to interest all our [wo]m-en, rich and poor alike, showing eac[h o]ne the privilege of taking part in [t]his United Offering?

If we are not doing these things[, y]ou and I, and should begin to-day, wh[at] do you suppose would happen? The r[es]ult would be *far* beyond our expectation[s f]or the glory of God and the fulfilmen[t] of that most important of all missio[na]ry prayers, "Thy kingdom come."

(690)

STUDY CLASSES

any other meetings, the hours have been chosen for that very reason, and they will be held on only seven days. Second, suppose it does mean sacrifice? If we go to Cincinnati unselfishly, not for our pleasure but for what we may gain for others, and if we are in earnest about our educational work, we shall surely seize this opportunity, and give up, if necessary, other meetings; and pleasures for these classes.

TRIENNIAL NOTES

THE members of the Woman's Auxiliary who hope to be in Cincinnati will wish to remember a few dates and special occasions:

October 5th, Wednesday: Morning, Public Service at opening of General Convention. Afternoon: Conference of *diocesan officers* of the Auxiliary.

October 6th, Thursday: Morning, it is proposed to hold an adjourned session of the *officers' conference.*

October 7th, Friday: Missionary Day in General Convention.

October 8th, Saturday: 8 A.M., Holy Communion, with United Offering, in Christ Church; 8:15, Holy Communion in St. Paul's Cathedral. Afternoon: General Meeting of the Woman's Auxiliary.

October 10th, Monday: Morning, there may be another adjourned session of the *officers' conference.*

On following days the hours between 10:30 and 12:50 will be occupied in informal conferences, open to all members of the Auxiliary, with prayers at noon followed by missionary addresses.

Officers who have not already notified the Secretary of their intention of being in Cincinnati will please do so as soon as possible.

Any, member wishing information about boarding places should write to Mrs. Mortimer Matthews, Glendale, O.

(691)

ACKNOWLEDGMENT OF OFFERINGS

Offerings are asked to sustain missions in thirty missionary districts in the United States, Africa, China, Japan, Brazil, Mexico and Cuba; also work in the Haitien Church; in forty-two dioceses, including missions to the Indians and to the Colored People; to pay the salaries of thirty-two bishops, and stipends to 2,253 missionary workers, domestic and foreign; also two general missionaries to the Swedes and two missionaries among deaf-mutes in the Middle West and the South; and to support schools, hospitals and orphanages. With all remittances the name of the Diocese and Parish should be given. Remittances, when practicable, should be by Check or Draft, and should always be made payable to the order of George Gordon King, Treasurer, and sent to him, Church Missions House, 281 Fourth Avenue, New York. Remittances in Bank Notes are not safe unless sent in Registered Letters.

The Treasurer of the Board of Missions acknowledges the receipt of the following from June 1st to July 1st, 1910.

* Lenten and Easter Offering from the Sunday-school Auxiliary.

NOTE.—*The items in the following pages marked "Sp." are Specials which do not aid the Board in meeting its appropriations. In the heading for each Diocese the total marked "Ap." is the amount which does aid the Board of Missions in meeting its appropriations. Wherever the abbreviation "Wo. Aux." precedes the amount, the offering is through a branch of the Woman's Auxiliary.*

Home Dioceses

Alabama

Ap. $150.00; *Sp.* $46.95

MONTGOMERY—*St. John's S. S.**: Gen.	150	00
MISCELLANEOUS—Babies' Branch, Sp. for missionary font, Alaska	46	95

Albany

Ap. $928.75; *Sp.* $56.27

ALBANY—*St. Peter's*: Colored, $61.65; Indian, $28.61; Dom., $110.54	200	80
Helen L. Wilson, Gen.	25	00
AMSTERDAM—*St. Ann's*: Gen.	77	55
BURNT HILLS—*Calvary*: Dom.	6	11
CANTON—*Grace*: Gen.	54	35
CLAVERACK—*Trinity Church*: Gen.	5	20
COOPERSTOWN—*Christ Church*: Dom., $45.14; Frn., $3	48	14
FAIRFIELD — *Trinity Church*: Dom., $3.56; Frn., $3.32	6	88
HUDSON—*Christ Church*: Sp. for Bishop Whipple Memorial, Havana, Cuba	10	00
JOHNSTOWN—*St. John's*: Gen.	150	00
LITTLE FALLS — *Emmanuel Church*: Charles Bailey, Sp. for Church Extension Fund, Porto Rico	5	00
MENANDS—*St. Margaret's S. S.*: Gen.	7	75
MIDDLEVILLE—*Memorial*: Dom.	10	96
OGDENSBURG—*St. John's*: Frn., $10; Wo. Aux., Sp. for Bishop P. T. Rowe, D.D., Alaska, $40	50	00
RAYMERTOWN—*St. Paul's*: Sp. for St. John's University, Shanghai	1	27
SARATOGA SPRINGS—*Bethesda S. S.**: Dom., $19; Frn., $18.30	37	30
SUMMIT—*"Crowe's Nest"*: Gen.	10	00
TROY—*St. Barnabas's*: Dom., $1.50; Frn., $1.50	3	00
St. John's: *Gen., $169.71; Cuba, $32	201	71
St. Luke's S. S.*: Gen.	10	00
WALLOOMSAC—*St. John's Chapel S. S.**: Gen.	4	00
MISCELLANEOUS—"Cash," Gen.	60	00

Arkansas

Ap. $788.42

ARKANSAS CITY—*St. Clement's*: Gen.	4	0
BATESVILLE—*St. Paul's*: Gen.	31	0
BERRYVILLE—*St. Paul's*: Gen.		6
BLYTHEVILLE—*St. John's*: Gen.	2	0
BOONEVILLE—*Ascension*: Gen.		8
BRINKLEY—*St. Luke's*: Gen.	1	0
CAMDEN—*St. John's*: Gen.	28	0
CLARENDON—*St. Cyprian's*: Gen.		8
DES ARC—*St. James's*: Gen.		8
DE VALL'S BLUFF—*St. Michael's*: Gen.	2	0
EUREKA SPRINGS—*St. James's*: Gen.	7	0
FAYETTEVILLE—*St. Paul's*: Gen.	36	0
FOREMAN—*St. Barnabas's*: Gen.	4	0
FORREST CITY—*Church of the Good Shepherd*: Gen.	24	0
FORT SMITH—*St. John's*: Gen.	96	0
FULTON—*Emmanuel Church*: Gen.	2	0
HARRISON—*St. John's*: Gen.	4	0
HOPE—*St. Mark's*: Gen.	14	0
HOT SPRINGS—*St. Luke's*: Gen.	96	0
JONESBORO—*St. Mark's*: Gen.	9	0
LAKE VILLAGE — *Emmanuel Church*: Gen.	9	0
LITTLE ROCK—*Christ Church*: Gen.	16	2
St. Mark's: Gen.	4	0
St. Paul's: Gen.	24	0
Trinity Church: Gen.	96	0
LONOKE—*St. Mark's*: Gen.	2	0
MAMMOTH SPRINGS — *St. Andrew's*: Gen.	2	0
MARIANNA—*St. Andrew's*: Gen.	24	0
MENA—*Christ Church*: Gen.	14	0
MONTICELLO—*St. Mary's*: Gen.	2	0
MORRILLTON—*St. Agnes's*: Gen.	4	0
NASHVILLE—*Church of the Redeemer*: Gen.	2	0
NEWPORT—*St. Paul's*: Gen.	38	0
OSCEOLA—*Calvary*: Gen.		2
PINE BLUFF—*Trinity Church*: Gen.	108	0
POCAHONTAS—*Ascension*: Gen.	2	0
RUSSELLVILLE—Gen.		0
SEARCY—*St. Thomas's*: Gen.	12	0
STUTTGART—*St. Alban's*: Gen.	2	0

(692)

9 60	Catechists' School Land and Building	
1 80	Fund, Shanghai......................	25 00
36 00	·PACIFIC GROVE—*St. Mary's S. S.**:	
2 40	Gen.	20 70
2 40	SAN FRANCISCO—*Advent*: Gen........	15 00
	Grace: William Mintzer, Sp. for Cate-	
	chists' School Land and Building	
	Fund, Shanghai....................	100 00
	St. Peter's: Wo. Aux., salary of Rev.	
	J. W. Nichols, Shanghai...........	1 00
	St. Stephen's: Gen.................	14 75
	"Anonymous," Gen...............	100 00
540 00	SAN RAFAEL—*St. Paul's*: Gen.......	24 45
5 00	VISALIA—*St. Paul's*: Gen...........	7 50
50 00	WALNUT CREEK—*St. Paul's*: Gen.....	3 25
4 00		

Central New York

10 00	*Ap.* $877.90; *Sp.* $337.15	
2 00	ADAMS — *Emmanuel Church*: Dom.,	
45 00	$2.22; Frn., 83 cts.; S. S.,* Gen.,	
2 00	$2.75	5 80
	BINGHAMTON—*Christ Church*: $31.28,	
	S. S.,* $46.79, Gen...............	78 07
	Trinity Church: Dom...............	25 00
	CAPE VINCENT—*St. John's*: Gen......	33 50
166 00	MEXICO—*Grace*: Gen...............	8 60
	NORWICH—*Emmanuel Church S. S.**:	
25 00	Gen.	82 05
	Clarence L. Parker, Gen...........	10 00
	ONONDAGA CASTLE—*Church of the*	
	Good Shepherd: Gen..............	1 00
	OWEGO—"A Member," Wo. Aux., Sp.	
14 67	for Miss Bristowe's personal use,	
75 05	Tokyo	5 00
5 00	PARIS—*St. Paul's*: Gen.............	10 00
5 00	SENECA FALLS—*Trinity Church S. S.**:	
25 00	Gen., $95; Sp. for Rowland Hall,	
10 00	Utah, $40......................	135 00
	SKANEATELES—*St. James's*: Lucy A.	
8 45	Fitch, Sp. for St. John's University	
	Expansion Fund, Shanghai........	10 00
	SYRACUSE—*Calvary*: Gen...........	20 53
10 00	In Memoriam, the mission work,	
17 91	Ichang, Hankow..................	6 00
12 07	(East)—Miss E. Van Heusen, Sp. for	
	Expansion Fund, St. John's Univer-	
	sity, Shanghai....................	3 00
187 68	UNION SPRINGS—*Grace*: Gen........	5 50
12 18	UTICA—*Calvary*: Gen..............	5 00
160 00	*Holy Cross*: Girls' Friendly Society,	
	Sp. for Girls' School, Bontok, Philip-	
	pine Islands....................	14 15
10 00	*St. George's*: Gen................	3 00
	WATERLOO—*St. Paul's*: Gen........	56 67
	WATERTOWN—*Church of the Redeemer*	
9 94	*S. S.**: Gen.....................	8 18
4 69	*Trinity Church*: Gen...............	300 00
17 15	MISCELLANEOUS—Second District Mis-	
	sionary Study Class, Wo. Aux., Sp.	
10 00	for industrial work in Julia C.	
5 00	Emery Hall, Africa, $62.50; Sp. for	
81 67	St. John's College, Shanghai, $62.50.	125 00
	Babies' Branch, Dom., $42; Frn.,	
	$47; Akita Kindergarten, Tokyo,	
25 00	$25; Angelica Church Hart Day-	
	school, Wuchang, Hankow, $10; Sp.	
	for kindergarten, Mayaguez, Porto	
10 00	Rico, $35; Sp. for "Arthur Selden	
	Lloyd" scholarship, Corbin, Lexing-	
	ton, $5.........................	164 00
	Through Lucy Carlisle Watson, Sp.	
	for "Utica" scholarship, Tortella	
9 10	Hall, Nenana, Alaska.............	100 00

Chicago

22 15	*Ap.* $962.43; *Sp.* $56.00	
6 70	CHICAGO—*Advent*: Gen.............	3 16
152 80	*Ascension S. S.**: Gen.............	8 33
6 60	*Atonement*: Frn.................	15 00
	Christ Church S. S.*: Salary of Rev.	
	Chi Hsui, Hankow...............	180 00

Epiphany: Gen...................... 20 00
  Choir boys of Epiphany Church, Boys' Day-school, Ichang, Hankow.. 5 00
Grace: Dom., $2.15; Frn., $87.20; Gen., $4.48.................... 93 83
Holy Nativity S. S.*: Gen............ 16 23
St. George's S. S.* (Grand Crossing): Gen.......................... 26 61
St. James's: $50, "A Member," $200, Gen.......................... 250 00
St. Peter's: Gen., $156.79; Sp. for Miss Jeffrey, St. Paul's School, Beaufort, East Carolina, to help pay debt, $50; Sp. for Miss Folsom, St. Mary's Mission, Honolulu, $5; Sp. for Oneida Mission, Fond du Lac, $1 212 79
EVANSTON—*St. Luke's*: Dom. and Frn., $37; S. S.,* Birthday Fund, Gen., $3.72................... 40 72
  Mrs. C. C. Poole, Gen............. 5 00
GENEVA—*St. Elizabeth's S. S.**: Gen. 15 00
HINSDALE—*Grace*: Gen............. 24 74
RIVERSIDE—*St. Paul's S. S.**: Gen... 30 00
WINNETKA—*Christ Church S. S.**: Gen. 72 02

Colorado

Ap. $382.34; *Sp.* $3.00

ALAMOSA—*St. Thomas's S. S.**: Gen... 6 02
COLORADO SPRINGS — *St. Stephen's*: Dom. and Frn.............. 252 00
DENVER—*Epiphany*: Junior Aux., Gen. 5 00
St. Barnabas's: Junior Aux., Gen..... 15
St. John's Cathedral: Junior Aux., Frn., $1; Gen., $5............. 6 00
St. Luke's (Montclair): Junior Aux., Gen. 6 00
St. Mark's: Mothers' Meeting, Sp. for Bishop Aves, Mexico............. 3 00
St. Stephen's: Junior Aux., Gen...... 5 00
MORRISON—*All Angels'*: Gen....... 2 00
MISCELLANEOUS—Wo. Aux., Gen...... 100 17

Connecticut

Ap. $4,151.94; *Sp.* $1,348.55

ANSONIA—*Immanuel Church*: Dom... 5 00
BANTAM—*St. Paul's*: Gen........... 24 50
  Mrs. W. N. Sanford, Gen.......... 5 00
BETHANY—*Christ Church*: Gen...... 11 57
BETHEL—Mrs. George A. Shepard, Gen. 5 00
BRIDGEPORT—*Christ Church*: Gen.... 39 75
  Mrs. Edward Wright Harral, Gen.. 25 00
BRISTOL—*Trinity Church*: Gen....... 16 58
BROOKLYN—*Trinity Church*: Gen..... 35 91
BYRAM—*St. John's S. S.**: Gen....... 3 70
DANBURY—*St. James's*: Gen........ 39 67
DANIELSON—*St. Alban's*: $12.65, Wo. Aux., $20, Gen............. 32 65
DARIEN—*St. Luke's*: Gen........... 42
DEEP RIVER—*St. Peter's*: Frn..... 2 61
EAST BERLIN—*St. Gabriel's*: Gen.... 24 55
ESSEX — *St. John's*: Dom., $3.21; Frn., $2.14................. 5 35
GREENFIELD HILL—"A Friend," Gen.. 10 00
GREENWICH—S. C. Talbot, Gen...... 5 00
GROTON—*Seabury Memorial*: Gen.... 27 00
HARTFORD—*Christ Church S. S.**: Gen. 100 00
Church of the Good Shepherd S. S.*: Gen. 60 00
St. James's: Gen............. 92 00
St. Monica's S. S.*: Gen.......... 4 00
Trinity Church: "A Member," Gen.. 5 00
  "A.," Gen.................. 3 00
HAZARDVILLE—*St. Mary's*: Gen..... 90
LIME ROCK—"L. C. B.," Gen., $50; "In Memory" of medical missions, $50 .... 100 00
MIDDLETOWN — *Holy Trinity Church*: Dom., $34.43; Indian, $31.36; Colored, $2.68; Frn., $10.95; Gen. (of which S. S.,* $159.36), $231.87... 311 29
St. Luke's: Gen................. 25 47
MILFORD—*St. Peter's*: Gen.......... 15 50

MYSTIC—*St. Mark's*: Gen...........
NEW CANAAN—"One who helps as she can," Gen..................
NEW HAVEN—*Ascension*: Gen.......
St. Paul's: Estate of Mary E. Baldwin, Dom. and Frn., $34.05; Miss Frances J. Baldwin, Sp. for Church Extension Fund, Porto Rico, $5; Junior Aux., Sp. for Girls' High School, Kyoto, $10..............
St. Thomas's: Gen...............
Trinity Church: Mrs. T. H. Bishop, Sp. for Church Extension Fund, Porto Rico...............
  Miss Mary E. Hollister, Gen.......
  Miss Sarah L. Mitchell, Gen.......
NOANK—*Grace*: Gen................
NORWALK—*Grace*: $85, S. S.,* $86.50, Gen. ....
NORWICH—*Trinity Church*: Gen......
NORWICH TOWN—Susan T. Adams, Gen. ....
OXFORD—*St. Peter's*: Gen.........
POMFRET CENTRE — *Christ Church*: Gen. ....
PORTLAND—*St. John Baptist's*: Gen..
Trinity Church: Dom., $60.50; Frn., $5; Gen., $116.76..........
QUAKERS' FARM—*Christ Church*: Gen.
RIDGEFIELD—Mrs. J. H. Bulkley, Sp. for Church Extension Fund, Porto Rico ....
RIVERSIDE—*St. Paul's*: Mrs. M. L. Lockwood, Sp. for Church Extension Fund, Porto Rico, $5; Sp. for Bishop Whipple Memorial Fund, Havana, Cuba, $6.................
ROCKVILLE—*St. John's*: Gen......
ROUND HILL—*Calvary S. S.**: Gen...
ROWAYTON—Mrs. E. F. Weed, Gen...
SIMSBURY—*Westminster School*: Gen.
SOUTHINGTON—*St. Paul's S. S.*: Gen..
SOUTH MANCHESTER—*St. Mary's*: Gen.
STAFFORD SPRINGS—*Grace*: Gen.....
STAMFORD—*St. John's S. S.*: "St. John's" scholarship, St. Hilda's School, Wuchang, Hankew, $50; "St. John's" scholarship, St. Elizabeth's School, Standing Rock, South Dakota, $60; Sp. for scholarship, St. Augustine's School, Raleigh, North Carolina, $25; Sp. for John and Mary, under the late Archdeacon Hughson, Asheville, $50; Sp. for Rev. Mr. Spurr, Moundsville, West Virginia, $25.................
UNIONVILLE—*Christ Church*: $3.85, S. S.,* $3, Gen.............
WAREHOUSE POINT—*St. John's*: Dom., $54.25; Frn., $5.50..........
WEST HARTFORD—*St. James's*: $13.40, S. S.,* $4, Gen.............
WESTPORT—*Christ Church*: Gen.....
WETHERSFIELD—*Trinity Church*: Gen.
WILTON—*St. Matthew's S. S.**: Gen..
WINDSOR—*Grace*: Dom. and Frn., $51.76; S. S.,* Gen. $40.13.......
WINSTED—*St. James's*: Gen.........
YALESVILLE—*St. John's*: Gen.......
MISCELLANEOUS—New Haven Archdeaconry, Gen...............
  Branch Wo. Aux., Gen., $1,500; Sp. for Foreign Insurance Fund, $100; Sp. for Rev. D. T. Huntington for Trade School, Ichang, Hankow, $500; Sp. for work under Bishop Partridge, Kyoto, $200; Sp. for work under Bishop Graves, Shanghai, $200; Sp. for work under Bishop Aves, Mexico, $100; Sp. for Mrs. Roots's class, Hankow, $8.55; Sp. for Bishop Rowe, Alaska, $20; Sp. for Bishop Brent, Philippine Islands, $15; Sp. for Domestic Contingent Fund, $19..................... 2
  Junior Aux., Japan, $50.42; work among the mountain whites, $50.42.

East Carolina

Ap. $19.00 ; *Sp.* $5.00

5 00

WILMINGTON—*St. James's*: "A Member," Wo. Aux., Sp. for Bishop Horner's work in the mountains, Asheville 5 00

St. Paul's: E. Watson, Alaska mission. 5 00

10 00   Mrs. Adam Empee, Gen.......... 10 00
25 00   Miss Theodore Le Grand, Gen..... 4 00
3 89

17 19

Easton

Ap. $316.18 ; *Sp.* $145.00

CAROLINE CO.—*Holy Trinity Church* (Greensboro): Wo. Aux., Gen...... 5 00

CECIL CO—*Trinity Church* (Elkton): Wo. Aux., Gen................. 2 00

14 32   (Port Deposit)—Wo. Aux., Gen...... 1 00
4 03   (Aikin)—Mrs. William Murphy and
10 00   Mrs. Richard Whittingham, Gen.... 5 00
15 00   DORCHESTER Co. — *Christ Church*
12 25   (Cambridge): Wo. Aux, Gen., $15;
         Sp. for Archdeacon Wentworth, Lexington, $1..................... 16 00

St. Paul's (Vienna): Wo. Aux., Gen.,
8 00   85 cts.; Sp. for Archdeacon Wentworth, Lexington, $1............. 1 85

13 64   KENT Co. —*St. Clement's* (North Kent): Wo. Aux., Gen............ 5 00
         (Shrewsbury)—Wo. Aux., "Shrewsbury" scholarship, St. Mary's
48 23   School, South Dakota............ 60 00
         QUEEN ANNE Co. (Kent Island)—
         *Christ Church S. S.** (Stevensville): Gen. 12 99
         (Kent Island)—*Fore Point Mission S. S.** (Stevensville): Gen........... 1 68
         St. Andrew's (Sudlersville): Wo. Aux., Sp. for Archdeacon Wentworth, Lexington, for work in the mountains.. 1 00
         St. Paul's (Kent): Wo. Aux., Gen.... 5 00
         *St. Paul's S. S.** (Centreville): Gen.. 34 00
         Wye Church (Queenstown): Gen..... 12 00
         SOMERSET Co.—*St. Andrew's* (Princess Anne): Wo. Aux., Gen............ 8 00
         TALBOT Co.—*All Saints'* (Easton): Gen. 1 54
         Christ Church (Easton): $4.68, S. S.,*
148 53 $1.50, Junior Aux., $1, Gen....... 7 18
4 00   *Holy Innocents'* (Claiborne): Wo. Aux., Gen....................... 75
47 60   *St. Paul's* (Trappe): Wo. Aux., Sp.
25 00   for Archdeacon Wentworth, Lexington 1 00
         (Easton)—Miss Minnie C. Henderson, Gen. 1 00
         WICOMICO Co.—*St. Peter's* (Salisbury): Wo. Aux., Gen., $5; Sp. for
120 29   Archdeacon Wentworth, Lexington, $1 .... 6 00
         WORCESTER Co.—*St. Paul's* (Berlin): Wo. Aux., Sp. for Archdeacon Wentworth, Lexington................. 1 00
         St. Paul's-by-the-Sea (Ocean City): Gen. 2 00
         MISCELLANEOUS—Wo. Aux., Sp. for
73 45   Miss Ridgely for work in Cape Mount, Africa, $50; Sp. for Mrs. Wetmore, Asheville, $25.......... 75 00
         Junior Aux., Gen., $20.19; Sp. for Holy Trinity Orphanage, Tokyo, $25; Sp. for Mrs. Wetmore, Asheville (of which from Babies' Branch, $5), $20................. 65 19
167 00   Babies' Branch, Gen., $86; Akita
42 25   Kindergarten, Tokyo, $15; Little Helpers' Day-school, Wuchang, Han-
18 90   kow, $5; Angelica Church Hart Day-school, Shanghai, $5; Sp. for
51 97   "Little Helpers'" cot, St. Agnes's Hospital, Raleigh, North Carolina, $3; Sp. for "Arthur Lloyd" scholarship, Corbin, Lexington, $5; Sp. for missionary font, $1; Sp. for Bishop Spalding for White Rocks Emergency
16 00   Fund, Utah, $10................. 130 00

Florida

Ap. $172.00 ; *Sp.* $47.00

FERNANDINA—*St. Peter's* : Wo. Aux.,
Sp. for Miss E. W. Thackara, Arizona 20 00
GAINESVILLE—*St. Augustine's S. S.* * :
Gen. 4 00
JACKSONVILLE—*St. John's* : Wo. Aux.,
Sp. for Miss E. W. Thackara, Arizona 25 00
St. Philip's S. S. * : Gen............. 7 00
St. Stephen's : Wo. Aux., Sp. for Miss
E. W. Thackara, Arizona.......... 2 00
MISCELLANEOUS — Babies' B r a n c h,
Dom., $78 ; Frn., $78 ; Gaylord
Hart Mitchell Memorial Kindergarten, Akita, Tokyo, $5............. 161 00

Fond du Lac

Ap. $124.53 ; *Sp.* $3.80

APPLETON—*All Saints'* : Gen.......... 25 00
ASHLAND—*St. Andrew's* : Gen........ 6 84
BERLIN—*Trinity Church* : Gen....... 2 18
MANITOWOC — *St. J a m e s's* : Dom.,
$10.98 ; S. S., Sp. for Sisters of
St. Mary, Sewanee, Tennessee, $1.40 ;
Sp. for Dr. MacWillie, St. Luke's
Hospital, Wuchang, Hankow, $1.40. 13 78
MARINETTE—*St. Paul's* : Dom........ 14 39
NEILLSVILLE—*St. Luke's* : Gen...... 1 80
STEVEN'S POINT—*Intercession* : Frn... 5 20
MISCELLANEOUS—Branch Wo. Aux.,
Gen. 46 84
Babies' Branch, Gen., $11.30 ; Sp.
for missionary font, $1............. 12 30

Georgia

Ap. $109.42 ; *Sp.* $4.00

AMERICUS—*Calvary* : Gen........... 41 12
AUGUSTA—*Church of the Good Shepherd* : Junior Aux., St. Luke's Hospital, Shanghai, $3 ; salary of Rev.
Robb White, Baguio, Philippine
Islands, $3 ; Sp. for "Sister Katharine" scholarship, Guantanamo,
Cuba, $2 ; Sp. for Holy Trinity Orphanage, Tokyo, $2............... 10 00
BURROUGHS—*St. Bartholomew's Mission* : Gen........................ 1 00
SAVANNAH—*Christ Church* : Wo. Aux.,
$6.30, In Memoriam, $5, Gen...... 11 30
THOMASVILLE — *St. Thomas's* : Wo.
Aux., "John Watrus Beckwith Memorial" scholarship, St. Mary's Hall,
Shanghai 50 00

Harrisburg

Ap. $232.46

BELLEFONTE—George F. Harris, M.D.,
Gen. 10 00
HARRISBURG—*St. Paul's S. S.* * : Gen.. 45 00
HOLLIDAYSBURG—*Holy Trinity Church* :
Dom. 8 91
LANCASTER—W. F. Humble, Gen..... 50 00
MECHANICSBURG—*St. Luke's Mission* :
Gen.................................. 17 08
MUNCY—Mrs. Jesse Lightfoot, Gen.... 10 00
SELINSGROVE—*All Saints'* : Gen..... 2 65
SHAMOKIN—*Trinity Church* : Dom.... 3 82
YORK—*St. John's* : Gen.............. 75 00
Miss Elizabeth Bonham, Gen....... 10 00

Indianapolis

Ap. $573.91

ALEXANDRIA—*St. Paul's S. S.* * : Gen.. 3 61
CANNELTON—*St. Luke's* : Dom., 69
cts. ; Frn., 34 cts................. 1 03
EVANSVILLE—*St. Paul's* : Gen....... 67 51
INDIANAPOLIS—*Christ Church* : Gen... 177 30
Grace Pro-Cathedral : Dom......... 7 20
St. David's : Gen.................. 15 47

St. Paul's : Gen...................
JEFFERSONVILLE—*St. Paul's* : Gen....
MADISON—*Christ Church* : $4, S. S.
Birthday Offering, $3.50, Gen......
TERRE HAUTE—*St. Stephen's* : $100,
S. S.,* $69.54, Gen. ; "St. Stephen's"
scholarship, Girls' High School,
Kyoto, $50..........................
WILLIAMSPORT—Mrs. E. D. Boyer, Gen.

Iowa

Ap. $46.63

DES MOINES—*St. Mark's S. S.* * : Gen.
St. Paul's : Gen...................
FORT DODGE—*St. Mark's S. S.* * : Gen..
KEOKUK—*St. John's* : Gen..........
MAPLETON—*Trinity Church S. S.* * :
Gen.................................
MUSCATINE—*Trinity Church* : Gen....

Kansas

Ap. $122.13

ABILENE—*St. John's* : Gen..........
HERINGTON — *St. James the Less* :
"Thank-offering," Gen.............
IOLA—*St. Timothy's* : Gen.........
OTTAWA—*Grace S. S.* * : Gen.........
TOPEKA—Miss Juliet C. Smith's S S.
Class,* Gen........................
WICHITA—*St. John's* : Gen.........
MISCELLANEOUS—Diocesan Convention,
held in Grace Cathedral, Topeka,
collection, Gen....................

Kansas City

Ap. $136.86

KANSAS CITY—*St. Paul's S. S.* * : Gen.
ST. JOSEPH—*Holy Trinity Church S.
S.* * : Gen...........................

Kentucky

Ap. $416.50 ; *Sp.* $1.00

LOUISVILLE—*Advent* : $120, Wo. Aux.,
$10, Gen............................
Christ Church : Mrs. William Heyburn,
support of "Margaret Lander" bed,
St. James's Hospital, Anking, Hankow ....
Grace : Gen........................
St. John's : Wo. Aux., Gen.........
St. Mark's : Dom.. $42.50 ; Frn., $19.50
St. Paul's : Wo. Aux., Gen.........
Miss M. S. Bonnie, Gen............
Mary E. Pine, Gen.................
MISCELLANEOUS—Babies' Branch, Sp.
for missionary font...............

Lexington

Ap. $96.75 ; *Sp.* $12.00

GEORGETOWN—*Holy Trinity Church* :
Gen.................................
LAWRENCEBURG—*Grace* : Gen........
LEXINGTON—*Christ Church* : Junior
Aux., Sp. for Bishop Van Buren,
hospital work, Porto Rico.........
St. Andrew's : Gen................
Mrs. James T. Smith, Gen.........
NICHOLASVILLE—*All Saints'* : Gen....
VERSAILLES—*St. John's* : Juniors, Gen.
WINCHESTER—*Emmanuel Mission* : Gen.
MISCELLANEOUS—Branch Wo. Aux.,
Gen. ....
Babies' Branch, Dom., $4 ; Indian,
$4 ; Colored, $4 ; Frn., $4 ; Gen., $4.

Long Island

Ap. $1,346.50 ; *Sp.* $359.78

ASTORIA—*Church of the Redeemer* :
Wo. Aux., salary of Rev. William
Loola, Alaska, $2 ; Sp. for St. Paul's

School, Lawrenceville, Southern Virginia, $2.......................... 4 00
St. George's: Wo. Aux., salary of Rev. William Loola, Alaska, $10; Sp. for St. Paul's School, Lawrenceville, Southern Virginia, $2.50; Sp. for salary of sewing teacher, St. Augustine's School, Raleigh, North Carolina, $1; Sp. for St. John's University Expansion Fund, Shanghai, $7. 20 50
BAY SHORE—St. Peter's: Gen........ 25 00
BROOKLYN—Ascension: $50, Chapel, $5, S. S.,* $48.89; Dom. and Frn.; Wo. Aux., work among Seminoles, Southern Florida, $1.............. 104 89
Calvary: Wo. Aux., salary of Rev. William Loola, Alaska............ 2 00
Christ Church (Bay Ridge): Wo. Aux., salary of Rev. William Loola, Alaska, $2; Sp. for Bishop Rowe's white work, Alaska, $5; Sp. for chapel among the Kroos, Liberia, Africa, $2; Junior Aux., Sp. for sewing teacher's salary, St. Augustine's School, Raleigh, North Carolina, $2.......................... 11 00
Christ Church (Eastern District): Wo. Aux, salary of Rev. William Loola, Alaska, $5; work among Seminoles, Southern Florida, $5.............. 10 00
Christ Church: Wo. Aux., salary of Rev. William Loola, Alaska, $5; work among Seminoles, Southern Florida, $5; Sp. for salary of sewing teacher, St. Augustine's School, Raleigh, North Carolina, $3; Sp. for St. Paul's School, Lawrenceville, Southern Virginia, $2; Sp. for chapel among the Kroos, Liberia, Africa, $5 20 00
Church of the Good Shepherd: Wo. Aux., salary of Rev. William Loola, Alaska, $5; work among Seminoles, Southern Florida, $5.............. 10 00
Church of St. Mark (Eastern Parkway): Wo. Aux., salary of Rev. William Loola, Alaska, $4; Sp. for salary of sewing teacher, St. Augustine's School, Raleigh, North Carolina, $1; Junior Aux., Gen., $16.... 21 00
Church of St. Matthew: Gen., $69.47; Wo. Aux., salary of Rev. William Loola, Alaska, $3; work among Seminoles, Southern Florida, $1; Bishop Payne Divinity-school, Petersburg, Southern Virginia, $3; Frn., $5; Sp. for chapel at Fort Yukon, Alaska, $1................. 82 47
Grace (Eastern District): Wo. Aux., salary of Rev. William Loola, Alaska, $2; work among Seminoles, Southern Florida, $1; Sp. for St. John's University Expansion Fund, Shanghai; $1.25...................... 4 25
Grace (Heights): Wo. Aux., salary of Rev. William Loola, Alaska, $5; work among Seminoles, Southern Florida, $5; Bishop Payne Divinity-school, Petersburg, Southern Virginia, $25; Sp. for St. Paul's School, Lawrenceville, Southern Virginia, $25; Sp. for St. John's University Extension Fund, Shanghai, $2; Junior Aux., Gen., $3............ 65 00
Holy Cross: Wo. Aux., Gen.......... 3 00
Holy Trinity Church: Wo. Aux., salary of Rev. William Loola, Alaska, $7; work among Seminoles, Southern Florida, $7; Bishop Payne Divinity-school, Petersburg, Southern Virginia, $10; St. Paul's College, Tokyo, $7; Sp. for Miss Thackara's work, Fort Defiance, Arizona, $10; Sp. for Rev. Malcolm S. Taylor, Yadkin Valley School, Asheville, $25; Sp. for St. John's University Extension Fund, Shanghai, $5...... 71 00

Incarnation: Wo. Aux., work among Seminoles, Southern Florida, $10; "A Friend of Missions," St. Luke's Mission Hospital, Shanghai, $25; S. S.,* $1.35, Junior Aux., $25, Gen. 61 35
Church of the Messiah: Wo. Aux., Sp. for St. John's University Extension Fund, Shanghai.................. 1 00
Church of the Redeemer: Wo. Aux., salary of Rev. William Loola, Alaska, $5; Sp. for salary of sewing teacher, St. Augustine's School, Raleigh, North Carolina, $2....... 7 00
St. Ann's: $20, Wo. Aux., $17, Dom.; salary of Rev. William Loola, Alaska, $2; work among Seminoles, Southern Florida, $2; Sp. for All Saints' Hospital, South McAlester, Oklahoma, $15; S. S.,* "Benjamin C. Cutler" scholarship, Orphan Asylum, Cape Palmas, Africa, $50; "Frederick T. Peet" scholarship, St. John's University, Shanghai, $70... 176 00
St. Augustine's: Wo. Aux., salary of Rev. William Loola, Alaska, $2; work at Cape Palmas, Africa, $2; Sp. for St. Paul's School, Lawrenceville, Southern Virginia, $2........ 6 00
St. Bartholomew's: Bishop Rowe's work, Alaska, $20.03; Wo. Aux., salary of Rev. William Loola, Alaska, $2; work among Seminoles, Southern Florida, $1.............. 23 03
St. George's: Wo. Aux., salary of Rev. William Loola, Alaska, $3; work among Seminoles, Southern Florida, $2; Gen., $2.................... 7 00
St. James's: Wo. Aux., salary of Rev. William Loola, Alaska, $4; work among the Seminoles, Southern Florida, $2...................... 6 00
St. John's: Junior Aux., Gen........ 50 00
St. Jude's: Wo. Aux., salary of Rev. William Loola, Alaska............ 2 00
St. Luke's: Wo. Aux., Sp. for Miss Woods, Alaska, $5; Sp. for Bishop Griswold's work, Salina, $10; Sp. for sewing-teacher's salary, St. Augustine's School, Raleigh, North Carolina, $5; Sp. for St. John's University Expansion Fund, Shanghai, $5...................... 25 00
St. Mark's: Dom. and Frn......... 53 28
St. Mary's: Wo. Aux., salary of Rev. William Loola, Alaska, $3; Bishop Payne Divinity-school, Petersburg, Southern Virginia, $1; Gen., $1; Sp. for St. Paul's School, Lawrenceville, Southern Virginia, $1; Sp. for salary of sewing-teacher, St. Augustine's School, Raleigh, North Carolina, $1.20............ 7 20
St. Michael's: Wo. Aux., salary of Rev. William Loola, Alaska, $2; Sp. for chapel, Fort Yukon, Alaska, $5 .... 7 00
St. Paul's (Flatbush): Dom., $11; Frn., $5; Wo. Aux., salary of Rev. William Loola, Alaska, $15; work among Seminoles, Southern Florida, $7.97; Gen., $7; Sp. for salary of sewing-teacher, St. Augustine's School, Raleigh, North Carolina, $2.80; Sp. for St. John's University Expansion Fund, Shanghai, $9; Junior Aux., St. Elizabeth's Hospital, Shanghai, $6............ 63 77
St. Peter's: Gen.................... 62 50
St. Philip's (Dyker Heights): Wo. Aux., salary of Rev. William Loola, Alaska 2 00
St. Stephen's: Wo. Aux., salary of Rev. William Loola, Alaska, $1.50; work among Seminoles, Southern Florida, $1.50; Sp. for Miss Thackara's work, Fort Defiance, Arizona,

$5; Junior Aux., Gen., $5......... 13 00
Trinity Church (East New York) : Wo.
  Aux., Sp. for chapel among the
  Kroos, Liberia, Africa............ 2 00
BROOKLYN MANOR — St. Matthew's:
  Junior Aux., Gen................ 5 00
ELMHURST—St. James's: Wo. Aux.,
  salary of Rev. William Loola,
  Alaska, $15; work among Seminoles,
  Southern Florida, $5; Dom., $3.50.. 23 50
FAR ROCKAWAY—St. John's: Wo. Aux.,
  salary of Rev. William Loola,
  Alaska, $1; Gen., $2............. 3 00
FLUSHING—St. George's: Wo. Aux.,
  salary of Rev. William Loola,
  Alaska, $2; work among Seminoles,
  Southern Florida, $2; Sp. for Rev.
  H. F. Parshall, Cass Lake, Duluth,
  $6.25; Junior Aux., Gen., $5..... 15 25
GARDEN CITY—Cathedral of the In-
  carnation: Wo. Aux., salary of Rev.
  William Loola, Alaska, $50; work
  among Seminoles, Southern Florida,
  $5 .... 55 00
GLEN COVE—St. Paul's: Wo. Aux.,
  salary of Rev. William Loola,
  Alaska 2 00
GREAT NECK—All Saints': Wo. Aux.,
  salary of Rev. William Loola,
  Alaska, $10; work among Seminoles,
  Southern Florida, $5; Gen., $60;
  Sp. for salary of sewing-teacher, St.
  Augustine's School, Raleigh, North
  Carolina, $6; Sp. for St. Paul's
  School, Lawrenceville, Southern Vir-
  ginia, $5; Sp. for St. John's Univer-
  sity Expansion Fund, Shanghai,
  $9; Sp. for chapel among the
  Kroos, Liberia, Africa, $6........ 101 00
GREAT RIVER—Emmanuel Church: Wo.
  Aux, salary of Rev. William Loola,
  Alaska, $3; Sp. for salary of sew-
  ing-teacher, St. Augustine's School,
  Raleigh, North Carolina, $3; Sp. for
  chapel among the Kroos, Liberia,
  Africa, $5...................... 11 00
HEMPSTEAD—St. George's: Wo. Aux.,
  salary of Rev. William Loola,
  Alaska 2 00
HOLLIS—St. Gabriel's: Dom.......... 5 00
HUNTINGTON—St. John's: Wo. Aux.,
  salary of Rev. William Loola,
  Alaska, $1.50; work among Semi-
  noles, Southern Florida, $1.50..... 3 00
MERRICK—Church of the Redeemer:
  (of which S. S.,* $4.40), $14.40;
  Gen., Sp. to found a scholarship,
  Tortilla Hall, Alaska, $105....... 119 40
OYSTER BAY — Christ Church: Wo.
  Aux., salary of Rev. William Loola,
  Alaska 2 00
QUEENS — St. Joseph's: Wo. Aux.,
  salary of Rev. William Loola,
  Alaska, $1; work among Seminoles,
  Southern Florida, $1............. 2 00
RICHMOND HILL — Resurrection: Wo.
  Aux., salary of Rev. William Loola,
  Alaska, $2.50; work among Semi-
  noles, Southern Florida, $2.50..... 5 00
ROCKVILLE CENTRE — Ascension: Wo.
  Aux., salary of Rev. William Loola,
  Alaska 2 00
ROSLYN—Trinity Church: Wo. Aux.,
  Rev. William Loola's salary, Alaska. 1 00
SAG HARBOR—Christ Church: Wo.
  Aux., work among Seminoles, South-
  ern Florida..................... 2 00
SETAUKET—Caroline: Wo. Aux., sal-
  ary of Rev. William Loola, Alaska,
  $4.50; Junior Aux., Gen., $6.10... 10 60
WEST ISLIP—Christ Church: Gen.... 100 00
MISCELLANEOUS—"For Christ," Gen.. 100 00
  Branch Wo. Aux., anniversary of-
  fering, salary of Rev. William Loola,
  Alaska, $10; work among Semi-

noles, Southern Florida (of which
  anniversary offering, $10), $11.51;
  out-of-town meeting, Gen., $44; Sp.
  for salary of sewing-teacher, St.
  Augustine's School, Raleigh, North
  Carolina (of which Good Friday offering, $38.70, anniversary offer-
  ing, $3), $41.70; "Cash," Sp. for
  St. Paul's School, Lawrenceville,
  Southern Virginia, $5...........

Los Angeles

Ap. $123.19; *Sp.* $5.00
ANAHEIM—St. Michael's S. S.*: Gen..
LONG BEACH—St. Luke's S. S.: Sp. for
  Miss Thackara's Hospital, Fort De-
  fiance, Arizona.................
LOS ANGELES—St. Athanasius's: Gen.
SANTA MONICA—St. Augustine's S. S.*:
  Gen. ....

Louisiana

Ap. $383.76; *Sp.* $5.00
LAFAYETTE—Ascension: Gen.........
NEW ORLEANS—Annunciation: Gen...
Christ Church: Gen., $40.16; Frn., $5.
Grace: Wo. Aux., for support of girl
  in St. Elizabeth's School, South Da-
  kota ....
St. Andrew's: Dom. and Frn.......
St. Paul's: $100, S. S.,* $102.50, Gen..
OPELOUSAS—Epiphany: Gen.........
MISCELLANEOUS—Babies' Branch, Gay-
  lord Hart Mitchell Kindergarten,
  Akita, Tokyo, $2; Angelica Church
  Hart Day-school for Boys, Wuchang,
  Hankow, $1; "Little Helpers' ' Day-
  school for Girls, Tsingpoo, Shanghai,
  $1; Alaska, $12; Cuba, $2; Mexico,
  $2; South Dakota Indians, $2; Colored Missions in the South, $2;
  work among mountain whites, Vir-
  ginia, $2; Sp. for missionary font,
  $1; Sp. for "Little Helpers'" bed,
  St. Agnes's Hospital, Raleigh, North
  Carolina, $2; Sp. for Bishop Spald-
  ing's Emergency Fund, Utah, $2...

Maine

Ap. $108.84; *Sp.* $15.00
BIDDEFORD—Christ Church S. S.*:
  Gen. ....
FORT FAIRFIELD—St. Paul's: Gen.....
GARDINER — Christ Church: Work
  among Indians.................
PORTLAND—St. Stephen's: Frn., $5;
  Gen., $13.10..................
WEST BALDWIN—Miss G. H. Peirce,
  Gen. ....
MISCELLANEOUS—Babies' Branch, Gen.,
  $23.60; Akita Kindergarten, Tokyo,
  $5; St. Paul's School, Lawrenceville,
  Southern Virginia, $5; Sp. for "Lit-
  tle Helpers'" cot, St. Agnes's Hos-
  pital, Raleigh, North Carolina, $5;
  Sp. for Children's Ward, Chinese An-
  nex, St. Luke's Hospital, San Fran-
  cisco, California, $5; Sp. for mis-
  sionary font, $5................

Marquette

Ap. $25.55
ESCANABA—St. Stephen's: Dom.......
MANISTIQUE—St. Alban's: Gen.......
MARQUETTE—St. Paul's: Gen.........
MENOMINEE—Grace: Gen...........

Maryland

Ap. $1,336.62; *Sp.* $78.00
BALTIMORE—Advent: Gen., $25; Girls'
  Friendly Society, Sp. for Girls'
  School, Bontok, Philippine Islands,
  $5 ....

5 00

St. Matthew's (South): Gen., $48.83; Wo. Aux., Nevada, $1; Western Colorado, $1..................... 50 83

10 00

St. Paul's: Wo. Aux., "Bishop B. H. Paddock" scholarship, St. Paul's College, Tokyo, $45; Sp. for Trade School in Liberia, West Africa, $40. 85 00

36 15
26 00
5 00

St. Stephen's: Frn., $25; Wo. Aux., Nevada, $2.50; Western Colorado, $2.50; Junior Aux., Gen., $24..... 54 00

25 00

20 00

17 00
57 00

5 00

60 00

10 00
1 00

Trinity Church: Sp. in memory of Bishop Whipple, to be placed in the new cathedral at Havana, $25; Miss S. H. Hooker, Gen., $50; S. S.,* Gen., $330.30; Wo. Aux., North Carolina, $27.30; Nevada, $44.76; Western Colorado, $44.75; "Members," "Swannanoa" scholarship, St. Mary's School, South Dakota, $60; "A- Member," Sp. for Rev. Mr. Gilman's personal use, Hankow, $5; Sp. for Aomori sufferers, Tokyo, $5; Sp. for St. Margaret's School, Tokyo, $5 .... 597 11

"Thank-offering," Gen............ 5 00

BRIDGEWATER—*Trinity Church*: Junior Aux., Gen.................... 2 00

3 00

BROCKTON—*St. Paul's*: Gen........ 15 00

55 00

BROOKLINE—*All Saints'*: Wo. Aux., Nevada, $9.25; Western Colorado, $9.25 .... 18 50

10 00

Church of Our Saviour (Longwood): Dom. and Frn., $28.07; Junior Aux., Gen., $10; S. S.* Gen., $67.82... 105 89

170 00

St. Paul's: Dakota League, Sp. for Miss Carter, Alaska............. 5 00
Mrs. James M. Codman, Gen....... 50 00

375 00
300 00

"L. M. M.," Gen.................. 2 00
CAMBRIDGE—*St. Bartholomew's*: Dom. and Frn...................... 9 10

5 00

St. James's: $33.35, S. S.,* $135.41, Gen. 168 76

2 32

CHELSEA—*St. Luke's*: Gen., $25; Wo. Aux., Nevada, $3.92; Western Colorado, $3.93..................... 32 85

5 00

COHASSET — *St. Stephen's*: Junior Aux., Gen...................... 2 00
Miss Muriel Crocker, Gen......... 5 00

87 00

CONCORD—*Trinity Church*: Dom. and Frn. 20 50

6 15
89 00

DEDHAM—*Church of the Good Shepherd*: Wo. Aux., Nevada, $2.50; Western Colorado, $2.50........... 5 00
St. Paul's: Junior Aux., Gen........ 71 00
FALMOUTH—*St. Barnabas's*: Gen..... 10 40
FALL RIVER—*Ascension*: Junior Aux., Gen. 15 00

3 11

St. John's: Wo. Aux., Gen., $10; Sp. for Bishop Roots, Hankow, $10; Sp. for Miss Wheeler, Hankow, $2..... 22 00

GROTON—Groton School Missionary Society, Sp. for Mr. George R. Bedinger, Akita, Tokyo............. 15 00

20 26

HAVERHILL—*Trinity Church S. S.*: Gen. 108 09

10 00

HINGHAM—*St. John the Evangelist's*: Dom. and Frn.................... 15 00

LAWRENCE—*Grace*: Gen............ 25 51

3 00

St. John's: Gen.................. 8 16
LYNN—*St. Stephen's*: Gen.......... 26 00

50 00
2 00

MALDEN—Miss H. M. Smith, Gen..... 50 00
MARBLEHEAD—*St. Michael's*; Frn... 20 00

8 50
30 00
21 00

MARLBOROUGH—*Holy Trinity Church*: Wo. Aux.; Nevada, $2.50; Western Colorado, $2.50................ 5 00
MAYNARD—*St. George's S. S.*: Gen... 9 57

200 00

MEDFORD—*Grace*: Wo. Aux., Nevada, $2.50; Western Colorado, $2.50; Sp. for Trade School, Liberia, West Africa, $5..................... 10 00

1 50
24 63
90 00

MELROSE — *Trinity Church*: Junior Aux., $2, S. S.,* $31.80, Gen....... 33 80

4 00
55 00
5 00

MIDDLESEX—*Suburban Pastorate*: $10, S. S.,* $10.13, Gen............... 20 13
MILLIS MOSS—*St. Paul's*: Gen....... 2 00

MILTON—*St. Michael's*: Junior Aux., Gen. 10 00
NEW BEDFORD—*St. James's S. S.**: Frn. 26 22
NEWBURYPORT—*Christ Chapel S. S.**: Gen. 18 14
*St. Paul's S. S.**: Gen. 42 65
NEWTON—*Church of the Messiah* (Auburndale): "A Member," Wo. Aux., Sp. for Bishop Rowe, Alaska, $5; Sp. for Rev. W. C. Clapp, Philippine Islands, $5 .... 10 00
*St. Paul's S. S.**: Gen. 172 28
SALEM—*Grace*: Gen. 21 65
SOMERVILLE — *Emmanuel Church S. S.**: Gen. 37 89
St. Thomas's (East): Wo. Aux., Rev. Mr. Matthews's salary, Africa 1 00
SOUTH GROVELAND—*St. James's*: Gen. 4 28
TAUNTON—*St. Thomas's*: Junior Aux., Gen. 5 00
WALTHAM—*Christ Church*: Gen. 170 73
WATERTOWN—*Church of the Good Shepherd S. S.**: Gen. 2 80
WELLESLEY—*St. Andrew's*: Dom., $1; Gen., $81. .... 82 00
MISCELLANEOUS—Wo. Aux., Nevada, $2.37; Western Colorado, $2.37.... 4 74
Dakota League, Indian work, Oklahoma, $100; Seminoles, Southern Florida, $50; Indian, North Dakota, $50; salary of Miss Sabine, Alaska, $100; salary of Miss Woods, Alaska, $50; salary of Mrs. Evans, Alaska, $100; Sp. for hospital work, Oneida, Fond du Lac, $100; Sp. for mission school, Ross Fork, Idaho, $50; Sp. for hospital work, Fort Defiance, Arizona, $75; Sp. for Indian work, Oklahoma, $25; Sp. for Indian work, Utah, $75; Sp. for Indian work, Wyoming, $50; "Members," "Grace H. Hamlen Memorial" scholarship, St. Mary's School, South Dakota, $60 Colored Committee, Wo. Aux., Sp. for salary of Miss Dickerson, St. Paul's School, Lawrenceville, Southern Virginia, $70; Sp. for salary of Miss Wheeler, St. Augustine's School, Raleigh, North Carolina, $73...... 143 00
"Junior Aux." scholarship, Girls' High School, Kyoto 50 00
Girls' Friendly Society, Sp. for Rt. Rev. A. C. A. Hall, Bishop of Vermont 515 00

Michigan

Ap. $497.85; *Sp.* $91 50

ALMA—Miss Emily Case, Gen. 2 00
ANN ARBOR—"A Friend," Gen 3 00
BAD AXE—*St. Paul's*: Gen. 5 00
CARO—*Trinity Church*: Wo. Aux., salary of Miss Bull, Kyoto. 1 00
DETROIT—*Mariner's*: Wo. Aux., Africa. 2 00
*Church of the Messiah S. S.**: Gen... 52 62
St. George's: Gen. 20 51
*St. John's S. S.**: Gen. 265 00
St. Matthias's: Gen. 40 00
St. Paul's: Junior Aux., Gen. 10 00
EAST LANSING—Through M. F. Brennan, Gen. 3 00
FLINT—*St. Paul's*: $9, S. S.,* $29.72, Gen. 38 72
MISCELLANEOUS — Babies' Branch, "Little Helpers'" Day-school, Shanghai, $2.50; Angelica Church Hart Day-school, Wuchang, Hankow, $2.50; Akita Kindergarten, Tokyo, $30; salary of Mrs. Giridet, Cuba, $10; House of the Holy Child, Manila, Philippine Islands, $10; Sp. for Bishop Spalding's White Rock Emergency Fund, Utah, $5; Sp. for Miss Lucy Carter, Utah, $15; Sp. for Missionary Font, $1; Sp. for

"Little Helpers'" cot, St. Agnes's Hospital, Raleigh, North Carolina, $2.50; Sp. for "A. S. Lloyd" scholarship, Corbin, Lexington, $5; Sp. for Rev. H. C. Parke, Asheville, for "Kate W. Minor" scholarship, $10; Sp. for Miss Routledge, Philippine Islands, $2.50; Sp. for Mr. Ziegler, Alaska, $2.50; Sp. for "George C. Thomas" scholarship, Fort Yukon, Alaska, $25; Sp. for Miss Bull, Kyoto, $2.50; Sp. for Mrs. Littell, Hankow, $2.50; Sp. for Bishop Ferguson, Africa, $5; Sp. for Miss Hayashi, for Widely Loving Society, Kyoto, $13................

Michigan City

Ap. $37.84

DELPHI—*St. Mary's*: Dom. and Frn..
ELKHART—*St. John's*: Junior Aux., Gen. ....
FORT WAYNE—*Trinity Church*: Dom. and Frn., $20; Babies' Branch, Gen., $4.50 ....
MARION — *Gethsemane*: Junior Aux., Gen. (of which Babies' Branch, $1.50) ....

Milwaukee

Ap. $660.81

EAU CLAIRE—*Christ Church* $5.50, S. S.,* 70 cts., Gen.................
JANESVILLE—*Christ Church*: Gen....
Trinity Church: Gen. ....
KENOSHA—*St. Matthew's*: Gen......
LAKE GENEVA—Mrs. C. C. Boyles, Gen.
LANCASTER—*Emmanuel Church S. S.**: Gen. ....
MADISON—*Grace*: Gen., $141.44; Wo. Aux., "Rev. Fayette Durlin Memorial" scholarship, St. Mary's Hall, Shanghai, $50...................
PEWAUKEE—George Burroughs, Gen...*
RICE LAKE—*Grace*: Gen. ....
RICHLAND CENTRE — *St. Barnabas's*: Gen. ....
STAR PRAIRIE—*St. John the Baptist's*: Gen. ....
SUPERIOR—*Church of the Redeemer*: Gen. ....
MISCELLANEOUS—Wo. Aux., Gen......
Junior Aux., supplies for Anvik, Alaska, $100; St. Luke's Hospital, Shanghai, $50; St. Augustine's School, Raleigh, North Carolina, $50; "Milwaukee" scholarship, St. John's School, Cape Mount, Liberia, West Africa, $25; work among mountain whites in Tennessee, $25.. Babies' Branch, work among mountaineers of the South..............

Minnesota

Ap. $719.71; *Sp.* $55.02

AUSTIN—*Christ Church*: Gen........
FAIRMONT—*St. Martin's*: Gen.......
FARIBAULT—*Cathedral of Our Merciful Saviour*: Sp. for Bishop Whipple Memorial at Havana, Cuba, $39.02; S. S.,* $143.29................
*St. James's School S. S.**: Gen......
*Shattuck School S. S.**: Gen........
GOOSE CREEK—*St. James's S. S.**: Gen. ....
MINNEAPOLIS—*All Saints'*: Gen.......
St. John the Baptist's (Linden Hills): Gen. ....
St. Mark's: Gen....................
RUSH CITY—*Grace S. S.**: Gen.....
ST. PAUL—*Ascension S. S.**: Gen.....
*Christ Church S. S.**: Gen...........

OMAHA—*All Saints' S. S.**: Sp. for
Rev. J. Philip Anshutz, White Sulphur Springs, Montana, $50; Sp. for scholarship, Archdeacon F. B. Wentworth, Winchester, Lexington, $25.. 75 00

15 00
25 00
17 50

TECUMSEH—*Grace S. S.**: Gen........ 65

Newark

Ap. $2,954.42; *Sp.* $450.00

ALLENDALE—*Epiphany*: Gen......... 22 00
BERGENFIELD—*St. John's Chapel S. S.**: Gen...................... 20 08
BLOOMFIELD — *Christ Church*: Miss Brooks's S. S. Class, support of St. Hilda's School, Wuchang, Hankow.. 1 50
CLIFTON—*St. Peter's*: 93 cts., S. S.* (additional), 38 cts., Gen......... 1 31
EAST ORANGE—Mrs. C. H. Skinner, Gen................................. 25 00

148 74   ENGLEWOOD—*St. Paul's*: James Barber, Sp. for Church Extension Fund, Porto Rico, $5; Bible-class, Bishop Rowe's work, Alaska, $3.25; St. Mary's Hall, Shanghai, $3.25...... 11 50
James Barber, Gen.............. 20 00

6 00   HACKENSACK—"A Friend," Gen...... 2 00
HARRISON—*Christ Church*: Gen...... 77 95

5 00   HASBROUCK HEIGHTS—*St. John the*
8 00   *Divine*: Gen., $26.85; Sp. for Zangzok Station Equipment Fund, Shanghai, $7......................... 33 85

4 00   JERSEY CITY—*Holy Cross*: Gen...... 7 50

25 00   *St. John's* (Heights): $137.50, N. L. Lothiedge, $50, salary of Rev. W. J. Cuthbert, Kyoto................ 187 50

13 50   LITTLE FALLS—*St. Agnes's*: Gen.... 30 00
7 00   MADISON—*Grace*: Junior Aux., Gen... 10 00
20 00   MONTCLAIR — *St. James's* (Upper): Gen............................... 137 30

8 10   *St. John's*: Gen................... 76 10
St. Luke's: "A Friend," Sp. for Church Extension Fund, Porto Rico....... 5 00

10 00   Miss C. B. Brown, Gen............ 10 00
3 50   The Misses Puffer (Upper), Sp. for Rev. R. E. Wood, Wuchang, Hankow, for purchase of land........ 10 00

2 50   MORRISTOWN — Mrs. Octavius Applegate, Sp. for American Church Institute for Negroes.................. 25 00

29 72   NEWARK—*St. James's*: Gen., $103; Dr. T. W. Corwin, Sp. for Church Extension Fund, Porto Rico, $5.... 108 00
5 00   *St. Paul's*: Gen................... 40 95

54 07   *Trinity Church*: H. T. Tichenor, Sp.
700 00   for Expansion Fund, St. John's University, Shanghai.................. 10 00
30 90
300 00   Mrs. Alfred Benjamin, Gen....... 10 00
75 00   Mrs. J. W. Howell, Gen......... 10 00

51 20   ORADELL—*Annunciation S. S.**: Gen.. 60 00
20 00   ORANGE—A. Appleton Packard and Mrs. Packard, work among Colored. 5 00
10 00   George H. Hogeman, Gen.......... 5 00
24 56   PHILLIPSBURG—*St. Luke's*: Gen...... 75 00
RIDGEWOOD—*Christ Church*: Sp. for Bishop Partridge, Kyoto, for his work in "The City of the Blessed Well"............................. 50 00

54 65   RUTHERFORD—*Grace*: "M. R. W.," Sp. for Miss Thackara for her work at hospital, Fort Defiance, Arizona (of
5 00   which for her personal use, $2.50).. 5 00
10 00
150 00   *Grace Chapel* (East): Junior Aux., Gen............................ 2 00
15 00
241 00   SUMMIT—*Calvary*: Frn., $25; Gen., $363.88......................... 388 88
100 00   Angeline Candee, Gen............ 5 00
10 00   Annie G. Chamberlin, Gen......... 20 00

150 00   MISCELLANEOUS — "Friends," evangelistic work, Gen................... 335 00
Wo. Aux., Sp. for "Bishop Leonard" scholarship, Rowland Hall, Salt
2 00   Lake, Utah...................... 50 00
16 00   Wo. Aux., Alaska, $100; Porto Rico, $85; Honolulu, $80; Philippines,

$90; Southern Florida, $10; Colored, $8; Shanghai, $100; Hankow, $100; Bible-women, Japan, $100; "Lewis Cameron" scholarship, St. Margaret's School, Tokyo, $50; Tokyo, $50; "Bishop Starkey" scholarship, Girls' High School, Kyoto, $50; "Bishop Odenheimer" scholarship, St. Mary's Hall, Shanghai, $50; Sp. for "Julius" scholarship, Tortella Hall, Nenana, Alaska, $100; Sp. for "Helena W. Dillingham" scholarship, Alaska, $25; Sp. for "Newark" scholarship, Tortella Hall, Nenana, Alaska, $33.50; Sp. for St. Margaret's School Building Fund, Tokyo, $119.50 .... 1,151 00

New Hampshire

Ap. $188.37; *Sp.* $8.00

CONCORD—*St. Paul's*: Gen............	30 00
Rev. J. K. Tibbits, Gen...........	50 00
DOVER—*St. Thomas's*: Gen.........	30 00
HANOVER—*St. Thomas's*: Dom...	22 62
KEENE—*St. James's S. S.**: Gen......	27 75
LINCOLN—*Church of the Messiah*: Gen.	3 00
MANCHESTER—*Grace S. S.**: Gen. (additional)	14 00
MISCELLANEOUS—Wo. Aux., Gen., $11; Sp. for Foreign Life Insurance Fund, $8	19 00

New Jersey

Ap. $1,624.29; *Sp.* $48.50

ASBURY PARK—Miss V. Nelson, Gen..	10 00
ATLANTIC CITY—Esther T. Harriman, Gen.	5 00
BASKING RIDGE—*St. Mark's*: Gen...	11 47
BERNARDSVILLE — *St. Bernard's*: St. Augustine's School, Raleigh, North Carolina, $1.03; Indian, $1.04; Alaska, $1.10; Philippines, 78 cts.; Colored, 52 cts.; Africa, $1.04; China, 80 cts.; Japan, 49 cts...	6 80
Somerset Inn Mission: Philippines, $1; St. Augustine's School, Raleigh, North Carolina, $1; Africa, $1; China, $1; Japan, $1........	
Children of St. Bernard's Parish (including St. Bernard's, Bernardsville, St. John's Chapel, Bernardsville, Somerset Inn Mission, Bernardsville, St. Mark's Chapel, Basking Ridge, Far Hills Mission, St. Luke's Chapel, Gladstone, St. Paul's Mission, Gladstone, and St. Bernard's School, Gladstone), Gen..........	5 00
BURLINGTON—*St. Mary's S. S.**: Gen.	166 79
St. Mary's Hall: Agape Society, Sp. for Mr. Ishii, Tokyo, for work among feeble-minded children......	100 00
CAMDEN—*St. Paul's*: Sp. for Rev. A. A. Gilman's work, Changsha, Hankow	5 00
CRANFORD—*Trinity Church*: Dom. and Frn.	39 50
ELIZABETH — *Christ Church*: Dom., $40.50; Wo. Aux., Sp. for Bishop Partridge's work in "The City of the Blessed Well," Kyoto, $13.50....	54 00
St. John's: Woman's Foreign Aid Committee, for "St. John's" bed, Elizabeth Bunn Memorial Hospital, Wuchang, Hankow, $40; Sp. for Aomori, Tokyo, $15; Sp. for Bishop Knight, Cuba, $10...............	65 00
Trinity Church: Gen..........	206 55
Miss E. C. Johnston, "John Dowers Memorial" scholarship, St. John's University, Shanghai............	50 00
FREEHOLD—*St. Peter's*: Gen.......	51 00
HELMETTA — *St. George's*: Charity	

Guild, St. Luke's Hospital, Shanghai, to help restore sight of six blind people ....

LAKEWOOD—*All Saints'*: Gen....... E. B. Haven, Gen..............	
LONG BRANCH—*St. James's*: Gen....	
MERCHANTVILLE—"K. P. H.," Gen....	
MOORESTOWN — *Trinity Church*: $15, Mrs. Henry Morrison, $10, Gen....	
MOUNT HOLLY—*St. Andrew's*: Gen...	
PLAINFIELD—Miss H. N. De Klyn, Gen.	
PLEASANTVILLE—Mrs. Emily W. Place, Gen.	
SEA GIRT—*St. Uriel's S. S.**: Gen....	
SOUTH AMBOY—*Christ Church S. S.**: Gen.	
SOMERVILLE—*St. John's*: Dom., $23.85; Gen., $23.75....................	
TRENTON — *Grace*: $63.44, S. S.* $42.20, Gen......................	
St. Andrew's: $10, S. S.,* $8.60; Gen..	
Trinity Church: $306, S. S.,* $104.52, Gen.	
WESTFIELD—*St. Paul's S. S.**: Gen..	
WOODBURY—*Christ Church*: Gen.....	

New York

Ap. $7,345.49; *Sp.* $1,279.31

ANNANDALE—*St. Peter's S. S.**: Gen..
BRONXVILLE—*Christ Church*: Gen....
CROTON—*St. Augustine's S. S.**: Gen..
DOBBS FERRY—The Misses Masters's School, "The Misses Masters" (Graduate) scholarship, South Dakota ....
GARRISONS — *St. Philip's-in-the-Highlands*: Gen......................
HARRISON—*All Saints'*: $34, Wo. Aux., $101.64, S. S.* $15, Gen......
HASTINGS—*Zion Chapel*: Wo. Aux., Sp. for Hospital of the Good Shepherd, Fort Defiance, Arizona....
HIGHLAND—*Holy Trinity Church*: Gen.
KINGSTON—*Church of the Holy Spirit S. S.**: Gen..................
LARCHMONT—*St. John's*: Gen........
MOUNT VERNON—*Ascension*: Gen....
Trinity Church: Wo. Aux., Sp. for Hospital of the Good Shepherd, Fort Defiance, Arizona................
John W. Hammond, Gen............
NEWBURGH—*St. Paul's*: Gen........
NEW PLATZ—*St. Andrew's*: Gen......
NEW YORK—*All Angels'*: Girls' Friendly Society. Sp. for Girls' School, Bontok, Philippine Islands..
Ascension: Gen., $80.80; Niobrara League, "Church of the Ascension" scholarship, St. Elizabeth's School, South Dakota, $60...............
Ascension S. S.* (West New Brighton): Gen. ....
Ascension Memorial: Jane C. Duff, Gen. ....
Beloved Disciple: Gen., $28.35; Sp. for Bishop Rowe, Alaska, $5......
Calvary: Wo. Aux., Missionary Society, Africa, $10; Brazil, $10; Cuba, $10; China, $10; Hooker Memorial School, Mexico, $10; Mexico, $15; Shanghai, $30; Mrs. G. Zabriskie, native work, Mexico, $200; Gen., $800............
Epiphany: Gen.................
Grace: Gen., $200; Sp. for Church Institute for Negroes, $25; St. Augustine's League, Committee on Missions for Colored People, Sp. for St. Agnes's Hospital, Raleigh, North Carolina, $10; Sp. for Hospital of the Good Samaritan, Charlotte, North Carolina, $5................
Grace S. S.* (City Island): Gen......
Grace Chapel S. S.*: Gen............
Heavenly Rest: Young Woman's

Foreign Chapter, scholarship, Deaconess House, Shanghai, $50; Mr. Tai's work, Tokyo, $50; Mexico, $30; Sp. for Church Building Fund, Walcamatsu, Tokyo, $25; Mission Junior Aux., Sp. for scholarship, St. James's Memorial School, Wuhu, Hankow, $25............ 180 00
Holy Apostles': Gen., $154.35; S. S.,* Gen., $45; St. Augustine's League, Sp. for Archdeacon Russell, St. Paul's School, Lawrenceville, Southern Virginia, $47.40............ 246 75
Holy Trinity Church (East 88th Street): Gen., $200.52; Sp. for St. John's College, Shanghai, $16.50; S. S.* "St. Christopher" scholarship, $1; St. John's University, Shanghai, $50; "St. Christopher" scholarship, $2; St. John's University, Shanghai, $170.91.. 487 93
Intercession Chapel: Gen........ 375 67
Church of the Mediator (Kingsbridge): Gen................. 33 03
Chapel of the Messiah S. S.*: Gen... 1 02
Mission S. S.* (New Dorp, S. I.): Gen......................... 24 34
St. Agnes's Chapel: Sp. for Bishop Rowe's work, Alaska, $25; Wo. Aux., Sp. for Bishop Robinson's work, Nevada, $18.............. 43 00
St. Andrew's (Richmond, S. I.): Wo. Aux., Gen.............. 25 00
St. Bartholomew's Swedish Mission S. S.*: Gen................. 27 00
St. Chrysostom's Chapel: Branch Wo. Aux., Sp. for Bishop Rowe's work, Alaska, at his discretion, $12.68; Sp. for Dr. Myers, St. Elizabeth's Hospital, Shanghai, $12.68....... 25 36
St. Esprit's: Gen............ 501 50
St. James's: "A Friend," Sp. for Church Extension Fund, Porto Rico, $5; S. S., Mission Study Class, Girls' Friendly Society Candidates, kindergarten work, China, $1..... 6 00
St. James's (Fordham): Junior Aux., Gen...................... 2 00
St. John's (Clifton, S. I.): Gen., $316; Bishop Rowe's work, Alaska, $20; S. S.,* "Scofield Memorial" scholarship, St. Mary's Hall, Shanghai, $40; Gen., $95.90........ 471 90
St. John the Evangelist's: Gen...... 50 00
St. Mark's: Gen., $18.71; Wo. Aux., Girls' Guild, Sp. for Archdeacon Spurr's work in West Virginia, $25. 43 71
St. Mary's (Mott Haven): Gen....... 2 70
St. Mary the Virgin: Gen........ 705 00
St. Paul's Chapel S. S.*: Sp. for Bishop Olmsted, Colorado.......... 84 70
St. Paul's (Bronx): Junior Missionary Society, Gen................. 10 00
St. Simeon's: Feeding Bishop Rowe's dogs, Alaska................ 2 00
Chapel of St. Priscilla: Gen....... 5 00
St. Thomas's S. S.*: Gen........ 189 02
Trinity Church S. S.*: Sp. for Rev. R. E. Wood, for purchase of land, Wuchang, Hankow............ 50 00
Trinity Chapel: Gen., $4; through Relief Society, Mrs. H. H. Cammann, Frn., $5.................. 9 00
Miss Agnes Lathers, Bishop Gray's work among Seminoles, Southern Florida, $10; salary of a missionary, South Dakota, $4; for a day in St. Luke's Hospital, Shanghai, $25. 39 00
Miss A. B. Halsted, "Marion E. Harsen" scholarship, St. Andrew's Seminary, Mexico............. 100 00
Miss K. Goold, St. Paul's College, Tokyo.................. 5 00
"A Member," Gen............ 400 00
Mrs. J. P. Morgan, Gen.......... 100 00
Francis Lynde Stetson, Gen........ 100 00

(New Brighton, S. I.)—Mary McK. Nash, Gen.................. 25 00
"A. L. P.," Gen.............. 25 00
Mrs. Charles C. Beaman, Gen...... 5 80
Miss Park, Gen.............. 5 00
Mrs. C. K. Griffin, Sp. for Bishop Thomas's work, Wyoming......... 300 00
"A Friend," Sp. for Bishop Rowe's work, Alaska.............. 21 00
"C. V. B. W.," Sp. for Catechists' School, Land and Building Fund, Shanghai.................. 5 00
"A Friend," Catechists' School, Land and Building Fund, Shanghai..... 2 00
OSSINING—All Saints' (Briarcliff): Gen...................... 25 00
Trinity Church: Gen........... 153 96
PEEKSKILL—St. Peter's: Wo. Aux., Sp. for Hospital of the Good Shepherd, Fort Defiance, Arizona..... 30 00
POUGHKEEPSIE—Christ Church: Gen.. 30 00
PORT CHESTER—St. Peter's: $75, S. S.,* $30.11, Gen.......... 105 11
RHINECLIFF—Ascension: Dom....... 5 00
RYE—Christ Church: Sp. for Bishop Partridge's work, Kyoto, $54.29; Wo. Aux., salary of woman missionary, Liberia, Cape Mount, Africa, $50; "Hope" scholarship, Collegiate and Divinity-school, Cuttington, Liberia, $40; S. S.,* $85.38, Junior Aux., $20, Gen........... 249 67
SUFFERN—Christ Church: Wo. Aux., Sp. for Bishop Partridge's fund, Kyoto................... 50 00
WAPPINGER'S FALLS—Zion S. S.*: Gen...................... 150 00
WHITE PLAINS—Grace: Gen....... 340 00
YONKERS—Christ Church: Wo. Aux., Sp. for Hospital of the Good Shepherd, Fort Defiance, Arizona...... 25 00
St. Andrew's: Gen............ 127 62
St. Johannes's (Swedish): Sp. for Rev. F. E. Lund, Wuhu, Hankow, $15.03; Sp. for Rev. C. F. Lindstrom, Kiukiang, Hankow, $15.03........ 30 06
St. Paul's: Wo. Aux., Sp. for Hospital of the Good Shepherd, Fort Defiance, Arizona................ 5 00
MISCELLANEOUS—Branch Wo. Aux., Archdeaconry of Dutchess County, Dom., $8.11; Frn., $8.11....... 16 22
Branch Wo. Aux., Gen.......... 2 00
St. Augustine's League, Sp. for Rev. P. P. Alston, Charlotte, North Carolina, $25; Rev. Richard Bright, Savannah, Georgia, $50; Sp. for St. Augustine's School, Raleigh, North Carolina, $100; Sp. for St. Paul's School, Lawrenceville, Southern Virginia, $100............. 275 00

North Carolina

Ap. $84.90; *Sp.* $87.00

CHAPEL HILL—Mr. and Mrs. K. T. Battle, Gen............... 5 00
DAVIE CO.—Ascension S. S.: Gen...... 2 50
GREENSBORO — Holy Trinity Church: Wo. Aux., Sp. for Rev. B. Ancell, Yang Chow, Shanghai, Dispensary Fund, Gay Chow.............. 5 00
St. Barnabas's: Gen........... 30 00
RALEIGH—St. Ambrose: Wo. Aux., Sp. for Bishop Ferguson, Africa........ 4 00
St. Augustine's S. S.: Sp. for Holy Trinity Orphanage, Tokyo, $4; Sp. for Dr. Glenton, Elizabeth Bunn Hospital, Wuchang, Hankow, $4.... 8 00
RIDGEWAY—Church of the Good Shepherd: Gen................. 4 65
SMITHFIELD — Transfiguration: Gen., $4; "A Parishioner," Frn., $2...... 6 00
SOUTHERN PINES—Emmanuel Church: Sp. for St. Paul's College, Tokyo.... 10 00
TARBORO—St. Luke's: Wo. Aux., Gen. 1 75

MISCELLANEOUS—Convocation of Charlotte, Sp. for Rev. Mr. Correll's Building Fund, Tsu, Kyoto......... 25 00
Convocation of Raleigh, Babies' Branch, Akita Kindergarten, Tokyo, $20; Gen., $15; Sp. for Bishop Rowe, Alaska, $10; Sp. for St. Luke's Hospital, San Francisco, California, $5; Sp. for "Bishop Atkinsen" cot, Holy Trinity Orphanage, Tokyo, $20..................... 70 00

Ohio

Ap. $218.47; *Sp.* $43.00

AKRON—*St. Andrew's*: Gen.......... 2 00
St. Paul's: Mrs. H. M. Houser, Frn., $5; Wo. Aux., Japan, $10........ 15 00
BEREA—*St. Thomas's*: Gen........... 1 00
CLEVELAND—*St. Mark's*: Wo. Aux., Philippines, $5; Japan, $15........ 20 00
St. Philip's: Wo. Aux., Sp. for scholarship, Anvik, Alaska........... 30 00
Trinity Cathedral S. S.: Porto Rico Class, Sp. for St. Luke's Hospital, Ponce, Porto Rico.............. 3 00
KENT—*Christ Church*: Gen.......... 7 50
LIMA—*Christ Church*: Gen........ 43 92
PAINESVILLE—*St. James's*: Gen...... 29 05
TOLEDO—*Trinity Church*: Gen., $100; Mrs. W. W. Bolles, Wo. Aux., Sp. for Christ School, Arden, Asheville, $10 .... 110 00

Oregon

Ap. $332.72; *Sp.* $210.50

EUGENE—*St. Mary's*: Junior Aux., $7, S. S.,* $14, Gen............. 21 00
FOREST GROVE—Gen.............. 3 50
HILLSBORO—*All Saints'*: Gen........ 5 50
McMINNVILLE—*St. James's*: Gen..... 6 50
MILWAUKEE—*St. John's*: Gen........ 4 00
PORTLAND—*Grace Memorial*: Wo. Aux., Gen. 15 00
St. Andrew's (Portsmouth): Junior Aux., Gen. 10 00
St. David's: Junior Aux., Gen..... 15 00
St. Mark's: Wo. Aux., Gen., $8; Sp. for Bishop Spalding, Utah, $4.50... 12 50
St. Matthew's: Wo. Aux., Gen., $2.77; Sp. for Bishop Spalding, Utah, $11. 13 77
St. Stephen's Pro-Cathedral: Gen., $143; Wo. Aux., Gen. (of which Junior Aux., $15), $27; Sp. for Bishop Spalding, Utah, $20....... 190 00
Trinity Church: Wo. Aux. (of which Junior Aux., $15), $45; Gen., Junior Aux., Sp. for Bishop Spalding's work among Indians, Utah, $175 .... 220 00
ST. HELEN'S—*Christ Church*: Wo. Aux., Gen................ 5 00
SALEM—*St. Paul's*: Wo. Aux., Gen... 5 00
WOODMERE—*St. Paul's*: Gen........ 13 00
WOODSTOCK—*Church of Our Saviour*: Gen. 7 45

Pennsylvania

Ap. $9,771.39; *Sp.* $8,482.40

ARDMORE—*St. Mary's*: Junior Aux., Gen. 5 00
BUCKINGHAM—*Trinity Church S. S.*: Gen. 12 00
BRYN MAWR—Miss Abby Kirk, Gen.. 5 00
CHELTENHAM—*St. Paul's*: Junior Aux., Gen., $30; S. S.* (additional), Sp. for Archdeacon Spurr for two scholarships, West Virginia, $50........ 80 00
CENTRE HILL—*Trinity Church S. S.*: Gen. 50
CLIFTON HEIGHTS — *St. Stephen's*: Junior Aux., Gen............. 50
CONCORDVILLE—*St. John's S. S.*: Gen. 5 52
CONSHOHOCKEN—*Calvary S. S.*: Gen. 50 00

DOYLESTOWN—*St. Paul's S. S.*: Gen.. 53
DOWNINGTOWN—*St. James's*: Junior Aux., "Faith" scholarship, St. Augustine's School, Monrovia, Africa. 21
Miss Frances E. McIlvaine, Gen.... 5
FALLSINGTON—*All Saints' Memorial*: Gen. 8
FORT WASHINGTON—Sarah A. Swain, Gen. 19
HONEYBROOK—*St. Mark's S. S.*: Gen. 12
JENKINTOWN—*Church of Our Saviour*: J. Conyngham Stevens, Gen., $25; Junior Aux., Sp. for St. Agnes's Hospital, Raleigh, North Carolina (of which for cot, $1), $6; S. S.* (additional), Gen., $3.24.... 39
KENNETT SQUARE—*Advent S. S.*: Gen. 5
LANSDOWNE—*St. John the Evangelist's*: $38, Junior Aux., $40.86, Gen. 78
MEDIA—*Christ Church S. S.*: Sp. for Mrs. L. S. Springer, Edneyville, Asheville 43
NEWTOWN—H. G. Reeder, Sp. for the expansion of St. John's University, Shanghai 1
NORRISTOWN—"B. S." Gen............ 50
NORWOOD—*St. Stephen's*: Wo. Aux., Frn. 5
PAOLI—*Church of the Good Samaritan*: Dom. and Frn........... 93
PERKIOMEN—*St. James's S. S.*: Gen. 3
PEQUEA—*St. John's S. S.*: Gen...... 27
PHILADELPHIA — *Advocate Memorial*: Junior Aux., Gen., $5; Sp. for scholarship for a girl, Philippines, $15; Sp. for scholarship for a boy, Philippines, $15.................. 35
All Saints' (Lower Dublin): Wo. Aux., Sp. for building, St. Elizabeth's Hospital, Shanghai, $10; Indian Hope Association, Indian, $20; Junior Aux., "Ruth Curtis" (In Memoriam) scholarship, St. John's School, Cape Mount, Africa, $25............. 55
All Souls' for the Deaf S. S.: Gen... 25
Calvary (Germantown): Diocesan Committee, Wo. Aux., Gen., $25; Indian Hope Association, Indian, $10; Junior Aux., Sp. for scholarship, St. Mary's Orphanage, Jessfield, Shanghai, $40.................. 75
Calvary Monumental S. S. (West): Gen. 50
Christ Church Chapel S. S.: Gen.... 12
Covenant S. S.: Gen............. 400
Crucifixion: Dom. and Frn., $33.37; Junior Aux., Gen. (of which No. 1, $5, No. 2, $5), $10........... 43
Emmanuel Church (Holmesburg): Junior Aux., "Rev. Daniel Caldwell Millett Memorial" scholarship, Boone University, Wuchang, Hankow, $50; Gen., $3..................... 53
Epiphany Chapel: Dom., $9.27; Frn., $16.31 25
Epiphany (Pelham) : Junior Aux., Gen... 10
Free Church of St. John S. S.: Gen... 40
Gloria Dei (Old Swedes') : Gen....... 50
Grace S. S.: Gen................. 194
Grace Chapel S. S.: Gen........... 91
Grace (Mt. Airy): Primary Branch, Junior Aux., Gen........... 10
Holy Innocents' S. S.: "Mary C. Currier" scholarship, Girls' Training Institute, Africa.............. 25
Holy Trinity Church: Junior Aux., Gen. (of which Saturday Morning School, $2), $3; St. Paul's School, Lawrenceville, Southern Virginia (of which from Vacation Bible-school, $5), $10.60 ; South Dakota, $5; "Sallie W. Ashhurst" scholarship, Girls' Training Institute, St. Paul's River, Africa, $25 ; Saturday Morn-

for Bishop Rowe, Alaska, $101; Sp. for Bishop Gray, Southern Florida, $100; Sp. for Bishop Funsten, Idaho, $100; Sp. for Bishop Spalding, Utah, $100; Sp. for Bishop Moreland, Sacramento, $100; Sp. for Rev. Mr. Thorn, Oneida, Fond du Lac, for hospital work, $100; Sp. for Oneida lace-workers, Fond du Lac, $50; Sp. for Miss Thackara's hospital at Fort Defiance, Arizona, $100; Sp. for Karok Indians, Sacramento, $75.84; Sp. for Miss Sibyl Carter's lace industry, $50........ 976 84
John E. Baird, Sp. for work of Rev. Lawrence B. Ridgely, Hankow..... 500 00
"Cash, A. F.," Gen............... 120 00
Mrs. A. J. Cassatt, Sp. for Shanghai Catechist School, Land and Building Fund.................. 50 00
(Torresdale)—"Cash," medical work.. 30 00
(Chestnut Hill)—Mrs. William A. Dick, work in Alaska............. 25 00
Mrs. J. S. Cox, Wo. Aux., "Grace" scholarship, St. John's University, Shanghai 25 00
G. W. Pepper, Sp. for St. Luke's, Kearney 25 00
Ellen S. Patterson, Gen........... 25 00
Mrs. Carl N. Martin, Gen......... 5 00
F. Cooper Pullman, Gen.......... 5 00
Miss L. S. Pechin, Gen.......... 5 00
Mrs. H. T. Tily, Gen............ 5 00
Foreign Committee, Wo. Aux., Sp. for Zangzok Station Equipment Fund, Shanghai................. 5 00
"F. E. McI.," Sp. for Expansion Fund, St. John's University, Shanghai 1 00
(Bustleton) — William S. Robinson, Dom. and Frn.................. 1 00
James Whittington, Gen.......... 1 00
PHOENIXVILLE — St. Peter's: Gen., $1,073.17; Sp. for Expansion Fund, St. John's University, Shanghai, $100 .... 1,173 17
RADNOR — St. Martin's: Helen C. Bunting, Gen..................... 5 00
ROSEMONT—Church of the Good Shepherd S. S.*: Gen................. 36 23
RYDAL—Mrs. William W. Frazier, Sp. for station class for women at Hankow, $25; Sp. for Widely Loving Society Orphanage, Osaka, Kyoto, $25; Sp. for David Tang, $25, Sp. for Guy School, $25, with Rev. T. K. Hu, Kiukiang, Hankow; Sp. to help start a chapel at Wusih, Shanghai, $25; work among the Kroos, Africa, $25 .... 150 00
SWARTHMORE—Trinity Church: $17.40, St. Margaret's Guild, Junior Aux., $15, S. S., $10, Gen............. 42 40
VILLA NOVA—Miss L. Frishmuth, Gen. 100 00
WAYNE—St. Mary's S. S.*: Gen...... 225 00
WHITEMARSH—St. Thomas's: Gen.... 64 23
WELDON—St. Peter's S. S.*: Sp. for Bishop Horner, Asheville, $10; Gen., $19.95 .... 29 95
WYNCOTE—All Hallows': (of which Wo. Aux., $10), $30, Sp. for Dr. Pott for St. John's College, Shanghai; Junior Aux., "All Hallows'" scholarship, St. Hilda's School, Wuchang, Hankow. $50.... 80 00
MISCELLANEOUS—"A S. S. Worker,"* Gen. 5 00
Through J. S. Newbold, Sp. for the erection and furnishing of a church at the American Church Mission, Soochow, Shanghai.............. 6,000 00
Missionary Mass Meeting, held in Academy of Music, May 9th, 1910, Gen. 191 73
"Y. D.," Gen.................... 100 00

Wo. Aux., Frn., $10.03; Domestic Committee, salary of Domestic missionary bishop, $1,218; Dom., $50; Sp. for Bishop Brent, Philippine Islands, $25; Sp. for Rev. W. C. Clapp, Bontok, $1; Sp. for St. Matthew's reading-room, Fairbanks, Alaska, $10..................... 1,314 08
Diocesan Committee, Wo. Aux., Gen. 6 00
Wo. Aux., Executive Board, Colored Committee, work among the Negroes 227 35
Junior Aux., St. Augustine's School, Raleigh, North Carolina, $45; support of native worker, Alaska, $100; "Pennsylvania" scholarship, Girls' High School, Kyoto, $50; "Helen Mackay-Smith" scholarship, St. Mary's Hall, Shanghai, $50.50; "Faith" scholarship, St. Augustine's School, Monrovia, Africa, $4; Gen., $2.95; Miss Anne M. Hubbard, Gen., $5; "S. C. B.," Junior Aux., Gen., $10 .... 267 45
Babies' Branch, Gen.............. 304 35

Pittsburgh

Ap. $1,080.17; *Sp.* $37.00

EMPORIUM—*Emmanuel Church*: Gen.. 8 16
GREENSBURG—*Christ Church*: Gen.... 13 92
HOMESTEAD—*St. Matthew's*: Frn..... 9 00
JOHNSTOWN—*St. Mark's*: Gen........ 5 00
McKEESPORT—*St. Stephen's*: Gen.... 5 05
PITTSBURGH—*Calvary*: $469.09, Mrs. John H. Bailey, $300, Gen........ 769 09
St. Margaret's Deaf-Mutes: Gen...... 8 50
St. Peter's: Gen................... 225 00
(Allegheny)—Eliza P. Byram, work in China 10 00
TARENTUM — *St. Barnabas's*: Gen., $1.45; S. S., Sp. for Rev. Robert E. Wood, Hankow, $2................ 3 45
TITUSVILLE—*St. James's*: Gen....... 25 00
WARREN—*Trinity Church*: Sp. for St. John's University, Shanghai....... 35 00

Rhode Island

Ap. $1,998.75; *Sp.* $65.00

ASHTON—*St. John's Chapel*: Gen.... 25 79
BARRINGTON—*St. Matthew's* (West): Gen............................ 1 55
BRISTOL—*St. Michael's*: Gen........ 50 00
CENTRAL FALLS—*St. George's*: Gen... 77 04
CENTREDALE—*St. Alban's*: $10, S. S.* $4.60, Gen.................... 14 60
EAST PROVIDENCE—*St. Mary's*: Gen., $17.76; Guild of Holy Child, Junior Aux., Alaska, $5; Colored, $3; Indian, $2...................... 27 76
GREENVILLE—*St. Thomas's*: Children's Lenten Mite-box,* Gen............ 5 30
MANTON—*St. Peter's*: Gen.......... 45 04
MIDDLETOWN—*Holy Cross*: Gen....... 14 02
NEWPORT—*Emmanuel Church*: Junior Aux., Alaska, $10; Colored, $10; China, $10.................... 30 00
St. John's: Colored............. 75 00
Trinity Church: $55.97, Junior Aux., $5, Gen..................... 60 97
PAWTUCKET—*Advent*: $2, Frn., Junior Aux., $2, Gen................. 4 00
St. Luke's Chapel: Frn........... 3 00
St. Paul's: Gen.................. 201 79
Trinity Church: Gen.............. 28 00
PORTSMOUTH AND MIDDLETOWN — *St. Mary's*: Gen.................... 8 82
PROVIDENCE—*All Saints'*: Dom. and Frn. 88 00
Calvary: Gen.................... 68 84
*Epiphany S. S.**: Gen............. 33 12
Grace: $460, Junior Aux., $5, Gen.... 465 00

St. James's: Gen...................
St. John's S. S.: "St. John's S. S." scholarship, in St. Mary's School, South Dakota.................
Mrs. Richards, Sp. for furnishings for St. Luke's Hospital, Shanghai...
WAKEFIELD—*Ascension S. S.**: Gen...
WARREN—*St. Mark's S. S.**: Gen.....
WESTERLY—*Christ Church*: Dom., $75; Frn., $75......................
MISCELLANEOUS—Wo. Aux., salary of Miss Bull, Kyoto, $290; "Susan Carrington Clarke" (Advanced) scholarship, $40, "Jessie H. Campbell" (Advanced) scholarship, $40, both in St. John's School, Cape Mount, Africa; Sp. for Foreign Life Insurance Fund, $50 ....

South Carolina

Ap. $223.39; *Sp.* $10.00

CHARLESTON — *St. Michael's*: $62.50, "Two Sisters," $5, Gen............
*St. Paul's S. S.**: Gen.............
St. Philip's: Gen.................; Mrs. K. C. Porcher, Dom., $5; Frn., $5
Mrs. Augustine S. Smythe, Sp. for work of Rev. Robert C. Wilson, Shanghai ....
Miss Mary Jervey, Gen...........
FLORENCE—*St. John's S. S.**: Gen...
HARTSVILLE—*St. Bartholomew's*: Gen.
LAURENS—"E. B. S.,". Gen..........
MT. PLEASANT—Mrs. M. C. Seabrook, Gen...........................
PRINCE FREDERICK—(Pee Dee), Gen..
SOCIETY HILL—*Trinity Church S. S.**: Gen...........................
STATEBURG—*Holy Cross*: Mrs. W. W. Anderson, Bishop Rowe's work, Alaska, $5; Gen., $5..............
SUMMERTON—*St. Matthias's*: Gen....
SUMMERVILLE—*St. Barnabas's*: Gen...

Southern Ohio

Ap. $82.37

CINCINNATI—*Epiphany*: Gen..........
Charles W. Short, Gen...........
Alice M. Lean, Gen.............
COLUMBUS—*St. Philip's S. S.**: Gen...
DELAWARE—*St. Peter's S. S.**: Gen...
HARTWELL — *Holy Trinity Church*: Gen...........................
Miss Helen A. Merrell, Gen......
PORTSMOUTH—Captain N. W. Evans, Sp. for Church Extension Fund, Porto Rico.................
TERRACE PARK—"Church Woman," Frn.

Southern Virginia

Ap. $415.11; *Sp.* $251.13

AUGUSTA Co.—Mrs. Joseph S. Cochran (Staunton), Sp. for Armistead M. Lee Memorial Chapel, Anking, Hankow ....
Edward Berkeley, Gen............
BOTETOURT Co.—*St. Mark's* (Fincastle): Wo. Aux., Gen..........
BRUNSWICK Co.—*St. Andrew's* (Lawrenceville): Miss Annie Price, Sp. for Alaska ....
St. Paul's Memorial Chapel: Gen....
BUCKINGHAM Co. — *Grace, Tillotson Parish*: Dom., 98 cts.; Frn., 98 cts.
CHESTERFIELD Co.—*Church of the Good Shepherd, Manchester Parish*: Gen. ....

5 00
5 00

16 13
5 00
1 00

10 00
2 00

9 09
2 50

38 66

2 75

1 00

30 00

16 25

64 64
5 00
16 94
4 00

205 00

179 00

83 23
1 65
15 00
1 65
3 30
7 90
8 50
7 50
63 90
5 00
26 38

2 00
75 00
2 75
1 00

Texas

Ap. $175.63

HOUSTON—*Christ Church*: Gen......	150 00
LUFKIN—*St. Cyprian's S. S.**: Gen..	14 16
NAVASOTA—*St. Paul's*: Gen.........	3 55
PALESTINE—*St. Philip's*: Gen........	7 92

Vermont

Ap. $327.25; *Sp.* $2.00

BELLOWS FALLS — *Emmanuel Church*: Gen.	113 10
EAST FAIRFIELD—*St. Barnabas's*: Gen.	7 00
LYNDONVILLE—*St. Peter's*: Gen......	5 00
PROCTORSVILLE—*Gethsemane*: Gen....	3 00
RICHFORD—*St. Ann's*: Gen...........	6 15
ST. JOHNSBURY—*St. Andrew's*: Gen., $30: Junior Aux., Sp. for Miss A. T. Wall, Hirosaki, Tokyo, $2.........	32 00
SPRINGFIELD—*St. Mark's*: Gen.......	10 00
WELLS—*St. Paul's*: Gen.............	3 00
MISCELLANEOUS—Wo. Aux., Gen......	150 00

Virginia

Ap. $884.74; *Sp.* $4,423.84

ALBEMARLE Co.—*Christ Church S. S.** (Charlottesville): Frn............	24 00
St. John Baptist's S. S.* (Ivy Depot): Gen.	1 56
St. Paul's S. S.* (Ivy Depot): Gen...	3 91
(Charlottesville)—Rev. H. B. Lee, Sp. for Armistead M. Lee Memorial Chapel, Anking, Hankow..........	10 00
Buck Mountain Chapel: Gen........	2 00
Sylvania Chapel: Gen..............	75
(Esmont)—Mrs. H. D. Forsyth, Dom., $10; Frn., $10............	20 00
ALEXANDRIA Co. (Alexandria) — "A Friend," Sp. for Church Extension Fund, Porto Rico...............	5 00
St. Peter's (Alexandria): John G. Bragan, Sp. for Church Extension Fund, Porto Rico..............	2 50
Episcopal High School (Alexandria): "Mary B. Blackford" scholarship, St. John's School, Cape Mount, West Africa	25 00
(Alexandria)—Mrs. N. S. Cummings, Gen.	2 00
(Alexandria)—Alice E. Colquhinn, evangelistic work in Alaska.......	1 00
ESSEX Co.—*St. Anne's Parish* (Occupacia): Gen....................	12 35
St. Luke's (Essex): Frn............	3 04
FAIRFAX Co.—*Theological Seminary*: Dr. and Mrs. L. M. Blackford, Sp. for Armistead M. Lee Memorial Chapel, Anking, Hankow..........	25 00
Theological Seminary: Students, Gen..	50 00
(Burke)—"A Friend," Sp. for Church Extension Fund, Porto Rico.......	25 00
Falls Church (Falls Church): Wo. Aux., Sp. for Bishop Rowe, Alaska..	2 00
St. John's (McLean): Mr. B. G. Foster, Gen......................	10 00
FAUQUIER Co.—*Whittle Parish*: Frn..	25 00
FREDERICK Co.—*Christ Chapel* (Winchester): Gen..................	2 75
Episcopal Female Institute (Winchester): China Missions' Guild, Sp. for Wuchang, Hankow..............	25 00
GLOUCESTER Co.—*Ware and Abingdon* (Gloucester): Wo. Aux., Alaska, $6; Mr. Sinclair's work, Shanghai, $6..	12 00
HENRICO Co. — *Grace* (Richmond): Brotherhood of St. Paul, $5, Wo. Aux., $14, Gen.................	19 00
Emmanuel Church (Brook Hill): Wo. Aux., Alaska, $10, Honolulu, $10...	20 00
(Richmond)—Brotherhood of St. Paul, feeding of Bishop Rowe's dogs,	

Alaska, $5; Gen., $5; Sp. for edu-
cating Chinese boy under Bishop
Restarick, Honolulu, $5........... 15 00
Epiphany (Richmond): Brotherhood of
St. Paul, feeding of Bishop Rowe's
dogs, Alaska.................... 7 58
Holy Trinity Church (Richmond):
Gen. 125 00
St. Paul's (Richmond): Brotherhood
of St. Paul, feeding of Bishop Rowe's
dogs, Alaska, $10; Gen., $5........ 15 00
St. Andrew's (Richmond): Girls'
Friendly Society, Sp. for "Pike
Powers Memorial" cot, Jessfield Or-
phanage, Shanghai................ 30 00
St. Mark's (Richmond): Gen......... 91 78
(Richmond)—L. M. Williams, Dom.
and Frn. 25 00
(Richmond)—John L. Williams, Gen. 100 00
(Richmond)—Mrs. Hubert Jackson,
Gen. 10 00
KING WILLIAM CO.—*St. John's* (West
Point): Frn.................... 2 25
LOUDOUN Co.—*St. James's* (Lees-
burg): Gen..................... 185 00
(Leesburg)—"A Friend," Sp. for the
Anking Building Fund, Hankow.... 4,280 00
MIDDLESEX CO.—*Christ Church* (Mid-
dlesex): Frn., $15; Sp. for St.
Paul's College, Tokyo (of which
Wo. Aux., $6), $14.34; S. S.,*
Gen., $2.05.................... 31 39
SPOTSYLVANIA Co. — *St. George's
Chapel* (Fredericksburg): Mission-
ary Society, China, $11; "A Fam-
ily," Hankow, $15............... 26 00
St. George's (Fredericksburg): Gen... 35 72

Washington

Ap. $1,213.79; *Sp.* $44.00

WASHINGTON, D. C.—*Advent*: Gen.,
$44.55; Wo. Aux., Frn., $5........ 49 55
Ascension: Dom. and Frn., $14.60;
Gen., $100..................... 114 60
Christ Church (Georgetown): L. M.
Zeller, Gen.................... 1 00
Epiphany: Tokyo, $300; Mrs. Lewis's
Class for Young Women, Sp. for
Miss Susan Higgins, medical mis-
sionary at Wuchang, Hankow, $12.. 312 00
Nativity Chapel S. S.: Gen.......... 5 92
St. Agnes's: Gen.................. 6 00
St. John's (Georgetown): Gen....... 94 52
St. Margaret's: Gen., $50; S. S.,*
"St. Margaret's" scholarship, St.
Margaret's School, Tokyo, $50; Gen.,
$48.84 .... 148 84
St. Stephen's: Gen. (of which S. S.,*
$107.01) 157 01
National Cathedral School: Bishop
Satterlee Memorial Missionary So-
ciety, Sp. for Building Fund, St.
Margaret's School, Tokyo......... 10 00
"A Friend," rent of mission house
at Santurce, Porto Rico, $10; Sp.
for Bishop Van Buren's use, Porto
Rico, $5....................... 15 00
"Hope," Gen.................... 100 00
Grace Willis, Sp. for Alaskan Hos-
pital Fund..................... 1 00
M. L. Perkins, Gen................ 2 00
Mrs. W. P. Young, Gen............ 20 00
Mrs. S. M. Jones, Sp. for Rev. Mr.
Nichols for house for training cate-
chists, Shanghai................ 3 00
In Memoriam, "A. L. T.," Gen...... 5 00
Miss Leila Mechlin, Gen........... 10 00
Miss Caroline C. Kirkland, Gen.... 5 00
PRINCE GEORGE CO.—*St. James's* S.
S.,* *Holy Trinity Parish*: Gen..... 3 56
St. Philip's S. S.,* (Woodville): Gen. 1 31
St. Thomas's Parish: $46.85, S. S.,*
$30.63, Gen.................... 77 48

ST. MARY'S CO.—*St. Mary's S. S.*,*
(Charlotte Hall): Gen............
MISCELLANEOUS — Wo. Aux., Sp. for
Rev. F. L. H. Pott, St. John's Col-
lege, Shanghai, $10; Sp. for Mrs.
Sharpe, Edneyville, Asheville, $3...
"Anonymous," Gen...............

Western Massachusetts

Ap. $692.00; *Sp.* $91.43

AMHERST—*Grace*: Frn.............
CLINTON—*Church of the Good Shep-
herd S. S.*,*; Gen................
MILFORD—*Trinity Church S. S.*,*: Gen.
NORTH ADAMS—*St. John's*: Gen......
NORTHAMPTON—*St. John's*: Gen.....
ORANGE—*Trinity Church*: Gen.......
PITTSFIELD—*St. Stephen's*: $177.64,
"A Friend," $5, Gen..............
"A Friend," St. Mary's School,
Rosebud, South Dakota...........
Mary C. Webster, Gen............
A. R. Childs, medical work........
John W. Thomson, Gen...........
SPRINGFIELD—*Christ Church*: Gen....
St. Peter's: Gen..................
WESTFIELD—*Atonement S. S.*,*: Gen..
WORCESTER—*All Saints'*: Gen......
St. Mark's S. S.,*: Gen., $48.42; for
scholarship, Boone University, Han-
kow, $32.84....................
St. Matthew's: Gen...............
MISCELLANEOUS—Girls' Friendly So-
ciety, Sp. for Christ School, Arden,
Asheville, for Mrs. Wetmore's use..

Western Michigan

Ap. $189.09; *Sp.* $5.00

BATTLE CREEK—*St. Thomas's*: Gen..
GRAND RAPIDS—*Grace*: Gen.........
St. John's S. S.,*: Gen............
HASTINGS—*Emmanuel Church S. S.*,*:
Gen., $28.49; S. S., Sp. for "Julia"
cot, St. Mary's Orphanage, Jessfield,
Shanghai, $5...................
HOLLAND—*Grace*: James Price, Gen..
IONIA—*St. John's*: Indian Mission....
KALAMAZOO—*St. Luke's*: Miss Minnie
Goodnow, Frn..................
NILES—*Trinity Church S. S.*,*: Gen..
STURGIS—*St. John's*: Gen...........

Western New York

Ap. $1,069.56; *Sp.* $383.25

ALBION—*Christ Church S. S.*,*: Dom..
BATH—Miss Elizabeth T. Brundage,
Gen., $5; St. John's College, Shang-
hai, $5........................
BUFFALO—*Ascension*: Gen...........
St. Andrew's: Sp. for Rev. R. N. Wil-
cox, Hendersonville, Asheville......
St. John's: $89.70, S. S.,* $77.15, Gen.
St. Jude's S. S.,*: Dom. and Frn.....
St. Mark's S. S.,*: Gen............
St. Mary's-on-the-Hill: Gen.........
St. Simon's: Frn.................
St. Thomas's S. S.,*: Gen..........
Cornelia Griesser, Sp. for St. John's
University Expansion Fund, Shang-
hai ....
CALEDONIA—*St. Andrew's S. S.*,*: Gen.
CHARLOTTE—*St. George's S. S.*,*: Gen.
GENESEO—*St. Michael's S. S.*,*: Gen..
Branch Wo. Aux., Gen., $9; Sp. for
Bishop Rowe, Alaska, $20........
GENEVA—*Trinity Church*: Gen. for
Bishop Rowe, Alaska, $17; Sp. for
Bishop Graves, Shanghai, $30; Sp.

MOUNDSVILLE—*Trinity Church*: Dom., $2; Brazil, $1.85; Cuba, $1.85; Honolulu, 71 cts.; Philippines, 72 cts.; Porto Rico, 72 cts.; Mexico, $1.90; Gen., $24; Frn., 85 cts.; Colored, $1.10; Indian, $1.25...... 36 95

PARKERSBURG—*Church of the Good Shepherd*: Gen., $6.97; Honolulu, $3.08; Philippines, $3.08; Alaska, $3.09; Indian, $8.62; Porto Rico, $1.87; Brazil, $1.87; Cuba, $1.87; S. S., Honolulu, $3.98; Philippines, $3.97; Alaska, $3.97; *Gen., $43.21. 85 58

89 75
20 00
20 00
11 00

Trinity Church: Junior Aux., Sp. for Miss Barber, Hankow............. 5 00

205 46

Mrs. W. H. Small, Gen............ 25 00

20 60

SHEPHERDSTOWN—Mrs. E. Lee Goldsborough, Sp. for Armistead M. Lee Memorial Chapel, Anking, Hankow.. 10 00

Mrs. Eleanor S. Potts, Sp. for Armistead M. Lee Memorial Chapel, Anking, Hankow.................. 25 00

25 00

TAVENNERVILLE—*Grace S. S.**: Gen... 6 79

MISCELLANEOUS — Wo. Aux., Gen., $122.45; Idaho, $1; "Henry Hobart Morrell" scholarship, St. Mary's Hall, Shanghai, $45; Elizabeth Bunn Memorial Hospital, Wuchang, Hankow, $6.50; Sp. for insurance of Rev. J. G. Meem, Brazil, $59.50.

12 00

255 00

Babies' Branch, Gen., $50; Akita Kindergarten, Tokyo, $15; Angelica Church Hart Day-school, Wuchang, Hankow, $5; Little Helpers' Day-school, Shanghai, $2; Sp. for Chilen's Ward, St. Luke's Hospital, San Francisco, California, $5; Sp. for Bishop Spalding for White Rocks Emergency Fund, Utah, $1; Sp. for "Little Helpers'" cot, St. Agnes's Hospital, Raleigh, North Carolina, $8; Sp. for missionary font, 92 cts.................... 86 92

234 45

50 00

Missionary Districts

Alaska

Ap. $67.10

CHENA—Gen. 32 10
FAIRBANKS—*St. Matthew's*: Gen...... 25 00
KATALLA—*S. S.**: Gen............. 5 00
SALCHAKET—*St. Luke's*: Gen........ 5 00

271 00

Asheville

Ap. $133.21; *Sp.* $11.00

ACTON—*St. Paul's*: Gen............ 1 00
ALEXANDER—*Missions*: Gen......... 1 00
BALSAM—*St. Peter's*: Dom.......... 26
BLOWING ROCK—*Church of the Holy Spirit*: Gen...................... 1 00
BESSEMER CITY—*St. Andrew's*: Gen... 50
BOONE—*St. Luke's*: Gen........... 50
BOWMAN'S BLUFF—*Gethsemane*: Gen. 1 00
BREVARD—Mrs. M. A. E. Woodbridge, hospital work.................. 10 00
CARITON—*St. Andrew's*: Dom., $1.26; S. S.,* Gen., $6.78............... 8 04
CASHIERS—*Church of the Good Shepherd*: Dom., 25 cts.; Frn., 25 cts.; Gen., $1..................... 1 50
CULLOWHEE—*St. David's*: Dom....... 26
FLETCHER—*Calvary*: Dom., $3; Frn., $3; Gen., $3................. 9 00
FRANKLIN—*St. Agnes's*: $2.75, S. S.,* 60 cts., Gen.................. 3 35
St. Cyprian's: Gen.............. 50
GRACE—*Grace*: Gen.............. 4 00
HENDERSONVILLE—*St. James's*: Ernest

20

2 36
7 40

8 50

2 50
1 50

4 50

3 00

L. Eubank, Sp. for Church Extension Fund, Porto Rico............ 1 00
"A Friend," Sp. for Church Extension Fund, Porto Rico............ 10 00
HIGH SHOALS—*St. John's*: Dom., $1; Frn., $1; Gen., $2............ 4 00
LEICESTER—*St. Paul's*: Gen........ 1 00
LENOIR—*Chapel of Peace*: Gen....... 50
St. James's: Dom., $4; Frn., $4; Gen., $4.................. 12 00
LINCOLNTON—*St. Luke's*: Dom., 50 cts.; Frn., $4; Gen., $3......... 7 50
MICADALE—*St. Mary's*: Dom........ 26
MORGANTON—*Church of the Good Shepherd*: Gen............ 1 00
Grace: Indian, $2; Colored, $2...... 4 00
MURPHY—*Church of the Messiah*: Dom., $1; Frn., $1; Gen., $1....... 3 00
OWENBY—*Church of the Redeemer*: Gen. 1 00
PRENTISS—*St. George's*: Gen........ 75
RONDA—*All Saints'*: Gen.......... 50
SHELBY—*Church of the Redeemer*: Gen. 25
ST. JUDE—*St. John Baptist's*: Gen... 50
SYLVA—*St. John's*: Dom., 27 cts.; S. S.,* Gen., $2............... 2 27
WAYNESVILLE—*St. Michael's*: Dom... 27
MISCELLANEOUS—Junior Aux., Gen... 50 00
"E. N. J.," Gen............... 2 50

Eastern Oregon

Sp. $23.72

THE DALLES—*St. Paul's*: Sp. for Mrs. L. P. Frederick's work, Shanghai... 23 72

Honolulu

Sp. $5.00

HONOLULU—*St. Andrew's Cathedral*: Junior Aux., Sp. for June 11th, in St. Agnes's Hospital, Raleigh, North Carolina 5 00

Idaho

Ap. $154.13

BLACKFOOT—*St. Paul's*: Gen........ 5 00
BOISÉ—*Grace*: $10, S. S.,* $30.70, Gen. 40 70
DE LAMAR—*S. S.*: Gen.......... 8 31
GOODING—*Trinity Church S. S.*: Gen. 5 00
KETCHUM—*St. Thomas's*: Dom., $1.85; Frn., $2.95; S. S.,* Gen., $1.62... 6 42
MACKAY—*Edith Reiss,* Gen......... 50
WENDELL—*St. Barnabas's S. S.*: Gen. 3 20
MISCELLANEOUS—Wo. Aux., Gen. (of which Junior Aux., $10, Babies' Branch, $5)............... 85 00

Kearney

Ap. $44.05

MERRIMAN—*St. Paul's*: Gen........ 3 25
NORTH PLATTE—*Church of Our Saviour*: Gen............... 25 00
O'NEILL—*St. Paul's*: Gen.......... 1 30
SIDNEY—*Christ Church*: Gen........ 14 50

Nevada

Ap. $7.45

BLAIR—*Mission*: Gen............ 3 50
DAYTON—*All Saints'*: Gen.......... 1 00
HAWTHORNE—*Mission*: Gen......... 45
MILLERS—*Mission*: Gen............ 2 50

New Mexico

Ap. $62.00

EL PASO—*St. Clement's* (Texas): Gen. 47
CARLSBAD—*Grace* (New Mexico): Wo. Aux., mission work in Liberia..... 15

North Dakota

Ap. $358.50; *Sp.* $20.00

BISMARK—*St. George's S. S.*: Gen...
BUFFALO—*Calvary*: Gen.......... 8
CRARY—*St. Barnabas's*: Gen......... 2
DEVIL'S LAKE—*Advent*: Gen.......... 50
DICKEY—*St. John's*: Gen.......... 4
FARGO—*Gethsemane*: Gen.......... 22
Wo. Aux., Sp. for work of Deaconess Routledge, Philippine Islands... 20
FORT YATES—*Mission*: Gen......... 5
LAKOTA—*Church of the Good Shepherd*: Gen. ....
LARIMORE—*St. John's*: Gen.......... 2
LISBON—*Trinity Church*: Gen...... 20
LIDGERWOOD—*Mission*: Gen......... 2
MILNOR—*Mission*: Gen.......... 1
MCHENRY—*St. Michael's*: Gen......... 4
OAKES—*Mission*: Gen.......... 5
PEMBINA—*Grace*: Gen.......... 2
RUGBY—*St. Paul's*: Gen.......... 20
RED HAIL—*St. Gabriel's S. S.*: Gen..
SARLES—*Mission S. S.*: Gen......... 2
VALLEY CITY—*All Saints'*: Gen...... 30
WAHPETON—*Trinity Church*: Gen.... 5
WALHALLA—*St. Peter's*: Gen......... 5
WISHEK—*Mission*: Gen......... 2
MISCELLANEOUS—*S. S.*: Gen......... 13
Wo. Aux., Gen............... 150

Oklahoma

Ap. $59.74

ENID—*St. Matthew's S. S.*: Gen..... 2
OKARCHE—*Mission*: Gen......... 2
OKLAHOMA CITY—*St. Paul's Cathedral*: Gen. 12
OKMULGEE—*Church of the Good Shepherd*: Gen. 4
SAPULPA—*Church of the Good Shepherd*: Gen. 2
SHAWNEE—*Emmanuel Church S. S.*: Gen. 5
TAHLEQUAH—*All Saints'*: Gen....... 2
TULSA—*Trinity Church*: For support of Boone University, Wuchang, Hankow 5
WANETTE—*All Saints'*: $5.25, S. S.,* $1.65, Gen............... 6
WELEETKA—*Mission*: Gen.......... 4
MISCELLANEOUS—Convocation at St. Luke's, Chickasha, Gen............ 10

Olympia

Ap. $66.26

DUNLAP—*All Saints' S. S.*: Gen..... 25
RENTON—*St. Luke's S. S.*: Gen..... 9
TACOMA—*Holy Communion*: Gen..... 10
Trinity Church S. S.*; Gen........ 21

Porto Rico

Ap. $15.00

MAYAGUEZ—*St. Andrew's*: Wo. Aux., Gen. 5
SAN JUAN—*St. John the Baptist's*: "A Member," Wo. Aux., Gen...... 5
VIRQUES—*All Saints'*: Wo. Aux., Gen. 5

Western Colorado
Ap. $31.74

COLONA—*S. S.**: Gen		2 75
CIMARRON—*S. S.**: Gen		2 50
GUNNISON — *Church of the Good Samaritan*: Ladies' Guild, Frn		5 00
LAKE CITY—*St. James's S. S.**: Gen		3 00
MONTROSE—*St. Paul's*: $3, S. S.,* $11.79, Gen		14 79
PLACERVILLE—*S. S.**: Gen		3 70

Wyoming
Ap. $105.15

EVANSTON—*St. Paul's*: Gen		9 15
RAWLINS—*St. Thomas's*: $41, S. S.,* $50, Gen		91 00
SUPERIOR—*Christ Church*: Gen		5 00

Foreign Missionary Districts
Ap. $111.30

Africa

CUTTINGTON—*S. S.**: Gen		10 00

China

HANKOW—Chinese school children,* Gen.		13 79

Cuba

BOLONDRON—*San Pablo*: $15, S. S.,* $9.50, Gen		24 50

New Brunswick

ST. JOHN—Miss Abbie H. Swinerton, Gen.		1 00

Greece

ATHENS—*Hill Memorial School*: Miss Bessie M. Masson, for Koyukuk, Alaska, $2; Nenana, Alaska, $1; Gen., $3; *Sp. for school at Anvik, Alaska, $6.26; Sp. for St. Mary's Orphanage, Shanghai, $6.25		18 51

Japan

KYOTO—Wo. Aux., Gen		40 00

Mexico

ENSENADA—Mrs. S. R. Sawday, Gen		3 50

Miscellaneous
Ap. $13,675.14; Sp. $1,069.77

Interest — Dom., $2,116.64; Frn., $1,564.69; Gen., $2,637.59; Sp., $989.64; Specific Deposit, $7.07		7,315 63
United Offering, Wo. Aux., 1907, on account of appropriations to September 1st, 1910, Dom., $3,500; Frn., $3,500		7,000 00
Daughters of the King, salary of Miss Richmond, Shanghai		187 50

(Left margin figures)

20 45
5 40
55
4 40
4 05
7 90
3 30
5 40

12 00

1 68
70
2 73
6 48

3 85
1 70
1 82
1 63

1 91
1 35
1 61
97
3 91

4 91

2 40
2 00
50 00
7 90
6 12
25 00

17 44
10 00
9 00

26 75

39 00

125 00
15 00

4 70
5 00

20 80
1 50

25 00
9 00

Atlantic Mutual Scrip., Frn........ 123 00
League of Eastern Oregon, Sp. for
Bishop Paddock, Eastern Oregon... 65 00
"K. C. B.," Gen., $38.65 ; : Sp. for
enlargement of St. John's College,
Shanghai, $5................ 43 65
Passengers on steamship *Philadelphia,* Sp. for Church Extension
Fund, Porto Rico................ 5 75
Sale of Bishop Van Buren's sermons,
Sp. for Church Extension Fund,
Porto Rico...................... 4 38

Legacies

W. N. Y., BUFFALO—Estate of Mrs.
Charles H. Smith, Dom.,-$177 ; Frn.,
$177 .... 354 00
MD., CARROLL Co. (Westminster)—
Estate of Miss Sallie Longwell, to
the Society...................... 145 84
WASH., MONTGOMERY Co. (Barnesville)—Estate of Mrs. Priscilla J.
Poole, Frn....................... 95 00

Receipts for the month..........$ 93,17 88
Amount previously acknowledged $1,270,236 95
Transferred from
Omnibus to Specials for St. Paul's
College, Tokyo,
f u n d received
from a committee appointed last
December in Philadelphia by the
Foreign Committee of the Wo.
Aux. (but without
any official connection with the
Wo. Aux.), for
detail see separate acknowledgment on page 602
of July SPIRIT OF
MISSIONS 36,366 22
             —————— 1,306,60 17

Total since September 1st...$1,399,78 05

SUMMARY OF RECEIPTS

Receipts divided according to purposes to which they are to be applied	Received during June	Amounts previously Acknowledged	Tot
1. Applicable upon the appropriations of the Board.	$70,985 88	$715,888 18	$786,87 06
2. Special gifts forwarded to objects named by donors in addition to the appropriations of the Board.	21,591 09	215,526 11	237,11 20
3. Legacies for investment......................	....	165,000 00	165,00 00
4. Legacies, the disposition of which is to be determined by the Board at the end of the fiscal year	594 84	89,295 96	89,89 80
5. Specific Deposit................................	7 07	120,892 92	120,89 99
Total...........................	$93,178 88	$1,306,603 17	$1,399,78 05

Total receipts from September 1st, 1909, to July 1st, 1910, applicable upon the appropriations, divided according to the sources from which they have come, and compared with the corresponding period of the preceding year. Legacies are not included in the following items, as their disposition is not determined by the Board until the end of the fiscal year.

OFFERINGS TO PAY APPROPRIATIONS

Source	To July 1, 1910	To July 1, 1909	Increase	Decrease
1. From congregations......................	$402,041 90	$348,514 26	$53,527 64	$....
2. From individuals........................	37,526 53	70,854 65	....	33,32 12
3. From Sunday-schools....................	137,220 89	134,315 97	2,904 92	....
4. From Woman's Auxiliary................	75,593 23	81,416 31	....	5,82 08
5. From interest..........................	62,970 34	58,387 24	4,583 10	....
6. Miscellaneous items....................	1,521 17	4,519 09	....	2,99 92
Total...........................	$716,874 06	$698,007 52	$18,866 54	....
Woman's Auxiliary United Offering........	70,000 00	40,000 00	30,000 00	....
Total...........................	$786,874 06	$738,007 52	$48,866 54	....

APPROPRIATIONS FOR THE YEAR

SEPTEMBER 1ST, 1909, TO AUGUST 31ST, 1910

Amount Needed for the Year

1. To pay appropriations as made to date for the work at home and abroad........ $1,214,63 07
2. To replace Reserve Funds temporarily used for the current work.............. 32,95 33

Total... $1,247,58 40
Total receipts to date applicable on appropriations......................... 786,87 06

Amount needed before August 31st, 1910.................................. *$ 460,71 34

* Through an oversight in the July SPIRIT OF MISSIONS the amount here stated as needed to August 31st, 1910, was $649,536.64 when it should have read $531,877.22.

THE
Spirit of Missions

AN ILLUSTRATED MONTHLY REVIEW
OF CHRISTIAN MISSIONS

September, 1910

CONTENTS

The Subscription Price of **THE SPIRIT OF MISSIONS** is **ONE DOLLAR** per year. Postage is prepaid in the United States, Porto Rico, The Philippines and Mexico. For other countries in the Postal Union, including Canada, twenty-four cents per year should be added.

Subscriptions are continued until ordered discontinued.

Change of Address: In all changes of address it is necessary that the old as well as the new address should be given.

How to Remit: Remittances, made payable to George Gordon King, Treasurer, should be made by draft on New York, Postal Order or Express Order. One and two cent stamps are received. To checks on local banks ten cents should be added for collection.

All Letters should be addressed to **The Spirit of Missions**, 281 Fourth Avenue, New York.

Published by the Domestic and Foreign Missionary Society.
President, RIGHT REVEREND DANIEL S. TUTTLE, D.D. *Secretary*, ———
Treasurer, GEORGE GORDON KING.
Entered at the Post Office, in New York, as second-class matter.

(714)

A SEMINOLE BRIDE AND GROOM

THE SPIRIT OF MISSIONS

AN ILLUSTRATED MONTHLY REVIEW
OF CHRISTIAN MISSIONS

VOL. LXXV.	**September, 1910**	No. 9

THE PROGRESS OF THE KINGDOM

ENCOURAGED by the kind reception which was given to the Japanese Semi-centennial Number issued last September, we are, in the same month of this year, concentrating upon a special field of work. There should be a definite value in devoting an occasional issue of THE SPIRIT OF MISSIONS to the more careful consideration of a particular field, and it is our hope that the readers of this magazine may find the present issue a useful one.

Our Indian Number

In Japan we had the distinction of being the pioneers of modern missions. While we cannot claim to have been the first in the Indian field, we may at least say that the Church has rendered therein a conspicuous and remarkably fruitful service. As far back as 1703, one of the very first missionaries sent by the newborn Society for the Propagation of the Gospel went to the Iroquois in New York; and then, at the consecration of John Henry Hobart, the Church in New York took a new life, the revival of the mission among these Indians was promptly begun. The remarkable work at Oneida, Wisconsin, is the fruit of these labors. It was James Lloyd Breck who began

The Church and the Indian

in the West that work which brought to the front Bishop Whipple as the champion of the Indian and Bishop Hare as his most conspicuous friend and apostle. What these contributed to the betterment of the red race and the peaceful solution of the problems surrounding them, can never be reckoned, but the Church was honored in their deeds.

The death of Bishop Hare and the appreciations of his work which were thereby called forth, are fresh in the memories of us all. But in an issue devoted to Indian missions we may well repeat that of the 25,000 Indians in South Dakota, 10,000 are baptized members of the Episcopal Church; that the congregations number 100, ministered to by twenty-six clergy and sixty catechists and helpers; that in the years of his service, Bishop Hare himself laid hands upon 7,000 Indians in confirmation, and that South Dakota has 4,000 living Indian communicants. When one realizes that there are less than 24,000 Christian Indian communicants of any name in the entire country, the significance of these figures becomes more evident. They mean that wherever the Church has gone with serious purpose, and has carried to the Indians the richness of her apostolic heritage, she has won their allegiance and found an opportunity for noble service.

The Government and the Indian

Future historians will be called upon to decide this rather complicated question: Which has been more abused, the Indian or the Government? Perhaps the decision may be influenced in some measure by the fact that the abuse which the Government received was largely verbal and oratorical, while that meted out to the Indian was definite and personal.

Censure and reproach the Government has undoubtedly deserved in many instances. Even so strenuous an upholder of the divine right of the white man as Colonel Theodore Roosevelt admits in his historical writings the aggression and the ruthlessness of the white man, encouraged by the supine and dilatory attitude of the Government. But that we as a nation have always abused and plundered the Indian, few are prepared to believe. It is useful in acquiring a true perspective to have such a statement of the many problems involved as that presented in the recent book by the Hon. Francis E. Leupp, an extensive review of which will be found in this issue. That there *are* honest Indian agents, and that—despite the cumbersomeness of our governmental machinery—there have been, and still are, high officials who are real friends of the Indian, this volume amply demonstrates.

The Perishing Indian

IT is exceedingly difficult, and practically impossible, to furnish anything like accurate figures concerning the fluctuations of Indian population. No trustworthy estimates were made in the earlier day, either by the Indians themselves or by the white man; and such guesses as are recorded probably represented exaggerations of from four to tenfold. There are men familiar with Indian affairs who believe that there are as many Indians in the country to-day as there were when Columbus discovered America. Though most of us would doubt this, it is certain that there has

JAMES L. HOUGHTELING, founder of the Brotherhood of St. Andrew, and from 1888 to 1900 its president, died at his home in Winnetka, Ill., July 28th. To him,

James Lawrence Houghteling under God, more than to any other layman, has been due the great awakening of the Church's laity during the last twenty-five years. He restored to the men of the Anglican Communion an almost forgotten ideal of

Christian citizenship and service. He combined in a remarkable degree the capacity for seeing visions of what men might be and do, the constructive ability to work them out in practical everyday life and the executive ability to rouse other men and set them to work. Thus he developed the vast latent resources of our laymen for missionary service among their fellows. In doing that he inevitably helped them to be more faithful Churchmen in all directions. Undoubtedly many a man who began to work for "the spread of His Kingdom among men," through the Brotherhood rules of prayer and service, has naturally come to realize that the Church's mission is to men everywhere—and not to *men* only, but to nations and races. So the Brotherhood has helped to train and develop some of the most devoted members of the Church's mission staff at home and abroad, as well as some of the staunch supporters of the enterprise in the home parishes.

In 1894, during Mr. Houghteling's presidency of the Brotherhood, it responded to Bishop McKim's call for help by sending Mr. Charles H. Evans to Japan as its representative to aid the laymen of the young Japanese Church to undertake Brotherhood work. In this connection Mr. Houghteling wrote to a Japanese layman: "Our hearts are warm toward the young men of Japan, a nation whose intelligence, courage and patriotism are known to all men. Our hearts' desire is that they shall have all the blessings which we enjoy, and that the richest of all blessings, the knowledge of God and citizenship in the Kingdom of Jesus Christ, may speedily be theirs."

As a Churchman in the ranks Mr. Houghteling took his part in meeting the missionary obligations of parish and diocese, while individual missionaries who asked him for special aid rarely had their requests refused. In 1904 Mr. Houghteling took a leading place in starting the Laymen's Forward Movement of the Middle West and formulated the simple platform upon which it proposed to work. This movement has had an important part in making possible that larger participation in the Church's general missionary work that in recent years has characterized most of the Western dioceses.

The Church can ill afford to lose from her militant ranks, at the early age of fifty-four, a man like Mr. Houghteling. The recollection of his life and its achievements will long remain an inspiring memory.

T HE treasurer's department cannot shut its eyes to the fact that it will probably be compelled to report to the coming General Convention a very serious deficit. How great this will be it

A Probable Deficit

THE committee to prepare a programme for the joint sessions of the two houses of the General Convention, when the Church's mission work will be reviewed and discussed, consists this year of the Bishops of Southern Ohio and Indianapolis, the Rev. Alexander Mann, D.D., of Boston, Dean Matthews, of Cincinnati, Mr. George W. Pepper, of Philadelphia, and Mr. Stephen Baker, of New York. The committee has had the help of Mr. George Gordon King and Mr. John W. Wood, who is acting as its secretary.

Missionary Meetings at the General Convention

As the committee cannot bind the Convention to accept its programme in advance, all announcements concerning plans are subject to revision when the Convention meets on October 7th to consider the committee's report.

Following the report of the committee on the morning of October 7th there will be a brief presentation of the Triennial Report of the Board of Missions and its auxiliaries. Then there will follow an address by one of the secretaries reviewing the "Progress of the Church's Mission at Home and Abroad," and an address by the Treasurer of the Board, giving "Some Facts about Missionary Offerings." The morning will close with discussion and questions upon the report of the Board.

Reports of Our Leaders

In the afternoon the session will be asked to consider "How the Church Can Better Discharge Her Duty to the American People." Bishop Francis, of Indianapolis, Bishop Horner, of Asheville, Bishop Brooke, of Oklahoma, and Bishop Nichols, of California, have been asked to treat different aspects of this subject in twenty-five-minute addresses.

The Committee on Programme proposes that four other afternoons shall be set apart for the consideration of missionary matters. On Monday, October 10th, it is hoped that "Achievements and Opportunities in the Orient" may be recounted by Bishops Graves of Shanghai, Roots of Hankow, McKim of Tokyo and Partridge of Kyoto.

The third joint session is scheduled for the afternoon of October 14th, when "Special Forms of Home Mission Work" are to be discussed by Bishop Johnson, of South Dakota, speaking for the Indians, Bishop Guerry, of South Carolina, for the Negroes, and Bishop Rowe for the work in Alaska.

For the afternoon of October 17th the general subject proposed is "The Church's Outposts in the Island World." The speakers selected are: Bishop Restarick, of Honolulu, Bishop Knight, of Cuba, and Bishop Brent, of the Philippines.

The fifth and last joint session is planned for the afternoon of October 19th, when it is expected that the Church's work in Mexico, Porto Rico, Brazil and Africa may be outlined by the bishops in charge.

Other Important Meetings Besides these distinctly official meetings there will be several others of great interest and importance.

On the evening of Sunday, October 9th, Bishop Morrison, of Iowa, is to preach the sermon before the Board of Missions. As September 25th marks the seventy-fifth anniversary of the consecration of Jackson Kemper as the first missionary bishop of the American Church, Bishop Morrison has been asked to commemorate the event by a sermon, more especially on the Church's work in the home land.

Four great missionary mass meetings have also been arranged for. They will be held in Music Hall, with accommodation for 4,000 or 5,000 people. The first of these will be on Tuesday evening, October 11th, with Bishop Vincent as chairman. The subjects and speakers are: "What the Church Can Do for the Western Frontier," by Bishop Robinson, of Nevada; "Brazil: The Land of Need and Opportunity," by Bishop Kinsolving, and "A Day's Work on the Arctic Trail," by Bishop Rowe.

THE SANCTUARY OF MISSIONS

B UT years rolled on—the sun
    beheld
Those savage chiefs again,
All gathered as at council fires,
  Or leagued with peaceful men;
    *   *   *
With laud and anthem rung the
    grove;
And here, where howled their yell,
I've heard their Christian litanies,
  And old Te Deum swell.

And when the golden Easter came
Again they gathered there,
All eager for the Christian name,
  And Christ's dear cross to bear.
Oh! forest-aisles, ye trembled then
  Like fanes where organs roll,
To hear those savage-featured men
  Outpour the Christian soul.
　　　　　　—Arthur Cleveland Coxe.

THANKSGIVINGS

"We thank thee"—
For the great names and the good
service of those who have stood as
the champions and friends of thy
Red children in this land.
For the renewed demonstration,
among an aboriginal people, of the
power of thy gospel to renew the
waste places of the earth.
For the shining examples of those
who, though born in pagan darkness, have, by the revelation of thy
truth, been transformed into the
likeness of thy Son.
That by means of the conferences
held this summer, more of thy children than ever before have been
studying how better they may serve
thee and advance thy kingdom.

INTERCESSIONS

"That it may please thee"—
To bring all those who are yet in
paganism and ignorance to the
knowledge of thee and of thy dear
Son; especially the unevangelized
Indians of this land. (Page 718.)
To raise up friends and helpers
for those who are ministering to thy
stricken children in mission hospitals; especially those among the
Indian race. (Pages 743, 746, 764.)
To go with those who have gone
forth in thy name to carry the light
of thy truth into the dark places of
the earth. (Page 719.)

To so move those who direct the
religious education of the young
that they may rightly instruct them
in the mission of thy Church and
inspire them to take their share in
furthering of that mission.
To so govern thy Church with
godly quietness and wisdom that
she may be enabled in the coming
General Convention to devise those
things which shall be for thy glory
and the salvation of all men.
To so direct the missionary instruction of the study classes at the
coming General Convention that the
minds and hearts of many may be
stimulated to better knowledge and
worthier service.

PRAYERS

FOR THE YOUNG

O GOD, who makest us think
    and do what is good, we
humbly beseech thee to implant in
the hearts of the young such gratitude for thy Gospel of Salvation as
will manifest itself in earnest endeavor to bring others to the
knowledge of thee and of thy Son,
Jesus Christ; so that many may be
brought out of darkness and the
shadow of death into the glorious
liberty of the children of God, to the
praise of thy Name; through Jesus
Christ our Lord. *Amen.*

FOR INDIAN MISSIONS
[Composed by Bishop Hare]

O MOST merciful God, who hast
    promised that all those who
dwell in the wilderness shall kneel
before thy Son; Remember, we pray
thee, the Indian tribes of our land,
and all those who have gone to
them in thy Name. Guide and govern all those who are put in civil
or military authority over them,
that the people may lead a quiet and
peaceable life in all godliness and
honesty. Set up and strengthen
thy Church among them, that they
may all come to know thee, the
only true God, and Jesus Christ,
whom thou hast sent. Endue its
ministers with heavenly love and
wisdom, and make them ensamples
to the flock. Hear us for the sake
of thy Son, Jesus Christ our Lord.
Amen.

THE INDIAN AND HIS PROBLEM*

Francis E. Leupp

NO. man of the present generation is bett
fitted to discuss the important and delic
questions involved in what is genera
called "The Indian Problem" than is t
author of the interesting volume which bears the abo
title. For twenty-five years Mr. Francis E. Leu
has been intimately acquainted with conditio
among our Indian tribes, and for five years of th
time he stood at the head of the Government servi
Without criticism or derogation of that which h
been previously accomplished, it may be said th
Mr. Leupp has contributed more toward the soluti
of this problem—so far as Government action c
solve it——than any other man who has ever held t
responsible position of Commissioner of Indi
Affairs, and he properly dedicates his book "To Th
dore Roosevelt, the President whose unwavering co
fidence and support enabled me to put into practi
operation most of the policies advocated in the f
lowing pages."

Written in a clear and simple style, and avoiding statistical and other prec
details, the book nevertheless gives in readable and attractive form a survey of t
subject which the reader will find both delightful and profitable. It is not oft
that one is taken so intimately into the confidence of a man who knows his subj
both inside and out—from the standpoint of the official, of the citizen, and
the Indian himself. Though the statement seems to us rather too modest, the pu
pose of the book may be best defined in the author's own words:

> "My little volume is not offered as a contribution to the literature of
> ethnology, of jurisprudence. or of political science in the narrower sense of
> that term. It expresses no opinions but my own, and neither represents
> nor commits any other person, either in or out of public life. In short,
> it is simply a message of friendly counsel from a white citizen of the
> United States, proud of his country, and anxious to see the members of
> our dominant race do their full duty toward a weaker element in the popu-
> lation who were Americans long before we were."

I

By the insertion in his title of a single and somewhat unexpected word, M
Leupp has cleverly pointed out the road he believes must be followed. He writ
not concerning "The Indian Problem," as most men would have done, but "T
Indian and *His* Problem"—which is a very different thing. As one reads on throu
the seventeen chapters which comprise the volume, the writer leads him more a
more to the conviction that the problem is one which must be worked out *by* t
Indian and not *for* him; that the white race owe to him an intelligent understan
ing, a sane sympathy, temporary protection against his weaknesses, even-hand
justice and a fair chance to make himself a man and a citizen.

His opening chapter, on "The Indian as He Was," is a discriminating and
luminating word-picture. The author quotes with appreciation the phrase of t

* "The Indian and His Problem," by Francis E. Leupp, formerly United States Commissioner
Indian Affairs. Charles Scribner's Sons.

ate Dr. William T. Harris, who referred to the Indian race as "Homeric children," and he shows the good qualities which underlie many of the traits which are so unintelligently, and sometimes savagely, criticised by writers upon Indian subjects. He gives us neither Cooper's Indian—the high-minded and statuesque hero of fiction, nor yet the Indian of the average school history—a bloodthirsty and devilish monster; but the real Indian as he is known, and can only be known, by the man who has seen beneath the surface and has lived near to him as friend.

He next shows us what happened to these Homeric children, and how the Indian as he was, became the Indian as he is—a person changed by his changed environments; the victim of a conquest which has brought him some good and much evil. This interesting parallel is drawn:

"Suppose a century or so ago an absolutely alien people, like the Chinese, had invaded our shores and driven the white colonists before them to districts more isolated, destroyed the industries on which they had always subsisted, and crowned all by disarming them and penning them into various tracts of land where they could be fed and clothed and cared for at no cost to themselves: to what condition would the white Americans of to-day have been reduced? In spite of their vigorous ancestry they surely would have lapsed into weakness of the mind and body and will, and become pauperized. No race on earth could overcome, by forces evolved from within themselves, the effect of such treatment. That the Indians have not been wholly ruined by it is the best proof we could ask of the sturdy traits of character inherent in them."

With the policy that would permanently shut the Indian away from contact with civilization and would perpetuate his status as a "ward of the Government" and a dependent upon the white man's bounty, Mr. Leupp has no sympathy. "We must end," he says, "the un-American absurdity of keeping one class of our people in a common lump. Each Indian must be recognized as an individual, and so treated, just as each white man is. We must strive, too, in every way possible, to make the Indian an active factor in the upbuilding of the community in which he is to live. The theory too commonly cherished on the frontier, that he is a useless survival from a remote period, like the sage-brush and the giant cactus, must be dispelled, and the way to dispel it is to turn him into a positive benefit."

This does not necessarily mean converting the Indian into a farmer, and certainly not the effort to make him something other than an Indian. From Mr. Leupp's point of view, to be the best kind of an Indian is to be something quite worth while. It means the possession of qualities and characteristics distinct and admirable—a contribution unique and useful to the general good of the Nation. His words are true of other races than the red when he says, "Nature has drawn her lines of race, which it is folly for us to try to obliterate along with the artificial barriers we throw down in the cause of civil equality. The man whom she has made an Indian, let us try to make a better Indian, instead of vainly struggling to convert him into a Caucasian." To the life of the frontier Mr. Leupp believes that the Indian who has been given an education which fits without unfitting him, can make a useful contribution; and work out thereby his own salvation, and in that of his race.

II

The breaking up of reservations by the allotting of lands in severalty is the first step toward bringing the Indian out of that communistic and patriarchal state from which our own race emerged so many centuries ago; and a simple and practical education for Indian children is the second. This education should be such as reaches back into the homes, influencing the parents through the children; and we

are therefore glad to find that Mr. Leupp's experience does not lead him to)u
mend the system of non-reservation schools.

For many years it has been the practice to send to the reservations repre :ntɛ
tives of institutions like Carlisle, Haskell and Hampton, who gathered chi re
from ten years upward, sometimes cajoling and wheedling unwilling paren i
order that the scholars obtained might be as many as possible, since the Gc rn
ment paid a stated sum for the care of each. For five, or it might be seven or to
years, these children did not see their homes, and when they did return to th)
was too often as strangers, educated out of all harmony with the surroundings of ie
earlier life, and quite unfitted to take any useful place in the primitive comm it
where they were born. For many of "the failures of education" which ai r
ported—for reversions to type and returns to the blanket—Mr. Leupp justly a;
that we ought not to blame the Indian; "for it is his unbalanced white fr n
who are accountable." They have sounded in his ears "the benefits of an e c
tion" until he has become convinced that if he can obtain this thing "he will ee
only to sit still and spread his lap, and let fortune fill it with prizes." In whic h
dream does not so greatly differ from that of the ambitious white boy; but the ii
boy after graduation has some chance to use what he has learned, to find out io
inadequate it is, and to add to his equipment that which may help in some me ur
to fulfil his dreams. Such chances do not come in equal measure to the Indiar

If there must be Indian boarding-schools, Mr. Leupp believes that they gh
better be on the reservations, where frequent returns of the children to their l ne
are possible, but he feels that the work done by the day-schools, which do not ak
the children away from their homes at all, has produced the better results, ai h
speaks with kindly appreciation of the service which has been rendered by m y
little mission school in giving the elements of an education and laying the fo da
tions of character. This has not been because they were better equipped or or
thorough in their instruction than the Government schools—indeed, the revers ha
been true—but because they began the new life as nearly as possible where th ol
left off, and also because, as he justly says, "a school is apt to be better cond te
under private control than as a part of the Government machinery."

Boarding-schools cannot be wholly dispensed with among certain tribes icl
are still nomadic in their habits and whose homes are widely scattered, bu Mr
Leupp declares them to be an anomaly in our scheme of popular instruction. H
calls them "educational almshouses," where everything is given to the Indian pi
during his entire period of enrolment, thus fostering "an ignoble willingne t
accept unearned privileges, with the result that in certain parts of the Wes th
only conception his white neighbors entertain of him is that of a beggar, as a es
sive as he is shameless. Was ever a worse wrong perpetrated upon a weaker y
stronger race?"

The remedy for this condition Mr. Leupp finds in the obliteration of exclu el
Indian boarding-schools by throwing them open to the white race as well, ar b;
requiring that some return be made for the education given. But most of ɛ h
believes in the simpler plan of the Indian day-school, with its schoolhouse n
teacher's cottage, on a small farm, where reading, writing and ciphering cɛ b
interspersed with practical instructions in raising vegetables and milking cov
mending fences and the care of poultry, in sewing, cooking, washing and iro
"For," he says, "the Indian needs practical rather than showy instruction
Gospel of Indian salvation, if I read it aright, puts industry at the top of h
virtues."

III

We have given much space to the matter of education, because the author
it to be fundamental, and insistence upon it permeates the book; but ther

other features which we must not overlook. Perhaps the chapters from which readers would be most likely to dissent are those dealing with questions of Indian Lands.

It is the assumption of many Indian advocates—an assumption not only unproved, but evidently considered as requiring no proof—that the whole country belonged of right to the Indian, and that every foot of it taken without some form of payment to him constituted sheer aggression—the insolent dominance of the race that had the strongest arm and the most grasping hand. But is this necessarily true? Mr. Roosevelt, in his "Winning of the West," discusses this question, and shows that vast tracts—as, for example, most of Kentucky and Tennessee—were never inhabited by the Indians at all, but were used only as hunting-grounds and battlefields—a sort of debatable no-man's land. It was impossible that the Indians of America, who probably numbered not over half a million when this country was discovered, and who, according to some reputable authorities, were not more numerous than the Indians of to-day, should have possessed and occupied the entire land. Daniel Boone and his comrades, after they had made their eight-months'-long hunt in Kentucky, had established as good a claim to the territory as any Indian tribe possessed, for none of them had done more than this.

This, of course, does not justify the wanton aggression which was often practised, nor the decree of exile which so frequently banished whole tribes from the home of their people. But it does not help the cause of justice or fairness to cry out against every instance in which the Government either removed a tribe or changed the terms under which its land was held. Many of the difficulties were inevitable, and Mr. Leupp holds "that what has been so sweepingly denounced as A Century of Dishonor might better be described, so far as the Government's operations are concerned, as an era of mutual misunderstandings."

He admits that there is something pathetic and appealing in the lament of an old Indian over the passing of the land of his ancestors into the hands of an alien people, but he points out that if large parts of our country were not to remain a wilderness, and if the Indian was ever to pass from the position of a nomad, roaming over vast fields, to that of stationary habitation and the development of the arts of civilization, such passing of the lands was unavoidable; and the most that could be asked of the advanced race was that it should deal justly with the backward races and give always a fair equivalent for the land which it invaded. "This," he says, "I believe the Government of the United States has uniformly striven to do, in spite of the cupidity of many of its individual citizens."

With the above statement some of us will hardly find ourselves in agreement, but we shall all agree with his conclusion that the Indian should be protected in the rights which have been granted him, and that "we should lay hold now on the means which are nearest to our hand, save all we can for the Indian, and nail it fast, while the times are still favorable for such an undertaking."

IV

Of special interest to us are the chapters in which the author treats of "Missionaries and their Methods" and "Philanthropy and Criticism." In the main his attitude is sympathetic, and no man appreciates more fully what may be accomplished for the Indian by religious and philanthropic agencies. But he also gives us many side-lights, with glints of humor now and then as he tells of the delicate situations in which he has found himself through the mistaken zeal or the narrow view of well-meaning people. His absolutely sound advice is that such agencies and individuals shall adopt toward the Government and its officials the attitude of confidence and coöperation, rather than criticism and suspicion.

It is pleasant to find in these pages the following statement:

"The best way to approach Indians with an appeal to consider Christianity is by furnishing them first with something on a level with their
understanding, which they can and will use as a bridge to carry them
into the domain of enquiry. The Catholic priests of old time who established their faith on the Pacific Coast, were experts in husbandry; they
taught the Indians how to raise, harvest and preserve important additions
to their food supply. The Society of Friends, in their operations in the
Mississippi Valley, used to start model stores, carpenter-shops and like
enterprises. The Mennonites of our generation have devoted much attention in the arid zone to agriculture and the improvement of water resources. The Protestant Episcopal mission to the Navajos set up an excellent hospital at Fort Defiance. Such illustrations show what I have
in mind. If you approach an Indian with the bare abstract proposition
that you are bringing him a religion better than that of his fathers, you
must prepare for either resentment or indifference; but if you show him
new ways of appeasing his hunger, or mend his broken leg, or save the
life of his fever-stricken child, you have given him something which locks
into his environment, as it were. When he sees you doing this for him,
not once or twice, but continuously, wonder begins to stir in his mind as
to what it all means. Then comes your opportunity for telling him that
your religion is a religion of love; that it is founded on the idea that all
human beings, of every name and race, are brothers; that you are trying
to do him good because he is your brother and you love him. And so your
chain of instruction can go on, one link being forged into another as fast
as his understanding will open to permit it.

"A hospital I consider a better channel of approach than any other,
because it accomplishes so many ends with one stroke. It confers a definite
and palpable benefit upon the patient; it confounds the sneers and
machinations of the native medicine men, when a sufferer they are unable to cure puts himself under the care of white physicians and recovers;
it is the most potent instrument for uprooting superstition, because in all
primitive religions the healing power is an attribute of divinity; it is an
intelligible evidence of the superiority of Caucasian culture generally, and
it paves the way for any further advances his white friends wish to make
to the Indian. I have always encouraged the establishment of hospitals by
private benevolence rather than by public appropriation. When set up by
the Government, half their interest is lost. The Indian has had his moral
perspective distorted so long by gratuitous favors from the Treasury that
he is apt to look upon a Government hospital as he looks upon a Government ration-house, mixing contempt with his appreciation of it."

V

Mr. Leupp's final chapter gives his answer to the question: "What is to be
ultimate fate of the Indians?" He believes that they will be absorbed and mer
with our own race. This will not necessarily come to pass by intermarrie
though he does not sympathize with the wholesale contumely which has been pou
out upon "squaw-men" and "half-breeds." Some of the former have doubtless n
ried Indian wives because of their land, but he suggests that these are not the o
men who have married heiresses for the sake of an idle life, and he also adds that
numbers among his best friends in the West many a hardy, fearless pioneer, v
is a true husband to an Indian wife, and a faithful father to his children. C
cerning the latter, he says that the child of one white and one Indian parent 1
mally inherits the shrewder and more self-seeking traits of his white ancestry, a

therefore, is more open to the temptation to act as a go-between for white grafters bent on getting hold of Indian property. But he does not feel—as is often asserted —that the half-breed inherits the worst traits of both races. "In my acquaintance, which is large," says Mr. Leupp, "the good mixed-bloods outnumber the bad. They stand up for the rights of their red kinsmen, while their broader intelligence saves them from irrational extremes. Moreover, it is not their ancestry which makes the vicious specimens what they are. We find the same over-reaching disposition among the better-educated, but normally ill-balanced members of all races, whether of pure blood or mixed. It is our common human nature, not Indian nature or white nature, which is to blame."

But whether by intermarriage or otherwise, the merging of the Indian with the general population of the country is inevitable. "He is losing his identity hour by hour, competing with whites in the labor market, mingling with white communities and absorbing white pioneers into his own, sending his children to the same schools with white children, intermarrying with whites and rearing an offspring which combines the traits of both lines of ancestry. In the light of his new day, which is now so near its noon, he need not be an inspired seer to discern the approaching end of his pure aboriginal type, and the upgrowth of another, which will claim the name 'American' by a double title as solid as the hills on his horizon."

VI

We have made a long review of this illuminating book. The volume will be welcomed by every student of Indian matters, and while not technically designed as missionary literature, it is such, in the best sense of the word. For it is written by a man of clear vision and large heart, who loves his fellows, whatever their color, and would help them to understand their heritage as children of the one Father and heirs of the kingdom of life.

This review cannot be closed more fittingly than with the incident which concludes the book:

"As I put aside my pen," says the author, "there comes to me the memory of another leave-taking. I had passed a whole day in an Indian council, arguing, urging, pleading, in an effort to induce the tribe to recede from what seemed to me an unwise stand. A battle of words in an unknown tongue had raged fiercely over my head, as the speakers who supported me and those who resisted fought the question out between themselves. The struggle ended in a victory for my champions.

"Meanwhile the day had waned, and the horses had been brought to the edge of the village preparatory to my departure. As the rank and file of the band pushed forward to shake my hand, one—tall, erect, dignified—remained aloof. He was a splendid-looking Indian, a proud figure among his fellows, who had fought me till overwhelmed, and then had surrendered with all the honors of war. When the last of the lesser men had dropped back and I had turned to go, he advanced and checked me. His face, though still earnest, had lost all its sternness. I read in it that he had put aside the animosities of debate and wished now to tell me so. Throwing his arm around me, he drew me toward him till we stood heart to heart, and then said with great impressiveness: 'Farewell, my friend. Do not forget us. We have now only God and you!'

"To the readers who have been patient enough to accompany me thus far, and whose purpose toward the superseded race is neither robbery nor charitable exploitation, but honest, unselfish, practical help, I pass on his appeal."

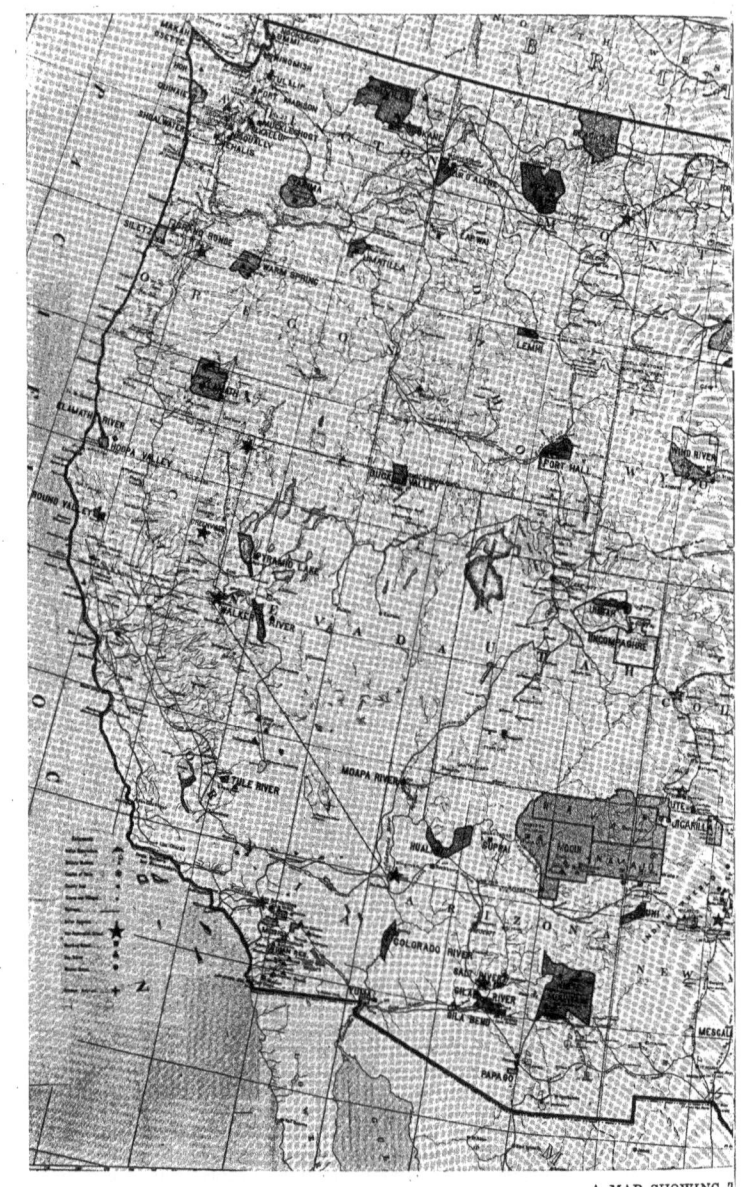

A MAP SHOWING 7
Compiled under the direction of th

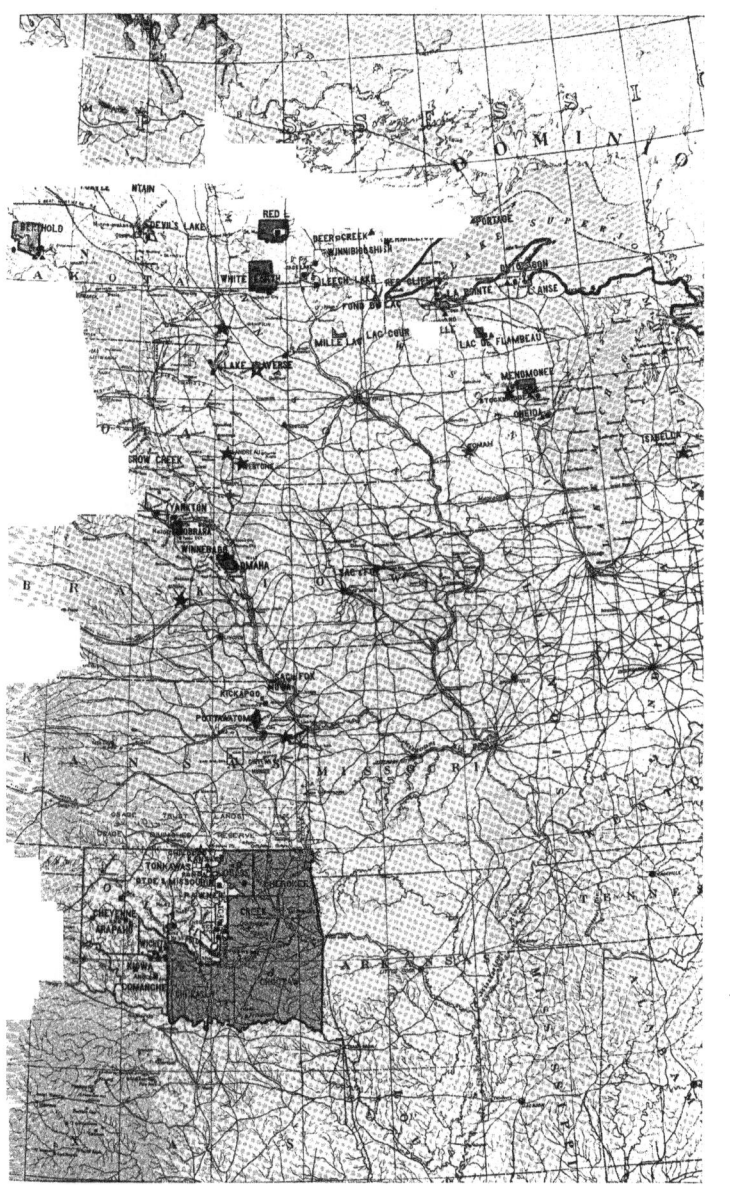

S OF THE WEST
ioner of Indian Affairs, 1907

OUR FIRST FOOTHOLD IN ALASKA

By Archdeacon Stuck

Our mission among the Indians at Anvik was our first foothold in Alaska. It was planted in 1887 by the Rev. Octavius Parker and the Rev. John W. Chapman. The latter is still our missionary at Anvik, having seen wonderful changes in the twenty-three years of his service. The following description by Archdeacon Stuck, though written some little time ago, gives a vivid picture of this interesting mission. Miss Sabine, of whom he speaks, has recently been transferred to Circle City.

THE steamboat from St. Michael's made the landing carefully in the darkness, picking up the spot with her searchlight, and a couple of deck hands leaped ashore and tied her up. A skiff was launched from the other side of the boat, into which the purser with his mail-bag tumbled, followed by me with my valises. Then the searchlight was swung around up the Anvik River and trained upon the mission landing, and a couple of the crew pulled us quickly over the intervening quarter of a mile. The mail bags exchanged, the skiff as quickly returned. There was a blast from the whistle, a churn of the wheel, a shower of sparks from the smokestack, and the steamboat was swallowed up in the night.

The next morning disclosed a beautiful situation. The wooded bluffs rise sheer from the water till the point of the confluence is well rounded; then a series of terraces breaks the abruptness of the ascent, and the mission buildings are crowded, not unpicturesquely, upon two of the terraces. Built boldly of hewn logs, with broad bases where the loose earth and rocks have been confined by timber, they have that dignity which solid construction always gives. The prospect from the mission is wide and fair, stretching many miles up the Yukon until the great river sweeps around distant palisades. To the left, the sinuous Anvik meanders about its low, green islands, with the native village in the middle distance, and the purpling mountains whence it rises closing the

view. A summer fishing camp lies i[m]-mediately before us, across the lim[i]d water, with tents that once were wh[it]e, and rows of split salmon that are [a]ll unmistakably red. Behind us the bl[uf]fs display everywhere the shimmer[in]g golden glory of the autumn birch, m[o]st beautiful of northern trees, in[te]r-mingling with the dark green of [th]e spruce.

The country is a sombre country [a]t best. For eight months in the year i[t i]s a black-and-white country. It has [it]s bursts of vernal and autumnal beau[ty]. But they do not last long. When [i]t comes to buildings, the country ne[ed]s all the enhancement that art can g[iv]e. A shingle roof with a mossy green sta[in], rough-hewn logs, or clapboards, with [a] dark-red stain, and window frames [o]f white, would speak of care and loving [in]-terest, and would set a most wonder[fu]l example to the natives. Whenever [a] native gets hold of a little paint he p[ro]-ceeds to daub it on the palings arou[n]d the family graves first, and then on [it]s front door. A little free paint and eve[ry] native village would blossom like a s[ea] anemone. Is there any generous pa[in]t dealer, of missionary impulse, w[ho] sympathizes enough with Eugene Fiel[d's] aspiration "to paint, without restrai[nt], creation redder still," to send us the m[a]-terial? Every traveller on the Yuk[on] wearied with the endless monotony [of] the prospect, would rise up and call h[im] blessed.

Anvik is our oldest mission in Alas[ka]. It has had twenty-three years of ha[rd] work, and there is much to show for [it.]

The smell, of which Mr. Spurr speaks
so strongly, is not worse at Anvik now
than at any native village. On entering any native cabin the first thing that
strikes you is the lintel of the door—and
that is no joke! I had many a bruise
before I acquired the habit of stooping.
The next thing is the smell. It is bad
enough at first, but one gets used to it
after a while. Mr. Chapman says the
smell does not bother him any more, except at Christmas time, when some of
the Eskimos from Unalaklik come
over with seal-oil, and the young men
and maidens purchase cheap perfumery
from the trader. Given a cold Sunday,
a red-hot stove and a crowded church,
says Mr. Chapman, and the normal dried
fish odor, combined with the festival
reek of the seal-oil and the perfumery,
is about as much as the stoutest
stomach can stand. He says there have
been times when he was glad that Christmas comes but once a year. After all,
there is something to be said for incense.

All the transformation that has come
to Anvik is the work of Mr. Chapman
and his assistants. If Mr. Spurr could
revisit the place he would admit that the
missionary whom he saw walking on the
beach took off his clerical coat to some
purpose. It has been a long, slow business, and it is not finished yet. I wonder
if other people realize as keenly as the
Alaskan missionary realizes, the para-
mount importance of improvement in
the conditions of life amongst the natives? We talk about their low standards
of conduct; their low esteem for female
virtue. How can it be otherwise? I
have tied myself up in a chain of deduc-
tions that is adamantine; I can see no
escape from it; I am as certain of it as
I ever was of anything in my life. Here
it is: There can be no chastity without
modesty, and there can be no modesty
without privacy. I have gone over that
again and again, and I hold that it is ir-
refragable. All the preaching and talking in the world will not have as much
effect as the providing of an opportunity
of privacy. I believe it is just as true
of the Negro in the South as it is of the

Yukon Indian in the North. I believe
it is true everywhere. Every step upward in material comfort among these
peoples renders possible a step upward
morally.

Besides the tremendous difficulties
which the character and condition of the
people imposed, Mr. Chapman's work
has suffered from numerous other drawbacks. Constitutionally, the people
seem peculiarly liable to disease, as Mr.
Spurr's description would lead one to
suppose. Twice the people have changed
the site of their village, abandoning their
old houses and building new ones, so that
now the main village is about a mile
away from the mission, but still the de-
stroying angel seems to follow them.
And the school has suffered greatly from
the many deaths among the children.

The school has suffered from another
thing—the unscrupulous competition of
the Roman Catholic mission at Holy
Cross, forty miles below. This place is
the show place of the river, and along
its own mediæval lines is admirably conducted. It has a staff of three priests,
four lay brothers and six sisters. It
has more ground under cultivation than
is under cultivation at any other point in
Alaska. It has horses and cows, a steamboat, a mowing machine and other
agricultural machinery—and there are
ninety children in the boarding-school.
I want to say everything good about
their work that I can, and there is very
much that is good. I have met their boys
working on steamboats again and again,
and I found them intelligent, well-
grounded in the rudiments of education,
writing and speaking better English
than nine-tenths of white boys of their
age, though weak enough when it comes
to figures, as is the case with most mis-
sion-bred boys. I visited the mission at
Holy Cross, and was most courteously
received. The priests struck me as
gentlemen—foreign gentlemen, of course,
for all the Roman priests I have met in
Alaska are Frenchmen or Italians.

Some time ago Mr. Chapman found
that the Holy Cross steamboat was coming up to his village, and that en-

e last of all its race—she goes from
ouse to house and sits down beside the
d aunties—they always remind me of
egro aunties--who whine and whimper
eir pleasure at her visit, and she tells
em in their own tongue of the love
f God and the wonderful things that
e has done. The children gather
und, the scrap-book is opened, and the
ctures that never fail to interest are
oduced; and while I cannot personally
stify to the contents of that black bag,
noticed that it went forth like one of
araoh's fat kine and returned like one
his lean ones. What a comforter she
! There was a poor old sick woman
o had crawled out-of-doors into the
nshine, and had built herself a little
e, and had piled up a brush wind-
reen, and there squatted, rocking and
aning. And Sister Bertha squatted
wn beside her on the ground, and took
r hand, and talked to her in her
ange, guttural vernacular—and how I
l regret that I had left my camera at
irbanks! Sister Bertha's success with
natives is the result of Sister
rtha's method, which is none other
n Christ's method—the method of
e. When she is not teaching she is
iting; and visiting or teaching I
ow that she is praying all the time.
e children flock around her, and well
y may, and even the most stolid and
len—and Anvik excels in stolid and

sullen natives (I gave one boy a quarter just to see if he would smile, and he
didn't!)—even the most stolid and sullen have a smile for her.

Fancy that dear lady keeping enough
interest in her culture and her reading
to send outside for "The Historians'
History of the World," in I know not
how many massive volumes; and when I
had pounced upon it and eaten the heart
out of its treatment of the Stuart period
(inadequate as usual) what else should
I find but Sven Hedin's latest book of
Asiatic travel! I had scarcely done the
first volume when I had to leave, but it
will be a long time before I forget the
pleasure that these new books gave me.
And fancy Miss Sabine's keeping up
like that!"

When I had finished preaching to the
natives on Sunday, with Mr. Chapman
as interpreter, he asked me to tell them
something about the natives at the other
missions, and one of their own number
interpreted while I sketched my visit to
our Yukon points last winter. But they
were especially interested in what I had
to tell them about the Tanana and the
Koyukuk Indians. They held a discussion amongst themselves after I had
done, and the upshot of it was that they
promised to give $1 apiece toward this
work at Christmas. I was very much
encouraged and pleased at this evidence
of interest and sympathy.

IN THE LAND OF THE OJIBWAYS

By the Venerable H. F. Parshall

AND of the Ojibways
Minnesota has always
been, so far as the
white man knows;
l they are names to conjure with
ch are associated with the early
istian work among those Indians.
nper and Breck, Whipple and Peake,
fillan and Appleby, each gave of his
ndid energies to build up the work
ng these red men,

First at Gull Lake in 1852, then at
Crow Wing, and after 1868 at White
Earth, the work was confined to a single
mission for twenty-five years. The Rev.
John Johnson (En-Ma-Gah-Bowh) was
the only Indian missionary. That these
early missionaries made their influence
felt is evidenced by the opposition of
the "traders." What part they may have
had in the framing of the treaty of 1855,
whereby a large tract of land was ceded

A TYPICAL INDIAN CHAPEL AT CASS LAKE MISSION

The Sunday-school is gathered in the foreground. The upper left-hand corner shows the old church; the right-hand corner the missionary, the Rev. C. T. Wright, one of our Indian clergy

to the Government with the understanding that no liquors should ever be sold within its boundaries, we cannot fully determine, but it is certain that the opposition of the traders to that part of the treaty referring to the sale of liquor was directed against the missionaries. Too cowardly to fight in the open, the traders appealed to the Pillager Indians. The bell was shot down from its place over the mission chapel and the lives of the missionaries were so threatened that it seemed the part of wisdom to abandon the mission until quiet should be restored. We can easily imagine the sense of failure with which Breck and his associates must have turned their backs upon the work for whose upbuilding they had struggled through four years. If it is given them to know of the splendid institutions built upon the foundations which they laid in Faribault in 1856, and that the bell once silenced by heathen hands is now being rung on each Lord's Day by one of those same Pillager Indians to call his people to the worship of God, they must at length understand that "God moves in mysterious way, His wonders to perform."

The policy of concentration for quarter of a century more than justified itself. Archdeacon Gilfillan came to the work in 1872. For five years he was storing up energies to meet the demands for expansion. His first task was to learn the language. His next work was to gather around him certain young men and train them for the ministry. He also prepared a Service Book that would be put into the hands of the people as they would accept it and as they could use it

Between the years 1877 and 18—several native deacons were ordained, and the work was extended to the Red Lake, Cass Lake, Winnebegosh, and Leech Lake Reservations, as also to other points on the White Earth Reservation. The chapel and school-house were placed side by side, and worked together for the uplift of these children of the forest who responded eagerly to the leadership of the "Paleface." But it was not long before the cry against "Government and

the Indian to sink into depths never
touched by him in his days of heathenism. I would not be unjust, nor would
I make sweeping charges without acknowledging that there have been some
splendid exceptions to the rule, yet we
must recognize the fact that the vast
majority of the white men who have had
dealings with the Indians have had no
reverence for God, have recognized no
law, have been profane and dishonest,
have looked upon the Indians, their persons and their goods, as their natural
prey, and have not hesitated to make
drunkards of men, women and children
in order that they might more easily rob
them of their virtue and despoil them of
their goods.

The approach of civilization has
worked other hardships to the Indian.
Many of their sugar-groves and berry
patches have been destroyed, and their
meadows appropriated by others. Under
the game laws of the State they may
hunt and fish for their own tables, but
may not offer anything for sale. To
each Indian has been allotted 160 acres
of land, but with his small knowledge,
and usually less inclination for farming,
the land represents no other value than
what he can realize from the sale of it,
or of the timber it bears. Fortunately
the right to sell does not extend to the
full-bloods, else the land-sharks would
have had it all.

I have purposely painted the dark side
of the picture first. We accept opposition as a challenge to greater activity,
and take account of the obstacles placed
in our way only that we may overcome
them. I know not one of those who are
standing on the firing-line who has ever
thought of giving up.

Three of the men who were ordained
in the '70's are still actively at work.
Only last week we laid to rest one who
for thirty years had spoken the Gospel
of Divine Love to his people. With the
exception of two men, whose impaired
health compelled their resignations, our
force of native missionaries has never
been depleted except by death.

We have now twelve chapels in which

An average congregation at the Church of St. Antipas, Redby

services are held regularly, and three other preaching stations. This work is at present in charge of five priests and one deacon working under the supervision of the archdeacon. This force we must increase as soon as possible. The call for the taking up of new work is urgent, but it must go unheeded until we are more secure in our present holdings.

The question is sometimes asked, "Are the Indian clergy really devoted to their work?" I can best answer this question by telling some things which I know to be true, and which might be duplicated many times. It was last November. A little girl was dying and wanted to see the missionary, who lived fourteen miles away. Although a fierce storm was raging, a messenger was dispatched to the home of the missionary. It was long after night-fall that the missionary returned from a trip that had entirely worn out his team. He learns of the child's sickness, stops at home only long enough to get a little food, and then sets off on foot. On his way he has to cross a bridgeless stream. Without a moment's hesitation he plunges into the water, nearly waist deep, crosses the stream, and with cloth-

ing frozen stiff goes on several mile to his destination. He reached the bed de of the child at 3 A.M. The knowlge of that experience came to me, not m the missionary, but from others. He had done what he felt to be his duty, d thought nothing more about it. he same self-forgetfulness and devotio is evident among all our missionarie in this work.

In spite of the temptations to w h they have been subjected, most of ur members have remained true to t ir Church. The services are always ll attended, and the evidences of reve t devotion are not more marked in an of our white congregations. Quick of visual perception, the Indian is by a-ture a ritualist. He seems stolid, t that is the result of his training and is environment. In reality he is emotic l, and loves expression. He believes in is religion, and he talks it to others.

In conclusion, let me say that we o know what has been, and is being, e by the Church among these poor d people, believe not only in the work, t in the people. Give the Indian a squ e deal and he will prove himself wo y of it.

SACRED TEPEE OF THE ARAPAHOES
Wherein is kept the sacred pipe called "The Chariot of God"

SOME INDIAN FOLK LORE

By the Reverend John Roberts

FORTY-TWO years ago, in the Big Horn Mountains in Wyoming, a little Arapahoe Indian boy was born. The tepee that sheltered [hi]m was pitched with others in a beauti[fu]l valley in which game and fish were [pl]entiful; and, in their season, berries [an]d roots. The Arapahoes being great [hu]nters, there was no lack of good things [to] eat at the camp-fires. They had plenty [of] buckskins and pelts to wear, and [hi]des for moccasins and tepees. One [m]ight suppose that this little Indian [bo]y had a happy home and pleasant [pla]ce to live; but it was not so, for in ad[di]tion to many other dangers there was [a] constant peril of attack from [ho]stile Indians who were hovering [aro]und. Brave and wary as the Arapa[ho]es were, many a time was the camp raided—their men killed and women and children carried off by enemies to other tribes—so that it was a fortunate thing for them when, in 1878, by the pressure of a strong military force, the United States Government compelled them to give up their roaming life in the hunting grounds, and to settle down on the Shoshone Reservation under the protection of the soldiers at Fort Washakie, Wyoming.

The little boy referred to was about six years old when he came to live on the reservation. Being a bright, thoughtful lad, the medicine men took pride in teaching him the past history of the *Henaunauānauan* (chosen people), as the Arapahoes call themselves, and all their ancient lore. The sacred order among them, the *Jenejehenane*—

(739)

An Arapahoe lad in native dress

corresponding to the Levites of the Jews,
has preserved a wonderful store of traditions that reaches back far into the dim
past. Through this sacred society he
learned that long, long ago, when the
Arapahoes lived on the "old earth," their
country was taken, they themselves cruelly treated, and their children slain by a
people they call the *Neanthan* (Gentiles,
aliens). That to escape oppression they
left the "old earth" and came to this
"new earth," crossing over on frozen
water, somewhere in the far northwest.
That while they were crossing the ice
broke up and the bulk of the tribe was
drowned; that the remnant which had
not reached the water returned whence
they came, while the few who had
reached land on this side, after bewail-
ing their great loss, continued their
journey, travelling toward the South.
(The Arapahoes call the South "Down
below"—the North "To windward.")
    They had with them in their journey-
ings only two kinds of animals, dogs
and reindeer; but as they travelled on
they found other animals, hitherto un-

ARAPAHOE SUN DANCE

gh places, of the offering of a piece
the skin of the fore-arm held up
ward the northwest, the sacred quarter
ence they came, as a ransom in case
severe illness of a son. They told him
the great sacrifice, made once in every
neration, when all the men of the
be offered themselves in solemn as-
ably, with bowed heads, before the cus-
lian of the Sacred Pipe, and one of
m was chosen by him to die for the
ple. They told him the history of
.t sacred pipe, which takes many,
ny days to tell. It is called the
eja (the flat pipe) because it is flat
appearance, and it is called *hodde*
aneauthau (the chariot of God) be-
se the spirits (shades) of dying
pahoes gazing on it are carried safe
"Our Home." It was given to the
t Arapahoe by *Hejevaneauthau* (the
ange Being on High, which is their
e for the Creator), when he created
earth. The elders told the lad that
must regard that pipe with awe, as
g most holy, for it was the token of
G's care for His chosen people, and it
h led them in their pilgrimage through
t ages. In the place where it rested
e they pitched their tents—when it
ed, they journeyed with it. At all
s, in behalf of their people, it had
rked wondrously" even to this day.
he elders told him that the *Hendu-*
inau (they cannot even pronounce

the word Arapahoe, "Nap-a-au" is the
nearest that they can come to it) were
the first created people; that for them
the earth was made. This is their story
of the Creation: In the beginning the
earth was covered by the waters of a
flood, except the topmost peak of a high
mountain, on which sat the first Arapa-

Blessing by an elder

(741)

hoe, weeping. Looking up, he saw *Jevaneauthau* coming to him, walking on the water. Being asked why he wept, he replied that he was lonely and homeless. *Jevaneauthau* then commanded a dove to find a country for the Arapahoe. Returning after a fruitless search the dove said, "The water is over all." A turtle was then bidden to go on the same quest. It dived at once into the water and presently brought up some mud in its mouth, and said, "The earth is under the water." *Jevaneauthau* then said, "Let the waters flow away to the big seas and let the dry land appear." Immediately a beautiful vision of mountains and valleys, hills and plains appeared before them, fresh and green as in spring, and He turned to the Arapahoe and said, "All this is for you and your descendants forever." Then as they walked about in this beautiful place, *Jevaneauthau* threw some pebbles in a deep lake. Seeing them sink into the depths the Arapahoe cried: "Oh, are my children to die?" To comfort him *Jevaneauthau* handed him the flat pipe, and said to him, "Preserve this most carefully, for it will be through the ages to your children during life a guide and blessing, and when they die it will carry their souls safe to 'Our Home'; and when at the last it wastes away their dead bodies will rise again, and then, with the great hosts of the dead, I, the Deliverer, will come from the Northwest to be Chief over my people for ever. Be kind to your friends, fight bravely your enemies. Farewell!"

With his mind full of such teaching, instilled into him from his earliest childhood, this Arapahoe boy one day, twenty-five years ago, stood watching the Indian pupils harvesting the grain on the school farm. Seeing a gap in the line of workers he threw off his blanket and unbidden, worked until evening. At supper time a suit of clothes was given him, his braided scalp-lock and long black hair was clipped by one of the older pupils, and he was enrolled as Michael—it being the feast of St. Michael and All Angels. He was a studious and apt pupil, but it was a long

"JAROPVILLE"

This name will not be found in the postal guides, and may never appear on any map; but here lives Jarop, and here our missionary goes on her errands of mercy

SOME OF MY UTE PATIENTS

By Mary Latimer James, M.D.

N the dry, invigorating climate of the Uintah Basin one might suppose illness would be rare. But the shiftlessness of the population, mbined with a disregard for all the ws of hygiene, including cleanliness, ake our Ute Indians a prey to all anner of disease. Even in a *wickiup* ent) it is possible to exclude fresh air d to build a hot, smoky fire that will ise the temperature to summer heat en when the thermometer outside vers around zero. Thus the germs of berculosis gain a foothold which they not relinquish during the hot summer months, when their victims naturally seek the fresh air. Diseases of the n and eyes also abound, due largely filth and contagion.

The Indians have long had a friendly ling for our missionaries out here. nsequently, on my arrival last fall, I found them far more ready to place confidence in my medicines than I had expected. Few of them can be trusted to carry out a treatment alone, but they nearly always let me do what I want to do for them.

"The box-clinic"

(743)

Little patients on the porch of the mission house

Already many are beginning to come here to be treated in the clinic, which I furnished almost entirely with cases, shelves, etc., constructed from boxes. My up-to-date, white-enamelled operating table lends a pleasing variety to the otherwise crude aspect of the room.

At present we have two little Indian patients staying with us—one with tuberculosis of the knee and the other with hip-joint disease, probably also tuberculosis. During the day they hobble around on crutches, one pair made by me from my usual source of lumber—boxes. At night one of these little girls sleeps on the porch by Miss Canfield's window, and the other in a tent close to my door. Two other Indian girls, one an orphan and one motherless, are spending the summer vacation with us.

But the greater part of my work is done in the camps. This old man, decked in feathers, is one of my special friends. One night he called me to his tent in terrible agony as a result of eye treatment from an Indian "medicine

A STURDY POLICEMAN

'He stalked proudly forth asking me to take him, and to tell people that I had made him well"

Weitch's squaw, who had trachoma for ten years

gave me another opportunity to tell the old story of the Virgin Mary's little Son, Jesus Christ, whom His Father, the Great Spirit, sent down to earth to teach men how to live and to help one another.

The Ute is so low in the scale of civilization that I fear it will take a genera-tion or two to change the tribe to any great extent. Yet it is possible even now to help these Indians a good deal in their illness and trouble, and to do a little to point them to the Saviour of the world.

mp about four or five miles from here, er a dreadful road paved with huge bble-stones, I can no longer visit her ily, as I used to do.

The chubby papoose, held up so proud-by her mother, scarcely resembles poor, little pneumonia patient whom almost despaired of last winter. For while I went to see her twice a day, ;h time scarcely daring to hope I ght find her alive when I reached re.

The group of wickiups, with sage-ish in the fore-ground and mountains the rear, is the home of several of my ients, relatives and connections of a old Indian named Jarop. One of m is Evangeline, the little girl, who, ugh so young, is the mother of a utiful little papoose. Evangeline my first Indian obstetrical case. other day her mother asked me my t name, suggesting that she give it to papoose. As my name is Mary, it

The chubby papoose who was cured of pneumonia

GLADE CROSS AND HOSPITAL

THE UNCONQUERED SEMINOLES

THE Seminole Indians, now resident in the Everglades of Florida, are the remnant of a once powerful tribe. Their origin seems to be indicated by their name. The word "Seminole" means "Seceder," and there is reason for accepting the theory that they are a branch of the Creek Nation, who left the main tribe before Indian history began to be written.

No Indian tribe has had a more gallant or a sadder history. From the beginning they withstood the encroachment of the white man, and were the victims of that terrific campaign which made a name for Andrew Jackson, but which, it is to be feared, was waged chiefly as a war of aggression, and for which even the Government of the United States—never too particular about its treatment of Indians—was unwilling to assume responsibility.

The incidents of this campaign had furnished cause for an undying enmity between these Indians and all white men,

and the smoldering fires broke out agai[n] in 1835, when the second Seminole Wa[r] was fought. In his life of Thomas [B]enton, Theodore Roosevelt says, con[n]cerning this war:

"The conflict with the Seminoles wa[s] one of the legacies left by Jackson t[o] Van Buren; it lasted as long as th[e] Revolutionary War, cost $30,000,00[0] and baffled the efforts of several gen[n]erals and numerous troops, who ha[d] previously shown themselves equal t[o] any in the world. As is usually the cas[e] in Indian wars, there had been wrong don[e] by each side; but in this instance we wer[e] the more to blame, although the Indian[s] themselves were far from being merel[y] harmless and suffering innocents. Th[e] Seminoles were being deprived of thei[r] lands in pursuance of the general polic[y] of removing all the Indians west of th[e] Mississippi. They had agreed to g[o] under pressure, and influenced, probabl[y] by fraudulent representations; but the[y] declined to fulfil their agreement. I[f] they had been treated wisely and firml[y]

As a result of this second Seminole
war a majority of the tribe were trans-
ported to the Indian Territory, where
over 2,000 of them live to-day, but a
small band defied their antagonists to the
end, and retreated into the fastnesses of
the Everglades, carrying with them few
memories of the white man which were
not associated with dread and loathing.

There they are to-day, 400 of them,
scattered through the impassable Everglades and subsisting as best they can.
These aborigines early attracted the attention of Bishop Gray, and he established a mission among them at Glade
Cross, far in the centre of the Ever-
glade country. Here we have a hospital
under the care of Dr. W. G. Godden.

These are perhaps among the most intelligent and moral of the Indian "rem-
nants" of our country. Their conversion to Christianity is said to have been
begun by a woman. A correspondent
tells us that "Miss Flossie Tippins, a
native of South Florida, and reared near
the Seminoles, married Bill Brown, an
English sailor who deserted his vessel at
Key West and landed years ago at Fort
Myers. They settled near the Indian
hunting-ground, eighty miles southeast
of Fort Myers, and opened up a small
trading post. Bill Brown and 'Queen
Flossie,' as she was called, have been
there all these years, and to-day are the
only traders that command the respect
and confidence of the Indians. Flossie
has learned their language and gained
their confidence; she found them the
only tribe of Indians who observed their
native customs and clung to the religion
of their ancestors. Missionaries had
been sent to them by Baptists, Methodists and others, but not until Flossie
embraced the Episcopal faith would an
Indian see religion in any other light
than that of their forefathers. She induced the Rev. Henry Gibbs, an English
clergyman, to accept a charge among
them, and for years he ministered to
their spiritual needs."

Mr. Gibbs's health failed, and since his
departure others have ministered to the

Seminoles; but, most of all, their friend is their bishop, who believes in them firmly, and speaks most strongly of their Christian possibilities.

It is a hard and self-sacrificing work which must be done to win them, but "the Big Man" (their designation for Bishop Gray) goes often among them. Upon a recent visit he tells us that "a congregation of more than a hundred bucks, squaws and piccaninnies were present at a service in the open air, when they not only listened to a sermon in simple and plain language, which many understood, but also witnessed the baptism and confirmation of some white candidates, there, seventy miles beyond Fort Myers. Convinced, at last, that we are not helping to have them caught and sent to Oklahoma or Indian Territory, they have had a meeting of the council, and commended us all as their *true* friends, and authorized *all who desire* to come to us for instruction, baptism and full membership. God be praised for the manifest advance! Already, a sub-chief leading the way, baptisms have commenced, and a number are being prepared for the Holy Rite of the Laying-on of Hands."

IN THE EVERGLADES

THE CHURCH AND THE IROQUOIS

By the Reverend William B. Thorn

EVERYONE knows something of that remarkable confederation of tribes whose council fires once flamed across the State of New York from the Hudson to Lake Erie. The Mohawks, Oneidas, Cayugas, Onandagas and Senecas were "The People of the Long House"—a reference to the form of their council lodges—or, as some writer has appreciatively called them, "The Romans of America."

It was among these splendid and somewhat civilized tribes, with their settled towns, palisades, forts, methods of agriculture and codes of law, that the Church began her first Indian work. The Society for the Propagation of the Gospel in Foreign Parts was but three years old when a missionary was sent, in 1702, among the *Onionta-augs*, "The People of the Stone"; or, as we have anglicized it, "The Oneidas." Seven years later we find four Iroquois sachem crossing the ocean to present an address and take belts of wampum to Queen Anne, saying, "Since we were in covenant with our great Queen's children we have some knowledge of the Saviour of the world. If our great Queen would send some to instruct us they would find

first church in the Northwest Territory, a
quaint log structure, and called it (after
their well-loved friend, the Bishop of
New York) Hobart Church. This in
time gave way to a frame building, and
that in turn to the present stately and
massive stone church, which holds 800
and is often uncomfortably filled.

The Rev. Eleazar Williams continued for some years his faithful and
self-sacrificing work among his people,
but into the quiet life of this pioneer
missionary there came the dazzling flash
of ancient royalties and the haunting
echo of past cruelties. It was no true
kindness which urged him to believe
that he was a scion of the Bourbon race.
The thought became a will-o'-the-wisp,
which he followed through an uneasy
life to an unhappy end.

After him came a line of faithful missionaries, who each in his day labored
for the Christianizing and civilizing
of the tribe. Conspicuous among these

The Cross on the Hilltop

HOBART CHURCH, ONEIDA MISSION

was the Rev. E. A. Goodnough, who for thirty-six years was their faithful friend and pastor. Under Fr. Goodnough the stone church and the mission house were built, and among the people whose loved friend he had been through so many years, his body rests in the hill-top cemetery, where practically every stone bears an Indian name.

The Rev. Solomon S. Burleson succeeded Fr. Goodnough as priest of the mission. He added to the church its chancel, and in response to an impera-

tive need built the hospital. After sev[eral] years of most arduous service—not on[ly] as priest, but as the physician of 2,0[00] persons scattered over a reservation ni[ne] miles by twelve—he succumbed to a d[is-]ease which was undoubtedly accentuat[ed] by overwork, and thus a second missi[on-]ary laid down his life for the Oneid[a] and slept on the hill-top among [his] people.

Concerning one other of the cler[gy] who have ministered to the Oneidas [I] must briefly speak. He, too, rests in t[he] Oneida burial ground, but it is the s[oil] of his fathers. Onan-gwat-go (bet[ter] known by his English name, Cornel[ius] Hill) was hereditary chief of this p[eo-]ple, and exercised great influence amo[ng] them. From the time of his young m[an-]hood he was an interpreter and catechi[st,] and under the Rev. Fr. Burleson he w[as] made a deacon. Later he was advanc[ed] to the priesthood—the first of his tr[ibe] to reach that honor. After long ye[ars] of faithful service he was called to [his] rest in the winter of 1906-7, thus closi[ng] a life devoted to the upbuilding of [his] people.

Since the death of the Rev. Fr. Bur[leson]

The Mission Hospital

The Mission House

n, in 1897, three different white missionaries have labored among these people and much material progress has been made.

*Cornelius Hill—
1st Chief and First
Priest of the Oneidas*

The Oneidas are a growing tribe. The rate of increase is not large — last year the births exceeded the deaths by fifty-four; but still it is an increase, and the Church's responsibility becomes greater each year. The official census of last year showed 2,259 persons connected with the tribe. Of these considerably over 1,200 are adherents of the Church and between 500 and 600 are active communicants.

The mission work is many-sided. The Church, of course, ministers to the spiritual needs of the Oneidas, but she seeks to advance their social interests and to help their physical wants. In the great stone church, named for the noble Hobart, there are three services each Sunday and one on Thursday. All the feasts and fasts are also observed. These services are well attended; on Sunday morning, at eleven o'clock, there is always a large congregation of earnest worshippers.

The Sunday-school is held in the Government Building. Only our own children attend, and no attempt is made to proselyte. This is under the care of the Sisters of the Holy Nativity, the missionary visiting the school twice each month, when he catechizes the pupils and gives an instruction. Religious instruction is also given, by one of the sisters, in our parish school.

The parish hall is a great factor in our work. It is the home of the guilds, the band and the library. Here entertainments are given from time to time and marriage feasts and social gatherings are held.

The hospital has been, and is, a great benefit to the people. It was built by the Rev. Solomon S. Burleson, and certainly should be sustained as a memorial to this noble man who laid down his life for his flock. At present, owing to the lack of funds, but few patients can be accommodated. We cannot go into debt. But it is hoped that in the near future some friends of the Indians, in view of the good accomplished by the institution, will rally to its support. Outdoor relief is carried on by the missionary so far as his limited resources permit. Formerly boxes of provisions, etc., were sent for the work and for the hospital, but during the past year nothing of this nature has been received.

The Guilds, Woman's Auxiliary and Junior Auxiliary meet regularly and are active and enthusiastic. The women give gladly of their time and work, making quilts and garments; these are sold to raise money, chiefly for the pledges made to diocesan and general missions.

There is a creamery in connection with the mission. This is not a good investment looked at from a business standpoint, but it helps the India. Of late years new creameries have be started around the edge of the reser tion, and ours, of course, can have o a limited patronage. It has, howev, taught the people much, and its supp t is not in vain.

The present missionary, with greatly reduced gifts, cannot carry the work as it was carried on in tir past. More funds should be placed t his disposal. Conditions are rapi changing. New needs are springing . The people are increasing in numb, and there is no corresponding incre in their resources. They look to Church for aid in their necessi. Hitherto she has not failed them; she fail them now?

The bishop-coadjutor has just mad visit to the mission and he had a delig ful day. The accompanying picture show how the Indians welcome th bishop. Nor is it by brass bands processions alone that they show th appreciation. The church was filled, forty-seven were confirmed.

ESCORTING THE BISHOP FROM THE STATION TO THE CHURCH

The Indians have what amounts to a genius for music. Instruments are handed down from father to son, and there are sometimes three generations in the same family who can play. It is not unusual at public gatherings (where the band is always present) to see one set of men lay down the instruments and another entirely new set take them up and go on, and when these are fatigued a third set do likewise

, *Special Government Agent*

yond what we now term the mission strip.

Upon the fall of the missions—that is, when the mission property was "appropriated" by the Mexican government— an attempt was made to secure to the Indians some rights in the land they occupied; but, it appears, ineffectually.

When gold was discovered in California, shortly after the American occupation, there occurred the most tremendous gold rush known in history. The exact number of the miners has not been accurately recorded. By 1852 the white population of California was supposed to be over 200,000. These were, for the most part, men, strong and masterful. Most of them had behind them the traditions of 200 years of Indian fighting, and a considerable number were under the necessity of fighting their way across the plains against some of the most warlike Indians of America. But the California Indians were not warlike. They were more nearly sedentary than any other Indians of America, outside of the Pueblos, and were a mild, inoffensive race. They made their living easily from the abundant supply of game, fish, wild fowl, native roots, fruits and various nuts, especially acorns. They had discovered how to separate the bitter principle from acorns, and the resulting meal was cooked in a variety of forms, palatable and nutritious. The miners very soon muddied the streams with their mining operations and shut off the Indians' supply of fish. Game also became scarce, and the little valleys where the roots grew were occupied by mining settlements. The agricultural lands were soon taken for grain raising, and the grazing lands for cattle and hogs. In many cases the Indians were even forbidden to pick up acorns, as the settlers desired them for their hogs. This procedure, of course, deprived the Indians of the greater part of their subsistence,

and they suffered severely—as you or I
would suffer if we lost three-fourths of
our income.

The Indians were armed only with
bows and arrows and the miners were
well armed with the best firearms of the
day. As the Indians were also heavily
outnumbered, especially in the mining
districts, their case was hopeless from
the start. Owing to the many languages
and dialects, united action on the part
of the Indians was impossible. No
general war resulted, but a great series
of skirmishes and misunderstandings
took place.

The Indians, of course, would meet any
aggression or insult in the usual
savage way, by retaliating on the first
white man whom they met; then the
miners would find it necessary to band
together and "wipe out" the offending
village. This was usually done by surrounding the Indian camp at day-break
and shooting everybody who appeared.
A man, about fifty years old, told me that
when a boy of ten he went with his parents to run cattle in a certain valley in
the Coast Range now known as Eden
Valley. There was a considerable Indian population in the valley and the
cattle-men were afraid the Indians would
run off their stock, so they sent some distance away for some Indian enemies of
the Eden Valley tribe and surrounded
the camp one morning. My informant
went along to "see the fun," as he
thought. An Indian came out of one
of the tepees and the man beside my boy-
friend shot him. The Indian gave a cry
and a leap, and fell over. Then as the
Indians poured out of the tepees they
were shot down from all sides. My informant said he saw 600 men, women
and children shot that morning, and
that he dreamed of massacres for weeks.

I have heard of one larger affair where
a punitive expedition was gotten up to
punish the Indians for the murder of
two white settlers who, according to all
accounts, fairly deserved what they got.
The punitive expedition went up into
the valley where the tragedy had occurred, but were unable to find any o
the Indians who had committed the mur-

In its dealings with the Indians elsewhere than in California the United States has recognized that they had a right to the land they actually occupied, and this right has been upheld in the Supreme Court of the United States, being termed the "Indian right of occupancy." This right has been cancelled only by payment therefor, except in California. The Government not only took the Indians' lands away without payment, but it also arranged the laws so that the Indian of California could not acquire title even to his own home, for a period of forty years after the American occupation. The Indian was not a citizen of the United States, and therefore could not homestead land. He was not an alien, and therefore could not be naturalized and acquire the right to take up land.

In 1875 an Act was passed for the purpose of allowing Indians to homestead land, but the restrictions were so many that the Act was of no value in California.

From the American occupation, in 1846, to the passage of the Indian Allotment Act, in 1887, it was impossible for an Indian in California to acquire land from the public domain, and in those sixty-odd years everything worth taking had been appropriated by white settlers, including, in most cases, the very lands which the Indians claimed as homes. At first it did not matter so much when a white settler filed on the land occupied by Indians and ejected them under due process of law, but as the years went on it became increasingly difficult for an evicted Indian to find any place where he might be welcome. There is hardly a band in Northern California that does not have its tale of repeated evictions.

The Indian was, of course, in all these years, subject to considerable race prejudice in California, and many people objected strongly to an Indian having a home, or legal rights, or school privileges; and, more strange still, to his having the right to learn of Christianity. This prejudice has moderated to a considerable extent, but it is still strong

enough to prevent an Indian from securing justice in the courts in many communities, and it still excludes more than
two-thirds of the Indian children from
the public schools, or from any schools.

For many years no missionary work
was done among the Northern California
Indians. Some fifteen years ago the
Northern California Indian Association
was organized as a branch of the National Indian Association. Its work began in a small way for one or two bands
only. Some years ago it was decided to
make a canvass of the field and find out
how many Indians there were in California, where they were located and
what their condition. The society was
appalled at the conditions revealed.

The Northern California Indians are,
for the most part, crowded into small
settlements of from twenty to 200 souls,
called *rancherias*. In these rancherias
the sanitary and moral conditions
prevailing are pretty bad. The Indians were all practically subject to
eviction at any moment, without any
apparent rights under the law, and
wholly ignored by the Christian people
of the state. Their own native religion, a form of Shamanism, has, to
a considerable extent, broken down, for
it has failed them in their hour of need.
The rising generation has little belief in
anything, and from the atmosphere of
despair which prevails in rancherias the
Indian has been truly described as a being without hope in this world or in the
next.

The Northern California Indian Association, now known as the California
Indian Association, found great difficulty in securing anyone to establish
missions or schools or do missionary or
school work among these Indians, who
were subject to eviction at any moment,
so that the work or fruit of the mission
might be jeopardized or destroyed at any
time. One of the main efforts of the
association, therefore, was to secure land
for the landless Indian, with the result
that an appropriation made by Congress
is now being expended in the purchase
of lands in small tracts for homes.

Missionary work among the Indians

he last sixty years, learned practically
othing of Christianity or the better side
f our civilization, and though he has, un-
rtunately, absorbed much of the seamy
ide of our life, he is not the absolute
avage which we meet on some reserva-
ons—or used to meet. A considerable
ortion of these Indians have adapted
hemselves in a measure to our civiliza-
on, and make their living as laborers
a civilized pursuits—usually as laborers
pon the ranches and farms. Nearly all
ppreciate the need and value of educa-
on for their children; and the majority
e willing and anxious to learn of
hristianity.

The California Indian has a very good
putation for honesty among his white
eighbors. It is almost unheard of for
a Indian to be arrested for, or convicted
, theft. He may be sent into the field
work alone, and will do his work, with-
t supervision, faithfully and carefully.

Indians do not put vines in their hops
or grapes when packing them. Indians
cutting wood can be relied on to pile
their logs fairly and honestly. There is
no class of labor in California so reliable
as Indian labor. It is a misfortune that
so few of them remain.

The Indian is naturally an intensely
religious person, and although the California Indians have, to some extent,
weakened in their devotion to their own
heathenism, those who have accepted
Christianity make Churchmen of whom
no one need be ashamed.

The efforts of the California Indian
Association to induce various Christian
bodies to enter the missionary field for
the Northern California Indians are producing some results, and it is hoped that
in a few years the entire field may be
covered and that the reproach of neglecting the heathen in our own back yard
may be removed.

JUST AN INDIAN
By the Reverend John W. Chapman

THE subject of this sketch is an
Indian. It was formerly the
custom to regard his people as
belonging in a class by them-
s ves, and as having but little in com-
1 1 with certain other well-recognized
f at divisions of mankind, as, for instance, sailors, organ-grinders and policemen, an exception being made, perhaps,
with regard to missionaries. Later on it
was discovered that there were more
points of resemblance between these different groups than was at first supposed,
and a new classification was adopted, the
greater part of mankind being separated
into two great divisions, the rich and
the poor, the Indians being assigned to
the latter class. It was felt, however,
that something was still wanting, and in
1895 a *savant* removed his pipe from his
mouth long enough to remark, in modest
appreciation of his own catholic sympathies, that he could "go" anybody but
the Chinese.

The subject being left in this somewhat unsettled condition, it is felt that
even a small contribution, serving to illustrate personal characteristics, may
help to clear the situation.

The individual to whom the accompanying picture bears a somewhat distant resemblance came in lately, as I

was having a quiet chat with a young
man who had just returned from an interesting trip through the country to the
eastward from the Yukon. He stopped
outside the window to peek in, and then
came in without knocking. Many of the
older people about us find it difficult to
acquire the habit of knocking, and to
overcome the habit of peeking.

He spoke to us. His manner was
somewhat apologetic, but not servile, and
he seemed glad to see us. He was tall
and gaunt and grizzled. His outer garment was made of bed-ticking, and he
had a piece of clothesline tied about his
waist. He had come some thirty miles.
He walked a little unsteadily, and said
that he did not feel very well, but he
often says that. He came over and sat
down near me, and then got up and
asked me how I was. His face expressed kindly feeling, and he came so
near that the thought crossed my mind
that he might be intending to kiss me,
but he sat down again.

He had some rabbits to sell, and said
that he would like to get milk for two
of them. A rabbit is worth a can of
milk. It appeared that he was not in-
dulging in luxuries for himself. He has
a married daughter who is taking care
of an infant which was exposed by its
parents, and the milk was for the baby.
His son-in-law, it seems, does not do
much for the family, and the old man
said that it had been all that he could do,
not feeling very well, to keep the baby
supplied with milk. Last fall he went
into debt with the storekeeper for five
dollars' worth of milk, but had not been
able to pay it yet, so he was going to try
to get an extension of time. That milk,
however, was gone, and that was why he
wished to sell the rabbits.

He also wished that he had some
ammunition, so that he might get some
more rabbits; but ammunition is nearly
gone now, and the best that we could do
for his muzzle-loading shotgun was rifle
primers with the little brass piece that
fits inside picked out. He did not think
that they would go very well. He used
them last year, but the constant con-
cussion of the hammer had broken the

THE RED MEN OF WYOMING

By the Right Reverend N. S. Thomas, D. D.

CHIEF WASHAKIE

JUST before his death, Chief Washakie, "the noblest Roman of them all," gave to the Church the 160 acres on which our school is located and through the kind offices of our senators and our representative at Washington, this gift was ratied by special act of Congress. A atent, granted the Domestic and Forign Missionary Society, has been sent) the Church Missions House, New ork, where it is now on file.
In the military post cemetery at Ft. Washakie there is this inscription:

WASHAKIE
1804-1900
CHIEF OF THE SHOSHONES
A WISE RULER
ALWAYS LOYAL TO THE GOVERNMENT
AND TO HIS WHITE BROTHERS

Washakie is said to have been the only Indian who was ever given a military funeral. He was buried in the military cemetery by order of the War Department, and a monument was erected by the Secretary of War.

Washakie was authorized to select his reservation as a reward for his loyalty. No one knew the ground better than he did. He chose the Wind River Reservation, because of its perfect climate and the abundance of water and grass. "A snug little nest," he called it, "for my people." It surely was. There his ponies were always fat, and there game gathered in winter for shelter, so that it was not necessary for his young men to go out into the mountains for meat. Washakie was born, not as the Secretary of War would have it, in 1804, but in 1799. He was, therefore, a centenarian. His father was a Flathead and his mother was a daughter of a chief of the Shoshones. Of all the able men who have been illustrious leaders of their

GEORGE WASHAKIE

(759)

One of the white man's lessons against which the Church has to contend.

people, whether in war or in peace, no chief ever held more complete sway than did Washakie, who was ever a friend of the Government and the Church.

There are two tribes on the Wind River Reservation, the Shoshones and the Arapahoes. Both have been under the care of our Church since General Grant's administration. As President, Grant's policy was to assign missionary work among the Indians to various religious denominations, and on different reservations. By reason of this policy, the Wind River Reservation in Wyoming was given to us, and for it we are responsible.

The Indians at present number some 1,800; and are about equally divided among the two tribes, who live apart and have nothing in common. Their languages are entirely different and they do not intermarry. They have been hereditary foes.

Some years after the reservation was laid out, the Commissioner of Indian Affairs proposed to put the Arapahoes, with Old Friday, their chief, on the

reservation. Washakie protested on t[?] ground that they were "bad Indian[?] and that Old Friday was "double-heart[?] and double-tongued" and would betr[?] the white people the first chance he h[?] The next year, as Washakie had p[?] dicted, Old Friday swooped down up[?] Miner's Delight, killed eight men a[?] wounded several others. The min[?] organized, attacked the Arapahoe villa[?] on Wind River and killed sixteen [?] them. The soldiers were compelled [?] interfere, with the result that t[?] Arapahoes were marched over to t[?] reservation, and Chief Washakie was [?] structed to look after Old Friday a[?] make him keep the peace. There w[?] about 900 Arapahoes at the time, a[?] the number has remained about t[?] same. The Arapahoes have lived [?] peace with the unwilling Shoshones, a[?] their children have been sent to the sa[?] industrial school, in charge of Major [?] E. Wadsworth.

Twenty-six years ago Bishop Spal[?] ing, of Colorado, sent the Rev. Jo[?] Roberts to this difficult, and then di[?]

OUR MAIN MISSION BUILDING AND THE MISSION HERD

ta field. A few months later the Rev. Sherman Coolidge, a native Arapahoe, was sent from Minnesota to assist Mr. Roberts in the work among the Arapahoe. Now there is a distinct division of the labor—Mr. Roberts has entire charge of the Shoshones and Mr. Coolidge of the Arapahoes.* From the very beginning it has been the policy of our missionaries to work shoulder to shoulder with the Indian agents, who in speaking in the large, have aided them in their efforts to uplift the two tribes. In addition to the Government day school, with which Mr. Roberts and Mr. Coolidge are both closely identified, we have a small boarding-school accommodating twenty pupils, called the Shoshone Indian Mission School, located on the 160 acres given us by Chief Washakie. Its work is to train the little girls too small for the curriculum of the Government school. But even should the work overlap the school would justify itself in that it is, so to speak, an anchor to windward, and by

* Since this article was written, Mr. Coolidge has moved to Oklahoma to work among his people there, and Mr. Roberts has the care of both tribes.

reason of it we can never be dispossessed of our heritage. The great need of the work has been for two women workers to follow up the efforts of the school among the young mothers—one to work among the Shoshones and one among the Arapahoes.

I am thankful to report that those two workers have been found—one of them, Miss Charlotte L. Briggs, of Marion, Mass., a trained business woman, and the summer secretary of the late George C. Thomas, will work among the Arapahoes; the other, Miss Adeline R. Ross, a graduate of Smith College and of the Philadelphia Training-school for Deaconesses, will work among the Shoshones.

In addition to this notable reinforcement the Sybil Carter Lace Association has for some months past had a representative on the ground, and the lace industry has been begun. It is hoped that this valuable adjunct of missionary work may be placed upon a permanent basis at no distant date. The great and present need of our Indian work is the support of these new workers.

Not so pressing, but equally important for the whites as well as the In-

(761)

THE REV. SHERMAN COOLIDGE

withdrew. Why, no one knew; but it was afterward said by one of the band of Sioux warriors that they supposed the villagers had been aware of the attack and had gathered in the strongest building of the place to withstand it.

Thus it happened that had not the bishop been present and the town people at church they would all have been massacred. No work so evident and signally blessed by God can fail of success.

But may our hospital come so. There is no hospital within a radius of 200 miles in any direction, save at Casper, more than 100 miles to the eastward.

In no spot in this, the least developed of our states, is a hospital so needed

dians upon the reservation is the building of our hospital in Lander. Unless some individual desires to make a memorial of this hospital, and therefore retains the privilege of giving it a name, it will be called the "Bishop Randall Hospital."

It was at Lander that Bishop Randall made his last visitation: It was a most difficult journey from Denver to Lander by stage—as far as from Boston to Washington, or thereabouts; but in the dead of winter the exposure must have been dreadful. It caused the death of the good bishop.

The place is further dedicated to his memory by a most remarkable event. On the bishop's first visitation, I have been told, his path into the town was lined with human heads from which the scalps had been recently torn. Services were held in the log church, which lies just behind the present Church of the Redeemer. During the services the Sioux attacked the village, but after encircling the church and delivering a running fire upon the building they

REMAINS OF THE SUN-DANCE TEPEE

In the background Bishop Thomas, the Rev. Sherman Coolidge and the Rev. Dr. Scher

VIEW FROM "THE WINDOW'

A bit of natural scenery near Fort Defiance, Arizona

GLIMPSES OF LIFE AT THE NAVAJO HOSPITAL

By Elizabeth W. Thackara

N the early days of the Hospital of the Good Shepherd the Indians used to bring their sick (those who were not able to ride on horse-) on litters made of poles. One er afternoon four Indians came, ging on one of these litters a boy of ve years. They had walked fully 100 s. The boy had hip disease and was st pitiable object. He remained at hospital for four years, so that he sixteen when he left—eight years g

ce a year his father came to visit him and was very glad that his boy had gotten almost well, and proud that he had learned to speak English and could read and write. It also pleased him that his son had become a Christian and was baptized.

Ya-Kee (the small boy) was the pet of the household. The older boys and men called him *Char-don-nay* (my little brother-in-law), which was expressive of their affection. He was very fond of a joke. One of the Indians on going to bed put his shoes near at hand. He occupied a small room by himself, the

A TYPICAL NAVAJO HOGAN

Yakee and his father

door being carefully locked and only th[e]
small transom left open. The next morn[n]-
ing one shoe was missing. Later in th[e]
day, after much search, it was found fa[r]
away under the wood-pile. How was i[t]
possible that the shoe got there! [A]
Chindi (a devil) must have taken it ou[t]
for was not the door locked? A medicin[e]
man was consulted, who took the sho[e]
away for a season to make it all righ[t]
before the owner could wear it agai[n]
The charge was "fifty cents." A wee[k]
or so later *Ya-Kee* showed how he ha[d]
gotten the shoe out through the tran[-]
som, while the Indian slept.

Dear *Ya-Kee* was most anxious to b[e]
allowed to go to school. It was the grea[t]
desire of his heart, and we—he and I—
used to talk about it. His father, he wa[s]
sure, would consent. *Ya-Kee* was ex[-]
pecting his father to come soon and [it]
would then be decided. The Fourth [of]
July came, but *Ya-Kee,* strangel[y]
enough, was late for breakfast. Whe[n]
he came in it was remarked how badl[y]
he looked, though he said there wa[s]
"nothing the matter." Immediately afte[r]
breakfast an Indian woman appeared [

prayers for their sick; and I thought it was their own form of prayers for which he asked. It happened at that time that a very noted medicine man was also at the hospital under treatment, who was an old friend—possibly a connection—of the family, and I thought the poor husband wanted him to be permitted to come in. "Yes," I said, "if you wish." "No," the old Indian said, "we want you to make the *Christian* prayers for her, as you make them every morning; all the days I have been here I have followed *very hard* the Christian prayers."

And so, all kneeling, we "made them" for her.

"OLD SINGING MAN"
He was lately at the hospital and successfully operated on for cataract. In spite of his forbidding appearance Miss Thackara says he was "a pleasant old patient"

CHIEF RED HAIL

*To his earnestness and devotion is due the building of St. Gabriel's Church. He refused to
content until he had secured for his people a Tipi-Waukan (House of God)*

AMONG THE SIOUX AT RED HAIL

By the Reverend John J. Cowan

HAD a strange white man, a few
decades ago, alighted on the
spot where Red Hail Camp
now is, on the banks of the
Cannon Ball River, and beheld the old
warrior, Chief Red-Hail, a battle-scarred
survivor of more turbulent times, with
his son, No Cow-Tail, surrounded by
Grey-Bear, Iron-Shield, Red-Eagle, Iron-
Rod, Shoot-Many, Red-Bull, Sea-Walker,
Bear-Paw, White-Cow-Walking, and
others, all in solemn conclave assembled,
he might have been pardoned for beating
a hasty retreat to a safer place. Yet

here they all were, in this year of g[...]e
1910, with pitched tents, in solemn [...]-
sembly, just as in former times, but [...]a
different business. It was the an[...]l
Christian convocation of the Sioux [...]-
dians of North Dakota.

After a drive of forty miles from [...]e
nearest railway station, the bishop [...]-
rived on Thursday, July 14th. Eac[...]f
the four days of convocation [...]e
crowded with services and meetings [...]a
business character. It is interestin[...]o
record that all the arrangements pert[...]-
ing to entertainment and business [...]e

de by the Indians themselves, and
it well they did the work.

ach evening after sunset informal
ices were conducted by the Indians
heir own language. In the centre of
stockade-line enclosure was a tall
staff, at the top of which floated a
with a large cross; around this the
ians squatted, as is their custom, the
along one side of the circle, the
en on the other. There was no
bting the earnestness of the speakers,
iously appointed. In eloquence rare
ny language—in terms teeming with
tion for the Gospel, they paid their
ute and rendered homage to their
our.

n Sunday morning the bishop con-
fied nine Indians and one white youth,
an the convocation closed in the after-
no with the farewell service to the bishop,
w h the Indians requested permission
to hold. This informal service was
to thing in its simplicity. Prayers were
of ed for his safe return home; the
bi op's buggy was brought to the en-
tr ce of the enclosure by William Cross,
th faithful Indian "coachman" who
cl s the right to drive the bishop on
hi Indian visitations, and before start-

ing on his long return journey each Indian was in line to shake the bishop's
hand and wish him "God speed."

These Sioux Indians appreciate what
is being done for them by their priest—
and he does more than will ever be recorded. To meet the expense of the convocation the sum, of $359.67 was sub-
scribed, and nine head of cattle were
given for provisions—all by the Indians
themselves.

¶

THE comprehensive plan for the conducting of mission study classes
under the direction of the Junior department in connection with its meetings in Cincinnati will do much to aid
the Board in stimulating missionary
study while there is as yet no Educational Secretary. It is hoped that many
will try to take advantage of this opportunity. The classes will be normal, intended to train the members for carrying on work in their own localities. The
leaders, who have all received a special
training in the work, have already
demonstrated their fitness by their success.

ST. GABRIEL'S CHURCH, RED HAIL
Where the services of the Convocation were held

MISSIONS IN THE SUNDAY-SCHOOL

THIS Department is created because of an expressed need which it will endeavor to fill. In steadily increasing numbers, letters come to the Church Missions House asking for detailed information about the study of missions in the Sunday-school. Rectors and Sunday-school leaders begin to see that not only does the future life of the Church depend on the leaders and members who are now being trained in the Sunday-school, but they also see that in the missionary motive, and in the history and description of missionary work, there is material not only helpful, but *essential* to the education of Christian character and the development of loyal Churchmen.

The Situation

This new demand within the Church is part of a national demand. In North America there are 15,000,000 scholars enrolled in Sunday-schools. It takes but little vision to imagine what advance might be made in the near future if that large army of young life could be equipped to meet with intelligence and enthusiasm the problems of the Church of to-morrow. In the Sunday-schools of the Church are 430,000 scholars and 35,000 teachers. These constitute our responsibility and our opportunity.

Our Aim

As soon as we ask the question: *How can the study of missions become a factor in the educational work of the Church?* it becomes clear that the greatest care and wisdom must be exercised in determining an answer. The question throws us into an uncharted educational sea. The deepest currents of the missionary motive in the individual are unknown. The power of the missionary enterprise as a world movement has not been estimated. Much depends on experiment. We must wait patiently for further development in child study. We must have a care that we do not over-emphasize passing motives and the im-

mediate events that interest us, ... these motives and events have no ... manent educational value. To gai... the wisdom which separates the trans... from the permanent factors in mi... study, must be the constant pray... of him who would use missions as an du... cational implement.

A cut-and-dried missionary cu... lum, providing material for every g... de, is quite impossible to-day. Stories... pictures and models to interest an in... struct the different grades have ... en provided; but let no one be dec... ed into thinking that these "put mis... ns into the Sunday-school." No Chr... ian educator will content himself in ... us touching the fringe of a great o... or-tunity. The student of missions i... the Sunday-school can have no smalle... im than the study of the beginnings o... the missionary motive in the child's lif... nd the right nourishment of that m... ve. This means the study of the hea... life of the child—that life in which a ... n-taneous and joyous sympathy in ch... ish things is intended by God to be ... el-oped by life into a joyous servic... nd sacrifice for His Kingdom.

First Steps

While this Department starts w... a high aim, it will endeavor to mee... m-mediate needs. (1) The first nece... ry step is to rightly understand the ... ed for mission study in the Sunday-sc... ol. Distinguish clearly between *intere... ng* scholars in pictures and tales of ... o-ism, and *educating* scholars in the ... is-sionary motive. Send to the Educat... nal Department, Church Missions Hous... 281 Fourth Avenue, New York, for... he pamphlet, "The Necessity for Mi... on Study in the Sunday-school." This ... n-tains a "Missionary Policy for the ... n-day-schools of the Episcopal Chu... h," This policy should be studied ... nd adapted, and then studied again b... he teachers and officers of the parc... ial school. Besides the policy, the pam... let contains three articles on the prin... les

stated intervals, the classes of the whole school, or of certain departments, are brought together in the church. Missionary hymns are sung, missionary addresses are made and a missionary catechism is recited.

(3) *The Weekly Missionary Address*—Each. Sunday the rector or superintendent, or some person prepared, tells a missionary story.

(4) *The Monthly Lesson*—One session is given each month to a definitely arranged series of lessons. The teachers are specially prepared by teachers' meetings. Books, pictures, scrap-books, etc., are provided.

(5) *The Weekly Ten-Minute Lesson*—Many teachers, with the consent of the rector, are using the last ten minutes of each period for a missionary story, or for the study of work in the field. Valuable use is made of the illustrated pamphlets published by the Board of Missions. Good lessons have been arranged by using the pictures and material published in current numbers of THE SPIRIT OF MISSIONS.

(6) *A Year's Course*—Some schools have found it wise to give a whole year to mission study. The subject fits the adolescent years of fourteen or fifteen, and has held many disappearing classes. Definite courses have been provided for this method.

RY LESSON

older grades emphasize the assignments and supplementary reading, but do not consider seniors and adults above the use of the scrap-book in some form.

These lessons contemplate a forty-minute period. This may be secured by giving one entire session each month to missions; or by dividing the material into four sections and spending ten minutes on each section each Sunday.

All teachers are advised to master the material and teach without notes.

Necessary Material The following should be secured by each teacher:

(a) Each issue of THE SPIRIT OF MISSIONS.

(b) Outline map of Western Hemisphere. A good assignment can be made by having a scholar trace a map from his school geography.

(c) A blank book for a class scrap-
book. Best size is 6¾ x 8¼
inches. Use an ordinary book,
and if the scholars take an interest, promise to have it bound
in covers when the lessons are
completed. This book can be
loaned to the sick of the parish
or sent to the hospital. Scholars
should be encouraged to bring
for this class scrap-book any
pictures or clippings that bear
on the subject.

(d) Pamphlets from the Church Missions House. For these address: Educational Secretary,
281 Fourth Avenue, New York.
Titles and numbers will be given
one month in advance.

Point of Contact On the Sunday before you begin this
course say to the
class: "An event of great importance is
now taking place at Cincinnati. Who can
can tell me what it is, and something
about it?" (Change the question to present, past or future as may be necessary.)
Many scholars will know about the Convention, but incomplete answers will be
given; therefore, assign the question to
one member of the class, and ask for a
short report next Sunday. To two other
members give these questions, asking for
reports: Who attends the Convention?
What meetings attract the largest au-
diences? Reports may be written ot
oral.

The Lesson The following Sunday
go to the class with
the pictures here
given cut out ready for mounting in the
scrap-book, and with any other material—
pictures or clippings—you may have collected. Have the aim clearly in mind:
*I am going to try to make real to my
class the missionary aspect of the General Convention, and to open their minds
to the extent of the mission work of the
Church.* Begin the session by asking for
the first report. Draw out and centre
attention upon the representative character of the Convention. "Our diocese
is represented by whom?" Draw out
names of diocesan bishop and the delegates; have pictures of each, if possible.
Impress that the whole American
Church is assembled and acting by representatives. With the second question
emphasize the presence of missionary

reason for the Convention, and the Board and the raising of the money by the whole Church. (2) Promise the next lesson as follows: "Let us suppose that Bishop Johnson, of South Dakota, asked the Board for $37,000 for work among the Indians in his diocese. The Board grants his request. In the next lesson we will follow the bishop to his diocese and see him working to do his part in carrying out Our Lord's Command."

At the conclusion of the lesson have the scholars mount the pictures in the scrap-book. Let them suggest the order. See that the outline map is first and that the journey from New York to Cincinnati is marked out.

Pamphlet to be used in connection with next lesson: Number 620.

Lesson I.   Picture 3

THE CHAPEL
Church Missions House, New York City

Lesson I.   Picture 4

THE BOARD ROOM
Church Missions House, New York City

A BANNOCK CAMP

OUR INDIAN WORK IN IDAHO.

By Bishop Funsten

ABOUT ten years ago the Board of Missions accepted a transfer from the Connecticut Indian Association of the property which they held on the Fort Hall Reservation in Idaho. This mission consisted of a frame dormitory and mission rooms, and 160 acres of sage-brush land. This was situated at Ross Fork, and the tribes among whom the work had been carried on were the Shoshone and Bannock. These people were at that time mainly living in tepees, doing very little cultivating of land; very indifferent to all improvement, and slow intellectually. They still kept up many of their wild, savage customs and costumes. They had advanced little in the knowledge of the Christian religion, and seemed very suspicious of any strangers, and of any effort by our missionaries.

We opened our school under some earnest missionaries, and gathered as many children as we could take care of in the small frame building that was already in existence. That work has been going on for years, with many changes in the *personnel* of our teachers. A good many Indians have been baptized, and some confirmed, and many have passed away. Meanwhile pupils have grown up and married, and the work has assumed new aspects. The Indian people themselves are awakening to the necessity of being instructed in religious truth, as well as in the ways of the white man. A generous family in Virginia have erected a neat little church near the Mission, where we have services conducted by clergymen from the neighboring towns. The Government has er[??]te its schools not far away, and our [??] sionaries have full access to the chi[??]re being trained in the commodious [??]ild ings at that point. We have a grea[??]op portunity of reaching a needy peop[??] i we now awaken to our responsi[??]ty The children are eager to get int[??]th mission school, and we have nee[??] o capable and consecrated missionari[??] t supply the vacancies that come in so[??]ff cult and discouraging a work. I [??]v secured a clergyman and his wife to [??]k up residence at the mission and [??]ke complete charge of the important [??]rk of leading these pagan people [??]m darkness to light.

The work is hard and discoura[??]ng. It is lonely and depressing to be o[??]on an Indian reservation, and in con[??]nt contact with the degradation and [??]is ease, with the ignorance and sup[??]ti tion, with the poverty, suffering [??]nd death that one sees on all sides. [??]ly brave-hearted, consecrated Chri[??]an people will continue at such a post,[??]nd carry on such a work. Surely they [??]ve a right to be sustained and supporte[??]by proper equipment. We need a small [??]s pital where the sick may be cared [??]r, and where the ravages of disease m[??]be prevented. It is sad to see a p[??]le among whom consumption is doing [??]ch a deadly and yet preventable work.[??]If we carried out our real mission [??]we would not only teach these Inc[??]ns about the blessedness of life beyond[??]he grave, but show them how to [??]ve practical, useful, clean lives in [??]is world.

NEWS AND NOTES

THE eighteenth annual session of the Colored Convocation of Southern Virginia met at Lynchburg on July 25th-27th. The sessions were well attended, only one of the clergy being absent, and he unavoidably so. Southern Virginia has the largest work among negroes of any southern diocese, and Archdeacon Russell, who under the bishop is the leader in the work, has cause to rejoice in its success. The address of the archdeacon—who in the absence of either bishop presided over the Convocation—was filled with excellent and practical suggestions for the furtherance of the general work. An intimation of what their congregations expect from our Negro clergy is contained in the following paragraph:

As a rule the Episcopal minister is expected to know something about any movement for the betterment of all the people with whom he comes in contact. He is expected to know very much about diseases and their cures, and so he is frequently appealed to by the poor in times of sickness in order to save life—as well as a doctor's fee. He is considered no less a wise counsellor, and is, therefore, eagerly sought after, at times when the meshes of the law gather about those who either ignorantly or wilfully disregard the principles of propriety and decency. He is consulted by the farmer as to the time of planting and the proper method of cultivating the crops grown in his community; his advice is sought by the mechanic and the business man. Hence the minister is to be little short of a walking encyclopedia, full of, and ready to give out, information on all topics."

¶

The Rev. Pierre E. Jones writes concerning the work at Constard, on the island of Haïti:

ON the 6th of August, 1903, the missionary and his family were stoned and driven away by the enraged mob of Romanists and heathens that took "counsel together against" the message of the Gospel. To-day the same missionary sees "the travail of his soul." One hundred and twenty men and women, besides their children, are worshipping the Lord and praising Him for His love toward the children of men. The very spot from which the missionary was driven away seven years ago has been purchased and consecrated to the service of the Living God by the laying of the corner-stone for the erection of church, school and parsonage. The Roman archbishop, who never thought of this place, has just sent his priests to destroy our mission by building a church in our neighborhood. If they build before we do, we shall have to abandon the place, as we were compelled to do at Eaugeau eight years ago. Now, what is to be done? We have done our utmost in beginning the building. Must seven years of continuous prayers and work be all in vain? Nay, the Lord, who has brought from darkness to light those 120 persons will not forsake them. From His treasure He will send us the means, through His servants whom He has blessed with the silver and gold which are His.

¶

A mutual friend of Miss Emberley and Miss Johnston, the first of whom is retiring from, and the latter taking up work at Fairbanks, Alaska, sends us the following information:

MISS EMBERLEY and Miss Johnston made a phenomenal trip into Alaska. They must have made the best possible connections at every point. The last letter from Miss Emberley was dated Skagway, July 28th, and she said they had several hours there and at Wrangell; for which she was glad, as it gave her an opportunity to introduce Miss Johnston to the workers at those places. A telegram from Miss Emberley stated that they arrived safely at Fairbanks, August 5th, and that she was to be married at St. Matthew's Church on the evening of August 6th, by the Rev. Charles W. Peabody, to Mr. Roy C. Hall.

BISHOP AVES writes under date of June 16th, telling of the death on the 11th of the Rev. Genero Melendez, one of our native priests. "Mr. Melendez," he says, "was one of the most active and successful of our younger clergy, and greatly beloved by his Indian congregations, to whose physical as well as spiritual welfare he devoted himself with assiduous, self-denying zeal. While visiting with me recently the mission at San Miguel el Alto, during an epidemic of typhus fever and small-pox, Mr. Melendez spent almost the entire night ministering to the sick and dying. Though not a regular physician, he used his little knowledge as best he could for the relief of the great numbers who, because of their extreme poverty, could have no other; and he will be sadly missed as a true and faithful pastor. His work was growing. At my last visit to El Oro there were nearly one hundred men in the congregation; and after the service they presented me with a petition to accept them as a mission and to allow the Rev. G. Melendez to minister to them.

"It is a grave question how we are to continue this good work, for by the death of three of our native clergy during the past two years our strength has been sadly reduced, and during the same period the field has been expanding by a steady natural growth."

ANNOUNCEMENTS

CONCERNING THE MISSIONARIES

Alaska

THE REV. CHARLES E. BETTICHER, JR., on furlough, left Fairbanks in July and reached his home at Haverford, Pa., on August 10th.

MISS MABEL H. PICK, deaconess, who sailed from Seattle by the steamer *Cottage City* on August 1st, arrived at Wrangell on the 6th.

MISS CLARA C. JOHNSTON left Boston on July 18th; sailed from Vancouver for Skagway by the steamer *Princess Royal* on July 23d, and arrived at St. Matthew's Hospital, Fairbanks, on August 5th.

MISS ISABEL M. EMBERLEY, whose resignation was accepted by the Board on April 12th, left Boston July 18th and was married to Mr. Roy C. Hall on August 6th in St. Matthew's Church, Fairbanks.

Brazil

BISHOP KINSOLVING, coming to attend the General Convention, with his wife and daughter, left Rio Grande do Sul July 8th, sailed from Rio de Janeiro by the steamer *Vasari* on July 18th and arrived at New York on August 3d.

THE REV. W. M. M. THOMAS, on furlough, with his family, sailed by the same steamer. His address is Pearson, Md.

THE REV. GUIDO A. ZUMBUHL was advanced to the priesthood in Rio de Janeiro on July 3d.

Cuba

THE REV. DAVID W. BLAND, who was appointed on April 12th, with his wife left Camden, N. Y. on August 17th and sailed from New York by the steamer *Olinda* on August 24th for Guantanamo.

Hankow

THE REV. T. P. MASLIN, on regular furlough, with his wife and two children sailed from Shanghai by the steamer *Empress of China* on June 28th, arrived at Vancouver on July 17th and proceeded to Alameda, Cal.

THE REV. FREDERICK G. DEIS, who was appointed May 10th, with his wife left Oshkosh, Wis., on August 9th and sailed from San Francisco by the *Tenyo Maru* on the 16th.

THE REV. ROBERT A. GOODWIN, JR., whose appointment took effect on June 1th, left his home at Richmond, Va., July 15th and sailed from Vancouver by the steamer *Empress of India* on August 17th.

DR. JOHN MACWILLIE, returning after furlough, with his wife and family left Toronto on August 8th and sailed from Vancouver by the same steamer.

MISS EMILY L. RIDGELY, deaconess, who was appointed on June 14th, left Trenton, N. J., on August 27th and is to sail from Vancouver by the steamer *Empress of Japan* on September 7th.

MISS SUSAN H. HIGGINS, returning to duty after furlough, left her home at Gholden, Pa., on August 11th and is to sail from Vancouver by the same steamer.

MISS SARAH E. HOPWOOD, whose appointment took effect on May 31st, left her home at Bridgeport, Conn., on August 27th and is to sail with Miss Higgins.

Mexico

THE REV. AND MRS. LELAND H. TRACY sailed from New York by the steamer *Antilles* on July 9th and, after spending a few days with Bishop Aves in Texas, arrived at Chihuahua on July 23d.

Shanghai

BISHOP GRAVES, coming to attend the General Convention, sailed from Shanghai by the steamer *Empress of India* on July 19th, arrived at Vancouver on August 6th and reached his home at Geneva, N. Y., on the 12th.

THE REV. DR. F. L. H. POTT, returning after furlough, left Wappingers Falls on August 11th and sailed from Vancouver by the steamer *Empress of India* on the 17th.

THE REV. ROBERT E. BROWNING, who was obliged to return to the United States on account of illness, sailed from Shanghai by the steamer *Empress of China* on June 28th, arrived at Vancouver on July 16th and proceeded to Portland, Ore.

THE REV. THOMAS K. NELSON, whose appointment took effect June 17th, left his home at Blacksburg, Va., on August 7th and sailed from Vancouver by the steamer *Empress of India* on the 17th.

MR. MONTGOMERY H. THROOP, on leave of absence for one year to take a special course at Yale University, left Shanghai by the steamer *Mongolia* on July 8th, arrived at San Francisco on August 4th and reached his home at Albany, N. Y., on the 10th.

MR. TRACY R. KELLEY, who was appointed on May 10th, with his wife sailed from San Francisco by the *Tenyo Maru* on August 16th.

DR. FRANCES F. CATTELL, who left New York on July 4th and sailed from San Francisco by the steamer *Manchuria* on the 12th, was married to the Rev. Benjamin L. Ancell, of Yangchow, on the 30th, at Yokohama, Japan.

The Philippines

BISHOP BRENT, coming to attend the General Convention, sailed from Southampton by the steamer *George Washington* on August 3d and arrived at New York on the 10th.

THE REV. JOHN A. STAUNTON, JR., and wife, who sailed from Manila on June 4th by way of the Suez Canal, arrived at New York by the steamer *Prinz Friedrich Wilhelm* on August 29th.

MRS. C. RADCLIFFE JOHNSON and son, who sailed from San Francisco May 3d, arrived at Manila on June 10th.

Tokyo

BISHOP MCKIM, coming to the General Convention, with his wife and two daughters sailed from Yokohama by the steamer *Minnesota* on August 20th, which is due to arrive at Seattle on September 3d. They will proceed to Nashotah, Wis. They were accompanied by Mrs. George Wallace, who brought the body of Mrs. A. D. Cole, her mother and Mrs. McKim's mother, for interment at Nashotah.

THE WOMAN'S AUXILIARY

To the Board of Missions

ST. LUKE'S MISSION BUILDINGS

THE YEAR AT ST. LUKE'S, WHIRLWIND

By Harriet M. Bedell

THIS has been a year of many discouragements on account of inefficient help; but our blessings have more than balanced the discouragements.

The school has been larger than ever before and for the first time the Indians have been enthusiastic in helping to spread Christ's Kingdom among their people and also among other nations. They themselves paid the apportionment and $10 for the work in Oklahoma; the Sunday-school sent $18 to the Board for General Missions, besides having collections at Sunday and Holy Communion services toward the current expenses of the mission. This is not much, but it shows a great step in advance. As Bishop Brooke says, "Heretofore they seemed to have no thought of giving, but rather of what they could get."

When I gave out the boxes at the beginning of Lent I at first gave to those only who I thought would be willing to give. This proved to be a mistake. Mrs.

Warpath came in, "You didn't [give] Bessie a box"; Mrs. Chicken Ha[wk], "Where's Paul's box?" etc. I rep[lied] that I would give out the others [in] school, so the next day I gave e[very] child a box, and every one came b[ack] with with an offering. In one family of [five] children even the baby had to have a [box].

The Guild met every Thursday [to] make bead-work for the new ch[apel], which we need so much. We hav[e a] large box full of work ready to [sell]. These meetings were always attractiv[e to] me. The women came in their bri[ght]-colored gowns with flowing sleeves. T[hey] are not used to sitting on chairs [or] benches, so there were groups here [and] there on the floor. I cut out wh[at I] wished them to make, but they m[ade] their own designs and chose what co[lors] they liked. As a result we have real [In]-dian things.

The Indians have learned not to [dis]-turb me in school except in case [of] illness, but after school they often c[ome]

dians were coming toward the trees near
the mission house from all directions.
There was beef with rice and raisins,
beans, bread and coffee. After prayers
and addresses the feast was soon an event
of the past. After visiting a while
everybody left pleased, to go to their
own allotments.

The scholars remain in Whirlwind all
winter, seldom asking to go, but immediately upon the close of school they
are gone.

Through the kindness of the Indians'
Hope I have a little tent, saddle and
bridle, and after a few days' rest I go
with Bishop Brooke to Chilocco Indian
Government boarding-school, where we
have about a hundred members; then
with David and his wife visit Indians,
staying a day or two in the different
camps. At Deer Creek I have been
promised a large gathering and the Indians are all delighted with my little
tent. David conducts the services in
Cheyenne direct from the Prayer Book.

This past year we have had several
baptisms but only four confirmations,
but these four are most valuable to us
and were won only through prayer, it being hard for them to give up many old-
time customs. When Mrs. Chicken
Hawk stood before the bishop great
drops of perspiration were on her fore-
head and temples. I believe she is very

ON THE WAY TO GUILD MEETING

much in earnest. Several times she has come to tell me how happy she is. "I'm happy now—different way. I will try to keep in the Jesus' road," etc.

During the year we have received many splendid boxes, so that our store-room is pretty well supplied. Every box contained things that were a real help. We have now plenty of material and shirts for the boys for the opening of school and also winter dresses and un-derwear. I have been supplied with all I asked for and more, and am most grate-ful. We receive regularly a number of magazines for our reading room, which is open every night after chapel until nine o'clock. The young people in the camp thoroughly enjoy this, for in many of the homes there is no light save from the fire in the ground, and the reading-room does away with much of the camp loafing. When we are finished with the magazines we send them to our white

neighbors living seven or more mil[away, who lease the Indian lands. Th(in turn promise to send them on.

Another year I hope our industri work may be resumed. This consists (teaching the girls who come to the hou: in turn every day to do the work th; each day brings and taking charge (the sewing-class and helping the gir with their dresses, etc. No one need l afraid of the Indians. Our mission beautifully located, the work is extrem ly interesting, and I have hardly know a sick minute since I came, though never worked so continuously or hard b fore. The climate is delightful, and don't see why it should be difficult to g(anyone to live here. While we are som what isolated from white people we nev(get lonesome, and can always drive town, which is about nine miles awa: Do what you can to get the helpe: needed.

THE STORY OF A PONCA INDIAN GIRI
Told by Herself
[A paper read by Mrs. Amos Ross at a meeting of women held on April 20th, 1910, at Sioux Falls, S. D.]

My dear Friends:

I FEEL grateful for the privilege of being allowed to say a few words in memory of our late beloved Bishop Hare.

I have known Bishop Hare for a great many years. The first time I saw him was when he came to Ponca Agency. I was at the missionary school then with my brother and sister. The Rev. Owen Dorsey and his mother had charge of the mission house then. I remember the first time the bishop asked us our names and we hardly answered him, as we did not know how to talk English then. He was very much pleased to see us. At that time a lady by the name of Miss Annie Baker taught the school. She is now Mrs. Gregory. After she left, Sis-ter Mary and Miss Ives came there to do missionary work. Sister Mary was the teacher and Miss Ives had charge of the work.

Bishop Hare was our guardian. I 1873 Sister Mary and Miss Ives wei placed in charge of Santee Mission an the bishop sent for us to go there, : we went and stayed with them at tl mission house. St. Mary's School we not built until the next year. When was done, they placed just a few gir there. I was one of the first girls th; went to St. Mary's School. I did n(go to school very long, as Mr. Ross use to come and see me quite often. Sist(Mary and Miss Ives told me that M Ross was a good man and they wei willing for me to marry him. Bisho Hare confirmed me before I was ma ried. In 1877, Mr. Ross was made de(con and helped the Church at Santee f(a while.

In 1880 Bishop Hare sent word to M Ross to come up to Pine Ridge to d missionary work and teach school. O our way to Pine Ridge, we stopped ε

Rosebud and attended the first convo-
ation held there by Bishop Hare. As
it was necessary for Mr. Cleveland to
leave, bishop requested us to take
charge of the mission at Rosebud for
two months. At the end of that time
we went on to Pine Ridge. Of course I
was very young then, with two small
children, Joseph and Oliver. We were
stationed at Wounded Knee. When we
first went to Wounded Knee, the In-
ans were wild yet, but they were glad
to see us and gave us a hearty welcome.
Mr. Ross taught school week-days, be-
ides doing missionary work. Every-
ing was new to the Indians then, and
they did not seem to realize what going
to church meant. Some old men would
sit there and smoke, while others would
be sleeping. Some evenings Mr. Ross
would try to teach them to sing Church
hymns in Indian, which they thought
very amusing. I always remember Hymn
No. 73 (Bethany) was the first one Mr.
Ross tried to teach them. Some of those
people that Mr. Ross taught at that time
are still living, and they are the best
church members we have.

The bishop wrote to us often and tried
to encourage us in every way. He used
to visit around once a year. He always
said when he came, "Mrs. Ross, I am
very glad to come to your house again."
I'm not a very fine cook, but he always
said he liked my cooking. He always
liked the jelly I make and so I used to
give him some. I am proud to say that
he asked me to mend for him twice.

The Indian men at that time did not
haul wood as they do now, and did not
believe in packing it, so the women used
to pack it on their backs. We had no
team yet, and Mr. Ross made a little
hand sled on which he hauled wood and
water for us to use at the house. I did
not try to have any women's meetings
yet because it seemed almost impossible
to get them together, but, as it was a
Government day-school, there was dress
material sent out there to them for the
children, and I used to cut out dresses
for the girls and tried to fit them on,
but I had a hard time, as they did not

want to take off their shawls, but they
soon got over it.

We stayed there for three years, then
we had a reason to go back to Santee,
so we went, as bishop let Mr. Ross go
back. After we got back to Santee,
bishop wanted Mr. Ross to take charge
of the church at Howe Creek, known as
"Blessed Redeemer." We were there for
a year, and in 1885 bishop asked Mr.
Ross to go back to Pine Ridge again.
He said the people out there were in the
dark yet. Then we came to Medicine
Root and took charge of St. Barnabas's
Church, which had just been finished.
The people were very glad to have Mr.
Ross there and helped cheerfully in the
Church work. They had already started
the women's meetings before we came,
so that made it easier for me. We were
at this station for six years. When the
trouble in 1890 and '91 occurred, it was
thought best that I should return to
Santee for a while. Mr. Ross stayed
at Pine Ridge. After the battle of
Wounded Knee the wounded and dying
were placed in our church at the agency.
Bishop came to visit and comforted the
poor people, staying with them for two
days. He also wanted to find out the
cause of the trouble and talked with the
agent in charge as to the best things to
be done. In 1892 bishop sent Mr. Ross
to Corn Creek to take charge of the
eastern half of the Pine Ridge Reservation, the Rev. Charles Cook having the
western half. We were stationed at the
Inestimable Gift Church, this being the
centre of all chapels and stations in his
district.

The women's meetings are well attended, and we hope they may do better
yet. We have been on the Pine Ridge
Reservation for thirty years now and I
do not know how much longer we will
stay. Mr. Ross and myself are now getting old, but we enjoy the Church work
as much as ever. God knows what is
best for us and may spare us a few more
years, but we cannot tell. We notice
a great difference for the better from
what was when we first came. There
are many Christians, but I think it is

THE UNITED GUILDS OF SANTEE BEFORE THE EDITH FRANKLIN MEMORIAL HOUSE

all Bishop Hare's work. I think the bishop was a great man and always think that he saved many souls and always did his duty wherever he was, and I know our dear Bishop Johnson will do the same. But now our good bishop is taking his much-needed rest, we all ought to try to follow his good example and keep up the good work which he started.

I attended the mission council here last October, but sorry to say, I missed some of the women's meetings. This the first white women's meeting I attended. I did not think I could get and talk in English, and so I have written down what I have to say this time.

I wish to say before I sit down what Sister Mary and Miss Ives said me about Mr. Ross being a good man was true, and I feel that I owe it them that I became a minister's wife.

I shake hands with you all. I remain your sister in Christ,

LUCY ROSS.

THE UNITED GUILDS OF SANTEE AGENCY
SOUTH DAKOTA

IN response to an inquiry with regard to the united guilds of Santee Agency, Mrs. William Holmes, wife of the Indian missionary at that place, writes us:

"I will send you a picture of the Edith Franklin Memorial House, and the United Guilds. The United Guilds select officers in April, at the agency church There are only three officers, president secretary and treasurer, one officer from each guild, and every year they change This year the agency has the treasure

"The United Guilds have service

ST. JOHN'S MEMORIAL CHURCH, CAMBRIDGE, WHERE THE CONFERENCE MET DAILY
IN THE EARLY MORNING

alf-past ten, in the church. The Rev.
[r. Holmes, the Rev. Mr. Saul, and Mr.
eorge Lawrence, catechist, and Mr.
arker and Abraham and Chapman,
ilpers, are present. After the singing
id prayers, if there is time, they all
ve us a short address, and before we
ng the last hymn the treasurer takes up
e offering. There is a United Offering
x and all the offering goes for that.
ometimes it is five dollars, and some-
nes six, and sometimes less.
The men come with their wives. Some
the people come twenty miles, some
teen, some seven, to attend this meet-
g. After the service we have a dinner
epared by the agency guild. They
ve two long tables; the men sit at one
d the women at the other. After din-
r is over they pile up the dishes and
women have their meeting. They
en with a hymn and creed and prayers,
d a chapter from the Bible, and then
president makes an address, and then
l-call, and then they pass the plate
und again, for there are always some
e, and then they count the money, and
secretary writes it down in her book.
en they vote on the time of the next
ting. Then the president calls upon
e of the women to make short ad-
sses; sometimes five or six women will
ak. They close with a hymn.

THE CAMBRIDGE
CONFERENCE

*How It Appealed to a Junior
Officer*

PERHAPS the most vivid impression of the conference was that
of opportunity—it was almost a
keynote. Those who met there
came with the idea that they were determined to make the most of those days.
It was distinctly a conference of hard
work. The few who came not knowing
just why, soon caught the spirit, and the
earnestness of purpose in each and every
member was very striking. Could any
one begin those days as we did with a
daily attendance at the Holy Eucharist
and not feel that there was given to us
an opportunity to look deeper into our
souls and to offer ourselves afresh that
in us might be accomplished His will in
whose Name we were gathered? And
then in each class was borne home again
to us the opportunity for the Church
and for us the privilege of service. In
the Bible study, the first hour, the revelation—God speaking at sundry times
to His people and using all things to accomplish His purpose; next, the study

of the work still to be done, and lastly,
the goodly heritage come down to us.

The conferences in the afternoon and
evening were perhaps the least helpful
part, as most of them had not been sufficiently planned out and prepared for;
there were two striking exceptions here,
however. One felt all through those days
that there were so many people with
whom one would like to share the privileges, so many whom one longed to have
there. Is there not some way by which
we can let more people know what a
power and strength the conference will
give them in their work, so that they can
already be planning to come next year?

The conference of 1910 is past in one
sense, yet it is surely very present in the
hearts and minds of every one of its
members and very much in the future in
its results. They will go on, reaching
for some unto the uttermost parts
of the earth in the insight they
there obtained of spiritual things and
the truth of the message they carry
with them to their field of active service,
and for all is a truer realization that
each day brings an opportunity to serve
and that the field is within as well as
without, at home and abroad, and that
the work is not ours and is successful
only in so far as we make our wills
obedient to the will of God.

Perhaps I ought to say the conference
meant so much to me that I cannot
really write any adequate impression.

A FIELD OR A FORCE?

A JUNIOR leader preparing for a
study class asked advice of a
mission study class leader. "The
first thing to decide," was the
answer, "is whether your future class is
to be a field or a force." In other words,
was the work to be done in and for the
members of the class, or were they to receive that they might pass on to others?

No one doubts that there is more inspiration in preparing a force than in
simply working a field. A study class
leader has hardly a more delightful
thought than to let her imagination

Before prayers informal conferences, on the United Offering, the Woman's Auxiliary and its Junior Departmnent, Missionary Information and Gifts, will be held; at one session a Question Box will be conducted, at two there will be a gathering of secretaries, at another of missionaries, and after prayers the missionary bishops in turn will address the Auxiliary. These sessions will close with a Review of the Triennial and a Quiet Hour.

On arrival in Cincinnati, go to Auxiliary Headquarters and register, stating the diocese from which you come, your address in Cincinnati, and, if a diocesan officer, your office in the branch. It is suggested that diocesan officers provide themselves with a bit of purple ribbon, one inch by four and a half, stamped with the name of their diocese.

THE UNITED OFFERING DAY

ON account of local conditions the date of the United Offering day has been changed, and it is to be Saturday, October 8th. At eight o'clock the Holy Communion will be celebrated in Christ Church and the United Offering will be made. In the afternoon the general meeting will be held in the Music Hall.

HOW ONE DIOCESAN OFFICER LOOKS UPON HER WORK

I AM looking forward to the Triennial services and meetings, my first attendance at such gatherings, with the greatest pleasure and expectation of receiving new inspiration and intelligence in the work which grows upon me day by day, and week by week. The possibilities of it are tremendous and sometimes overwhelming in the sense of responsibility that underlies it all. I wish I could make others feel as I do the opportunity and privilege of service for the Master offered by Auxiliary work. The vision and the joy of service are the two things I like to dwell upon.

ACKNOWLEDGMENT OF OFFERINGS

Offerings are asked to sustain missions in thirty missionary districts in the United States, Africa, China, Japan, Brazil, Mexico and Cuba; also work in the Haitien Church; in forty-two dioceses, including missions to the Indians and to the Colored People; to pay the salaries of thirty-two bishops, and stipends to 2,253 missionary workers, domestic and foreign; also two general missionaries to the Swedes and two missionaries among deaf-mutes in the Middle West and the South; and to support schools, hospitals and orphanages.

With all remittances the name of the Diocese and Parish should be given.

Remittances, when practicable, should be by Check or Draft, and should always be made payable to the order of George Gordon King, Treasurer, and sent to him, Church Missions House, 281 Fourth Avenue, New York.

Remittances in Bank Notes are not safe unless sent in Registered Letters.

The Treasurer of the Board of Missions acknowledges the receipt of the following from July 1st to August 1st, 1910.

* Lenten and Easter Offering from the Sunday-school Auxiliary.

NOTE.—*The items in the following pages marked "Sp." are Specials which do not aid th* Board *in meeting its appropriations. In the heading for each Diocese the total marked "Ap." is th* amount *which does aid the Board of Missions in meeting its appropriations. Wherever the abbrevia* tion *"Wo. Aux." precedes the amount, the offering is through a branch of the Woman's Auxiliary.*

Home Dioceses

Alabama

Ap. $291.89 ; *Sp.* $3.08 '

HUNTSVILLE — *Nativity*: Wo. Aux., Gen.	10 00
MINTER—The Misses Lockwood and Miss Reynolds, Gen.	2 00
MOBILE—*All Saints' S. S.*: Gen.	34 89
*Christ Church S. S.**: Gen.	100 00
St. James's: Work in Porto Rico, $3; Brazil, $12	15 00
Mrs. Ripley, Gen.	5 00
Mrs. William A. Gould, Gen.	1 00
MONTGOMERY—*St. John's*: $51.50, Wo. Aux., $50, Gen.	101 50
Mrs. J. J. Mayfield, Gen.	5 00
TALLADEGA—*St. Peter's*: Gen.	7 50
WHISTLER—*St. Paul's*: Gen.	10 00
MISCELLANEOUS—Babies' Branch, Sp. for font, for Alaska	3 08

Albany

Ap. $516.35 ; *Sp.* $49.74

ALBANY—*All Saints' Cathedral S. S.**: Gen.	54 52
St. Andrew's: "A Friend," Gen.	5 00
St. Paul's: "A Friend," Mexico.	50 00
St. Peter's: "A Friend," Sp. for Church Extension Fund, Porto Rico, $10; S. S., Gen., $33.46	43 46
BURKE—Mrs. E. C. Wiley, Dom. and Frn.	15 00
CAMBRIDGE—*St. Luke's*: Gen.	15 78
CATSKILL—*St. Luke's*: Gen.	2 00
CHAMPLAIN—*St. John's*: Gen.	13 32
CHERRY VALLEY—*Grace*: Gen., $1.30; S. S.,* Frn., $7.25	8 55
COHOES—*St. John's*: Gen.	11 95
COOPERSTOWN—*Christ Church*: Gen.	57 20
ILION—*St. Augustine's S. S.**: Sp. for Rev. J. M. Cuthbert, St. Mary's, Kyoto	39 74
MADRID—Miss Zella B. Stevens, Bishop Rowe, Alaska	1 50
MALONE—*St. Mark's*: Gen.	60 00

POTSDAM—*Trinity Church S. S.**: Gen.	25 0
SALEM—*St. Paul's*: Frn.	21 0
SARATOGA SPRINGS—*Bethesda*: Dom. and Frn.	58 0
SCHENECTADY—*St. George's*: Miss M. A. Towell, Gen.	5 0
Mrs. A. Van Nostrand, Gen.	5 0
SIDNEY—*St. Paul's*: Gen.	14 0
TROY—*Ascension*: Men's Union, Gen.	30 0
St. Barnabas's: Gen.	5 0
WALTON—*Christ Church*: Dom.	15 0
WESTPORT—Mary Caroline Keith Hayner, Gen.	10 0

Arkansas

Ap. $26.00 ; *Sp.* $11.00

CAMDEN—Mrs. A. A. Tufts, Gen.	5 0
LITTLE ROCK—*Trinity Cathedral*: P. K. Roots, Sp. for Church Extension Fund, Porto Rico	10 0
P. K. Roots, Gen.	20 0
Miss Mary Knox Gatlin, Junior Aux., Gen.	1 0
MARIANNA—*St. Andrew's*: Dudley S. Clark, Sp. for Church Extension Fund, Porto Rico	1 0

Atlanta

Ap. $208.48

ATLANTA—*Incarnation*: Gen.	40
St. Paul's: Gen.	25
CALHOUN—*St. James's*: Gen.	2
CARROLLTON—*St. Margaret's*: Gen.	2
CAVE SPRING—*Church of the Good Shepherd*: Gen.	2
COLUMBUS—*St. Christopher's*: Gen.	3
Trinity Church: Gen., $5; Wo. Aux., Caroline Day-school, Shanghai, $50.	55
DECATUR—*Holy Trinity Church*: $4.50, S. S.,* $21.48, Gen.	25
EAST POINT—*St. Paul's*: Gen.	5
EATONTON—*All Angels'*: Gen.	3
MARIETTA—*St. Barnabas's*: Gen.	1
MILLEDGEVILLE—*St. Stephen's*: Gen.	30
NORCROSS—*St. Thomas's*: Gen.	5
UNION POINT—*Mission*: Gen.	4
WASHINGTON—*Church of the Mediator*: Gen.	5

Chicago

Ap. $1,078.06 ; *Sp.* $235.03

AURORA—*Trinity Church* : Wo. Aux.,
Gen. 1 00
BELVIDERE—*Trinity Church* : Wo. Aux.,
Sp. for St. Elizabeth's Hospital
Building Fund, Shanghai......... 6 59
All Saints' : Wo. Aux., Gen........... 2 00
Ascension : Wo. Aux., Gen........... 2 00
Atonement (Edgewater) : S. S.,* Gen. 50 00
Christ Church (Woodlawn Park) :
Gen. 50 00
Epiphany : "H.," Gen.............. 2 55
Grace : Wo. Aux., "J." (In Memoriam).
St. John's School, Cape Mount, Af-
rica, $40 ; "Frank" scholarship, St.
John's School, Cape Mount, Africa,
$40 ; Sp. for St. John's College,
Expansion Fund, Shanghai, $100... 180 00
Church of the Good Shepherd : Wo.
Aux., Gen........................... 2 00
Holy Cross : Frn.................. 7 00
Incarnation (Fernwood) : "M.," Gen.. 1 00
Church of Our Saviour : Wo. Aux..
Gen. 2 50
St. Ambrose's : Wo. Aux., Gen....... 1 00
St. Andrew's : Wo. Aux., Gen......... 10 00
St. Bartholomew's : Wo. Aux., Gen.... 17 08
St. James's : Dom. and Frn., $205.32 ;
Morning Primary and Afternoon Sun-
day-school, Children's Birthday Of-
fering, Sp. for Bishop Graves, Shang-
hai, $7.44..................... 212 76
St. Philip's : Wo. Aux., Gen......... 1 00
Miss Marion P. Warren, Gen....... 10 00
Mrs. W. C. Wheelock, Gen......... 5 00
J. F. Pendleton, Gen.............. 5 00
Miss Agnes E. Kraft, Gen......... 1 00
EVANSTON—*St. Luke's* : Dom. and Frn.,
$26.50 ; Sp. for St. John's Univer-
sity, Shanghai, $2 ; Wo. Aux., Gen.,
$10 .... 38 50
GALENA—*Grace* : Wo. Aux., Gen...... 2 00
GLENCOE—*St. Elizabeth's* : Wo. Aux.,
Gen. 7 00
HIGHLAND PARK—*Trinity Church* : Gen. 58 00
HINSDALE—*Grace* : Gen., $58.53 ; Sp.
for St. Luke's Hospital, Shanghai,
$5 .... 63 53
LA GRANGE—*Emmanuel Church* : Wo.
Aux., Gen., $10 ; Junior Aux., Sp.
for Miss Stewart's work, Hankow,
$5 .... 15 00
LAKE FOREST—*Church of the Holy
Spirit* : Dom., $50 : Gen., $389.58.. 439 58
MAYWOOD — *Holy Communion* : Wo.
Aux., Gen...................... 1 00
OTTAWA—*Christ Church* : Wo. Aux.,
Gen., $1 ; Sp. for Bishop Rowe,
Alaska, $2..................... 3 00
STERLING—*Grace* : Wo. Aux., Gen.... 2 00
STREATOR—*Christ Church* : Wo. Aux.,
Gen. 1 00
MISCELLANEOUS — Wo. Aux.. Dr.
Myer's work, Shanghai, $6 ; Sp. for
American Church Institute for
Negroes, $25 ; Sp. for St. Paul's
College, Tokyo, $25 ; Sp. for Build-
ing Fund, St. Elizabeth's Hospital,
Shanghai $57 (of which from offer-
ing of Quiet Hour, $7, offering of
annual meeting, $50)............. 113 00

Colorado

Ap. $137.56

BOULDER—Mrs. Robert Fenton, Gen.. 1 00
CANON CITY—*Christ Church* : Junior
Aux., $7.88, A. R. Livingston, $15,
A. P. Livingston, $25, Gen........ 47 88
COLORADO SPRINGS — *St. Stephen's* :
Dom. and Frn.................. 16 63

DENVER—*St. Barnabas's*; Gen....... 47 05
St. John's: "A Member," Gen........ 15 00
 Mrs. Alfred Brown, Gen........... 4 00
PUEBLO—*St. James's* (Bessemer): Frn. 5 00
 Mrs. Joseph A. Hill, Gen.......... 1 00

Connecticut

Ap. $2,418.42 ; *Sp.* $175.00

BRIDGEPORT—*St. George's*: Gen...... 10 00
St. John's: "Glover Sanford Memorial"
 scholarship, St. Margaret's School,
 Tokyo 12 50
BRIDGEWATER—*St. Mark's*: Gen...... 40 76
DANIELSON—*St. Alban's*: Gen....... 40 25
EAST HADDAM—Rev. Dr. F. C. H.
 Wendel, for Bishop Rowe's work in
 Alaska, $1; Bishop Roots's work in
 Hankow, $1.50; Mrs. F. C. H.
 Wendel, Sp. for Archdeacon At-
 wood's work in Arizona, $2........ 4 50
FORESTVILLE — *St. John's Mission*:
 Gen. 14 00
GREENWICH—*Christ Church*: $48, E.
 M. C. Leonard, $15, Sp. for Expan-
 sion Fund, St. John's University,
 Shanghai 63 00
HARTFORD—*Christ Church*: "J. E. K.,"
 Sp. for Rev. R. E. Wood, Wuchang,
 Hankow, for purchase of land...... 5 00
St. John's: Frn................... 113 40
Trinity Church: "A Member," Gen.... 1,000 00
 Mrs. J. Garrett, Gen.............. 5 00
 Mrs. A. C. Goodman, Sp. for Expan-
 sion Fund, St. John's University,
 Shanghai 100 00
 "S. M. B.," Gen................... 50 00
IVORYTON—"A subscriber to THE
 SPIRIT OF MISSIONS," Gen......... 15 00
LITCHFIELD—*St. Michael's*: Wo. Aux.,
 Mrs. F. M. McAllister, Gen........ 5 00
LONG HILL—*Grace*: Gen............. 12 88
LYME—"A Friend," for the services of
 a nurse for one day.............. 2 00
MIDDLETOWN—Miss E. A. Barry, Gen. 10 00
 Mrs. A. D. Medlicott, Gen......... 5 00
MILFORD—*St. Peter's S. S.*: For Alaska 2 60
MYSTIC—*St. Mark's*: Gen........... 12 00
NAUGATUCK—Mrs. Maria N. Pond,
 Gen. 5 00
NEW BRITAIN—*St. Mark's*: Gen..... 10 00
NEW CANAAN—*St. Mark's*: Gen...... 219 06
NEW HAVEN—*St. James's* (Westville):
 Gen. 15 75
Trinity Church: Miss Sarah G. Hotch-
 kiss, for medical work among women
 and children in China............ 50 00
 Miss Jane N. Bishop, Gen......... 20 00
NEW LONDON—*St. James's*: "Lega,"
 Gen. 10 00
NEW MILFORD—*All Saints' Memorial*:
 Gen. 130 00
St. John's: Miss Lena A. Botsford,
 $3.75, C. Elmer Beach, $1, Gen.;
 Girls' Friendly Society, for work
 among children in Alaska, $2.44.. 7 19
NORFOLK—Elizabeth V. Sage, Gen.... 10 00
NORWALK—*St. Paul's*: Gen......... 62 87
PORTLAND—*Trinity Church*: Dom..... 56 25
RIDGEFIELD—Mr. Albert N. Stone, Gen. 5 00
SALISBURY—*St. John's*: Gen........ 2 00
SHARON—*Christ Church*: Gen....... 61
SHELTON—*Church of the Good Shep-
herd*: In memory of Elizabeth Sea-
 bury Nichols, Gen................ 10 00
SOUTH KENT—Mrs. R. J. Boyd, Gen.. 2 00
SOUTH NORWALK — *Trinity Church*:
 Bethany Guild, for "Bethany" schol-
 arship, St. Margaret's School, Tokyo 25 00
STAMFORD—James H. Burdick, for
 work in St. Matthew's Mission,
 Alaska 1 00
 Miss Susan Leeper, Gen........... 1 00
 Miss L. Le Roy, for settlement house
 work, Manila..................... 5 00
STRATFORD—*Christ Church S. S.*:

Gen. ....
TARIFFVILLE—*Trinity Church*: Gen....
TASHUA—*Christ Church*: Gen......
THOMASTON—*Trinity Church*: Gen....
WALLINGFORD—*St. Paul's*: Gen......
WASHINGTON—Mrs. Orville H. Platt,
 Gen. ....
WESTON—*Emmanuel Church*: Gen....
WINDSOR—*Grace S. S.*: Sp. for child's
 bed, St. Luke's Hospital, Ponce,
 Porto Rico.......................:....
YANTIC—*Grace*: Gen...............
MISCELLANEOUS—In memory of Mr.
 John G. Floyd, Gen...............
"W.," Gen...........................

Dallas

Ap. $76.05

ABILENE—*Heavenly Rest*: Gen......
BROWNWOOD—*St. John's*: Gen......
CORSICANA—*St. John's*: Dom.......
DALLAS—*Incarnation*: Juniors, No. 1,
 Gen. ....
FORT WORTH—*St. Andrew's*: Dom. and
 Frn. ....
Trinity Church: "A Member," Gen..
 Mr. Rochester Haddaway, Gen.....
MISCELLANEOUS—Junior Aux., Gen....

Delaware

Ap. $89.00 ; *Sp.* $31.50

MIDDLETOWN—*St. Anne's*: Gen., $6;
 Junior Aux., Mountain District of the
 South, $2 ; Gen., $5.............
NEWARK—*St. Thomas's*: Junior Aux.,
 Gen., $1 ; Sp. for Bishop Rowe,
 Alaska, $2.......................
 Miss Fannie L. Shapleigh, Gen.'....
NEW CASTLE—Mrs. H. H. Hay, Gen..
REHOBOTH—*All Saints'*: Gen.......
SMYRNA—*St. Peter's*: Junior Aux.,
 Mountain District of the South, $3 ;
 Sp. for Bishop Rowe, Alaska, $2...
STAUNTON—*St. James's*: Gen., $25;
 Junior Aux., Mountain District of the
 South, $1........................
WILMINGTON—*Calvary*: Junior Aux.,
 Mountain District of the South.....
Holy Trinity Church: Junior Aux.,
 Mountain District of the South.....
St. John's: Junior Aux., Mountain Dis-
 trict of the South................
Trinity Church: Junior Aux., Moun-
 tain District of the South.........
MISCELLANEOUS—Junior Aux., "Bishop
 Lee" scholarship, St. Andrew's Sem-
 inary, Mexico, $16.50 ; Sp. for Miss
 C. J. Neely, Tokyo, $5.50 ; Sp. for
 Rev. E. L. Woodward, Anking, Han-
 kow, $13; Sp. for Rev. S. H. Littell,
 Hankow, $9......................

Duluth

Ap. $13 79

DULUTH—*St. Paul's*: Wo. Aux., Gen..
 "C. A. K.," Gen..................
GLENWOOD—*St. Paul's*: Gen........

East Carolina

Ap. $35.00

BEAUFORT Co.—*St. James's* (Bel-
 haven): Gen......................
HYDE Co.—*St. George's*: Gen.......
WILMINGTON—*St. Mark's S. S.*: Gen..
 "A Friend," Gen..................

Easton

Ap. $99 69

CECIL Co.—*St. Stephen's* (Earleville):
 Junior Aux., for "Shasi Day" schol-
 arship, Hankow, $10 ; Bishop Hare,
 Indian, South Dakota, $2..........
CECIL Co.—*St. Mark's S. S.* (Near
 Perryville): Gen..................

Indianapolis

Ap. $318.10 ; *Sp.* $10.00

ALEXANDRIA—*St. Paul's* : Gen........	2 00
ATTICA—*Grace* : Gen..............	4 00
COVINGTON—Mrs. T. Q. Brookes, Gen..	1 00
CRAWFORDSVILLE—*St. John's* : Frn....	2 00
ELMWOOD—*St. Stephen's* : Gen.......	5 00
FRANKFORT—*St. Luke's* : Gen........	3 00
INDIANAPOLIS—*Grace* : Men's Auxiliary Association, Gen.................	147 07
St. Alban's : Gen.................	3 00
St. Paul's : Gen..................	25 00
St. Philip's : Gen................	14 00
JEFFERSONVILLE—*St. Paul's* : J. V. Reed, Sp. for Church Extension Fund, Porto Rico...............	10 00
MT. VERNON—*St. John's* : Gen.......	3 00
MUNCIE—*Grace* : Gen.............	25 00
PRINCETON—*St. Andrew's* : Gen......	80
SHELBYVILLE—*Christ Church* : Gen....	3 00
TERRE HAUTE—*St. Luke's* : Gen.......	3 20
St. Stephen's : Gen..................	72 03
Wilbur O. Jenkins, Gen............	5 00

Iowa

Ap. $203.98

CEDAR RAPIDS—*Grace* : Gen.........	46 05
CHARITON—*St. Andrew's* : Gen.......	48 67
CLINTON—*St. John's* : Gen..........	16 06
INDEPENDENCE—*St. James's* : Gen....	17 20
Wo. Aux., Miss Babcock's salary, Tokyo, $8 ; Gen., $5 ; Junior Aux., Gen., $5...................	18 00
IOWA CITY—Wo. Aux., Miss Babcock's salary, Tokyo...................	10 00
OSKALOOSA—*St. James's S. S.** : Gen.	48 00

Kansas

Ap. $517.81 ; *Sp.* $52.00

ATCHISON—Sarah G. Walton, Settlement House, Manila..............	10 00
CHANUTE—*Grace* : Gen.............	8 80
CHERRYVALE—*St. Stephen's* : Gen.....	2 70
EMPORIA—Mrs. O. B. Hardcastle, Gen.	5 00
FORT RILEY—Gen...................	11 50
FORT SCOTT—*St. Andrew's* : Ladies' Guild, Gen....................	5 00
FRONTENAC—Gen.	1 50
INDEPENDENCE—*Epiphany* : Gen.......	12 24
JUNCTION CITY—*Covenant* : Gen......	16 00
PITTSBURG—*St. Peter's* : Gen.........	3 11
TOPEKA—*Grace* : Frn..............	64 00
WAMEGO—*St. Luke's* : Dom. and Frn..	11 00
WICHITA—*St. John's S. S.* : Sp. for "Honolulu" scholarship, for Hannah Cummings and Bishop Restarick...	40 00
MISCELLANEOUS — Wo. Aux., "Bishop Thomas Memorial" scholarship, St. John's University, Shanghai (of which Juniors, $5), $50 ; Gen. (of which Juniors, $12.95, Babies' Branch, $6), $316.96 ; Sp. for Bishop Nelson, Atlanta, Georgia, scholarship in school for poor whites, $12.	378 96

Kansas City

Ap. $382.55 ; *Sp.* $156.50

CARTHAGE—*Grace* : Through Wo. Aux., Frn.	10 00
KANSAS CITY—*Grace* : Frn., $56 ; Wo. Aux., Gen., $27.75 ; S. S.,* Gen., 50 cts.	84 25
St. Augustine's : Wo. Aux., Gen., $5 ; Sp. for Bishop Rowe, Alaska, $2....	7 00
St. George's : Gen.................	25 00
St. John's : Wo. Aux., Gen.........	2 00
St. Mary's : Wo. Aux., Sp. for St. Mary's-on-the-Mount, Sewanee, Tennessee, $25 ; Sp. for Rev. A. DeR. Meares, Biltmore, for church building, Asheville, $2.50..............	27 50
St. Paul's : Wo. Aux., $25, Junior Aux., $5, Gen...................	30 00

Trinity Church: Wo. Aux., $20, Junior Aux., $10, Gen. ... 30 00
MARSHALL—"A Friend," Gen. ... 3 50
ST. JOSEPH—*Christ Church*: Wo. Aux., native Bible-women, Wusih, Shanghai, $50; Juniors, Gen., $7.50. ... 57 50
SPRINGFIELD — *Christ Church*: Gen., $18; Junior Aux., Gen., $6; Sp. for Bishop Aves, Mexico, $2. ... 26 00
MISCELLANEOUS—Wo. Aux., "Margaret Atwill" scholarship, Girls' High School, Kyoto, $50; Gen., $42.82; Sp. for "Mary F. Eaton" scholarship, Honolulu, $50. ... 142 82
Junior Aux., Sp. for Edward Atwill Nearing Memorial, for educational work in Mexico. ... 65 00
"Little Helpers'" kindergarten, Akita, Tokyo, $10; Gen., $8.48; Sp. for hospital, Raleigh, North Carolina, $3; Sp. for children's ward in Chinese Hospital, San Francisco, California, $4; Sp. for missionary font, Sewanee, Tennessee, $1; Sp. for Emergency Fund, Whiterocks, Utah, $2 ... 28 48

Kentucky
Ap. $349.25; *Sp.* $5.00

BOWLING GREEN—R. W. Covington, Gen. ... 5 00
HENDERSON—George Lyne, Gen. ... 3 00
LOUISVILLE—*Advent*: Gen. ... 3 00
Christ Church Cathedral: Mrs. Sidney Hewett, Indian. ... 3 75
Grace S. S.: Gen. ... 25 00
Church of Our Merciful Saviour: Gen. ... 12 00
St. Andrew's: Gen., $150; Mrs. C. C. Mengel, Gen., $75; J. C. Loomis, Sp. for Church Extension Fund, Porto Rico, $5; Wo. Aux., "Nellie Rogers Robinson" scholarship, St. Elizabeth's School, South Dakota, $60; Brazil, $12.50. ... 302 50

Lexington
Ap. $14.50

DANVILLE—*Trinity Church*: Gen. ... 2 50
Mrs. J. R. Cowan, Gen. ... 10 00
FRANKFORT — Miss Lillian Lindsey, Alaska ... 2 00

Long Island
Ap. $802.24

BROOKLYN—*Ascension* (Eastern District, Greenpoint): Rev. J. A. Denniston, Gen. ... 1 00
St. Matthew's: Gen. ... 3 00
Grace (Heights): Gen. ... 150 00
Church of the Holy Comforter: Gen. ... 1 00
St. John's: Gen. ... 5 00
St. Luke's: Dom. and Frn., $100; Mrs. W. H. Bolton, Gen., $10; "Anonymous," Dom. and Frn., $50. ... 160 00
FLUSHING—*St. George's*: Gen. ... 114 04
GREAT RIVER—*Emmanuel Church*: Gen ... 75 00
ISLIP—*St. Mark's*: Gen. ... 100 00
MASSAPEQUA — *Grace*: $100, Chapel, $10, Dom. and Frn. ... 110 00
MERRICK—*Church of the Redeemer*: In memory of "C. N. K.," Gen. ... 50 00
MINEOLA—*Nativity*: $7.42, S. S.,* $6.24, Gen. ... 13 66
RICHMOND HILL—*Resurrection*: Gen. ... 14 54
MISCELLANEOUS—Rev. W. H. Weeks, Gen. ... 5 00

Los Angeles
Ap. $184.05

LA JOLLA—Mrs. E. C. Rock, Gen. ... 5 00
LOS ANGELES—*Christ Church S. S.**: Gen. ... 117 70
Epiphany: Gen. ... 41 85
Miss Oma Cooke, Gen. ... 5 00

SANTA BARBARA—Mrs. Hannah Ude, Gen. ...
SIERRE MADRE—Mrs. M. A. Webster, Gen. ... 1

Louisiana
Ap. $143.81

CROWLEY—*Trinity Church*: Gen. ...
DONALDSONVILLE—*Ascension*: Gen. ... 1
HOUMA—*St. Matthew's S. S.**: Alaska, $23.89; Porto Rico, $9.75; China, $4.02; St. Luke's Hospital, Shanghai, $4.84; Miss Suthon's work, Kyoto, $8.78. ... 5
LAUREL HILL—J. B. McGehee, Gen. ...
MONROE—*Grace*: Gen. ...
NEW ORLEANS — *Annunciation*: Gen., $25; Wo. Aux., Miss Suthon's salary, Kyoto, $1.65. ... 2
Christ Church Cathedral: Gen. ... 2
St. George's: Wo. Aux., Miss Suthon's salary, Kyoto. ...
St. John's: Gen. ... 1
Trinity Church: Wo. Aux., Miss Suthon's salary, Kyoto. ...

Maine
Ap. $238.38

AUGUSTA—*St. Mark's*: Mrs. J. W. Freese, Gen. ... 2
BAR HARBOR—*St. Saviour's*: Gen. ... 9
LISBON CENTRE—Mrs. Alice Dickens, Gen. ...
NORTH HAVEN—Mrs. W. N. Bullard, medical work, China. ... 10
PORTLAND—*St. Stephen's S. S.*: $5.88, "A Friend," $10, Gen. ... 1
SACO—*Trinity Church*: Gen. ... 1

Marquette
Ap. $52.96

CEDARVILLE—Gen.
CRYSTAL FALLS—*St. Mark's*: Gen.
DETOUR—*St. Stephen's*: Gen.
ESCANABA—*St. Stephen's*: Dom.
GLADSTONE—*Trinity Church*: Gen.
IRON RIVER—*St. John's*: Gen.
PAINESDALE—*St. Mary's*: Gen.
STAMBAUGH—*St. Mary's*: Gen.
WILSON—*Zion*: Gen.
WINONA—Gen.
MISCELLANEOUS—Gen.

Maryland
Ap. $414.46; *Sp.* $10.00

ALLEGHENY CO.—*St. Philip's Chapel*: $3.50, S. S.,* $3.31, Gen.
Holy Cross Chapel (Cumberland): $3, S. S.,* $2, Gen.
ANNE ARUNDEL CO.—*St. Peter's Parish, Ellicott Chapel* (Patuxent): Gen.
St. Anne's Parish (Annapolis): Colored, $10; Gen., $15.
All Hallows' Parish: Dom. and Frn.
St. Alban's Chapel (Glen Burnie): Gen.
BALTIMORE—*Advent Chapel*: Gen.
St. James's: Gen.
St. Margaret's: China.
Mrs. E. S. Bowne, Gen.
Miss Virginia Bolton, Gen.
"Two sons of Mrs. Horace Hills," Bishop Rowe's work, Alaska.
"H. W. A.," Sp. for Rev. Mr. Ancell, Shanghai.
Edward L. Gernand, Gen.
Miss M. D. Williams, Gen.
BALTIMORE Co. — *Holy Comforter* (Lutherville): Gen.
Church of the Redeemer: Dom. and Frn.

56 55	
2 50	
10 00	
20 00	
3 60	
2 00	
25 00	
50 00	
9 14	
3 00	
40	
85 00	
32 87	
5 00	
104 00	
28 93	
10 00	
10 00	
*	
25 00	
50 00	
25 00	
10 00	
10 00	
20 00	
5 00	
5 00	
5 00	
5 00	
5 00	
3 00	
2 00	
5 00	
5 00	
193 66	
50 00	
50 00	
10 00	
10 00	
21 28	
18 70	
5 00	
2 00	
50 00	
10 00	
5 60	
444 95	
2 00	
2 00	

FALL RIVER—*Ascension*: Dom. and Frn. ...

St. James's: Wo. Aux., Sp. for rebuilding St. Margaret's School, Tokyo... 263 09

GLOUCESTER — Miss M. Humphreys, Mexico ... 2 00

GROTON AND AYER—*St. Andrew's*: Gen. ... 5 00

HAVERHILL—*Trinity Church*: $62.30, S. S.,* $3.62, Gen. ... 10 06

IPSWICH—*Ascension*: Gen. ... 65 92

LAWRENCE—*Grace*: Gen. ... 163 00

Miss Maria Packard, Gen. ... 16 06

LEXINGTON—*Church of Our Redeemer*: Gen. ... 2 00

LYNN—*St. Stephen's*: Gen. ... 18 56

MANCHESTER—*Emmanuel Church*: Sp. for St. John's Expansion Fund, Shanghai ... 32 37

MARLBORO—*Holy Trinity Church*: Wo. Aux., Hooker School, Mexico, $5; China, $2 ... 125 00

MEDFORD—*Grace*: Gen. ... 7 00

MEDWAY—*Christ Church*: Gen. ... 36 10

MELROSE—*Trinity Church*: Gen. ... 11 73

MILLIS—*St. Paul's Mission*: Gen. ... 13 50

NATICK—*St. Paul's*: Dom. and Frn., $45; Wo. Aux., Gen., $22.15 ... 2 00

NEWBURYPORT—*St. Paul's*: "Members," South Dakota League, "Bishop Bass" scholarship, St. Elizabeth's School, South Dakota, $60; Wo. Aux., Sp. for "Mary J. Woart Memorial" scholarship, St. Paul's School, Lawrenceville, Southern Virginia, $26 ... 67 15

NEWTON CENTER—"A Friend," medical work ... 86 00

NEWTON—*Grace*: Dom., $111.97; Frn., $1 ... 50 00

Church of the Messiah (Auburndale, West): Wo. Aux., Sp. for Rev. Mr. Gilman's personal use, Changsha, Hankow ... 112 97

NORWOOD—*Grace Mission*: Gen. ... 5 00

PLYMOUTH—Miss Elizabeth T. Crehore, Gen. ... 5 00

QUINCY—*Christ Church*: Gen. ... 5 00

SHARON—*St. John's Mission*: Gen. ... 50 00

SIASCONSET—Mrs. C. I. Meeker, Gen. ... 23 70

SOMERVILLE — *St. James's S. S.** (West): Gen. ... 5 00

St. Thomas's (East): Wo. Aux., Hooker School, Mexico ... 13 15

SOUTH GROVELAND—*St. James's*: Gen. ... 1 00

TAUNTON—*St. Thomas's*: Mission Class, Sp. for Bishop Kinsolving, Brazil ... 1 61

WALTHAM—*Ascension*: "E. E. S.," Gen. ... 25 00

WELLESLEY—*Wellesley College*: Christian Association, Sp. for Miss Alice M. Fyork, Tokyo, for piano ... 2 00

WINCHESTER—*Epiphany*: Circle City, Alaska, $25; "native clergyman," Anking, Hankow, $25 ... 25 00

WINTHROP—*St. John's*: Gen. ... 50 00

WOBURN—*Trinity Church*: Wo. Aux., Sp. for rebuilding St. Hilda's School, Wuchang, Hankow ... 32 64

MISCELLANEOUS—Wo. Aux., "A Member," Sp. for St. Paul's College Building Fund, Tokyo ... 6 00

"A Sunday-school," Sp. for St. John's University Expansion Fund, Shanghai ... 500 00

Through Dr. Augustus Thorndike, Foreign Committee, mite-box belonging to the late Mrs. Augusta Thorndike, for Frn. ... 15 00

Through Wo. Aux., Mrs. C. S. Tuckerman and friends, salary of Rev. Julian L. Meade, Jr., Wusih, Shanghai ... 5 91

Wo. Aux., Nevada, $40; Western Colorado, $40 ... 400 00

80 00

Through Wo. Aux, "A Friend," Gen.   25 00
Through Wo. Aux., "A Friend," Sp.
for Miss L. J. Woods's work with
children, Fort Yukon, Alaska......   10 00
Wo. Aux., Foreign Committee, for
"Nancy Long" scholarship, St.
John's, Cape Mount, Africa, Mrs. E.
D. Seldon......................   25 00

Michigan
Ap. $130.27; *Sp.* $15 00
ANN ARBOR—Mrs. Charles B. G. De
Nancrede, Gen...................   5 00
BIRMINGHAM—*St. James's*: Gen.....   40 55
CLINTON—*St. John's*: Gen.........   16 70
DETROIT—*St. Andrew's S. S.**: Gen..   13 83
St. John's: Michael F. Pfau, $2, Mrs.
G. Hargreaves, $10, Gen..........   12 00
St. Joseph's: Gen.................   4 69
St. Matthias's: Gen...............   35 00
SAGINAW — *Calvary Memorial*: Dom.
and Frn.......................   2 50
MISCELLANEOUS—Wo. Aux., for Dea-
coness Routledge, Philippines......   15 00

Michigan City
Ap. $282.49; *Sp.* $8.00
EAST CHICAGO—*Church of the Good
Shepherd*: Gen..................   5 88
ELKHART—*St. John's S. S.**: St. Luke's
Hospital, Shanghai, $8; Gen., $8;
Sp. for Sisters of St. Mary's,
Sewanee, Tennessee, $8..........   24 00
FORT WAYNE—*Trinity Church*: Gen..   30 00
GOSHEN—*St. James's*: Gen.........   48 30
HAMMOND—*St. Paul's*: Gen.......   24 60
KOKOMO—*St. Andrew's*: $33.60, Wo.
Aux., $5, Gen..................   38 60
PLYMOUTH—*St. Thomas's*: Gen.....   72 80
SOUTH BEND—*St. James's*: $25, S. S.*
$19.31, Gen....................   41 31
MISCELLANEOUS—Wo. Aux., Gen.....   5 00

Milwaukee
Ap. $164.35; *Sp.* $5.10
BARABOO—Mrs. Louisa M. Gowan, Gen.   3 00
CHIPPEWA FALLS — *Christ Church*:
Frn., $3; Gen., $25.56..........   28 56
COLUMBUS—*St. Paul's*: Sp. for work
at leper colony, San Juan, Porto
Rico 3 10
ELKHORN FALLS—*St. John's*: $15.15,
S. S., $10, Gen.................   25 15
HARTLAND—*Grace*: Gen..............   3 50
JANESVILLE—*Trinity Church*: Gen....   14 33
MADISON—Mrs. W. A. P. Monis, Gen..   5 00
MILWAUKEE — *St. Andrew's S. S.**:
Support and education of Julia Red
Eye, St. Mary's School, South Dakota   30 73
St. Edmund's: Sp. for work at leper
colony, San Juan, Porto Rico.....   2 00
St. James's: Gen.................   23 31
RACINE—*Holy Angels' Chapel S. S.**:
For Rev. R. E. Woods's work, Wu-
chang, Hankow.................   2 08
Holy Innocents' S. S.*: Rev. R. E.
Woods's work, Wuchang, Hankow..   12 69
St. Luke's: "H.," Gen.............   10 00
St. Stephen's: Gen...............   6 00

Minnesota
Ap. 464.57
ALBERT LEA—*Christ Church*: Gen....   73 53
BELLE CREEK—*St. Paul's*: Gen.......   6 00
BENSON—*Christ Church*: Gen.......   41 75
LAKE BENTON—*St. John's S. S.**: Gen.   7 06
LITCHFIELD—*Trinity Church*: Gen....   18 87
MAZEPPA—*St. Andrew's*: Gen.......   3 00
MINNEAPOLIS—*All Saints'*: Gen......   105 00
Mrs. J. T. Wyman, Gen..........   2 20
ROCHESTER—Mrs. Margaret Bracken-
ridge, Dom....................   100 00
ST. PAUL—*Christ Church*: Gen.......   96 16
Miss Eunice D. Peabody, Gen......   10 00
Mrs. F. B. Millard, Gen...........   1 00

Mississippi
Ap. $224 56
ABERDEEN—*St. John's*: Miss Julia E.
Eckforel ....
BOLTON—*St. Mary's*: Gen...........
BRANDON—*St. Luke's*: Gen..........
COLUMBUS—Mrs. C. B. Whitfield, Gen.
HATTIESBURG—*Trinity Church*: Gen..
INDIANOLA—*St. Stephen's*: Gen......
NATCHEZ—Mrs. George F. Greene,
Gen. ....
Mrs. Ernest E. Brown, Gen........
PANTHER BURN—Mrs. J. W. Johnson,
St. Mary's School, Rosebud, South
Dakota ....
PASS CHRISTIAN—*Trinity Church*: $38,
Wo. Aux., $1.90, Gen...........
RAYMOND—*St. Mark's*: Gen.........
TERRY—*Church of the Good Shep-
herd*: Gen....................
TUPELS—*All Saints'*: Gen...........
VAIDEN—*St. Clement's*: Gen........
VICKSBURG—*Holy Trinity Church*: Wo.
Aux., Gen.....................
YAZOO CITY — Miss Katherine B.
Mazyck ....

Missouri
Ap. $751.53; *Sp.* $35.00
ST. LOUIS—*All Saints'*: Sp. for work
of Rev. W. T. Cleghorn, St. Philip's
Church, Los Angeles............
Emmanuel Church (Old Orchard):
Frn. ....
Mt. Calvary: Dom. and Frn.........
St. Augustine's: Gen..............
St. Augustine's: Gen..............
St. Peter's: Dom. $25; Frn., $100...
Trinity Church S. S.*: Gen.........
Mrs. H. N. Davis, Gen............
M. Bryan Tompkins (Kirkwood),
Frn. ....
G. H. Ten Broeck, Gen...........
MISCELLANEOUS—Junior Aux., Sp. for
Miss Woods's Library, Wuchang,
Hankow ....

Montana
Ap. $143.77
BOZEMAN — *St. James's*: "Bishop
Brewer" scholarship, Girls' Training
Institute, Africa................
BUTTE—*St. John's*: "Bishop Brewer"
scholarship, Girls' Training Institute,
Africa ....
DILLON—*St. James's*: "Bishop Brewer"
scholarship, Girls' Training Institute,
Africa, $5; "Dillon" scholarship, St.
Augustine's School, Africa, $25....
FORSYTHE—*Ascension*: Gen..........
HELENA—*St. Peter's*: "Bishop Brewer"
scholarship, Girls' Training Institute,
Africa ....
LEWISTON—*St. James's*: Gen........
McDONALD—*St. Paul's*: Gen........
MISSOULA—*Church of the Holy Spirit*:
"Bishop Brewer" scholarship, Girls'
Training Institute, Africa........
VIRGINIA CITY—*St. Paul's*: Gen......

Nebraska
Ap. $82.26
FREMONT—*St. James's*: Gen.........
HARTINGTON—*Grace*: Gen..........
HARVARD—*St. John's*: Gen.........
MADISON—*St. Matthew's*: Gen......
RANDOLPH—*St. Philip's*: Gen.......

Newark
Ap. $636.50; *Sp.* $924.50
ALLENDALE—*Epiphany Mission*: Gen..
EAST ORANGE—*St. Agnes's*: Gen......

5 00	ROCHESTER—*Church of the Redeemer*: Gen. 2 00
50 00	SANBORNVILLE—*St. John the Baptist's*: Junior Aux., Gen................. 3 00
5 00	WALPOLE—Helen D. Bridge, Gen..... 5 00
	WILTON—Mrs. Edward Abbott, Gen.. 25 00
50 00	Branch Wo. Aux., Frn., $5; Gen., $26 .... 31 00
3 00	
5 00	**New Jersey**
43 91	*Ap.* $620.47 ; *Sp.* $11.25
	ASBURY PARK—*Trinity Church*: Gen.. 20 00
	BOUND BROOK—*St. Paul's*: Dom., $6; Frn., $6; Mrs. Eliza Dean Post, Sp. for Church Extension Fund, Porto Rico, $10 .... 22 00
85 10	BURLINGTON—*St. Mary's*: Gen...... 106 00
	CRANFORD—*Trinity Church*: Wo. Aux., Gen. 75 00
25 00	DUNELLEN — *Holy Innocents'*: Dom., $2.80; Frn., $2.80; Gen., $5; Junior
5 50	Aux., Sp. for Bishop Partridge's work in Kyoto, $1.25 .... 11 85
	ELIZABETH—*Trinity Church*: Gen..... 4 00
137 50	FREEHOLD—*St. Peter's*: Gen......... 95 00
1 00	LINDEN—*Grace*: Gen............... 5 00
21 45	MOORESTOWN — Mrs. Horace Roberts,
4 32	Gen. 5 00
	NEW BRUNSWICK — *Christ Church*: Gen. 3 00
630 00	*St. John the Evangelist's*: Wo. Aux., Gen. 22 00
2 00	OCEAN CITY—Florence S. Shaler, for Dom. and Frn................. 10 00
	PALMYRA—*Christ Church*: "A Member," Gen...................... 10 00
44 00	PLAINFIELD—*Heavenly Rest*: $15, S. S.,* $6.42, Gen............... 21 42
50 00	*Grace*: Wo. Aux., "L. T.," $10, "I. T.," $10, Gen................. 20 00
1 15	PRINCETON—Mrs. H. N. Russell, for St. Margaret's School, Tokyo, $30; Gen.,
5 00	$50 .... 80 00
25 00	RUMSON — *St. George's-by-the-River*: Gen. 30 00
	SOUTH AMBOY—*Christ Church*: Dom., 74 cts.; Alaska, Rev. Mr. Chapman's work, $2.29, Asheville, Bishop Horner's work, $3.03; Indian, $9.32;
30 00	Frn., Rev. Mr. Woods's work, Hankow, $2.08; Gen., $17.43 .... 34 89
2 00	MISCELLANEOUS—Branch Wo. Aux., for
3 00	"Clarkson" scholarship, in the Hooker Memorial School, Mexico... 56 56
61 47	**New York**
	Ap. $4,390.69 ; *Sp.* $5,347.63
	BEDFORD—"K.," medical missions.... 2 00
257 50	BREWSTER—*St. Andrew's*: $120, S. S.,* $70.07, Gen.................. 190 07
	St. Paul's Chapel: $4.40, S. S., $8.47, Gen...................... 12 87
	BRONXVILLE—*Christ Church*: "A Member," support of girls' schools, Manila, Philippine Islands, $37.50;
5 00	two beds, Elizabeth Bunn Hospital, Wuchang, Hankow, $25; "Divinity" scholarship, Boone University, Wuchang, Hankow, $25; Wo. Aux., Sp.
200 00	for Good Shepherd Hospital, Fort Defiance, Arizona, $28.08...... 115 58
55 00	CROTON FALLS—Miss Frances H. Close, Dom., $5; Colored, $5; Indian, $5;
50 00	Haiti, $5; Porto Rico, $5; Philippines, $5; Alaska, $5; Africa, $5;
4 50	Japan, $5; China, $5............. 50 00
	GARRISON—*St. Philip's*: Dom. and Frn. 41 00
	GOSHEN—*St. James's*: Dom., $85;
10 00	Frn., $85.................... 170 00
	GREENWOOD LAKE—*Church of the Good Shepherd S. S.*:* Gen......... 5 25
10 00	H'GHLAND—*Holy Trinity Church*: Gen. 2 00
2 00	IRVINGTON—*St. Barnabas's*: Dom., $50;
10 45	Bishop Brown's work, Arkansas,
5 00	

$25; work in Alaska, $25; Dom. and Frn., $325.65 .... 425 65
KINGSTON—*St. John's*: Dom., $7.04; Frn., $5.77 .... 12 81
LARCHMONT—*St. John's*: Gen 169 00
MT. VERNON — *Ascension*: Bishop Brent's work, Philippines, $30; Wo. Aux., Sp. for Good Shepherd Hospital, Fort Defiance, Arizona, $20 .. 50 00
NEWBURGH—*Church of the Good Shepherd*: Gen 50 00
NEW ROCHELLE—*Trinity Church*: Gen. 3 00
NEW WINDSOR—*St. Thomas's*: $50, S. S.,* $16, Gen. 66 00
NEW YORK CITY—*Advocate*: Dom., $5; Frn., $5 .... 10 00
Beloved Disciple: Gen 24 90
*Christ Church S. S.**: Gen 41 20
Grace: "A Friend," Sp. for Church Extension Fund, Porto Rico, $10; St. Augustine's League, Committee on Missions to Colored People, Sp. for St. Agnes's Hospital, Raleigh, North Carolina, $10; Sp. for Good Samaritan Hospital, Charlotte, North Carolina, $5 .... 25 00
Grace (City Island): Wo. Aux., Sp. for Good Shepherd Hospital, Fort Defiance, Arizona 11 05
Church of the Holy Comforter (Eltingville, Staten Island): Gen. 14 00
*Resurrection S. S.**: Bishop Partridge, Kyoto 38 00
St. Agnes's Chapel: "A. B. T.," Gen.. 10 00
St. Bartholomew's: Mrs. E. H. Van Ingen, Gen., $100; "A Friend," Sp. for Church Extension Fund, Porto Rico, $10 .... 110 00
St. James's: Everett P. Wheeler, Frn., $10; Wo. Aux., "Mrs. E. W. W.," Sp. for boarding-school on Lion Hill, Wuhu, Hankow (In Memoriam, "Rev. E. W. W."), $3,500 .... 3,510 00
St. Luke's Chapel: Gen 100 00
St. Mark's: Gen 15 00
St. Mary's (Manhattanville): $87.71, S. S., $27.98, Afternoon S. S., $36.79, Gen. 152 48
*St. Michael's S. S.**: Salary of Rev. Alfred A. Gilman, Changsha, Hankow 218 33
St. Simeon's (Bronx): Gen 12 00
St. Simon's: Junior Aux., Sp. for Christmas festival, Gate School, Shanghai 3 00
St. Stephen's: Gen. 60 00
Transfiguration: "A Member." Gen.... 5 00
Trinity Church: Gen., $5; Wo. Aux., Sp. for scholarship, Anvik, Alaska, $34.50 .... 39 50
Miss Ellen King, Dom., $500; Frn., $500 .... 1,000 00
Mrs. Mary C. Scrymser, Sp. for St. Paul's College, Tokyo, Fund 1,000 00
Miss Julia Livingston, Gen 500 00
Mrs. Eastburn Benjamin, Dom. and Frn. 300 00
Miss Grace H. Dodge, Sp. for St. John's Expansion Fund, Shanghai, China 250 00
"M. M. H.," Brazil, $100; natives, Mexico, $100 .... 200 00
W. Willis Reese, Sp. for Expansion Fund, St. John's University, Shanghai, China 100 00
Francis Lynde Stetson, Sp. for St. John's Expansion Fund, Shanghai, China 100 00
"Miss Mary E. Cox Memorial" scholarship, St. Hilda's School, Wuchang, Hankow 50 00
Miss A. L. Horn, $25, Miss S. L. Horn, $25, Gen. 50 00
"Layman," Frn. 50 00
Mrs. Francis W. Paris, Gen 30 00
"A Thanksgiving, June 29th," Gen .. 25 00

Miss Henrietta M. Schwab, Gen ....
Mr. Joseph D. Holmes, Gen ....
Miss I. Lawrence, Gen ....
Miss J. Henrietta H. Rhoades, Gen.
"A Thank-offering," for improvement of health, Gen ....
Society of Busy Workers, Sp. for Turtle Mountain Indians, North Dakota ....
Mrs. Ellen V. Caesar (West New Brighton, Staten Island), Gen ......
"W. A.," Deaconess Nichols, Gen..
Wo. Aux., Sp. for Bishop Hare Memorial Fund, South Dakota ......
Through Wo. Aux., "A Friend," Sp. for Domestic Contingent Fund ....
OSSINING—*St. Paul's*: $100, S. S., $51.07, Gen. ....
Trinity Church: "A Member," Gen ...
PATTERSON—*Christ Church*: Sp. for Good Shepherd Hospital, Fort Defiance, Arizona ....
PEEKSKILL—Thomas J. Powers, Jr., Gen. ....
"A Friend," Gen ....
PELHAM MANOR—Mrs. G. R. Talboys, Gen. ....
PORT CHESTER—*St. Peter's*: Gen ....
POUGHKEEPSIE—*Christ Church*: Gen..
RHINEBECK—*Church of the Messiah*: China Mission and educational work, $60; Gen., $134.56 ....
RYE—*Christ Church*: Gen., $52; Wo. Aux., Sp. for Rev. A. A. Gilman, Changsha Equipment Fund, Hankow, $100 ....
SCARSDALE—Mrs. A. B. Cram, Gen ...
YONKERS—*St. Andrew's*: Sp. for Good Shepherd Hospital, Fort Defiance, Arizona ....
Mrs. J. H. Clark, Dom., $15; work among natives in Mexico, $15 .....

North Carolina

Ap. $283.14

CHARLOTTE—*St. Peter's*: Asheville...
COOLEEMEE—*Church of the Good Shepherd*: Dom. and Frn., $6; S. S.,* Gen., $21.84 ....
HALIFAX—*St. Mark's*: Gen ....
LAWRENCE—*Grace*: Gen ....
MAYODAN—Junior Aux., Gen ....
MIDDLEBURG—*Heavenly Rest*: Gen....
RALEIGH—*Christ Church*: Gen......
Church of the Good Shepherd: Gen....
Mrs. F. H. Busbee, Gen ....
SALISBURY—*St. Luke's*: Gen..........
John Hill, Gen ....
SPEED—*St. Mary's*: Gen ....
SPRAY—*St. Luke's S. S.*: Gen ....

Ohio

Ap. $963.90; Sp. $103.75

AKRON—Miss Eleanor Francis, Gen...
BOARDMAN—*St. James's*: Dom. and Frn. ....
BOWLING GREEN—*Annunciation*: Gen..
CLEVELAND—*Christ Church*: Gen.....
St. Paul's: Dom. and Frn ....
Trinity Church: Dom., $184.87; Colored, $143.40 ....
Mrs. Katherine L. Mather, Sp. for St. John's College Expansion Fund, Shanghai ....
CROSS CREEK—*St. James's*: Gen......
CUYAHOGA FALLS—*St. John's*: Frn...
DELPHOS—Esther Hampton, Gen.....
ELYRIA—*St. Andrew's*: Frn ....
FREMONT—Mrs. John B. Rice, Gen....
LIMA—*Christ Church*: Gen..........
MONROEVILLE—*Zion*: Gen............
STEUBENVILLE—*St. Paul's*: Gen......
St. Stephen's: Sp. for St. Paul's College, Tokyo ....

30	hai	5	00
	St. Luke's (Kensington): Gen........	100	00
20	St. Mark's: Junior Aux., Gen........	5	00
	St. Martin's: "X. Y. Z.," China.......	100	00
	St. Martin's-in-the-Fields: Frn., $15; Gen., $17.96; "Members," Gen.,		
44	$1,000; Henry H. Bonnell, Frn., $25.	1,057	96
	St. Mary's (West): St. Agnes's Guild, Junior Aux., Gen................	10	00
	St. Matthew's: $85.43, Junior Aux., $9, Gen........................	94	43
	St. Paul's (Aramingo): Gen.........	37	00
	St. Paul's (Chestnut Hill): Arthur E.		
00	Newbold, Sp. for St. John's College		
00	Expansion Fund, Shanghai........	1,000	00
00	St. Paul's Memorial (Overbrook):		
19	Dom., $2.25; Gen., $413.30; "A		
73	Member," Gen., $5............	420	55
	St. Peter's: S. Davis Page, Gen., $100; "A Member," Gen., $500; "A Member," Rev. R. A. Walke's salary, Tokyo, $375; Philippines, $35 Wo. Aux., "A Member," Gen., $500..	1,510	00
65	St. Thomas's: Wo. Aux., Bishop Ferguson's work, Africa, $5; Junior Aux., Gen., $1....................	6	00
00	St. Timothy's (Roxborough): Junior Aux., Gen...................	5	00
	Church of the Saviour (West): "A S.," Dom., $5; Sp. for Expansion Fund,		
17	St. John's University, Shanghai, $5;		
49	"A Member," Gen., $5; Junior Aux.,		
20	Gen., $5......................	20	00
25	Zion; Gen....................	5	00
	"A Philadelphia Woman," Gen.....	5,000	00
	"A . T. A.," Gen................	10,000	00
00	S. S.: Philadelphia, Gen............	500	00
82	Mrs. John Markoe, Sp. for St. Luke's Hospital, Shanghai, Furnishing		
00	Fund	250	00
	"R. R.," $100, Evan Randolph, $5, Gen.	105	00
00	Mrs. J. S. Cox, Gen.............	100	00
	Miss Linda H. Pancoast, training of native helpers in China..........	50	00
	Mrs. Evelyn McGowan, Sp. for		
00	Aomori, Tokyo..................	25	00
00	Miss Nora Davis, Gen.............	16	64
	Miss L. C. Rodney (Germantown):		
00	Gen.	10	00
	"A Friend," Gen.................	10	00
	Lloyd M. Smith (Germantown), Sp.		
00	for St. John's University, Shanghai.	10	00
65	Miss Elizabeth H. Brown, Gen.....	5	20
	Mrs. C. M. Brown, Gen...........	5	00
00	"M. C. B." (Wissahickon), Gen....	5	00
00	Mrs. S. Porcher (Chestnut Hill), medical work....................	5	00
	Miss E. Demuth (West), Gen......	5	00
08	Mrs. Mary G. Foster (Germantown), Gen.	5	00
	Mrs. J. B. Cooper (Mt. Airy), Gen..	2	00
00	PHOENIXVILLE — St. Peter's: "A Friend," Sp. for Extension Fund.		
00	Porto Rico....................	25	00
	ROCKLEDGE — Holy Nativity: Junior		
50	Aux., Gen.....................	1	00
	SWARTHMORE—Mrs. A. B. Harrower,		
27.	Gen.	3	00
	WAYNE—St. Mary's: Junior Aux., Gen.	7	50
00	WEST WHITEHEAD—St. Paul's: Gen..	10	00
00	WHITEMARSH—St. Thomas's: Gen....	100	00
56	WILLOW GROVE—St. Anne's: Gen......	3	43
	WYNCOTE—All Hallows': Dom. and Frn., $20.30; Junior Aux., Gen., $5.	25	30
00	WYNNEWOOD—Miss Mary K. Gibson,		
00	medical work..................	100	00
	MISCELLANEOUS—"Y. Z.," Gen........	100	00
	Miss M. P. McBlair, Dom., $5; Frn., $5; Gen., $5..................	15	00
	Wo. Aux., salary of Domestic Mis-		
00	sionary Bishop.................	502	50
00	Junior Aux., "St. James" scholar-		
00	ship, Girls' Training Institute, St. Paul's River, Africa, $25; Miss Mary K. Gibson, "St. James" scholarship, St. Mary's Hall. Shanghai,		

$50; Gen. (of which Miss Elizabeth N. Brock and Miss Violet P. Walsh, $5), $7.95 .... 82 95

Pittsburgh
Ap. $864.67; *Sp.* $10.00

BROWNSVILLE — *Christ Church*: Miss Mary A. Hogg, Gen 50 00
BUTLER—*St. Peter's*: Dom. and Frn.. 10 60
EMPORIUM—Josiah Howard, Gen..... 100 00
FAIRVIEW—*St. Paul's*: Gen 70
FRANKLIN—*St. John's*: Gen 106 76
GEORGETOWN—*St. Luke's*: Gen....... 2 50
GREENSBURG—*Christ Church*: Gen.... 20 00
JEANNETTE—*Advent*: Gen........... 5 16
NEW KENSINGTON—*St. Andrew's*: Gen. 3 95
PITTSBURGH — *St. James's Memorial*: Gen. 15 00
Trinity Church; Dom.............. 500 00
John S. McCormick, Sp. for Expansion Fund, St. John's University, Shanghai 10 00
Mrs. Ormsby Phillips (Allegheny), Josephine Hooker School, Mexico... 50 00

Quincy
Ap. $238.02

CANTON—*St. Peter's*: $5.40, Wo. Aux., $5, Gen. 10 40
CARTHAGE—*St. Cyprian's*: Wo. Aux., Gen. 2 50
FARMINGTON—*Calvary*: Wo. Aux., Gen. 5 00
GALESBURG—*Grace*: Wo. Aux., Gen ... 10 00
St. John's: Wo. Aux., Gen.......... 10 00
KEWANEE—*St. John's*: Wo. Aux., Gen. 5 00
KNOXVILLE—*St. Alban's*: Gen........ 15 00
St. Mary's: Wo. Aux., Gen.......... 10 00
MOLINE—*Christ Church*: Wo. Aux., Gen. 13 00
OSCO—*Grace*: Branch Wo. Aux., Gen. (of which Ministering Children's League, $2) 5 00
PEORIA—*St. Paul's*: $25.77, Wo. Aux., $20, Gen. 45 77
St. Stephen's: Wo. Aux., $5, Junior Aux., $1, Gen.................... 6 00
QUINCY—*Church of the Good Shepherd*: Wo. Aux., Gen.................... 3 00
St. John's Cathedral: $66.85, Wo. Aux., $11, Gen.................... 77 85
ROCK ISLAND—*Trinity Church*: Wo. Aux., $15, Holy Child, Juniors, $1, Dorcas Juniors, $1, Gen.......... 17 00
RUSHVILLE—*Christ Church*: Wo. Aux., Gen. 2 00
MISCELLANEOUS — Branch Wo. Aux, Gen. 50

Rhode Island
Ap. $650.74; *Sp.* $505.00

APPONAUG—*St. Barnabas's*: Gen..... 21 40
BRISTOL—*St. Michael's*: Gen........ 50 00
CRANSTON—Mr. Walter Hirst, Gen.... 5 00
EAST GREENWICH—Mrs. A. S. Hodgman, Sp. for Church Extension Fund, Porto Rico............... 10 00
LONSDALE — *Christ Church*: Junior Aux., for work in Alaska, $3; Colored work, $3; Indian work, $3; work in China, $3............. 12 00
NEWPORT — "A Churchwoman," for work in Alaska, $5; Sp. for the Southern Mountaineers of Virginia, $5 .... 10 00
Mrs. Ezra A. Howard, Gen.......... 25 00
NORTH PROVIDENCE—*Church of the Holy Spirit*: Gen............... 11 00
PAWTUCKET—*Advent*: Dom. and Frn.. 17 95
PHILLIPSDALE—*St. David's*: Gen...... 5 00
PROVIDENCE—*Church of the Redeemer*: Junior Aux, for Alaska.......... 3 00
St. Andrew's: Gen................ 8 39
St. John's: Dom., $75; Frn., $75; Indian, $20; "M. L. C.," Gen., $100.. 270 00

St. Stephen's: S. H. Woodcock, Gen... 1
Mrs. Albert Babcock, Gen.......... 3
Mrs. Charles Bradley, Gen......... 50
Miss M. L. Corliss, Sp. for Church Extension Fund, Porto Rico........ 100
Miss Julia Grinnell, Gen.......... 11
"R.," Gen., $100; China, $25...... 125
SAYLESVILLE—Mr. and Mrs. J. W. Turner, Gen..................... 5
WARREN—*St. Mark's*: Miss Alice Wheaton, Gen.................. 10
WICKFORD—Miss C. Newton, Gen..... 1
MISCELLANEOUS—Branch Wo. Aux., Sp. for American Church Institute for Negroes, $240; Sp. for Rev. A. A. Gilman, Hankow, $150; Junior Aux., Gen., $11...................... 401

South Carolina
Ap. $345.69; *Sp.* $41.00

AIKEN—*St. Augustine's Mission*: Gen. 7
St. Thaddeus's: Wo. Aux., for salary of assistant for Miss McCullough, Porto Rico, $1; N. S. Wilson's Dayschool, Hankow, $1; Sp. for "Bishop Howe" cot, St. Mary's Orphanage, Shanghai, $5.................. 7
BATESBURG—*St. Paul's*: Gen........ 1
BLUFFTON—*Church of the Cross*: (of which 1908-09, $2.50)........... 5
CHARLESTON — *St. Michael's*: Junior Aux., Bishop Capers Day-school, Wuchang, Hankow, $5; Sp. for R. Ishii, Tokyo, $36............... 41
Mr. D. C. Hayward, Gen........... 5
Mrs. Isaac Hayne, Gen........... 1
COLUMBIA—*Trinity Church*: Gen..... 100
Trinity Chapel: "M. C. P.," Gen... 10
EASTOVER—Mrs. James Schoolbud, Gen. 20
EDGEFIELD—*Trinity Church*: Gen..... 3
GEORGETOWN—Mr. Walter Hazard, Gen. 2
GREENVILLE—*Christ Church*: Gen..... 125
GREENWOOD—*Resurrection*: Gen...... 6
LAURENS—"E. B. S.," Gen.......... 4
McPHERSONVILLE — *Sheldon Church*: Gen. 7
PINOPOLIS—*Trinity Church*: Gen..... 20
STATEBURG—*Holy Cross*: Wo. Aux., Frn. 5
WILTON—*Christ Church*: Gen........ 15

Southern Ohio
Ap. $754.73; *Sp.* $41.00

CINCINNATI—*Advent*: Wo. Aux., Gen., $7.50; Sp. for Maintenance Fund, St. Luke's Home, Phoenix, Arizona, $5 12
Grace (Avondale): Gen............ 32
Nativity (Price Hill): S. S.,* Gen.. 6
St. Mark's Deaf-Mute Mission: Gen.. 1
St. Paul's Cathedral: "E. M.," Gen.. 100
St. Stephen's (Winton Place): Gen., (of which S. S.,* $45.87)........ 55
Mrs. Frederick Harmeyer, for work among sick and crippled children in China 10
Mrs. Elizabeth Irwin, Gen......... 10
Mrs. B. B. Whiteman, Gen......... 100
Calvary (Clifton): Wo. Aux., Gen..... 5
COLUMBUS—*Trinity Church*: Wo. Aux., Sp. for Maintenance Fund, St. Luke's Home, Phoenix, Arizona........... 30
Mrs. Rufus W. Clark and children (In Memoriam), Gen.............. 135
Mr. William T. Magruder, Gen...... 10
HILLSBORO—*St. Mary's*: Gen., $7.52; Wo. Aux., Sp. for Maintenance Fund, St Luke's Home, Phoenix, Arizona, $5.................... 12
NEWARK—*Trinity Church*: Gen....... 49
POMEROY—*Grace*: Gen............. 2

1 00	Church (Lexington): Gen., $70; Wo. Aux., 'Sp.' for Armistead Lee Memorial Chapel, Anking, Hankow, $10 .... 80 00
30 50	TAZEWELL Co. (North Tazewell)— Mr. B. H. Stras, Frn............ 10 00
10 00	WARWICK Co.—St. Paul's (Newport News): Gen.. $16.94; Junior Aux., St. Luke's Hospital, Shanghai, $15.................... 31 94
	WASHINGTON Co. (Abingdon)—Miss Gay R. Blackford, Gen.......... 10 00
55 00	(Abingdon)—Mrs. James L. White, Gen. 6 00
127 24	**Springfield**
	Ap. $69.69
	ALTON—St. Paul's: Gen............ 20 49
	CARROLLTON—Trinity Church: Gen... 2 10
	CHESTERFIELD—St. Peter's: Gen..... 1 35
12 00	JACKSONVILLE—Trinity Church: Gen.. 25 00
	METROPOLIS—St. Alban's: Gen....... 1 80
	PARIS—St. Andrew's: Gen.......... 7 05
	SPRINGFIELD—St. John's: Gen....... 8 90
40 00	Miss Lucy H. Archer, Gen......... 3 00
25 00	**Tennessee**
	Ap. $289.10
	CLEVELAND—St Luke's Memorial: Frn. 4 25
81 99	JACKSON—St. Luke's: Wo. Aux., Gen.. 5 50
	MEMPHIS—Calvary: Dom. and Frn., $77.38; Wo. Aux., Gen., $80...... 157 38
1 00	Grace: Junior Aux., Gen........... 5 00
2 00	NASHVILLE—Advent: Wo. Aux., Gen.. 2 50
	Christ Church: $103, S. S.,* $6.47, Gen........................ 109 47
16 51	MISCELLANEOUS—"A Helper," Gen.... 5 00
50 00	**Texas**
11 00	*Ap.* $169.16: *Sp.* $1.00
	AUSTIN—All Saints': "A Communicant," Indian missions, $1.41; Sp. for Rev. Robert E. Wood, Wuchang,
5 00	Hankow, for purchasing of new
17 57	property, $1.................... 2 41
39 35	GALVESTON — Trinity Church: Wo. Aux., Gen................... 10 00
13 00	GEORGETOWN—Grace: Gen........... 13 50
	HOUSTON—Christ Church: Wo. Aux., Gen. 10 00
1 00	Trinity Church: Gen.............. 60 00
	NACOGDOCHES—Mrs. John H. Cox, Gen. 5 00
10 00	TEMPLE—Christ Church: Gen........ 10 25
5 02	WACO—Mrs. Flora B. Cameron, Gen... 50 00
15 00	**Vermont**
1 93	*Ap.* $139.00
	NEWPORT—St. Mark's: "A Friend," for work among mountain people of
19 76	Asheville 20 00
4 54	RICHFORD—St. Ann's S. S.*: Gen.... 24 00
	ST. ALBANS—St. Luke's: "A Communicant," Gen.................. 20 00
3 35	MISCELLANEOUS — Branch Wo. Aux.,
19 95	Gen. 75 00
2 00	**Virginia**
10 00	*Ap.* $651.98; *Sp.* $144 00
2 20	ALBEMARLE Co.—Grace (Campbell): Gen. 44 21
10 00	(Charlottesville)—Miss S. R. Hauckel, Gen. 5 00
12 00	(University)—Mrs. John B. Minor and friend, Gen................... 8 00
5 00	ALEXANDRIA Co.—Christ Church: "A Friend," Gen.................. 25 00
1 00	Post Chapel (Fort Myer): Sp. for Miss Ridgely, Cape Mount, Africa...... 15 00
5 00	East Fal's Church—Mrs. Charles A. Marshall, Gen................. 1 00
18 00	ESSEX Co.—St. John's (Tappahannock): Gen..................... 27 00

St. Paul's (Tappahannock) : Gen...... 7 60
(Tappahannock)—Mrs. B. B. Bircken-
brough, Gen.................... 15 50
FAIRFAX Co.—*St. John's* (McLean) :
B. G. Foster, Sp. for Church Exten-
sion Fund, Porto Rico............. 5 00
(Burke)—G. W. C. Lee, Gen........ 50 00
FAUQUIER Co. (Marshall)—Mrs. J. M.
Ramey, Bishop Rowe's work, Alaska. 10 00
FLUVANNA Co. (Bremo Bluff)—Mrs.
Charles Wilkinson, Sp. for Rev. B. L.
Ancell, Yangchow, Shanghai........ 50 00
GLOUCESTER Co.—*Abingdon* (Glouces-
ter) : Gen....................... 15 40
Ware Church : Dom., $5 ; Gen., $18.25. 23 35
Ware and Abingdon : Sp. for Rev.
T. L. Sinclair, Shanghai.......... 27 00
HENRICO Co. — *Emmanuel Church*
(Richmond) : "Two Virginia Church-
women," Gen., $80 ; Mrs. M. A.
Stewart, Gen., $50 ; Junior Aux., Sp.
for work in Bontok, Philippine
Islands, $5...................... 135 00
Holy Trinity Church (Richmond) :
Mrs. M. C. Patterson, Gen......... 5 00
St. James's (Richmond) : Wo. Aux.,
Gen. 20 00
St. John's (Richmond) : Captain John
F. Mayer, Sp. for Church Exten-
sion Fund, Porto Rico............. 2 00
St. Mark's (Richmond) : Gen......... 10 00
(Brook Hill)—"A Virginia Church-
woman," Gen..................... 30 00
(Richmond)—Mrs. Joseph Bryan, Gen. 25 00
(Richmond)—Mrs. H. E. Weed, Gen... 2 00
(Richmond)—Miss M. S. Stringfellow,
Gen. 1 00
KING WILLIAM Co. — Mrs. V. M.
Heaton, Gen..................... 4 00
LANCASTER Co.—*White Chapel and
Emmanuel Church* (Bertrand) : Gen. 8 57
Trinity Church : Gen................ 2 43
LOUDOUN Co.—*St. James's* (Lees-
burg) : Gen...................... 25 00
Belmont Chapel : Gen............... 3 61
MATTHEWS Co. — *Kingston Parish*
(Matthews) : Mrs. C. C. Murray,
Gen. 5 00
ORANGE Co.—*St. Thomas's* (Orange) :
Gen., $39.20 ; Wo. Aux., support of
native workers, Bishop Williams's
church, Kyoto, $10............... 49 20
PRINCE WILLIAM Co.—*St. Paul's S. S.*
(Haymarket) : Gen................ 10 87
WARREN Co.—*Calvary* (Front Royal) :
Dom., $6.46 ; Frn., $6.88......... 13 34
MISCELLANEOUS — Babies' Branch,
Miss Carter's work for Indian chil-
dren, Whiterocks, Utah, $5 ; Bishop
Rowe's work for children, Alaska,
$15 ; Bishop Restarick's work for
children, Honolulu, $10 ; Bishop
Brent's work for children, Philip-
pine Islands, $10 ; Bishop Funsten's
work for children, Idaho, $5 ; kinder-
garten, Akita, Tokyo, $5 ; Angelica
Church Hart Day-school, Wuchang,
Hankow, $5 ; Gen., $20 ; Sp. for
Deaconess Drant's work for children,
San Francisco, California, $5 ; Sp.
for Mr. Ishii's orphanage, Tokyo,
$30 ; Sp. for "Little Helpers' " cot,
St. Agnes's Hospital, Raleigh, North
Carolina, $5..................... 115 00

Washington

Ap. $1,096.66 ; *Sp.* $159.88

WASHINGTON (D. C.) — *Ascension* :
Alice S. Hobbs, Gen.............. 10 00
Christ Church (Georgetown) : $75,
Mrs. F. W. McReynolds, $5, Gen... 80 00
National Cathedral School : Bishop Sat-
terlee Memorial Missionary Associa-

tion, Sp. for Expansion Fund, St.
John's University, Shanghai.........
St. John's (Georgetown) : "A Mem-
ber," China....................
St. Alban's : Wo. Aux., support of
Bible-women, Shanghai............
St. Andrew's : "A Member," Gen.....
St. Paul's : "A Member," $5, S. S.,*
$49.97, Gen.....................
St. Thomas's : Wo. Aux., Sp. for Ne-
vada ....
Through Mrs. H. Randall Welch,
Sp. for Bishop Roots's work, Han-
kow, at his discretion.............
Mrs. Alfred Holmead, Sp. for Arch-
deacon Stuck, Alaska, $10 ; Sp. for
Miss Carter, St. John's-in-the-
Wilderness, Alaska, $10..........
"A Friend," rent of mission house at
Santurce, Porto Rico, $10 ; Sp. for
Bishop Van Buren, Porto Rico, at
his discretion, $5................
Miss Mary G. Talcott, Gen.........
Mrs. Agnes Chase, Gen............
Mrs. J. Rook, Gen................
Tench T. Marye, Gen..............
Mrs. W. F. Koenig, Oregon.........
Mrs. L. M. Zeller, Gen............
MONTGOMERY CO. (Bethesda)—"M. B.
N.," Gen........................
PRINCE GEORGE'S Co.—*Holy Trinity
Church* : Gen....................
ST. MARY'S Co.—*All Saints' Parish* :
Frn. ....
MISCELLANEOUS — Miss Anna Mc-
Gowan, Sp. for Bishop Rowe's work,
Alaska, $15 ; Dr. I. H. Correll's
work in Tsu, Kyoto, $10..........
Wo. Aux., "A Member," salary of
Deaconess Stewart, Hankow.......
Babies' Branch, Porto Rico, $5.58 ;
Honolulu, $5.58 ; Akita kindergarten,
Tokyo, $6.38 ; Angelica Church Hart
Day-school, Wuchang, Hankow,
$6.38 ; Little Helpers' Day-school,
Shanghai, $6.38 ; Mexico, $6.38 ;
Africa, $6.38 ; Brazil, $6.38 ; Sp.
for "Little Helpers' " cot, St.
Agnes's Hospital, Raleigh, North
Carolina, $5.58 ; Sp. for Bishop
Spalding for Emergency Fund,
Whiterocks, Utah, $5.58 ; Sp. for St.
Margaret's School for girls, Boise,
Idaho, $5.58 ; Sp. for school for na-
tive children, Ketchikan, Alaska,
$5.58 ; Sp. for St. Luke's Hospital,
San Francisco, California, $5.60 ;
Sp. for Boerne, West Texas, $5.58 ;
Sp. for missionary font, $6.38......

Western Massachusetts

Ap. $1,539.03 ; *Sp.* $63.00

AMHERST—*Grace* : Wo. Aux., Sp. for
Foreign Missionary Insurance Fund.
BALDWINSVILLE — Mildred A. Libby,
M.D., Gen......................
EASTHAMPTON—"In Memoriam," Gen..
FITCHBURG—Mrs. A. S. Tyler. Gen...
HOLYOKE—*St. Paul's* : Wo. Aux., Phil-
ippine insurance, $1.47 ; Sp. for
Building Fund, St. Margaret's
School, Tokyo, $1...............
LANCASTER—Miss H. M. Swasey, Gen..
LENOX—*Trinity Church* : Dom., $100 ;
Frn., $50 ; Gen., $1,061.89....... 1,
Mrs. M. E. Zimmerman, Sp. for In-
dian work in Idaho...............
Miss Charlotte Cram, mite-box, Frn.
LEOMINSTER—*St. Mark's* : Gen........
MOUNT WASHINGTON—Miss Ella E.
Russell, one hospital day..........
NORTH ADAMS—Gabriel Abbott, Gen..
ORANGE—*Trinity Church S. S.** : Gen.,

5 00
2 00
50 00
5 00
1 00
39 00
5 00
1 00
10 00
2 00
23 16
..
65 00

83 09
3 00
2 00
5 50

35 00

4 00

28 00

5 00

18 00

13 00
65 00

98 00

10 00

10 00
3 70

School, Tokyo, $5; Colored Salary Fund, $10............................ 15 00
KALAMAZOO—*St. Luke's*: Wo. Aux., "Dr. Cuming" scholarship, St. Elizabeth's School, South Dakota...... 15 00
MANTON—Gen. 3 00
MARSHALL—*Trinity Church*: Gen.. 5 00
NILES—*Trinity Church*: Gen. $31 52; Wo. Aux., "Ellen E. Robinson" scholarship, St. Elizabeth's School, South Dakota, $10.............. 41 52
PETOSKEY—*Emmanuel Church*: Wo. Aux., Gen., $5; Sp. for Rev. F. B. Wentworth, Winchester, Lexington, mountain missions, $1............ 6 00
TRAVERSE CITY—*Grace*: Wo. Aux., Colored Salary Fund, $5; "Josephine E. Wheelock" scholarship, Girls' Training-school, St. Paul's River, Africa, $10.................... 15 00
WEQUETONSING—John G. Magee, Gen.. 5 00
WHITEHALL—Gen. 1 85
MISCELLANEOUS—Wo. Aux., "Dr. Cuming" scholarship, St. Elizabeth's School, South Dakota............ 3 00

Western New York

Ap. $342.28; Sp. $100.00

ALFRED—Mrs. William C. Burdick, Sp. for Expansion Fund, St. John's University, Shanghai.............. 100 00
BATH—*St. Thomas's*: Gen........... 3 30
BUFFALO—*All Saints' S. S.**: Gen..... 14 13
Grace: Dom. and Frn.............. 85 00
St. Jude's: Gen..... .... 25 00
St. Mark's S. S.*: Gen............. 9 25
St. Simon's S. S.*: Gen............. 50 00
Miss Arabella Riley, Gen.......... 1 00
GENEVA—*Trinity Church*: Wo. Aux., "Harry W. Nelson" scholarship, St. Hilda's School, Wuchang, Hankow... 50 00
LOCKPORT—Richard E. Norton, $1. M. E. H. Norton, $5, St. Paul's School, Lawrenceville, Southern Virginia 6 00
OAKFIELD—*St. Michael's*: $10, S. S., $4.60 (additional), Gen............. 14 60
PALMYRA—"A Friend," Gen......... 5 00
ROCHESTER—*Ascension S. S.*: Bishop Coxe Day-school, Shanghai........ 4 00
Christ Church: Wo. Aux., Gen...... 10 00
Epiphany S. S.: Bishop Coxe Day-school, Shanghai................. 3 00
St. Andrew's S. S.: Bishop Coxe Day-school, Shanghai................ 5 00
St. James's S. S.: Bishop Coxe Day-school, Shanghai................. 5 00
St. Luke's S. S.: Bishop Coxe Day-school, Shanghai................. 8 00
St. Mark's S. S.: Bishop Coxe Day-school, Shanghai................. 5 00
St. Paul's S. S.: Bishop Coxe Day-school, Shanghai................. 8 00
Trinity Church S. S.*: Bishop Coxe Day-school, Shanghai.............. 10 00
Mrs. A. B. Smith, Gen............. 5 00
Miss E. M. Moser, Gen............. 5 00
Mrs. W. Horton, Gen.............. 1 00
MISCELLANEOUS—Junior Aux., "Helen M. Halsey" scholarship, Girls' Training Institute, West Africa, $5; "Sybil Carter" scholarship, St. Hilda's School, Wuchang, Hankow, $5 .... 10 00

West Texas

Ap. $26.20

ALFRED—*St. Thomas's*: Gen......... 2 50
COMFORT—*St. Boniface's S. S.*: Gen.. 3 00
FALFURRIAS—*Grace*: Gen........... 2 50
GONZALES—*Church of the Messiah*: Junior Aux., Gen................ 1 00

HALLETTSVILLE—*St. James's*: Gen.... 7 60
SAN DIEGO—*Atonement*: Gen......... 50
YOAKUM—*Church of the Holy Communion*: Gen..................... 9 10

West Virginia
Ap. $345.73
CHARLES TOWN—Miss S. M. Keyes, "C. E. Ambler" scholarship, Hooker Memorial School, Mexico.......... 15 00
FORT SPRING—*Church of the Holy Communion*: Gen................. 5 92
LEWISBURG—*St. James's*: Honolulu, 33 cts.; Philippines, 33 cts.; Porto Rico, 34 cts.; China, $2.91; Gen., $8.75 .... 12 66
NEW MARTINSVILLE—*St. Ann's*: Mexico 3 40
PARKERSBURG—*Church of the Good Shepherd*: Gen............... 200 00
Trinity Church: Mrs. M. E. Rathbone, Gen. 15 00
RONCEVERTE—*Incarnation*: Philippines, 89 cts.; Porto Rico, 88 cts.; Cuba, 88 cts.; China, $2.............. 4 65
ST. ALBANS—*St. Mark's*: Gen....... 1 40
SHEPHERDSTOWN—*Trinity Church*: Dom. and Frn................. 31 49
WHEELING—*St. Luke's*: Gen......... 35 00
WHITE SULPHUR SPRINGS — *St. Thomas's*: Gen.................. 21 21

Missionary Districts

Alaska
Ap. $135.00
CIRCLE CITY—*Heavenly Rest*: Gen.... 10 00
FORT YUKON—*St. Stephen's*: Gen..... 20 00
NOME—*St. Mary's Mission*: Gen...... 100 00
VALDEZ—*Epiphany S. S.*: Gen........ 5 00

Arizona
Ap. $30 00
TUCSON—*Grace S. S.**: Gen.......... 26 00
WICKENBURG—*Mission*: Gen.......... 4 00

Asheville
Ap. $43.25; *Sp.* $6.75
BELLE—*Trinity Church* (Haw Creek): Dom............................
BILTMORE—Mrs. L. W. Elias, evangelistic work in the foreign field..... 7 00
CANDLER—*St. Clement's*: Dom....... 30
GLEN ALPINE—Rev. James Joyner, Gen. 1 00
GREEN RIVER—*St. Andrew's*: Gen..... 1 00
St. Joseph's: Gen................. 1 00
LINCOLNTON—*St. Cyprian's*: Frn., 50 cts.; Gen., $1............... 1 50
YADKIN VALLEY—*Chapel of Rest*: Dom., $1.37; Frn., 55 cts.; Gen., $2. 3 92
MISCELLANEOUS—Wo. Aux., Gen., $27; Sp. for Whiterocks Indians, Utah, 50 cts.; Sp. for St. Anne's Embroidery School, Kyoto, $3.25; Sp. for church at Wheatland, Wyoming, $3.. 33 75

Eastern Oregon
Ap. $4.44
THE DALLES—Wo. Aux., Gen........ 4 44

Honolulu
Ap. $50.00; *Sp.* $66.00
MISCELLANEOUS—Wo. Aux., "Honolulu Missionary Union" scholarship, Sp. for St. Mary's Orphanage, Shanghai. 50 00
Wo. Aux., Gen., $50; Sp. for Foreign Missionary Life Insurance Fund, $16 .... 66 00

Idaho
Ap. $90.41; *Sp.* $11.80
BONNER'S FERRY—Gen. ....
CALDWELL—*St. David's*: Gen.........
CŒUR D'ALENE—*St. Luke's*: Gen.....
KETCHUM—*St. Thomas's*: Gen.......
LAKE—Mrs. George Garner, Gen......
LEWISTON—*Nativity*: Gen...........
MOSCOW—*St. Mark's*: Gen..........
NAMPA—*Grace S. S.*: Sp. for Rev. R. C. Wilson, Zangzok, Shanghai, $11.80; *Gen., $16.26............
POCATELLO—*Trinity Church*: Gen.....
WALLACE—*Holy Trinity Church*: Gen.

Kearney
Ap. $35.76
HASTINGS—*St. Mark's*: Gen.........
HOLDREGE—Gen..................
KEARNEY—*St. Luke's S. S.**: Gen...
KIMBALL—*St. Hilda's*: Gen..........

Nevada
Ap. $2.35
TONOPAH—*St. Mary's S. S.*: Gen.....

North Dakota
Ap. $1.78
ASHLEY—*Mission S. S.*: Gen.........

Oklahoma
Ap. $162.25
ATLAS—*Mission*: Gen..............
DEWEY—Mrs. John G. James, Gen...
HOBART—*Grace*: Gen..............
MANGUM—*Mission*: Gen............
McALESTER—*All Saints'*: Gen.......
NEWKIRK—*St. John's*: Gen.........
OKLAHOMA CITY—"Thankful," Gen...
PAWHUSKA—*St. Thomas's*: Work in West Africa...................
PAWNEE—*Ascension*: Gen...........
TULSA—*Trinity Church*: "Three Members," work at Boone University, Wuchang, Hankow............
WATONGA—*St. Stephen's*: Gen......
MISCELLANEOUS — Branch Wo. Aux., Gen. ....

Olympia
Ap. $226.18; *Sp.* $10.00
BLAINE—*Christ Church*: Gen........
BUCKLEY—*St. Paul's*: Gen..........
CHEHALIS—*Epiphany*: Gen..........
Mrs. Kate C. Millett, Gen........
EAST SOUND — *Emmanuel Church*: Gen. ....
MONTESANO—Mrs. A. D. Bishop and son, Gen.....................
OLYMPIA—*St. John's*: Gen..........
PORT ANGELES—*St. Andrew's*: Gen...
SEATTLE—*St. Andrew's*: Gen........
St. Mark's Settlement S. S.: Sp. for Rev. Mr. Clapp, Bontok, Philippine Islands ....
SNOHOMISH—*St. John's*: Gen........
TACOMA—*St. Luke's*: Gen. (of which "A Friend," $5)...............
Miss Sarah M. Trowbridge, Gen....

Sacramento
Ap. $62.15
BURNS VALLEY—*Mission*: Gen. (of which Apportionment, 1908-09, $1.10)...
COLUSA JUNCTION — Miss Martha Arvedson, Gen..............
ELK GROVE—*Mission*: Gen..........
FERNDALE—*St. Mary's*: Gen........

13 40
2 70
13 40

5 00
1 35
2 10

7 00

1 18
35
1 10
14
32
1 61
92
92
1 69
42
2 25
1 13
1 01
2 06
50
.93
2 17

21 00

30 02

2 50

8 00
18 00

2 38

5 59
33 00

5 00
42 00
2 50

39 86

24 90
25 01

5 54

53 45

20 78
2 00
4 00
5 00
12 50
45 00

5 98

Spokane
Ap. $118.02

COLFAX—*Good Samaritan*: Wo. Aux.,
Gen. 3 00
DAVENPORT—*St. Luke's*: Wo. Aux.,
Gen. 1 00
KENNEWICK—*St. John's*: Wo. Aux.,
Gen. 3 00
NORTH YAKIMA—*St. Michael's*: Wo.
Aux., Gen........................ 10 00
SPOKANE—*All Saints'*: Wo. Aux., Gen. 50 00
Brunot Hall: Junior Aux., Gen..... 10 00
St. David's: Wo. Aux., Gen..... 4 00
Epiphany: Guild, Wo. Aux., Gen..... 3 00
St. John's: Wo. Aux., Gen......... 4 00
St. Matthew's: Wo. Aux., Gen...... 5 00
St. Peter's: Wo. Aux., Gen........ 1 50
St. Thomas's: Wo. Aux., Gen....... 5 00
MISCELLANEOUS — B. C. Washington,
Gen. 10 00
Branch Wo. Aux., Gen............ 8 52

Utah
Ap. $179.69

SALT LAKE CITY—*St. Mark's Cathedral*: Gen.................. 107 50
St. Paul's: (of which S. S., $49 04)
Gen. 66 54
Sp. for Convocation Offering, Gen.. 5 65

Western Colorado
Ap. $62.53

GLENWOOD SPRINGS—*St. Barnabas's*:
Gen. 18 26
GRAND JUNCTION—*St. Matthew's*: Gen. 7 88
MONTROSE—*St. Paul's*: Gen........ 3 50
OURAY—*St. John's*: Gen............ 7 50
SILVERTON—*St. John's*: $6.64, St.
John's Guild, $15, Gen........... 21 64
STEAMBOAT SPRINGS—*St. Paul's*: Gen. 3 75

Wyoming
Ap. $56.20

ATLANTIC CITY—Andrew M. Adger,
Gen. 25 00
CAMBRIA—*St. David's*: Gen......... 2 70
EVANSTON—*St. Paul's*: Wo. Aux., Gen. 2 50
GILLETTE—*Holy Trinity Church*: Gen. 3 00
LARAMIE—*St. Matthew's*: Junior Aux.,
Gen. 10 00
SHERMAN—Mrs. C. W. Taylor, Gen.... 1 00
Convocation of the District of Wyoming, Gen..................... 12 00

Foreign Missionary Districts
Ap. $536 18; *Sp.* $125.00

Africa

EDINA—*St. Luke's S. S.**: Gen...... 35 00
LIBERIA—"A Friend," Wo. Aux., for
salary of Miss Ida N. Porter, Shanghai 112 50

Canada

NORTH HATLEY—Miss Jennie H. Davis,
for "Mary Wyman" scholarship, in
Mary Hooker School, City of Mexico. 80 00

England

ASHBOURNE—Mrs. W. C. Alderson,
Gen. 10 00

Hankow

Gen., $178.93; Wo. Aux., Gen. (of
which Juniors, $5; Babies' Branch,
Frn. children, $13.64)............ 242 57

Panama

COLON—*Christ Church*: Sp. for Church Extension on the Isthmus of Panama, for the new church at Bas Obispo, Canal Zone, $70; Mrs. Wooldridge and Rev. Edward J. Cooper, "A Thank-offering," Sp. for Bishop Rowe, Alaska, $30............... 100 00

Shanghai

Dr. and Mrs. Jefferys, Sp. for St. Luke's Hospital, Shanghai, Furnishing Fund....................... 10 00
Apportionment, current year, Gen.. 56 11
Miss A. B. Richmond, Sp. for scholarship, Mr. Ishii's Orphanage, Tokyo. 15 00

Miscellaneous

Ap. $24,309.37; *Sp.* $965.48
Specific Deposit $32.19
Interest, Dom., $3,913.44; Frn., $3,359.93; Gen., $9,919.17; Sp., $813.05; M. T. O., $32.19........18,037 78
United Offering, Wo. Aux., on account of appropriations to September 1st, 1910, Dom., $3,500; Frn., $3,500 .... 7,000 00
Girls' Friendly Society, Sp. for Mrs. Wetmore, to maintain Christ School, Arden, Asheville, as a Holiday House; Holiday Houses in Chicago, New York, Ohio, New Jersey, Michigan, Connecticut, Rhode Island,

Washington, and St. Andrew's Church, Elizabeth, New Jersey, and St. Andrew's Church, Wilmington, Delaware 8 93
Conference for Church work held in Cambridge, Massachusetts, Gen..... 6 37
League for Eastern Oregon, Sp. for Bishop Paddock, Eastern Oregon.... 6 00
"Cash," Gen..................... 2 46
S. E. Monroe, Gen............... 1 00
Mrs. S. D. Ely, Gen............. 1 00
"A. B. G.," support of a deaconess or nurse...................... 00
"One who wants to help"......... 00
Mrs. Holliday, Sp. for Expansion Fund, St. John's University, Shanghai 50

Legacies

ALBANY, SCHENECTADY—Estate of Mrs. Eliza E. Anderson, for Dom. missions, with the request that the same be used especially for work in Western Texas and Northern Texas and for work among Indians..........20,24 68
CONN., NEW HAVEN—Estate of Sarah M. Rowland, to the Society......... 9 68
VT., MIDDLEBURY—Estate of Mrs. Elizabeth H. Platt, Dom., $155.05; Frn., $155.05................... 31 10

Receipts for the month.........$ 115,5 36
Amount previously acknowledged.. 1,399,7 05

Total since September 1st......$1,515,3 41

SUMMARY OF RECEIPTS

Receipts divided according to purposes to which they are to be applied	Received during July	Amounts previously Acknowledged	Tot
1. Applicable upon the appropriations of the Board.	$ 81,785 63	$ 786,999 06	$ 868,78 69
2. Special gifts forwarded to objects named by donors in addition to the appropriations of the Board.	12,219 08	236,992 20	249,2 28
3. Legacies for investment.....................	....	165,000 00	165,00 00
4. Legacies, the disposition of which is to be determined by the Board at the end of the fiscal year	21,507 46	89,890 80	111,3 26
5. Specific Deposit.............................	32 19	120,899 99	120,9 18
Total...........................	$115,544 36	$1,399,782 05	$1,515,3 41

Total receipts from September 1st, 1909, to August 1st, 1910, applicable upon the appropriations, divided according to the sources from which they have come, and compared with the corresponding period of the preceding year. Legacies are not included in the following items, as their disposition is not determined by the Board until the end of the fiscal year.

OFFERINGS TO PAY APPROPRIATIONS

Source	To Aug. 1, 1910	To Aug. 1, 1909	Increase	Decrease
1. From congregations.....................	$423,089 78	$379,258 96	$43,830 82	$... ..
2. From individuals......................	65,858 12	82,420 85	....	16,5 73
3. From Sunday-schools..................	139,638 31	139,852 38	....	2 07
4. From Woman's Auxiliary...............	81,447 06	87,060 78	....	5,6 72
5. From interest........................	80,162 88	71,232 81	8,930 07	... ..
6. Miscellaneous items..................	1,588 54	7,573 07	....	5,9 53
Total......................	$791,784 69	$767,398 85	$24,385 84	... ..
Woman's Auxiliary United Offering........	77,000 00	45,000 00	32,000 00	... ..
Total........................	$868,784 69	$812,398 85	$56,385 84	... ..

APPROPRIATIONS FOR THE YEAR

SEPTEMBER 1ST, 1909, TO AUGUST 31ST, 1910

Amount Needed for the Year

1. To pay appropriations as made to date for the work at home and abroad........ $1,214,6 07
2. To replace Reserve Funds temporarily used for the current work.............. 32,9 33

Total... $1,247,5 40
Total receipts to date applicable on appropriations......................... 868,7 69

Amount needed before August 31st, 1910..................................... $ 378,8 71

THE
Spirit of Missions

AN ILLUSTRATED MONTHLY REVIEW
OF CHRISTIAN MISSIONS

October, 1910

CONTENTS

The Subscription Price of THE SPIRIT OF MISSIONS is ONE DOLLAR per year. Postage is prepaid in the United States, Porto Rico, The Philippines and Mexico. For other countries in the Postal Union, including Canada, twenty-four cents per year should be added.

Subscriptions are continued until ordered discontinued.

Change of Address: In all changes of address it is necessary that the old as well as the new address should be given.

How to Remit: Remittances, made payable to George Gordon King, Treasurer, should be made by draft on New York, Postal Order or Express Order. One and two cent stamps are received. To checks on local banks ten cents should be added for collection.

All Letters should be addressed to The Spirit of Missions, 281 Fourth Avenue, New York.

Published by the Domestic and Foreign Missionary Society.

President, RIGHT REVEREND DANIEL S. TUTTLE, D.D. *Secretary,* ——— ———
Treasurer, GEORGE GORDON KING.

Entered at the Post Office, in New York, as second-class matter.

OLD ST. PETER'S, PHILADELPHIA
Where Bishop Kemper was consecrated, September 25th, 1835

HE SPIRIT OF MISSIONS

AN ILLUSTRATED MONTHLY REVIEW
OF CHRISTIAN MISSIONS

VOL. LXXV. **October,** 1910   No. 10

THE PROGRESS OF THE KINGDOM

After Seventy-five Years

THIS year, and the very month in which this is written, is rich with memories of events which made an epoch in our missionary history. It was the General Convention of 1835 which established our Missionary Society on a foundation wide as the Church itself; which declared the sphere of its responsibility to be as wide as the world; and which devised for the conducting of this campaign of service the order of missionary bishops. A fuller account of these events will be found in the historical articles which appear in the following pages. We comment editorially upon this anniversary chiefly that we may call attention to the conditions existing seventy-five years ago as compared with those of to-day.

In the first place, THE SPIRIT OF MISSIONS was not yet born. Its infant life began the following January, 1836. Of course we can hardly imagine what the Church could have been like without THE SPIRIT OF MISSIONS, and we trust our readers find the conception an equally difficult one.

Secondly, the number of missionaries in the employment of the Board at that time consisted of 33 clergy, 4 laymen and 9 women. This covered both the domestic and foreign field, which, viewed from our modern standpoint, were strangely mixed. Texas, for example, which had not yet been admitted to the Union, counted as a foreign field, while Chicago stood for the "Far West." To-day we number 1,050 clergy at home and abroad, 680 laymen and 750 women.

Thirdly, the receipts of the infant society, as they appear in the pages of THE SPIRIT OF MISSIONS during the first year of its life were $25,528.33. To-day we appropriate over $1,200,000 and find even that insufficient for the demands from the field.

Three-quarters of a century of marvellous growth the Church of to-day looks back upon. At the General Convention of 1835 she counted 36,416 communicants and 763 clergy, while to-day her numbers are 929,117 communicants and 5,516 clergy. Much as we realize things unaccomplished and see opportunities which have not been grasped, there is still great cause for thanksgiving in what, by the grace of God, has been accomplished.

(805)

THE record of the Church's giving
for the past year is complete. The
books of the treasurer were balanced on
the first of Septem-
Final Figures   ber, at which time
of the   the fiscal y e a r
Deficit   closed. We rejoice
to say that the re-
sult is more satisfactory than at one time
seemed possible. The deficit which we
must report to the General Convention
amounts to $74,532.55. Of this $33,000
was brought over from last year, being
an inheritance from the still larger deficit of the previous year. The actual
shortage, therefore, of the current year
is about $40,000, while the appropria-
tions are more than $66,000 in excess of
the previous year. This means that,
while we have used $136,000 in legacies
at the disposal of the Board in reaching
this result, the Church has given considerably the largest sum in her history.

It is gratifying to
Whence It   note that $30,000 in
Came   excess of last year
has come through
increased giving to the regular apportionment. This we wish specially to
emphasize, as it is the common experience that congregations which have once
been educated to consider their apportionment as a moral obligation and a
spiritual opportunity, do not readily unlearn the practice of giving.
A second source, which will touch the
hearts of all friends of the missionary
cause, was in certain unexpected legacies
—particularly the generous gift of the
late Bishop McVickar (a legacy of
$20,000) which, at the request of his
family, has been applied to help in meeting the deficiency. This magnanimous
act will be greatly appreciated, but it is
sad that the living Church should depend
upon the gifts of the dead to carry on
her living work. Shall the day not come
when we provide so adequately for the
current expenses of the Church's mission that the pious bequests of those who
are at rest may be used for the planting of permanent memorials in the mission field?

service, and who, with their five assistants and seventy-five pupils, will lose
practically all their possessions in the
burning of the *Tipi-Tonka,* "Big
House," as the Indians call it.

The Church at large will sympathize
with South Dakota and its bishop in this
calamity, and will echo the sentiment
of a local newspaper, the Valentine *Re-
publican,* which declares that it "joins
with the citizens generally in hoping
the Church authorities will decide to rebuild, believing that an institution of
this kind, conducted as St. Mary's has
been, is a substantial and praiseworthy
one which should not be lost to the
country."

Bishop Johnson estimates that not
less than $15,000 will be required to re-
store the school to its former state of
efficiency.

The Centennial of the First American Board of Foreign Missions

IN October the American Board of
Commissioners for Foreign Missions will celebrate the centennial of its
organization. It was
the first missionary
society formed in
this country for the
extension of God's
Kingdom in non-
Christian lands. For
the first few years of its existence it was
the channel through which American
Christians of various communions expressed their missionary zeal. But as
the religious life of the nation grew
stronger the "American Board," as it is
generally known, became identified almost exclusively with the Congregationalists and is now controlled by the
authorities of that denomination. Its
career has been an honorable and useful
one. It was the pioneer in sending the
Gospel to the Hawaiian Islands and to
other parts of the South Seas. Its work
in Turkey has had no small part in
creating the conditions which at last
seem to hold out hope for ultimate reform to that long-suffering people. In
India, China and Japan the missions of
the American Board have long stood for
effective service by well trained men and

women. Its staff now numbers nearly
six hundred Americans, who are making
known the Christian message in twenty-
seven different languages, with the help
of 4,500 native assistants. The 584 congregations established as a result of this
work include 74,000 living communicants, while the adherents number 132,-
000. In its 1,500 schools and colleges.
the Board is training more than 70,000
pupils. Over 300,000 cases are treated
annually by able doctors and nurses in
its seventy-one hospitals. In its large
use of native helpers, in its industrial
and literary work, in its effort to develop self-supporting and missionary-
hearted congregations, the American
Board is worthily maintaining the best
traditions of missionary service. It has
made large contributions to the peace
and progress of the world. Its achievements deserve to be known and applauded
by all. Upon the invitation of the
American Board many of the mission
boards of the country will be represented
at the centennial exercises in Boston
October 11th-14th. Our Board of Missions has appointed the Rev. Dr. Leonard
K. Storrs as its representative.

I T is certain that the approaching
General Convention will be more
strongly ruled by the missionary motive,
and will direct more
Missions at the   attention to dis-
General   tinctively mission-
Convention   ary matters, than
has any previous
session. Such a result would naturally
have followed upon the awakening consciousness of our duty to Christ and
His world, which we, in common with
Christians of other names, have experienced during the last two years. As
never before, a world-wide mission has
been brought before the eye and impressed upon the mind of the Church.
It would, therefore, be impossible for
the Church to meet in Council without
stressing those things upon which her
attention has been fixed.

But there is a further reason for fore-
casting a distinctly missionary convention. Some of the most important

The Need of
Prayer

In view of all these, and many other questions, which the General Convention will be called upon to decide, the prayers of our faithful Church folk should be many and constant, that the Divine Spirit will grant wisdom and understanding, a large sympathy and a larger love, to those who are the Church's representatives in her great council. Let us ask especially that both they and we may increasingly realize that it is the one business of the Church to make her Lord known to those whom He seeks to win, and that all "business" which does not aid in doing this is worse than a waste of time.

ONE of the most effective and far-reaching influences of St. Paul's Normal and Industrial School, Lawrenceville, Va., is that

Negro Farmers
in
Conference

which it exercises through the yearly meeting of what is called the Farmers' Conference. This is just what its name indicates, and its membership is confined to the Negroes within the county. The sixth annual session of this Conference took place in the closing week of July, and for two days 2,500 persons were in attendance, representing all sections in the community. Archdeacon Russell, who is the head of St. Paul's School, was the father of the Conference and has from the beginning been its president. In his address at this latest session he told some things which are well worth noting.

In the six years since the first gathering met, the progress within the county was indicated by the following facts: The total valuation of real and personal property then was $325,000; now it is $515,209.15. Number of acres owned then, 40,550; to-day, 54,000. The Negroes of the county own a little over one-seventh of its land area and one-sixth of its taxable values. Three years ago criminal prosecutions were 24; last year, 18. Criminal expenses then, $1,944.20;

now, $954—a decrease of more than half.
The speaker also said that the jail stood
open for half a year, and until March of
this year there were only two prisoners.
Only one murder was committed in the
county during the year, and neither victim nor murderer was a native of the
county, or even of the state. The lack of
prisoners has caused such a reduction in
the revenue of the sheriff for feeding
prisoners that he declares the Conference
is about to starve him out. "Yet," said
the speaker, "in some of the much-ad-
vertised 'Negro Edens' and 'Gardens of
Paradise' the sheriffs are still doing a
thriving business in feeding prisoners,
with no immediate prospect of starvation; the jails are not lacking inmates,
and the criminal expenses show a decided
tendency to hold their own."

These results Archdeacon Russell at-
tributes to the good work done by the
Farmers' Conference. If he is right in
this—as in a measure at least he must
be—this Conference should draw to itself
the attention of all those who are interested in the betterment of conditions
among Negroes. It certainly marks a
way by which lasting results are to be
obtained, and it suggests a means of education for adult members of the population which will. to some extent, be a substitute for the more thorough training
given to the younger Negroes in our industrial institutions.

Such efforts must lead to progress, not
only in methods of agriculture, but in all
that makes for betterment in the life of
the Negro and his family. We are not
surprised, therefore, to find its president
urging, and the Conference adopting,
plans for the extension of the school opportunities; the Negroes themselves furnishing the money to provide a longer
term. There are also sound and straight-
forward words about manliness and self-
reliance, the paying of taxes, the rotation
of crops and the establishing of bank accounts. A significant statement is that
which declares that the number of such
accounts has in six years increased from
none to 200, with outstanding certificates
of deposit aggregating over $25,000.

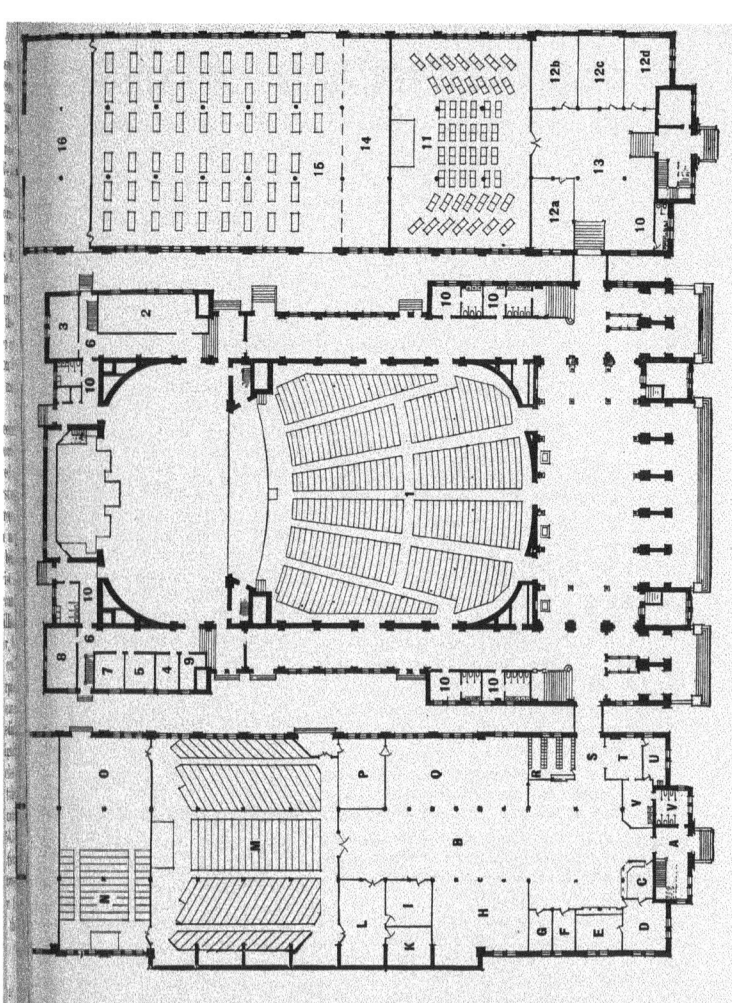

First Hall—A—Elm Street Entrance. B—Lobby. C—Registration. D—Office. E—Information and Post-office. F—Church Periodical Club. G—Daughters of the King. H—Reception and Writing Rooms. I—Girls' Friendly Society. K—Junior Auxiliary Rest-room. L—Junior Auxiliary Exhibit. M—Woman's Auxiliary Hall. N—Conference Hall, Sunday-school, etc. O—Sunday-school Exhibit. P—Serving Kitchen. Q—Tea-room. R—Check-room. S—Passage to Main Building. T—Rest-room. U—Hospital. V—Toilets. X—Store-room.

Second Hall—1—House of Deputies. 2—Information. 3—Postoffice. 4—Telegraph and Telephone. 5—Committee Room. 6—Stairways to Committee Rooms on Floor Above. 7—President's Private Room. 8—Secretary's Office. 9—Storage Room. 10—Toilets.

Third Hall—11—House of Bishops, Assembly Room. 12a, 12b, 12c, 12d—House of Bishops, Committee Rooms. 13—House of Bishops, Lobby. 14—House of Bishops, Lunch Room. 15—General Lunch Room. 16—Kitchen.

(811)

THE SANCTUARY OF MISSIONS

THY task may well seem over-
hard
Who scatterest in thankless soil
Thy life as seed, with no reward—
Save that which duty brings to
toil.

Yet do thy work; it shall succeed
In thine, or in another's day,
And if denied the victor's meed
Thou shalt not lack the toiler's
pay.
—*Anon.*

THANKSGIVINGS

"We thank thee"—
For the increasing realization of
our duty and privilege in giving life,
or influence, or wealth, for the extension of thy Kingdom. (Page 806.)

For the leaders who have been
raised up to arouse the Church to a
sense of her Mission, and to fight
her wars of conquest. (Pages
813, 817.)

For the guidance and growth
vouchsafed during the seventy-five
years of the Church's conscious life
as The Missionary Society.

For the light which shines from
our Christian schools in non-Christian lands. (Page 836.)

For the men and women who are
bearing faithful witness for thee
among the peoples of our own land.

That the fruits of righteousness
are the common proof of the power
of thy Gospel, by whomsoever it is
preached. (Page 828.)

For the good examples of thy servants who, having finished their
course in faith, do now rest from
their labors. (Pages 642-43.)

That thou hast set us in this good
day of opportunity, with power in
our hands, and loyalty to thee in
our hearts.

INTERCESSIONS

"That it may please thee"—

To guide by thy Holy Spirit the
action of the General Convention in
choosing a leader for our missionary
work and devising plans for its development. (Page 808.)

To raise up friends who in this
time of need shall rally to the aid
of the Indian schools in South
Dakota. (Page 807.)

To guide and bless those who are
aiding the Negro people to grow in
industry, integrity and the fear of
God. (Page 809.)

To keep sweet the hearts and lives
of Christian men in foreign lands
that by their righteous living they
may bless themselves and honor
thee. (Page 822.)

To call others who shall close up
the vacant places in the ranks of the
missionary army and add the reinforcements needed for success

To make fruitful the teaching of
missions among the young.

PRAYER

FOR GENERAL CONVENTION

REVEAL thy will, O Lord, to
thy servants, the bishops,
presbyters and laymen of thy
Church in General Convention assembled; and so direct all their
words and works that in them thy
holy Name may be glorified and the
bounds of thy kingdom enlarged
through Jesus Christ our Lord.
Amen.

¶ Persons wishing to join the "Church Prayer League" of intercession
for missions should address the Rev. Harvey Officer, O.H.C., Holy Cross,
West Park, Ulster County, N. Y.

THE MISSIONARY AWAKENING OF 1835

By the Reverend Hugh L. Burleson

SEVENTY-FIVE years ago this fall the General Convention met in Philadelphia. In some respects this was the most momentous gathering which the Church has ever known, and it may justly be said to mark an epoch in missionary history.

Few of us realize through what difficulties and discouragements the Church struggled into being and finally gained a foothold among the religious influences of this country. The Convention of 1789 adopted the Prayer Book and the Constitution, harmonizing some hitherto discordant elements and marking the beginning of united action in the life of the Church. But the growth which followed was pitiably small. This has been called the period of the great stagnation. Yet during this time foundations were laid, and a machinery of administration devised which has met remarkably well the demands and the stress of the years that have followed.

With 1811 began the new era of internal growth. For the twenty-four years

Bishop G. W. Doane

following the Church was so greatly engaged in "strengthening her stakes" as to have little opportunity for "lengthening her cords." Churches were built, missions established, and state after state elected its bishop. At the General Convention of 1835 the two bishops of 1811 had become fourteen, the twenty-five clerical deputies had become sixty-nine, and the twenty-two laymen fifty-one. The nine states represented were now twenty-one.

Bishop McIlvaine

But the missionary idea had not yet taken hold upon the consciousness of the Church. Largely and necessarily concerned in previous years with the great problems of her own internal growth—indeed of her very existence in the new land where circumstances had been so tremendously against her—it was not strange that the American Church should not earlier have understood herself. She was, in the eyes of the Nation,—and largely in her own eyes—a respectable and exclusive sect of English origin and Tory proclivities. Her missionary enterprises—such as they were—had been the efforts of a volunteer society embracing a small number of people; a society which men joined as they might any other association for the promotion of any enterprise—wise or otherwise. Loosely organized, a suppliant for the Church's casual bounty, such a society could not gain a serious hold upon the Church's consciousness. The vision was narrow and the results were meagre.

And then the Church awoke and set herself about her task! Two great things happened in the Convention of 1835: First, the Church learned that she herself the Missionary Society; Second, she created her Missionary Bishops.

I

A committee had been appointed to consider and report on missionary re-
organization. It consisted of Bishop G. W. Doane, the representative High
Churchman of his day; Bishop McIlvaine, the leading Evangelical, and Dr.
Milnor, rector of St. George's Church. To them, in their deliberations, it came like
a revelation that there was a simple and vital basis for membership in the missionary society. They found themselves instantly agreeing to the suggestion of
Dr. Milnor that the Church herself was such a society, and that every
baptized child of hers was a member thereof. A report embodying these principles was immediately prepared and unanimously adopted, and the whole scope
of the Church's missionary enterprise was thereby transformed and enlarged.
Instantly the new conception took its place among the religious conviction of
the Church, and with it there came an enlarged view of responsibilities, which
were seen to be not only nation-wide, but world-wide.

The two great sermons preached in connection with that Convention sound
a note which has echoed throughout the years, and is still a guiding principle of
our work. Bishop McIlvaine in his missionary sermon before the Convention
said:

> "The Church is a great missionary association, divinely constituted,
> for the special work of sending into all the world the ministers and mis-
> sionaries of the Word.
>
> "But if such be the cardinal object of the whole Church, it must be
> alike the cardinal object and duty of every part of that Church, so that
> whether a section thereof be situated in America or in Europe, or the re-
> motest latitudes of Africa, it is alike required to attempt the enlightening
> of all the earth; and though it be the smallest of the local divisions of the
> Christian household; and though just on its own narrow boundaries there
> may be millions of neglected pagans swarming with the horrors of heathen-
> ism, still that little section of the Church is to embrace within the circle of
> its zeal, if not of its immediate labors, the destitute of all the earth."

With such words as these echoing in their ears, the members of the Convention adopted a Constitution for the guidance of the Church's Mission in
which it was declared that "This Society shall be considered as comprehending
all persons who are members of the Church," and "for the guidance of the Committees it is declared that the missionary field is always to be regarded as one—
The World; the terms Domestic and Foreign being understood as terms of locality, adopted for convenience. *Domestic* Missions are those which are established *within*, and *Foreign* Missions are those which are established *without* the
territory of the United States."

At last the Church had found herself! Thus she took her first step in a
glorious advance.

II

The first question had involved principles and ideals; the second was one
of practical efficiency. If the words of her declaration were true, the Episcopal
Church in America, as a national branch of the Catholic Church, immediately
became responsible for planting her faith and order throughout the nation and
the world. How was this to be done?

We must not fail to recognize that the situation was a difficult one. That
which is the ultimate strength of the Church was for the time her immediate

weakness. An Episcopal Church without a bishop is like a body without a head. It is a marvel that under the conditions of Colonial times the Church could grow at all. Only the distant and somewhat vague connection with the See of London served to fill the great void and create a technical sense of unity. Yet how was the episcopate to be established in distant places where priests and parishes were not? Such a thing had not been heard of. The only ideal of a bishop which existed was that of a man who ruled over parishes already established, and with dignity and aristocratic pomp controlled a Church already brought into being. It is not strange that the apostolic conception of a bishop as the first missionary, carrying with him to distant places the fulness of the Church's ministry of grace, had long been obscured.

It is true that one or two had grasped this idea. Philander Chase, the born pioneer and sturdy man of God, had heard the call of the wilderness and gone out into it. He had himself felt, and had inspired in others, a conviction of the futility of an Episcopal Church without a bishop. Going to Ohio in 1817 he was, in the following year, elected bishop by a so-called convention of two clergymen and nine laymen, and in 1819 was consecrated as bishop of that western wilderness. After heroic labors and hardships, leaving behind him as a monument Kenyon College, whch he established at Gambier, he went on in 1831 to the Territory of Michigan, which then included practically all the known Northwest. Plunging once more into the trackless forests, he reappears four years later in Illinois, where, in this memorable year of missionary awakening, 1835, by a corporal's guard he is again elected bishop of a diocese which has in all four presbyters, one church building and thirty-nine communicants.

PHILANDER CHASE
Bishop of Ohio and Illinois

No doubt such as he had unconsciously been shaping the convictions of the Church. It could not but be seen how sharp was the dilemma. On the one side was the Church's responsibility—certainly for the entire nation, and after that for the world; on the other, the ineptitude of the Church unless equipped with her apostolic ministry in its three orders. How, then, could the episcopate reach the United States and the world? Ohio and Illinois had solved the question by a most desperate resource—by electing, in their feebleness, a man to whom they could give no support, and for whom there was not even a parish of which he could be rector. This plainly was an impossible burden, which only a few daring souls would take up. And no man so elected could hope to do his work as it should be done.

It was at this time that there flashed upon the mind of the Church another solution. Bishops must be *sent*, not called. Students of ecclesiastical polity reminded themselves that the episcopate is committed, not to a single man but to a body, the *episcopatum in solidum*. It was not the individual bishops, but the House of Bishops, to which was entrusted the preservation of faith and order, and therefore the jurisdiction over the national Church. If the *jurisdiction* lay with them, then the power of *mission* also was theirs. It was competent for them to choose and create a bishop who should be their vicar, and represent the American Episcopate in places where its constituent members could not go. And thus there emerges the missionary bishop, exercising jurisdiction under the House of Bishops in such places outside the limits of organized dioceses as it shall decree. This was a perfectly sane and logical solution of the problem—

and it was also a *revolution*. It was the opening of a door of opportunity so great that the Church of that day could not possibly have understood the consequences which were to follow.

Yet some forecast of that which God was doing through them must have stirred the hearts of these good fathers of the Church. Many of them had stood faithful in the sad day of disappointment and in the trying day of internal growth. Now their vision seemed suddenly enlarged, and the whole Convention breathed a hope and an enthusiasm such as had never been known in the Episcopal Church.

The great sermon preached by Bishop Doane at the consecration of Bishop Kemper was a noble utterance. "What," he said, "is meant by a missionary bishop? A bishop *sent forth* by the Church, *not sought for* of the Church; going *before* to organize the Church, not waiting till the Church has partially been organized; a leader, not a follower, in the march of the Redeemer's conquering all triumphant Gospel; sustained by their alms whom God has blessed both with the power and will to offer Him of their substance, for their benefit who are not blessed with both or either of them; sent by the Church, even as the Church is sent by Christ.

"To every soul of man, in every part of the world, the Gospel is to be preached. Everywhere the Gospel is to be preached *by, through* and *in* the Church. To bishops, as successors of the Apostles, the promise of the Lord was given to be with His Church 'always, to the end of the world.' . . . Open your eyes to the wants, open your ears to the cry, open your hands for the relief of a perishing world. Send *the Gospel*. Send it, as you have received it, *in the Church*. Send out, to preach the Gospel, and to build the Church—to every portion of your own broad land, to every stronghold of the Prince of hell, to every den and nook and lurking place of heathendom—a missionary bishop!"

At last the Church had found herself! Great trials, many disappointments, even sad discouragements, lay before her, but she had taken up her task and faced her problem. The events of this memorable year had determined the ideals by which she was to be guided. She knew herself set to be a missionary throughout the length and breadth of this land, and the lands beyond—and she never lost the vision. She was at last true to the commission of her Lord, and her reward came according as she was faithful.

BISHOP KEMPER IN HIS OLD AGE

JACKSON KEMPER:

OUR FIRST MISSIONARY BISHOP

By the Reverend Hugh L. Burleson

*Bishop Kemper
as a young man*

IT was on the first day of September, 1835, that the House of Bishops, assembled in General Convention, pursuant to a canon just passed, announced to the House of Deputies that they had elected the Rev. Francis L. Hawks, D.D., Bishop of the Southwest, and the Rev. Jackson Kemper, D.D., Bishop of Indiana and Missouri, to which title was afterwards added that of Missionary Bishop of the Northwest. Dr. Hawks declined his election, and the Southwest had to wait for its bishop, but with soldierly promptness Jackson Kemper, having seen a duty, hastened to perform it. He accepted the call and was consecrated at St. Peter's, Philadelphia, on September 25th—the last man upon whom the patriarchal Bishop White laid hands in consecration. In this act there also joined that bishop, twice technically a diocesan, but really a veteran missionary—Philander Chase. It was a good strain from which to derive his spiritual lineage.

Within six weeks Bishop Kemper was on his way to his distant field. Not altogether as a stranger did he go, for in company with Dr. Milnor he had the year before visited the Indian mission at Green Bay, and through his activity as a member of the Board of Missions he was already familiar with such work as was being carried on in the West; while in the twenty-four years he had spent, not only as a parish priest in Philadelphia but as an active missionary making yearly tours throughout western Pennsylvania, he had learned many lessons of border work and life.

Consecrated for Indiana and Missouri (between which two jurisdictions lay the vast territory of Illinois), Bishop Kemper found on arriving in his field that he was possessed of the following equipment: one clergyman but no church building in Indiana; one church building but no clergyman in Missouri! And here he began to lay foundations. Accompanied by the Rev. Samuel Roosevelt Johnson, who had come with him from the East, he traversed the southern portion of Indiana, visiting towns of a thousand inhabitants which had no place of public worship. Across the southern part of Illinois they drove in an open wagon with the trunks serving as seats, and toiling through a swamp fitly named "Purgatory" arrived at St. Louis the middle of December.

To follow the journeyings of this apostle and trace the history of his achievements would be impossible. Let us rather try to realize what he was confronting.

His Task

The performance of his work was beset with serious difficulties, some of which may be indicated thus:

(1) The vast territory and the means of communication. There was no a single railway west of the Alleghanies. Over a region comprising the great states of Indiana, Missouri, Iowa, Minnesota, Wisconsin and parts of Kansas and Nebraska, he was compelled to travel by stage coach or lumber wagon, in the saddle or on foot, except where he could use the Mississippi and its confluents. His greatest luxury was the cabin of a river steamer of the early day.

(2) The lack of helpers. Enthusiastic as the Church had been in sending out its missionary bishops, they were very rarely followed by missionary priests. A few devoted men like Breck, Adams and Hobart at Nashotah, or the little band that began pioneer work in Minnesota, were his chief reliance. For years in many places he was not only bishop, but the whole band of clergy. Failing to secure helpers in the East he turned with energy to the field itself, and in the hope of eventually developing a trained body of laymen and some future clergy within his own territory, he founded Kemper College, St. Louis, and persuaded Breck and his companions to give themselves for the establishment of an associate mission out of which grew Nashotah, and later, Seabury. But the clergy raised from the soil were still a long way off.

(3) The people. The settlement of the Middle West was largely from the East. The problem was—if we may so style it—the problem of the Pilgrim Children. Literally so, for the vast majority were Puritans, or sectarians of some sort—if they could be said to have any religion at all. The Church in the East had appealed chiefly to the more cultured and wealthier people. Few of these migrated to the West, which was given over, so far as religion was concerned to extravagant forms of revivalism; the sect spirit was rampant, and the born ministers were frequently lacking in education, and sometimes in qualities most important for one who is to stand as a Christian example. Men living in a region burned over by the fires of religious sensationalism were repelled by the lack of correspondence between religion and morality. Freed from the religious restraints of their earlier home, and eager chiefly to seize material opportunity and acquire sudden wealth, thousands had grown careless or abandoned all religious practices.

(4) The crudities and uncertainties of a new land. The material out of which, and the instruments by which, a religious life such as the Church inculcates could be formed, were largely lacking. Schools were few; churches there were none. Many of the settlers had little but their clothing and their optimism—not much of the former but plenty of the latter, as is usually the case in new land. Each little hamlet was certain that it would become a great metropolis. A thousand other communities, far more promising than that frontier trading-post set in the mud at the foot of Lake Michigan, dreamed of themselves a Chicago. And how could one foresee the drift of the future? Who could know where railways would run and great cities spring up?

Such was the task, but over against the difficulties there were fundamental elements of success. There was the certainty of Christ's promise to be with those who go in His name to win His children; there was the bishop's supreme faith in his own apostolic mission; and there were, scattered throughout the vast area over which he travelled, the scores of faithful souls who still loved the Church of their early days, and whose touching gratitude for his ministration made his pilgrimages and his hardships a joy. Out of this seed the Church of the Middle West was born, and by men who were worthy followers of this great leader the foundations were laid.

His Personality

The following estimate from the pen of the Hon. Isaac Atwater, editor of the St. Anthony paper, appeared after a visitation of the bishop in 1852:

"Bishop Kemper appears something over fifty years of age. Although his hair is assuming a silvery gray, time has in other respects dealt lightly with him; for his frame is erect, his step is as firm, and complexion as ruddy as thirty years ago. His countenance bears the unmistakable impress of benevolence and kindness of heart. You cannot look upon his bland, open face and portly frame, strong with vigorous health, without feeling that the heart within dwells in perpetual sunshine.

"In action he is not a disciple of the Demosthenean eloquence. His gestures are few and not remarkably graceful, though generally appropriate and well-timed. He has a voice of great sweetness, musical in its intonations, which he manages with skill and effect. There is something in the tone, inflections and volume of his voice as he reads a hymn, or the sublime service of the Church, that convinces you there is heart, soul, feeling, there.

"Bishop Kemper displays in his sermons nothing of the subtle metaphysician. It requires no careful thought or intense application to follow him in his train of reasoning. Sentence after sentence, big with important truth, rolls from his lips and falls with most irresistible persuasion and convincing eloquence on the heart of the hearer. He does not inform the intellect and leave the heart unaffected.

"In the social circle Bishop Kemper is at once dignified and affable, frank and open in conversation, perfectly at ease him-

The altar and pulpit of St. Peter's Church, where Bishop Kemper was consecrated

self, and possessing the happy faculty of making all within his influence feel the sunshine of his presence. It is in the interchange of the 'gentle courtesies and sweet amenities' that some of the loveliest and most striking traits of his character are displayed. In him are blended the varied characters of the faithful minister, the kind neighbor, the disinterested friend, the patriotic citizen and the refined gentleman."

Such was the man who went up and down the western valleys, visiting feeb missions and presiding at convocations and councils. Said a prosperous wes ern man, pointing to Bishop Kemper: "Yonder is the richest man in Wisconsin "To the worldly," says Bishop Whipple, "he showed the beautiful simplicity of life of self-denial; yet he was always and everywhere the bishop. In the lumbe man's camp, in the Chippeway lodge, in the log-cabin or the city home, men sa in the simple grandeur of his holy life 'the sign and seal of his apostleship.' "

His Achievement

For nearly thirty-five of the sixty years during which he served at the alta Bishop Kemper traversed the land to which he had been sent. One after a other dioceses were erected out of his vast jurisdiction, and at last, when i 1859 the election of Bishop Whipple was approved by the General Conventio he reluctantly surrendered the title of missionary bishop, which he had so nobl borne, and became the diocesan of Wisconsin.

"What had been accomplished? Twenty-four years had passed away, and by God's blessing on the Church he now saw Missouri a diocese, with its bishop and 27 clergy; Indiana a diocese, with its bishop and 25 clergy; Wisconsin, his own diocese, with 55 clergy; Iowa, a diocese, with its bishop and 31 clergy; Minnesota an organized diocese, with 20 clergy; Kansas but just organized a diocese, with 10 clergy; and the territory of Nebraska, not yet organized as a diocese, with 4 clergy; in all six dioceses where he began with none, and 179 clergymen where he at first found one."

As though this were not enough, he devoted himself for another ten year to the administration of his diocese. He was spared to see his eightieth birthday on Christmas Eve, 1869, but with the coming of the New Year his strength be gan to fail. Still for several weeks he discharged his official duties, oftentime writing his own letters, and to the end—which came on May 24th—he was serv ing the Church to which he had already given a service almost unparalleled i Christian history. He sleeps well in the cemetery at Nashotah, surrounded b many who were his staunch helpers in that early day; and of him his biographe has justly said:

"The Napoleon of a spiritual empire had passed away—and who would not prefer Kemper's crown to Bonaparte's? The missionary bishop of a jurisdiction greater than any since the days of the apostles—and St. Paul himself had not travelled as widely and as long, for Kemper had gone 300,000 miles upon his Master's service—was gone to his reward. Well had his life borne out the meaning of his name: 'Kemper: A Champion.' With the great Apostle to the Gentiles he could say: 'I have fought a good fight; I have finished my course; I have kept the faith.' "

THE GERMAN BANK, HANKOW

TREATY PORT CITIES IN CHINA:
THEIR RELATION TO MISSIONARY WORK

By the Reverend Arthur M. Sherman

DOWN the coast of China, up her great rivers, even to a thousand miles inland, exist the port cities. These important places have been opened by the Chinese to foreigners at intervals during the last seventy years by treaties between China and other nations. China has been unwilling to have foreigners live and trade promiscuously in the empire, but being forced by various wars to open China for the residence and trade of aliens, she has allowed them to live in certain specified cities. These are known as "treaty-port" cities, and foreigners in China other than missionaries (who are allowed to live anywhere) are compelled to live together in these centres.

Even in the port cities the Europeans (as all foreigners are called) do not live in the native settlements. Concessions of land have been accorded foreign nations, and in them the foreign residents live, trade and find recreation. These concessions are almost as much under the control of the nation to which they have been rented as if they actually existed in a colony of their respective governments. They are governed by a local municipal council. These councils lay out wide, clean streets and establish their own police force—khaki-clad Cossacks in a Russian concession, red-turbaned Seiks in the British. Here the merchants from the West build their foreign offices, residences, factories, storehouses, churches and recreation grounds. In fact, these foreign concessions are clean, well-kept little cities of England, Germany, Russia or France, set down by the side of a great Chinese mart bearing the same name.

The settlement is sometimes an international one, as "the model settlement" of Shanghai, the Paris of the East.

There the magnificent banks, hotels, plazas, drives and parks entirely eclipse the small Chinese city. In fact, many visitors go to Shanghai and never see the native town. In Hankow—the Chicago of China—the concessions are separate in government, although to the eye they appear to be one continuous foreign city, extending for two miles along the Yang-tse River. The boundaries between the concessions are well established and defined, but invisible, and a stranger walking along the spacious "Bund" does not know when he has crossed the line from Great Britain to Russia.

Character of the Population

The foreign population of these port cities varies from the 10,000 or more in Shanghai to a little handful in some lonely interior port. But whether few or many, these foreigners form a very important part of the city's population. They are the Commissioners of the Chinese Imperial Customs, with large staffs of foreign and Chinese officers. They are the consular representatives of foreign powers. They are merchants of large interests and of a high grade of intelligence, with the English, German, Japanese or Russian assistants, as the case may be. They are far from being a negligible quantity, and though there are always some who are the flotsam and jetsam of human society from their native lands, many are men who would be leaders in their own lands and are sent to the East because men of large capacity are needed in China to deal with important situations and opportunities.

These port cities are the points of contact between China and the outside world. A strong impression is given in these centres of the character of Western civilization, education, morality and religion. The whole nation is often judged by the few representatives the Chinese see in these treaty ports, and the foreigners resident there are accepted as exponents of the things for which their nation stands.

CHURCH OF ST. JOHN THE EVANGELIST, BRITISH CONCESSION, HANKOW

agues and acquaintances. And he is urged to the same sort of life by men in whom he sees much to admire—men of ability, and a polish that has come from good education and a wide knowledge of the world. He is told that it is necessary in a tropical climate to live just such a life as they are living. Many a downward step has been taken during that fatal first month in an Eastern port city.

If ever a man needs a good friend it is when he first comes to live in the strangely fascinating life of a treaty port in China.

Floating Population

In addition to the more fixed population of these cities, the larger ports with good harbors, such as Shanghai, Hankow, Chefoo, etc., have their numbers greatly augmented by the foreign men-of-war that constantly come and go, and by the officers of the many foreign merchant ships that ply between the various ports. Apart from a very few of the larger places, practically nothing is done for the sailors whom we send to China. The "lure of the East" combined with the very worst from the West awaits them. On shore leave, in little knots, the sailors along up and down the streets. Some-

times thousands of various nationalities are in the harbor at once. They are out for a good time—they have no shore friends. They have no clubs, like the resident foreigners; there are no recreation grounds open to them except on special occasions. Who is to befriend these lads and hold out before them the help and strength of the religion of their home, so far away? Many are the pitfalls spread for unwary feet. Cheap drinking saloons, gambling dens and other places of iniquity bid for the patronage of generous Jack Tar.

America's Share in Demoralizing the East

It is sad to notice that America is sending influences to China to complicate the dangers of the East. The writer had as a fellow-passenger on the Pacific an American who kept a gambling house in the city of Tien-tsin. In the same city the site of the Y. M. C. A. had to be changed because the street that led to it was lined with vile dens, floating the American flag. In Hankow women walk up and down our streets, bearing the name of Americans, and bringing the blush of shame to one proud of his heritage. This is a part of our contribution to China.

Interior of St. John's. This church was recently erected by the foreign community

Relation to the Missionary Problem

Such are the conditions the missionary in these hybrid cities sees. He is trying to tell the Chinese—and to live before them—one thing; while all around him the lives of scores and hundreds of his own race speak more loudly than anything he can say.

To the ordinary Chinese all foreigners are Christians. Is it any wonder that he concludes that his religion is as good as theirs? Is it any wonder that missionaries who are away from the treaty ports and from other foreigners find their work easier, and the character of their native converts better? In the ports the missionary sees his work for the Chinese being daily undone, and he also sees his own people in sore need of help.

Although the Church has gone to China primarily for the Chinese, we cannot leave our own blood unshepherded—both for their own sakes and for the sake of the effect of their lives upon the Chinese. We are in China to advance the Kingdom of God. Anything which is involved in that work is part of our mission. We cannot be interested in Chinese missions and ignore this great al-

lied work which we are now inadequately handling. We *must* work for the men and women of our own race who can do so much to advance or retard the progress of Christ's Kingdom among the Chinese. In Christianizing our own people in China, we will do much toward the Christianization of China. As Mr. William T. Ellis, the Philadelphia journalist has said in his very stimulating recent book, "Men and Missions," "the bearing of the port city upon missionary operations has been hitherto grievously underestimated or else ignored. Few more difficult tasks are before the men of the churches of America and Europe than this one of making the port cities truly representative of the highest civilization of the West, especially in respect to ethical, moral and spiritual phases."

Responsibility of the American Church

The American Church has a peculiar responsibility for the cities along the Yang-tse River. The Church of England is at work in North, South and West China, leaving this as the field for the Episcopal Church of the United States. The port cities in this section

GRAVE OF THE FIRST BISHOP OF HANKOW IN THE ENGLISH CHURCHYARD

have a large proportion of Englishmen in their population. Many of them are nominally Church of England men. The Anglican Church has a prestige which opens many doors to its missionaries. At one time the English Church maintained services in various ports. The government built an occasional church, and chaplains were sent out. These were withdrawn many years ago, and now the American Church is responsible for Chinese and foreigners alike— so far as the Anglican Church is concerned. Bishop Roots, realizing this responsibility, has appointed in each port city one of his missionaries as port chaplain, and wishes them to give as much time as they can spare from the pressure of other districts to the work among the foreign residents.

In Wuhu the foreign community are raising money to build a church for themselves. In Hankow, the largest port city in this district, the English-speaking community have recently built in attractive and convenient church building (to replace an older one); they pay part of the chaplain's salary, and have now begun in the churchyard a house for his residence. They greatly appreciate the time given and the work done on their behalf.

The Present Need

We cannot yet, perhaps, send out men to give their time exclusively to port city work, but we should send well-qualified men to give at least a part of their time to this work. Most missionaries are overworked; many of them doing the work of two or three men. By sending more workers to relieve them, some of the older missionaries here and there can be in a measure released for this work among the foreigners. This can, however, be only a temporary arrangement. We look forward to the time when in the larger ports, and especially in Hankow, there will be a chaplain who will not have to be a double-barrelled man, but can give all his time and strength in the work for English-speaking people. Money is also needed to help in the support of men for this kind of work. Parish houses are needed for the maintenance of work for sailors and others. And a pressing need in Hankow is for a library to circulate wholesome literature among the port residents.

KEEPING COOL IN JAPAN

This is the famous Gojo bridge over the Kamo-Gawa (Wild-duck River). In the bed of this stream, just beyond the bridge, they crucified the early Christians, and in the middle of the bridge began the struggle which overthrew the Shogunate and introduced the history of modern Japan. A unique use of the bridge is here shown: Platforms with short legs are placed in the bed of the shallow river; a bamboo shield overhead protects from dust and rain. Here the Japanese drink tea and hold social converse during the hot weather

CHRISTIAN UNITY IN JAPAN

By the Right Reverend Sidney C. Partridge, D. D.

I WISH to express a few thoughts on this all-important subject, which have been called forth by recent evangelistic experiences in the Missionary District of Kyoto, and to try to make it clear that there is one form, at least, in which that which we are all so earnestly longing for, working for and praying for has already, by God's grace, been actually obtained.

Quite naturally, there is no place where the subject is brought more vividly to the minds and hearts of all Christian people than in the foreign field. "Here, if anywhere," men say, "is the place where we should present a united front to the foe. Sad as our divisions are at home, in nominally Christian lands, they are inexpressibly more so, when we stand side by side in the darkened Orient, with the one on Word of God clasped in our hands, and the One Faith in our Divine Lord proclaimed upon our banners." "Let us all," they say, and say truly, "strive to unite our forces there. Let us make one great and final effort for our own creed, for our own protection and, above all, for our own success, in the concentration of missionary strength and effort."

In this connection, it is always important to remember three things, which, while not making the call for unity any less urgent, yet may serve to modify the subject somewhat in people's minds at home and restrict a certain amount of criticism passed upon those who, with love and charity for all, are trying to be loyal to the great commission in preaching the Gospel to every creature.

Christendom are the greatest bar to the success of missions. An experience of over a quarter of a century in two of our largest mission fields has convinced me that this is largely a misconception, and that the state of things abroad which arises from our ecclesiastical divisions is grossly exaggerated in people's minds at home. It is based, in the first place, upon a wrong system of reasoning, and it overlooks, if it does not ignore, that very vital and effective unity which practically is ours, by God's mercy, already.

There are always, let us remember, two kinds of Orientals that we have to deal with when we come to discuss missions or any other kindred and international subject. There is the real creature of flesh and blood whom the missionary meets face to face, and whom he has to deal with day by day, and there is the ideal creature who is conjured up in the mind and imagination of Church-folk at home. The former is the one who actually lives in the Orient, who tills its soil, eats its food, wears its garb, and inherits all its traditions of the past. He is the product to-day of all the blended systems of philosophy, ethics and religion that have swayed and guided his ancestors, and it is to him, and not to the ideal personage who springs from the fertile American Christian's brain, that we are commissioned to bring the Gospel. He worships his own idols and —it is all important to remember—he does his own thinking, both about his own religion and about the one that we bring and offer to him. He claims the right and privilege of doing this, and he is most surely, by God's permission, entitled to it. Yet this is the very thing that we at home are constantly denying him. We insist, in spite of the continued protests of missionary and convert alike, in doing our Oriental brother's thinking for him. We attempt, by a sort of telepathic system, to project our Western logic into his Eastern brain, and we draw his conclusions for him. Then we go ahead and erect an elaborate structure of arguments on this foundation—and smile complacently when we finish our reasoning and are confident that we "know it all."

As a matter of fact we know little or nothing about it. The Oriental, whom we have treated as little better than an automaton, will either look stolidly indifferent or smile that historic smile of his ancestors as he recognizes the utter unfairness and absurdity of our position. Let us, just for once, come to our senses, and do him at least the justice—if not pay him the compliment—of asking him to tell us honestly and candidly just what he thinks about it all.

Out of the myriad questions and subjects to which all this applies, let us choose just this one before us. Let us ask honestly and frankly whether it is actually true that he cannot accept Christianity because of its divisions and whether he really says to us—as thousands of American Christians believe he does: "I cannot accept the teachings of Christ because all is in such confusion. Your voices and messages are so different that I am bewildered and cannot tell which is right. Go home and agree first of all among yourselves, before you come out here to preach a new religion to me. In the meantime I will abide peacefully in the faith of my fathers, where all is peace and harmony and the sectarian spirit is unknown. What was good enough for the old folks is good enough for me," etc., etc.

Does he actually talk like this—ever or under any circumstances? Yes, under one circumstance only, and that is when the European has hypnotized him and put these ideas into his head. Not otherwise. He doesn't talk that way himself because he knows perfectly well that his own religions are split up into divisions infinitely worse than ours. Buddhism, for instance, presents before his daily life a vision of sectarianism that is unknown in Christian America and can only be paralleled in the nearer Orient in the spirit and scenes that we witness around the Holy Sepulchre in Jerusalem.

Did any Asiatic seeker after truth ever

THE UNDERGROUND STORE OF THE OVERLAND POST

WITH THE OVERLAND MAIL

By the Reverend Maxwell W. Rice

SELDOM was the missionary more agreeably surprised than when the mail stage which had picked him up from the train Ajax, Utah, drew up at an old ranch. he corrals and stockyards were empty d dilapidated, but the adobe and log uses seemed in good repair, though ly one of them appeared to be occu- d. The low buildings with either dirt thatched roofs, all covered with the ite alkali dust, presented so foreign appearance to the missionary that he mped out of the stage to take pictures the rambling outlay of buildings, ds and fences. His surprise grew as looked over the establishment. Con- ted with the occupied building is a e underground store. As the travel- climbed back into the stage he asked driver what it all meant; what so e an outfit was doing among the scat- d ranches in Rush Valley. The er was a Civil War veteran—with a den leg, of course—a driver of the

A snapshot at the missionary

good old type that takes considerable personal interest in the passenger. "You ought to have told me you were a tenderfoot," he replied with a twinkle in his eye. "I thought you had been over the line before. We are on the old 'Overland Route,' and this post was one of the important stops of the 'Overland Mail.'"

A minute later he asked, "How far did you say you were going?" The missionary said that he was going right through to Ibapah in the Deep Creek Valley. "I guess you are not going right through," the old fellow answered; "no stage runs out of Vernon until to-morrow, and Deep Creek is 120 miles from Vernon. What are you going way into that country for? Mining prospector; I guess that's what you are." He said this eyeing my wide felt hat, corduroy shirt, khaki trousers and leggings. It is sometimes unwise to let men know at once what your business is, but realizing that seldom, if ever, did missionaries go through this country it was only fair to let the route know that once at least a missionary had been a comrade. I gathered along the line that Deep Creek did not have a very good reputation; it is too remote from law. A valley whose mail arrives three times a week by staging 130 miles of desert is a place where hot temper and quick act have the right of way; where the people still cling to that rough, lawless, violent way of life once prevailing in the west.

But what interested me more at the time was the fact that the entire 130 miles of stage line was itself part of the old "Overland Route," and I was to travel the whole way with the "Overland Mail." It is perhaps the only part of the "Overland Route" over which the mail stages still run.

It was past noon when I reached Vernon, where I was to spend the night. Vernon is the agricultural centre of Rush Valley. (It lies about seventy miles southwest of Salt Lake City.) The thirty houses of the town proper provide for a population of over a hundred. Ranches are to be seen thinly

Ready for the desert

ind hosts and started on the 120-mile rive to Ibapah. There were three of s in the stage. Mr. Walters, who has e mail contract, and a man wearing chauffer's cap, occupied the front seat. had the second seat, but not to myself, r mail bags and water-bottles took up eir share of the canyon wagon. A nyon wagon is a strong cart with akes, and with a white canvas top as otection against the sun.

The range between Rush Valley and cull Valley is low and not hard to ss, but high enough to give at Point okout a fine view of the mountains and desert valleys to the west. As we descended into Skull Valley the sun set over a desert as flat as the ocean. It is rightly named the "skull" valley, for bleached bones of various animals lay along the roadside, showing plainly what happens when one gets too far from water. Range upon range of desert mountains rose blue against the sunset; some of the mountains showing those strange shapes seen in pictures of the desert.

At Simpson Spring we ate a faint supper, changed horses and driver and set off in a dust storm. Columns of

CLIMBING THE DESERT RANGE

CALLAO, ON THE EDGE OF THE DESERT

alkali dust travelled past us like water-spouts at sea. Our new driver was a typical cowboy. He stuttered so badly, however, that conversation was impossible. But he could swear without difficulty. Consequently his sentences began smoothly and ended equally well.

We reached the Dugway Mountains about midnight, and lay down in the brush under the stars, glad to rest our backs from the jolting and wrenching of the wagon, while the driver watered and fed his horses. Then on foot we climbed the pass, experiencing no difficulty in finding our way, because starlight on the desert is exceptionally bright. The long descent was made at a lively pace. About one in the morning the nigh horse fell in a heap and was dragged before the brakes took effect. We jumped, and found the wagon tongue broken off midway. It was soon spliced with rope and once more we were rattling down the mountain.

Once upon a time to ride with the "Overland Mail" was an exciting experience. The man on the seat beside the driver carried a gun across his knee, and all were on the look-out for Indians or for hold-ups! That night it was exciting, for we were twenty-five miles from water, going down a mountain range in the dark with our wagon-tongue broken in such a way that another all would probably have driven it into the horse's side.

At five in the morning we reached sh Springs, where John Thomas gave a hearty breakfast. The man with the chauffeur's cap went no further, a he here recovered the motor cycle he ad come in search of. The way now ay over the Fish Springs Mount ns. Hitherto we had given the Great A er-ican Desert a wide berth; we ow descended directly upon it, and ur after hour jogged across its sout rn shore; for it lay like a great ocea to the north. At times we could see es with islands, and trees, and even ffs rise from its expanse, apparently b a few miles away. It seemed hard to e-lieve that such sights could be illu n. One cannot blame the traveller for l v-ing the road and following the lur of these desert mirages to quench is aching thirst.

Callao lies on the edge of the d rt a few miles east of the Deep C ek Range. It is over eighty miles fro a railroad. Now came the most tires e part of our journey. Stage-riding er desert valleys and mountain range is bad enough when the traveller is f h, but after a night of it, in fact after re than a solid twenty-four hours, it e-

A mining camp in the desert; the ore is carried 70 miles

comes slow torture. And, furthermore, each hour of torture took the missionary miles further from civilization, toward a destination where he had not to expect kindness or courtesy in any form. The driver was perhaps a type of the people to whom he was going. Fearless and independent and strong—the kind that will do hard work for months, and then go on a debauch that spares neither himself nor the people who get in his way. From sitting half asleep he would start up, swear at his horses, lashing them so suddenly that the seat went over more than once into the back of the wagon. These drivers size up their passengers in five minutes, and a nervous passenger has a hard time of it. But if one snores gently through the maddest lunging of the horses the show is the sooner over. It was just dark when we rolled, in clouds of dust, down the western slope of Deep Creek Range into Sheridan's ranch at Ibapah. Sheridan took me at once to supper, which was my first square meal since leaving Vernon. The sun was long up and the day hot before I awoke in my cabin next morning. I had reached my journey's end,

but I had not come to Deep Creek for the sake of that stage-ride, even though it was quite an experience to travel in 1910 with the "Overland Mail," much as my predecessors had done in the fifties. No! My mission was not to search out the "Overland Route," but to hunt up the teacher of the Ibapah school, who had written Bishop Spalding that she had herself started a Sunday-school in a valley where there had never been one—nor a church within one hundred miles. She wrote that she was leaving, and hoped he could find some way of carrying on the work. It was a bit disheartening to learn that she had already gone over into Nevada to "Eight Mile Ranch" for a visit. So I found myself once more on the "Overland Route," travelling this time with an Irish ranchman. He was looking for his cattleman, who had gone off on a spree. We found him in the saloon, with a broom for a crutch and a huge bottle in his hip pocket. He had been thrown while riding wild horses, and "kicked up" a bit. The Irishman was quick-witted. He laughed hugely over the man's crutch, set him up to all the drinks he wanted, and a few more,

just to make sure he would not want to
go back for more. Then he brought the
crowd out for me to take their picture.
Once more he took them in for drinks.
When they came out I saw that if I
wanted to reach "Eight Mile Ranch" in
a hurry I would best change my method
of travel. I exchanged my seat in the
wagon for the cattleman's horse—a
change that met with welcome all
around. So I rode off across the Nevada
line to the ranch where the teacher was
staying. I found her not lacking in
weight, wit or energy. She had lived in
four continents, and she was quite positive that no place she had lived showed
greater need of a church than Deep
Creek. We planned to hold a special
Sunday-school service at three o'clock
Sunday afternoon.

My hosts of the "Eight Mile Ranch"
made me welcome, and showed me over
the ranch house. Like the first ranch I
came upon after leaving the train, this
too, the end of my journey, was a post
house of the "Overland Mail." They
showed me the doorway by which the
stage entered the house before the passengers were unloaded, because more passengers were killed in getting in and out
of the coaches than in any other way.
So this ranch house was built something
like a fort—the old loop-holes in the
walls could still be seen, through which
rifles were trained upon the Indians.
The graves are outside, where the murdered were laid away.

The next day I was up at five, and
spent the day in the saddle, visiting the

*Where "the stage entered the house before
the passengers were unloaded"*

EIGHT-MILE RANCH

We rode together—Indian and white. Tying our horses to a cart-wheel, we entered a yard in which the people had gathered to play cards. A blanket was spread on the ground for a table. At the corners the players were seated with their money piles. All looked up as the white man entered.

It was 6:20 P.M.—two hours of daylight left. The Indians wanted to finish their game. But as I had had a hard time to find their village even by daylight I did not want to find the "Eight Mile Ranch" by starlight. So I pulled out my watch and said: "I go back at seven. I came all the way from Salt Lake. May be so you don't have preacher come again." There were low grunts from the players. Slowly one of them rose, kicking over his cards as a signal that I could have the floor. The game was at once cleared away. I sat; they stood and sat around me. A woman came out of the hut and laid her papoose against the wall. Many of these Indians had never heard the story of Jesus Christ, but they had seen a picture of the Crucifixion. When I spoke of this they wanted to know what it meant. They had never heard the Lord's Prayer, so I tried to teach it to them. They seemed much interested. They had no Bibles, but none of them could read, so they did not want any. I knew they had

a school, so I asked about it. They handed me, with great ceremony, a sealed letter. I rose to receive it, broke the envelope, and sat down to read it to them. It was the report of the school teacher, Charley Broom. There had been school in the village just one month. Charley Broom had fourteen pupils. I tried to read their names, to the huge delight of my audience.

Then I rode away, stopping at the chief's hut to say good-by. He charged me to tell Salt Lake people that "Gosiute he good Indian. White man like Gosiute, Gosiute like white man." The reason for this commission is that they are afraid of being put on the reservation. I thanked them for their courtesy, and told the chief I would carry his message to the outside world. That meant once more 140 miles with the "Overland Mail"!

Simpson Spring in a dust storm

(835)

A LIGHT SHINING IN DARKNESS
WHAT A CHRISTIAN UNIVERSITY IS DOING IN THE HEART OF CHINA

T HE past year will always be regarded as one of the most important in the history of the development of the educational work of the American Church Mission in Central China. The great event of the year was the incorporation of Boone College, Wuchang, as a university—an event which marks a culminating point in the plans and work of nearly forty years past. Step by step the school advanced from very small beginnings, and this year of incorporation has been a year of growth in all directions, the numbers in residence, including the Boone preparatory school, being by far the highest recorded.

In 1901, after the Boxer outbreak, Boone School was reopened with less than 100 boys. This term we have reached a total of 420 students, all resident. The total number of *Christian* students in residence during the spring term, 1910, was 131, much larger than the whole school ten years ago.

The Future of Mission Colleges

There has been much uncertainty in the minds of many people as to what would be the fate of mission colleges in view of the development of government institutions. Up to the present time there has been no falling off in the numbers attending mission colleges in this centre. The Wesleyan High School, situated about a mile away from Boone, has more than doubled its numbers during the last five years. Whatever the future may have in store for us, at present the demands upon us are greater than ever. The probabilities are that the fate of our mission colleges will depend upon the value of the education provided, and the efficiency of the work done. As yet, the most efficient educational institutions are the missionary colleges. As the government schools

grow in efficiency there may be m[..] competition, but there is not likely to [..] any falling off if the standard of edu[..] tional efficiency is maintained. Pare[..] and friends of students appreciate t[..] better discipline of our institutions, a[..] the fact that we are Christian and requ[..] attendance at Christian worship on t[..] part of all our students has not as [..] created any difficulty. Parents who [..] not Christian appreciate the moral val[..] of the training given in Boone, and th[..] prefer the stricter discipline of a Chr[..] tian College to the laxity of many g[..] ernment schools.

Extension

A most important development h[..] taken place this year in the closing [..] St. Peter's Hospital, and the handi[..] over of its buildings for college purpos[..] It is proposed to reopen the hospital [..] another and more suitable part of t[..] city, where its usefulness to the peop[..] in general will be greatly enhanced, whi[..] at the same time giving to Boone an o[..] portunity of greater development. T[..] step taken this year is part of a poli[..] adopted by the bishop with the unan[..] mous approval of the mission some thr[..] or four years ago; a policy which has f[..] its object the strengthening not only [..] Boone, but of the work of St. Hilda[..] School, and all our educational wor[..] The whole of the mission compoun[..] which formerly domiciled all our inst[..] tutions, is to be given up to the un[..] versity, and the other institutions are [..] have separate compounds in more a[..] vantageous situations, where the work [..] each can have more room for expansio[..] A fine plot of ground of over four acr[..] has just been purchased for St. Hilda[..] School, outside of the city and abo[..] fifteen minutes' walk from our prese[..] compound. It is proposed in the ne[..] future to remove St. Hilda's to this be[..]

ing forward to taking courses in American and European universities.

We also need a man able to teach philosophy—a subject most important at the present time for the young men of China. A great work of reconstruction in Chinese thought, and the comparison, criticism and, where possible, the harmonizing of Chinese philosophy with Christian philosophy, will be called for in the near future. Such a teacher will need to make a thorough study of the Chinese language, and especially to master Confucian thought in order to be effective as a teacher and lecturer. China at the present time needs the trained philosophic and ethical teacher even more than the scientist. Our students are beginning to take a great interest in ethical and historical studies, and these studies should be encouraged, for they will afford light and leading in the great work of reconstruction which must take place when China enters in real earnest upon the path of reform.

For the school department we should have trained teachers, able especially to teach the English language. It may be regarded by some as unfortunate that so much work has to be done through the medium of English. This, however, is a matter over which we have no control. English is demanded, and the students go where they can best obtain it. It is essential that the teaching of English in the preparatory departments should be as efficient as possible, in order that students may enter upon the higher departments of study with a good working knowledge of the English language. So far as now appears there is not likely to be any falling off in the demand for English. Certainly the student who has taken his college course in English has great advantages over the one who knows no language but his own. Such men at present are taking the lead in all departments of work, whether in Church or State. They are the most influential among the young men of China to-day, and they will have much to do in shaping the China of to-morrow.

Again, we need more buildings. Our college chapel is too small to accommodate all our students. We have always made our Church service a most important part of our work. Although so many of our students are non-Christian, all attend regular church services daily. During the past term the chapel has been very crowded, and in the hot weather the necessity for close seating made it very uncomfortable, which was a great drawback to the interest and profit of the services. The boys of the preparatory school are not able to attend service in the chapel, as there is not room for them. We should double the accommodation at present existing.

Also, we urgently need a science hall equipped for teaching all branches of physical science. Our work is done at present under great difficulties for lack of proper laboratories and apparatus. Then, too, we need a large assembly hall, in which students and visitors can gather on public occasions. The new library affords at present a place for public lectures and for ordinary meetings, but it is too small for the purposes of a general assembly room, and was not intended permanently for such purposes.

The Outlook

Much is being said and written in all parts of the world about the outlook in China. There are certainly many things to discourage the true friends of China. It is generally believed that the educational system of China has undergone a complete reform. This is perhaps true, on paper, but those who know most intimately the educational conditions at present existing are not by any means optimistic. In giving up the old much has undoubtedly been lost, and the new is as yet so crude and imperfect that one is disposed to think that the losses in transition have outweighed the gains. One thing, however, is certain: that the old regime in education cannot be restored, though the new is so very unsatisfactory. There is greater need than ever for well-equipped Christian universities. Our American Church col-

HOW THEY OPENED THE CHAPEL AT MACAGUA

By Archdeacon Steel

ALL readers of THE SPIRIT OF MISSIONS (and that should mean every man and woman and child in the Church) will remember the vivid picture of Bishop Knight's service at Macagua-Arabos, which was printed in 1908. At that time the good bishop wrote below his picture an appeal for a sum of money large enough to erect at this place a modest chapel. A quick response came from the Sunday-school of Trinity Church, New Haven, Conn. Work was begun at once, and the work on the edifice was completed and the building was formally opened for divine service on August 7th. Not only the inhabitants of the pueblo, but all the countryside, turned out *en masse*. The roads and lanes leading to the little town were filled with men, women and little children, some on horseback, many on foot. According to the custom of the country the manes of the little Cuban ponies were trimmed short, and their tails were plaited, tied with colored ribbons and fastened to the skirts of the saddles. The men were dressed in white, their heads shaded by the great *sombreros*, or broad Panama hats of all shapes; from their belts were swinging their *machetes*, or broad swords, which every Cuban farmer carries.

Had you seen them filling the roads and lanes in every direction, and heard the clanging of their *machetes*, you would have been sure that another "revolution" was beginning; and it was indeed so! But the war-cry this time was not "*Vive Cuba libre*," but "Onward, Christian Soldiers," and "Fight the Good Fight." It was a "revolution" in morals and in the habits of a lifetime. A new people was awakening to the beauty and the glory of "The Church of the Living God," for which they will some day be ready to live and die if need be. Their war-cry will be "*Vive la Yglesia libre y pura.*" (Life to the pure and free

Church!) "Thank God for a pure branch of the Catholic Church, in which there is a clean priesthood, the Apostolic Faith 'once delivered,' the Gospel preached and the Sacraments administered unmutilated to the poor as well as the rich! Praise God from whom such blessings flow!"

To announce the hour of the service the little bell jangled in the belfry, and the air was filled with the *whissssh-boom* of rockets.

A procession was formed in the sacristy, consisting of the members of the choir, and the clergy, preceded by the crucifier, but it was with great difficulty that they could enter the chapel because of the crowd. All the people of the pueblo were there, in addition to the multitudes of *guajiros* (country people); also the alcalde (mayor), and the chief of the police, with other notables. The great congregation overflowed the building and the people stood at the doors and windows trying to catch some of the "words of life" which fell from the lips of the consecrated priest. The Rev. Francisco Diaz, who originated the work at Macagua, was the chief ministrant, delivering the sermon and celebrating the Blessed Sacrament, at which fifty-one people received. Mr. Diaz was assisted in the service by the Rev. Sergio Ledo, the missionary in charge of this work.

After the recessional hymn the national hymn of Cuba was sung, in which the whole great multitude without and within the chapel united with ringing voices.

At the close of the service the little bell tinkled away, the rockets sped and cracked, and the roads and lanes leading from the pueblo filled with the *guajiros* and their families homeward bound, echoed with Cuba's hymn, and snatches from "The Songs of Zion." It was a red-letter day in the annals of Macagua-Arabos.

PLANTING THE UNKNOWN CHURCH

By the Reverend F. W. Crook

The writer is stationed at Ukiah, Cal., in the District of Sacramento.
The account he gives is typical of much of our Western mission work.

MY work covers a population of 26,500 souls scattered over the whole of Mendocino County, Northern California, containing 3,780 square miles. I am the only clergyman of our Church that has ever labored in this county, and until ten years ago the Episcopal Church was as unknown to the great majority of people in this county as is the Grand Lama of Thibet, or the doctrines of Buddha—absolutely so! Yet in this county, intensely un-Roman, that Church has six Capuchin fathers, and is vigorously pushing on with an eye to the future.

It is often asked—not unreasonably, on the surface—"Why send men and money to California, Oregon and the Far West, when right at our door are millions unconverted?" The answer can best be given by an object lesson. Thirty to sixty years ago the same was said regarding Missouri, Kansas, Tennessee. When Bishop Tuttle first went to Missouri he showed me a long list of towns having then from 1,500 to 3,000 inhabitants, which never had services. In those days his diary for Missouri read: "Tuesday, held services in the South Methodist Episcopal Church, Podunk. Friday, held service in the Campbellite meeting house, Skookum," etc., which meant that these Christians, more alert, because more earnest than we (there's the truth) had not disdained the common folk in these 1,500 and 3,000 towns, while we, in those states, were an "unknown tongue."

Come now with me to Mendocino County. Here are well-to-do men of forty, fifty and sixty, children of the sturdy, plain folk whom we neglected in Missouri, Kansas and Tennessee. They are leaders here in wealth and education. They are staunch Baptists, Methodist

Episcopal (South) and Campbell[es] They assume a patronizing air to[r] us as a mere "city religion," a [c] man's creed. Hence here, to this [y] the Presbyterian Church is an ex[i] and ours a mere seedling just plante[o] difficult soil. Are we to repeat in[h] smaller towns and sparsely-settled [ot] of California the grave neglect of w[c] we were guilty elsewhere? If s[c in] twenty years we shall be dignified [m-] balmers of a Church that is dead *in he State*, whatever it may be among th[re-] fined in the cities.

The headquarters of our Church [or] this county are at Ukiah, the co[ty] seat. We have built, by the *actual le-* *nials*—and my experience is that [w] places make *real* denials—a neat ch[h], 24x50, costing nearly $2,000. Our [o-] ple here are *poor*, spelled all in do[le-] sized capitals—except one or two [m-] ilies.

From Ukiah I go by rail to Willi[a] small agricultural town of about 1[0]. Here a South-Methodist pastor alo[is] resident. Our Church people are [n-] istered to in the ration of time I [an] spare. From Ukiah we go over [mountains, up, up, by four-horse s[ge,] until from the pass 2,400 feet above [a-] level you look, about 4 P.M., across [n-] limited square miles of redwood tin[r;] while far away, on a clear day, lie[he] Pacific Ocean, with the coast of [li-] fornia stretching away to the n[h.] After riding till evening we reach [it-] tle logging railway, and are wh[ed] down through glorious scenery to [rt] Bragg, a lumber town by the sea. [ur] years ago we were utterly unknown [re] I opened our work in a hall, and as [re] happened to be descendants of eas[rn] and Wisconsin people here, the preju[ce]

(840)

tury. The time will never come when we can say to the Church at large, "Now our missionary work is completed; you good people who have been so generous all these years may henceforth be relieved. Be more generous with yourselves in the future and make your personal religion delightfully comfortable." There will always be too much Church extension in sight ever to give this questionable hope.

On the other hand, it may be reasonably expected that the large and increasing additional yearly appropriations shall not always be necessary. As time passes many places at present wholly or partially maintained by the Board will be self-supporting, thereby relieving the Church at large. We are rapidly getting the Church planted in all parts of the world, and as sections become able to take care of themselves they will relieve the Church and become *contributing* factors. This has been done in the past, and the future is even more hopeful.

While we are not satisfied with what we are doing in many places—in that diocesan apportionments are not paid in full, for instance—yet compared with twenty years ago there is much cause for rejoicing. Dioceses that then were assisted to the extent of $3,000 each year have relieved the Board of responsibility and now pay $4,000 into the general treasury. That is, they give up the price of a missionary bishop's salary, and are now paying the price of one. We have a heavy responsibility upon us now, because we are doing big things, and these big things must continue. Yet many parts now assisted will soon become a help instead of a charge.

So to those who may say, "How long?" we may say, in respect to missionary work in general, *forever,* because we cannot rest until we have made the name of Jesus Christ a praise and a power in all the world; but in respect to those parts now in our care perhaps for *half a century* to come.

W. R. BLACKFORD.
Caro, Mich.

BEREAVEMENT IN THE SHANGHAI MISSION

LILLIS CRUMMER, TEACHER

MISS LILLIS CRUMMER died at Omaha on the 27th of August. The news will bring deep sorrow to her fellow-workers in China. One of them wishes to place on record his sincere regard and his deep respect for her memory by these few lines.

Miss Crummer joined the mission at Shanghai in 1894. She was a well-trained teacher, and had further spent a year in the Deaconess House at Philadelphia. After getting a start in Chinese she began her work among the women, and during her time of service she had experience in all parts of it. Engaged at first in evangelistic work and in charge of girls' day-schools, she gained rapidly in experience, and when the Training-school for Bible-women was established she became its first head.

After years of active and useful work she was obliged to retire on sick leave, and when she came back to China she was placed in charge of the English department in St. Mary's Hall. Here she effected great improvements in organization, and inaugurated several changes which are greatly to the advantage of the school. To our great regret her sickness returned, and under doctors' orders she was obliged to return again to the United States early in 1909. Most of the time since then was passed in the hospital; and in great weakness, till she was called to rest.

Miss Crummer impressed one at once by the force of her character, which was evident in her very look and bearing. She did not bring weakness and timidity to the mission field, but a strong will, energy and activity, combined with earnest devotion to the cause of Christ

and His Church. Whatever she undertook she did well and thoroughly. She could be relied upon to do her duty at all times. Very often such strong characters become autocratic and self-assertive in their relations with fellow-missionaries or with the Chinese, but it was not so with her. I never had occasion to consult with her about the work for women without finding her advice help-

ful, and I came to rely very much upon her good judgment and strong common sense. And she was absolutely loyal to the Church and to the mission. One could always be sure of finding her on the right side.

Always cheerful and good-natured, she was an example of how to live with others. Perhaps her quick sense

umor was a help to her in this, as in
ll the relations of mission life. She was
ot at all the sort of woman that is often
upposed to be the typical missionary.
trength, courage, cheery good-humor,
n absence of all pretence and of that
eak piety which is so often mistaken
r goodness—these were the qualities
hich all could see in her. But under
ese there was a deep sense of duty and
steady religious zeal, and the convic-
on that she was meant to work in
hina. Her last regret, when she was
most at the end of life, was that she
as not allowed to go back to that work.
ese are the marks of real saintliness
d godliness—the marks of those who
ve done great things for God. Yet no
e would have been so astonished as she
she had been told that she was one of
e best of Christ's servants, for she
s as humble as she was strong.

In this imperfect way I have tried to
tch her character as it appeared to us
o worked with her side by side. None
us who knew her will ever forget her,
l, seeing how God so often calls the
t missionaries away, one cannot but
l that the work that they leave un-
shed here is meant to be completed
ond, or that a greater work is given
n to do.

F. R. GRAVES.

LLIAM HENRY STAND-
RING, PRIEST

EWS was received by cable on
the 19th of September of the
death of the Rev. W. H. Standring at Nagasaki, Japan. Mr.
Mrs. Standring had gone to Japan
fo month's rest, leaving Shanghai in
th last days of July and intending to
g to Unzen, a place in the hills near
While at Nagasaki he was taken ill
w typhoid fever, and died.

. Standring came from the parish
of e Good Shepherd in Newburgh,
N. . In school he stood at the head of
his lass and then entered Cornell Uni-
ve y. His education for the ministry

was at the General Theological Seminary, and he went out after graduation
to join the Shanghai mission.

After a short time at Shanghai he
was detailed for work at Soochow and,
when Mr. Ancell took up the work at
Yangchow, Mr. Standring succeeded
him as head of the Soochow station.
Under him the school work was developed and the Church and evangelistic
work extended.

Mr. Standring was of a cheerful disposition and beloved by all his associates. As a worker he was not only
zealous but wise. I think the prominent
characteristic he showed in all the relations of mission life was faithfulness.

I had come to depend upon him very
much as to things in the Soochow station. This last year he had been over-
burdened with work, the Zangzok District having fallen to him while Mr.
Wilson was absent on furlough. When
I visited that station with him in
June I was struck by the thoroughness
with which he was doing everything.

As a missionary and as a clergyman
he was true to his calling. Can one say
more?

To his young wife and to the mission
our sympathy goes out in fullest
measure. Who will come out to carry on
his work?

F. R. GRAVES.

BISHOP HARE'S BOARDING-SCHOOLS

By the Right Reverend Frederick Foote Johnson, D.D.

CLOTHED IN HIS
GLORY

Facing the rising sun

T is now almost five years ago that I journeyed over for the first time to make a visitation as assistant to the beloved Bishop of South Dakota among our Sioux Indian brethren of the Church west of the Missouri River. Thirty miles from any railway point, in the midst of the unbroken prairie, in the evening when the Chapel service was over, in a rude, one-roomed log cabin lighted by a dingy lamp, with a fringe of Indian men about me on the cabin floor, I sat and listened for the first time to the Sioux Indian tongue.

I shall never forget the weirdness of the cabin nor the native dignity of the several speakers as each stood up to address me, nor the picturesqueness of the language as it came to me through my interpreter. Presently, after many had told out their hearts, an old Indian chief arose to tell me something of the story of the coming of the Gospel to the people of the Dakotas. "A few years ago," said he, "we Indians just like this cabin if you put out that light. We all dark and desolate and dreary. Bishop Hare, he come to us. He build us schools for our children. He bring us Holy Baptism and Confirmation and Holy Communion. He give us Bible and Prayer Book. He build us churches and chapels. He send us teachers and ministers of Jesus. Now we Indians like this cabin with that lamp upon the wall; *we all getting light*."

As I look out from my window Sioux Falls to-day upon the covered mound above the grave in which the body of the Bishop of South Dakota rests—"The inn of a pilgrim journey to Jerusalem"—I say to myself When the new series of the stories the triumphs of Christian faith written, it will tell the story of how young man, gently born, finds himself delicately reared, splendidly educated gat him out of his country, and from kindred, and from his father's house unto a land which God would show him It will tell how, leaving the attractive intellectual atmosphere and social vantages and opportunities of a certain eastern city, he built his cabin-home the Dakota Territory, a waste of bare prairie, roamed over by wild bands buffaloes and wild nomad Sioux. It will tell how, when many good people were saying, "What's the use of preaching Gospel to a perishing race?" he persisted in his mission, because he heard the call of them that were in captivity and longed to deliver a people appointed unto death. It will tell how, when people everywhere who had no experimental knowledge of the proposition were saying, "No good Indian but a dead Indian," he, with a noble band of clergy and other teachers whom he grappled to his heart with hooks of steel, in the land of the Dakotas builded out of almost hopeless material a spiritual house able to resist storms; settled the roving Sioux Indian in families, and made

OLD WIND

Facing the s

BISHOP HARE AND HIS INDIAN CHILDREN

untless numbers of them earnest and evoted and consistent followers and eachers of the gentle Jesus.

On the white-metal cross which the shop used to give to each person on hom he laid his hands in confirmation nong the people of the Dakotas is inscribed the words, « Ἵνα ζωὴν ἔχωσι. » That they might have life." He, following his Master, gave life. Six-and-irty years of life he joyously gave for e spiritual and moral and physical d intellectual and material upbuilding the Sioux—for no interest of the ux to him was foreign. And when, in t October, God's finger touched him d he slept, I verily believe that the al paragraph of the most splendid pter in the history of nineteenth century missions in America was closed.

n 1873 Bishop Hare came out to this ern land as the Missionary Bishop of rara. He found 6,000 Indian chil-running wild, like jack-rabbits on plains. It was before the Government began to make provision for the ation of the Indian. Bishop Hare mediately appealed to the Church for acial help, and boarding-schools e built, whose names are house-words in the homes of many of devoted and generous Churchfolk our land—St. Mary's and St. Eliza-b's.

St. Mary's is for girls only. It is situated on the great Rosebud Reserve, thirty-five miles from the nearest railway point, which is a point called Valentine, in Nebraska. This year the enrolment at St. Mary's is seventy-five. The report for the month of March has just this moment come to my desk, and shows an average attendance of seventy. One girl enrolled is seventeen; two are sixteen; the others are aged from five to fifteen. Some of the little people who read this article may be interested to hear the names of some of the girls of St. Mary's. Here they are: Nellie At-the-Straight, Julia Bear-Doctor, Nellie Brave-Boy, Millie First-in-Trouble, Carrie Gunhammer, Louise Picket-pin, Clara Points-at-Him, Nellie Pretty-Voice-Eagle, Rosa Quick-Bear, Mabel Six-Shooter. There are other names which you would think just as queer.

The principal of St. Mary's, Mr. L. K.

St. Mary's School

(845)

THE LITTLE BOYS OF ST. ELIZABETH'S

Travis, and his good wife, are just completing their ninth year of efficient service at that splendid lighthouse out on the billowy South Dakota prairie. There are seven assistants to the principal at St. Mary's, two of whom are also pupils of the school. The following extract from a letter of Mr. Travis may be of interest:

"The school keeps five or six horses; four cows, which furnish milk for the school and sufficient cream and butter for cooking and family use; hens enough to supply eggs during nearly all the year, and about twenty hogs. Four heifers are now being raised to replace the milch cows as they are needed.

"A kitchen garden is cultivated which yields an abundance of vegetables during the season. Several hundred bushels of potatoes are grown, which abundantly supply the school the entire school-year.

"In the last two years considerable new ground has been broken, so that the general farming land for the growing of oats, corn, millet, etc., now includes about fifty acres. We cut and store for winter use fifty or sixty tons of tame hay.

"As we have no boys at St. Mary's, these outside operations depend upon the labor of the regular farmer, with the as-

sistance of the principal and a small amount of outside help required at harvest time."

I have told you that St. Mary's School is in the south part of South Dakota, about twenty-five miles from the Nebraska line. It is for Indian girls only. St. Elizabeth's school is away up in the northern end of the state, on the Standing Rock Reserve, about twenty-five miles from the North Dakota line. It is for Indian boys and girls. A monthly report which falls under my eye as I write gives an enrolment of twenty-five boys and thirty-seven girls; a total of sixty-two, with an average of 60.5. I am tempted to ask whether the averages in white schools at the East put us very much to shame? Two boys at St. Elizabeth's are seventeen years of age. The youngest lad is eight. The oldest girl is

St. Elizabeth's Mission

(846)

St. Elizabeth's is seventeen, and the youngest is six. And these boys and girls have just the same kind of names as the St. Mary's girls—I mean just as funny. The principal of St. Elizabeth's, Mr. J. L. Ricker, has completed his third year of efficient service. In addition to his good wife he has a staff of five assistants. In a recent letter Mr. Ricker says: "Our children have all returned to school well and happy and everything is running as smoothly as it is possible to run. Everybody is working hard, for at this time of the year there is so much to be done in a school of this kind."

St. Elizabeth's has a railway station of the new Chicago, Milwaukee & Puget Sound Railway about two miles distant. In a few weeks through trains from Chicago to Seattle will pass almost through the front yard of the school. This sometimes seems to some of us a doubtful benefit. But the youngsters don't agree with us on that point, for they like to sit on the fence and watch the train whiz by.

But I would not have you think that all the time is spent in sitting on the fence. The boys have many busy hours each day—farming, gardening, splitting and fetching wood and hauling water. The girls (both at St. Elizabeth's and at St. Mary's) learn bread-making, cooking, laundering, general housework, sewing, mending, dressmaking, and fancywork. In both schools faithful and painstaking class-room work is done under the patient and gentle guidance of the kindly teachers. Reading, writing, arithmetic and geography are taught.

There are hymn-singing, and Bible lessons, and Catechism drill. There is bright and happy worship morning and evening in the school chapels. And on Sundays the children and their teachers meet with the congregations which assemble regularly in the nearby church. Well-dressed, bright-faced, clean-bodied, happy-hearted children are they all; learning lessons and forming habits which will make them useful citizens of the state; and learning also those things which a Christian ought to know and believe to his soul's health.

To help in the support of these Indian boarding-schools, Bishop Hare instituted the system of scholarships, which has been in use for many years. He estimated that the annual payment of $60 would cover the expenses of a pupil in the schools. Parishes, Sunday-schools, branches of the Auxiliary and the Juniors, and individuals here and there, have generously taken many scholarships and carried them on from year to year.

In the example of the noble Bishop Hare, who in this western field laid down his life for his friends, we have a compelling illustration of what one man considered the cause of Christian missions was worthy of in the way of personal service, personal sacrifice; in the way of life, and love, and labor.

Are there not many who read these lines who will make glad thank-offerings to God for this choice vessel of His grace, and who, from their "much" or from their "little," will send their gifts to carry on the work from which he rests?

Since the above was written, St. Mary's School has been totally destroyed by fire. See description of the calamity on page 807.

ST. MARY'S GIRLS AT PLAY

OUR LETTER BOX
Intimate and Informal Messages from the Field

Our pioneer missionary in Alaska, the Rev. John W. Chapman, under date of July 7th, writes as follows:

THE school at this mission has been remembered this year by so many friends with gifts of clothing, toys and money, that I cannot hope to reach them all by personal letters. I trust, therefore, that you will allow me space in the columns of THE SPIRIT OF MISSIONS to express my appreciation. I can, perhaps, best do this by telling something about our school children, and the aims that we have in view.

We are caring for twelve boys and girls, most of whom have been with us for a number of years. It is not, as it was in early times, difficult to retain the children. They come willingly and leave us reluctantly, and would usually be glad to return. They are growing up into sturdy, helpful young men and women, and try to please us in every way.

It has been my aim to teach them self-support, and with that end in view we have established a small herd of cattle and have broken up ground and made gardens. We have also taken advantage of the summer run of salmon to add to our food supply. The yield of the garden has increased year by year, and last year we harvested enough vegetables to furnish our tables daily throughout the winter. All the children take a great deal of pleasure in gardening, and all have their own garden beds.

The herd is also successful, after several years of effort, and an error in introducing a breed which did not prove to be hardy. It has been a strain upon our resources to develop these features, build a barn and sheds, enclose our gardens and make necessary repairs and improvements; and last year, except for

the food which we raised upon [t]e premises, we should have gone hung[ry]. We are in the same position this ye[ar], and are hoping for a prosperous seas[on]. A failure in the gardens or in the he[rd] would be a serious matter for us.

The children have been too young [for] heavy tasks, but they are now growi[ng] into strong, hardy boys and girls from twelve to fifteen or eighten yea[rs,] and equal to any of the ordinary work [of] the mission. They are also learning [to] think for themselves. A steamboat [ar]rived this week, and discharged freig[ht] at the mission. Many passengers we[re] strolling about the yard, and a you[ng] man approached one of the older gir[ls] offering her a present of money. She [re]fused, and so did one of the young girls, to whom he next offered it. The refusal was a polite one, and their e[x]ample seemed to be contagious, for [he] tried to give his money to one of t[he] village women, and to one of the lit[tle] boys, and even to an imbecile—but with out success. The girls did not know th[at] they were being observed.

I am told the young man remark[ed] that it was the first time that he had ev[er] known an Indian to refuse a prese[nt.] Unfortunately, it is not the first ti[me] that a white man has exhibited bad ma[n]ners in the presence of our Indians. [I] am sure that those who have helped us maintain the school will share in th[e] pleasure that the conduct of our childr[en] gave us.

*

OUR readers will remember t[he] graphic account by the Rev. A. [J.] Gilman in the June number of T[HE] SPIRIT OF MISSIONS of the destruction [of] his personal effects in the Changsha ri[ot]

WORLD'S CHRISTIAN CITI-ZENSHIP CONFERENCE

THE National Reform Association, with headquarters in Pittsburg, Pa., is projecting a world's conference on the Bible principles of civil government, to be held in Philadelphia, Pa., November 16th-20th, 1910. At this conference it is proposed, to have read authentic reports of the respective attitudes of the sixty different nations of the world toward the Christian religion, and also toward the prevailing religion or religions in each country.

The great problems of all countries—such as the weekly rest-day, capital and labor, public education in its relation to morality and religion, laws relating to the family, war, and how to abolish it, vice and crime, and the means of their suppression—will be discussed by the speakers from this and other countries. The fundamental principles of government in their relation to Christianity will also be the subject of discussion, and especially the place and power of the Christian religion in our American national life. Among the speakers from America are the Hon. W. J. Bryan, Ex-Governor Hanly, of Indiana; Commissioner McFarlane, of Washington, D. C.; the Rev. Dr. Francis E. Clark, of Boston; John R. Mott and Robert E. Speer, of New York; Drs. Stevenson and Brumbaugh, of Philadelphia; Governor Stuart, of Pennsylvania; Drs. Wylie and McCrory and Wishart, of Pittsburg; Dr. Scovel, of Wooster University, O., and Dr. Parsons, of Portland, Ore.

Delegates will be present from all lands, especially long-resident missionaries in foreign countries. Many delegates have already been appointed in this country. Congregation, Missionary Associations, Men's Brotherhoods, Christian Endeavor and other young people's societies, Ministerial Associations, Church Conferences, Presbyteries, Synods, General Assemblies, Mission Boards, Sabbath, W. C. T. U., and other reform organizations, are entitled and requested to appoint delegates.

NEWS AND NOTES

AN interesting departure in mission work has recently been undertaken in the diocese of Montana. Mr. Paul Tajima, a Japanese who came to this country some years ago to learn English, fell in with our missionary at Havre, Montana, and has since made his home there. He was confirmed two years ago, and now, under the supervision of the Rev. L. J. Christler, missionary, with headquarters at Havre, he has not only begun a Japanese work in that town but is extending it along the line of the Great Northern, which railway employs a considerable number of Japanese. The work takes the form of clubs, which have certain beneficiary features, but which exist avowedly for the investigation of the Christian faith. A most sympathetic message from the Rev. Mr. Christler has been translated into Japanese and published on a large sheet, which also contains a considerable number of other suggestions and items of information. This is being distributed by Mr. Tajima, concerning whom Bishop Brewer says: "He is undertaking a work among his own countrymen which I hope may have good results. I confirmed one Japanese last spring at Havre, and others will probably be presented at my next visitation."

¶

THE twenty-fifth anniversary of Bishop Ferguson's episcopate in Liberia was fittingly commemorated by the congregations of Trinity Parish and its Kroo chapel in Monrovia. A most appreciative address, signed by the rectors, wardens and vestrymen of both congregations, was presented to the bishop. It concluded thus:

"The congregations we represent have decided to present to you a memento in silver, in such form as may be most agreeable to you, and suitably inscribed, and they pray that God may add to this

(850)

token of their esteem and affection the choicest and richest blessings on your work, yourself, and those nearest and dearest to you."

¶

A member of the Church, whose summer holiday has been used for a visit to Alaska, was supplied with letters of introduction to some of the missionaries. This message comes by way of acknowledgment:

I SHOULD like to thank you, while I am still on Alaskan soil, for having been so very good as to interest others in our plan of a "mission tour" in Alaska. Everyone has been most kind, and we have met all or most of the active workers here, and are returning with such a definite idea of this immense field of labor, its needs and its opportunities. To our regret, we have not met Bishop Rowe, but we knew, in advance, that he would be up the Yukon beyond the limits of our present journey. He is truly beloved by all classes here. Let the field be visited by one of the Church Missions House people. You will then better understand what I mean.

¶

IN THE SPIRIT OF MISSIONS for July appeared an item, under the diocese of N——, acknowledging the sum of $25 sent by a parish branch of the Junior Auxiliary for school work in Liberia. This would attract little attention among the hundreds of other offerings unless the fact were known that this branch is composed entirely of young colored girls who have been stimulated to great activity by the knowledge of what is being done for their own race in that distant land. It is their determination to provide a sum sufficient to maintain one child in a mission school for a limited number of years. Up to this time they have never dreamed of raising so much as $25 a year, but with such an object they feel confident of success.

the first cause of Christ in the first place and to keep it there. Missions are simply the Church going on the errand of God to interpret the Gospel to all nations. This is the highest expression of Christian service and of the spiritual life of the Church. It is safe to say that the growth of a diocese, as of a parish, is measured by its missionary activity.

¶

Deaconess Sabine, of Alaska, who was recently transferred by Bishop Rowe from the Anvik Mission to Circle City, sends us what she calls a "small item," which we commend to the attention of white parishes in the United States:

LAST week I received a printed notice from Bishop Rowe, asking that Circle City mission pay its apportionment of $10. When the Indian layreader finished the service on Sunday I told the people, through an interpreter, what it meant and what the bishop asked. Sunday evening I had the first gift of 50 cents. All Monday, Tuesday and Wednesday they kept coming, almost every one with 50 cents, some with a little more. One man brought his wife and little child, and the tot had her 50 cents, which she ran and gave me herself. One man, who was quite poor and had been sick, told me he had no money but wanted to give; would I let him split wood for me for cash (as I always pay in trade for work). Of course I would. So now I have in hand $16 to give the bishop when he comes. I think if every parish did the like there would be quite an ingathering this year.

¶

LAST summer a note appeared in THE SPIRIT OF MISSIONS asking if one of our readers had a second-hand typewriter to spare, or would be willing to buy a new one, for the use of one of our missionaries in Japan. A generous-minded correspondent writes that she will send $25 toward buying one if any other person or persons will help in the matter. Who will respond?

THE MISSION STUDY LEADER

MISSIONARY instruction in the Sunday-school does not depend so much on literature as on a leader. By "leader" we mean the person to whom the *rector assigns the responsibility* of the missionary instruction of the school. *There must be one person* who has the ability, knowledge and vision to plan a course for the entire school. He may create a *cabinet*, consisting of the leaders of departments and grades, who may advise and execute, but upon *one person*, regardless of the size of the school, must be placed squarely and openly the leadership of the school in missionary instruction.

Qualifications

The first necessary qualification of this leader is that he or she has the ability to teach. A faithful and earnest member of one of the parochial missionary societies is not always the most desirable person for a Mission Study Leader in the Sunday-school. Extensive knowledge about missions or enthusiasm for missions by no means constitutes the first qualification of the leader. The Sunday-school is an educational agency, its success depends on teaching personalities; the Mission Study Leader must have a teaching personality, *i.e.*, the spontaneous ability to adapt himself and his subject to the class; to present the subject in hand in terms familiar and attractive to the class.

Some of the best Mission Study Leaders to-day are teachers who have demonstrated their ability to teach in Sunday-school and whose interest in missions is newly developed because they have lately come to regard missionary instruction as one of the best implements for religious instruction.

(852)

The second qualification is *comprehension of the missionary motive.* Does the leader realize that *missions is the Church demonstrating God's Love?* Bishop Lloyd says: "We go that men may know what their Father is like." Love cannot be demonstrated without sacrifice. *Does the Leader in Mission Study realize that his own demonstration, his own sacrifice, is the first requisite for successful missionary teaching?* The teachers in the school will not value missionary instruction, will not give up time and sacrifice pleasure in order that it may be the best, unless they are inspired by the leader, and they cannot be inspired unless the leader leads by sacrifice.

Sunday-school success waits for the growing capacity of the teacher to give up.

There are other necessary qualifications, but we will not consider them now, because there are other points that must be mentioned in this limited space.

Methods

(1) The Leader should have an *appropriation.* Books, maps, pictures, THE SPIRIT OF MISSIONS, must be used in abundance. Tools must be provided if the teachers are to do work that will command the respect of the scholars.

(2) The Leader should attend all accessible *conferences* of Sunday-school workers whenever missionary instruction is considered on the programme. He should go not only to get, but to give of his own experience. He should be sent by the school or the parish to one of the summer conferences.

(3) The Leader should *get in touch*

with other Leaders. Send name and address and brief description of situation and plans to the Editor of this Department. From time to time lists will be published with descriptions of methods that have worked successfully.

(4) The Leader should realize that his chief work is *adaptation*. There are no complete systems of missionary instruction provided for every possible Sunday-school situation. It is a time of experimentation. Have a clear idea of the end to be sought. Master the "Policy" found in the pamphlet "The Necessity of Mission Study in the Sunday-school." (For which apply to the Church Missions House, sending 6 cents in stamps.) Determine the steps possible in each grade.

Concentrate attention on a few steps at a time. Work with the individual teacher. If the teachers cannot be gathered at a teachers' meeting, or in small groups, get an appointment at their homes. There make clear the great opportunity that the teacher has; then show the particular thing that the teacher can do with the particular class. A few such interviews, at a cost of time and energy to the Leader, will accomplish ends of inestimable value: the teacher will be impressed by the Leader's devotion, the task will take on new valuation, and the whole work of the Sunday-school will be given new life. This is one step in the Leader's *demonstration*.

A MISSIONARY LESSON

General Subject: "Missions on Our Side of the World."

(Note.—For a description of the methods to be used in teaching these lessons see THE SPIRIT OF MISSIONS, September, 1910, page 769.)

Point of Contact On the Sunday before you give this lesson say to the class: Who inhabited and possessed this land before Columbus came to it? What has become of them? Draw out briefly the reservation method of the government and the unfortunate life of the Indians. Do they have any churches? Do you think that any of our Bishops who were at Cincinnati are sent by our Church to the Indians? Some of the scholars may remember that Bishop Johnson and his Indians was announced as the subject of the next lesson.

Inform and teach the class by drill that

(1) Bishop Johnson (South Dakota) to the Sioux Indians represents the *largest work*.

(2) Bishop Grafton (Wisconsin) to the Oneidas represents the *oldest work*.

(3) Bishop Brooke (Oklahoma) to mixed tribes represents work carried on *under the hardest circumstances*.

(4) Bishop Rowe (Alaska) to the Alaskans represents the work *farthest away*.

(Work among the Indians is carried on in fifteen dioceses and missionary jurisdictions. The above classfication is not to be taught as exhaustive, only as an easy method of remembering some of the interesting facts of our Indian work.)

We cannot visit all of these tribes, but next Sunday we will go with Bishop Johnson back to South Dakota and see what the Church is doing under his direction to help the Sioux Indians.

Ask three scholars to remain after the session, or, better, come to your home, or meet you at a certain time at one of their homes. Ask them to help you in next Sunday's lesson by being ready to tell about Bishop Johnson's work. Give to each a copy of pamphlet No. 620, written by Bishop Johnson. Ask one to tell about Bishop Hare, another about St. Margaret's School, and the third about St. Elizabeth's School. Read over the pamphlet with them, and point out to each the particular facts that belong to his assignment.

The Lesson Go to the class with the aim clearly in mind: *I will try to show my class that the Church is helping*

*the Indian to become a good citizen and
a good Christian.*

Start the lesson by asking: What Bishop do we study about to-day? The
class ought to be able to answer; Bishop
Johnson, because you have promised to
study about him, once in connection with
the Convention and again last Sunday,
when you announced this lesson. Where
is his diocese? Locate on outline map.
If you went out there, which do you
think you would find, the Indians living
in houses or wigwams? If you had gone
thirty-six years ago you would have
found them roving about, living in wigwams, but to-day they live in houses—
some of them pretty good ones. Do you
know who greatly influenced them to
make the change? Let me show you his
picture. (Produce Bishop Hare's picture.) Then announce the scholar who
will report on Bishop Hare. At the conclusion of the report draw out from the
class the following points and fix them
by repetition.

(1) He lived with them.

(2) He carried the services of the
Church to them.

(3) He trained them to be his helpers
(to-day of the twenty-two clergy sixteen
are Indians).

(4) He organized and built schools.

Do not fail to emphasize the contrast
before and after Bishop Hare's work.
When he died there were ten thousand
baptized Indians and four thousand communicants.

Taking up the next report, introduce
it by "Let us visit the two schools Bishop Hare organized, one in the South, St.
Mary's, and one in the North, St. Elizabeth's.

From the report on St. Mary's draw
out the reasons for calling St. Mary's a
"splendid light-house on the billowy
South Dakota prairie." Tell the story
the old Indian chief told on pages 2 and
4 of the pamphlet. Ask: Why is education like a light? What do you see better
because of your school life? What do
the girls at St. Mary's see better because
of their school life? Draw out: The
value of learning how to make good
bread, mending clothes properly, of
reading, writing, arithmetic, geography,
of worship by hymns, Prayer and Bible
reading.

Lesson II. INDIAN LIFE AS IT WAS WITHOUT THE CHURCH Picture 1

Lesson II. Picture 2

THE RIGHT REV. FREDERICK
FOOTE JOHNSON, D.D.
Bishop of South Dakota

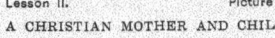

Lesson II. Picture 3

A CHRISTIAN MOTHER AND CHILD

(855)

MEETING OF THE BOARD OF MISSION

September 20th, 1910

THE Board of Missions met at the Church Missions House on Tuesday, September 20th, the Bishop of West Virginia in the chair. The following members were present: The Bishops of Pittsburgh, Ohio, Massachusetts, Minnesota, Indianapolis, Long Island, Newark, and the Bishop-coadjutor of Virginia; the Rev. Drs. Eccleston, Anstice, Alsop, Perry, McKim, Parks, Storrs, Smith, the Rev. Mr. Miel and the Rev. Dr. Manning; Messrs. Low, Mills, Chauncey, Goodwin, Mansfield, Butler, King, Morris and Pepper; of the honorary members the Bishops of Shanghai, Hankow, Springfield, The Philippines, Cuba and the Bishop-in-charge of South Dakota.

Announcement was made of the death of the Rt. Rev. Dr. McVickar, and the chairman, Bishop Peterkin, called the Board to prayer.

The treasurer's report showed receipts and legacies applying on the appropriations of $1,121,162.94; offerings from congregations had increased $43,756, but individual offerings were $13,051 less. Also there were small decreases in the receipts from the Sunday-school, the Woman's and Junior Auxiliary, and miscellaneous items. As compared with nine years ago, when the apportionment plan was inaugurated, the contributions have more than doubled; the number of contributing congregations (4,968) is also more than double. This year 36 dioceses and 27 missionary districts completed their apportionment, 16 more than last year.

The total expenditure for central expenses and making the work known to the Church, including department secretaries, was six and nine-tenths per cent. of the gross receipts; last year it was seven and two-tenths per cent. The treasurer said: "Another way of stating this is that approximately one-half of the total expenditure in central expenses

is for administration purposes, or and one-half per cent. of the rec and the other half is expended on a business house would term 'p tion,' also amounting to three and half per cent." The deficiency on tember 1st was $74,532.55. Of amount $33,000 was the deficiency (last year. Since the books were ($7,312 had been received toward r ing this deficit.

At the request of Bishop Rowe mission was given the Rev. Mr. Bett to secure scholarships for To Hall. Mr. Betticher will also see: to erect a modest log chapel and a firmary for the Indians of the Ta district.

A resolution was adopted expre appreciation of the action of Bishop of Eastern Oregon in linquishing the appropriation mad past year for his travelling expe and also in proposing that the appo: ment of his district be increased to The Bishop of Duluth was gr: permission to allow his archdeacc other clergyman in his stead to pr the work of the district in the East ing the coming year, without end ment. Permission was given to the John W. Heal to make an appea $600 to free from debt Grace Ch Olathe, a memorial to Bishop Ed J. Knight. The necessary resolu were adopted to take effect upor recognition by the General Conve of the missionary district of Sacran as a diocese, directing the treasur pay into the Episcopal Fund of the new diocese $10,000 from the H Brown Fund, $1,000 from the gi: James Saul, and $9,000 from the eral funds.

An appropriation, out of the amount assigned, was made for Negro work in Delaware and Lexin

The Standing Committee on Aud: ported that they had caused the l

MISSIONARY SPEAKERS

FOR the convenience of those arranging missionary meetings, the following list of clergy and other missionary workers available as speakers is published:

When no address is given, requests for the services of these speakers should be addressed to the Corresponding Secretary, 281 Fourth Avenue, New York.

Secretaries of Departments

I. Rev. William E. Gardner, 1 Joy Street, Boston, Mass.

II. Rev. John R. Harding, D.D., 692 Genesee Street, Utica, N. Y.

III. Rev. Thomas J. Garland, Church House, Philadelphia.

IV. Rev. R. W. Patton, care of the Rev. C. B. Wilmer, D.D., 412 Courtland Street, Atlanta, Ga.

V. Rev. John Henry Hopkins, D.D., 703 Ashland Boulevard, Chicago.

VI. Rev. C. C. Rollit, 4400 Washburn Avenue, South, Minneapolis, Minn.

VII. Rev. H. Percy Silver, Box 312, Topeka, Kan.

VIII. Rev. L. C. Sanford, 1215 Sacramento Street, San Francisco, Cal.

Alaska

Rev. C. E. Betticher, Jr., of Fairbanks.

Brazil

Bishop Kinsolving. (Until about February 1st.)

Rev. W. M. M. Thomas, of Rio Grande.

China

Shanghai:

Rev. Gouverneur F. Mosher, of Wusih.

Rev. John W. Nichols, of Shanghai.
(Available for Department VIII.)
(Address 1215 Sacramento Street, San Francisco, Cal.)

Hankow:

Bishop Roots.

Rev. T. P. Maslin, of Hankow.

Rev. Amos Goddard, of Shasi.

Harry B. Taylor, M.D., of Anking.

Deaconess Katherine E. Phelps, St. Hilda's School, Wuchang.

Mary V. Glenton, M.D., Elizabeth Bunn Hospital, Wuchang.

Japan

Tokyo:

Rev. Charles H. Evans, of Maebashi.

Porto Rico

Bishop Van Buren.

The Philippines

Rev. John A. Staunton, Jr., of Sagada.

Work Among Negroes in the South

Rev. S. H. Bishop, Secretary of the

American Church Institute for Negro
500 West 122d Street, New York.
Archdeacon Russell, of St. Paul
Lawrenceville, Va., and the Rev. A.
Hunter, of St. Augustine's, Raleigh, N.
are always ready to take appointmen
especially when a number of engag
ments in the same neighborhood can
grouped.

ANNOUNCEMENTS
CONCERNING THE MISSIONARIES

Africa

BISHOP FERGUSON, *en route* to the
General Convention, with his wife and
grand-daughter, sailed from Monrovia
on August 14th, and arrived at Hamburg on the 29th. He left Liverpool by
the steamer *Celtic* on September 24th.

AT the meeting on September 20th
the Board approved the appointment of
Miss Emily de Wint Seaman, of Fishkill-on-Hudson, N. Y., under the Woman's Auxiliary United Offering, for
work at Bethany House, near Cape
Mount.

BISHOP FERGUSON'S appointment of
Mr. William Harold Woodruffe as teacher in the Girls' Training Institute, Bromley, in place of Miss Ruth M. Dodge; his
appointment of Mrs. E. Louise Ware, as
teacher in Trinity Parish Day-school,
Monrovia, *vice* Mrs. M. F. Hilton, retired, and the transfer of the Rev. R. C.
Cooper from Buchanan to Grace Church,
Clay-Ashland, were approved.

Alaska

THE Board of Missions, at its meeting on September 20th, approved the appointment by Bishop Rowe of Dr.
Edgar A. Loomis, of Dallas, Tex., as
missionary physician at Tanana, and
the appointment of Miss Clara C. Johnston, of Parrsboro, Canada, as nurse in
St. Matthew's Hospital, Fairbanks.

ON August 6th, at St. John's-in-the-
Wilderness, Allakaket, Bishop Rowe
married Miss Clara M. Heintz to Graf-

ton Burke, M.D., both missionaries und
the Board.

THE REV. GEORGE E. RENISON a
family, who sailed from Seattle by t
steamer *City of Seattle* on August 7
arrived at Juneau on the 11th.

THE resignation of Mr. Harry
Strangman, dated August 31st, was
cepted.

Canal Zone

AT the meeting on September 20th t
Board accepted the resignation of t
Rev. William Cross, of Cristobal.

Cuba

THE REV. C. B. COLMORE, being a de
gate to the General Convention, sai
from Havana September 20th.

THE REV. DAVID W. BLAND and wi
who sailed from New York on Aug
24th, arrived at Guantanamo on the 31

Hankow

AT the request of Bishop Roots,
September 20th, the Board approved
appointment of Miss Edith Kay,
Malden, Mass., to act as his secreta
Miss Kay left Boston on September 5
and sailed from San Francisco by
steamer *Siberia* on the 13th.

THE Board also approved his appoi
ment of Miss Lucy Fish Baker,
Jamestown, N. Y., under the Woma
Auxiliary United Offering.

THE REV. ARTHUR M. SHERMAN,
turning after leave of absence beca
of illness, with his family left Ba
more, Md., on September 5th and sai

from San Francisco by the steamer *Siberia* on the 13th.

THE REV. AMOS GODDARD, on regular furlough, with his wife and two children, coming by way of the Suez Canal, arrived at Philadelphia on August 2d.

MISS KATHERINE E. PHELPS, Deaconess, on regular furlough, left Shanghai by the steamer *Mongolia* in July 5th, sailed from Yokohama by the steamer *Empress of Japan* in August 16th, arrived at Vancouver on the 28th, and reached New York on September 14th.

Honolulu

MISS SARAH J. SIMPSON, who was appointed by the Board on June 14th, sailed from San Francisco by the steamer *Sierra* on August 20th, and arrived at Honolulu on the 26th.

Kyoto

DR. AND MRS. GEORGE M. LANING, who sailed from San Francisco on July 19th, arrived at Osaka August 9th.

Mexico

BISHOP AVES reported the death, on June 11th, of the Rev. Genero Melendez, of El Oro, and his appointment of the Rev. Louis Amalric in his place.

Porto Rico

AT the meeting on September 20th the Board approved the transfer by Bishop Van Buren of the Rev. Leonard Read from Ponce to Vieques and accepted the resignation of Miss L. R. Kennedy, of San Juan, to date from August 31st.

MISS IVA MARY WOODRUFF, who was appointed as missionary teacher at the meeting on May 10th, sailed from New York by the steamer *Ponce* on September 10th and arrived at Mayaguez on the 16th.

Shanghai

THE REV. WILLIAM HENRY STANDRING, of the Soochow Mission, died at Nagasaki, Japan, on September 18th, of typhoid fever.

MISS LILLIS CRUMMER, a missionary in the Shanghai District from 1894 until April, 1909, died in her home at Omaha on August 27th.

AT the meeting on September 20th the Board approved the appointment by the Bishop of Shanghai of Miss Elizabeth Selden, of New York City, and Miss Caroline Fullerton, of Minneapolis, Minn., under the Woman's Auxiliary United Offering.

THE Board accepted the resignation of the Rev. R. E. Browning of his appointment as a missionary in the Shanghai District.

The Philippines

AT the meeting on September 20th the Board approved Bishop Brent's appointment, under the Woman's Auxiliary United Offering, of Miss Frances E. Bartter, of Maidstone, England, as a worker in the Settlement House. Miss Bartter will sail from England on October 8th for Manila.

MISS LILLIAN M. OWEN, who sailed from San Francisco on June 28th, arrived at Manila July 24th.

Tokyo

AT the meeting on September 20th Miss Caroline M. Schereschewsky, daughter of the late Bishop Schereschewsky, was given the status of a woman serving under appointment by the Board, she having been heretofore employed in the field. Miss Schereschewsky, who is on furlough, arrived at her brother's home, Baltimore, July 10th.

THE REV. CHARLES H. EVANS and wife, who sailed from Liverpool on August 11th, arrived at Montreal on the 19th, and reached St. Paul, Minn., on the 23d.

THE REV. JAMES CHAPPELL, returning to duty after furlough, with his wife and two children sailed from London by the *Tango Maru* on August 20th, which is scheduled to arrive at Yokohama about October 5th.

DR. R. B. TEUSLER, returning to duty after furlough, with his family left Basic City, Va., on August 12th, and sailed from San Francisco by the steamer *Siberia* on September 13th.

The Woman's Auxiliary

To the Board of Missions

ONE OF OUR OREGON MINING TOWNS

SEEKING IN EASTERN OREGON

Three years ago a parish priest on the Atlantic coast was chosen to be th
first Missionary Bishop of Eastern Oregon. He had spent his previous min
istry in the city of New York, and largely in that district of which *Th
World's Work* for September tells us, the census for 1900 records in a sma
portion of Manhattan Island south of Fourteenth Street and east of th
Bowery, "a population of more than half a million—more than that of Ar
zona, Delaware, Montana, Nevada, New Hampshire, New Mexico, Utah, Ve
mont or Wyoming, almost as large as North Dakota, and denser than th
densest parts of Calcutta or Bombay."

In that crowded district Bishop Paddock had passed his days, one of th
tumultuous throng, going in and out among his people, visiting the depth an
darkness of their cellars, climbing to their attics beneath the blazing roof
thus seeking his sheep and learning to know them by face and name. S
when called to the far distant field of Eastern Oregon, it was most natural fc
him to continue to seek out his flock, there so sparse and scattered, and t
spend the earliest years of his episcopate in pastoral care.

On September 2, the Bishop writes to the Secretary of the Woman
Auxiliary:

It is approaching three years since I left New York. I can say very hoi
estly that I have acquired a lot of experience since then. I have tried to wor
very quietly, and have almost hoped that temporarily we might be forgotte

by the Church outside until I knew the field intimately and could see the right solution of our great problems. Though we still have so small a staff of clergy, yet it is a comfort to be able to report that we know now of twice as many confirmed persons as when the district was set apart. * * * The people are beginning to give property and money to build little houses of worship, or guild halls with prophets' chambers attached, and are learning to expect only so much of a missionary's time as they can approximately pay for. I believe the results already, as I see them, have justified what might seem to some a rather unreasonable expectation.

THE WORK OF A UNITED OFFERING MISSIONARY
By Alice J. Knight, Deaconess

A February Report:

I WANT to tell my friends in the Auxiliary something of the places in Eastern Oregon which are becoming familiar to me in my missionary journeyings. This, from which I am now writing, is a frontier town at the terminus of a little branch railroad. There has been a bad washout on the road and no trains are expected to go out before Thursday. As I am due elsewhere to-night for a few days' office work with the bishop, this is serious. I have been trying to find some way to get out, and, by taking the stage to-morrow morning and spending a night on the way, hope to arrive by the next evening. This will save one day. The railroad and stage lines have all been uncertain this winter, and there have been delays at every point. This place is one of those mushroom towns which spring up rapidly out here. It is in the sheep country, and there is a great wool warehouse, from which the wool is shipped. This year railroad lines are being built down into the interior, not more than fifteen or twenty miles away, so this has become for the present a railroad town. All the supplies for this line come through the place, and the hospital tents are here.

Last week I was here for a night and visited the sewing society, where I talked to the women, and, later, as there is no church and no minister in the town, I gave an illustrated talk on the life of Christ. Two good women, Presbyterians, have carried on a Sunday-

school here for several years and are doing well with it. I visited it yesterday and spoke to the children and was much pleased with them. Directly after Sunday-school I had a little service, to which all the children stayed, and about fifteen grown persons came. I have also called upon a number of the people here, but I think that this is really a man's town and that the work which needs most to be done is to open a place to which the men can go evenings. The women would help to fix up a room, but that is all we could expect of them, and they would probably have to use a tent, for there are no buildings, not much but shacks, anyway. A Young Men's Christian Association man could do something, I think. I am going to try to see if one cannot be sent. It is not likely that the town will be permanent when the railroads get down into the far interior, for then the most of the business that this little road has done will go on the other lines.

Between my first and second visits here I spent a week at a neighboring hamlet in the sheep country. There we have a few people, but as there is no minister of any kind there is missionary work to do for all, so I spoke principally of what the Christian life really means and said but little, except incidentally, about the Church. I gave one talk only on Baptism and Confirmation, and the people came out nicely and were interested. Being without a minister and so far from any place where there is one, they are in great need when sor-

row and death come. A little boy died,
the child of a Scotch rancher, the day
I arrived. They wanted some kind of
Christian burial, and asked me if I
would take the funeral. This is the
third time I have had to read the
Church prayers on such an occasion. I
do not like to do it, but cannot refuse.
How hard it is for these poor people, no
one to pray with them or give them comfort! Nobody knows, who has not seen
it, the great need of these isolated
communities.

Another place which I visited lately
is also a sheep town and at the terminus
of another branch road. The only minister there is an Irish Roman Catholic
priest, who ministers to his own people
only. We have the merest handful who
belong to us, but a good many came out
to my evening talks and a few to the
little house meetings in the afternoons.
At another place on the main line, between two of our parishes, there is quite
a number of Church people who show a
good deal of interest, and there will be a
small class for confirmation the next
time the bishop visits them. There I
was able to organize a guild, and to arrange for their accepting a neighboring
clergyman's offer to come once a month
and give them a service. They are also
going to try to secure a lot for future
building.

December I spent between two other
towns, one of them very encouraging,
but needing the regular visits of a
clergyman; the other is full of young
people and if the right man would only
come we would sweep them all in. In
the fall I went up into the Wallowa
Valley, and hope to go again in the late
spring. In January, as the bishop insisted upon it, I took a ten days' rest,
after which I felt as fresh as at the beginning of the year, and really believe
I am growing more of a Samson every
day! Cold, long rides, cold rooms and
beds, and ice-water to wash in, do not
harm a person at all! Plenty of fresh
air—there is an abundance of that in
Eastern Oregon—hard work and a clear

In another place we have twenty-four communicants and a number of families nominally connected with us, and there I spent the most of two weeks, in calling on the people, and arousing them to some effort. Twice they came out for instruction, and then to Evening Prayer on Sunday. I had private talks with several who might be candidates for baptism and confirmation and left them some reading. In the fall, if I go down again, I may be able to get the little Seventh Day Adventist church rented for Sundays, and start lay-reading services, if the bishop thinks it a good plan. In still another place I organized a society, and set the ball rolling for active measures in the fall.

In all these visits, what is accomplished is not to be set down in figures. It is seed-sowing and one must not look for immediate results. But such a field as this has a great need. All this country will, at some not distant day, be filled with settlers. This Pacific Coast is going to be the scene of great activities, and because of its situation, sooner or later, is going to be brought into close contact with the nations of the Orient, and is going to

wield a tremendous influence, not only upon the government and policy, the customs and education and religion of our own country, but presumably upon those nations coming into contact with the West. Now, it seems to me a question of vital importance: What is this great Northwest going to be, Christian or unbelieving? What sort of influence is it to exert? Shall it be for good or evil?

I hope the Church may wake up in time to the great needs of this western field. I believe myself that much depends upon the next ten or fifteen years. If men care more about mining advancement and big salaries, and having an easy time and a comfortable home, than they do about having our land a righteous land, where God is honored and where men recognize His claims, then, with that spirit at the base of supplies, the work out here will be like trying to bale out the ocean with a teaspoon; but if once our candidates for the ministry can be brought to feel their responsibility, and to be glad to go, not where life is easy, but where they are *needed*, great things will be accomplished. As far as this district goes, I think we have a right to feel distinctly encouraged.

A UNITED OFFERING DEACONESS IN OKLAHOMA

By Katherine L. Patterson, Deaconess

IN my first two years in this district I succeeded in putting the little church, which was in a very neglected condition, into almost entire repair. This was done through the aid of the barrels and boxes of clothing that were sent me, using for this purpose the money which was received from the sale of their contents. After these two years I was transferred to Oklahoma City.

Oklahoma City is practically a city of strangers, as people have come and still are coming from nearly every State of the Union, though most of them from

the near by States; many of them from small towns where they have had little or no Church privileges and Church training. These naturally lack interest, and others, giving up their old church connections, find it difficult to feel at home again under new conditions, particularly from a social standpoint, saying they don't know any one and feel strange and lonely. Then also many have come here to make a new home and a fresh start in life, and this is the one absorbing interest.

So I feel that my special work is to bring them together socially, and so to

AN OKLAHOMA CHURCH

get them interested in the Church, that they may feel that once more they have a Church home. The Church must go or reach out to them in order to get their interest and devotion, which can best be done through the parish house, which is at present being built and possibly will be finished by the first of September.

It is impossible for one priest and a deaconess to do all that could and should be done, owing to the rapid growth of the city. Missions should be started in various parts of the town, and these eventually would be independent parishes, but this cannot be done for lack of equipment.

My work for the cathedral is principally through guilds and calling, though the calls must necessarily be short, as much time must be given to the missions that we have. In the Colored mission I can give the time only for an industrial class Saturday morning, though I should like to do more. At Capitol Hill I am trying to keep the little flock together until the place grows, which it surely is

doing, and a man can take charge, wh is needed. St. Andrew's Mission is c I have started recently in the south a poorer part of the town, where there a few of our families and where there a great opportunity for social work, l it needs one's whole time for it, with sistance. To show how ignorant the p ple are of our Church, when I fi started the mission, seeing the al through the window of the store wh service is held, we were taken for Ron Catholics, and I a Sister; others sa "What is the Episcopal Church? never heard of it." Much tea ing is needed, and I am hoping that n winter an effort may be made in that rection through the help of Daughters of the King.

A great drawback to the work, wh is perhaps more so here than elsewhe is the lack of helpers who can be pended upon. This is not so much lack of interest, but from the fact tl many of the members are young marr people with families and homes to t care of—many women doing their o work.

A MASSACHUSETTS OFFICER TRAVELLING

ONE of our Massachusetts officers has just returned from a journey round the world which her interest has made in a great part a missionary journey. She writes:

"Six weeks in China and two months in Japan gave me abundant opportunity to see much of our work and to meet many of our workers. I went up the Yangtse to Hankow and Wuchang and stopped at Kiukiang, Anking and Wuhu on the way down. At Shanghai I saw only the work in and around the city, but that kept me busy. My time in Japan was divided equally between Kyoto and Tokyo. In Kyoto I made my headquarters with Miss Suthon, going out to Tsu on the east coast and to Maidzuru on the west coast, and to Nara and Otsu on my way north. In Tokyo I saw the work in and around the city and went from there to Nikko and to Sendai. Everywhere I had a warm welcome.

I go home with my interests greatly widened and an enlarged stock of enthusiasm. No one could help being proud of our plant and the work that is being done, and the fine body of workers. Everywhere there are needs to be met and opportunities waiting to be grasped, and in some places the weakness of the medical work is appalling—the men's side of the hospital at Anking closed, at St. Luke's, Shanghai, Dr. Tucker struggling alone, and just before I left Tokyo he had come utterly worn out to be with his brother.

Of all the places I visited, Sendai naturally interested me the most, because of its connection with the United Offering. The training-school is well established, with a very attractive class of girls, whose training is bound to mean so much for the Church. The buildings are most satisfactory, and the compound gives good light and air for the students, and already has been laid out with shrubs and trees. I was the first officer of the Auxiliary to visit the school since the new buildings were finished.

A CALL FOR LEADERS FROM THE FRONT
By Bishop Roots, of Hankow

I SUPPOSE most of those Juniors who think about the missionary work done by Churchwomen in foreign lands, but who have not specially studied the subject, would picture to themselves the ignorant women and girls who have to be taught, and the families waiting to be made bright with the intelligent recognition of woman's high place in the home and with an appreciation of the sacredness of the life of every woman and even of little girls, as well as of boys and men. They would doubtless picture to themselves, also, the suffering women and girls whom missionary doctors and nurses can relieve of much pain. And I think most of the Juniors would have an imagination vivid enough to picture to themselves other things our Churchwomen do abroad.

And do we realize how important it is in all the departments of life to cultivate a true and vivid imagination? The pictures we have in our minds of the things we do not yet see with our eyes are more important than anything else about us; for they make or mar our whole life. If the imagination is cultivated as it ought to be, the Juniors will know that ignorance and pain are really not the worst things suffered by the great multitudes in non-Christian lands, and they will picture to themselves the spiritually blind eyes of the many, many women and children who are waiting to be enlightened by the word and example of that Churchwoman who shall go out as a missionary of the Cross of Christ.

Now such pictures are true and right, however imperfect they may be. The

needs of women and children in Africa
and China, and even in modern Japan,
are very, very great, and it should be the
ambition of many of our best Juniors
to help supply these needs by going to
live the whole-hearted and wholesome life
of a missionary among them. This would
be nothing unnatural; it would just be
living out in the wide, wide world the
life of sane and vigorous unselfishness
and helpfulness which Christian children learn first at their mother's knee,
in their own homes, and then practise
and learn more and more in the church
their parents attend, until they have
reached the stage where they can look
on the whole world as their Master did,
who came to give His life a ransom for
the whole world.

But in most of the great mission
fields to-day our task is not simply to do
the work of teaching and healing, ourselves, but to train and supervise the native workers and Christians till they are
able to minister effectively—far more effectively than the foreign missionary—
to the need of their fellow-countrymen.
This fact is recognized more and more
clearly as we find how, especially in
Japan and China, the native Japanese
and Chinese are able to learn almost anything and bear almost any responsibility, if only they are given a fair chance
by patient and generous help from those
who know how. And we are finding that
the principle involved applies to the
work for women as well as to that for
men. The work now being done by
Churchwomen in all our great mission
fields is not simply to teach the ignorant, but to train teachers; not only to
relieve women and children who suffer,
but to train doctors and nurses who can
minister to their own race in their suffering and pain; not only to bear witness
to the light, and to bring the blessed
truth of God's love in Christ home to
those whose eyes have been spiritually
blind, but to encourage and build up native workers, who can meet the spiritual
needs of their own fellow-countrywomen.

In China it has been said that the

OF MISSIONS and mite-chests for both general missions and the United Offering. At the end of the year these individual members could be again approached, and where a parish branch of the Auxiliary is already formed be encouraged to connect themselves with that branch; parishes where there is no branch be encouraged to form a branch in the parish. We are sure that much work of this sort is waiting to be done, with results we can hardly estimate.

OCTOBER MINUTES

THE first conference of the season was held at the Church Missions House, on Thursday, September 29th, Mrs. Sawyer, president of the Newark branch, presiding.

Twenty-one officers were present: Albany, 1; California, 1; Connecticut, 2; Kentucky, 1; Long Island, 1; Louisiana, 1; Newark, 6; New York, 7; Hankow, 1.

The secretary called attention to the Annual Report of the Woman's Auxiliary, which it is hoped may be read at an early meeting of every parish branch. Miss Lindley announced that a separate record of the work of the Junior Department is being presented.

Good reports of the United Offering of 1910 came from California and Connecticut, the story of a delightful open-air summer meeting from Long Island, and from Hankow the account of the last annual meeting of that branch, held in the assembly hall of the new Boone Library, the first public library established in China, through the efforts of Miss Wood, of Wuchang.

THE NOVEMBER CONFERENCE

THE November Conference of Diocesan Officers of the Woman's Auxiliary will be held on Thursday the 17th, from 10:30 to noon in the Church Missions House. Subject: "Fruits of the Triennial."

ACKNOWLEDGMENT OF OFFERINGS

Offerings are asked to sustain missions in thirty missionary districts in the United States, Africa, China, Japan, Brazil, Mexico and Cuba; also work in the Haitien Church; in forty-two dioceses, including missions to the Indians and to the Colored People; to pay the salaries of thirty-two bishops, and stipends to 2,253 missionary workers, domestic and foreign; also two general missionaries to the Swedes and two missionaries among deaf-mutes in the Middle West and the South; and to support schools, hospitals and orphanages.

With all remittances the name of the Diocese and Parish should be given. Remittances, when practicable, should be by Check or Draft, and should always be made payable to the order of George Gordon King, Treasurer, and sent to him, Church Missions House, 281 Fourth Avenue, New York. Remittances in Bank Notes are not safe unless sent in Registered Letters.

The Treasurer of the Board of Missions acknowledges the receipt of the following from August 1st to September 1st, 1910.

* Lenten and Easter Offering from the Sunday-school Auxiliary.

NOTE.—*The items in the following pages marked "Sp." are Specials which do not aid the Board in meeting its appropriations. In the heading for each Diocese the total marked "Ap." is the amount which does aid the Board of Missions in meeting its appropriations. Wherever the abbreviation "Wo. Aux." precedes the amount, the offering is through a branch of the Woman's Auxiliary.*

Home Dioceses

Alabama

Ap. $260.86

ANNISTON — *St. Michael and All Angels'* : Gen	34	00
MOBILE—*Christ Church* : Gen	81	25
MONTGOMERY—*St. John's* : Gen	145	61

Albany

Ap. $3,125.03 ; Sp. $6.50

ALBANY—*All Saints'* : Gen	87	55
St. Peter's : $774.63, Edward S. Davis, $5, Gen	779	63
BALLSTON SPA—*Christ Church* : Gen	91	94
BURNT HILLS—*Calvary* : Frn	5	00
CAMBRIDGE—*St. Luke's* : Gen	100	00
CHESTERTOWN—*Church of the Good Shepherd* : Gen	2	12
COOPERSTOWN—*Christ Church* : Gen	106	00
EAST SPRINGFIELD—*St. Paul's* : $10, S. S., $8; Gen	18	00
ELIZABETHTOWN—*Church of the Good Shepherd* : $46, S. S., $2, Gen	48	00
GLENS FALLS—*Church of the Messiah* : Frn., $50 ; Gen., $125	175	00
GOUVERNEUR—*Trinity Church* : Frn	10	00
HAINES FALLS—*All Angels'* (Twilight Park) : Gen	40	00
HERKIMER—*Christ Church* : Gen	42	80
Countryman S. S. : Gen	1	44
HOOSICK FALLS—*St. Mark's* : Gen	15	00
HUDSON—*Christ Church* : Gen	47	26
ILION—*St. Augustine's* : Gen	10	00
KINDERHOOK—*St. Paul's* : Dom. and Frn	60	00
LAKE GEORGE—*St. James's* : Gen	108	63
MORRIS—*St. Luke's* (Butts Corners) : Gen	3	00
Zion : Gen	42	80
OGDENSBURG—*St. John's S. S.* : Gen	52	00
SALEM—*St. Paul's S. S.* : Young Foreign Missionaries, Frn	18	50
SARATOGA SPRINGS — *Bethesda* : Dom. and Frn	103	21
SCHENECTADY—J. Campbell Close, Gen	5	00

SHARON SPRINGS — *Trinity Church* : Dom. and Frn	1	81
SOUTH GLENS FALLS—*Chapel of the Good Shepherd* : Gen	10	00
SPRINGFIELD CENTRE—*St. Mary's* : $50, S. S.,* $15, Gen	65	00
STAMFORD—M. B. Whitaker, Gen	2	00
TROY—*St. John's* : Junior Aux., Gen	19	00
Louis S. Crandall, $5, Mrs. John I. Thompson, $5, Gen	10	00
WADDINGTON—*St. Paul's* : Gen	15	00
WALLOOMSAC—*St. John's Chapel* : Gen	3	00
WARRENSBURGH—*Holy Cross* : Gen., $26.34 ; S. S., Sp. for work of Rev. R. E. Wood, Wuchang, Hankow, $6.50	32	84
MISCELLANEOUS—Dudley Tibbits, Gen.	1,000	00

Arkansas

Ap. $1.50

FORREST CITY—*Church of the Good Shepherd* : Junior Aux., Gen	1	50

Atlanta

Ap. $875.05 ; Sp. $1.00

ATLANTA—*Epiphany* (Inman Park) : Gen	53	00
St. Luke's : Frn	100	00
St. Paul's : Gen	15	00
St. Philip's Cathedral : Dom. and Frn	275	00
AUSTELL—*Church of the Good Shepherd* : Gen	3	48
CARTERSVILLE—*Ascension* : George L. L. Gordon, M.A., Frn	1	00
CLARKSVILLE—*Grace* : Gen	5	00
COLUMBUS—*Trinity Church* : Gen	66	15
DALTON—*St. Mark's* : Rev. G. L. L. Gordon, Frn	1	00
DECATUR—*Holy Trinity Church* : Gen	7	00
EATONTON—*All Angels'* : Gen	3	00
MACON—*St. Mark's* : Gen	7	00
St. Paul's : Dom., $6.42 ; Frn., $31..	37	42
MARIETTA—*St. James's* : Dom. and Frn	25	00
TALBOTTON—*Mt. Zion* : Gen	6	00
WINDA—Junior Aux., Sp. for Rev. Mr. Betticher's school, Alaska	1	00

AUGUSTA—*St. Andrew's*: Gen........ 4 68
BIG FLATS—*St. John's*: "A Friend,"
 Gen. 2 46
BINGHAMTON—*Trinity Memorial*: Gen. 50 00
BRIDGEWATER—*Christ Church*: Gen... 7 00
BROOKFIELD—*St. Timothy's*: Gen..... 1 00
BROWNVILLE—*St. Paul's*: Gen........ 3 00
CAMDEN—*Trinity Church*: Gen....... 5 00
CANASTOTA—*Trinity Church*: Gen.... 1 05
CAPE VINCENT—*St. John's*: Gen...... 5 00
CARTHAGE—*Grace*: Gen............. 11 20
CAYUGA—*St. Luke's*: "A Friend," Gen. 16 00
CAZENOVIA—*St. Peter's*: Gen........ 3 00
CHENANGO FORKS—*St. John's*: "A
 Friend," Gen.................... 3 00
CHITTENANGO—*St. Paul's*: (of which
 "A Friend," $6.93) Gen........... 8 68
CLARK'S MILLS—*St. Mark's*: Dom.,
 $14.43; Frn., $14.42.............. 28 85
CLAYTON—*Christ Church*: Gen....... 2 86
CLAYVILLE—*St. John's*: Gen......... 4 00
COPENHAGEN—*Grace*: Gen.......... 7 00
DEERFIELD—*St. Paul's*: (of which S.
 S,* $7) Gen..................... 13 00
DRYDEN—*Trinity Church*: Gen....... 11 00
DURHAMVILLE — *St. Andrew's*: (of
 which "A Friend," $4) Gen........ 8 00
EAST ONONDAGA—*St. Andrew's*: "A
 Friend," Gen.................... 9 00
ELLISBURG—*Christ Church*: Gen...... 1 00
ELMIRA—*Trinity Church*: (of which
 S. S., $25) Gen.................. 50 00
EVANS MILLS—*St. Andrew's*: Gen.... 5 00
FREDERICKS CORNERS—*St. Paul's*: Gen. 1 15
FORESTPORT — *Christ Church*: "A
 Friend," Gen.................... 12 60
FULTON—*Zion*: Gen................. 12 32
GLEN PARK — *Olin Memorial Chapel*:
 (of which "A Friend," $1.08) Gen.. 6 08
GREAT BEND — *Trinity Church*: (of
 which "A Friend," $4.10) Gen..... 7 10
 Mrs. C. N. Hewett, Gen.......... 1 00
GREENE—*Zion*: Gen................. 68 83
GREIG—*Trinity Church*: (of which "A
 Friend," $6.41) Gen............. 9 41
GROTON—*St. Andrew's*: Gen......... 2 00
HOLLAND PATENT—*St. Paul's*: Gen... 16 28
HORSEHEADS — *St. Matthew's*: "A
 Friend," Gen.................... 5 90
ITHACA — *St. John's*: Wo. Aux., $2,
 S. S.,* $78.07, Gen.............. 80 07
JAMESVILLE—*St. Mark's*: Gen........ 5 00
KENDAIA—*St. Andrew's*: Gen........ 1 00
KIDDERS—Gen...................... 5 00
LACONA—*Emmanuel Church*: (of which
 "A Friend," $7.50) Gen........... 12 50
LA FARGEVILLE—*St. Paul's*: Gen...... 3 95
LOWVILLE—*Trinity Church*: Gen..... 14 00
MARCELLUS—*St. John's*: (of which "A
 Friend," $4.03) Gen............. 12 71
McDONOUGH—*Calvary*: Gen......... 4 00
MEMPHIS — *Emmanuel Church*: "A
 Friend," Gen.................... 5 35
MILLERS BAY—Gen.................. 2 16
NEW HARTFORD—*St. Stephen's*: Gen.. 3 42
NEW YORK MILLS—*St. James's*: Gen .. 4 00
ONEIDA—*St. John's*: Gen........... 7 50
ONONDAGA CASTLE—*Church of the Good
 Shepherd*: Gen.................. 3 80
ORISKANY—*St. Peter's*: Gen......... 7 00
OSWEGO—*Christ Church S. S.*: Gen.. 29 00
Evangelist's: Mrs. H. F. Wallace,
 Gen. 5 00
PIERREPONT MANOR—*Zion*: Gen....... 90
PORT BYRON—*St. Paul's*: Gen........ 2 00
PORT LEYDEN—*St. Mark's*: Gen...... 5 00
PULASKI—*St. James's*: Dom., $6.89;
 Frn., $9.12..................... 16 01
 Dr. Charles E. Low, Gen.......... 1 00
REDFIELD—*Emmanuel Church*: Gen... 9 00
ROME—*St. Joseph's*: Gen........... 2 00
Zion: Dom., $6.01; Frn., $6.47; Gen.,
 $59 95 .... 72 43
ROMULUS—*St. Stephen's*: Gen....... 10 00
SACKETT'S HARBOR — *Christ Church*:
 Gen. 36 50

SKANEATELES—*St. James's*: Gen...... 148 40
SLATERVILLE SPRINGS—*St. Thomas's*: (of which "A Friend," $1.50) Gen.. 10 50
SPEEDSVILLE—*St. John's*: Gen....... 3 50
SPENCER—*St. John's*: Gen............ 3 00
SYRACUSE—*Emmanuel Church* (East): (of which "A Friend," $3) Gen.... 9 00
St. Andrew's: Gen.................. 75
St. Mark's: Gen.................... 115 00
St. Paul's: Dom., $40.28; Frn., $63.52; Gen., $119.12............. 222 92
St. Philip's S. S.*: Gen........... 50
Church of the Saviour: Gen......... 45 42
- "A Friend," Gen....,.............. 1 00
Mrs. Wallis Wadsworth, Frn....... 1 00
TRENTON—*St. Andrew's*: Gen........ 5 00
TRUMANSBURG—*Epiphany*: Frn....... 16 50
UNION SPRINGS—*Grace*: Gen......... 5 00
UTICA—*Calvary*: Gen................ 80 00
Trinity Church: Gen............... 125 53
Mrs. E. J. Wolcott, Gen............ 100 00
Mrs. C. G. Irish, Gen............. 5 00
VAN ETTEN—*St. Thomas's*: Gen...... 5 00
WARNERS—*St. Paul's*: (of which "A Friend," $3.14) Gen.............. 9 10
WATERLOO—*St. Paul's*: Gen........ 48 06
WATERTOWN—*Olin Memorial Chapel*: Gen. 2 00
St. Paul's: Gen.................... 133 62
WATERVILLE—*Grace*: Gen........,.... 2 19
WEEDSPORT—*St. John's*: "A Friend," Gen. 4 00
WELLSBURG — *Christ Church*: "A Friend," Gen 3 00
WESTMORELAND — *Gethsemane*: "A Friend," Gen..................... 10 00
WILLARD—*Christ Church*: Dom. and Frn............................... 5 00
WILLOWDALE—*Grace*: Gen.......... 10 00
MISCELLANEOUS—Diocesan Convention, Gen. 26 75

Chicago

Ap. $1,082.64; Sp. $15.15

BATAVIA—*Calvary*: Gen............. 16 50
BERWYN—*St. Michael and All Angels'*: Dom. and Frn.................. 30 00
CHICAGO — *Atonement* (Edgewater): Dom. and Frn.................... 15 18
Epiphany: (of which "H.," $2) Gen.. 7 00
Grace: Dom., $9.95; Frn, $79.96; Mr. Meacham, $100............ 189 91
Church of Our Saviour: Gen........ 10 00
St. Barnabas's: Gen................ 5 20
St. Bartholomew's: Wo. Aux., Sp. for Valle Crucis, Asheville............ 4 55
St. John's (Irving Park): Dom. and Frn. 6 00
St. Luke's: Gen.................... 20 00
St. Simon's: Girls' Friendly Society, Sp. for Bishop Rowe, Alaska, for door and windows in native hut, Alaska 10 00
M. Lester Coffeen, Gen............. 5 00
DIXON—A. H. Tillson, Gen........... 1 00
DUNDEE—*St. James's*: Gen........ 18 00
ELMHURST—Mrs. F. and Miss Jannette C. Sturgis, Gen................ 5 00
EVANSTON—*St. Luke's*: Dom and Frn. 144 54
FREEPORT—*Grace S. S.**: Gen...... 30 00
GENEVA—*St. Mark's*: Gen.......... 4 00
GLEN ELLYN—*St. Mark's*: Gen..... 5 00
HINSDALE—*Grace*: Gen............. 31 89
KENILWORTH—*Church of the Holy Comforter*: Gen.................. 107 32
LA GRANGE—*Emmanuel Church*: Dom. and Frn......................... 100 00
LAKE FOREST—*Church of the Holy Spirit*: In memory of J. N. D., Bristol, Maine, Gen................. 100 00
LOCKPORT—*St. John's*: Gen......... 10 00
MARSEILLES—*St. Andrew's*: Gen..... 4 10
OTTAWA—E. C. Swift, $10, Mrs. Helen V. Swift, $5, Gen.............. 15 00
SYCAMORE—*St. Peter's*: Gen........ 5 00

MISCELLANEOUS—"A Friend," Gen.... 2 0
Juniors for "Bishop McLaren" scholarship, St. Mary's School, South Dakota, $60; "McLaren" scholarship, Hooker School, Mexico, $80; "Bishop Philander Chase" scholarship, St. John's School, Cape Mount, Africa, $25; "Charles Palmerston Anderson" scholarship, Girls' High School, Kyoto, $30.............. 195 0
Babies' Branch, Sp. for missionary font ...., 1 0

Colorado

Ap. $64.11; Sp. $3.65

DENVER—*St. Peter's*: Gen.......... 3 7
William B. Berger, Gen............ 5 0
Gertrude M. Denison (Montclair), Gen. 5 0
EVERGREEN—*Transfiguration*: Gen.... 15 0
GEORGETOWN—*Grace*: Gen.......... 1 0
MT. MORRISON—*St. Michael and All Angels'*: For deaf-mute missionary at St. Louis.................... 3 4
TRINIDAD—Miss Amelia White, Gen... 10 0
MISCELLANEOUS—Babies' Branch, Gen., $15; Angelica Church Hart Day-school, Hankow, $2; for "Little Helpers'" Day-school, Shanghai, $2; for Gaylord Hart Mitchell Kindergarten, Akita, Tokyo, $2; Sp. for "Little Helpers'" bed, St. Agnes's Hospital, Raleigh, North Carolina, $1; Sp. for Indian work, White Rocks, Utah, $1.65; Sp. for a missionary font, $1.............,...... 24 6

Connecticut

Ap. $4,134.57; Sp. $330.15

BANTAM—*St. Paul's*: Gen............ 16 8
BETHEL—*St. Thomas's*: Gen........ 66 8
BETHLEHEM—*Christ Church*: Gen.... 31 4
BRANFORD—*Trinity Church*: $17.75, Miss Ellen M. Palmer, $1, Gen..... 18 7
BROAD BROOK—*Grace*: Gen.......... 20 0
BROOKLYN—*Trinity Church*: Gen.... 11 2
BYRAM—*St. John's*: Gen.......... 12 0
DURHAM—*Epiphany*: Gen........... 22 6
EAST HADDAM—*St. Stephen's*: Gen.... 68 5
Rev. F. C. H. Wendel, Bishop Spalding's work, Utah, $1; Mrs. F. C. H. Wendel, Sp. for work in Logan, Utah, $2....................... 3 0
EASTON—*Christ Church*: Gen........ 4 0
FAIRFIELD—*St. Paul's*: Gen........ 155 0
GUILFORD—*Christ Church*: Gen...... 12 8
HADLYME—*Grace Chapel*: Gen...... 5 2
HAMDEN—*Grace S. S.**: Gen....... 15 0
HARTFORD—*St. John's*: Gen........ 120 3
St. Monica's Mission: Gen......... 9 9
Trinity Church (of which "A Friend," $15); Gen., $113.93; Rev. Dr. Trumbull Huntington's work, Hankow, $5; "E. B.," Sp. for Rev. R. Ishii, Tokyo, $50....................... 168 9
HUNTINGTON—*St. Paul's*: Gen...... 20 0
LIME ROCK—*Trinity Church*: Bishop Brent's work, Philippines......... 29 0
MERIDEN—*All Saints'*: Gen......... 50 0
MIDDLE HADDAM—*Christ Church*: Gen. 60 0
MIDDLETOWN—*Christ Church*: Gen... 25 0
Holy Trinity Church: Dom., $24.75; Frn., $20; Gen., $40............ 84 7
MILFORD—*St. Peter's*: Gen......... 19 4
MONROE—*St. Peter's*: Gen......... 21 3
MYSTIC—*St. Mark's*: Gen......... 24 6
NAUGATUCK—"A Friend," Gen...... 2 0
NEW HAVEN—*St. James's* (Westville): Gen. 38 2
St. John's: Gen.................... 177 5
Chapel of the Epiphany: Gen...... 8 0
Forbes Memorial Chapel: Gen...... 359 2
All Saints' Chapel: Gen........... 10 0
NEWTOWN—*Trinity Church*: Gen..... 132 7

MORA—*St. James's*: Gen............ 1 00
PINE CITY—*Grace*: Gen............. 2 86
PRINCETON—*Hope Church*: Gen....... 4 62

East Carolina
Ap. $57.00; Sp. $2.00

ATKINSON—*St. Thomas's*: Wo. Aux.,
Gen. 1 50
ELIZABETH CITY—Mrs. Elizabeth Mar-
lin, Gen.......................... 5 00
LEWISTON—*Grace*: "A Friend," Gen.. 1 00
EDENTON—*St. Paul's*: Wo. Aux., Gen.,
$10: "Bishop McKim" scholarship,
Tokyo, $2......................... 12 00
ROXOBEL—Mrs. I. G. Powell, Gen..... 2 50
WILMINGTON — *St. James's*: Eliza
Munds, Gen., $10; Wo. Aux., "A
Member," Sp. for Bishop Horner's
work in mountains of Asheville, $2.. 12 00
MISCELLANEOUS—Jones-Gordon Memor-
ial, for Indian work, South Dakota. 25 00

Easton
Ap. $133.05; Sp. $5.00

CAROLINE Co. — *Epiphany Mission*
(Preston): Gen................... 2 25
CECIL Co.—*St. Mary's* (North East):
Gen. 14 00
North Sassafras Parish: Gen.......... 11 00
Parish House Congregation (Perry-
ville), Gen....................... 2 00
St. Mark's Chapel (Near Perryville):
Gen 4 00
DORCHESTER Co.—Miss S. A. Hirst
(Cambridge), Dom. and Frn....... 5 00
St. Stephen's (East New Market):
Gen. 3 31
St. Paul's (Vienna): Gen............ 1 34
QUEEN ANNE'S Co.—*Christ Church*
(Stevensville): Dom. and Frn..... 34 64
Mr. and Mrs. Edwin H. Brown, Jr.
(Centreville), Gen................ 10 00
SOMERSET Co.—*Princess Anne*: "A
Friend," Gen..................... 1 00
TALBOT Co. — *Trinity Cathedral*
(Easton): Gen................... 16 00
WORCESTER Co.—*All Hallows' Parish*
(Snow Hill): Men's Aux., Gen..... 12 50
MISCELLANEOUS—Junior Aux., Gen.,
$12; Sp. for Bishop Spalding, Utah,
$5 .... 17 00
Babies' Branch, Gen.............. 4 00

Florida
Ap. $939.97

GAINESVILLE—C. R. Layton, Gen...... 10 00
JACKSONVILLE—*St. John's*: Gen...... 286 67
St. Philip's: Gen................... 55 00
LAKE CITY—*St. James's*: Gen........ 14 00
PENSACOLA—*Christ Church*: Gen..... 168 00
ST. AUGUSTINE—*St. Cyprian's*: Gen... 16 80
Trinity Church: "J. H. H.," Gen..... 245 42
TALLAHASSEE—*St. John's*: Gen....... 72 80
St. Michael and All Angels': Gen..... 6 00
MISCELLANEOUS—Gen. 65 28

Fond du Lac
Ap. $261.48

ALGOMA—*St. Agnes-by-the-Lake*: Gen. 2 00
ANTIGO—*St. Ambrose's*: Gen......... 6 91
APPLETON—*All Saints'*: Gen.......... 25 00
BERLIN—*Trinity Church*: Gen........ 2 00
BIG SUAMICO—*St. Paul's*: Gen...... 6 68
FOND DU LAC—*St. Michael's*: Gen.... 5 00
GRAND RAPIDS—*St. John's*: Gen..... 20 00
GREEN BAY—*Blessed Sacrament*: Gen.. 7 60
Christ Church: Gen................. 7 56
MARSHFIELD—*St. Alban's*: Gen...... 50 00
MENASHA—*St. Stephen's*: Gen........ 6 13
OAKFIELD—*St. Mary's*: Gen.......... 8 60
OCONTO—*St. Mark's*: $20, S. S., $10,
Gen. 30 00
OSHKOSH — *Trinity Church*: Mrs.

Charles W. Radford, $5, Miss Emily
C. Haff, $2, Mr. and Mrs. Frank
W. Radford, $5, Gen............. 12 00
RHINELANDER—*St. Augustine's*: Gen... 70 00
MISCELLANEOUS—Babies' Branch, Gen.. 2 00

Georgia
Ap. $252.13

AUGUSTA—*St. Paul's*: Gen........... 100 00
BRUNSWICK—*St. Athanasius's*: Gen... 15 00
FREDERICA—*Christ Church*: Gen...... 20 00
PINEORA—*Holy Trinity Church*: Gen.. 5 00
QUITMAN—*St. James's*: Gen.......... 10 00
TIFTON—*St. Anne's*: Gen............ 2 13
MISCELLANEOUS—Wo. Aux., Julia K.
Miller Memorial, for hospital work in
Alaska 100 00

Harrisburg
Ap. $604.66; *Sp.* $10.00

BELLEFONTE—*St. John's*: $32, S. S.,
$10, Gen...................... 42 00
BLOSSBURG—*St. Luke's*: Gen........ 5 32
BLUE RIDGE SUMMIT—Miss Edith
Duer, Sp. for flood sufferers in To-
kyo 10 00
CARLISLE—Mrs. Robert Grosvenor,
medical work in foreign fields..... 5 00
COLE's CREEK—*St. Gabriel's*: Gen.... 1 98
COLUMBIA—W. T. Garrison, Gen...... 30 95
COUDERSPORT—*Christ Church*: Gen... 5 00
HANOVER—*St. George's*: Gen........ 3 00
HARRISBURG—*St. Stephen's*: Gen..... 213 60
JERSEY SHORE—*Trinity Church*: Gen.. 5 00
MANHEIM—*St. Paul's*: Gen.......... 5 00
MILLERSBURG—*St. Bartholomew's*: Gen. 3 15
MONTOURSVILLE—*Church of Our Sa-
viour*: Gen................... 8 67
PARADISE PARK—*All Saints'*: $8, S.
S.,* $7.15, Gen................ 15 15
RIVERSIDE—*Grace*: Gen............. 3 19
SHAMOKIN—*Trinity Church*: Gen..... 12 06
SUNBURY—*St. Matthew's*: Gen....... 51 29
ULYSSES—*Church of the Holy Spirit*:
Gen.......................... 1 20
UPPER FAIRFIELD—*Church of the Good
Shepherd*: Gen................ 1 58
WATSONTOWN—*St. Jude's*: Gen...... 2 20
WELLSBORO—*St. Paul's*: $10, S. S.,
$10, Gen...................... 20 00
WILLIAMSPORT—*Christ Church*: Frn.,
$4.66; Gen. $4.66............. 9 32
Trinity Church: Gen............... 100 00
YORK—*St. John's*: Gen............. 60 00

Indianapolis
Ap. $443.95

ANDERSON—*Trinity Church*: Gen..... 1 45
BLOOMINGTON—*Trinity Church*: $20,
S. S.,* $14.72, Gen............ 34 72
COLUMBUS—*St. Paul's*: Gen......... 5 90
CRAWFORDSVILLE—*St. John's*: Gen... 8 00
EVANSVILLE—*Holy Innocents'*: Gen... 5 90
INDIANAPOLIS—*Christ Church*: Wo.
Aux., Gen.................... 8 00
Grace: Dom., 25 cts.; Frn., $21.65;
Men's Aux., Gen., $52.46...... 74 36
Holy Innocents': $27.75, S. S.,* $8.40,
Gen.......................... 36 15
St. George's: Gen................. 15 35
LAWRENCEBURG—*Trinity Church*: Gen. 10 00
MADISON—*Christ Church*: Gen....... 16 25
NEW ALBANY—*St. Paul's*: $52, Wo.
Aux., $5; Gen................. 57 00
VINCENNES—*St. James's*: Gen., $10;
W. P. Gould, Dom., $25; Frn., $25.. 60 00
W. P. Gould, St. Augustine's School,
Raleigh, North Carolina, $25; St.
Paul's School, Lawrenceville, South-
ern Virginia, $25.............. 50 00
WORTHINGTON—*St. Matthew's*: Gen... 8 00
MISCELLANEOUS—"A Friend," Gen.... 5 00
Wo. Aux., Gen................. 47 87

Iowa
Ap. $527.28

BELLEVUE—*St. Paul's*: Salary of Rev.
Mr. Nieh, Hanch'uan, Hankow..... 3
CHARLES CITY—*Grace*: Gen.......... 23
DAVENPORT—*Trinity Church*: Gen.... 17
DES MOINES—*St. Paul's*: Dom. and
Frn. 248
DUBUQUE—*St. John's*: For the Bishop
of Olympia, for a missionary, $29.10;
salary of Rev. Mr. Nieh, Hanch'uan,
Hankow, $4.50................. 33
DYERSVILLE—*Christ Church*: Salary of
Rev. Mr. Nieh, Hanch'uan, Hankow. 8
KEOKUK—*St. Mary-the-Virgin*: Gen.. 7
MAQUOKETA—*St. Mark's*: Gen........ 3
MARSHALLTOWN—*St. Paul's S. S.*: Gen. 17
MT. PLEASANT—*St. Michael's*: Gen... 27
SIOUX CITY—*St. Paul's*: Dom., $6.50;
Frn., $6.50................... 13
St. Thomas's: Gen................. 125

Kansas
Ap. $145.23

ABILENE—*St. John's*: Gen........... 4
COLUMBUS—*St. Paul's*: Gen......... 2
FRONTENAC—Gen................. 2
GIRARD—*St. John's*: Gen........... 16
KANSAS CITY—*Ascension*: Gen....... 3
MANHATTAN—*St. Paul's*: Gen....... 12
OTTAWA—*Grace*: Dom............. 16
PARSONS—*St. John's*: Gen.......... 4
PITTSBURG—*St. Peter's*: Gen....... 6
TOPEKA—*Grace*: Gen.............. 17
St. Simon-the-Cyrenian: Gen........ 11
Miss Ardelia B. Wayne, Gen........ 25
H. L. P. Hillyer, Gen............ 10
WINFIELD—*Grace*: Gen............. 5
MISCELLANEOUS—Gen. 8

Kansas City
Ap. $265.53

CAMERON—*St. John's Mission*: Gen... 10
HIGGINSVILLE—Gen................ 3
KANSAS CITY—*Grace*: Frn.......... 131
St. Augustine's: Gen.............. 4
St. George's: Gen................ 25
Trinity Church: Gen.............. 40
NEOSHO—*St. John's*: $17.40, S. S.,*
$15.08, Gen.................. 32
SPRINGFIELD—*Christ Church*: Gen.... 20

Kentucky
Ap. $456.27

ANCHORAGE—*St. Luke's*: Gen........ 15
J. E. Hardy, Gen............... 5
ELIZABETHTOWN—*Christ Church*: Gen 5
HOPKINSVILLE—*Grace*: Gen......... 77
LOUISVILLE—*Advent*: Gen.......... 45
Christ Church: Dom.............. 300
J. C. Loomis, Gen............. 1
SHELBYVILLE—*St. James's*: Gen...... 5
UNIONTOWN—"J. H. D.," Gen........ 3

Lexington
Ap. $165.75

COVINGTON—Robert C. Simmons, Gen. 5
FRANKFORT—Miss Caroline A. Selbert,
Gen. 1
HARRODSBURG—*St. Philip's*: Gen.... 5
LEXINGTON—*Christ Church*: Dom. and
Frn. 137
St. Andrew's: Gen................ 2
MAYSVILLE—*Nativity*: Gen.......... 12
PARIS—*St. Peter's*: Gen............ 2

Long Island
Ap. $2,626.11; *Sp.* $21.00

ASTORIA—*Church of the Redeemer*:
Dom., $5; Gen., $80............ 85
St. George's: Gen................ 5

SOUTH PASADENA—*St. James's*: "A
Parishioner," Gen 25 00
TERMINAL — *St. Michael and All
Angels'*: Gen 1 80
MISCELLANEOUS—Dom. and Frn 90
"A Little More," Gen 5 00
"A Friend," Gen 5 00

Louisiana

Ap. $554.84

ALGIERS—*Mount Olivet*: Gen 14 00
BUNKIE—*Calvary*: (of which S. S.,
$8.26) Dom. and Frn 22 26
GRAND PRAIRIE—*Mission*: Gen......... 2 85
HAMMOND—*Grace*: Dom. and Frn.... 12 10
HOUMA—*St. Matthew's*: Gen 47 54
JENNINGS—*St. Luke's*: Gen 4 75
LAKE CHARLES—*Church of the Good
Shepherd*: Gen 35 00
LAKELAND—*St. Paul's*: $4.90, Mrs. J.
B. Churchill, $5, Gen 9 90
LAKE PROVIDENCE—*Grace*: Gen 4 95
LAUREL HILL—*St. John's*: Wo. Aux.,
Mrs. Evans's salary, Alaska, $10;
Miss Suthon's salary, Kyoto, $10;
Gen., $10 .... 30 00
MARINGOUIN—*St. Stephen's*: Dom. and
Frn 9 90
MARKSVILLE—*St. Peter's*: Dom...... 2 10
MELVILLE—*St. Nathaniel's*: Gen...... 7 55
MINDEN—*St. John's*: Gen............ 5 00
NAPOLEONVILLE—*Christ Church*: Gen. 5 00
NEW ORLEANS—*Christ Church*: Gen.,
$36.28; Wo. Aux., for Miss Suthon's
salary, Kyoto, 30 cts 36 58
Grace: Wo. Aux., Mrs. Evans's salary,
Alaska, 80 cts.; Miss Suthon's sal-
ary, Kyoto, 80 cts 1 60
St. Andrew's: Dom. and Frn 25 16
St. Anna's: Dom. and Frn 7 15
St. George's: Wo. Aux., Mrs. Evans's
salary, Alaska, 75 cts., Miss Suthon's
salary, Kyoto, 50 cts., "V. Q. E. W.,"
$10, "A Member," $5, Gen 16 25
St. Paul's: $115, Wo. Aux., $15, Gen.;
Wo. Aux , Frn., $5; Miss Suthon's
salary, Kyoto, $7; Mrs. Evans's sal-
ary, Alaska, $4 .... 146 00
Trinity Church; Wo. Aux., Mrs. Evans's
salary, Alaska, $2; Miss Suthon's
salary, Kyoto, $5 .... 7 00
"A Friend," Gen 1 00
OPELOUSAS—*Epiphany*: Gen.......... 26 75
SHREVEPORT—*St. Mark's*: Gen....... 95 00
UNION SETTLEMENT—*Church of the
Good Shepherd*: Gen 2 65
WASHINGTON—*St. John's*: Gen....... 6 50

Maine

Ap. $1,733.92

BIDDEFORD—*Christ Church*: Gen 15 00
BRUNSWICK—*St. Paul's*: Gen 12 00
DEXTER—*Church of the Messiah*: Gen. 5 00
DRESDEN—*St. John's*: Gen 6 00
FRYEBURG—"Anonymous," Gen........ 1 00
GARDINER—*Christ Church*: Gen 157 55
KINGMAN—*St. Luke's*: Gen.......... 3 00
LISBON FALLS—*St. Matthew's*: Gen... 5 00
LITTLETON—Gen. 4 00
MADISON—Gen. 5 00
NEW CASTLE—*St. Andrew's*: Gen..... 48 00
NORTH EAST HARBOR—*St. Mary's-by-
the-Sea*: Gen 919 45
OLD TOWN—*St. James's*: Gen 15 00
PORTLAND—*St. Luke's*: Gen......... 250 00
St. Paul's: Gen 3 00
WATERVILLE—*St. Mark's*: Gen 30 00
WINN—*St. Thomas's*: Gen........... 3 00
WISCASSET—*St. Philip's*: Gen 23 12
YORK HARBOR — *St. George's-by-the-
Sea*: Gen 228 80

Marquette

Ap. $498.45

BERGLAND—Gen.	1 50
BESSIMER—Gen.	3 00
CALUMET—*Christ Church*: Gen......	9 50
CHARMING—Gen.	2 14
DIABATE—Gen.	2 42
ESCANABA—*St. Stephen's*: Dom.....	4 50
EWEN—*St. Mark's*: Gen.:..........	2 79
FRONT CREEK—Gen...................	1 01
HOUGHTON—*Trinity Church*: Gen...	59 40
HUMBOLDT—Gen.	2 10
IRON RIVER—*St. John's*: Gen.......	7 35
ISHPEMING—*Grace*: Gen............	17 70
LAKE GOGEBIE—Gen.	8 36
MARENISCO—Gen.	2 24
MARQUETTE—*St. Paul's*: Gen........	220 05
MENOMINEE—*Grace*: Gen...........	11 20
PAINESDALE—*St. Mary's*: Gen.......	2 00
ROBER—Gen.........................	4 00
ST. IGNACE—*Church of the Good Shepherd*: Gen......................	3 00
SAULT STE MARIE — *St. James's*: Duluth, $5; Alaska, $5; Gen., $118.80	128 80
SIDNAW—Gen.	1 20
SPENCE'S—Gen.	2 00
WAKEFIELD—Gen.	2 19

Maryland

Ap. $2,102.47; *Sp.* $256.50

ALLEGHENY CO. — *Emmanuel Church* (Cumberland): Gen.............	118 31
ANNE ARUNDEL CO.—*St. Anne's Parish* (Annapolis): Gen..............	178 94
St. James's Parish (Jewell): Gen..:.	50 00
BALTIMORE—*Advent*: Gen...........	43 50
All Saints': Gen...................	30 00
Church of the Holy Comforter: Dom. and Frn.........................	5 00
Holy Innocents': For work at Changsha, Hankow...................	5 00
Church of the Messiah: Dom. and Frn.	102 00
St. Barnabas's and St. George's: Frn.	8 25
St. Bartholomew's: Gen............	92 39
St. John's (Huntington): Gen.......	52 00
St. Luke's: Dom. and Frn..........	91 23
St. Michael and All Angels': Dom., $150; Frn., $150; Wo. Aux., Mrs. Julia M. Burton, Gen., $5..........	305 00
St. Paul's: Gen....................	50 00
St. Peter's: Gen...................	445 42
E. A. Lycett, Gen...................	100 00
Randolph Barton, Gen.......:......	10 00
"H. W. A.," Sp. for Rev. Mr. Ancell, Shanghai...................	20 00
Thomas W. Hall, for Bishop Rowe's work, Alaska....................	2 00
BALTIMORE CO.—*St. James's* (Monkton): Gen., $2; Sp. for church building at Han Yang, Hankow, under care of Rev. A. M. Sherman, $11.50	13 50
St. John's (Mt. Washington): Frn., $7; Gen., $17...................	24 00
*St. Paul's S. S.** (Avalon): Gen.....	3 26
St. Thomas's (Garrison): Gen........	138 56
St. Timothy's (Catonsville): Gen....	7 50
Sherwood Parish: Gen..............	20 00
"A Friend" (St. George's), Frn.....	38 00
FREDERICK CO.—*All Saints'* (Frederick): Gen., $33.76; China Mission Chapter, Wo. Aux., Sp. for Bishop Roots, Hankow, $225; Five-cent Collections, Indian, $4.65; Frn., $4.65; Mexico, $4 70....................	272 76
HARFORD CO. — *Churchville Parish* (Churchville): Dom., $10; Frn., $20.	30 00
HOWARD CO.—*Grace* (Elkridge): Frn., $50; Deaf-mutes, $7.35............	57 35
St. Alban's (Alberton): Gen..........	15 00
St. John's: Frn....................	10 00
QUEEN ANNE'S CO.—Miss Elizabeth Neall Brown and Mrs. Edwin H. Brown (Centreville), Gen.........	20 00

Massachusetts

Ap. $5,454.26; *Sp.* $85.75

ALBERTON—*Church of Our Saviour*: Gen.	
ARLINGTON—*St. John's*: Gen.......	
BEACHMONT—*St. Paul's*: $11, S. S.,* $24.42, Gen	
BEVERLY—*St. Peter's*: Gen........	
BEVERLY FARMS—*St. John's*: Gen....	
BOSTON—*Advent*: Wo. Aux., Sp. for St. John's Expansion Fund, Shanghai..	
All Saints' (Ashmont): Wo. Aux., Hooker School, Mexico...........	
Ascension: Gen., $25; Sp. for Rev. R. E. Wilson, Shanghai, $6.......	
Christ Church: John D. Bryant, $5, "A Member," $5, Gen..........	
Church of the Messiah: Wo. Aux., Hooker School, Mexico...........	
Church of Our Saviour (Roslindale): Gen.............................	
St. Augustine's and St. Martin's: Gen.	
St. James's (Roxbury): Dom. and Frn.	
St. John the Evangelist's: Gen......	
St. John's (East): Dom. and Frn., $10; "Towards Spreading the Kingdom," Dom., $48.33; Frn., $96.67; "A Friend," Wo. Aux., "Frances Lathrop Fiske" scholarship, St. Mary's School, South Dakota, $60; S. S.,* Gen., $6..............	
St. John's (Orient Heights): Dom., $25; Frn., $29; S. S.,* Gen., $14.34; "Towards Spreading the Kingdom," Dom., $48.33; Frn., $96.67....	
St. Margaret's (Brighton): Gen......	
St. Mary's-for-Sailors (East): Gen...	
St. Peter's (Jamaica Plain): $165.86, George O. Currier, $10, Gen......	
St. Stephen's: "A Member," Gen., $20; Wo. Aux., Isle of Pines, Cuba, $5...	
Trinity Church: Gen., $93.09; Miss Helen Paine, Gen., $200; Wo. Aux., Hooker School, Mexico, $15; Isle of Pines, Cuba, $15.................	
Grant Walker, Gen..............	
Miss Cornelia A. French, Gen......	
BRIDGEWATER—*Trinity Church*: Gen..	
BROOKLINE—*Church of Our Saviour*: Dom., $18.50; Wo. Aux., Hooker School, Mexico, $27; San Gabriel, Brazil, $2; Isle of Pines, Cuba, $12; Haiti, $5....................	
CAMBRIDGE—*Christ Church*: "A Member," Gen., $25; Wo. Aux., Sp. for Rev. J. P. McCullough, Isle of Pines, Cuba, $5.....................	
St. Bartholomew's: Gen., $11.90; Wo. Aux., Hooker School, Mexico, $1...	
St. James's: Gen.................	
St. John's: Mrs. Alexander O. G. Allen, $15, Mrs. Robert D. Smith, $50, Gen.	
St. Peter's: Gen.................	
St. Philip's: Gen.................	
Archdeacon and Mrs. S. G. Babcock, Dom. and Frn..................	
Church Work Conference, Sp. for St. John's University, Shanghai.......	
CANTON—*Trinity Church*: Gen.......	
CHELMSFORD—*All Saints'*: Gen......	
CHELSEA—*St. Luke's*: Dom. and Frn., $22.50; "A Friend," Gen., $85......	
DEDHAM—Mrs. Augustine H. Amory, Gen.	
DUXBURY—*St. John's*: Gen.........	
EDGARTOWN—*St. Andrew's*: Gen......	
EVERETT—*Grace*: Gen..............	
FALL RIVER—*St. James's*: Gen......	
St. John's: Gen..................	
St. Luke's: $20, Wo. Aux., $3, Gen...	
St. Stephen's: Gen...............	
FALSMOUTH — *St. Barnabas's*: Gen., $76.63; S. S.,* $13.04..........	
FRAMINGHAM—*St. Andrew's* (South): Gen	

WINTHROP—*St. John's*: "A Friend,"
Gen. 30 00
WRENTHAM—*Trinity Church*: Gen.... 2 00
MISCELLANEOUS—"Mass," Gen....... 300 00
"Anonymous," Gen............... 120 00
Miss C. A. L. French, Gen........ 100 00
Wo. Aux., "A Member," Sp. personal
for Deaconess C. M. Carter, Alaska. 50 00
Wo. Aux., "A Friend," Isle of Pines,
Cuba, $20; Sp. for Rev. J. P.
McCullough, Isle of Pines, Cuba, $5. 25 00
Wo. Aux., "A Member," Gen........ 25 00
Wo. Aux., Western Colorado, $10;
Nevada, $10..................... 20 00
"A Friend," Gen................. 10 00
Wo. Aux., "A Friend," Isle of Pines,
Cuba 2 00

Michigan

Ap. $1,156.80; *Sp.* $62.50

BAY CITY—*Trinity Church*: Gen...... 16 00
CARO — *Trinity Church*: Wo. Aux.,
Alaska 1 00
DETROIT—*Christ Church*: Gen........ 415 38
Epiphany: Gen................... 20 00
Ephphatha Deaf-mute Mission: Gen.. 1 50
Church of the Messiah: Gen.......... 205 32
Church of Our Saviour: Gen......... 2 80
Church of Our Saviour (Leesville):
Gen. 8 75
St. John's: Gen., $207.88; Young
Woman's Aux., Sp. for Priory
School, Honolulu, $50; Charles C.
Zabriskie, Gen., $30; "A Member,"
Gen., $10...................... 297 88
St. Peter's: Gen................... 45 00
St. Thomas's: Gen................ 83 50
"Lithe," Gen................... 25 00
John B. Howarth, Gen............ 10 00
Mrs. Stevens, Wo. Aux., Sp. for Rev.
H. C. Parke, Asheville, in memory
of Mrs. Miner.................... 10 00
J. F. Wiber, Gen................ 5 00
DURAND—*St. John's*; Gen........... 3 20
GROSSE ILE—*St. James's*: Wo. Aux.,
St. Paul's School, Lawrenceville,
Southern Virginia, $5; Philippines,
$3; Sp. for F. E. Adams Memorial,
Good Shepherd Hospital, Arizona,
$2; Gen., $3................... 13 00
LEXINGTON—*Church of the Good Shep-
herd*: Gen....................... 12 00
OWASSO—*Christ Church*: Wo. Aux.,
Miss Thomas, Sp. for F. E. Adams
Memorial, Good Shepherd Hospital,
Arizona 50
PONTIAC—*All Saints' S. S.*: Gen.... 4 35
PORT HURON—*Grace*: Florence H.
Avery, Frn...................... 3 00
TECUMSEH—*St. Peter's*: Gen........ 25 62
TRENTON—*St. Thomas's*: Wo. Aux.,
Gen. 5 00
UNION CITY—A. J. Ackley, Gen....... 5 00

Michigan City

Ap. $328.12

BRISTOL—*St. John's*: Gen........... 12 60
ELKHART—*St. John's*: Wo. Aux., Gen. 5 00
FORT WAYNE—*Trinity Church*: Gen... 131 02
GARY—*Christ Church*: Gen.......... 22 26
GOSHEN—*St. James's*: Gen.......... 10
MISHAWAKA—*St. Paul's S. S.*: Gen.. 8 30
PERU—*Trinity Church*: Gen.......... 55 44
PLYMOUTH—*St. Thomas's*: Wo. Aux.,
Gen. 5 00
VALPARAISO—*St. Andrew's S. S.*:
Gen. 6 40
WAWASEE—*All Saints*': Dom. and Frn. 20 00
MISCELLANEOUS—Wo. Aux., Gen...... 5 00
"A Friend," Gen................. 57 00

Milwaukee

Ap. $308.59; *Sp.* $74.59

BRADHEAD—*St. Martin's*; Gen........ 3 00
DELAFIELD—"A Memorial from Five
Sisters," Sp. for Miss Farthing's
work in Alaska................ 25 00
DELAVAN — *Christ Church*: Dom.,
$11.70; Frn., $18.46; S. S.,* Gen.,
$25 .... 55 16
EVANSVILLE—*St. John's*: Miss Pearl H.
Campbell, Gen.................... 3 00
JANESVILLE—*Trinity Church*: Gen.... 1 00
LA CROSSE—*Christ Church*: Gen..... 15 00
St. Peter's: Gen................. 1 00
LANCASTER—*Emmanuel Church*: Gen.. 5 00
MADISON—*Grace*: Wo. Aux., "A Mem-
ber," $2, Woman's Service, $2.01,
Gen. 4 01
MILWAUKEE — *All Saints' Cathedral*:
Gen., $10.15; Sp. for purchase of
land, Wuchang, Hankow, $9........ 19 15
G. Y. Wilkinson, Gen............. 1 00
NASHOTAH—*St. Mary's*: Gen........ 28 00
OCONOMOWOC—*Zion*: $38.03, S. S.,*
$19 48, Gen................... 57 51
PLATTEVILLE—*Trinity Church*: Gen... 5 30
RACINE—*St. Luke's*: $10, "G.," $2,
"R.," $5, Gen.; Mrs. Harriet C. W.
Root, Frn., $1; Miss Catharine
Warner, Gen., $1................ 19 00
RICE LAKE—*Grace*: Gen............. 1 00
SHARON—*St. Mary's*: Gen.......... 5 00
STAR PRAIRIE—Gen................. 61
STOUGHTON—*St. Stephen's*: Gen..... 3 00
SUPERIOR—*St. Alban-the-Martyr*: Gen. 5 00
TURTLE LAKE—*St. Philip's*: Gen..... 5 00
WATERTOWN—*St. Paul's*: Gen....... 4 45
WAUKESHA—*St. Matthias's*: Gen..... 13 40
WHITEWATER—*St. S.*: Gen.. 4 00
MISCELLANEOUS—Rev. G. W. Dunbar,
Dom. and Frn.................. 25 00

Minnesota

Ap. $1,995.44; *Sp.* $.50

ANNANDALE—*St. Mark's*: Gen........ 2 00
AUSTIN—*Christ Church*: Gen........ 17 40
BELLE PLAIN—*Transfiguration*: Gen... 4 00
BIRCH COULEE—*St. Cornelia's*: Gen... 8 00
BLUE EARTH—*Church of the Good
Shepherd*: Gen.................. 1 50
BRAHAM—*Mission*: Gen............. 50
BROWNTON—*St. Mary's*: Gen........ 3 23
CALEDONIA—*Trinity Church*: Gen.... 6 00
CANNON FALLS—*Church of the Re-
deemer*: Gen....................
DELANO—*Church of the Holy Spirit*:
Gen. 2 31
FARIBAULT—*Cathedral of Our Merciful
Saviour*: Gen.................. 300 00
GOOD THUNDER—*St. Luke's*: Gen.... 2 00
GOOSE CREEK—*St. James's Mission*:
Gen. 1 00
HENDERSON—*St. Jude's*: Gen........ 6 00
JACKSON—*Christ Church*: Gen....... 6 00
KENYON—*Ascension*: Gen.......... 10 00
LE SUEUR CENTRE—*St. Paul's*: Gen.. 8 00
LITCHFIELD—*Trinity Church*: Gen.... 23 13
MANKATO—*St. John's*: Gen......... 18 50
MANTORVILLE—*St. John's*: Gen...... 7 00
MINNEAPOLIS—*Gethsemane*: Gen..... 600 00
Grace: Gen..................... 10 00
St. Mark's: Gen.................. 400 00
St. Matthew's S. S.:* Gen......... 17 05
St. Paul's: Gen.................. 100 00
Brewer Goodsell, Gen............ 5 00
MORRISTOWN—*St. John's*: Gen...... 50
MORTON—*Ascension*: Gen.......... 2 50
NEW ULM—*St. Peter's*: Gen........ 12 00
OLIVIA—*St. John's*: $4, S. S., $1.90,
Gen. 5 90
OWATONNA—*St. Paul's*: "A Friend,"
Gen. 10 00
RED WING—*Christ Church*: Wo. Aux.,
for "Clara B. Copel Memorial" schol-

arship, St. John's School, Cape
Mount, West Africa..............
ROCKFORD—*Breck Memorial Church*:
Gen. ....
RUSH CITY—*Grace*: Gen...........
ST. PAUL—*Ascension*: Gen..........
Christ Church: Gen...............
Church of the Good Shepherd: Gen...
St. Clement's: Gen., $165; J. F. A.
Williams, for Archdeacon Dray's
work in Wyoming, $4.............
St. John's (White Bear): Gen........
St. Peter's: Gen.................
St. Philip's: Gen................
St. Stephen's: $2.50, S. S., $2.50,
Gen. ....
Arthur W. Partridge, Gen.........
ST. PETER—*Church of the Holy Com-
munion*: Gen..................
SHAKOPEE—*St. Peter's*: Gen........
SPRING CREEK—H. Bruxvoort, Sp. for
St. Paul's College, Tokyo..........
STILLWATER—*Ascension*: Gen.......
WARSAW—*St. Thomas's*: 50 cts., S. S.,
$1.27, Gen.....................
WATERVILLE—*St. Andrew's*: Gen.....

Mississippi

Ap. $376.88; *Sp.* $5.00

ABERDEEN—*St. John's*: Gen.........
BAY ST. LOUIS—*Christ Church*: Gen..
CARROLLTON—*Grace*: Children's Mis-
sionary Society, Sp. for Bishop
Rowe's work, Alaska.............
CHURCH HILL—*Christ Church*: Gen...
COLUMBUS—*St. Paul's*: Gen........
GLASS—*Church of the Holy Com-
munion*: Frn....................
GRENADA—*All Saints'*: Gen.........
GULFPORT—*St. Peter's-by-the-Sea*: Gen.
HERNANDO—*Ascension*: $5, Ethel S.
Cooke, $10, Gen.................
HOLLY SPRINGS—*Christ Church*: Dom.
LONG BEACH—*All Saints'*: Gen......
McCOMB CITY—*Church of the Media-
tor*: Gen......................
MAGNOLIA—*Church of the Redeemer*:
Gen. ....
MISSISSIPPI CITY—*St. Mark's Mission*:
Ladies' Guild, Gen...............
MOSS POINT—*St. Alban's*: Gen......
OCEAN SPRINGS—*St. John's*: Gen.....
OKOLONA—*Grace Mission*: Gen.......
PASCAGOULA—*St. John's*: Gen.......
SUMMIT—*Christ Church*: Gen.......
MISCELLANEOUS—"A Friend," Gen....

Missouri

Ap. $1,282.33

IRONTON—*St. Paul's*: Gen..........
LOUISIANA—*Calvary*: Gen..........
OVERLAND PARK—*St. Paul's Mission*:
Gen. ....
POPLAR BLUFF—*Holy Cross*: Gen.....
ROLLA—*Christ Church*: Gen........
ST. CHARLES—*Trinity Church*: Gen..
ST. LOUIS—*Ascension*: Gen.........
Christ Church Cathedral: School work
in China, $10; Gen., $150.........
Emmanuel Church (Old Orchard):
Laymen's Missionary Society, for
Foreign Missions................
Church of the Good Shepherd: Gen...
Holy Communion: Mrs. P. C. Moffitt,
Gen. ....
Mt. Calvary: Dom. and Frn........
St. Andrew's: Gen...............
St. George's Chapel: Gen..........
St. Peter's: Dom., $32.49; Frn.,
$32.49
St. Paul's: Dom. and Frn..........
L. F. Jones, Gen.................
J. H. Thompson, Gen.............

MISCELLANEOUS — Branch Wo. Aux., Colored, $100.50; "Frederick B. Sheetz Memorial" scholarship, St. John's School, Cape Mount, Africa, $25; Gen., $107.50............. 233 00

Montana

Ap. $118.98

CHINOOK—*St. Timothy's*: Gen.......	10 00
COLUMBUS—R. J. Brennan, Gen......	5 00
CULBERTSON—*Church of the Good Shepherd*: Gen..................	10 00
GLENDIVE—*St. Matthew's*: Gen.......	50 00
HAVRE—*St. Mark's*: Gen............	32 58
HELENA—*St. Peter's*: Gen..........	1 40
WIBAUX—*St. Thomas's*: Gen.........	10 00

Nebraska

Ap. $223.83

FALL CITY—*St. Thomas's*: Gen......	2 60
HARVARD—*St. John's S. S.**: Gen....	4 25
NORFOLK — *Trinity Church*: Dom., $8.25, S. S., $7, Gen...........	15 25
OMAHA—*St. Paul's*: "Miss A.," Gen..	10 00
St. Philip-the-Deacon: Gen.........	12 00
Trinity Cathedral: Dom. and Frn....	120 33
PALMER—*St. Mark's*: Gen..........	3 85
SOUTH OMAHA—*St. Martin's*: Dom. and Frn.	52 89
WYOMING—*Christ Church*: Gen......	2 66

Newark

Ap. $3,544.61; *Sp.* $78.00

ALLENDALE—*Epiphany*: Gen..........	21 50
BLOOMFIELD—*Christ Church*: Gen....	139 36
DOVER—*St. John's*: Gen...........	10 00
EAST ORANGE—*Christ Church*: Gen...	132 55
St. Agnes's: Gen.................	15 00
St. Paul's: $63.95, S. S.,* $62.23, Dom. and Frn...................	126 18
Mrs. E. J. Marsh, Sp. for Bishop Horner, Asheville..............	50 00
ENGLEWOOD—*Junior Aux.,* Gen.......	5 00
HACKETTSTOWN — *St. James's*: Rev. William J. Cuthbert, Tokyo......	4 37
HOBOKEN—Mrs. Lillian Brain, Gen....	1 00
IRVINGTON—*Trinity Church*: Gen....	35 00
JERSEY CITY—*Holy Cross*: Gen......	7 33
St. John's (Heights): Rev. William J. Cuthbert, Tokyo................	137 50
St. Paul's: Gen., $50; Wilhelmina F. Rhode, Gen., $2...............	52 00
LYNDHURST—*St. Thomas's*: Gen......	2 54
MAPLEWOOD — "Thank-offering," work at St. Margaret's School, Tokyo....	2 00
MILLINGTON—*All Saints'*: Gen.......	17 21
MILLBURN—*St. Stephen's*: Gen.......	30 00
MONTCLAIR—*St. John's*: Gen........	4 73
MONTVALE—F. C. Ackerman, Gen.....	5 00
MORRISTOWN—*Church of the Redeemer*: Gen..................	826 90
St. Peter's: Archdeacon Stuck's salary, Alaska.........................1,030 05	
NEWARK—*Grace*: Rev. Elliott White, Sp. for Rev. W. J. Cuthbert, Kyoto.	25 00
St. Paul's: Gen..................	70 97
Trinity Church: Rev. Mr. McNulty's salary, Shanghai.................	100 00
PASSAIC—*St. John's*: Junior Aux., Gen. (of which Miss H. P. Simmons, $10)	25 00
Minnie I. Maclagan, Gen............	10 00
PATERSON—*St. Paul's*: Gen..........	300 00
Trinity Church: Gen..............	22 25
SWANHOPE—*Christ Church*: Rev. John A. Staunton, Jr., Sagada, Philippine Islands	3 22
SUMMIT—*Calvary*: Gen.............	152 95
MISCELLANEOUS—"A Friend," Gen....	5 00
Junior Aux., Gen................	50 00
Babies' Branch, Gen., $200; Sp. for "Little Helpers'" cot, St. Agnes's	

Hospital, Raleigh, North Carolina, $3 .... 203 00

New Hampshire

Ap. $398.93; *Sp.* $25.00

BERLIN—*St. Barnabas's*: Gen........	25 00
CLAREMONT—*Union Church* (West): $6, S. S.,* $4, Gen.............	10 00
CONCORD—*Grace S. S.** (East): Gen..	2 00
St. Luke's: Junior Aux., Gen......	5 45
*St. Mary's S. S.**: Gen...........	3 00
St. Paul's School: "A Friend," Sp. for Easter School, Baguio, Philippine Islands	25 00
St. Timothy's: $20, S. S.,* $16.76, Gen.	36 76
DANBURY—*Church of the Holy Spirit*: $2, S. S.,* $1, Gen.............	3 00
EXETER—*Christ Church*: Gen........	3 92
FRANKLIN—*St. Jude's*: Gen.........	15 00
HOLDERNESS—*Holy Cross*: Dom. and Frn.........................	25 00
JAFFREY—Clara N. Parker, Gen.....	15 00
LANCASTER—*St. Philip's*: Gen......	2 80
MEREDITH—*Resurrection*: Gen.......	1 00
NASHUA—*Church of the Good Shepherd*: Gen.....................	111 00
NEWPORT—*Epiphany*: Gen..........	6 00
PETERBOROUGH—*All Saints'*: Gen....	1 00
PORTSMOUTH—*Christ Church*: $20, S. S.,* $20, Gen................	40 00
St. John's: Gen.................	75 00
SALMON FALLS—*Christ Church*: Gen..	5 00
WILTON—*Transfiguration*: Gen.......	2 00
MISCELLANEOUS—Wo. Aux., Gen.....	11 00

New Jersey

Ap. $2,341.77; *Sp.* $209.00

ASBURY PARK—*Trinity Church*: Wo. Aux., Sp. for salary of Mrs. William Holmes, South Dakota........	5 00
ATLANTIC CITY—*St. James's*: Gen....	65 00
BASKING RIDGE—*St. Mark's*: Gen....	8 95
BAY HEAD—*All Saints'*: Gen.......	35 00
BEACH HAVEN—*Holy Innocents'*: Gen.	18 00
BELMAR—"Friends," Gen............	5 00
BERNARDSVILLE—*St. Bernard's*: Gen.	458 58
Somerset Inn School: Gen..........	1 20
BEVERLY—*St. Stephen's*: Dom. and Frn.	89 33
BURLINGTON—*St. Barnabas's*: Gen....	55 00
CAMDEN—*St. Paul's*: Gen., $168.38; Wo. Aux., Sp. for salary of Mrs. William Holmes, South Dakota, $30; "A Member," Koyukuk Indian Mission, Alaska, $6; Frn., $10.......	214 38
St. Stephen's: Gen..............	25 00
(In Memoriam), J. H. Carpenter, Gen.	4 00
CAPE MAY—*Advent*: Gen...........	10 00
CRAMER HILL—*St. Wilfrid's*: Gen....	77 00
ELIZABETH—*Christ Church*: Wo. Aux., "A Member," Dom...........	40 00
St. John's: William T. Day, $3, Mr. Gales, $2, Sp. for St. John's University, Shanghai, $5; Wo. Aux., Sp. for salary of Mrs. William Holmes, South Dakota, $5.............	10 00
Trinity Church: Gen..............	2 00
FLORENCE—*St. Stephen's*: Wo. Aux., Sp. for salary of Mrs. William Holmes, South Dakota.........	5 00
GIBBSBORO—*St. John's-in-the-Wilderness*: Frn., $5; Gen., $5.........	10 00
HADDONFIELD—*Grace*: St Anne's Guild, "A Member," Wo. Aux., Sp. for salary of Mrs. William Holmes, South Dakota..................	3 00
HELMETTA—*St. George's*: $144.97, S. S.,* $20, Gen................	164 97
HIGHLANDS—*Mary Trash*, Gen......	3 00
KEYPORT—*St. Mary's S. S.*: Gen.....	12 00
LAMBERTVILLE—*St. Andrew's*: Gen., $20; Wo. Aux, Sp. for salary of	

Mrs. William Holmes, South Dakota, $4 .... 24 00
LUMBERTON—St. Martin's: Gen...... 3 00
MANTOLOKING—St. Simon's: Gen..... 18 00
MERCHANTVILLE—Grace: Wo. Aux., Sp. for salary of Mrs. William Holmes, South Dakota............ 5 00
MONMOUTH BEACH — St. Peter's-in-Galilee: Wo. Aux., Frn., $50; Sp. for the Patterson School, Yadkin Valley, Asheville, $15; Sp. for St. Hilda's School, Wuchang, Hankow, $25; Sp. for Rev. A. M. Sherman, for his work in Hankow, $10...... 100 00
MOORESTOWN — Trinity Church: "A Friend," "Trinity Memorial" scholarship, St. Elizabeth's School, South Dakota, $60; S. S., "Rev. H. Hastings Weld Memorial" scholarship, St. John's School, Cape Mount, Africa, $25 .... 85 00
MOUNT HOLLY—St. Andrew's: Wo. Aux., Sp. for salary of Mrs. William Holmes, South Dakota............ 10 00
NAVESINK — All Saints': $176.43, "Members," $100, Gen............... 276 43
NEW BRUNSWICK—St. John's: Wo. Aux., Sp. for salary of Mrs. William Holmes, South Dakota, $5; "A Member," Sp. for St. Agnes's Hospital, Raleigh, North Carolina, $1.. 6 00
John N. Carpender, Gen.......... 50 00
OCEAN CITY—Holy Trinity Church: Gen................................ 10 00
"A Friend," Sp. for erection of new building, for St. Hilda's Girls' School, Wuchang, Hankow................ 3 00
PERTH AMBOY—St. Peter's: Gen..... 5 00
RAHWAY—St. Paul's: Gen.......... 1 00
RED BANK—Trinity Church: Mrs. William S. Jones, Sp. for "Mary Grace" scholarship, St. Hilda's School, Wuchang, Hankow.................. 50 00
RIVERTON—Christ Church: Gen...... 34 38
ROSELLE PARK—St. Luke's: "A Member," Gen....................... 5 00
RUMSON—St. George's: Wo. Aux., Dom., $30; Frn., $50........... 80 00
SCOTCH PLAINS—All Saints': Gen.... 4 00
SEA GIRT—St. Uriel's: Gen......... 32 00
SHREWSBURY—Christ Church: Junior Aux., scholarship at Boone College, Wuchang, Hankow................ 49 69
SOMERVILLE—St. John's: Gen........ 86 25
SPOTTSWOOD—St. Peter's: Gen...... 29 95
SPRING LAKE—Holy Trinity Church: Gen................................ 85 00
SWEDESBORO—Trinity Church: Gen... 73 00
TOM'S RIVER—Christ Church: Gen.... 12 84
TRENTON—Grace: Gen.............. 7 51
St. Michael's: Gen................. 35 00
St. Paul's: Dom., $10; Frn., $10.... 20 00
Trinity Church: Wo. Aux., Sp. for salary of Mrs. William Holmes, South Dakota....................... 3 00
WOODBURY—Christ Church: Gen...... 2 25
MISCELLANEOUS—Babies' Branch, Sp. for salary of Mrs. William Holmes, South Dakota.................... 25 00

New York

Ap. $19,137.34; Sp. $1,072.31

ANNANDALE—Mrs. G. A. Dean, Gen... 5 00
BEDFORD—St. Matthew's: Wo. Aux., Sp. for Hospital of the Good Shepherd, Fort Defiance, Arizon........ 42 50
DOBBS FERRY—Zion: Gen........... 61 85
EAST CHESTER—St. Paul's: Gen..... 56 00
GOSHEN—St. James's S. S.*: Dom... 13 85
HARRISON—All Saints': Gen......... 15 65
HIGHLAND—Holy Trinity Church: Gen. 1 50
KINGSTON—Church of the Holy Spirit: Gen. 5 75

LAKE MAHOPAC—Holy Communion: $41, S. S.,* $9.57, Gen........... 50
MAMARONECK—St. Thomas's: Gen.... 282
MT. VERNON—H. W. Greene, Gen..... 10
NEW HAMBURGH—Irving Grinnell, Gen. 25
NEW ROCHELLE — Trinity Church: Gen. 187
NEW YORK—All Saints': Gen........ 57
All Souls': For St. Margaret's School, Tokyo, in memory of "C. L. E.," $20; for Elizabeth Bunn Memorial Hospital, Wuchang, Hankow, in memory of "Dr. S. E.," $10....... 30
Ascension: Gen.................... 370
Ascension (West New Brighton): For Bishop Partridge's Mission in Kyoto, $63.34; Gen., $122............... 185
Beloved Disciple: Gen............. 28
Calvary: Dom., $1,200; Frn., $1,000.. 2,200
Church Missions House Chapel: Farewell Service, Frn................. 28
Grace: Gen., $1,761.51; Committee on Missions for Colored People, St. Augustine's League, Sp. for St. Agnes's Hospital, Raleigh, North Carolina, $10; Sp. for Good Samaritan Hospital, Charlotte, North Carolina, $5 1,776
Holy Apostles': Gen............... 72
Holy Communion: $325, Mrs. Charles W. Ogden, $500, Gen........... 825
Holy Faith: Colored, $15.20; Gen., $80.30 95
Holy Nativity: Gen................ 6
Holy Trinity Church (Harlem): Edith M. Bond, Violet H. Bond, Gen..... 200
Incarnation: Francis Lynde Stetson, Gen. 800
St. Agnes': Wo. Aux., "A Member," Gen., $5; S. S.,* Gen., $625.33; "Rev. E. A. Bradley, D.D." scholarship, Girls' Training Institute, Africa, $25; Sp. for "Rev. Edward Bradley, D.D." scholarship, St. Augustine's School, Raleigh, North Carolina, $25; Sp. for Archdeacon Russell, Lawrenceville, Southern Virginia, $50; Sp. for Rev. Primus P. Alston, Industrial School, Raleigh, North Carolina, $50; Sp. for St. Mary's-in-the-Mountains, Sewanee, Tennessee, $50; Sp. for Rev. Mr. Hughson's Boys' School, Sewanee, Tennessee, $50; Sp. for Bishop Rowe, Alaska, $100; Sp. for Expansion Fund, St. John's University, Shanghai, $50; Sp. for Rev. R. C. Wilson, Zangzok, Shanghai, $25........... 1,055
St. Augustine's Chapel: Gen........ 107
St. Bartholomew's Swedish Chapel: Gen. 16
St. Cyprian's: Gen................ 5
St. George's: Gen................. 4,000
St. James's: Gen.................. 250
St. John the Evangelist's: Miss Elizabeth H. Wisner, Gen............. 25
St. Luke's: Gen................... 48
St. Mary-the-Virgin: Rev. A. G. van Elden, Dom. and Frn.............. 5
St. Michael's: Gen., $120; Sp. for Rev. A. A. Gilman, Changsha, Hankow, $32 152
St. Stephen's: For work in Asheville.. 163
St. Thomas's: "A Friend," Gen...... 300
Trinity Church (New Dorp): Mrs. William Mason Smith, Gen........ 25
Mary W. B. Alexander (New Brighton), for China................. 5
August Belmont, Gen.............. 800
L. C. Benedict, Gen............... 5
W. Bayard Cutting, Gen........... 800
G. W. Dix, Gen................... 10
Maynard C. Eyre (Clifton), Dom.... 25
Miss Annie Frazier, Dom. and Frn... 400
Frank Le G. Gilliss, Gen........... 6
Mrs. Francis W. Johnston, $20, Miss

Chapel of Hope: Dom., $1; Frn., $1;
Gen., $1............................ 3 00
St. Andrew's Chapel: Dom. and Frn.. 3 00
St. Michael's S. S.*: Colored, $4; Gen.,
$4 17 .... 8 17
DURHAM—*St. Titus's Mission*: Gen.... 1 35
GERMANTON—*St. Philip's*: Gen......... 2 00
GREENSBORO—*St. Andrew's*: Gen...... 11 00
St. Barnabas's: Frn................. 30 00
LEWISTON—"M. B. U.," Gen............. 7 00
LEXINGTON—*Grace Mission*: Gen..... 30 00
LITTLETON—*St. Anna's Chapel*: Gen.. 3 00
MILTON—*Christ Church*: Gen........ 1 00
Cunningham Chapel: Gen............. 1 00
MONROE—*St. Paul's*: Dom. and Frn.. 12 00
ROCKINGHAM—Wo. Aux., for the sup-
port of Misses Cheshire, China..... 12 00
PITTSBORO—*St. James's Mission*: Gen. 2 00
RALEIGH—*Christ Church*: Gen...... 10 90
ROANOKE RAPIDS—*All Saints' Mission*:
Gen. 1 25
ROWAN CO.—*St. Jude's*: Gen........ 1 02
SALISBURY—*St. Luke's*: Gen........ 1 50
WELDON—*Grace*: Gen............... 5 00
WILLIAMSBORO—*St. John's*: Gen...... 4 00
MISCELLANEOUS — "Anonymous," the
Argola Fund income, only to be used
in payment of the salary of some
foreign missionary clergyman, to be
designated by the Board of Missions
(additional) 1,000 00

Ohio
Ap. $2,951.97

AKRON — *Grace*: Deaf-mute Mission,
Gen. 4 00
St. Andrew's: Gen.................. 5 00
ALLIANCE—*Trinity Mission*: Gen..... 5 00
ASHTABULA—*Grace*: Gen............. 11 10
St. Peter's: Gen.................. 10 00
BARBERTON—*St. Andrew's*: Gen...... 4 08
BELLEFONTAINE—*Trinity Church*: Gen. 5 00
BELLEVUE—*St. Paul's*: Gen......... 5 00
BEREA—*St. Thomas's*: Gen.......... 3 50
BOARDMAN—*St. James's*: Gen........ 10 00
BOWLING GREEN—*Annunciation*: Gen.. 4 00
BRYAN—*Trinity Church*: Gen........ 4 00
BUCYRUS—*St. John's*: Gen.......... 5 00
CANTON—*St. Paul's*: $20.75, "A Mem-
ber," $5, Gen..................... 25 75
Epiphany: Deaf-mutes, Gen.......... 4 00
CARDINGTON—*Church of the Good Shep-
herd*: Gen....................... 4 00
CATAWBA ISLAND — *Holy Sacrament
Mission*: Gen.................... 10 00
CLEVELAND—*All Saints'*: Gen....... 10 00
Atonement: Gen.................... 4 00
Christ Church: Gen................ 25 00
Church of the Good Shepherd: Gen... 10 00
Grace (South): Gen................ 10 00
Grace: Gen....................... 113 39
Church of the Holy Spirit: Gen...... 10 00
Incarnation: Gen.................. 10 00
St. Agnes's: Deaf-mutes, Gen........ 6 35
St. Alban's: Gen.................. 10 00
St. Mark's: Gen.................. 10 00
St. Andrew's: Gen................ 25 00
St. Matthew's: Gen............... 10 00
St. Paul's (East): Dom. and Frn..... 25 00
St. Philip's: Gen................. 10 00
Trinity Cathedral: Dom., $1,061.80;
Gen., $225.42..................... 1,287 22
William G. Mather, Gen............ 250 00
CLYDE—*Grace*: Gen................ 5 00
COLLINWOOD—*St. Stephen's*: Gen...... 5 00
CONNEAUT—*St. Paul's*: Gen......... 5 00
COSHOCTON—*Trinity Church*: Gen.... 10 00
CROSS CREEK—*St. James's*: Gen..... 3 00
DEFIANCE—*Grace*: Gen............. 5 00
DENNISON—*St. Barnabas's*: Gen...... 5 00
EAST LIVERPOOL—*St. Stephen's*: Gen.. 10 00
EAST PLYMOUTH—*St. Matthew's*: Gen. 5 00
FINDLAY—*Trinity Church*: Gen...... 35 82
FOSTORIA—*Trinity Church*: Gen..... 18 00

FREMONT—*St. Paul's S. S.*: Gen..... 3 51
GALION—*Grace*: Gen................ 10 00
GENEVA—*Christ Church*: Gen........ 5 00
HICKSVILLE—*St. Paul's*: Gen....... 5 00
HUDSON—*Christ Church*: Gen....... 20 45
HURON—*Christ Church*: Gen........ 10 00
JEFFERSON—*Trinity Church*: Gen.... 10 00
KENT—*Christ Church*: Gen.......... 5 00
KENTON—*St. Paul's*: Gen........... 10 00
KINSMAN—*Grace*: Gen.............. 5 00
LAKEWOOD—*St. Peter's*: Gen....... 5 00
LISBON—*Trinity Church*: Gen...... 5 00
LORAIN—*Church of the Redeemer*:
    Gen............................ 5 00
St. David's: Gen.................. 5 00
LYME—*Trinity Church*: Gen........ 5 00
MADISON—*St. John's*: Gen......... 5 00
MANSFIELD—*Grace*: Gen........... 10 00
    H. M. Alvord, Gen.............. 2 00
MARION—*St. Paul's*: Gen.......... 10 00
MARYSVILLE—*St. Mary's*: Gen...... 5 00
MASSILLON—*St. Timothy's*: Gen.... 74 82
MAUMEE—*St. Paul's*: Gen......... 20 02
MEDINA—*St. Paul's*: Gen......... 10 00
MILAN—*St. Luke's*: Gen.......... 10 00
MILL CREEK—*St. Mark's*: Gen..... 5 00
MONROEVILLE—*Zion*: Gen......... 5 00
MT. GILEAD—*Transfiguration*: Gen... 5 00
NAPOLEON—*St. John's Mission*: Gen.. 5 00
NEW PHILADELPHIA—*Trinity Church*:
    Gen............................ 5 00
NILES—*St. Luke's*: $10, S. S.,* $5.25,
    Gen............................ 15 25
OBERLIN—*Christ Church*: Gen...... 10 00
PERRY—*St. Ann's*: Gen........... 10 00
PORT CLINTON—*St. Thomas's*: Gen... 20 00
RAVENNA—*Grace*: Gen............ 10 00
SALEM—*Church of Our Saviour*: Gen. 10 00
SANDUSKY—*Calvary*: Gen.......... 20 00
Grace: Colored.................... 50 50
St. John's: Gen................... 5 00
St. Luke's: Gen.................. 5 00
SHELBY—*St. Mark's*: Gen......... 5 00
SIDNEY—*St. Mark's*: Gen......... 5 00
TIFFIN—*Trinity Church*: Gen...... 20 00
TOLEDO—*All Saints'*: Gen......... 5 00
Calvary: Gen..................... 10 00
Grace: Gen...................... 10 00
St. Andrew's: Gen............... 5 00
St. John the Evangelist's: Gen.... 5 00
St. Martin's: Gen................ 5 00
St. Paul's (East): Gen........... 10 00
St. Thomas's: Gen............... 5 00
Trinity Church: Gen............. 190 00
UNIONVILLE—*St. Michael's*: Gen... 5 00
UPPER SANDUSKY — *Trinity Church*:
    Gen............................ 5 00
WARREN—*Christ Church*: Gen...... 10 00
WELLSVILLE—*Ascension*: Gen...... 10 00
WILLOUGHBY—*Grace*: Gen......... 11 21
WINDSOR MILLS—*Christ Church*: Gen. 5 00
WOOSTER—*St. James's*: Gen....... 20 00
YOUNGSTOWN — *Emmanuel Church*:
    Gen............................ 5 00
St. James's: Gen................. 5 00
St. John's: $40, S. S., $50, Gen..... 90 00
St. Andrew's: Gen............... 10 00
St. Augustine's: Gen............. 7 00
Emmanuel Church: Deaf-mute, Gen... 5 00

Oregon

Ap. $354.14; *Sp.* $30.00

COQUILLE—Mrst S. D. Sperry, Gen.... 5 00
MEDFORD—John W. Smitzer, Gen...... 2 00
OREGON CITY—*St. Paul's*: Gen...... 25 15
PORTLAND—*Church of the Good Shep-
    herd*: Gen..................... 18 80
St. David's: Gen................. 65 00
St. Mark's: Gen................. 57 19
*Trinity Church S. S.**: Gen., $41; Sp.
    for Widely Loving Society of Osaka,
    Kyoto, $30..................... 71 00
"C. P. S.," Gen................... 50 00
MISCELLANEOUS—Gen............... 90 00

Pennsylvania

Ap. $19,100.51; *Sp.* $545.25

AMBLER—*Trinity Memorial*: Gen..... 25
ARDMORE—*St. Mary's*: Gen.......... 35
BRISTOL—*St. Paul's*: Gen.......... 30
BRYN MAWR—*Church of the Redeemer*:
    Gen (of which Junior Aux., $11),
    $573.13; Miss Gertrude Ely, Sp. for
    Rev. Mr. Staunton, Philippine Isl-
    ands, $10....................... 583
CENTREVILLE—*Trinity Church* (Buck-
    ingham): Gen................... 20
CHELTENHAM—Mrs. A. F. Parks, "A
    Thank-offering," for work in Mex-
    ico............................. 2
CHESTER—*St. Luke's*: Gen......... 2
COATESVILLE—*Church of the Trinity*:
    Gen............................ 60
CONSHOHOCKEN — *Calvary*: Dom.,
    $7 64; Colored, $6.15; Indian,
    $3.75; Frn., $6.55; Gen., $11.39... 35
DEVON—Mrs. Anna N. Lloyd, Gen.... 5
DOYLESTOWN—*St. Paul's*: Gen..... 21
EDDINGTON—*Christ Church*: Gen.... 80
GREAT VALLEY—*St. Peter's*: Gen.... 5
GWYNEDD—*Church of the Messiah*:
    Gen............................ 201
HATBORO—*Advent*: Gen........... 7
HONEYBROOK—*St. Mark's*; Gen..... 12
HULMEVILLE—*Grace*: Gen......... 5
JENKINTOWN—*Church of Our Saviour*:
    Gen............................ 228
KENNETT SQUARE—*Advent*: $10, S. S.,
    $5, Gen........................ 15
LANGHORNE—*St. James's*: Gen...... 5
McKINLEY—*St. Andrew's*: Gen..... 5
MEDIA—Mrs. Charles J. Dougherty,
    Gen............................ 5
MILFORD SQUARE—Elizabeth Kingston,
    Gen............................ 10
NEW LONDON—*St. John's*: Gen..... 3
NORRISTOWN—*All Saints'*: Gen..... 50
    "E. S.," Gen................... 40
NORWOOD—*St. Stephen's*: $70, S. S.,
    $10, Gen....................... 80
OAKS—Mrs. F. M. Cresson, Gen...... 20
PAOLI—*Good Samaritan*: Dom. and
    Frn............................ 42
PENLLYN—Andrew A. Blair, Gen..... 500
PEQUEA—*St. John's*: Gen.......... 13
PHILADELPHIA — *All Saints'* (Lower
    Dublin, Torresdale): Gen........ 10
Atonement Memorial: Sp. for Nevada. 22
Calvary (Germantown): Gen. (of
    which Junior Aux., $10), $60; Sp.
    for Nevada, $10................. 70
Calvary (West): For Alaska........
Christ Church (Germantown): Dom.. 26
Christ Church Hospital: Gen....... 9
Church of the Covenant: "A Member,"
    Gen............................ 300
Crucifixion: Dom. and Frn........ 10
Emmanuel Church (Holmesburg):
    Gen............................ 35
Epiphany (Sherwood, West Philadel-
    phia): "A Friend," Gen.......... 5
Grace (Mt. Airy): Junior Aux., Gen. 10
Holy Apostles': Mrs. Mary A. Todd,
    Gen............................ 300
Holy Comforter Memorial: Gen...... 25
Holy Trinity Church: Dom., $600;
    Frn., $403; Gen. (of which "K.,"
    $50, Junior Aux., $3), $1,128; Wo.
    Aux., Frn., $10; Sp. in memory of
    "E. M.," for Mrs. L. H. Littell,
    Hankow, $60; Christian Endeavor,
    Sp. for Bishop Root, for Ichang,
    Hankow, $25.................... 2,226
Home for Consumptives (Chestnut
    Hill): Gen..................... 5
L'Emmanuel: Gen................ 10
Prince of Peace Chapel: Gen., $80.50;
    Wo. Aux, Frn., $5.............. 85
Church of the Redeemer: Gen....... 5
St. Alban's (Roxborough): Gen...... 15

WEST WHITELAND—*St. Paul's* (Glen Lock): Gen...................... 19 05
YARDSLEY—*St. Andrew's*: Gen........ 32 65
MISCELLANEOUS—"Cash, A. F.," Gen. 500 00
Right Rev. Alexander Mackay-Smith, D.D., Gen................. 500 00
Interest on Lenten Offering, funds in bank, Gen.................... 37 27
"M. C. M.," Gen................. 10 00
Wo. Aux., "An Officer of Wo. Aux.," Gen. 10 00
Junior Aux., Gen................ 3 36

Pittsburgh

Ap. $2,072.91 ; *Sp.* $35.00

BROWNSVILLE—*Christ Church*: Gen... 10 00
CONNELLSVILLE—*Trinity Church*: Frn. 5 00
DU BOIS—*Church of Our Saviour*: Gen. 20 65
DUNBAR—*St. John's-in-the-Wilderness*: Frn. 4 00
ERIE—*St. Paul's*: Dom., $21.25; Frn., $20.70 ; S. S., Sp. for purchasing one lamp for Calvary Church, Cape Mount, Africa, $10.............. 51 95
FAIRVIEW—*St. Paul's*: Gen.......... 4 95
FOXBURG—*Memorial Church of Our Father*: Church Guild, Sp. for "Sarah Lindley Fox" scholarship, Mrs. Littell's work, Hankow...... 25 00
FRANKLIN—*St. John's*: Gen.......... 90 30
GEORGETOWN—*St. Luke's*: Gen 6 60
HOMESTEAD—*St. Matthew's*: Frn...... 10 91
KITTANNING—*St. Luke's*: Dom....... 8 88
MEADVILLE—*Christ Church*: Gen..... 51 57
NEW BRIGHTON—*Christ Church*: Herford Hope, Gen.................. 10 00
NORTH GIRARD—*Grace*: Gen.......... 24 05
OAKMONT—*St. Thomas's Memorial*: Gen. 356 75
PITTSBURGH—*Ascension*: Dom. and Frn. 30 00
Calvary: $495.52, "E. M. D.," $2, Gen. 497 52
Christ Church (Allegheny): "E. S. C.," Gen. 100 00
Church of the Good Shepherd: Dom. and Frn 50 00
St. Mark's: Dom. and Frn........ 16 55
St. Mary's Memorial: Gen.......... 20 00
St. Peter's: Gen................. 100 00
Miss Mary Burgwin, for medical work 10 00
Henry A. Phillips, Gen............ 10 00
"A. M.," Gen.................... 25 00
"A Friend," Gen................. 50 00
SHARON—*St. John's*: Gen........... 39 95
TITUSVILLE—*St. James's*: Gen....... 26 78
WARREN—*Trinity Memorial*; Gen...... 320 94
WEST BROWNSVILLE—*St. John's*: Gen. 3 00
WILKINSBURG — *St. Stephen's*: Dom., $9.50 ; Frn., $88.06 ; (In Memoriam), "C. T. H., Jr.," Dom. and Frn., $5 .... 102 56
Susan Jones, Gen................ 25 00

Quincy

Ap. $85.00

CARTHAGE—*St. Cyprian's*: Gen....... 5 00
GALESBURG—*St. John's*: Gen......... 5 00
PEORIA—Cyril B. Clark, Gen........ 5 00
ROCK ISLAND—*Trinity Church*: Gen.. 55 00
RUSHVILLE—*Christ Church*: Gen..... 5 00
TISKILWA—*St. Jude's*: Gen......... 10 00

Rhode Island

Ap. $1,144.09

ASHTON—*St. John's*: Gen........... 14 45
AUBURN—*Ascension*: Gen............ 34 50
BARRINGTON—*St. John's*: Gen........ 5 00
St. Matthew's (West): Gen.......... 6 45

BRISTOL—*St. Michael's*: Gen......... 78 00
Trinity Church: Dom................. 1 20
MIDDLETOWN—*Holy Cross*: Gen...... 1 61
NARRAGANSETT PIER—*St. Peter's*: "A
Friend," Gen...................... 5 00
NEWPORT—*Emmanuel Church*: Gen... 318 07
St. George's: "A Friend," Gen...... 5 00
St. John's: Dom................... 100 00
Albert L. Chase, Gen.............. 20 00
PHENIX—*St. Andrew's*: "A Friend,"
Gen................................. 5 00
PHILLIPSDALE—*Grace Memorial*: "A
Friend," Gen...................... 5 00
PONTIAC—*All Saints'*: "A Friend,"
Gen................................. 5 00
PORTSMOUTH—*St. Mary's*: Gen....... 10 18
St. Paul's: Gen..................... 8 65
PROVIDENCE—*Christ Church*: Dom. and
Frn.............................. 17 95
St. Ansgarius's: Salary of Rev. J. G.
Hammarskold, $38.02; Rev. F. E.
Lund, Wuhu, Hankow, $25; Gen.,
$89.70............................. 102 72
St. Stephen's: Gen.................. 10 00
"A Friend," Gen.................... 200 00
RIVERSIDE—*St. Mark's*: "A Friend,"
Gen................................. 5 00
SAUNDERSTOWN—*St. John's*: Gen.... 10 00
TIVERTON—*Holy Trinity Church*: Gen. 5 00
WAKEFIELD—*Ascension*: Gen......... 19 83
WARREN—*St. Mark's*: Gen.......... 98 26
WICKFORD—*St. Paul's*: Frn., $4.80;
Gen., $47.37...................... 52 17

South Carolina
Ap. $714.49; *Sp.* $15.00

ALLENDALE—*Holy Communion*: Gen... 6 00
ANDERSON—*Grace*: Gen............. 15 67
BENNETTSVILLE—*St. Paul's*: Gen..... 15 00
BERKELEY—*St. John's*: Gen......... 4 76
CAMDEN—*Grace*: Gen.............. 27 00
CHARLESTON—*Grace*: "A Member," $5,
"A Friend," $3, Gen.; Wo. Aux.,
Gen., $5; Sp. for Bishop Horner's
Appalachian School, Asheville, $5.. 18 00
Holy Communion: Wo. Aux., Sp. for
scholarship at Anvik, Alaska...... 10 00
St. Luke's: Wo. Aux., assistant for
Miss McCullough, Porto Rico, $5;
Japanese Bible-women, Kyoto, $5;
Chinese Bible-women, Hankow, $5;
Gen., $8.98; Junior Aux., Bishop
Capers Day-school, Hankow, $5.... 28 98
St. Philip's: Gen................... 62 50
St. Michael's: Wo. Aux., N. S. Wil-
son's Day-school, Hankow, $5; M. E.
Pinkney, Bible-women, Tokyo, $3;
Bible-women, Hankow, $10; Bible-
women, Kyoto, $10; assistant to Miss
McCullough, Porto Rico, $2; Gen.,
$5.32.............................. 35 32
St. Philip's: Wo. Aux., N. S. Wilson's
Day-school, Hankow, $5; M. E.
Pinkney, Bible-women, Tokyo, $5;
Chinese Bible-women, Hankow, $10. 20 00
CHERAW—*St. David's*: Wo. Aux., N.
S. Wilson's Day-school, Hankow... 1 00
COLUMBIA—*Church of the Good Shep-
herd*: Gen......................... 20 00
Trinity Church: Gen................ 121 61
C. H. Preston, Gen................ 10 00
EASTOVER—*Zion*: Wo. Aux., Gen.;
Junior Aux., assistant for Miss Mc-
Cullough, Porto Rico, $1; Bishop
Capers Day-school, Hankow, $5;
Gen., $1; M. E. Pinkney Fund, for
Bible-women, Tokyo, $2........... 9 00
EDISTO ISLAND—*Trinity Church*: Gen. 30 00
FLORENCE—*St. John's*: Gen......... 85 40
GLENDALE—Miss E. L. Tew, Gen..... 5 00
GLENN SPRINGS—*Calvary*: Gen...... 25 00
HAMPTON Co.—*Heavenly Rest*: Gen... 17 50
JAMES ISLAND—*St. James's*: Gen.... 15 00
JOHN'S ISLAND—*St. John's*: Gen..... 25 00

LAURENS—*Epiphany*: Wo. Aux., assist-
ant for Miss McCullough, Porto Rico.
Mrs. A. C. Haskell, Gen...........
"E. B. S.," Gen.....................
McPHERSONVILLE — *Sheldon Church*:
Miss M. M. Colcock...............
MANNING—*Mission*: Gen.............
MARS BLUFF—*Christ Church*: Gen....
OKATEE—*Mission*: Gen..............
RIDGE SPRING—*Grace*: Gen.........
RION—*Mission*: Gen................
SANTEE—*St. James's*: Wo. Aux., Gen.
SPARTANBURG—*Advent*: Wo. Aux., Gen.
SUMMERVILLE—*St. Paul's*: Wo. Aux.,
assistant for Miss McCullough, Porto
Rico, $1; Japanese Bible-women,
Kyoto, $2; Chinese Bible-women,
Hankow, $5........................
SUMTER—*Church of the Holy Com-
forter*: Gen........................
STATEBURG—*Holy Cross*: Gen........
TIMMONSVILLE—*Church of Our Sa-
viour*: Gen.........................
WILLINGTON—*St. Stephen's*: Gen....
YORKVILLE—*Church of the Good Shep-
herd*: Gen.........................
MISCELLANEOUS—"A N. C.," Gen.....
"Anonymous," Gen..................

Southern Ohio
Ap. $965.00; *Sp.* $525.00

CINCINNATI—*Christ Church*: Gen.....
Epiphany: Gen.....................
Epiphany (Walnut Hills): Gen.......
St. Andrew's: Gen.................
St. Luke's: Gen....................
St. Paul's: Miss Fidelia Coffey, $250,
Wo. Aux., $25, Gen................
Mrs. G. H. Thomas, Sp. for Church
Extension Fund, Porto Rico........
E. Worthington, Gen...............
W. H. Davis, Gen..................
William Irwin, Gen.................
DAYTON—*St. Clement's*: Gen........
GLENDALE—*Christ Church*: Rev. C. H.
Benedict, Sp. for Church Extension
Fund, Porto Rico..................
(In Memoriam), Gen...............
HARTWELL — *Holy Trinity Church*:
Gen................................
MARIETTA—*St. Luke's*: Wo. Aux., sup-
port of Bible-women, Hankow......
J. A. Gallaher, Gen.................

Southern Virginia
Ap. $1,188.27; *Sp.* $71.37

ALLEGHANY Co. — *Alleghany Parish*:
Gen................................
AUGUSTA Co. — *Trinity Church*
(Staunton): Gen....................
BATH Co.—*Christ Church* (Warm
Springs): For Deaf-mute Missions..
BOTETOURT Co.—*St. Mark's* (Fin-
castle): Gen........................
CAMPBELL Co. — *Grace Memorial*
(Lynchburg): Gen...................
Mrs. Winthrop G. Stevens, Gen....
DINWIDDIE Co.—*Church of the Good
Shepherd* (Petersburg): Gen.......
St. Paul's: Wo. Aux., Sp. for Alaska,
$10; Sp. for Indians, Oklahoma (of
which Junior Aux., $10.74), $20.74;
Junior Aux., Sp for Cuba (of which
Babies' Branch $10), $15; Sp. for
Mexico (of which Babies' Branch,
$7.63), $12.63; Sp. for Rev. Mr.
McRae's work, Shanghai, $10......
ELIZABETH CITY Co.—*St. John's*
(Hampton): Gen....................
HALIFAX Co.—*Christ Church* (Mt.
Laurel): Gen........................
St. John's (Houston): Gen., $22; "F.
C. C.," Frn., $50..................

CLEVELAND—*St. Luke's*: Gen......... 29 75
KNOXVILLE—*St. John's*: Gen......... 200 00
MEMPHIS—*Calvary*: Gen............. 174 47
Grace: Wo. Aux., "Bishop Quintard"
  scholarship, St. Mary's Hall, Shang-
  hai, $2; Mrs. W. A. Gage, Gen., $10. 12 00
Holy Trinity Church: Gen........... 1 10
  John Pritchard, Gen............. 5 00
NASHVILLE—*Advent*: Wo. Aux., "Bish-
  op Quintard" scholarship, St. Mary's
  Hall, Shanghai.................. 50
St. Ann's: Gen.................. 43 20
SEWANEE—Wo. Aux., "Bishop Quin-
  tard" scholarship, St. Mary's Hall,
  Shanghai 1 25
SOUTH PITTSBURG — *Christ Church*:
  Gen. 10 00
TATE SPRING—D. Mosby, Gen........ 10 00
TRACY CITY—*Christ Church*: Wo. Aux.,
  Gen. 1 50

Texas
Ap. $154.85

BELLEVILLE—*St. Mary's*: Gen........ 9 25
BRENHAM—*St. Peter's*: Dom. and Frn.. 8 05
HOUSTON—*Christ Church*: Gen....... 85 00
Trinity Church: Gen............... 20 00
  Sarah J. Payne, Gen............. 3 00
NACOGDOCHES—*Christ Church S. S.*:
  Gen. 15 00
NAVASOTA—Ewing Norwood, Gen.... 2 00
PALESTINE—*St. Philip's*: Gen........ 2 45
SAN AUGUSTINE—*Christ Church*: Gen. 4 10
TAYLOR—Mrs. Kate Rayburn, Gen.... 1 00
WHARTON—Miss Kate Rugeley, Gen.... 5 00

Vermont
Ap. $180.46; *Sp.* $3.00

ENOSBURG—*Christ Church*: Gen...... 94
FAIR HAVEN—*St. Luke's*: Gen........ 2 00
GRAND ISLE—*Vantines*: Gen......... 20 52
RICKFORD—*St. Ann's*: Gen.......... 4 00
SHOREHAM—*All Saints'*: Gen........ 1 00
WINDSOR—*St. Paul's*: Mrs. Sheldon,
  Sp. for Rev. R. C. Wilson, Shanghai. 3 00
MISCELLANEOUS—Wo. Aux., Gen...... 95 00
  Junior Aux., Gen................ 57 00

Virginia
Ap. $542.01

ALBEMARLE Co.—*St. Paul's* (Ivy De-
  pot): Gen..................... 12 00
ALEXANDRIA Co.—*Christ Church* (Al-
  exandria): $15, Wo. Aux., $15,
  Gen. 30 00
CHARLES CITY Co.—*Westover Parish*:
  Mrs. M. C. Oliver, toward salary of
  Deaconess Carter, Alaska........ 10 00
CLARKE Co.—*Grace* (Berryville): Gen. 1 75
Wickliffe Parish: Gen............. 21 00
CULPEPER Co.—*All Saints' Memorial
  Chapel* (Rapidan): Dom. and Frn.. 9 91
FAIRFAX Co.—*Truro Parish, Pohick
  and Olivet Churches*: Gen......... 20 00
*Truro Parish, Zion and Good Shepherd
  Churches*: Gen.................. 6 00
FAUQUIER Co.—*Whittle Parish, Church
  of Our Saviour*: Gen............. 9 20
Leeds Parish: Gen................ 15 00
Piedmont Parish, Emmanuel Church:
  Gen. 3 00
GLOUCESTER Co. — *Abingdon Parish,
  Abingdon Church*: Gen.......... 1 50
Ware Parish, Ware Church: Gen..... 9 50
HANOVER Co. — *St. James-the-Less*
  (Ashland): Gen................. 40 40
HENRICO Co. — *Emmanuel Church*
  (Brook Hill): Gen.............. 130 87
Monumental (Richmond): Wo. Aux.,
  Gen. 10 00

O. S. Morton (Richmond), Gen..... 5 00
KING WILLIAM CO.—*St. David's S. S.* (Aylètts) : Gen.................. 3 53
LOUDOUN CO.—*St. James's* (Leesburg) : Gen.................. 30 00
PAGE CO.—*Christ Church* (Luray) : Gen. 4 00
Calvary (Shenandoah) : Gen.......... 3 50
PRINCE WILLIAM CO.—*St. Paul's* (Haymarket) : Gen.................. 54 00
Miss Jeanie S. Herrell (Manassas), Gen. 15 00
RAPPAHANNOCK CO. — *Trinity Church* S. S. (Washington) : Gen.......... 4 00
RICHMOND CO.—*Lunenberg Parish, St. John's* : Gen.................. 15 09
ROCKINGHAM CO. — *Lynwood Parish, Grace* : Gen.................. 2 00
St. Stephen's : Gen.................. 5 00
WESTMORELAND CO.—*Washington Parish, St. Peter's* : Gen.......... 55 76
MISCELLANEOUS—Babies' Branch, Gen. 15 00

Washington

Ap. $1,392.03 ; *Sp.* $10.00

WASHINGTON—*Ascension* (D. C.) : Dr. William C. Rives, $200, Mrs. William C. Rives, $50, Gen. ; Chinese School, for work in China, $10.......... 260 00
Christ Church Parish (Georgetown) : Gen. 25 00
Epiphany : Frn., $200; Miss Isabel C. Freeman, $100, Mrs. H. B. Buckingham, $100, Gen.................. 400 00
Grace (Georgetown) : Gen.......... 20 00
St. James's : Frn., $1.63 ; Gen., $37.65 ; S. S., Gen., $3.38.................. 42 66
St. John's Parish : William J. Boardman, Gen. 25 00
St. Mark's : Indian, $37.75 ; Colored, $27.44 ; Porto Rico, $21.35 ; Dom., $51.58 ; Frn., $51.59 ; Gen., $24.44.. 214 15
St. Alban's (Mt. St. Alban) : Gen.... 141 97
St. David's Chapel (Tenleytown) : Gen. 4 00
Miss Ellen King, "H. M. Beare" (Graduate) scholarship, South Dakota 60 00
"A Friend," for rent of mission house at Santurce, Porto Rico, $20 ; Sp. for discretionary use of Bishop Van Buren, Porto Rico, $10........ 30 00
D. McN. French, Gen.................. 10 00
George Y. Worthington, Gen....... 5 00
W. F. Koenig, Gen............... 5 00
R. N. Mason, Dom. and Frn....... 5 00
R. E. P. Kreiter, Gen........... 1 00
CHARLES CO.—*Port Tobacco. Parish* : Gen. 60 00
PRINCE GEORGE CO. — *St. Philip's* (Laurel) : Frn., $20; Mrs. C. E. Butler, Gen., $2.............. 22 00
St. Thomas's (Croome) : Gen......... 13 76
Zion Parish : Gen.................. 27 49
ST. MARY'S CO.—*Trinity Parish* : Dom. and Frn.,' $10 ; Brazil, $20........ 30 00

Western Massachusetts

Ap. $798.55 ; *Sp.* $25.00

CLINTON—*Church of the Good Shepherd* : Gen.................. 69 44
DALTON—*Grace* : Gen.................. 20 00
GREENFIELD—*St. James's* ; $45, S. S.,* $44.67, Gen............... 89 67
HOLYOKE—*St. Paul's S.* S.* : Gen..... 40 00
LEE—*St. George's* : Gen.............. 33 00
NORTH ADAMS—*St. John's* : Gen..... 19 05
NORTH GRAFTON—*St. Andrew's* : Gen. 50 00
PITTSFIELD—*St. Stephen's* : Gen....... 50 25
Mrs. E. A. Bradley, Gen.......... 2 00
SPRINGFIELD — *Christ Church* : "A Friend," Gen.................. 24 00
St. Peter's : Gen.................. 116 00

WILLIAMSTOWN — *St. John's* : Cuba,' $7; Gen., $166.57.............. 173
Rev. Robert Scott, for orphanage, Manila, $25 ; Sp. for Rev. Mr. Mayo's work in the mountains of Virginia, $25 50
WORCESTER—*St. Matthew's* : Gen..... 58
All Saints' : Frn.................. 8
MISCELLANEOUS—Mrs. Cara D. Chase, Gen. 25

Western Michigan

Ap. $756.48

ALLEGAN—"C. R. W.," Gen............ 10
BENTON HARBOR — *Holy Trinity Church* : Gen.................. 15
CHARLEVOIX—*Christ Church* : Gen...., 14
ELK RAPIDS—*St. Paul's* : Gen........ 8
GRAND HAVEN—*St. John's* : Gen....... 8
GRAND RAPIDS—*Grace* : Gen.......... 60
St. Mark's : Dom. and Frn.......... 182
Church of the Good Shepherd : Gen.. 7
St. Bede's : Deaf-mute Mission, Gen.. 1
St. John's : Gen.................. 6
GREENVILLE—*St. Paul's* : Gen........ 5
HASTINGS—"J. W. B.," Gen.......... 5
HOLLAND—*Grace* : Gen.............. 12
HORNER—*Christ Church* : Gen........ 8
IONIA—*St. Paul's* : Gen.............. 11
KALAMAZOO—*St. Luke's* : Gen...... 150
LELAND—*Summer Congregation*, Gen.. 16
LUDINGTON—*Grace* : Gen............
LUTHER—*Christ Church* : Gen........ 3
MANCELONA—*Nativity* : Gen..........
MANISTEE—*Holy Trinity Church* : Gen. 18
MT. PLEASANT—*St. John's* : Gen...... 12
MUSKEGON—*St. Paul's* : Gen.......... 115
NEWAYGO—*St. Mark's* : Gen..........
NORTHPORT POINT—Summer Congregation, Gen.................. 5
OMENA—Summer Congregation, Gen... 5
PETOSKEY—*Emmanuel Church* : Gen... 24
ROCKFORD—*St. James's* : Gen........
SAUGATUCK—*All Saints'* : Gen........ 3
SCHOOLCRAFT—*St. Stephen's* : Gen....
SOUTH HAVEN—*Epiphany* : Gen....... 4
ST. JOSEPH—*St. Paul's* : Frn., $20 ; Gen., $21................ 41
TRAVERSE CITY—*Grace* : Gen.......... 8

Western New York

Ap. $1,228.61 ; *Sp.* $17.00

BROCKPORT—*St. Luke's* : Frn., $1.05 ; Gen., $18.42.................. 19
BUFFALO—*All Saints'* : Gen.......... 70
St. Mary's-on-the-Hill : Dom., $125 ; Frn., $125 ; Dom. and Frn., $12.50 ; George H. Boxall, Sp. for Church Extension Fund, Porto Rico, $2...... 264
St. Thomas's : Gen.................. 1
Trinity Church : Dom., $181.13 ; Frn., $96.23 277
Walter Devereaux, Gen............ 5
CANANDAIGUA—Miss E. K. Kraemer, Gen. 10
CANASERAGA—*Trinity Church* : Dom., $5 ; "A Friend," Sp. for St. Hilda's School for Girls, Wuchang, Hankow, $5................ 10
CLYDE—"A Friend," S. S.," Gen...... 5
EAST AURORA—*St. Matthias's* : Dom.. 15
GENESEO—*St. Michael's* : "Members," Gen. 20
GENEVA—*St. Peter's* : Gen.......... 20
"E. R. C.," Gen.............. 2
"C.," Gen. 100
JAMESTOWN—*St. Luke's* : $25, "A Friend," $10, S. S., $10, Gen........ 45
LOCKPORT—*Grace* : Juniors, Sp. for St. Andrew's Priory, Honolulu... 10
MANCHESTER—*St. John's S. S.* : Gen.. 1
NORTH TONAWANDA—*St. Mark's* : Gen.. 56

Gen., $63; Sp. for Miss Barber's
work, Anking, Hankow (of which "A
Friend," $10), $40; Mrs. H. H.
Small (In Memoriam), Sp. for Miss
Barber's Women's School, Anking,
Hankow, $10...................... 113 00

Missionary Districts

Alaska
Ap. $38.25

CIRCLE CITY—*Heavenly Rest*: Gen....   6 00
FAIRBANKS—*St. Matthew's*: Gen..... 27 25
TANANA—Miss Florence G. Langdon,
Gen. 5 00

Arizona
Ap. $26.30

BISBEE—*St. John's*: Gen............. 26 30

Asheville
Ap. $21.10

ASHEVILLE—*St. Matthias's*: Gen......   5 00
EDNEYVILLE—*St. Paul's*: Gen........   2 00
FRANKLIN—*St. Cyprian's*: Gen.......   50
HENDERSONVILLE—*St. James's*: Gen...   6 00
RONDA—*All Saints'*: Gen............   50
SHELBY—*Church of the Redeemer*:
Frn. 1 10
UPLAND—*St. John the Baptist's*: Gen..   1 00
VALLE CRUCIS—*Holy Cross*: Gen......   5 00

Eastern Oregon
Ap. $396.25

BEND—*Mission*: Gen................   5 00
CANYON CITY—*St. Thomas's*: Gen.... 10 00
CASCADELOCKS—*Mission*: Gen........   3 00
CONDON—*Mission*: Gen..............   3 00
HERMISTON—*Mission*: Gen...........   3 00
HOOD RIVER—*St. Mark's*: Gen....... 20 00
KLAMATH FALLS—*Mission*: Gen...... 10 00
LAKEVIEW—*Mission*: Gen............   3 00
NYSSA—*Mission*: Gen...............   5 00
ONTARIO—*Mission*: Gen.............   3 00
PRAIRIE—*St. John's*: Gen............   3 00
PRINEVILLE—*Mission*: Gen..........   1 25
SHAMIKO—*Mission*: Gen............   5 00
SUMPTER—*St. Paul's*: Gen..........   3 00
COVE—*Ascension*: Gen..............   5 00
WALLEO VALLEY—*Mission*: Gen......   3 00
UNION—*St. John's Memorial*: Gen....   3 00
VALE—*Mission*: Gen................   5 00
WESTON—*All Saints'*: Gen...........   3 00
MISCELLANEOUS—Gen. 300 00

Idaho
Ap. $8.70

BELLEVUE—*St. Paul's*: Gen..........   5 00
COEUR D'ALENE—*St. Luke's*: Gen.....   3 70

Kearney
Ap. $127.70

ANSELMO—*Mission*: Gen.............   2 00
BROKEN BOW—*St. John's*: $14.50,
Junior Aux., $10, Gen............ 24 50
CHADRON—*Grace*: Gen............... 27 00
CRAWFORD—*St. Monica's*: Gen.......   8 00
HASTINGS—*St. Mark's*: Gen.........   4 20
MERNA—*Mission*: Gen...............   2 00
MISCELLANEOUS — Branch Wo. Aux.,
Gen. 60 00

Nevada
Ap. $20.00

CARSON CITY—St. Peter's: Dom...... 20 00

New Mexico
Ap. $157.38

ALBUQUERQUE—St. John's: Gen.......	35	00
LAS VEGAS—St. Paul's: Gen.........	25	00
RATON—Trinity Mission: Gen.......	5	00
SOCORRO—Epiphany: Gen...........	5	00
EL PASO — St. Clement's S. S.* (Texas): Gen....................	87	38

North Dakota
Ap. $47.05

CASSELTON—St. Stephen's: Gen......	12	05
DRAYTON—Gen.	2	00
FARGO—W. C. Macfadden, Gen......	5	00
Mrs. A. E. Camerfold, Gen.........	5	00
GLADSTONE—Gen.	2	00
LINTON—Gen.	3	00
TOWNER—St. Mark's: Gen...........	18	00

Oklahoma
Ap. $107.24

ARDMORE—St. Philip's: Gen.........	5	55
CHELSEA—Church of the Redeemer: Gen.	4	25
CHICKASHA—St. Luke's: Gen., $15.25; Junior Aux., Gen., $5........	20	25
CLAREMORE—St. Paul's: Gen.......	3	00
GUTHRIE—Trinity Church: Gen......	9	65
LEHIGH—St. Andrew's: Gen........	2	10
NORMAN—St. John's: Gen..........	1	60
OKLAHOMA CITY—St. Paul's Cathedral: Gen.	23	59
PAWNEE—Mrs. E. G. Gray, Gen......	5	00
PAUL'S VALLEY—St. Mary's: Gen.....	3	65
SAPULPA—Church of the Good Shepherd: Gen.	3	00
SHAWNEE—Emmanuel Church: Gen...	10	00
TULSA—Trinity Church: "Three Members," Boone University, Wuchang, Hankow	5	00
VINITA—St. John's: Gen............	3	10
MISCELLANEOUS—Juniors, Gen........	7	50

Olympia
Ap. $570.47

ANACORTES—Christ Church: Gen.....	15	75
EVERETT—Trinity Church: Gen......	33	60
KENT—St. James's: Gen.............	34	00
RENTON—St. Luke's: Gen..........	8	40
SEATTLE—All Saints': Juniors, Gen...	3	00
St. Andrew's: Gen..................	2	28
St. Clement's: Gen.................	25	00
St. Mark's: Gen...................	204	25
Trinity Church: Gen................	239	19
TACOMA—Trinity Church: Juniors, Gen.	5	00

Porto Rico
Ap. $33.00

MISCELLANEOUS—"A Friend," Gen.... 33 00

Sacramento
Ap. $173.20

BENICIA—St. Paul's: Gen............	21	50
COLLINSVILLE—St. James's: Gen.....	5	40
ELK GROVE—Gen..................		20
LOOMIS—All Saints' Mission: Gen...	10	60
NEVADA CITY—Trinity Church: Gen...	28	60
PLACERVILLE—Church of the Saviour: Gen., $24.60; S. S.,* Dom., $3.60..	28	20

RED BLUFF—St. Peter's: Gen........	24
SACRAMENTO—Trinity Mission: Gen...	37
MISCELLANEOUS — Branch Wo. Aux., Gen.	17

Salina
Ap. $57.85

BENNINGTON—Gen.................	10
DODGE CITY—St. Cornelia's Mission: Gen..........................	7
FORMOSO—Gen...................	5
HARPER—St. James's: Gen.........	10
KINSLEY—Holy Nativity: Gen......	10
MEDICINE LODGE—St. Mark's: Gen....	10
WAKEENEY—Mrs. J. P. Lohman, Gen..	5

South Dakota
Ap. $335.41; Sp. $1.97

BLUNT—Mission: Gen., $3; Sp. for St. Paul's College Building Fund, Tokyo, $1.97	4
BROOKINGS—St. Paul's: Gen........	9
BRISTOL—St. John's: Gen..........	3
DE SMET—St. Stephen's: Gen........	15
ELK POINT—Church of Our Saviour S. S.*: Gen.....................	10
ELWOOD—Mary P. and Annie R. Dealtry, Gen.......................	5
FORT PIERRE—St. Peter's Mission: Gen., $6.23; Sp. for St. Paul's College, Tokyo, $2.35.............	8
HOT SPRINGS—St. Luke's: Gen......	20
HURLEY—Grace Mission: Dom. and Frn.	13
MITCHELL—St. Mary's: Gen.........	24
SELBY—Christ Church: Gen.........	5
SIOUX FALLS—Calvary: Gen.........	37
WEBSTER—St. Mary's: Gen.........	13
WOONSOCKET — St. Luke's Mission: Gen...........................	4
LOWER BRULE—Church of the Holy Comforter: Dom., $21; Frn., $21...	42
Holy Faith: Dom., $3; Frn., $2.60...	5
Holy Name: Dom., $3; Frn., $2.47...	5
St. Alban's Chapel: Dom., $1.33; Frn., $1.30	2
St. Peter's Station: Dom., $2; Frn., $2	4
Church of the Saviour: Dom., $1.50; Frn., $1.50	3
Church of the Messiah: Dom., $6.52; Frn., $6	12
PINE RIDGE—Grace: Gen...........	1
Church of the Messiah: Gen.........	
St. Alban's: Gen..................	
St. John's: Gen...................	
St. Julia's: Gen..................	
St. Mark's: Gen..................	
St. Mary's: Gen..................	
St. Mary's (Sand Hill): Gen.........	1
St. Matthew's: Gen...............	
St. Paul's: Gen..................	1
St. Peter's: Gen..................	1
St. Philip's: Gen.................	5
St. Thomas's: Gen................	
ROSEBUD MISSION—Ephphatha Chapel: St. Mary's School, Dom. and Frn..	5
SANTEE FLANDREAU—St. Mary's: Indian School, Gen.................	2
Church of Our Most Merciful Saviour: Dom., $5; Frn., $5............	10
Chapel of the Holy Faith: Dom., $5; Frn., $5......................	10
Church of the Blessed Redeemer: Dom., $5; Frn., $5............	10
PONCA AGENCY—St. John's: Dom., $2.50; Frn., $2.50............	5
STANDING ROCK—St. Elizabeth's: Junior Aux., Dom., $12.50; Frn., $12.50.	25
YANKTONNAIS MISSION — St. Peter's: Gen...........................	1
All Saints': Gen..................	

	MILFORD—Gen. 2 00
	POWELL—Gen. 2 00
	RIVERTON—St. James's: Gen......... 2 15
5 00	SARATOGA—St. Barnabas's: Gen...... 1 89
6 00	WIND RIVER—Church of the Redeemer:
6 50	Gen. 5 00

25 00 *Foreign Missionary Districts*

10 00
21 55

Ap. $1,302.86 ; *Sp.* $2.50

Africa

25 00
4 00 "A Friend," Gen.................... 224 00
8 00
3 25

Brazil

	BAGE—Church of the Crucified: Gen.. 5 17
	JAGUARO—Christ Chapel: Gen....... 8 05
	LIVRAMENTO—Chapel of the Nazarene: Gen. 3 45
	PORTO ALEGRE—Trinity Church: Gen.. 8 70
25 00	PELOTAS—Church of the Redeemer: Gen. 22 07
	RIO GRANDE—Church of the Saviour: $8.07, S. S,* $10.22, Gen....... 18 29
10 00	RIO JANEIRO—Redeemer Chapel: Gen. 6 90
	Trinity Chapel: Gen............... 6 03
	SANTA MARIA—Church of the Mediator: Gen. 12 41
	SANTA RITA—Calvary: $4.21, S. S.* 71 cts., Gen.... 4 92
	SAN GABRIEL—Chapel of the Redemption: Gen.... 1 72
50 00	SAN LEOPOLDO—Messiah Chapel: $2.66, S. S,* 56 cts., Gen........ 3 22
	SAN JOSE DO NORTE—Resurrection: $2.57, S. S.* $1.11, Gen...... 3 68
	VIAMAO—Grace: Gen.............. 3 79

Cuba

41 80
7 50   Gen. 369 47

2 70
45 00
2 50
7 50   ### England
25 00
6 22 LONDON—Brother and sister of Miss
Lisa Lovell, Gen.................. 33 33
M. Lloyd Woolsey, Gen., $2.50; Sp.
for Rev. Robert Wood, Wuchang,
Hankow, for the purchase of land,
$2.50 .... 5 00

Hankow

13 86
2 15 S. S.* : Gen...................... 14 00
75
75
8 44
75   ### Kyoto
2 25
18 75 Rev. J. J. Chapman, $4.95, Rev. C.
5 25 S. Reifsnider, $9.90, Rev. W. J.
1 76 Cuthbert, $4.95, Rev. R. H. McGin-
4 50 nis, $4.95, Dr. Henry Laning and
5 60 family, $29.70, Mr. J. Reifsnider,
1 88 $9.90, Miss L. Bull, $9.90, Miss G.
3 50 Suthon, $2.48, Miss M. Aldrich, 25
cts., Miss J. Kimball, $2.47, Miss M.
E. Laning, $2.48, Miss H. L. Tetlow,
$1.48, Miss Hasu Gardiner, $2.47,
Miss A. B. Cahusac, $1.49, collections
at foreign service, $18.59, Gen.... 105 96

Mexico

2 24
16 50
2 13 GUADALAJARA—St. Mark's: Gen...... 9 98
4 60 CHIHUAHUA—St. Mary's: Gen........ 19 90
3 75 CUERNAVACA—San Miguel: Gen....... 3 98
6 05 MEXICO CITY—Christ Church: Gen.... 128 33
3 00 San Pedro: Gen................... 18 67
1 55 R. M. Raymond, Gen............. 200 00

RINCON ANTONIO—Gen.............. 12 44
SALTILLO—Missionary work, Mexico.. 8 45
SAN. LUIS POTOSI—*Grace*: Gen....... 7 50
St. Andre's Seminary: Gen.......... 2 49

Tokyo

TOKYO—*Holy Trinity Church*: Wo.
  Aux., Gen.................... 30 00
KANDA—*Christ Church*: "Thank-offer-
  ing," Gen........................ 3 46

Miscellaneous

Interest, Dom., $3,748.82; Frn.,
$1,341.63; Gen., $2,994 66; Sp.,
$730.88; Men's Thank-offering,
$156.80; United Offering, Wo. Aux.,
$1,253.76 ....10,226 55
United Offering, Wo. Aux., on ac-
count of appropriations to Septem-
ber 1st, 1910, Dom., $4,109.65;
Frn., $590.35...................... 4,700 00
American Church Missionary So-
ciety income, Christian Education
Fund, Brazil...................... 483 60
Legacy, Miss Henrietta Martin, for
salary of clergyman, Indian field,
South Dakota...................... 960 00
Wo. Aux., "A Friend," in loving
memory of Kate S. Nelson, September

12th, 1910, Sp. for Miss Thackara,
  Navajo Hospital, Arizona.......... 2
League for Eastern Oregon, Sp. for
  Bishop Paddock, Eastern Oregon... 6

Legacies

CONN., NEW HAVEN—Estate of Rev.
  George Brinley Morgan, to the So-
  ciety 1,00
R. I., PROVIDENCE—Estate of Rt. Rev.
  William N. McVickar, to the Society.20,00
WASH. (D. C.), WASHINGTON—Estate
  of C. Oliver Buck, to the Society... 1,22
WASH., P. G. CO. BLADENSBURG—
  Estate of Benjamin O. Lowndes,
  Dom. 2,48

Receipts for the month..........$ 148,78
Amount previously
  acknowledged $1,515,326 41
Less a m o u n t ac-
  knowledged in Sep-
  tember SPIRIT OF
  MISSIONS u n d e r
  miscellaneous U.S.
  interest, returned to
  Standing Commit-
  tee on Trust Funds   948 21
                    ——————— 1,514,37

Total since September 1st.......$1,663,17

SUMMARY OF RECEIPTS

Receipts divided according to purposes to which they are to be applied	Received during Aug.	Amounts previously Acknowledged	Tot
1. Applicable upon the appropriations of the Board....	$117,213 32	$867,836 48	$985,04
2. Special gifts forwarded to objects named by donors in addition to the appropriations of the Board..	4,456 73	249,211 28	253,66
3. Legacies for investment...........................	....	165,000 00	165,00
4. Legacies, the disposition of which is to be determined by the Board at the end of the fiscal year	24,714 88	111,898 26	136,11
5. Specific Deposit.................................	2,410 56	120,932 18	123,34
Total	$148,795 49	$1,514,378 20	$1,663,17

Total receipts from September 1st, 1909, to September 1st, 1910, applicable upon the appro
tions, divided according to the sources from which they have come, and compared with the
responding period of the preceding year. Legacies are not included in the following items, as
disposition is not determined by the Board until the end of the fiscal year.

OFFERINGS TO PAY APPROPRIATIONS

Source	To Sept. 1, 1910	To Sept. 1, 1909	Increase	Decr
1. From congregations...................	$490,509 16	$446,752 89	$43,756 27	$ ....
2. From individuals...................	95,002 66	108,054 25	....	13,05
3. From Sunday-schools.................	141,703 02	144,483 42	....	2,78
4. From Woman's Auxiliary, annual offering	85,803 04	96,520 97	....	10,71
5. Woman's Auxiliary United Offering, 1907	81,700 00	87,410 77	....	5,71
6. Woman's Auxiliary United Offering, 1892 and 1895	3,552 34	3,787 60	....	23
7. From interest...................	83,747 44	76,545 66	7,201 78	....
8. Miscellaneous items................	3,032 14	18,127 09	....	15,09
Total	$985,049 80	$981,682 65	$3,367 15	....

After applying all legacies received during the year that were at the discretion of the B
$136,113.14, the receipts failed of meeting the net appropriations of the year by $41,577.21.
this must be added the shortage of September 1st, a year ago, $32,955.34, so that the
deficiency at the close of the year amounted to $74,532.55.

During 1909-1910 there was an increase of $30,700 in contributions toward the apportion
Sixteen additional dioceses and missionary districts completed their apportionments, maki
total of sixty-three. About 372 more parishes and missions this past year completed
apportionments, making a total of 2,772, while 4,968 parishes and missions sent either the v
or a part of the apportionment, a gain of 168 over the year before. The dioceses and dist
completing their apportionments were: Arkansas, Atlanta, California, Connecticut, Dallas,
ware, Duluth, East Carolina, Florida, Indianapolis, Kansas, Kentucky, Lexington, M
Marquette, Massachusetts, Michigan City, Mississippi, Missouri, Montana, New Hampshire,
York, North Carolina, Oregon, Pennsylvania, Quincy, Rhode Island, South Carolina, Spring
Texas, Vermont, Virginia, Washington, Western Massachusetts, West Texas and West Virg
Alaska, Arizona, Asheville, Eastern Oregon, Honolulu, Idaho, Kearney, Nevada, New Mexico, N
Dakota, Oklahoma, Porto Rico, Salina, South Dakota, Southern Florida, The Philippines, 1
Western Colorado, Wyoming, Africa, Brazil, Cuba, Hankow, Kyoto, Mexico, Shanghai and Toky

THE

Spirit of Missions

AN ILLUSTRATED MONTHLY REVIEW
OF CHRISTIAN MISSIONS

November, 1910

CONTENTS

The Subscription Price of THE SPIRIT OF MISSIONS is ONE DOLLAR per year.
This is prepaid in the United States, Porto Rico, The Philippines and Mexico. For other countries in Postal Union, including Canada, twenty-four cents per year should be added. Subscriptions are continued until ordered discontinued.

Change of Address: In all changes of address it is necessary that the old as well as the new address should be given.

How to Remit: Remittances, made payable to George Gordon King, Treasurer, should be made draft on New York, Postal Order or Express Order. One and two cent stamps are received. To checks on local banks ten cents should be added for collection.

All Letters should be addressed to The Spirit of Missions, 281 Fourth Avenue, New York.

Published by the Domestic and Foreign Missionary Society.
President, RIGHT REVEREND DANIEL S. TUTTLE, D.D.   Treasurer, GEORGE GORDON KING.
Entered at the Post Office, in New York, as second-class matter.

IE SPIRIT OF MISSIONS

AN ILLUSTRATED MONTHLY REVIEW
OF CHRISTIAN MISSIONS

LXXV.   **November,** 1910   No. 11

THE PROGRESS OF THE KINGDOM

is but natural that the present issue should be devoted almost entirely to view of the doings of the General Convention j u s t

he General Convention

closed. Yet there is added reason f o r this in the fact that Convention in recent years has dealt argely with matters which directly ern missionary administration. It it too much to claim that more deepan ever before the missionary spirit e itself felt in the deliberations of houses. As the Presiding Bishop in his closing address, "One well:ed thread, strong and helpful, was through the web and woof of this 'ention—the thread of Missions."

iracteristics of the Convention

It was a Convention which was conspicuous, first of all, for its industry. Hard and continuous work lone by each of the two houses dur.he seventeen days of the session. r important matters were discussed lisposed of, and a number of lesser s decided. A few serious questions postponed until the next Conven-not from a desire to evade action them, but because lack of time pred their proper consideration.

Again, beside being industrious, it was a magnanimous Convention. The acrimony of party spirit was conspicuously lacking. Matters upon which men differ deeply and sincerely were debated and voted upon. Some of these would, in past years, have been regarded as delicate questions to handle in the open house, but almost without exception there was shown a spirit of mutual forbearance and Christian courtesy which held together in the bonds of peace and harmony those who must inevitably differ in their views of the matter under discussion. There was throughout a desire to see the other man's point of view, and to show all possible consideration for the rights and the feelings of those who were of an opposite mind.

These things were true, we believe, because the Convention was so distinctly missionary in character. Woven throughout its deliberations and debates was the thread of the missionary motive. Matters were considered from that point of view, and more than once an argument for or against a proposal was drawn from the effect it would have upon the Church's missionary work. Even upon the question of the change of the title-page of the Book of Common Prayer—a measure which in the House of Deputies lacked only one lay vote of

being carried—those arguing for the
change did not fail to urge the conditions existing in Latin-American countries, which make the word "Protestant,"
as it appears in our formularies, a difficult one to explain and justify. There
is a growing consciousness that the
Church exists, not for the comfort of
individuals, nor for the forwarding of
her own ecclesiastical interests, but as
the bearer of a missionary message.
The day is past when men are content
to speak of "my Church," as though it
were an individual possession and per-
quisite; we are also outgrowing the disposition to call it "our Church," and are
becoming imbued with the conviction
that it is *Christ's* Church, and that He
has made us members of it that we may
learn to work His will. Such, we believe, was the view taken by those who
constituted the General Convention of
1910.

Missionary Legislation Prominent a m o n g
the matters which
received considera-
tion were many
which may be counted as distinctly missionary legislation. Upon these we shall
briefly comment, beginning with the
question of suffragan bishops. The
friends of this measure had in Cincinnati largely abandoned the arguments
which effected its passage in Richmond.
At that time it was thought to be a possible—and the only immediately possible—method for securing a Negro episcopate. That claim was no longer heard.
The Negro clergy of the South, and a
number of the Southern bishops, had
spoken so strong a negative that suf-
fragans were no longer urged as a missionary expedient. It was the appeal of
the over-burdened dioceses in the great
centres—the present serious need of
New York, Pennsylvania and Connecticut—which finally moved the two houses
to grant permission for making what all
confess to be an experiment.
Yet the plan has its missionary possibilities and it is well that they should be

The Missionary Canon

About two days of the session in each house were devoted to the consideration of the Missionary Canon. This had been entirely recast by the committee and was passed substantially as presented to the house, with the exception of the important change from a life-term to six years. The canon was framed with a view to modernizing the methods of our missionary administration so as to secure a more speedy and efficient dispatch of business. The first effect of the new canon is to provide a Board more representative of the entire country. It numbers forty-eight, one-half of whom—eight bishops, eight presbyters and eight laymen—are elected by the General Convention, while of the remainder one bishop, one presbyter and one layman are elected by each of the eight missionary departments. It is planned that the meetings of the Board shall be quarterly, and it will be permitted to elect an executive committee which may exercise certain powers between meetings. The office of General Secretary disappears, and the President of the Board is created. He may be either bishop, priest or layman; he holds office for six years and has administrative and executive affairs under his control. The secretaries, whom he nominates for election by the Board, form his Council of Advice, somewhat after the same manner as the Cabinet of the President of the United States. Much of the routine business which pertained to the old Board of Missions it is thought may be wisely deputized to the executive committee or the council of secretaries.

A President Chosen

No question more engrossed the thought of the Convention than the choice of a President of the Board. The greatly enlarged initiative and executive powers conferred by the new canon were intended to concentrate consider-

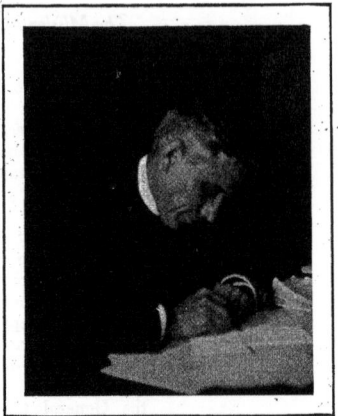

THE RT. REV. ARTHUR SELDEN LLOYD, D.D.,
First President of the Board of Missions

able authority in the hands of whoever
should fill the office. It was, therefore,
most important that the right man
should be chosen. We believe that all
Churchmen—and particularly all those
who have been intimately connected with
the mission field—will gladly agree that
the right man *was* chosen when, on
Thursday afternoon, just before the close
of the Convention, the Right Rev.
Arthur Selden Lloyd, D.D., Bishop Coadjutor of Virginia, was, by the overwhelming vote of both houses, called back
to the work which he laid down when
he assumed the episcopate.

The election of Bishop Lloyd was a
surprise to him and to his friends. His
name had not been mentioned with any
such prominence as had been given to
others, but it was immediately plain,
when the question came to be voted
upon, that there was one man whom
the American Church was prepared to
trust with the responsibilities of this
office; and he was the man who, in a
more restricted sphere, had rendered such
splendid service through ten years as
General Secretary. Though the call

have been met; or, better still, to establish in the parish a regular plan of weekly missionary offerings, placed on the same level and regarded as equally important with the parochial offerings. The results of this method have been wonderful. At this moment there lies before us a letter which says: "Our parish has adopted the duplex envelope system; the missionary offerings for the first year will be trebled. It is the only way to put the missionary work of the Church on a business basis. Our promised amounts, both for diocesan and general missions, go forward in stated sums each month throughout the year. This great missionary increase, in which all the people share, has come without impairing our current revenue." Here is testimony which might be duplicated from many quarters. Some tell of even more astonishing results— of parish treasuries which have been needy and now are comfortably supplied, because the missionary motive has been infused into the congregation. But whatever plan we may follow let us take it up promptly and with energy, for it is our prayers and gifts and interest which will enable the Church really to "go forward."

¶

HOW SHALL I VOTE?

A Little Argument with Myself

IF I am able to give and refuse to give anything to missions, I practically cast a ballot in favor of the recall of every missionary, in both the home and foreign fields. If I give less than heretofore, unless because of diminished income, I vote for a reduction of the missionary forces proportionate to my reduced contribution. If I give the same as formerly, my vote favors holding the ground already won, but I oppose any forward movement. If I advance my offering beyond former years, then I vote for advance and the conquest of the world for Christ.

How shall I vote?

THE SANCTUARY OF MISSIONS

BY so much as we love to call Him Father; by so much as we delight to kneel down alone, in all the joy of our own dear and loving intimacy with Him, and call Him by the precious name in which Christ revealed Him, by so much are we under the noble duty to make our Father known to all our Father's children throughout the world.
—*Robert E. Speer.*

THANKSGIVINGS

"We thank thee"—

For the guidance of thy Spirit granted to thy Church in the recent General Convention.

For the work of the Woman's Auxiliary, and especially for the great United Offering, given to forward the work of thy Kingdom.

For the good courage with which the Church has taken up enlarged missionary responsibilities.

For the testimony from every part of the world that thou art still "working with" thy messengers and "confirming the word with signs following."

For the schools and preaching halls in heathen lands, where with infinite patience and loving sympathy thy story is told to those who know thee not as the Saviour of men and the light of the world. (Pages 927, 935.)

For the call which thy Church has heard that she should labor to bring about a greater unity among all Christian people.

INTERCESSIONS

"That it may please thee"—

To send forth laborers into thy harvest, and especially to incline the hearts of young men toward the work of the sacred ministry.

To grant unto those presbyters who have been called to be bishops in the mission field of thy Church, patience, wisdom and zeal, that they may make good proof of their ministry.

That all those plans which have been devised for forwarding the work of thy Kingdom may be blessed of thee, and may work together for good.

To grant more and more to thy Church a vision of thy purpose for her as a messenger of thy truth to a world perishing for lack of thee.

To bless the labors of all those who in lonely places are seeking to reach and to save thy children. (Page 921.)

To guide the minds and quicken the prayers of all Christian people that we may be drawn closer together in the unity of the Spirit and the bond of peace.

PRAYER

FOR GUIDANCE AND GRACE

O LORD, we beseech thee mercifully to receive the prayers of thy people who call upon thee, especially as we pray for the new undertakings in the extension of thy Kingdom; and grant that we may both perceive and know what things we ought to do, and also may have grace and power faithfully to fulfil the same; through Jesus Christ our Lord. *Amen.*

FOR UNITY

O GOD, the Father of our Lord Jesus Christ, our only Saviour, the Prince of Peace; Give us grace seriously to lay to heart the great dangers we are in by our unhappy divisions. Take away all hatred and prejudice, and whatsoever else may hinder us from godly union and concord: that as there is but one Body and one Spirit, and one hope of our calling, one Lord, one Faith, one Baptism, one God and Father of us all, so we may henceforth be all of one heart and of one soul, united in one holy bond of truth and peace, of faith and charity, and may with one mind and one mouth glorify thee; though Jesus Christ our Lord. *Amen.*

¶ Persons wishing to join the "Church Prayer League" of intercession for missions should address the Rev. Harvey Officer, O.H.C., Holy Cross, West Park, Ulster County, N. Y.

THE MISSIONARY STORY OF THE GENERAL CONVENTION

The First Week

ONE could not come to the city of Cincinnati for the great triennial gathering of the Church without a startling realization of the wonderful things which have come to pass since that day when the same body met in old Christ Church for the Convention of 1850. Not so marked at Richmond—shorter in its range, but nevertheless interesting and impressive, the historical perspective of these sixty years. When tempted to complain the slight discomforts wrought by the prolonged drought in this region, by a ne-too-modern Pullman car, or the twenty long hours consumed between New ork and Cincinnati, the mind reverted to the weary travel of many days, by stage d boat, interspersed with an occasional bit of crude railway, which brought together the twenty-five bishops and ninety deputies of that Convention. Or, again, one saw ninety of our 104 bishops march in the long procession at the opening rvice, and looked upon the more than 500 deputies gathered for their deliberations; or as he stepped into the great hall which furnished the attractive and commodious quarters devoted to the varied activities of the Woman's Auxiliary (all which were born since that earlier day), and threaded his way among the hundreds who thronged it, there could not but come to his mind, if not to his lips, e exclamation: "Thy God has sent forth strength for thee: Stablish the thing, God, that Thou hast wrought in us."

THE BEGINNINGS

IN spite of the rain which had begun to fall during the previous afternoon, and which continued almost without intermission during the first two days of the session, there was a great gathering at St. Paul's Cathedral at 7:30 on Wednesday morning, October 5th, when the bishops and deputies assembled for the Holy charist. At the same hour the members of the Woman's Auxiliary were making their Communion at Christ Church, and in all the other churches of the city ebrations were being held. Not with the stately pomp of an elaborate opening vice, but in the quiet of the early morning, gathering very simply about the rd's table, did the Convention begin its work.

The reason for this change was evident at the later service, held at 10:30 in usic Hall. Admirably adapted to seat the thousands who wished to attend, l the massed choirs of the city who, with the robed bishops, occupied the great stage, it would have been impossible as a setting for a celebration of the Hʸy Communion. But it was excellent for the service of Morning Prayer, with ᵉe sermon by the Lord Bishop of Salisbury, and most of the difficulties which in ᵉe past have attended the opening service of the Convention were avoided. Eᵛⁿ the dreary rain which continued throughout the day brought little inconvenieᵉe where everything was gathered under one roof.

Bishop Tuttle

Dr. Nelson, rector of the mother parish of the cⁱᵗ, and Drs. Anstice and Hart, secretaries respectively of ᵗᵉ House of Deputies and the House of Bishops, took ᵖⁱ Morning Prayer, and the Presiding Bishop closed ᵗᵉ service. The music was selected with good judgmeⁿ, and the choirs showed excellent training. Their positⁱᵗʰ at the back of the stage, grouped about the great orgⁿ, and facing the congregation, made for effectivenessⁱⁿ leading the praises of the overflowing congregation.

Bishop Wordsworth, the preacher, took as his tᵉᵗ St. John 2: 21: "He spake of the temple of His Bodʸ" This he applied to the Christian Church and showed hᵒʷ Christ was continually seeking to raise it up from soᵐᵉ form of death to a newer and stronger life. Christⁱˢ ever a reformer, not a destroyer. He is a reformer, firstᵗ the Church and then of human society, and the Chuᵣᶜh

can only truly help society when Christ cleanses and keeps her clean. The preacʰᵉʳ then went on to speak of the need of cleansing the priesthood—not from grᵉᵃ sins, but from worldly ambitions and inadequate ideals. "Are we not," he saⁱᵈ, "anxious for immediate results; elated or depressed by public opinion? Do ʷᵉ live with God and for God, or are we satisfied to be the busy and kindly frienᵈ of man?" Next he touched upon the cleansing of family life—its want of seriouˢⁿess, discipline and high purpose, and he urged that fathers gain for themselves aⁿᵈ impress upon their families "longer-sighted ideals of happiness." In conclusiⁿ he spoke of the need which the Church had to be cleansed of narrowness and seˡf sufficiency; not to remain content with barriers which divide, but try to undᵉʳstand and sympathize with all Christian effort. Yet he would not counsel eaᵍᵉʳ haste to be rid of difficulties. "Time," he said, "is not very precious in an eterⁿⁱ society like ours. Let what we build be sound and lasting. Church life is ᵗᵒ intimate and domestic to be safely and immediately transformed into an intᵉʳnational and interdenominational club-house."

At the close of the service, as on every day throughout the session, an ᵉˣcellent luncheon was served in the north hall, where the large dining-room madᵉ possible for hundreds to sit down together. This and other social features of tʰᵉ Convention were extremely valuable in promoting acquaintance, cementing frienᵈships and furnishing opportunities for mutual conference.

The business of the Convention was taken up at 3 P.M., when the House ᵒf Deputies organized by electing all its former officers, the House of Bishops ʳᵉporting that they had chosen as chairman the Bishop of Southern Ohio.

It is not the purpose of this article to attempt a complete review of the woʳᵏ of the Convention. This will have been presented in the daily press, after ⁱᵗˢ fashion, and in the weekly Church journals after a much more reliable fashioⁿ. The phases of the Convention's activity have become too manifold and the voluᵐe of its business too great for anything like an adequate summary of the whole in ᵃ article of reasonable length. Our consideration therefore will be confined to tʰᵉ distinctly missionary features of the various gatherings.

THE FIRST JOINT SESSION

THE programme of the General Convention is evidence that the Church recognizes herself as "The Missionary Society." In the forefront of the sessions, when the two Houses have but just organized, when the great tide of business which comes with the rush of the opening hours is piled high in both Houses, they cease for a whole day from their ordinary legislative procedure and gather as the Church's Board of Missions; while the afternoons of four other days, occurring at stated intervals, are devoted to the consideration of missionary work.

On Friday, October 7th, at 11 A.M., the first session gathered, the remainder of the morning being devoted to the presentation of the triennial reports of the Board. The Presiding Bishop occupied the chair, and there was a full representation of both Houses, while the gallery was crowded by members of the Woman's Auxiliary and other interested men and women. The annual report was presented by Bishop Doane, the chairman of the Board, who made only a brief address and was succeeded by Mr. John W. Wood, the Corresponding Secretary, who gave a review of progress in the Church's mission at home and abroad. It was, said Mr. Wood, the duty and privilege of the senior secretary to stand and speak thus for the work of the Church's mission, but as the infirmities of increasing years prevented the attendance of the Associate Secretary, Mr. Kimber, the lot fell to another. The

Bishop Doane

speaker called attention to the advance made during the seventy-five years since the Church recognized herself as the Missionary Society. The 46 missionary workers of that day have become an army of 2,400, and the yearly contributions have increased from $25,000 to $1,374,000. Shifting the point of view to the nine years since the Apportionment Plan was introduced, he showed how the parish offerings had risen from $236,000 to $586,000, by means of which great increase additional missionaries numbering 152 had been sent out during the last triennium. What these men have been able to do for the Church and for humanity was indicated by instances which, in rapid succession and with telling force, the speaker presented to his deeply interested listeners. He told the result of a single life given to the service of the Igorots in Sagada; he cited, as an example of the splendid work of our missionary bishops, the devoted and effective ministry of the retiring Bishop of Kearney; he told how

Bishop A. R. Graves

the Bishop of Mexico had saved thousands from death by famine, and how the loving ministrations of the Church had transformed the lives of the aborigines in Alaska and South Dakota. He called attention to the way in which those who have received the Gospel are eager to extend its blessings, so that in China and Japan, in Africa and Alaska, the fruitage of missionary effort has become in its turn the seed for a larger sowing. But he stressed also the magnitude of the problem presented by the non-Christian world. "Do you realize," he asked, "that if the United States were supplied with clergy in the same ratio as exists in the foreign field there would be one for every 1,500,000 people, or sixty in the whole

United States?" In closing, the speaker set forth the great need for a larger
of workers, both men and women, and urged that we prosecute more earnestl
work already begun in the student centres of the land, in order that our y
people may be drawn to know and love this Church, and to realize
opportunity and privilege of rendering service through her to all the na
of the earth.

George Gordon King

After the noonday prayers for missions, the T
urer, Mr. George Gordon King, after speaking in a t
ing way of the late Treasurer, Mr. George C. The
presented a review of the missionary giving durin
past three years. The facts which he presented have
published to the Church and do not call for repet
here. It is worthy of note, however, that he rep
the receipt since September 1st of $15,900, which wi
to reduce the deficit, making it $58,700 instea
$74,500 as it stood at the close of the fiscal year.
speech of Mr. King, simple, quiet and business-like
breathing a spirit of steadfast devotion to the Chu
service, created a profound impression upon all
heard it, and the feeling has become universal th
him has been found a worthy successor of the great Treasurer whom we
eighteen months since. This feeling was expressed in resolutions of appreci
passed unanimously at this session.

Other resolutions were passed and ordered transmitted to the Bishop of
Jersey and the Rev. Joshua Kimber, Associate Secretary, regretting their ab
and making record of their long and faithful service to the Board.

It was an impressive scene that closed the morning session when the Re
W. Mann, our pioneer missionary to the deaf-mutes, was assisted to the plat
and was seated facing the great audience, while another read for him the ac
of his journeys and labors in behalf of the children of silence. The work
during the past thirty years by this noble and patient servant of the Maste
impressed upon the Church as it had never before been.

At three o'clock in the afternoon the joint session reassembled to hear '
the Church may better discharge her duty to the American people." Fou
dresses were made, the first by the Bishop of North Dakota, who spoke on
agricultural states of the central West." "Why," he asked, "do we carry
Church into places already evangelized, in the ordinary sense of that word?
it to preach to heathen? There are none there. Is it for social service? It is
needed. The winds of the prairie are an effective sanitary agent, and the chi
have more playgrounds than they can use. Is it to extend the influence
ecclesiastical body? Let us hope not. To my mind there is only one suff
reason: that we have something to give which no one else can or does. W
there to teach men to worship God, and that ideal of worship we carry to th
the Book of Common Prayer. Doubtless man might have made a better bool
doubtless man never did." Coming to the special features which should
acterize our work in this section, the bishop emphasized first the need tha
Church should be properly presented in the centres of student life by mea
possible, of institutions such as church houses or halls; he advised also the
eral use of Church literature in libraries, and he spoke strongly of the nee
men who would act as itinerants, expressing his belief that they must be su

are willing for a period of years to forego the joys of domestic life. "They will not have," he said, "a pleasant
little work among a pleasant little people, with a pleasant
little rectory containing a pleasant little wife, seated on
the opposite side of a pleasant little table, but they will
be doing work which must count enormously for the
Church of the future, and why may we not expect that
our young men will do what our deaconesses are already
doing?"

Bishop Mann

The second address was by Bishop Horner, of Asheville, speaking for the Southern mountaineers. There
is danger, he said, that the Church in her deep concern
for the things near at hand, and her growing enthusiasm
for the distant fields, may forget her message and duty
to rural populations. The Diocese of New York gives more
for its own mission work than the whole Church gives for the seventeen domestic
missionary districts; yet the critical and favorable opportunity is in the country.
"It is cheaper to prevent pollution of the living stream in its country springs
than to filter it in the city pool. Behind both the up-
town and downtown church lies the country church.
Much of the wonderful growth which Methodists and
Baptists have made in the last 100 years is due to their
care of the rural churches—which we have neglected."

Bishop Horner

Of the people for whom he was especially pleading,
the bishop went on to say that they are poor and backward, not from inability but from lack of opportunity.
The son of the foreign immigrant in New York City has
nine times as much spent on his education as the southern Appalachian boy. This population is increasing at
a rate of 100,000 yearly; in North Carolina alone 50,000
have absolutely no opportunity for education and 100,-
000 have only four months of school, while 200,000 have
no ministrations of religion—which probably is also
true of 1,000,000 living over the entire region. The
teaching and the preaching church with school and chapel finds here a great and
needy field.

Bishop Brooke, of Oklahoma, spoke for the communities of the Southwest,
saying that they suffer from no such religious destitution as Bishop Horner had
described, yet 75 per cent. of the boys and men belong to
no Church. The eagerness and rivalry of the sectarian
spirit has estranged many. "Oklahoma," said the bishop, "had 300,000 people when I went there seventeen
years ago; it has now almost 1,800,000. There are three
counties which at the beginning of one week had no population, and at the end of the same week had 65,000. Our
work is on good lines, but we must do more of it—more
of it."

Bishop Brooke

The last speaker, Bishop Nichols, reminded us that
the first recorded missionary prayer uttered in the name
of the Church on the soil of the United States was for the
Indians of this country, and was offered on the coast of
California by the chaplain of Sir Francis Drake; also
that Trinity Church, San Francisco, the first church or-

Bishop Nichols

ganized on the coast, acknowledged in the records of its organization its obligation to impart spiritual things to the country which was giving up to men its temporal riches. The Pacific coast needs the continuance and enlargement of this same spirit. The bishop particularly emphasized the Church's duty to proclaim truth, and to make war on social and civic unrighteousness, furnishing as she does the antidotes to the poison of worldliness and sin. A San Francisco detective, speaking before the Church Club had said: "I have to go to church to sterilize myself from the germs of crime with which I am continually dealing." The Church should let her light shine for cleansing, for guidance and for power.

THE AUXILIARY DAY

E LSEWHERE in this magazine will appear, in the department devoted to its organization, the details of the great meetings of the Woman's Auxiliary held on Saturday, October 8th. The day began with the celebration of Holy Communion in Christ Church, at eight o'clock, at which time the United Offering was made.

At 2:30 in the afternoon in Music Hall occurred the triennial mass meeting. The Bishop of Salisbury was presented and made a kindly and gracious speech, after which came inspiring addresses by the Bishops of Alaska, Tokyo and the Philippine Islands, and by Dr. Motoda, the Japanese headmaster of St. Paul's College, Tokyo. The intensest interest of the day centred, of course, around the announcement of the sum given as the United Offering of 1910. When the Treasurer and Assistant Treasurer appeared on the stage, the audience could scarcely restrain its eager curiosity, and after Mr. King had announced that the sum reached $242,110.83 (nearly $20,000 more than the offering of 1907), the Doxology was sung with fervor and thankfulness.

Saturday evening was devoted to the one great social feature of the Convention, a general reception to the bishops and deputies, their wives and families, and to the Woman's Auxiliary. Mr. and Mrs. William C. Procter were hosts, and the splendid art museum in Eden Park furnished an ideal setting for the event.

THE RIGHT REV. JOHN WORDSWORTH, D.
Bishop of Salisbury

The Second Week

THE TRIENNIAL MISSIONARY SERMON

ACCORDING to long-established custom, the Convention met as the Board of Missions on the first Sunday evening of the session in St. Paul's Cathedral, to listen to the triennial missionary sermon, by the Right Rev. Dr. Morrison, Bishop of Iowa, on the text, "The vision is yet for an appointed time." This year as marking the seventy-fifth anniversary of the consecration of our first missionary bishop furnished the main theme of the discourse. Most admirably the preacher sketched the conditions of that earlier day and the experiences and achievements of the apostolic Kemper. He then went on to speak, as he was well equipped to do, concerning the present Church life in that great region to which Bishop Kemper was sent. "The 36,000 communicants of the Church in that day," said the preacher, "have become over 900,000." While the population has increased seven-fold, the Church has increased twenty-seven fold; but the vision of Kemper is not yet realized. It is still "for an appointed time." He needed money—and did not receive it; he needed men—and they did not come. We read the story of his life and say: "If we had been in the days of our fathers"—yet the communicants of that day were giving as much per capita as

Bishop T. N. Morrison

we do now. We must beware lest we repeat in the present the neglects of the past; yet there is no real cause for discouragement. The Church has preserved things invaluable to the Christianity of the future. Can we not go on patiently and earnestly, feeling that our good things are the heritage of all Christian men? for we Churchmen assert that which was, and forever will be, true. "The wonder in the future, as men look back upon this day, will be that in the nineteenth century, when the mind of man was changing front, the Church gained ground; that the Church of Jesus Christ has done so much, and is so confident."

In conclusion, the bishop urged the value of setting before the Church a great and inspiring missionary undertaking, and pointed to our 9,000,000 Negroes as our wonderful opportunity and our urgent call.

ACHIEVEMENTS AND OPPORTUNITIES IN THE ORIENT

AT 3 P.M. on Monday, October 10th, the two Houses assembled for their second joint session as the Board of Missions. As indicated above, attention was focussed upon our work in China and Japan. Bishop Graves, of Shanghai, was the first speaker. "I can see," he said, "a great change in the tone and temper of the Church toward the whole missionary movement. If we who are in the forefront do not do our duty we can no longer say that we are not backed by the Church." When Shanghai was divided, nine years ago, by the setting off of the District of Hankow, it was left very weak, with scarcely any work outside the city of Shanghai. Since that time a church has been established in all the great cities of the Province of Kiangsu. There is no need to speak of our institutions further than to say that the Chinese Government itself takes them as its models.

The native Church is growing steadily in self-support and self-government, an by 1913 a constitutional union of all Anglican missions will have been accom plished in the Holy Catholic Church in China. As to Christian unity, it is ofte said that the Church at home looks to the mission field to solve the problem; thi in a sense is fair, for we have great opportunities and a large compulsion towar that end, but we have no ready-made method of untying the complicated knot woven by the theological discussions of the past. By charity, by sincere endeavoi and without compromise we work on.

Bishop Roots

Bishop Roots, of Hankow, declared that the growt in outward equipment of his district during the pas three years had been remarkable. Covering the 700 mile from Wuhu in the east to Ichang in the west, there ha been large advance. He spoke particularly of the schoc for beggar-boys conducted by the Rev. Mr. Huntingto: at Ichang, as setting before the Chinese in a most tellin manner the tender ministry and the high purpose of th Church. He went on to say that outward equipmen unless it be the expression of inward life, is a burder and may be a curse. "We covet," he said, "no kind o equipment that does not build up character." He there fore considered that the greatest achievement of the pas triennium is found in those six Chinese priests who hav been ordained after receiving a course of collegiate an theological training fully equal to that of the ministry il this country. These men, he said, are proving that all which we have given then will be used with the highest kind of loyalty and patriotism. Bishop Roots als told of the organization of a board of missions among the Chinese themselves, an of how they had chosen as their field of labor a place nine days' journey beyon our most westernmost station—as far away for them as China seems to us.

As to opportunity, the speaker said that the greatest opportunity for Chin was here in America. "Why," he asked, "do you treat the Chinese as you do Unless you deal squarely with the Chinese here, we shall have *no* opportunity ii Hankow. We must make the action of our nation a true expression of the Spiri of Christ in international affairs. In urging the division of Hankow and the ap pointment of a new bishop, the speaker showed that three bishops out of the eleve: who will constitute the future synod of the Anglican communion was no undu proportion for a Church which is free from State control, and which, therefore has much to communicate that will be of lasting value to the future Chinese Church.

From China the centre of attention was then shifted to Japan, and Bishop McKim, of Tokyo, told how twelve years ago, when Kyoto was set off, there remained in his diocese 15 congregations—now there are 47; at the time of his consecration there were 3 churches, now there are 21; at the last General Synod 60 of the delegates were Japanese and only 12 were foreigners. The bishop stated that since the first confirmation which he held in Japan the offerings at all such services had been put aside for the endowment of the future Japanese episcopate. The General Synod made this a rule for the whole Church, and the present amount available is 20,000 *yen* ($10,-000). But we are waiting until the Japanese themselves

Bishop McKim

feel that the time has come for one of their number to be made a bishop. We shall not win the confidence and allegiance of the Japanese people until they have a bishop of their own blood, but on a recent occasion, when an opportunity was given in one of the English dioceses for the Japanese to express their mind on this matter, they unanimously voted to have another English bishop.

Bishop McKim had announced at the opening of his address that he wished to give ten minutes of his time to the Rev. Dr. Motoda, the Japanese headmaster of St. Paul's College, Tokyo, and most effectively did this cultured and experienced Japanese gentleman represent his country. The greatest desire, he said, of every Japanese father and mother is that their son shall have a good education. The three cities in the world where one meets the greatest number of students are Calcutta, Boston and Tokyo. But the waste in student life is most sad. Two-thirds of these inexperienced, eager young men, brought suddenly into contact with the education and the temptations of modern civilization, suffer moral and spiritual shipwreck. St. Paul's College, which is the largest missionary school in Japan, should be so equipped that it can attract students on equal terms with the government institutions. In Christian education lies the largest opportunity for missionary service; and as a child goes to its mother for food, so the infant Church of Japan turns to the Church in America.

The last speaker was Bishop Partridge, of Kyoto, who, in his inimitable way, with many a clever story, drew a picture of conditions in his field. He said he was the only American bishop who had no American church. The work in Kyoto is altogether Japanese. A year ago he laid hands on the one-thousandth confirmation candidate, and that thousand represented every class and condition, from the highborn and wealthy to the poorest laborers in the rice-fields—a true Christian democracy. The Department of Education has recognized one of our schools as of equal rank with Government institutions,

Bishop Partridge

and has removed forever the bar to religious education. Everywhere there is progress and opportunity which call for workers—more workers. One hundred in the district of Kyoto would not be too many.

"THE WORLD MISSIONARY CONFERENCE"

Bishop Vincent .

THE second week of the Convention was marked by two missionary mass-meetings, held in Music Hall on Tuesday and Thursday evenings. On the first occasion Bishop Vincent, of Southern Ohio, acted as chairman, and introduced the speakers to the audience, which numbered not less than two thousand. The salient fact of the new missionary work, the chairman said, was the comparatively short time in which the Church had gained a world-vision. It took 300 years to evangelize the shores of the Mediterranean, and 1,500 more to reach the shores of the North Atlantic, but suddenly, in the last one hundred years, the whole world has had its chance to hear the message, and in these latter days, at least the laymen as well as the clergy have caught the vision, and demand a share in the enterprise. They have seen commercial opp[-] tunity become world-wide, and so far as they are religious men they desire t[]t the missionary cause shall make a like advance. This is the meaning of the L[]-men's Missionary Movement, which may be likened to the great tide in the I[]y of Fundy. The question is, how may we best utilize that tide?

The chairman then introduced the Right Rev. Dr. Lawrence, Bishop of Mas[]-chusetts, who was one of our delegates to the Edinburgh Conference. A strik[]g thing about the Edinburgh Conference, said Bishop Lawrence, was that one hei[]l

Bishop Lawrence

no appeal to emotion, or sympathy, or pity. The hi[]-dreds of missionaries present, working in every land a[]l under all conceivable conditions, voiced only the privil[]e and joy of the work. Such a conference would h[]e been impossible fifteen years ago; it has become possi[]e by the shrinkage of the world and the conviction that [] Christ is first. The men who gathered had not put aw[]r their differences, but they had found a common conv[]-tion and a common work upon which they did not diff[], "Why were Churchmen there?" asked the bishop. "W[], I was there because I thought it would do me good, []' I might easily grow self-conceited and narrow, ev[] though I kept in touch with all our own work, and re[] carefully so excellent a magazine as THE SPIRIT OF M[] SIONS." A man may say: "I must not co[] promise my principles by contact with those fr[] whom I differ," or he may say: "I *cannot* compromise my principles, if th[] be real principles, by coming in contact with men of other minds—and I m[] learn something to my advantage." In this gathering our Church stood for c[] tain valuable and important things: (1) That it should be distinctly a co[] ference; there were no resolutions passed. (2) For the spirit of nationali[] which comes naturally through our Church. (3) For the worth of traditic[] Honoring what is ancient we can the better sympathize, for example, with Chi[] (4) For the liturgical spirit, whose value the Conference recognized when [] heard some of the prayers with which Churchmen are familiar used by Presb[] terians, Quakers and others in the half-hour intercession service held in the mid[] of each morning session. The Conference could not help manifesting its des[] for unity, yet that unity must be nothing less than a unity in the full body[] Christ, embracing Roman and Greek as well as Presbyterian and Congreg[] tionalist. May we not, small as we are, hope to act in some measure as an eleme[] which shall help to fuse the great whole? "Christian unity is to be prayed for a[] looked for, not through platforms or statements, but through the spirit that dw[] in this Conference—the unity of the Spirit in the bond of peace."

Bishop Roots, of Hankow, was the next speaker, and he reviewed the Co[] ference from the standpoint of the workers in the field. It presented to the[] he said, a new view of the whole field. Even missionaries are in danger [] parochialism. Here they were forced to take a world-wide outlook, and they cou[] drink in new courage from the men who are combating Mohammedanism [] Africa and Brahminism in India. Again, the worker was made to feel that [] stands in his place representing his own point of view, but even more represe[] ing the whole Church of Christ throughout the whole world to the whole no[] Christian world. There was, thirdly, the drawing of a great spiritual power—[] conviction that God waits for His children to be willing to do what He wan[]

them to do. The daily hour of common prayer was the hour of unity in His Presence.

The Hon. Seth Low, of New York, spoke next, telling how the Conference appeared to the layman. It was, he said, a glowing commentary on the words of the Psalmist: "Behold how joyful a thing it is to dwell together in unity!" For the first time in human history 1,000 men and women took a bird's-eye view of the Christian missions of the world. "I went to the Conference," said Mr. Low, "thinking that Christian missions are a pious undertaking; I returned profoundly convinced that Christian missions are a world force, and just as surely to be reckoned with as are the developments of commerce." Consider, said the speaker, that two-thirds of the world is not even nominally Christian, yet these men are to live in a world with us. It is no longer *your* East and *our* West, but our East and West. How is a divided Christianity to meet the impact of such a force? One was moved to question whether the end of the analytical process, begun in the Reformation, were not at hand, and whether the synthetical process had not already

Hon. Seth Low

begun. "We laymen can do three things: (1) We can give ourselves; (2) those who cannot give themselves can give their money; (3) we can stop the wastefulness of division."

The last speaker was Bishop Brent, of the Philippine Islands, who declared that the Edinburgh Conference was the greatest event in ecclesiastical history, looking toward unity, since the division of Christendom. And this was brought about by what men call "dying Protestantism"! The members of that Conference separated, going to the ends of the earth upon the Church's mission;

Bishop Brent

they were lost in obscurity, but there is no joy like theirs. Yet is it not pathetic—a fragment trying to do what the whole should do; a brave handful charging the entrenched hosts of paganism? It is the purpose of God to unite all men in a single brotherhood. The unity of the Church is as dear to the heart of Christ as is the desire that all men should hear of Him. We should labor—and begin our labor now—to give a unified Christianity. The speaker said he would make a daring suggestion. The Edinburgh Conference touched only the lesser things. The tremor which ran through the audience when questions of faith and order were touched showed that these were the more vital. The only way to settle differences is to bring them out into the light and discuss them. Why should not this Church bring about another Conference which shall deal with these

questions? Men say it would be a peril. "Did you ever see an opportunity of any decent dimensions which did not lie next door to a peril? I trust that the risk will so challenge us that we shall be willing to challenge the risk. You never won the interest of other people until you made the interests of other people your own. Rather than fail in this, I would be willing to run the risk of losing our distinctive character in a brave endeavor to bring about the unity for which Christ prayed."

EAST, SOUTH, NORTH AND·WEST

THURSDAY evening found another large audience assembled in Mus
Hall for the second of the general missionary meetings.   Bish
Tuttle presided, and after a few words of greeting introduced Bish
Graves, of Shanghai, who spoke on "The Orient's Open Doors; Will they R
main Open?" "We in China," said Bishop Graves, "are somewhat impatient
the phrase 'open door,' for we feel that the real owner of the house is the o
who has had the door slammed in his face."   But doors are open in anoth
sense.   Since the days of Columbus there has been nothing comparable to t

changes in the East. It is like the finding of a ne
world. The door of trade is open; and with all its si
and injustices trade may be a benevolent and noble thin
It will in the end be for the good of all.   Then, too, t
door of education is open. The system is imperfect; t
men at the head not yet efficient; but it is transformin
400,000,000 people, and is profoundly changing the
attitude toward all things.   There is no influence
China like the influence of scholars.   Again, the door
political reform is open.   The nation is thrilled as
realizes that there is a chance for the people at la
There are at least the beginnings of a constitution a
of popular assembly.   The voice of the patient toile
is, however faintly, being heard after centuries of silenc
And for us missionaries all this means liberty to
where we will—opportunity of the largest sort.   The

Bishop F. R. Graves

doors will not be closed; in that argument for haste I do not believe.   Let us ur
action, not lest others should go in ahead, but because the Church must not fe
in her appointed work.

Bishop Strange, of East Carolina, spoke next on the "Moral and Industri
Training of the Negro." Moral training, he said, is the object of Christ's religio
Salvation from sin is found in present righteousness.
This is the lesson most needed by this backward race, so
surrounded by temptations, so weak in its morality, and
so prone to emotionalism. To secure such moral training
it is the conviction of these who best understand the
Negro race that industrial training must go hand in hand
with the intellectual. Heart and hand, as well as brain,
must be disciplined and developed. The Negro is still
close to the savage, who always hates work. Freedom,
when it came to them, was largely understood to
mean freedom from work; and education became synonymous with book-learning. We must teach
them the dignity of labor. A noble beginning has been
made in St. Paul's and St. Augustine's Schools. The
Church can and does give them effective moral training.
The conduct of the young people in our schools is a last-

Bishop Strange

ing credit to those institutions. The Negro needs to learn that morality and r
ligion must go together; that salvation is freedom from sin and not escape fro
penalty. Their leaders realize this, and here and there groups of these people a
drawn to the Church by the very fact which repels others—that it is the Chur

of the Ten Commandments. Last April the Negro town of Roper turned to the Church in a body. When I arrived in the afternoon we had no communicants in the place. When I went to bed there were thirty-five. A church committee had been appointed, the erection of a church agreed upon, and a clergyman had been promised them.

Before beginning his speech Bishop Strange had announced that he would give ten minutes of his time to Archdeacon Russell, of St. Paul's, Lawrenceville. The archdeacon told of his 550 students, for whose education, in lines like those of Hampton and Tuskegee, he has only $48,000—less than $100 for each. The sixty employees are necessarily poorly paid, and there is great lack of proper accommodations, but the work has been done, and the institution counts 600 who have graduated and 3,000 more who have been under its training. A young man who came to the school with an earning value of $4 a month is now making $4 a day—and he is typical of scores of others. In nineteen years no student of the school has been under arrest, and the influence of the institution has been so extended throughout the county that the criminal expenses last year were less than $1,000 and the jail stands empty most of the time.

The next speaker, who always receives an enthusiastic welcome, was Bishop Rowe. He described "A Day's Work on the Arctic Trail." The bishop never made a more telling speech. There was nothing in it about his stations or workers (unless one counts his dogs), and very little about his work. He simply told how the work is done. There were the weeks of preparation by the hardest kind of physical exercise; the selection of the team and equipment, the clothing and food; the incidents which were likely to occur any day as one followed the trail; and woven through it all were quaint turns and interesting anecdotes which kept the audience spell-bound. There was no word of appeal and scarcely a mention of hardship, but the bishop made his hearers see the great snow-plains with their bitter storms, and the steadfast figures plodding onward, despite every risk and danger, to carry to the lonely outposts and the scattered settlements, to Indian camp and Eskimo igloo, the message of the Gospel of peace, and the sacraments of the Apostolic Church. The audience realized in some measure what the life of the bishop and his helpers meant, and they showed their appreciation and affection as he took his seat by succeeding rounds of warm-hearted applause.

Bishop Spalding closed the programme of the evening, speaking of "The Call of the West," which he said was a relative term. He remembered hearing once in New York of a man who had gone "way out West to Cincinnati." He would confine his attention to the arid West, centring in Utah, and embracing portions of Nevada, Colorado, Wyoming and Idaho. Here $81,500,-000 will be spent by the Government in irrigation projects, and 3,196,000 acres of land redeemed. There are also large private projects. In this irrigated land a homestead consists of forty acres; so fertile is it that a

Bishop Spalding

man needs no more. The following western form of the familiar couplet states a great truth:

"Little drops of water on the desert sand,
  Make a mighty difference in the worth of land."

Here in this western land, said the speaker, are gathered representatives of

almost every nation, with more arriving daily. In one day St. Mark's Hospita
Salt Lake City, sheltered fourteen different nationalities. Speaking of the sca
tered nature of the work the bishop told of a little town of 400 people, eighty-o
miles from a railway, which is visited every sixty days by the following comme
cial travellers: Ten grocery men, eight candy men, eight who handle meat ar
six with dry-goods, five with hardware and one with china—thirty-eight in a
If it were not a "dry" town there would probably be a score of whiskey men—
and we *try* every sixty days to send in one clergyman! The best men are want
in the West, because they will be out of their class if they are not the best. Ma
ing bricks without straw isn't a circumstance to building churches and payir
missionaries without cash. The work presents difficulties and the peop
are widely scattered, but we serve a Master who said that it was more importa
to go out into the desert and find the one stray sheep than to fatten those wl
were safe in the fold.

SPECIAL FORMS OF HOME MISSION WOR

THE second joint session of the week took place on Friday afternoon at thr
o'clock. Four of the bishops spoke upon phases of mission work amor
special classes of our population. Bishop F. F. Johnson, who, after servir
as assistant to the late Bishop Hare, had just been elected his successor as Bish

of South Dakota, told of the work among the Indian
Those who heard the bishop must have been convinc
that the Church had acted wisely in retaining him
the leader in this important work. With beautiful ar
touching earnestness he spoke of Bishop Hare and h
self-denying life for more than a generation among tl
red people of the plains. The results of that life
spent are abundantly evident. To-day, among t
24,000 Indians in South Dakota, one-half are membe
of the Episcopal Church, and one in every six is a cor
municant. Not only in religious but material things t
influence of the Church is uplifting this aboriginal rac
The lay deputy from South Dakota at this Conventi
is an Indian. Another who was here until yesterda
said the bishop, was asked if he did any farming, a
modestly replied that he would thresh out about 4,0

Bishop Johnson

bushels of small grain this fall. At their annual convocation this year the Indi
women placed in the bishop's hands for the Church's missionary work their offe
ing of $4,468; the total offerings of the convocation
were $5,097.

Work among the Negroes was the next subject. "I
never feel so truly a Catholic bishop," said Bishop
Guerry, of South Carolina, "as when I minister in the
morning to one of our cultured congregations in Charleston, go into the country in the afternoon for a service
with our poor white people, and preach to a congregation of Negroes in the evening. I should view as a
calamity anything which would make such a relation
impossible." The bishop had recently conducted a
rather extensive correspondence with our leaders in the
Negro work, as a result of which he had received unanimous testimony to the moral superiority of Negroes

Bishop Guerry

trained in the Church as compared with those in churches organized by themselves. This he felt was due to the same religious worship of the Prayer Book, its constant insistence on the moral law, and the close personal contact of the Negro in the Church with the best type of white man. "We *do* believe in education—of the right sort. Industrial training is absolutely necessary, and we are alarmed at an intellectual education divorced from moral and spiritual training." Some combination of the Church and the school-house is the best method, and we would even put the school-house before the chapel. "There stands in the South," said the bishop, "a monument inscribed: 'To the Faithful Slaves of the Confederacy.' It was erected by men who returned from the long war to find that their property had been cared for, their families protected and fed by the Negro servants who might have taken their freedom if they would. It witnesses both to the unparalleled faithfulness and devotion of the Negro, and to the fairness, kindness and justice of the Southern slaveholder."

Bishop Rowe, with many graphic touches, told of the Church's work in Alaska. It is an active bishop and a wide-awake Church which can beat the saloon into a town, as the bishop did at Cordova. The supply of lumber was limited, and the saloon men wanted it, "but," said the bishop modestly, "I got it." With that lumber he built, not a church, but a club-room, which stood for a year and a half as the only competitor of fourteen saloons. It is called the Red Dragon, and is used both as club-house and church. So successful has the venture been that the bishop hopes for the means to repeat it else-where. He sketched the work among the natives, telling of our schools at many points, where devoted women are training the Eskimo and Indian children. One shuddered a little at the description of the "igloo church" at Point Hope, inside the arctic circle, where the atmosphere was so thick that the lights went out, and the condensation hitting the roof dropped to the floor and froze there. But shut your eyes, said the bishop, listen to the

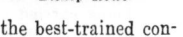

Bishop Rowe

responses and the singing, and you might think yourself in the best-trained congregation in the States.

Bishop Spalding, of Utah, gave a remarkable summary of the founding, organization, and progress of Mormonism, declaring that if the Church had done her duty in the Middle West in the early part of the nineteenth century the country might have been saved from this religious fanaticism. He believed there was in Mormonism a blind groping after, and missing of, the truths which the Church has in her keeping. After a graphic account of the organization, theology and ritual of this grotesque but powerful sect, the bishop called attention to the fact that the Church in Utah, in the midst of a Mormon population, a pioneer combating forces as impregnable as heathenism, can no more support itself than can the Church in China. He viewed as most hopeful the work among young Mormons in college towns, where church and club-house stand together.

The Third Week

THE LAYMEN'S MISSIONARY MEETING

THE mass-meeting on Sunday night, October 16th, brought out the greatest audience since the opening service. Our churches in the city had omitted their evening services and urged their congregations to be present in Music Hall. It certainly looked as though they had done so.

Mr. Samuel Mather, of Cleveland, acted as chairman of the meeting, and in his brief opening address set forth something of the history and purposes of the Laymen's Missionary Movement. He then introduced the first speaker, the Rev. George Craig Stewart, of Evanston, Ill., who told of the Chicago Missionary Congress. Chicago and Edinburgh, said the speaker, are associated with a great movement, which has been sweeping over the world, teaching men that they cannot be converted to Christ without being converted to His cause. Why have we been so slow in responding? Because we have been too busy deciding how we shall organize, and march, and who shall lead. Yet now there is a spirit pervading every Christian body looking toward unity. Shall the vision become vapor? How shall we go about the King's business? By using business methods. A man once said of us: "When I look over your congregations I say, 'Where are the poor?' but when I reckon up your missionary offerings I say, 'Where are the rich?'" The speaker then gave some practical examples of how the weekly missionary offering and the every-member canvass had again and again resulted not only in paying all missionary obligations, but in placing on a more substantial footing the local finances and benevolences of the congregation.

The second speaker was to have been Mr. W. R. Stirling, of Chicago, who is well known to Churchmen of the Middle West. A great and recent bereavement prevented his attendance, but he sent the following telegraphic message, which was read to the audience:

GENERAL CONVENTION, CINCINNATI, O.:

I very greatly regret it is impossible for me to keep my engagement to speak upon "Business Methods Applied to a Man's Task." May I be permitted to make one or two suggestions?

First: Interest follows knowledge. Business men should be more systematically, frequently, and intelligently informed about the work that is being carried on all over the world by the many heroes among the bishops and clergy of our Church.

Second: No general would leave his post or his army and come home to buy supplies to clothe and feed his men; no manager of a large corporation would do a clerk's work. We men should discourage our missionary bishops from leaving their posts to become mere solicitors for funds, by encouraging them with liberal gifts, proportional to the needs in their fields. These needs should be made plain to us from pulpit and chancel by clergy and lay speakers; the latter, I believe, would be frequently the most effective.

Third: Familiarize us with the work of our great corporation, the Church (in which we are all stockholders), all over the world, by means of geographical charts, showing vital and startling facts; show us and tell us facts that perhaps we are too lazy or indifferent to read; make our shortcomings clear to us in no uncertain language.

Fourth: Our failures and shortcomings are partly due to our inadequate policy; ask us for something worth the attention of a business man. Aim high. Challenge every soul that has the ability to give in hundreds and thousands of dollars to do so. Urge every soul to ask the question, "What is my share?" not in proportion to what some other soul gives, or fails to give, but in proportion to my own means. There can be no evasion, no proxy, no substitute in this business of the Master. Establish the principle of the "every member" canvass and a weekly pledge, and aim at a minimum offering of ten

cents per week from every soul, not merely communicants, and the resulting
millions will evangelize the world in this generation.

Fifth: Be bold and be systematic, get close to the people through Department Missionary Councils and the Laymen's Forward Movement. Use us;
demand our personal service; advertise and follow up as men do in ordinary
business. Adopt the Ohio plan of dividing the congregation among a group
of men to follow up.

Sixth: If it be possible adopt this plan of publicity: at the top of every
page of every number of every Church paper, whether general, diocesan or
parochial, print some such challenge as the following, for at least the next
twelve months: "A minimum weekly gift is desired of ten cents per week
from every soul in the Church ten years of age and over. Those who can
give in tens and hundreds of dollars are expected to do so. Give what *costs*,
according to your ability, and receive the blessing." I earnestly hope that the
Convention will adopt a forward policy worthy of the task, namely: "To tell
it out among the heathen that the Lord is King."

"Money and the Kingdom" was the subject of Mr. Alfred E. Marling, of
New York, a member of the Presbyterian Church and chairman of the great
Missionary Congress that met in Chicago. He talked as a business man to business men, in what he described as the plain and homely
language which men of the street use to one another.
I have just been reading, said the speaker, of a road in
Iowa, 180 miles long, which was built in one hour. By
a concerted plan bodies of men turned out all along the
line, set to work at the same moment, and at the end of
the hour the road was finished. Can't we get together
and build a highway for the King? Money is stored-up
personality. If not linked with personality it is useless.
A pile of gold dollars has no power until someone takes
hold of them. The question is not what I make of my
money, but what I let it make of me. Making money
is a good game, but using the money you have made, that
it may be turned into power, is a better one. Link it with
the Kingdom. A man without a vision is only a drudge,
and the best vision is that which our Master shows us.
His Kingdom can't advance without us. We have Him whom we call life eternal;
shall we not share Him? "I say to you men, and especially to the younger ones
among you (for I'm sorry that the vision came to me so late): You've got only one
life to live for your Master. Live it!"

Alfred E. Marling

No one is more eagerly listened to, wherever and whenever he may speak,
than Mr. George Wharton Pepper, of Philadelphia, who made the closing address of the evening. Our Christian responsibility in these last days, said Mr.
Pepper, is to demonstrate that our Lord's philosophy is the solution of the age-
long problem of how to live a noble and a happy life. It is because we are so sure
it will stand this test that we have left parish and counting-room and office, and
have come here to spend many days in planning how we may make that demonstration more effective. But let us not be so busy Christianizing the other fellow that we don't take time to be real Christians ourselves. No amount of giving—even if it reached the point of sacrifice—will take the place of personal
service. If we are not making a thing our own, we cannot really share it with
others. Christian doctrines are not merely ancient symbols or undisputed truths;
they are formulas for solving the eternal problems of daily life. Personal devotion and the sacraments of the Church are the source and spring of unselfish
social service. The missionary enterprise is only the world-wide application of
the love and helpfulness which we have learned close at hand. He loves all children better who better loves his own. The speaker then went on to give concrete

instances of work which men might do, and the mission field to which he call
attention was one close at hand. He urged their interest in the young life of r
land; a better support for our Church schools and colleges; a personal and Chi-
tian interest in the students who crowd our undenominational institutions. Th,
he said, may seem a domestic problem, but it touches foreign missions as w..
Students from China and Japan are crowding into our universities. Shall e
make Christians of the men who are here in training to become leaders of thr
nations? He told of a young Chinaman in the University of Pennsylvania, w,
after being brought under sympathetic Christian influence, had stood up ce
night and said: "I see now what my country needs. My people might acque
all your learning, might use all your machinery and surround themselves with l
your comforts, but they would be the same people still. What they need is
great enthusiasm. Not enthusiasm for a truth, but for a sublime leader; and
know of no Leader who can awaken it except your Christ. I shall become
Christian."

OUTPOSTS IN THE ISLAND WORLD

THE missionary events of the concluding week were the joint sessions of the tw
Houses on Monday and Wednesday afternoons. The first was devoted
hearing from our leaders in the island world. The man who stands at th
cross-roads of the Pacific, Bishop Restarick, of Honolulu, said: "Outposts shou
be strong, not weak; and we whom the Church has set in them are trying to ma
them as impregnable as possible." Such an outpost
the Hawaiian Islands. They may be called an expe-
ment station in foreign missions. The bishop told
the Church's effective work among the native Hawaiian
of how we are reaching the large Chinese populatio
and training from among them men who return
China, carrying an earnest Christianity with them;
the Japanese also, who crowd the five missions whi
we maintain among them, eager to be taught; of t
Koreans who in one mission alone number thirty-eig
communicants. One of these, when baptized, asked
be named "Jubilate." When told that this was not
personal name, he replied, "I know that; but it is
the Prayer Book, and it is the way I feel in becoming
Christian." Since going to the Islands, nine years ag

Bishop Restarick

the bishop has seen the lay-workers increase fro
one to twenty-nine. The seven clergy have become twenty, and the offerings ha
grown from $7.000 to $37,000, while the value of Church property has increas
more than fourfold.

Perhaps the most striking feature of the session was the speech of Mr. Y.
Kong, a Chinese presbyter working among his own people at St. Peter's, Honolul
to whom the bishop had given ten minutes of the time allotted to Hawaii. M
Kong, who has been twenty years in the Hawaiian Islands, emphasized the gre
influence which the Chinese there are exerting upon the Orient. "Foreign-bo
Chinese," he said, "are affecting all China in education, commerce and religion
He told of the generosity of the poor folk in his mission, and of the large sacrific
they make in thankfulness for their Christian faith. His 150 communican
give more in proportion to their means than any congregation in America.
woman who earns $2 a week pledged $30 for the Church; a man who sells peanu

on the corner gives $50; with an average income of $1 a day many are giving from $100 to $150. "They do all what they can," said the speaker, "but of many things we still have need."

Bishop Knight spoke concerning Cuba and the Canal Zone. He said that the weather which the committee was furnishing in Cincinnati made the dweller in the tropics feel at home. He told first of the Isthmus and its great work; of how the Church is trying to care for the great army of 25,000 laborers and 8,000 virile Americans, who are engaged in the greatest work which a government ever undertook. Of Cuba, he said that the United States Government had given these people much, but could not give all they need. They need instruction in the principles of right living. The Church of liberty must complete the work begun by the government of liberty. He told of the splendid growth of the work in the last six years. Where there were then two

Bishop Knight

clergy we now have twenty, assisted by thirty other workers. The property then valued at $10,000 is now conservatively estimated at $168,000. Of our 1,500 communicants more than one-half are natives.

Last upon the programme was Bishop Brent, of the Philippine Islands, who said that he had no such story of inspiring progress to bring to the Church at home; yet much had been accomplished in the Philippines. The work there is peculiarly diversified and difficult. First, of course, we must provide for our own; and upon the large body of young Americans throughout the Islands the work centring about the cathedral in Manila is a great influence for good. "We are striving to be," he said, "in these islands the Church of the reconciliation." Only recently a body of Methodists and Baptists in one of the principal ports had urged him to send them a spiritual leader. But it is the glory of our Church that she does not confine herself to great and populous nations. We have gone among the shy folk of the mountains, and at Baguio, Sagada and Bontoc are bringing the Igorots to the knowledge of Christ; and we are finding in them, especially in the children, the possibility of a Christian culture equal to our own. He showed how here, as elsewhere, the great hope of the future is in the children, and the Church which would serve must be the teaching Church. "I was once," he said, "an enthusiast for secularized education, but that time is past. I venture to say that education is a menace to man's truest welfare unless conscience and character are being lifted up day by day. We hope for a Christian nation, but shall not have it unless somehow, *somewhere*, we have Christian education."

MEXICO, PORTO RICO, BRAZIL, AFRICA

"IN the great chess-game where human beings are the pieces," said Bishop Aves, of Mexico, in the opening address at the last joint session Wednesday afternoon, "the king, the queen and the bishop have disappeared, but the knights and castles are still on the board, and the pawns remain pawns. A representative republic is only now slowly emerging in Mexico. Spain's 00 years of rule put the mark of feudalism upon the nation. There are only wo classes—the few who rule, and the many who obey. Humboldt said that Mexico was a beggar sitting on a bag of gold. The saying is true to-day. The peon has een in succession slave and serf and soldier, but none of the gold has ever reached he beggar. It is the peon for whom I plead; for the poor creatures in their mud uts. Ambition is the child of hope. How can men be thrifty or ambitious who re born and live and die without hope? It is to such that much of our work in

Mexico is directed. We have given them corn to dull the mortal edge of fami[,]
and blankets to cover their nakedness; we have a house of industry where a f[w]

Bishop Aves

of the women can earn enough to exist upon; we sh[l]
try to reach some of them with physicians and to deve[o]
our settlement work in the City of Mexico. Yet n[e]
of these touch the cause of the evil. They need a cha[n]
for self-support. Our only great and lasting serv[e]
must be rendered through education, by raising up[a]
middle class out of the eleven millions of peons who fo[r]
so terrible a majority of Mexico's fifteen millions. [t]
has been said that we exterminated the Indian, a[n]
Mexico enslaved him. Who shall say which was t[e]
greater shame? But to the ruling class also the Chur[h]
has a mission. Their successful revolt against [t]e
tyranny both of the foreigner and of the Church has l[t]
many of them alienated from religion. The message[:]
Him whose Kingdom was not of this world, brought b[y]
Church free from political alliances, may meet th[e]

need and win their allegiance.

After Bishop Aves had spoken, a few moments were given to Bishop Greer,[ ]
New York, whose name did not appear upon the printed programme. He ask[d]
leave to say a word concerning the American Church Institute for Negro[.]
Established four years ago, it is gathering up and correlating our scattered a[d]
sporadic efforts toward education. Five schools, in different parts of the Sou[h],
are united under its supervision. Church people do not seem to know, but th[y]
should be made to know, that we have an institute which in the number of [ ]
students and in the scope of its work ranks with Hampton and Tuskegee. [W]
can help mightily to solve the problem of the colored race. "The Roman Chur[h,]
awake to the need, is raising $1,000,000 for this purpose. I ask from the Chur[h]
not one dollar less."

Bishop Van Buren, of Porto Rico, drew a touching picture of the embarra[s]
ments and difficulties against which a missionary bishop contends. He told [ ]
the school where a little child comes, bringing his own
chair, in the hope that he may be admitted, but must be
turned away because there is no room. He told of the
hospital which had been built as a witness to the tender
mercy of Christ through His Church. There was, he
said, in that island more than enough work for all the
Christian forces represented there, in the fight which
must be waged against sin, Satan and death; and he
urged his need for volunteers—young men, good men,
who are without family ties.

"I claim," said Bishop Kinsólving, of Brazil, "a
share in the distinction wherein a missionary bishop who
spoke at a former session believed that he stood alone.
I, too, am an American bishop without an American
congregation." Remember, as you think of the 1,200

Bishop Van Buren

communicants in Brazil, that each one represents an absolute gain to the Church. They were not received by transfer, but we[ ]
won by the message. Our equipment and work are evangelistic. As yet [w]
have neither hospital nor educational institution; we are simply preaching t[e]
Gospel. What have we accomplished? There are nine churches, worth $150,00[ ]
which are as sufficient for the needs of the cities where they are located as are o[r]
churches in Cincinnati. We have also focussed our effort upon a native ministr[y]

I went to Brazil twenty-one years ago and have multiplied myself by twenty-one. Of this number seventeen are native clergy, fourteen of them priests; splendid men and living epistles of their countrymen. And still we are extending the work. Recently we planted the Church in Rio de Janeiro with its 1,000,000 people. Our two missions there, under Dr. Brown, have doubled since July. Up toward Pernambuco we are now extending the firing-line, a distance of 2,000 miles. You talk about the size of Texas. What is little Texas compared with Brazil? I sent some prayer books to a band of Christian folk at the head-waters of the Amazon. They travelled 5,500 miles after leaving my door. What do we need? The time has come for schools. Having sown far and wide we must begin to plant deep. We have our vision for Brazil, and I believe that this dear Church, which in the present Convention is doing such great things to extend the Kingdom, will help us to realize that vision.

Bishop Kinsolving

This final session of the Convention as a missionary body was fittingly closed by one who directed our thought far across the ocean to that which was so long called the Dark Continent. Bishop Ferguson, our devoted Negro bishop in Liberia, reminded us that sixty years ago in Cincinnati, the first missionary bishop for Africa, John Payne, was elected by the General Convention. "I come to you," he said, "as a fruit of his labors, as one raised up in the field, who owes what he is to the work this Church has done in Africa." Twenty-five years ago Bishop Ferguson was called to the episcopate. What has been accomplished since then under an African bishop? Then 1,800 had been baptized, since then nearly 7,000; to the 1,035 confirmations then recorded, 3,367 have been added; the 419

Bishop Ferguson

communicants have become 2,400; the nine schools of that day are now forty-one, and the six churches twenty-two; the clergy, lay-readers and catechists which then numbered thirty-two, are now ninety-six; and the Church property has increased from $23,000 to $121,000. The people, said the bishop, are more and more learning self-support, and give generously when they have the money, but most of them are very poor. It is his conviction that the establishment of industrial schools, where trades may be learned and the young people taught the dignity of labor, is of first importance to the work. Little beyond agriculture is now possible for them. For the schools already established and for those which should be built the gifts of the Church are needed. He asked also for two women who would teach the girls how to work. In closing he told of the Kroo chapel near Monrovia, whose congregation is so eager for an adequate building that the men are quarrying stone, and the women are carrying it upon their heads to the site of the new building.

The story of Liberia brought the missionary sessions to a close, but the last words were those of the Presiding Bishop, who acted as chairman. With the earnestness and fire which always characterize the admonitions of this veteran missionary he dismissed the assembly to their allotted tasks, far and wide throughout the world, urging patient work and confident courage, and praying God's blessing upon their labors undertaken in His Name.

With the words of the benediction the joint session stood adjourned until 1913.

STATISTICS FROM THE EDINBURGH CONFERENCE

SHOWING WORK DONE IN BEHALF OF THE NON-CHRISTIAN WORLD

General and Evangelistic Summaries

Ordained missionaries	5,522
Physicians (men)	641
Physicians (women)	341
Lay missionaries not physicians (men) . . .	2,503
Married women, not physicians	5,406
Unmarried women, not physicians	4,988
Total foreign missionaries (physicians who are ordained not counted twice)	19,280
Ordained natives	5,045
Unordained natives (preachers, teachers, Bible-women and other workers)	92,918
Total of ordained and unordained workers . . .	98,388
Principal stations	3,478
All other sub-stations	32,009
Church organizations	16,671
Communicants added during year 1907 . . .	127,875
Total communicants	1,925,205
Total baptized Christians (living)	3,006,373
Total native Christian adherents, including baptized and unbaptized, all ages	5,291,871
Sunday-schools	24,928
Sunday-school membership, including teachers and pupils .	1,198,602
Native contributions	$2,726,900

Contributions for One Year for Work among Non-Christians

American and Canadian societies . . .	$10,037,275
Australasian societies	390,000
British and Irish societies	10,483,755
Continental societies	3,334,260
South African societies	488,855
West Indian societies	6,000
Societies in Africa, except South Africa . .	80,685
Societies in Asia	524,665
Societies in Malaysia	10,630
	$25,356,125

THE CHURCH WAGON EN ROUTE

A CHURCH WAGON IN SOUTHERN
WYOMING

By the Reverend Theodore Sedgwick

WHEN Bishop Thomas was chosen to lead the Church in Wyoming he was given a difficult and, at the same time, a most interesting work. It is difficult, because the people are scattered and inaccessible, and interesting because they are a fine type. They seem like the survival of the fittest. The softer and less determined have stopped where the soil would quickly respond to effort. The men in Wyoming, whether raising sheep on the sage-brush prairies or cattle on the boundless ranges or establishing farms by bringing water from a distance to their land in great irrigating ditches—they all are determined to make good, and "win out" in a life which soon becomes fascinating. The women go with the men, and endure hardness by living on lonely ranches, five or forty miles from their neighbors, with smiling faces and without complaint. People who will overcome the difficulties of a country capable of a

drought in summer which makes the stretches of treeless prairie a veritable desert, and which in winter often freezes the sheep and cattle by the thousand (as it did last winter, when they were caught without feed by the deep snows), are a people of character and purpose.

There is a railway across the south of Wyoming, another that goes two-thirds across the middle of the state, and a third which runs across the north. Along the eastern edge you can get by rail from the first to the second, and soon another railroad will connect the second with the third—everywhere else horses are your only resource.

To reach these scattered settlements and ranches Bishop Thomas fitted out a wagon, which has spent the summer zigzagging across the state, bringing the Church to a people who welcome her. On July 1st four of us started from Laramie, which is close to the Colorado line, and travelled 350 miles to Shoshoni, about the centre of the state, which we reached toward the end of the month, and where Bishop Thomas met the wagon on August 1st. He then covered the northern part, going through the Yellowstone Park, and finishing this interesting trip in Jackson's Hole, among the Teton Mountains.

The Rev. Robert M. Beckett drove the wagon. He has charge of a country sixty miles by forty, of which Jackson is the centre, where he lives and is building a church. He is ninety miles from the railroad, and the pioneer in this notorious region. The other two were students at the University of the South, who are looking forward to the ministry. They had been brought up in the Church of the Holy Apostles, Philadelphia, and had received their vision of the ministry from the bishop when he was their rector. In a few years they will be with him again in his splendid work, and now are getting a foretaste of what is to come.

We had a complete outfit, so that we were free to go where we would, camping where we could find water and feed for the horses. We called at each ranch and were always welcomed. The hospitable

people were glad for every opportunity that the Church offered them. I took their names, also the ages of the children, and in very few cases were any of them baptized. As, in most cases, the houses are far from the school-houses they have little chance for a common Sunday-school, and would be glad to receive lesson papers and study them. These should be simple and attractive with the Bible text on them, as they do not, in most cases, know how to use the Bible. At one ranch a bright-looking boy of fourteen came to the door. After making his acquaintance, I asked him if he had a Bible. His face lighted, and he said, "I was reading it when you came." He was fifteen miles from the nearest church and Sunday-school, but the mail could bring him weekly a lesson leaflet.

The second day brought us to a town where lately a church had been built. It was church and school-house in one. They had services whenever a minister chanced to come. I asked permission to officiate, as it was Sunday. I was directed to the home of a good woman who lived in a barn; the house had not been built. I found she kept boarders, and four teen were sitting about the table after the dinner. It was a chance to invite them to the service that evening. I then started on a round-up, visiting every house. At eight o'clock we had thirty-five p r e s e n t ; good organist played our hymns, which were sung with spirit. All were grateful for the service, and some had walked several miles to be present. They begged us to stay with them for a little. We, however, had to push on to another town —twenty miles — which we reached at six o'clock

PITCHING OUR NIGHTLY TENT

HOSPITALITY AT A LONELY RANCH

on the night of the Fourth of July. No festivities were to take place; why not a service? At a saloon, the central building of the town, were a lot of drunken men. Up and down the village street, bareback, the men were running their ponies, yelling and cracking their whips. Whose ear could I get? I called at the hotel; the good woman, a kind of mother in Israel, said, "I am an Episcopal; of course we want a service." She told me to see the gentleman who kept the saloon (he was the school commissioner) and to ask for the use of the school-house. The service was soon arranged. Then we rounded up the people. Like the wise virgins, they brought their lamps with them, as the lamp in the schoolhouse had no oil in it and had gone out. The organ, of which they boasted because it had cost $165, was found, unfortunately, to have been put out of commission by the school children; the hymn books, which were always kept for such occasions, were gone. We could start the hymns, as we had our own books, and, in spite of the small boy who said, "Tell the man to sit down and be quiet," we had a service in which many shared heartily—some of them members of our own Church.

After leaving the towns, sometimes, we would go great distances without passing even a ranch. One day we went thirty-two miles to find water, reaching at nightfall the log-cabin of a man who lived alone and had for six years "bached it." He had lost his wife and child. With only his few horses and his dog he seemed happy and content. He welcomed us; his stove was ours to cook on, his pasture was ours for our horses. So it always was; there never was a more hospitable people.

These separate ranches can only be ministered to by mail. A paper can be sent, and books, so necessary in a lonely

"I'm an Episcopal"

HUNGRY MISSIONARIES

life. The people who live in little settlements can be reached by the parson
on horseback during the week, while he
gives his Sunday duty to his parish. For
instance, Caspar is an interesting and
enterprising city, with its large court
house, and streets with pretty houses
and well-watered lawns, in spite of the
sand and the sage-brush. We have a
good church there, and a genial and hospitable rector. Up the Platte River are
four settlements which can well be cared
for from Caspar. At the first, Bessemer
Flats, fourteen miles, we had service in
a log school-house with a most intelligent and grateful people, who came
through a driving thunderstorm to be
present. Then on to Bates Creek, nineteen miles, where there is another group
of families. Beyond is Alcova, about
forty miles from Caspar. When we held
service there one man came to me and
said, "I was baptized in the Episcopal
Church, and this is only the second time
in twelve years I have had the opportunity of sharing in a service." Another said, "It is seven years since I
have attended church." It was the same
with the women; all are anxious for
regular services. Fourteen miles still
farther on, over a high mountain, with a
road of heavy sand, we reached the Path-
finder Dam, where the Government Reclamation service has been at work for
several years, with a force of three or
four hundred men. They have had no
religious worship. The number at work
now is about two hundred, as the con-

miles long, can be reached by the parson during the week on horseback, and on his return trip he can stop at the ranches with lesson leaflets for the children, often hearing the lessons already learned. So the scattered people can be ministered to.

The unexpected in this country creates added interest. The people are never commonplace. The men have travelled all over the West. After the crops are harvested they often hitch their horses to a "prairie-schooner" and, with their families, are gone for months, gaining an intelligent knowledge of the people and the country. They are posted on all the questions of the day.

On one occasion we had lost our way. It was toward the second day of wandering without much food and no water. We had travelled fifty miles, when, to our great satisfaction, we saw a distant building. It meant water. At this lonely ranch, in the midst of a sandy desert, we found a young woman. Her husband had gone for the day over the range. Around her neck hung a gold chain with a Phi Beta Kappa key. She was a graduate of Wellesley College, and was now a Wyoming bride. She knew her Greek and Latin, and loved her horse on the care-free prairie.

This work needs men like the bishop able to move easily at the call of the few. The Church that is interested enough to go to the people is the Church that wins the interest of the people. They do not care so much who you are, but rather whether you care for them. Such work will fascinate men. It requires endurance, it forgets hardships, but most of all it demands faith, mixed with ordinary common sense.

COMMUNICANTS OF THE AMERICAN CHURCH IN DISTANT MISSION FIELDS

	Established	Communicants
Africa	1835	2,594
Brazil	1889	1,120
Canal Zone	1906	1,852
China	1836	2,206
Cuba	1888	1,355
Haiti	1861	651
Japan	1859	3,190
Mexico	1904	1,187
Philippines	1901	590
Porto Rico	1901	459

THE TEACHERS RELAXING THEMSELVES

CONFIDENCES OVER THE HIBACHI
NO. III
By C. Gertrude Heywood

THE spring vacation had really begun. The dormitory was empty and quiet, for most of the girls had returned to their' homes, and those who were left had gone out to see the cherry blossoms. We teachers were gathered in one of the rooms, allowing ourselves the full measure of relaxation after the effort of promoting four classes and graduating one. An alumna, whose first baby had been born a week ago, had sent the usual present of *"o mochi"*[1] in acknowledgment of the congratulatory gifts that we had sent her on the announcement of the baby's birth.

The *"hibachi,"*[2] unnecessary now for warmth, had been called into service to toast the *"o mochi."* Yoshida San,

much advised by the others, presided over the important task, skilfully turning with chopsticks the flat square pieces, which, little by little, swelled out like inflated marshmallows and took on a warm brown hue. Sugi San grated the *"katsuobushi"*[3] with a sharp kitchen knife; Imai San, armed with another pair of chopsticks, immersed the toasted *"o mochi"* in their bath of *"shoyu"*;[4] while the rest of us helped by suggestions and all ate freely of the delicious cakes. Our little cups of pale green tea sat in front of our knees and were frequently replenished, and with it all, and most freely of all, a lively conversation was circulating.

We had been discussing the graduating class; what changes the five years in the school had wrought in them; their individual capabilities and the probabili-

1. *O mochi:* a cake made of rice flour and used at congratulatory times, such as New Year, births, etc.
2. *Hibachi:* a box of wood, brass or china filled with ashes, in the middle of which are placed a few red coals of charcoal.

3. A dried fish grated and used for seasoning.
4. Japanese soy—a sauce.

ties of their future. From them we gradually drifted to stories of graduates of former years, and at last Kurokawa San said, "But if you want the best story of downright pluck and unwavering determination, you should hear about Hiyama San; how she came to the school and what she did here." They all agreed, and my various questions brought out the facts that Hiyama San, whose father, a "samurai,"[5] died when she was a little girl, came to the school as a servant, worked her way through, and was now teaching mathematics in the Girls' University in Tokyo. "But," they said, "you must ask Hiyama San herself the details; we have never heard them."

Just then, according to the good old proverb, we heard the flap, flap of somebody's "zori"[6] coming down the long corridor, and who should appear in the open "shoji"[7] but Hiyama San herself, come in for an afternoon visit. She was greeted with shouts of laughter, and on demanding the reason was told that she must forthwith tell the story of her life. But in Japan hospitality consists largely in feeding a person, and for some time Hiyama San was busy disposing of the "o mochi" that was toasted for her and the tea that was freely poured. At last, for the fifth or sixth time, but this time with an air of finality, she protested that she could not possibly eat another mouthful or drink another drop, and then her kind hostesses took pity on her and the remains of the feast were sent down to the kitchen. One by one the others went off with various excuses and Hiyama San and I were left alone.

"They were all making jokes about the story of your life, Hiyama San," I said, "but I really wish you would tell me about yourself, if you don't dislike to."

"Oh, no, indeed," she answered, "of course I don't dislike to. I am like most people and enjoy talking about my-

self, but there is really nothing very interesting to tell. What kind of things do you wish to know?"

"I want to know everything about you that you are willing to tell, from the very first that you can remember up to the time that you graduated from St. Margaret's School," was my modest request, and we settled ourselves one on each side of the "hibachi," not because we needed its warmth, but because the few glowing coals, almost lost in their bed of soft ashes, always seem to light the fires of sympathy and confidence in the hearts of those who talk across them.

After a brief pause, Hiyama San began, stopping often to answer my requests for explanations and expansions, and the following is the gist of her story:

"My earliest recollections go back to our home in ———, when my father, mother, brother, sister and I were all together. My father was a very devout man, a follower of the Monto sect of Buddhism. My memories of that time are not very distinct, but one that stands out clearly is of my father going to a temple of Kwannon to worship. The Montoists are supposed to worship only Amida, and I am not sure why my father went to the temple of Kwannon, but I remember perfectly that every day, rain or shine, no matter how late it might be when he came back from the town office where he was employed, he always went to worship. And almost every day I went with him, and on the way he would talk with me, and the burden of his talks, judging from the impression that it left on my mind, was that if I were honest and sincere I might have perfect faith in being protected by—something—Amida, I suppose he called it; as for me, my idea of that protecting power was no more definite than to call it Something. But in spite of that indefiniteness, from those early days, I learned to have faith, and that faith never deserted me. It was so strong, that when my father died, when I was ten years old, I went by myself to that same temple and prayed for him.

---

5. A knight in the old feudal system.
6. Straw sandals worn in the house on the wood floors, but not on the straw mats.
7. Paper sliding doors.

HIYAMA SAN

as long as I were honest and faithful, I should be protected, I made up my mind to leave my aunt and try my fortune in some larger place.

"I packed up just the few clothes that belonged to me and set out one day, meaning to stop first at my mother's and tell her my plan. I persuaded a 'kuru-maya,'[8] who had been employed by my aunt, to take me there—a ride of some twenty miles. My mother was exceedingly surprised to see me. She tried her best to dissuade me, and messengers came from my aunt urging me to return. But nothing could change my mind, and after a short visit I left my mother and went to Osaka.

"In Osaka there were friends and relatives of the family, and I went first to one of them, hoping that I could find some way of supporting myself and studying at the same time. But, although they were very kind to me, I soon saw that it would be impossible for me to accomplish my purpose there. I was continually being urged to get married, and I could not take up any profit-

8. A man who pulls a jinrikisha.

able kind of work because it would be considered as bringing disgrace upon my relatives. But my faith in my ability finally to succeed, and my faith in some protecting power, did not desert me, and I decided that, if Osaka were impossible, I must go to Tokyo.

"There was one circumstance in my Osaka experience that is interesting now as I look back upon it. Next to the house where I lived there was a small Christian church and we could hear the singing of the hymns at the services. My only idea at that time about the 'Yaso'[9] religion was that it was one that taught its followers to be unfaithful to their country and their ancestors, and I regarded it as something to be avoided as carefully as the plague.

"My mind was soon made up to go to Tokyo, and I began to plan the ways and means. I had no money, but I had the few clothes that I had brought with me from my aunt's. Money was more essential than clothes, and after much persuading I finally prevailed upon the woman in whose house I was staying to let me send for a second-hand dealer and sell all but the clothes I needed to wear. If I remember correctly, they brought about twenty yen. In a few days I started for Tokyo, where I knew not a soul, with the clothes on my back, a small parcel containing a few little things and the munificent sum of twenty yen.

"I could not afford to travel by the railway, and when the friend with whom I was staying took me to the boat-landing, there happened one of those strange incidents that justified my never-wavering faith in a protecting power. The man who sold me the ticket (it seems strange to tell now in this busy time when nobody trusts anyone) asked me if I would take a package to a friend of his in Tokyo, and with that package and my own small bundle for baggage I boarded the boat for Yokohama. I don't remember very much about the trip, but even when I reached Tokyo I don't

think I was very much frightened. I had no other place to go, and so I inquired my way to the address on the package given me by the ticket man in Osaka, intending after delivering that to find some place to board until I could get work. The address on the package was No. 38 Tsukiji, the present home of Bishop McKim, then occupied by two women missionaries, and the person to whom the package was addressed was a Japanese woman, who was working for them. After I delivered the package and was about to leave, she asked me where I was going to stay, and when I said I was going to look for a boarding-house, she insisted upon my staying with her for that night at least.

"I told you that I knew no one in Tokyo, but I had known one girl who had come to the Girls' Higher Normal School, and, more or less unconsciously, I had been counting on getting, if not help, at least advice from her. The next morning I started out for the school, but when I reached there I found she had graduated some years before and no one could tell me where she was. I remember that day—there was a drizzling rain and the streets were slimy with mud, and as I turned away with this one faint hope gone, I began to feel the forlornness of my position and to wonder if I had made a mistake. I went back to 38 Tsukiji, because I had no other place to go, and told my new friend about my disappointment. I wonder now how she trusted me so, but she never seemed to doubt my story, and she invited me to stay with her until I should find something to do and some place to stay.

"In just a short time I did find something—work in a factory for weaving the strings of 'haori,' 'obi,'[10] etc., and with much gratitude I left Tsukiji and went to live in the boarding-house of this factory. The people there were very kind to me, and I worked with might and main to learn to do the weaving, receiving in return my board and lodg-

9. Vulgar word for Christian.

10. Articles of Japanese dress.

SOME TEACHERS AND PUPILS OF ST. MARGARET'S SCHOOL

ing, but believing that when I had attained a certain degree of skill they would pay me regularly and I should be able to save, and eventually get the education which was my aim and end. As I think of it now, the people running that factory must have been delighted to find a simple little country girl who would work day after day, from the rising of the sun until the short twilight was nearly gone, and then accept gratefully board and room and a few kind words as a just reward.

"On the first holiday—there were two in a month, the first and fifteenth—I went to Tsukiji, as I was in duty bound by Japanese custom, to tell the woman who had befriended me how I was fixed and to carry her as a token of my gratitude a string for a *haori*, which the forewoman had given me.

"O Cho San, my friend, asked me in detail about my work, and when she learned that I was working without any wage she was exceedingly indignant and said that the factory people were only working on my ignorance and innocence, and that I must not stay there

any longer. She said that the foreigners with whom she lived had told her to get someone to help her, and she asked me to accept the position. I was very loth to do so. I had a strong prejudice against foreigners, and, in addition, I hated and was afraid of the Christian religion. But when O Cho San urged me, remembering my indebtedness to her, I could find no excuse for refusing, and so finally went to live with her.

"The very first Sunday my fears about the Christian religion were realized, for I was told by O Cho San that I would better go to Sunday-school, just to hear what it was like. Courtesy forbade me to refuse, but I went with the determination to let as little as possible of this religion, which taught disloyalty to one's ancestors and country, pass the portals of my ears. Of course I was without a shadow of fear that any of it would ever enter my heart. The teacher gave a simple talk about the protecting love of the one true God. The metaphorical mufflers I had put over my ears were soon snatched off, and my supposedly impenetrable heart was opened

(931)

wide as the firm conviction flashed into my mind, 'Why, this is the God I have been trusting in all my life, and this is the God who has protected me so far in my efforts to rise. But this is the Christian God—am I then a Christian?' It did not take me long to find the answer to this question; I attended Sunday-school regularly, and the more I heard the more I was convinced that the Christian faith was the faith which I must make mine.

"All this time I was living with O Cho San and helping her, but after a few months I came to the conclusion that I could not stay there any longer. O Cho San gave me to understand that I was very unpopular with all of her friends and acquaintances among the cooks, because I worked too hard and so set a higher standard than they wished to live up to. Besides this, I myself had realized, almost from the beginning, that —although some of course were exceptions, and I am sure one could not find a kinder Christian than O Cho San had been to me—association with other cooks and servants was not a refining influence, and I was accomplishing nothing toward realizing my final aim. So I made up my mind that I must try to find something else, and I began to consider possibilities.

"But just then the Providence that was guarding me again intervened; this time in the form of one of the teachers of the mission school for girls next door —St. Margaret's School. The windows of the school looked down on the garden of the house where I lived, and Mrs. Komiya, one of the teachers, looking out every morning early, saw me pulling weeds in the garden. This was not part of my work, but I liked to get up early and go out in the garden to work. So Mrs. Komiya went to O Cho San and asked her about the country girl who seemed to be working so hard, and when O Cho San told her for what purpose I had come to Tokyo she immediately arranged for some of the teachers in the school to give me lessons in the evenings.

I was very happy and grateful, but exceedingly sad, because I did not see how I could keep on living with O Cho San, whose hints about the jealousy of other servants I felt sure were meant as hints that we would better part.

"When Mrs. Komiya heard that I wished to leave she offered me the position, just then vacated, of cook in St. Margaret's School. I accepted at once, feeling that now truly my port was in sight, and that no matter how many reefs of hard work were between me and the dock I should finally land safely. Truly, there was hard work and plenty of it, but it was all overshadowed for me by the fact that every night I was having regular lessons, and was really progressing toward my goal. There were about thirty people to cook for, besides a good deal of cleaning to do. Never did I stay in bed later than four o'clock in the morning and very, very seldom did I go to bed before twelve; often it was one or two before I had finished the day's work; for many things still undone when it came time for my lessons had to be finished after everyone else had gone to bed. Such a life would have been impossible for many people, but I was very strong and have always been able to get along with very little sleep. The thought that I was really succeeding kept me from realizing much bodily weariness.

"One day Mrs. Komiya called me to her and told me that she had seen how much in earnest I was, and as there were scholarships in the school which were for the purpose of helping just such girls as I, she had decided to let me enter the school as a regular pupil on a scholarship. For my answer to this offer I was very much censured at that time by all the teachers. They considered that I showed only rank ingratitude and obstinacy in my refusal to accept the proffered help. Perhaps I was wrong, but I certainly was not ungrateful. I felt that I had set out to accomplish a certain purpose—that I put my faith in God to help me through—that He had done so, so far, and that it would be doubting Him to accept other aid. That is the way I reasoned then, but as I look back now I think perhaps it was just false pride—wanting to do it all myself, without being under obligations to anyone.

"Mrs. Komiya was angry with me for my obstinacy at first, but finding me determined she gave up the idea and then suggested to me that I give up my work as cook and take the position of bell-ringer—that is, ringing the bells for the classes, answering the door and doing various odd jobs. This would bring me much less money, but I should have more time for study and could enter most of the regular classes. I was very glad to do this, and as soon as a new cook was secured I entered on my new duties. Life seemed very easy and very pleasant after that, and I kept that position until I was able to graduate from the school.

"When I came to the school my faith had been strong, but very ignorant and elementary. While I was there I was taught by Mrs. Komiya and others, and learned even more from their lives than their words, and at last was baptized and confirmed—a real Christian.

"The first thing I did after graduation was to write a letter to my mother. I had come to Tokyo seven years before, but during that time had sent no word to and received none from any member of my family or any friend at home. I had come with the determination that if I did not accomplish my purpose it would be because I had died in the attempt, and while there was any doubt I did not want my relatives to know. It was with great relief that I learned my mother was still alive, and her joy over news from me, whom she had thought dead, or worse, was unbounded.

"I began to teach at once in a mission school in Kyoto, but the first summer vacation I went home for a visit, and from that time on was able to help my mother quite a little. I hoped in a few years to carry out my purpose of making a home for her with me, but just as

O Cho San and Hiyama San

I was ready to do so, she was taken sick and died.

"Also, my ambition to be famous has gone the way of most child dreams, but I am happy—oh, so happy! and, although I am not teaching now in St. Margaret's School, I am always ready to give up any position I may have to serve in whatever way I can the school that enabled me not only to get my education, but to know the God in Whom I had believed."

The leaves on the trees in the school garden rustled softly in the gentle spring breeze as Hiyama San's story came to a close. The short twilight had come and was almost gone; the *shoji* was pushed back and we could see the moon just beginning its night's journey across a cloudless sky. Two swallows suddenly chased each other across its bright face and disappeared into the blue depths. All was as quiet as if we were in the lonely country instead of a busy capital.

Hiyama San sighed. "This," she said, "is like a picture of the peace of heart which I found in this school, after a tumult of restless ambition and worldly trouble."

"Do you think," I asked, "that if you had not come to St. Margaret's School, you would have accomplished your purpose just the same?"

"Yes," she answered after a moment's thought, "I should have succeeded in getting my education. Such determination as mine could not have failed. It probably would have taken longer and meant greater hardships. But I cannot bear to think what kind of woman I should have become. My education I could have won, but my character and Christianity are gifts of God through this school. I thank God for it."

Hiyama San is only one of many Japanese women who are thankful for the St. Margaret's School of the past. In the future this same school will have even greater opportunities of doing as much or more for Japanese girls. Will not you, who have read this true story of one of the graduates of the school, help to make its future certain? Fifteen thousand dollars are still lacking for the building of a new recitation hall. Unless this is put up, the Government will withdraw its license and St. Margaret's School, the only school for girls maintained in the district of Tokyo by the Church in America, will be discredited in the eyes of the public and will be obliged to give up its work. Will you not help to make other Japanese girls thankful?

WHAT A PRAYER BOOK DID
By a Florida Missionary

DURING the past winter an invalid woman, as a last attempt to regain health, was sent with her husband, an old soldier and also an invalid, down to the pine woods of Florida. Interested army people provided the expense, which had to be light. The husband was sent to a hospital and died in a few weeks. The wife was sent to the pioneer homestead county to board. She only lived a month and never knew of her husband's death. In the scattered primitive settlement the people of various religions had been too indifferent to gather for worship, and, as they expressed it, "too poor and busy getting a foothold to afford the means to fight the devil with."

This invalid was a good Church-woman and had a prayer book, so while she lived she had a service every Sunday at her bedside and invited the people to come. One Lord's Day while the new-born day was early filling the woods with its sunshine and call to life, she fell asleep, but her well-worn prayer book and Bible were left—a silent witness for the Faith and Truth which had guided her life.

I only knew of this incident after her death when, as missionary on the east coast, I was asked for prayer books and hymnals. A visit soon followed. I found about thirty people, who met on Sundays in continuation of the bedside service, a woman leading them. Since then a number of Episcopalians have been "discovered" within a radius of five miles, who have joined with the others. A church building is imperative now if the work is cared for. The bishop has at their request assumed spiritual oversight and named it All Saints' mission, and I have added it to my several other missions or kindergartens, as a point for monthly visitation. An acre of land to be planted with a hundred grape-fruit trees and cared for and fertilized as long as the donor lives has been given and will in a few years yield an income.

During the past year I completed my twelfth church in the mission field and concluded I would stop. I have said that often before, and yet when the call came I had to start anew and meet the same old discouragements. But the chapels come and are paid for and we give thanks for some loyal souls who realize that the mission appeal is a part of their salvation also.

A TAICHOW FAMILY WHO ENTERTAINED THE MISSIONARY AT DINNER

A PREACHING HALL IN TAICHOW
By the Reverend T. L. Sinclair

TAICHOW is a walled city of 150,000 inhabitants lying east of Yangchow and constituting its first out-station. To reach Taichow one travels by chair, bicycle, wheelbarrow, donkey, or on foot, six miles across country to Hsien Nu Miao, and thence by launch to Taichow. We have had one resident catechist there since March, while a part of the time of a foreigner is given to this work. As yet we have little of which to boast, for we have not been able to start institutional work of any kind, but our preaching hall is open daily, except Saturday, and he who will may hear.

The term "preaching hall" is perhaps misleading. It suggests a service with singing, prayers and reading of Scripture; but that is. not the case in China. If there are any prayers they are few and short. There is no reading of Scripture except that which is to be expounded, and I am afraid many of our friends at home would say there was no singing.

Besides talking, little else is done. Nevertheless there is much of interest to be seen in a preaching hall. The hall is usually a room in a Chinese house, with doors opening on the street; a table, a few chairs, and a number of benches constitute about all the furniture, some scrolls and pictures being added for adornment. At 8 P.M. the doors are opened, and we begin to sing a hymn. The Chinaman being by nature well supplied with curiosity, a head is soon poked in to see what all this noise is about. If the singing is not enough to make him take a seat, a sight of that strange looking, curiously dressed foreigner proves too strong an attraction to be passed by lightly. Curiosity, like misery, loves company, and soon the hall is filled.

After we have asked and exhorted them to be seated, and not to stand in the door, blocking those who want to come in or those going out, we have a short prayer. Meanwhile one or two babies have begun to cry; several children are holding an animated conversation; some man has seen fit to remark to his neighbor that the foreigner's clothes are not like theirs; and somebody else is reading aloud the scrolls on the wall. After we have managed to get a certain degree of quiet, preaching begins. Here we have no limit. The preacher may safely go on as long as there is any one to listen, for he may rest assured that his congregation feel at liberty to leave whenever they are so inclined. He must not be disturbed if some old gentleman attempts to light his pipe over the lamp hanging from the wall, or if someone calls to his neighbor across the street, or if a noise is heard outside and the whole crowd rush out to see the cause of the disturbance. All this happens as a matter of course in China, and must be so regarded.

Next comes what the Chinese call *tan tan* (chat, chat). The preachers come and sit among the people to answer any question they may ask and discuss anything they may wish to discuss. This is a most important part of the work in a preaching hall. As a rule the people

LAUNDRY WORK IN PROGRESS

are willing to stay as long as we are willing to talk to them. I have known them to stay as late as 11:15 P.M., and that night they went because the lamp went out. Although we talk about anything and everything, yet this part of our work is productive of much good. Kindly feeling is produced, friends are made, and we hope some Gospel seed is sown.

It is interesting to study the faces of those who come into the hall. I often wish I could show my American friends our preaching hall in Taichow. Our congregations are of many and varied types. Here is one who with smooth words and smiling face says that he wants to be a Christian. You wonder why he thus declares himself so soon but if you accept him you are not left long in doubt. Here is another whose forbidding face seems to proclaim hardened villainy. Here is one whom you might imagine had just stepped out of one of Dickens's novels; or another with a smile which never comes off. He tells you the preaching is too long, but he stays until eleven o'clock and you know he has come to have a good time. Here are two young ladies who insist on talking while you are preaching. Here is a boy with a fine face whom you wish you might have in your Sunday-school. Here is a baby with rings in its nose and ears who looks at the "foreign devil" and wonders what he is making all that noise about.

One of the most interesting, and most to be pitied, is an old opium smoker. His clothes are ragged; he is dirty and unkempt. He begs us to give him some medicine to stop the craving for opium. Willingly would we do this, but we know the medicine needed is

OUR CATECHIST AND HIS FAMILY

gazing crowd, or if I leave the doors to my room open there is soon a crowd standing in the courtyard gazing in. Moreover, the interest never seems to flag. I believe many of them would stand looking for an hour at a time. Immovable, silent, with blank, expressionless faces they stand and stare, and if they see you every day it is just the same. Although their faces look blank, their minds are not so. They can describe the dress of the foreigner as well as a lady can that of a bride. One often wishes he could look into the brain of a Chinaman, and find out about what he is thinking. There surely is a mechanism there which fits into the skull of no other human. His blank stare is a problem too intricate for the foreigner. but even that stare has its advantages, for it indicates a curiosity which makes us always sure of a congregation. The preaching hall is to them a sort of circus —and the foreigner is the elephant which draws the crowd.

In our talks after the preaching is over the questions asked are enough to test the patience of a Job: What is your honorable name? is the first, of course; then: What is your business? How old are you? What country did you come from? How long did it take to get here? How much did it cost? Did you come on a steamer or by railway? How long

HUTS OF THE FAMINE REFUGEES

have you been here? How much did your clothes cost? Were they made in America or, in China? Why don't you shave your head? How often do you have your hair cut? How often do you bathe? And so on, *ad infinitum.*

They know nothing about our Lord and Saviour, and care less; but as water can penetrate the most hardened soil, so we hope, by the help of Jesus Christ, to plant the Gospel in the hardest heart, and have it bring forth fruit. The same cause which brought them the first time brings them again and again, until at least some come for a more worthy cause. Yet it is, and necessarily must be, slow. Often, as one looks at them and sees how sin and superstition are a part of their very life, the thought comes: What is the use of it all? Can I hope to change the hearts of these people, to remove their ancient traditions, to take away their old customs? Can I take them out of the rut they have been travelling for centuries and make them follow a new path? Can I do this? And then the answer comes: No, not I, but Jesus Christ working through me! Thus one coming in contact with the Chinese day after day has it impressed

upon him that to hope to convert the Chinese to Christianity without the intervention of a higher Power would be absurd, and to attempt it the height of folly. Every true Christian Chinaman is thus a living witness to the divinity of Christ.

Thus we run our preaching hall. Thus we hope to win men for Christ. There is a great need for just such work as this in China to-day. The masses can only be reached in this way. If China as a nation is ever to become Christian this must be our method. If one wants to work for Christ there is a great opportunity here, and there is a great need. East of Taichow is another city of about the same size without a single missionary; north and west there are others, and towns and villages without number. Let us, therefore, "pray the Lord of the harvest that He will send forth laborers into His harvest."

¶

THE new missionary district of Wuhu, set apart from Hankow by act of the General Convention, is the eastern part of the old district, which lies next to Shanghai. It includes the Province of Ngan-whei and the northern part of Kiang-si.

A GROUP OF THE FAMINE SUFFERERS

VIEW OF EAST SOUND

AMONG THE SAN JUAN ISLANDS

By the Reverend J. W. Hard

SET in the midst of the blue waters of Puget Sound, our parish comprises a whole county in this wonderful State of Washington, and is one of the most beautiful and healthful. The San Juan Islands, which comprise the county between the mainland of Washington and Vancouver Island, range in size from several miles in length to mere points of rock, and number somewhere in the hundreds, if you can count them all. Our Church has missions upon Orcas Island, the largest of the group, where I have four stations. Church work was started here in the early days, and we have two church buildings, one at East Sound and another at West Sound, seven miles away. About six miles further on is Deer Harbour, where we hold service in the public school. Olga is about eight or nine miles in another direction from East Sound, and here we hold service in the hotel dining-room. Until I came here there had been nothing but occasional lay services for a period of five years, and I have an uphill task before me in trying to gather what remains into Church work again—far harder than starting a new work in a new district.

DRAWING THE NET
The foam which appears at the bottom of the net is a struggling mass of salmon

The catch. There are 3,000 salmon aboard this scow

Sundays are busy days. On one Sunday I preach in East Sound at eleven, and walk to West Sound for service at three; then at Deer Harbour for service at eight, returning the next day by steamer. The next Sunday I preach at Olga at eleven, getting there by a boat which leaves at 7:45 A.M., and returning to East Sound at seven in the evening, where I have service at eight. As the island is mountainous, the roads are of necessity rather steep, and not always straight, and I have to "pack" books for services in an old army knapsack on my back. I am promised more books to avoid this, but I have carried them for many months now; and in hot summer weather, when roads are dusty, you can imagine I have enough healthy exercise, to say the least.

Our population is scattered, there being nothing like a town or even a village of any size except at Friday Harbour, the county seat on San Juan Island.

The industries of the place are fruit and dairy-farming, lumber and salmon fishing. I am sending pictures of a salmon trap, and you will gather from them something of what happens. In a week or so now the boats will be loaded down with pears and apples, and this will continue until the spring. Farms for the most part are not large, as help is hard

to get, and orchards need constant and untiring attention to keep down the pests of one sort and another. We grow the finest cherries in the world. One of our neighbors sent some to the Japanese Emperor last year. Our apples are not as fine in color as those raised in eastern Washington, but we think them of superior flavor. Of course this may be insular prejudice, but they are the best we get.

Our scenery is simply beyond compare. There are mountains and valleys, deep bays and steep cliffs, alternating with smooth stretches of water and distant islands, tall firs and cedars and tiny flowers, eagles and humming birds, together with almost all varieties of feathered folk between these two extremes.

I had hoped when I came here to have a small launch, in order to reach other islands, but I have not realized my hope and have made up for it by walking to as many places as I can reach on foot. It is a fairly strenuous life, to say the least. Congregations vary a great deal: at Deer Harbour, from fifty to seventy-five; at West Sound about twenty to thirty; at East Sound from fifteen to twenty, and at Olga according to the number of summer visitors, for it is but a summer resort.

The Deer Harbor school-house, where service is held

B. Richmond

struction in them. And in spite of the many, often well-equipped, native schools which are opened all around us from year to year we are encouraged by an increase; a small school grows large enough to warrant being divided into two grades, or a new school is opened in some out-station.

The course of study is carefully laid out to lead up to the work of the higher schools. The general rules are the same for all day-schools, except as they have to be modified to suit local conditions. It is our aim to employ as teachers our own communicants, though this is not always possible.

A mission day-school forms the most striking contrast to the old-fashioned native school, of which plenty still remain. Just outside the Grace Church compound, in the native city of Shanghai, is a school of the true, old-fashioned type. In a small, dirt-floored room, with no light except from the door, some twenty small boys gather daily. They keep long hours, from somewhere between seven and eight in the morning to five or six at night, and it is a relief to know that the poor little urchins are very irregular in attendance and have a long recess for breakfast at odd times in the forenoon. They can be heard from afar, studying at the top of their voices, memorizing Chinese classics, which they do not understand; they may be seen, standing with their backs to the teacher, "backing the book," that is, reeling off page after page at lightning speed. The small boy whose ambitious parents have sent him to school at the age of three or four, disconsolately dangles his poor little feet from his stool and learns characters written out on small squares of red paper. The teacher is often not to be found in the school-room, and there is no discipline except that of blows.

Now come inside the Church compound. Here is a girls' school of two grades, fifty little girls, with two teachers, and on the other side of the compound a boys' school of the same size, also with two teachers. Though by no means ideally equipped, the school-rooms are light and clean; there are black-boards, maps and pictures, and the children are supplied with slates. School begins at nine o'clock with prayers in the church, and closes at four, an hour's recess being given at noon and a recess of fifteen or twenty minutes in the middle of the morning and afternoon sessions. The pupils are divided into classes and everything they learn is carefully explained. They are taught arithmetic, geography, and elementary science, and every day they sing and have physical drills. They are controlled by firm, but just and gentle means, and every effort is made to inculcate habits of regular, punctual attendance. Clean hands, faces and garments, and smooth hair are required. They come to church and Sunday-school on Sundays. In most of our boys' schools English is taught, and in some places it is necessary to teach it in the girls' school, that we may not lose desirable pupils. The children are mostly from the respectable middle-class, with a few from wealthy families, and some from the very poor. This of course varies with the locality of the school. Generally the parents are deeply interested in the school, coming on invitation to visit it, and then perhaps being induced to come to church. In a number of cases women have been brought in through a little son or daughter in the school. Chinese mothers are proud of their children, and when they say with great humility that "little brother" or "little sister" is very stupid and troublesome, they are yearning to be assured that quite the opposite is the case.

Now and again incidents come to our knowledge which prove that good is done by these schools: Some years ago, a lady worker in one of the missions in Shanghai, visiting a little country village, came across an old woman who listened eagerly, and at last exclaimed that she herself was a Christian, and knew the Lord's Prayer, the Creed and the Ten Commandments. She proved that

OUR LETTER BOX

Intimate and Informal Messages from the Field

A TYPICAL MOUNTAIN FAMILY

A correspondent sends us the story of her visit to one of the little churches hidden away in the coves of the Virginia mountains:

OUR week in the Blue Ridge Mountains was nearing its end when, on a lovely Sunday afternoon, we set out in search of "the chapel-in-the-mountains" of which we had heard. For a mile and a half we followed a winding road bordered with trees and ferns, while the little mountain rivulets tinkled their way over the rocks toward the Shenandoah River. Presently we came in sight of the pretty frame church recently erected at this spot—the first of its kind among these hills, and peculiarly the mountaineers' own. How they value their place of worship could be judged from the throng of men, women and children — perhaps a hundred — who crowded about the door and filled the attractive interior.

We were impressed with the earnestness of the mountain people, and there seemed to be especially good material in the dozen or so young men who took part in the service, joining heartily in

Some Sunday-school pupils

(943)

the singing of the simple hymns led by one of their number. One could but wonder whence came and how lived those many little children and their elders who come from forest hamlets to gather in the chapel at "Sunday afternoon preaching." One of the chief workers at this chapel is a poor woman, the mother of a large family, who lives near by in a tiny, whitewashed cabin, better kept than most of its kind, with a little patch of garden and a few fruit trees for shade. She it was who said to us: "Ain't it a *grand* church? We are all trying to help pay for the pews ($72); next month's to be a feast day, when the bishop comes. I think the Episcopalians do things just right! We're real proud of it all, whether we belongs or not."

It was the earnest hope of the rector that the debt on the church (about $200) might be paid, in order to consecrate the building "when the bishop

came," and we trust his labors w crowned with success. Nowhere, think, could there be greater need the Church than in this mount region of old Virginia, known by old-fashioned name of Snicker's Gap.

¶

An eye-witness writes us about a farewell party in China:

WELCOMES and farewells are m much of in China and Japan. it was natural that Deaconess Phe after five years of devoted service in Hilda's School, Wuchang, should rece from the teachers and pupils an unus send-off before starting home on furlough.

It was on a hot summer's day tow the end of June that the comp gathered in the main school-room for formal exercises connected with t particular farewell. First came a hyr then a prayer by Mrs. Tsen, the matr (In the picture she is standing at D coness Phelps's right.) After that one the girls read a farewell address writ in high classical Chinese, inscribed "Lady-Scholar" Phelps. Then came great item of the programme, when newly-organized Chorus Class sang v nicely in English the greater part Stainer's "Crucifixion." This was tended to be as far as possible a surpr to the principal, who had been wish in vain until quite lately for some who would take hold of the music of school.

Then came an affecting little Chin poem recited by one of the small gi But the thought of the poem—that saying farewell to "Fay Hsiao Ji (Chinese for Miss Phelps) who was ing so far away across the ocean, v too much for the little speaker, w could only finish in a torrent of tea wherein most of the other girls join Miss Phelps then responded in a sh Chinese speech, reminding all that was coming back again soon, and th though her body would be in Amer her heart would be in Wuchang.

Home of the chief church worker

After this every one adjourned for the taking of a photograph, and there were tea and sandwiches and many good-bys on the lawn. The little girl who had recited the poem begged that she might go with Miss Phelps to her house and spend with her the last night in Wuchang.

One can only add that when Deaconess Phelps does return it is earnestly to be hoped that she may bring back with her the few thousands of dollars which will make it possible to take in more of the many girls who now must be turned away; $15,000 will enable the School to double its numbers. Another $15,000 would almost give room for the 300 girls who could soon be assembled—if there were enough teachers from America. How long, how long is it to be before the women and the means materialize?

¶

The Rev. B. L. Ancell, the leader of the North Kiangsu Mission, with its headquarters at Yangchow, China, writes:

WE have secured a large building lot here in Yangchow, on which we propose to build a school for boys. A house has been rented in Nanking, and a native priest will be located there at once. We already have a small band of communicants in that city. Prayers are asked for the Nanking work."

A young lay-reader, who during the summer has been doing missionary work in Eastern Oregon, tells of a trip with Bishop Paddock:

A SHORT time ago the bishop wrote suggesting that I meet him at Mitchell, seventy-five miles distant, and drive there from Canyon City. I started early Wednesday morning and drove all that day over dusty roads, reaching Dayville that evening. Here I spent the night, finding one woman who knew something of our Church. She secured the schoolhouse for our meeting on the following evening—when we were to come back that way—and unearthed an old Church Hymnal, which she had owned for many years; but she had no prayer book.

I drove on over very steep roads, making one stop at midday, and reached Mitchell at 7:30 P.M. After "putting up" my horses I started to find the bishop and discovered him just coming in at the other end of town on the stagecoach. It was now 7:40 P.M. We had secured the Baptist Church for our meeting (the only church building in the town) and the Baptist minister came to meet us. About 8:15 the service began with a hymn sung by the Baptist choir from their own hymn books. In the meantime I had distributed copies of "The Evening Prayer Leaflet" to the gradually-arriving congregation. Sixty copies were given out, and less than a dozen returned at the close of the service. There were about sixty-five people present, including a goodly proportion of men. There had never been a prayer book service there before.

We left Mitchell at 5:30 the next morning and arrived at Dayville about 6:30 P.M. After a hurried supper we held the arranged-for service in the school-house. There is no church building of any kind here. Nineteen people were present—five women and fourteen men. Of the two saloons in town one closed, but the other refused to do so.

Left Dayville at 5:45 next morning (Saturday) and after driving all day reached Canyon City at 5:30 P.M. After supper the bishop met the guilds, and at 8 P.M. held service in St. Thomas's Church, baptizing one person and confirming two. Next morning (Sunday) the bishop celebrated the Holy Communion and preached the sermon. That afternoon we drove fifteen miles to Prairie City and had service in the public hall, to which many men came. Next morning the bishop celebrated Holy Communion and baptized a small boy, both at a private house. That same afternoon we drove twelve miles to a local camping resort. Some of our communicants there had secured the dance hall (the only large structure on the grounds) and had decorated it with wild flowers and greens. Nearly the entire camp came to the service that evening. The dance hall proprietor could let us have the hall only for an hour, so at the close of the service the bishop baptized an infant out under the trees, with everyone standing around—and reverent too. I held a lantern for the bishop to see, and someone else held another lantern for the godparents. The next morning, after a celebration at eight in the dance hall, when fifteen people communicated, we drove back to Prairie City, and the bishop started for Burns, some eighty-five miles away, by stage.

Now this is a good sample of what the bishop has been doing for the last three months. Since June 1st he has travelled about two thousand miles by stage, being on the road nearly every day and holding services almost every night.

It is a mystery to me how he is able to stand it. Oregon has more post-offices fifty miles away from the railroad than any other state or territory in the Union. This makes hard, long and difficult journeys a necessity.

¶

A young Presbyterian layman, engaged in railroad construction work in Alaska, writes to a friend at home:

I SPENT Sunday in Cordova and as there were two steamers discharging their cargoes at the pier, I passed several hours at the dock, watching them. The bridge steel for the bridges formed a large part of one cargo, and it was interesting to watch the unloading.

Then Cordova contains a place known as the "Red Dragon," maintained by the Episcopal Church. Prayers are said there on Sundays. There are comfortable chairs and seats, a good collection of books and magazines, and a pool table. The place is a sort of outpost of practical Christianity in the Copper River country; a good place in which to spend a few hours, and I enjoyed being there while in Cordova. Cordova contains no resort, aside from twenty or more saloons, or worse places; and the "Red Dragon" is very popular among quite a number of men who work in, or near, Cordova.

I do not know who was responsible for the "Red Dragon," but whoever built that place did a good work.

¶

The call to the ministry as a young Japanese Christian heard it is suggested by this message:

A STUDENT told me a week ago that during his vacation at home, where he is the only Christian in the town the people came in such numbers to ask about his new religion, that he came to devote most of his time to them, and moreover, became so impressed with the vastness and ripeness of the field and his own responsibility to help reap it, that he decided to give his life to the Christian ministry. He is now entering the seminary.

THE WORLD IN BOSTON

By the Reverend William E. Gardner

IN the summers of 1908 and 1909, two expositions on a very large scale were held in the Royal Agricultural Hall in the north of London. The first of these, in connection with the London Missionary Society, was entitled "The Orient in London"; the second, in connection with all the societies of the Church of England, "Africa and the East." Many people in America visited one or both of these expositions and a much larger number have read accounts of them. Each of them attracted at least half a million of people, and the results were especially notable in the attendance of large numbers of people who do not read missionary literature or attend missionary meetings.

A number of Christian men in Boston have formed a committee to hold a similar exposition there, and so to introduce the movement into the United States. Bishop Lawrence is one of the vice-presidents of the exposition, and Professor P. M. Rhinelander, of the Episcopal Theological School, is the Educational Secretary. The clergy and laity of the Church of Greater Boston are giving the movement their support. A guarantee fund of $60,000 has been raised, and the Rev. A. M. Gardner, the organizer of "The Orient in London," has been invited over to become the General Secretary. The name of the exposition is "The World in Boston," and it is to be held in the largest building of the city—Mechanics Building—from April 24th to May 20th, 1911.

A committee of gentlemen in New York, including several devoted laymen of the Church, have formed a company called "The Missionary Exposition Company," whose business it will be to construct such expositions wherever held in the United States and Canada, and to charge a rent for the material used. This company has been formed for the express purpose of making it possible to hold an exposition anywhere at a minimum of cost. Already Toronto, Detroit, Buffalo and Cleveland have formed committees to consider the possibility of holding expositions in those towns. It is not expected that the exposition anywhere will result in a financial loss; the entrance money and other income in England has always paid expenses, and the profits have yielded a considerable income to the Missionary Societies. The object of the exposition, however, is educational and not financial, and "The World in Boston" has been organized for the sake of the interest it will excite, and the enthusiasm it will arouse in home and foreign missions.

The plans for Boston include too many features to be recapitulated here. Both home and foreign missions are largely represented, and all the great fields at work in North America and throughout the non-Christian populations of the world are included. The idea is so to reproduce the field of missionary labor as to put those who visit the exposition in the same position and to give them the same opportunity of recognizing the need of heathenism and the progress of the Gospel as they would have if they were to visit fields in person. An army of voluntary workers called "stewards" will be enrolled and trained to explain the exposition and to drive home the missionary moral. Ten thousand of these will be needed in Boston and are being enrolled in the churches now.

It will be seen that a missionary exposition is not a mere show, but a spiritual enterprise designed to bring to those who do not recognize it at present their responsibility for spreading the Gospel through the world. The great problem of every missionary society, both home and foreign, is not so much to secure larger contributions and further sympathy from those who already sympathize and give, as to enlarge its constituency by interesting those who at present are indifferent or even hostile.

THE RIGHT REVEREND FRANCIS KEY
BROOKE, D.D.,

Bishop of Oklahoma

THE GROWTH OF A WESTERN TOWN

*The upper picture shows the town on August
6th; the middle one on August 16th;
the lower one on November 6th
of the same year*

A LONELY RANCH HOUSE IN WESTERN COLORADO

SUNDAY-SCHOOL DEPARTMENT

Rev. William E. Gardner, Editor

(Address all correspondence to the Editor, at 1 Joy Street, Boston, Mass.)

MISSION STUDY IN THE PRIMARY DEPARTMENT

❜ HE primary department is the strategic point in the Sunday-schools of to-day. Unless a good ındation is laid in religious edu-:ion during the most impressionable ars, the best results cannot be secured er. Two facts must be taken most ·iously by the Mission Study Leader the Sunday-school. (See October is- ꞓ of THE SPIRIT OF MISSIONS, page 852.) ꞁ It will always be true that the best ssionary impulses will be in those men d women who had their sympathy ;htly appealed to and carefully nur- ·ed in the primary period of their es. With this fact goes another: (2) ꞓ sympathy of a little child cannot be :rectly developed by stories and pict- ꞓs alone. The greatest educational ·ce in the child's life, the force or- ined by the Father, is in the *child's* *n activity.* Along with the story ıst go a constant training in acts ıich express sympathy. In seeking · such acts as will nurture sympathy, : teacher must have two rules in mind: ꞏ1) Any activity is valuable that has it the aim of helpfulness. ꞏ2) Helpfulness must be directed first the immediate sphere of the child's ꞏ, the Sunday-school class, the primary ꞏartment, the home, the child's inti- te friends and playmates, etc., and n widened out in ever enlarging :les as the experience of the child will ke possible. ꞏhe concrete suggestions given below therefore grouped under two heads: ivity that will train sympathy, and ries and pictures that will widen the on.

Activity

l) A little baby commands the deep- interest of a child. That interest is of the best foundations for develop- sympathy. Request the children to ort the coming of a little baby in r neighborhood. See that a few flow-. (in some cases only three) are sent by the children, with a card bearing the greetings of the school.

(2) Have the children carry a card with the school's greetings to all babies enrolled on the Font Roll. Have them re- member children shut in at Christmas and Easter, and occasionally some older person.

(3) Remember with fruit or flowers all sick children who are members of the school; also teachers who are ill.

(4) Describe, not too often, a certain cripple—blind, deaf, or maimed in limb— and ask concerted aid.

(5) Explain the need of kindness to animals and stimulate kindly acts.

(6) If there is a Day Nursery or a Home for Children in the community, tell the children about it and call upon them at stated intervals for such interest and gifts as they can give. If there is no institution, the teacher should select a poor family or families and interest the children concretely in the needs and happiness of the children of that family.

The shoes and stockings, the grocer- ies and toys, etc., should be brought by the children; they should be allowed to help in packing the basket or box. This requires great patience on the part of the teacher, who should keep ever in mind the blessing that comes to "little hands that help by hindering." These suggestions may be indefinitely in- creased. Only a few are given, with the intention of bringing out the ingenuity of the teacher.

Pictures and Stories

(1) Hang up a large blank card of some attractive color. Paste on it a pretty border. Print an appropriate text: "Go ye into all the world." The first Sunday put a picture of an ocean steamer in the centre. Tell the class that it is *their* ship in which they will visit boys and girls in far away lands. Describe features of ship life that will interest class. Each Sunday take them to different lands, and tell one story of

Lesson III.   Picture 3

Lesson III.   Picture 4

Lesson III.   Picture 7

(950)

the child life of that land, and mount one or two pictures illustrating the story. One card can be made to last a year, and gain increasing attention as the year passes. It is wise to let the children by turns cut out the pictures and mount them. Material for the work can be found in any of the children's numbers of THE SPIRIT OF MISSIONS. At another time the picture of a bishop may be used, and pictures of the schools and churches in his diocese added. Whatever is done in this way should be accompanied by some expression on the part of the child. In one school a tiny

basket was brought into the class, and to the delight of the children it was each Sunday filled to overflowing with the pennies given to help the children in the land described.

The editor requests primary teachers to report to him all successful methods, and he urges them to make (1) helpful activity, and (2) widening vision, the aim of the missionary instructions in the Primary Department, and to realize that in these concrete ways they are helping the children to *become* members of Christ, children of God and inheritors of the Kingdom of Heaven.

A MISSIONARY LESSON

General Subject "Missions on Our Side of the World."
Lesson No. 3. Going to the Coast.

(For a description of the methods to be used in teaching these lessons see THE SPIRIT OF MISSIONS, September, 1910, page 769.)

Point of Contact and Assignments On the Sunday before you give this lesson ask the class, by way of review, to name the largest, oldest, hardest and farthest away Indian missions. Then ask: If we could visit only one more Indian mission which one ought we to go to? Wait for individual opinion, but convince the class that we should go to the *hardest*. Why? (1) To encourage. (2) To make our knowledge broad. Promise next Sunday: (1) a trip to Oklahoma (show on map), not only to see the Indians, but to see the interesting and difficult work that Bishop Brooke has to do; (2) then a rapid journey to Seattle. What States shall we go through? Take map and draw an imaginary line from Oklahoma to Seattle. Ask them to name the States touched: Oklahoma, Colorado, Wyoming, Idaho and Washington. Five states, but *eight dioceses:* Oklahoma,* Eastern Oklahoma, Colorado, Western Colorado, Wyoming, Idaho, Spokane and Olympia. First assignment: How many clergymen are in these eight dioceses? How many square miles of area? Compare these with local diocese. Send scholars to the Church Year Book in the rector's study.

Second assignment: Ask a scholar to bring in a short account of the rapid

* During the General Convention of 1910 Oklahoma was divided.

growth of Oklahoma. He can get it from his school geography or an encyclopedia. See also Bishop Brooke's address before the General Convention, page 903.

Third assignment: Steamboat Springs and the life of W. D. Harris, at Oak Creek, Western Colorado. This assignment might be worded in another way, *i.e.,* describe a missionary journey of Bishop Brewster in Western Colorado. Tell where he went and what he did.

The Lesson Go to the class with this aim clearly in mind: *I want to show my class*: (1) *the bigness of the West;* (2) *the things that are being done, and* (3) *what the Church must do, to make it as good as it is great.* Start the lesson by turning to the outline map in the note book and asking the class to tell where we were in the last lesson. Where do we go to-day? How many states do we touch? How many dioceses? Call for the first assignment, by asking: How many square miles are there in these dioceses? How many in our diocese? How many clergymen in the eight dioceses? Compare with the number in our diocese.

In some of the Eastern dioceses the comparison will be startling. Ask the question: Is it fair to ask a few ministers to cover a large area, when in another section of the United States a

large number of ministers cover a small
area? See if some scholar will be sufficiently interested to suggest that the
largest number of ministers should be
where there is the largest number of
people; agree with him, but ask: should
we then be satisfied to have only a few
ministers in the Great West? Test the
class with the question: Why should we
put many ministers into the Great West?
Wait for answers, and draw out expressions of opinion, then say: Let us
leave South Dakota, where we were in
our last lesson and go south (use map)
and visit Oklahoma. There we will try
to see why many more ministers are
needed in the West.

See the diocese on the map. It used
to be the Indian Territory. Bishop
Brooke (picture 1) is the bishop, and his
work is very hard (1) because there are
not only more Indians there than in any
other diocese, but there are more tribes
and therefore a great many different
languages and a great variety of customs. With all these difficulties Bishop
Brooke has only been able to secure
enough money and men to establish two
missions among all these Indians.
(2) The second reason why his work is
difficult is because the people are coming
in so fast that he cannot get enough
money or men to start new churches for
the new people. Now call for the second
assignment and show picture No. 2,
illustrating the rapid growth that follows the opening of the new land.

We must now start on our journey
northwest to Seattle. As we pass
through Colorado, we might stop and
hear Bishop Brewster, of the diocese of
Western Colorado, tell about Steamboat
Springs and Oak Creek in his diocese.
Call for third assignment. Emphasize:
(1) reason it was called "Steamboat
Springs"; (2) the incidents of the bishop's journey: miles travelled, temperature; (3) population: compare with a
local town, well known to class, of 1,200
inhabitants; (4) church life: thirty communicants, no church building, needs;
(5) story of the life of Mr. W. D. Harris
at Oak Creek: with his own hands built
part of church, lived in the vestry-room,
taught school.

Leaving Bishop Brewster we would
rush along in the train through the beautiful state of Wyoming. If we had time
we might visit Bishop Thomas. He

Lesson III.   Picture 6

ANNOUNCEMENTS CONCERNING THE MISSIONARIES

Africa

Bishop Ferguson, who sailed from iverpool on September 24th, arrived at ew York on October 2d, and pro-eeded immediately to Cincinnati. Re-rning from the General Convention, he ill leave New York by the steamer Kaiserin Auguste Victoria" on Novem-er 5th for Hamburg.

Mrs. Nathan Matthews, coming to e United States for reasons of health, iled from Cape Mount on September I; arrived at New York by the steamer Mesaba" on October 18th, and pro-eded to her home at Shipman, Va. Mr. atthews accompanied her as far as ngland.

Alaska

The Rev. L. H. Buisch and wife, ho sailed from Seattle August 11th, ar-ved at Fairbanks on August 29th.

Miss Lizzie J. Woods, returning to e States because of illness, left Fort ukon on September 18th; arrived at Seattle on October 6th, and reached Portsmouth, N. H., on the 20th.

Haiti

The Rev. Pierre E. Jones, on leave of absence granted by the Board, sailed from Port-au-Prince with his daughter, Marianne, by the "Prins Frederik Hendrik" on September 25th and arrived at New York on October 2d.

Hankow

Bishop Roots, returning after the General Convention, left Boston on October 31st, intending to sail from San Francisco by the steamer "Korea" on November 8th.

The Rev. Robert A. Goodwin, Jr., and Dr. John MacWillie and family, who sailed from Vancouver on August 17th, arrived at Shanghai on September 5th and reached Wuchang about September 22d.

Miss Emily L. Ridgely, deaconess,

(953)

Miss Susan H. Higgins and Miss Sarah E. Hopwood, who sailed from Vancouver on September 7th, arrived at Shanghai on September 26th and reached Hankow October 1st.

Miss Lucy Fish Baker left Jamestown, N. Y., on October 30th, and is to sail from San Francisco by the steamer "Korea" on November 8th.

Miss Annie J. Lowe, of Boston, Mass., was appointed as a missionary nurse at Anking on October 25th, and is to sail by the same steamer.

Kyoto

The Rev. Isaac Dooman, returning after furlough, left New York on October 17th, and sailed from San Francisco by the steamer "Mongolia" on the 25th.

Shanghai

Bishop Graves, returning after the General Convention, left Chicago on October 27th, and is to sail by the steamer "Korea" on November 8th.

At the meeting on September 20th, on the request of Bishop Graves, Mr. Percy L. Urban, of Lansdale, Pa., was appointed as a missionary in the Shanghai district. Mr. Urban left his home on October 24th, and is to sail from San Francisco by the same steamer.

The Rev. Dr. F. L. H. Pott and the Rev. Thomas K. Nelson, who sailed from Vancouver on August 17th, arrived at Shanghai on September 5th.

The Rev. Robert C. Wilson and family, returning after furlough, left Bethel, Vt., on October 18th, and sailed from Seattle by the "Awa Maru" on the 25th.

Dr. Angie M. Myers, who returned to duty by way of Europe, arrived at Shanghai on September 11th.

Miss Caroline Fullerton, who was appointed on September 20th, left Montpelier, Vt., on September 29th, and sailed by the "Awa Maru" on October 25th.

Mrs. Pott left Wappingers Falls on October 18th, and sailed by the same steamer.

Tokyo

Mrs. George Wallace, returning to Tokyo, sails from San Francisco by the steamer "Korea" on November 8th, and is due to arrive at Yokohama on the 25th.

MISSIONARY SPEAKERS

FOR the convenience of those arranging missionary meetings, the following list of clergy and other missionary workers available as speakers is published:

When no address is given requests for the services of these speakers should be addressed to the Corresponding Secretary, 281 Fourth Avenue, New York.

Secretaries of Departments

I. Rev. William E. Gardner, 1 Joy Street, Boston, Mass.

II. Rev. John R. Harding, D.D., 692 Genesee Street, Utica, N. Y.

III. Rev. Thomas J. Garland, Church House, Philadelphia.

IV. Rev. R. W. Patton, care of the Rev. C. B. Wilmer, D.D., 412 Courtland Street, Atlanta, Ga.

V. Rev. John Henry Hopkins, D.D., 703 Ashland Boulevard, Chicago.

VI. Rev. C. C. Rollit, 4400 Washburn Avenue, South, Minneapolis, Minn.

VII. Rev. H. Percy Silver, Box 312, Topeka, Kan.

VIII. Rev. L. C. Sanford, 1215 Sacramento Street, San Francisco, Cal.

Alaska
Rt. Rev. P. T. Rowe, D.D.
Rev. C. E. Betticher, Jr.

Eastern Oregon
Rt. Rev. R. L. Paddock.

South Dakota
Rt. Rev. F. F. Johnson, D.D.

The Philippine Islands
Rev. J. A. Staunton, Jr.

Western Colorado
Rt. Rev. Benjamin Brewster, D.D.

Brazil
Rt. Rev. L. L. Kinsolving, D.D.

China
Shanghai:
Rev. G. F. Mosher, of Wusih.
Hankow:
Dr. Mary V. Glenton, of Wuchang.
Rev. Amos Goddard, of Shasi.
Rev. Paul Maslin, of Wuhu.
Deaconess Katharine Phelps, of Wuchang.

Japan
Tokyo:
Right Rev. John McKim, D.D.
Rev. C. H. Evans, of Mayebashi.
Rev. J. S. Motoda, of Tokyo.

THE WOMAN'S AUXILIARY

To the Board of Missions

THE EVOLUTION OF THE TRIENNIAL

ON October 14, 1874, sixty-six women from six dioceses assembled in Calvary Sunday-school room, New York City; during the days between October 5 and 11, 1910, many hundreds of women from ninety diocesan branches met together. Both gatherings were the general representative meetings of the Woman's Auxiliary to the Board of Missions, and the change between the two assemblies is more than that of numbers merely.

These meetings began with the understanding that the Auxiliary, being auxiliary to the Board of Missions, should meet when and where the Board of Missions met. In 1877, when it was decided that the Board should meet triennially instead of annually, at the time and place of General Convention, the Auxiliary followed their lead. Later, when the General Convention resolved itself into the Board of Missions, the Auxiliary arranged its meetings so that its members might always attend those missionary sessions.

Gradually the growing interest and intelligence called for more frequent meetings. To the one day's gathering of 374 in 1883 was added an introductory Communion Service and a conference of diocesan officers, which, in 1889 and 1892, had its adjourned session. In Minneapolis, in 1895, was held a series of small meetings in St. Mark's Parish House, the first headquarters of the Auxiliary throughout Convention time. In 1898, in Washington, St. John's Parish House became Headquarters, and we still remember the first Auxiliary exhibit, the bags and cases that contained the United Offering, then made in gold, the Alaska nuggets and the shawl of olden hue sent from Brazil to be sold

for the offering; the early days of conferences, the bishops' visits, the loving tribute paid to Bishop Hare, the introduction of that pleasant feature which has been the occasion of beginning so many lasting friendships, the Auxiliary teas.

In 1901, in San Francisco, to the conferences and talks and teas were added the historical exhibit of the churches in different dioceses, and the display of envelopes which pictured on their faces the earliest building in which the Church's service had been held in each diocese, and which had contained the checks for the United Offering, now grown so large it could no longer be offered in gold.

In San Francisco, for the first time, a building other than a parish building was used for headquarters, a house being rented for that purpose; and in this house accommodation was offered to other societies of women also, where they might receive their members and circulate information. Three years later, in Boston, the Massachusetts branch gave a large hall with its connecting rooms to the use of the Auxiliary, repeating and extending this larger hospitality, as the Virginia and Southern Ohio branches have done since then.

It was in 1904 that the Secretary of the Auxiliary, realizing that large numbers of women would be coming to Boston, and that it would be impossible for all to attend the sessions of General Convention, and also that, while there, because of their missionary interest, those sessions were largely devoted to other subjects, planned a programme which gave at Headquarters a succession of busy days. The programme filled the morning with conferences; prayers at noon were followed by visits from mis-

sionary bishops, and in the afternoon till
five o'clock, the women sat unweariedly
listening to these and other missionary
visitors. And the days closed with the
pleasant Auxiliary teas.

It was in Boston that first a group of
Junior leaders lodged under one roof,
and began to draw together in the close
association which a common home so
naturally and happily affords.

So, in 1907, when coming to Richmond, a similar programme was planned,
except that continued conferences took
the place of the bishops' visits, and the

THE TRIENN

LAST February the Secretary of
the Woman's Auxiliary went
prospecting in Cincinnati. Everyone was most kind, showing
churches, parish houses, hotels and the
Music Hall which since then has become the familiar centre of so much of
interest and value.

It is useless to try to picture all that
the clergy and laity, the Woman's Auxiliary of Southern Ohio, and men and
women within and without the Church
have done for the pleasure and help of
their Convention guests. We shall leave
it to Miss Lindley to tell of the beautiful
Junior House, and of that work in study
class and with Junior leaders, conducted
through her initiative and under her
guidance, so significant in its beginnings, so rich in promise, and which
marks this triennial in the life of the
Auxiliary with an importance that cannot now be estimated.

The mere mention of Auxiliary headquarters at the Music Hall recalls at
once to hundreds of readers of THE
SPIRIT OF MISSIONS a succession of delightful days; if sometimes too absorbing and too distracting, this must be ascribed to conditions which had never existed before. Never before had the meetings of the Auxiliary been held under
the same roof as those of General Convention. The Convention assembled in
a hall which at any session afforded
ample room for every person who wished

Girls' Friendly Society occupied the Auxiliary Assembly Hall on certain afternoons.

This hall was at the end .of the wide corridor. A special request from the Southern Ohio branch confined our sessions to the morning hours, and those were crowded full. The only exceptions were the business conferences held on the afternoon of Wednesday, the 5th, and Thursday, the 6th, when a second adjournment extended the time to five o'clock, when the business was completed to the great satisfaction of all.

It would be impossible in the limits of our space to give in detail all that filled those animated hours.

The Michigan Branch gave us the presiding officer of our business conferences; Michigan City, Long Island, Milwaukee, Kansas City, Pittsburgh and Pennsylvania contributed the officers who presided over Conferences on the "United Offering as a Gift," first of "Life," then of "Means"; "Missionary Information and How to Get It," "The Junior Department," "The Woman's Auxiliary" and "Gifts"; Massachusetts gave the officer who opened the Question Box: Virginia presented to us the Secretaries, Treasurer and Assistant Treasurer of the Board of Missions; while New York, Kansas, Ohio, Georgia, South Carolina, Iowa, Louisiana, California and Arkansas in turn introduced to us our missionary bishops at the close of noonday prayers. Those prayers were read by our two Priest-Secretaries of the Board, and by the Department Secretaries, while, on one occasion, the Corresponding Secretary presented to us, in a space of less than two hours, some twenty missionaries from almost as many different fields.

On one day Deaconess Goodwin, the Student Secretary, conducted a programme meeting, and on another Miss Fiedler, of California, did a like work. The United Offering Treasurers gathered for two extra sessions; the Juniors held three sectional meetings; the leaders among the Little Helpers of the Babies' Branch held one.

On Friday, the 21st, from Oklahoma we had the review of our Convention days from the standpoint of one to whom all was new, and from Southern Ohio the portrayal of what the Convention and the Auxiliary had brought to the people among whom our gatherings had been held; and these all closed with a parting message from the Rev. H. L. Burleson, of the Board of Missions.

THE UNITED OFFERING DAY

FOR the first time our United Offering Service was an early one, and at its close one veteran officer said: "It has been perfect; this settles it for all the future."

It was the first time, and no one could estimate how large the attendance would be, so provision was made in the basement chapel for those crowded out from Christ Church. Here Mr. Burleson celebrated, assisted by the Student Secretary, Mr. Gravatt. Only a few gathered there, but they asserted that there was a special charm and blessing attendant upon their quiet service, to which the notes of distant music came, and from which their share in the great offering was sent to be presented with the rest in the church above.

There most careful attention had been given to all details. The Bishop of Southern Ohio was the celebrant, assisted by the rector of the parish, and the Secretaries of the Fifth and Eighth Missionary Departments. The clergy of the city and neighborhood were our ushers; selected members from the different women's choirs formed the choir; and the women of the Auxiliary, filling the church, enjoyed in that early hour the quiet, reverent hush that it had sometimes seemed impossible to gain at a later time. In the seats were scattered a leaflet prepared in Cincinnati, giving the texts:

"This is none other than the House of God; this is the Gate of Heaven."

"And there was silence in Heaven by the space of half an hour."

"The Lord is in His Holy Temple; let all the earth keep silence before Him."

These texts were followed by a request for reverent silence, and quotations from the "Imitation," and suggestions for reading of Hymns and Psalms.

Bishop Vincent spoke a few earnest, loving words; as we sang "Onward, Christian soldiers," and "Holy offerings," the United Offering of 1910 was gathered, and with the Doxology the loving United Offering gift—the expression of three years of thankful service—was offered on God's Altar.

Then the hundreds of privileged women, representatives of thousands and tens of thousands absent, in reverent ranks approached to offer themselves again to God, to render to Him the highest act of worship, and to receive Himself in whom they are joined with all His people, struggling on earth to-day and through all the ages called to rest in Him, to share in His high work of constant intercession.

For the United Offering mass meeting held at 2:30 on the afternoon of Saturday, the 8th, some three thousand women met in Music Hall, and Bishop Vincent welcomed them to Cincinnati and presented the Bishop of Salisbury, our English guest. The Secretary made the triennial report; and the speakers followed—Bishop Rowe, of Alaska, on "Women Pioneers"; Bishop McKim (who shared his time with the Rev. J. Motoda, Japanese Vice-Principal of J. Paul's College, Tokyo), on "Mission Women and Their Influence in the Upbuilding of Christian Womanhood in Japan," and Bishop Brent, on "The Philippines as a Battle Ground of Christian Unity." Bishop Cheshire, who was to have told us of the Negro in America, was prevented by an accident from attending the meeting.

Mr. King, our Treasurer, announced the amount of our United Offering of 1910—$242,110.83, and the disposition of the $15,000 for buildings was told—$10,000 for St. Hilda's School, Wuchang, $5,000 for St. Augustine's School, Raleigh. The Presiding Bishop gave his blessing, and another United Offering Day for the Auxiliary was happily closed.

THE OFFICERS' CONFERENCE IN CINCINNATI

ON Wednesday, October 5th, at 3:30 P.M., the business conference of diocesan officers of the Woman's Auxiliary met in the Auxiliary assembly room of the Music Hall, Cincinnati, and on the nomination of the Secretary, Mrs. Stevens, president of the Michigan branch, was elected its presiding officer. Mrs. Stevens took the chair, and called the meeting to order.

In the absence, through illness, of Mrs. Irwin, president of the Southern Ohio branch, Mrs. Mortimer Matthews, chairman of the Committee on Hospitality, welcomed the Auxiliary.

Miss Brady, of West Virginia, and Miss Knight, of Milwaukee, were appointed to receive the cards of registration; Miss Hutchins, of Massachusetts, and Miss Spalding, of Utah, to assist Miss Lindley in keeping the roll as called by the Secretary; Miss Rand, of Southern Florida, and Miss Stoney, of California, to whom later was added Miss Triplett, of Missouri, to keep the minutes of the meeting.

The roll was called by dioceses, and as the delegations stood and were counted, the Secretary handed them checks for amounts sent direct to the Mission

ern Ohio branch, and of hope for her
speedy recovery, was adopted by a rising
vote, and the representatives of the
Bethlehem branch were asked to convey
this message to Mrs. Irwin.

On motion the meeting adjourned to
Thursday, October 6th.

ADJOURNED SESSION

The adjourned session of the Officers'
Conference was called to order at
10:45 A.M. on the 6th of October, when
the minutes of the preceding session were
read, and additional names added to the
roll.

A resolution on organization was
moved by Milwaukee and referred to the
committee on miscellaneous resolutions.
Mrs. Monteagle, of California, asked
leave to withdraw a resolution upon the
United Offering of 1910 offered from
that diocese on October 5th, and to substitute another. Consent being obtained,
this substitute for a previous resolution
was also referred.

Mrs. Soule, chairman of the committee
on resolutions on the United Offering of
1913, made the report of that committee
offering the resolution prepared by them.
This resolution, moved by California
and variously seconded, after discussion
(broken by an interval for noon-day
prayers), and amended on motion from
Oklahoma and Virginia, was finally
adopted as follows:

THE UNITED OFFERING OF 1913

Resolved: That the United Thank-
Offering of 1913 be given to the Board
of Missions for woman's work in the
mission field, including the training.
testing, sending and support of wom-
en workers, also the care of such
workers when sick or disabled; but
that a sum not exceeding $20,000 be
devoted to buildings for the use of
women workers, approved by the
Board of Missions on the recommendation of the General Secretary and
the Secretary of the Woman's Auxiliary. Also, that to our united gifts
there shall be added our united and
earnest prayers that God will put it

into the hearts of many faithful
women to give themselves to the
work of the Master in the Mission
field, or, if they cannot go themselves,
to give of their substance gladly as
the Lord hath prospered them.

On the passing of this resolution the
Doxology was sung.

On motion of Miss Stuart, of Virginia, it was

Resolved: That the request made to
the Board of Missions, in 1895, as to
the training of women candidates
for the Mission field be renewed.

On motion of Nebraska, the report of
the Committee on Resolutions on Representation was postponed till Monday,
October 10th, but later on it was resolved to adjourn to 3 P.M. of the day of
the present meeting.

On motion of Southern Virginia,
seconded by Maryland, the Secretary was
asked to report on the reservation of
seats for those bearing the United Offering at the United Offering Service, and
at her request Miss Johnston, United Offering Treasurer of the Southern Ohio
branch, was appointed to act with herself, as a committee upon this matter.
After a brief interval for consultation
with Miss Johnston, the Secretary reported on the arrangement decided upon,
which was that one person from each
diocesan branch, presenting the envelope
bearing the offering of that branch to the
usher at the door, should be given a seat
in the church.

On motion the meeting adjourned to
3 P.M.

SECOND SESSION ON OCTOBER 6TH

The meeting reassembled at 3 P.M., and
was opened with prayers. After the
reading and correction of minutes, and
various notices, Mrs. Adams, chairman
of the Committee on Resolutions on
Triennial Representation, read the report of that committee, which, as
amended by Mrs. Sioussat, of Maryland,
was adopted as follows:

I. *Resolved:* That representatives
at the Triennial Meeting of the Wom-

JUNIOR AUXILIARY REPORTS FROM THE TRIENNIAL

IT would be impossible to tell in one page all that the days in Cincinnati meant to the Junior leaders fortunate enough to be there. Even to restrict the report to that which pertains to actual Junior happenings would demand much more space than can be given. Perhaps we may be able to use the Junior page for several months for reports from the Triennial and suggestions growing out of them, but for this month we must be content merely to report briefly on a few of the most important points.

We should all agree that our first word must be one of grateful appreciation for all that the Juniors of Southern Ohio did to make us happy and comfortable. Eighteen Junior Officers were lucky enough to live in the "Junior house"—a house rented and furnished for this purpose, and a place which will be long remembered with pleasure and profit. And outside our Junior House many other opportunities were given for our enjoyment.

Coming to that which was done in the line of work we omit again all mention of the general meetings and conferences where seniors and juniors met together, and for the present confine our report to what was accomplished among the Juniors meeting by themselves.

The Juniors held five conferences, three for discussion, one on the Babies' Branch work, and a final one for the reports of committees and adoption of resolutions. The mission study classes were under the direction of the Junior Department, though their membership was not confined to Junior leaders. And best of all were the two services on October 15th, the Corporate Communion for all Junior leaders and members of the study classes, and the Quiet Hour conducted by Bishop Lloyd. It is not possible to report this, only those of us who were

there will see that our winter's work is
better because of those services.

The informal conferences discussed
many problems and questions which are
of interest to all Junior leaders: The
question of Baptism as an essential to
membership in the Junior Auxiliary, the
having boys' branches, the gaining and
keeping of the younger women, co-operation between the Junior Auxiliary and
other societies, the possibility of having
one new Junior collect rather than the
two at present in use, were some of the
questions discussed. Committees were
appointed to consider all these suggestions and report at the last conference,
held on October 17th. As these meetings
were simply Junior conferences it was
not of course possible to legislate, but
recommendations were made, and while
these recommendations have no binding
power upon any officer or branch, still, in
that they represent the opinion of those
Junior leaders who were attending the
Triennial, they should commend themselves to the careful consideration of all
Junior officers, and so we print them
here.

On Membership

We, your Committee on Membership of the Junior Department, although recognizing that by Baptism
we are members of the Church and
eligible as members of the Auxiliary
feel that it would be contrary to the
Church's Mission to debar any child
from attendance at meetings.

We recommend that in no case
shall an unbaptized child hold office
in a Parish Branch, or be considered
a full member, and that each leader
shall use her influence to bring such
children to Baptism.

On Co-operation with the Girls' Friendly Society

We recommend that a Committee
of Junior Diocesan officers with Miss
Grace Lindley be appointed to confer with the national President, and
the Missions Associate, to bring
about closer union between the
Junior Auxiliary and the Girls'
Friendly Society in their Missionary
work.

ACKNOWLEDGMENT OF OFFERINGS

Offerings are asked to sustain missions in thirty missionary districts in the United States, Africa, China, Japan, Brazil, Mexico and Cuba; also work in the Haitien Church; in forty-two dioceses, including missions to the Indians and to the Colored People; to pay the salaries of thirty-two bishops, and stipends to 2,253 missionary workers, domestic and foreign; also two general missionaries to the Swedes and two missionaries among deaf-mutes in the Middle West and the South; and to support schools, hospitals and orphanages. With all remittances the name of the Diocese and Parish should be given. Remittances, when practicable, should be by Check or Draft, and should always be made payable to the order of George Gordon King, Treasurer, and sent to him, Church Missions House, 281 Fourth Avenue, New York. Remittances in Bank Notes are not safe unless sent in Registered Letters.

The Treasurer of the Board of Missions acknowledges the receipt of the following from September 1st to October 1st, 1910.

* Lenten and Easter Offering from the Sunday-school Auxiliary.

NOTE.—*The items in the following pages marked "Sp." are Specials which do not aid the Board in meeting its appropriations. In the heading for each Diocese the total marked "Ap." is the amount which does aid the Board of Missions in meeting its appropriations. Wherever the abbreviation "Wo. Aux." precedes the amount, the offering is through a branch of the Woman's Auxiliary.*

Home Dioceses

Alabama

Ap. $203.96; *Sp.* $2.00

BIRMINGHAM—*St. Mark's*: Gen.......	3 00
CARBON HILL—*St. James's Mission*: (Apportionment, 1909-10) Gen......	3 00
CARLOWVILLE—*St. Paul's*: (Apportionment, 1909-10) Gen............	5 47
COALBURG—(Apportionment, 1909-10) Gen..............................	3 00
COAL VALLEY—(Apportionment, 1909-10), Gen..........................	3 00
DEMOPOLIS—*Trinity Church S. S.*: Stiles Ulmer, Sp. for Rev. Mr. Betticher, for Alaskan Indian Christmas tree......................	2 00
DORA—*Mission*: (Apportionment, 1909-10) Gen......................	3 00
JASPER — *Mission*: (Apportionment, 1909-10) Gen............	3 00
MOBILE—*Trinity Parish*: Junior missionaries, for St. Mary's Hall, Shanghai	40 00
Mrs. William A. Gould, Gen.......	50
MONTEVALLO—*St. Andrew's*: (Apportionment, 1909-10) Gen.......	15 00
MONTGOMERY—*Church of the Holy Comforter*: Junior Aux., Gen......	5 25
St. John's: (Apportionment, 1909-10) Gen........................	98 24
PATTEN AND CORONA—(Apportionment, 1909-10) Gen.............	5 00
UNIONTOWN—*Holy Cross*: (Apportionment, 1909-10) Gen...........	16 50

Albany

Ap. $420.15; *Sp.* $16.50

ASHLAND—*Trinity Church*: (Apportionment, 1909-10) Gen...........	8 00
BALLSTON SPA—*Christ Church*: Wo. Aux., Gen.........................	30 00

CANTON—*Grace*: Sp. for R. E. Wood, Wuchang, Hankow, for purchase of land	6 50
COHOES—*St. John's*: Gen...........	7 14
COOPERSTOWN—*Christ Church*: (Apportionment, 1909-10) Gen.......	15 50
ESSEX—*St. John's*: $26.75, S. S.* $7.79 (Apportionment, 1909-10), Gen.	34 54
FRANKLIN—*St. Paul's*: Gen.........	2 13
GILBERTSVILLE—Miss E. J. Hughes (Apportionment, 1909-10), Gen....	3 00
HAINES FALLS—Mrs. Caroline D. Booraem (Twilight Park) (Apportionment, 1909-10), Gen..........	5 00
HUDSON—*Christ Church*: (Apportionment, 1909-10) Gen..........	50 00
ILION—*St. Augustine's*: Gen.......	10 00
INDIAN LAKE—Summer services, Gen..	2 50
JOHNSTOWN—*St. John's*: "A Parishioner" (Apportionment, 1909-10), Gen................................	5 00
LAKE PLACID—Mary E. Burleson (Apportionment, 1909-10), Gen........	1 00
MECHANICVILLE—*St. Luke's*: (Apportionment, 1909-10), Negroes, $1.19; Gen., $38.93.......................	40 12
MIDDLEVILLE—*The Memorial*: Dom...	2 27
ONEONTA—*St. James's*: Gen........	33 30
SANDY HILL—*Zion*: Frn............	40 51
SCHENECTADY—*St. George's*: Wo. Aux., Gen...........................	35 00
SCHUYLERVILLE—*St. Stephen's*: (Apportionment, 1909-10) Gen........	5 00
SIDNEY—*St. Paul's*: (Apportionment, 1909-10) Gen....................	3 07
TROY—*Holy Cross*: Wo. Aux., Sp. for Miss Annie W. Cheshire, Shanghai..	10 00
WALTON—*Christ Church*: (Apportionment, 1909-10) Gen..........	50 00
WILLSBORO—*St. Mary's*: (Apportionment, 1909-10) Gen..........	7 62
MISCELLANEOUS—Right Rev. W. C. Doane, D.D. (Apportionment, 1909-10), Gen........................	29 45

(963)

Atlanta

Ap. $27.00 ; *Sp.* $50.00

ATHENS—*St. Timothy's*: (Apportionment, 1909-10) Gen.............. 5 50
ATLANTA—*Church of the Holy Comforter*: (Apportionment, 1909-10) Frn. 15 00
DECATUR—*Holy Trinity Church*: (Apportionment, 1909-10) Gen........ 1 50
MORIETTA—"A Friend," work among Indians (Apportionment, 1909-10).. 5 00
MISCELLANEOUS—Junior Aux., Sp. for "Sister Katherine" scholarship, Mrs. Brooks's School, Guantanamo, Cuba. 50 00

L

Bethlehem

Ap. $629.60

CARBONDALE—*Trinity Church*: Gen..... 37 50
CORNWALL—"A Friend," Bishop Rowe's work, Alaska.................. 100 00
HAZLETON—*St. Peter's*: (Apportionment, 1909-10) Gen.............. 15 00
READING—*Christ Church*: (of which Apportionment, 1909-10, $15) Gen.. 475 00
WILKES-BARRE—*Calvary*: S. S. Class No. 7, Gen.................... 2 10

California

Ap. $11.00 ; *Sp.* $10.00

MILL VALLEY—*Church of Our Saviour*: (Apportionment, 1909-10) Gen..... 10 00
OAKLAND—*St. John's*: "A Communicant" (Apportionment, 1909-10), Gen........................... 1 00
SAN FRANCISCO—*Trinity Church*: Mr. and Mrs. Bryant Grinwood, Sp. for Shanghai, Catechist School Land and Building Fund.................... 10 00

Central New York

Ap. $214.33 ; *Sp.* $54.13

AFTON — *St. Ann's*: (Apportionment, 1909-10) Gen................. 12 07
ALEXANDRIA BAY—"A Friend" (Apportionment, 1909-10), Gen......... 30 00
CLAYTON—*Christ Church*: (of which Apportionment, 1909-10, $27.51) Gen. 31 45
COPENHAGEN—*Grace*: Gen........... 1 00
ELMIRA, — *Emmanuel Church*: Gen. (Apportionment, 1909-10).......... 1 55
ENDICOTT—*St. Paul's*: Gen.......... 5 00
HARPERSVILLE—*St. Luke's*: Gen....... 8 00
NEW HARTFORD—*St. Stephen's*: (Apportionment, 1909-10) Gen....... 13 00
NEW BERLIN—*St. Andrew's S. S.*: Gen. 27 19
PULASKI—*St. James's S. S.*: Bontoc Mission, Philippine Islands........ 2 25
REDFIELD—*Emmanuel Church*: Gen... 1 82
SYRACUSE — *All Saints'*: (Apportionment, 1909-10) Gen.............. 12 40
Grace: Dom., $10 ; Frn., $10 ; Gen., $5.60 (Apportionment, 1900-10) ... 25 60
(In Memoriam), "A. P. W." (East), Gen. (Apportionment, 1909-10)..... 1 00
UTICA—*Grace*: (Apportionment, 1909-10), "A Member," Gen., $5 ; "A Thank-offering," Wo. Aux., for St. Luke's Mission Hospital, Shanghai, $25 .... 30 00
St. Luke's: (Apportionment, 1909-10) Gen. 12 00
MISCELLANEOUS—Second District, Wo. Aux., Sp. toward completion of hospital at Sagada, Philippine Islands.. 16 28
Babies' Branch, Sp. for Deaconess Drant's work among sick Chinese children, San Francisco, California. 37 85

Chicago

Ap. $925.84

AURORA—*Trinity Church*: Dom. and Frn. 125
BELVIDERE—*Trinity Church*: Gen. (Apportionment, 1909-10)........... 5
CHICAGO—*Ascension*: Dom., $37 ; Bontoc, Philippine Islands, $2.50 ; Frn., $31.16 70
Epiphany: Gen. (Apportionment, 1909-10) 1
Grace: Dom........................ 32
St. Barnabas's: Gen............... 21
St. James's: (Apportionment, 1909-10) Dom. and Frn.............. 27
Transfiguration: Anna P. Kellogg, Dom. and Frn. (Apportionment, 1909-10). 20
Trinity Church: G. S. Blakeslee, Gen. (Apportionment, 1909-10)......... 25
Henry E. Bullock, Gen............. 100
"L," "William H. Hare" (Graduate) scholarship, South Dakota......... 60
Rev. D. W. Wise (Apportionment, 1909-10), Gen.................. 5
EVANSTON—*St. Luke's*: Dom. and Frn. 133
St. Mark's: Gen. (Apportionment, 1909-10) 74
FARM RIDGE—*St. Andrew's*: Wo. Aux., Gen. 1
HINSDALE—*Grace*: Gen............. 53
KANKAKEE—*St. Paul's*: Gen. (Apportionment, 1909-10)............. 20
MANHATTAN—*St. Paul's*: Gen........ 5
OAK PARK—*Grace*: (Apportionment, 1909-10) Gen................. 5
WAUKEGAN—"A Churchwoman," Gen. (Apportionment, 1909-10).......... 5
WESTERN SPRINGS—*All Saints'*: Gen. (Apportionment, 1909-10)......... 2
WINNETKA—*Christ Church*: Gen...... 5
MISCELLANEOUS — Wo. Aux., "Silver Thank-offering," $8.64, Junior Aux., $105, Gen...................... 118
Junior Aux., "Charles Palmerston Anderson" scholarship, Girls' High School, Kyoto................. 20

Colorado

Ap. $6.50

DENVER—*Church of the Redeemer*: Gen. (Apportionment, 1909-10)..... 6

Connecticut

Ap. $747.68 ; *Sp.* $74.38

BETHEL—"A Friend," Gen............. 5
BRIDGEPORT—*St. Paul's*: Dom. and Frn. 50
CHESHIRE—*St. Peter's*: Gen......... 10
COLLINSVILLE—*Trinity Church*: Dom., $1.98 ; Gen., 10 cts............ 2
DEEP RIVER—*St. Peter's*: Gen....... 6
EAST HADDAM—Dr. F. C. H. Wendel, Archdeacon Bryan's work in Panama 2
FARMINGTON—C. C. Griswold (Apportionment, 1909-10), Gen.......... 25
GALES FERRY—Mrs. H. S. Bisbing, Sp. for St. John's-in-the-Wilderness, Allachakat, Alaska.............. 5
GREENWICH—*Christ Church*: Sp. for Expansion Fund, St. John's College, Shanghai 30
HARTFORD—*Christ Church*: "A Communicant" (Apportionment, 1909-10), Gen. 2
Church of the Good Shepherd: "A Member," (Apportionment, 1909-10), Gen., $5 ; Sp. for Land and Building Fund of Shanghai Catechist School, $1................... 6
Trinity Church: "A Lady," Sp. for

East Carolina

Ap. $368.75

2 00	
300 00	
50 00	GATESVILLE—*St. Mary's*: (Apportionment, 1909-10) Gen.............. 8 00
3 00	ROXOBEL — *St. Mark's*: (Apportionment, 1909-10) Gen.............. 5 25
26 00	WILMINGTON — *St. James's*: (Apportionment, 1909-10) Gen.......... 329 50
4 00	WINDSOR—*St. Thomas's*: (Apportionment, 1909-10) Gen.............. 18 00
40 00	WINTON—*St. John's*: (Apportionment, 1909-10) Gen.............. 7 00
10 00	WOODVILLE — *Grace*: (Apportionment, 1909-10) Gen.............. 1 00
1 00	

Easton

Ap. $75.17

26 38	CECIL Co.—*St. Andrew's* (Andora): Gen. 2 25
10 00	*Trinity Church* (Ekton): Gen........ 5 57
10 00	QUEEN ANNE'S Co.—*Wye Parish*: (Apportionment, 1909-10) Gen........ 4 37
5 00	TALBOT Co.—*All Saints'* (Easton): Gen. 5 16
2 15	*Christ Church*: (Apportionment, 1909-10) Gen.................. 47 82
1 75	MISCELLANEOUS—"W. S.," Gen....... 5 00
	Mrs. J. B. Gray (In Memoriam), Gen. 5 00
87 70	

Florida

Ap. $12.00

100 00	JACKSONVILLE—Mrs. A. N. Mitchell (Apportionment, 1909-10), Gen.... 12 00

Fond du Lac

Ap. $65.49

17 00	CHILTON—*St. Boniface's*: Gen........ 2 00
5 00	SHEBOYGAN—Mrs. Thomas A. Lang (Apportionment, 1909-10), Gen..... 50 00
1 00	WAUPACA—*St. Mark's* (Apportionment, 1909-10) Gen.................. 9 34
3 07	MISCELLANEOUS—Babies' Branch, Gen.. 4 15

Georgia

Ap. $68.99; *Sp.* $5.00

21 93	AUGUSTA—*Church of the Good Shepherd*: (Apportionment, 1909-10) Gen. 40 00
17 50	*St. Mary's*: Gen.................... 3 00
	BLACKSHEAR—*All Saints'*: (Apportionment, 1909-10) Gen.............. 1 00
	SANDERSVILLE — *Grace*: (Apportionment, 1909-10) Gen.............. 12 05
11 00	SAVANNAH—*St. Paul's*: Wo. Aux., Dom. 6 94
6 12	MISCELLANEOUS—Branch Junior Aux., for Rev. Robert White's salary, Philippine Islands, $3; St. Luke's Hospital, Shanghai, $3; Sp. for Holy Trinity Orphanage, Tokyo, $2; Sp. for "Sister Katherine" scholarship, Guantanamo, Cuba, $2; Sp. for Nenana School, Alaska, $1........ 11 00
60 00	

Harrisburg

Ap. $334.52; *Sp.* $5.00

12 00	ALTOONA—*St. Luke's*: Gen.......... 15 00
25 00	COUDERSPORT—*Christ Church*: (Apportionment, 1909-10) Gen.......... 25 00
	EAGLESMERE — *St. John's-in-the-Wilderness*: (Apportionment, 1909-10) Frn. 5 00
	HARRISBURG—*St. Paul's*: (Apportionment, 1909-10) Gen.............. 5 00
250 00	MARIETTA—*St. John's*: Gen.......... 3 14
4 00	NEWPORT—*Nativity*: (Apportionment,

1909-10) Gen............
PHILIPSBURG—*St. Paul's*: (Apportion-
ment, 1909-10) Gen..............
SHAMOKIN—F. W. V. Lorenz (Appor-
tionment, 1909-10), Gen..........
WILLIAMSPORT—*Christ Church*: Dom.
and Frn...................
MISCELLANEOUS—Babies' Branch (Ap-
portionment, 1909-10), for "Little
Helpers'" Day-school, Shanghai,
$5; for kindergarten at Akita,
Kyoto, $5; Gen., $136.23; Sp. for
"Little Helpers'" bed, St. Agnes's
Hospital, Raleigh, North Carolina,
$5; Sp. for Emergency Fund, White-
rocks, Utah, $5; Sp. for a mission-
ary font, $5; Sp. for a font at
Pueblo, Mexico, where Miss Karcher,
of St. Matthew's, Sunbury, is serving,
$20 ....

Indianapolis

Ap. $133.72

GREENSBURG—*Trinity Church*: Gen...
INDIANAPOLIS—*Christ Church*: (Appor-
tionment, 1909-10) Gen..........
Grace Pro-Cathedral: Gen..........
MUNCIE—"A Friend" (Apportionment,
1909-10), Gen....................
TERRE HAUTE—*St. Mark's Mission*:
(Apportionment, 1909-10) Gen.....
St. Paul's: (Apportionment, 1909-10)
Gen. ....
WASHINGTON—*St. John's*: (Apportion-
ment, 1909-10) Gen..............

Iowa

Ap. $240.57; *Sp.* $10.00

ALGONA—*St. Thomas's*: Gen.........
BOONE—*Grace*: Gen................
BURLINGTON—*Christ Church*: (Appor-
tionment, 1909-10) Gen...........
DAVENPORT—*Trinity Church*: (Appor-
tionment, 1909-10) Gen...........
DES MOINES—*St. Mark's*: (Apportion-
ment, 1909-10) Gen..............
DUBUQUE—*St. John's*: Salary of Rev.
Mr. Nieh, Hankow..............
DYERSVILLE—*Christ Church*: (Appor-
tionment, 1909-10) for salary of
Rev. Mr. Nieh, Hanch'uan, Hankow.
GARDEN GROVE—*St. John's*: (Appor-
tionment, 1909-10) Gen...........
GLENWOOD—*St. John's*: Gen.........
INDEPENDENCE—*St. James's*: C. D.
Jones, Sp. for Church Extension
Fund, Porto Rico.................
LYONS—*Grace S. S.*: Gen..........
SIOUX CITY—*St. Paul's S. S.*: (Appor-
tionment, 1909-10), Dom., $3; Frn.,
$3 ....

Kansas

Ap. $18.95

EUREKA—*St. Thomas's Mission*: Gen..
MANHATTAN—Rev. J. H. Sage (Appor-
tionment, 1909-10), Frn..........
TOPEKA—Mrs. E. Hempsted (Appor-
tionment, 1909-10), Gen..........
WICHITA—*St. Stephen's* (East): Gen..

Kansas City

Ap. $131.00

BRUNSWICK—*St. Paul's*: (Apportionment, 1909-10) Gen..............
FAYETTE — *St. Mary's*: (Apportionment, 1909-10) Gen..............

Massachusetts

Ap. $1,154.89 ; *Sp.* $100.00

ANDOVER—*Christ Church*: Gen., 51 02
BOSTON—*Advent*: "A Member," Gen. (Apportionment, 1909-10), 100 00
Church of the Messiah: Gen. (Apportionment, 1909-10), 5 00
St. Paul's: Mrs. Herbert H. Eustis, Gen. (Apportionment, 1909-10), 150 00
St. Stephen's: Gen. (Apportionment, 1909-10), 10 00
Anna T. Reynolds, Gen. (Apportionment, 1909-10), 50 00
Olga E. Monks, Gen. (Apportionment, 1909-10), 25 00
Percival Chittenden (Dorchester), Gen. (Apportionment, 1909-10), 2 00
A. G. Clark, Gen., 1 00
BRADFORD—Mrs. W. B. Kimball, Gen., 5 00
BRIDGEWATER—*Trinity Church*: 65 cts., Altar Guild, $5, Gen. (Apportionment, 1909-10), 5 65
BROOKLINE — *All Saints'*: "Churchwoman," Gen. (Apportionment, 1909-10), 1 00
CAMBRIDGE—*Christ Church*: "A Member," Gen. (Apportionment, 1909-10), 100 00
St. John's: Frn., 100 00
CHATHAM—Miss Grace Nugent, Dom., $1; Frn., $2, 3 00
CONCORD—*Trinity Church*: Gen. (Apportionment, 1909-10), 10 00
DEDHAM—*Church of the Good Shepherd* (East): per Rev. F. Pember, Frn., 9 00
FALL RIVER—*St. Stephen's*: Gen. (Apportionment, 1909-10), 35 00
FALMOUTH—*Church of the Messiah* (Wood's Hole): Gen., 30 43
LEXINGTON—*Church of the Redeemer*: "M. D." (Apportionment, 1909-10), $25, S. S.,* $28.66, Gen., 53 66
LINCOLN—*St. Anne's*: Dom. and Frn., 11 61
MARBLEHEAD—*St. Michael's*: Gen., 60
MATTAPOISETT — *St. Philip's*: Gen., $10; Children's Service, for work under Bishop Horner, Asheville, $5; for the Elizabeth Bunn Memorial Hospital, Wuchang, Hankow, $5, 20 00
MEDFORD—*Grace*: Gen., 12 19
NEWTON—*Church of the Redeemer* (Chestnut Hill): Gen. (Apportionment, 1909-10), 154 00
St. John's (Newtonville): Gen., 21 15
*St. Mary's S. S.** (Lower Falls): Gen., 20 00
SOMERVILLE—*St. Thomas's*: Gen. (Apportionment, 1909-10), 8 58
WESTON—Mrs. Charles Dean, Gen. (Apportionment, 1909-10), 10 00
MISCELLANEOUS—Dakota League, Sp. for supplies for St. Mary's School, Rosebud, South Dakota, 100 00
Branch Wo. Aux., "A Member," Dom., 50 00
Branch Wo. Aux., Domestic Committee, for Western Colorado, $50; Nevada, $50, 100 00

Michigan

Ap. $488.12 ; *Sp.* $15.50

ALGONAC—*St. Andrew's*: Gen. (Apportionment, 1909-10), 14 00
CAMBRIDGE — *St. Michael and All Angels'*: Gen., 12 77
DELRAY—*St. Mark's*: Junior Aux., Alaska, $4; Sp. for Miss Routledge, Manila, Philippine Islands, $4, 8 00
DETROIT—*St. Andrew's*: St. Agnes's Guild, Junior Aux., Gen., $15; Sp. for Miss Routledge, Manila, Philippine Islands, $3, 18 00
Mariners' Church: Gen. (Apportionment, 1909-10), 4 23

Left-margin column amounts:
10 00
4 85
23 00
1 50
6 75
7 41
6 10
25 00
3 00
3 90
5 00
5 00
40 00
10 00
3 00
5 07
37 50
2 00
5 00
50 00
2 31
3 49
40 00
6 52
10 00
5 00
3 00
1 00
2 00
18 00
10 00
7 00
25 50
38 00

St. *Barnabas's*: Gen..............   12 77
St. *John's*: Colored educational work,
$18.05; Mrs. George Beck, Gen.,
$10; (Apportionment, 1909-10),
Junior Aux., Alaska, $5; St. Augus-
tine's School, North Carolina, $5;
Gen., $5; Sp. for Miss Routledge,
Manila, Philippine Islands, $2.....   45 05
St. *Joseph's*: Junior Aux., St. James's
Hospital, Anking, Hankow, $1.50;
Sp. for Bishop Rowe, Alaska, $5;
Sp. for Miss Routledge, Manila,
Philippine Islands, $5; Sp. for Bish-
op Horner, Asheville, 50 cts.......   12 00
St. *Peter's*: Gen. (Apportionment,
1909-10) 25 00
St. *Stephen's*: Gen., $4.18; Junior
Aux., Alaska, $3; Sp. for Bishop
Horner, Asheville, $2; Sp. for Wide-
ly Loving Society, Osaka, Kyoto, $3.
George Hargreaves, Gen. (Appor-
tionment, 1909-10).............   12 18
Mrs. C. B. Grant, Gen. (Apportion-
ment, 1909-10).................   20 00
JACKSON—*St. Paul's*: Gen. (Apportion-
ment, 1909-10).................   10 00
MACKINAC ISLAND — *Trinity Church*:   131 32
Dom. (Apportionment, 1909-10)...,   20 00
OWOSSO—*Christ Church*: "Personal,"
Wo. Aux., Gen..................   5 00
PONTIAC—*All Saints'*: Gen., $25;
Junior Aux., "Bishop C. D. Wil-
liams" scholarship, St. John's
School, Cape Mount, Africa, $25....   50 00
PORT HURON—*St. Paul's*: Gen........   2 80
WILLIAMSTON—*St. Katherine's S. S.*:
Gen.   50
YPSILANTI—*St. Luke's*: Gen..........   100 00

Michigan City

Ap. $103.44

ELKHART—*St. John's*: Dom. and Frn..   3 00
HAMMOND—*St. Paul's*: Gen. (Appor-
tionment, 1909-10).............   34 62
HOWE—*St. Mark's*: $1, Junior Aux.,
$1, Gen.; Junior Aux., Dom., $1;
Frn., $1.......................   4 00
LIMA—*St. Mark's*: Wo. Aux., Gen.....   4 50
LOGANSPORT — *Trinity Church*: "A
Communicant," Frn.............   2 00
SOUTH BEND—*St. James's*: Gen. (Ap-
portionment, 1909-10)...........   55 32

Milwaukee

Ap. $82.36; *Sp.* $45.00

CUMBERLAND—*All Souls'*: Gen. (Appor-
tionment, 1909-10)..............   80
EAU CLAIRE—*Christ Church*: Gen.
(Apportionment, 1909-10).......   24 04
EVANSVILLE—*St. John's*: Gen. (Appor-
tionment, 1909-10)..............   5 00
HAYWOOD — *Ascension*: Gen. (Appor-
tionment, 1909-10)..............   2 35
MILWAUKEE—*All Saints' Cathedral*:
Gen., $10; Sp. for purchase of land,
Wuchang, Hankow, 45 cts........   10 45
R. O. Wooster, Gen. (Apportion-
ment, 1909-10).................   5 00
"A Subscriber," Gen. (Apportion-
ment, 1909-10).................   1 00
PORTAGE—*St. John's*: Frn..........   7 10
RACINE—*St. Luke's*: Frn..........   26 00
SHELL LAKE—*St. Stephen's*: Gen. (Ap-
portionment, 1909-10)..........   52
SPOONER—*St. Alban's*: Gen. (Appor-
tionment, 1909-10)..............   55

Minnesota

Ap. $133.85

BECKER—*Trinity Church*: Gen.......   2 00
ELYSIAN — *Grace*: (Apportionment,
1909-10) Gen....................   2 00
GLENCOE—*Christ Church*: Gen.......   5 00

HASSAN—*St. John's*: Gen...........
LUVERNE—*Holy Trinity Church*: (Ap-
portionment, 1909-10) Gen.........
LITCHFIELD—*Emmanuel Church*: Gen,.
MINNEAPOLIS—*Church of the Messiah*:
Gen. ....
St. *Ansgarius's*: Gen...............
St. *Johannes's*: Gen...............
St. *Paul's*: Gen. (Apportionment, 1909-
10) ....
NORTHFIELD—*All Saints'*: $5, S. S.,*
$12.50, Gen. (Apportionment, 1909-
10) ....
ST. PAUL—*St. Mary's S. S.* (Merriam
Park): Gen. (Apportionment, 1909-
10) ....
A. W. Partridge, Gen.............
ST. PETER—*Holy Communion*: Gen.
(Apportionment, 1909-10).........
SLAYTON—Mrs. Mark Tisdale, Gen...
WASECA—*Calvary*: Gen.............
WORTHINGTON — St. *John's*: Gen.
(Apportionment, 1909-10).........

Mississippi

Ap. $83.35

BILOXI—*Church of the Redeemer*: Gen.
(Apportionment, 1909-10) ....
GRENADA—*All Saints'*: A. C. Leigh,
Gen. (Apportionment, 1909-10)....
GREENWOOD—*Nativity*: Gen.........
LELAND—R. S. Porter, Frn..........

Missouri

Ap. $1,539.83

ST. LOUIS—*Emmanuel Church* (Old
Orchard): "A Member," Dom......
St. *Andrew's*: Gen. (Apportionment,
1909-10) ....
St. *Peter's*: Dom., $15; Frn., $1,300... 1
St. *Stephen's House S. S.**: Gen. (Ap-
portionment, 1909-10)...........

Montana

Ap. $5.00

TOWNSEND—Miss Orlena Coggeshall,
Gen. ....

Nebraska

Ap. $123.29

CENTRAL CITY—*Christ Church*: Dom.
and Frn. (Apportionment, 1909-10).
CREIGHTON—*St. Mark's*: Gen. (Appor-
tionment, 1909-10)..............
NELIGH—*St. Peter's*: Gen. (Appor-
tionment, 1909-10)..............
NIOBRARA—*St. Paul's*: Dom. and Frn.
(Apportionment, 1909-10).......
OMAHA—*St. Andrew's*: Gen. (Appor-
tionment, 1909-10) ....
St. *Philip's*: Gen. (Apportionment,
1909-10) ....
Trinity Cathedral: Dom. and Frn. (of
which $25, Apportionment, 1909-10)

Newark

Ap. $401.76; *Sp.* $8.00

ALLENDALE—*Epiphany*: Gen.........
CLIFTON—*St. Peter's*: (Apportionment,
1909-10) Gen..................
EAST ORANGE—*Christ Church*: (Ap-
portionment, 1909-10) Bishop Rowe's
work, Alaska..................
HASBROUCK HEIGHTS — *St. John-the-
Divine*: (Apportionment, 1909-10)
Gen. ....
JERSEY CITY—*Holy Cross*: (Appor-

9 06	
137 50	
10 00	
42 60	
29 78	
33 55	
11 42	
10 00	
30 00	
3 00	
8 00	
2 43	
50 00	
3 42	
4 00	
50	
8 50	
1 00	
35 42	
10 00	
15 00	
180 00	
4 71	
12 00	
66 09	
47	
25 00	
1 00	
70 83	
12 00	
10 00	
59 00	
37 05	
5 00	
5 00	
16 85	
5 00	
60 00	

New York

Ap. $10,830.52; *Sp.* $431.75

BRONXVILLE—*Christ Church*: Sp. for Expansion Fund, St. John's University, Shanghai............... 22 00
CARMEL—Marion C. Tracy (Apportionment, 1909-10), Gen............. 10 50
CORNWALL—*St. John's*: (Apportionment, 1909-10) Gen............ 20 00
DOBBS FERRY—*Zion* (Greensburgh): (Apportionment, 1909-10) Gen..... 125 83
FISHKILL—*St. Andrew's*: Gen........ 35 00
FISHKILL VILLAGE—Miss A. I. Vandervoort, Gen...................... 10 00
GREENWOOD LAKE—*Church of the Good Shepherd*: Sp. for Expansion Fund, St. John's University, Shanghai..... 13 75
KINGSTON—*St. John's*: Dom., $6.60; Frn., $6.11; Junior Aux., Gen., $2.. 14 71
MARLBORO—*Christ Church*: (Apportionment, 1909-10) Gen.......... 16 00
MATTEAWAN—*St. Luke's*: Wo. Aux., Gen., $5; Sp. for Foreign Life Insurance Fund, $5; Sp. for Deaconess Routledge's work, Manila, Philippine Islands, $5...................... 15 00
MOUNT VERNON—Mrs. J. W. Shepard (Apportionment, 1909-10), Gen.... 1 00
"A Friend," Sp. toward the purchase of a donkey for the Rev. Mr. Matthews, Cape Mount, Liberia........ 21 00
NEW YORK—*All Angels'*: (Apportionment, 1909-10) Gen............. 846 42
All Souls': (Apportionment, 1909-10) "G. R.," Gen., $20.25; "A and G.," Gen., $115; St. John's University, Shanghai, $15; Bishop Partridge's work, Kyoto, $10; S. S.,* Gen., $38.51 .... 198 76
Ascension (West New Brighton, Staten Island): (Apportionment, 1909-10) Gen. 82 00
Beloved Disciple: Gen............... 24 60
Christ Church (Riverdale): (Apportionment) Gen................... 60 00
Grace: (Apportionment, 1909-10), "A Member," Gen., $100; St. Augustine's League, Committee on Missions for Colored People, Sp. for St. Agnes's Hospital, Raleigh, North Carolina, $10; Sp. for Good Samaritan Hospital, Charlotte, $5............. 115 00
Holy Communion: Miss Mary L. Ogden, $100, Charles W. Ogden, $50, Gen.. 150 00
Holy Apostles': Gen., $67.70 (Apportionment, 1909-10); "A Member," Wo. Aux., Sp. for Christmas gifts, for Kyoto, $5; Sp. for Christmas gifts, for Hankow, $5............. 77 70
Church of the Messiah: (Apportionment, 1909-10) Gen............. 2 50
St. Andrew's (Richmond, Staten Island): Wo. Aux., Sp. for Elizabeth Bunn Memorial Hospital, Wuchang, Hankow, $50; "A Member," Gen., $25 .... 75 00
St. George's: $1,109.40, Wo. Aux., "A Member," $50 (Apportionment, 1909-10), Gen...................1,159 40
St. John's (Clifton, Staten Island): Gen. 20 00
St. Mary's: Brazil.................. 50 00
St. Peter's (Westchester): (Apportionment, 1909-10) Dom............. 16 91
St. Philip's: (Apportionment, 1909-10) Gen. 150 00
Trinity Chapel: Domestic Missions in the United States, $1,823.52; missions in Africa, China, Japan, $1,881.35 ....3,704 87
"J. M. L.," medical mission work in China, $700; work in Oklahoma, $700; work in Eastern Oregon, $600; (Apportionment, 1909-10)... 2,000 00

970 Acknowledgments

"A Friend" (Apportionment, 1909-10), Gen.... 1,000 00
Mrs. E. Benjamin (Apportionment, 1909-10) Gen.... 300 00
"Birthday Offering," Gen.... 100 00
Miss E. Shriner (New Brighton, Staten Island) (Apportionment, 1909-10), Gen.... 1 00
General Theological Seminary "Divinity" scholarship, Trinity Divinity-school, Tokyo, $70; "Divinity" scholarship, Boone Divinity-school, Wuchang, Hankow, $100.... 170 00
Girls' Friendly Society, Sp. for salary of deacon, the Rev. S. C. Hughson, O.H.C., St. Andrew's School, Sewanee, Tennessee.... 10 00
NYACK—Grace: Gen.... 94 00
OSSINING — All Saints' (Briarcliff): Mrs. D. B. Plumer, Sp. for Expansion Fund, St. John's University, Hankow.... 5 00
Trinity Church: Wo. Aux., Sp. for Hospital of the Good Sheperd, Fort Defiance, Arizona, $75; S. S., Gen., $40 115 00
PEEKSKILL—St. Peter's: (Apportionment, 1909-10) Gen.... 59 00
Mrs. John J. Cox (Apportionment, 1909-10), Gen.... 10 00
POUGHKEEPSIE—Christ Church: Gen.. 30 00
RYE—Mrs. George P. Titus, Gen.... 6 17
SPARKILL—Christ Church (Piermont): Gen.... 2 00
WHITE PLAINS—Grace S. S.: "Grace Church" scholarship, St. John's University, Shanghai, $50; Gen., $52.15. 102 15
YONKERS—"Mrs. J. H. C.," Gen.... 10 00
Miss Alice I. Gilman (Apportionment, 1909-10) Gen.... 10 00
MISCELLANEOUS—Niobrara League, Sp. for supplies for St. Mary's School, Rosebud, South Dakota (of which Mrs. George A. Ward, $100).... 200 00

North Carolina
Ap., $127.91; *Sp.* $3.00

CHARLOTTE—St. Michael's: Wo. Aux., Sp. for Bishop Ferguson, Africa (of which Junior Aux., $1).... 3 00
St. Peter's S. S.*: Gen.... 50 50
GREENSBORO—St. Cuthbert's Chapel: (Apportionment, 1909-10) Gen.... 1 00
HALIFAX—St. Mark's: Gen.... 1 25
JACKSON—Church of the Saviour: (Apportionment, 1909-10) Gen.... 5 00
RALEIGH—Christ Church: (Apportionment, 1909-10) Gen.... 16 90
ROWAN CO.—St. Mark's: (Apportionment, 1909-10) Gen.... 26
St. Mary's: (Apportionment, 1909-10) Gen.... 1 00
St. Matthew's: (Apportionment, 1909-10) Gen.... 1 00
SOUTHERN PINES—"A Friend" (Apportionment), Gen.... 1 00
MISCELLANEOUS — "Anonymous" (Apportionment, 1909-10), Gen.... 50 00

Ohio
Ap. $357.12

ASHTABULA—St. Peter's: Gen.... 10 60
CLEVELAND—Emmanuel Church: Miss Maude L. Kimball (Apportionment, 1909-10), Gen.... 12 00
Incarnation: Gen., $27.86; Wo. Aux., salary of Miss Elwin, Shanghai, $5.. 32 86
St. Andrew's: Wo. Aux., salary of Miss Elwin, Shanghai.... 1 41
St. John's: Junior Aux., salary of Miss Elwin, Shanghai.... 5 00
Harriet P. Hutchinson (Apportionment, 1909-10), Gen.... 1 00
JEFFERSON—Trinity Church: Gen.... 10 00

MAUMEE—St. Paul's: Gen....
OBERLIN—Christ Church: Gen....
SANDUSKY—Grace: Wo. Aux., Philippines, $5; salary of Miss Elwin, Shanghai, $10; "Sandusky" scholarship, St. John's University, Shanghai, $40....
TOLEDO—St. Andrew's S. S.* Gen....
UNIONVILLE—St. Michael's: Gen....
WELLSVILLE — Ascension: Wo. Aux., salary of Miss Elwin, Shanghai....
WOOSTER—St. James's: $4, S. S., 58 cts. (Apportionment, 1909-10), Dom.
MISCELLANEOUS—"A Friend" (Apportionment, 1909-10), Gen....

Oregon
Ap. $38.50

ASTORIA — Holy Innocents': (Apportionment, 1909-10) Gen....
CORVALLIS—Good Samaritan: (Apportionment, 1909-10) Gen....
EUGENE—E. L. Blossom (Apportionment, 1909-10), Gen....
TOLEDO—St. John's Mission: Gen....

Pennsylvania
Ap. $2,101.94; *Sp.* $696.05

ARDMORE — St. Mary's: Wo. Aux., Sp. for nurses' salary in St. Luke's Hospital, Shanghai....
BRYN MAWR—Church of the Redeemer: Mrs. Perot's Bible Class, Sp. for Nevada....
CHELTENHAM—St. Paul's: Wo. Aux., Sp. for Bishop Roots, Hankow....
ITHAN—St. Martin's Chapel: Frn....
MERION STATION—Mrs. S. Burns Weston (for 1909-10), Gen....
NORWOOD—St. Stephen's: (Apportionment 1909-10) Gen....
PHILADELPHIA — Atonement (Memorial): Apportionment 1909-10) Gen....
Calvary (Germantown): Girls' Friendly Society, Sp. for salary of teacher, St. John's Mission, Battle Creek, Tennessee....
Christ Church Chapel: Wo. Aux., Sp. for Bishop Roots, Hankow....
Christ Church (Franklinville): Gen....
Emmanuel Church (Holmesburg): D. M., $5; Miss Disston, $1 (Apportionment 1909-10), Gen....
Epiphany Chapel: "A Member," Gen., $5; Girls' Friendly Society, Sp. for salary of teacher, St. John's Mission, Battle Creek, Tennessee, $5....
Epiphany Mission (Sherwood): (Apportionment 1909-10) Gen....
Holy Apostles': Wo. Aux., salary of Miss Sarah H. Reid, Shanghai....
Holy Trinity Church: Wo. Aux., Missionary Bible-class for Hooker Memorial School, Mexico....
Children of the House of the Holy Child (Apportionment 1909-10), Gen.
Messiah Chapel: Girls' Friendly Society, Sp. for salary of teacher, St. John's Mission, Battle Creek, Tennessee
Prince of Peace: Wo. Aux., "Foreign Committee" scholarship, St. Hilda's School, Wuchang, $2.50; "Foreign Committee" scholarship, $2.50....
Resurrection: Girls' Friendly Society, Sp. for salary of teacher at Battle Creek, Tennessee, St. John's Mission....
Church of the Saviour: Wo. Aux. (In Memoriam), M. A. C. Ireland, Sp. for evangelist's salary, St. Luke's

75 00	In memory of "A. F. P.," Sp. for
23 00	Utah 25 00
	Wo. Aux., Domestic Committee, salary of a domestic missionary bishop. 100 00
	Miss Ellen Morris, $1, "A Friend,"
50 00 ·	$2, collection at candidates' annual service, $23.45, Girls' Friendly Society, Sp. for salary of teacher at Battle Creek, Tennessee, St. John's
61 00	Mission 26 45

Pittsburgh

Ap. $211.00; *Sp.* $60.00

25 00	AMBRIDGE—*St. Matthias's*: Gen...... 2 00
25 00	BUTLER—*St. Peter's*: Dom. and Frn... 2 60
38 52	FOXBURG—*Church of Our Father*: Rev. A. A. Benton, D.D. (Apportionment, 1909-10), Gen.......... 10 00
	FRANKLIN—*St. John's*: Gen.......... 18 50
178 49	McKEESPORT—*St. Stephen's*: Dom. and
5 50	Frn. 4 56
	OAKMONT—*St. Thomas's*: Sp. for Expansion Fund, St. John's University, Shanghai................... 10 00
50 05	PITTSBURGH — *Christ Church*: Anglican Young People's Association, Sp. for Utah..................... 50 00
	SEWICKLEY — *St. Stephen's*: (Apportionment, 1909-10) Gen.......... 153 66
15 00	SHARON—*St. John's*: Gen.......... 9 68
	MISCELLANEOUS—Rev. Dr. Dyess (Apportionment, 1909-10), Gen........ 10 00

Quincy

Ap. $51.41

10 00	CANTON—*St. Peter's Mission*: (Apportionment, 1909-10) Gen........ 2 00
87 00	CARTHAGE—*St. Cyprian's*: (Apportionment, 1909-10) Gen.............. 5 00
245 00	FARMINGTON — *Calvary*: (Apportionment, 1909-10) Gen.............. 2 70
200 00	KEWANEE—*St. John's*: Gen.......... 5 00
125 00	QUINCY—*Cathedral of St. John*: (Apportionment, 1909-10) Gen........ 27 55
50 00	*Church of the Good Shepherd*: (Apportionment, 1909-10) Gen........ 9 16

Rhode Island

Ap. $716.78

50 00	BRISTOL—*St. Michael's*: "Mrs. H.,"
50 00	Gen............................ 10 00
50 00	NEWPORT—*Trinity Church*: Gen..... 691 78
15 00	PHILLIPSDALE—*Grace Memorial*: (Apportionment, 1909-10) Gen........ 10 00
10 00	PROVIDENCE—Eliza A. Peckham: (Apportionment, 1909-10), Gen........ 5 00
10 00	
5 00	

South Carolina

Ap. $158.50; *Sp.* $68.00

5 00	AIKEN—*St. Thaddeus's*: (Apportionment, 1909-10) Gen............... 50 00
4 00	ANDERSON — *Grace*: (Apportionment, 1909-10) Gen.................. 2 00
9 00	BEAUFORT—*St. Helena's*: Junior Aux., for Bishop Capers Day-school, Wuchang, Hankow................... 5 00
126 62	CLEMSON—*Holy Trinity Church*: Junior Aux., assistant for Miss McCullough, Porto Rico, $1; Bishop Capers Day-school, Wuchang, Hankow, $1........................... 2 00
9 75	EASTOVER — *St. Thomas's*: (Colored),
8 15	Gen. 10 00
	HAGOOD—*Ascension*: (Apportionment, 1909-10) Frn................... 5 00
100 00	LAURENS — *Epiphany*: $17.50, Wo. Aux., $10, "A Friend" (Apportionment, 1909-10), $20, Gen.......... 47 50
7 16	"C. B. S.," Gen................. 4 00
100 00	

RIDGE SPRINGS—*Grace*: Wo. Aux., assistant for Miss McCullough, Porto Rico, $1; N. S. Wilson's Day-school, Hankow, $1; Gen., $3...... 5 00
ROCK HILL—*Church of Our Saviour*: Junior Aux., Bishop Capers Day-school, Wuchang, Hankow......... 5 00
SANTEE—*St. James's*: Wo. Aux., M. E. Pinkney Fund, Bible-woman, Tokyo, $2.50; N. S. Wilson's Day-school, Hankow, $2.50; Sp. for "Bishop Howe" cot, St. Mary's Orphanage, Shanghai, $3.................... 8 00
SPARTANBURG — "Personal," Sp. for Valle Crucis Mission, Asheville, $50; Sp. for prayer room at Valle Crucis, Asheville, $15............. 65 00
SUMMERVILLE—*St. Paul's*: Dom., $5; Frn., $5; Junior Aux., assistant for Miss McCullough, Porto Rico, $1.... 11 00
SUMTER—*St. Augustine's*: (Apportionment, 1909-10) Frn............... 7 00

Southern Ohio

Ap. $155.65; *Sp.* $312.00

BELLAIRE—*Trinity Mission*: (Apportionment, 1909-10) Gen............. 10 00
CINCINNATI — *Calvary*: (Apportionment, 1909-10) Gen................ 25 00
Christ Church: (Apportionment, 1909-10) Gen.................... 25 00
Epiphany: (Apportionment, 1909-10) Gen.......................... 20 00
Church of Our Saviour: (Apportionment, 1909-10) Gen............. 50 00
Trinity Missionary Guild, Wo. Aux., Sp. for "Helen T. Memorial" scholarship, St. Peter's School, Honolulu. 12 00
COLUMBUS—*All Saints'*: Mission for Deaf-mutes 2 00
DAYTON—*Christ Church*: Mrs. E. E. Parker, missions in China......... 10 00
DRESDEN — *Zion*: (Apportionment, 1909-10) Gen.................... 2 00
GLENDALE—Mrs. C. K. Benedict, Sp. for the enlargement of St. Elizabeth's Hospital, Shanghai......... 300 00
MADISON TOWNSHIP — *St. Matthew's Mission*: (Apportionment, 1909-10) Gen. 1 10
MARTIN'S FERRY—*St. Paul's*: (Apportionment, 1909-10) Gen.......... 5 00
MILFORD—*St. Thomas's*: (Apportionment, 1909-10) Gen............. 5 55

Southern Virginia

Ap. $514.91; *Sp.* $70.00

AMHERST Co.—Mrs. Hugh S. Worthington (Sweet Briar) (Apportionment, 1909-10), Gen............ 1 00
APPOMATTOX Co.—*St. Paul's, Patrick Parish*: Dom., 50 cts.; Frn., 50 cts. 1 00
BEDFORD Co. (Bedford City)—Wo. Aux., Second Circle, Sp. for "Lucy Griffin" scholarship, Anvik, Alaska. 50 00
CAMPBELL Co.—*St. Paul's* (Lynchburg): (of which Apportionment, 1909-10, $294) Gen............. 299 00
ELIZABETH CITY Co.—*St. John's* (Hampton): (Apportionment, 1909-10) Gen..................... 79 75
HALIFAX Co.—*Christ Church* (Houston): Colored (Apportionment, 1909-10) Gen................. 2 00
St. John's (Houston): Wo. Aux., St. Mary's Hall, Shanghai............ 25 00
Trinity Church (South Boston): Frn... 15 00
ISLE OF WIGHT — *Christ Church* (Smithfield): Wo. Aux., Sp. for support of Sei Kobayashi, in Mr. Osuga's Orphanage, Tokyo................. 20 00
LEE Co.—*Keokee Mission*: Gen...... 8 25

MONTGOMERY Co. — *St. Thomas'* (Christiansburg): Gen...........
Ethel A. L. Lacy (Blacksburg) China missions.................
NORFOLK Co.—*St. Mark's* (Lambert' Point): (Apportionment, 1909-10 Gen. ....
St. Paul's (Norfolk): (Apportionment 1909-10) Gen...............
PITTSLYVANIA Co.—"A Friend" (Danville), Gen.....................
PRINCE EDWARD Co. — *St. John' Memorial* (Farmville): (Apportionment, 1909-10) Gen...........
ROANOKE Co.—*St. John's* (Roanoke) (Apportionment, 1909-10) Gen...
St. Paul's (Salem): Gen...........

Springfield

Ap. $67.50

ALBION—*St. John's*: (Apportionment 1909-10) Gen................
ALTON — *St. Paul's* (Apportionment 1909-10) Gen................
CARLINVILLE—*St. Paul's*: (Apportionment, 1909-10) Gen.......
JACKSONVILLE—*Trinity Church*: (Apportionment, 1909-10) Gen.......
PETERSBURG—*Trinity Church*: (Apportionment, 1909-10) Gen.........

Tennessee

Ap. $129.15

CHATTANOOGA—*St. Paul's*: (Apportionment, 1909-10) Gen.......
FRANKLIN — *St. Paul's*: (Apportionment, 1909-10) Gen.......
GALLATIN—*Immanuel Church*: (Apportionment, 1909-10) Gen.......
JACKSON—*St. Luke's S. S.**: Gen....
PULASKI—*Church of the Messiah* (Apportionment, 1909-10) Gen....
SEWANEE—Rev. William S. Bisho (Apportionment, 1909-10) Gen....
SOUTH PITTSBURGH — *Christ Church* Wo. Aux., Gen.................
SPRING HILL—*Grace Chapel*: (Apportionment, 1909-10) Gen.......
WINCHESTER—David Driver, Gen.....

Texas

Ap. $108.00

ANGLETON—*Church of the Holy Comforter Mission*: Gen.............
HOUSTON—*Christ Church*: (Apportionment, 1909-10) Gen..........
WASKOM—*St. Mary's Mission*: Gen...

Vermont

Ap. $15.01; *Sp.* $102.00

ENOSBURG FALLS — *St. Matthew's*: (Apportionment, 1909-10) Gen.....
GRAND ISLES—*Vantine's*: Gen......
MANCHESTER CENTRE—E. L. Wyman, M.D. (Apportionment, 1909-10), Gen.
MIDDLEBURY—"A Friend," Sp. for Rev. J. W. Chapman, Alaska, to be used for family described in "Just an Indian" ....
MISCELLANEOUS—"A Friend," Sp. for work of Rev. Robert C. Wilson, Shanghai ....

Virginia

Ap. $400.79

ALBEMARLE Co.—*Christ Church S. S.* (Charlottesville): for the "Hilga

50 00	portionment, 1909-10)............ 14 00
	HARBOR SPRINGS—*St. John's*: Gen.
5 00	(Apportionment, 1909-10).......... 16 52
	HOLLAND — *Grace*: Gen. (Apportion-
20 75	ment, 1909-10)................. 3 75
	IONIA—*St. John's*: Gen. (Apportion-
14 24	ment, 1909-10)................. 3 00
14 10	KALAMAZOO—*St. Luke's*: Gen. (Appor-
9 15	tionment, 1909-10)............... 29 18
1 75	MANISTEE — *Holy Trinity Church*:
	Gen. (of which Apportionment,
	1909-10, $1).................. 2 00
3 80	MARSHALL—*Trinity Church*: Gen. (Ap-
10 00	portionment, 1909-10)............ 2 00
	MUSKEGON—*St. Paul's*: Gen. (of which
	Apportionment, 1909-10, $5)....... 18 70
260 00	NILES—*Trinity Church*: Gen (Appor-
	tionment, 1909-10)............... 3 00
	OMENA—*Summer Congregation*: Gen.
	(Apportionment, 1909-10)......... 4 05
12 00	PETOSKEY — *Emmanuel Church*: Gen.
	(Apportionment, 1909-10).......... 51 72
	MISCELLANEOUS—Through the bishop,
	from individuals in St. Mark's Pro-
	Cathedral, Grand Rapids and St.
12 00	Paul's, Muskegon, Gen. (Apportion-
	ment, 1909-10)................. 80 98
	Rev. J. N. Rippey, Dom. and Frn.. 2 00
63 29	
	Western New York
30 06	*Ap.* $734.14 ; *Sp.* $30.00
25 00	BELFAST—*Grace*: Dom. and Frn...... 6 57
	BRANCHPORT—*St. Luke's*: Gen....... 10 00
7 70	BUFFALO—*Church of the Good Shep-
	herd S. S.**: Gen.............. 61 74
115 50	*Grace*: Dom. and Frn........... 80 00
4 00	*St. James's*: Gen............... 30 00
1 00	*St. Mary's-on-the-Hill*: Dom. and
	Frn. 12 50
	St. Paul's: George F. Plimpton, Sp.
	for Expansion Fund, St. John's Uni-
	versity, Shanghai.............. 5 00
	St. Simon's: Frn. (Apportionment,
50 00	1909-10) 35 00
	George F. Plimpton, Gen. (Appor-
2 00	tionment, 1909-10).............. 5 00
	Elbert B. Mann, Sp. for Expansion
29 85	Fund, St. John's College, Shanghai. 25 00
	"A Friend," Gen................ 100 00
10 00	GENEVA—*Trinity Church*: Wo. Aux.-
	Gen. 5 00
	HORNELL—*Christ Church*: Dom., $25;
	Gen., $50; Frn., $18 (Apportion-
25	ment, 1909-10) ; Dom., $20 (Ap-
	portionment, 1910-11)............ 113 00
	NORTH TONAWANDA—*St. Mark's*: Gen.
	(Apportionment, 1909-10).......... 14 83
11 50	OAKFIELD—*St. Michael's*: Gen........ 5 73
25	OLEAN—*St. Stephen's*: Dom., 25 cts.;
20 00	Frn., $21.34 ; Gen., $39 (Appor-
54 12	tionment, 1909-10).............. 60 59
	PALMYRA—"A Friend," Gen. (Appor-
2 75	tionment, 1909-10).............. 4 00
	ROCHESTER — *Christ Church*: Gen.
	(Apportionment, 1909-10).......... 100 00
	St. Luke's: "Elizabeth," Gen........ 25 00
	SOUTH PHELPS—*St. Paul's*: Gen...... 1 68
	WESTFIELD—A. B. Ottaway, Gen. (Ap-
	portionment, 1909-10)............ 1 00
	Miss Lillian M. Skinner. $10, Miss
45 00	Annie Hullenbacher, $1, Misses York,
	50 cts., Miss Laura A. Skinner, $1,
	Gen. (Apportionment. 1909-10).... 12 50
	MISCELLANEOUS—Mrs. C. H. Boynton,
	Wo. Aux., for the "W. F. C. Memor-
	ial" bed, Elizabeth Bunn Hospital,
	Wuchang, Hankow.............. 50 00
10 00	**West Texas**
50 00	*Ap.* $121.93
	KARNES CITY—Gen. 3 00
36 00	KENVILLE—E. Galbraith, Frn......... 50 00
5 50	SAN ANTONIO—*St. Mark's*: $35, S. S.,
	$33.93, Gen.................. 68 93

West Virginia

Ap. $245.85 ; *Sp.* $63.00

ANSTED—*Church of the Redeemer*: Dom. 3 65
BECKLEY—Gen. (Apportionment, 1909-10) 6 85
BLUE RIDGE—*St. Andrew's*: Gen. (Apportionment, 1909-10) 3 00
Christ Church: Gen. (Apportionment, 1909-10) 3 00
CHARLES TOWN—*Zion*: Gen., $131.67 ; St. Andrew's Guild, Sp. for the Church paper in Brazil, $60 ...... 191 67
FORT SPRING — *Greenbrier Parish*: Gen. 1 82
HARPER'S FERRY — *St. John's*: Gen. (Apportionment, 1909-10) 5 00
MOOREFIELD — *Emmanuel Church*: Dom. and Frn. 2 65
MIDDLEWAY—*Grace*: Brazil. 3 11
NEW MARTINSVILLE — *St. Ann's*: Brazil 5 80
PAGE — *Epiphany*: Gen. (Apportionment, 1909-10) 7 34
POWELLTON—*St. David's*: Gen. 3 37
ROMNEY—*St. Stephen's*: Dom. and Frn. 13 30
RONCEVERTE—*Incarnation*: Deaf and Dumb and Blind, $1.97 ; Frn., $1.52. 3 49
WESTON — *St. Paul's*: Gen., $27.40 ; S. S., Cuba, $2.20 ; Brazil, $2.20 .. 31 80
WELLSBURG — *Christ Church*: Gen. (Apportionment, 1909-10) 20 00
MISCELLANEOUS—Wo. Aux., Sp. for Miss Barber's work, Anking, Hankow 3 00

Missionary Districts

Alaska

Ap. $90.00

DOUGLAS—*St. Luke's*: Gen. 10 00
FAIRBANKS—*St. Mark's*: Gen. 50 00
NOME—*St. Mary's*: Gen. 25 00
SALAKAKET—*St. Luke's*: Gen. 5 00

Asheville

Ap. $1.00 ; *Sp.* $1.50

LINCOLNTON—*St. Luke's*: (Apportionment, 1909-10) Gen., $1 ; "A Member," Sp. for Fair Fund, for St. Matthew's Mission, hospital at Fairbanks, Alaska, $1 .... 2 50

Honolulu

Ap. $50.00

MISCELLANEOUS—Wo. Aux., Gen. (Apportionment, 1909-10) 50 00

Idaho

Ap. $2.00

BOISE—Miss L. A. Putnam, Gen. (Apportionment, 1909-10) 2 00

Kearney

Ap. $2.80

HASTINGS—*St. Mark's*: Gen. 2 80

New Mexico

Ap. $7.00

ALAMOGORDO—*St. John's*: Gen. 5 00
CARLSBAD—Rev. N. T. Tracy, Gen. ... 2 00

North Dakota

Ap. $38.47

JAMESTOWN—*Grace*: For deaf-mute work ....
LANGDON—*St. James's*: Gen. ....
MINOT—*All Saints'*: Gen. ....
OSNABROOK—Gen. ....
PEMBINA—*Grace*; Gen. ....

Oklahoma

Ap. $27.50

MCALESTER—*All Saints'*: (Apportionment, 1909-10) Gen. ....
OAK LODGE—*St. John's*: (Apportionment, 1909-10) Gen. ....
TULSA—*Trinity Church*: "Three Members," toward support of Boone University, Wuchang, Hankow ....

Olympia

Ap. $20.00 ; *Sp.* $5.00

BELLINGHAM—*St. Paul's S. S.*: (Apportionment, 1909-10) Gen. ....
SEATTLE—Wo. Aux., Sp. for St. Hilda's Building Fund, Hankow ....
TACOMA—*St. Peter's*: (Apportionment, 1909-10) Gen. ....

Porto Rico

Ap. $5.00

MISCELLANEOUS—Wo. Aux., Gen. ......

Sacramento

Ap. $146.50

COLFAX—*Church of the Good Shepherd*: Gen. ....
FOLSOM — *Trinity Church*: (Apportionment, 1900-10) Gen. ....
GRASS VALLEY — *Emmanuel Church*: (Apportionment, 1909-10) Gen. .....
MARYSVILLE—*St. John's*: (Apportionment, 1909-10) Gen. ....
NAMPA—*St. Mary's*: (Apportionment, 1909-10) Gen. ....
SANTA ROSA—*Incarnation*: (Apportionment, 1909-10) Gen. ....
WOODLAND—*St. Luke's*: (Apportionment, 1909-10) Gen. ....

Salina

Ap. $.50

MEADE—*St. Augustine's*: Gen. ....

South Dakota

Ap. $519.77

DALLAS—*Incarnation Chapel*: (Apportionment, 1909-10) Gen. ....
FAIRFAX — *Trinity Church*: (Apportionment, 1909-10) Gen. ....
FLANDREAU—*Church of the Redeemer*: Gen. ....
CHEYENNE RIVER MISSION—*St. John's*: Wo. Aux., Dom., $5 ; Frn., $5 ....; *St. Stephen's*: Wo. Aux., Dom., $5 ; Frn., $5 ....; *Ascension*: Wo. Aux., Dom., 75 cts. ; Frn., 50 cts ....; *St. Mary's*: Gen., 75 cts. ; Wo. Aux., Dom., $2 ; Frn., $1.50 ....; *Emmanuel Church*: Wo. Aux., Dom., $1.25 ; Frn., $1.25 ....; *St. Paul's*: Gen ....; *St. Barnabas's*: Wo. Aux., Dom., 50 cts. ; Frn., 50 cts ....

2 50	School, South Dakota, $5; St. Mary's School, South Dakota, $5; Japanese Babies, $3...................... 36 00
2 00	St. Luke's: Gen................... 1 00
2 50	STANDING ROCK MISSION—St. Elizabeth's: Wo. Aux., Dom., $20; Frn., $16 .... 36 00
2 00	St. Thomas's: Wo. Aux., Dom., $15; Frn., $10..................... 25 00
8 00	Church of the Good Shepherd: Wo. Aux., Dom., $10; Frn., $6.75..... 16 75
2 00	St. John the Baptist's: Wo. Aux., Dom., $20; Frn., $15............. 35 00
2 00	YANKTON MISSION—Holy Fellowship: Wo. Aux., Dom., $12.37; Frn., $11; Daughters of the King, Frn., $3.65. 27 02
10 00	St. Philip's: Wo. Aux., Dom., $5; Frn., $5 .... 10 00
	CROW CREEK MISSION—Christ Church: Wo. Aux., Dom., $5; Frn., $5..... 10 00
17 50	St. John the Baptist's: Wo. Aux., Dom., $3.25; Frn., $3.25.......... 6 50
50	All Saints': Wo. Aux., Dom........... 5 00
50	St. Peter's: Wo. Aux., Dom., $3; Frn., $2.50....................... 5 50
55	MISCELLANEOUS — Collections during convocation (Apportionment, 1909-10), Gen...................... 33 91
1 50	
50	**Southern Florida**
50	*Ap. $12.85*
1 10	KEY WEST—St. Paul's: (Apportionment, 1909-10) Gen.............. 12 85
90	
1 00	**Spokane**
1 00	*Ap. $14.50*
1 15	ROSLYN—Calvary: Gen............. 4 50
25	SPOKANE—Holy Trinity Church S. S.*: Gen. 10 00
3 25	
5 70	**Wyoming**
	Ap. $9.15
20 50	LANDER—Trinity Church: (Apportionment, 1909-10) Gen.............. 7 40
10 00	SARATOGA—St. Barnabas's: Gen...... 1 75
90	
2 50	
1 25	*Foreign Missionary Districts*
5 00	**Africa**
2 00	LIBERIA—St. Philip's (Gardenersville): (Apportionment, 1909-10) Gen...... 3 00
1 70	
1 00	**Canada**
9 00	TORONTO—Mrs. Kemp, Sp. for St. Hilda's Building Fund, Wuchang,
17 00	Hankow 5 00
	P. W. T. Ross, Sp. for Rev. R. E. Wood, Wuchang, Hankow, for purchase of land.................... 1 00
9 50	QUEBEC—Ayers Cliff Inn: Miss K. L.
1 50	Patterson (Apportionment, 1909-10), Gen. 10 00
37 50	**Mexico**
	GUADALAJARA—Rev. A. L. Burleson (Apportionment, 1909-10), Gen... 4 99
45 00	**Tokyo**
	TOYKO—Trinity Cathedral: (Apportionment, 1909-10) Gen.......... 50 00

Miscellaneous

Ap. $1,526.07; *Sp.* $1,514.89
Specific Deposit, $18.91
Interest, Dom., $856.61; Frn., $443.68; Gen., $174.68; Sp., $686.89; Men's . Thank-offering, $18.91 .... 2,180 77
St. Leger Fund, Sp. for Bishop Rowe, for Cordova, Alaska, $500; Sp. for Bishop Roots, for Boone Library, Wuchang, Hankow, $150; Sp. for Rev. Mr. Gilman, Hankow, for personal library, $50 .... 700 00
"A Friend," Sp. for Archdeacon Neve's work in the Diocese of Virginia 125 00
"Friends," Gen 50 00
Travellers aboard the S. V. Luckenbach, from Porto Rico, Sp. for work among sailors in San Francisco, California 3 00
Through *The Living Church,* Gen... 1 10

Legacies

L. I., GREAT NECK—Estate of Miss Mary Rhinelander King, for investment for John Alsop King and Mary Colden King Fund, for Colored Missions, $20,000; for investment for Colored Missions, $10,000; for investment for the "Cornelia King" scholarship, Anvik, Alaska, $2,500; for the Bishop of Alaska, for his work in said diocese, $10,000; for the Bishop of Oklahoma, for his work in said diocese, $3,000......45,500 00
L. I., BROOKLYN—Estate of Rev. Isaac Maguire, to the Society.......... 500 00
W. MASS., PITTSFIELD—Estate of Parker L. Hall, Dom., $50; Frn., $50 .... 100 00

Total received during September, 1910 ....$81,079 57

THE SUNDAY-SCHOOL TEACHERS' MANUAL

Designed as an Aid to Teachers in Preparing Sunday-school Lessons

THE

Spirit of Missions

AN ILLUSTRATED MONTHLY REVIEW
OF CHRISTIAN MISSIONS

December, 1910

CONTENTS

The Subscription Price of THE SPIRIT OF MISSIONS is ONE DOLLAR per year.
Postage is prepaid in the United States, Porto Rico, The Philippines and Mexico. For other countries
in the Postal Union, including Canada, twenty-four cents per year should be added.
Subscriptions are continued until ordered discontinued.
Change of Address: In all changes of address it is necessary that the old as well as the new
address should be given.
How to Remit: Remittances, made payable to George Gordon King, Treasurer, should be made
by draft on New York, Postal Order or Express Order. One and two cent stamps are received. To
checks on local banks ten cents should be added for collection.
All Letters should be addressed to The Spirit of Missions, 281 Fourth Avenue, New York.

Published by the Domestic and Foreign Missionary Society.
President, RIGHT REVEREND DANIEL S. TUTTLE, D.D.   *Treasurer*, GEORGE GORDON KING.
Entered at the Post Office, in New York, as second-class matter.

THE SPIRIT OF MISSIONS is regularly on sale
   In Philadelphia: By Jacobs' Book Store, 1210 Walnut St.
   In Milwaukee: By The Young Churchman Co., 412 Milwaukee St.
   In Boston: By Smith & McCance, 38 Bromfield St.
   In Elizabeth, N. J.: By Franklin H. Spencer, 743 Jefferson St.

WANTED

From every person in the Church over ten years of age, for the work of the Church's Mission, a minimum gift of

10 CENTS A WEEK

Those who can give in tens and hundreds and thousands of dollars are expected so to do.

Give what *costs*, according to your ability, and receive the blessing!

See the Message from the Board of Missions,
page 991

THE MISSIONARY DISTRICTS OF THE CHURCH

I. AT HOME

Alaska: Right Rev. Dr. Peter Trimble Rowe.

Arizona: Rev. Julius W. Atwood, Bishop-elect.

Asheville: Right Rev. Dr. Junius Moore Horner.

Eastern Oklahoma: Rev. Theodore Payne Thurston, Bishop-elect.

Eastern Oregon: Right Rev. Dr. Robert L. Paddock.

Honolulu: Right Rev. Dr. Henry B. Restarick.

Idaho: Right Rev. Dr. James Bowen Funsten.

Kearney: Right Rev. George Allen Beecher.

Nevada: Right Rev. Dr. Henry Douglas Robinson.

New Mexico: Right Rev. Dr. John Mills Kendrick.

North Dakota: Right Rev. Dr. Cameron Mann.

North Texas: Rev Edward A. Temple, Bishop-elect.

Oklahoma: Right Rev. Dr. Francis K. Bro

Porto Rico: Right Rev. Dr. James H. Van

Philippine Islands: Right Rev. Dr. Charle: Brent.

Salina: Right Rev. Dr. Sheldon Munson G

San Joaquin: Rev. Louis Childs Sanford, elect.

South Dakota: Right Rev. Dr. F. F. Johns

Southern Florida: Right Rev. Dr. William Gray.

Spokane: Right Rev. Dr. Lemuel Henry W

Utah: Right Rev. Dr. Franklin Spencer Sp

Western Colorado: Right Rev. Dr. Benjami ster.

Wyoming: Right Rev. Dr. Nathaniel S. Tl

Though not a missionary district the Panama Canal Zone has been placed under the care of t Bishop of Cuba.

II. ABROAD

Brazil: Right Rev. Dr. Lucien Lee Kinsolving.

Cape Palmas: Right Rev. Dr. Samuel David Ferguson.

Cuba: Right Rev. Dr. Albion Williamson Knight.

Hankow: Right Rev. Dr. Logan Herbert Roots.

Kyoto: Right Rev. Dr. Sidney Catlin Partr:

Mexico: Right Rev. Dr. Henry D. Aves.

Shanghai: Right Rev. Dr. Frederick Rogers

Tokyo: Right Rev. Dr. John McKim.

Wuhu: Rev. F. L. Hawks Pott, D.D., Bisho

III.

HAITIEN CHURCH : Right Rev. Dr. James Theodore Holly.

IMPORTANT NOTES

THE CLERGY

THE Clergy are requested to notify "The Mailing Department, 281 Fourth Av New York," of changes in their post-office addresses in order that the B publications may be correctly mailed to them.

SUBSCRIBERS

SUBSCRIBERS will observe that the address label indicates the time to which sub tions are paid. Changes are made in the labels on the 15th of each month. I scriptions are received later than the 15th, the change in the label will appear a month

CONCERNING WILLS

IT is earnestly requested that inquiries be made concerning Wills admitted to pr whether they contain bequests to this Society, and that information of all suc quests be communicated to the Treasurer without delay. In making bequests for mi it is of great importance to give the exact title of the Society, thus:

I give, devise, and bequeath to The Domestic and Foreign Missionary Society of the Prot Episcopal Church in the United States of America, for the use of the Society..........

If it is desired that the bequest should be applied to some particular department o work, there should be substituted for the words "FOR THE USE OF THE SOCIETY,' words "FOR DOMESTIC MISSIONS," or "FOR FOREIGN MISSIONS," or "FOR WORK AI THE INDIANS," or "FOR WORK AMONG COLORED PEOPLE," or "FOR WORK IN AFRI or "FOR WORK IN CHINA," etc.

(980)

HE SPIRIT OF MISSIONS

AN ILLUSTRATED MONTHLY REVIEW
OF CHRISTIAN MISSIONS

LXXV. **December,** 1910   No. 12

The Christmas Contrasts

The countless stars, each one a world, look down;
A few sheep huddle on the hillside brown.

Angels, archangels, cherubs, seraphs blaze;
Some simple shepherds listen in amaze.

A maid fulfils what mighty prophets said,
Man, weak, and lying in a cattle-shed.

Almighty Love upon this earth appears,
But shows Himself through baby smiles and tears.

—*Cameron Mann*

THE PROGRESS OF THE KINGDOM

E of the most striking proofs of the universality of the Christian on is found in the intimate appeal which Christ makes to the men of every race. We speak of Him, most truly, as the Saviour and er of all men, yet we picture Him culiarly our own—an Anglo-Saxon ur.

he Desire of l Nations

may be, therefore, that some will feel a slight shock as they look at the picture opposite, wherein a Chinese Christian artist has set forth his idea of the Nativity. The distinctly Oriental baby and the quaint, slant-eyed shepherds seem to us incongruous. Yet is there not herein a beautiful lesson, and a new and larger vision of what Christmas means?

In the paintings of the old masters we are already familiar with an interpretation which depicts the Virgin and the

(981)

Child, the shepherds and the wise men,
with the physiognomy of the race and
clothed in the costume of the artist's
age and country. It is a Dutch, or
Spanish, or Italian mother that broods,
with eyes of love, over her child, and
across the canvas, with jingling spurs,
clad perhaps in mediæval armor, ride
the kingly visitors from the East.

All this would be merely an amusing
anachronism did it not set forth, in striking fashion, how Christ and Christmas
belong not to one race, or age, or clime,
but to all. For He is indeed the Desire
of the nations, and seeks to be continuously incarnate in the sacred and
secret places—the hearts and homes of
all people.

So the picture is true. The Child of
Bethlehem *is* that stolid Chinese baby,
just as truly as He is the radiant infant
in the arms of the Sistine Madonna.

A Bethlehem
n Every
Land
Among the great
lessons which the
missionary motive
teaches there is none
greater than this—
that our Christ is really and intimately
the Christ of all men. Strange nations,
to whom we go with His message, who
never quite understand *us,* can and do
understand *Him.* He enters into their
lives as deeply as He has entered into
ours; they clothe Him with their own
ideals; He becomes bone of their bone
and flesh of their flesh. He has crossed
a barrier which still holds us back; for
He *is* the message—larger than any
word of ours, more manifold in His appeal than our circumscribed vision can
picture. We can only bow with truer
and humbler worship before those things
in Him which, though hidden from us,
other eyes have seen, and pledge ourselves anew to the great service which
seeks to plant a Bethlehem in every land,
and to make the Christ-Child the dear
Guest of every heart. May the day be
hastened when the Desire of all Nations
shall come to all the nations of His
heart's desire!

commodating 5,000 persons and filled every Sunday, had been destroyed as in a moment. For only seven years has this notable building stood upon its present site, a third successor of the earliest structure, but during those years it has been a material witness to all the world that the Gospel is indeed "the power of God unto salvation."

The story of Uganda is too well known to need repetition here. To that work, more than to any other conducted by the Anglican communion, may we fittingly apply the words of the hymn, "A Nation in a Day"; for it is indeed within the day of a single human life that the work has been done. The first white presbyter to find his way into the forbidden land of the Waganda lives and works to-day in a quiet English parish and is not yet an old man. It was only last August that the body of Mwanga, "proud, perjured, fleeting" Mwanga, who seven years ago died in exile—whose cruel lips decreed the death of Hannington—was brought back to rest in the soil of his forefathers, and was buried with Christian words in the tomb of King Mtesa.

How these facts help us to realize the wonderful transformations which the Christian message can produce under the power of the Spirit of God! Beside the Uganda of thirty years ago— Uganda in its barbarism, its degradation and its seeming hopelessness—we place the Uganda of to-day, with its 70,000 Christian men and women, and its native ministry of over 2,000—a centre of light and missionary activity in an erstwhile Dark Continent.

THE work of our mission in Mexico, always difficult, will undoubtedly be made more so by the events which *The Unrest in Mexico* have just taken place there. Never, since our ruthless invasion in 1845, and our plundering of a defenceless people, has the Mexican nation felt any cordial kindness for Americans. Doubtless the things which have since been suffered at the hands of thousands of exploiting Americans have not tended to make the *gringos* more welcome. What is in store in that inevitable day when the strong hand of the present president is removed, no one can say. That there will be reprisals again, many Americans believe, and we, as an American Church, may perhaps find our position accordingly difficult.

Yet our mission there is in a unique sense a great trust. Not only are we seeking to shepherd our own expatriated countrymen and keep about them in a new land the sacred influences of the Church of their baptism and confirmation, but we are also called upon to exercise a fostering care over the *Iglesia Catolica Mexicana*. Into this *ecclesia*, as in apostolic days, "not many wise, not many mighty," are called. It is the Church of the poor, the home of the *peon*, and the only comfort and resource of many to whom life seems desolate indeed and the future a hopeless blank. We must at all hazards bless ourselves in blessing them, and sustain with greater earnestness than ever before the efforts of our bishop and his faithful little band of workers.

THE Church at large may perhaps be startled by the action of the new Board at its first meeting in deciding upon a Forward Movement and calling for very large additional gifts. Yet the Church herself was, in fact, the first to proclaim the Forward Movement. That was necessarily involved in the legislation passed at the General Convention. Although a deficit of $74,000 was reported, and although the apportionment now in force, if paid in full, would not meet the present appropriations—much less provide for a deficit— the Convention was not daunted. It courageously determined that much greater things must be undertaken. It admitted new dioceses, it established new missionary districts at home and

Call for a Forward Movement

On November 17th the new diocese, which comprises the northwestern part of the state, met for its primary council and elected for its diocesan the Rev. Dr. Rogers Israel, rector of St. Luke's Church, Scranton. The bishop-elect has been conspicuously successful as a parish priest and has the respect and confidence of the Church. He has been a deputy to a number of General Conventions and has served on many responsible and important committees. Best of all, he has inspired his parish with missionary zeal and so demonstrated that he may be looked to as a leader in these days when the Church has set her face toward the better fulfilment of her Master's trust.

FOLLOWING closely upon the completion of the list of our department secretaries by Dr. Harding's acceptance of the Second Department, two vacancies have occurred, one by the election of the Rev. Mr. Sanford, of Department VIII., as Bishop of San Joaquin, and the other by the retirement of the Rev. Dr. Hopkins, of Department V., who becomes rector of a parish in Chicago. Both have done effective work, and their loss makes the Church realize more fully the value of this office so recently created, and the power it has already become in missionary expansion.

The Department Secretaries

Mr. Sanford, of course, still remains in the active missionary work of the Pacific Coast. It is due to Dr. Hopkins to record the fact that his retirement takes place because of the insistence of his physician, who assures him that he cannot, without grave danger, continue the work which he has been so aggressively conducting throughout his department. The Executive Committee, in accepting his resignation, desired to record its deep appreciation of his untiring service. They felt that the admirable way in which the department has responded to his efforts indicated more clearly than could any words of theirs the quality of his work.

MORE than once in recent years an alarm has been sounded concerning the decrease of candidates for the ministry. The question has become one of the topics frequently discussed in clerical assemblies and Church journals, but it is evidently a matter which will not be cured by debate. One of the most seriously important statements in the report of the Committee on the State of the Church, made to the recent General Convention, was found in the paragraph which set forth the following facts: In 1904 the candidates for Orders were 510; in 1907 they were 469; in 1910 they were 423. With a very large advance in the Church's membership and a tremendous demand for workers in the foreign field, the number of men studying for Holy Orders has fallen off in the last six years nearly 20 per cent.

Men for the Minisry

Is it strange that bishops and clergy seek in vain for helpers? And is it not time that we all should rouse ourselves to a sense of responsibility in this matter? Are we using the opportunities which we certainly have to set young men face to face with the good vision of the glory of Christian service in the ranks of Christ's ambassadors? It will not do for us to disclaim responsibility. We each have our human contacts with others—with parents and young men and boys. We each have our share in moulding Christian public opinion; we each can do something to dignify the office of the ministry in the minds of Christian people; and, most of all, we can each pray distinctly and definitely that God may call certain ones to this good work. Clubs and convocations will accomplish little by papers and resolutions and speeches. In the lives of our communicants, in the atmosphere of our homes, in an inadequate view of the ministry, and in our lack of definite personal intercession, the difficulties will be found —and here they must be overcome. To this service for the Church, so urgently needed, we should one and all immediately devote ourselves.

THERE were those who, while admiring the enthusiasm developed last year by the Laymen's Missionary Movement, were wont to remark that the world is not going to be converted by enthusiasm and that movements of the same sort had been kindled gloriously, had flamed splendidly, and had then died away into very cold ashes. All of which is undoubtedly true, and was frankly recognized by the leaders of the Movement.

The Laymen's Missionary Movement

Their intention to prevent such a result is made evident by the campaign of the present season, which has already opened. This year they purpose to put the emphasis upon the training of about 10,000 members of missionary committees, by conducting a series of conferences in about seventy-five cities where the conventions were held last year. This is "follow-up" work of the most practical sort, and in the conferences already held ample proof has been presented of fruitful results. At Greensboro, N. C., for example, a conference was held on October 3d and 4th. It was shown that the convention last January led the churches of Greensboro to increase their offerings for missionary work from $7,304 for a year to $20,000 —that is, from $1.20 per member to $3.28. Nor was this all. A like splendid increase had been made in contributions to various other causes. The money for a Y. M. C. A. building, worth $65,000, was subscribed within a single week. Yet in this place not over 60 per cent. of the Church members are even now systematic contributors to the work of missions.

The conditions at Greensboro are no doubt typical of those existing elsewhere. An awakening has taken place. Striking results have been accomplished by the telling of the missionary story, and the adoption of systematic methods for securing gifts. But the things accomplished are only a promise of even greater things which may be done when the whole Church is reached with the Message and responds to its appeal.

THE SANCTUARY OF MISSIONS

HE stooped to bless,
And stoop ng, raised us
And the tenderness
Which looked in pity on a world of
sin,
Long years ago,
Still waits in love to call the
nations in;
Till all shall know
How men may rise in Him to holi=
ness,
Because He stooped so low.
—*A. R. G.*

THANKSGIVINGS

"We thank thee"—

For the great gift of Him who "for us men and for our salvation came down from heaven, and was incarnate."

For the missionary message of the Christmas-tide and the appeal it makes to every heart.

For the signs of leadership manifested among those charged with the care of our missionary work. (Page 991.)

For the inspiring examples of missionary success which mark our own time. (Page 983.)

For the lives of men and women consecrated to carrying thy message into all the earth. (Pages 995 and 1017.)

For the privilege of blessing the lives of the needy and making glad the hearts of little children by gifts at Christmas time. (Pages 999 and 1027.)

INTERCESSIONS

"We pray thee"—

To move thy Church to join more earnestly in bringing to all men the knowledge of the Great Christmas Gift.

To bless the lives of little children, helping them to grow into the image of the Child of Bethlehem.

To send forth laborers into thy harvest and to stir the consciences of Christian men and women that they may use their influence toward this end. (Page 986.)

To guard and protect our missionaries in Mexico, and to guide the feet of all thy children into the way of peace. (Page 983.)

To prosper the work of those who have been called by thy Church to take up the burdens of the missionary episcopate, and give them strength according to their task. (Page 995.)

To give to all teachers a vision of the divine childhood within every soul, that they may minister to those committed to their care as unto thee. (Pages 1011 and 1037.)

To send to the isolated people of the southern mountains more Christian friends and helpers in their need. (Page 1008.)

To be with those who spend their Christmas in the northern night and cause the Daystar to shine upon their souls. (Page 999.)

To move the hearts of thy people to supply the present need of St. Hilda's School, Wuchang. (Page 1014.)

PRAYER

O DAY-SPRING, Splendor of the eternal Light, and Sun of Righteousness; Come and enlighten those who sit in darkness and the shadow of death.

O King of Gentiles, thou Whom they long for, and Corner-stone that makest both one; Come and save man, Whom thou formedst out of the clay.

O Emmanuel, our King and Lawgiver, the Expected One of the Gentiles, and their Saviour; Come to save us, O Lord our God.—*Sarum Antiphons.*

THE WORK OF THE BOARD OF MISSIONS

By the Right Reverend Arthur Selden Lloyd, D. D., President

[Immediately after the organization of the new Board, President Lloyd, who had taken the chair for the first time, read to the Board a statement of the things for which, in his judgment, the Board should stand, and of the purposes for which, as he believed, its members had been elected by the Church. This document, which created a profound impression and has elicited wide comment, is given below.]

THE change made by the General Convention just ended in the Canon having to do with the missionary work of the Church indicates that the Church expects new and more comprehensive service from its Board of Missions.

This Canon is the first step toward coördinating all the forces that have been developed in recent years by the rapid growth of the American Church. The Church seems to have felt that the time has come when in the Church as in the nation these questions must be answered: How may its national interests be conserved without encroaching on diocesan rights? How may the dioceses be brought into such harmonious relation and coöperation as will make it possible to apply the Church's united strength to the development of its national and world-wide interests? And the Board of Missions seems to have been constituted for the purpose of finding an answer.

If this is the Church's intention in framing its new Canon, then the Board of Missions becomes, so to speak, the Church's Board of Strategy, whose duty it will be to study the conditions and progress of the work, as well as to acquaint itself with the obstacles to be overcome; to inform itself as to the resources of the Church so that it may have definite knowledge of what it can depend on for its work of extension; and to shape such a policy as can be applied everywhere by all the dioceses contributing, so that these may work together, adding strength to strength. That something like this was the purpose of the Church in framing the Canon seems to be borne out by the fact that the Board has been authorized to intrust committees with the routine business that formerly was brought to the Board itself, and no doubt the Board will be glad to avail itself of this relief.

If the Board is to reduce to practical terms the task confronting the Church it will be necessary, as I have said, for the Board to inform itself exactly with regard to the conditions to be taken into consideration, e.g., it must know:

1. The conditions surrounding American citizens in isolated or congested districts, so that the Church may be informed what ought to be done toward improving their state.

2. The movements of population throughout the country and their significance.

3. The immigration of foreigners, their nationality, social development and ecclesiastical relations, as well as their places of settlement, with a view to telling the Church how it may help the State to enable these to become good citizens.

4. The conditions surrounding the Indians, so that the Church may be told what help it can render the State in building them up in citizenship.

The Work of the Board of Missions 989

5. The relation of the Black people in America to the conditions surrounding them, so that the Church may learn how they can be helped to attain that which a worthy ambition is driving them to find.

6. The conditions abroad, especially where the American Church has been planted, that the American Church may be told what help it ought to render these Churches to enable them to become established.

And all such questions ought to be studied with a view to deciding how much f the work the Church ought to undertake along with a working plan for doing t. Thus the formulation of what may be called a national policy for the Church eems to be no less incumbent upon the Board than the obligation to know what he Church's task is.

But before the Church will consider such questions as these with any intenion of trying to solve them, it must first be sure that its resources are adequate. ind it will not believe it is able on any showing until it has been taught to think f itself as an Organism filling the land, every member of which is called to labor or the health and strength and growth of the whole Body; nor yet before it learns o regard it as definite dereliction, not on the part of a diocese but of the whole Body, if any of its resources are unprofitable because undeveloped.

To help the Church thus to know itself and to meet courageously the obliations our Lord Jesus Christ has laid upon it is the most difficult because the nost delicate task confronting the Board. I confess my chief ground of hope ests in the assurance that it has to be done, and therefore there must be a way or doing it which can be found. In the meantime it is quite possible to meet that seems to be a primary obligation of the Board, viz., to secure exact information as to the financial strength of the Church, not only as exhibited in its diocesan nd parochial reports, but as it really is. For this it will be necessary to get into ouch with the large number of individuals in the Church who are concerned in he great undertakings of the Nation. The Board should be able to give these deailed information about the Church's work, that they may determine whether hey desire to have part in it. The Board should be equally careful to be able to ive to all such subscribers an itemized statement of the use made of their money, nd what has been accomplished. In a word, the Board ought to know what the Church is able to spend on its work of extension, and devise means for gathering iat amount into the Board's treasury.

When the Board has intelligently informed itself with regard to the quesons that confront the Church and which challenge it to real service, it will be rident that the Church unaided (however willing it may be) cannot render all ie service the Nation has a right to expect from organized Christianity in buildig up among us a Christian civilization; to say nothing of what must be done to elp the nations know the Revelation of the Father. The Board must therefore ecessarily inform itself with regard to every force that makes for righteousness in ir land, that it may avail itself of every help.

1. It will lend all its power to forward the epoch-making movement among laymen.

2. It will realize the importance of coming into close working contact with every Missionary Board doing work in this and other lands, glad to count these as friends and allies.

3. Especially will it welcome every opportunity of conference with other Boards, that from all sources it may gain light on the hard questions the Church has called upon it to answer.

I confess I have a high ambition for this Board in such relation that—frankly confessing the Church must share with others the work for mankind which, if it might, it would gladly do unaided—this Board may become the unifying force among all the forces working to establish His Kingdom in the earth, and so become a practical factor in making possible that organic unity of Christendom which must be regained before the Kingdom of God can be established everywhere.

To do these things will require systematic and arduous and self-denying work. The question is how to go about doing them. Perhaps the Board may think it wise to appoint Committees who shall study the questions about which the Board must be informed in order that it may act intelligently. This is my hope; and that their labor may be so useful and illuminating that the Church will form the habit of looking to its Board of Missions for guidance and for suggestion in everything relating to its national development.

I have no doubt if the Board will go about its work on some such basis as here suggested, it will result first of all in the Church's realizing its strength as it never has done, and in making it confident that it can carry forward the work it has to do with system and with power. But the most blessed result will spring of the enlarged sympathy that is born of working together at a common task. The Church will know itself as one—the very Body of Christ, and so will become worthy to lead the servants of our Lord and Master in their labor to bring back to Him all His redeemed ones.

ᴸ MESSAGE FROM THE BOARD OF MISSIONS

[The new Board of Missions, recognizing the urgency of an immediate and adequate Forward Movement, outlined a general policy at its first meeting and instructed its Executive Committee to put forth to the Church its call for the carrying out of that policy. The following message has been sent to all the bishops and clergy, through whom it is hoped to reach every member of the Church.]

o the Members of Every Congregation of the Church:

THE General Convention is over. A new Missionary Canon has been adopted. The new Board of Missions has been elected. It has met and organized for work, and now sends the following message to the Church:

As we review the present missionary situation we are impressed by the wide :tent and high quality of the work already under way. During the last ten ars especially, there has been notable progress in the Church's work at home ad abroad. This has been made possible by the decided growth of the mission-y spirit in hundreds of our congregations. The Board feels that what has been me is an earnest of still greater things that may be done.

We are also deeply impressed by the need for an immediate and vigorous orward Movement.

In all the home fields the leaders are pointing out work to be done and are king for the means and the men to do it. Every man who loves his country ll wish to share in meeting these needs.

Abroad the situation is one of critical opportunity. The World Conference Edinburgh recorded its conviction that "the next ten years will, in all probability, constitute a turning point in human history, and may be of more critical portance in determining the spiritual evolution of mankind than many centuries of ordinary experience. If those years are wasted havoc may be wrought at centuries are not able to repair. On the other hand, if they are rightly used, ey may be among the most glorious in Christian history."

We rejoice that the Cincinnati General Convention was dominated by a ase of unity in one blood, and that more vital unity, which springs from our lowship in the Gospel and our share in One Living Christ. Differences of rty, of section, even of nationality, were relegated to their proper place, and a natural consequence the record of the Convention shows that it was a Conven-n of missionary progress.

It was determined by the Convention that no methods which have stood the t in the affairs of men of progress should be overlooked, but that agencies auld be multiplied so that all parts of the Church may be reached to secure requisite force for new ventures. Plans must be made to reach every man, man and child in the American Church, and make of them in fact what they by name and profession, members of the Missionary Society—the Church.

The Convention plainly expected that the members of the Church would dly undertake great things for God. Accordingly it instructed your Board of ssions to perfect plans for enlarging the missionary staff. It recommended t throughout the Church men be enlisted in diocesan and congregational com-tees for Church Extension. It created five new missionary districts—four in United States and one abroad—and elected six missionary bishops.

992   A Message from the Board of Missions

The action of the Convention largely increased the obligations of the Church, so that for the fiscal year September 1st, 1910, to August 31st, 1911 they amount to $1,370,000.

We realize that, as your Board of Missions, we must endeavor to fulfil the will of the Church as expressed in the General Convention. To do this adequately we need the co-operation of every bishop and clergyman, and of every member of every congregation.

We therefore call upon all members of the Church to join in a Forward Movement, and we ask for at least $500,000 in addition to the appropriation of $728,000 announced last September, and the usual offerings from the Woman's Auxiliary and the Sunday-schools.

The additional offering is needed for these purposes:

1. To provide for the appropriations already made in excess of the apportionment, and for the additional expenses ordered by the General Convention in the erection of new missionary districts, the election of bishops and the admission of new dioceses ....$125,00(

2. To enable the Board to use the legacies, left at its discretion, for constructive purposes—the building of churches, residences for missionaries, schools and hospitals—and not for paying debts or salaries .... estimated 100,00

3. To wipe out the existing deficit, incurred during the last three years 75,00

4. To enable the Church to do adequately some of the work waiting to be done, especially in our own country, and to make good some of the crying deficiencies of the past.......... 200,00

$500,00

HOW CAN THIS FORWARD MOVEMENT BE REALIZED?

We believe the people are ready in love and loyalty to our Lord to undertake large things. They need information and organization. The needed organization is made possible by the new missionary canon. The Board is representative of the entire Church, and upon its members in their respective departments, with the Department Secretaries, is laid the responsibility of co-operating with the bishops and clergy in making this Forward Movement effective.

It is, of course, recognized that no one plan is applicable in all its detail to the varying conditions throughout the Church. In the absence, however, of some plan which the local authorities are convinced would be more effective, we urge that the following may with advantage be put into operation:

1. Let a diocesan committee of clergymen and laymen be appointed by the bishop, to take, under his direction, the oversight of the Forward Movement in his diocese.

2. Let this diocesan committee be divided into sub-committees of two members each.

3. Let a certain number of congregations be assigned to each sub-committee

4. Let each sub-committee present the message of this Forward Movement to the authorities of each congregation assigned to it.

5. Let the sub-committee secure the appointment of a committee in each congregation to make a personal canvass of every individual for subscription on a weekly basis.

This is the method that has been followed with marked success in many parishes throughout the country. In recommending that it be generally employed the Board is complying with the following resolution, adopted by the House of Deputies at Cincinnati, and concurred in by the House of Bishops:

Resolved: The House of Bishops concurring, that the Board of Missions be, and is hereby recommended to further the formation in all dioceses and districts of missionary committees of laymen auxiliary to the Board. The duty of such committees shall be to organize missionary committees in all congregations of the dioceses and districts, to foster and develop the interest of laymen in the missionary work of the Church, and to co-operate with the Board of Missions and the Department Secretary.

We therefore ask every clergyman in charge of a congregation to form a missionary committee of men to aid him in enlisting every member of the congregation as a supporter of the Church's mission by regular prayer and systematic gifts.

The first duty of this congregational committee would be to make a list of the members of the congregation, from which a certain number of names would be assigned to each two members of the committee. The members of the committee, going two by two, would then make a careful canvass of the congregation, in order that every individual may have the privilege of supporting the Church's mission offered him, personally and adequately. This is a method that men understand and use for other important undertakings. Its value and success have been demonstrated repeatedly and strikingly in the last two years. Wherever intelligently applied, whether in the large city congregations or in small town and country congregations, it has greatly increased the gifts.

The reason for this is plain to anyone who will take the trouble to analyze the usual missionary offering. Inquiry indicates that not more than one-fifth of the communicants—to say nothing of the baptized members—give anything at all, and that not more than one-tenth give in proportion to their ability. The offering usually represents the love and devotion of a small fraction of the congregation. The need is not so much for an increase in the amount given by the few already enlisted as for a great increase in the number of givers. This the canvass will accomplish.

A simple plan of putting the canvass into operation is outlined in leaflet No. 1,102, enclosed herewith. This plan is the result of much experience. It has been tested many times. We urge that it be given a fair trial.

In making the parish canvass, the clergy are urged to impress upon their people these principles:

1. It is due to every individual that the privilege of supporting the Church's mission should be offered him personally and intelligently.
2. Each person should be asked to give in proportion to his means, in tens or hundreds or thousands of dollars, and not in proportion to what someone else gives or fails to give.
3. Almost every individual can give a minimum sum of ten cents a week, if a larger amount be not possible.
4. Everyone should be asked to name a weekly gift, though some who give in large amounts may prefer to make payments monthly, quarterly, semi-annually, or annually. Whatever plan of payment is selected by the donor, it is urged that all subscriptions should be based on a certain amount per week.
5. For the convenience of those who prefer to give weekly, the duplex envelope is strongly recommended.

In order that proper care may be given to the missionary funds, and tha
subscriptions may be carefully followed up, the Board recommends the appoint
ment of a missionary treasurer in every congregation.

If the question be asked, "Can our parish afford to adopt a method that i
sures larger missionary giving?" we reply: Can your parish afford *not* to ado
it? The evidence is in hand to prove that a congregation which follows th
system is enriched rather than impoverished. The adoption of the canvass f
missionary offerings has almost invariably resulted, not only in increased missio
ary giving, but in a larger income for parochial and all other purposes. It h
led in some cases to the clearing off of debts of long-standing, to parish improv
ments, to a more adequate salary for the clergyman, and to increased offerings f(
diocesan work and all other extra-parochial objects. The fact is that no congr
gation can afford not to adopt improved methods for securing more missionar
givers and larger missionary gifts.

The Board of Missions is prepared to supply literature and to give all othe
aid in its power to insure the success of this Forward Movement.

Whether or not the plan of weekly offerings be adopted, we urge that th
canvass method of securing subscriptions be used. The Department Secretarie
report their unanimous conviction that no method is so effective as the canvass
Wherever it has been tried under their observation it has produced notable result

Finally, we ask that frequent prayer be offered for the Church's missio
and for the success of this effort to provide the means for its advancement, "tha
in all things God may be glorified through Jesus Christ, Whose is the glory an
the dominion for ever and ever."

By order and on behalf of the Board of Missions.

ARTHUR S. LLOYD,
WILLIAM LAWRENCE,
JOSEPH M. FRANCIS,
DAVID H. GREER,
HENRY ANSTICE,
REESE F. ALSOP,
WILLIAM T. MANNING,
GEORGE GORDON KING,
BURTON MANSFIELD, .
HENRY LEWIS MORRIS,
GEORGE WHARTON PEPPER,
WILLIAM F. COCHRAN, .
W. R. STIRLING,
         Executive Committee.

THE NEW MISSIONARY BISHOPS

T HE last General Convention saw the election of six missionary bishops. This, together with the erection of the four new districts, constitutes a notable forward step and is a significant indication of what the Church wishes to accomplish in the way of expansion. These trusted leaders go out to take up the work in their several fields, but it is one of the essential elements of their success that the sympathy and support of the entire Church shall go with them. They are our representatives at the front, sent to do our work and looking to us for equipment and encouragement. The election of a missionary bishop and his establishment in a new district does nothing beyond creating a new obligation for the Church. Her sympathetic remembrance, her fostering care, her prevailing intercessions must be behind him and with him and about him as he goes on his mission.

Here, then, are six new men whom the Church must take into her heart and remember at her altars. Not all of them have yet accepted the solemn trust offered to them, but they are such men as will inevitably do so unless positively deterred by some greater and more imperative duty.

The most honored post in the Church's campaign is, of course, the foreign field, and the most commendable act of missionary advance was the division of the District of Hankow and the election of a new bishop for Wuhu. The Church is to be congratulated on the quality of the man so chosen. It would be difficult to name a presbyter on the roll of our foreign missionaries better fitted by nature, ability and long experience to inaugurate the work in a new field than is the honored and able president of St. John's University, Shanghai, the Rev. Francis L. Hawks Pott, D.D. He is the son of the late James Pott, the famous bookseller of New York, and is a namesake of that distinguished clergyman who at the same time with Jackson Kemper was elected a missionary bishop, but felt impelled to decline the call. Dr. Pott graduated at Columbia University and the General Theological Seminary. He was ordained deacon in 1886 and has given his entire ministerial life to China, in evangelistic and educational work. He is the leading presbyter in the District of Shanghai, and was among the distinguished delegates to the Edinburgh Conference. He spent last winter and spring in this country and made many telling addresses in connection with the Laymen's Missionary Movement, and also to individual congregations of the Church. He has translated many theological books into Chinese and is the author of an English history of China. Nothing is as yet known about the arrangements for his consecration.

FRANCIS L. HAWKS POTT
Bishop-elect of Wuhu

The Very Rev. George Allen Beecher, Dean of the Cathedral at Omaha, Neb., was the first of the new bishops to be consecrated. This service took place in his cathedral on St. Andrew's Day, and he will at once take up his work in the District of Kearney. Bishop Beecher is a son of the middle West, thoroughly familiar with the conditions prevailing there. He was born and reared on a farm in Monmouth, Ill., and is a graduate of the University of Nebraska and the Philadelphia Divinity-school. Bishop Graves, whom he succeeds, ordained him both to the diaconate and the priesthood, and the entire work of his ministry has been done within the State of Nebraska, over the western portion of which he now becomes bishop.

GEORGE ALLEN BEECHER
Bishop of Kearney

The Rev. Julius W. Atwood, chosen for Arizona, is already archdeacon of that district and rector of

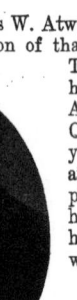

JULIUS WALTER ATWOOD
Bishop-elect of Arizona

Trinity Church, Phœnix, where he has established a home for the treatment of tuberculosis sufferers, Mr. Atwood is a graduate of Middlebury College and the Cambridge Theological School. The first thirteen years of his ministry were spent in New England, and the next thirteen in Columbus, O., from which place he went to Arizona three years ago. There he has been the trusted helper of Bishop Kendrick, who has heretofore had charge of that district, together with New Mexico.

To help in solving the tremendous problem which Oklahoma presents it was well that a young and vigorous man, of experience in the middle West, should be chosen, and the lot fell upon the Rev. Theodore Payne Thurston, rector of St. Paul's Church, Minneapolis. Mr. Thurston is also a son of the West, having been born in Illinois and receiving his early education at Shattuck School. He is a graduate of Trinity College and Cambridge Theological School, and has spent his entire ministry in the State of Minnesota, where he has built up, with remarkable energy and ability, the three parishes which he has served. So invaluable has he become in his present work that he has found it difficult to decide where his duty lay. Should he accept the election his going will be a great loss to the Church in Minnesota. The district to which Mr. Thurston is called embraces the old Indian Territory and is that portion of the state which in recent years has received such an astounding influx of settlers.

THEODORE PAYNE
THURSTON
Bishop-elect of Oklahoma

LOUIS CHILDS SANFORD
Bishop-elect of San Joaquin

For the new District of San Joaquin, which includes that part of the Diocese of California lying east of the Coast Range, one has been chosen who is familiar with the missionary work of the entire Pacific Coast. The Rev. Louis Childs Sanford is known to the Church as the first secretary of the Eighth Department. He graduated at Brown University and Cambridge Theological School and his entire clerical work has been done in California. Thus again has the Church chosen a man who is on the ground, and thoroughly familiar with the problems to be faced. Mr. Sanford has made a wide circle of friends in his work during the past two years as Department Secretary.

The Rev. Edward A. Temple is elected for the new District of North Texas, which includes what is known as the Panhandle and embraces 64,000 square iles. Mr. Temple is a Virginian by birth and a graduate of the Virginia Seminary. His early ministry was given to his native ate, but he is at present the rector of St. Paul's urch, Waco, Tex. He is a man of energy and missionary ideals. In the early days of the missionary partments Mr. Temple was asked to act as department secretary but found it impossible to do so.

CHANNING MOORE WILLIAMS: BISHOP

CONSECRATED, OCTOBER 3D, 1866

N December 2d, in Richmond, Va., Channing Moore Williams, our pioneer missionary in pan, and afterwards Bishop of Yedo, passed to his ward. This announcement will mean little to many our readers. Patient and faithful in his labors,

EDWARD ARTHUR TEMPLE
Bishop-elect of North Texas

iet and inconspicuous to the point of self-effacement, Bishop Williams was ver a prominent figure in the eye of the Church, but the results of the more in fifty years which he gave to her service—all of them in Japan—are written the Lamb's Book of Life. As a pioneer, facing with unswerving purpose the irs of seeming failure; as bishop, helping to gather in the harvest when the at opportunity came; and last of all, as the quiet missionary retired from epis- al dignity and responsibility, he lived only for Japan and the Church. The d of his adoption became the home of his heart and into her Christian fabric wrought with lavish generosity all that he possessed of character, knowledge d purpose. The people of Japan will understand, as the people of America haps can never do, how much is due to this simple, sincere, self-forgetting, ient man of God. May he find light and peace in the presence of the Master om he served.

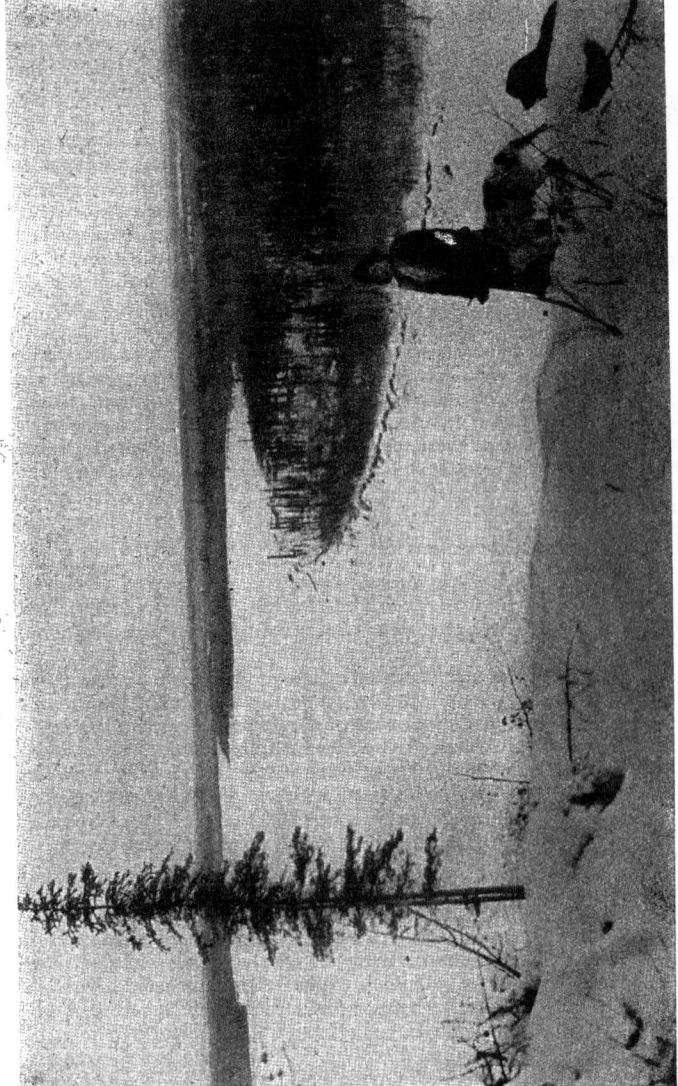

THE MISSION ON OR NEAR YOUNG'S OLD WILDERNESS ATLAKEET

The group of buildings is plainly discernible on the point across the frozen river

CHRISTMAS MORNING AT ST. JOHN'S IN THE WILDERNESS

On either side of Archdeacon Stuck stand the interpreters, one a Koyukuk and the other a Kobuk; each in turn translates into his own language the English words as they are read or spoken

CARRYING CHRISTMAS TO ALLAKAKET

By Archdeacon Stuck

A year ago at this time Archdeacon Stuck was hurrying northward from Fort Yukon to Allakaket, combating for many weary days storms almost unprecedented, that he might carry to that little band at the mission under the Arctic Circle the best gift of the Christmastide, by making it possible for them to receive their Christmas Communion. What such a visit meant to those two faithful women living alone among the natives, many miles from the nearest white settlement, and deprived for months of the ministrations of the Church, we leave our readers to imagine. That the expedition was worthy the making, they will certainly be convinced after reading the brief, but vivid account which follows:

THE Allakaket is always an interesting place. And what native mission is not interesting at Christmas? For Christmas is the great native festival. They came from far and near, Kobuk and Koyukuk. Old and young, first and last, there were upward of one hundred and fifty natives here at Christmas. And they listened ever so intently, ever so eagerly, as by the mouths of the inevitable two interpreters the sweet story of the Nativity was told to them over and over again, morning and night, week-day and Christmas Day and Sunday, during the whole season. On the morning of Christmas Day we took our first missionary offering. The first year here we were most anxious that the natives should be disabused of the impression industriously sowed by certain white men of the baser sort that the mission had come to take

THE FAMILY AT HOME

The interior of the Mission House at Allakaket, Christmas, 1909

A KOYUKUK AND A KOBUK GIRL

from them. The second year was a year of great scarcity and hardship. The salmon did not "run" in the summer; there was no game in the winter. We thought it wisest to defer the offering. This year, by the goodness of God, has been a fat year. The caches are full of dried fish, and game has been fairly abundant. So we asked for the offering; not for us; not for Alaska—for building other missions far away and sending men and women to people who had no one to care for them. We put it to them: "If you are glad the mission has come to you, give something to help send it to others."

There were about one hundred and twenty-five people in church that morning, and the offering amounted to upwards of $130—I do not know exactly how much yet, as there were several mink skins and ermine skins put in the alms-basin that have not yet been disposed of.* But I was pleased with the first missionary offering from St. John's-in-the-Wilderness, and am proud to send it to

---

* The total offering of these native people for the cause of the Church's Mission was $142.

THE TOP OF THE GREAT BLUFF WHERE THE TWO KOBUKS WERE BURIED

the Missions House. It spells gratitude and appreciation.

The Christmas tree, the "potlatch," the native dance, the fire-balloons we sent up (and the ones that wouldn't go up), the glee of the children of the house over their stockings, the ten Christmas baptisms, the great football games—though the weather spoiled out-door sport—yes, and the sad notes struck by the death of our oldest Kobuk, Mesuk the snowshoe maker, and the death that followed rapidly of a strong, stalwart, splendid young Kobuk man, of double pneumonia, the picturesque burials on the top of the great bluffs that overlook the mission, the birth of two Christmas babies—I could write many pages about these things, but I must quit.

I will not quit, however, until I have spoken of the high esteem in which the mission stands with almost all the white men in the country. I had no more than touched the Koyukuk at Coldfoot when I began to hear of Miss Carter's adventurous journey to attend a white woman in childbirth, and at Wright City and Nolan Creek I heard her praise sung

A KOBUK BRIDE AND GROOM

Married at Allakaket in Christmastide, 1909

(1001)

MOSES, CHIEF OF THE KOYUKUKS

by everyone. Nor was it confined to praises. Here is a whole quarter of beef that one man has sent as a present; here is a box containing twenty-five pounds of candy made by an upper-river road-house keeper who used to be a confectioner; here is a patent nickel-plated range with all sorts of new-fangled contraptions that several of them clubbed together to buy, and another one undertook to haul. Miss Carter has been overwhelmed and embarrassed by the multitude of her Christmas gifts. And those miners on Nolan Creek and the folks at Wright City are talking of getting up a petition to the bishop to send Miss Carter up there to start a mission and a reading-room and a hospital. But it would take a great deal more than that to make her budge from the Allakaket and the cherished isolation that makes so greatly for its success.

ON St. Andrew's Day, November 30th, in the midst of her beautiful work for the Indian children at Nenana, Alaska, Annie Cragg Farthing "fell on sleep," leaving a void in the ranks of our missionaries in Alaska and in the hearts of her children at Nenana which it will indeed be hard to fill. A more extended appreciation of her character and work will appear in the next issue.

SOME ALLAKAKET CHILDREN

Where our missionary slept while among the Indians in Washita

AN INDIAN DANCE IN OKLAHOMA

By Harriet M. Bedell

OUR work is chiefly centred among the Cheyenne blanket Indians on the South Canadian River, where we have a Church day-school, which goes hand in hand with work in the tepees. The Indians live in a most primitive way and we begin with conditions as we find them, working up to higher standards. From this our work radiates out to other camps.

The Indians are encouraged to cultivate their own allotments, so that they may have one place which they can call home. Many are doing this, and doing it well, but the inwrought traits of character are still prevalent and they do wander from place to place, camping in groups here and there; occasionally assembling for an Indian dance, or some other religious ceremony.

The only thing for the Church to do is to follow, and I feel this part of our work to be very important. I go with our Indian deacon and his wife. We have services under the trees, though in the camps assembled for dances this is not always possible; but even there the Church has a work to do.

The care of the sick, the evening camp fire, and familiarity with the inner camp-life of the Indian affords many opportunities for the spread of Christ's Kingdom.

I have just returned from the Washita River, where about 3,000 Indians were assembled—Cheyennes, Arapahoes, Comanches, Kiowas and Pawnees. They camped around a fifty or sixty acre space. The scene was very picturesque—the white tepees with men and women in gay attire going in and out.

They gathered for the Willow Dance, which was held in a tent erected with much ceremony in the centre of the above space—the purpose was to invoke the Great Spirit's blessing on the medicine men, and their medicine, which they

MRS. ANTELOPE SKIN AND HER YOUNGEST

*The mother has recently been confirmed
and is a devout communicant*

made in a large tepee, erected for them and carefully guarded while they were there.

Early in the morning the squaws went to the woods near by to cut poles for the dance tepee; and later the men, dressed in feathers and other finery, in four companies, went out on horseback, coming back on the gallop from four points of the camp and bringing willow branches, etc., for decorating the tent. The dash of hundreds of Indians toward the centre of the camp was a sight not soon forgotten. Those reaching the site first brought special blessings and received much honor.

The centre pole was erected with great ceremony; then the women put up the other poles and canvas drawn over these completed the structure.

A large buffalo head, in which the Great Spirit was supposed to be, was placed in the tent reverently, and the medicine men came from their tepee to the tent. There were drummers and singers, both men and women. The dancers, twenty in number, and chosen only from a certain clan, were painted with care by certain ones chosen for the work.

After a parade the dance began. It consists of just the bending of the knees. They danced for nearly two days, fasting, stopping only five times to have the paint changed on their bodies and faces. Those who endured longest brought special blessings.

The medicine men, drummers and singers, had to be continuously feasted, and it was an interesting sight to see the women in their bright-colored dresses and shawls carrying food from the camp to the tent.

Presents of tepees, ponies, etc., were presented to the dancers and others. This is a deplorable condition. Many returned to their homes destitute, having given away even their tepees.

These dances, I am glad to say, will soon pass into history. The younger Indians, especially the Christians, show little interest. I did not witness the dance itself, because of its deplorable nature; and I was pleased to find that many of our young people did not witness it, but were there for the social intercourse.

The Indians made me very welcome, and several have promised to send their children to our school this coming winter. The Indian is suspicious of the white man until he knows him to be a friend. I went into one strange home, but was not greeted very cordially. In the course of the conversation the Indian girl who was with me told who I was. Two of the old men came forward and shook hands the second time — this

*The Rev. David P.
Oakerhater*

THE CHURCH DAY-SCHOOL OF ST. LUKE'S MISSION, WHIRLWIND ALLOTMENT,
FAY, OKLA.

The adults from left to right: Turkey Legs, chief; David Oakerhater, Indian deacon; Mrs. Tall
Meat, a communicant; Rev. J. J. H. Reedy, priest-in-charge; Harriet M. Bedell,
assistant missionary and teacher

time very heartily—saying, "Hamstow" (sit down).

I found a sick baby in one home and asked if I might do something for it. An old Indian there said, "Nope, go home." I turned to the mother and said, "Your baby is very sick. I think I can make her better. I shall be glad to come any time."

The next day I called again. The old Indian was very pleasant and shook hands saying, "How!" The baby was still sick with fever. I had a thermometer, which I showed them. They were all much interested and finally let me see how much fever the baby had—which was very high. I told them I always asked God to bless my medicine and I was sure He would now help this baby. The old man said nothing, but the mother consented, and after a prayer I left. The next morning when I called the baby was better and I was made very welcome. They have promised to come to our mission. These are only two of the many daily experiences.

School opens the first week in September. About the middle of August the Indians begin to come back to Whirlwind (named from the original allottee). Very soon all are settled for our winter's work. The Rev. Sherman Coolidge, a full-blooded Indian priest, with his wife, are to be with us. We ask your prayers that God will use us as effective instruments in His service.

¶

The rector of a parish in Missouri writes:

OUR Sunday-school is out to make a record this next year with its Easter Offering for missions. One class of boys is working overtime to beat the record for classes. They have earned already over $13 by work of various kinds and put that into their treasury for the Easter Offering.

A CHRISTIAN FAMILY WHOSE YOUNGEST WERE PERHAPS AMONG THE MARCHERS

PREPARING FOR "KURISUMASU"

By the Rev. J. J. Chapman

ONE day in the middle of December I was walking between Matsuyama and Haibara, two stations on a mountain plateau eight miles from the railroad. It was Sunday, and service at Matsuyama was over. That afternoon there was to be Sunday-school at Haibara and preaching and service at night. Sunday is a holiday for school children, just as in America, and as the Sunday-school is dignified with the name of school, old and prejudiced parents don't seem to object to their children attending. So in this small town of 2,000 people most of the children come to school on Sunday. Those that don't come during the year begin to take interest the first part of December, when talk of Christmas is again going around. So practically all the children in town come to the Christmas celebration and take part.

As I approached Haibara, while still a mile away, I heard a strange sound of trumpets, drums and fifes, slightly resembling music. It came echoing up the valley at the foot of which lay the village. The winter air was still, and all was quiet as I listened. It was not the voice of them that shout for victory, but it was plainly the noise of them that sing which I heard. I turned to the coolie who was carrying my baggage and asked an explanation of this strange noise of rejoicing coming from the usually quiet and sober little hamlet. Being a man of the neighborhood he knew all about it and explained to me as we walked along together that the children were practising for a Christian festival called "Kurisumasu," which came at this time of the year just before New Year's, and that it was their custom to practise their songs with the accompaniment of drums, fifes, trumpets and horns. There was a foreign "orugan," he said, in the church, which the catechist played, and with which he taught them when he came (for there is

no resident catechist to direct their youthful energy), but the rented building was so small that the children took to marching in the streets. All could not get into the building, but all could follow the procession and sing. Gradually drums and other accessories were called into use.

It was hard to recognize the tune amidst the rattling and booming of the old drums (they were drums from the temples), but it served to advertise the Sunday-school to all the town. For miles around there is no one but knows that there is a "Jesus preaching place" in Haibara, and that once a year the "Jesus people" have a big festival, which stirs up more talk than any of the old-time festivals at the temple.

It is a pity we cannot give more personal attention to these children. There should be a resident Bible-woman to lead them and keep them from running all over the church and beating the drums in the sanctuary when no one is there. We do not spend much money on this lonely mountain spot. The house rents for $1.50 a month and seats forty people. The communicants are only five, and so not able to do so much. Neither the mission nor the Japanese Church owns a foot of land there, and the house owner may turn us out at any time.

When I reached the preaching place there they were, having finished the procession around town, and I was greeted by the strains of "Hark, the herald angels sing." If the original "herald angels" heard them, I know that, unless they are foreign to human nature, they were touched by the humor of the situation. A motley crowd of two hundred children, with drums, trumpets and fifes, diligently, earnestly and seriously singing *at* a tune which the teacher had once taught them. None but those versed in country singing in Japan could have guessed the original.

THE MISSION HOUSE AT JUMP OFF

UMP OFF: WHERE SANTA CLAUS MAKES HIS FIRST VISIT

By Archdeacon Windiate

EVERYONE has heard about "the jumping-off place" — wherever that may be. In our minds it stands for the most hopeless and isolate and impossible locality imaginable. But whatever the origin of s name, "Jump Off" is not that place. ; is a beautiful spot in the Tennessee ountains not many miles from ewanee, in a section whose picturesque-ess has become a sort of proverb in the ate. But while all around was beauful the condition of the people was deorable. The neighborhood was typical : the life of those isolated and backard people whom we are wont to class gether as southern mountaineers.

Some years ago, when the present ean Colmore of Cuba was a student , Sewanee, he started a work in the ighborhood of Jump Off, which after s departure was somewhat fitfully carred on. The Rev. W. S. Claiborne, rec-r of Otey Memorial Church, Sewanee, d what was possible for these people, id touching signs of appreciation ac-mpanied even the small work which uld be thus accomplished. For ex-nple: A man living near the mission as baptized. Though what one would ll uneducated, he seems to have alized the gift of spiritual life in that crament, and the responsibility placed on its recipient. When next the rec-r visited that station this man had thered about him twenty men, whom had brought in from the country und that they might learn about the hurch and her sacraments.

But it was within the present year at the greatest impulse was given to is work. A young woman who had been an active worker in the Church of the Incarnation, New York City, offered for service among the mountaineers of Tennessee. Last summer she took charge of the work at Jump Off, solicited about $1,000 and constructed the Mission House shown in the accompanying picture upon plans of her own. Under her superintendence the work went forward, and the story is told that when difficulties in securing labor had presented themselves this resourceful young woman built with her own hands. The great fireplace of hewn stone in the main room is pointed out as a monument to her energy.

The building has a large common room, used also for services, containing an altar which can be screened off. There also are living rooms, and very wide porches, which in themselves make attractive teaching and working apartments for the summertime. A variety of industries flourish at the Mission House. There are sewing and cooking classes, there are visits for conferences over domestic needs and difficulties, and the new missionary and her assistant are constant in their ministrations to the sick of the neighborhood. There is no doctor near, but the Church Hospital at Sewanee helps those who are most seriously ill, and many a tramp over the mountains is taken by the young women to carry medicine to the sick babies—by no means few in number.

The Church service is a revelation and a joy to these people. On Sundays the room will scarcely hold the congregation. They are responsive and learn the service readily. The things which the Church is bringing into their narrow lives arouse an interest which is remarkable. Even the men and boys come to the sewing meetings and, of course, never miss a cooking meeting—if they can get in.

They are a splendid people, these stalwart mountaineers, from whom have sprung some of the ablest men of the nation, and they need only to be touched with the stimulus of education and religion in order to respond abundantly to the highest influences.

The most promising department of work, and one which demands much time and thought, is, of course, the Sunday-school. Already some sixty children are gathered, who show themselves eager pupils. It can scarcely be believed that they had never heard of Santa Claus, never seen bananas—or many other things dear to the childish heart and palate—until the new teacher came. Under the stimulus of this teacher they are making astonishing progress, and through the children the parents are reached and stirred to greater ambition. Signs of betterment are to be seen in the homes, and the long-neglected country cemetery has been transformed. The brush is cleared; the fence rails—which used to be laid across the graves as their sole protection—have disappeared. The trees are trimmed and the grass cut, and enclosing all there is a wire fence. On All Saints' Day it will be consecrated. They are learning also the meaning of Memorial Day, the Fourth of July, and the great Feast Days of the Church, which now make new and bright spots in the lives which formerly were only stirred by the latest shooting affray or the annual "sanctification" revival. Best of all will be the Christmastide—that joy of children and all who love them—the first one for these children of the mountains.

Is it true, as our missionary claims, that her people are of higher and more interesting type than other mountaineers, or is it only that there has been uncovered in them, by the loving service rendered, a rich vein of golden character which underlies the humanity of these people reared among the everlasting hills and living close to nature's heart?

¶

THE MOSLEM LAYMEN'S MOVEMENT

IN Burma (where Indian merchants are the Moslem missionaries) the Moslem population increased thirty-three per cent. in the past decade. In the western Soudan and on the Niger whole districts once pagan are now Mohammedan, and this has been, to a large extent, the work of lay missionaries—merchants, travellers, and artisans. It would be an exaggeration to say that every Moslem is a missionary, but it is true that, with the exception of the Dervish orders (who resemble monks), the missionaries of Islam are the laymen in every walk of life, rather than its priesthood. For example, a pearl merchant at Bahrein, East Arabia, recently, at his own expense and on his own initiative, printed an entire edition of a Koran commentary for free distribution. On the streets of Lahore and Calcutta you may see clerks, traders, bookbinders, and even coolies, who spend part of their leisure time preaching Islam or attacking Christianity by argument.

The merchants who go to Mecca as pilgrims from Java return to do missionary work among the hill tribes. In the Soudan the Hausa merchants carry the Koran and the catechism wherever they carry their merchandise. No sooner do they open a wayside shop in some pagan district than the wayside mosque is built by its side. And is it not a remarkable proof of the earnestness even of the Arab slave-dealers, that, in spite of the horrors of the traffic, the very slave routes became highways for Islam, and the Negroes adopted the religion of Mohammed to escape the very curse which brought it to them?—*From Zwemer's "Islam: a Challenge to Faith."*

"Such physical exercise as the limited playground and the traditions of Chinese girldom permit"

IN THE HEART OF THE MIDDLE KINGDOM

By the Reverend Dudley Tyng

AFTER the self-satisfied slumber of millenniums, Great China awaking and reaching out after some good which she now realizes that she has not—that is the interesting spectacle which goes on before the eyes of the Occidental dweller in the "Middle Kingdom." Of all the phenomena of this awakening none equals in interest the widespread desire for a new type of education. Everywhere men, and now women, are demanding a new sort of culture, such as this ancient land of the scholar has not known until this day. To meet this new demand on the part of Chinese women, in the vast District of Hankow, we have reared St. Hilda's School.

It occupies about an acre of land, adjoining what is called Boone University Compound. As is proper in this coun-try, it turns its back on Boone College with a lofty exclusive wall, and looks down on the rest of the world from a wall almost equally high. The school building is about the size of a large American dwelling. As we enter the front door we see that its two stories are built around a little open-air court. In this house are living seventy-two girls. Who would think it! The place was built for forty pupils, but such is the pressure for entrance that over seventy are squeezed in, most of them sleeping two in a narrow bed in dormitories meant for half the number; sitting three on a bench built for two; crammed into the commonplace room they call a chapel, till the last resource of turning aisles about and selecting small stools to sit on instead of large ones has been tried, and not one more can be gotten in. The only comment one need make on this is that the girls have plenty of ventilation and are less crowded than in their own houses; and that, being like the rest of the Chinese nation, they can sleep soundly anywhere.

St. Hilda's School has had a long and chequered history. It was founded in 1875 as the Jane Bohlen School for girls. In these thirty-five years it has never had more than one foreign teacher to give her whole time to the school. From 1883 to 1894 and from 1897 to 1899 it had no foreign unmarried lady teacher at all. Yet, in spite of all these drawbacks, the school has turned out Christian workers, and has given to a large number of Christian wives the only possible chance for an education in a land where ignorance is such a foe to Christianity.

St. Hilda's is distinctly a school for Christian girls. It has little room for the many others who apply. Deaconess Phelps, the present principal, wrote, several years ago, as follows: "The desire for education has at last reached the women of our district. The only way in which I could make room for four very important girls (future wives of clergy, etc.) for the next term was to drop the four laziest girls. They naturally did not like it, but there was nothing else to do. It had a good effect on the whole school, however, as all the others were afraid it might be their turn next, and they began studying furiously." And again: "In planning for this new term it was hard to choose between the new applicants. Of course, clergymen's daughters must be taken in, and those engaged to divinity students, and there were a number of nice heathen girls of Mandarin class, whom we greatly desired to receive, and whom Mr. Ridgely, our chaplain, thought it our special duty to take in. But, if determined to be educated, they could go to other schools in Shanghai, whereas our Christians are poor, and St. Hilda's is their only chance to make anything of their lives. So we usually gave the preference to those en-gaged to Boone School boys. But again I had to remember that we must produce teachers, and that these must come from the unengaged girls. So I must keep room for some of them. Then of course, when I got my list satisfactorily made up, some foreigner would write that the orphan daughter of some faithful old Christian must come to school, or her relatives would marry her to a heathen to get rid of supporting her. So I had to revise my list and see which girl to sacrifice. And one can never tell what will become of the girl who is refused admission. Had St. Hilda's accommodation for 150 girls, it would not cost any more to run the school, but there really should be accommodation for 300, with new buildings outside the city, where land is cheap." So by refusing thirty or forty applicants a term the principal manages to take in the most urgent cases. This leaves entirely out of account those who do not apply because they know it is of no use.

The present curriculum at St. Hilda's School covers eight years of work. Next year a class of girls will be ready to advance to a high school course, but this will be possible only if another qualified teacher can be secured. In the present primary and grammar course a main study is, of course, Chinese. This is a long and difficult study for natives as well as foreigners. For besides the great labor of learning to read and write the characters, the acquiring of the written style is a considerable study. To the Chinese boy or girl the writing of compositions in Wenli, the written language, is as great a task as the Greek and Latin exercises of school children at home. Besides Chinese, the girls study English for six years, geography, science, Chinese and foreign history, hygiene, physiology and arithmetic. This last study the children find difficult, for it involves thinking and reasoning. But it forms a valuable antidote to a long heredity of memorizing without thought.

So much for the mental training of the students. St. Hilda's tries to do as much

"They are not by any means so stolid as they look"

for the body as its limited playground and the traditions of Chinese girldom will permit. In the first place, of course, the school forbids foot-binding. A strong stand was made in this direction about ten years ago. All girls with bound feet must unbind them. Nevertheless the Chinese matron discovers not infrequently that girls who have free feet by day bind them up by night, when they hope not to be discovered. So imperious in beauty's eyes is fashion's command! However, in spite of free feet the girls do not have much variety or intensity of exercise. The physical drill is the chief form of exercise. The principal looks longingly for the time when the school may have tennis courts.

Another important feature is its religious work. This lies mainly not in converting or influencing heathen girls, but in training those already baptized. How important is this work of implanting high ideals, of developing character and spiritual life, only those in the mission field can adequately realize. For a Christian school in a heathen land has in most cases to do the work of a parent, as well as a teacher; to give the training in Christian knowledge and habits which in America most homes will furnish. Thus the personal influence of the teacher counts here for even more than in Christian lands.

Apart from the personal influence or work of its teachers, St. Hilda's tries to accomplish this end by its various classes for baptism, confirmation and Bible study, by the work of a branch of the Y. W. C. A., and by its Sunday and daily services. It is stimulating both to sight and to faith to watch the girls of St. Hilda's filing two by two, the smallest first, into the Church of the Holy Nativity, looking, as is proper in this country, neither to left nor to right. For to the eye of faith that double line—which could easily be made three or four times longer, were the accommodations larger—is the promise and prophecy of China's multitudinous womanhood, redeemed and transformed in Jesus Christ.

So much for St. Hilda's School as it was and is. Let us imagine for a moment what it might be. Just outside the "Little East Gate" of Wuchang, near us and the city, is a tract of land which the interest and generosity of some ladies in Philadelphia has converted into the site for a new St. Hilda's. From the city wall near by we can see the green fields, soon, we hope, to become greensward and college lawn. There will be the new school with its buildings,

DAUGHTERS OF OUR CHINESE CLERGY

chapel and playground. There will stand the school, with its high school and normal courses, with its 300 bright-faced girls drawn from many cities along a thousand miles of the yellow Yangtse, and from Honan to the north and Hunan to the south. It will be *the* higher educational institution for women, so far as our Church is concerned, in a region with a hundred million people, in a district where the Church is growing rapidly. From the portals of the new St. Hilda's, as the years pass by, will go forth a continuous stream of young women, trained in body, mind and soul. Many of these will go out to meet the call which comes from everywhere for teachers and nurses. More, and probably nearly all in the end, will become educated Christian wives, sources of light and centres of power in their respective communities. Others will go forth, not Christians in name, perhaps never to be such; but these will find that St. Hilda's has changed their lives and led them into a new world. How fancy kindles as one looks forward

and sees the far-reaching beneficent influence of the St. Hilda's that is to be, in the new China which is slowly emerging before our eyes!

That is the vision. Its realization depends on two things—teachers and buildings. Six women from America as teachers for St. Hilda's! What a career they may look forward to! And the buildings? $15,000 gold will put up a building with complete accommodations for at least one hundred girls, and every other $15,000 will do as much more.

Bishop Roots in his last two annual reports calls the need of St. Hilda's the most important need of his diocese, with its 80,000,000 people. For the great need of the work as a whole is the development of the work for women. That is far behind the work for men, and necessarily so, because of the scarcity from the beginning of woman workers. The work will never be on a satisfactory basis until we have *women* competent to instruct the Chinese women, and schools to educate the Christian mothers of the next generation.

. IN THE CARPENTER SHOP
A scene in St. Augustine's School, Raleigh, N. C.

THE AMERICAN CHURCH INSTITUTE:
NOTES ON ITS WORK

THE report of The American Church Institute for Negroes contains among other interesting items a declaration of the Southern bishops respecting the Institute and its work. This declaration has been published in the Church papers and is therefore not news; but the following "circular," signed by all the Southern bishops having Negro work, is worthy of special note as indicating the measure of confidence in the Institute entertained by those bishops:

"WE, the undersigned Bishops of Southern dioceses, having schools for the education of Negro children and youth, believing a Christian and a practical education of these children and youth to be an absolute necessity to the moral safety of our civilization and to the good citizenship of the Negro race, and believing also in the purpose and efficiency of The American Church Institute for Negroes as visitor to our schools and as trustee of funds, do appeal to all loyal Churchmen for small and large gifts for the work of the Institute. We ask the sum of $1,000,000 for the development of our present work and for greatly needed extension of the same kind of work to all the dioceses of the South."

OF the twenty-three graduates from St. Augustine's School, Raleigh, last May, eight girls are teaching in public and parochial schools, one is studying domestic science at Hampton, and two boys are studying for the ministry. In other words, nearly half the members of the graduating class have within five months engaged in social and religious service or in further preparation therefor. It is also worthy of notice that two of the girls are teaching domestic science, and one is taking a further course in that science with a view to teaching. This is a thoroughly healthful symptom, and indicates that the Negroes are obeying the same practical impulse which is animating the most intelligent education of white girls.

The attendance at St. Augustine's this year is not as large as for some years previous; but that is not a discouraging fact because it is probably due to the necessity of adjustment of the sentiment and purpose of both parents and students involved in the year added to the school course. This means higher standards of work, and it means also increased expense to our students and to their parents. The purpose of this added year is to devote more time to normal work, properly so-called, for those who are to teach.

Work on the new girls' dormitory, which has been made possible by the generosity of the Woman's Auxiliary, will be immediately begun. We are securing plans for the proposed building and shall begin work on the foundations at once.

ST. PAUL'S SCHOOL, Lawrenceville, Va., has opened with the largest attendance in its history.

Before work could be begun on the new domestic science building at St. Paul's it was necessary to move two other buildings and to build a store. The store is practically completed, and work on the new domestic science building will be shortly begun.

THE repairs to the plant of the Vicksburg Industrial School, Vicksburg, Miss., made possible by the application of a portion of the Men's Thankoffering, have been completed and the school has begun its work. The Rev. W. H. Marshall, who came to us from Texas, has been manifesting intelligence and energy in studying the needs and purposes of the school, and the best methods of realization of those purposes.

LET us close this month's notes by quoting from a letter received from one of our St. Augustine's graduates— one who completed his course at Yale— in response to an invitation to leave the work he is now doing for something

OFF TO THE FRONT

BRIEF SKETCHES OF RECENTLY APPOINTED MISSIONARIES

WITHIN the past year a rather unusual number of persons have gone out to recruit the Church's forces beyond the confines of our own country. We who remain at home naturally desire to follow them with our sympathy and our prayers, as well as our gifts, and we shall do this better if we know something of them and see their faces—if only on the printed page. Therefore we present in this issue portraits of some of those most recently appointed, together with brief notes concerning them.

For Alaska

FOUR helpers have gone to assist Bishop Rowe and his band on duty in Alaska. It stands to the credit of the new deaconess school in the Diocese of California that one of its first graduating class goes to the mission field in the person of Miss Mabel Howard Pick. Miss Pick, who was set apart as a deaconess before leaving for Alaska, is English by birth, but has been living for nearly ten years in Canada and the United States. In addition to her training as a deaconess she has had considerable experience in church and institutional work. She is stationed at Wrangell.

The Rev. Louis Herman Buisch, who graduated from the General Theological Seminary in 1905, goes to Alaska with his wife, as missionary to Fairbanks, thus relieving the Rev. C. C. Betticher, Jr., who is now on his furlough, and who plans, after his return, to give

MR. BUISCH

all his time to the work among the Tanana Indians, in which he has been so successful. Mr. Buisch entered the ministry in Western New York and has since done faithful and conscientious service there. He was appointed at the May meeting of the Board and is already in the field.

The Rev. George Edward Renison, the second priest to go to Alaska, is in a sense "to the manor born." He is the son of a Canadian missionary priest who has been a life-long friend of Bishop Rowe, and the brother of another. He has seen active work as a layman in both eastern and western Canada and was a missionary in the Diocese of Duluth while it was still a missionary district. For two years he worked among the Cree Indians of Hudson Bay, living with his family 400 miles from civilization. He then went to the Diocese of California, where he worked for a short time before responding to the call of Bishop Rowe for the work in Alaska.

MR. RENISON

Foremost among the splendid helpers who have made the work in Alaska possible, is the little band of missionary nurses. No work could be more telling than that accomplished by the Christian nurse in this primitive country, where hardship is inevitable, and accident and suffering are frequent. When Miss Emberley gave notice of her retirement from the work at St. Matthew's Hospital, Fairbanks, she immediately set about searching for a substitute, whom she found in Miss Clara C. Johnston, a trained nurse working in Roxbury, Mass. Miss Johnston was born in Canada, but received her training and practised her profession in New England. She goes to the work in Alaska with the highest testimonials as to her fitness and faithfulness. Miss Johnston returned in company with Miss Emberley and was introduced by her to the new work.

MISS JOHNSTON

For Hankow

SIX recruits—two men and four women—have gone to the District of Hankow to work under Bishop Roots. At the April meeting of the Board the Rev. Robert A. Goodwin, Jr., was appointed to assist the Rev. Mr. Lindstrom in his work at Kiukiang. Mr. Goodwin's father is the rector of St. John's Church, Richmond, Va., and he is a graduate of that fine mother of missionaries, the old Virginia Seminary. It is needless to say that his ancestry, education, and natural abilities mark him as one to whom the Church may look for faithful and effective service in the mission field which he has chosen.

MR. GOODWIN

At the same meeting of the Board

Miss Sarah Elizabeth Hopwood was appointed as a teacher at St. Hilda's School, Wuchang. This to her was the fulfilment of a long standing ambition. For years it had been her conviction that she was definitely called to work in the Orient. It is a cause for great encourage-

MISS HOPWOOD

ment when such bright young lives are freely given to the Church's high service.

The Rev. Frederick G. Deis, appointed for evangelistic work in the District of Hankow at the May meeting of the Board, was a student in the General Theological Seminary, New York, and the Nashotah Seminary. He has thus far done his work in the middle West. When applying for appoint-

MR. DEIS

ment he was engaged in work at the Church of the Epiphany, Chicago. He sailed with his wife in September for his distant field.

All those familiar with the work of the China mission are acquainted with the Rev. Lawrence B. Ridgely, of Wuchang, who has taken so active and

DEACONESS RIDGELY

burden, goes Miss Annie Jane Lowe, who also sailed with Bishop Roots on November 8th, immediately after her appointment. Miss Lowe graduated at the Boston City Hospital in 1902, and since has rendered service in several of the important Massachusetts hospitals and in private nursing. Miss Lowe has the distinction of being the first person appointed to what will henceforth be known as the District of Wuhu.

Nothing shows more clearly the practical nature of the modern missionary campaign than d o e s the variety of workers which it enlists. The idea of a missionary stenographer would have been startling a few years ago, but it is in this capacity that Miss Edith Kay goes to the district of Hankow. T h e w o r k of the Church's mission is a great business, a n d its leaders need the same helpful subordinates as do executives in other large enterprises. The service which the secretary of a foreign missionary bishop can render to the cause is no slight one.

MISS KAY

For Shanghai

TO the district of Shanghai four persons have gone. Three of them are young men, the first of whom to receive appointment was the Rev. Thomas Kinloch Nelson. Mr. Nelson is a graduate of the University of Virginia and of the Virginia Theological Seminary. Not only is he a graduate of the latter institution, but he may be called in a peculiar sense the child of the seminary. As the son of the late Professor Kinloch Nelson he was born and reared within its walls. He is spoken of as a man of rare fitness and promise, with a

MR. NELSON

sound judgment which should make him a particularly valuable servant of the Church in the mission field.

Mr. Harold B. Barton, who was appointed at the May meeting for work in St. John's University, is the son of an old Church family of Worcester, Mass. He graduated from Harvard College, where he did admirable work in connection with the St. Paul's Society and the Phillips Brooks Association. He later became a teacher in St. George's school, Newport, where he rendered most satisfactory service.

Mr. Percy L. Urban goes also to reinforce the staff at St. John's University. Never adequately manned, this school will now need more than ever the help of the Church in the way of workers and gifts, because it is likely soon to lose its president, Dr. Pott, who has been elected bishop of the new District of Wuhu. Mr. Urban is a graduate of Princeton Uiversity, where he took highest honors in classics and graduated *summa cum laude* in the department of English. After his graduation he served as a teacher in the university and during the short episcopate of Bishop Knight in Western Colorado he worked under him as a lay missionary. He therefore goes to the field equipped by an experience both in the mission field of the West and as a teacher in the East.

MR. URBAN

Dr. George M. Laning, who goes to the District of Kyoto, is returning to his native land. He is the son of Dr. Henry Laning, our long-time faithful missionary at St. Barnabas's Hospital, Osaka. Miss Serena Laning, his

DR. LANING

sister, is already under appointment as a worker in the district. Dr. Laning is a graduate of Kenyon College and took his medical degree at the University of Michigan. It is the conviction of those who know him best that, like his father, he is fitted to render faithful service in the mission field.

Miss Una F. Dudley, of Long Branch, N. J., received an appointment for work in Porto Rico at the June meeting of the Board and sailed with Bishop Van Buren to take up her work in that field on November 20th. She has long cherished the desire to enter the mission field and had this object in mind while taking her course as a nurse at the Monmouth Memorial Hospital, Long Branch. Miss Dudley was born and reared a Baptist, and came into the Church from conviction. Her energy, experience and sound health are good auguries for success. She will be stationed temporarily at Mayaguez, taking up the work of a district nurse, and will probably go later to St. Luke's Hospital, Ponce.

Miss Iva M. Woodruff has gone to take up the work of a kindergartner at Mayaguez, Porto Rico. She has already had a considerable experience in this work, and is spoken of in the highest terms by those who have been associated with her. She is a graduate of St. Mary's School, Knoxville, Ill., and

MISS WOODRUFF

had her kindergarten training in Chicago and Cleveland. She also took a course in the Teachers College and Columbia University, New York. She has had six years' practical experience in teaching in the public schools and spent one summer travelling in Europe.

The Rev. Leland Howard Tracy has been appointed by the Bishop of Mexico as missionary at Chihuahua. Mr. Tracy was in the ministry of the Presbyterian Church, but his convictions led him to resign therefrom and receive confirmation at the hands of Bishop Burgess of Long Island. He was placed in charge of St. Lydia's Church, Brooklyn, where he did excellent work and was ordained on Trinity Sunday. He started almost immediately for his work in Mexico, accompanied by his wife and child, and has begun his service in that largest of our mission fields.

BOOK REVIEWS

THE MODERN MISSIONARY CHALLENGE. By John P. Jones D.D. Fleming H. Revell Co., New York. Cloth, $1.50.

Dr. Jones has made himself known throughout the country as one of the most telling speakers in the recent campaign of the Laymen's Missionary Movement. Anything therefore which comes from him will be accorded unusual consideration. He has placed the missionary cause under a decided obligation in putting forth "The Modern Missionary Challenge." The book is an expansion of a course of lectures delivered this autumn before the Yale Divinity-school and at the Bangor and Oberlin theological seminaries. It is a discriminating and vivid treatment of the whole missionary idea, illuminated by the personal experience of one who has himself been a part of the great movement. His personal testimony, drawn from the experience of many years in India, forms a particularly telling feature, though he writes for a much larger purpose than the telling of his own story. The chapters on new conditions, new problems and new methods in mission work are particularly suggestive, as are also the review of the present forces and agencies and the startling situation set forth by his chapter on the magnitude of the task to be accomplished. Dr. Jones has woven into his treatise many findings of

the several Commissions of the Edinburgh Conference, so that his book possesses an authoritative character quite beyond that which might be given it by his well-known personal ability. We are glad to note that among the statistics given he includes, so far as he can, those of the Roman and Greek Catholic Churches, thereby presenting a fairly comprehensive view of the whole Christian campaign in non-Christian lands.

While we do not give unqualified assent to Dr. Jones's conclusions, we are convinced that the book will be of great interest to those who read it, and that it will be particularly helpful to any clergyman wishing to present in his sermons the vital and stimulating facts and appeals of modern missions.

THE DECISIVE HOUR OF CHRISTIAN MISSIONS, By John R. Mott. Student Volunteer Movement, New York.

No one is better qualified to write on such a striking subject than the author, who, to a greater degree than any other man, has come into personal touch with the world field, and, as chairman of Commission I. of the Edinburgh Conference, has had access to voluminous correspondence, giving the latest information from missionary work in all non-Christian lands.

In an interesting, instructive and inpiring way the book deals with the opportunities, difficulties, methods of attack and possibilities of the Christian rmy in its world battle. Bringing the atest news from the whole battle-line to adividual soldiers in one part of the eld, it must arouse them to action to meet this unprecedented world opportunity, one that, it would seem, can ardly be so great again. The book rould be read by every Christian, and specially by each ordained officer in the rmy. It is splendidly adapted for use a mission study classes.

[EMOIR OF GEORGE HOWARD WILKINSON, BISHOP OF ST. ANDREWS. By A. J. Mason, D.D. Longmans, Green & Co., New York.

One of the events of the year 1908 was he appearance of the two-volume biography of the Right Rev. George Howard Wilkinson, D.D., sometime Bishop of ruro and afterward the Primus of the cottish Church. Dr. Arthur J. Mason, ho was one of Bishop Wilkinson's chaplains, wrote this most admirable work hich he modestly calls a memoir. It oved to be one of the most effective ographies written in recent years, and et with instant and widespread appreciation. Dr. Mason has just produced a e-volume edition, printed in much less etentious form and containing practically all the important material of the nger edition. The chief compression s been obtained by the omission of cerin collections of letters written by the rimus, which, though deeply interestg, are not absolutely necessary to the rtrayal of his character. To all those 16 wish to look in upon the life of a vout, inspiring and virile man of God heartily commend this volume.

"ECHOES FROM EDINBURGH"

FOR a fortnight last June Edinburgh was the focus of the thought and npathy of a large part of the Christian rld. The World Missionary Conference then in session in the ancient and picturesque Scotch capital has been fairly characterized as one of the most notable gatherings in Christian history. Its purpose, its personnel and its methods all gave promise of an occasion of great significance and influence. This promise was amply fulfilled by the sessions of the Conference and the spiritual forces it released.

Unfortunately, only a mere handful of the mighty Christian host that looked sympathetically toward Edinburgh could attend the Conference. Many thousands will no doubt study the nine alluring volumes just published and containing the full official report of the Conference. But for everyone who will do this ten thousand others will lack the time, the opportunity or the inclination for such exhaustive study. The Conference Committee decided wisely, therefore, when it determined to publish in a single volume a popular account of the great meeting. *Echoes from Edinburgh* (F. H. Revell Co., New York, $1 net) bids fair to be deservedly the most popular and useful missionary book of the year.

The committee was fortunate in securing as the writer of the book the Rev. W. H. T. Gairdner, a member of the staff of the English Church Missionary Society. Mr. Gairdner typifies the fine ability, thorough training and ardent missionary spirit of many of the younger clergy of the Church of England. An Oxford man, still under forty, he is recognized as one of the missionary statesmen in Egypt, where most of his working life has been spent. He has already made notable contributions to missionary literature in the biography of Douglas Thornton and in a brilliant study of Mohammedanism under the title of *The Reproach of Islam*.

Mr. Gairdner has succeeded in putting a large amount of information into a hand-book of 270 pages. Going back to the very beginning, he traces, in the opening chapters, how the thought of the leaders about the Conference and the preparations for it gradually developed. Then a chapter on "Edinburgh" and its historical associations aptly voices the affection that every Conference delegate must feel for the city where some of the most stimulating days of his life were spent.

The great meeting on the opening evening of the Conference, June 14th, is vividly described with special emphasis upon the address of the Archbishop of Canterbury, and particularly upon its close, when, after asserting that "the place of missions in the life of the Church must be the central place and none other," he concluded: "Secure for that thought its true place in our plans, our policy, our prayers, and then—why then, the issue is His, not ours. But it may well be that, if that come true, there be some standing here to-night who shall not taste of death till they see the Kingdom of God come with power."

Some of the notable delegates are then introduced. Mr. Gairdner has done this in a clever fashion, of which one instance must suffice: "Seated among the members . . . was Kajinosuke Ibuka, in whose face, immobile as a Buddha, lurked the suspicion of an enigmatic twinkle of an Eastern image when some missionary delegate, in a confidential moment, tells the Conference what missionaries think about the Japanese, or what they suppose the Japanese think about them. This man is one of the foremost Christians in Japan, a theologian, a college principal, one of the nine who were formed into the first Protestant communion in Japan."

Then Mr. Gairdner passes to the most difficult part of his task in the nine chapters which summarize the reports of the Commissions on the subjects considered by the Conference and its discussion of the reports. On the whole, Mr. Gairdner has done this work well. If some find his style occasionally badly involved, bearing the evident marks of a mystical and poetic temperament, it must be admitted that he seems to have caught the

spirit of the occasion. To interpret that is no less important than to give a well-balanced summary of the discussion.

We hope that every reader of THE SPIRIT OF MISSIONS will read this book and commend it to others.

As the Churchman follows the discussions of the great gathering, he will share Mr. Gairdner's regret that a shattered Christendom prevented the proceedings of the Edinburgh Conference from being hallowed and consecrated by a celebration of the Holy Communion. Then let him turn to the chapter summarizing the discussion on "Co-operation the Promotion of Unity." There he will find abundant ground for the conviction that our Lord's ideal and prayer will some day be realized.

Here is a passage from the report of the Commission:

"Unity, when it comes, must be something richer, grander, more comprehensive than anything which we can see at present. It is something into which and up to which we must grow, something of which and for which we must become worthy. We need to have sufficient faith in God to believe that He can bring us to something higher and more Christlike than anything to which a present we see a way."

Here are the words of an Englis bishop spoken in the tense discussion o an ever memorable day:

"We have no use for the least com mon denominator of Christianity. W look with hope to its greatest commo measure some day, a day not yet i sight. . . . One day we shall be on but it will be effected by a higher unio than is in sight at present, when ou deepest convictions and needs are me and satisfied, not whittled away."

Here are the words of an Italia bishop, written as a message to the Con ference and read to it: "My desire fo you is but the echo of Christ's word which have resounded through the cen turies—'Let there be one flock and on Shepherd.'"

OUR LETTER BOX
Intimate and Informal Messages from the Field

The Rev. E. P. Newton writes the following vivid description of last Christmas Day in Alaska. How many hungry, lonely men would have been thankful for such Christian fellowship as the Valdez rectory extended!

CHRISTMAS DAY was ideal. I was out at 7:30 without a coat, wearing only a light cardigan jacket, more to keep dry than for warmth. Mushing about in the deep snow sets the blood going. Do you know this word "mush"? It is the regular trail term here from the French *"marche,"* by way of Canadian patois, and then plain United States "mush.". When we say "mush" to the dogs they hustle and get out of the way. How would it sound, "I mushed out to the park" or "I mushed down Broadway"! but I mushed up to the hospital and left a Christmas present in the vestibule.

We had a good service at 10 A.M. Early celebrations are almost impossible in this country; people are such late risers. Nine o'clock would be like seven in New York in relation to the habits of people.

Christmas afternoon at four, fifteen men sat down for a Christmas dinner at the rectory. I aimed to invite the most solitary men I could find. They were all ages, from sixty to twenty. One of them was *chef*—though the twenty-seven-pound turkey was cooked at a restaurant, as the pan would not go into my oven—and the nurses made the plum pudding, and the mince pies were given to me, and another lady made the cranberry jelly—but our *chef* baked the finest of hams basted with sherry, and we had potatoes and rice and onions, and abundance of gravy. It was a fine meal. The Yule candle of 1905 I brought to Alaska and it has done duty for three Christmases. It's getting pretty short. I put it on the top of a candy pail covered with tissue paper for our centre piece, laying bunch raisins about the edge and piling nuts within. Then we had two seven-branch candlesticks for light and turned out the electric lights. After dessert we cleared away the tables, for they extended into the front room, and sat about the library for our coffee and cigars. One man sang well, and recited, and I read two of O. Henry's short stories from the book you sent me, and we talked, and finally played cards. One of the men said, "I haven't had so good a time since I came to Alaska." It was a great privilege to spread some cheer that day and made a very happy Christmas for me.

* *

The wife of one of our missionaries in Cuba sends the following from Santiago:

"SUMMER in the Tropics" is a phrase which makes our friends back in the snug heart of civilization throw up their hands in horror! But, as a matter of fact, Mr. A—— and I were as comfortable in the old school-house in Guantanamo this summer as we have ofttimes been in our apartment in New York.

The teachers departing to their various

Eight of the reasons why we stayed

(1025)

Our little choir

homes in "the States," we decided, instead of paying some stranger to come
and stay with the orphans for the summer, to go over and take care of them
ourselves, for we were too busy recover-
ing from our last vacation to entertain
any thoughts of going North this year.
So we closed the rectory and took over
the care of our numerous family. From
Juan Antonio and Carmita, the "littlest"
baby, to Dolores and Teresa, the oldest;
who are quite big girls, my little flock
kept decidedly busy. I gave them practical dressmaking lessons and they progressed rapidly. Though little Mercedes
will tell you, I am sure, that they were
not at all good lessons, for she bewailed
the relentless justice which made her rip
out a sleeve when she had made two for
the same arm.

We planned to do a great deal of pic-
nicing with the children during the summer. They love nothing so much as to
set out on foot before the dawn, and walk
up hill and down dale in the glory of
awakening morning till they find an
arroyo (small stream) and there spend
the day, returning at sunset—that marvellous sunset of the tropics! But we
were obliged to forego this sort of thing
when the news came from the bishop
that we were to move to Santiago. Also
that the school—that is to say, the boarding department—was to be moved, and

among the Laboring Classes," by the Rev. Y. Suguira, who has devoted himself unstintedly to this work in Tokyo.

One day, given up to an all-day excursion to Chuzenji, the charming lake 2,000 feet higher up among the mountains, was most enjoyable. A row on its deep blue waters was provided by the generosity of the bishop. When we met in the evening some feet were blistered and many limbs were stiff, yet all agreed that we had had, in school-boy language, a "rattling good time."

Early on Saturday morning the bustle and excitement betokened the dispersing in all directions of those who had gathered for a time of united prayer and counsel. They went back, in some cases, to lonely outposts, with joy in their hearts and renewed strength to fight the battle of the Cross, and to win new victories for the faith which is overcoming the world.

* *

Deaconess Lawrence, writing from among the Virginia mountains, says:

SEVEN girls stayed in residence for the summer term, and, like the creatures of the wood and field, we have garnered in our provender for the winter. We are still working hard, though school began last week. Five of the girls are being prepared for confirmation—at their own request and without any solicitation on my part. Two of them are my god-children, baptized the first year I came here, and it is such a pleasure to have them confirmed. I gave notice at morning prayers that I would meet any of them who wished to be confirmed, at a later hour in the chapel—and it was such happiness to have all five that I hoped for come at the time appointed. They are taking their preparation so intelligently—so reverently—as to make me very hopeful as to their steadfastness in the future. When I asked one why she wished to be confirmed, she said, "To make me *stronger*," which was about as good an answer as many of her superiors could have given.

I started a little Sunday-school over

in Honeytown, some three miles across the nearest ridge, in the middle of June. We have to meet in a grove and sit on unplaned planks, but some sixty or seventy people come out to "preaching" and we have a regular Sunday-school attendance of twenty-five. They *have* *never* had such a thing as a Sunday-school before. As winter comes on we will have to close up for a while unless, as I am hoping, some one of the congregation offers land for a little church. They are all so interested that this is very likely to occur.

In August we took the children to Luray Cavern—quite an undertaking— a thirty-two-mile trip by wagon and two hours on the train. Some of the girls had never seen a train before. One had never seen a town, and the little village of "Elkton" was a wonderful sight. The Cavern itself was awe-inspiring, and for the first time since I have been in the work I nearly collapsed under the weight of my responsibilities as half a dozen robust girls flung themselves simultaneously upon me for protection. I entered the cave with two clinging to each hand and others holding on to my dress. Their fear was soon overcome, however, and they enjoyed everything.

* *

Miss Elizabeth Upton, writing from Kawagoe, Japan, tells of Christmas parties among her Japanese children:

I WRITE to explain why your generous gifts have remained so long unanswered. Immediately after the Christmas parties I was plunged into a most strenuous three months. Besides keeping up the regular work, I had to train a new kindergartner to take the place of our other who started the kindergarten, as she was to be married. As I knew very little about kindergartening and had to study it all first and then teach it, you can imagine it took all my spare energy.

You sent $25 for a Christmas Party. How many people do you think that provided for? Perhaps 250, you say. Well, with the help the Christians could

give, and our Sunday-school children, and $2 from a lady in America, we had five different parties in five different towns, for about 700 people in all.

The Sunday before Christmas the children brought their gifts for children poorer than themselves, some money, some oranges or cakes, or peanuts, and we had enough to give all the oranges and peanuts to one of our outside country Sunday-schools.

Our first party was on Christmas night, at the pretty Japanese hall in Kawagoe. Some of the children were there three hours ahead of time.

We tried a new plan this year—having each class sing a Christmas hymn or carol, and then we had a magic lantern, showing many slides giving scenes from the life of our Lord, so that everyone there knew a little bit more why we were having this celebration. As we cannot get good kerosene, the lantern got very hot and we had to stop showing the pictures and let it cool off.

During the wait we gave out the real presents, promised for regular attendance. To one child who had never missed —a little boy from the kindergarten—we gave a foreign cotton umbrella just as tall as he was; which, of course, made him the envy of all his friends. His two sisters had also been very regular, so one had a prayer book and the other a hymnal. The other presents will seem funny—wooden clogs, a string to fasten a Japanese coat, wooden boxes covered with pretty paper for use as work-boxes, a gay knitted thing for the neck and woollen mitts. Then everyone had either a little toy, a note-book or a writing-brush, as well as a package of cakes and three tangerines. The grown-up visitors had such pretty cakes, pink and green and white in pretty shapes of pine-tree or crescent, but if you had eaten one you would have found the outside just like the starch paste you use for scrap-books, only a little stiffer, and inside a heavy, wet, dark-brown paste, very sweet, made of crushed beans.

Everyone seemed to have enjoyed their Christmas party, and we felt glad that more people had heard the Christmas message.

Monday night we went to another town where one of our catechists had been stationed for about six months, travelling on a funny little train, the windows of which have a streak of paint across them to make the people know they are of glass, as otherwise they would stick their heads right through.

We went to the house where the Monday school is held, and met the Christmas tree and trimmings, the cakes, presents and phonograph that a man had dragged on a kind of two-wheeled push-cart. About twenty-five people came. Everyone was early and helped to trim the tree and then sat on the floor in rows to listen to the Christmas story, and to look at the big pictures we had to show. They stood up and sang the Christmas hymn learned by heart, and said the Creed most reverently.

This little country Sunday-school, started by Miss Heywood, has the most faithful and most reverent of all our children. One of the boys, thirteen years old, said, when his father told him to go to the temple: "No, I can only worship the True God, Jesus."

At the next station the theatre was decorated with flags made by a boys' club. The programme took five hours to finish. The theatre was so cold we had to have fire-boxes on our laps and under our feet. About 300 were present.

The next party was given in the upper room that an old farmer had built especially for Christian meetings, although he himself has not yet been baptized. Here were gathered nearly fifty.

The next day our guests were poor little nurse girls and boys, who came with their babies tied on their backs. The 150 other children who came at first to the Sunday-school were forbidden to continue by the principal of the day-school. Some of these children did come, as well as the most influential man of the town and a policeman. Everyone seemed to enjoy the party, although all the babies cried at once. The children of this school lost their homes or had their homes damaged by the recent floods (August, 1910). Many of them have to live in the government school-house. We have started a kindergarten to help them.

NEWS AND NOTES

THE teacher of a Bible-class writes: "I wish to give fourteen members of my Bible-class a year's subscription to THE SPIRIT OF MISSIONS. May I have copies of the Christmas number, with presentation cards, in my hands in time to give them to these scholars at the Christmas tree on December 28th? I will send you a list of their addresses so that you can send the magazine to them for the following year."

If any teachers want to follow this example we will send them a copy of the Christmas number, with presentation card, to give to their pupils at the Christmas festival, with a receipt for a year's subscription, for $1. This means that they will get thirteen issues of the magazine for a year's subscription.

THE Pacific Mail steamer *Korea*, sailing from San Francisco on November 8th, carried quite a party of missionaries. It included Bishop Graves, of Shanghai; Bishop Roots, of Hankow; Bishop Restarick, of Honolulu; Miss Lucy F. Baker, of St. Luke's, Jamestown, N. Y., who goes to St. Hilda's School, Wuchang; Miss Annie J. Lowe, who goes from the Boston City Hospital to similar service as a nurse at St. James's Hospital, Anking, and Mr. Percy L. Urban, a graduate of Princeton, who is to become one of the faculty at St. John's University, Shanghai. In accordance with the kindly custom of the Church people of San Francisco, a missionary meeting was held for the outgoing party on November 7th, with addresses by the three bishops. On the sailing day there was an early celebration of the Holy Communion at the pro-Cathedral, followed by a breakfast.

¶

THE apportionment to Alaska for last year was $100. To September 1st the congregations have given $874.41. The apportionment made to Alaska for the coming year is $300. Bishop Rowe has already made out his detailed apportionment list and distributed it through the district. He asks the congregations to give $1,105 for the coming year instead of the $300 apportioned by the Board of Missions.

¶

A CHURCH deaconess in charge of three small hospitals, in the government Indian service in the West, writes from the midst of a scarlet fever epidemic:

"As all three hospitals are under my supervision, and are quite long distances from one another, there are times when I feel inclined to want to be a centipede. Then some pairs of feet might be resting occasionally, while others could keep going. However, when one is well—as I am—there is only gratitude for the privilege of work, even while very sorry anyone must be in pain."

¶

The Rev. Robert A. Griesser, one of the junior members of the staff at Soochow, China, writing of the death of the Rev. W. H. Standring, says:

I CANNOT begin to tell you the sense of loss that comes over us as we realize that Standring will not come back to us. He was a man who gave himself so whole-heartedly to everyone that all loved him. You appreciate this as well as we who worked with him.

I wish you could have been at the service this morning to see how the Chinese feel about his death. The church was filled at nine o'clock. It was one of the most impressive services I have ever attended. It was very simple, but the sense of oneness among all the congrega-

tion could be felt. If the Chinese are hard to move, then they must have been under a very strong emotion this morning. The sobbing of the women was pitiful, especially during Mr. Woo's splendid address, which touched every heart. We all felt with the faithful proctor, Mr. Woo, who went out during the service and returned with his smoked glasses on —lest the boys should see his emotion.

We feel that Standring sacrificed his life for these people in a very real way. He worked so hard that he was exhausted this summer when school closed, and so had not the strength to fight the disease. He gave his life for these people, and this morning we saw the result partly revealed. Can a man ask for any finer investment of his life? Would that more of our men at home could realize this. I am well, and enjoying my work so much."

¶

Here is one result of the Laymen's Movement Convention in Houston, Tex., last February. The rector of Christ Church says:

WE already have a regular subscription list of $2,200 for missions— diocesan and general—and we have not yet secured the co-operation of at least 40 per cent. of the men of the parish. We are determined to have them, or the most of them, before next Easter.

¶

THE Church Club of Milwaukee held a notable missionary dinner in connection with the sixty-fourth annual council of the diocese. Just over 100 men were present. The occasion was a stimulating one. Mr. Frederic C. Morehouse, editor of *The Living Church*, presided. Addresses were made by the Rev. Holmes Whitmore, rector of St. Paul's Church, Milwaukee, on "The Church in the Middle West"; by the Rev. John H. Hopkins, D.D., on "The Signs of the Times"; by the Right Rev. William W. Webb, D.D., Bishop of Milwaukee, on "Our Diocese"; and by the Right Rev. R. H. Weller, D.D., Bishop-coadjutor of Fond du Lac, on "Forward."

MEETING OF THE BOARD OF MISSIONS

November 3d, 1910

THE first meeting of the Board of Missions elected under the new Missionary Canon was held on Thursday, November 3d, at the Church Missions House. In spite of the fact that only ten days' notice was given, and that the membership is now scatered over the entire country, only eleven of the fifty members failed to answer to their names and no missionary department was without its representation.

Archdeacon Emery represented the Pacific Coast; the Bishop of Kansas, and Dean Davis, of St. Louis, the Department of the Southwest; Bishop Williams, of Nebraska, and the Rev. Mr. Sedgwick, of St. Paul, were present from Department VI. From the South came the Bishops of Florida and Atlanta, Dean Capers, the Rev. E. E. Cobbs and Mr. J. H. Dillard, of New Orleans; the Middle West was represented by Dean Matthews, of Southern Ohio, Mr. Stirling, of Chicago, and the Bishop of Indianapolis; while almost the entire membership resilent in Departments I., II. and III. was present. The Bishops of Pittsburgh, Eastern Oregon and South Dakota attended as honorary members and the department secretaries of the first, second and third departments, together with the Missions House staff, completed the number which crowded the Board room.

After the adoption of a suggested Order of Business the president read his inaugural statement to the Board, in which he set forth the ideals which he had for the Board's work in the future. This will be found printed in full on page 988.

A Committee on By-Laws was then appointed, consisting of the Bishop of Indianapolis, the Rev. Dr. Alsop, Mr. Pepper and Mr. Pruyn, who retired for consultation.

The Board then heard with satisfaction the report of the treasurer showing that receipts from all sources to November 1st were $62,345, as compared with $38,091 for the same period last year.

Formal communications from the secretary of the House of Bishops concerning the erection of four new missionary districts and the addition of six missionary bishops to the staff at home and abroad forcibly reminded the Board of the additional responsibilities laid upon it by the progressive policy of the last Convention. The salaries of the new bishops were voted to date from their consecration.

A balance of $3,118.65, remaining from the Men's Thank-offering of 1907, was voted to the Bishop of Nevada, to be used as the nucleus of a fund for the erection of an episcopal residence at Reno.

Dr. Harold Morris, of Philadelphia, was appointed to St. Luke's Hospital, Shanghai, and Miss Annie Jane Lowe, of the Boston City Hospital, was added to the nursing staff of St. James's Hospital, Anking. Miss Elizabeth Nichols, of Ithaca, N. Y., was also appointed to the Shanghai mission, where she will serve as a teacher in St. Mary's School. The resignation of the Rev. Henry B. Bryan from the Panama mission was accepted to date from November 1st.

Bishop Lloyd having been elected as a member of the Board by the General Convention before his choice as president—which office carries with it an *ex-officio* membership—the Bishop of Washington was elected to fill the vacancy thus created. The president then nominated as secretaries of the Board Mr. John W. Wood, the Rev. Hugh L. Burleson and the Rev. Joshua Kimber, which latter will continue to be known as the associate secretary. The treasurer nominated Mr. E. Walter Roberts as his assistant. All these were duly elected, the Board expressing to Mr. Roberts its appreciation of his thirty-four years of service. Under the new canon the secretaries, treasurer, and assistant treasurer form a Council of Advice for the president, whose duties he is asked to define. At his request the

Board adopted a standing resolution providing that the Council of Advice should have the management of the office of the Board, together with authority to provide for the payment of all obligations coming under the standing rules of the Board; to arrange in cases of emergency for appointments and furloughs; to consider all matters requiring action by the Board or the Executive Committee, and to submit the same to the Board or the Executive Committee with its recommendation; to consider and make recommendation to the Executive Committee concerning requests for permission to make appeals for special purposes, and to make recommendations to the Board or Executive Committee concerning any matter connected with the work of the Board.

The Committee on By-Laws then reported, and, after the making of some minor changes, their report was adopted. There will be four stated meetings of the Board in each year, on Wednesdays, the second in February, the first in May, the fourth in September, and the second in December.

An Executive Committee of three bishops, three presbyters and five laymen will exercise the powers of the Board in the interim between its meetings, but may not make appropriations aggregating more than $10,000 between any two meetings unless specifically authorized to do so. It will meet monthly, except in July and August, and will report its acts to the Board. The membership of the committees elected was as follows:

Executive Committee: The Right Rev. Dr. Lloyd, president; Mr. George Gordon King, treasurer; the Right Rev. Dr. Lawrence, the Right Rev. Dr. Greer, the Right Rev. Dr. Francis; the Rev. Dr. Anstice, the Rev. Dr. Alsop, the Rev. Dr. Manning; Mr. Pepper, Mr. Morris, Mr. Cochran, Mr. Stirling, Mr. Mansfield.

Trust Funds Committee: Mr. Morris, Mr. Chauncey, Mr. Pruyn, Mr. King, Mr. Newbold.

Audit and Finance Committee: The Right Rev. Dr. Lines, the Rev. Dr. Mann, Mr. Low.

So far the meeting had been largely of a routine character. It was toward the end of the afternoon, when adjournment seemed about to be taken, that Mr. W. R. Stirling, of Chicago, rose and suggested that something more should be done. The machinery had been constructed, should it be left standing still? Was not the Board created to put the spirit within the wheels? Could not every member be sent back to his department to accomplish something toward this end? The obligations already in sight greatly exceeded the entire apportionment, even if it were raised in full; what would the Board do about it?

Mr. Stirling's challenge deeply stirred the meeting. It was the note of leadership for which the new members had been waiting, and they responded. A motion was passed extending the session to include the morning of the following day, and the appointing of a committee which should sit in the evening to prepare a plan of action. This was done, and at the session on Friday morning Bishop Nelson, on behalf of the committee, presented a stimulating report calling for a general Forward Movement, and naming the sum of $500,000 as that which the Board should ask the Church to raise in addition to all apportionments. Not only did this report suggest a goal, but it outlined the process by which it was to be reached, and it instructed the Executive Committee to put the entire plan into immediate operation. The substance of this epoch-making report is embraced in the message sent out to the Church by the Executive Committee as a result of its meeting on November 18th, published on page 1033 of this issue.

When the Board next meets, on February 8th, 1911, it will first of all participate in the service of the Holy Communion to be held in the chapel, which by the new By-Laws becomes the first order of all stated meetings.

SPECIAL MEETING OF THE EXECUTIVE COMMITTEE

ON Friday, November 18th, the Executive Committee met at the Church Missions House at the call of the president, to carry out the instructions of the Board in sending a message to the Church concerning the Forward Movement. All but two members were present, together with all the officers of the Board. As the result of their deliberations a message to the Church, based on the report presented by a special committee of the Board of Missions, was prepared and ordered sent to all the bishops and clergy. Various means for carrying the plan into effect were discussed and action taken thereon; chief among these was a request that the president nominate for election a special secretary for the Forward Movement.

The committee passed the following resolutions:

I.

Resolved: That the retiring allowance of the Right. Rev. A. R. Graves, D.D., be fixed at $2,000 per annum.

II.

The Executive Committee having been informed that the consecration of the Bishop-elect of Kearney will take place on St. Andrew's Day, at which time the responsibility of the Right Rev. A. R. Graves, D.D., as Bishop of Kearney will cease:

Be it resolved: That this committee desires to place on record, and to express to Bishop Graves its profound appreciation of the heroic and fruitful service which he has rendered to the Church, hoping that he may still find opportunity to give to the work of the general Church the benefit of his large experience, in arousing interest and otherwise setting forward the progress of Christ's Kingdom.

The resignation of the Rev. John Henry Hopkins, D.D., as secretary of Department V., to take effect on November 30th, was presented and the following resolution was passed:

Resolved: That the Executive Committee of the Board of Missions has received with great regret the resignation of the Rev. John Henry Hopkins, D.D., as secretary of the Fifth Department.

In accepting the resignation at Dr. Hopkins's request, the committee, on behalf of the Board, desired to record its deep appreciation of the untiring service rendered by Dr. Hopkins since his entrance upon the office in February, 1909, and regrets that the heavy round of work that he has undertaken has impaired his health. The admirable way in which the Department has responded to his efforts indicates more clearly than could any words of the committee the quality of his work. The committee desired to assure Dr. Hopkins of its hearty good wishes for his future usefulness in parochial work, and thanked him for his expressed willingness to be of further service to the Board as opportunity may offer.

Several other matters of routine business were disposed of, among them a resolution to reduce the salary of the Bishop of Western Colorado from $3,000 to $2,000, and to increase the Board's appropriation for the support of missionaries in that district by the sum of $1,000. This action was taken at the request of the bishop and convocation of the district.

The Executive Committee adopted the following resolution, setting forth the status of contributions to the Forward Movement Fund:

Resolved: That contributions to the $500,000 Forward Movement Fund do not constitute payments upon apportionments, but shall be regarded as a special fund and so reported.

The committee then adjourned to meet on December 13th.

ANNOUNCEMENTS

CONCERNING THE MISSIONARIES

Alaska

Miss Annie C. Farthing, of Tortella Hall, Nenana, died suddenly on November 30th.

Bishop Rowe has transferred Miss Margaret C. Graves from Fairbanks to Anvik.

Hankow

The Rev. A. S. Cooper, on regular furlough, left Hankow on October 4th and arrived at New York by the steamer "Mauretania" on November 3d.

Kyoto

Bishop Partridge, returning after the General Convention, with his wife and little daughter, left New York on October 29th and sailed from Vancouver by the steamer "Empress of Japan" on November 9th.

Porto Rico

Bishop Van Buren, returning after the General Convention, sailed from New York by the steamer "Philadelphia" on November 20th.

Miss Una F. Dudley, whose appointment to Mayaguez was approved by the Board at its meeting on November 3d, sailed by the same steamer.

Shanghai

At the request of Bishop Graves, at the meeting on November 3d, the Board of Missions approved the appointment of Dr. Harold H. Morris, of Villa Nova, Pa., and the appointment of Miss Elizabeth Nichols, of Ithaca, N. Y., as workers in the District of Shanghai.

The Rev. B. L. Ancell and wife sailed from Japan on August 20th and arrived at Yangchow on the 29th.

Dr. Jefferys with his wife and two children sailed by the steamer "Minnehaha" on November 12th. Dr. Jefferys is to take a special course at the London School of Tropical Medicine and proceed to China later.

The Philippines

Bishop Brent, returning after the General Convention, sailed from New York by the steamer "Mauretania" on November 30th en route to Manila.

Tokyo

Bishop Channing Moore Williams died at Richmond, Va., on December 2d.

The Rev. James Chappell, who, with his wife and two children, sailed from London on August 20th, arrived at Tokyo October 6th.

The Rev. R. W. Andrews and family, on regular furlough, sailed from Yokohama by the "Nippon Maru" on October 26th and arrived at San Francisco on November 12th.

MISSIONARY SPEAKERS

FOR the convenience of those arranging missionary meetings, the following list of clergy and other missionary workers available as speakers is published:

When no address is given requests for the services of these speakers should be addressed to the Corresponding Secretary, 281 Fourth Avenue, New York.

Secretaries of Departments

I. Rev. William E. Gardner, 1 Joy Street, Boston, Mass.

II. Rev. John R. Harding, D.D., 692 Genesee Street, Utica, N. Y.

III. Rev. Thomas J. Garland, Church House, Philadelphia, Pa.

IV. Rev. R. W. Patton, care of the Rev. C. B. Wilmer, D.D., 412 Courtland Street, Atlanta, Ga.

V. ———— ————

VI. Rev. C. C. Rollit, 4400 Washburn Avenue, South, Minneapolis, Minn.

VII. Rev. H. Percy Silver, Box 312, Topeka, Kan.

VIII. Rev. L. C. Sanford, 1215 Sacramento Street, San Francisco, Cal.

Alaska

Rev. C. E. Betticher, Jr.

Eastern Oregon

Rt. Rev. R. L. Paddock.

Honolulu

Rev. Y. T. Kong.

South Dakota

Rt. Rev. F. F. Johnson, D.D.

provided for from the income of the Indemnity Fund returned to China by this Government on the suggestion of President Roosevelt. Of the seventy successful candidates, twelve were from St. John's University, Shanghai.

¶

A LOCAL official in Japan recently issued these instructions to the people under his care:

It is hereby decreed:

That people shall not crowd around foreigners in the streets, or in front of shops.

That shop-keepers shall not charge any excessive price to foreigners for goods sold.

That another dog shall not be set on, or sticks or stones thrown at dogs accompanying foreigners.

That in the street, park, or any other public places, such words as "keto" (hairy stranger), "Akaluje" (red beard), shall not be uttered.

That staring shall not be made at foreigners except when necessary.

That it shall be borne in mind that the foreign missionary, like the Japanese, Shinto and Buddhist priest, deserves respect.

That impediment shall not be given to the foreigners at play or on bicycles, by throwing fragments of tiles, stones or sticks, or by arranging many children in the streets.

That no disrespect shall be displayed toward foreign religions, or words to the same effect shall not be written in the sign-boards of shows.

That it shall be borne in mind that foreigners are disgusted with the habit of spitting everywhere, and of scattering about the skins of fruit and cigarette ends in the train or on ship.

That those who are learning foreign languages shall not try unnecessary talk with foreigners for the mere purpose of practising their tongues.

That the age of a foreigner shall not be asked, unless some special necessity demands it.

That the collars, cuffs, gloves and shoes shall be kept clean.

That it shall be understood that when a foreigner looks at his watch, he suggests that he has some urgent engagement.

Lesson IV.   Picture 1

ESKIMOS AT CAPE NOME

Lesson IV.   Picture 2

A congregation assembled for service in a store in Bettles

MISSION STUDY IN THE JUNIOR DEPARTMENT

IN the Junior Department the principles of activity and vision described for the primary department (See THE SPIRIT OF MISSIONS, November, page 949) are still operative.

Principle of Activity

(1) The greatest educational force is the child's own activity.

(2) Any activity that has helpfulness for its aim is valuable in training the mission spirit.

To these should now be added a third:

(3) As the joy of doing things with others is now appearing, all activity should be co-operative; by groups of two or more, or by the class.

Principle of Vision

All stories and pictures must now have a larger purpose than an appeal to the emotions. There must be a definite attempt to increase the scholar's information and prepare him for an ever-deepening consciousness of a world-wide Christian responsibility and loyalty.

Activity

In order that there may be co-operative activity, the class must have some money of its own. In some schools, where the current expenses are met by the vestry, the scholars are taught that the weekly offerings are class money to be used as the class directs, it being understood that such money must always be expended *in helping, or making someone happy.* This method not only trains the missionary spirit of the class, but it trains the scholars in stewardship and accustoms them to the responsibility of religious finance. Under this method each class should have a treasurer who, in a small book, will keep an account with the treasurer of the school. In this book, Sunday by Sunday, he should enter the amount of each offering and also the expenditures when voted by the class. In schools, where the offerings are needed to support the school,

an extra offering might be asked for class work. With the help of this money the following activity can be directed for the purpose of training the missionary spirit:

1. The class remembers a sick pupil by flowers or fruit, bought with some of the class money. (One class of boys met each week after school, bought the materials necessary and made a box of candy for a boy shut in with a broken leg.)

2. By appointing groups of twos, a convalescent member can be daily visited, and a small gift carried.

3. Classes can combine and buy a suit of clothes, shoes, etc., for a pupil, who for want of clothes is kept at home. Superintendent or rector does not give the name of such a child.

4. Direct the interest in the welfare of school associates and emphasize the fulfilment of responsibility to school, class or choir; regular and punctual attendance, glad performance of tasks assigned.

Emphasize team play whenever possible.

Visits to the hospitals, Day Nurseries, playgrounds, Newsboys' Home should be preceded or followed by some kind of a gift.

Concrete information on needs in mission fields, by use of pictures and stories, should be followed by appropriations from class money.

The making and selling of articles to earn money for the Lenten Offering. The gathering of things that the scholars value to be sent in boxes or barrels to the mission field.

Arrange exchange letters between Sunday-school scholars and boys and girls in the mission fields, especially in the mission schools.

Direct scholars to make for the Parish Bulletin Board, or for class use, posters, picturing and describing missionaries, schools and scholars, hospitals and customs of various people.

Such activity can be increased according to local circumstances and the activ-

Lesson IV.   Picture 3

Bishop Rowe preaching to Indian fishermen on the banks of the Yukon

Lesson IV.   Picture 4

CHRIST CHURCH, ANVIK

ity of scholars and the ingenuity of the teacher.

Pictures and Stories

In order that the scholar may be trained to a world-wide vision, the teacher of each class should see that during the year the class gains information about and contributes to (a) the local church; (b) some philanthropic institution in the city or town; (c) some good work in the state or diocese; (d) some mission work in the United States; (e) the mission work abroad. In the last two cases, always make the genuine call definite by describing some particular field. A teacher may begin: "Suppose our money went to China, what would it do?"

The rector or superintendent at times should come before the school and ask the classes to contribute toward some definite need at home or abroad, which he then describes. This should be done early in the session, so that the classes

may vote, and turn in a slip to the treasurer bearing the name of class and the amount voted. The treasurer can then report the total amount to the school at the end of the hour and forward check to its proper destination.

Beside the lessons now appearing in THE SPIRIT OF MISSIONS, other courses can be secured from the Church Missions House. A good book on China is Miss Sturgis's "Overcoming of the Dragon" (paper, 35 cents; postage, 8 cents). On the Negro work, send for "Pickaninnies' Progress" (paper, 15 cents; postage, 2 cents). Miss Haywood's "Torchbearers on the King's Highway" (paper, 20 cents; postage, 8 cents) and "Winners of the World" (paper, 30 cents; postage 7 cents) give biographical material. Valuable courses can be secured from the Church Missions Publishing Company, 211 State Street, Hartford. Send for "The Kingdom Growing" (25 cents) or "The Missionary Leaflet" (15 cents).

A MISSIONARY LESSON

General Subject: "Missions on Our Side of the World."
Lesson No. 4. Alaska.

(For a description of the methods to be used in teaching these lessons see THE SPIRIT OF MISSIONS, September, 1910, page 769.)

Methods of Review This course is now sufficiently developed to place emphasis on the *review*. Ask a certain scholar to open the note book at the place where the pictures of Lesson I. are mounted; then inquire: What was the first lesson about? Encourage other scholars to tell any facts about the lesson suggested by the pictures. Try to unify these suggestions under the "aim" as given in the lesson. In this way the sets of pictures for each lesson can be made to suggest the review exercise for each lesson, but in each case strive to impress the particular "aim."

Sometimes a whole period can be profitably spent on review work, at another time have a running and rapid review of all the lessons. The more frequent the review the more quickly can the exercise be conducted.

Point of Contact and Assignment On the Sunday before you give the lesson ask the class such questions as:

What is the general subject of our missionary lessons?

What missions have we visited?

Where did our railroad journey end?

What missionary district shall we visit next?

In describing the sea voyage from Seattle to Alaska each teacher can emphasize as much detail as will interest and hold the class. In younger classes it is good to bring in a picture of an ocean steamer and mount it in the note-book. Ask some such questions: If you were going to seek for gold, what would you take? If you were going as a missionary, what would you need?

State that next Sunday you will need the help of four scholars in order to have an interesting lesson. Produce the four sets of assignment questions as found below, which you have prepared by copying on separate sheets of paper. Give out with each set a copy of pamphlet 805 and ask those to whom you have given slips to come next Sunday prepared to give these assignments to the whole class:

1. The Land. (Pamphlet, pages 3 and 6, left column.)

What is the size of Alaska? (Use maps on page 3.)

Why is it part of the United States? What is the great river and why are most of the towns located on this river?

Where are the gold fields?

2. The Beginnings of Church Work. (Page 5.)

Who were the first missionaries and what did they accomplish?

Tell the story of Dr. Driggs at Point Hope.

Who were the first women missionaries?

3. The Bishop. (Pages 6 and 13, 14, 15.)

What in Bishop Rowe's early ministry fitted him for the work in Alaska?

What sacrifices did Bishop Rowe make when he was elected bishop?

Describe one of his winter visitations.

What do you think Bishop Rowe has accomplished?

4. The Work of the Church. (Pages 7, 8' 9, 10 and 11.)

What people does the Church at Tanana try especially to reach?

Describe the buildings.

Tell them to name things that the Church has done to improve the life at Point Hope.

What do they do in the Church at Fairbanks besides worship?

What other building is at Fairbanks?

The Lesson Go to the class with this aim clearly in mind: I want to show my class that Alaska is the land of wealth and opportunity; (2) that the people who go there need the Church, and (3) that great heroism is demanded from Christian soldiers there and here if the need is to be met.

Centre the first assignment around the map on page 4 of the pamphlet. Locate Sitka and the Klondike region. Trace the Yukon to its mouth. Show the distance between Fairbanks and Valdez—500 miles—this was the hard trip taken by the bishop in 1904. Point out Point Hope, the Church's mission farthest north. Emphasize that Alaska is a land with rich opportunities for fishing, mining and agriculture as well as gold digging; that in one year it yields three times the price paid for it by the United States.

In the second assignment point out the hardships endured by the early missionaries. Ask: What was it that made Dr. Driggs persevere? Emphasize the conditions as described by Lieutenant-Commander Stockton and show how it made an appeal to Christian manhood. In describing the development of Anvik show Lesson Picture 4, and the picture on page 11 of the pamphlet. With classes of girls emphasize the work of Deaconess Sabine, who has given generously of her life to Alaska.

The third assignment is a splendid chance to appeal to heroism. The pamphlet is rich with material on Bishop Rowe, and little difficulty will be experienced with this assignment. Make much of the pictures on pages 2, 12 and 15, also of Lesson Picture 3.

With the fourth assignment draw out the definite characteristics of each of the four missions:

Tanana Mission to the Indians.
Point Hope Mission to the Eskimos.
Nome Mission to gold seekers.
Fairbanks Mission to the miners.

Use the pictures in the pamphlet and also Lesson Pictures 1 and 2.

Gather the lesson together by asking: What can we do to help those men and women who are working for the Church in Alaska? We can pray. We can prepare to give more in our mite-boxes during the next Lent. We can tell others about the work in Alaska, so that they will be interested and give. When we are older we may be able to go ourselves and help the Church in the new North land.

Promise of Next Lesson Show on the map the long sea trip down the western coast to Mexico.

Note Book and Pictures Trace the voyage from Seattle to Sitka and then to Fairbanks, Tanana, Anvik and Point Hope. Mount in the note book the pictures cut from the pamphlet as well as the Lesson Pictures.

Material for Lesson 5: Pamphlet, "The Church in Mexico." Send to 281 Fourth Avenue, New York City.

THE WOMAN'S AUXILIARY

To the Board of Missions

THE SCHOOL BUILDING AT SOOCHOW

A GREETING FROM SOOCHOW

WHAT OUR CHINESE CHRISTIAN WOMEN THINK OF THE VALUE OF CHRISTIAN EDUCATION

THE women of the Auxiliary, who have just devoted $10,000 from their latest United Offering to the new building for St. Hilda's School, Wuchang, will be interested in the greeting which the women of the Soochow Mission gave the Secretary when she visited them in 1908. Although this visit was made so long ago, it was only this fall that the translation of this message reached the Missions House, together with a letter from Deaconess Paine.

DEACONESS PAINE'S LETTER

You have probably forgotten that such a document as the enclosed was ever promised you, but on reading it over perhaps the circumstances will gradually come to your mind. Mrs. Tsang wrote it all out in her best style, and I have translated it as literally as possible.

The training-school will open again in about a month, and I hope the mainspring of it, Miss Lok, will be enough better to come back at that time. She has been suffering with a nervous trouble which is her old enemy, and she feels almost discouraged about herself. I do not know how the school can go on any longer without her, but I take it that that is one of the things I am not expected to know. Since the school came to Soochow we have not as many substitute teachers as they used to have at St. John's.

As for the girls' school, while there is so much about it to encourage us to feel that it ought not to be closed, yet the sad news has just come that Mrs. Dan, the faithful little second teacher, cannot return, and where to look for someone to help Mrs. Tsang will be a question. Then, too, the Chinese house which we rent for the school will not accommodate the girls whom it is our duty to educate, and the new building, whose prospects seemed so bright a little while ago, has sunk below the horizon out of sight. But difficulties were made to be overcome, and these are not great ones compared with what most missionaries meet. When I read the story written by Miss Rich- mond of the toils and struggles of the pioneers of our mission, I feel unworthy to be counted among their successors, and it seems as if perhaps we need more trials and difficulties to call out our faith, and so ought to be glad of them. I know you have us always on your heart, and I hope you will pray not so much for our prosperity in an outward sense as for an increase of spiritual strength for us all. That is our greatest need.

THE WOMEN'S MESSAGE

Translation of the address made by the Soochow Branch of the Woman's Auxiliary to Miss Emery, on the occasion of her visit to Soochow.

Miss Emery (May Sian-tsia):

NOTHING could exceed our happiness in having you with us to-day and in having a reception for you to show our respect and admiration. Last year at the General Meeting we consulted about the matter of inviting you to China, and were all of one mind. But thinking of the great distance dividing us, we could hardly hope for a favorable answer. How could we know you would not fear the myriad miles, the difficulties and dangers of deep sea and barred mountains, but would give a favorable response to our invitation? In kindly coming to our humble country, you truly show your affection for us to be deep and of long standing.

But in your presence we feel like apologizing, because last Friday at the reception for you at St. Mary's in Shanghai, we could not be present, because some of us were sick and unable to come, others, either because of home affairs or on account of their children, were prevented from coming to welcome you. We hope you will pardon us.

But now that you have come to us, we shall surely receive a great benefit, for you are able to broaden our affection, so that it will go out to far-away people whom we have never seen and whose language we do not understand, but with whom we yet should be in sympathy and toward whom we should show affection like that which you have shown to us.

Our Soochow branch of the Woman's Auxiliary is the smallest and weakest of all the branches; and when the General Meeting is held, we are ashamed to make our report before the meeting. Our society was established just three years ago under not very promising conditions, and the number of communicants is a little larger now. When the society was first started there were eight members altogether, seven of these being our own Church-workers. This year we count altogether twenty-one, eleven of them being those who in these three years have

DEACONESS PAINE

contribute two or three cash and help to do a little work with our hands, gives the believers whose ability is small a part in the great good work.

In calling to mind the great favors our humble country has received from the Church in America, we see that the benefits to women have been especially great. The women of our humble country have formerly been like caged birds; birds by nature are meant to fly high and seek food, but shut up by men in cages they can do nothing, but can only depend upon others to give them food. The women of our humble country may have ambitions to help the world and ability to be independent, but fathers and mothers cherish one-sided views in dealing with girls, do not consider their education a matter of importance, so that the customs with regard to women grow worse daily.

Since Christianity entering China was first to establish girls' schools and train women to become useful members of society, for this favor and virtue we are grateful and cherish it forever in memory. From recent times girls' schools in our humble country have flourished extensively, and have done away with the wretched and ignorant customs of several thousand years' standing. Parents. have gradually come to realize that it is important also to teach daughters. If we investigate these benefits, we see it truly is the doing of the Church. Since the Holy Church entered China, the condition of our humble country has become better every month and every day.

From these considerations is it not clear that the Holy Church is the doctrine of perfect excellence, benefiting the world and the souls of men? So we continually pray the Heavenly Father to help us believers always to have our missionary duty on our hearts, and to look for the gradual increase of the Church, so that we may not slight the grace of the Lord Jesus in suffering to save and redeem the world, nor disappoint the hope of all the believers of your honorable country. We also hope that your honorable country will send more missionaries to China to help us in our weakness. Alas that the citizens of our humble country are like infants, as regards knowledge of the true faith, and know nothing! Though there are those who understand and try to lead others, these are too few; especially as our humble country is populous and large, if there are not many missionaries, how can we bring the truth to all? As regards all the missionaries of your honorable country in China, they are deeply respected, not only by us; but those also who do not understand the doctrine, having seen their good works, are already learning to honor them. After the eminent person returns to her country, if she meets relatives and

friends of missionaries in China, and they ask about the affairs of China, please repeat to them the foregoing, and it may be of comfort to them in thinking of those who are far away.

We have prepared here a few common little pieces of hand-work on purpose to offer to you as a slight token of our respect and love. We humbly hope you will graciously receive them.

The Soochow Branch of the Woman's Auxiliary in China respectfully welcomes with these words The General Secretary of the Woman's Auxiliary in Great America, Teacher Emery, Eminent Person.

Date by Western Calendar, 1908, 10th mo. 28th da.

WHAT THE UNITED OFFERING WAS IN 1907 AND IN 1910

[Compare these figures and study why your own branch lost, or gained, or did not gain more. Plan for a great increase in 1913.]

	1907.	1910.		1907.	1910.
Alabama	$1,083.56	$1,344.77	Marquette	392.00	410.50
Alaska	407.17	288.15	Maryland	5,299.25	5,592.71
Albany	3,814.14	3,425.92	Massachusetts	13,492.01	14,253.94
Arizona	118.35	59.80	Michigan	3,027.74	3,635.53
Arkansas	490.75	700.20	Michigan City	382.00	409.94
Asheville	1,061.49	1,106.18	Milwaukee	1,414.66	1,905.00
Atlanta	......	1,196.14	Minnesota	2,584.37	3,371.60
Bethlehem	3,593.56	4,307.38	Mississippi	520.00	842.88
California	2,097.77	2,628.16	Missouri	1,510.03	2,000.00
Central New York	5,399.33	3,126.00	Montana	518.91	563.57
Chicago	5,209.50	5,029.23	Nebraska	827.00	756.25
Colorado	1,028.84	1,130.12	Nevada	......	120.00
Connecticut	9,703.64	6,886.25	Newark	6,301.00	7,700.00
Dallas	414.12	608.00	New Hampshire	753.51	755.49
Delaware	1,733.30	1,925.00	New Jersey	4,211.13	4,533.81
Duluth	357.88	292.72	New Mexico	400.46	338.50
East Carolina	1,684.51	2,524.05	New York	32,160.95	31,186.52
Eastern Oregon	......	102.00	North Carolina	1,573.20	1,782.69
Easton	1,149.36	1,401.38	North Dakota	393.45	515.69
Florida	500.50	506.14	Ohio	4,515.59	6,503.00
Fond du Lac	261.56	220.66	Oklahoma	113.40	309.35
Georgia	*1,686.57	836.01	Olympia	443.00	712.57
Harrisburg	1,580.11	1,639.61	Oregon	*402.70	520.06
Honolulu	415.06	440.60	Pennsylvania	33,425.30	36,076.57
Indianapolis	731.00	761.81	Philippines	229.00	119.58
Idaho	300.00	330.00	Pittsburgh	3,182.16	3,306.00
Iowa	1,079.39	1,375.67	Porto Rico	58.15	101.95
Kansas	300.00	477.00	Quincy	372.29	471.00
Kansas City	533.27	560.66	Rhode Island	4,500.00	6,056.00
Kearney	......	214.56	Sacramento	150.04	190.45
Kentucky	1,000.00	1,600.00	Salina	40.00	105.00
Laramie	†147.22	......	South Carolina	1,744.25	2,581.30
Lexington	761.86	867.82	South Dakota	1,171.98	1,477.70
Long Island	5,264.00	7,000.00	Southern Florida	331.40	400.20
Los Angeles	2,100.00	2,640.40	Southern Ohio	3,526.44	8,114.42
Louisiana	1,248.70	1,410.08	Southern Virginia	3,900.50	3,167.94
Maine	1,187.80	1,722.51	Spokane	156.50	240.00
			Springfield	252.00	384.25
			Tennessee	1,595.08	1,487.94

* Including in 1907 what is now the Diocese of Atlanta.
† Divided into the Districts of Kearney and Wyoming.

* Including in 1907 what is now Eastern Oregon.

	1907.	1910.		1907.	1910.
Texas	561.61	653.71	Hankow	202.97	188.19
Utah	481.00	162.70	Kyoto	87.75	88.81
Vermont	762.81	795.20	Mexico	56.41	68.92
Virginia	6,115.57	4,633.95	Shanghai	222.43	305.33
Washington	2,526.50	2,696.53	Tokyo	197.00	140.82
Western Colorado	....	154.00	European Churches ..	251.58	300.00
Western Massachusetts	2,092.64	3,108.74	Greece	10.00	15.00
Western Michigan ...	704.72	1,045.00	Haiti	12.00	....
Western New York...	6,366.16	6,104.55	Canada	10.00	....
West Texas	783.66	1,029.37	England	5.00	....
West Virginia	2,217.59	2,305.79	Church Periodical Club	....	26.00
Wyoming	....	170.09	St. Barnabas' Guild		
Africa	110.05	56.88	(for Alaska nurse).	600.00	....
Brazil	231.15	100.00	Miscellaneous	779.49	463.49
Canal Zone	....	60.00			
Cuba	47.70	4.00	Total $224,251.55		$243,361.45

A PARISH BRANCH IN EASTERN OREGON

WE have just started a branch of the Woman's Auxiliary with nine members; more will come. They will meet once a month, and the president, who is deeply interested and who two years ago cared nothing about these things, will prepare a programme, and thus they will learn something about the Woman's Auxiliary and the work the Church is doing. They pledge ten cents each year, and will have the little blue box at each meeting to receive free-will offerings. At Easter the offering and the pledge will go to make up their part of the apportionment. St. Agnes' Guild is also studying missions, and has a blue box and will also help toward the apportionment end; so I think it will be given. As these women work hard to give toward the expenses of the Mission, I think that, small as this effort seems, it is really all that we can ask.

To-night I give a lecture on Africa and African Missions. I have the dolls that belong to the set for children, sold at the Missions House, and I have adorned them with bead anklets and necklaces and bracelets, painted some other little dolls black and rigged them up in various ways, and made four or five African huts, using bunch grass for the thatched roofs, so that we have an African village as an illustration. I could find no maps, so I made some on cotton cloth. Our girls from the Guild are just coming into the Church. Only two now are unbaptized and nearly all are confirmed.

The next letter says: "I take great pleasure in enclosing $2 toward the United Offering, the first return from any of the blue boxes that I gave out a year ago. It comes from this place, where we have just organized the first branch of the Auxiliary in any of our mission stations. Small as it is, it is an earnest of better things to come and is a great encouragement to me.

IMPRESSIONS OF A DIOCESAN OFFICER AT HER FIRST GENERAL CONVENTION

I HAVE just returned from the Convention, with hardly time as yet to assort my impressions. As first experiences often are, it was all very wonderful, and I have brought back, among other things, what I am sure is going to prove an unfailing antidote for any discouragement in the future—a little of that atmosphere of splendid optimism which pervaded everything. Even where results were few and resources pitifully small, there was never a suggestion of doubt that it was all very much worth while.

And next to that, the Convention brought home to me the sense of the urgency of the need everywhere. There was not a report from the field which did not tell us of waiting opportunities, sometimes amounting to a crisis in the affairs of the mission. There seemed to be no "most important" field, but just a great universal call for immediate re-enforcement. If I can manage to put a little of those two impressions into my work—missionary optimism, and the endeavor to *do quickly* what is given us to do, my first Triennial will not have been one of enjoyment merely.

THE NOVEMBER CONFERENCE

THE November Conference was held on Thursday, the 17th, and there was an excellent representation: From California, three; Connecticut, one; Easton, one; Long Island, five (one Junior); Louisiana, one; Massachusetts, one (Junior); Montana, one; Newark, two; New York, twenty (one Junior); Pennsylvania, three; Western Massachusetts, one; Hankow, one; and visitors from New Jersey, one; the Philippines, one—forty-two.

Mrs. Warren, president of the New York branch, presided, and opened the meeting with prayer. The subject of the conference was "The New Year's Responsibilities," and during the first hour the advance work of the women and Juniors was brought forward.

The secretary referred to the organizing of the new Board of Missions, and commended the reading of the organization of the new Board, the report of its first meeting and the president's message to its officers and members. She called attention to the fact that the stated meetings of the Board are to be prefaced by a celebration of the Holy Communion, and asked if this practice might not be adopted before the first officers' conference each year. This proposition received the very earnest assent of the officers present.

She then commented on Bishop Lloyd's message, suggesting that as he called the Board to inform themselves as to conditions of the peoples in this country, and of opportunity in other lands, the Auxiliary members should do the same; beginning with the united study of the subject now being urged from the Educational Department—the Negro in America; and that as he recommended the study of resources, so the Auxiliary should suggest a similar study, holding itself in readiness to follow any plan which may be recommended to it by the Board, but not waiting for such recommendation, rather acting at once in a forward movement. The following advance movements were suggested:

1. A study of present conditions in dioceses and branches where parishes and missions have no Auxiliary branch, and the giving one such parish or mission into the care of a diocesan officer to work at for a year.

2. A study of parish conditions. When a parish branch consists of a few women to plan together that such members, after conference together, each devote herself for a year to gaining the interest and co-operation of some one other designated woman.

3. A study of one's own gifts and then of the gifts in the parish and diocesan branches, and a carefully thought out plan to get individual gifts which shall be made not only at stated times, as weekly, but also of such amount as shall be in proportion to individual ability.

It was especially suggested that in all this individual work there should be definite prayer made at the beginning, and at the close of each year that the officers—diocesan or parochial—should come together for the purpose of reporting definitely as to their efforts and their results.

Miss Lindley then made her report, mentioning the value of personal experience, of personal work for the advancement of Christ's kingdom, of study and prayer, and pausing to emphasize the work lying before us of enlisting the young women between twenty and forty, still unreached. Miss Lindley asserted the readiness of Junior leaders to take hold of this work and to try to form groups of such young women which, after being gathered and influenced by the Juniors, ought by the next Triennial to be ready to be passed on bodily into the ranks of the Woman's Auxiliary.

This subject and that of missionary study were of such interest to the officers that they resolved to return to the Board room after prayers at noon, and to continue the conference till 1 P.M. It was also resolved to call future conferences at 10 instead of 10:30 A.M.

In the interval between 11:30 and noon a committee of three—Miss Delafield, Mrs. Hobart and Miss Warren— conducted a half-hour of thanksgiving and intercession.

After noon prayers, Mrs. Warren gave her place to Miss Delafield, and Miss Lindley spoke of the value of the discussion system of missionary study, and the necessity of training normal classes that teachers might be trained for the work of conducting such classes in all our branches.

By request, Deaconess Phelps, of Hankow, told of St. Hilda's School, Wuchang, and, after prayers, the conference adjourned.

NOTES AND QUESTIONS

A WORD or two about this Junior page. Its only excuse for existence is its use to Junior leaders. We are very anxious to make it of real service to the leaders and we shall be glad to have suggestions as to how this may be done. In the months in which it has been used there have been articles on various subjects of Junior work, the apportionment for last year, the United Offering, hints to leaders, and, through the kindness of the Junior leaders of Massachusetts, New York and Pennsylvania, articles on organization, the value of Junior headquarters in a diocese, suggestions on finding missionary volunteers, and, on the last subject an article by Bishop Roots. At first the plan was that when possible the same subject should be discussed in the Woman's Auxiliary pages for Seniors and Juniors, but it is not necessary to keep

to this plan. What we want now is to know the desire of the Junior leaders. This is your page; what do you want in it? When the request for topics for discussion in the Junior conferences in Cincinnati was made, more subjects than could be treated in those conferences were sent in. One left out for want of time was this question from Michigan, "Could not the Junior page in THE SPIRIT OF MISSIONS be made into more of a question and answer department?" What do the Junior leaders think of this? We shall welcome answers sent as promptly as possible.

If you think it helpful to use this page for this intercourse between Junior leaders we might begin at once. Will as many Junior leaders as possible answer the two questions given in this number, sending in their replies very promptly?

QUESTIONS

1. How often should the Junior leaders of a diocesan branch meet together?

2. What should be done at these meetings?

WHAT JUNIOR BRANCHES MAY DO WITH THE RESOLUTIONS ADOPTED IN CINCINNATI

As told in the last SPIRIT OF MISSIONS the Junior leaders, meeting in informal conference in Cincinnati, could not legislate. Their resolutions only embodied the opinion of the majority of those at this Triennial. What seemed a very good plan was followed by the Junior leaders of the New York branch. At their first conference this year, part of the time was given to a report of the "Juniors in Cincinnati" and a discussion of the resolutions which the Juniors passed there. Each resolution was taken up, discussed and voted upon. In this way the resolutions on Baptism and the "older girls" were adopted, thus making them a part of the policy of the New York branch. The resolutions on "co-operation between societies" and the new Collect were deferred until more had been done by the committee in charge of the carrying out of these resolutions. The one on boys' work was left for special discussion. The discussion of the question of "older girls" proved so important that it was voted to give the entire time of the next New York Conference to a discussion of this problem.

A SUGGESTION FROM ONE AUXILIARY BRANCH

We of the Woman's Auxiliary have asked our first vice-president in the parish to take an especial interest in the Junior work and to be a link between the two bodies and foster the Junior work, especially in cases where the Juniors are left without a head in the parish. They are also asked to use efforts toward the appointment of a head in such a case; and I am now considering the wisdom of asking in turn from the Juniors a similar fostering care of the Babies' Branch work. The first plan works well; logically, the second should work well also.

Our Corresponding Secretary suggests that the triennial meetings awakened more interest in missionary study. I myself feel that the strongest (or perhaps the freshest) impression I received at the meetings was that the Juniors and Junior helpers provide us with our missionaries. That thought influences me constantly, but I think it might be carried down another step, and that we might see that the Little Helpers of the Babies' Branch are to be the recruits of the Junior Department. They have a training peculiarly suited to them (and to their mothers), but no one will deny that they are better fitted to begin Junior work, when old enough for it, on account of that training.

LITTLE HELPERS' NEW KINDERGARTEN

The new object for the Little Helpers this year is for the kindergarten at Mayaguez. Their gift for this is to be $500, which will count on the appropriations of the Board of Missions. At Mayaguez, Miss Woodruff has about twenty-five "very attractive little people who love the kindergarten." There, as in almost every country, the hope of the future rests in training the children. It

seems especially appropriate that the help needed for the Porto Rican kindergarten should be sent through the Board by the members of the Babies' Branch.

ST. MARY'S GRADUATES OF 1910

WHEN we look back to the days when Miss Jones gathered the first girls about her in the early days of the China Mission, it seems marvellous to read what Miss Mitchell writes from St. Mary's, Shanghai, to-day:

"Last year's graduates have returned to continue their studies and to take up Latin and French. As we had the Life of Christ for our subject last year, I let the girls choose between several subjects, and they all wanted to study Comparative Religions. As several girls in the class are nominally heathen, it is a great chance to help them to the truth. The girls are all about twenty years of age, and they seem to understand the instruction given very well. I have had individuals prepare short papers on Prayer, Forgiveness, and several such subjects, which they have done very well.

THE DECEMBER CONFERENCE

THE December Conference will be held at the Church Missions House, on Thursday, December 15th, at ten o'clock.

Please notice this change in the hour of meeting.

The subject will be, "The Problem of the Young Woman and the Woman's Auxiliary: How the Junior Department Would Try to Solve It."

All diocesan officers of the Junior Department of the Woman's Auxiliary attending the officers' conference on December 15th, are asked to return to the Church Missions House at 2:30 that afternoon for an informal Junior conference to discuss details for carrying out the plans for the "older Juniors and younger women." The subject of the January conference will be "Leaders."

ACKNOWLEDGMENT OF OFFERINGS

Offerings are asked to sustain missions in thirty missionary districts in the United States, Africa, China, Japan, Brazil, Mexico and Cuba; also work in the Haitien Church; in forty-two dioceses, including missions to the Indians and to the Colored People; to pay the salaries of thirty-two bishops, and stipends to 2,253 missionary workers, domestic and foreign; also two general missionaries to the Swedes and two missionaries among deaf-mutes in the Middle West and the South; and to support schools, hospitals and orphanages. With all remittances the name of the Diocese and Parish should be given. Remittances, when practicable, should be by Check or Draft, and should always be made payable to the order of George Gordon King, Treasurer, and sent to him, Church Missions House, 281 Fourth Avenue, New York. Remittances in Bank Notes are not safe unless sent in Registered Letters.

The Treasurer of the Board of Missions acknowledges the receipt of the following from October 1st to November 1st, 1910.

* Lenten and Easter Offering from the Sunday-school Auxiliary.

NOTE.—*The items in the following pages marked "Sp." are Specials which do not aid the Board in meeting its appropriations. In the heading for each Diocese the total marked "Ap." is the amount which does aid the Board of Missions in meeting its appropriations. Wherever the abbreviation "Wo. Aux." precedes the amount, the offering is through a branch of the Woman's Auxiliary.*

Home Dioceses

Alabama
Ap. $200.00

SELMA — St. Paul's: (Apportionment, 1909-10) Gen.................. 200 00

Albany
Ap. $222.75

AMSTERDAM—St. Ann's: Gen........ 17 00
DUANESBURGH—Christ Church: (Apportionment, 1909-10) Gen......... 20 00
GLENS FALLS—Church of the Messiah: Gen. 50 00
LEBANON SPRINGS—Church of Our Saviour: Gen..................... 2 50
TROY—Christ Church S. S.: Gen...... 20 00
Holy Cross: $43.25, in memory of "T. S.," $5, Gen..................... 48 25
SARANAC LAKE—St. Luke the Beloved Physician: (Apportionment, 1909-10) Gen..................... 50 00
UNADILLA—St. Matthew's: Gen....... 15 00

Arkansas
Ap. $22.50

FAYETTEVILLE—St. Paul's: Gen....... 22 50

Atlanta
Ap. $161.94; *Sp.* $1.00

ATLANTA—St. Luke's S. S.*: Gen..... 161 94
St. Philip's Cathedral: Rev. C. T. A. Pise, Sp. for Bishop Rowe, Alaska, for new Red Dragon............. 1 00

Bethlehem
Ap. $215.87; *Sp.* $100.00

LEBANON — St. Luke's: (Apportionment, 1909-10) Gen., $45.87; Sp. for Rev. Robert E. Wood, Wuchang, Hankow, for purchase of land, etc., $100 .... 145 87
MAUCH CHUNK—St. Mark's: Gen..... 125 00

READING—Christ Church: Gen....... 20 00
SAYRE—Church of the Redeemer: Frn. 25 00

California
Ap. $15.00

OAKLAND—Mrs. Z. J. Hatch, for the salary of Bible-woman in China.... 15 00

Central New York
Ap. $182.31; *Sp.* $50.00

CAZENOVIA—St. Peter's: Gen........ 2 00
PULASKI—St. James's: Dom., $4.30; Frn., $6.61..................... 10 91
UTICA—St. Andrew's: Gen........... 4 40
MISCELLANEOUS — Wo. Aux., native helpers, Alaska................. 125 00
Wo. Aux., Fourth District, "Jane Dows Westcott Memorial" scholarship, Cuttington Collegiate and Divinity-school, Africa, $40; Mrs. Charles Tyler Olmsted, Wo. Aux., Sp. for Bishop Ferguson, for Kroo Chapel, Liberia, Africa, $50........ 90 00

Chicago
Ap. $450.30; *Sp.* $102.15

AURORA—Trinity Church: Wo. Aux., Gen. 1 00
CHICAGO — Christ Church: Girls' Friendly Society. Sp. for Girls' School, Bontoc, Philippine Islands.. 3 00
Church of the Epiphany: Wo. Aux., Gen., $15; Girls' Friendly Society, Sp. for Girls' School, Bontoc, Philippine Islands, $2.90.............. 17 90
Grace: Frn., $14.71; Mrs. L. B. Hibbard, Sp. for Bishop McKim, Tokyo, $75 .... 89 71
St. Barnabas's: Gen., $6.04; Girls' Friendly Society, Sp. for Girls' School, Bontoc, Philippine Islands, $5 .... 11 04
St. James's: Dom. and Frn.......... 54 80
St. Martin's: Wo. Aux., Gen........ 1 00

(1049)

St. Simon's Mission: Dom. and Frn., $27.30; Girls' Friendly Society, Sp. for Girls' School, Bontoc, Philippine Islands, $5...................... 32 30
JOLIET—*Christ Church*: Wo. Aux., Gen. 5 00
LAKE FOREST—*Church of the Holy Spirit*: Gen...................... 300 00
LA SALLE—*St. Paul's*: Frn............ 5 00
LIBERTYVILLE—*St. Lawrence's Mission*: Gen. 16 50
STIRLING — *Grace*: Bishop McKim's work, Tokyo.................... 3 95
MISCELLANEOUS—Girls' Friendly Society, Sp. for Girls' School, Bontoc, Philippine Islands................ 11 25

Colorado
Ap. $20.00
DENVER—*St. Thomas's S. S.**: Gen... 17 75
PUEBLO—*St. James's Church and S. S.*: (Apportionment, 1909-10) Gen..... 2 25

Connecticut
Ap. $1,136.09; *Sp.* $166.00
BRIDGEPORT—*St. John's*: "Glover Sanford Memorial" scholarship, St. Margaret's School, Tokyo........ 12 50
EAST HADDAM—Rev. Dr. F. C. H. Wendel, work in Philippines..... 1 00
HARTFORD—*Christ Church*: "A Member," Gen..................... 600 00
"A Friend," Gen................. 3 00
MILFORD—*St. Peter's*: Gen.......... 5 00
NEW HAVEN—*Christ Church*: Women's Missionary and Home Work Chapter of the Guild, Sp. for Rev. Mr. Cuthbert, Kyoto............... 21 00
"In memory of two dear relatives," work in Alaska (1909-10)........ 50 00
"Anonymous," Sp. for Utah........ 20 00
NORWALK—*Grace*: Gen............. 75 00
RIDGEFIELD—*St. Stephen's*: Gen...... 230 00
SAYBROOK—*Grace*: Gen............. 39 00
STAFFORD SPRINGS—*Grace*: Gen..... 15 80
STAMFORD—Miss E. D. Ferguson, Sp. for Utah..................... 100 00
WATERBURY—*St. John's*: Frn., $65.45; Sp. for St. John's College, Shanghai, $25...................... 90 45
WESTPORT—William L. Coley, Gen.... 1 00
WOODBURY—*St. Paul's*: Dom. and Frn. 38 34

Dallas
Ap. $70.80
FORT WORTH—*St. Andrew's S. S.**: Gen. 66 03
St. Michael and All Angels' (North): S. S.,* Gen..................... 4 77

Delaware
Ap. $5.50
DELAWARE CITY—*Christ Church*: Mrs. Mary Fawkes, Gen.............. 50
NEWARK — *St. Thomas's*: (Apportionment, 1909-10) Gen............. 5 00

East Carolina
Ap. $5.00
NEW BERN—*Christ Church*: In memory of "J. G. H.," Gen........... 5 00

Erie
Ap. $25.00; *Sp.* $100.08
ERIE—*St. Paul's*: $89.94, Mrs. Jennie Festing, $5, S. S., $5.14, Sp. for work in Utah...................... 100 08
FRANKLIN — *St. John's*: (Apportionment, 1909-10) Gen............. 25 00

Fond du Lac
Ap. $5.00
ONEIDA—*Holy Apostles'*: Juniors, Gen. 4 00
WAUPUN—"A Friend," Gen.......... 1 00

Georgia
Ap. $130.50
BAINBRIDGE—*St. John's*: Frn........ 26 50
SAVANNAH—*St. Paul's*: "A Member" (Apportionment, 1909-10), Alaska, $50; Japan, $50................. 100 00
WAYCROSS—*Grace*: Gen............. 4 00

Harrisburg
Ap. $56.92
BEARTOWN—*Calvary S. S.**: Gen..... 9 55
BLOOMSBURG—*St. Paul's*: (Apportionment, 1909-10) Gen........... 20 00
WILLIAMSPORT—*Christ Church*: Dom. and Frn...................... 27 37

Indianapolis
Ap. $12.90; *Sp.* $326.24
INDIANAPOLIS—*Christ Church*: Sp. for Bishop Van Buren's work, Porto Rico (of which from "A Friend," $250). 326 24
LAWRENCEBURG—*Trinity Church*: Gen. 10 00
MT. VERNON—*St. John's*: Gen....... 2 90

Iowa
Ap. $29.58
ALGONA—*St. Thomas's*: (Apportionment, 1909-10) Gen............. 6 20
COUNCIL BLUFFS—*St. Paul's*: Gen.... 17 38
CRESTON—*St. Paul's*: Gen.......... 2 00
LE MARS—*St. George's*: Gen......... 4 00

Kansas
Ap. $23.52
HIAWATHA—*St. John's*: Gen......... 12 00
PARSONS—*St. John's*: Gen.......... 10 81
WICHITA — *All Saints'*: (Apportionment, 1909-10) Gen............. 71

Kansas City
Ap. $77.86
ATCHISON CO.—*St. Oswald's*: Gen.... 10 86
KANSAS CITY—*St. George's*: Gen..... 25 00
ST. JOSEPH—*Christ Church*: Gen..... 25 00
TRENTON—*St. Philip's*: Gen........ 5 00
WARRENSBURG—*Christ Church*: Gen.. 12 00

Kentucky
Ap. $152.00; *Sp.* $10.00
LOUISVILLE—*Calvary*: Sp. for Bishop Van Buren, Porto Rico......... 10 00
St. Andrew's: Gen................. 150 00
Mrs. William Rodman, Gen........ 2 00

Lexington
Ap. $51.00
COVINGTON—*Trinity Church*: Gen..... 51 00

Long Island
Ap. $195.95; *Sp.* $31.75
BROOKLYN—*St. Ann's*: Gen......... 10 00
St. Paul's (Flatbush): Dom., $51.75; Frn., $44.25.................... 96 00
St. Stephen's: Gen............... 21 68
MERRICK—*Church of the Redeemer*: Gen. 54 29
QUEENS—*St. Joseph's*: Gen......... 3 98
RICHMOND HILL—*Resurrection*: Sp. for St. John's University Expansion Fund, Shanghai................ 31 75
SEA CLIFF—*St. Luke's*: Gen......... 10 00

Los Angeles
Sp. $5.00
LOS ANGELES—Rev. Benjamin Hartley, Sp. for Rev. S. D. Ferguson, Jr., Cape Palmas, Liberia........... 5 00

Louisiana
Ap. $31.57; *Sp.* $10.00
GIBSON—*St. Anna's Mission*: Gen., for 1909-10 .... 5 30
NEW IBERIA—"Individual," Domestic

Missions in the United States...... 3 00
NEW ORLEANS—*Christ Church Cathedral*: (Apportionment, 1909-10) Gen. 10 77
St. Paul's S. S.: Gen............. 12 50
MISCELLANEOUS—Babies' Branch, Sp. for the support of Sunia Ozawa, in St. Agnes's School, Kyoto........ 10 00

Maine
Ap. $45.11; Sp. $5.00
AUGUSTA—*St. Mark's*: Gen......... 29 06
HOULTON—*Church of the Good Shepherd*: Gen...................... 6 10
NORTH EAST HARBOR—Margaret H. Nelson, Sp. for University Hospital Furnishing Fund, Philippine Islands. 5 00
RICHMOND—*St. Matthias's Mission*: Gen. 1 00
YORK HARBOR—*Trinity Church*: Gen.. 8 95

Marquette
Ap. $34.79; Sp. $10.00
CRYSTAL FALLS—*St. Mark's*: Gen.... 2 80
HERMANSVILLE—Gen. 2 80
MANSFIELD—*Mission*: Gen.......... 2 19
MARQUETTE—*St. Paul's*: Gen., $26; Girls' Friendly Society, Sp. scholarship for girl in school at Rutherfordton, Asheville, $10.............. 36 00
POWERS—Gen. 1 00

Maryland
Ap. $423.15; Sp. $2,010.00
BALTIMORE — *Ascension S. S.*: For "Alice Fair" scholarship, St. Mary's Hall, Shanghai.................... 40 00
Chapel of the Guardian Angel: (Apportionment, 1909-10) Gen........ 5 00
Prince of Peace S. S.: For Brazil... 229 57
Grace: Miss Elizabeth L. Clark, for "W. V. Clark Memorial" scholarship, St. John's School, Africa........... 25 00
"H. W. A.," Sp. for Rev. Mr. Ancell, Shanghai 10 00
BALTIMORE Co. — *Trinity Church* (Towson): S. S., for work of Bishop Kinsolving, Brazil............. 10 00
FREDERICK Co.—*All Saints'* (Frederick): Gen., $33.76; Sp. for Rev. Dr. Osborne, "Ingle" (Divinity) scholarship, Boone University, Wuchang, Hankow, $2,000; Wo. Aux., Indian, $4.66; Frn., $4.68; Mexican, $4.66. 2,047 76
St. Paul's (Point of Rocks): Dom. and Frn. 7 08
St. Stephen's (Thurmont): Gen...... 4 24
HARFORD Co. — *Emmanuel Church* (Bel Air): Gen................... 50 00
WASHINGTON Co.—*St. Anne's* (Smithburg): Gen..................... 4 50

Massachusetts
Ap. $157.92; Sp. $5.00
BOSTON—*St. John's* (East): Sp. for Logan, Utah................... 5 00
Through Miss E. A. Clapp (Dorchester), Gen. (Apportionment, 1909-10) 1 25
FALMOUTH—*St. Barnabas's*: Gen.... 12 75
FRAMINGHAM—Alice J. Monk, Gen. (Apportionment, 1909-10)........ 1 00
LYNN—*St. Stephen's*: Gen......... 24 00
MALDEN—*St. Paul's*: Wo. Aux., Nevada 25 00
NEWTON—*Church of the Redeemer* (Chestnut Hill): Dom. and Frn. (Apportionment, 1909-10)........ 50 00
SALEM—*Grace*: Miss Frances R. Kilham (Apportionment, 1909-10), Gen. 10 00
SANDWICH—*St. John's*: Gen........ 18 42
WELLESLEY—*Dana Hall School*: Gen.. 13 50
MISCELLANEOUS—Wo. Aux., Massachusetts Juniors, Gen............... 2 00

Michigan
Ap. $158.27; Sp. $20.00
ADRIAN—*Christ Church*: Wo. Aux., Gen. 4 00
DETROIT—*Christ Church*: Gen. (Apportionment, 1909-10)............. 131 52
St. John's: "A. H.," Sp. toward equipment for the Julia C. Emery Hall, Africa 20 00
Mrs. C. B. Grant, Gen. (for 1909-10) 10 00
GREENFIELD—*St. Paul's*: Gen....... 2 75
LANSING—*St. Paul's*: Gen. (Apportionment, 1909-10)............... 10 00

Michigan City
Ap. $8.80
MARION—*Gethsemane*: Wo. Aux., Gen. 5 00
PERU—*Trinity Church*: Gen........ 3 80

Milwaukee
Sp. $3.00
MILWAUKEE—Mary S. L. Myers, Sp. for Bishop McKim, Tokyo............ 3 00

Minnesota
Ap. $47.22; Sp. $500.00
ANOKA—*Trinity Church*: Gen....... 12 00
MINNEAPOLIS—Miss Frances S. Weller, Sp. for Tsu property, for Dr. I. H. Correll, Kyoto.................. 500 00
ST. PAUL—*Church of the Messiah S. S.*: Gen.................... 35 22

Mississippi
Ap. $20.00
HERNANDO—*Ascension*: Gen......... 5 00
INDIANOLA—*St. Stephen's*: Gen...... 15 00

Missouri
Ap. $181.10
KIRKSVILLE—*Trinity Church S. S.*: Gen............................ 1 10
ST. LOUIS—*Emmanuel Church* (Old Orchard): Laymen's Missionary Society, Gen...................... 30 00
Grace (Kirkwood): Frn., $100; Gen., $50 .... 150 00

Montana
Ap. $5.00
JOLIET—*Church of Our Saviour*: Gen. 5 00

Nebraska
Ap. $50.00
LINCOLN—Mrs. George Worthington, Wo. Aux., for the "Bishop Worthington" scholarship, in Orphan Asylum, Cape Palmas, Africa.............. 50 00

Newark
Ap. $262.94; Sp. $142.08
EAST ORANGE—M. Douglas Cole, Sp. for Building Fund, St. Paul's College, Tokyo 50 00
JERSEY CITY—*St. John's*: Salary of Rev. W. J. Cuthbert, Kyoto........ 137 50
Holy Cross: Gen.................. 9 06
MILLBURN—*St. Stephen's*: Gen. (Apportionment, 1909-10)............. 107 79
MONTCLAIR—*St. John's*: Gen........ 8 59
St. Luke's: H. St. John Webb, Sp. for Expansion Fund, St. John's University, Shanghai................ 25 00
MORRISTOWN—Miss E. M. Applegate, Sp. for Vernal, Utah............. 25 00
SUMMIT—*Calvary S. S.*: The Chapman Class, Sp. for Rev. J. W. Chapman, for his work in Anvik, Alaska...... 42 08

New Hampshire

Ap. $29.78; *Sp.* $1.00

CONCORD—*St. Paul's*: Babies' Branch, Gen., $7.78; Sp. for missionary font, $1 ....   8 78
EXETER—Friendly Society, Gen........   2 00
KEARSARGE—"In Memory," for St. Mary's School, South Dakota.......   10 00
SANBORNVILLE—*St. John the Baptist's*: Gen.....................   10 00

New Jersey

Ap. $164.21; *Sp.* $156.00

ATLANTIC CITY — *Ascension*: Junior Aux., Gen., $2; Sp. for Building Fund, St. Margaret's School, Tokyo, $1 ....   3 00
HADDONFIELD—*Grace S. S.*: Gen......   50 00
MERCHANTVILLE—"K. P. H.," Gen....   4 00
METUCHEN—*St. Luke's S. S.*: Sp. for Bishop Brewster, Western Colorado.   5 00
MIDDLETOWN—*Christ Church*: Gen...   13 01
MT. HOLLY—*St. Andrew's*: Colored, $15.20; Brazil, $30.............   45 20
PRINCETON—*Trinity Church*: Wo. Aux., "Louisa C. Tuthill" scholarship, St. Mary's Hall, Shanghai.........   40 00
RUMSON — *St. George's-by-the-River*: Wo. Aux., Sp. for Bishop Roots, Hankow 100 00
SHREWSBURY — *Christ Church*: "A Friend," Sp. for Divinity-school Building, St. Paul's College, Tokyo..   50 00
WENONAH—*All Saints'*: Gen.........   10 00

New York

Ap. $3,159.93; *Sp.* $1,757.85

BREWSTER—*St. Andrew's*: Sp. for Rev. Charles E. Crusoe, Corbin, Lexington 5 00
BRONXVILLE—*Christ Church*: "A Member," "Divinity" scholarship, Boone University, Wuchang, Hankow, $25; two beds, Elizabeth Bunn Hospital, Wuchang, Hankow, $25; Girl's School, Manila, Philippine Islands, $87.50; Sp. for Bishop Ferguson, Africa, for enlarging church, $50...........   137 50
MATTEAWAN—*St. Luke's*: "C. F. G.," Gen., $2.06; Wo. Aux., "Mrs. Winthrop Sargent" scholarship, St. John's University, Shanghai, $100..   102 06
MOUNT VERNON—*Ascension*: Wo. Aux., Sp. for Good Shepherd Hospital, Fort Defiance, Arizona................   20 00
John W. Hammond, Indian Schools, South Dakota, $2.50; Bishop Gray's work among Seminoles, Southern Florida, $2.50; Gen., $5..........   10 00
NEW ROCHELLE—*Trinity Church*: Wo. Aux., Sp. for Good Shepherd Hospital, Fort Defiance, Arizona......   26 00
NEW YORK—*All Angels'*: Gen........   61 84
Beloved Disciple: Gen.............   86 42
Calvary: "A Member," Gen........   600 00
Grace: Committee on Missions for Colored People, St. Augustine's League, Sp. for St. Agnes's Hospital, Raleigh, North Carolina, $10; Sp. for Good Samaritan Hospital, Charlotte, North Carolina, $5...................   15 00
Holy Apostles': Gen..............   27 65
Incarnation: Wo. Aux., Mrs. Hooker's School, Mexico, $8; "A Member," Wo. Aux., Gen., $5.............   13 00
St. Bartholomew's: Brazil, $250; Cuba, $250; S. S., Sp. for St. Agnes's Hospital, Raleigh, North Carolina, for "Little Helpers'" cot, $61; Sp. for Rev. C. E. Betticher, Fairbanks, Alaska, for school at Nenana, $100.   661 00
St. James's: Frn. (Apportionment, 1909-10), $1,345; St. Augustine's League, Mrs. E. W. Warren, Sp. for

education of Beatrice Small, St. Augustine's School, Raleigh, North Carolina, $80....................   1,425 00
St. Michael's: Salary of Rev. A. A. Gilman, Changsha, Hankow (Apportionment, 1909-10)...............   151 00
St. Paul's (Morrisania) : (Apportionment, 1909-10) Gen..............   26 00
St. Paul's (Tompkinsville) : S. S.,* Gen. 14 13
St. Peter's (West Chester) : (Apportionment, 1909-10) Dom., $7.26; Wo. Aux., Sp. for Bishop Morrison, Duluth, at his discretion, connection with forest fires, $15; Sp. for Rev. S. C. Hughson, O.H.C., Sewanee, Tennessee, for St. Andrew's School, $10 ....   32 26
Mrs. R. T. Auchmuty, Sp. for Church Extension Fund, Porto Rico........   500 00
Ethel M. Strange, Sp. for Bishop Thomas's Hospital for Sioux Indians, Wyoming 10 00
"A Friend" (Apportionment, 1909-10) Gen.....................   5 00
Mrs. Nicholas and Friend, through an Associate of Girls' Friendly Society, Sp. for fund for piano at Changsha, Hankow................   1 25
"A Member of King's Daughters," Frn. 1 00
NYACK—S. E. Rosedale, Elizabeth Bunn Hospital, Wuchang, Hankow..   5 00
PEEKSKILL—*St. Peter's*: Girls' Friendly Society, Sp. for salary of missionary curate, Rev. S. C. Hughson, O.H.C., St. Andrew's School, Sewanee, Tennessee 5 10
POUGHKEEPSIE—*Christ Church*: Gen..   30 00
Church of the Holy Comforter: (Apportionment, 1909-10) work of Bishop Partridge, Kyoto...............   22 07
Wo. Aux., "Poughkeepsie Memorial" scholarship, St. John's School, Cape Mount, Africa....................   40 00
SAUGERTIES—*Trinity Church S. S.*: Gen. 25 00
SCARSDALE—*St. James-the-Less*: Sp. for Good Shepherd Hospital, Fort Defiance, Arizona................   34 50
WAPPINGERS FALLS—*Zion*: Sp. for St. John's College Building Fund, Shanghai 100 00
MISCELLANEOUS — St. Augustine's League, Sp. for St. Paul's School, Lawrenceville, Southern Virginia, $100; Sp. for St. Augustine's School, Raleigh, North Carolina, $100.....   200 00
Wo. Aux., Sp. for Bishop Spalding, for Church House, Vernal, Utah, $125; Sp. for Bishop Funsten, Idaho, $100; Sp. for Bishop Thomas, Wyoming, $25; Sp. for St.Paul's School, Lawrenceville, Southern Virginia, $25; Sp. for Bishop Rowe, Alaska, $25; Sp. for Bishop Graves, Shanghai, for starting dispensary at Gunchow, $75; Sp. for Bishop McKim, St. Paul's College, Tokyo, $75; Sp. for Bishop Brent, Philippines, $25......   475 00
Wo. Aux., Sp. for Bishop Ferguson's work, Liberia, $25; Sp. for Mrs. Kinsolving's organ, Brazil, $25........   50 00

Ohio

Ap. $46.12; *Sp.* $25.37

CLEVELAND—*Atonement*: Dom. and Frn. 3 87
St. Matthew's: Gen..............   5 25
ELYRIA—*St. Andrew's*: Dom.........   12 00
MONROEVILLE—*Zion*: Sp. for Rev. Mr. Kong, Chinese church in Honolulu..   3 67
NORWALK—*St. Paul's*: Sp. for Rev. Mr. Kong, St. Peter's Church, Honolulu..   6 70
STEUBENVILLE—*St. Stephen's*: Sp. for

St. Hilda's Building Fund, Wuchang,
Hankow 15 00
TOLEDO—*St. John's*: Miss Alice M.
Thorne, Bontoc, Philippine Islands,
$5; Gen., $5.................. 10 00
St. Paul's (East): Gen............. 15 00

Olympia
Ap. $40.65
BELLINGHAM—*St. Paul's*: Gen........ 9 70
CENTRALIA—*St. John's*: (Apportion-
ment, 1909-10) Gen.............. 16 95
SEATTLE—*All Saints'*: Gen.......... 14 00

Oregon
Ap. $1.50; *Sp.* $30.00
CORVALLIS—*Good Samaritan*: (Appor-
tionment, 1909-10) Gen.......... 1 50
PORTLAND—*Trinity Church*: Sp. for
Widely Loving Society, Osaka,
Kyoto 30 00

Pennsylvania
Ap. $1,443.07; *Sp.* $1,603.31
ANDALUSIA—*Church of the Redeemer
Chapel*: Gen.................. 4 90
ARDMORE—*St. Mary's*: Wo. Aux., "For-
eign Committee" scholarship, St.
Hilda's School, Wuchang, Hankow,
$5; "Foreign Committee" scholar-
ship, Girls' High School, Kyoto, $5.. 10 00
BALA—*St. Asaph's*: Wo. Aux., Sp. for
Foreign Insurance.............. 4 00
CLIFTON HEIGHTS—*St. Stephen's*: Wo.
Aux., "Pennsylvania Wo. Aux."
scholarship, Hooker Memorial School,
Mexico 2 00
DOWNINGTON—*St. James's*: Dom...... 15 00
KELTON—*St. John's*: Mrs. J. W. Gib-
son, Sp. for St. John's University,
Shanghai 1 00
ITHAN—*St. Martin's Chapel*: Dom..... 2 05
MEDIA—*Christ Church*: Wo. Aux., Sp.
for Foreign Life Insurance Fund.... 2 50
PHOENIXVILLE—*St. Peter's*: Wo. Aux.,
Sp. for Bishop Knight, for school
supplies in Cuba................ 5 00
PHILADELPHIA — *Advocate Memorial*:
Wo. Aux., for Training-school, Sen-
dal, Tokyo, $1; Sp. for Foreign Life
Insurance Fund, $3.............. 4 00
Chapel of Prince of Peace: Wo. Aux.,
for "W. Beaumont Whitney" schol-
arship, Havana, Cuba, $2; "Penn-
sylvania Wo. Aux." scholarship,
Hooker Memorial School, Mexico, $2;
S. S., Gen., $18.89; Sp. to Bishop
Johnson, South Dakota, $10.50.... 27 89
Christ Church Chapel: Wo. Aux., Sp.
for Bishop Knight, for school sup-
plies in Cuba, $2; Sp. for Foreign
Life Insurance Fund, $2.......... 4 00
Grace: Frn.................... 91 59
Grace (Mt. Airy): Wo. Aux., for "Kin-
solving" scholarship, Brazil, $2;
Elizabeth Bunn Hospital, Wuchang,
Hankow, $1; Sp. for Foreign Life
Insurance Fund, $3.............. 6 00
Holy Trinity Church: Wo. Aux., Mis-
sionary Bible-class, for Bible-reader,
China 25 00
St. James's (Kingsessing): Wo. Aux.,
Sp. for Foreign Life Insurance Fund. 2 00
St. Luke's and Epiphany: Wo. Aux.,
"Kinsolving" scholarship, Brazil... 5 00
St. Mark's: "A Parishioner," Sp. for
St. John's University, Shanghai.... 100 00
St. Martin's-in-the-Fields (St. Mar-
tins): Dom., 50 cts.; Frn., $30.50;
Gen., $59.87.................. 90 87
St. Mary's: Wo. Aux., "Bishop Whit-
aker" scholarship, St. John's School,
Cape Mount, Africa, $20; Sp. for
Miss Bull, for orphanage, Kyoto, $25. 45 00
St. Matthias's: Wo. Aux., Sp. for

Bishop Knight, for school supplies in
Cuba 2 00
*St. Michael and All Angels' Mission
Chapel*: Frn.................. 10 00
St. Paul's (Aramingo): Gen......... 32 00
St. Paul's Memorial (Overbrook):
Dom., $3.25; Gen., $125.19; Wo.
Aux., "Kinsolving" scholarship,
Brazil, $5; Sp. for Foreign Life In-
surance Fund, $5.............. 138 44
St. Paul's (Chestnut Hill): Dom.,
$337.63; Gen., $500............ 837 63
St. Peter's (Germantown): Wo. Aux.,
Sp. for Foreign Life Insurance
Fund 1 00
Church of the Saviour: Wo. Aux., Sp.
for Foreign Life Insurance Fund... 5 00
Wo. Aux., "A Member," Sp. for hos-
pital, Nopala, Mexico, $100; Sp. for
Medical Mission, New Mexico, $200. 300 00
Estate of George C. Thomas, Sp. for
Archdeacon Stuck's reading-room at
Fairbanks, Alaska.............. 500 00
Misses Blanchard, Sp. for Church
Extension Fund, Porto Rico....... 300 00
Miss Mary K. Gibson, Sp. for Utah.. 100 00
Miss Frishmuth, Sp. for Vernal,
Utah 25 00
Miss Elizabeth H. Brown, Sp. for
Mr. L. H. Travis, St. Mary's School,
Rosebud Agency................ 5 31
"Anonymous," Sp. for Vernal, Utah. 200 00
RADNOR—*St. Martin's*: Dom......... 91 20
UPPER PROVIDENCE—*St. Paul's Memor-
ial*: Gen.................... 1 00
WHITE MARSH—*St. Thomas's*: "Thank-
offering," $15, "X. Y. Z.," $35,
Gen. 50 00

Pittsburgh
Ap. $111.93
BARNESBORO—*St. Thomas's*: Gen..... 4 50
HOMESTEAD—*St. Matthew's*: Frn..... 12 45
WILKINSBURG—*St. Stephen's*: Dom.,
$11.50; Frn., $83.48............ 94 98

Quincy
Ap. $5.00
PITTSFIELD—*St. Stephen's*: Gen...... 5 00

Rhode Island
Ap. $172.35
BRISTOL—*St. Michael's*: Gen........ 75 00
NEWPORT—*Trinity Church*: Dom.,
$75; Gen., $8.85............... 83 65
WICKFORD—*St. Paul's*: Frn......... 13 70

Sacramento
Ap. $12.00
Wo. Aux., Gen. (of which Juniors,
$8) 12 00

South Carolina
Ap. $107.51
CHARLESTON—*St. Michael's*: Gen..... 62 50
CHERAW—*St. David's S. S.**: Gen..... 29 51
LAURENS—"E. B. S.," Gen.......... 4 00
RIDGE SPRINGS—*Grace*: Gen........ 1 50
STATEBURG—Mrs. W. W. Anderson,
Gen. 10 00

Southern Ohio
Ap. $222.79; *Sp.* $750.00
CHILLICOTHE—*St. Paul's*: (Apportion-
ment, 1909-10) Gen............ 5 00
CINCINNATI—*Calvary* (Clifton): John
C. Sherlock, $100, Mrs. John C.
Sherlock, $50, Sp. for Vernal, Utah. 150 00
Epiphany: Gen................ 181 30
GALENA—*Church of Our Saviour*: (Ap-
portionment, 1909-10) Gen....... 5 00
GLENDALE—Mrs. Mortimer Matthews,
Sp. for enlargement of St. Eliza-
beth's Hospital, Shanghai......... 300 00

St. Paul's (Greenville) : Gen.......... 15 00
"A Friend," Wo. Aux., salary of
Miss Ida N. Porter, Shanghai...... 112 50

Miscellaneous

Ap. $17,117.80 ; *Sp.* $3,123.53
  Specific Deposit, $243,380.73
  Specific Deposit, $19.28
Interest, *Dom.,* $1,862.99 ; *Frn.,*
$1,109.20 ; Gen., $1,258.77 ; *Sp.,*
$2,433.42 ; Men's Thank-offering,
$19.28 .... 6,683 66
The United Offering of the Wo. Aux.
for 1910, for woman's work in the
mission field ; including the training,
sending and support of women workers ; also the care of such workers
when sick and disabled ; also for the
erection of buildings in the mission
field as memorials to our late Treasurer, Mr. George C. Thomas, $10,000
for St. Hilda's School, Wuchang,
China ; $5,000 for St. Augustine's
School, Raleigh, N. C...........243,361.45
United Offering, Wo. Aux., 1910, on
account of appropriations to September 1st, 1911, Dom., $6,000 ;
Frn., $6,000..................12,000 00
Offering at opening service of General Convention, Gen 242 04
Wo. Aux. meetings, Cincinnati, Sp.
for Southern Florida, $22.33 ; Sp. for
Oklahoma, $22.18 ; Sp. for Nevada,
$22.20 ; Sp. for Kearney, $29.41 ; Sp.
for Spokane, $31.91 ; Sp. for Wyom-
ing, $37.91................... 165 94
Wo. Aux. in Cincinnati, Sp. for Idaho,
$9.43 ; Sp. for Kyoto, $14.43 ; Sp.
for Cuba, $12.29 ; Sp. for North Da-
kota, $8.50 ; Sp. for Olympia, $8.50 ;
Sp. for Mexico, $5.50 ; Sp. for Porto
Rico, $8.74 ; Sp. for Honolulu, $8.74 ;
Sp. for Utah, $8.75 ; Sp. for Salina,
$14.82 ; Sp. for Hankow, $5.81.... 105 51
Collection at St. Paul's Cathedral,

Cincinnati, O., at Triennial Mission-
ary Service, Gen.................. 159 28
Wo. Aux. meetings, Cincinnati, Sp.
for Bishop Ferguson, Africa, $61.33 ;
Sp. for Bishop Kendrick, Arizona,
$59.33 ; Sp. for Bishop Brewster,
Western Colorado, $55.34 ; Sp. for
Brazil, $16.64 ; Sp. for Sacramento,
$16.64 ; Sp. for South Dakota,
$17.65 ; Sp. for Shanghai, $12.95 ;
Sp. for Asheville, $13.95 ; Sp. for
Eastern Oregon, $12.95 ; Sp. for
Cuba, 15 cts................... 266 93
Junior Aux. Triennial Corporate
Communion Service, held in Cincin-
nati, Gen...................... 23 13
Services during meeting of General
Convention, held in Christ Church,
Cincinnati, Gen., $238.39 ; Sp. for
Building Fund, Grace Mission, San
Luis Potosi, Mexico, $151.73...... 390 12
Junior Department, through Mission-
ary Exhibit in Cincinnati, Gen.... 5 50
Daughters of the late Cortland W.
Starr, for the "Cortland W. Starr"
scholarship in St. John's University,
Shanghai 25 00
Daughters of the King, for Miss
Richmond's salary, Shanghai...... 187 50
"A Friend," Gen................. 1 00
"A Friend," Gen................. 5 00

Legacies

$1,253.75

PA., PHILADELPHIA—Estate of David
Roberts, Dom................... 41 25
W. N. Y., BUFFALO—Estate of Mrs.
Charles H. Smith, Dom.,- $606.25 ;
Frn., $606.25................. 1,212 50

Receipts for the month..........$287,598 12
Amount previously acknowledged.. 81,079 57
                                  ――――――――
                                  $368,677 69

Lightning Source UK Ltd.
Milton Keynes UK
UKHW051851211118
332720UK00023B/578/P